W9-CAG-562

A HISTORY
OF CIVILIZATION

A HISTORY OF CIVILIZATION

The Mid-seventeenth Century
to
Modern Times

SECOND EDITION

The Story of Our Heritage

By ARTHUR J. MAY, University of Rochester

CHARLES SCRIBNER'S SONS *NEW YORK*

C-7.66 [J]

PRINTED IN THE UNITED STATES OF AMERICA
Library of Congress Catalog Card Number 64–13271

TO CHRIS AND STEVE

undergraduates while this book
was in the writing

"It is the duty of every man to endeavour that something may be added by his industry to the hereditary aggregate of knowledge and happiness. To add much can indeed be the lot of few, but to add something, however little, every man may hope."

—Samuel Johnson, *The Rambler*,
number 129, June 11, 1751

PREFACE TO THE SECOND EDITION

Since the appearance of the first edition of this work, huge developments impinging upon the Western heritage have taken place. To record and interpret the transit of current affairs into history, the last chapters have been fully recast.

Due attention has been given to such fundamental topics as the exploding world population, the winning of national independence on the colored continents, Soviet cultural advances, and the fierce, ongoing rivalry between West and East—merely to cite certain examples.

Fresh illustrations have been introduced in the final sections and the maps have been revised in keeping with political changes. Suggestions "For Further Study" at the end of each chapter have been brought up to date and in most instances expanded. The term "paperback" accompanies important titles that are available in inexpensive editions.

Uncertainties that attend historical writing are multiplied in reconstructing the recent past. Much essential information has not yet been disclosed. Sequels are veiled in the future. Perspectives are dim. And, however lofty one's ideals of impartiality and honesty may be, personal convictions and preconceptions are likely to cast shadows across his pages. In the tentative treatment of the post-Hiroshima period, a studied effort has been made to hold these obvious limitations to a minimum.

No less than endless process, history—or its interpretation—is unending debate.

Mrs. Margie Redmond of Rochester expertly typed the manuscript.

A. J. M.

Rochester, New York

PREFACE AND ACKNOWLEDGMENTS TO THE FIRST EDITION

Edmund Burke proclaimed to his confused and anxious age that no people can look forward to posterity which does not look backward to its ancestors. That axiom has been kept steadily in mind in preparing this comprehensive survey of Western civilization and its planetary impact from Peter Stuyvesant to Albert Einstein. From the age of the Renaissance into the twentieth century, the West of Europe reigned supreme over the globe; since then the political leadership of the region has given way to the United States and the Soviet Union, yet the cultural preeminence of Western Europe persists.

It is the larger trends and tendencies over three centuries of time, the fundamentals in the spacious western inheritance —the spirit of free inquiry, faith in reason, civil liberties, the democratic creed, and industrial technology, to mention certain conspicuous elements—that are evoked in these pages. Civilization is a living organism, constantly changing, shedding a cell here, adding fresh tissue there. Sometimes change has been so gradual as to be apparent only after the passage of many generations; sometimes change comes more rapidly and is therefore more noticeable as has been strikingly true since about 1800.

Whether students entering our colleges and universities are less familiar than their predecessors with the historical and cultural roots of contemporary civilization need not be debated here. It seems evident, in any case, that growing emphasis upon the study of United States history in pre-college training has deprived many a youthful learner of adequate acquaintance with the rich diversity of Western society—the institutions, treasures, traditions and social creativity that have been heaped up and are now under challenge by the Soviet colossus as never has that heritage been menaced before. That consideration and the necessities of a liberalizing and enlightening education have largely dictated the subject matter of this book.

While an older school of historians looked upon the sphere of the state as of transcendant significance, it is now widely accepted that other realms of endeavor possess comparable importance. Science and technology, consequently, music and literature, currents in philosophy and religion, art and architecture have been allotted their places among the main manifestations of Western genius, without, however, slighting political happenings.

Despite all vicissitudes, Europe, which is nothing other than the western cape of the Eurasian continent, remains the heart of contemporary western culture. So the accent in the book rests on the West, but the whole of humanity is in fact brought into some sort of focus—the transit of European ways of doing and thinking to other societies, the action and influence of the West of Europe upon the Americas, the Moslems, the Indians and the Orientals. As a glance at the chapter titles will show, an unusual amount of attention has been assigned to the Americas, to Russia and to the Far East.

In matters of structure, the book reflects more than a quarter of a century of experience and experiment in introducing undergraduates to the contemporary world by way of history and in encouraging them to independent reflection about their own times. One quarter of the chapters deals with developments since 1919. At every turn the arrangement has been designed to facilitate the grasp of sequence, to exhibit the historical "law of continuity," to fix attention on what has endured, always with an eye to the present generation. An array of specially prepared maps and a profusion of illustrations, carefully integrated with the text itself, are intended to clarify historical processes and to make outstanding personalities more real and interesting.

In this adventure in long-term synthesis it has not been possible, alas, to set forth great themes with the fullness that one would wish or to recreate in detail the men and women of earlier generations, who were as actual as we are, moved by kindred emotions and aspirations, groping for answers to the eternal mysteries, tormented by insecurities and swayed by ideas and ideals like unto ourselves. To counteract those limitations a list of books of solid attainment for further study accompanies each chapter.

The author, it needs hardly be said, has approached his task with a minimum of passion and the maximum of objectivity that he could muster. That attitude, whatever its imperfections, appears to be more than ever desirable at a time when prophets of gloom and doom seem to be more than normally vocal, and when facile preachers exploit the evidences of the past to prove with cheeky assurance the inevitable decline of the West, or the inevitable superiority of the Nordics, or the inevitable class war and proletarian dictatorship. The perspective afforded by reasonably impartial history should make the transient present more intelligible, less vexing, more meaningful. Historical learning, it is true, seldom serves well in foretelling the future, and yet it can and in fact should reinforce a sense of values and thus should help in shaping the things to come. Perhaps we can agree that "no man who is correctly informed as to the past will be disposed to take a morose or desponding view of the present." That conviction, at any rate, was come to by an eminent British historian, Thomas Babington Macaulay.

It is a pleasure to record obligations to men and women who have nourished and inspired, consciously or not, my labors. First in line must be recalled the several generations of undergraduates in the University of Rochester who have been confronted with almost every page of the volume in one form or another and, perhaps, by reason of that experience are more intelligent, tolerant, and responsible members of society. The editor of the series in which this book appears, Professor Arthur C. Bining of the University of Pennsylvania, gave unwearied and perceptive counsel all along the way and offered innumerable recommendations for the improvement of the content. That master of all of us who teach undergraduates about Western civilization, the late Professor Laurence B. Packard of Amherst College, and Professor Kent Forster of Pennsylvania State College, each read half the chapters and proposed constructive criticisms.

Learned and generous colleagues at Rochester searchingly examined sections of the manuscript bearing upon their own specialties and saved the writer from errors in fact or interpretation: the late Professor Neil C. Arvin (French and Comparative Literature), Professors Willson H. Coates (British History), Dexter Perkins (American History), and Glyndon G. Van Deusen (French and American History). Professor C. Harold King of the University of Miami, author of the first volume of this set, made fruitful suggestions and helped me to avoid excessive overlapping with his own book.

My best thanks go to Mr. Samuel Bryant for his maps, and to all those who helped to make the distinguished selection of illustrations truly a complement to the text, notably to Dr. Karl Küp, Miss Elizabeth E. Roth and Mr. Wilson G. Duprey of the Print Room, New York Public Library; Mr. Lewis M. Stark and his assistants in the Reserve Room of the same institution; Miss Elizabeth Fuller and Miss Dorothy C. Miller of the Museum of Modern Art, New York; the staff of the Picture Research section and the several Curators of the Metropolitan Museum of Art, New York; Mr. John Walker of the National Gallery of Art, Washington, D.C.; Bradbury, Agnew and Company, Ltd., and Mr. Peter Agnew; to Mr. Frederick A. Sweet of the Art Institute of Chicago; to Miss Florett Robinson and the Scribner staff; and to many other ladies and gentlemen, both here and abroad, whose zeal and learning in their work as conservers and students of art is exceeded only by their kindness.

Especial tribute must be paid to the ingenuity and skill of Mrs. Frederic W. Gleichman of Rochester in rendering my muddy long-hand sheets into clean typescript. At every step on the long road, my wife, Hilda Jones May, lent invaluable encouragement.

ARTHUR J. MAY

Rochester, New York

TABLE OF CONTENTS

PART V: THE WORLD IN FERMENT

PART I

THE LATE SEVENTEENTH AND EIGHTEENTH CENTURIES

CHAPTER I

THE WORLD OF PETER STUYVESANT

ASCENDANCY OF THE DUTCH

BEST known as a portly Dutchman with a wooden leg, Peter Stuyvesant is almost a legendary figure in the folklore of America. In 1646, this tough-textured soldier, who had won honor and lost a limb, landed in the New World as director-general of New Netherland. A quarter of a century earlier, the headquarters of Dutch enterprise in North America had been planted at New Amsterdam on the tip of Manhattan Island. A tyrannical spirit, full of plans for imperial expansion, Stuyvesant quarreled sharply with the small band of colonists, fought three regular wars with neighboring Indians and conquered the Swedes in Delaware. His dominions corresponded broadly to New York, New Jersey and Delaware of today, though Dutch pretensions extended as far east as Cape Cod. But in 1664 Stuyvesant was obliged to surrender the Dutch holdings to England.

Peter Stuyvesant

For our present purposes, Stuyvesant may serve as an informed man of experience looking out upon the world at the mid-seventeenth century from the isolation of New Amsterdam. At that point, none could have dreamed that this primitive community would mature as the turbulent, sophisticated New York of three centuries later. Inside a protective fort nearly a thousand inhabitants occupied rather more than a hundred frail dwellings; a wooden church, several taverns, a marketplace and harbor facilities rounded out the village. Almost from the beginning New Amsterdam possessed a cosmopolitan flavor, with eighteen languages in use in Stuyvesant's day. Farms had been laid out to meet local food requirements and to raise hemp and flax for export; but furs made up the principal traffic of the busy port, especially beaver pelts which Indians exchanged for liquor and other delights brought over from Holland.

Old Amsterdam in the Seventeenth Century

New Netherland was a prosperous daughter of Old Netherland or the United Provinces, then the most envied and probably the richest of European states.[1] Long subject to Spanish domination, the sturdy Dutch nation, intensely patriotic and fiercely Protestant, secured formal acknowledgment of its independence in the Peace of Westphalia of 1648. Eighty years defiance of the mightiest of empires had been carried to a triumphant conclusion. Seven provinces, each with its own government, but with a central administration to look after common affairs and to carry on dealings with the external world, made up the Dutch Republic. The wealthiest of all, Holland, contained Amsterdam and half a dozen other major communities; so important was Holland in the Dutch confederation that its name was commonly used for the state as a whole. An affluent merchant patriciate determined the policies of Holland and of the Dutch Republic itself much of the time.

This little nation of about 2,000,000 people relied upon its splendid navy for defense and for expansion of its overseas interests. Not many soldiers could be recruited from the small native population, a weakness that soon cost the Dutch their primacy. Remarkably tolerant for the day, the Dutch burghers welcomed the persecuted and dissenters from other countries and the nation benefited materially and intellectually from these newcomers. The eminence of the United Provinces in the things of the mind and spirit was no wise inferior to their supremacy in trade and their political prestige.

The greatness of the Dutch rested upon the sea, upon commerce, shipping, colonies and the capital accumulated in these enterprises. Dutch shipyards at the peak of their activity built half the ocean-going vessels of Europe; eight of her skillful seamen, it was said, could do the work of twenty sailors of other countries. That competitive advantage helped the Dutch to capture more than half of the oceanborne commerce of the globe; in 1650 the Dutch merchant navy boasted over 10,000 vessels. Aside from building ships, Dutch craftsmen developed thriving textile, leather and diamond cutting industries. And as merchants, the Dutch prospered from transactions in a wide variety of wares, especially sea products (notably the herring monopoly which was the foundation of national wealth), spices and slaves.

In the first half of the seventeenth century, the commerce of the United Provinces had expanded at a fabulous pace. It was a real asset for the Dutch that throughout the period the

[1] See C. Harold King, *A History of Civilization: The Story of Our Heritage* (New York, 1964), Chap. XXXII.

New Amsterdam, 1679. A view from the north

New York City today

The Exchange (the "Bourse") in Amsterdam, a nerve center for the trade of the Netherlands

other maritime powers were engaged in international or internal strife. As an English investigator properly concluded, the United Provinces had grown wealthy because of "the vastness of their trade, into which their religion, their manners and dispositions, their situation and the form of their government were the chief ingredients."

Combining valor with lust for gain, sturdy Dutchmen established trading stations and colonies around the globe. In the New World, apart from New Netherland, the Dutch had footholds in the West Indies and in Guiana. At the southern extremity of Africa, convenient as a stopping place on the long dreary voyage to Asia, Capetown was founded (1652); presently Dutch families settled permanently in the area. Best of all, the Dutch ruled most of the East Indies, rich in spices, as well as the Malay Peninsula and Ceylon.

Farther east, Formosa provided a base for business with the Orient; trade with China was opened up about 1656. The Dutch—and only the Dutch—were allowed to trade with Japan

The Council of the Guild of Clothmakers at Amsterdam, by Rembrandt van Rijn

in a restricted way. And sea captains of Holland proved that Australia was an island and discovered Tasmania and New Zealand. In literal truth, the empire of which Peter Stuyvesant was a servant girdled the globe. While intent upon monopolizing the business of their own possessions, the Dutch cut avariciously into the commerce of the colonies of other West European countries.

OUTSIDE OF EUROPE

Vast areas of the globe, as matters stood at the mid-seventeenth century, remained unknown to Europe, untouched by the customs and the institutions of the West. Latin America, it is true, belonged almost entirely to Spain and Portugal, the pioneers in overseas expansion. More exactly, Spanish authority prevailed over northern South America, extended along the west coast to southern Chile and inland across the province of Upper Peru (Bolivia). Portugal claimed Brazil, though only the seaboard had been visited; the interior was an unexplored "no-man's land" and to this day the Amazon basin is the largest of the world's unmapped regions. The Dutch shared with France sovereignty over Guiana.

Except for a tenuous English foothold in Honduras, Central America was exclusively the domain of Spain. The enormous Spanish Empire also embraced Mexico and Florida, and stretched round the Gulf of Mexico into the southwestern section of the present United States. Most of the islands of the West Indies, Cuba for one, belonged to Spain. For the rest of North America, permanent English settlements had been planted on the fringes of Virginia, Maryland and New England, the Dutch controlled New Netherland, the Swedes New Sweden and French explorers had raised their national flag and founded villages in the area to the west and north of New England.[2] Other than these European holdings, North America was still a happy hunting ground for semi-nomadic Indians.

Turning to Africa, Spain and Portugal owned archipelagoes off the west coast and each of them claimed thin strips along the coasts of the continent. Several nations had set up slave stations at strategic points on the western seaboard. The Dutch flag had been hoisted at the southern tip of Africa, and the writ of the Turkish sultan ran across the Mediterranean littoral almost to the Atlantic; the portion of Africa north of the Sahara Desert had long been in contact with Europe. Apart from these areas, Africa was a sealed book to the West and would largely remain mysterious for two centuries more.

Already Portuguese, English, and Dutch interests had staked out trading zones in India and the Dutch had established themselves in the East Indies. Western merchants had started a small business with China, where, in 1644, conquering Manchus had seated themselves on the dragon throne. Shortly before the mid-seventeenth century, Russian explorers and fur traders had pressed along the riverways of the Siberian wastes to the Pacific and in 1652 a stockaded fortress was raised at Irkutsk, just west of Lake Baikal; the Muscovites, that is to say, had come to stay. As has been pointed out, Japan (Cipangu) preferred to live aloof from the West, save for very modest commercial rights granted to the Dutch. Spain held sovereignty over the Philippines and over island clusters farther south in the Pacific, while the Dutch advanced claims to Australia and other islands in the South Seas.

By 1648, then, the range of European activity and interests had become global; but for Peter Stuyvesant's generation ignorance concerning the outside world—its peoples and cultures, its potentialities—was enormous.

HOW EUROPE WAS GOVERNED

Western Europe constituted, of course, the heart of Western civilization. There the modern nation-state had by now been established on firm foundations. Surveying governmental forms, Peter Stuyvesant would have been impressed by the prevalence of royal and princely absolutism. Despotism, the oldest and most persistent pattern of government known to

[2] By the mid-seventeenth century French adventurers had learned the general character, though not the precise limits, of the Great Lakes system.

Austrian cavalry in action against the Turks near Vienna

man, stood in fact on the threshold of one of its golden eras. Kings and princes wielded their scepters, it was believed, by the sanction of God; as such they were infallible, beyond good and evil, indispensable for the preservation of civilized order in society and for physical security. Rulers were to be blindly obeyed. Even so the most nearly absolute governors of the time commanded only a fraction of the power available to a Hitler or a Stalin in the twentieth-century state. In one of the most discussed of all treatises on government, *Leviathan, or the Matter, Form and Power of a Commonwealth,* published in 1651, Thomas Hobbes vigorously argued the case for despotism and the all-controlling state, only he reasoned that authoritarian government was a secular affair of practical necessity rather than an instrument of God's will.

In the main royal and princely crowns were transferred by hereditary right, though in Poland and the Holy Roman Empire, the right of electing the sovereign belonged to the nobility (or part of it) and the higher dignitaries of the Church. Already, however, the republican principle had captured slender bridgeheads in Europe; the small Swiss confederacy, the Dutch Republic and the merchant-republics of Venice and Genoa in Italy loomed up as islands in the sea of absolutism. For a decade, commencing in 1649, England, too, experienced the republican regime of Oliver Cromwell.

As in the past—and in the future—a primary responsibility of the state was to maintain law and order and to protect itself against external aggression. For purposes of defense or of conquest, military services had recently been improved. About the middle of the seventeenth century, the permanent professional army became a standard feature of European affairs. Hitherto only the Ottoman Empire had maintained a standing army and that example may have inspired Christian countries to imitation, Sweden setting the pace. Troops were equipped with swords, pikes or matchlock muskets with a rope of match to set off the powder, and soon after 1650 with bayonets. Before a shot could be fired the soldier had to perform many operations, requiring no little training. Cavalry forces figured prominently in the equipment of war.

Everywhere foreign mercenaries, men who chose soldiering as their vocation, made up the larger part of the standing armies. By present-day standards, armies were surprisingly small; a Swedish force of 100,000 caused chroniclers to pause and take note. If armies were not large they were active; taking the seventeenth century as a whole Europe was entirely free of fighting for only four years. Operations ceased, to be sure, during the inclement winter months and probably campaigning was never too arduous; the thinker René Descartes entered military service so that he might pursue philosophy with a minimum of interruption!

An important innovation of the century was the creation of strong sea forces by the western maritime countries. Men-of-war protected cargo carriers, which were themselves armed against piratical raids; in time of formal war these vessels could be turned to preying upon enemy commerce. Before the century was over wars had been fought wholly or largely at sea.

However able and energetic a monarch or a prince might be he could not manage the whole machinery of government alone. It was the rare ruler who did not have a few competent ministers at his side. Administration was entrusted to highly organized bodies of officials reinforced by police services. As economic activity grew and the control of the state over the economy increased, bureaucracies expanded correspondingly. Each country, moreover, had an assembly (or diet) of sorts usually representing churchmen, nobility and middle-classes; but in most cases these bodies were merely decorative, if indeed they came together at all. Except in the little republics where the wealthy burghers dominated, the ruling class comprised the aristocracy and the great landed proprietors.

EUROPE'S POLITICAL MAP

In the autumn of 1648, the Peace of Westphalia put an end to warfare that had tormented central Europe for thirty years. An obscure Silesian poet voiced sentiments that welled up in many a weary heart:

> Full thirty years and more we've known,
> Bloodshed and plague and riot;
> What bliss if now there should ensue
> Thirty rich years of quiet.

To a remarkable extent, after the arrangements of Westphalia, the boundaries of states in the west of Europe paralleled those existing at the mid-twentieth century. The Dutch Republic and Switzerland, for instance, and even France occupied nearly the same areas as today. French prestige, it is true, stood much higher and France commanded extensive colonial possessions.

The Spanish state, on the other hand, was quite different, for in addition to Spain proper, the kingdom included the southern Netherlands (Belgium) and large holdings in Italy—Sardinia, the Duchy of Milan, Naples and Sicily; Spain also owned, as has been noted, far-flung dominions overseas. Portugal, which in 1640 had permanently broken away from Spain, had lost most of its once vast Oriental empire, but it still exercised lordship over Brazil. Together with Wales, England constituted a separate kingdom; political bonds with Scotland were intimate and England held sovereignty over Ireland. Just before the mid-century, the island realm was immersed in civil war, but it was on the verge of becoming a leading factor in the affairs of Europe.

Off to the north lay the little, though relatively populous, kingdom of Denmark to which Norway was attached. Danish predominance in this region declined in proportion as the prestige of its rival, Sweden, increased. Respected for military prowess and allied to France, Sweden had risen rapidly in international stature; the Westphalian peace had converted the Baltic Sea into a Swedish lake, as the phrase ran, with Finland, an appendage of Sweden for centuries, as the eastern outpost of the kingdom.

At 1648 the political situation in "Germany" diverged widely from that of the mid-twentieth century. Nominally, most of central Europe was ruled by the Holy Roman Emperor of the German Nation; in point of fact, however, public authority rested in some three hundred and fifty sovereignties, many of them ludicrously small. Tradition decreed that the head of the Austrian branch of the Hapsburgs should be elected to the dignity of emperor; but his real power derived from his hereditary possessions, not from the Empire. The Hapsburg realm embraced the kingdoms of Bohemia and Hungary as well as the German-inhabited duchies of Austria itself—an array of diverse lands and peoples subject to a common sov-

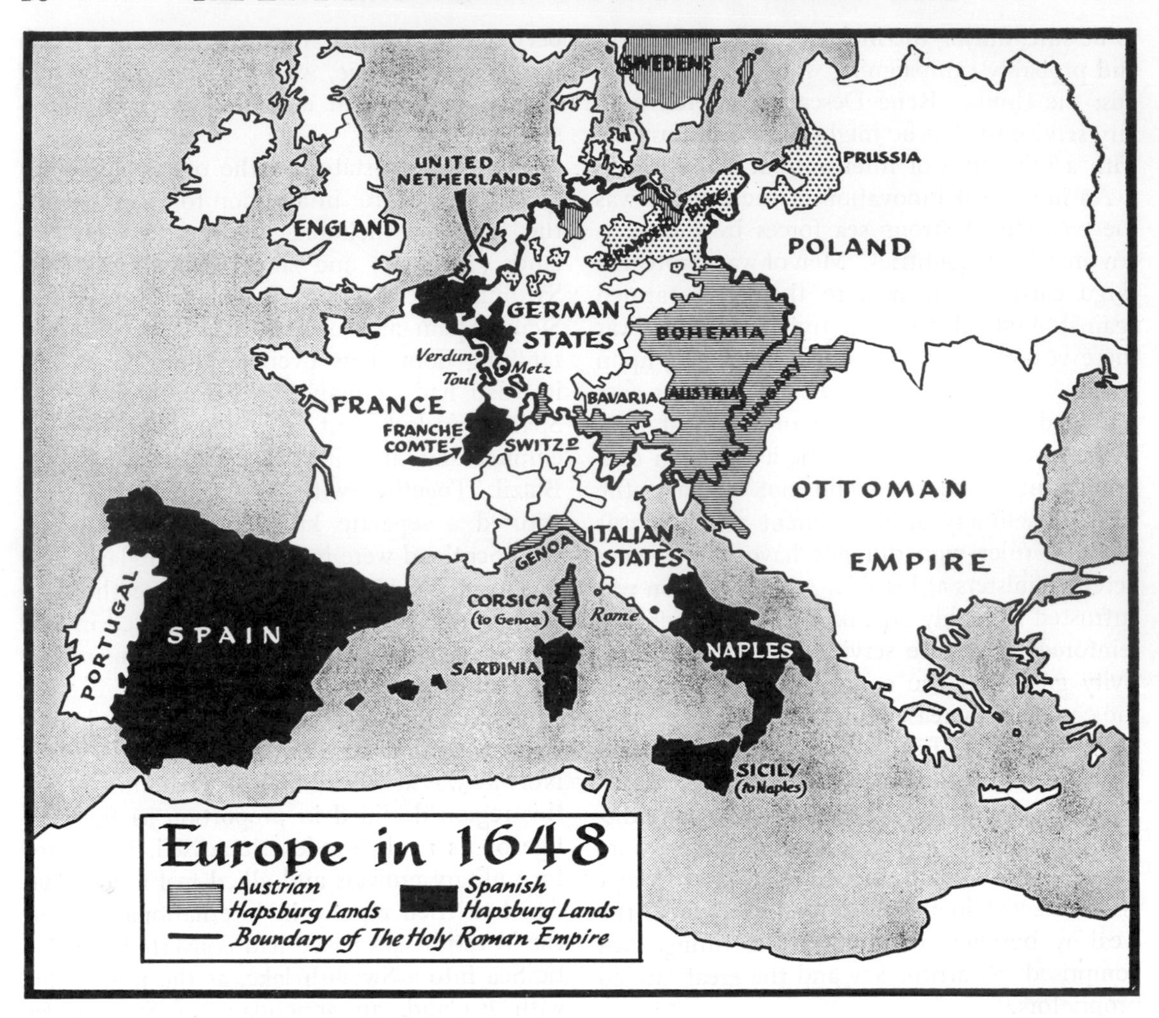

ereign. This state barred the road to the progress of the Turk into central Europe and fought with might and main to restrain the expansionist instincts of France. As the emperor headed the Catholic princes of "Germany," so the ambitious electors of Hohenzollern Brandenburg gained recognition as spokesmen of the Protestant forces.

Like Germany, Italy was simply a geographical expression, which would not achieve nationhood until the third quarter of the nineteenth century. Straight through the center of the peninsula, from sea to sea, lay the papal States of the Church. The mercantile republics of Venice and Genoa, though they had fallen from their former eminence as business centers, still retained their places on the map and Venice owned trading stations in Dalmatia (Zara, Ragusa, Cattaro) and on the island of Crete. Virtually all the rest of Italy was subordinate to Spain.

Three large states held sway in the east of Europe: Poland, Russia and the Ottoman Empire, the last two alien to the traditions and manners of the West. Whereas the greatness of Russia lay in the future, the most glorious and exciting chapters in the history of the Pole and the Turk had already been written. Poland —or more exactly the dual kingdom of Poland-Lithuania—surpassed any other European country in area. It was bounded on the west by the Holy Roman Empire, on the south by the Ottoman dominions, on the east, seventy-five to a hundred and seventy-five miles beyond the Dnieper River, by Russia, and on the north by the Baltic Sea and provinces of Sweden.

Dominantly Roman Catholic in faith and thus Western in cultural orientation, Poland contained large bodies of religious and political minorities. Most disturbing of these at the moment were the Cossacks of the Ukraine who in 1648, rebelled against Polish administration, overran sections of the kingdom and soon afterward transferred their allegiance to the tsar of Russia. The easy successes of Cossack insurgents advertised the fact that Polish military strength was ebbing. And there were other symptoms of Poland's mortal illness; the strong-willed nobility reduced the national assembly close to anarchy and insisted on the maintenance of the principle of elective kingship. Foreign powers, Sweden, France and Austria, interfered in Polish politics, seeking thus to further their own selfish purposes and ambitions.

An even greater potential menace to the integrity of Poland was tsarist Russia, as yet scarcely European at all, untouched by the intellectual and scientific currents of the age. Commercial and technological influences from the West were growing, it is true, and at the middle of the seventeenth century a section of Moscow was set aside for the residence of Western merchants and artisans. Yet essentially Russia was an Oriental country with customs and institutions peculiar to itself. "What needs hast thou, O miserable Rus," inquired a religious spokesman scornfully, "of Latin customs and German fashions?"

Boasting an impressive army and considerable seapower, Ottoman Turkey was a standing threat to Christendom in 1648, as it had been for two centuries. Ruled by Moslems and composed of diverse national groups, this empire ranged across three continents. The hard core of the state was Asia Minor up to the line of Persia; it included the Arabian Peninsula and extended across northern Africa almost to the western limit of Algeria. In Europe the authority of the sultan covered the Balkan Peninsula, and half of Hungary, while vassals ruled most of the rim of the Black Sea.

Taken all in all, the Ottoman Empire was a formidable state, though signs of degeneracy were not lacking. Slender diplomatic and commercial ties linked Turkey to France, and warfare with Venice to determine the mastery of the eastern Mediterranean (symbolized by the island of Crete) was recurrent.

Such in broad outline was the European political map in the day of Peter Stuyvesant. To the west, the map closely resembled that of our own time, but the picture in the center and in the east of Europe was radically different.

By 1648 European international relations had taken on characteristics that persisted into the twentieth century. Management of foreign affairs was the prerogative of the sovereign guided by ministers and influenced by the wishes or whims of the ruling class, whether the aristocracy or the mercantile interests of Venice or Holland. Exchange of diplomatic representatives to handle political and commercial transactions had become a fairly well established institution; these agents were extremely sensitive, jealous of the prestige of their princes, quick to take offense at a slight or any transgression of the amusingly elaborate etiquette. Diplomatists earned a reputation for dark secrecy, dissimulation, recourse to bribery and, on occasion, they were not above stirring up dissension in the country to which they were accredited. If not yet quite a definite profession, diplomacy was moving toward that dignity. The arrangement of the Peace of Westphalia by negotiations between diplomatists set a precedent for concluding wars that future centuries followed.

The principle of the balance of power had by now emerged as the master doctrine of European statecraft. For political stability, that is, and the security of the nations, no one state or combination of states should be permitted to become so strong as to imperil the freedom and independence of the rest. This concept, which underlay treaties of alliance and directed diplomacy in its intricate and devious course, might be described in language later used by the poet Alexander Pope:

> Now Europe balanc'd, neither side prevails:
> For nothing's left in either of the scales.

Before the mid-seventeenth century, an occasional thinker had set himself to puzzling out ways of combatting the barbarities of war and curbing international anarchy. Best known and most respected of them was the learned and versatile Dutch jurist, Hugo Grotius. For his writings he is often referred to as the "father of international law." And several plans to unite Christian Europe in some kind of a federation to maintain peace were prepared. The most interesting of these projects was probably drafted by the Duke of Sully, first minister of the French king Henry IV, and known by the latter's name. Sully proposed that the boundaries of states should be permanently fixed along lines that he sketched and that each country should have full freedom in choice of religion and in form of government. A general assembly, or senate, representing the Christian states, and in session at all times, would be charged with adjusting international quarrels and organizing the defenses of Christendom against a possible Moslem attack. An international armed force would be created and placed under the control of the assembly. This blueprint attracted only limited support in European official circles, for it was interpreted as a shrewd stratagem to make France the arbiter of Europe. Certain of the ideas of Sully, however, reappeared in later projects for an international league to further peace and progress.

Neither the teachings of Grotius nor the plans of Sully and others made much of a dent upon the thinking of their age and generation. Yet it is of interest, and not without significance, that more than three hundred years ago, a few intelligent and far-sighted men were brooding on ways and means of conquering the ogre of war.

Inside a French peasant cottage, late Seventeenth Century

ECONOMIC AND SOCIAL FABRIC

At the mid-seventeenth century an overwhelming majority of Europeans depended upon the soil for their livelihood. Peasants and serfs resided in thousands of compact villages, not in separate farmsteads, and rarely ventured far from the place in which they were born. Due to fundamental conditions of climate and soil and to local traditions, products varied a good deal; cereals and a few vegetables were the standard crops. Much of the land was covered with moors, marshes, and forests, and customarily plowing fields lay fallow one year out of three. As a rule, farming was of the subsistence type intended to satisfy the food and clothing needs of a household. Tools and methods of cultivation were primitive with oxen as the principal draught animals. Farming involved a maximum of human labor with women and children toiling beside the men. As cultivators and dairymen, as in so many other activities, the Dutch ranked at the top and their superior techniques were copied, bit by bit, in England and in neighboring areas on the Continent.

In England, Holland, Northern Europe, most of France, western Germany and northern Italy the rustics were largely freemen. But elsewhere they were serfs obligated to work three days a week or more for the benefit of the landlord. Serfs were subject in body, if not indeed in soul, to their lords and masters. A wide social abyss separated the West and eastern Europe, where serfs were callously exploited, treated as cattle, bought and sold; serfdom as a legal institution of Russia was formally defined in a codification of laws completed in 1649 and destined to survive for nearly two centuries.

Naturally there were variations in rural levels of living, but ignorance, cruelty, and degradation of women prevailed universally. Food ordinarily consisted largely of black rye bread, likely to be heavy and indigestible; when crops failed a sort of bread was baked out of acorns and roots. Oatmeal porridge, soup, cheese, peas

A public letter-writer and other street types, early Eighteenth Century

and lentils were common foods. Wheat bread and even meat were eaten by English peasants, but these foods were rarities on the Continent. Fish supplemented the meager diet of peasants living near rivers or seas and of others during Lent and on religious holidays.

Clothes on the Continent were made of linen and rough canvas—occasionally, of wool—and wooden shoes were the rule. Rude cottages were built of wood and clay, smoky and with the bare earth serving as the floor. Professional medical care was seldom available to the rural masses; concoctions of herbs or superstitious rites were relied upon to cure sickness and disease while artless mid-wives eased the pains of child-birth. Perhaps one child out of three died before reaching his first year. Famine and plague periodically ravaged the countryside and devastation by warring armies was an ever-present peril. Simple living, frugality, hard work during the farming months, enslavement to stupid superstitions, obedience to authority, resignation to the prevailing social order characterized the way of life of the unlettered and underfed country millions.

Nothing more valid than learned guesses, alas, are available on the population of Europe at the mid-seventeenth century. England and Wales contained about 4,500,000 inhabitants, Scotland and Ireland approximately a million apiece—altogether, fewer than reside in London today. France may have had as many as 17,000,000 people, Spain around 7,000,000, Italy 13,000,000, the "German empire" about the same as France, Poland about 11,000,000 and Russia somewhat less than that. It is a safe assumption that the whole of Europe was home for not more than 90,000,000, and very nearly nine out of ten of them could be classified as rural.

A striking difference between the mid-seventeenth century and the mid-twentieth was the relative scarcity of cities. In all of Europe not a dozen communities boasted a population in excess of 100,000. London was approaching half a million, but no other English city was greater than 30,000. Paris, long since acclaimed as "the eighth wonder of the world," was slightly smaller than the English capital; an enthusiastic traveler pictured Paris as a city "exceeding great, being no less than ten miles in circuit, very populous, and full of very goodly buildings, whereof the greatest part are of fair white freestone."[3] Holland had several substantial cities of which busy and opulent Amsterdam, "the Venice of the north," had about 300,000 inhabitants. Venice itself, now past its prime, was still saluted as "the queen of the Christian world."

No city of central Europe approached the 100,000 mark; once flourishing communities such as Augsburg and Nuremberg suffered severely during the Thirty Years' War, while Frankfurt-am-Main and Hamburg gained in stature. As yet Berlin was only a large village and Vienna was hardly more than a frontier capital. Russia's Moscow was merely an untidy conglomeration of wooden shops, dwellings and churches sprawled out in the vicinity of the walled Kremlin. Under Turkish rule, the ancient metropolis of Constantinople had declined so greatly that it was probably no larger than Amsterdam.

Cities and large towns differed very much from their twentieth-century descendants. Streets were narrow, indifferently paved, if paved at all, and a gutter to remove rain and debris ran down the center; the lighting of streets with torches or lanterns was an innovation of the late seventeenth century. In city as in country, police protection left much to be desired. Comparatively few law-breakers were apprehended, but inhumane punishments were inflicted upon criminals who were caught. Recourse to torture to obtain confessions was still in vogue; prisons were earthly hells and convicted culprits were often broken on the wheel.

Many city buildings and houses were constructed of wood, easily ravaged by fire. Dutch burghers, however, favored houses of brick and stone, high and narrow with steep gables; normally these buildings served as offices and warehouses as well as homes. Dwellings of the prosperous were illuminated with candles, pictures decorated the walls, and the furniture was

[3] Quoted in W. F. Reddaway, *A History of Europe from 1610 to 1715* (London, 1948), p. 18.

turned out by expert craftsmen. The diet of the well-to-do townsman was more diversified than in the countryside. Alcoholic beverages were consumed almost from cradle to grave; tea and coffee were just becoming known.

Public welfare institutions—schools, hospitals, almshouses and asylums—appear to have been more generously supplied in Dutch cities than in others. Sanitary facilities in cities were so primitive that water-borne diseases, such as cholera and typhoid fever, and smallpox frequently decimated the inhabitants. Someone called Paris "the dirty theater of all nations," while a poet wrote of the French metropolis,

> How strange it is, I need not tell it,
> For all the world may easily smell it,
> As they pass up and down.

Urban communities relied primarily upon the country districts for food and industrial raw materials and for newcomers to enlarge population.

Cities and towns lived, of course, on trade, industry and finance. The Dutch paced the field in these activities with imitative Englishmen and Frenchmen close on their heels. As yet, weights, measures and coins had not been standardized, even within a country; in consequence, the progress of business was hampered. The economic theory of the time, spoken of as mercantilism—and finding an echo in the economic nationalism of the twentieth century—taught that it was the duty of government to regulate and promote industry and commerce. In that way, it was reasoned, the state would be strengthened for purposes of power politics, for war and expansion. Fallaciously it was imagined that gold and silver represented the real wealth of a nation. From that it followed that a state must strive to enlarge its stores of precious metals, dominate routes of commerce and compel colonies to produce commodities required by the mother country.

Cloth, grain, timber, liquid and food specialties and colonial productions comprised the principal cargoes of commerce. Woolens were the major manufactured goods of England, while in France linens and silk fabrics for noble

Woman weighing gold, by Jan Vermeer

A French tinsmith's shop, Eighteenth Century

and plutocrat held top place. Imitative Europeans copied Oriental wares such as Chinese porcelain and calicoes of India. A large part of English industry was of the household variety, an entire family participating, but dependent primarily on farming for its livelihood.

On the Continent, in contrast, the medieval guild institution flourished; a skilled craftsman, plying his vocation, knew the thrills of individual creativity. The farther east one journeyed, the cruder grew the tools and the methods of the artisan (as of the agriculturist), with Russia the most backward of all. Some large manufacturing plants were operating in Lille, France, and northern Italy.

As in the medieval period, trade and industry labored under heavy transportation handicaps. Roads were so poor and rutted, muddy much of the year and dusty the remainder, that horses could seldom move at more than a walking gait. Upkeep of roads was a local responsibility—or irresponsibility. The splendid highways bequeathed by imperial Rome had long since become worn and neglected, while east of the Vistula in Poland there were only tracks, not roads at all. As with roads so with bridges; some fine old Roman bridges continued to carry traffic but newer bridges were often only planks laid on beams supported by wooden piles. The standard vehicles were coaches drawn by four to six horses, low four-wheeled wagons or carts hauled by oxen. Travelers needed two days to make a journey from Paris to Orléans, while freight transport required twice as long; wares frequently spoiled on long journeys.

In addition to these limitations, nobles exacted tolls on roads and governments on the European mainland levied fees on commodities entering towns or crossing provincial boundaries. Quite frequently brigands plundered wagons, making travel dangerous—and exciting. Nevertheless, about 1650, rudimentary public postal services began to be operated. Couriers on horseback riding the clock around and frequently changing their mounts averaged 120 miles a day. That novelty speeded up the circulation of business information and fostered the growth of newspapers, just then making their appearance.

Water-borne commerce had greater importance than land transport. France, endowed with excellent rivers, was especially favored. The Netherlands had a unique network of canals; a horse drawing a boat could pull as much as fifty horses hitched to carts. Packets sailing the oceans were small, two hundred tons or so, and often they were delayed for days by adverse winds.

Unprincipled men added to the perils of seafaring; sailors of one country greedily raided and robbed ships sailing under another flag, so that merchant vessels ordinarily were armed and they were often accompanied by a naval convoy. On the Mediterranean the danger of piracy was so great that insurance premiums customarily equaled forty per cent of the value of the goods a ship carried. Ability to fight as well as commercial astuteness were prerequisites for success in seaborne trade.

The growing accumulation of capital undergirded economic activities of a non-agricultural character. Thrifty merchants plunged savings into joint stock companies, financed manufacturing or invested in overseas enterprises. The medieval aversion to taking interest on loans had fallen into oblivion; the great Bank of Amsterdam, the leading financial institution of Europe, granted loans for as little as four per cent interest. Some rich capitalists purchased land and carried on commercial farming. In styles of living, prosperous businessmen vied with the nobility and marriages between members of these two social classes were not uncommon. Yet the almost Hindu view of society, with sharply defined classes, which had long prevailed in Europe was still in the ascendant.

The nobility rarely engaged in business, much preferring the profession of arms, or the church, and diplomacy or administration—though these last responsibilities were more often entrusted to middle-class men. The wealthier aristocrats in the West resided in spacious palaces or manor houses and, as a mark of conspicuous consumption, dressed in silk garments. An enormous wig, heavily cuffed and embroidered coat, ruffled breeches and high-heeled shoes distinguished the wearer as a man of substance and leisure.

At sumptuous banquets in high vaulted dining halls adorned with armor, family portraits and tapestry, aristocratic hands were plunged into food—forks were only just coming into vogue. In lieu of a bath, then an event rather than a habit, nobles sprayed themselves generously with perfume; the use of soap and water for personal cleanliness was a peculiarity of sober bourgeois households. Dancing, hunting game and dueling were popular pastimes of bluebloods.

WISDOM OF THE AGE

Except in Holland and Scotland where schooling was furnished to a large proportion of children, formal education in the era of Peter Stuyvesant was largely restricted to the wealthy and the aristocracy. Children of those classes were taught by private tutors or attended academies, noted for their severe discipline, which frequently invited rioting by the pupils. Commonly horizons were broadened after school days by travel to other countries and perhaps a stay at a royal court. Schools and colleges operated by Jesuit fathers enjoyed the best reputation.

In Protestant circles, Johann A. Comenius, a genial Czech who lived in several countries, was interested in raising Protestant schooling to the Jesuit level. It was his faith that universal education would promote the cause of domestic and international peace as nothing else could do. He prepared the first picture-book for the instruction of children, urged that the strict discipline of his time in the school room should be relaxed and that subject matter should be broadened; even science, he argued, deserved to be taught. The educational treatises of Comenius were translated into several languages and his ideas, too revolutionary to be accepted at the time, eventually found considerable application.

Countries to the west of Russia were well supplied with universities, though student enrollment at any of them seldom exceeded four hundred. Professors were more interested, it would seem, in molding the character of students than in the advancement of learning.

The Library of the University of Leyden, Holland, in the Seventeenth Century

Curricula heavily emphasized literary, classical and theological studies with an eye to training clergymen and teachers in particular. In the Netherlands, intellectual freedom extended to the lecture hall as well as to publication and that was a boon to learning, notably in the famous University of Leyden.

University lectures were presented in Latin and Latin was also the language of learned literature and diplomatic intercourse. Yet Latin was on the decline due to the competition of the vernacular tongues in which great poetry and prose were being created in all the countries of Western Europe. Authors of distinction were in inverse proportion to the small reading public—the exact reverse of the relationship in the twentieth century. Language frontiers in Europe, incidentally, have shifted very little since the mid-seventeenth century.

If the pursuit of pure science had not quite become respectable by the mid-seventeenth century, the notion was winning acceptance certainly that by humbling itself the human mind could conquer unknown worlds. Physics, chemistry, astronomy and, above all, mathematics engaged the energies of inquisitive, original intellects. One of the foremost scientists of all time, Christian Huygens, anticipated the spirit of the future when he wrote, "The world is my country, science my religion." By inventing the pendulum clock (1656), this Dutchman sharply lowered the cost of clocks, putting them within reach of the many.

René Descartes

New aids to mathematical knowledge, such as logarithms and analytical geometry, were devised. With its emphasis on precision, mathematics exerted a pervasive influence upon mature learning and thought in general. That point was well illustrated in the case of Descartes, a singularly versatile spirit, best known as a philosopher, but also honored as "the father of modern mathematics"—the man who mated algebra and geometry to create analytical geometry. At the same time, the microscope, a new instrument of research, together with the skeptical, intelligent studies of Dutch and English medical scientists began to liberate the treatment of sickness and disease from grim superstitions that had enchained it for hundreds of years.

The aura of the Italian Renaissance still hovered over the domain of the fine arts. During the lifetime of Peter Stuyvesant, the Spanish and Dutch schools of painting, the former best represented by the pictures of Velasquez, attained the high-point of their excellence. Rembrandt, Frans Hals and Ruysdael, to mention only the outstanding Dutch artists, painted permanently popular canvases. Architecture, like art, reflected Renaissance tastes, though it was somewhat more dignified and clear-cut in design, as shown in the new churches, public buildings, chateaux and homes of the burghers of the period. It is probably fair to say that music was as yet in its infancy, but opera, emerging in Italy, hinted at the majestic progress that was soon to come.

After the tumultuous "wars of religion," which had harassed Europe since the onset of the Reformation, Christian creeds were settling down to the unexciting, but salutary maxim of "live and let live." During the fighting each protagonist believed the best of itself and thought its opponent was cursed with a double dose of original sin—the enemy of God and the enemy of the human race. Arguably, the agonizing strife had been won neither by Catholic nor by Protestant, but by a third element which held that truth was uncertain, that the pursuit of truth invited ruinous conflict and that it was prudent, therefore, to concentrate on the achievement of order and peace. On the practical side, the peacemakers of Westphalia had resolved the religious dissension in central Europe with their formula that each prince might himself choose the religion of his subjects.

That minority of Europeans which concerned itself actively with the riddle of the universe accepted one or another version of the Christian interpretation of life—except, of course, for Jews and Moslems. Despite the fundamental doctrines that they shared, each Christian communion was rigid, authoritarian, dogmatic about its special emphases and interpretations. From Ireland to the Urals, religion formed almost the exclusive intellectual and moral influence for the masses of mankind; in their everyday affairs, men had—as they had long had—a lively sense of the presence of God and the devil.

Old folk fantasies and weird superstitions were deep-rooted in the Western mentality. Consider, for instance, the belief in witchcraft; though the craze had passed its peak, it had by no means been vanquished. Even reputable intellectuals uncritically accepted charges that wretched old hags worked their black arts as accomplices of the devil and deserved, therefore, to be punished. So late as 1634 a Frenchman was roasted to death on the charge that he had afflicted a group of nuns with demoniac possession. The occult in the form of magic and astrology haunted the mind of the age: comets were superstitiously interpreted as divine warnings of impending calamity. An eminent lawyer of Leipzig compiled exhaustive tables based on the Bible, demonstrating that God actually used heavenly bodies to instruct the devout on the shape of things to come. To question the efficacy of prayer to bring down rain would have caused all but the most sophisticated to turn pale with terror. Alchemy had lost its universal appeal, it is true, yet practitioners of that pseudo-science glibly promised to produce gold by a secret, miraculous process and they attracted plenty of gullible clients. Quite by accident, some alchemists, honestly seeking the truth, discovered some basic facts of chemistry.

Rembrandt van Rijn

By the middle of the seventeenth century, the distribution of Catholics and Protestants in Western Europe had been stabilized on lines that persisted. Catholicism was displaying fresh vitality, especially in France where new monasteries and charitable foundations were flourishing. Monastic orders, above all members of the militant and powerful Society of Jesus, by their labors as schoolmasters and confessors, contributed uniquely to the revival of the drooping spirit of the mother church. Zealous missionaries, moreover, working in the colonies of the Catholic powers, brought natives into the fold to compensate for the Protestant secessions. As apostles to pagans, Jesuits carried the Cross around the globe—to the colonies in America, to Africa, and to China where a quarter-million converts were reported.

Little needs to be said in a general way about Protestantism. By the mid-seventeenth century, the initial energy of that epochal movement had been dissipated. Competitive sectarians argued endlessly and aridly about their theological peculiarities. As a reaction to the coldness and sterility of German Protestantism, pietistic, mystical sects appeared which professed a simple religion of the heart; quite similar was the Quaker group in England, dating from 1647. It was at just this point that the pioneer Protestant missionary society was organized in England—the Society for the Propagation of the Gospel in New England. Now and then partisans of Christian Reunion brought forth unification schemes, conferences were assembled and areas of agreement explored, without, however, making any progress toward reknitting "the blessed company of all faithful people."

In the east of Europe, the Orthodox Eastern Church—the faith of Russia and the Balkans—languished in blissful somnolence. But in 1652 Russian churchmen were passionately aroused when the patriarch of the day introduced minor liturgical and literary innovations; dissenting "Old Believers" (*Raskolniki*) seceded from the official church and formed a sect that endured in spite of fierce persecutions.

Though few in numbers when compared with Christians, Jews dwelt in scattered communities from England to Constantinople, but mostly in Germany and Poland. In these latter countries as in the Italian Peninsula, destructive waves of anti-Jewish fanaticism time and again imperiled lives and property of ghetto-dwellers. Alleged messiahs recurrently appeared among the Jews promising to liberate their coreligionists from affliction, and projects for the return to the ancient homeland of Palestine repeatedly cropped up.

So long as the Christian Church frowned upon moneylending as sinful and reproached the merchant as only slightly better than a bandit, businessmen, Jews and others, operated under a cloud. But by the mid-seventeenth century, attitudes had radically changed and in the course of the century Jews in many sections of Germany were granted greater freedom and unprecedented security. Much favored were "Court Jews," thrifty, energetic, adventuresome men, who served as army contractors or advisers and financiers of princes. By reason of their strategic position at court they were able to intercede on behalf of fellow Jews.

Progressive and tolerant Holland offered sanctuary to oppressed Jews, who, in turn, contributed richly to the material and intellectual prosperity of their adopted country; a few Jews drifted off to the Americas, settling, for example, in the New Amsterdam of Peter Stuyvesant and even in Pernambuco.

The Netherlands also welcomed creative thinkers who dared to be unfashionable, notably the Frenchman René Descartes and his influential disciple, Benedict Spinoza. Individual yet impersonal in their speculations, rationalistic, secular and naively confident in the capacity of the human mind, these subtle intellectuals introduced new mental attitudes into Europe. They raised and then answered in untraditional ways the traditional problems of philosophy. The welfare of philosophy, it seemed to them, depended on complete independence from theology. For them wisdom began, not with faith, but in experience. They disputed, for instance, the idea of a transcendant God sitting in judgment on mortal men. It seemed to them, too, that the universe, far from being regulated by supernatural authority, was a mechanism responding to unchanging laws.

In a *Discourse on the Method of Rightly Conducting the Reason and Seeking Truth in the Sciences* (1637), Descartes laid the ground plan of modern philosophical naturalism. He adopted as his watchword, "Never to accept anything for true which I do not clearly know to be such." Spinoza, on his part, aspired, "Not to laugh at men or weep over them or hate them but to understand them." Together, these two intellectuals exerted an unparalleled impact upon thinking on the upper levels about the principles that guide and the springs that inspire personal and social action. Generation after generation of philosophers and the philosophically minded have turned to their writings for solutions of religious, moral and individual problems. Yet impeccably orthodox critics flayed Descartes and Spinoza as destructive of all that was valid and worthy in thought, and Spinoza was harried out of his Jewish community. Nevertheless, they carved for themselves a permanent niche in the gallery of ideas.

CONCLUSION

This or something like this was the picture of the age as it might have appeared to crotchety Peter Stuyvesant brooding in an inn on the lower end of Manhattan Island. As would be true for just short of three centuries to come, the throbbing heart of civilized society was the western half of Europe. The fascinating and endless process of transplanting European ways and institutions—political, economic and religious—to other continents and peoples had fairly commenced.

On many counts, as this compressed sketch has sought to suggest, the world of 1648 in its varied aspects diverged from the contemporary scene of three centuries later. Immense transformations occurred in the interval as this book seeks to clarify and explain.

At 1648 Europe stood on the edge of far-reaching changes in the whole conception of the state, in science and manners, in religious points of view. Intellectual and aesthetic sensibilities were entering upon a new age. Explosive ideas of reason and the conquest of material nature would presently challenge time-hallowed traditions.

What actually impended has been authoritatively explained by the Regius Professor of History at Cambridge University. "Somewhere about the middle of the seventeenth century," he writes, "European life was so completely transformed in many of its aspects that we commonly think of this as one of the great watersheds of modern history, comparable with the Renaissance or the Reformation or the French Revolution." [4]

[4] G. N. Clark, *The Seventeenth Century* (2nd ed., Oxford, 1947), p. ix.

FOR FURTHER STUDY

George N. Clark, *The Seventeenth Century* (2nd ed., Oxford, 1947) PAPERBACK

David Ogg, *Europe in the Seventeenth Century* (new ed., London, 1954) PAPERBACK

John N. L. Baker, *A History of Geographical Discovery and Exploration* (rev. ed., New York, 1937)

Leslie Stephen, *Hobbes* (new ed., London, 1928)

Georges Renard and Weulersse, G., *Life and Labour in Europe, XV to XVIII Century* (Eng. trans., New York, 1926)

William F. Reddaway, *A History of Europe from 1610 to 1715* (London, 1948)

Violet Barbour, *Capitalism in Amsterdam in the Seventeenth Century* (Baltimore, 1950)

Herbert Butterfield, *The Origins of Modern Science, 1300–1800* (New York, 1951)

Wilhelm von Bode, *Great Masters of Dutch and Flemish Painting* (Eng. trans., New York, 1911)

Sydney H. Mellone, *The Dawn of Modern Thought* (London, 1930)

CHAPTER II

THE SUPREMACY OF FRANCE (1648-1715)

THE AGE OF LOUIS XIV

TWICE within the range of modern times the history of not only Europe but of the world has revolved around the history of France. In the first instance, King Louis XIV ruled; the second occasion was the era of the French Revolution and Napoleon at the end of the eighteenth century. So overshadowed was each epoch by a single personality that it has become fashionable to apply his name to the period.

And yet in a precise sense "the Age of Louis XIV" is something of a misnomer. Chance designated this man to preside over a large and richly endowed kingdom of hard-working, intelligent and gifted people whose energies and talents made possible the achievements of the reign. France placed at the disposal of the king the finest military establishment of Europe, an array of trained administrators, diplomatists and commanders, and a solid foundation of resourceful business men, thrifty peasants and ingenious craftsmen. The monarch himself, to be sure, imprinted a personal stamp upon his country and time.

The Sun King: Emblem of Louis XIV

In a kingdom, which had been grievously wracked by the warfare of preceding generations, Louis XIV promoted a fresh and vigorous conception of national solidarity. France appeared to be a land of order and decorum when compared to turbulent England—where King Charles I had perished on the scaffold, where Cromwell after a republican experiment was officially branded a usurping traitor, where James II fled abroad to die in exile and Christian creeds contended with one another.

The reign of Louis XIV admirably illustrates the nature of hereditary authoritarian government, its strengths and its frailties. By the standards set in the French monarchy at this

Louis XIV

time other absolutist regimes deserve to be measured—and have indeed habitually been measured. Not since the disintegration of the realm of Charlemagne, whose successor Louis XIV fancied himself, had the French kingdom attained such distinction or invited such imitation. It is not too much to say that Western Europe was "bourbonized" by France. Neighboring countries aped French administrative procedures, mimicked the gayety and immorality of the royal court (or tried to do so), copied French economic policies, envied French architectural and cultural achievements, and intrigued and fought to escape domination by France.

Frenchmen at later epochs in the national history, moreover, drew inspiration from the pre-eminence which France enjoyed while Louis XIV was king and from the powers of resilience the nation then displayed. The age of Louis XIV, whatever its discomforts and hardships for those who lived through it, was certainly not lacking in dramatic excitement.

QUALITIES OF THE KING

In any variety of authoritarianism the traits, the convictions and habits of mind of the supreme executive have large, if not decisive, significance. Louis XIV, who ascended the throne in 1643, assumed personal management of public affairs in 1661, and continued to rule until his death in 1715. He belonged to the breed of outstanding monarchical despots. And it was with him, during more than half a century of French ascendancy, that every European concerned with public matters, whether as statesman or official, had to reckon as the ultimate maker of policy.

Called a "God-given child" because he was the first offspring of his parents' twenty-three years of marriage, Louis XIV exhibited more than ordinary human traits. Contemporaries were impressed by his proud, dignified bearing and his personal charm which persisted to the end. He was so exquisitely polite that he would not pass even a chambermaid without raising his hat. Time, as is its way, impaired his physical attractiveness; his face was pitted with the marks of smallpox, his teeth dropped out and dyspepsia plagued him, the penalty for excessive indulgence at the table. "I have often seen the king," the memoirist Saint Simon tells us, "eat four large plates of different soups, an entire pheasant, a partridge, a large plate of salad, two large slices of ham, some mutton with gravy and garlic, a plate of pastry and then some fruit and hardboiled eggs."

Not obliged to win friends to retain power, Louis XIV never unbent or deliberately tried to make himself popular. And he lacked the saving grace of humor. Along with diligent application to duty, which kept him toiling away at state affairs as few monarchs have worked, the Grand Monarch developed a strong sense of piety as he grew older. Uncommonly fond of the ladies and surrounded by a succession of colorful butterflies in his younger days, he turned puritan at middle age, finding relaxation only with the shapely Madame de Maintenon, whom he secretly married.

The first marriage of Louis XIV to a Spanish princess, a union dictated by political calculations, yielded little happiness. Toward his immediate family the king was frequently cold to the point of inhumanity. The death of his only brother and of his only son, for example, evoked no more emotion within him than the departure of a discarded mistress or minister. On the other hand, he showered honors on two illegitimate sons and rejoiced over the birth of grandsons and great grandsons. As long as physical vigor permitted, he sought diversion in dancing, gaming and hunting.

Although he never benefited from a broadening "liberal" education, Louis XIV learned from experts the essentials of administration, the manners of diplomacy and military strategy. Gaining confidence with experience he personally chose leading public servants, bourgeoisie preferred, and instructed generals and diplomatists on how to manage their affairs. In selecting top counsellors he showed, at least in the first half of the reign, remarkably shrewd judgment. He readily accepted advice from advisers, provided they did not exhibit too much independence. Novelties and unorthodoxies annoyed a monarch who prided himself on being the "Sun King."

From first to last, Louis XIV was bent on advancing the fortunes of France, to gain for his country (and its king) unexampled splendor and moral respect. "In working for the State," he wrote, "a king is working for himself. The good of the one is the glory of the other." The price that had to be paid was almost perpetual warfare (or its equivalent) and the impoverishment of the masses over whom he ruled.

KING AND GOD

The personal views of Louis XIV on the right and proper form of government harmonized with the deeply-rooted theory that kings ruled by divine right—a philosophy symbolized by the religious ceremonial at the time of coronation. None other than God had summoned the king to his exalted office and responsibilities; and to God, not in any sense to his subjects, was the anointed monarch responsible for his stewardship. In reaching decisions, in issuing decrees and in choosing war or peace, the king merely acted as the instrument of a Higher Power.

"Holding as it were the place of God," Louis XIV declared, "we seem to participate in His knowledge." Or again, "God has set me up that I may serve as an exemplar to others, not that I may follow their example." Reinforcing the faith of their master, leading French churchmen extolled the supernatural authority of the crown. In the language of Bishop Jacques Bossuet, an eloquent apologist of kingly authoritarianism, "the royal throne is not the throne of a man, but the throne of God himself. Princes act as ministers of God, and as His lieutenants on earth." As Bossuet read the Old Testament, divinely appointed sovereigns had exercised unlimited authority in ancient Israel and comparable power must therefore be accorded to the monarch of any state resting upon Christian foundations.

To dispute or resist the authority of the crown was sheer blasphemy. Scriptures and church teaching alike enjoined citizens to undivided loyalty and obedience. The prevalent ideology taught that if misfortune befell the nation because of royal decisions, God would in due course punish the ruler; either that, or God had simply used the king as His tool to punish subjects for their shortcomings. For wickedness on the part of the monarch, one remedy alone was available to the governed: petitions to God imploring Him to show the king the error of his way. As a French saying runs, "*On peut tout faire pour regner*"—"everything is permitted to one who rules."

Small wonder then that Louis XIV freely identified himself with the state and believed that the king could do no wrong. Divine sanction authorized arbitrary violation of pledges or ruthless treatment of dissent. On taking over the actual direction of public affairs at the age of twenty-two, the king announced that "hitherto I have been content to let my affairs be managed for me. In the future I shall be my own prime minister."

Extensive travels over the realm must have acquainted the Grand Monarch with the miserable plight of multitudes of his subjects, yet he remained callously apathetic to their welfare. He distrusted the upper nobility and feared the inhabitants of Paris, for skeptical spirits had already cast doubts upon the validity of the hallowed God-King doctrine. Even murmurings of republicanism cropped up now and again.

THE VERSAILLES FOLLY

Partly to escape popular pressures in Paris, partly to display the splendor and opulence of his person and country, Louis XIV caused a modest hunting lodge at Versailles, a dozen miles from the capital, to be transformed into a magnificent palace. This establishment served as the royal residence until the French Revolution. The tourist of today sees Versailles much as it was when the great king here breathed his last at the age of seventy-seven.

No expense in brain or brawn or gold was spared in raising this magnificent monument of royal absolutism. Thousands of workmen and horses toiled year after year on the buildings and grounds, under the careful gaze of the king himself; the unhealthy environment exacted a heavy toll in artisans and laborers. Architects, artists and landscape gardeners in an epoch of singular brilliance expended their finest talents upon the Versailles folly.

When completed the royal apartments could accommodate ten thousand guests while a staff of some fifteen thousand servants was required to keep the estate in order. Twenty-two servants looked after the infant granddaughter of the king alone. Pavilions, halls and apartments were richly decorated with choice Gobelin tapestries, marble sculptures, bronzes and paintings, many of them celebrating notable events in the career of the Grand Monarch. World-renowned is the *Galerie des Glaces* (the Hall of Mirrors) through whose large, arched windows peered from time to time the ornamental aristocracy of Bourbon France, the German conquerors of France in 1871 as they proclaimed the king of Prussia emperor of Germany, and Allied statesmen of 1919 as they placed their signatures on the treaty of peace with defeated Germany.

Roundabout the imposing palace were huge stables, kennels housing nearly a thousand hunting dogs, coach houses, menageries and a famous hall of orange trees. Gardens of unmatched symmetry, covering a broad acreage and dotted with ponds and fountains, sculptures and noble terraces furnished an exquisite setting for lavish entertainments and cere-

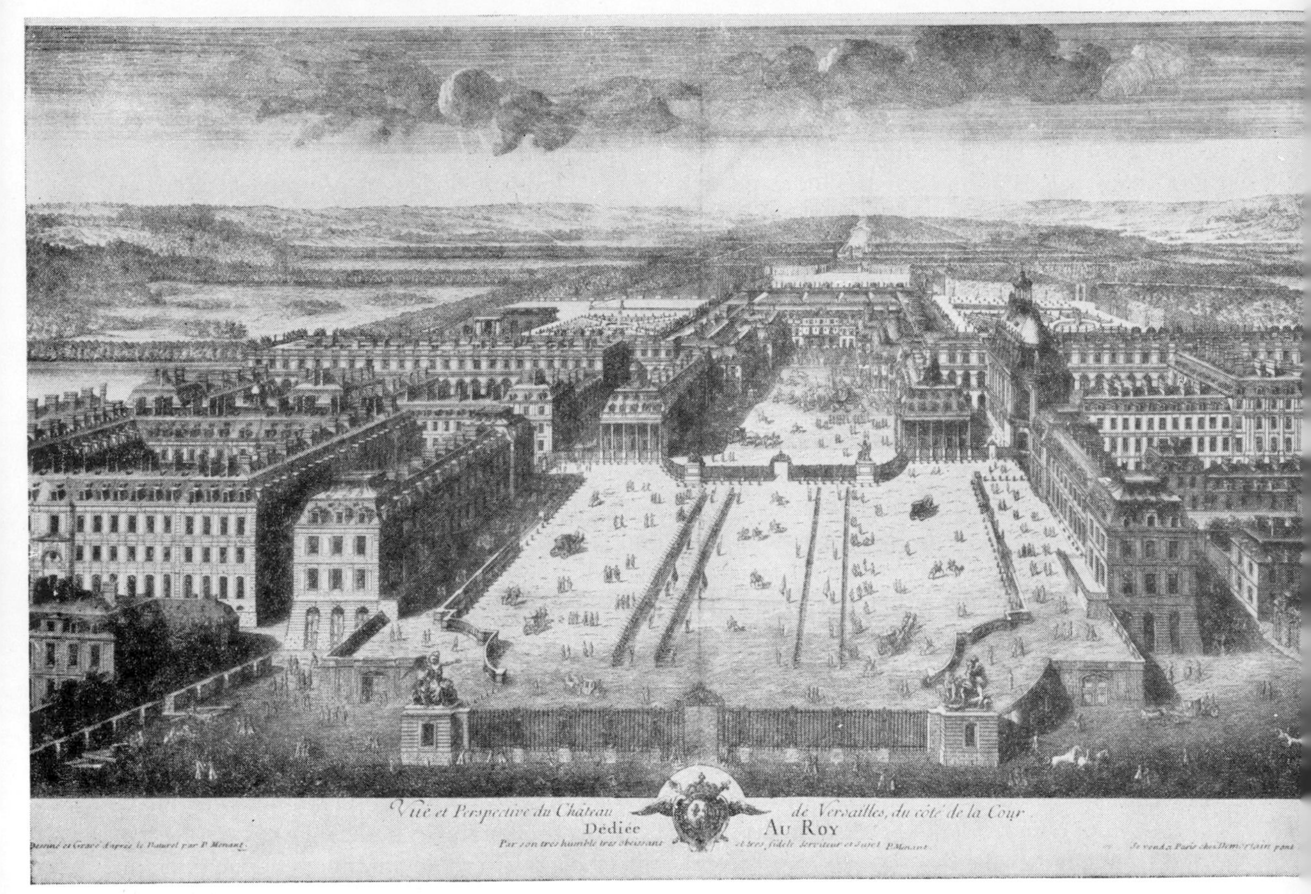

Perspective view of the Palace of Versailles

monies. To furnish water to palace and park an aqueduct from a nearby river was started but was soon abandoned in favor of a pumping system from the Seine and an intricate tracery of reservoirs on the estate itself; a highway was constructed to Paris. On the edge of the royal acres, a town arose for retainers and servants. And, as a retreat for Madame de Maintenon, a sumptuous villa was built within walking distance of the palace.

Thither in 1682 Louis XIV transferred the official headquarters, aloof from the workaday world of Paris. There business of state was transacted, and there gorgeous balls and fêtes were staged, milling crowds of aristocrats dancing attendance on their lord and master. On occasion, parties were enlivened by theatrical performances; at gaming tables men lost and won fortunes and in adjacent bed-chambers women bartered their persons amid luxurious glamor. For all its grandeur Versailles left a good deal to be desired. Food, for instance, fetched from remote kitchens turned cold before it could be eaten, while in the winter months wine in glasses froze into solid blocks. Candles in lavish profusion furnished such illumination as was available in the palace.

Even as trees from across the kingdom were uprooted and planted in the royal gardens, so the leading French aristocrats, who might cause trouble if left without surveillance, were compelled to congregate at Versailles. To the élite of the courtiers was reserved the privilege of participating in the punctilious ritual which attended Louis XIV as he retired for the night or arose for the day. Aristocrats were expected,

Bedchamber of the Sun King

required indeed, to hold aloof from serious occupations, the fighting services excepted.[1] Economic parasites, without political responsibilities, the court nobility sought to divert themselves in aimless frolics and prodigally wasted their substance in riotous living. Nevertheless, they set standards of behavior for the admiration and imitation of the nobility in the rest of Europe. In spite of appearances, Louis XIV succeeded only imperfectly in integrating the aristocrats in his regime of disciplined order; they retained their wealth and a spark of independence which one day would flare up anew.

All in all the Versailles establishment had few equals in history and no superiors. Rulers of German states, of Austria and of England hastened to emulate the Bourbon extravagance and palace frivolities in the same way that they aped the French language and court etiquette. In the 1830's the government of the day converted Versailles into a national museum of "all the glories of France." But long since Louis XIV's folly had contributed its full share to the bankruptcy of the House of Bourbon. A learned French historian has concluded that Versailles had more ruinous consequences "than any of Louis XIV's wars or all of his wars combined . . ."

[1] A few nobles engaged in maritime commerce without, however, achieving much success.

BOURBON GOVERNMENT

From the past Louis XIV inherited a bureaucratic machine to execute the laws and keep the kingdom operating. Departments of government were entrusted to a series of councils, of which the most influential was the *Conseil d'Etat* (Council of State). Composed at most of five members, this body resembled a ministry and met frequently, the king presiding, to deliberate on large questions of public policy, more particularly on diplomatic and military issues. The final word on moot points was spoken by the monarch.

On many counts the most important single royal officer, at least in domestic affairs, was the Controller-General, who had jurisdiction over raising and disbursement of revenue. A strong personality in this post was only a little less powerful than the king himself; and frequently he interfered in other branches of government. Part of the income of the state accrued from royal properties scattered indiscriminately about the kingdom. And from subjects, or more exactly from the nonprivileged elements, the government obtained funds in the form of direct and indirect taxes, which were numerous, inequitably levied and increased as the reign of

Louis XIV moved along; popular protestations over high taxes caused, however, no serious consternation at Versailles. Gaping deficits in the state budget were closed by borrowing from financiers at exorbitant rates of interest.

Attached to each department of government was a staff of civil servants, large or small as the volume of business or tradition required. For the more responsible positions the king decidedly preferred middle-class men, crowding their way upward, though not above lining their own pockets as occasion offered. Churchmen and aristocrats were deliberately excluded from the bureaucracy; not that they were too smart, but rather that Louis XIV distrusted them politically or doubted their competence.

From the "vile bourgeoisie," as one noble diarist complained, were also recruited the principal agents of the king in the provinces of France, the intendants, thirty-four in all. These indefatigable and faithful watchdogs of the crown were appointed by and responsible directly to the monarch. It was their assignment to keep a sharp eye on the condition of agriculture and industry in their districts, to see that transportation facilities were kept in trim and that royal revenues kept flowing, as prescribed in the capital. Aside from these economic responsibilities, intendants supervised police officers in village and town and kept tabs on local nobles who might foment trouble. Very busy-bodies indeed, these agents, instruments of administrative centralization, contributed significantly to the consolidation of royal authoritarianism.

Of other institutions of French government little need be said. In Paris and many provinces gatherings of lawyers, called *parlements,* handled certain kinds of legal disputes. The Parisian body possessed the right to register royal edicts, but, if it balked, a writ from the crown normally overrode it; *parlements* might also draft "humble remonstrances" against abuses, without, however, much prospect of having grievances remedied. For the time being, Louis XIV virtually eliminated the *parlements* as a political force. On paper, the Estates-General, a national assembly representing all ranks of French society, still existed. But in fact this body was never summoned, though at a desperate point in the War of the Spanish Succession, presently to be discussed, when the fortunes of France were at a low ebb the Court at Versailles considered calling the Estates together. Equally, provincial assemblies had little beyond decorative importance, puppets of the local intendants.

From top to bottom, the French despot and his bureaucracy operated the machinery of state. They determined taxation and religious policies, ordained laws and economic measures, charted the course of diplomacy, decided whether the nation should engage in war and when the moment had arrived to seek peace with enemy powers. Having said that, it must also be remarked that more than once government decisions were successfully resisted. Unorganized opposition blocked, for instance, the establishment of universal direct taxation, a royal drive for complete religious uniformity failed in its realization and certain of the economic innovations associated with the name of Colbert were partly nullified. Monarchical totalitarianism, in short, like other varieties of totalitarianism, proved to be less than total in practice, whatever the theory.

SERVANTS OF THE "GRAND MONARQUE"

Of all the ministers of Louis XIV two attained exceptional distinction and eminence: Cardinal Jules Mazarin and Jean Baptiste Colbert. An Italian by birth, cunning, ruthless and avaricious, Mazarin graduated from the diplomatic corps of the Pope into the service of France, headed then by another clever and crafty churchman, Cardinal Richelieu. After the death of Richelieu, Mazarin, his heir and executor, carried forward foreign policies aiming at the humiliation of Austria and of Spain. Leading counsellor of the mother of Louis XIV during the latter's childhood, Mazarin performed also as the trusted and fatherly mentor of the teen-age king, who learned his lessons well.

In the middle of his French career, Mazarin

was challenged by uprisings spoken of as the Fronde. This agitation enlisted the support of the *parlement* of Paris, of unruly elements in the capital and, in its closing phase, of disgruntled aristocrats—the last open revolt of this class against the crown. The demands of the original Frondeurs of 1648 included downward revision of taxes, abolition of the intendants and the right of prompt jury trial. Loyalist troops crushed the insurgents, who had, however, the satisfaction of forcing Mazarin to flee temporarily to Germany.

That revolutionary episode burned itself deeply into the memory of the young king and largely accounts for the everlasting apprehension he had of the upper nobility and of his Parisian subjects. As for Mazarin, he moved from strength to strength, exploited his exalted office for personal profit and at his death turned over a powerful and respected state to Louis XIV.

Colbert, who succeeded Mazarin as chief officer of the crown, was a man of very different mold. The Cardinal, a son of sunny Naples, was courteous, conciliatory, communicative; Colbert, who hailed from the north, was austere, aloof, decisive, routineering, nicknamed "the north wind." Mazarin was schooled in diplomacy, but Colbert's training lay in law and finance. The Cardinal shone most brilliantly in the manipulation of foreign affairs while Colbert concentrated primarily on domestic matters. Both men could be unscrupulous and mendacious if that seemed likely to promote the interests of king or country, to which both were devoted.

Of bourgeois stock, Colbert climbed the bureaucratic ladder rung by rung, under the benevolent patronage of Mazarin, reaching in 1665 the post of Controller-General. He owed his elevation to demonstrated abilities and to advantageous family connections. Louis XIV recognized his capacity and allowed him remarkably wide latitude in implementing an impressive list of projects.

Colbert's chosen sphere was the national economy; his genius lay in planning fiscal reforms and the promotion of business. But he attempted to accomplish too much too quickly. Hard-working and conscientious, he managed bureaus that are presided over by nine ministers in the more complex France of the twentieth century. He drove his corps of subordinates as though they were a four-in-hand. Colbert imagined that all Frenchmen should reflect his own private virtues: love of detail, frugality, industry and orderliness. But Frenchmen in the mass were not fond of these puritan qualities and never had been.

French official thinking on economics may be summed up in the words "paternalism" and "mercantilism." That creed taught that the wealth of a nation consisted in hard money. Export trade should, therefore, be encouraged by means of subsidies and the manufacture of quality products at attractive prices. To prevent the draining away of bullion, foreign-made goods should be kept out of the country as much as possible by tariffs and allied devices. According to the mercantilists, colonies resembled cows, which should be milked for the benefit of the mother country, the suppliers of rawstuffs and the consumers of manufactured wares; homeland and overseas possessions should together comprise a self-sufficient economy. For the transportation of goods, a merchant marine was necessary and to safeguard commerce and empire a strong fleet was indispensable.

Ideas of this order kept racing through the fertile brain of Colbert. If only France emulated the maritime states of England and the Netherlands, in which merchants and manufacturers were respected and business prospered, France might be able to draw ahead of these rivals. What riches, what honor would then accrue to the monarchy! The power of the state, not the welfare of its inhabitants, was the supreme concern of Colbert. He never understood, nor did his contemporaries, that the object of economic activity should be to enable the ordinary fellow to enjoy a better living with less effort.

At certain stages in his career Colbert concentrated on overhauling state finance, whose administration was extremely deficient. Grafting officials, evasion of taxes and extortion of the poor were only the more flagrant abuses.

Colbert managed to root out certain evils in the collection of taxes and recommended more equitable assessment of taxes. Public revenues increased in response to rising business and commercial activity. By insisting upon order in keeping records, compelling more honesty in fiscal officials, raising indirect taxes and scaling down the public debt, Colbert contrived to stabilize national finance temporarily and even balanced the budget. That condition of affairs was seldom duplicated thereafter in France, or any other major nation for the matter of that. Imposition of heavier taxes made the name of Colbert a byword and a reproach. Unhappily, the extravagant demands of the Versailles court and the lavish outlays for the fighting services emptied the national cupboard almost as rapidly as the expedients devised by Colbert filled it—sometimes even faster.

This practical-minded statesman devoted special care to the encouragement of manufacturing, under stringent regulation by the authoritarian state. Infant industries were nourished with royal subsidies and shielded from foreign competition by protective tariffs. Government bureaus prescribed in minute detail the sizes, quality and designs of manufactures. A formidable swarm of inspectors watched over business enterprises, circulating through mill and workshop to enforce standards, and bringing violators of the rigid codes to book. But plans to establish uniformity in weights and measures throughout the kingdom fell far short of the goal.

In time, excessive interference by government agents discouraged initiative, stifled enterprise and chilled the spirit of adventure. Against regulation of business within reasonable limits there could be no complaint, but the French administration overstepped the bounds of common sense and impeded economic progress.

Foreign artisans were welcomed in France and foreign manufacturing methods were brought in from as far away as Persia. The famous royal Gobelin tapestry mills prospered in a manner without precedent. To supply industry with rawstuffs the raising of hemp, flax and silkworms was fostered, and mining and lumbering too responded to the restless zeal of Colbert. French industrial leadership was not effectively challenged by Great Britain until about 1800; and in luxury goods of silk, lace, linens, tapestry and porcelains, the pre-eminence of France has prevailed to the present time.

Except for materials required by industry, agriculture received scant attention from the French government. But military needs encouraged the breeding of better horses, and means of inland communication, roads and waterways were improved. The *Canal du Midi*, which was opened to traffic in 1681, moved barges across France between the Mediterranean and the Atlantic; it was a major success and inspired the construction of other canals. The city of Paris was "modernized," so to speak, more adequate police protection was provided, streets were improved and lighted at night.

Commercial and imperial expansion lay close to the heart of Colbert. French shipbuilders benefited by grants from the royal exchequer and mercantile tonnage grew rapidly. Vessels of war were turned out in such quantity that in 1677 the French fleet drew abreast of the English or the Dutch navies; Toulon, Calais and Dunkirk, the last ceded by England, were developed as naval stations. Sailors were recruited in the many coastal communities, taken from jails or snatched up on city streets. Colbert is often called the father of the French navy, doubtless his most enduring accomplishment. France now possessed the resources to contest mastery of the seas with the English and the Dutch and even perhaps to outstrip them in the fight for overseas markets. It was a source of pride to Colbert that ships sailing the Mediterranean were obliged to salute the Bourbon flag.

Beyond the range of Europe, the energetic minister keenly desired to build up trade, especially by means of chartered commercial companies and the exploitation of colonial areas. A company for the West Indies, for example, and another for the East Indies were awarded monopolies in their respective regions; neither, however, produced much of value for France. In North America the French flag had been hoisted by hardy explorers, fur traders and

A visit of Louis XIV (at left) to the Gobelin tapestry mills, as memorialized in a contemporary tapestry

Jesuit missionaries over Canada, the Great Lakes region and the gigantic storehouse of concealed wealth in the valley of the Mississippi and her tributaries. The great heart of North America, that is, was French. The vast and undefined Louisiana territory, claimed for the French crown by René de La Salle in 1682 and named for Louis XIV, witnessed to the magnificent potentialities of new France. The Senegal coast of Africa yielded slaves, and French trading posts had been erected in distant India. But uniformly the development of colonies was retarded by the scantiness of the French population and by the strait-jacket regime imposed by the authoritarian government and the church of France.

The Grand Monarch and his military chiefs never warmed up to overseas enterprise. They were army men, unsympathetic to expenditure of funds to open up colonies and valuing foreign commerce only as it reinforced capacity for war; and prospects of large returns from America or the Indies seemed remote and dim indeed. The negative posture of the court blasted the dreams of French world expansionists.

Colbert served his king better than his country and died a spent volcano, wealthy, but despised by Frenchmen whose backs were bent beneath tax burdens.

CULTURAL GLORIES

For all the diligence Colbert displayed in building up the material fabric of the kingdom, he nonetheless took time to promote the higher living—literature, the fine arts and science. His splendid private library was enriched by books and manuscripts from all over Europe. Put in charge of the ministry of arts, he generously patronized culture, fostered the organization of half a dozen learned or artistic academies and bestowed gifts and pensions upon master craftsmen, native or foreign.

It would be wrong, however, to place too much emphasis on the patronage of Colbert and Louis XIV in bringing fresh luster to France in the realm of the intellect and spirit. A lush flowering of national genius displayed itself, to be sure, but it was not at all sudden. Richest, most varied and most versatile in literature, the mind of France set its stamp upon foreign countries and gave to the French language a distinction and prestige never lost. French writers in later periods and authors in other nations willingly paid tribute to the literary greatness of the age. Yet an atmosphere of authority pervaded the republic of letters, as the economy, and the fighting services. It was obligatory for writers who desired royal gold to sing royal praises, to eulogize and advertise the glories of Louis XIV, real and imagined.

Never has freedom of expression been a hallmark of authoritarianism. Before a book could appear in France, the publisher was obliged to secure approval by an official censor; ideas that deviated from conventional norms seldom appeared in print or if they did they were likely to be suppressed with alacrity. In literature, furthermore, as in other departments of culture, the royal academies, conservative and orthodox, frowned upon originality in the interpretation of human concerns.

It is neither possible nor indeed desirable to recall all the excellent French men of letters in the age of Louis XIV. History is long and life is short. Judged by time, the sternest and least emotional of critics, the contributions in drama were outstanding, and Jean Baptiste Molière, the foremost playwright, ranks with the greatest figures of world literature.

The father of Molière intended that he should follow the family tradition of upholsterer to the king, but the lure of the theater proved irresistible. With a company of actors, he traveled about France for years playing anywhere an audience could be assembled, and picking up miscellaneous snippets about human nature, which he later wove into comic farces. Many of his human types and incidents, Molière appropriated from the "improvised comedy" of Italy; that is, stock characters of contemporary society, amusing dialogue and mimicking of local peculiarities of costume and custom. In 1658 he ceased being a vagabond and became the favorite at the royal court. His

Jean Baptiste Poquelin, called "Molière"—a youthful portrait by an unknown painter

Louis XIV watches a performance of Molière's Le Malade Imaginaire*—the year, 1676; the place, the gardens of Versailles.*

troupe of players and the comedies they performed amused the Sun King and his entourage.

There is a preachy tone in much that Molière wrote. He ridiculed the vain, the hypocritical and the pompous in bourgeois professional circles and the nobility in the hope of encouraging more natural behavior. *Le Malade Imaginaire,* for instance, pokes fun in a distinctly urbane manner at current eccentricities and antiquated methods favored by physicians. Since the plays of Molière portray the manners and foibles of French social classes, except the peasants, they have retained a popularity approaching the dramas of Shakespeare.

Inferior to Molière yet much prized and read are Corneille and Racine. The former, a key figure in the evolution of the French theater, was at his best in describing the traits of strong, stoical men and in analyzing motives and passions. Called the most French of authors, Racine earned renown through tragedies stressing the primitive emotions, especially the passion of love, which animate mankind; his most admired characters are women. Convinced that human nature was inherently evil, he delighted in portraying the triumph of wrong over right, vice over virtue. *Athalie,* a richly poetic play of unusual distinction and inspired by biblical tales, is acclaimed as Racine's masterpiece. As a sideline, so to speak, he served as the official historian of court and crown. Rare intuitive qualities, witty dialogue and melodious language characterize the productions of Racine. Invited to evaluate Racine as a literary artist, Voltaire replied: "There is no commentary needed in this case. All that I could do would be to write at the bottom of each page: beautiful, harmonious, admirable, pathetic, sublime."

Among French prose writers, Blaise Pascal and Pierre Bayle have exerted a large and lasting influence upon Western letters and thought. Pascal, a precocious and many-sided genius, inventor and scientist as well as a distinguished thinker and author, embraced the pessimistic religious heresy of Jansenism, explained below. Passionately devoted to the search for truth and a master in the use of irony, Pascal composed fierce polemics against the Jesuits. These attacks took the form of letters, written under a pseudonym, and addressed to a friend in the countryside. *Lettres provinciales*, flawless in style, attained immediate popularity and intensified general distrust of the Jesuits. "Let us endeavor to think well," Pascal implored, "this is the principle of morality." In this masterpiece and in *Pensées (Thoughts)*, the author disclosed his personal religious experiences and opinions.

Questions which Pascal raised and tried to answer have permanent interest for students of religion, and the secular tone of his writing makes him readily intelligible even today. His belief in the necessity of Christianity, for example, and in the existence of God reveal fresh insights. His approach is decidedly constructive; wisdom, humanity, cutting satire and sharp logic emerge on every page. The frontal assaults of Pascal on the Jesuits, while often unfair and caricatured, have furnished arguments for anticlericals ever since.

The writings of Bayle were even more challenging to Christian orthodoxy. Born in a Huguenot parsonage, Bayle ended up a deist, though vilified by enemies as an incorrigible atheist. His faith in reason and his satirical treatment of theological and moral questions profoundly influenced French skeptics of the eighteenth century. Freedom in matters of conscience was the sole theme that warmed his frigid spirit. For flaying intolerance and condemning popular religious customs, Bayle was eventually driven out of France.

Jacques Bénigne Bossuet, Bishop of Meaux

Bayle amply revealed his skeptical outlook and his vast erudition in a *Historical and Critical Dictionary* (1697). Therein he undertook to reconstruct the past in the form of sketchy biographies, wholly free of theological presuppositions. Partly in the nature of a polemic against the political and religious policies of Louis XIV, the *Critical Dictionary* proved to be a serviceable weapon in the warfare of reason against tradition, of "enlightenment" against obscurantism and persecution. It served as a model and inspiration for Voltaire and other French rationalists of the next century.

On the opposite side of the fence, Bishop Bossuet upheld with learning and pugnacity the cause of Catholic conventionalism. Specialist in rhetorical eulogies of royalty and aristocracy, he dogmatically defended the status quo, lauded the divine-right creed and the Sun King, yet was not afraid of upbraiding his royal master for moral lapses. The leader of the French Church in the prime of his life, Bossuet engaged in fervent controversies with heretics and staunch partisans of the Papacy alike.

Drawing upon extensive reading, Bossuet composed for the enlightenment of the heir to the throne a wide-ranging *Discourse on Universal History*. He was not one to confuse historical scholarship with the dreary accumulation of detail. Very different from Bayle, he argued that history merely portrayed the operation of divine purpose in the affairs of earth. The fortunes of a nation, that is to say, were directly proportional to its observance of the Christian pieties. Prosperity was the certain reward of virtue while Divine Providence would unerringly punish wrongdoing. Bossuet grasped the essential idea of the unity of all history, though he passed over the Orient, of which he was ignorant. His theological interpretation of the human pageant, a recurrent theme in Christian literature, long held the field and still commands devoted adherents.

In François La Rochefoucauld, French letters had a coiner of moral *Maxims* par excellence. Embittered by events and disillusioned by contacts with his aristocratic class, this soldier turned cynic summed up in polished epigrams the wickedness and selfishness of the society in which he moved. Someone has said that his epigrams contained never a word too many or too few and their popularity has endured. In a kindred vein Jean de la Fontaine, an author of warm and generous instincts, was noted for fables in poetic form. Animals were invested with the virtues and defects of human beings; the role of the lion was reserved appropriately for Louis XIV. For a time La Fontaine was the toast of the royal court and his productions have been read with delight by succeeding generations who shun Aesop's tales as childish and sugary.

It was an epoch, finally, prolific in entertaining and informing letter and memoir writers of whom Madame de Sévigné and the Duc de Saint Simon were most distinguished. An assiduous correspondent, Sévigné painted a vivid picture of aristocratic living, though, true to her class and century, she neglected the rural masses. Saint Simon circulated in court society, storing away in his capacious memory or on notepaper what he saw, heard and thought. Inasmuch as most of his voluminous memoirs were actually written long after the events described, questions are raised concerning their accuracy and balance. Sévigné and Saint Simon mixed frothy anecdotalism and solid interpretative comment with fascinating pen portraits of celebrities. Taken together, a whole age, perhaps, a whole civilization, is reproduced colorfully and not without realism.

It is easy to understand why cultivated Europeans were bedazzled by the vigor, the variety and charm of phrase of French literature. But in art and music France borrowed from other peoples; styles responded to the tastes and whims of king or courtiers. French artists drifted to Rome to learn their lessons, returning home to raise national standards modestly. The leading painter, Charles Le Brun, was brought into prominence by Colbert. Attracting the favorable notice of the king, he was assigned chief responsibility for decorating the Versailles palace. Though a skilful designer, the paintings of Le Brun are scarcely more than mediocre. Colors appear as superficial additions and paint was applied insensitively.

Portraitists endeavored to reproduce on canvas the uneasy mood of influential court celebrities. Although the France of Louis XIV had many musicians, there was only one composer of outstanding merit, Jean Baptiste Lulli. Born in Florence, Lulli popularized opera, hitherto an unimportant art form in France, writing over twenty works for the diversion of the court and the upper class. Friendly with Molière, Lulli composed music for several of his plays, and into dance music he introduced lively rhythms which crowded the stately formalisms of tradition aside.

RELIGIOUS RIGORS

France was, of course, overwhelmingly a nation of Roman Catholics, the "eldest daughter of the Church." And one of the oldest traditions of the French state was intimacy with the Church, the linkage of crown and altar. Louis XIV felt personally responsible for the welfare of the souls of all his subjects and, as became an authoritarian, he strove to subject French Catholicism to the state as fully as possible and to impose religious uniformity upon the whole population. Pursuit of those objectives brought on acrimonious disputes with the Vatican, controversy with the Catholic sect of Jansenists and heartless repression of Protestant Huguenots.

Friction between king and Pope has a long history in France. Secular authorities and most churchmen in the age of Louis XIV were intent upon safeguarding the independent heritage of the French Church. When Louis XIV reasserted the royal right to appoint bishops and lesser clerics and laid claim to the revenues of vacant bishoprics, quarreling between the state and the Papacy came into the open. Under the guidance of Bishop Bossuet (and on the urgings of the king) the French bishops in 1682 prepared a formal statement on the relations of the French Church to the Vatican—a "Declaration of the Liberties of the Gallican Church." It proclaimed the autonomy of French Catholicism in administrative matters, endorsed the royal pretension on selection of bishops and flatly asserted that a general council of the church took precedence over the Pope in ecclesiastical questions.

The Vatican tartly repudiated this declaration of independence, but only a minority of French churchmen sided with Rome. Foreign observers were stunned that the Vicar of Christ should so much as defy the Sun King. "It was so to speak," remarked an Italian diplomatist, "like resisting heaven itself." Eventually the dispute was adjusted in a compromise that substantially approved the royal claims; and the concept of an autonomous French Church persisted.

A sharp division of mind, in the meantime, had arisen in Catholic circles over the teachings of Bishop Cornelius Jansen. He argued for a vital and deeply personal spiritual experience and insisted that everlasting life was reserved to a small number of chosen Christians; other individuals, regardless of their merits, would be condemned to destruction. His followers demanded more simplicity in religious devotions, practiced austere ethical ideals and contended for a minimum of papal authority over the French Church. For their aversion to compromise, their stern moral standards and gloomy theological emphases, Jansenists were tagged the Calvinists of Catholicism, a designation which they firmly rejected.

Certain French clergymen, even some bishops, sympathized with the Jansenist heresy. Many laymen, too, were attracted to the cause and for them Blaise Pascal was the most influential spokesman. No friend of innovations, Louis XIV, who was embittered by Jansenist criticism of his private conduct and persuaded that the movement contained anti-monarchical inclinations, endeavored to stamp out the sect. Aligned with him were Jesuit fathers, who preferred a less rigorous morality than the Jansenists and who held that salvation would not be restricted to a selected few; rather each individual could himself freely determine his ultimate destiny. Jesuits had stressed these views in theological warfare with Protestantism, and they argued that if standards of human behavior were set too high, believers would be alienated. That position laid the Jesuits open to charges of moral laxity, which Pascal, for example, exploited with eloquent satire.

Beyond that, the Jesuits were allies of the Vatican, ardent exponents of a strictly international interpretation of Catholicism. Without difficulty they secured papal condemnation of the schismatic Jansenists. Repressive measures were ordained but persecution advertised the heresy which, instead of fading away, prospered. For over a century strife between Jesuit and Jansenist disturbed French Catholicism and as late as 1905 a papal directive roundly denounced Jansenist tenets.

Quite different was the fate of another Christian minority, the Huguenots, who followed the Calvinist version of Protestantism. Tolerated under a royal decree published at Nantes in 1598, the Huguenots freely worshiped in prescribed districts, maintained schools and courts of their own and were eligible to hold public offices. As a group they were noted for piety, industry and thrift. At the beginning of the reign of Louis XIV, the Protestants exceeded a million, some of them wealthy, some of them prominent in the armed forces of the kingdom. Being a conspicuous minority, Huguenots were disliked and suspected by the majority, as is the way with men. Their material prosperity, moreover, excited jealousy, and devout Catholics, the king for one, detested the sect as heretical. Beyond that, it was reported that the Huguenots constituted a "Fifth Column" for Protestant England and the Netherlands and as such menaced the security of France.

Any country has the right, of course, to protect itself against espionage or traitorous behavior, but of these crimes the Huguenots were guiltless. Suspicions, alas, turned surmises into actualities. In French circles which counted it was felt that the country would be safer if the Protestant million was eliminated. The lofty principle that neither government nor any other institution should coerce the private conscience had no standing in the time of Louis XIV.

From the mid-1660's onward, Huguenots were kept under close supervision and were victims of all manner of discrimination. Taxes were unfairly levied upon them, marriage with Catholics was forbidden, schools, courts and churches were closed, and, worst of all, beastly soldiers were billeted in Huguenot households with instructions to make themselves as obnoxious as possible. On the other hand, a Huguenot who professed conversion to Catholicism escaped tax disabilities and billeting. Much the larger part of the Huguenots had actually entered the Catholic communion before Louis XIV yielded to the temptation to silence Protestant convictions forever. In 1685 the Edict of Nantes was arbitrarily canceled. By that gesture His Most Christian Majesty intended to demonstrate his faith by his works, perhaps to make amends for youthful shortcomings and for recent bickerings with the Pope and to achieve more perfect religious solidarity in the nation.

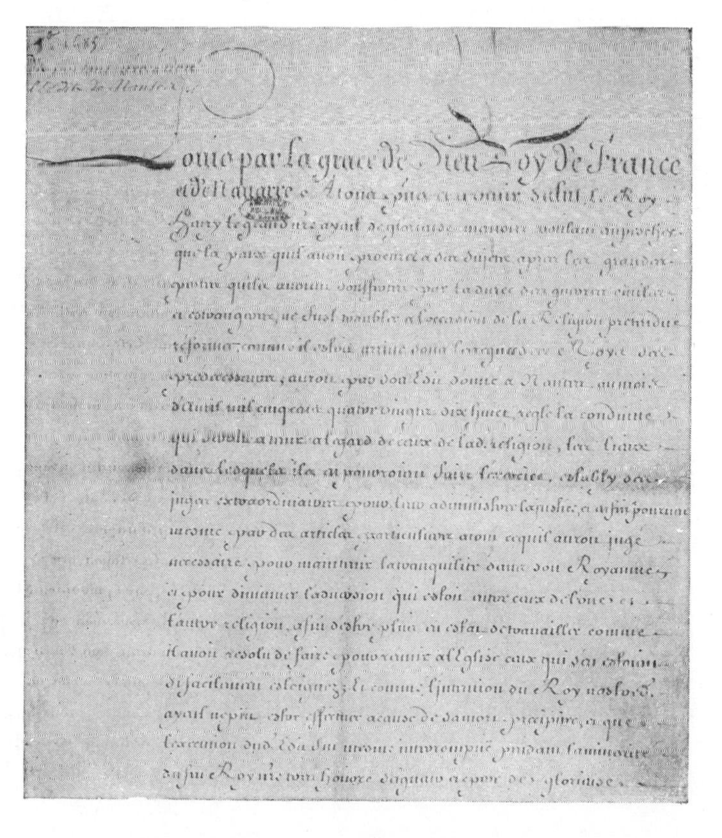
Louis par la grace de Dieu Roy de France

In 1685, the Edict of Nantes was revoked by the document shown at the right.

Protestants could no longer carry on worship, their churches would be thrown down and their clergy had either to go into exile or join the navy. Children born to Protestants were considered illegitimate and might not inherit property. Although the Pope spoke out against forced conversion of the Huguenots as contrary to the dictates of Christianity, Catholic France generally applauded the royal initiative. Declared Bishop Bossuet to the king: "It is a work worthy of your reign . . . Through you heresy is no more," and added, "God alone has performed this miracle."

Although it was unlawful to flee abroad, upwards of 200,000 Huguenots nonetheless sought sanctuary in England, in Holland, in German states and in English America; over thirty Huguenot churches were built in London alone. That exodus robbed France of excellent economic and military talent and strengthened by so much the resources of the countries in which the refugees took root.[2] Besides, wherever persecuted Huguenots wandered they roused hatred of His Most Christian Majesty and of Catholicism. Yet, in spite of all, Protestantism was not thoroughly uprooted in France. Worship was conducted in secret, and in the twentieth century a million Protestants lived in France, one of their number, Gaston Doumergue, being chosen a president of the Third Republic.

It is evident, in retrospect, that intolerance toward Jansenism and the Huguenots damaged the Bourbon monarchy and French Catholicism alike. The spectacle of the crown hounding citizens for religious convictions caused sensitive French spirits to writhe and rebel. In the next century Christian enemies of the dynasty joined forces with anticlericals in undermining the status quo.

AN ERA OF VIOLENCE

During the reign of Louis XIV, France was involved in four major and convulsive wars, the last of which brought the country to the edge of ruin. It was in truth an era of violence, yet neither the first nor the last.

Western Europe had not known peace for any prolonged period since the emergence of assertive national states in the fifteenth century. Courts and aristocracy, at any rate, relished fighting which seemed natural, glorious and exciting. Warfare appeared indeed to be the normal order of society, ordained by the Great Architect of the universe Himself.

At the close of the Thirty Years' War in 1648 France stood supreme among the powers of Europe and her ascendancy was not seriously challenged for two generations.[3] Richelieu had transmitted to Mazarin and Louis XIV the classical design of French foreign policy, an inheritance that persisted into the twentieth century. As Richelieu explained: "I wished to restore to Gaul the limit which nature designed for her . . . and identify Gaul with France." Quite simply, that program implied the extension of French frontiers to the Pyrenees, the Alps and the Rhine. More than that, Louis XIV was determined that Spain and Austria should not unite, for then France would have been encircled as in the sixteenth century. As a sort of corollary, German disunity was systematically fostered as essential for French predominance in Europe. For these ends, wars of conquest could be glibly interpreted as wars for national security—defensive struggles.

Overweening ambition impelled the Grand Monarch in the concluding phase of his career to try to reach beyond natural frontiers. He dreamed in fact of merging Spain with France, of erasing the Pyrenees, that is. Another purpose of French foreign policy was glory, dynastic glory, which would somehow inflate the prestige and the pride of king and courtiers and perhaps bring psychological rewards to bourgeois and peasant. It is impossible to say where the quest for French national security and the lust for national aggrandizement, respectively, began and ended.

[2] Many a prominent German military leader of the future boasted a Huguenot ancestry as did Count Camillo Cavour, a distinguished Italian statesman of the nineteenth century.

[3] France and Spain fought on until 1659 when a treaty fixed the Pyrenees as the boundary between the two nations, an arrangement that has lasted.

Commercial ambition and ideological passions, too, carried some weight, at times considerable weight, in deciding French behavior in the family of nations. Frenchmen who shared the vision of Colbert wished to wrest commercial advantages from the Netherlands, England and Genoa. And in the realm of ideas, France detested Dutchmen and Englishmen who made sport of the divine right philosophy and prized personal liberties. The Dutch deliberately baited the proud Sun King by publishing a cartoon showing the sun undergoing eclipse behind a huge Dutch cheese. It was a grievance, too, and an incitement, in some measure, that the Netherlands and England were intensely Protestant nations and offered asylum to French refugees.

The power of a country and its standing among the nations depend first and last upon the fighting services—the ability and skill of commanders, the size and esprit of army and navy and the quality of military equipment. All that in turn reflects the economic strength of the country and its martial traditions. While Louis XIV reigned France prided itself on the foremost military establishment and the most respected diplomatic corps in the world. Stately aristocrats served the crown as special agents on political errands abroad, but career diplomatists were more important, residing in foreign capitals, carrying on official negotiations with governments and reporting on current conditions and prospects. Louis XIV himself, who spoke the final word on war or peace, acquired a wide understanding of international statecraft, as befitted a pupil of Mazarin.

Despite his religious professions Louis XIV had no scruples against arranging partnerships with heretical (Protestant) princes or teaming up with Moslem Turks against the adversaries of France. In his management of foreign affairs the king combined prudence and boldness in about equal proportions with firmness and guile. Before launching an attack Louis XIV felt no obligation to proclaim his reasons for taking up arms; quick, unheralded invasion of an enemy country, then as now, brought obvious advantages in aggression.

However much control the Grand Monarch exercised over diplomacy, he entrusted the actual conduct of war to military specialists. It was rare for the king to assume direction of troops though he thoroughly relished watching army operations, sieges of fortified towns preferred. In the person of Marquis François de Louvois, France possessed a first-class army administrator, an invaluable and devoted servant of the crown and the successful competitor of Colbert for the ear of the king.[4] The efficient

[4] Louvois also took an active interest in diplomacy, especially in dealings with petty Italian states which he endeavored to terrorize into subservience.

The plundering of a village—a common incident in the wars of the Seventeenth Century.

organization of the French army under the guiding intelligence of Louvois largely explains the military reputation of France in the age; foreign countries, however, copied French methods, even improved upon them, with results that were disastrous for the innovator. French pre-eminence in the art of war is revealed in one way by the military terms which passed into the English language: artillery, infantry, battalion, battery, lieutenant and maneuvers, for example.

Appointed minister of war in 1666, Louvois carried through a series of reforms. Up to a point, for example, financial jobbery was removed from the officers' corps, the preserve of the more energetic aristocrats. Frenchmen and foreigners were attracted into the military service by higher and regular pay, better living quarters and they were equipped with uniform clothing. By 1679 France boasted a standing army of 280,000 officers and soldiers, a very considerable force by the standards of the day.

For the scientific study of strategy and tactics, schools were founded and campaigns were carefully planned and plotted in advance. More deadly weapons, especially muskets and cannon, were manufactured and unexampled efficiency was achieved in the service of supply. Ordinarily soldiers were idle during the winter months and war matériel was then piled up for the next year's operations. Strict discipline prevailed; the name of one French commander, Martinet, has entered the English language as the synonym for rigorous, arbitrary discipline.

Side by side with Louvois worked Marshal Sébastien Vauban, who was mainly responsible for improvement of the engineering branch of the armed services. A resourceful military brain, Vauban specialized in the fortification of towns and in breaching the defenses of enemy communities.[5] Seapower was the particular province of Colbert, as noted above; with him as sponsor and prod the French navy moved up with the best in Europe. Altogether Louis XIV commanded vast military resources, on land and water, to enlarge the Bourbon realm or to protect it.

On the other side, the economy of France was poorly organized for prolonged warfare. After the death of Colbert sound methods of accounting were dropped and plans to finance military operations out of booming exports collapsed. Burdensome taxation hampered manufacturing while money-lenders exacted exorbitant interest rates for loans. To meet state financial requirements, civil service posts were multiplied and sold with abandon. Battening upon the needs of the government, corrupt speculators accumulated large fortunes.

THE EARLY WARS OF LOUIS XIV

It is neither necessary nor profitable to recount the diplomatic and military record of Louis XIV in detail. If the sovereign authority of France was to extend to the natural boundaries, then the Spanish Netherlands (Belgium), Spanish-ruled Franche Comté, a district due west of Switzerland, and the cluster of principalities called Alsace and Lorraine belonging to the Holy Roman Empire would have to be annexed.

Directly to gain these areas France fought three desultory wars. In the first conflict (1667–1668) Spain was the major adversary. Unable to conquer the Spanish Netherlands, the supreme war aim, the Grand Monarch settled for a dozen strategically attractive fortresses on the northern border of France. In a second contest waged from 1672 to 1679, acquisition of the Dutch Republic was the largest object of French aggression. If the Netherlands passed to France, then the power equilibrium of the West of Europe would have been gravely upset—the liberties and security of other countries would have been placed in jeopardy. To dispel that nightmare, Spain, Austria and German Brandenburg rallied alongside of the Dutch; for a time, England was the ally and then the foe of Louis XIV.

Although the Dutch fleet scored victories, the fighting on land, though costly, was inconclusive. In a word, France could not subdue

[5] Vauban was more than a gifted militarist. He was interested in the public welfare and boldly published a program of reform, for which the enraged Louis XIV dismissed him from the public service.

Louis XIV watches his troops as they cross the Rhine into Germany, 1689.

the coalition, nor could the coalition overcome France. Peace by negotiation closed the struggle, France picking up Franche Comté in the process. The elated subjects of Louis XIV now saluted their master as Louis the Great; he had reached in fact the high point of his career. Presently French troops nibbled away at Alsace and Lorraine, seizing the city of Strassburg, for instance, in 1681, and holding on to it. That annexation consolidated the French position in Alsace and assured French control over German principalities on the Left Bank of the Rhine. As Louis XIV said, Alsace provided "a passage for our troops to Germany."

War set Western Europe ablaze again in 1689, dragging along for eight years. France and her satellites confronted a formidable partnership, organized to deny dominance over the Continent to Louis XIV. The alliance embraced Austria, several German states, Spain and ultimately the Netherlands and England, whose common sovereign, William the Third stood forth as the mortal enemy of the French design for hegemony. The armies of France wrote another dark chapter in the long and bitter Franco-German blood feud, fearfully ravaging the Left Bank of the Rhine. The broken shell of the princely castle at Heidelberg still stands as mute testimony to French depredations. Germans long remembered these spoliations and nursed desires for revenge; during the Franco-German War of 1870, for example, the most respected German historian of the day, Leopold von Ranke, declared: "We are still fighting Louis XIV."

As a kind of side show, French and English colonists, each reinforced by Indian mercenaries, waged King William's War in faraway America. Cruel and savage raids were conducted by each party on the settlements of the other; struggles for power in Europe invariably cycled into world wars. The ambitions of Louis

XIV at sea were shattered by Anglo-Dutch fleets which administered a severe drubbing to the French navy in 1694; half a century passed before French sea power recovered from the defeat. And on land at Namur the proud troops of Louis the Great suffered their first major reverse since his accession. By 1697, however, all belligerents had tired of the indecisive sparring and a peace settlement, dictated by sheer war weariness, was arranged at Ryswick, near the Hague.

How then had these recurring conflicts profited the French kingdom? The lilies of France waved over Franche Comté, parcels of Alsace and Lorraine and fortified towns along the southern boundary of the Spanish Netherlands. But temporary French control in the Italian peninsula was broken and the enemies of France, moreover, had imposed precise limits upon the territorial expansion of the Bourbon monarchy. In America, France and England returned each other's holdings which had been captured in the course of the fighting.

THE WAR OVER THE SPANISH SUCCESSION

After making peace with the Allies in 1697, French statecraft concentrated on the destiny of Spain, whose childless monarch, Charles II, stood on the brink of the grave, as in fact he had been for a quarter century. Who then should succeed to the Spanish crown? In spite of the sharp decline of Spain in the preceding century, it was still accounted a Great Power. Apart from Spain proper, the realm included the Spanish Netherlands (Belgium), much of Italy and half the globe outside of Europe. Spain was indeed a surpassingly attractive prize.

By reason of dynastic ties, the leading claimants to the Spanish patrimony were Emperor Leopold I of Austria and Louis XIV, who coveted the kingship for a grandson, Philip. Instead of waiting for Charles II to die, French diplomacy proposed to divide up his lands with some show of equity, but no formula satisfactory to Austria could be discovered. At long last, in 1700, Charles the Bewitched passed away, bequeathing his dominions to Philip. Not without misgivings, Louis XIV approved his acceptance and French officials promptly took over the management of Spanish affairs. It appeared certain that Spanish military forces and the overseas empire would be integrated with the might of France. To prevent that consummation, to preserve a balance of power and to further the imperial ambitions of England and the Netherlands, another imposing anti-French coalition was organized; the maritime nations united with Austria and German states against the Grand Monarch.

The War over the Spanish Succession started in 1702 and lasted nine years. The Allies benefited magnificently from greater naval strength and from two superior generals, an Austrian commander, Prince Eugene of Savoy, and the English Duke of Marlborough, whose descendant of the twentieth century, Winston Churchill, would recount his career with learning and eloquence. Major battles, to be told and retold in song, story and patriotic school book, were fought at Blenheim in Bavaria in 1704 and at several points in Belgium. Compared with twentieth-century warfare, these engagements were puny affairs; at Blenheim, for example, the Allied soldiers numbered only 45,000 and battles of that dimension took place only once in two years on the average. In the North American phase of this global war, French forces drove the English from the Hudson Bay region and won the race for mastery over the mouths of the Mississippi River.

When his armies faltered, the Sun King sought to end hostilities by recourse to diplomacy. First, he tried to break up the Alliance, which was tormented by internal divisions as is customary with coalitions, by buying off individual allies. That failed. Then he tried to negotiate peace with the Alliance as a whole. That, too, came to naught. French morale and military resources touched bottom in 1708. Famine gripped the richest provinces; heavy casualties had decimated the armies; the royal treasury was bare; riots and demonstrations broke loose; there were ominous rumblings of revolution.

Driven to desperation, Louis XIV solicited terms of peace once more from the Allies. But

The Porte Saint-Antoine, Paris, with the Bastille shown at the left

the price asked—the cooperation of France in ousting Philip from Spain—was too steep. A wave of patriotic fervor, hot and indignant, swept the French kingdom. As was true repeatedly in the future, France exhibited remarkable qualities of resilience, the hallmark of a fundamentally strong nation. More fighting, no decisive encounters on land, more diplomatic dickerings and by 1711 all combatants were ready to lay down their arms. Behind the backs of her allies, Britain entered into secret negotiations with France, which formed the prelude to a general settlement of 1713–1714, spoken of as the Treaty of Utrecht.[6]

The Utrecht agreements stand as a milestone in the political history of Europe and the wider world. The distribution of the immense properties of Spain formed the principal items in the treaty. The candidate of Louis XIV, Philip V, received the Spanish crown and the colonial possessions. But he renounced all rights to the French throne and promised, as did the French government, that the two countries should never be united. Austria annexed the southern Netherlands (Belgium) and the major part of the former Spanish holdings in Italy—Lombardy, Naples and Sardinia—decent compensation indeed for the sacrifice of Austrian claims to the Spanish kingship. Sicily was awarded to Savoy, but it was traded in 1720 to Austria for Sardinia. On a larger view, the Treaty of Utrecht meant that no single European combination was powerful enough to dominate the Continent. Something like an equilibrium of strength, in other words, had been preserved.

As for Great Britain it emerged from the contest definitely stronger in moral prestige and political power. She had triumphantly demonstrated the influence of seapower upon history in a way that grew into a habit. Her fleet had captured and her statesmen retained the Rock

[6] The damaging epithet of "perfidious Albion" appears to date from British undercover dealings with France at this time.

of Gibraltar, key point for the mastery of the western Mediterranean. And Britain contrived to prevent any major rival from bolstering its position along the Middle Sea. In America Britain deprived France of the Hudson Bay territory, Nova Scotia and smaller parcels of territory, while Spain conceded to British merchants limited trading privileges with South American colonies. As never before, it became apparent that the future of the island kingdom lay upon the water.

The sun of the Sun King had now set and would not rise again. His grandson wore the crown of Spain, to be sure, but that did not mean even friendship with France; actually, in a few years the two nations were at war with each other. More important, France had been considerably weakened in manpower, in material resources and in financial strength; accumulated war debts would help in time to break the back of the Bourbon dynasty forever. Without regrets, Louis XIV took leave of the world in 1715. The world on its part chose not to mourn his departure; ordinary Parisians, we are told, "openly returned thanks to God."

LEDGER OF A REIGN

Casting up a balance sheet of the Grand Monarch and his rule the first point to be made is that Louis XIV thoroughly understood the philosophy and practices of royal absolutism and helped to standardize them. He exemplified the ruler whose daily round was meticulously planned to the minute and who toiled hard and long at the business of being king. His reign witnessed modest advances in French manufacturing and commerce and would be forever glorious for scintillating literary achievements. Frank imitation of many features of French civilization by other countries proved the respect in which France was held.

Political despotism demands intelligent, resourceful hands on the tiller, but the royal successors of Louis XIV turned out to be incompetent weaklings so that his reign appeared extremely brilliant by contrast. It may be, too, though this is more debatable, that France was militarily more secure at the end of the reign than at the beginning.

But important items must also be posted in the debit column of the ledger. Royal extravagance, crushing taxation and bleeding wars left France prostrate and exhausted. Appalling wretchedness held commoners in thrall. Making allowances for changes in values, it has been estimated that the French national debt of 1715 exceeded by seven times the debt of 1914. The potentialities of France, furthermore, in America and in international commerce had been seriously impaired. And religious intolerance had embittered many a sensitive French spirit. Seeds of the epochal French Revolution of 1789—or some of them—were sown or germinated in the age of Louis XIV. Last, but not at all least, French diplomatic practices and political objectives, Bourbon lust for military grandeur bequeathed evil traditions to the Europe of the future.

On his death-bed Louis XIV is reported to have murmured to his five-year-old heir: "Try to keep the peace with your neighbors. I have loved war too well; do not copy me in this; nor in the lavish expenditures I have made." That counsel, alas, fell on stony ground.

FOR FURTHER STUDY

LAURENCE B. PACKARD, *The Age of Louis XIV* (New York, 1929)

MAURICE ASHLEY, *Louis XIV and the Greatness of France* (New York, 1948) PAPERBACK

DAVID OGG, *Louis XIV* (new ed., London, 1944)

VOLTAIRE, *The Age of Louis XIV* (many editions, New York, 1901)

JOHN B. WOLF, *The Emergence of the Great Powers* (New York, 1951) PAPERBACK

JAMES F. FARMER, *Versailles and the Court under Louis XIV* (New York, 1905)

CHARLES W. COLE, *Colbert and a Century of French Mercantilism* (2 vols., New York, 1939)

ALBERT L. GUÉRARD, *The Life and Death of an Ideal: France in the Classical Age* (New York, 1928)

FREDERICK L. NUSSBAUM, *The Triumph of Science and Reason* (New York, 1953) PAPERBACK

WINSTON S. CHURCHILL, *Marlborough, His Life and Times* (6 vols., New York, 1933–1939)

CHAPTER III

OLIGARCHIC RULE IN BRITAIN (1660-1789)

BRITAIN IN HISTORY

THERE appear to be mystifying if not indeed miraculous elements in the large role which the small British isle has played in global affairs. Insularity is the key to much of British history. Detached from the Continent, Britain enjoyed comparative security, exemption from invasion even in the dark years of the Second World War. On occasion the island kingdom has experienced the alarms and pangs of military peril, it is true, but it has been free from that constant sense of danger which has haunted continental countries.

Instead of large and costly armies, such as European powers maintained, Britain depended upon the fleet primarily for defense and offense. With the exception of the War of American Independence Britain has always been on the winning side in the great struggles of modern times. Britons developed a feeling of excellence, a certain haughtiness of temper which infuriated or made envious continentals less favored by geography. At home, the island character of the kingdom encouraged qualities of individualism, personal enterprise and daring.

Insularity alone cannot of course account for the eminence of Britain; Greenland, as an example, is a much larger island but inconsequential in human affairs. The British Isles, however, benefited from a salubrious climate, natural riches in fertile farmlands and in iron and coal resources beneath the soil. Communication, furthermore, was relatively easy on land or water. Standards of material comfort in all ranks of society surpassed those of the Continent, at any rate in the modern age.

Into the island, moreover, successive waves of population flowed from Europe. Coming either as conquerors or as peaceful immigrants, the newcomers brought fresh energy, intellectual talents and manual skills. Like other nations of Europe, Britain has been a melting pot, which inspired Daniel Defoe to write:

> Thus from a mixture of all kinds began
> That heterogeneous thing an Englishman.

Shakespeare in *Richard II* speaks of "England, bound in with the triumphant sea." But that is precisely what the sea did not do; rather the open water invited adventure, exploration and trade and fostered enterprise, initiative and a disciplined freedom. Concerning the crucial importance of the sea and seapower a late seventeenth-century English pamphleteer declared: "To the question, What shall we do to be saved in this world? there is no other answer but this, Look to your moat. The first article of an Englishman's political creed must be that he believeth in the sea; without that there needeth no general council to pronounce him incapable of salvation. . . . We are confined to an island by God Almighty not as a penalty but as a grace, and one of the greatest that can be given to mankind."

By happy accident Britain was located at the very center of the oceanic commercial operations which started to expand in the Renaissance centuries. Earlier and more thoroughly than some other peoples, Englishmen appreciated that national vitality and prosperity could be bettered by the exchange of commodities with foreigners. About the middle of the seventeenth century, Thomas Mun, foremost English writer on mercantilist doctrine, proclaimed this gospel in ringing accents which have sounded down the years. "Foreign trade," he wrote, "is the great revenue of the king, the honour of the kingdom, the noble profession of the merchant, the school of our arts, the supply of our wants, the employment of our poor, the improvement of our lands, the nursery of our mariners, the walls of the kingdom, the means of our treasure, the sinews of our wars, the terror of our enemies."

Native captains or foreigners in the national service hauled British wares to every corner of the globe, fetching back food, rawstuffs for manufacturing and the specialties of Europe, Asia and the Americas. British adventurers landed on every shore of the globe, staking out imperial claims, preparing the way for colonists and building a great empire (two of them really) which evolved into the strangest partnership of peoples which history records. It was an empire, in the effusive grandiloquence of one Briton, "whose morning drum-beat, following the sun and keeping company with the hours, encircles the globe with an unbroken chain of martial airs."

Implicit in the expansion of British business and commerce was the growth of the mercantile and manufacturing classes, proportionately much stronger than in France or Germany and keenly alert to combine with elements in the aristocratic ruling caste to advance bourgeois fortunes. Middle-class pressures contributed substantially to the growth of governmental institutions which ensured civil freedoms, personal dignity and broadened public participation in state affairs. In contrast to France and other continental countries, Britain experimented in political forms leading the way from royal authoritarianism to parliamentary ascendancy.

That road to freedom was not at all a smooth one, but milestones along the route had been raised before the arrival of modern times. Traditions of vigorous self-government reach back to the Anglo-Saxon epoch. That inheritance was enlarged by later developments like the Great Charter, the jury system and the rise and progress of a national assembly, the Parliament, whose authority fluctuated but never entirely disappeared. Fair and open discussion of public issues, which has gone on uninterruptedly for centuries, is a unique British contribution to the Western way of living. From the longer past Englishmen inherited, too, a lively consciousness of community, that attitude of mind called nationalism, which internal convulsions might shake but could not basically impair.

In modern Europe, England pioneered in subverting the will of the crown to the wishes of an elected élite, backed by the aggressive and ambitious middle classes. A full century and a half before the guillotine severed the head of

Beachy Head on the southern coast of England. "The first article of an Englishman's political creed must be that he believeth in the sea—"

Louis XVI of France, an English king had been brought to the scaffold. Another English monarch, who entertained divine-right convictions, discreetly fled to France and only thus escaped expulsion by force. After that, Britain settled down to a slow-paced moderation in politics, which must have been disconcerting to continentals who had written her off as an unstable, unreliable and rebellious island.

Slowly the tradition deepened that Britain handled public affairs cautiously, pursuing a rule-of-thumb, one-step-at-a-time behavior pattern. Although other peoples in their adventures in government never imitated British models fully, they nevertheless copied, sooner or later and in greater or lesser degree, British institutions and the broad British ideals of the good life, politically speaking. That legacy is a supreme gift of Britain to history.

In the material realm, Britons energetically promoted international trade and blazed the trail in that vast and unending transformation spoken of as the industrial revolution. As with British political principles and practices, so machine industrialism spread from the island into the two hemispheres. British merchants, British machines, British finance, like British settlers and missionaries, penetrated into every corner of the globe.

And Britain in history involves more than all that. It implies choice riches in literature and philosophy, extraordinary achievements in science, dynamic religious enthusiasms and more modest attainments in the fine arts. The genius of Britain has run more to the practical and the utilitarian than to the aesthetic and the speculative, more akin to ancient Rome than to Greece, though the point may easily be exaggerated.

THE STUART RESTORATION

For the third of September, 1658, John Evelyn, cultivated English monarchist, tersely confided to his diary: "Died that arch-rebel, Oliver Cromwell, called Protector."[1] The Cromwellian interruption in the continuity of the English constitution had in truth come to an end. As his successor, Cromwell designated his son Richard, who was so little a chip off the old block that he was ridiculed as "Tumbledown Dick." Incapable of coping with the authority entrusted to him, he resigned his powers to the army and the Parliament.

The legitimate claimant to the throne of England was Prince Charles, son of the decapitated Charles I, and an exile in Europe. Bidding for the crown, Charles promised that if chosen king he would allow Parliament freely to decide larger state questions and he would uphold broad liberty of conscience. Those assurances set a strong tide of opinion flowing in his favor. Parliament voted that "the government is and ought to be by King, Lords, and Commons," and invited Charles to mount the throne. Amidst tumultuous enthusiasm Charles II recovered the crown of his Stuart father.

Evelyn tells us in his *Diary* ". . . his Majesty, Charles II, came to London . . . with a troop of above 20,000 horse and foot, brandishing their swords, and shouting with inexpressible joy; the ways strewn with flowers, the bells ringing, the streets hung with tapestry, fountains running with wine . . . such a restoration was never mentioned in any history . . . since the return of the Jews from their Babylonish captivity . . ."

Charles II was clever, shrewd, calculating, a merry monarch, fond of fun, fond of the bowl, fond of the ladies. Reacting against the hard austerity of Puritanism, court and country indulged in a season of frivolous dissipation. And yet the portrait of shocking depravity in high places and of sexual pathology painted by historical novelists of the twentieth century, grossly overemphasizes the wickedness of the Restoration.

[1] For the dramatic career of Cromwell, consult C. Harold King, *A History of Civilization: The Story of Our Heritage* (New York, 1956).

While a refugee at the court of his august cousin, Louis XIV, Charles learned to admire the ways of French royal despotism, Roman Catholicism and French culture. He patronized science and scholarship, but he knew his history too well to suppose that France could be copied in matters of government or religion, however much he wished that could be brought to pass. He had the English crown, which made him almost giddy with delight, and he intended to cling tightly to it. Parliament doled out funds to the king only in niggardly amounts, so he took subsidies from Louis XIV to the hour of his death.

Not only was the Stuart dynasty restored, but the landed aristocracy returned to its historic place and the Established Church regained her traditional standing. As the king had pledged, public business was managed by Parliament which was moderately royalist and staunchly Anglican in outlook. The king dissuaded the lawmakers from wholesale revenge upon the partisans of Cromwell, though ten men who had a hand in the execution of Charles I were brought to the block.

Coercive, discriminatory legislation, too, was enacted against non-Anglicans. All clergymen, for example, were ordered to subscribe to the tenets of the Established Church; one out of five declined to obey and was cast out of his living. Others submitted with their lips but not their heads. Another measure restricted appointment to local offices to Anglicans. Intermittent persecution of dissenters, in harmony with the temper of the century, lasted until 1688. Among the upper classes Roman Catholic proselytism was active, being abetted by the known Catholic inclinations of the king.

POLITICAL PARTIES

Within Parliament, marked cleavages of opinion developed, most conspicuously over the treatment of religious dissenters. One faction desired ecclesiastical uniformity and wished to dragoon all citizens into the state church. This group was also inclined to allow the crown relatively broad powers, and in foreign policy, it shared the Francophile sympathies of the monarch.

Composed overwhelmingly of landed aristocrats, this faction came to be known as the Tory Party, an epithet originally used for Catholic brigands in Ireland. As a term of reproach, Tory was applied to partisans of the king in English America before and during the American Revolution. The word took on and retained sinister connotations in the political vocabulary of the United States. President Franklin D. Roosevelt was wont to label his political opponents as "Tories," while his bosom friend, Winston Churchill, prided himself on being a Tory.

Competing with the Tories in the reign of Charles II were the advocates of religious toleration. They were intransigently opposed to a Roman Catholic on the throne and ardent believers in the subordination of the crown to Parliament. They were impressed, too, with the menace of France to the security of their island. Reflecting the outlook and interests of the business community, this group was called the Whig Party, after the most blue-blooded Scottish Calvinists. The emergence of distinct and competing political parties was a significant feature of the era of Charles II; time would demonstrate that vigorous and rival parties were an essential component of representative government.

Toward the end of the 1670's wild rumors raced across the kingdom of a gigantic conspiracy, "a popish plot," to replace Charles II by his brother, James, an avowed Catholic, and to massacre Protestants who resisted. The faith of Rome would then be made standard in the country. The plot was exploited if not invented by a charlatan named Titus Oates. His reports were readily believed by the more gullible members of society.

Frightened Englishmen worked themselves into ecstasies of hysterical emotion. Roman Catholics were thrown into jail, some were put to death and the Whigs took command of Parliament; and yet a bill to exclude Roman Catholics from the throne failed of adoption. It was now, however, that the Habeas Corpus Act was incorporated (1679) into English fundamental law. That measure prescribed additional safeguards for the principle that arrested citizens would be promptly tried and on a specific charge—another protection against arbitrary government.

Passions were so violently inflamed over the Catholic exclusion issue that it appeared as though another civil war impended. Memories of the devastating decade of the 1640's were still exceedingly green. The prospect of a repeat performance bolstered the prestige of the king and enabled him to govern in the last years of his reign without parliamentary restraint. At his death in 1685, Charles II was hardly less popular than when he was welcomed to the throne.[2]

FOREIGN RELATIONS

In foreign affairs, the main threads in the Restoration epoch were the enlargement of empire and tortuous maneuverings with France. Charles II married a Portuguese princess who brought as dowry the island of Bombay which soon blossomed into a leading center of English commerce with India. Under pressure of the business community and in line with mercantilist dogma, England warred upon the Dutch Republic, "fought for the fairest of all mistresses, trade." As the fruit of a quick and easy victory England annexed the colony of New Netherland, which was renamed New York, in honor of the Duke of York, brother of the king. England now controlled the entire eastern seaboard of central North America, and new colonies were carved out in Carolina, New Jersey and Pennsylvania.

English relations with France fluctuated. Of the Francophile convictions of Charles II, reinforced as they were by the concrete of hard cash from Louis XIV, which the monarch used in turn to bribe Parliament, there is no doubt. But he could not always control English external policy. Twice England fought and weakened the Dutch (1665–67, 1672–74), which indirectly benefited France. The second struggle however, was so unpopular that Charles II was forced to pull out of the war. England even threatened to fight against

[2] On his deathbed, the king formally entered the Roman Catholic Church.

France, which persuaded Louis XIV to make peace with his enemies (1678), as a similar English diplomatic gesture had done a decade earlier. Charles II decidedly failed to appreciate the peril to English security and freedom of an overwhelmingly powerful France.

JAMES II—AND LAST

Charles II accurately predicted that his brother James, if he became monarch, "would lose his kingdoms because of his religious zeal." Alike in their affection for France and French culture, the Stuart brothers differed in other respects. Instead of being shrewd, gay and debonair, James was obvious and obstinate, and unwilling to conceal his sincere attachment to Catholicism and to royal authoritarianism. He valued his creed more than the crown. Although when he took the throne the future looked rosy indeed, James II made himself universally execrated in a surprisingly short space of time.

In the face of the known attitude of Parliament and country the king was resolved to return England to the Roman Church. And that at a time when the remorseless persecution of the Huguenots in France had fanned anti-Catholic passions to white heat. Through the influence of James II Catholics displaced Anglicans in public offices, the army included, which roused the suspicion that the king intended to employ the army as the tool of tyranny.

Heedless of loud protests, university chairs and even positions in the church were staffed with professing Catholics; prohibitions on Catholic worship and other bans were lifted. James II, in Olympian oblivion of realities, fancied that he was indispensable for domestic tranquility and could, therefore, win through in his Romanizing purposes.

Actually the royal policy alienated virtually all sections of the population. The English had no intention of swallowing the Roman pill. But the parliamentary opposition, afraid of unloosing civil tumult, held its hand, for James was elderly and upon his death the crown would pass, it was supposed, to his Protestant daughter, Mary. She was the wife of William of Orange, the head of the United Netherlands and the acknowledged champion of Protestant Europe and of representative government.

Those consoling reflections were, however, rudely shattered when a son was born to James II. The prospect of a Catholic dynasty induced prominent Whig and Tory spokesmen alike, to call upon William of Orange for help; he was invited, indeed, to lead an army to England and expel the detested and discredited king. Plainly, in the thinking of the politicans, another ruler was acceptable but there was no acceptable alternative to the English Church.

The Prince of Orange responded affirmatively and promptly. Not that he had any lively desire to wield the English scepter, but he very much wanted the cooperation of England in an impending conflict with Louis XIV. He came, he was seen, he did not need to conquer, for he was welcomed as a deliverer. The forces sympathetic to James II melted away and the king betook himself across the Channel. Flight might be contrary to honor and to royal dignity but it was healthy. Thereupon Parliament declared that James II had in fact abdicated and that the throne was vacant. England had witnessed a bloodless revolution which the future would salute as glorious.

THE "GLORIOUS" REVOLUTION

Parliament, Whigs and Tories together, asked William and Mary to take the crown jointly. Implicit in their acceptance was the confirmation of the principle that Parliament possessed the right to dismiss a king and appoint a successor, the same as any other state servant—no vestige of the sanction of God here.

Presently Parliament approved the celebrated Declaration of Rights which restated, in the main, historic liberties of Englishmen which James II had arbitrarily infringed. Kings were forbidden to levy taxes or keep a standing army without the consent of Parliament. Kings were obligated to summon Parliament frequently and permit untrammeled debate. It was declared unlawful for the crown to deny trial by jury or to exact excessive bail of a citizen

The Coronation of William III and Mary in Westminster Abbey, April, 1689

charged with wrongdoing. The only really novel feature in the document debarred any person who professed Catholicism, or who married a Catholic, from occupying the throne.

The Declaration of Rights forms an integral part of the British Constitution. The essence of constitutionalism is the existence of legal restraints upon governmental authority. In Britain these limitations are firmly embedded in precedent and national tradition and the principles on which they are based are no less constitutional because they are not collected in a single document.

Another law of 1689 allowed freedom of worship to all Christians except Roman Catholics, who cherished too much of historical Christianity, and Unitarians who accepted too little. While substantially admitting that no sect possessed a monopoly on religious truth, this law did not cancel all existing discriminations against men outside of the Established Church. Barriers to non-Anglicans in public offices and in attendance on universities, for example, went untouched. If full religious liberty had not yet been realized, praiseworthy progress toward the goal had nonetheless been

John Locke

achieved, persecution had ceased and the advance proved to be permanent. In the same channel of freedom, legislation imposing reservations on freedom of publication was permitted to lapse. Before long the first permanent newspaper (1702) made its début in London and polemical political pamphleteering took on fresh zeal.

All in all the gains of the Glorious Revolution represented extremely modest deviations from the English heritage. It was in truth a decidedly conservative business. But the long and turbulent rivalry between Stuart kings and Parliament had been triumphantly resolved in favor of the latter. Whatever shadow of authority still resided in the crown, the substance belonged to Parliament. So severely limited in fact was the power of the monarch that England was well along the road to becoming the "crowned republic" which it is today.

Parliament governed England, and the politically articulate oligarchy, largely landowning aristocrats, governed Parliament. By recourse to bribery and corruption one king of the future, George III, would try to rule as well as reign, but his adventure suffered speedy shipwreck. Aside from the ascendancy of Parliament, the events of 1688 and 1689 had confirmed basic personal and civil rights to the individual Englishman. From England these concepts radiated throughout the world. English principles were seized upon by the politically discontented everywhere, most importantly in English America and in France. Quite commonly English principles were exported in the writings of John Locke.

THE WRITINGS OF LOCKE

Locke is sometimes described as the founder of psychology. Thinkers had long debated whether men were naturally good, or innately wicked, as Christian theology taught. Locke argued in his epochal *Essay Concerning Human Understanding* (1690) that neither view was valid. Rather, at birth the mind of man resembled a blank tablet and experience alone molded one's qualities and personality. Or, put otherwise, social environment determined the character and beliefs of the individual. From which it was reasoned that if the environment were improved society would proceed logically to perfection.

Allow man freedom, insisted Locke, within the orbit of established law, and he would mature intellectually and business would prosper to the advantage of the state. As a sort of corollary Locke favored freedom and variety in the training of youth.

But the larger reputation of Locke stems from his interpretation and justification of the political happenings of 1688 and 1689, put forth in *Two Treatises of Government* (1690). The *Second Treatise* ranks with the most influential political tracts of the Western tradition. Although accustomed to grappling with large constitutional problems, Locke had little that was original to say about the revolutionary events of 1688–89. Yet his explanation is prized for the form in which it was cast and for lucidity of expression.

According to Locke, government is an artificial creation, an indispensable convenience, resting upon a contract between ruler and ruled. To quote the philosopher: government is necessary in order to avoid the "inconvenience of the State of Nature which follows from every man being a judge of his own case." It is the responsibility of government to safeguard the natural rights of man, that is, to insure the safety of citizens and to protect their property. The sanctity of private property was a basic postulate in Locke's thinking.

Government, wrote Locke, must exercise control by "established standing laws, . . . by indifferent [i.e. impartial] and upright judges . . . and all this is to be directed to no other end than the peace, safety, and Public Good of the people." Arbitrary taxation or imprisonment of citizens was unlawful.

As Locke read the record, government derived its authority from the governed. Government must be carried on by discussion and in harmony with the desires of the majority. The decisive word on public questions should be spoken by an elected legislature. If and whenever a government violated the inherent rights of man, citizens were privileged to change the government, as in truth the English had done in 1688. On the subject of Church and State, Locke strongly urged that they should be wholly separate institutions; because the business of the State lay in the secular sphere—the preservation of natural rights, while the task of the Church was to guide the soul of man to the world beyond. "Toleration," Locke asserted, "is agreeable to the gospel of Jesus Christ, it is also dictated by the genuine reason of mankind. The care of each man's salvation belongs only to himself."

The treatises of Locke clearly outlined the governmental principles of the island kingdom. They served as textbooks on political philosophy in Britain and were eagerly studied in Europe and in English America. Somewhat refined by later thinkers in New World and Old, the philosophy of Locke supplied an ideological framework for the revolutions of 1776 in English America and of 1789 in France. Lockian teachings, in time, insinuated themselves into the texture of rational and democratic thought all over the globe.

WORLD POLICY

The calculation of William of Orange (or William III) that England would bolster up the anti-French coalition was not disappointed. Under the leadership of the king and with the resolute backing of Whig politicians, England twice entered the lists against Louis XIV (1689–97, 1702–13). For that policy there were three persuasive reasons: the prevention of French predominance in the west of Europe, the advancement of English commercial and colonial interests, and, ideologically, the protection of Protestantism and enmity toward the autocratic regime of the Grand Monarch, which supported Catholic pretenders to the crown of England.

In the prosecution of the wars England relied upon seapower, fighting the fleets of the enemy and imposing an economic blockade on his ports. Only small English contingents participated in the land warfare, though English commanders acquired an enviable reputation; the Duke of Marlborough is probably the ablest military leader the island has ever produced. And English subsidies were awarded to any prince on the Continent who would turn his soldiers against Louis XIV or his allies. England emerged from the wars as the leading naval and commercial power and with a broader colonial empire; the challenge of Louis XIV was wholly frustrated, as is explained in another place (pp. 42 and 43). For a full generation after 1715 Britain experienced the blessings of peace which enabled her to consolidate the world position which victory had earned.

While the fortunes of England soared, the strength of King William's original princedom, the Netherlands, steadily declined. This small state, peopled though it was with men of heroic and exemplary qualities, could not stand up under the buffetings of English commercial rivalry and wasting conflicts with France. Amsterdam yielded to London as the foremost seaport and financial community of the world.

As by-products of the struggle against Louis XIV two enduring English institutions were founded: the Bank of England (1694) and the national debt. To finance the war, beyond income from taxation, the government had recourse to borrowing on long term. Funds were channeled largely through the Bank of England, organized under state charter by a company of merchants. Profits arising out of foreign trade, especially sales of cloth to Portugal, enabled the English capitalist class to lend money to a government which prosecuted war in the interest of still greater exports.

The establishment of the Bank testified in itself to the growing importance of finance and trade in Britain. But at first the operations of the Bank were directed to supplying funds to the government rather than to making loans for business undertakings. Britain benefited from financial stability while France was the victim of appalling confusion, a heavy drag upon the military arm of the government. The strength of the Bank of England became a matter of proverb. Serving as a model for similar institutions in other countries, the Bank remained under private management until taken over in 1946 by the state.

THE UNITED KINGDOM

Long since, Scotland had merged with England under the title of Great Britain. Prior to 1603 each half of the island possessed a king and institutions of its own, but in that year both crowns were taken by James I. A century later, in 1707, the union of the crowns was converted by treaty into a union of the two kingdoms. It was a unique piece of political integration, and among the most successful of modern times.

The great hall of the Bank of England

Scotland contained a population of about a million, comparatively poor, but proud of national traditions, of the Presbyterian faith and of a mature educational system. Full partnership between Scotland and England promised mutual advantages, on the principle that in union there is strength. Scotch producers would have free access to English and colonial markets—an independent Scottish adventure in empire-building, incidentally, had collapsed ignominiously. For the English, on the other side, the union would ensure the collaboration of Scotch brains and brawn in expanding national power, and it would also increase the sense of security against foreign invasion.

But there was another aspect to the merger. The historic Parliament of Scotland was abandoned, representatives instead being sent to London, and lesser curtailments on the jealously cherished Scottish independence were enforced. Large sections of Scotland hotly resented the sacrifice of political independence, and twice within the ensuing forty years Scotland served as a base for military operations against the British king. But rising prosperity and the healing salve of time tempered indignation. A Scottish National Party, dedicated to home rule, was organized, but it failed to excite much enthusiasm and was several times divided by schisms.

Based upon general consent, the bond of England with Scotland has endured. But endless storms and turbulence studded relations with Ireland, or rather with the larger section of Ireland, until 1949 when the final political link with England was at last severed. Ireland had been claimed by England since the twelfth century. English rulers, notably James I and Cromwell, had attempted to transform this incorrigibly rebellious island of Catholics into a loyal satellite by planting Protestant settlers from Scotland and England in the northern provinces, called Ulster. Landed properties had been freely bestowed upon immigrants with the result that though Irish Catholics made up three-quarters of the population, they owned less than a quarter of the soil.

Irish longing for independence created an opening for the exiled James II. Accompanied by French troops and wearing the livery of Louis XIV, James landed in Ireland in 1689. Immediately fighting broke out between Catholics and Protestants. William of Orange crossed over to Ireland and decisively vanquished the Catholic forces in the Battle of the Boyne.[3] Once more James II took up residence in France, where he was joined by some Irish soldiers.[4]

Protestant subjugation of the Emerald Isle was swiftly completed and the Irish danger to the safety of England was eliminated or at any rate greatly diminished. Native Irish institutions were sternly repressed and the position of the Protestant minority fortified; none but Protestants, for instance, might be elected to the Irish Parliament, which in fact merely echoed the voice of London. Catholics could not marry outside their faith, nor own weapons, nor take employment as teachers. Moderate restrictions were laid upon Catholic worship; the Church, nevertheless, served as the rallying ground of Irish resistance to England and to Protestantism.

Treatment of Catholics in Ireland was far less severe than the abuse of Huguenots in France but the two intolerances ran parallel in part, and both nourished burning memories. Betterment in the primitive Irish living conditions, instead of mitigating animosities, heightened demands for national freedom. While Scottish energies and resources strengthened British power, Ireland remained an Achilles heel.

CABINET GOVERNMENT

A salient feature of British constitutional growth in the eighteenth century was the establishment on firm foundations of the cabinet scheme of government. Coupled with that was the emergence of the prime ministership, and the custom that a ministry held office only so long as it commanded a majority of the votes in the House of Commons. These institutions,

[3] Commemorating the triumph of William of Orange, Irish Protestants are still called Orangemen.

[4] Marshal MacMahon of the nineteenth century was one of many prominent French citizens of Irish descent.

so vital to the whole British system of government, had been developing over the years and in fact did not attain full flower until the nineteenth century. All alike reflected conditions and traditions peculiar to this island and were shaped to the requirements of a compactly unified nation.

The trend toward cabinet government was aided by the accession to the throne, in 1714, of George I, elector of the German principality of Hanover. Parliament had conferred the crown upon his family since it was the Protestant dynasty most closely related to the British royal house. George I became king amidst the hearty applause of the Whig Party and the monarch reciprocated the cordial sentiments. For nearly half a century the Whigs dominated the British political stage.

A German to the marrow of his bones (he even imported his mistresses from Germany), George I cared more for his native Hanover than for Britain. He concentrated on diplomatic affairs, allowing ministers authority in domestic matters, including the distribution of offices in State and Church. Since the king spoke no English, whenever he attended ministerial conferences conversation had to be carried on in a debased Latin. But he seldom appeared at meetings and a committee of ministers accordingly took responsibility for the management of state business.

That body was called the cabinet because the number of ministers was so small that they could assemble in a little room. Gradually it became unwritten convention that the king must appoint as ministers the recognized leaders of the stronger party in the Commons and that the cabinet was collectively responsible for the conduct of public affairs. A cabinet resigned, moreover, whenever a majority of the Members of Parliament (M. P.'s) rejected any important ministerial proposal. The king reigned as the legal and titular head of Britain, but real executive authority belonged to the royal advisers in the cabinet.

At the time, M. P.'s were chosen under a bewildering variety of old traditions and not more than one out of ten adult males could vote. Some 6,000 electors could actually choose more than half of the M. P.'s. As a rule, however, elections were decided by polite agreement among gentlemen, not by strident electioneering and counting of heads. At the election of 1754, to illustrate, the expense and inconvenience of a contest had to be incurred in only forty-two districts.

Certain towns (or boroughs), moreover, which by long tradition had representation in the Commons, belonged to landed proprietors who themselves appointed the M. P.'s. The practice, which is anathema to mathematical concepts of representative government, was not without some merit, for it opened the door of Parliament to men of ability who lacked the personal qualities that appeal to an electorate.

As for the upper house, the Lords, it consisted of nobles sitting by hereditary privilege, and of prominent ecclesiastics of the Established Church, all members of the landowning aristocracy. A court of law declared that "those who own the land should rule the land," and that was the reality in eighteenth-century Britain. Parliament was spoken of as the best club in London, the rendezvous of aristocratic country gentry, the ruling oligarchy of island and empire.

It was during the long ministerial leadership of Robert Walpole, from 1721 to 1742, that the cabinet institution hardened into something approaching its present-day form. Walpole in fact was the first man to be generally recognized as Prime Minister. An energetic country squire of commanding personality, uncouth and venal, Walpole excelled as a skilful manipulator of men and as an astute financier. His favorite authority was common sense which he habitually invoked. He was put in charge of the public treasury at a moment when a speculative mania had suddenly burst and the kingdom was in the grip of a severe financial crisis. Prudential economic measures which he sponsored quickly righted matters.

While mainly concerned with financial affairs, Walpole also headed the Whig Party, domineered over ministerial colleagues (dismissing any who quarreled with him), and he explained and defended legislative proposals in the Commons. He assured himself of majority backing by flattering M. P.'s, by judiciously calculated distribution of patronage or by open bribery and corruption. Habits of public morality were not exactly those of the twentieth century. Defeated in the Commons in 1742, Walpole resigned at once and thus solidified the custom that a ministry must retire when it no longer commanded the confidence of the lower house.

SOCIETY AND MIND

The era of Walpole was a period of peace, progress and prosperity. Some part of the British reputation for orderliness and moderation was fashioned at this time. With one trifling exception, Britain held aloof from international wars; Walpole once smugly boasted to his Queen, "50,000 men killed this year in Europe and not one of them an Englishman." By mid-eighteenth century population had reached about 6,000,000.

It is prescribed in the catechism of the Anglican Church that every Englishman should work to keep himself and his family according to the usual standard of that state of life unto which it had pleased God to call him. There were, however, several "states of life" in British society.

Some seventy families, large landed magnates, occupied the summit of the social pyramid. Directly beneath the patricians were well-to-do squires, belonging to the governing class too. This proud, ruling oligarchy was politically divided, as noted before, into Whigs and Tories. Unlike France or Prussia, England had no military aristocracy and the upper caste casually absorbed wealthy tradespeople who purchased landed property or married into "society." Country gentlemen were free to enrich themselves by bourgeois methods, though to engage in a full-time commercial pursuit was generally frowned upon as undignified and degrading. The Church, the law, the university, however, were "respectable" professions.

Aristocratic families, like their counterparts on the Continent, patronized arts and letters, and were voracious and, in general, discerning collectors of paintings. In the wake of "grand tours" much that was finest in French, Italian, Dutch and Flemish schools of art arrived in England. Domestic and foreign craftsmen were employed in building and decorating London residences and handsome country seats. Rural mansions ranged from the palatial Blenheim Palace of the Marlboroughs to modest manors set in luxuriant parks. Large and distinctly pompous rooms matched the elegant social etiquette of the age; they were daintily ornamented, and color was supplied by rugs, draperies and mahogany furniture. The best of the great country houses, some of them to be sure older than the eighteenth century, are the choicest English contribution to the visual arts.[5]

Sir Robert Walpole in the House of Commons, London

As a class the English country gentlemen kept a watchful eye on their estates, ever eager

[5] Due to economic changes, over half a hundred of the historic mansions have now passed into state possession. They have been made accessible to the public as hospitals, museums, youth hostels or educational institutions. A few of the great residences have been turned into country clubhouses or divided into apartments.

to enlarge them, and they devoted a good deal of time to gaming, hunting and boorish high living. Hearty fellows that they were, they loved to eat, drink and be merry. Lord Byron hit off the landed gentry this way:

> For what were all these country patriots born?
> To hunt, and vote, and raise the price of corn? . . .
> They roar'd, they dined, they drank, they swore they meant
> To die for England—why then live?—for rent.

Many an aristocrat was a "free-thinker" because his mind was too indolent or too crude to probe into speculative matters; some aristocrats, however, contributed modestly to literature and science.

Living was decidedly less pleasant for ordinary English rustics, who eked out a subsistence from small farms, raising grain and livestock for their own needs. Villages were still the principal units of society and perhaps three-quarters of the English depended upon the land for their daily bread. The class of small landowners declined rapidly in the eighteenth century as opulent landlords bought up little farms.

For the future welfare of Britain the onward march of the mercantile classes was of the utmost importance, as observant foreigners duly noted. Commented the Frenchman Voltaire on British society, "The bottom dregs, the top, the froth, and the middle excellent." Prospering on trade, finance and to a degree on manufacturing, the bourgeoisie represented gathering power and exerted considerable influence, mostly indirect, on state policy. It is said that Louis XIV contemptuously dismissed England as a nation of shopkeepers.

Foreign commerce expanded six-fold in the course of the eighteenth century. Trade with colonies or traffic in slaves piled up many great fortunes. Woolen goods topped industrial production and handicraft wares were turned out in profusion; mining and metal-working as yet employed only a few hands. For the greater part, manufacturing was carried on by artisans in their cottages with a journeyman perhaps and a couple of apprentices toiling alongside. This type of industrial organization, since it centered in the home, was called the domestic system. The master often owned the simple tools, and obtained raw materials or semi-finished goods to be worked up from capitalist middlemen. Ordinarily artisans cultivated plots of ground as a side-line.

London was of course the incomparable metropolis, in 1700 the home of perhaps 700,000 if the suburbs and encircling villages are reckoned in. No other British community had a twentieth of that population and only Paris among Occidental cities approached London in size. So rapid was the rebuilding of London after the devastating Great Fire of 1666, which caused more damage than German bombing in the Second World War sweeping away 13,000 houses and ninety churches, that Defoe wrote exultantly: "New Squares, and new Streets rising up every Day to such a Prodigy of Buildings, that nothing in the World does, or ever did, equal it."

Later generations lamented that the opportunity for intelligent replanning of London after the fire had been missed. But perhaps the glory of the city was its disorder, its narrow and awkward streets, its creaking shop signs and vendors noisily hawking their wares. As Samuel Johnson, dean of London lovers, sagely remarked, "When a man is tired of London, he is tired of life, for there is in London all that life can afford."

Daily living for the London poor as for their rustic fellows was hard and drab, relieved in many cases by intemperate consumption of cheap gin which, until the imposition of heavy taxes at the middle of the century, competed effectively with ale and beer as the favorite stimulant of commoners. Drunkenness and brawling were spoken of as national curses. Consumption of tea (and sugar) was on the rise and diet could be diversified by citrus fruits, bananas and potatoes—if the pocketbook permitted.[6] Ordinary Londoners dearly loved to

[6] Although the potato was known to Shakespeare, it was not until well along in the eighteenth century that the homely root was established as a decent food for gentlemen. For generations the now friendly and indispensable potato was regarded with alarm and suspicion; even men of learning fancied that it would cause leprosy and other diseases or incite to wickedness.

The rise of the mercantile interest in the Eighteenth Century is expressed in the opulence and charm of this family portrait by George Stubbs. It represents the Wedgwood family, whose potteryware was alike distinguished for practicality and artistic taste.

watch the hanging of criminals which custom prescribed as legitimate entertainment. It cost spectators nothing—and surely was unwholesome.

Capital of the realm and the headquarters of the Established Church and high society, London was also the intellectual center of the kingdom and had a virtual monopoly on the printing industry. It prospered as the leading English port and as a veritable bee-hive of trade, finance and varied kinds of domestic handicrafts. London then occupied a distinctly larger place in the national economy than would be true a century later. After the Great Fire, houses and other structures of red brick replaced the traditional wooden buildings. Homes in newly developed residential districts stressed solid comfort more than beauty, smugness and symmetry rather than artistic grace.

So prodigious was the industry of Sir Christopher Wren in the reconstruction of London, that a worshiper could attend a different church designed by him every Sunday in the year. The masterpiece of this greatest of British architects is grave and dignified St. Paul's Cathedral. Symbol of London, this church, once white but now grimy from smoke and soot, is distinguished for its graceful spires and towers in front of a majestic dome.

In the realm of the fine arts, Great Britain borrowed extensively from France and Italy. At the middle of the eighteenth century wealthy young Englishmen were as much Parisians as Londoners. Fashionable Britons bought their clothes in Paris, and their coaches, objects of art and some of their books. French tastes, French wit, French *savoir vivre* were admired and imitated by British aristocrat and scholar

At left, St. Paul's Cathedral, London

Below are shown two views of another London church designed by Sir Christopher Wren—St. Mary-le-Bow (whence the expression "the sound of Bow Bells"), an engraving of 1754; and at right, a photograph taken in December, 1944 after bombing by Nazi planes.

alike. Late in the century, English craftsmen earned an international reputation for mahogany furniture. Supreme as designers were Thomas Chippendale and George Hepplewhite, expert cabinetmakers with shops of their own, while Thomas Sheraton was best known for his writings on patterns of furniture. Among English-speaking peoples the designs of these masters have increased in popularity with the years.

Simultaneously, an English school of painting evolved, steady and balanced in its principles. Artists specialized in portraiture, the best-liked expression of painting in the island, and in exquisite landscapes and woodland scenes. Acute perception of subjects characterized the portraits of Sir Joshua Reynolds. The romantic Thomas Gainsborough and George Romney were also prized masters with the brush, while William Hogarth satirized coarse and frivolous

English Eighteenth Century furniture. From left to right across the page: Chippendale side-chair; Hepplewhite shield-back chair. Below, at left, a Chinese Chippendale curio cabinet; at right, a Hepplewhite commode of mahogany with satinwood marquetry.

A scene from John Gay's play The Beggar's Opera, *painted by William Hogarth*

social habits in distinctly original paintings and engravings. Curious characters seem almost to have walked straight from the sidewalks of London on to his canvases; social and political satire as an art form found a genius in Hogarth. Sculpture in England never rose above mediocrity.

Apart from the compositions of Henry Purcell, a gifted artist born out of time, British musical productions attracted little attention until the Saxon genius George Frederick Handel settled in England. He was distinguished as a composer of Italian-type opera, of which he had learned while a student in Italy, and of religious oratorios. Handel's *Messiah* (1741), with its enthralling Hallelujah chorus and soprano solo, "I know that my Redeemer liveth," is often pointed to as opening a new era in English vocal music. Not only in Britain, but wherever British cultural tastes have taken root, this masterpiece has retained its hold upon music-lovers. The remains of Handel, fittingly, were laid to rest in Westminster Abbey, the British "Hall of Fame."

Literature, perhaps the loftiest manifestation of English intellectual talent, increased in quantity and quality in this "classical" age of writing. Timeless works appeared which everyone praises and few read, as is the fate of classics. Wealthy aristocrats with literary pretensions generously subsidized writers. Among the poets Alexander Pope ranked at the top by reason of impeccable beauty of form, the coldly satirical cast of his thought and his finely chiseled verses (*The Rape of the Lock; Essay on Man*). No doubt Pope influenced contemporaries more than any other literary artist, and he was the first professional writer in England who freed himself from private patronage.

The English novel was launched on its lush career with *Robinson Crusoe* (1719) by Daniel Defoe. Immediately popular in the realm of sentimental fiction were Samuel Richardson's *Pamela* (1740) and *The Vicar of Wakefield* (1766) by Oliver Goldsmith, the latter an entrancing portrayal of eighteenth-century moods and habits and not without traces of witty satire. Jonathan Swift excelled in prose writing, winning enduring honor with his last major piece, *Gulliver's Travels,* a sharp-barbed critique of the follies and foibles of men; opulent in its detail, this story of lusty adventure has been an unforgettable reading experience for many generations.

The literary essay engaged the suave pen of Joseph Addison and of the many-sided and irascible Samuel Johnson, who in his prime dominated London literary circles. An epitaph on the pew of the church which Johnson attended proudly describes him as "the philosopher, the poet, the great lexicographer, the profound moralist, and the chief writer of his time."

Even newspapers and fugitive political pamphlets responded to the current vogue of good style in British writing. The rise of magazines in the 1730's created a medium through which writers who were able to please the public fancy

The Exhibition of the Royal Academy, 1771. Growing British interest in the collecting of paintings and the encouragement of painters was given further impetus by these yearly shows.

could earn a living with their pens; certain publishers and booksellers contrived to amass fortunes. Of passing interest, as a handy source of historical information, is the *Annual Register*, a yearly survey of the outstanding developments in all countries, with emphasis upon Great Britain. Appearing first in 1758 with Edmund Burke as editor, the *Register* has been regularly published ever since. Burke, however, is better known for controversial political writings, some of them familiar to every schoolboy in the United States, and as a classical philosopher of political conservatism.

At the end of the century, English authors of distinction switched from conventional and rational emphases to more emotional and romantic themes. The noble "Elegy in a Country Churchyard" by Thomas Gray heralded the oncoming popularity of romanticism in British poetry.

Universities in eighteenth-century England contributed little to the advancement of learning. The ancient foundations of Oxford and Cambridge resembled monasteries at low ebb, lifeless, somnolent, easy-going. On the other hand, vital and enlightened nurseries of education, called academies, sent forth men who attained renown in literature, science and industry. Although religious studies bulked large in the curricula, fundamental instruction was offered in mathematics and the expanding sciences. Scotland possessed, at the time, the finest system of primary education in the world. And the Scottish universities—the Glasgow of Adam Smith and James Watt, and Edinburgh with its celebrated medical school—kept the torch of scholarship burning brightly. Cultivation of scientific inquiries at these exploring seats of learning yielded discoveries of great value for technological progress.

TRENDS IN RELIGION

In the course of the eighteenth century Christianity in England experienced interesting and instructive changes. At the outset of the century the angry theological controversies of the preceding period lost their vigor and rationalistic ideas invaded Christian thought as they did secular literature. Writers on religion had much to say about the "reasonableness of Christian teachings"; according to staunch friends of Christianity, a reasoned faith was more logical and rational than disbelief.

That approach to religion was calculated to appeal to the head, nothing more; for the heart is seldom obedient to the mandates of reason. More than that, tolerance in religious matters fostered indifference and torpor, while accumulating speculations on findings in science, disturbed conventional theological ideas. A species of Christianity called deism, which denied the miraculous and the supernatural in the historic creed, won many adherents among the intellectual classes.[7] Attendance upon divine worship fell off, ceased to be fashionable; higher churchmen succumbed to the apathy and the skeptical spirit of the time and lived and thought like the aristocracy, the class from which they came. Clergymen often performed better as gentlemen farmers than as ministers of religion.

Parish priests, frequently poor in purse and indolent in temper, preached solid sermons on elevated moral themes, but short on vitality or persuasiveness, and containing precious few grains of social sympathy. Public worship was formal, frosty, lifeless, and ordinary fellows, the poor and disinherited, were neglected or ignored.

But the stodgy Christianity of the island kingdom was turned somewhat dramatically into novel channels by Methodist evangelism. This movement originated among a group of students at the University of Oxford whose reputation for piety, concern for forgotten men and an ordered routine of daily living set them apart from other undergraduates. Scorned and ridiculed for their methodical way of living, they were labeled Methodists in derision and the name lingered. Leaders of the group were John and Charles Wesley and George Whitefield, all of whom became ordained ministers of the Established Church.

While attending a religious meeting in 1738, John Wesley experienced a remarkable and transforming "rebirth," in which, as he recounts it, "my heart strangely warmed. I felt I

[7] The nature of deism is explained on p. 173.

did trust in Christ, . . . and that an assurance was given me that He had taken away my sins . . . and saved me from the law of sin and death." Belief in sudden conversion assumed a prominent place in Wesley's Christianity and to that was joined the conviction that men must cultivate a vital personal faith, untrammeled by doctrinal details. Wesley would win men to salvation by faith in the crucified Christ.

It was possible, Wesley taught, for Christians to attain perfection on this earth, if they willed to do so. True believers should shun the theater, dancing, strong drink, observe the Sabbath strictly and be sober in dress and deportment. On the moral side, Methodism represented a revival of the stern imperatives and inhibitions of old-fashioned Puritanism.

Allied with Whitefield, a tremendously compelling popular orator, Wesley set to work convincing ordinary Englishmen of a sense of sin and persuading them to his vision of the good life. Public appeals were couched in warmly emotional language and were strongly democratic in accent. In time the Methodist movement made itself felt in nearly every department of English life.

For half a century Wesley energetically carried on his evangelical labors, gathering con-

The Methodist "Tree of Life"—a popular contemporary engraving which expresses the gist of Wesley's teaching

John Wesley

verts into religious societies and commissioning laymen to preach the good tidings. Lay preachers were an immense source of strength to the Methodist cause; some of them were largely unlettered, but they preached none the worse sermons for that, save as they encouraged religious terrorism. Decorous Anglican churchmen denied their pulpits to the Methodist enthusiasts, whom they derided as rabid fanatics, so the unconventional revivalists held forth on the streets and in the fields, attracting thousands of converts among the unprivileged and depraved. Methodism encouraged men in the gutter to look at the stars. Eventually Wesley founded a church wholly independent of Established Anglicanism.

Hearty congregational singing supplemented earnest extemporaneous preaching in Methodist meetings. The illiterate convert could sing hymns and follow the message of the preacher even though he could not read. Charles Wesley composed hundreds of devotional verses, simple and satisfying in artistry, which were set to attractive music. Asking why the devil should have all the good tunes, Wesley proceeded, with success, to equip the devil's opponents. He belongs to the group of eighteenth-century English hymn writers to whom tribute is paid Sunday after Sunday in the Protestant churches of Christendom.

Upon popular manners and habits the impact of "the people called Methodists" was profound, encouraging sobriety, self-discipline and diligence. Methodism powerfully counteracted the appeal of extremist political and social doctrines and helped to impart to British working-class movements a quality of moderation not duplicated on the Continent. As a humanitarian force, Methodism helped set the wheels of social change revolving, and in the nineteenth century promoted the material interests of industrial workers. Methodist enthusiasts fostered elementary education in Sunday Schools, teaching not only gospel truths but how to read and write. They actively engaged, too, in agitations against slavery and intemperance, pushed missionary enterprises in foreign parts and exerted a leavening influence upon older Protestant sects.

Wesley's religion was carried to Wales, Ireland and to North America, where, in 1784, an independent Methodist Church was organized. Methodist circuit riders were familiar figures on the landscape of the youthful United States; they planted seed that grew into the largest Protestant communion of the New World.

KING AND OLIGARCHY

King George III took the helm of Great Britain and Ireland in 1760 at the age of twenty-two. When he had reached forty-five he and the governing oligarchy had started to learn lessons in political wisdom never since forgotten. The fairest jewel in the British colonial crown, English America, had been permanently lost, and the constitutional prerogatives of the monarch had been defined in a manner that no later British sovereign dared to dispute.

At his accession, George III was extremely popular among broad sections of the British community. Unlike his immediate predecessors, the new king loved Britain, his birthplace, and he spoke the English language. He worshiped in the state church and won popular applause by the wholesome character of his personal behavior. But George III cherished outmoded conceptions of the role of the monarch in affairs of state. As heir-apparent he had been taught and came to believe that the long monopoly of the Whig Party in government must be broken; and through his mind ran the admonition of a doting mother: "George, be king." Courageous in a home-spun sort of way, George III was somnolent when he imagined he was awake. He was obstinate, too, and yet willing to back down when he realized that the opposition was too strong to be overborne.

As king, George III applied himself to state business with the industry of a Louis XIV. It was his ambition to recover for the crown prerogatives that had been whittled away during the Whig ascendancy; more exactly, he would assert the right of the king to pick ministers and to influence the deliberations of the cabinet. Put in other language, he wanted to obtain for himself about the same measure of authority that the Constitution of the United States assigns to the President. By bribery and patronage, devices which Whig oligarchs had fruitfully exploited, the king would try to secure a House of Commons obedient to the royal will.

Implementation of these designs, which of course cut athwart recently established constitutional practices, brought on acrimonious quarrels with the Whig oligarchy. No fewer than six ministries came and went in the first decade of the reign. Unable to impose upon the Commons a cabinet of his own choosing, George III literally purchased a set of M. P.'s who were ready to vote as he wished. That procedure flew in the face of the theory that the monarch was only a political cipher.

In 1770, with Lord North as nominal first minister, George III at last controlled a cabinet of pliant pygmies. Assuming leadership in the ministry, the king made himself the prime minister in effect. To consolidate his authority he took up with an extremely popular cause: the right of Parliament to levy taxes on English America. Quite in keeping with mercantilist dogma, British politicians in large majority felt

The Eighteenth Century was prolific in political caricature. Here, Charles Fox (center) and Edmund Burke (at right) are shown joining hands with Lord North, whose policies they bitterly opposed.

that colonies should be economically beneficial to the mother country. Standard economic theory was reinforced by the necessity of raising additional revenue; the national debt and interest charges had been substantially increased because of warfare with France, fought in part to protect the English colonies in the New World.

Coercive measures against English America were enacted in Parliament by thumping majorities. And equally strong support was forthcoming for military policies intended to crush the rebellious colonists in the War of American Independence. Criticism of the official course was expressed by only a thin minority of Whigs, with Edmund Burke as principal spokesman. Responsibility on the British side for the American Revolution rested by no means upon George III alone, but upon a large majority of the ruling oligarchy.

The march of events which exploded in the American Revolution is described in another place. Here it is sufficient to point out that British interest in the prosecution of the war dwindled when Bourbon France allied itself in 1778 with the colonial insurgents and Spain and the Netherlands joined in the struggle. By surrendering at Yorktown (1781), General Cornwallis not only assured victory for the Revolutionary cause, but ruined the pretensions of George III to rule as well as to reign. Lord North retired from the thankless task of posing as chief minister. Whigs took effective command of the parliamentary machine and pressed the monarch to yield to the logic of military defeat. Obliged to eat crow, George III did so without too wry a face. By the Treaty of Paris of 1783 the victorious colonies were recognized as a free and independent nation.

Ever since, executive authority in Britain has belonged to the prime minister and his cabinet, responsible to the Commons. Party competition, only tepid in the eighteenth century, became and has remained the transcendent fact in British politics. Clamor had arisen, in the meantime, for drastic revision in the franchise laws, for elimination of the "spoils systems" in the selection of M. P.'s and for redistribution of seats in the Commons. These demands, if passed into law, would have made Parliament more responsive to the public will. But the violent and terrifying eruption of the French Revolution and the subsequent and protracted warfare with France postponed British parliamentary reform, except for curtailment of the "spoils" system," for two generations.

SUMMARY

Glancing back over the period since the Restoration of Charles II, several developments of substantial and lasting importance for world civilization are seen to have transpired in the island kingdom. The crown had been permanently subordinated to the elected Parliament, which was managed by a cabinet chosen from the ranks of Parliament and responsible to it. Freedom of conscience, freedom of press and other civil liberties had been placed on firm foundations.

The British government, even though controlled solely by men of property, contrasted sharply with the autocratic regimes on the Continent. As a British publicist put it (1807), "all civilized governments may be divided into free and arbitrary; or more accurately into the government of England and the other European governments."

The British aristocracy had passed through its golden age. Tomorrow belonged to the middle classes. Men of letters brought fresh distinction to English literature and meritorious creations had been achieved in architecture and art. Novel religious and humanitarian currents, best identified perhaps with John Wesley, had been set flowing. Business, trade and industry had grown at an unprecedented pace. The national economy was still primarily agricultural and commercial, it is true, but far-reaching changes were coming over industrial processes that would convert the island kingdom into the unique workshop of the world.

Abroad, British enterprise and British arms had accumulated a gigantic empire, only to lose the choicest portion during the reign of George III. By reason of fierce competition for power and colonial dominion Great Britain became involved in desperate struggles with continental countries. For a time the outcome of those contests enhanced British international prestige, though later it declined; but these matters are better reserved for discussion elsewhere.

FOR FURTHER STUDY

GEORGE N. CLARK, *The Later Stuarts, 1660–1714* (Oxford, 1934)

GEORGE M. TREVELYAN, *England under Queen Anne* (3 vols., New York, 1930–1934)

BASIL WILLIAMS, *The Whig Supremacy, 1714–1760* (Oxford, 1939)

WALTER T. SELLEY, *England in the Eighteenth Century* (2nd ed., London, 1949)

JAMES BOSWELL, *The Life of Johnson* (new ed., 6 vols., Oxford, 1934–1950)

JOHN GLOAG, *English Furniture* (London, 1944)

ERIC NEWTON, *British Painting* (London, 1945)

MALDWYN L. EDWARDS, *John Wesley and the Eighteenth Century* (London, 1933)

CHARLES R. RITCHESON, *British Politics and the American Revolution* (Norman, Okla., 1954)

MAURICE ASHLEY, *England in the Seventeenth Century* (London, 1960) PAPERBACK

HESKETH PEARSON, *Merry Monarch: The Life and Likeness of Charles II* (London, 1960)

DAVID OGG, *England in the Reigns of James II and William III* (Oxford, 1955)

JOHN H. PLUMB, *England in the Eighteenth Century* (London, 1950) PAPERBACK

DOROTHY MARSHALL, *Eighteenth Century England* (London, 1962)

JOHN H. PLUMB, *Sir Robert Walpole* (2 vols., London, 1956, 1961)

ESMÉ C. WINGFIELD-STRATFORD, *The Squire and his Relations* (London, 1956)

RICHARD PARES, *King George III* (Oxford, 1953)

CHARLES G. ROBERTSON, *Chatham and the British Empire* (new ed., London, 1948) PAPERBACK

CHAPTER IV

THE HEART OF EUROPE (1648-1740)

THE HARVEST OF WAR

AT THE middle of the seventeenth century, France and England were—and had long been—united countries, capable of vigorous participation in international affairs and global commerce. Radically different was the situation in the heart of Europe where the two principal groupings, the Germans and the Italians, were politically divided. Germany and Italy were geographical expressions, nothing more, and were to remain so for two hundred years longer. The contrast between the west of Europe and the center has bearing upon the discontents and the convulsions of the twentieth century.

The largest and most respected of German states was Austria, whose Hapsburg sovereign also wore the phantom crown of the Holy Roman Empire. By reason of the disparate peoples inside sprawling Austria, it was less a German state than an ethnographical museum under a single dynasty. Its principal territories lay in the mid-Danube valley, making Austria the natural defender of Christendom against Turkish subjugation. At the time, Turkey, in a measure, resembled Communist Russia after the Second World War, for it threatened to overrun central Europe and impose its peculiar institutions and customs. As matters worked out, the menacing Ottoman flood was checked, and Austrian armies marched victoriously southward disseminating Western light and learning.

And Austria did more. She was the principal force preventing the France of Louis XIV from dominating the heart of Europe. She was the main barrier against inundation by the Russians to the east, who, under the dynamic will of Peter the Great, were presently to attain unprecedented European importance. At the same time, the emergence of a powerful kingdom of Prussia, an outstanding event of the eighteenth century, bolstered the security of central Europe against west and east.

After the terrible ordeal of the Thirty Years' War "Germany" presented a picture of human misery almost as chaotic and depressing as at the close of the Second World War. Marching armies had ransacked and ravaged; hunger and distress prevailed on every side. Uprooted folk in the thousands roamed the countryside; disease and starvation claimed far more victims than had shot and shell. The German population of nearly twenty millions had fallen by almost a third as a result of the catastrophic warfare. Not until late in the eighteenth century would Germany recover from the human costs of the war.

Over wide areas immense physical destruction had taken place. Villages and towns by the hundred were reduced to heaps of rubble, and capital equipment and means of communication had been wrecked with baleful consequences for commerce and manufacturing. It is easy, however, to exaggerate the ruinous impact of the war upon urban life. German cities had been on the downgrade before the fighting started, due to the shift in trade routes from sea and land to the Atlantic Ocean after the great geographical discoveries. The eclipse of Venice and the rise of Holland as a commercial power had adversely affected the German economy.

But the Thirty Years' War accelerated the impoverishment of the once powerful German middle class at precisely the period when the bourgeoisie in the west of Europe was strengthening its position. Rather than engage in business or a learned profession many a German middle class man took employment in civil administration. It was well along in the eighteenth century before Germany ceased to be essentially a land of peasants. Agriculture of course was the principal means of livelihood. In the war years vast tracts of land and vineyards had been damaged by military operations or by improper cultivation; herds and flocks had been

The destruction of agriculture in Germany during the course of the Thirty Years' War is the background for this contemporary etching of a peasant and a soldier.

cut down by about two-thirds. Yet farming could and did revive much faster than commerce and industry.

Standards of personal behavior had been gravely impaired by the prolonged and brutalizing warfare. Respect for the rights of others and for property was weakened. The landed aristocracy, moreover, was definitely estranged from the rural masses. And degradation in the things of the mind paralleled the moral morass left behind by the war; a full century elapsed before German culture began to move forward again. To the informed and sensitive German of 1648 the future must have looked as bleak and foreboding as to his descendants in 1945, following the Second World War.

A HOUSE DIVIDED

Aggravating the German tragedy was the course pursued by the masters of the principalities into which "Germany" was divided—over three hundred of them, almost all small. Legally, it is true, the ancient Holy Roman Empire of the German nation still existed, but practically it was a hollow fiction; men marveled that this picturesque survival was able to hold together at all. The assembly (diet) of the Empire had degenerated into an impotent conference of envoys, in which the French ambassador frequently spoke the decisive word. Only in time of grave emergency could an imperial army be assembled and then it was too awkwardly organized to count for much. The supreme court, to adjust disputes among member states, was little more than a cipher and there was no imperial currency or common standards in weights and measures. The Holy Roman Empire, in short, was dead generations before it was buried.

Public authority in Germany was lodged in a multitude of princes, who considered themselves as emperors in the small, and resembled landed proprietors administering private estates. Princely power extended over the whole range of daily living, regulating everything needful for the material and moral health of subjects. With minor exceptions, old local assemblies lapsed into desuetude.

Princes published laws, levied and disbursed revenues, maintained standing armies of their own and diplomatic corps. They created ornate bureaucracies whose members were rewarded with ever more resounding titles as they moved up the official ladder. Since individual enterprise had been sadly depleted by the long warfare, the German states passed under the direction of powerful bureaucracies which undertook to solve technical questions and economic problems. It was assumed that public officials possessed greater wisdom in such matters than private citizens; and once the ascendancy of the bureaucratic apparatus had been established, it was not thereafter significantly lessened. However petty, the German princedoms were in truth "Leviathan" states operated on authoritarian principles with Prussia boasting the tightest discipline of the lot.

The military and administrative services together with the moral weight of the Church upheld and fortified the authority of the despots. Unquestioning submission of the governed to an authoritarian ruler, which is often singled out as a hallmark of the German people, became part of the German heritage. The governments of Germany in this era of mercantilism minutely supervised commercial and industrial transactions. They raised tariff barriers against neighbors, coined money and had distinctive systems of weights and measures. These practices, coupled with the ravages of the late war, prevented Germany from progressing economically as Britain and France were doing. Only the peasantry was productive in a major way and upon that class was saddled the heavy load of financing governments. Noble properties in sections of Germany were greatly enlarged and the workers on them reduced to servile chattels. A rigid caste society solidified.

To the north, especially, the "earth people" were unfree, owning no tools and toiling on large estates. But in the west the status of rustics approached that of France, for although they paid dues to overlords, they were permitted to sell surplus products (if any) in the towns and they possessed a considerable measure of personal freedom. Peasants clung to the antiquated three-field tradition of farming without experimentation. In the course of the eighteenth century the potato assumed the place in the diet of Germans, as of other poor people in the west of Europe, that rice held for the Chinese masses. Yield per acre was abundant, and the potato could be easily cultivated, stored and prepared for the table. The peasant's patch of potatoes attenuated the age-old dread of starvation. Few peasant properties, however, raised more food than the families consumed themselves and it was unlawful for peasants to engage in trade or manufacturing.

Petty German tyrants deliberately patterned their courts on the French model. The customs of France, French literature and language became fashionable, and gold from the purse of Louis XIV was greedily accepted in return for political support. French diplomacy profited, too, from the sharp antagonism toward Austria which existed in Bavaria and some of the lesser German states. Certain small German principalities, primarily in Alsace, passed wholly under French sovereignty, while Sweden governed another group of states, and Denmark, a third. Beyond that, the king of Saxony accepted (1697) the crown of Poland, while the elector of Hanover in 1714 assumed the kingship of Great Britain and Ireland.

Germany, to repeat, was simply a geographical phrase, very much divided against itself. Nowhere was there consciousness of common nationality (though sporadically, anti-French passions flamed up), nowhere was there a vision of German national unity. A German's Fatherland meant his own petty state, the rest of Germany was commonly referred to as "foreign parts."

THE AUSTRIAN HAPSBURGS

Alone among the German states, Austria commanded sufficient manpower and physical resources to pursue a fully independent rôle in foreign affairs. By election, the head of the Austrian state held the coveted dignity of Holy Roman Emperor, but his real power depended upon his own dominions. Once admitted to the circle of Great Powers, Austria retained that rank until the end of the First World War.

The growth of the Hapsburg realm in the heart of Europe contains more bizarre and fortuitous chapters than the story of any other country. The original nucleus of the state was an area along the Danube on which Vienna stands. Dynastic marriages and military conquests added territories adjacent to Vienna, and in 1273, a German nobleman, Rudolph of Hapsburg, came into possession of this small German-speaking duchy; his descendants reigned over Austria, with slight interruptions, to 1918. Further annexations, more astute marriages extended the frontiers, and from the fifteenth century onward Austrian sovereigns were habitually elected as Roman Emperors. The most momentous of the Hapsburg marriages, solemnized in 1496, linked that family with the dynasty of Spain. The crowns of Spain and Austria rested for a time on the same Hapsburg head, who was monarch of the broadest empire ever presided over by a Christian prince.

But the immense empire was split up in 1556, the Austrian estates and the dignity of emperor passing together to one branch of the Hapsburg House. In the meanwhile, in 1526, the Austrian Hapsburgs, who were in fact as much Spanish as German, had acquired the adjoining Kingdoms of Bohemia and Hungary. Known after the First World War as Czechoslovakia, Bohemia prided itself on a rich and virile tradition. It was peopled mainly by Slavic-speaking Czechs, but also by men of German speech, and was included in the Holy Roman Empire. The last of the independent kings of Bohemia had also been elected ruler of Hungary; he perished in 1526 fighting the Ottoman Turks.

The hard core of the population of Hungary was Magyar, descendants of marauding conquerors who had thrust into the Danube valley from their Asiatic homeland in the ninth century. Their language, their literature, their pride were peculiar to themselves. Surrounding peoples, mostly Slav in tongue, were subjugated by the Magyars to form the kingdom of Hungary. Early in the sixteenth century, as has been indicated, the fortunes of Hungary, as of Bohemia, were tied to the Hapsburg dynasty in Vienna, a relationship that prevailed until 1918,

Turkish janissaries, or shock troops recruited from among the Christian children of the lands subject to the Sultan

Much the larger part of the inhabitants in the Hapsburg realm spoke languages other than German, but that had little significance before the upsurge of patriotic nationalism. Periodically, Czechs and Magyars of an independent cast of mind struggled to liberate their countries from Hapsburg control, or at least to obtain home rule.

The Austrian empire, then, was in reality several nations governed by the House of Hapsburg, and steadily knit more tightly together by economic interests. Another linch-pin was Roman Catholicism, to which the great majority of the subjects were attached. Austria proper, though not Bohemia, escaped the worst ravages of the Thirty Years' War. Thereafter Hapsburg energies and expansionist zeal switched from central Europe to the Balkan peninsula, a deviation, which among other consequences, enabled France to exert unprecedented influence in German politics.

THE RISE OF THE OTTOMAN TURKS

Austria concentrated her attention on the East, half because of the Turkish peril and half because of the opportunities for territorial aggrandizement in that direction if the armies of the sultan could be broken. It may seem surprising that Turkey, which after the Second World War depended desperately upon the help of the United States to preserve her independence, should once have caused terrifying apprehensions in Christian Europe. But such in fact was the case.

Open an atlas to a map of the age of Louis XIV and across southeastern Europe and western Asia is printed "Ottoman Empire." That realm stretched over northern Africa, too, almost to the boundary of Morocco. Like Austria, the farflung Ottoman realm contained disparate peoples and tongues—and differing religious creeds to boot.

The original Turks, the Seljuks—yellow men—moved out of western Asia in the eleventh century. They easily wrested Asia Minor (Anatolia) from the enfeebled and degenerate grasp of the Byzantine or East Roman Empire, which for generations had been "drying up like a puddle in the sun." Although the newcomers adopted Mohammedanism as their religion, they assimilated in other respects—and that fast—with conquered Christians.

Turkish subjugation of the Christian Holy Land inspired the romantic Crusades of the late Middle Age. Though failing to recover Palestine, the Crusaders, nonetheless, retarded the march of the Moslem into Europe. Presently a tribal chief, Othman—whence the name Ottoman—asserted his power over neighboring tribes and founded a ruling house which for two centuries produced talented administrators and skilful strategists. From the first the Turkish government and the army were indistinguishable, and therein lay a vital source of Ottoman strength. The top figure, or sultan, exercised autocratic authority.

Shortly after the middle of the fourteenth century Ottoman troops crossed into Europe just south of the venerable Christian bastion of Constantinople. The last of the medieval invaders of Europe, the Turks were soon embarked upon an intoxicating career of conquest. Small Christian nations in the Balkan peninsula, mostly Slav in speech and culture, bowed before the seemingly invincible Moslems. All Europe trembled.

For their time, the Turks were relatively humane conquerors. Peoples whom they overpowered were not compelled, for instance, to accept the faith of Islam, though some, out of expediency or conviction chose to do so. On the other hand, the conquered were outrageously taxed and forced to hand over their finest young men for service in the Ottoman army. Brought up as Moslems, thoroughly disciplined, well equipped and provided for these soldiers, called *janissaries,* were the "West Pointers" of Turkey. They carried everything before them. Appealed to by the Pope, Hungary and Poland despatched regiments to check the Turkish flood, but the most they could accomplish was to hold up the advance. The thorny and complex Near Eastern Question now entered European diplomacy, persisting into the twentieth century.

As the crowning achievement of their operations in the Balkans the Turks captured Constantinople in 1453 after a memorable siege and a heroic defense by utterly inadequate Christian forces. Once incomparably the greatest of Christian cities, the home of matchless wealth, grandeur and culture, Constantinople was now rededicated as the Ottoman capital under the name of Istamboul, and served as such until after the First World War. The triumph of the Turk at Constantinople had most alarming and depressing reverberations in Christendom. Historians were long accustomed to date the dawn of modern history from this melancholy event.

Victory whetted the Turkish appetite. Troops overran the east Mediterranean area and, finding resistance light and booty attractive, pushed recklessly onward. The sultan added the title of caliph to his dignities, assuming thus the headship of the Moslem religion. Sea warfare with merchants of Venice, who almost monopolized business between the eastern Mediterranean and western Europe, resulted in fresh successes for the Turks. Ottoman interference with East-West commerce stimulated the search for an alternate route to the sources of Oriental luxuries, leading on to the chance discovery of the Americas and the finding of an all-sea route to Asia around southern Africa.

Under Sultan Suleiman the Magnificent, who died in 1566, the Ottoman Empire ranked as the largest, the most powerful and probably the best governed state in the world. Imperial boundaries were pushed out in western Asia and great armies drove deep into Hungary. On the battlefield of Mohács in 1526, the Turks broke the Hungarian chivalry and the king of Hungary lost his life, the crown, as has been noted, passing to the Hapsburgs in Vienna. In 1529, Ottoman forces of 200,000, a strength unheard of in Christendom, hammered upon the defenses of Vienna. Repulsed and driven back, the Turks nevertheless retained their grip on Hungary, save for the western district, which Austria recaptured.

John Sobieski, King of Poland

THE OTTOMAN DECLINE

The Turkish empire had touched and in fact passed its zenith; a long and very gradual decline set in. It was still very extensive, however, covering southeastern Europe, the northern rim of the Black Sea, western Asia and the southern shores of the Mediterranean. The Turkish element in Europe itself was never more than a thin veneer laid upon a heterogeneous array of subject nationalities. For stability, the Ottoman realm required a continuous line of supermen as sultans, competent and dedicated officials, loyal troops and, not least, political disunity in Christendom. None of these prerequisites of strength availed in the century after the departure of Suleiman the Magnificent.

Quite otherwise, a league of Christian nations, formed under papal guidance, defeated the Turks on land and sea (Lepanto, 1571). But in the second half of the seventeenth century, reinvigorated and inspirited Ottoman armies resumed the assault upon Christian Europe. Abetted by Hungarian insurgents, a huge Turkish attacking force marched upon Vienna in 1683, and laid siege to that outpost of Chrisendom. Shellfire damaged buildings in the Austrian capital, which was only defended by an improvised citizen army. It seemed improbable that the city could survive Turkish pressure. To the rescue, happily, rallied soldiers from Germany and a Polish force commanded by King John Sobieski. After a single day of desperate fighting, the Turks pulled back in headlong flight, leaving their booty behind them.

It was now the turn of Christian Europe to carry war into the possessions of Turkey. Austria teamed up with Poland and Venice in what is spoken of as the last Crusade. Toward the close of the fighting Russia joined in the contest, a momentous event for that intervention marked the beginning of antagonism between Austria and Russia over the Balkan peninsula which flared up, intermittently, until both monarchies perished in the First World War.

Badly thrashed, the Turks tacitly acknowledged their declining vigor in the Treaty of Carlowitz of 1699. Thereby Turkey was confined to the south of the Danube; Austria recovered nearly all of Hungary and Poland annexed lands north of the River Dniester. Two subsequent wars underscored the decline of Turkey, without however producing important transfers of territory. No longer could the Ottoman Empire be regarded as a real danger to the safety of Christendom, although it still ruled a large area of Europe. Austria stood guard on the Danube, but prospects of driving the Turk from the Continent were shattered by a Prussian attack upon the Hapsburg lands.

In the heart of Vienna stands an equestrian statue of that colorful cavalier, Prince Eugene of Savoy, organizer of victory over the Turks. Of Italian descent, he learned the arts of war in the army of Louis XIV. After taking part in the relief of Vienna in 1683, Prince Eugene advanced to supreme command of the Hapsburg forces, introducing military methods he had been taught in France. Morale of troops, for instance, was bolstered by good food and barracks and veterans were allotted farms on land recovered from Turkey. The martial exploits of the Prince, against the French as well as the Turks, made him the most famous man in continental Europe.

INSIDE AUSTRIA

In addition to territorial aggrandizement to the east, the Austrian House of Hapsburg secured sovereignty over the southern Netherlands (Belgium) and large sections of Italy by the Peace of Utrecht, 1713. It would appear, on balance, that the Italian holdings were a political liability, for they diverted Austrian energies from the east, the logical path of expansion, and were vulnerable to attack by France.

Vienna was the focal point of the widely dispersed Hapsburg realm of peoples. Nature herself intended that a proud city should arise at this point on the Danube, most picturesque of European rivers, and the crossroads of trade thoroughfares from every direction. Once the Turkish tidal wave had receded, Vienna, previously not much more than a frontier fortress, expanded into a considerable city. It was the capital of Catholic Germany as well as of the House of Hapsburg; about a fourth as large as London, Vienna was protected by stout walls and fringed by quaint suburban villages. As though drawn by a magnet, the landed aristocracy of the realm concentrated in the capital, artists and tradesmen, too, from Hungary, Bohemia, Italy, Belgium and southern Germany.

Something of the reputation of Vienna for tolerance, charm and lightheartedness, which was created at this time, is traceable to the cosmopolitan character of the community. Viennese were more likely to enthuse over a musical celebrity than over a topflight statesman or commander. In the mellow atmosphere of Vienna it was easy to enjoy the present and allow the Church to look after the future; allegiance to Catholicism had been deepened by the desperate struggles with the Turkish worshipers of Allah.

Rising commerce, incomes from the broad fields and forests of the nobility and public revenues enhanced the material prosperity of Vienna. Church, Court and High Society brought beauty and brilliance to the community. The rigid social protocol, the pomp and ceremony of the Spanish court surrounded the imperial household; rulers of Austria surpassed even Louis XIV in ceremonial ritual. For each day of the week, their functions were prescribed in minute detail. Commented an English traveler: the Austrian Court is "a mixture of French elegance and levity with coarseness and heaviness, Spanish solemnity and vacuity, Hungarian pride and love of display, oriental splendour and misery, and Italian love of art . . ."

Churches, monasteries and aristocratic town residences were built on a sumptuous scale, often in the baroque style of architecture, an importation from Italy. Ornate and stately, baroque nevertheless expressed individualism and afforded opportunity for touches of merriness. Best souvenir of this type of architecture is the massive Charles Church, designed by an extraordinary baroque master, Fischer von Erlach, a church that took twenty years to build. On either side the façade is flanked by enormous Doric columns; the church proper is surmounted by a spacious dome and the ceiling is richly decorated with exquisite frescoes. This edifice and Gothic St. Stephen's Cathedral, the symbol of Vienna and begun in the fourteenth century, were the dazzling ecclesiastical showpieces of the city.[1]

Fischer von Erlach also applied his rare creative gifts to the enlargement and beautification of the Hapsburg palace and mansions for the upper nobility in Vienna. Ornate establishments of white stone rose as much as six stories. Like their counterparts in England, artistically designed rooms were adorned with fine carvings, tapestries, statuary and tasteful furniture. In the finest baroque pattern was the extensive

[1] Retreating Nazis almost ruined St. Stephen's in April of 1945 with incendiary bombs, the worst blow the noble building ever sustained in its long history.

The Belvedere Palace, once on the outskirts of Vienna

summer palace, Schönbrunn, on the edge of Vienna, whose parks and formal gardens outdid even Versailles.[2] At elegant aristocratic dinners half a hundred dishes were served by lackeys in full livery, and washed down by a score of choice vintages. In regal splendor if not in suavity of manners the Austrian aristocracy matched that of France—and outlived it.

Court and nobility patronized the arts and music and assembled famous collections of art treasures. Artists and musical masters were mostly Italians or responded to Italian influences. Native folk music, for which Vienna achieved international celebrity, was cultivated in bourgeois taverns. Foundations were laid which were to make Vienna incontestably the musical capital of Europe.

Government in the Hapsburg realm was of course in the pattern of absolutism. Nobles exercised powers, however, which were denied the French aristocracy, for example, and the various provinces had assemblies (diets) which occasionally caused real concern in Vienna. The machinery of state was directed by a pettifogging bureaucracy, though provincial administrations had local peculiarities. Dispersed

[2] For Prince Eugene, the magnificent Belvedere Palace, on the outskirts of Vienna, was designed by Lukas von Hildebrandt—evidence, incidentally, that the morbid feeling of insecurity against the Turks had disappeared.

as its domains were, Austria was inescapably implicated in every major European diplomatic convulsion that arose. A great and respected power, Austria possessed large armies and resources, and martial traditions which had been quickened by wars with France and wearing struggles with the Turks. Foreign commerce was promoted; a company to trade with India, for instance, was organized in the Belgian possession.

Emperor Charles VI, who took the helm of government in 1715, was not a strong ruler. He lacked the tough, masculine virtues expected of an autocrat. Not blessed with a son and heir he dreaded lest the empire might be despoiled upon his death. To avoid such a calamity, he devoted years of assiduous bargaining to secure the assent of provincial assemblies and of foreign governments to his daughter, Maria Theresa, as his successor. In that objective he succeeded, though several princes concurred in the imperial wish with their fingers crossed. The death of Charles VI in 1740 was soon followed by a general European conflagration.

Maria Theresa as Archduchess

THE ORIGINS OF PRUSSIA

The assault upon Austria was delivered by the tough-textured kingdom of Prussia. The appearance of this formidable power is a controlling fact of modern history. One day Prussia was to become the core of a united Germany, the strongest nation of Europe.

Prussia originated in the electorate of Brandenburg which in 1415 was acquired by the unimportant German noble family of Hohenzollern. Brandenburg was a singularly unattractive patrimony, no larger than Vermont, with infertile soil, and sparsely peopled. It lay, however, close to the geographical center of Germany and was the meeting place of trade highways. The walled town of Berlin, a business community of sorts, was picked as the residence of the elector. During the Reformation the Hohenzollerns turned Protestant and practiced religious toleration. The ruling oligarchy of the little state were aristocratic Junker landlords; in local assemblies the Junkers wielded the power of purse and by grants of money they purchased concessions which reinforced their hold on administration.

Marriage arrangements added tiny duchies in the Rhine valley to the Hohenzollern state, and in 1618 the elector inherited the province of East Prussia, high up on the Baltic, which very nearly doubled his square mileage. East Prussia had been subjugated in the thirteenth century by German crusaders—the Order of Teutonic Knights—who had appeared in the area to convert the pagan population and to establish feudal baronies. Streams of German peasants and merchants flowed in after the conquest and they laid out towns of which the largest was Königsberg. East Prussia, which was separated from Brandenburg by a broad belt of Polish territory, acknowledged Poland as overlord before its transfer to the Hohenzollerns.

The elector coveted Pomerania, on the rim of the Baltic adjoining Brandenburg, and under the Treaty of Westphalia of 1648 he annexed the eastern and poorer half. At the same time he picked up several promising ecclesiastical princedoms in Germany proper, so that the Hohenzollern holdings stretched from beyond the Vistula up to the Rhine. All these principalities had their own special institutions, assemblies and privileges.

HOW BRANDENBURG BECAME PRUSSIA

The real founder of Hohenzollern greatness was Frederick William, "the Great Elector," who ruled from 1640 to 1688. A man of robust physique and boundless energy, rough and coarse, he aspired to consolidate his small possession within and enlarge it without. He could be as perfidious as a Mazarin if that seemed necessary to advance state interests. Throughout his reign the Great Elector spent himself in creating a first-class standing army, useful both for defense or to compel international respect. An impressive military establishment, he well knew, would reinforce and amplify the voice of diplomacy. At his death, his regiments contained 31,000 well-disciplined soldiers, or over five times as many as at his accession, and next to the Austrian, the finest army in German Europe. Compared with the army of France, the Hohenzollern forces were still small, though large in relation to the population of fewer than 1,500,000.

Frederick William I, Elector of Brandenburg and King of Prussia

Other enduring Prussian institutions dating from the era of the Great Elector were a highly centralized despotism and an efficient administration. Local assemblies lost their power, bit by bit, to shape the course of public affairs, and thus the possibility of assemblies maturing as institutions of representative government was prevented.

On the other hand, the social and economic privileges of the Junker aristocracy were extended and guaranteed. Not only were members of this caste assigned the prominent places in public administration and the army, but they were exempted from taxation. A working alliance, mutually advantageous, bound the absolute ruler and the senior officials together. Deep into the nineteenth century the Junkers constituted the governing class of Prussia-Germany and their economic and social power persisted into the twentieth century. All citizens from the king down applied themselves to the advancement of state welfare to a degree unapproached in other German principalities. Prussia became indeed Sparta born again.

The huge army and an expansionist foreign policy entailed heavy taxation, but the government pursued policies calculated to keep the economy stable. Public finance, as an example, was managed with scrupulous care; manufacturing was fostered by state subsidies and shielded from outside competition by tariffs. Immigrants equipped with industrial skills were greeted with open arms; among others, 20,000 Huguenots found a hospitable environment in this Protestant land. Some of them settled in Berlin whose population in the reign of the Great Elector jumped from six to thirty thousand. To raise agricultural production more land was brought under cultivation by reclamation and drainage projects, and roadways were somewhat improved.

On the diplomatic front Frederick William achieved the objective of freeing East Prussia from Polish sovereignty; yet, hard though he tried, he failed to snatch western Pomerania from Sweden. In pursuit of that aim, he lined up with Louis XIV, accepting subsidies from the French exchequer; the funds were largely squandered on a little navy and on a colonial misadventure in western Africa. But Swedish Pomerania eluded his grasp. Later Hohenzollern rulers esteemed the Great Elector as the finest exemplar of princely virtues and achievements. Frederick the Great, after gazing at his remains, blurted out, "Shut up the coffin; he has done great deeds."

Although the head of the House of Hohenzollern commanded a fairly broad domain, he bore only the name of elector. That anomaly was changed in 1701 when, with the concurrence of the Holy Roman Emperor, the Elector Frederick III was elevated to royal dignity as king in Prussia. That title brought greater moral prestige in international society, and the ambition of the dynasty was whetted for still grander distinction.

Intending to emulate Louis XIV, the first Prussian king generously encouraged learning and science. On his order the Royal Academy of Sciences was organized in 1701, with the universal genius Gottfried Leibnitz as presiding officer; in time this Academy took rank with the most respected scholarly bodies of Europe. And the University of Halle, opened in 1694, introduced fresh and vivifying currents into intellectual work. Instead of dry scholasticism, studies having practical implications were emphasized; almost all the prominent Prussian civil servants of the next century were educated at Halle and the example it set inspired reforms in other universities. Continuous warfare with France filled the reign of Frederick I and the heritage of authoritarian government was in no wise impaired.

THE ADVANCE OF PRUSSIA

It was during the kingship of Frederick William I (1713–1740) that Prussia unmistakably raised herself above other north German states. Purposes and ideals which the Great Elector had favored were more intensively applied. "Kings are made for work," declared Frederick William I, "and if they want to reign with honor they must look after their affairs for themselves"—precisely the language of Louis XIV of France.

What the king preached, he practiced. "I am the finance minister and the field marshal of the king of Prussia," he proclaimed. His daughter tells us that dining-room conversations were limited to economic and military topics. It was the intention of this grim and emotionless monarch to have his subjects mirror in their lives his own preferences and qualities: hard work, devotion to the public weal, parsimony, obedience to duty, no gayety nor frivolity, few comforts and little culture.

In an amazing measure the wishes of the monarch became realities. Prussians high and low, rich and poor learned as never before to serve the state with body and soul in life or death. Austerity, discipline and self-denial were firmly established as basic elements in the Prussian tradition. That was clearly evident in the army, the special pet of the "drill sergeant" king, the symbol and guarantor of his unfettered authority. The size of the military forces was doubled, reaching 83,000, and was exceeded by only three other armies of Europe; in training, in discipline, in esprit de corps, the Prussian regiments had no peer.

As already explained, officers were drawn from Junker families of the northern provinces who cherished raw and predatory martial traditions and who prided themselves on technical efficiency and fidelity to the crown. Their feeling of superiority as aristocrats was heightened by membership in the officers' corps; in their sight civilian officials were distinctly inferior clay. Rank and file troops were recruited principally from the Prussian population under a regime of almost universal service; some foreigners who made soldiering their vocation, were also enrolled. Frederick William I was inordinately proud of a regiment of Potsdam giants—all over six feet—and collected from everywhere in Europe. No gift from a fellow sovereign evoked as much gratitude in Berlin as a consignment of towering guardsmen. The king stood with his gun cocked, foreigners were heard to say, but would never pull the trigger.

The Prussian army was maintained out of royal revenues, principally by the income from crown lands, while many another German state depended upon foreign subsidies for its army. At the same time that public income was increasing, expenditures were held at an irreducible minimum and superfluous officials were dismissed. Frugality, expertness and conscientious devotion to duty were strong traits of the Prussian civil bureaucracy.

Efforts were put forth to keep the economy on a high level and to enhance state income by typically mercantilist legislation. Frankly imitating the practices of Colbert, the Prussian government encouraged industries and subjected them to elaborate regulation and inspection; foreign goods were shut out by tariffs and it was declared unlawful to export raw materials needed in native manufacturing. The royal army was clothed in Prussian-made cloth, which Berliners, too, were required to wear. Foreign craftsmen were joyfully welcomed and exempted from restrictive guild rules.[3]

Protestant or Catholic refugees were assured religious freedom in a country whose royal family worshiped in the Calvinist tradition while the bulk of the population was Lutheran. Tolerance of religious opinions in Prussia stood in shining contrast to the political compulsions of authoritarianism. By law, moreover, children were supposed to receive elementary schooling, but the legislation was wretchedly enforced. New land was opened to cultivation by extensive drainage enterprises, rivers and roads were improved to facilitate the movement of crops and manufactures.

All in all, the Prussian despotism was admirable in its way and in its day. This rather parvenu kingdom not only drew ahead of its German neighbors but was prepared to challenge Austrian leadership in German Europe. At his death in 1740 Frederick William I bequeathed to his son and successor, Frederick II, surnamed the Great, a well-ordered governmental machine, a large army, a prosperous economy and a submissive population of two and a half millions, fully a quarter of them immigrants or descendants of immigrants. With that inheritance the new master would lead Prussia to a pinnacle of greatness never before reached.

[3] The functions of guilds were whittled down to the supervision of the quality of products and of working conditions.

CROWN PRINCE FREDERICK

Like other conspicuous and dynamic political personages Frederick II is a highly controversial figure. Judgments on his methods and accomplishments vary widely among historical specialists; few deny, however, that he was the ablest of Hohenzollerns and the foremost monarch of his century, a first-class general and an autocrat who tempered his despotism with a measure of benevolence. Frederick II took over the kingship full of soaring ambitions for himself and his country. Already he had familiarized himself with the dynamics of national aggrandizement and with the strong points and the shortcomings of contemporary governments. Someone has described him as an "unamiable youth, with the aspirations and vanity of a minor poet," yet "the most consummate practical genius, who, in modern times has inherited a throne."

Frederick's pathway to the throne was no bed of thornless roses. His father intended that the crown prince should be an exact replica of himself and, accordingly, issued detailed instructions for the training of the boy, even to the precise content of his prayers! The paternal determination to train up the child in the way that he should go soured the soul of the crown prince. Son and Hohenzollern sire held contrasting and clashing opinions on the nature of the good life.

Precocious, sensitive to the things of the mind, studious, the young Frederick struck out along independent lines. He learned and loved the French language, for example, and wrote in that tongue by preference. He eagerly devoured good literature, enjoyed penning odes to daffodils and such and cultivated a taste for music, playing a flute on the sly. His fondness for the ladies was not always bounded by strict convention; and his theological outlook strayed from the narrow orbit of Protestant orthodoxy.

Frederick the Great in youth

The youthful Frederick, moreover, disliked the military profession and he let his aversion be known.

Small wonder, then, that his hidebound and unlovable father felt that he had hatched a worthless dilettante and rake. In hot anger the king repeatedly and harshly reprimanded the heir-apparent. Frederick decided, at the age of eighteen, to escape from bondage by fleeing abroad, but the king discovered the plan. A friend and accomplice of Frederick was put to death before his very eyes and he himself was threatened with similar punishment; instead, however, he was confined for a term in prison. Bitterly and boldly Frederick complained, "You treat me not as your son but as a miserable slave." Hard-bitten teachers, selected by the king, were set to work instilling orthodox notions of government and religion in the mind of the crown prince.

After his release from prison, Frederick exhibited a considerable change of heart. Not that he abandoned his intellectual pursuits, for he gathered round him a company of mellow and cultivated spirits and struck up a correspondence with Voltaire, which fast blossomed into mutual admiration; as king, Frederick often entertained the witty Frenchman at the royal palace, but after a generation of intimacy they became estranged. Frederick discovered an opiate in hard work, and he dutifully married the insipid and awkward daughter of a lesser German dynasty, as ordered by his father.

In public the reformed prince affected the gravity of an elder statesman and manifested lively interest in the royal army. As a colonel, he reinforced in the field what he had learned about the science of war from books. He pored over the pages of history and arrived at his own conclusions on the way that nations had made themselves strong and men got their names into history books. At length father and son were so thoroughly reconciled that the king could say: "I die contented since I leave such a worthy son and successor." How Frederick as monarch applied his conceptions of statecraft is explained later.

DIVIDED ITALY

Even as Prussia was to become the kernel of a united Germany so Piedmont (or Sardinia) was to fill a like role in the destiny of Italy. At the mid-seventeenth century, Italy was partitioned into a bevy of principalities, some of them managed by foreign powers. National unity had been insistently demanded by Dante and other fine Italian spirits as the indispensable prologue to freedom and prosperity in the peninsula, but stubborn obstacles barred the road to that goal.

For one thing, alien governments, Spain, France and Austria, kept poking their fingers into the Italian pie, pulling out a plum now and then. The fate of the peninsula was actually shaped in the foreign offices and on the battlegrounds of northern Europe. Public spirit in Italy was so feeble that international sparring over the country was viewed with frigid apathy, seldom with resentment. A popular poet sang:

> If France should win, what matters it to me?
> If Austria loses, does it better thee?
> They do not fight for either thee or me;
> Rather indeed they scoff at me and thee;
> Yet they will bring a thousand woes on thee.

Another standing barrier to unification was the Papal States of the Church presided over by a prince who at the same time was the Chief Shepherd of international Roman Catholicism and as such a considerable moral force in Europe. Alongside of all this were deep-rooted jealousies between the several principalities,

The heart of Berlin in the time of Frederick the Great. The Royal Opera House is in the center, the Royal Palace at the extreme left of the view. The church of St. Hedwig is at the right.

differing historical and social traditions and the inertia of little governments whose first and last interest was self-preservation. To cross those hurdles to unity would require generations. Italy, consequently, continued to be as long it had been, a piece of geography, a pawn of diplomacy. Its history was redeemed, however, by distinguished accomplishments in the fine arts and science.

Ranging from south to north the major Italian states of the seventeenth and eighteenth centuries were: the Two Sicilies (the island of Sicily and the adjacent mainland with the capital of Naples); the States of the Church; the commercial republics of Venice and Genoa; Lombardy (the Milanese) and the Kingdom of Savoy-Piedmont. A few comments will identify each of them.

Spain, at the middle of the seventeenth century ruled the Two Sicilies. Administration was extremely corrupt and incompetent. Onerous taxation, which weighed more burdensomely on peasants than on townsmen, paralyzed economic activity, and neither group benefited much from taxes paid to the state. Brigandage cursed the countryside, landed proprietors often allying with outlaws for mutual gain. Shortages of food were recurrent while plague periodically decimated the population of the Two Sicilies. Uprisings in protest against wretchedness and poverty occurred repeatedly, but never displayed much vitality. After 1715 Austria replaced Spain as master, yet administrative abuses went unremedied. In 1738 the Two Sicilies passed to a branch of the Spanish dynasty which managed to retain the crown until 1860.

Chief executive of the Papal States was of course the Pope. By long established custom a new Pope was elected on the death of an incumbent by the Cardinals, their most important duty. Apart from the Papal Republic, centering on Rome and stretching across the middle of the peninsula, the Pope owned properties in other Italian states; those holdings were a fecund source of friction and jealousy. From the standpoint of administration and the economic welfare of the inhabitants, the Papal domains were scarcely superior to the degraded Two Sicilies; public officials without exception were professional churchmen. The voice of the Pope, once so decisive in European politics, no longer carried weight. But Rome itself continued to attract cultivated Europeans, who there could study at their leisure memorials and treasures from the several stages of Western civilization.

As one would expect, over a century and more of time the Popes were individuals of varied personality. All were Italians by birth and most of them elderly when elected. Certain Popes allowed themselves to be swayed by favorite nephews or foreign diplomatists, while others boldly defied the designs of a Louis XIV and resisted the encroachments of covetous neighbors. As a rule, Popes furnished funds for the cultivation of arts and letters, combatted the heretic inside the Church and tirelessly preached warfare against the Ottoman infidel without.

For Catholicism as a whole, the crucial problem of the late eighteenth century was the future of the ubiquitous Society of Jesus. Historically, this order had been the militant and resourceful ally of the Papacy. Jesuit fathers were the victims of an accumulation of animosities. By their aggressiveness they incurred the hostility of other Catholic orders and parish priests; and by dabbling in politics and business they excited the suspicion and antipathy of secular governments. As champions of the principle of papal supremacy, moreover, Jesuits antagonized Catholic "deviationists," such as the French Gallicans, while freethinkers, for obvious reasons, were strongly enlisted against the Society of Jesus. For Protestants, of course, the Jesuits were the arch enemy, the main agents of Rome in winning back to Mother Church large sections of Europe which had swung into the Protestant camp. And it was widely believed that Jesuits were forever plotting the destruction of Protestant kingdoms. All manner of evil doings were attributed to the Society; enmity mounted in intensity.

After prolonged and prayerful deliberations Pope Clement XIV, in 1773, suppressed the Jesuit order as he had been urged to do by statesmen who had already expelled the

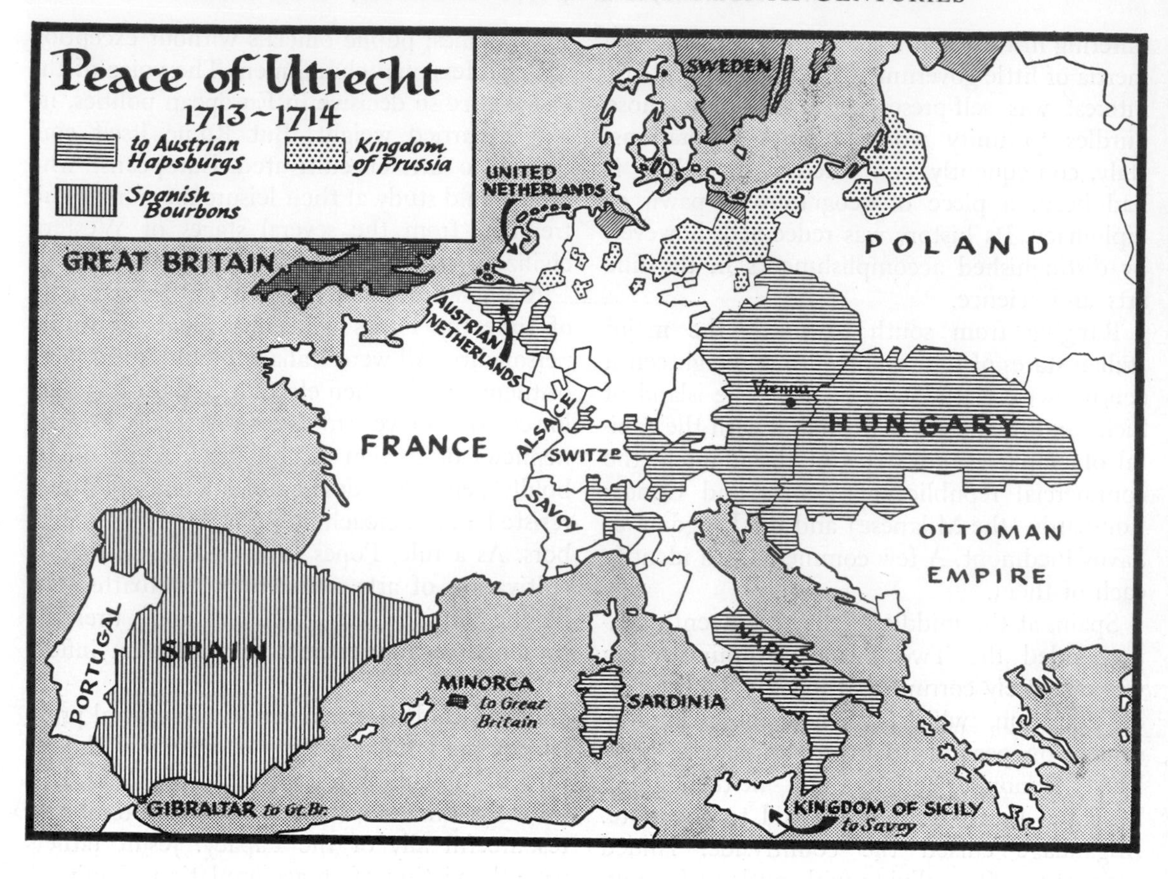

Jesuits from their countries. The decision, which the Pope thought necessary in order "to remove a source of trouble and to restore peace in the Church," provoked fierce controversies. Indeed, many Jesuits declined to accept the papal verdict as final; headquarters of sorts were set up in faraway Russia, against the time when the Society might be restored to papal favor. That day arrived in 1814.

On opposite sides of northern Italy lay the venerable republics of Genoa and Venice, which had long since experienced their best days. Yet Genoese citizens owned considerable capital and the "City of Palaces" struggled manfully to retain a place in the commercial sun. The prosperity of her sons as moneylenders and merchants invited envy and some emulation in other Italian principalities. Venice embraced not alone the famous "Queen of the Adriatic," but also a stretch of territory on the mainland and Dalmatia along the eastern shore of the Adriatic. Changes in routes of trade from the Mediterranean to the Atlantic had sealed the doom of Venice; year by year trade argosies grew smaller and fewer. Crippling struggles with the Turks, the penetration of French and British merchants into Near Eastern business, destructive raids upon shipping by pirates, the encirclement of the Republic by Austria after the Treaty of Utrecht (1713) and injurious mercantilist devices marked the visible stages in the economic decay of Venice.

Nonetheless, to an extent unapproached by other Italian states, the Venetian government allowed citizens to think and write as they pleased and to worship as seemed proper to the individual conscience. Painters and skilled craftsmen, moreover, contrived to uphold the rich Venetian traditions in art. And Venice continued to attract European holidaymakers; during the famous annual carnival the city teemed with guests bent on fun and excite-

Francesco Guardi, a pupil of Canaletto, painted this atmospheric view of the Rialto, Venice.

ment.[4] But this was merely froth. The glory of Venice had departed, had woven itself into a history of perennial fascination.

Westward from Venetia was Lombardy, centering upon Milan. Long a dependency of Spain, Lombardy was ceded to Austria in the Utrecht settlement of 1713 and it remained in the Hapsburg realm until absorbed by the Italian kingdom in 1859. Human conditions in Lombardy were not much better than in the Two Sicilies, though the fertile soil yielded a better living for the peasantry. Milan and the towns contained a class of enterprising manufacturers and merchants but tariff policies and trade regulations imposed brakes on growth. The advent of Austrian administration brought some improvements in government. Austrian officials, however, were detested as Germans, popularly identified with the northern barbarians who had stormed into Italy in the twilight of antiquity. Late in the eighteenth century, Lombardy turned more prosperous and intellectual activity took on fresh vigor.

Last of all, a small principality, known interchangeably as Savoy, Piedmont or Sardinia was located in the northwestern corner of the peninsula. In 1601, the dwarf duchy of Savoy had annexed adjoining Piedmont with Turin, which was adopted as the principal residence of the rulers. The barren isle of Sardinia and

[4] A respectable part of Venetian income came from the 30,000 Englishmen who visited the city each year to see the sights, gamble and flirt.

Venetians at Carnival time, as a Venetian painter of the Eighteenth Century saw them

the title of king were acquired by a Duke of Savoy early in the eighteenth century. Bordering on France, this state was ever in danger of inundation and French influences were paramount, as was illustrated in one way by the gay court at Turin, a miniature Versailles.

The history of the Savoy dynasty paralleled that of the Hohenzollerns in Prussia. At the outset of the eighteenth century, Piedmont was classed as an European power and it stood forth as spokesman on Italian affairs, a role never thereafter lost. A line of spirited kings, benevolently despotic, revered by many and respected by all, built up the prestige of their little country. Piedmont in the 1860's, as is explained later on, gathered the other Italian principalities into the kingdom of Italy.

ITALIAN CULTURE

Despite political division and apathy, mass illiteracy and economic stagnation, Italy occupied an enviable place in the domain of the mind and spirit. The lush bequests of the Renaissance had been allowed to tarnish, it is true, but they had not been entirely squandered. Italian genius instructed Europe in architecture, painting and music, hit upon fundamental findings in science and contributed, though less generously, to the republic of letters.

Italian architects of the period rejected the simple Renaissance designs which had so long been popular. For critics who consider restraint the trade-mark of good architecture, they debased the profession. Styles called baroque and later rococo became fashionable in Italy; designers stressed extravagant ornamentation, masses of odd statues, heavy columns and irregular lines—in short, the complete absence of simplicity.[5] Baroque architecture gives the impression of ornate and massive turbulence.

Originating in Rome, baroque conceptions attained popularity throughout much of Europe and affected the decoration and furnishings of households as well as exteriors. Most gifted of the Italian masters was Giovanni Bernini who designed the celebrated colonnade of St. Peter's in Rome and ornamental fountains there and elsewhere in the Eternal City. In his exuberance he created heroic groups of nymphs, river gods, satyrs and monsters, altogether admirable examples of baroque tastes. Many palaces and churches in Venice and Rome, notably Jesuit churches embody baroque ideals.

Italians made their mark in sculpture and painting, too, and it was customary for budding foreign artists to study with teachers in Italy or seek inspiration there. The robust Salvator Rosa founded a famous school of landscape painting. Prominent in the eighteenth century were two Venetian artists, Giovanni Tiepolo, who painted acres of canvas and fresco in the turbulent baroque style, and Antonio Canaletto (or Canale) who excelled in almost topographic reproductions of buildings and canals of Venice. English patronage proved a boon to this brilliant though not especially talented artist. Italian painters carried their skills and enthusiasms to the capitals of Europe and foreign collectors bought up masterpieces of Italian artistic genius.

Until well along in the eighteenth century, Italians remained supreme in music, being particularly renowned for opera, or drama enlivened by songs and dances. Florence in 1600 witnessed the first authentic opera and from there it passed to the rest of Europe. The operatic aria, or solo part, severely diminished the importance of the play in theatrical productions. Incomparable master of the aria was Alessandro Scarlatti, a Neapolitan, who wrote more than three hundred pieces and dispatched pupils and talented disciples to all the courts of Europe. Italian princes competed with each other for the best in operatic presentations; temperamental prima donnas were petted and rewarded with magnificent salaries. The eighteenth century was a golden age of Italian vocalists, several of whom, like Farinelli and Cafarelli, toured the musical centers of the Old World. It was at this time, too, that Stradivarius perfected the violin and Cristofori of Florence devised "a hammer to strike strings," the forerunner of the piano.

Men of letters in Italy were outclassed by musicians, though some were patronized by noble families. Intellectual originality was discouraged by governments and, except for Padua, the universities of Italy were in a torpid state. Only barristers were intellectually active as a class and in the eighteenth century their outlook was colored by the fashions and novelties which flourished in France. In philosophy a figure of great originality was Giambattista Vico, who, in *Scienza Nuova* (New Science) (1725) attempted to explain the laws of social evolution.

But the Italian mind seemed to prefer physics to metaphysics, the practical and utilitarian to the speculative and hypothetical. At any rate, the impetus imparted to scientific study by the researches of Galileo carried over into the next century; after that the scepter of scientific leadership was handed to other peoples. Always Italian men of science were haunted by the fear that ecclesiastical wrath might descend upon them, as upon Galileo. Florence and Padua excelled as centers of scientific study, with mathematics as the favored subject. Torricelli, a student of Galileo, invented the barometer and Grimaldi propounded the undulatory theory of light in an elementary form. The distinguished biologist Malpighi was probably the first investigator to study minute organisms through a microscope. His findings, many of which were published by the Royal Society of London, pointed the way to several specialized branches of biology.

To promote scientific researches, botanical

[5] Baroque is a term of Spanish origin meaning a large, imperfectly formed pearl.

gardens were laid out in the principal cities and university towns of Italy. Archaeological investigations were stimulated by excavations at ancient Pompei and Herculaneum, on the edge of Naples. Studies in alchemy marched hand in hand with legitimate science; searching for a cheap and certain method of making gold, curious Italians blundered upon modest morsels of sound chemical knowledge.

ADDING THINGS UP

For the century after Westphalia, the outstanding political phenomenon in central Europe was the prevalence of a maze of separate states, governed on authoritarian principles. The moribund Holy Roman Empire, the expansion of Austria and its struggles with the Turks and the making of a strong Prussia loom large on the historical chart. Sardinia (Piedmont) carried the political dreams of a sadly divided and foreign-dominated Italy.

Gradually the northern regions recovered from the Thirty Years' War. But heavy taxation and the application of mercantilist doctrines interfered with economic prosperity. War, plague and pestilence kept population down. In the many petty states of Germany and Italy, oppressive and repulsive absolutism prevailed. The social ostentation and debauchery of the ruling classes stood in glaring contrast to the poverty and wretchedness of the many. Millions of Germans and Italians, in consequence, welcomed the intoxicating doctrines of freedom and equality proclaimed by the French "Enlightenment."

Progress in the cultivation of the arts and science was registered, it is true, much of it in response to forces that emanated from France. German culture lagged well behind that of Italy, to say nothing of France and Britain. Frederick the Great ascribed German backwardness to warfare, which condemned princes and peoples alike to poverty. The absence of a great capital city in which cultural workers could congregate and stimulate one another was another obvious handicap. Rather than a Paris or a London, many courts competed for whatever cultural talent appeared in Germany. With the exception of Leibnitz, German intellectuals tended to be learned pedants; for the finer things of mind and spirit Germans borrowed from foreign sources, France, above all.

FOR FURTHER STUDY

CICELY V. WEDGEWOOD, *The Thirty Years' War* (New York, 1939)

WALTER H. BRUFORD, *Germany in the Eighteenth Century* (Cambridge, Eng., 1935)

FRANK L. CARSTON, *The Origins of Prussia* (London, 1954)

PAUL WITTEK, *The Rise of the Ottoman Empire* (London, 1938)

ROGER B. MERRIMAN, *Suleiman the Magnificent* (Cambridge, 1944)

FREDERICK L. NUSSBAUM, *The Triumph of Science and Reason* (New York, 1953) PAPERBACK

DOROTHY M. VAUGHAN, *Europe and the Turk* (Liverpool, 1954)

PAUL FRISCHAUER, *Prince Eugene* (New York, 1934)

GEORGE P. GOOCH, *Maria Theresa and Other Studies* (New York, 1951)

SIDNEY B. FAY, *The Rise of Brandenburg-Prussia to 1786* (New York, 1937)

FERDINAND SCHEVILL, *The Great Elector* (Chicago, 1947)

KATHERINE D. VERNON, *Italy from 1494 to 1790* (Cambridge, Eng., 1909)

CHAPTER V

THE AWAKENING OF RUSSIA

RUSSIA AND THE WORLD

EACH passing year heightens the role of Russia in the world pageant. As everyone knows, this vast country, occupying a sixth of the land surface of the globe, served as the stage for the Communist or Bolshevik Revolution of 1917. Thereafter the leaders of the new Russia proceeded to set up a totalitarian regime and economic institutions unexampled in any large way in recorded history. They extolled a set of human values, too, conceptions of the good life, which were sharply at variance with standards and tastes that had evolved in western society across the centuries.

If the Communist way of life had been confined to huge Russia alone, the subject would have to be assigned considerable attention in any faithful account of modern world civilization. But Communism appealed powerfully to the discontented, the frustrated, the oppressed and the poor around the globe; parties dedicated to Communist dogmas appeared in every country. As the headquarters of the new ideology, Moscow exerted the pull and commanded the allegiance of a new Mecca or a new Rome.

After the Second World War, at the dawn of the atomic age, police regimes patterned on the model of Soviet Russia and politically allied to it, seized control in the countries of eastern Europe and in populous China. Energetic, thoroughly disciplined parties in other countries, Italy, France, Germany and Japan, for instance, sought to push their nations along the Moscow road; they were "Fifth Column" weapons of Soviet expansion. Nothing less than lordship over the great globe itself was the declared goal of Communism.

Behind Communism as an international revolutionary force stood the Russian colossus equipped with a formidable military machine, commanding enormous human and material resources and directed by a small group of all-powerful

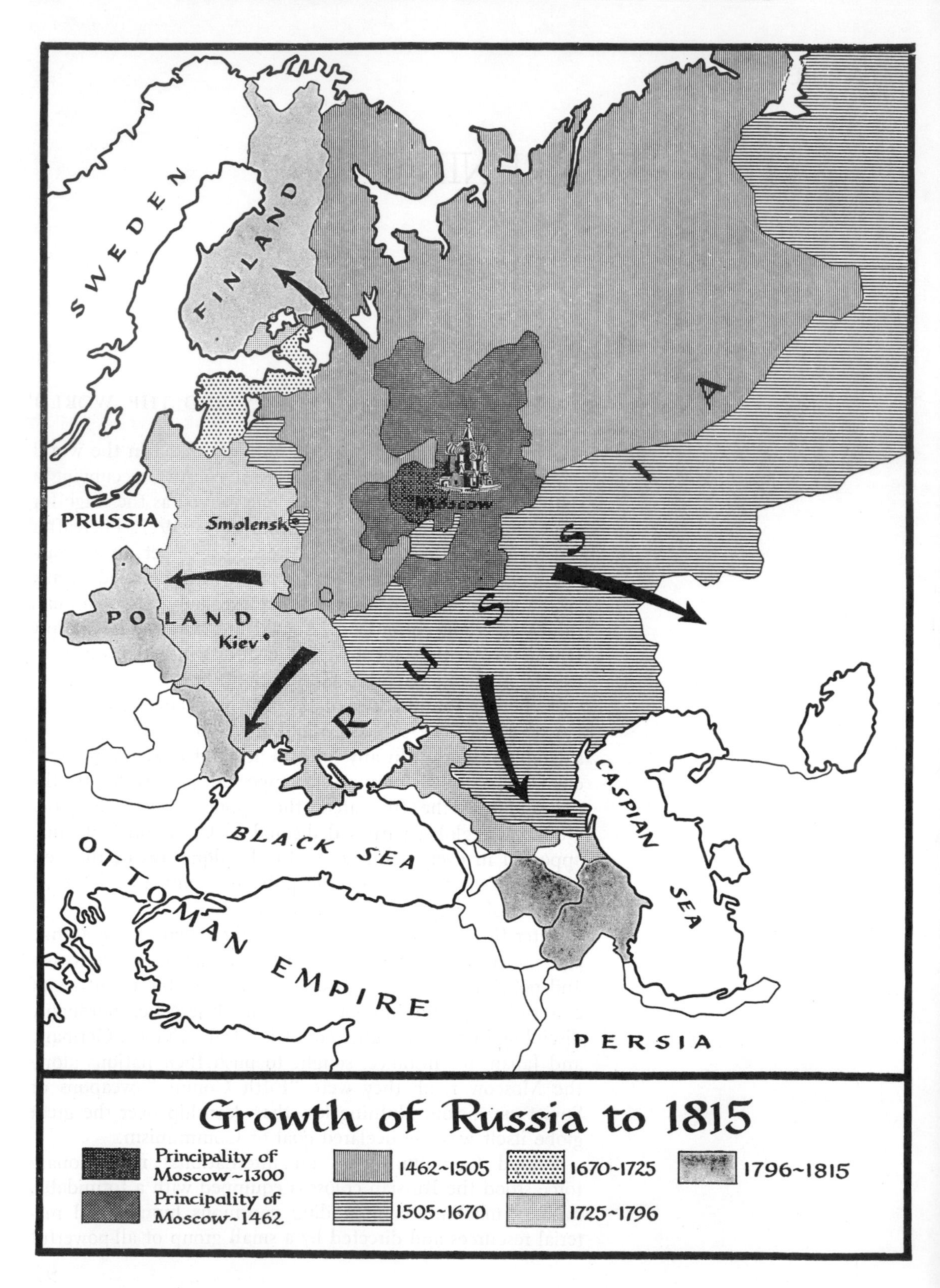

Growth of Russia to 1815

leaders. Glance at a map and the disparity between Russia together with Russian dominated eastern Europe and the balance of the Continent becomes quickly apparent. Faced with the Soviet threat to the peace of the world and to the security of every nation, Western Europe, spurred on and reinforced by the United States, slowly groped its way toward some form of organic unity.

Winston Churchill, British Prime Minister in the Second World War, once described Russia as "a riddle wrapped in a mystery inside an enigma." In all truth the Russians seem a strange and bewildering folk, outside the range of Western comprehension, as far away nearly as the moon. At one moment the Russian appears to be on top of the world shouting and dancing, then at the next he seems on the verge of self-destruction, sinking into a gloom as limitless as his steppes and as deep as his winter snows. He prefers to do nothing by halves. Once Russia was synonymous with religious piety and devotion, but under the Soviets it became the very paradise of the uncompromising and militant atheist.

Russian history explains a good deal about the Russians which otherwise would remain utterly mysterious. Soviet Russia by no means represents a clean break with the national tradition; autocracy in government, for instance, conforms to a deeply rooted Russian heritage. And, looked at in perspective, Soviet foreign policy has inherited much from Imperial Russia.

The pattern of Russian territorial growth is surprisingly similar to that of the United States. Both developed into immense countries which for generations stood on the margins of Western civilization; but in the twentieth century these young and virile nations moved closer and closer to the center of affairs. They emerged in fact as super-powers, dwarfing the countries which historically had shaped the course of world affairs. Stretching, after the Second World War, from the Carpathians to the Pacific, the Soviet Union was three times larger than the United States, and more populous, though much of the Russian land had slight or no value for human habitation.

Throughout much of their national history both of these giants were primarily agricultural countries and then both were rapidly transformed by industry. Both were human melting pots containing diverse races, colors and creeds. But, unlike the United States, Russia was traditionally open to land invasion and for long centuries she was virtually excluded from sea and ocean. In their cultural and ideological evolution, moreover, the two super-powers of the atomic age differed radically.

CONCERNING THE SLAVS

The Russians are the largest branch of the broad and prolific Slav linguistic family. At the mid-twentieth century about 250,000,000 people of Slavic speech lived in Europe, 15,000,000 more of Slavic descent in the United States and Latin America. The Slavs, remarked an eighteenth-century German savant, Johann Gottfried Herder, "hold a larger place on the map than in history." He confidently predicted that they were "destined to say the last word in the development of European humanity." "The past belongs to the Latins," someone else said in the nineteenth century, "the present to the Teutons, the future to the Slavs."

The origins of the Slavs are shrouded in obscurity. Until the ninth century they had no written language so that information about them to that point comes from accounts by outsiders or from archaeological remains. Early in the Christian era they resided beyond the Carpathian mountains in a belt of territory running eastward to the Dnieper River. In their rude economy, farming was carried on collectively, as was so frequently the case in simple societies. Substantial economic equality seems to have prevailed.

Religious ideas of the Slavs were extremely primitive. They believed, however, that a Supreme Being manipulated a host of lesser divinities. Objects of worship included sun, moon and stars, and the idea of immortality was present. A priestly class presided over ritualistic ceremonies and sacrifices (human sometimes). Monogamy was the accepted principle of family life.

The early Slavs were divided into clans and

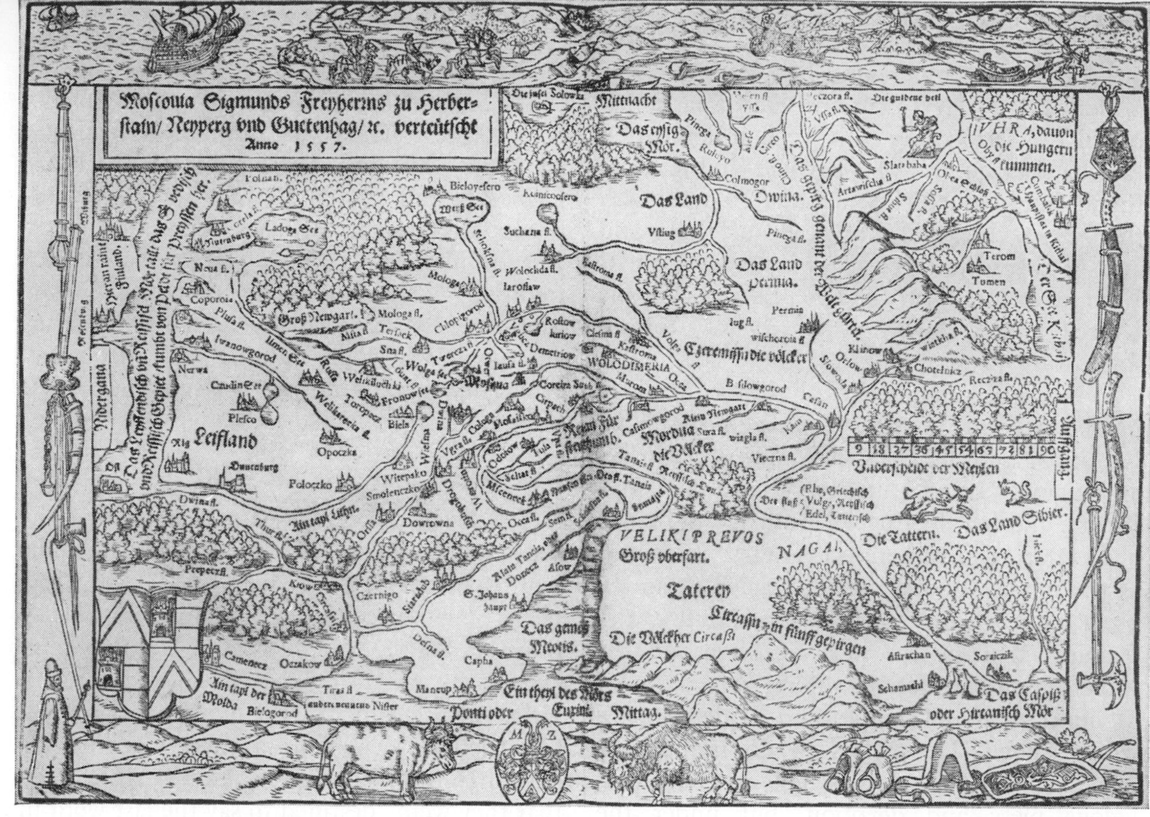

The woodcut frame about this Sixteenth Century map of Russia illustrates various phases of Russian life.

tribes without any overarching central authority. A sixth-century Byzantine chronicler tells us, "The Slavs live scattered widely in wretched huts and often change their place of abode . . . they are not ruled by one man but have lived from the earliest times in democracy." This peace-loving folk, unschooled in warfare, borrowed terms like helmet and sword (and presumably military equipment) from neighboring German tribesmen. Weakly organized for defense, Slavs were easy victims of plundering man-hunters who condemned captives to slavery; the word slave indeed is derived from Slav.

Just before 600 A.D. the Slavs in small tribal bands began to radiate in every direction. Most of the Balkan peninsula was peopled by them. Their descendants there are known as Serbs, Slovenes and Croats, together the Yugoslavs, and the Bulgars, although the original Bulgar stock came out of Asia. A heavy Slavic admixture is found in the Rumanian and Greek populations.

Other Slav companies migrated northward and westward into lands vacated by German tribesmen who had drifted into or toward the Roman Empire. They planted themselves along the Vistula Valley and the Baltic coast as far west as the Elbe River; history knows the children of these Slavs as Poles, Czechs and Slovaks. From this occupation dates the struggle between Slavs and Teutons which has repeatedly and profoundly affected the tide of European history.

The two World Wars of the twentieth century, for example, issued directly out of burning feuds between Teutons and Slavs. The savage fulminations of Adolf Hitler against the Slavs and the bestial horrors inflicted upon conquered Slavs by Nazi troopers in the Second World War are only very modern manifestations of the long-standing German antagonism toward Slavs.

A third group of Slavic tribesmen trekked off to the broad plains of eastern Europe. They were the ancestors in large measure of the Great Russians, sometimes spoken of as the Muscovites, of the Little Russians or Ukrainians, and of the White Russians, a smaller dialectic fragment.

Community of language, not "blood" uniformity was (and is yet) the binding tie of Slavdom, for these folk have mixed physical characteristics. Slavic tongues, at bottom, are variants of the Indo-European language, as are Greek, Latin and German. Two alphabets, in time, came into vogue among the Slavs. Poles and Czechs, for example, use the Latin alphabet, with diacritical marks for sounds peculiar to them. Russians and Balkan Slavs, on the other hand, have a Cyrillic alphabet whose symbols are based upon Greek characters.

The term Cyrillic is derived from the name of a Christian missionary, St. Cyril, a Greek. With his older brother, St. Methodius, Cyril wandered, in the second half of the ninth century, from the Byzantine Empire to present-day Czechoslovakia for the purpose of evangelizing the pagan Slavs. These apostles to the Slavs attracted many converts and for their use Cyril devised an alphabet; he translated Greek books into the Slav language and chanted the mass in Slavic. Eventually the Cyrillic alphabet was displaced in "Czechoslovakia" by Latin, but it was adopted by Serbs, Bulgars and Russians.

Of decisive significance in the history of Slavdom was the penetration into Middle Europe of the conquering Magyars, who separated the Slavs of the west and north from those of the east and south. Consequently, Slavdom was split along religious and cultural lines that have survived. Whereas the Slavs to the north gravitated into Roman Catholicism, almost all the rest, and numerically the larger part, adhered to the Orthodox or eastern version of Catholic Christianity. Northern Slavs, in other words, affiliated with Rome and the West, their cousins with Constantinople and the East. Slavs who were beneficiaries of Latin institutions and Latin culture by reason of their religious attachment developed habits of thought and standards of conduct that varied from the Byzantine norms of the East.

Each of the Slavic nationalities has a history of its own, its unique record of achievement and humiliation, its particular prides and prejudices, its own aspirations and antipathies. Nationalistically intoxicated intellectuals of the nineteenth century, historians and men of letters especially, exploited the past triumphs and tribulations of their own folk with unblushing romanticism—and melancholy consequences.

BULGARS AND YUGOSLAVS

Something may be said here about the two main bodies of Slavs in the Balkans, the Bulgars and the Yugoslavs.

The original Bulgars, who came from Asia, were yellow in skin and marauding in disposition. They pushed into the eastern Balkans at the end of the seventh century, overcoming Slav tribes without much difficulty. By intermarriage the conquering Bulgars were absorbed by the Slav majority. As a single nationality united in language and habits, the Bulgars entered the Orthodox Church about 863.

The Bulgar state experienced ups and downs. At one point Bulgaria appeared on the verge of bringing the whole Balkan peninsula under its rule. Decadence then set in, later a revival of power, and a final era of impotence. Golden memories of medieval grandeur were strummed upon by Bulgar patriots of the nineteenth century.

When the Ottoman Turks spread their rule over the Balkans, Bulgaria was degraded into a geographical term. Similar was the fate of the Yugoslavs of whom the Serbs had the largest importance.[1] This Slavic folk settled in the western Balkans and embraced Orthodox Christianity. Their loose tribal society succumbed to Bulgar assaults and later the Serbs passed under Greek vassalage. Freeing themselves, the Serbs enjoyed an era of greatness in the fourteenth century, when it seemed for a time that they might become sole lords of the peninsula. That prospect had faded, however, even before the Turkish conquest. After that, until the nineteenth century, the Serbs like the Bulgars had no independent history.

From time to time isolated voices were raised

[1] For historical reasons, the Croat and Slovene branches of the Yugoslavs became Roman Catholics and subjects of Hungary, Austria and Venice.

on behalf of a united Slavdom. A pioneer, seventeenth-century preacher of the doctrine that Slavs of all countries should unite was Yuri Krzhanich. A Roman Catholic priest and a scholar of ability, this Yugoslav was an ardent partisan of Slav solidarity. He wished, too, to attract the Slavs of Russia into the Roman Church.

On behalf of his Yugoslav fellows Krzhanich, about 1650, dispatched a piteous appeal for relief to the Tsar of all the Russias: "The western Slavs," he wrote, "are in terrible slavery . . . You, Great Tsar, ought to watch over the Slavic peoples, and as a good father, you ought to care for your scattered children." In a general history of the Slavs which Krzhanich compiled, he begged Russia to deliver the Balkan Slavs from domination by Turkish Moslems. His exhortations evoked no positive response, though they may have quickened official Muscovite interest in the forgotten Slavic brethren. The Pan-Slav gospel, composed of varied themes, attained prominence only in the nineteenth century, and it was reserved to Soviet Russia to merge all the Slavs in a general partnership after the Second World War.

Russian Noble, Sixteenth Century

FOUNDATIONS OF RUSSIA

The Slavs who drifted from their original habitat to the eastern plains came to be known as Russ. The word comes apparently from the Finnish Ruotsi, a name for mariners. It recalls that the semi-legendary Rurik, first political chieftain of Russia, was a Viking from eastern Sweden. Cousins to the Northmen who occupied French Normandy and other districts of western Europe, the Vikings passed across Russia to Constantinople in search of trade or plunder.

Slav tribesmen lived in villages and small towns. The Vikings established themselves first in Novgorod, not far from the present Leningrad, which developed into a considerable merchant community. They huckstered furs and slaves (Slavs) in the Byzantine empire. About 862 the Vikings under Rurik won control of Kiev on the Dnieper, the major Slav town. They founded a city commonwealth, which is regarded as the real beginning of the Russian state; Russian organized existence, in other words, may be traced for over a thousand years.

Commerce and war bound Kiev and Constantinople in close intimacy. As one result, Prince Vladimir of Kiev picked Orthodox Catholicism about 989 as the religion of his subjects. Ties with Constantinople were tightened by the marriage of the Prince, who was already surrounded by five wives and eight hundred concubines, to a Byzantine princess. As soon as Vladimir adopted Christianity, he ordered the destruction of heathen idols and compelled his subjects to undergo baptism en masse. Time-honored pagan beliefs and customs were not, however, so easily washed away. At Kiev, on a hill high above the Dnieper, a towering statue of the Prince holding aloft a cross stands, undisturbed by the Soviets, near the place where the wholesale baptism is reputed to have taken place. From Kiev the Christian gospel was carried to neighboring Russian principalities.

Byzantine Christianity had crucial importance in the formative centuries of the Russian nation. Culturally the Russians passed into the orbit of the Byzantine Empire, and influences emanating from Constantinople modified the pagan, primitive and barbarous Slavic society. Byzantine principles of autocracy, for example, and legal concepts, both secular and ecclesiastical, were transmitted to the Kievan princedom. Greek architects and artisans laid out churches and monasteries on Byzantine models, though the well known onion-shaped dome of Russian houses of worship appears to have been invented by natives in this land of heavy snows.

From Constantinople, too, came the custom of adorning churches with mosaics and ikons, which were calculated to inspire an otherworldly tranquility in the minds of worshipers. The alphabet of Cyril was adopted for the Russian written language and almost all the early books were religious in content. Until nearly the end of the sixteenth century indeed, Russian men of letters were very largely monks and priests.

Church and State formed an alliance for mutual benefit. Clergymen extolled princes as the anointed of God. Princes, in turn, showered gifts of land on the church and financed the construction of monasteries. The wealthy "monastery of caves" on the edge of Kiev developed into a famous shrine, attracting devout pilgrims from all across Russia; the monastic buildings, architectural showpieces and treasuries of art, were converted into anti-religious museums by Soviet Russia. Monks were prime agents in diffusing Byzantine culture among the Russian millions. From monastic ranks the governing ecclesiastics were chosen, but the supreme dignitary of Russian Christianity was long appointed by the Patriarch of Constantinople. For all its shortcomings, the Russian Church served as the major unifying, uplifting, and civilizing institution in this primitive country.

THE MONGOL IMPACT

Early in the thirteenth century rough and terrifying Mongol (or Tartar) horsemen from Asia raced over Russia. The weak princedoms scarcely offered token resistance. In 1240, Kiev, which was suffering from internal dissension and attacks from outside, was mercilessly ravaged. Presently the city and much of southwestern Russia passed under the scepter of the aggressive kingdom of Lithuania.

Mongols dominated the rest of Russia and for over two centuries exacted homage and tribute. Native princes, or some of them, took Mongol brides, though commoners seldom intermarried with the conquerors. The familiar adage "scratch a Russian and you'll find a Tartar" possesses little accuracy in any biological sense. Sections of southern and eastern Russia were set off as independent Mongol khanates. Despite Mongol ascendancy, the Russians were allowed to keep their traditional customs and religion, their language and their land.

Two hundred years of servile vassalage to these Asiatics left their mark upon the texture of Russian life. Christianity, throughout the period, afforded the chief solace and popular allegiance to the national faith deepened. Religious motives, possibly more than anything else, inspired conscious opposition to the Tartar yoke. Political authoritarianism seems to have taken deeper root and the indestructible soil-people became more subservient than before to their overlords. Cut off from European influences, Russia underwent a process of partial orientalization. That is seen, for example, in the introduction of flowing civilian garments, the exclusion of women from social functions and brutal punishment of trouble-makers by flogging or execution.

THE EMERGENCE OF MUSCOVY

It was the small duchy of Muscovy, encircling the town of Moscow, which took the lead in breaking the Mongol mastery. It became the kernel of Imperial Russia. Situated at the headwaters of several rivers, Moscow prospered as a commercial center. Her princes curried favor with Mongol potentates, entering into marital alliances, and obediently gathering tribute money. After the devastation of Kiev, the headquarters of the Russian Church was transferred to Moscow, which bolstered the prestige of the local prince.

Grand Duke Ivan III, called the Great, is saluted as the real founder of modern Russia. Artful in statecraft, cunning and ambitious, he resembled his Renaissance contemporaries, Louis XI of France and Henry VII of England. Under his leadership the hold of the Mongols over Muscovy was broken and nearby principalities were annexed; altogether the patrimony of Ivan was tripled in extent. The high point in the expansion was the capture of the flourishing republic of Novgorod, larger than Muscovy itself, and ranging off to the White Sea.

Ivan III married a Byzantine heiress and added the two-headed eagle of the Byzantine Empire to the coat-of-arms of Muscovy. Since Constantinople had been captured by Moslem Turks, he contended that his family was the legitimate Christian claimant to the city. The idea of a national mission to gain Constantinople has haunted the imagination of Russian rulers, Imperial and Soviet, ever since. As a sign of his pretensions Ivan adopted the title of Tsar, a Russian variant of the legend-encrusted Roman Caesar. He also invited Italian architects and craftsmen to reconstruct and beautify the governmental buildings in Moscow's Kremlin. Even physicians were invited in from western Europe and native scholars were granted subsidies from the state treasury. Muscovy was moving out of Oriental isolation.

When the Mongol ascendancy came to an end, Muscovy was hemmed in by strong states on every side. German communities and Swedish provinces were strung along the Baltic coast, while to the west the large kingdom of Poland-Lithuania barred the road to expansion. On the south and east Turks and Mongol khans ruled. Future Muscovite rulers would overcome every one of these neighbors.

The tsarist autocracy was consolidated by Ivan IV. Soviet authors who have been reinterpreting the career of this ruler as "the people's tsar" have had a trying experience, for history has pinned upon him the surname of the "Ter-

A partial view of the Kremlin, the ancient citadel of Moscow

Ivan Vasilievich, known as "the Terrible."

rible." Cruel and barbarous, at any rate by Western standards, he ordered critics and opponents to be massacred, smashed restless feudal landlords (boyars) and even murdered his son and heir with his own hands. Ivan's principal instrument of power was the *oprichnina,* in some ways the prototype of the political police of Soviet Russia.

The council of nobles, or duma, which had showed symptoms of independence, was drastically overhauled; in the future, members of this body would be hand-picked by the tsar. No institution existed thereafter which might exert restraining influences upon the autocratic will of the ruler. Here, in more than embryo, was the tyrannical police regime which has so long been synonymous with Russia. The "terrible" tsar made his reign memorable by enlarging the national domain. Successful crusades against Mongol chieftains added the whole Volga valley to the tsardom. That acquisition paved the way for Muscovite expansion into the Siberian vastness.

Maritime contacts with Western Europe likewise increased. English merchant adventurers, for instance, carried on a small business through modern Archangel and a conventional Anglo-Russian commercial treaty was arranged. Ivan the Terrible solicited a diplomatic alliance with Queen Elizabeth, upon whom he lavished gifts of jewels and furs, and even applied for an English wife—in vain.[2]

Not long after the death of Ivan IV in 1584 the Russian connection with the Orthodox patriarch at Constantinople was dissolved. The chief religious official in Moscow was invested (1589) with the dignity of patriarch and the church organization was more closely tied to the purposes of the state. Revered as the defender of the faith, the tsar regulated religious institutions and controlled ecclesiastical policies. "As God is in heaven, so is on earth the tsar," the proverbial philosophy asserted. Religious fervor buttressed the autocracy and supplied ideological pretexts for warfare against Moslems or non-Orthodox Christian believers.

A grave schism in the seventeenth century rent Russian Orthodoxy in twain and proved to be permanent. A patriarch of the time audaciously ventured to introduce textual modifications in church ritual and in the sacred books, which provoked impassioned outcries from hide-bound clergymen. They insisted on following time-hallowed usages and were therefore labeled "Old Believers." Fanatical persecution, sanctioned by the government, failed to subdue these hardy dissenters.

Russian Christianity was of course only one facet of the peculiar Muscovite way of life. Since exchange of goods was small, towns were few and scattered and the mercantile class unimportant. Learning was monopolized by the clergy, who trained men for the priesthood in their schools; Russian laymen were innocent of book-learning. Books, to be sure, were rarities and almost wholly devoted to religious interests. A printing press which somehow was brought into the country operated for only a short while.

[2] Shakespeare introduced "frozen Muscovites" into *Love's Labour's Lost.* (Act V, Scene 2.)

What then of the Muscovite masses, the myriad toilers on the soil? By about 1600, every peasant family was definitely bound to a particular estate. Rulers required a class of "duty men" for military service and to meet fiscal and administrative necessities. To maintain this class its members were assigned land and the services of the laborers on it. The Russian nobility and serfdom originated together. The state held some rustics under its immediate control, while others lived on ecclesiastical properties.

Bit by bit, the earth-people lost every vestige of freedom. Patriarchal landlords could impose fines or condemn serfs to bodily punishment without fear of governmental interference. If proprietors cared to do so, they might pick mates for their serfs, and they were responsible for the collection of taxes and recruiting soldiers for the army. Flight from an estate was corrected by severe penalties if the fugitive was caught. An edict of 1675, moreover, permitted a proprietor to sell his serfs, so that their status was indistinguishable from slavery; the state even collected a tax on transactions in serfs. Occasionally the bondsmen openly rebelled against their degraded existence, but in the main they were as submissive as they were rugged and credulous.

Russia was a land of villages and serfs. Certain fields attached to a village were worked by peasant families, each cultivating several strips of land. Periodically the strips were redistributed in keeping with the number of mouths in each household, a custom that was conducive to economic equality. Proprietors (or the state) appropriated a share of the village crops as remuneration for the use of strips of ground. Besides, serfs spent about half their working hours cultivating the fields of the landlord and the products belonged exclusively to the proprietor.[3]

The institutions of serfdom and manorial farming were conspicuously strengthened in

[3] Some serfs paid money or gave goods to their masters in lieu of field labor (*obrok*), while others worked in the home of the proprietor as domestic servants (*dvorovie*).

Russian noblemen in field costume, Sixteenth Century

Interior of a Russian peasant's house, Eighteenth Century

Russia at just the time when they were completely disappearing in England and were on the way out in France. Russian serfdom lasted until the 1860's and not a little of the heritage and psychology of that institution passed over into the twentieth century.

Foreigners who visited Muscovy carried away a low estimate of the savage ignorance and squalid poverty of the population, as this piece of Elizabethan doggerel reveals:

> Wild Irish are as civil as the Russes in their kind
> Hard choice which is the best of both, each bloody rude, and blind,
> Drink is their sole desire, the pot is all their pride,
> The soberest head doth once a day stand needful of a guide.

ADVENT OF THE ROMANOVS

Upon the extinction of the reigning dynasty at the beginning of the seventeenth century, chaos descended upon Russia. The state police broke into pieces, the centralized government fell a prey to confusion and ever new pretenders to the throne rode in and out of the Kremlin. At one point an ambitious nobleman, Boris Gudunov, half Mongol by descent, seized the crown with his own hands. He sent young men to western countries to study and in other ways sought to identify Russia with the West. He and his reign have been a fecund source of inspiration for Russian men of letters and musical composers.

Following the death of Gudunov general anarchy returned, which was an invitation to foreigners—Poles, Swedes, Tartars—to swoop down upon Russia. Polish troops actually occupied Holy Moscow and conferred the office of tsar upon a candidate of Polish choosing. In this "Time of Troubles," as Russian historians call the period, it seemed an open question whether the tsardom would survive.

A fierce national pride, however, generated in particular by the Orthodox clergy, delivered the country from destruction and expelled the foreigners. Then in 1613 a loosely organized assembly, or duma, of nobles, churchmen and merchants bestowed the crown upon Michael Romanov, who came of an old-line aristocratic family; until 1917 his house ruled Russia. Never did the duma develop into an influential organ of government, its advice was seldom solicited and in 1649 it passed out of existence. Over 250 years elapsed before another assembly representing the nation was created.

Not only did the first Romanovs restore a semblance of discipline inside the tsardom, but they lashed out against the would-be despoilers of their country. As a phase of the reconstruction, Russia imitated the West in army organization and in building up a military industry. Foreign army instructors, some German, some Irish, trained an effective fighting force.

In struggles with the Poles, doubly hated as invaders and as Roman Catholic heretics, Russia had the help of rough and tumble frontiersmen to the south, the romantic, independently minded Cossacks. Military triumphs over Poland (with which Lithuania was united) added to the tsardom in 1667 the larger part of the Ukraine, as far west as the Dnieper, along with historic Kiev beyond the river. From that heavy territorial amputation, Poland never fully recovered.

Through an institution of higher learning in Kiev a lively and sustained flow of Polish and Latin cultural influences quickened the intellectual life of Muscovy. And there were other indications of westernization. Foreign artisans, for example, brought in crafts and manufacturing techniques which were of especial value in meeting army requirements. Merchants encouraged commercial enterprise in Moscow, which took on an air of busy activity. With its many churches, Moscow was likened by travelers to the capitals of smaller European countries. One section of the city was reserved as a residential quarter for foreigners, Germans predominantly. Somewhat similarly, Dutch immigrants fostered the growth of industry in Tula, to the south of Moscow. The impact of the West, in short, had already been felt in Russia before the arrival of Peter the Great.

Something more should be said about the

Crossing the Moscow river on sledges, Sixteenth Century

Peter the Great

Cossacks, famed in history and romance. Dwelling in the southern river valleys they formed a human barrier against Turk and Mongol or an instrument for offensive operations. The mark of the Mongol lay heavy upon the Cossacks, although they possessed elementary institutions of self-government. Doughty fighters, they were long too undisciplined to be relied upon as soldiers of the tsars.

It was not indeed until the nineteenth century that the Cossacks submitted fully to the central government and served as its dread agents. As colonizers, Cossacks settled in the great open spaces of Siberia; and they were drawn into the cavalry branch of the national army, eventually earning a terrible notoriety as "bulldogs of the tsar," always ready to crack down on challengers of the status quo. Whatever the capacity, Cossacks were bold, ruthless, incredibly tough-textured.

Out of the Cossack community emerged in the seventeenth century a picturesque champion of the oppressed serfs, Stenka Razin. Miserable living conditions excited mass irritation which flared up spasmodically in primitive outbursts of savagery. The most violent of the risings occurred in the valley of the Volga with Razin directing insurgents in the pillage of properties and the slaughter of landlords. As was true of earlier serf risings in England and France, the better organized levies of the government suppressed the rebels and Razin was caught and killed (1671). Sometimes likened to Robin Hood, Razin's memory was kept green in the folk tales of the peasantry.

PETER THE GREAT

When Peter I, a man of almost unique genius and drive, assumed the throne in 1689, he had to govern a young nation in the throes of awakening, not a senile country in a state of decay. On many counts, the new master splendidly personified the people whom destiny had summoned him to rule. A huge man, over six feet six inches tall and amply proportioned, he had an inexhaustible store of energy and an iron physique equal to every kind and amount of exertion. The greatest of the tsars displayed a legendary capacity for hard, unremitting work.

We are told that he could wallow in his cups for two days on end and then after three or four hours of sleep appear sober and alert. Ease, luxury, cultural refinements Peter disdained. As brutal as he was coarse, he imperiously drove Russia toward civilized living, ruthlessly thrusting aside human obstacles to his designs.

As a boy the future tsar was keenly interested in technical learning, more particularly in skills related to war and commerce. He showed considerable dexterity in handling tools and mechanical contrivances. First and last he mastered the fundamentals of a dozen trades and even set himself up as court dentist carrying about in a bag the teeth of noblemen which he had extracted. Quite naturally this curious youth wandered into the foreign suburb of Moscow to learn what he could. Those experiences, coupled perhaps with the counsel of his mother, who had a veneer of Western culture, persuaded Peter that semi-oriental Muscovy must be remodeled along the lines of the progressive nations of the West—and that swiftly.

At the age of twenty-five, Peter, accompanied by half a hundred young men of leading families set off on a grand educational tour of the West. "I am among the pupils and seek those who can teach me," the ambitious tsar explained. Everywhere they went, these youths from a primitive and mysterious land attracted universal attention. But they had gone abroad not to be seen but to see and learn, and that they did.

The Russian travelers were chiefly interested in the maritime nations of Holland and England. Peter, as is well known, worked in disguise as a shipwright in Holland. He and his companions inspected mills, counting houses, shipping, institutions of learning, studied foreign administrative and fighting services; and thousands of artisans were enrolled for work in Russia. Withal the Russians could not shrug off the Muscovite heritage. For instance, their favorite pastime on an elegant estate they leased in England was to hurl one another from wheelbarrows through yew hedges!

Peter returned home fired with the determination to apply with swift thoroughness what had been picked up abroad. By copying Western manners he would strengthen Russia and purchase for this raw newcomer a place of respect in the family of nations. But first he felt it necessary to obtain outlets by sea to the West; as matters stood Russian frontage on the open water was restricted to the bleak Arctic north. Peter's unquenchable enthusiasm for territorial aggrandizement pushed his country into constant warfare. Russia in fact was at peace in only two of the thirty-five years of the reign.

The Ottoman Empire blocked the approach to the Black Sea and to expansion into the Balkan cockpit. The Turks were despised by Russians as heathen Moslems and as relatives of the medieval Mongol oppressors. Peter first claimed the rights of protector over Christians in the Ottoman empire and appealed to Balkan Christians to rebel—standard items in Russian foreign policy of the future. War upon Turkey won Azov (1700), the key to the Crimea, but the Russians retained it only temporarily. Other tests of strength accomplished little save to intensify Turkish hatred and to heighten Muscovite antagonism toward the infidels; in 1711 Peter while trying to evict the Turks from Moldavia, only narrowly escaped destruction.

In another direction, lands along the Caspian Sea and the town of Baku were annexed and Russian armies pressed hard upon Persia. Adventuresome explorers accumulated valuable data on the flora and fauna of the uncharted Siberian wilderness and penetrated to the Bering Strait. Armed clashes with Chinese forces preceded the demarcation of the frontiers in 1689 between the Russian and Chinese empires, which stood for nearly two centuries.

But the principal military campaigns were conducted against Sweden, the neighbor to the north. Able Swedish kings backed by an excellent army had hoisted their country into the category of Great Powers. For practical purposes the Baltic Sea had been converted into a Swedish lake. Peter was bent upon acquiring a strip of the Baltic coastline as a window to the West through which commerce and Western civilization might flow into Russia. That ambition was in fact the supreme objective of his foreign policy.

Sweden, on its part, was determined to keep what it had and in Charles XII it possessed an extraordinarily competent commander. Voltaire made him the hero of one of his most popular books. At the outset of the long duel with Russia—called the Great Northern War—Swedish troops, though greatly outnumbered, easily whipped their enemy. Disasters, instead of disheartening Peter, impelled him to improve the quality of his fighting services.

Charles XII marched against Moscow in 1708, following the route subsequently taken by the armies of Napoleon and Hitler—and with equally calamitous results. Invoking their classic pattern of defense against a stronger opponent, the Russians avoided pitched battles, retreated and wore down the enemy by guerilla tactics. The Swedes turned south into the Ukraine to hook up with rebellious Cossacks.

The weather, more than once an ally of Russia, became so cold that even vodka froze. With his army decimated and short on military supplies, Charles XII engaged Peter at Pultowa (1709), and suffered inglorious defeat.

On that decisive encounter, Lord Byron wrote:

> 'Twas after dread Pultowa's day,
> When fortune left the royal Swede,
> Around a slaughter'd army lay,
> No more to combat and to bleed.
> The power and glory of the war,
> Faithless as their vain votaries, men,
> Had pass'd to the triumphant Czar,
> And Moscow's walls were safe again. . . .

But more than Moscow was at stake—much more. The Tsar followed up the Pultowa victory by seizing the harbors of Tallin (Reval) and Riga on the Baltic and the lands adjacent to them. The fighting in the area was ruinous in the extreme; "there is nothing left to destroy," ran a report, "not a cock crows."[4] A portion of Finland, too, succumbed to Muscovite arms.

The Treaty of Nystadt of 1721 finally closed the Great Northern War. By its provisions, Russia relinquished Finland but retained the southern Baltic coastlands. The iron curtain to the west had been dramatically lowered. It was now that loyal Muscovites hailed Peter as "the Great" and now that he assumed the title of emperor. The verdict at Nystadt underlined the decay of Sweden and heralded the emergence of Russia as a topflight power.

THE WORK OF EUROPEANIZATION

In the meantime Peter had been forcing his semi-civilized subjects, or rather the nobility and the townsmen, along the road to Europeanization. Internal reformation was decidedly opportunistic rather than carefully thought out and planned, and many of the innovations were introduced only in the last decade of the reign.

On land at the mouth of the Neva River, taken from Sweden, a new capital called St. Petersburg (Leningrad) was built. Nature never intended that a great city should arise at that point, for the ground was swampy and had to be filled in and pilings had to be sunk to support heavy structures. Building elsewhere in Russia came to a standstill while St. Petersburg was being built. Serfs by the thousands were dragooned into raising this symbol of the new Russia. Peter optimistically fancied that the old and dismal traditions of Moscow would quickly be obscured by his shiny new creation. When finished, St. Petersburg compared favorably with leading German cities, though it fell short of the old Western capitals, Paris and London.

The great Tsar believed that autocratic paternalism was the best type of government. Very religious, though unsympathetic to the ceremonialism of the Russian church, he thought himself chosen by God to promote the welfare of his country. In language which might have fallen from the lips of Louis XIV, he asserted that "His Majesty is an autocratic monarch, responsible to no one for his policies. He has power and authority to govern his state and lands as a Christian ruler according to his will and understanding."

Imitating the West, Peter created a centralized bureaucracy and set up ten boards of ministers to supervise public affairs. Foreign experts were normally attached to the ministries. To recommend legislation a small advisory council or Senate was established and to keep an eye on officials, a system of national inspectors was set up, but it failed to root out bribery and corruption. Local administration, too, was reorganized. The empire was divided into eight divisions or "governments," presided over by governors, each assisted by a council elected from the nobles. Elected assemblies in the larger towns were controlled by an officer appointed by the tsar.

Nobles were compelled to serve the state either in the civil administration or in the military forces. The army which finally overcame the Swedes was frankly patterned on Western models, the troops being requisitioned from the villages. A navy, English-style, paralleled the large army in size but not in quality.

[4] These areas, known as Estonia and Latvia, were lost to Russia by the First World War and reclaimed by the Soviets during the Second World War.

Peter's armed services devoured nearly three-quarters of the state income. Taxes were repeatedly increased and new ones added until even beards and coffins were not exempt. Like his royal contemporaries, Peter was an orthodox mercantilist in his thinking on economics, and he wished Russia to be as self-sufficient as possible. Accordingly, it was forbidden to export wool or precious metals and the state controlled foreign trade by means of tariffs and subsidies. Skilled foreign artisans were heartily welcomed and young Muscovites were sent abroad to study commercial and manufacturing methods.

Aided by the government, scores of mills were built to manufacture weapons, cloth and other supplies for the fighting services. A few large-scale plants appeared. Workmen were recruited from the serf population, in the main; it is estimated that 1,500,000 serfs were employed in mills and mines in the eighteenth century. The mercantile and business classes rose to unprecedented social standing. Road-building was rather neglected, though the streets of major cities were paved and provided with stone sidewalks; canals were a special hobby of the "sea-minded" Tsar.

Peter wished to have a nobility comparable in every respect to the aristocracy of Western countries. Compulsory public service was only one of the rules laid down for this privileged set. Nobles were ordered to wear European garments and to shave off their beards and a textbook on etiquette instructed them not to spit on the floor, not to gnaw bones noisily at the dinner table and not to dance in high boots. Attendance at formal court parties, fancy balls and masquerades, was made obligatory and noblewomen were released from seclusion. Kowtowing before the Tsar was forbidden.

Learning was another interest close to Peter's heart. Elementary schools were established for the upper classes and considerable care was given to facilities for technical education. Military academies and schools for systematic instruction in medicine, navigation and engineering were organized. Foundations were laid for a learned Academy of Sciences on the Prussian model. Important foreign books were translated and the Tsar personally corrected and simplified the alphabet. He participated too in editing the pioneer Russian newspaper and ordered a revision of the calendar. Works of art were imported from abroad and a theater was opened on the Red Square in Moscow, but Peter rather neglected the aesthetic side of civilized living. He was too much the technocrat, too little the artist.

TREATMENT OF DISSENTERS

The ambitious reforms sponsored by the Tsar violated age-old traditions, cut athwart cherished prejudices and disturbed vested interests. Dignitaries of the Orthodox Church loathed Westernizing innovations and secretly denounced Peter as anti-Christ. Concluding that the hierarchy had grown too haughty, the Tsar proceeded to subject the Church completely to civil authority.

The office of patriarch was superseded in 1721 by a Holy Synod, composed of a lay chairman (or procurator) and prominent bishops, all selected by the emperor. Through the lay procurator, "the Tsar's eye," Peter called him, the state could manipulate the ecclesiastical establishment in the interests of autocracy. Freedom of worship, on the other hand, was granted to everyone except "Old Believers," Jesuits and Jews.

It was not only churchmen who felt that the pace of reformation was too furious and too far-reaching. Lay dissenters bristled with rage over the importation of foreign ways and foreign men. They much preferred traditional Muscovite customs and tastes; the rule banning beards, for instance, provoked angry protests. "With the beard one felt oneself to be made in the likeness of God," muttered conservative standpatters. "Without a beard one is degraded to the level of cats and dogs." Peter was the target of a swelling chorus of criticism and invective.

Enemies of the new and the different came to be called Slavophiles. They loved all that was distinctively Russian and struggled manfully against ideas and institutions bearing the stamp of the West, which they abominated. Slavophilism became a permanent force in Russian life. Later on Slavophiles interpreted the Petrine innovations as an unmitigated disaster for Russia and an encouragement to revolutionary tendencies. Unassimilable and alien forms of life and culture, they contended, strangled the free and natural development of the country. It is true, beyond doubt, that the Petrine reforms widened the social gulf.

Peter uncovered several plots against his life and had to contend with four major insurrections, the most dangerous of them among the incorrigible Cossacks. Against all and sundry, the strong-willed Tsar struck hard and irrevocably. His wife was banished to a convent and he was responsible for the death of his son after brutal torture. He personally hacked off the heads of mutinous guardsmen in Red Square. Those acts were intended as a warning to all who might dare to resist the reforming autocrat. They testified, too, to the savage qualities of the tyrant and the terroristic character of his authoritarian regime.

PETER'S PLACE IN HISTORY

Imperial Russia, apart from the more ardent Slavophiles, and Soviet Russia have alike revered the memory of Peter the Great. Stalin, it is reported, hung only a single portrait on the wall of his Kremlin office—that of Peter, another autocrat, another hurried, unsystematic and ruthless innovator.

To the Russia of the future, Peter I bequeathed a strong tradition of territorial expansion. Conquests on the Baltic and struggles with the Turks whetted the Muscovite appetite for further aggrandizement. Russia had vaulted swiftly into the Great Power circle and would doubtless have been a grave peril to European security if Prussia had not emerged as a bulwark against expansionist instincts. The main fabric of governmental institutions fashioned by Peter prevailed until the revolutions of the twentieth century.

Peter I created St. Petersburg, greatly expanded the national military resources and urged Russia toward the West in many directions. For the great Tsar, Europeanization implied material things rather than the ideological and cultural values of Western society. And three observations must be made about his domestic reforms. First, the process of Westernization had started before Peter was born; he merely accelerated trends that were already under way. Second, many changes were quite superficial—a thin Western coating laid upon the ancient Muscovite heritage, with little effect upon Russian society. Third, many projects were unfinished at his death and were never fully put into operation.

And yet the reign of Peter I was a shining landmark in Russian experience, an unfailing inspiration to later champions of change. The spirit of progress and the zest for Western learning which Peter personified were well expressed by an admiring subject, Michael Lomonosov, the son of humble fisherfolk, who pioneered in scientific and literary fields. "You whom the Fatherland expects to use from its own body and whom it wishes to equal men of foreign lands, be of good cheer! Show by your exertions that Russia is able to give birth to Platos of her own and quick-witted Newtons."

RUSSIA IN THE EIGHTEENTH CENTURY

For nearly half a century after the departure of Peter I, Russia seemed almost paralyzed. So much depended on the rulers, and the successors of Peter were a decidedly mediocre lot—three irresponsible women, two neurotic boys and an idiot. Court life was punctuated by palace coups and incessant intrigue, which weakened the authority and prestige of the crown. On occasion, ministers of German extraction virtually managed state business. But much of the time cliques of nobles were in charge and it is a matter of surprise that the higher nobility made no attempt to assume public power on a permanent basis and transform the autocracy into a limited monarchy.

Russia in this period only once exhibited real vigor in international politics, that in connection with the Seven Years' War. The Empress Elizabeth unsheathed the sword against the Prussia of Frederick the Great and her rough soldiers even raided Berlin. Almost certainly Prussia would have been thoroughly overwhelmed had not Elizabeth died in 1762, the victim of good liquor and bad men. Her heir, Peter III, a fanatical admirer of the Prussian king, withdrew his troops from the war. A diplomatic entente, indeed was arranged between the two countries which lasted with slight interruptions until 1890. In spite of heavy sacrifices in men and money, Russia gained only international prestige by taking part in the Seven Years' War. When hostilities ceased the army of the tsardom surpassed, no doubt, any other in Europe.

The real successor of Peter I was one of the most remarkable women of modern history, Catherine II (d.1796), often called "the Great." She is a perennially intriguing personality, the heroine of an engrossing success story, a woman of extraordinary versatility and vitality. Endowed with the mind of a philosopher and the will of one born to rule, Catherine displayed unusual courage and resourcefulness and keen insight into human nature. Not at all a genius, she understood that the best substitute for talent was hard work.

Born into an undistinguished German princeling family, Catherine at the age of fourteen married the Russian heir-apparent, who became Peter III. She easily and quickly acclimated herself to the Russian environment, professed conversion to Orthodox Catholicism, learned the Russian language and became more Russian than the Russians. She put her German past into cold storage; her prim and grim upbringing was rapidly shrugged off. Catherine had a knack for ingratiating herself with "the right people." A biographer tells us that this vivacious parvenu aspired to be a man, "not just any man but the greatest man in the world." Voltaire called her "that great man, who is Catherine." "It is to the north that we go for light," he exclaimed in a paroxysm of admiration for the Empress.

With the connivance of Russian noblemen, Catherine in 1762 deposed her utterly incompetent husband (who was soon mysteriously assassinated) and proclaimed herself the autocrat of all the Russias. Lacking a legitimate title to the crown, the Tsarina was forever plagued by conspiracies and pretenders. To fortify her authority she cultivated the good will of the nobility, exempting that class from military duties and personal taxation. Her era was the golden age of the Russian aristocracy.

Catherine II, called "the Great."

Lusty and amorous, she had an endless succession of lovers, and bore children to several of them. Some of these men were her consultants on state business, nothing more, for nobody dared tell this hard and calculating realist how to manage affairs.

Catherine II was intent upon enhancing the might of Russia and her own fame. As will be explained in another connection, she is customarily ranked with the benevolent despots. An admiring pupil and an avid correspondent of eminent literary figures of the French "Enlightenment," she toyed with the notion of reconstructing Russia on rational principles, without at all appreciating the magnitude of such an undertaking. Extremely sensitive to cultivated opinion in the West, she generously subsidized publicity agents to circulate her humanitarian dreamings in foreign capitals. The

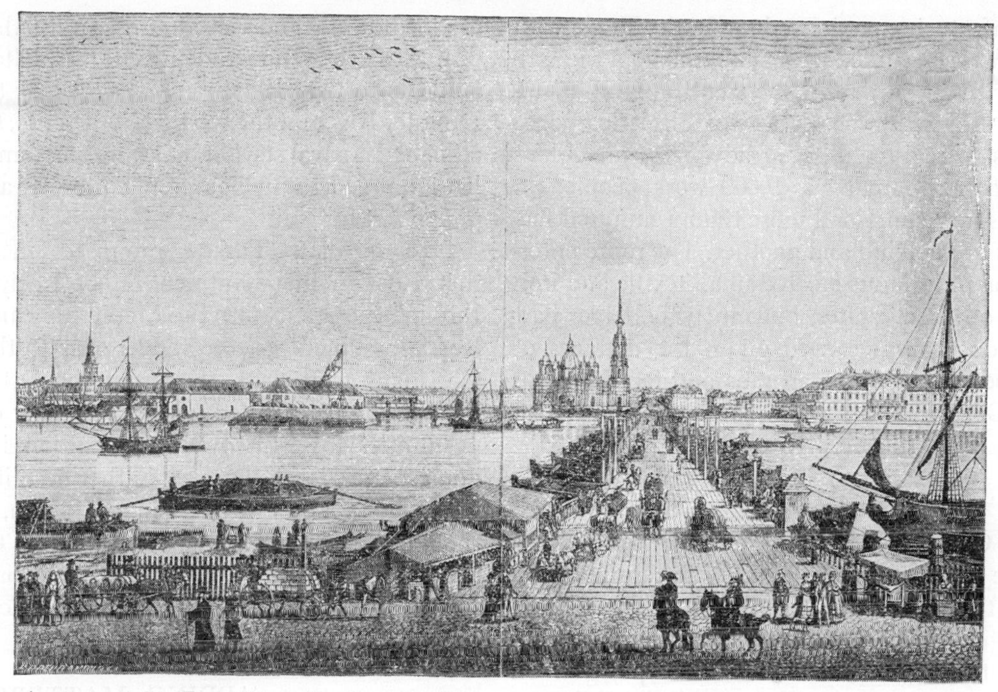

A view of St. Petersburg in the late Eighteenth Century, looking across the St. Isaac Bridge. The spired building at the extreme left is the Admiralty.

Russian "Minerva" pictured her own reign as a brilliant period of enlightenment and tolerance.

But the "enlightenment" of Catherine II was in fact only skin deep as her shabby handling of the serf problem vividly illustrates. Encouraged by the Empress, Russian men of letters, whose thinking had been stimulated by Western ideas, protested vehemently against the wretched condition of the peasants, and the venality of officials. At one point she contemplated the liberation of the serfs, but actually their lot deteriorated progressively. By order of Catherine nearly 2,000,000 bondsmen on church properties were transferred to the state. At the end of the reign the imperial government owned almost 15,000,000 serfs and about 20,000,000 belonged to noble proprietors; only slightly more than 3,000,000 inhabitants of Russia were legally freemen.

Serf resentment against uphill going in daily life manifested itself in the flight of thousands to the east and in the most destructive of Russian peasant insurrections, the Pugachev uprising of 1773. Pugachev, a Cossack, collected a considerable following of peasants and soldiers in a widespread rebellion centering in the valley of the Volga. It was the intention of the rebels to expel Catherine from the throne, exterminate the landed proprietors and release the serfs from their chains. A veritable jacquerie ravaged the Volga region in the course of which hundreds of landlords were butchered and their estates seized. For a time the insurgency threatened to cycle into an empire-wide rural revolution.

Catherine calmly hurled her armies against the insurgents. Short on discipline and morale, the rebels were decimated by famine. Pugachev himself was apprehended, dragged to Moscow in an iron cage and barbarously executed; thousands of his followers were slain and many more were despatched to the depths of Siberia.

If the Empress ever sincerely entertained thoughts of freeing the serfs, the Pugachev episode caused her to change her mind. It was 130 years before rural Russia was rocked again by widespread disturbances, though minor disorders were endemic.

While Catherine reigned, commerce and

manufacturing progressed modestly. Trade with the West expanded through harbors on the Baltic, with Britain as the best customer and supplier, and with Asia, by way of Black Sea ports. Industry registered some advances, one plant employing as many as 9,000 work people; St. Petersburg contained more than a hundred factories of one kind and another. The more enterprising proprietors erected small textile and iron mills on their estates, but much the larger part of industry was carried on in the cottages of the peasants. Skilled artisans and farmers from the German states were planted in the Volga valley or in southern Russia.

EXPANSION

If Catherine is at all entitled to the surname of Great, it is because she resumed in a sensational way the extravagant and predatory foreign policies of Peter I. She desired to consolidate and extend the national position on the Baltic and to expand the state at the expense of Poland. But her supreme aim, doubtless, was to add to Russia territories once in the Byzantine Empire and to convert Constantinople into a Muscovite harbor.

Those extravagant ambitions brought on recurrent fighting with the Ottoman Empire. Russian troops, under the greatest of her generals, Suvorov, whom Soviet Russia venerates, fought brutally and victoriously against the dispirited Turks. Russia deprived the sultan of lands up to the Black Sea and eventually to the Dniester River on the west; at Sevastopol, Catherine had a naval station built and a commercial harbor at Odessa, which grew rapidly as a shipping point for grain.

Beyond that, Turkey promised in 1774 that Russian merchantmen might freely pass through the Straits into the Mediterranean, and Russia assumed a protectorate over Orthodox Christians who were citizens of the Ottoman Empire. That right presented all manner of opportunities for Muscovite intervention in the domestic affairs of Turkey. Catherine failed to realize wholly her dreams in the south, even though the bear's share of Poland passed to the tsardom. Russia profited handsomely from the weakness and degeneration of both Turkey and Poland.

ADDING MATTERS UP

At the death of Catherine II in 1796 the Russian state had traveled far since its humble beginnings in the Norse principality of the ninth century at Kiev. Successive streams of Byzantine, Mongol and West European influence had played significantly upon the simple rustic Slav society of the East.

Stage by stage, lasting traditions of Russia

Note in this late Eighteenth Century picture of a street in Moscow how the ornate French style of some of the buildings sits uneasily alongside the log huts in the foreground.

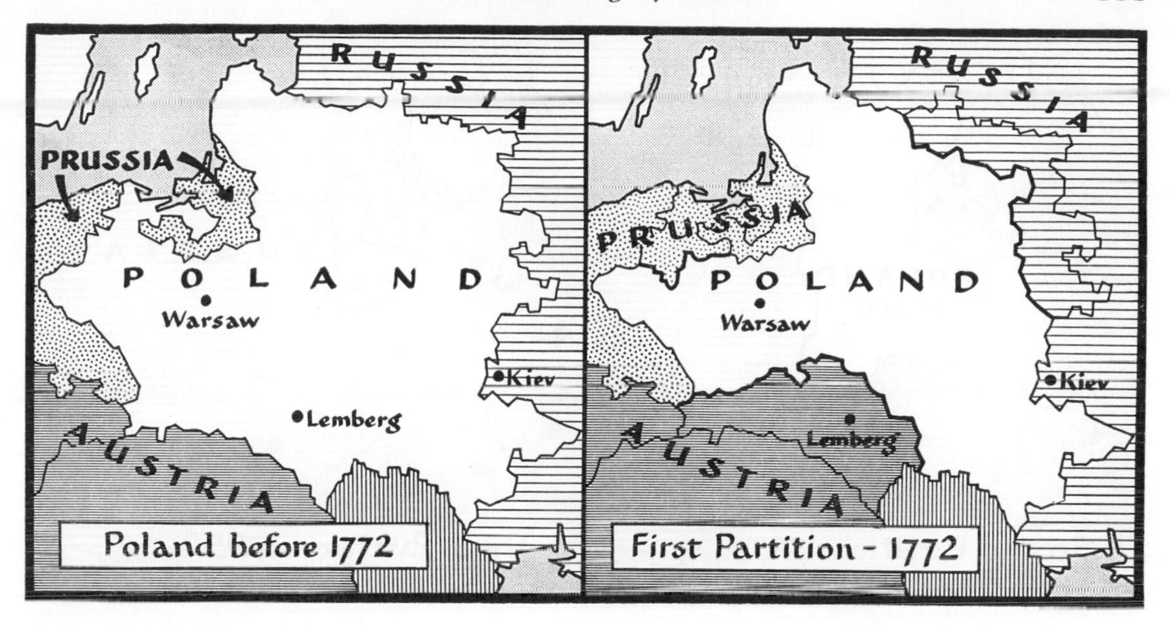

had been created. First of all, a highly authoritarian pattern of government had evolved in which the will of the tsar was tantamount to the voice of the Almighty and in which dissenters were arbitrarily liquidated or banished to Siberia. An uninspired, thoroughly conservative bureaucracy handled the actual administration of this gigantic police state.

Top officials to a considerable extent were drawn from German baronial families residing in the Baltic provinces. Down to 1905, at least, Baltic Germans held a commanding position in the varied life of Russia. In a later day Adolf Hitler would claim that Russia in truth had been built up by his German supermen. "For many centuries," he cries in *Mein Kampf*, "Russia lived at the expense of a directing superior class having a German nucleus."

From the acorns of Kiev and Moscow the Russian empire had grown into a formidable and an unwieldy colossus. Lesser principalities and then parcels of territory belonging to the weak neighbors Sweden, Turkey and Poland had been merged with the older Muscovite patrimony; when Catherine the Great passed away European Russia was very nearly as extensive as in 1914. And, off to the east, the writ of the tsar ran across northern Asia and over to Alaska in the New World. Sheer size, immense manpower (by the standards of the day) and capacity for war had elevated Russia to an undisputed place among the major powers of the world.

The authority of the ruler was upheld by nobility, bureaucracy and army, and buttressed by the Orthodox Church. Churchmen largely controlled intellectual and cultural affairs, though in the eighteenth century, secular universities were founded. Nothing of European stature in literature or the fine arts had as yet come out of Russia.

More than mere beginnings had been achieved, however, in Western-style commerce and manufacturing. St. Petersburg and Moscow were thriving cities; yet the business classes and the industrial workers comprised only a very small fraction of the population, the latter mostly serfs at that. The masses of Russia dwelt in abject servitude, illiterate and acquiescent. The privileged nobility had largely freed itself from Slav, Byzantine and Mongol traditions.

The upper nobles of Catherine's time had become cosmopolitan, foreigners in fact in their own country. French culture was the hallmark of aristocratic breeding. Lace ruffles and extrav-

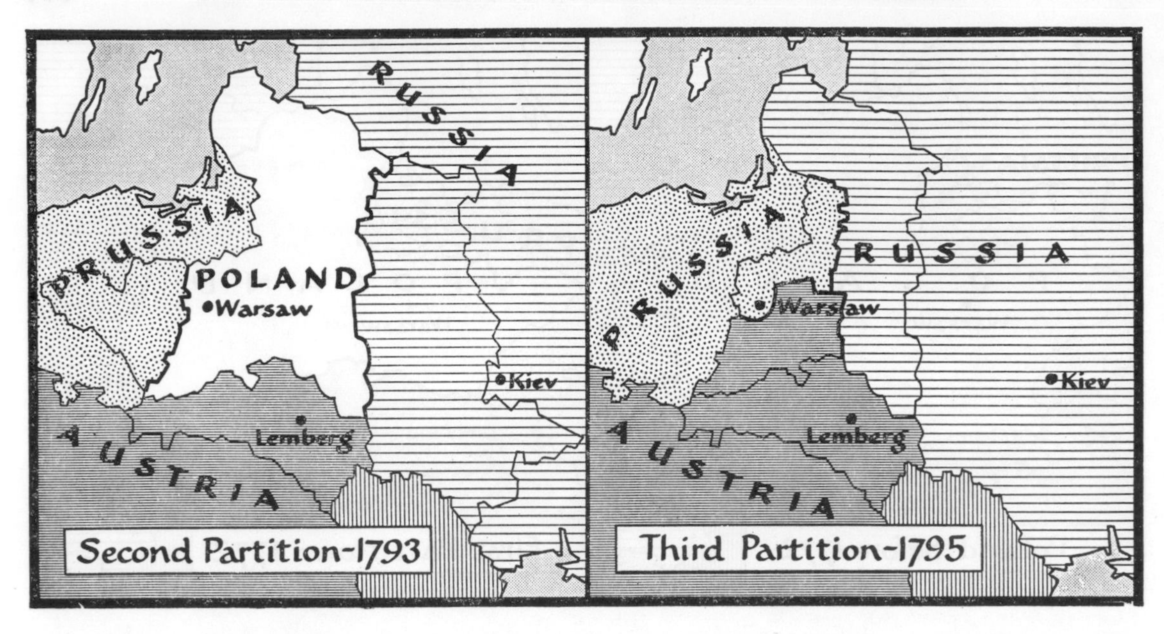

agant frolics, the literature and language of France were standard in the world of fashion. Tutors brought from France sometimes taught republican and revolutionary ideas to their pupils.

Someone has said that the Russian higher aristocracy wished that "in default of their bodies, their souls might be French." The gulf between the nobility and the masses had broadened profoundly. Aristocratic affection for France suffered a rude jolt, however, with the coming of the great French Revolution, and disintegrated when the armies of Napoleon invaded Russia in 1812.

FOR FURTHER STUDY

GEORGE VERNADSKY, *Ancient Russia* (New Haven, 1943)

GEORGE VERNADSKY, *Mongols and Russia* (New Haven, 1953)

FRANK NOWAK, *Medieval Slavdom and the Rise of Russia* (New York, 1930)

ROBERT N. BAIN, *Slavonic Europe: a Political History of Poland and Russia from 1447 to 1796* (Cambridge, Eng., 1908)

WILLIAM E. D. ALLEN, *The Ukraine* (New York, 1941)

EUGENE SCHUYLER, *Peter the Great* (2 vols., New York, 1884)

BENEDICT H. SUMNER, *Peter the Great and the Emergence of Russia* (New York, 1950) PAPERBACK

PETER PUTNAM, ed., *Seven Britons in Imperial Russia, 1689–1812* (Princeton, 1952)

ROBERT N. BAIN, *Charles XII and the Collapse of the Swedish Empire* (New York, 1895)

GLADYS S. THOMSON, *Catherine the Great and the Expansion of Russia* (New York, 1950) PAPERBACK

BENEDICT H. SUMNER, *A Short History of Russia* (new ed., New York, 1949) PAPERBACK

ANATOLE G. MAZOUR, *The Rise and Fall of the Romanovs* (New York, 1960) PAPERBACK

JEROME BLUM, *Lord and Peasant in Russia* (Princeton, 1961)

JOHN L. I. FENNELL, *Ivan the Great of Moscow* (London, 1961)

CONSTANTINE DE GRUNWALD, *Peter the Great* (Eng. trans., New York, 1955)

GEORGE P. GOOCH, *Catherine the Great and Other Studies* (New York, 1954)

CHAPTER VI

STRUGGLES FOR POWER AND EMPIRE

ON THE STUDY OF WAR

AN ALERT undergraduate once complained that the importance of war in the story of world civilization has been grossly neglected. "We ought to learn more about wars," he protested, "for men have done so much fighting." [1] Undoubtedly the bearing of war upon historical development has of late been complacently underestimated.

Traditionally the pendulum stood, in a manner of speaking, at the opposite extreme: the role of war was overvalued and historical reconstructions made the past seem "a mere record of butchery of men by their fellow men." Revolting against "drum and trumpet" emphases, and impressed with the irrationality of armed combat to settle disputes, certain historians after 1870 treated war as a pathological abnormality. They emphasized, over-emphasized economic, social and cultural developments to the neglect of military narrative. Present-day historians living in a more unsettled and less secure age appreciate more vividly that the sword as well as the plowshare has shaped the course of history.

Deprecation or ignorance of war offers no safeguard against its recurrence, and may indeed operate in the other direction. Although the United States has been involved in seven major wars (not reckoning Indian conflicts) in its relatively short history, disparagement of war has been particularly vocal in this country. The significance of war in carrying the United States to preeminence in the Americas has not always been faithfully evaluated. However desirable peace may be,

[1] An analysis of 278 wars involving the countries of Europe between 1480 and 1940 indicates that England took part in 28 per cent, France 23 per cent, Russia 22 per cent and Germany, including Prussia, 8 per cent. Quincy Wright, *A Study of War* (2 vols., Chicago, 1942), I, p. 221, n. 1. This exposition should temper the widespread impression that Germans have been uniquely bellicose in the modern age.

the record of history casts doubt on the thesis that armed conflict is unnatural to man.

Taking history in a broad sweep it is evident that man has been at war with man for thousands of years. Armed strife appears indeed to have afflicted mankind since human beings first peopled the earth. "Shall the sword devour forever?" Abner inquired of Joab in a small Palestinian war over 2,000 years ago. In historical antiquity and in the medieval centuries, for instance, men fought to the best of their ability with weapons that nowadays seem ludicrously primitive. War is by no means merely a thing of yesterday.

Warfare has exerted a profound, and perhaps an increasing, impact upon the course of human events. It is not necessary nor informed, however, to endorse the dictum of a Greek philosopher that war "is the father of all things." Fighting calls forth the worst and the best in humanity; calumny, cruelty, intolerance, profiteering and downright bestiality, on the one hand, and on the other courage, loyalty, endurance of physical and mental anguish, faithfulness to duty. For many, wars have meant sacrifice even unto death, and that when fighting was still the province of the professional soldier.

War has enriched the literature and fine arts of some peoples and degraded the cultures of others. It has exercised deep and lasting effects upon the economic fabric and has diverted social and moral habits into novel channels. It has brought about boundary shifts, exalting some countries, as in the case of Prussia and Russia in the eighteenth century, and condemning others to comparative impotence, as the history of Spain or Turkey sufficiently illustrates. The total wars of the twentieth century affected all citizens, whether actors or victims, and their effects will be felt for generations to come.

Study of military strategy and tactics, though disclosing a good deal about the technology and political standards of a period, is less rewarding and instructive than the search for the dynamic forces that have brought on struggles. There is no universal agreement on the circumstances and conditions that lead to war; causes are highly mixed and as complicated as the nature and interests of man. Pessimistic, cyclical theories of war have had their partisans. A sixteenth-century Italian belonging to that school wrote, ". . . peace brings riches; riches bring pride; pride brings anger; anger brings war; war brings poverty; poverty brings humanity; humanity brings peace; peace . . . brings riches, and so the world's affairs go round."

"War is a scourge," wrote (1765) Frederick the Great of Prussia. "It is a necessary evil because men are evil and corrupt, because it has always existed and perhaps because the Creator desires revolutions to convince us that there is no stability under the sun."

Economic considerations have often been vital in bringing on war: strains and stresses of commercial competition, imperialist expansion or population pressure. So have dynastic appetites, nationalist ambitions and religious or ideological enthusiasms. In modern times the common denominator of wars has often been the desire of one human group to expand its territories or resources, or to impose its will or doctrine upon another group. A strong country might be tempted by the evident weakness or disunity of neighbors to seek to absorb or despoil by means of force. Peace depended, in turn, upon superior strength on the part of countries that had no desire to annex or coerce others—power plus enlightened good will.

Hostilities were common enough in the eighteenth century, though less exhausting than in the preceding century or than the total warfare of the future. These wars were not wars of passion; neither the religious zealotry of the past nor the national enthusiasm of the future were evident. In the midst of war, it was possible for the English writer Laurence Sterne to wander blithely around France uncertain whether his native land was actually fighting France. And an American painter was the beneficiary of British royal patronage while the American Revolution was being fought.

At 1715 the Great Northern War was still on, with Russia and Sweden as the principal adversaries. But other European countries, economically distraught by the wars of Louis XIV, wished for a long peace. Having financed the late struggles on loans, all governments were burdened by debt; financial instability was especially acute and bothersome in France. Nevertheless, neighboring states greatly feared and mistrusted France.

Statesmen uniformly believed that the way to keep the peace was through an equilibrium of strength among the nations. Each country should seek safety in its own armaments and in alliances, in keeping with well-established practice. For a full generation after 1715 Europe escaped general wars. Armed conflicts took place, it is true, but they were localized affairs, fought to determine the destiny of Poland or the Italian and Balkan peninsulas. An intricate network of diplomatic alignments, coupled with war-weariness, spared Europe from universal conflagrations.

Frederick the Great in later life—a contrast with the portrait in Chapter IV

THE FACTOR OF EMPIRE

Directors of policy in Europe generally appreciated the value and potentialities of colonies and tropical commerce. Orthodox mercantilists all, statesmen were concerned to make their countries as economically self-contained as possible and to enhance national or princely power. One leading personality of the century, however, Frederick the Great, considered colonies more a liability than an asset. Writing in 1768, he explained, "If we have no colonies in Africa or America I congratulate my successors, for distant possessions drain a mother country of population, require a large fleet for their preservation, and provide endless occasions for war, as if we had not plenty of the latter already. . . ." More than a century passed before Prussia, having become Germany, struggled to obtain a place in the warm colonial sun.

Growing commercial and colonial rivalry was a hallmark of the eighteenth century. The main objects of colonial interest were African slaves, West Indian sugar and indigo, Virginia tobacco, Canadian furs, and the spices, tea, coffee and cocoa of Asia. To pay for these products Europe exported hardware, woolens and as a last resort precious metals. Slaves were often an important item in balancing transactions with the Americas; colonies depended upon slaves for labor power. The government of France offered a bounty for every "piece of ebony" that was landed in French dependencies, and sober British economists subtly defended the traffic in slaves as indispensable for commercial health. Work was hard and life short for the luckless African who fell into the grasp of a predatory slave-merchant.

The English and the French were the leading protagonists in the struggle for markets and empire, with the Dutch trailing along. North America, the West Indies, India and the Pacific were theaters of Anglo-French competition. Whenever wars in Europe involved these states they cycled into global conflicts to extend or defend imperial dependencies. Spain possessed the most extensive overseas realm. British merchants cut into the business of Spanish America, partly as permitted by treaty, more so by unlawful smuggling. Portugal drew material advantages from the huge colony of Brazil. Russia, not very active as a colonial power, confined its operations to northern Asia and the territory of Alaska.

Prior to the eighteenth century imperial rivalry had repeatedly envenomed international relations. But in that century, overseas enterprise became more aggressive, competition took on keener intensity, and as never before, states

View of shipping in the harbor of Calcutta, late Eighteenth Century

attempted to capture colonial markets in order to compel foreigners to buy or to prevent them from selling. Those activities wrought with melancholy force upon European tranquility. Surveying the record, the temperate and informed British economist, Adam Smith, concluded (1776): "Commerce, which ought to be among nations, as individuals, a bond of union and friendship, has become the most fertile source of discord and animosity. The capricious ambition of kings and ministers has not, during the present and preceding century, been more fatal to the repose of Europe, than the impertinent jealousy of merchants and manufacturers."

THE SUB-CONTINENT OF INDIA

Writing thus, Smith had especially in mind the titanic Anglo-French struggle over India. This huge area, 10,000 miles from Europe, was too warm to attract white settlers, but it produced a pleasing variety of soil products and minerals and precious stones as well. Native craftsmen wove simple textiles for the rural millions and rich brocades for the wealthy. From time immemorial Indians lived in thousands of villages, each a little world unto itself. From time immemorial great landlords owned huge estates and exercised police power over the peasants, who were contented with a few basic necessities, a little mud hut, a strip of loincloth, a helpmate and a bowl of rice.

Poverty, illiteracy and dirt disfigured Indian existence. Bodies of the peasants were chronic hosts to maladies that enervated and killed. While the plowman plodded contemplatively behind the bullock cart, often uncertain of his next meal, the affluent proprietor, perhaps a lordly maharajah, rode along on his painted elephant happy in his strongboxes of jewels, gold bullion and silver spangles.

Possibly two Indians out of three were attached to the religious traditions of Hinduism. This faith possesses neither a central administration nor congregational worship, no universally recognized scriptures nor even universal beliefs. A polytheistic religion, it stresses austerity, pessimism and resignation; it fosters attitudes of repose and gentleness and a severely fatalistic outlook. Hinduism conceives of the present life as only one link in a chain of existences. The social station into which a person is born is the inescapable consequence of behavior in a previous life. The Hindu must suppress all desire in order to merit re-absorption into the godhead.

Into such a mental environment the idea of castes fitted easily; asceticism and passivity seemed more vital than the Western customs of hard work, thrift and material incentives. The Indian caste system had infinite compartments and complications. Highly revered Brahmin priests, scholars and lawgivers formed the upper crust of society; below them ranked warriors, peasants, merchants and at the bottom a large population of outcastes. Outcastes were shunned by their social superiors and condemned to perform the most menial and disagreeable jobs. They might not enter Hindu temples or share food and water with castes above them; their very shadows were believed to radiate evil influences. Each caste pursued the even tenor of its way, worshiping its own deities, eating its special foods. It was not possible for a Hindu to move up from the caste into which he was born.

Arch rivals of the Hindus were the Moslems

The masterpiece of the Mogul style of Indian architecture—the Taj Mahal, or tomb of Mumtaz Mahal, wife of the Shah Jahan

of India, descendants of conquering invaders and steeped in prideful memories. Buddhists made up a third religious grouping, whose revered teacher and prophet lived in India contemporaneously with Confucius in China. Though a powerful force in other sections of Asia, Buddhism counted only a small following in its homeland, being in that respect similar to Christianity in Palestine.

When Europeans first appeared in India a Great Mogul emperor, residing in Delhi, ruled the sub-continent. Hundreds of native potentates or nabobs, managed local government, and many of them were practically exempt from central control. Political disunities facilitated the establishment and the extension of European power.

THE COMING OF THE WHITE MAN

At the end of the fifteenth century Portuguese pioneers began trading with India, but a hundred years passed by before Dutch, English and French merchants put in an appearance. Under charter of the crown in 1600 the English East India Company was awarded a monopoly of eastern business; to protect its interests or to promote them, the Company might acquire property and make war upon traders operating under other flags. It was hoped that this small band of Elizabethan merchants would supply Oriental commodities to England at lower prices than the Dutch. This business venture of unpromising beginnings laid the groundwork for the great British colony of India.

After failing to thrust into the Dutch preserve of the East Indies, the English East India Company concentrated its energies on India proper. Portuguese merchants were crowded aside by the militarily superior Britons. The walls on the way to the central lobby of the British House of Commons are lined with eight frescoes, one of which depicts a European in the midst of the gorgeous trappings of an Oriental court. The inscription beneath reads, "Sir Thomas Roe, Envoy from King James the First of England to the Moghul Emperor, succeeds by courtesy and firmness in laying the foundation of British influence in India, 1614." Actually, five years before that episode, agents of the English East India Company had laid out a trading station at Surat high up on the west coast.

Fortified English "factories" were erected at Calcutta in Bengal near the mouth of the Ganges, at Madras a thousand miles down the coast and at Bombay on the western side of the peninsula. English mercantile operations, which yielded very large profits, radiated from these three centers. The Company received little assistance from the government in London.

A rival for the wealth of India arose in the form of the French East India Company, sponsored by the great Colbert. With headquarters at Pondicherry in the southeast, trading stations were founded near Calcutta and Bombay. Initially, French and British merchants plied their business in peace, for India seemed big and populous enough to afford abundant opportunities for all concerned. British trade greatly exceeded the French, though in neither case did transactions begin to approach the business with the West Indies. Both groups held aloof from Indian domestic politics, but the "hands-off" attitude lasted for only a brief time.

RIVALRIES IN THE NEW WORLD

While engaged in developing trade with India, England and France had not ignored the lands beyond the Atlantic. Both nations held extensive dependencies in the New World. The French empire covered Canada and the broad valleys of the Mississippi and its feeders, while Newfoundland was shared with England. France also owned, besides smaller islands, lucrative Guadeloupe and Martinique in the West Indies, sources of sugar, molasses and rum.

Relatively few Frenchmen took up homes overseas and none but Roman Catholics were admitted to French colonies. Affairs of government were rigidly reserved to the authorities in Paris. Fur trading in the Canadian wilderness, small commercial and agricultural operations in and around Quebec and Montreal, and plantations in the West Indies afforded opportunities for French initiative. But at the middle of the eighteenth century French residents in America probably did not exceed 50,000.

At that point a radically different situation prevailed in English America where white settlers were thirty times more numerous than in the French colonies. Vigorous agriculture and handicraft industries nourished busy trading communities along the Atlantic. Generally tolerant in religion, English America welcomed immigrants of many faiths or none, and settlers were allowed considerable latitude in deciding local and provincial questions.[2] England also owned West Indian islands such as the Barbadoes, which Spain had overlooked, and Jamaica snatched away in 1655 from Spain; as suppliers of sugar and other tropical products, these holdings were highly prized. Bermuda, settled by the English early in the seventeenth century and organized as a Crown colony in 1684, possessed little more than scenic attraction.

Anglo-French conflicts in Europe after 1689 were invariably attended by petty though murderous wars between the two sets of colonists in America. Once started, the duel between these ambitious countries for world dominion persisted until the elimination of Napoleon Bonaparte in 1815. Under the Treaty of Utrecht of 1713, France relinquished her claims to Newfoundland, Nova Scotia and the Hudson Bay country to the English, retaining the broad basins of the St. Lawrence and the Mississippi. To hem the English in along the seaboard, French officials erected forts at strategic points in the New World empire, which excited apprehensions in English America and in Britain itself. Seeds of a new war germinated.

Resumption of Franco-British hostilities resulted from British quarrels with Spain, the ally of France. British merchants and navigators trading with Spanish America flagrantly transgressed commercial privileges extended to them at Utrecht. Smuggling was rife. To stop that illicit traffic Spain seized British lawbreakers, inflicting atrocities upon some of them. Injured British mercantile interests set up a loud clamor for vengeance, and standing national grievances against Spain were paraded in public. Passions boiled over after Spanish authorities boarded the ship of Captain Robert Jenkins on the high seas, appropriated the cargo and barbarously hacked off the mariner's ear.

The government responded by declaring war on Spain in 1739, much against the judgment of Prime Minister Walpole. Sometimes called the War of Jenkins's Ear, it was strictly a war for markets in which France fought alongside of Spain. Fighting was confined to South American waters and might have ended there had not a grave crisis arisen in Europe because of the invasion of the Austrian province of Silesia by the armies of Prussia, King Frederick II in command.

PRUSSIA SEIZES SILESIA

The year 1740 witnessed momentous happenings. In June the Prussian sovereign died leaving the kingdom to his twenty-eight-year-old son, Frederick II, whom statesmen looked upon as a gentle and inoffensive spirit. At Vienna, three months later, the Emperor Charles VI passed away after eating mushrooms, and his buxom daughter of twenty-three, Maria Theresa, succeeded to the Hapsburg patrimony. Before the year had closed, Frederick II launched his war machine against Silesia, the fairest jewel in the Austrian crown. "A dish of mushrooms changed the destinies of Europe," mused Voltaire.

Charles VI went to his grave confident that a sheaf of understandings which he had signed with foreign countries, Prussia among them, would assure the authority of his daughter over the whole disjointed Hapsburg realm. And yet half the princes of Europe, craving patches of that inheritance, stood to profit by the dismemberment of Austria. More specifically, Frederick II wished to annex Silesia. If that tempting prize were won upwards of a million subjects would be gained along with flourishing textile and iron industries. On top of that, the standing of Prussia in the European family

[2] For fuller treatment of English America, see Chapter VII.

Maria Theresa as Empress-Queen, shown with her children

would be improved, and Austria debased. Frederick II would not only add luster to his dynasty but achieve personal glory and fame.

These calculations spurred the Hohenzollern monarch to invade Silesia, without any provocation, without a declaration of war. His action resembled the German march into Belgium in 1914 and the Nazi thrust at Poland in 1939. Prussia, it is true, had certain legal claims to sections of Silesia, mostly of dubious validity. And since more than half the Silesians were Protestants, an ideological pretext for removing the province from Catholic and intolerant Austria was uncovered.

Nevertheless, in going to war, Frederick cared little for legal or moral arguments. As he himself brusquely said, "I take what I want. I can always find pedants to prove my rights." His faith rested on the Prussian army and the military resources of his allies, for eventually France and several of the smaller German states, bent on plunder at the expense of Austria, came into the struggle. The cold, calculating Machiavellian spirit of the ambitious Hohenzollern, it must be said, harmonized with the temper of the age. "From an ethical point of view," a seasoned judge has written, "Frederick was little better or worse than his neighbors. He differed from them in that he was able to succeed where they failed." [3]

The Prussian invasion of Silesia caught Austria by surprise. Military operations at first were in the nature of a Prussian parade, for the Hapsburg armies had not recovered from wars with Turkey, commanders were uninspired, the imperial treasury was bare. Only two pitched battles were fought, one at Mollwitz in 1741 ending in a sensational victory for Prussia. A startled Europe learned that Prussia possessed a topflight war machine. France and the German allies of Prussia harried the Hapsburg realm on every quarter. Young Maria Theresa, certain that right was on her side, stubborn and indomitably courageous, appealed in this dark hour to the honor of her noble subjects in Hungary. Promised tangible rewards, the spirited Magyars responded loyally to the appeals

[3] Sidney B. Fay, *The Rise of Brandenburg-Prussia to 1786* (New York, 1937), p. 120.

of their Queen. Britain also rallied to the side of Austria with money first and men later. Alone among the major countries Britain had nothing to gain from the dismemberment of Austria, and the security of the island kingdom would be placed in jeopardy if the balance of power should be tilted in favor of France.

Despite Hungarian fidelity and British help, Austria was worsted in the fighting and in 1742 sued for peace; most of Silesia was ceded to Prussia. Recalling the earlier seizure of Lorraine by Louis XIV, Frederick II wrote: "Lorraine and Silesia are like two sisters, of whom one has married the King of France, the other the King of Prussia." Neither Austria nor Prussia considered the treaty of peace as anything more than a mere truce. Maria Theresa was determined to recover Silesia, while, equally, Frederick intended to hold on to it. Warfare was presently resumed. Prussia, after experiencing reverses, won a string of victories, costly ones, which earned for the king the sobriquet of "the Great." By a second peace settlement of 1745, Austria again recognized Prussian sovereignty over most of Silesia, but once more it was simply a pause between rounds. Anglo-Austrian hostilities, meantime, against France and her German pawns, whom Frederick II twice deserted, were being waged to the point of universal impoverishment.

GLOBAL WAR

And the contest had taken on world dimensions extending to India and America. French ambitions for a commercial monopoly in India and competition for territories in the New World had blended into the war in Europe. As expressed in the florid rhetoric of Macaulay, "In order that he [Frederick II] might rob a neighbor whom he had promised to defend, black men fought on the coast of Coromandel and red men scalped each other by the Great Lakes of North America."

Fresh energy was infused into French enterprise in India with the appointment of François Dupleix in 1741 as governor of the East India Company. This smart and audacious proconsul aspired to nothing less than French lordship over the sub-continent. To carry out this grand design he and his agents dabbled in Indian politics, backing friendly nabobs against other princes and enrolling native soldiers in the French army with European officers, weapons and discipline. That force proposed to expel the British from India and in 1746 the French actually captured Madras. But the exploits of Dupleix roused little interest and no enthusiasm in governing circles at home, and Madras was soon handed back to the British. Unabashed, Dupleix plunged along with his exciting imperial scheme, attracting the potentates of all of southeastern India into his orbit.

In the American phase of the war, English colonial troops occupied the French stronghold of Louisbourg on Cape Breton Island, yet, oddly enough, proposals to unite the colonists in a common front against the French and their Indian mercenaries came to naught. French privateers raided shipping in American and European waters, but the more powerful British fleet imposed a blockade upon the ports of France and seized a large number of French merchantmen. British command of the sea was of vital importance in bringing the general war to an end.

At Aix la Chapelle, a treaty of peace was drawn up in 1748 which settled very few of the causes of international discord. Britain and France handed back conquests outside of Europe and British trading rights in Spanish America were reaffirmed. Austria recovered the southern Netherlands which French armies had occupied and Europe officially approved Prussian lordship over Silesia. Events quickly disclosed that these settlements amounted to nothing more than an armistice between world wars.

Austria utilized the breathing space for a heroic reconstruction of her domestic affairs. If Hapsburg resources were more intelligently and more effectively employed, Silesia, it was argued, might yet be reclaimed. None felt the insult and injury administered to Austria more keenly than Maria Theresa whom her mortal enemy, Frederick II, called sardonically "the ablest man in Austria." Devoted to the interests of the dynasty and a tireless worker, the

Louisbourg fortress on Cape Breton—a symbol of French empire in North America from 1713 until its fall in 1758 when this sketch was made.

His Britannic Majesty's troops were active also to the southward. Above, we see a British force disembarking to attack Spain's colonial city of Havana, Cuba, in the summer of 1762.

young Empress quickly divined the techniques of government and displayed unusual talent in picking advisers. As a rule she readily fell in with the judgments of experts; of them the ablest was Prince Wenceslaus Kaunitz, possibly the shrewdest diplomatist of the century, who in 1753 was entrusted with the management of foreign affairs. With an eye to bettering Austria's diplomatic standing, the Empress married off her children—or such of the sixteen as reached maturity—to foreign courts.

A lofty monument in downtown Vienna proudly recalls the great Empress. Statues of marshals and statesmen stand on the pedestal; in niches above are representations of accomplished Viennese musicians and other worthies of the reign; at the top, sixty feet in the air, Maria Theresa sits serenely on her throne.

Paying tacit tribute to Frederick II, the Austrian army, public administration and financial policies were remodeled along Prussian lines. Waste, duplication and overstaffing, commonplaces of Old World bureaucracy, were reduced and the autonomous rights of provinces were sharply curtailed so as to concentrate authority more fully in Vienna.

THE SEVEN YEARS' WAR (1756–1763)

In 1756 fighting on the grand scale was resumed. That struggle, which lasted seven years, had two distinct phases: Anglo-French jockeying for supremacy in America and India, and war in Europe due directly to Austrian unwillingness to accept the loss of Silesia. Other countries shared the view of the Court of Vienna that Prussia must be cut down to size and they coveted parcels of the Prussian domain; that line of reasoning shaped the policies of Russia, Sweden and Saxony. And France never forgot her standard objective of keeping central Europe in a condition of political disunity. Britain faithfully obeyed the dictates of the balance of power dogma.

On the eve of the renewal of hostilities, Europe witnessed sensational diplomatic revolutions. First, Prussia arranged a partnership with Great Britain, aimed in reality against Austria and France. Then, these latter countries, proverbially deadly enemies, submerged their differences and formed an alliance. That amazing sequence was primarily the handiwork of the astute Austrian foreign minister, Kaunitz, who presently inveigled Russia into a general coalition against upstart Prussia; Sweden and Saxony were likewise attracted into the anti-Prussian camp.

Despite the immense superiority of the encircling coalition Frederick II began the fighting. Supremely confident of Prussia's capacity for war, it seemed wise to strike at the allies before they attacked. In the spring of 1756 Prussian troops swept into Saxony, thus unleashing the bloodiest war of the century. Dazzling Prussian triumphs alternated, for six years, with grave reverses. Britain assisted her ally with raids on the French coast, the sleepless pressure of seapower and financial aid, which, however, was cut off shortly before the war closed. Prussian soldiers fought with rare valor, and profited from operating on internal lines and from the division of mind in the enemy camp.

The genius of Frederick the Great as a field commander was superbly exhibited in two resounding victories of 1757. His army defeated the French and Austrians at Rossbach, west of Leipzig, and at Leuthen near Breslau. The Leuthen campaign in particular was a masterpiece of military skill and made the Prussian king the most talked about man in Europe. British admiration for the "Protestant hero" knew no bounds; taverns, both in Britain and in distant Pennsylvania, appropriated his name.

The Russian steamroller clanked across East Prussia in 1758 but was halted at Zorndorf in the Oder Valley near Küstrin. Prussia purchased victory there at a heavy price in men and equipment; and next year Russian and Austrian armies disastrously routed Frederick at Kunersdorf, hard by Frankfurt on the Oder. Allied troops stormed triumphantly into Berlin. It is hard to see how Prussia could have escaped destruction if the enemy partnership had coordinated its resources effectively. So bleak in fact was the outlook that the iron temperament of the king nearly cracked; he even contemplated taking his life as the alternative to being captured.

But the Prussian sky brightened a bit in 1760. What proved to be the last major battle of the war was fought by Prussia and Austria at Torgau on the middle Elbe, the place at which American and Russian soldiers clasped hands toward the end of the Second World War. Casualties in both armies were prodigious and the Austrians fell back in retreat. Prussia, however, was on the edge of exhaustion, her great army having been whittled down by heavy blood-letting to a mere shadow of its former self. The warrior king moodily observed, "The outlook is as black . . . as at the bottom of a tomb." Multiplying his worries, the British government quit furnishing subsidies at this point, a defection which Frederick II called treachery and never forgot nor forgave.

Outwardly the king hewed to the principle that a commander's job was always to appear as a pillar of strength to the soldiers. But he kept turning over in his mind the desirability of seeking peace by negotiation. Then a lucky accident dramatically altered the military situation. Empress Elizabeth of Russia, Frederick's implacable foe, died suddenly (1762), and her successor, Peter III, broke off the fighting and agreed to a peace which left Prussia intact; Sweden also pulled out of the war. That piece of history, incidentally, was recalled by Nazi chieftains in the last stages of the Second World War. In their desperate dilemma they waited for something to turn up and wreck the Allied coalition; Hitler liked to have the story of Russian withdrawal in 1762, as told by Thomas Carlyle, read aloud.

Britain in the meanwhile had been carrying the war victoriously against France in America and in India. Hostilities had in fact started in the New World before the beginning of the conflict in Europe; French and English colonists clashed over ownership of the Ohio Valley. As a barrier against English pressure the French in 1754 erected an outpost at Fort Duquesne, within today's Pittsburgh. They haughtily declined to pull out as requested by young George Washington, who had gone thither on order of the Virginia assembly which claimed that the area rightfully belonged to Virginia.

Smoldering embers of hate and jealousy quickly flamed into a blaze. War hawks in Britain persuaded the government to despatch military forces to expel the French, but the latter, with the aid of Indian allies defeated the expedition. Formal war on France was declared by Britain in 1756. At the outset French arms achieved inconsequential successes. Then British and colonial troops stormed Louisbourg, Fort Duquesne and other French strongpoints. William Pitt, the Elder, prime minister in 1758, assumed the management of British war energies; austere and domineering, this inspired patriot and compelling orator practically dictated public policy. As was so true of Winston Churchill in another day, Pitt infused dynamic energy into the prosecution of the fighting. Frederick II remarked that England was long in labor until at last it brought forth a man.

Pitt maintained that the future of Britain lay outside of Europe, principally in North America. Consequently, he insisted that his country must subsidize Prussia, which would keep France pinned down in the Old World, while the French empire in America was broken; Britain must "conquer Canada in Germany," Pitt laconically explained. Sensational victories accrued to the British forces in 1759, crowned by the taking of Quebec, which settled the fate of Canada. After that, French resistance petered out in trivial encounters. The British navy, furthermore, ruled the waves. Ports of France were blockaded, her merchantmen driven from the seas and her fleet nearly annihilated. Working with military contingents, British sea forces conquered the French West Indies and Spanish colonial holdings, too, after Spain became (1762) a belligerent. And British naval supremacy denied reinforcements to French interests fighting for their very life in India.

A foeman worthy of the steel of Dupleix appeared in the person of Robert Clive. This chubby bookkeeper in the employ of the English East India Company withdrew from the counting-room in 1744 to enter the arena of politics and war. Imitating French methods, Clive organized Indian warriors (*sepoys*) in

The stages in the taking of Quebec, displayed in a single contemporary print. The blockading fleet, the scaling of the heights and the struggle on the Plains of Abraham are all shown.

Western style military formations, and at Plassey these levies scored decisively over the nabob of Bengal. Clive assumed virtual lordship over that productive province. French power in India was destroyed in 1760 at Wandewash near Madras. British successes in India, that is, broadly reproduced the record in America.

PEACE AND ITS CONSEQUENCES

Without effective support from France, which was lamed by intense factionalism in top governing circles, Austria could scarcely hope to whip Prussia. Frederick II for his part was quite ready to admit military stalemate. Accordingly, terms of peace were drafted in 1763 at Hubertusburg, a hunting lodge in Saxony. The Prussians agreed to evacuate Saxony, while Austria again acquiesced in Prussian sovereignty over Silesia; not an acre of land changed flags as a result of the bitterly contested war.

But the struggle, against great odds, had elevated the international prestige of Prussia, vindicated Prussian ownership of Silesia and enhanced the reputation of Frederick II. Those were precisely the objectives which the king had in mind on the eve of the first Silesian war back in 1740. The Hohenzollern war lord had shown surpassing talents as a strategist, military administrator and leader of men—and that when nearly all Europe was pitted against him and his kingdom of 4,000,000. Hard-worked

Robert Clive

soldiers and Prussians in general developed something akin to filial respect for "old Fritz."

The triumphs, the techniques, the resourcefulness of this superman made a profound and enduring imprint upon the German mind. As no one before him, Frederick II taught Prussia to worship military prowess and to rely upon armed strength. For the first time since Luther, Germans could point to a national hero, a patron saint, who was to become an inspiration in good seasons and ill. "It was Frederick the Great and the Seven Years' War," remarked the cosmopolitan Goethe, "that first gave German literature a subject with real greatness and living interest."

Prussia had definitely emerged as a Great Power and as a potential barrier to Russian pressure in central Europe. For the might of Muscovy, the late war had taught Frederick healthy respect; Prussian security, he felt, required the good will of the eastern colossus. On a longer view he concluded that the only way to survival against "this infamous and devastating horde of savages" was "the eventual formation of a league of the great sovereigns to oppose this dangerous torrent."

Just before Prussia and Austria came to terms, the Western belligerents Britain, France and Spain drew up the Treaty of Paris in 1763. That document underlined the painful humiliations which France had suffered. To Britain, France ceded all of Canada and the territory to the east of the Mississippi, except for New Orleans. To Spain, it transferred the huge Louisiana territory including New Orleans, as compensation for Spanish cession of Florida to Great Britain. Those arrangements assured British predominance from the far north to the Gulf of Mexico and from the Mississippi to the Atlantic.

Britain returned the French islands of Guadeloupe and Martinique in the West Indies, which provoked a storm of protest from British mercantile interests. They regarded these producers of sugar as infinitely more desirable than "the acres of snow" which was Canada. France was also permitted to carry on business with India but denied the right of maintaining armed forces, a stipulation that ruined forever the dream of French empire in India. Britain came out of the war with heightened moral prestige, supremacy at sea, an immense realm in America and an unchallengeable position in India; the balance of power in Europe, too, had been preserved. "Burn your Greek and Roman books," cried Horace Walpole exultantly, "histories of little people."

THE FORTUNES OF IMPERIAL BRITAIN

"Nothing," a distinguished historian of the British Empire has written, with less than literal accuracy, "Nothing great that has ever been done by Englishmen was done so unintentionally, so accidentally, as the conquest of India." After the expulsion of France, the British position in India was fruitfully consolidated. In 1761 Clive virtually withdrew from the Great Mogul the lingering remnants of his sovereignty. For practical purposes, the East India Company was master over large districts of the sub-continent, maintaining administrative and military services and collecting taxes; other European commercial interests were crowded into obscurity. Stockholders in the Company reaped rich harvests as did British business interests and their Indian counterparts.

Gains in India were more than offset by the loss of the choicest portions of English America (Chap. VII). Yet that humiliation in turn was compensated for, in a measure, by fresh British annexations in the Pacific. The hypothesis that

Captain James Cook

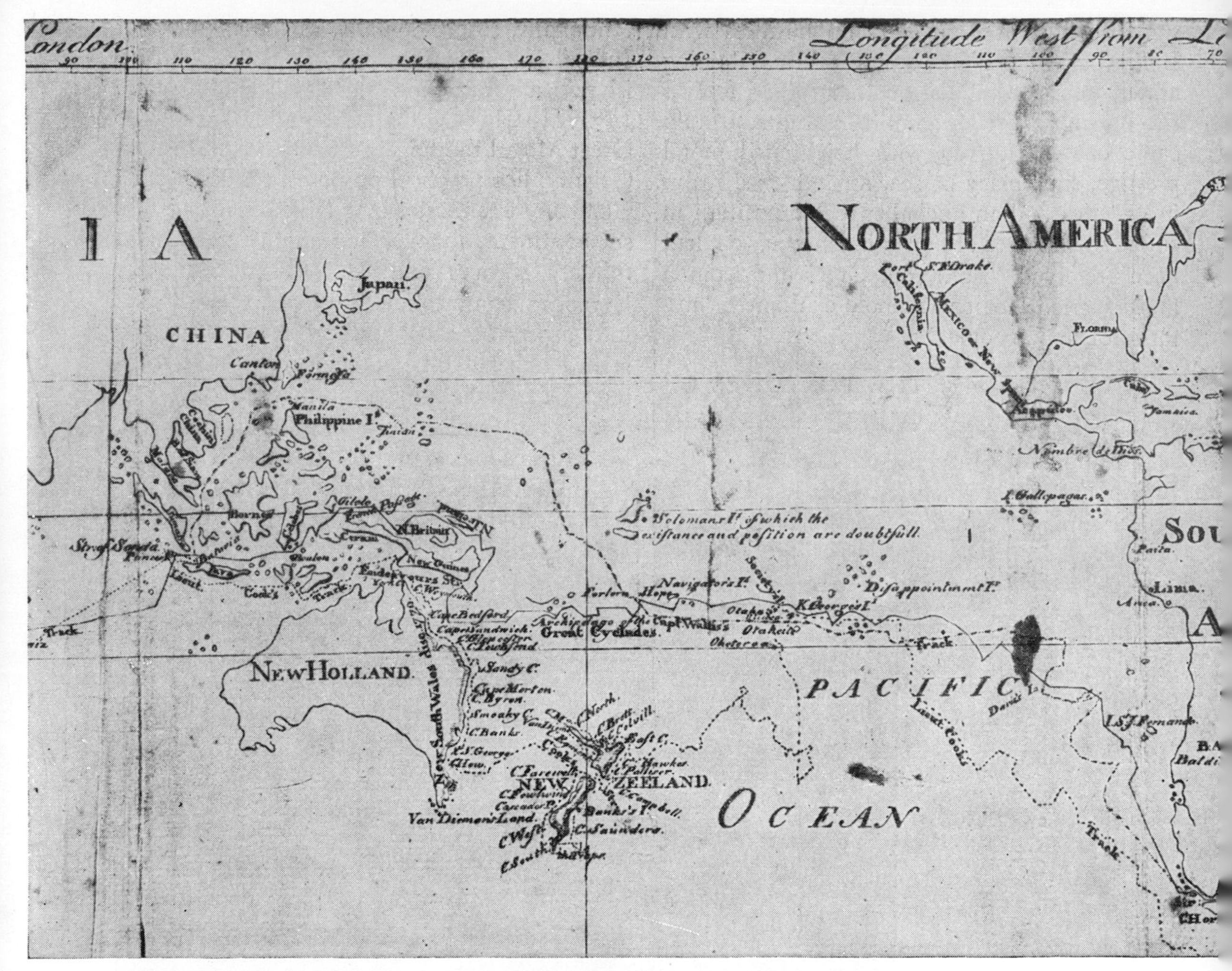

Detail from a map illustrating Cook's explorations in the Pacific

a continent of great extent existed in the South Seas, wealthy beyond the dreams of avarice, had perennially haunted the mind of Europe. Bold Dutch navigators had actually blundered upon Australasia in the seventeenth century, but their voyages had been ignored. The relentless Anglo-French feud inspired a series of rival expeditions into the Pacific; many small islands were discovered, at the cost of thousands of seamen, yet *Terra Australis* proved elusive.

It was a British captain, James Cook, fearless, tenacious of purpose and tactful, a product of the "age of reason" and of progress in navigation, who unveiled the mysteries of the Pacific. By taking infinite pains this foremost sailor in a nation of seamen transformed the map of the Pacific, removing territories from the realm of myth to the realm of knowledge. On the first of three explorations (1768) Cook touched upon New Zealand and Australia claiming them for the British crown. After investigating the customs and habits of native peoples he was not disposed to share the current illusions about "noble savages." He found them diseased, licentious, rashly pugnacious—cannibals often and given to human sacrifices. At Sydney, on the rim of a splendid harbor (Botany Bay), a British penal colony was established in 1788, the foundation stone of the great Dominion of Australia.

THE DOOM OF POLAND

The dismemberment of Poland by greedy neighbors crowned the perfidious diplomacy of the eighteenth century. That event—or series of events—ranks with the rape of Silesia as a revealing commentary on the political standards of the time, the absence of conscience when state interests were involved.

No country of Europe can point to a more colorful or a more turbulent history than Poland. About the year 1000 several Slavic tribes were merged to form an independent Polish state in the Vistula Valley, and Roman Catholic Christianity was adopted as the creed of this people. Religious and cultural influences from the West lifted the Poles out of semi-savagery. Thereafter epochs of sunshine and Polish political vigor alternated with periods of darkness and distress, often the result of warfare with Germans or Mongols. Persecuted Jews flocked from central Europe to Poland where a tolerant government afforded them a haven of sanctuary.

By reason of dynastic union with Lithuania in 1386, Poland emerged as the largest and most powerful country of eastern Europe.[4] It extended from the Baltic to the Black Sea, and attained international respect for culture, literature and architecture, much of which reflected the connections with Catholicism and the West. Cracow, the holy of holies of Poland, was famed for fine public buildings and for its university, at which Copernicus studied; Warsaw subsequently replaced Cracow as the capital.

Many Polish noble families embraced Protestantism in the age of the Reformation, but Jesuit fathers lured most of them back to the mother Church. As an instrument to win Eastern Orthodox Christians to the Polish way of life, Catholic clergymen organized (1596) the Uniate Church, which acknowledged the primacy of the Pope, retained the Slavic liturgy in public worship, and permitted priests to marry. With fire and sword spirited Polish noblemen—the *szlachta*—warred upon neighboring peoples—Germans, Swedes, Turks and Russians. Toward the end of the sixteenth century Poland reached the zenith of its power, prosperity and cultural grandeur; at one point a Polish puppet wore the crown of Russia.

But already the seeds of national decay and ruin had been sown. Poland transferred her rights in East Prussia to the rising state of Brandenburg and later ceded the larger part of the Ukraine to Russia (1667). The process of dismembering Poland had in fact begun. Participation of Polish chivalry, King John Sobieski commanding, in the relief of Vienna from the Ottoman Turks in 1683, marked the final demonstration of the military greatness of the nation.

The glory of Poland, and its chief enemy as well, was the aristocratic warrior caste. A surprisingly high proportion of the Poles had been ennobled in the course of time, and to that class were accorded two distinctive political privileges. Only representatives of the aristocracy were eligible for places in the national assembly and in that body any deputy might veto not only a single piece of legislation, but all laws that previously had been approved in a given session. This *liberum veto*, as it was called, crippled legislative processes and converted lawmaking into a ludicrous farce.

In the second place, the nobles, after 1572, possessed the right to elect the king, making Poland in practice a crowned republic. There was a marked tendency to choose as king a candidate who was unlikely to interfere with the prerogatives or the properties of the aristocracy. The elective principle invited bribery and intrigue, or military pressure by foreign powers which desired a friendly ruler on the throne. On one occasion, with about 64,000 nobles participating in the election, no fewer than eighteen candidates competed for the crown!

Politically speaking, then, Poland entered the eighteenth century as a picturesque medieval survival. And there were other glaring deficiencies in the Polish state, still the largest of Europe except for Russia. As part of the great east European plain, the country was extraordinarily hard to defend, without natural frontiers and with only precarious access to the

[4] The two states were fully combined in 1569.

Baltic Sea. And the social structure was another weakness for a wide chasm separated the *szlachta* from the rural masses. Comprising nearly 1,000,000 in a population of some 12,000,000, members of the aristocratic caste were individualistic, proud, conservative, jealous of their privileges and politically irresponsible. Nobles were, however, obligated to serve in the army and they preferred the cavalry, which was more ornamental and colorful than effective.

Most noble families were miserably poor, owning little or no land, ignorant and indolent. A score of large landed proprietors, the great magnates, constituted the real ruling class of the country. They maintained luxuriant establishments and lived prodigally, competing with one another in conspicuous consumption and for political influence. Allied to the patricians in temper and in fact were the leading dignitaries of the Roman Catholic Church. As for the country people, they had been fully enserfed in the sixteenth century. Living at a lowly level, they were undernourished, brutish, fleeced by the owners of the land which they worked. A saying ran, "If the nobles kill a peasant, they say they have killed a dog." The middle classes were small and composed largely of Jews and Germans, for authentic Poles felt it beneath their dignity to engage in business.

About half the inhabitants of the kingdom were Poles, a third Ukrainians and White Russians, and the remainder Lithuanians, Jews and Germans. But nationality counted for less, very much less, than religious affiliations. Although the population was preponderantly Roman Catholic (or Uniate) there was a large minority of Orthodox Catholics and a scattering of Jews and Protestants. Intolerance toward minorities and religious antipathies weakened the fabric of the Polish state.

Frederick the Great pictured the Poland of his time in colors that were by no means misleading. "This kingdom," he wrote, "is in a state of perpetual anarchy. The great families are at loggerheads. They prefer their own interests to the public welfare, and agree only in their harshness toward dependents, whom they treat less as human beings than as beasts of burden. The Poles are vain, arrogant in good fortune, broken in adversity . . . frivolous, without judgment, capable . . . of ruining themselves by their inconsequence . . . the King sells posts. A single member of the Diet can veto its decisions."

Rich in traditions, Poland was poor, fatally poor in resources of national power and an easy victim of her despoiling neighbors Russia, Prussia and Austria. Russia after 1733 exerted a decisive voice in the selection of Polish kings, and Catherine the Great even installed (1764) a discarded lover, Stanislaus Poniatowski, on the throne. Growing Russian control inspired a clique of lesser Polish nobles to break out in guerilla war, but Muscovite soldiers put down the insurgency.

It seemed as though Poland was fated to become the merest satellite of Russia—as after the Second World War. Catherine II reasoned, however, that Prussia and Austria would never tamely acquiesce in Russian absorption of the kingdom, and recommended collective partition, a proposal that Frederick II promptly approved. He coveted a section of Poland that would join East Prussia to Prussia proper, and he wished, also, to solidify political relations with Russia whose power and ambitions he genuinely dreaded. Months of secret bargaining ensued, Austria participating. Hapsburg interests, it was argued in Vienna, would best be served if Poland were to remain intact and independent; and Empress Maria Theresa disliked on moral principle the idea of cutting up the country. Nonetheless, Austrian soldiers marched into southern Poland while negotiations for partition were going on.

The world was apprized in 1772 that the three powers had worked out a treaty to partition Poland. Russia annexed the eastern provinces with 1,750,000 people, poor but Orthodox. Austria obtained Galicia (except Cracow), a region double the size allotted to Prussia and very much more populous. Prussia took over coveted West Prussia (without the port of Danzig), containing 600,000 souls, "Iroquois" Frederick derisively tagged them. None of the three robbers was entirely satisfied with what each had pilfered. All told, Poland

The sovereigns divide Poland in 1772—a contemporary French allegorical engraving. From left to right, Catherine II, Stanislas of Poland, Joseph (son of Maria Theresa), and Frederick II

was shorn of over a quarter of its territory and fully a third of its population. The national assembly dumbly acquiesced in the amputations and the rest of Europe looked on without raising a finger; the British foreign minister, indeed, dismissed the spoliation as "a curious transaction."

In spite of losses Poland remained an extensive state and it was faced with the necessity of starting afresh from a painfully low level. Awakened to the fact that they had been dwelling in a fool's paradise, leading Polish nobles undertook to reconstruct their country. Administrative innovations were matched by secularization of the schools and some betterment in economic affairs. Discussions on governmental reform matured in a Constitution of 1791, which removed the evils of elective kingship and the *liberum veto*; the principle of ministerial responsibility to the legislature was asserted, though nothing was done to uproot the institution of serfdom.

The Polish changes came too late, alas, to effect a thoroughgoing reformation. And a set of aristocrats, complaining that the Constitution was a manifesto of radicalism, begged Catherine II to intervene. The Tsarina was pleased to respond to the invitation; Russian soldiers and then Prussian troops, advanced into Poland without meeting any real resistance. In 1793, as the sequel to an understanding between Russia and Prussia, half of rump Poland was lopped off. Prussia secured the province of Posen and the city of Danzig, while Russia took a generous slice on the east, which moved her Polish boundary to about the same line as was fixed after the First World War. Again the Polish assembly, under duress, submitted to the inescapable, but a band of patriots rebelled.

Leading the insurgents was Thaddeus Kosciuszko, a militant partisan of freedom in the Old World and the New. Of humble parentage, he had received a military education in France and had placed his sword at the disposal of the American Revolution; Thomas Jefferson spoke of him as "as pure a son of liberty as I have ever known." Back in Poland, Kosciuszko raised an army of sorts, many of the volunteers being equipped merely with scythes and sickles. It was a heroic insurrection but futile; Kosciuszko was apprehended and the rebellion stamped out. Kosciuszko bequeathed to his countrymen a colorful legend which later generations cultivated.

What remained of Poland was parcelled out in 1795 among Russia, Prussia and Austria. In the era of captivity which followed, memories of the Polish past and dreams for the future were kept alive by priest, pedagogue and patriotic writer, until at the close of the First World War Poland was at last resurrected.

SUMMING UP

Reviewing the course of international affairs in the eighteenth century, it is evident that competition for commerce and empire was of crucial importance. The grim Anglo-French duel for global power ended in the spectacular triumph of Britain in both India and America. After that, Britain suffered a severe setback when English America broke away, but the realm in Asia and the Pacific was enlarged. Spain and Holland continued to be colonial powers of considerable stature, while Russia moderately extended her hold on northern Asia.

The diplomacy of the century was notoriously Machiavellian and crystalized in conceptions of the balance of power and *raison d'état* as principles of statecraft. The diplomatic heritage of Louis XIV, that is, became common European property. A greatly respected Swiss jurist, Emeric Vattel, alluded to "the principle of the balance of power, by which is meant an arrangement of affairs so that no state shall be in a position to have absolute mastery and dominate over the others." "England," Vattel pointed out, "has the honor to hold in her hands the balance of power, and she is careful to keep it in equilibrium. . . . It was this policy, aiming of course primarily at the security of Great Britain and her Empire, which inspired Pitt and his successors in their implacable struggle against French imperialism. . . ." [5]

The avarice of princes, lust for territorial expansion, self-interest and fear — all were summed up under the fluid term "reason of state." No falsehood, no deception, no breach of trust whether against outsiders or one's own subjects was reproached as wrong if the ends of the state seemed likely to be served thereby. Solemn treaties were cavalierly reduced to scraps of paper and rulers were quick to engage in what they invariably interpreted as preventive wars.

With the possible exception of Empress Maria Theresa, monarchs cared nothing for the moral rightness of their moves on the international chessboard. Crisp aphorisms of Frederick the Great, such as, "truth to tell, treaties are only oaths of deception and faithlessness," epitomized the prevailing cynicism. Prussia and Russia advanced to the stature of Great Powers, but Poland vanished, bringing Prussia and Austria into direct contact with Russia. Sweden and Turkey, though they escaped dismemberment, dropped out of the company of strong and influential nations.

Statesmen and their monarchs understood that diplomatic achievement and military potential were intimately interlocked. As Frederick II pithily remarked, "Negotiations without arms produce as little impression as musical scores without instruments." Each state, in consequence, maintained as large a fighting establishment as it could afford—or even beyond that; armies devoured much the biggest part of public expenditures. Armaments, on the

[5] In a celebrated book, *Le droit des gens, ou principes de la loi naturelle* (1758), Vattel set forth his views on the conduct of war and diplomacy, urging moderation so as to avoid a legacy of hatred and a desire for revenge on the part of the defeated.

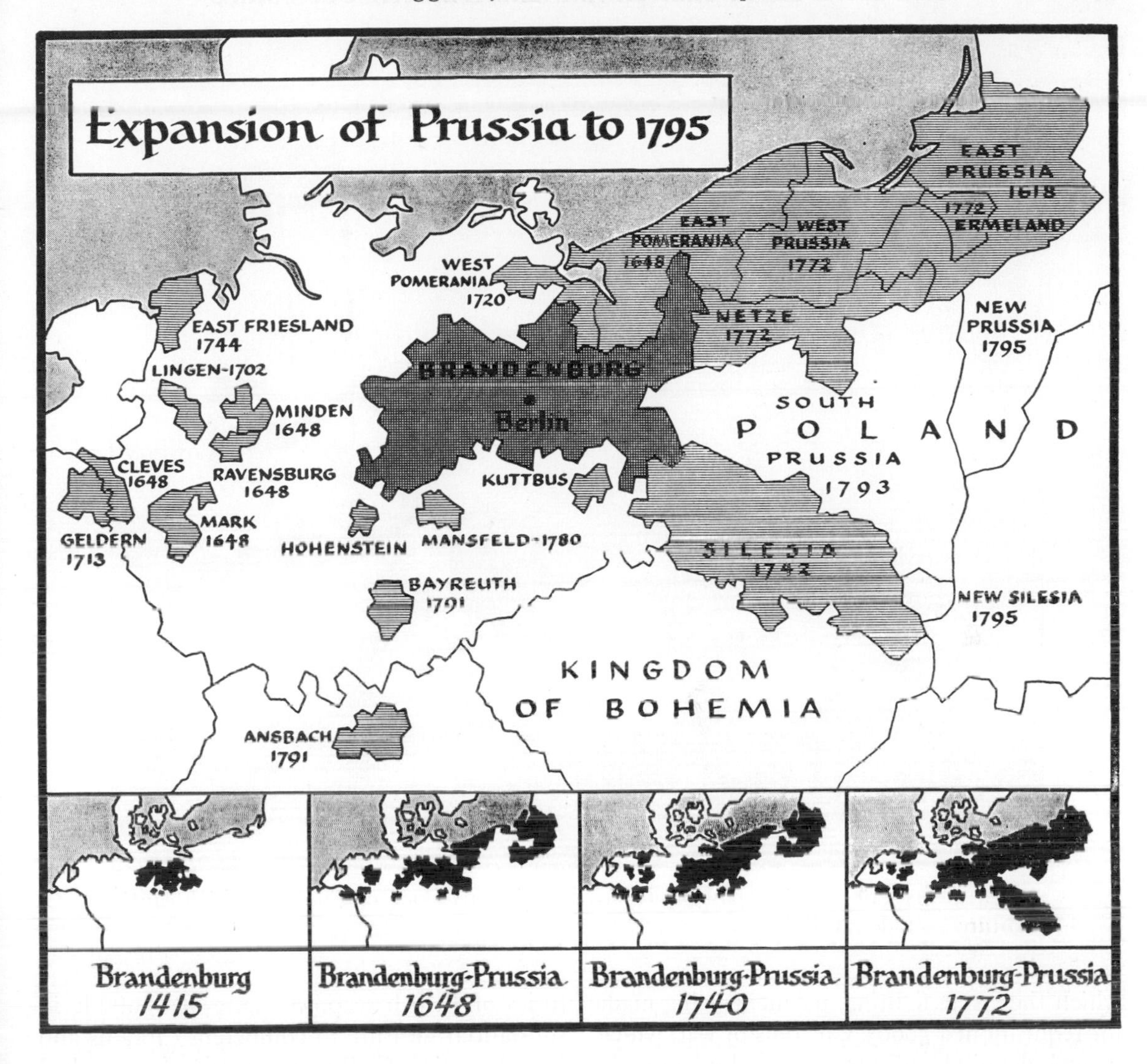

other side, stimulated the growth of manufacturing and shipbuilding.

Standing armies were made up of professional soldiers, who enrolled for long terms. Countries, such as Prussia and Russia, raised troops by a rudimentary type of conscription, but all armies contained a substantial proportion of foreign mercenaries. The soldier of the eighteenth century was neither respected nor glorified, considered rather as a shiftless ne'er-do-well. Punishment for violation of military rules was harsh and awkward equipment necessitated elaborate training and drill. Despite severe discipline, esprit de corps was low and little was done by way of indoctrination to raise morale; wholesale desertions usually accompanied reverses on the battlefield.

The officers' corps differed radically from the army rank and file. Officers were recruited, except in the case of Russia and Turkey, almost exclusively from their own country. Commissions in the French army were largely monopolized by the aristocracy, who purchased them; but sons of burghers were increasingly numerous as officers. In technical finish and social standing Prussian officers excelled all rivals. Service of supply was so poorly organized that in wartime soldiers lived off the countryside in

A British first-rate warship, possibly H. M. S. Britannia—one of England's Eighteenth Century "wooden walls"

which they were fighting, payment being made for requisitioned goods. Customs of war, which turned definitely toward greater humanity in the eighteenth century, and strict discipline of troops normally held plundering and atrocities at a minimum. Civilians, private property, military hospitals and their inmates were instinctively respected.

The object of war was to destroy the opposing army, not the physical annihilation of an enemy country. More commonly than not battles were indecisive affairs. Infantry operations, waged at short range, were conducted in accordance with orthodox tactical principles; Prussian commanders were the most flexible and sympathetic to experimentation.

Just as the Prussian armies benefited greatly from the high quality of the officers, so the victories of British seapower were attributable in substantial measure to competent captains and iron discipline. Ordinary seamen were snatched up in city and on highway or in wartime taken from the merchant marine. Battleships looked very much like commerce carriers and sea-fights as a rule were duels between individual vessels. British naval supremacy, much strengthened in the eighteenth century, enabled the island kingdom to sweep rival fleets from the ocean, blockade enemy harbors and appropriate colonial possessions.

The ideal of lasting peace among the nations attracted only minor attention in the literature of the period. William Penn, to be sure, published an enlightened *Essay Towards the Present and Future Peace of Europe* (1693). He proposed an overarching European assembly to preserve peace, without infringing upon the sovereign rights of the nations in domestic affairs. Going beyond that the Abbé de Saint-Pierre, something of a diplomatist and an optimistic believer in reason as the certain cure for the ailments of society, composed in 1713 an elaborate *Project for Perpetual Peace.* Essentially, this plan summoned the countries to organize a permanent league of nations to straighten out international disputes without recourse to arms. Each member would appoint a delegate to an international senate, sitting permanently at Utrecht, Holland, and each would furnish a quota of troops for an international army. Whenever a quarrel arose, countries not directly implicated would seek adjustment by mediation. Should mediation fail, then the international senate would study the dispute and recommend a peaceful settlement. If one party to the quarrel rejected the decision of the senate, the international army would then apply coercive measures. Diplomatic negotiations would be carried on in the open.

Other isolated thinkers sketched blueprints for perpetual peace founded on the treatise of Saint-Pierre, but embodying refinements. Jean Jacques Rousseau, as an example, brought forward in 1756 a plan for an alliance among the European rulers, who would send representatives to a permanent assembly. The rights and territories of all members would be guaranteed against attack, and violations would be corrected by soldiers from the other countries. Aside from the maintenance of peace, the assembly would seek to advance human welfare in general. These and other writings formed the starting points and the stimulus for later international schemes for keeping the peace, culminating in the foundation of the United Nations in 1945.

FOR FURTHER STUDY

PENFIELD ROBERTS, *The Quest for Security, 1715–1740* (New York, 1947) PAPERBACK

WALTER L. DORN, *Competition for Empire, 1740–1763* (New York, 1940)

LAURENCE H. GIPSON, *The Great War for the Empire* (New York, 1954)

GERALD S. GRAHAM, *Empire of the North Atlantic, the Maritime Struggle for North America* (Toronto, 1950)

ALFRED T. MAHAN, *The Influence of Sea Power upon History, 1660–1783* (new ed., New York, 1944) PAPERBACK

JOHN R. SEELEY, *The Expansion of England* (2nd ed., London, 1895)

RICHARD LODGE, *Great Britain and Prussia in the Eighteenth Century* (Oxford, 1923)

GEORGE P. GOOCH, *Frederick the Great* (New York, 1947)

GORHAN D. SANDERSON, *India and British Imperialism* (New York, 1951)

JAMES A. WILLIAMSON, *Cook and the Opening of the Pacific* (New York, 1948)

WILLIAM F. REDDAWAY, ed., *Cambridge History of Poland* (Vol. II, Cambridge, Eng., 1950)

MAX BELOFF, *The Age of Absolutism* (London, 1954) PAPERBACK

J. O. LINDSAY, ed., *The Old Regime* (Cambridge, Eng., 1957)

HENRY H. DODWELL, *Dupleix and Clive* (London, 1920)

JOHN F. C. FULLER, *A Military History of the Western World* (3 vols., New York, 1954–1956)

ZENAB E. RASHED, *The Peace of Paris, 1763* (Liverpool, 1952)

CHAPTER VII

BEGINNINGS OF THE AMERICAS

OLD WORLD AND NEW

UP TO this point, attention has been focused on the unfolding of Western civilization in Europe. Of that culture in all its fascinating complexity the peoples of the New World have been heir. On a steadily increasing scale the institutions, the products and the customs of the Americas, most importantly of the middle zone of North America, which in the fulness of time evolved into the United States, have been woven into the broad pattern of world history.

Ever since the epochal geographical discoveries of the fifteenth and sixteenth centuries the history of the Americas has been intimately intertwined with the march of events on the other side of the Atlantic. Columbus was in fact the first man to entangle America in European affairs. Although separated by an ocean, whose breadth diminished as ever swifter means of transportation appeared, the interaction of Old World upon the New and New World upon the Old has been a cardinal fact of modern history. As a nineteenth-century observer put it, Europe meant so much to the Yankee because "it is the home of his protoplasm, of the long succession of forces which made him what he is."

For two centuries and more, every major war in Europe, every large convulsion in economic affairs, has had repercussions upon the Americas. Every European cultural and religious innovation of significance, every important European scheme for social betterment, has been felt on the western side of the Atlantic. It was directly because of European appetites and vicissitudes that the New World was discovered, explored and colonized. By reason of competitive rivalries and jealousies in Europe the United States and later the twenty republics of Latin America managed to win political independence, without however detaching themselves from the social, economic and cultural fabric of the Old World.

During the rise and growth of machine-industry in Europe, the United States witnessed the reign of King Cotton, the perpetuation of Negro bondage, leading on to the War between the States and its melancholy aftermath of reconstruction. Varied circumstances in the Old World impelled Europeans to leave home and strike out anew across the Atlantic; the immigration of the colonial era multiplied greatly in the nineteenth century. In literal truth, the United States portion of the Americas grew into "a nation of nations," and the population of the other countries in the western hemisphere was only less cosmopolitan.

Looked at in world perspective the rapid advance of the United States to the stature of a Great Power forms one of the arresting and instructive narratives of recorded history. The span of time since the achievement of independence is short indeed, as history runs, but how immensely man has wrought in those few generations! Between the Atlantic and the Pacific and sloping southward from the Canadian snowfields to the blue Gulf of Mexico lie 3,000,000 square miles of land inhabited at the beginning of the 1960's by upwards of 190,000,000 people.

Only three hundred years before, that vast region had been the home and haunt of scattered and roving tribes of Indian savages. In the combination of raw materials, power resources, manufacturing plant and equipment the United States, at the dawn of the atomic era, ranked incomparably first among the nations of the world.

Walt Whitman pictured the lush riches of the United States in his poetic cadences:

> Interlink'd, food yielding lands!
> Land of coal and iron! land of gold! land of cotton, sugar, rice!
> Land of wheat, beef, pork! land of wool and hemp! land of the apple and the grape!
> Land of the pastoral plains, the grassfields of the world! land of those sweet air'd interminable plateaus!
> Land of ocean shores! land of sierras and peaks!
> Inextricable lands! the clutch'd together!

THE WESTWARD IMPULSE

Everyone knows that the Americas were blundered upon by European explorers in the final decade of the fifteenth century, though substantial settlements came only much later. For more than three generations after the discovery, the Americas were considered primarily as an obstacle on the route to the fabulous treasures of the Orient. Previously, migrations of Europeans had taken place almost exclusively overland; in the future the main movements would be over the ocean. It is relevant, first of all, to survey the circumstances in Europe which inspired exploration and subsequently occupation of the Americas.

The finding and subsequent staking out of territorial claims in the Americas was the unexpected by-product of the European search for direct access to the sources of spices, silks, drugs, precious stones and other luxury wares of Asia. As someone has observed, America was never deliberately discovered, but rather was stumbled upon, like a bedroom chair in the dark. Coupled with that impulse was the desire to exchange European goods for Eastern products by means of barter, which would stop the draining off of gold and silver to Asia in order to balance commercial transactions.

Columbus himself summed up the economic motive of exploration when he wrote: "Gold is the most precious of all commodities . . . he who possesses it has all that he needs in this world, as also the means of securing souls from purgatory and restoring them to the enjoyment of Paradise."

That utterance splendidly illustrates the inseparable linkage of the material with the spiritual in the thinking of the Age of Discovery. For it would be quite erroneous, superficial indeed, to imagine that the lure of worldly goods alone motivated explorers and conquerors. Piety and religious purpose were allied to commerce. The urge to evangelize pagan peoples, whom it was a virtue to pity and a duty to convert, made bold pathfinders of some men—or helped to do so. That instinct carried especial weight in Spain and Portugal, where agelong and militant crusades against Moorish infidels were approaching a triumphant conclusion.

The enthronement of Protestantism in England and Holland added a competitive edge to the conversion of the heathen. Christian insurgents, like the Roman Catholics, were anxious to deserve the favor of the Almighty by carrying forward the work of evangelization. A holy obligation rested upon English Protestantism, the chronicler and clergyman Richard Hakluyt records, to "Instill into the purged myndes [of the natives] the swete and lively liquor of the Gospell."

The idea of empire to enhance the prestige and revenues of one's monarch or country imparted a persistent impulse to overseas operations. Competition among European maritime states quickened the scramble for a favorable place in the colonial sun. Each country claimed for itself a share of "Father Adam's legacy," as a French king expressed the matter. In some degree, pioneer navigators were animated by sheer love of high adventure or spurred on by ambition for personal fame, fortune or glory. That dynamic, too, has persisted, as is so well exemplified in the twentieth-century adventures in unmapped polar regions of Admiral Richard E. Byrd, for instance. Active curiosity about strange lands and exotic peoples had been whetted, the imagination excited by the intellectual awakening of the Renaissance centuries. For intrepid mariners, moreover, the terrors with which the medieval mind had invested uncharted seas gradually dissolved. Each successful trip to foreign parts by sailors of one country stimulated seamen of other nations to emulation. The work of discovery and exploration, that is, was imitative and cumulative.

Men of Italy hold a fair place in the European background of early American history. In the age of the Renaissance, alert, secular-minded Italians pioneered in improving the techniques of seafaring and in the enlargement of the stock of geographical knowledge. The fabulous tales of Marco Polo, devoured by generation after generation, were a constant goad to Italian cupidity and adventuresomeness. The records of global discovery are studded with the names of hardy Italian navigators, among whom Christopher Columbus merits highest honors. And yet, the famous Italian commercial commonwealths, Venice and Genoa, Milan, Naples and the rest, had no direct share in overseas operations, whether discovery, or commerce or colonization.

Set well back from the Atlantic the Italian states concentrated on the established and lucrative trade with the Near East. And in the great age of global acquisition the peninsula was distracted by internal feuds and by desperate, strength-sapping struggles with the aggressive Ottomans. Politically disunited as it was, Italy possessed no royal dynasty to finance and otherwise promote extra-European enterprises.

That responsibility and opportunity fell to the rising national kingdoms along the Atlantic seaboard. Pioneering honors belong to Portugal, which profited from the far-sighted and courageous leadership of Prince Henry the Navigator—who was in fact a director of explorers rather than a navigator. Portuguese expeditions threaded their way down the flank of Africa and with gathering courage rounded the southern tip of the continent and dauntlessly pressed on to India (1498), treasure house of Oriental commodities.

That exciting discovery, or rather series of discoveries, fired the ambitions of mariners in the employ of other seaboard countries. Captains wearing the livery of Spain, Columbus and Magellan, most prominently, for England, the Cabot brothers and later William Hawkins and Francis Drake, Giovanni da Verazzano and Jacques Cartier sailing in the interest of the king of France, and Henry Hudson under the Dutch flag, plowed across unknown waters and revealed to an astonished and bewildered Europe the real nature of the globe. Immortal heroes all, they prepared the way for the conquest, settlement and exploitation of the *Mondo Novo*, the New World of America.

It was a fortunate happenstance that the Western Hemisphere was thinly peopled. Had large populations existed as in India and China, for example, human history would have run into far different channels. As matters turned out, small companies of conquering Spaniards bowled over picturesque and cultivated native states in Mexico and Peru without much trouble. In the middle part of North America "in-

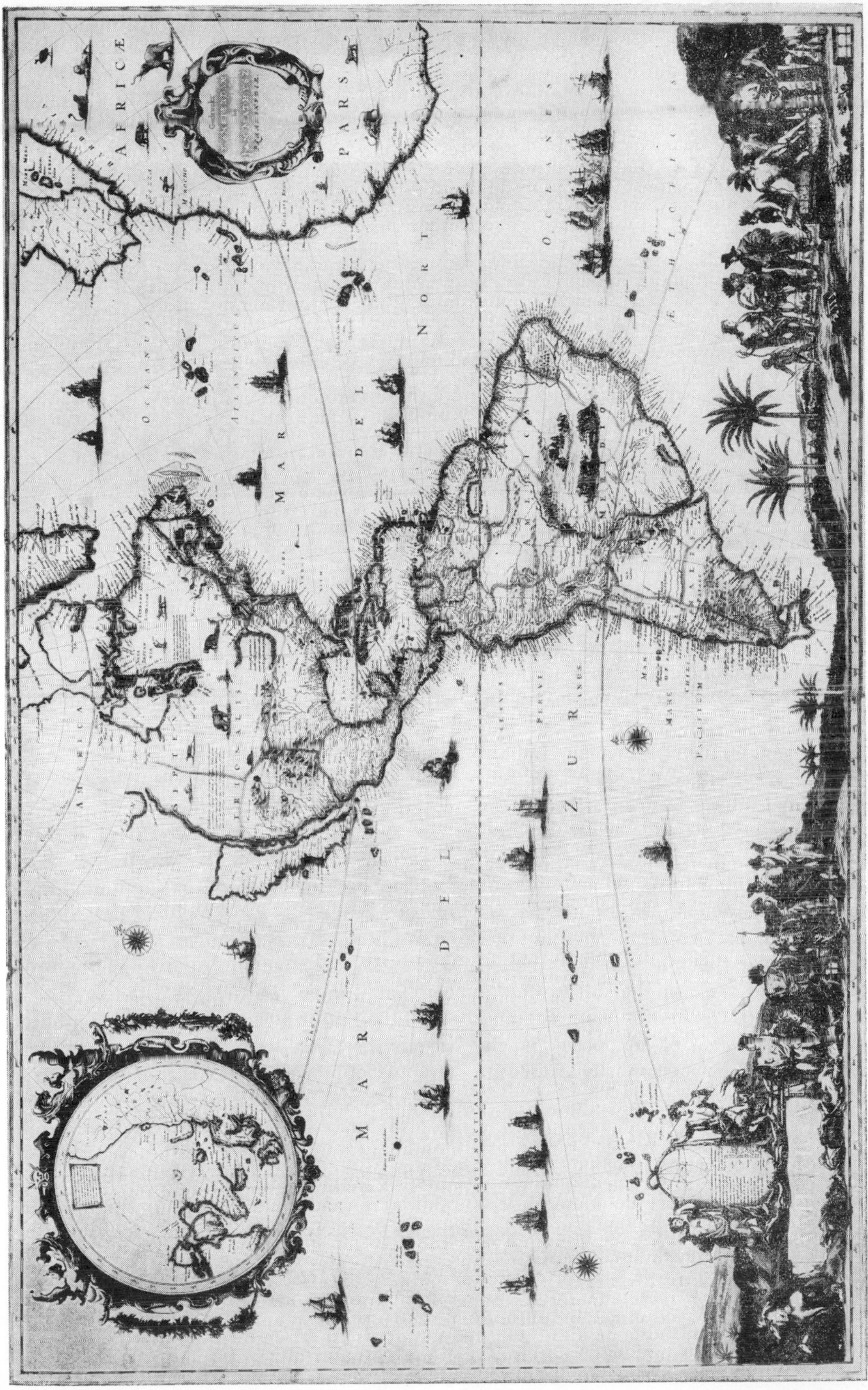

The Americas—a Dutch map of the mid-Seventeenth Century

This ruined Inca city, high in the Peruvian Andes, testifies to the building skill of the pre-Columbian Americans.

digenous" peoples probably did not much exceed 300,000 in the pre-Columbian age.[1]

The origin of these "first Americans" is an intriguing puzzle which has made an armchair archaeologist out of many a layman. Indians did not originate on this continent; no early anthropoidal remains have been unearthed in the Western Hemisphere. Reliable evidence points to the conclusion that the ancestors of the Indians crossed from Asia to America, by way of the Bering Strait, some 15,000 or more years ago. It is certain that "red men" had lived in North America for thousands of years before organized societies arose in the valleys of the Nile and the Tigris-Euphrates. With fire and sword or the persuasions of diplomacy and religion the simple Indians eventually yielded to restless and predatory Europeans.

SOUTH AMERICA BECOMES LATIN AMERICA

Much the larger half of the New World passed under the sovereignty of the Iberian nations, Spain and Portugal. In the sixteenth-century heyday of their greatness they planted their institutions and customs upon the broad lands south of the Rio Grande, and the mark of Spain was long evident in the southwest of the United States and Florida; indeed, even now the Spanish heritage has not been wholly effaced from those regions. By reason of discovery, exploration and conquest of primitive tribesmen, the vast colony of Brazil, about as large as the United States, became a prized trophy of the Portuguese crown.[2] Governing officers, headed by a viceroy, laid out administrative headquarters at Bahia (1567). Later Rio de Janeiro, acquired from the French, was incorporated in the Portuguese empire.

All the rest of Latin America, the Caribbean islands, the area from Florida to Venezuela, and, parcel by parcel, the balance of the mainland of South America submitted to the lordship of Spain. So extensive were the Spanish dominions and so fast were they accumulated that the administrative resources of the homeland were inadequate to organize and govern them effectively. Functionaries, clergymen and

[1] Some estimates place the figure at nearly 850,000.

[2] From 1624 to 1662, Dutchmen were masters of Brazil and their country fastened on to a slice of Guiana permanently.

Detail of Inca stonework. The fitting and bonding of the stones without the aid of modern devices is almost incredible.

colonists from Spain and Portugal, never large in numbers, monopolized the political stage and dominated the economic, social and cultural affairs of the Latin possessions. Immigrants from other European countries were unwelcome; they were rigidly debarred from the Spanish colonies.

Beneath the Europeans were the toiling millions, conquered and converted Indians, hardly more than slaves, Negroes hauled over from Africa and the mixed offspring of conventional or illicit unions, half-caste folk and mulattoes. Even at the middle of the twentieth century, Indians predominated in four of the twenty Latin republics; in Ecuador under ten per cent of the inhabitants were of white stock.

Supreme governmental authority was lodged, of course, in the kings of Spain and Portugal. But European officials on the spot enjoyed no little freedom in deciding public issues, more so in the Portuguese than in the Spanish holdings. To the inferior posts in the swollen provincial and local bureaucracies, colored citizens were slowly admitted in keeping with demonstrated capacity. The prevailing pattern of administration was authoritarian, mildly tempered by enlightenment—the iron hand concealed in a velvet glove. Although representative assemblies had no place in the Spanish scheme of things, councils were set up in the larger towns and cities in which a few natives gained experience in the management of public business.

From the beginning of occupation, arrogant and pugnacious Spaniards searched principally for precious metals and discovered them. Exports of gold and silver wrought with revolutionary force upon the economy and social habits of Europe. And even before the supplies of precious metals had been exhausted, white intruders switched to farming and cattle-breeding on an impressive scale.

Spanish and Portuguese lords of the universe staked out great landed properties, plantations and ranches. From their homelands, the Europeans imported tools, plants and seeds, such as wheat, sugar cane and citrus fruits, as well as horses, cattle, sheep and hogs. Besides shipping surpluses of these commodities abroad, the landlords enriched the diet of Europeans with plants native to the New World, such as corn, tomatoes and potatoes. By all odds the common potato, of which hundreds of varieties were raised in Bolivia and Peru, was most important; it was brought to Europe toward the end of the sixteenth century.

On the social side, an atmosphere of patriarchal feudalism pervaded Latin America. Indians and Negroes quarried the precious metals, cultivated the soil and cared for the livestock. Exploitation of the masses by white masters, outrageous everywhere, was rather less ethically repellant in the Spanish dominions than in Brazil. Thanks to the intervention of churchmen, the worst of the human abuses were in time somewhat mitigated.

Throughout the colonial era the trading and professional classes remained small in numbers and languid in spirit. Commerce inside the Spanish provinces was hindered by difficulties of transportation, though trade argosies regularly carried goods back and forth to Europe. Mexico City in the colonial epoch ranked first among communities of the Western Hemisphere in size and magnificence.

From the beginning of white hegemony the Roman Catholic Church and her clergy constituted a powerful force in the civilization of Latin America. The quest for pagan souls, waiting for conversion, was a strong and enduring impulse in the Iberian occupation. Devoted sons of St. Francis and zealous Jesuit fathers taught the red men to venerate the God of the white man, without always imbuing them with the inner spirit of the alien creed and ethic.

The scope of the Church in Latin America, as in medieval Europe, ranged far beyond religious responsibilities and ministrations. Churchmen obtained and kept jurisdiction over learning and intellectual affairs in general; a brisk trade in books from Spain satisfied the needs of natives who had learned the Castilian language. Under Christian auspices universities were operating in Mexico City and Lima by the mid-sixteenth century and primary schools taught European manual skills.

Aside from softening the rapacity of white masters, churchmen inculcated respect and loyalty to the mysterious monarch in far-off Europe. They also promoted the primitive arts and architecture; the house of worship, invariably ornate and massive, white and golden in the sun, was the prominent structure of every substantial community of Latin America. Inside the church, native communicants marveled at the gold decoration, the candles and the sacred mysteries of Catholic Christianity. In time the church amassed great wealth in movable treasure and landed estates. Beyond any comparison, the church was the channel through which the elements of the Western way of living, Iberian-style, were conveyed to Latin America.

The dissemination of Spanish culture over an area larger than Europe, surpassed the achievement of the colonizing countries of northern Europe. And whereas the latter overcame the problem of natives by brushing them aside, as again in Australia, the Spaniards brought about a cultural and physical fusion of peoples.

So it came to pass that all the Americas south of the United States took on, and still retain, the languages, the customs and something of the culture of Catholic Spain and Portugal.

EUROPE IN NORTH AMERICA

While South America was being molded into Latin America, the wilderness to the north was undergoing transformation by Dutch, French and above all, English influences. Much of the story of the imperial rivalries over North America has already been recounted, so that here brief recapitulation alone is necessary.

The monopolistic place of Spain and Portugal in the colonial sphere depended upon Spanish supremacy on the ocean. In the spacious age of Queen Elizabeth, England, impelled by mixed commercial and ideological (religious) motives, shattered Spanish maritime power. The epochal destruction of the great Armada in 1588 heralded the decline of Spain; the notion that the New World was essentially a private Spanish preserve was dealt an irreparable blow. England became ruler of the waves and initiated her remarkable expansion overseas. English buccaneers and freebooters merrily sacked Spanish colonies and pirated Spanish treasure, while English trading companies, ready to run risks in the hope of rewards, financed the planting of settlements beyond the stormy Atlantic.

Unlike the enterprises of Spain and Portugal, English colonialism was curiously haphazard, little controlled, relatively, by the government at home. As Edmund Burke remarked (1757): "The settlement of our colonies was never pursued upon any regular plan, but they were formed, grew, and flourished as accidents, the nature of the climate, or the dispositions of private men happened to operate."

The first permanent English community was started in 1607, at Jamestown, Virginia. An earlier experiment in settlement in the Roanoke region as well as enterprises in Maine and Newfoundland had quickly come to grief. Under charter of the crown, a company of London merchants laid the foundation of the Plymouth Colony, and before the seventeenth century was out, it united with the colony of Massachusetts which stretched off to Canada.

The Cathedral and the Plaza de Armas, Lima, Peru, show how thoroughly the Latin culture was impressed on South America.

This view of Quebec in 1758 is a fine example of American Colonial engraving as well.

In rapid succession other English colonies were established in Connecticut, Rhode Island and New Hampshire. To the south, Maryland and the Carolinas; and in the center, out of the colony of New Netherland, snatched from the Dutch, New York and New Jersey. They were soon joined by Pennsylvania and Delaware.

At the mouth of the river discovered by Hudson in 1609 Dutch interests had built New Amsterdam as the headquarters of New Netherland. Up the Hudson a hundred and fifty miles an outpost of trade was founded at Fort Orange, now Albany, and assertive Dutchmen pushed their claims toward the Connecticut on the east and the Delaware on the west. A Swedish settlement on the Delaware, containing fewer than a thousand Swedes and Finns, was absorbed into the Dutch dominions in 1655, but all were lost to the English in 1664, as has been indicated.

With Spain humbled and the Dutch eliminated, only France remained to contest with England for North America. After several ill-starred gestures at settlement, a lasting French colony had been founded at Quebec in 1608. Selected as the capital of New France, Quebec always held top place in French imperial strategy. Missionaries, fur traders and explorers claimed for Royal France the huge valley of the Mississippi and its tributaries. Warfare with England, however, robbed France of Hudson's Bay, Nova Scotia (Acadia) and Newfoundland.[3]

The decisive verdict on French America was rendered by British and colonial troops in the American phase of the globe-wide Seven Years' War, better known in the United States as the French and Indian war (p. 123). The Peace of Paris in 1763 sheared off the whole vast French empire in the New World, except for Guadeloupe, at the time a most lucrative supplier of sugar, other small West Indian islands, two small fishing islands off Newfoundland and a chunk of Guiana in South America. Britain took ownership of Canada and the Mississippi country and obtained Florida, to boot, from Spain. The first British empire had marched to greatness over the prostrate form of France, but the prolonged Anglo-French duel for world empire had not yet entered its last round.

Among the leading peoples of western Europe, the Germans exerted least influence upon the fortunes of North America in the formative centuries. Split into many political fragments like Italy, in the great age of discovery and occupation, and fearfully ravaged by the Thirty Years' War, "Germany" was incapable of taking part in the opening up of the New World. Several small trading adventures were launched by Germans in South America, it is true, but they collapsed either because of Spanish hostility or German negligence. With the notable exceptions remarked upon later, emigrants from Germany chose to trek off to eastern or southeastern Europe rather than to North America.

[3] Treaty of Utrecht, 1713.

THE PEOPLING OF ENGLISH AMERICA

The motives which impelled Europeans to leave home and start out afresh in the New World were as diverse almost as human behavior itself. It required strong convictions and a considerable sense of discontent in the pioneers who voluntarily forsook the homes and familiar scenes of their fathers and adventured overseas. The ocean voyage lasted six to ten weeks in cramped quarters, the passengers always in danger of contracting loathsome diseases and, awaiting them at journey's end a raw, untamed country.

The strongest driving force behind emigration, undoubtedly, was the longing for better economic opportunities, the allure of new wealth and new homes in a new world. Resplendent visions of America as a land of abounding promise captivated many an unhappy European. Virgin America beckoned, for instance, to Englishmen who had been displaced by the enclosure of fields to provide grazing ranges for sheep. And the belief that England was in fact over-populated and so afforded small chance to get ahead made recruits for America. English restraints upon exports persuaded hosts of Scotch-Irish to move overseas where they were joined by families from the Continent who faced insuperable barriers to land ownership in the country of their birth.

It was believed that on the other side of the Atlantic Europeans could build an earthly paradise and secure release from the countless restrictions of law and custom and the humdrum monotony of existence in the older Continent. Political oppression, such as attended the civil war in the England of Cromwell, induced merchants, farmers and a few country gentlemen to set off for English America. It is one of the glories of the United States that even in the colonial period it was a place of refuge for the oppressed and displaced.

Blending with secular urges, the desire for religious freedom, which sometimes has been inflated to legendary proportions, diverted Europeans to the New World. There they might worship without molestation as their consciences dictated. In German Europe, for instance, pietistic Protestant minorities, Mennonites, Amish and others, all step-children of the Reformation, were persecuted by Lutheran orthodoxy and by Catholics. Intolerance together with severe economic distress resulting from destructive French invasions of the Rhineland set a tide of German emigration flowing principally to Pennsylvania—a new Canaan—to the Mohawk valley of New York and into the southernmost colonies by way of the back country. To speed the departure of these troublesome sectarians, German governments relaxed the rigid rules against emigration.

From France (or by way of England) came small contingents of harried Huguenots to settle in every colony, though principally in South Carolina. There they formed in time a tenth of the colonial population. Unlike the German immigrants, the French Protestants were fast assimilated to colonial society. And Great Britain itself supplied quotas of settlers motivated in part by the desire to escape religious discrimination: Pilgrims to New England, Catholics to Maryland, Quakers to Pennsylvania, especially. Mild religious oppression was partly responsible also for the emigration of Scotch-Irish Presbyterians and of some thousands of Catholics from the southern counties of Ireland. A sprinkling of Jews found new havens in the cosmopolitan and urbane coastal cities.

The lure of distant adventure and the urge to carry the gospel message to heathen red men persuaded some Europeans to leave home. Incalculable was the influence, moreover, of high-pressure advertising through promoters, press and pulpit, describing the equable climate and the good earth beyond the Atlantic. The imagination of Europe was stirred by vivid portrayals of America as an earthly paradise, the "New Found Eden," certain to have a rosy future. Attractive pamphlets prepared by William Penn telling the virtues of his colony and printed in several languages played their special part in attracting pioneers to Pennsylvania.

Indentured servants and apprentices sailed for America, having mortgaged their brawn for as long as seven years to pay for transportation. Though free of the moral stigma attaching to slavery, this indenture practice was, nonetheless, a species of bondage. Deserters from merchant ships and from the British army in America—later from the Hessian mercenaries—also contributed to the peopling of the English dominions. Some settlers landed in the New World without having any say at all in the transaction. To supply laborers kidnapped children, insolvent debtors and political offenders were shunted overseas. Benjamin Franklin once recommended that rattlesnakes should be exported to England in return for unsavory jailbirds shipped to the colonies.

Among the involuntary immigrants were Negroes fetched from the forests of Africa. It was in 1619 that a Dutch vessel unloaded the first fateful cargo of "twenty negars" in English America. Until well along in the seventeenth century indentured whites outnumbered colored workers in the Southland, but by the close of the century, Negro slavery had struck deep root. Of the 400,000 Negro bondsmen in the colonies as of 1775 nearly nine out of ten were employed on Southern plantations; the minority in the North generally worked as household servants or craftsmen.

At that point about two million whites inhabited English America, almost a third as many as lived in England itself. Obedient to the biblical command to multiply and replenish, the colonists prided themselves on large families, and the natural growth was, of course, reinforced by the ceaseless flow of immigration.

Out of the heterogeneous mélange of tongues, traits and varieties of Christian experience in the colonies, there emerged a society of men somewhat different from their relatives an ocean away. "Here individuals of all nations are melted into a new race of men," proclaimed Crèvecoeur, a French visitor at the end of the colonial period, "whose labours and posterity will one day cause great changes in the world. Americans are the Western pilgrims, who are carrying along with them that great mass of arts, sciences, vigour, and industry which began long since in the East; they will finish the great circle."

COLONIAL LIVING

In the span of time between the establishment of bridgeheads in English America and the Declaration of Independence, the character of colonial living underwent considerable changes. In a very real sense English America was a projection of British civilization overseas. But Old World institutions, habits and traditions were slowly "Americanized" in the freer milieu of the Atlantic frontier.

Throughout the colonial era the inhabitants depended for the most part upon the soil and the forests for their livelihood. Agricultural conditions varied considerably from the subsistence farms on the poor soil of New England and the ever-advancing frontiers to the capitalistic plantations of Virginia and South Carolina. Immigrants brought with them seeds and plants of the kinds of crops traditionally raised in Europe livestock, too. From the Indians, palefaces learned how to grow corn, potatoes and tobacco—the last of which became the staple money crop of Virginia and Maryland. Red men also imparted to newcomers their time-tested techniques of agriculture and taught lessons in the most effective ways of felling trees or snaring fur-bearing animals.

Farm tools of course were rude and crude as in Europe itself. In every phase of farming the accent was on brawn and hard labor. Unlike the plodding peasant of the Old World, however, the American farmer "mined" the land rather than tilled it, the more enterprising moving on to greener pastures when the surface wealth had been skimmed off. Hard, unremit-

An American rural landscape in the Eighteenth Century, as sketched by a Royal Governor

ting work was the rule for the small independent farmer and his family on their limited acreages, while on the large Southern estates owners directed the operations of Negro bondsmen. Conditions of colonial agriculture fostered a spirit of rugged individualism and sublime self-confidence.

With the onward march of time, a surprisingly complex economy matured in the English possessions. Commerce, shipbuilding and water transportation attained considerable importance in New England and the middle colonies. Yankee traders were known up and down the coast and in the ports of western Europe a full century before the term Yankee came into use.

Boston, New York, Philadelphia and, in the south, Charleston to a lesser extent, blossomed and bloomed into prosperous commercial centers. They transacted business for the colonists and exchanged wares with Europe, Britain mostly, and with the West Indies. In payment for imported manufactures, colonial producers shipped abroad materials for the making or the repair of ships, timber, fish and furs, and from the South tobacco, rice and indigo. It was cheaper to build ships in America than in England so that on the eve of the Revolution a third of the British merchant marine bore the stamp of Yankee yards. Along the rim of white settlement and beyond, itinerant traders in quest of furs carried on a brisk barter business with the Indians, always in competition with French rivals.

The establishment and growth of handicraft industries enriched the variety of economic activity. Output of iron wares, for example, expanded greatly in the eighteenth century and by 1775 colonial forges accounted for a seventh part of the world's production. Household necessities and comforts and even some luxury wares, were manufactured in farmhouse, on plantation or in small shop. When the need appeared, native industries would be able to turn out a substantial proportion of the military equipment to win independence.

As in any new country, the progress of manufacturing was hampered at every turn by scarcities of capital and skilled artisans, by the high cost and slowness of transportation and by the instability of currencies. British laws, moreover, designed to regulate and restrict trade and industry, retarded expansion, though that handicap was somewhat offset by British subsidies paid on rawstuffs for which there was an urgent demand. Opportunities for professional men in the church, in medicine, in law and government kept pace with the maturing economy. Early in the eighteenth century an aristocracy of wealth had arisen in the older seaboard communities and successful Southern planters had become a landed aristocracy.

Throughout the colonial era emphasis was placed upon material welfare, but the things of the mind and spirit were not neglected. On many counts, English America was more cosmopolitan, less provincial, than the United States later on. Citizens of a global empire—many of them only recently arrived from Europe—Americans in a measure adhered to the fashionable cult which believed that humanity was one and perfectible. Germs of nationalism had not as yet deeply invaded the intellectual blood-stream.

British versions of Christianity and sects of Continental origin flourished in English America. Religion claimed a larger place in New England and Pennsylvania than in New York and the Southern colonies. The church served not only as a place of worship but as a focus of social activity, and frequently as schoolroom and forum for the discussion of secular problems; missionaries carried the gospel to "heathen" Indians. Clergymen commanded great respect, often being the most influential community leaders, especially in the colonies where church and state were most closely interlinked. Freedom of conscience prevailed in Pennsylvania and Rhode Island to a degree unmatched abroad, save possibly in Holland.

In coastal cities where wealth had accumulated and in manor houses of the South a cultured and urbane society came into being, comparable to that in provincial towns of Britain itself. Sophisticated affluent Charleston, indeed, frankly patterned itself on London. But on farm and frontier strenuous toil left little time or energy for the cultivation of the refining niceties. And in the north the Puritan legacy, nourishing though it was to the life of the spirit and to learning, taught men to be contemptuous of, or indifferent to, aesthetic enjoyments.

Book learning and the rudiments of education were furnished to some children in schools or by tutors. Ability to read, write and figure probably ranged higher in New England than anywhere else in the world. It was fashionable for Southern planters, in the late colonial period, to send their sons and occasionally a daughter to England to be educated and polished. On the other hand, during the Puritan Revolution some dour Englishmen sent sons to Harvard as a purer fountain of Puritanism than the homeland possessed. Colonial colleges, nicely distributed geographically, attracted a larger proportion of young men than similar institutions in the Old World. The popular American convictions that literacy would ensure earthly bliss and that learning would raise one's earning capacity were firmly rooted in the colonial epoch.

Books of all descriptions were brought in from Britain and the Continent, and American authors themselves composed some works of note. Philadelphia and Boston were busy centers of printing and book markets. Libraries, either privately owned or kept up by public subscription or local government, loaned out their volumes; by the time of the Revolution colonial libraries outnumbered, it would seem, those in Britain itself. And colonial newspapers in the eighteenth century built up a respectable reputation as literary vehicles and as agencies for the circulation of political opinions. In the major cities audiences witnessed English drama and music, the artists themselves frequently coming from Europe.

Harvard in the early Eighteenth Century

Nothing illustrates more impressively the improving quality of living in the New World than the architecture. It was a far cry indeed from the rough cabins or even tents of the original settlers to the palatial mansions on Southern plantations and the stately brick edifice in Philadelphia in which the spokesmen of the colonial insurgents affixed their signatures to the Declaration of Independence.

Out of the colonial population came accomplished painters of portraits. They covered acres of canvas with pictures of the "best people," which still decorate homes, clubs and public buildings in coastal communities. The American Benjamin West, for instance, succeeded Sir Joshua Reynolds as president of the British Royal Academy. And for their scientific attainments, several colonials, one as early as 1663, were elected as fellows of the Royal Society in London. No doubt the most significant American cultural contribution was in the domain of science; Franklin in the eighteenth century was hailed as the Newton of the New World. British and other European learned societies contained a much higher percentage of American members in the eighteenth century than in the twentieth.

The American Philosophical Society of Philadelphia, founded in 1744, was the first important learned academy on New World soil. Foreign scholars eagerly accepted invitations to membership. Benjamin Franklin and Thomas Jefferson are properly classed with the enlightened "philosophers" of the eighteenth century. Jonathan Edwards, of an earlier generation, the first profound religious philosopher in the New World, earned a place among the solid thinkers of his time by terrifying interpretations of the terrifying hell-fire tenets of John Calvin.

On the economic and cultural fronts, then, the adventure in the New World had netted sound returns for those who had dared to invest their futures in it. Colonial self-assurance, once the initial rigors of making a living in the raw, new country had been surmounted, gathered momentum, helped along by cultural and material accomplishments. All that had vital bearing upon the course of politics in the Thirteen Colonies.

HOW THE COLONIES WERE GOVERNED

Government in English America resembled the pouring of old wine into new bottles—with explosive consequences in time. Articulate colonists of British origin or descent carried in their memories the choice heritage of Magna Charta, the Declaration of Rights, a passion for freedom and home-rule for localities. Under one name or another the institutions of English local government, counties and towns, and their officers, such as sheriffs and justices-of-the-peace, were reproduced across the ocean.

Neither uniform nor static, provincial governments were defined in charters granted by the king which seldom delimited areas of authority with precision. These documents, however, promised citizens freedom of expression, rights of petition, jury trial and habeas corpus—standard British customs. A governor appointed by the crown in most colonies and a nominated council of advisers exercised the executive function. Responsibility for making laws belonged to colonial representatives controlled by the propertied minority, just as was the case with the British House of Commons. Assemblies grew to be self-governing in virtually all strictly provincial affairs; above all else, they held power over the public purse. Governor, council and elected legislature resembled in miniature king, lords and commons in London.

Since the functions of the branches of government were not sharply defined, and since colonists were quick to resist arbitrary rulings of royal agents, verbal duelling between assembly and governor were stock features of provincial public life. Late in the colonial era, governors posted a steady stream of despairing despatches to London recounting the aggressive spirit of assemblymen; more often than not, royal officials yielded to pressure.

With the years the jurisdiction of the assemblies expanded, paralleling in a way the growing authority of the British Parliament. Gain upon gain achieved by assemblymen, schooled in the strategies of politics, whetted appetites for further advantages and fostered faith in the uniqueness of "Americanism."

It was generally acknowledged that king (or governor) might veto certain acts of an assembly, for he was sovereign over the whole British realm. "The fealty and allegiance of Americans," declared John Adams in 1774, "is undoubtedly due to the person of King George III, whom God long preserve and prosper." If there was no question of allegiance to the crown, obedience to the British Parliament was something else again. In the thinking of many colonists Parliament possessed no warrant to enact legislation for English America, except navigation laws to regulate the trade of the Empire. Parliament, however, contended otherwise and therein lay the seeds of an irrepressible conflict.

BONDS OF UNITY

Down to the middle of the eighteenth century, at any rate, feeling of "national" consciousness in English America, though deepening, was neither widespread nor ardent. Rather, as in Canada nowadays, colonists cherished a dual loyalty: allegiance to the British crown, allegiance to their own colony. When visiting England, Americans seem to have felt almost as much at home as though they were in the New World itself. Not unlike the principalities of Italy, the several colonies differed considerably by reason of historical and social evolution and the residents prided themselves on local loyalties. Competing claims to western lands, moreover, roused mutual suspicions and petty prejudices in the Thirteen Colonies.

Powerful influences, on the other hand, nourished a sense of community and challenged divisive tendencies. For one thing, four out of five of the colonists spoke the English language and shared directly in the heritage of Britain, not least in the concept of the good society, politically speaking, which Parliament had vindicated in the seventeenth-century struggle with the Stuart Kings. Proud of colonial achievements and made aware of their increasing strength by press, pulpit and politician, many colonists believed that the New World was capable of charting its own destiny without benefit of or interference by the parent country three thousand miles away.

A small extremist minority by mid-eighteenth century was already preaching secession from the motherland and that agitation was reinforced by French propaganda which painted British rule in ugly colors. On the other side, however, the standing peril of the French and their Indian allies and warfare with them persuasively argued the need for a common colonial front. The desirability of political union of the colonies captured many and warm partisans, though opinions diverged as to just how the merger should be effected. Declared Franklin: "Everybody cries, a union is absolutely necessary, but when it comes to the manner and form of the union, their weak noddles are perfectly distracted." A decisive impetus toward unity was given by the stricter commercial policies pursued by the British government after the victorious conclusion of the Seven Years' War.

THE DOGMA OF MERCANTILISM

When European colonial empires were in the making, the economic philosophy spoken of as mercantilism was rising to high noon. British policymakers believed and applied without hesitation the universally accepted notions on the operation of colonies. Overseas possessions, in a word, should assist the motherland to become self sufficient, as independent of foreign sources of supply as possible. Colonial raw materials should close the gaps in the economy of the homeland. In that way "wealth" would accumulate when a nation was at peace and the country would be stronger in case of war with a foreign rival.

Once colonial supplies had satisfied the necessities of the imperial owner, surpluses might be sold to foreigners. Foreign stores of precious metals would in consequence be drained off to the colonial parent. Mercantilist logic prescribed a nice division of production. Put briefly, producers in the home country would profit from a monopoly in the colonial market on manufactures, while colonists would have access to the home market free of foreign competition. That arrangement, instead of profiting one party alone, would be mutually advantageous.

In the light of history, however, the British attempt to force the colonies into an inflexible economic strait jacket had fateful consequences. Rigidity proved disastrous in dealing with the healthy, growing organism in English America, though it must be added that Britain allowed its colonies greater latitude than did imperial countries of the Continent.

How in fact did the British government translate the prevalent mercantilist doctrine into legislation? First, laws restricted the transportation of goods to or from colonies to British-owned ships (colonial included). Second, certain designated colonial productions could be exported only to Britain or a British colony, though other commodities might be freely disposed of in markets outside of the empire.

Third, most foreign goods for colonial consumption might not be bought directly from the producing country but had to pass through Britain which raised the cost of the commodity. A Molasses Act of 1733, for instance, placed a heavy tariff on molasses and other sugar products from non-British possessions. And, again, hindrances were imposed upon manufacturing in the colonies. It was unlawful, for example, to build new mills to turn out iron or steel products. Membership in the British imperial system, on the other hand, netted special advantages to the Thirteen Colonies. Subsidies were paid for certain classes of goods needed in Great Britain, colonial merchants enjoyed unique trading privileges in the British Isles and colonial shipping interests profited from the rule restricting the carrying trade of the Empire to British vessels.

Laws on the statute books, moreover, and the execution of laws are not always identical. Enforcement of the British carrying and trade regulations was at best sporadic. Customs officials and indolent governors often winked at evasions; smuggling developed into an exact science and a lucrative one. When, after 1763, British authorities presumed to carry out commercial regulations strictly they infuriated diverse and influential elements in the colonial community.

Victory over France (and her Indian hirelings) added Canada and the Mississippi country, as has been noted, to the British Empire. Elimination of the French flag from the continent fanned colonial pride and undermined the notion that the British protective shield was indispensable for colonial safety. Government, the government in Britain, furthermore, was blamed for a sharp depression and "hard times" in the post-war years. Nearly a generation earlier an astute French statesman, Turgot, remarked that "colonies are like fruits which cling to the tree till they ripen," and, he added prophetically, "As soon as America can take care of herself, she will do what Carthage did." The "Revolutionary Generation" witnessed the fulfillment of that bit of smart prophecy.

ROAD TO REVOLUTION

After 1763 the British government pursued two broad policies in English America. It tried to enforce imperial regulations with vigor and it passed new laws especially to raise more revenue from the colonists. For one thing, settlers on the frontier and land speculators were antagonized by a proclamation of 1763 reserving territory west of the Appalachians to the Indians and ordering white squatters to move off. By this move, Great Britain intended to retard white occupation until a sound Indian policy was devised in London, but spirited frontiersmen felt that their interests had arbitrarily been trampled upon. Somewhat similarly, Southern planters who wished to pay off debts to Britons with cheap colonial currency flared up violently when a measure (1764) prohibited the printing of legal tender paper money.

British statesmen reasoned that the prospering colonials ought to share in carrying the financial burden bequeathed by the late war. After all, that conflict had been fought in part to remove the French menace to the security of English America—and to stop Indian raids that for generations had drenched frontier settlements with blood. For defense in the future against savage Indians or French intrigue, it was also contended, the colonists should bear part of the expense of maintaining British armed forces.

Since the colonial assemblies would not themselves vote funds, Parliament passed the Revenue (or Sugar) Act of 1764, which replaced the moribund Molasses Act. Intended to raise a substantial revenue, the law cut the duty on molasses from non-British sources in half and laid tariffs on white sugar, coffee and other commodities. Stricter regulations to collect duties were provided and any trader caught smuggling would be severely fined. Aware that efficient execution of the law would be financially damaging, New England mercantile interests protested though without special spirit and without attracting much general applause.

On the heels of the Revenue Act came the notorious Stamp Act of 1765, prescribing that stamps should be purchased and affixed to legal documents, newspapers, bills of lading, liquor licenses and other documents. Similar legislation, it should be noted, existed in the British Isles and the revenues that were collected would be spent in the Thirteen Colonies for their defense and security. By implication, at any rate, the law underlined the parliamentary claim to tax the colonists, a principle which cut squarely athwart New World theory. Since the tax would fall on nearly all groups in the colonies, it gravely increased resentment to the authority of Parliament. From north to south colonial resistance was prompt, almost universal and violently hostile. The bolder spirits organized demonstrations and riots and imperiled the lives of the collectors.

In actual fact the law was nullified and, as another method of protest, colonists quit buying British products, causing sales to fall off sharply; at the time British exports to America normally formed nearly a third of foreign trade. Nine colonies, moreover, despatched delegates to an historic assembly held in New York, which flatly repudiated the validity of taxes not authorized by colonial assemblies. That gathering of 1765 is often pointed to as the initial event in the American Revolution.

Under the twin pressure of British business interests that suffered because of the colonial boycott, and, less so, of popular opposition in English America, Parliament revoked the Stamp Act. At the same time, the lawmakers, many of them the merest marionettes of King George III, approved a Declaratory Act, asserting the unqualified power of Parliament to legislate for the colonies on any and all subjects. Individual British voices spoke up, it is true, on behalf of the colonists; William Pitt and Edmund Burke in particular lectured their countrymen with the honest fervor of medieval homilists, but they won few converts. Repeal of the Stamp Act gladdened colonial hearts, ordinary trade with Britain was resumed and the omens appeared good for reasonable harmony between mother and offspring.

But the sky soon darkened again. Still in quest of additional revenue, Parliament enacted in 1767 a set of measures called the Townshend Acts. Tariffs (indirect taxes) were imposed on glass, paper, lead, tea and some other imports; under older statutes these commodities could be imported only from British sources. To ensure effective collection of the new duties, the British customs service would be toned up. As the crowning thrust, part of the revenues would be applied to paying the salaries of British civil officials in English America, thus placing them beyond the financial control of local assemblies. The Townshend legislation evoked fresh colonial protestations, though on a less energetic scale than in connection with the Stamp Act. Clashes between citizens and British redcoats caused the shedding of blood.

Americans once more boycotted British products, but this time British exporters found alternate markets with which to trade. Nonetheless, Parliament reversed itself, canceling the Townshend duties, save the levy on tea; the exception advertised the right of Parliament to lay taxes on the colonies. Colonial passions quickly subsided, though militant extremists kept chanting the battle cry "No taxation without representation."

Parliament stoked the fires of secession by conferring upon the East India Company in 1773 a monopoly on the importation of tea into the Thirteen Colonies. That arrangement threatened to reduce if not wholly to empty the wallets of certain colonial mercantile interests. And if a monopoly on tea importation were enforced might not similar concessions be awarded British firms for other classes of goods and so strangle colonial merchants? Colonists replied with direct action either preventing tea ships from unloading their burdens or, more audaciously, destroying tea as occurred in the harbor of Boston. That piece of violence swept the feud with Great Britain to a climax: to wilful transgression of law, destruction of property had been added.

By way of punishment, Parliament imposed a ban on shipping to Boston which robbed thousands of employment and jeopardized the prosperity of the entire community. The Massachusetts constitution, moreover, was altered so as to enlarge the powers of the king and billeting of soldiers in Boston homes was authorized. General Gage, commander of His Majesty's troops in English America, was appointed royal governor. Impassioned and sober patriots alike vociferously condemned these "intolerable acts," which in truth were little short of a declaration of war.

On top of all this, in 1774, Parliament voted the Quebec Act, which had been under discussion for several years. Thereby freedom of worship was assured to Roman Catholics of Canada (Quebec), fulfilling a promise Britain had made in the Treaty of Paris of 1763. Yet to many a New England Protestant this enlightened action seemed nothing less than blasphemous; fevered brains even imagined that the British ministry was preparing to hand the empire over to the Pope! And the Quebec Act also extended the boundaries of Canada south to the Ohio and west to the Mississippi, the whole province to be administered by a military governor. It was suspected in colonial circles that this maneuver presaged the establishment of authoritarian rule in English America generally. The hour of revolution drew nearer.

HOW WAR CAME

Not all politically active colonists by any means were prepared to rebel against British authority. Many an intelligent and respectable American, preferring loyalty to liberty or apprehensive of rule by radical insurgents, deplored the opposition to the revenue laws and

The Boston Tea Party

the Boston "tea party." In each colony, two antagonistic factions confronted one another: the Tories or Loyalists over against the patriots or revolutionaries. Loyalists comprised an impressive and formidable company, coming mostly from the comfortably situated. Conservative in outlook, wedded to the status quo, Loyalists were terrified at the very suggestion of physical violence. On the other hand, certain aristocratic landed proprietors, personified and inspired by George Washington, drifted into the revolutionary camp.

But the main body of insurgents were middling and homespun folk. Though a minority the partisans of revolution were well-organized and had persuasive orators and writers who harped upon the iniquity of British tyranny and the blessings of freedom and independence. Among them, passion for liberty soared to lyric heights.

Under radical and moderate auspices the first Continental Congress came together in Philadelphia in the autumn of 1774. It was a body without any constitutional sanction, meeting to recover "just rights and liberties" and to restore "union and harmony" with Great Britain. Conciliatory voices were drowned out by the roar of revolutionaries. Rehearsing the manifold grievances of the colonists in a "declaration of rights," the Congress virtually denied that Parliament possessed sovereign authority in America. A ringing summons to colonists to quit doing business with Britain caused imports to tumble almost to zero.

Before the Congress convened a second time the Battle of Lexington dispelled the chance of averting civil war. That clash occurred when a British expedition was despatched from Boston to get hold of military stores which colonists had accumulated at Concord, some twenty miles inland. On the way, at Lexington, early on the morning of April 19, 1775, the redcoats were confronted by a contingent of "minutemen," drawn up on the Common and ready to fight. Someone pulled a trigger—whether a Briton or an American has never been determined—and a deadly skirmish ensued. Greatly outnumbered, the colonials quit the fateful green, leaving some of their fellows on the ground. Up to that point only a small minority of articulate colonists wished to strike off on the path of independence. But actual bloodshed greatly increased sentiment favorable to an open breach with the British Empire.

Of utmost importance in crystallizing separatist feeling was a short but widely circulated tract for the times, *Common Sense*, penned by a militant idealist Thomas Paine, recently arrived from England. In accents calculated to stir even the sluggish, Paine pleaded for independence, extolled the natural rights of man,

George Washington at Princeton

pointed up the material advantages of separation and prophesied, with robust faith, a glorious destiny for an America freed from "the royal brute of Briton." "Independence is the only Bond," cried Paine, "that can tye and keep us together."

In May of 1775, meanwhile, a second Continental Congress had assembled in Philadelphia. Defiantly that body launched preparations for war and sanctioned the creation of an army, entrusting Washington with the supreme command. It was presently learned that Britain had contracted with German Hesse for 20,000 mercenaries to crush the New World insurgency. So at long last, after many twists and turnings, the way was made straight for an outright declaration of independence. In the opinion of John Adams, the friends and the opponents of separation from Great Britain were about equally divided while another third of the colonists was unconcerned.

INDEPENDENCE PROCLAIMED

On July 4, 1776, the men of the Continental Congress cut the Gordian knot by proclaiming that the Thirteen Colonies had broken away from the British Empire. In the celebrated Declaration, Thomas Jefferson, aged 33, an inveterate foe of tyranny wherever found, rehearsed the grievances and the ideological faith of the insurgents. As the document itself belongs among the masterpieces of political literature, so Jefferson ranks not alone as a founding father of the American Republic but as a figure of universal political importance. And yet only the composition of the Declaration was Jefferson's, the ruling ideas stemmed largely from the teachings of John Locke and the philosophy of the "Enlightenment."

On the negative side the Declaration set forth the causes which impelled the colonies to "this mighty resolution" of throwing off allegiance to Britain. Scalding invective was poured upon the head of George III. Positively, the document enumerated the grand concept of the Revolution: the insurance by government of life, liberty and the pursuit of happiness, the last item a novel principle in political thought. All men were said to possess natural rights which Britain barred the way to attainment. It was not the purpose of the American revolt to create a powerful state but rather to establish a political environment in which the ordinary fellow would have fuller scope for his talents. Here was the ideological blueprint for Americans of the future, an immortal parchment whose principles have ever since been invoked as rallying cries by men everywhere struggling to escape oppression.

Upon the publication of the Declaration the struggle with Britain assumed the character of a "national" conflict against a foreign power. Loyalist dissenters became traitors and thousands fled penniless to Canada or to the motherland itself in order to go on living under the British flag. Colonial governments were easily and naturally converted into state governments. It remained, however, to vindicate in the fierce ordeal of battle the declaration of independence which many articulate colonists, if not indeed most, had accepted with extreme reluctance. Freedom had been bought, it had yet to be paid for—on the installment plan.

In summary, then, it is crystal clear that the causes of the American Revolution, as of other large historical processes, were many and intricate. Simple explanations satisfy only simple minds. It is altogether too easy and considerably less than half the truth to tell the story of American independence merely as a fight for liberty against the authoritarian and stupid King George III.

Patent economic grievances, quarreling about trading regulations, about taxes and tariffs, about currency laws and the occupation of lands to the west—these disputes coupled with irreconcilable interpretations of constitutional prerogatives contributed basically to the birth of the new nation. Each party to the controversy marshaled plausible arguments to uphold its contentions, and the more the arguments were reiterated the more compelling they appeared. Without common agreement on fundamentals, political compromise is impossible and no such agreement existed on the eve of the Revolution.

American aggressiveness, it may be said, collided with British obstinacy. And undergirding

IN CONGRESS, JULY 4, 1776.

A DECLARATION

BY THE REPRESENTATIVES OF THE UNITED STATES OF AMERICA, IN GENERAL CONGRESS ASSEMBLED.

WHEN in the Course of human Events, it becomes necessary for one People to dissolve the Political Bands which have connected them with another, and to assume among the Powers of the Earth, the separate and equal Station to which the Laws of Nature and of Nature's God entitle them, a decent Respect to the Opinions of Mankind requires that they should declare the causes which impel them to the Separation.

WE hold these Truths to be self-evident, that all Men are created equal, that they are endowed by their Creator with certain unalienable Rights, that among these are Life, Liberty, and the Pursuit of Happiness—That to secure these Rights, Governments are instituted among Men, deriving their just Powers from the Consent of the Governed, that whenever any Form of Government becomes destructive of these Ends, it is the Right of the People to alter or to abolish it, and to institute new Government, laying its Foundation on such Principles, and organizing its Powers in such Form, as to them shall seem most likely to effect their Safety and Happiness. Prudence, indeed, will dictate that Governments long established should not be changed for light and transient Causes; and accordingly all Experience hath shewn, that Mankind are more disposed to suffer, while Evils are sufferable, than to right themselves by abolishing the Forms to which they are accustomed. But when a long Train of Abuses and Usurpations, pursuing invariably the same Object, evinces a Design to reduce them under absolute Despotism, it is their Right, it is their Duty, to throw off such Government, and to provide new Guards for their future Security. Such has been the patient Sufferance of these Colonies; and such is now the Necessity which constrains them to alter their former Systems of Government. The History of the present King of Great-Britain is a History of repeated Injuries and Usurpations, all having in direct Object the Establishment of an absolute Tyranny over these States. To prove this, let Facts be submitted to a candid World.

HE has refused his Assent to Laws, the most wholesome and necessary for the public Good.

HE has forbidden his Governors to pass Laws of immediate and pressing Importance, unless suspended in their Operation till his Assent should be obtained; and when so suspended, he has utterly neglected to attend to them.

HE has refused to pass other Laws for the Accommodation of large Districts of People, unless those People would relinquish the Right of Representation in the Legislature, a Right inestimable to them, and formidable to Tyrants only.

HE has called together Legislative Bodies at Places unusual, uncomfortable, and distant from the Depository of their public Records, for the sole Purpose of fatiguing them into Compliance with his Measures.

HE has dissolved Representative Houses repeatedly, for opposing with manly Firmness his Invasions on the Rights of the People.

HE has refused for a long Time, after such Dissolutions, to cause others to be elected; whereby the Legislative Powers, incapable of Annihilation, have returned to the People at large for their exercise; the State remaining in the mean time exposed to all the Dangers of Invasion from without, and Convulsions within.

HE has endeavoured to prevent the Population of these States; for that Purpose obstructing the Laws for Naturalization of Foreigners; refusing to pass others to encourage their Migrations hither, and raising the Conditions of new Appropriations of Lands.

HE has obstructed the Administration of Justice, by refusing his Assent to Laws for establishing Judiciary Powers.

HE has made Judges dependent on his Will alone, for the Tenure of their Offices, and the Amount and Payment of their Salaries.

HE has erected a Multitude of new Offices, and sent hither Swarms of Officers to harrass our People, and eat out their Substance.

HE has kept among us, in Times of Peace, Standing Armies, without the consent of our Legislatures.

HE has affected to render the Military independent of and superior to the Civil Power.

HE has combined with others to subject us to a Jurisdiction foreign to our Constitution, and unacknowledged by our Laws; giving his Assent to their Acts of pretended Legislation:

FOR quartering large Bodies of Armed Troops among us:

FOR protecting them, by a mock Trial, from Punishment for any Murders which they should commit on the Inhabitants of these States:

FOR cutting off our Trade with all Parts of the World:

FOR imposing Taxes on us without our Consent:

FOR depriving us, in many Cases, of the Benefits of Trial by Jury:

FOR transporting us beyond Seas to be tried for pretended Offences:

FOR abolishing the free System of English Laws in a neighbouring Province, establishing therein an arbitrary Government, and enlarging its Boundaries, so as to render it at once an Example and fit Instrument for introducing the same absolute Rule into these Colonies:

FOR taking away our Charters, abolishing our most valuable Laws, and altering fundamentally the Forms of our Governments:

FOR suspending our own Legislatures, and declaring themselves invested with Power to legislate for us in all Cases whatsoever.

HE has abdicated Government here, by declaring us out of his Protection and waging War against us.

HE has plundered our Seas, ravaged our Coasts, burnt our Towns, and destroyed the Lives of our People.

HE is, at this Time, transporting large Armies of foreign Mercenaries to compleat the Works of Death, Desolation, and Tyranny, already begun with circumstances of Cruelty and Perfidy, scarcely paralleled in the most barbarous Ages, and totally unworthy the Head of a civilized Nation.

HE has constrained our fellow Citizens taken Captive on the high Seas to bear Arms against their Country, to become the Executioners of their Friends and Brethren, or to fall themselves by their Hands.

HE has excited domestic Insurrections amongst us, and has endeavoured to bring on the Inhabitants of our Frontiers, the merciless Indian Savages, whose known Rule of Warfare, is an undistinguished Destruction, of all Ages, Sexes and Conditions.

IN every stage of these Oppressions we have Petitioned for Redress in the most humble Terms: Our repeated Petitions have been answered only by repeated Injury. A Prince, whose Character is thus marked by every act which may define a Tyrant, is unfit to be the Ruler of a free People.

NOR have we been wanting in Attentions to our British Brethren. We have warned them from Time to Time of Attempts by their Legislature to extend an unwarrantable Jurisdiction over us. We have reminded them of the Circumstances of our Emigration and Settlement here. We have appealed to their native Justice and Magnanimity, and we have conjured them by the Ties of our common Kindred to disavow these Usurpations, which, would inevitably interrupt our Connections and Correspondence. They too have been deaf to the Voice of Justice and of Consanguinity. We must, therefore, acquiesce in the Necessity, which denounces our Separation, and hold them, as we hold the rest of Mankind, Enemies in War, in Peace, Friends.

WE, therefore, the Representatives of the UNITED STATES OF AMERICA, in GENERAL CONGRESS, Assembled, appealing to the Supreme Judge of the World for the Rectitude of our Intentions, do, in the Name, and by Authority of the good People of these Colonies, solemnly Publish and Declare, That these United Colonies are, and of Right ought to be, FREE AND INDEPENDENT STATES; that they are absolved from all Allegiance to the British Crown, and that all political Connection between them and the State of Great-Britain, is and ought to be totally dissolved; and that as FREE AND INDEPENDENT STATES, they have full Power to levy War, conclude Peace, contract Alliances, establish Commerce, and to do all other Acts and Things which INDEPENDENT STATES may of right do. And for the support of this Declaration, with a firm Reliance on the Protection of divine Providence, we mutually pledge to each other our Lives, our Fortunes, and our sacred Honor.

Signed by ORDER *and in* BEHALF *of the* CONGRESS,

JOHN HANCOCK, PRESIDENT.

ATTEST.
CHARLES THOMSON, SECRETARY.

PHILADELPHIA: PRINTED BY JOHN DUNLAP.

The Declaration of Independence

all the ferment was a growing feeling of distinctiveness among colonials, a dynamic awareness of uniqueness that had matured in the half century preceding 1775. The Revolution was in fact an evolution and in its finished form the handiwork of a militant, liberty-intoxicated minority. Its course was marked by mob violence, the destroying of property and the abuse of the innocent by enemies bent on feathering their own nests. But above and beyond the tangible and the unlovely shone the resplendent purposes for which the insurgents fought, under the direction of far-seeing, spirited and principled leadership.

WAR AND PEACE

Readers of these pages will be familiar with the way in which the war for independence was eventually won. From the bleak and dreary period of 1776 through the darkness of Valley Forge and of 1780, when even Washington "almost ceased to hope," until the sunny autumn of 1781, the armies of independence suffered an agonizing succession of defeats and retreats. Yet the British triumphs were somewhat akin to the victories of Pyrrhus. Throughout it all the insurgents were cheered by the assurance of Tom Paine that "what we obtain too cheaply we esteem too lightly; it is dearness only that gives everything its value."

Independence would scarcely have been achieved without the assistance of France. The Bourbon government first shipped supplies to the rebels through a dummy business corporation, and in 1778 entered into a formal alliance with America and declared war upon the common enemy. In deciding to ally openly with the colonists the French regime was motivated primarily by the intention to split the British empire and so square accounts with the ancient and hereditary foe.

Outside of French governing circles, active sympathy for the American cause was manifested by men who dreamed of liberty and freedom for their own country and who pictured the Thirteen Colonies as the Utopia envisioned by their "philosophers." Yet the autocratic Bourbon government itself could hardly have been expected to enthuse over a struggle for liberation or the paeans to liberty which ascended beyond the Atlantic. No more could the patriots of 1776 warm up to the obsolescent French monarchy; ideologically, it was an incongruous match, a marriage of convenience, but assistance was desperately needed and there was no disposition in America to require character references from the prospective benefactor.

French help moving over the Atlantic in the shape of arms and other equipment generously subsidized the American military effort. Trained soldiers, too, the young nobleman, Marquis de Lafayette conspicuously, placed their talents at the disposal of Washington. The Bourbon navy and Bourbon troops rendered yeoman service in the closing episodes of the war.

The intervention of France was shortly followed by the entry of Spain and Holland against Britain. And a combination of other Continental nations—the Armed Neutrality League—threatened to fight if Britain did not call a halt to the seizure of neutral merchantmen on the high seas. The struggle took on very nearly the dimensions of a global war, Britain against the world. The ineptitude of France and Spain, however, averted the worst disasters for Britain. Friendless Britain was never in quite so perilous a plight again until the somber year of 1940 in the Second World War. In the American theater, British commanders, mostly complacent mediocrities, were plagued with problems of supply and shortage of troops. Nearly half the soldiers at that were mercenaries shipped over by the German lord of Hesse. The lowering of the British flag at Yorktown by General Cornwallis symbolized the virtual end of hostilities—and of George III's adventure in personal government.

Formal treaties of peace were signed at Paris in 1783. Americans realized their maximum expectations, for in addition to recognizing independence, Britain conceded that the boundary of the new nation should run to the Mississippi and in the north to the Great Lakes and the St. Lawrence approximately. Spain reclaimed Florida from Great Britain, only to transfer it thirty-six years later to the United States.

For her contribution to the common triumph

France was rewarded with only a few small colonial gains. But the Bourbon monarchy had the psychological satisfaction of recovering lost prestige at the expense of Britain and the Court of Versailles had assumed that the alliance with the young trans-Atlantic Republic would last—a false calculation as the event presently disclosed. Worse than that, the French national treasury was disastrously impoverished and revolutionary sentiments were quickened by events across the Atlantic. A mere six years after the making of the American peace, the French volcano erupted.

As for Britain, small wonder that knowing Europeans concluded that her sun had set, defeated as she was in war, bereft of her choicest colonial properties and deeply in debt. Emperor Joseph II of Austria ranked the island kingdom alongside of Denmark, "completely fallen and forever." However grudgingly, British statecraft accepted the verdict of the facts as final. Chastened in mood, George III extended his hand in friendship to the first minister from the New World Republic, though he refused to send a minister in return for a decade.

Many an acute controversy between the two leading members of the English-speaking community would flare up and die away, radical changes would come over the British world position, before a serene statue of George Washington would be planted in front of the National Gallery in London and a British Prime Minister would say, as Clement Attlee did in 1946, that "the name of Washington is respected and honored," in Britain as in the United States.

A MORE PERFECT UNION

In the panorama of world history the success of the American nation in setting up republican and durable institutions of government takes rank with the winning of independence. During the war each of the thirteen republics adopted constitutions impregnated with the "spirit of 1776," with ideas of natural rights and popular sovereignty. Elected governors supplanted the crown-appointed chief executives and the supremacy of the legislatures was emphasized. But otherwise traditional governmental forms were little altered. Property and religious qualifications for the suffrage, for instance, varying from state to state, restricted the electorate to much less than half the adult white males.

Traditions of states' rights, parochial prides and prejudices militated against the organization of a strong central government. A union of the states was formed, it is true, in the Articles of Confederation, effective in 1781. But that was a frail reed, for the jurisdiction of the legislature was so narrowly defined that it could neither levy taxes, nor regulate commerce, nor did it show itself capable of smoothing out feuds between the rival states. There was no distinct executive body, moreover, to see that laws were carried out. If peace and security were to prevail the individual states would have to federate, surrendering much of their sovereignty.

Turmoil and tumult forced growth. Representatives of twelve of the republics, fifty-five delegates in all, men of property and station, converged upon the tranquil Quaker community of Philadelphia in the summer of 1787 to frame a more effective charter of unity. After four months of tough-minded discussion, much pulling and hauling, and compromises and concessions on every hand, the famous federal Constitution of the United States was drafted. It was speedily amplified by amendments guaranteeing civil liberties, spoken of as the Bill of Rights. Here was a novel framework of government. Here were enshrined the gains of the Revolution.

Searchingly debated in the state legislatures and approved by them, the Constitution went into operation in 1789 upon the inauguration of General Washington as President. A national constitution in written form is the most original contribution of the United States to the fine art of government. Ever since, the Constitution has been scrupulously studied by foreign statesmen and scholars when engaged in the building of constitutions, and sections of the unique document have been copied or adapted in the fundamental law of many countries.

A central feature of the American instrument, which is among the most complicated arrangements on earth, was the division of sovereign authority between the federal government and the governments of the states. Then too, the executive and legislative branches of the federal government were sharply separated. The British principle of cabinet responsibility to the legislature, in other words, was not adopted by the United States; instead the President was allowed to choose his own advisers, or cabinet officers. Actually more real power was lodged in the President than was exercised by the king whom he superseded.

In preparing the Constitution the delegates at Philadelphia endeavored to answer an old dilemma of government—a problem which Abraham Lincoln phrased this way: "It has long been a grave question whether any government not too strong for the liberties of its people can be strong enough to maintain its own existence in grave emergencies." To protect popular liberties against encroachment by the central government, the Constitution created a Senate and a House of Representatives representing state and local interests, rather than overarching national concerns. The country as a whole was represented by the President, but he was not clothed with authority to impose his will upon the legislature.

It was reasoned that in periods of tranquility the division in federal authority would ensure a minimum of government. When grave emergencies appeared, on the other hand, the President, it was assumed, would be able to persuade the legislature to support the policies he espoused. In actual practice the President can act fast and without a responsible cabinet. It might almost be said that it is a part of the Constitution that the President can ignore the Constitution; subsequently Congress asserts itself, restoring its own supremacy. Curious and awkward though these arrangements may appear, they have successfully satisfied the acid test: they have worked.

In making the Constitution, the men of 1787 decided that responsibility for the maintenance of peace between the states rested upon the federal government. Turning aside proposals for consolidation by gradual stages, they asserted the supremacy of the central authority. And yet the line of demarcation between the rights of the states and of the national government was not strictly drawn. Wrangling over this issue has persisted in one form or another to the present day.

SHOTS HEARD ROUND THE WORLD

The events leading to the birth of the United States form one of the most pregnant developments of the modern age. Their world meaning has grown with the years. A body blow had been struck at the hoary institution of monarchy and the principles of popular government had been given a decided impetus. The age of revolution had in reality dawned, and the next chapter would be written in France.

Partisans of freedom in Europe took heart from the trans-Atlantic achievements. The revolt against oppression, the victory of insurgency, the triumph of the republican ideology and institutions, free from aristocracy and serfdom, leavened the fermenting lump from Ireland to Russia. As John Adams sagely observed the American Revolution became a world-wide force.

It seemed that in America liberty and equality—the acme in human association—had come to fulfillment. Many a European, then or later, subscribed to the Utopian vision of America painted by Jean Pierre Brissot, a French journalist: ". . . I see this whole extent of continent . . . covered with cultivated fields, little villages, and country houses. (America will never have enormous cities like London and Paris . . . property will be more equally divided . . . happiness more universal.) I see Happiness and Industry, smiling side by side, . . . Liberty and Morals rendering almost useless the coercion of Government and Law, and gentle Tolerance taking [the] place of the ferocious Inquisition. I see [Americans, north and south] embracing each other, cursing tyrants, and blessing the reign of Liberty, which leads to Universal Harmony."

Leaders of colonial or other subject peoples,

eager for freedom, have since drawn inspiration from the example of the United States. Within a generation or so the nations of Latin America had cut loose from Spain and Portugal. Paradoxically enough, the triumphant revolt in English America preserved the "second" British Empire. British statesmen had learned the hard way the perils of administrative coercion and the wisdom of governing with the consent of the governed. As the ripened fruit thereof, the British Empire in time ceased being British, ceased being an Empire and became in truth a league of nations, the British Commonwealth.

FOR FURTHER STUDY

EDWARD P. CHEYNEY, *The European Background of American History* (New York, 1904) PAPERBACK

HERBERT I. PRIESTLEY, *The Coming of the White Man* (New York, 1929)

ROGER B. MERRIMAN, *The Rise of the Spanish Empire in the Old World and the New* (4 vols., New York, 1918–31)

BAILEY W. DIFFIE, *Latin American Civilization: The Colonial Period* (Harrisburg, Penna., 1945)

GEORGE M. WRONG, *The Rise and Fall of New France* (2 vols., New York, 1928)

CHARLES M. ANDREWS, *The Colonial Period of American History* (4 vols., New Haven, 1934–1938)

CARL BRIDENBAUGH, *Cities in the Wilderness* (new ed., New York, 1955)

EVARTS B. GREENE, *The Revolutionary Generation* (New York, 1943)

CARL L. BECKER, *The Declaration of Independence* (new ed., 1948) PAPERBACK

JOHN F. JAMESON, *The American Revolution Considered as a Social Movement* (new ed., New York, 1950) PAPERBACK

SALVADOR DE MADARIAGA, *The Rise of the Spanish American Empire* (New York, 1947)

LOUIS B. WRIGHT, *The Cultural Life of the American Colonies* (New York, 1957) PAPERBACK

PERRY MILLER, *The New England Mind* (new ed., Cambridge, Mass., 1954) PAPERBACK

LAWRENCE H. GIPSON, *The Coming of the Revolution* (New York, 1954) PAPERBACK

CARL BRIDENBAUGH, *Cities in Revolt* (New York, 1955)

EDMUND S. MORGAN, *The Birth of the Republic* (New York, 1956) PAPERBACK

CLINTON L. ROSSITER, *Seedtime of the Republic* (New York, 1953)

MICHAEL KRAUS, *North Atlantic Civilization* (New York, 1957) PAPERBACK

CHAPTER VIII

THE MIND OF THE EIGHTEENTH CENTURY

OLD IDEAS AND NEW

THE MIND of the eighteenth century had many facets. Alongside of the mass of inherited ideas on religion and philosophy, on learning and morals, on government and economics, novelties emerged and these the historian is bound to dwell upon. The onward progress of science, impressive in its variety and quality, reacted powerfully upon the outlook and actions of the century.

Professional literary men circulated new ideas, or old ones refurbished, which shaped or sharpened the opinions of their readers and in time of even some ordinary fellows. The age was distinguished by fresh thinking about the larger and ultimate problems of society and destiny. Critically minded intellectuals unintentionally smoothed the way to the epochal French Revolution at the century's end.

Significant changes in history, in the very nature of the case, follow from criticism of things as they are. Omelettes are not made without breaking eggs. If effective means of preserving the status quo had existed, men would probably still be hunting one another with clubs, drinking blood from the skulls of their victims and living on the economic and intellectual plane of ignoble savages.

Yet it would be false and inaccurate to imagine that Europeans in general eagerly accepted new ideas. Most men were too busy earning their daily bread or living out their customary round to be touched by the innovations of science or the fashions of the intellectuals. Ability to read was confined to a thin minority in any country, but some of the novel ideas were transmitted to some of the "plain people" by word of mouth.

The British Museum, as it appeared in the mid-Eighteenth Century; and an earlier scientific enterprise, the Botanic Garden at Oxford, shown in an engraved plan made towards the end of the Seventeenth Century.

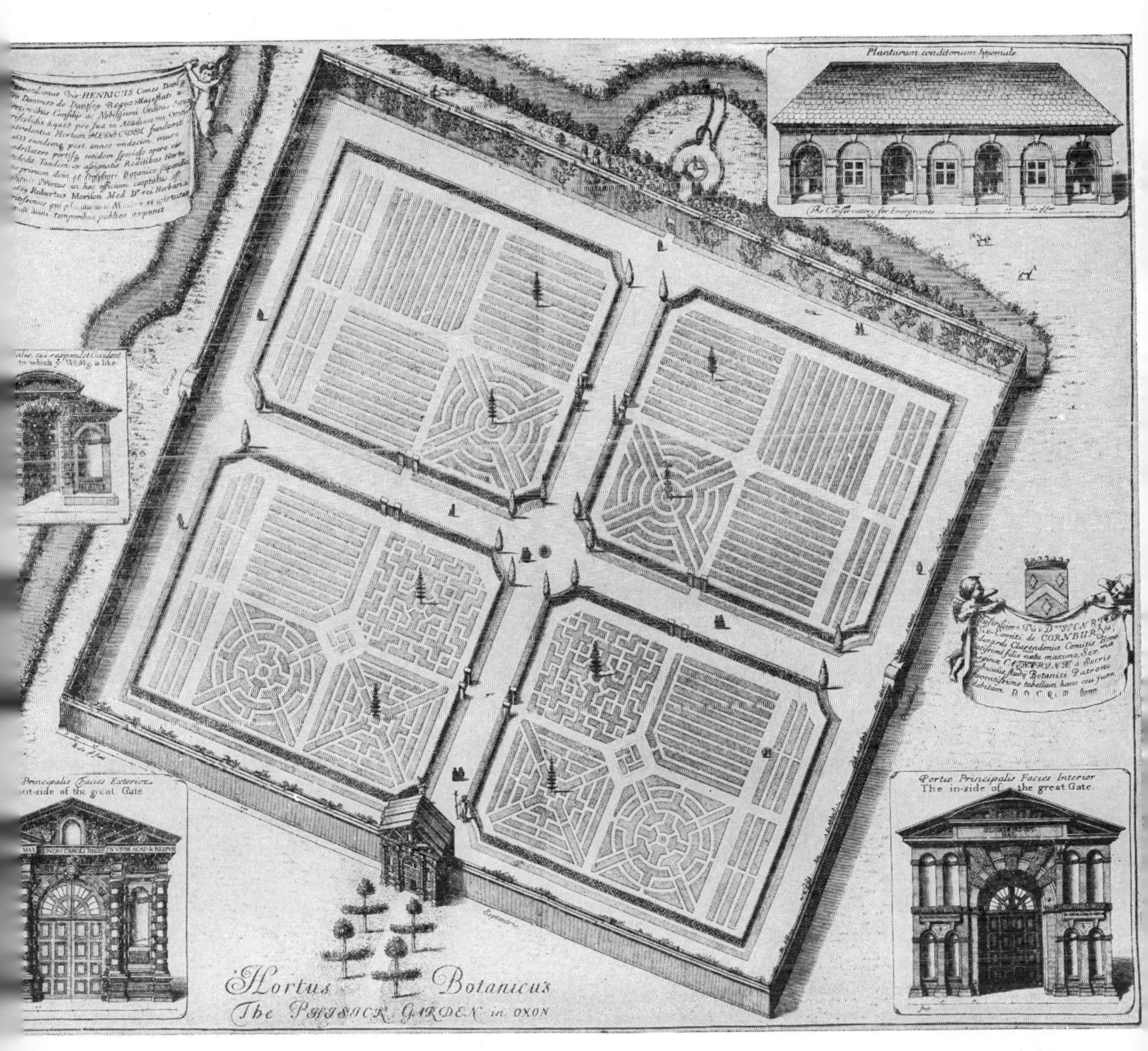

THE PATHWAY OF SCIENCE

In the realm of science the eighteenth century, to which the later seventeenth century is indissolubly joined, witnessed bold and fruitful advances. A remarkable number of "fathers" in this or that department of science appeared. Searching the ways of nature by experiment finally became intellectually respectable and the traditional practice of hounding scientists slowly went out of fashion. The conviction indeed gathered headway in circles which counted that science would unlock the mysteries of the universe and lead mankind to happiness on this earth.

"The first distemper of learning," Francis Bacon had written, "is when men study words and not matter." For that malady science provided the effective remedy. The critical spirit of science subtly invaded nearly all branches of scholarship and rescued learning from the idolatry of words.

Subsidies from public treasuries financed museums housing collections of birds, reptiles, geological specimens and the like for scientific study, laid out botanical gardens, and dispatched expeditions to unexplored areas to find new knowledge on the earth's flora and fauna. Learned societies or academies were created in the leading European capitals and in many a lesser city. Their purposes were to promote experimentation, to discuss scientific and mathematical problems, and to publish findings. Most prominent of them was the Royal Society of London, organized in 1662, "to increase the power of all mankind and to free men from the bondage of errors." Precision and uniformity in the exchange of ideas were furthered by these societies. Savants in their laboratories and studies, obscure amateurs, too, wonderfully enlarged the stock of scientific data and diffused the scientific spirit.

As the century moved along, science competed energetically with older and rather exhausted studies for the attention of creative minds. And scientific discoveries led to novel views regarding the world and man, encouraged criticism of established institutions and beliefs, and in some instances had practical application in mechanical contrivances or in bettering conditions of living. Not least in importance, the gains in science fostered an optimistic faith in human progress. It came to be believed that clogging inheritances which had long enchained mankind would melt away like mists before the warm sunshine of science.

ISAAC NEWTON

Head and shoulders above the other scientists of the age, perhaps of any age, stood the rather eccentric Englishman, Isaac Newton. On him Professor Albert Einstein, most eminent of twentieth century physicists, passed this magnificent verdict: "It is just two hundred years ago that Newton closed his eyes. It behooves us at such a moment to remember the brilliant genius who determined the course of Western thought, research, and practice to an extent that nobody before or since his time can touch."

Newton's genius flowed along three major channels. His far-ranging scientific interests led him to discoveries in several divisions of science, which stimulated further investigations by men of lesser stature. His findings, some of them the result of extremely simple experiments, strengthened respect for the scientific method of thinking. And his formulation of the law of gravitation was the first great physical synthesis in world history.

The son of a farm family little above the ordinary, Newton as a schoolboy displayed unusual mechanical aptitude. His biographers fondly describe models of clocks, sun dials and windmills which he constructed. As a scholarship student he attended Trinity College, Cambridge, without distinguishing himself. During a quiet sojourn in the country his ripening genius grasped the essential principles of his larger scientific discoveries. Mature at twenty-four, he hesitated, nonetheless, to reveal his conclusions on integral and differential calculus, the composition of light and the law of gravitation.

Nevertheless his abilities earned him in 1669 a professorship in mathematics at Cambridge, which he held for over thirty years. Since teach-

Sir Isaac Newton

ing responsibilities were light, he had an abundance of time for study and meditation. A bachelor and a recluse, indifferent to fame or social contacts, Newton was a perfect model for the cartoonist's conception of a university professor. He devoted himself chiefly to studies in optics and chemistry (more nearly alchemy), hitting upon novelties in both.

But most important of all he published in 1687 the *Principia,* incorporating the greatest triumph, it may be, of the human mind.[1] Therein Newton proved that the force which pulled planets toward the sun was the same as the force which caused objects to fall to the ground. Put otherwise, he showed that gravitation was a force operating uniformly throughout the universe. Thus he bound together with one sovereign principle all physical bodies, the great and the little, the myriad stars in their courses and the fall of an apple. The law of gravitation accounted for the operation of the whole universe in relatively simple mechanical terms. It furnished a solid foundation for a scientific interpretation of the world of nature in opposition to the traditional miraculous interpretation.

Newton himself, it is evident, was not impressed with the magnitude or importance of his accomplishment and turned to theological and chronological researches. He candidly acknowledged his debt to earlier scientists, Copernicus and Galileo, among others. "If I have seen further than others," he modestly wrote, "it is by standing on the shoulders of giants."

Admiring contemporaries lavished unstinted praise upon Newton and the stupendous achievement and adaptability of his mind. "No mortal," declared one of them, "could come nearer to the gods," while the poet, Alexander Pope, penned the celebrated epigram:

> Nature and Nature's Laws lay hid in night;
> God said, Let Newton be! And all was light.

[1] The full English title of the book is *The Mathematical Principles of Natural Philosophy.*

Gottfried Leibnitz

At his death, an appreciative nation laid the author of *Principia* to rest in Westminster Abbey. With the passing of time the reputation of Newton has risen steadily, as the tribute by Einstein bears witness.

Along with Newton must be mentioned his contemporary and in some respects his rival, Gottfried W. Leibnitz, a German savant. A scholar of exceptionally wide interests gifted with a fine command of philosophical resources, he contributed to scientific knowledge, aided in founding the famous Berlin Academy of Sciences and served as a public official. In his major work on philosophy, *Essays on the Goodness of God,* Leibnitz put forth the thesis that this world was the best of all possible worlds. By the middle of the eighteenth century, his principle of harmony between individuals in society and his thoroughly optimistic outlook had captured the educated classes. In keeping with his concern for theology and politics, Leibnitz strove to merge the disparate creeds of Christianity and to bring the quarrelsome states of Germany together. As a mathematician, he invented symbols still in use and, independently of Newton, he discovered the calculus, though Leibnitz had priority in publication. He ranks with the great Englishman as the last of the European minds whose knowledge encompassed virtually everything that was established in the department of science.

PROGRESS IN MATHEMATICS

No clearer illustration of the cumulative character of scientific learning can be found than the eighteenth-century history of mathematics. Building on the researches of Newton and Leibnitz, a brilliant array of mathematicians formally developed the calculus and its application to mechanics and astronomy. Original minds struck off in all directions in a resolute attempt to elaborate and perfect the law of gravitation. As a rule these scholars were attached to learned academies and royal courts more than to universities.

Probably the most distinguished family in the history of mathematics is the Bernoulli of Swiss Basle, whose members absorbed the enthusiasms and methods of Leibnitz. Johann Bernoulli, an extremely fertile experimentalist, made his mark in work which still appears in elementary books on differential and integral calculus. His pupil, Leonard Euler, is hailed as the most accomplished mathematical scholar of the century, a prodigious writer on pure mathematics and its applications to astronomy, artillery and shipbuilding.

When Euler retired as mathematician in the Berlin Academy, his place was taken by Joseph L. LaGrange, the top-ranking geometer of his generation. Frederick II in his letter of invitation to LaGrange expressed the desire that "the greatest geometer of Europe should live near the greatest of kings." A remarkable analyst, Euler made many original discoveries and in his celebrated *Mécanique analytique* (1788), he summarized and enlarged upon the mathematical progress of his century.

The claim that French writers held the scepter in mathematics was fortified by the studies of Pierre S. Laplace. A Parisian professor and a dabbler in politics as well, Laplace carried out a long series of original investigations on the mystery of the heavens, little disturbed by the convulsions of the epoch of the French Revolution and Napoleon. In his massive *Mécanique céleste* in five volumes, which almost deserves to be shelved alongside of the *Principia* itself, he demonstrated the stability of the solar system.

Called the "French Newton," Laplace brought to culmination the astronomical studies of the Englishman and of three generations of diligent mathematical investigators, to whom he assigned little credit. The *Système du Monde* (1796) contains Laplace's brilliant "nebular hypothesis," the point of departure for subsequent speculation on the origin of planets. Laplace admirably typifies French men of science who, without sacrificing thoroughness of research or finish of workmanship, prided themselves on qualities of clearness, order and literary skill.

British students of mathematics haughtily kept aloof from the stream of thought on the Continent. Unless an exception may be made in the case of Abraham de Moivre, a Huguenot refugee, who radically revised the study of higher trigonometry, Britain produced no mathematician of the first order of ability. After the publications of Laplace, mathematicians pessimistically concluded that their subject was on the verge of exhaustion, but the next century brought fresh interests and novel perspectives.

MEDICAL SCIENCE

Experimentalism in medical science yielded a notable harvest. A Dutchman, Hermann Boerhaave, earned international fame as a clinical instructor and his lecture hall at Leyden became a mecca for students from Europe and English America; the inquisitive Peter the Great sat at the feet of this master. From Leyden, Boerhaave's rational approach to medical problems and his zest for investigation were carried to other centers. For example, Gerhard van Swieten, a Dutchman, reorganized the school of medicine in Vienna, starting it on the way to becoming the most respected institution of medical learning in the world. Eccentric cults, too, flourished in Vienna, for there Franz A. Mesmer, an early exponent of hypnotism and F. J. Gall, founder of phrenology carried on their investigations.

A Swiss disciple of Boerhaave, Albrecht von Haller, achieved European stature by researches in botany and anatomy, being particularly esteemed for discoveries on the functions of nerves. Obstetrics, hitherto the preserve of midwives, was raised to a scientific level by William Smellie, a London practitioner. Even more accomplished was another Englishman, John Hunter, best known for his studies in surgical pathology. Previously, surgery had been identified with "the art and mystery of barbers" and it was taught—if taught at all—by anatomists, as a diverting sideline. By his tireless researches and pioneering instruction, Hunter established surgery as a scientific discipline. Through studies in comparative anatomy he acquired unusual eminence and authority as well as burial in Westminster Abbey.

Hunter splendidly expressed the spirit of inquiry, of which he was a shining symbol, in a note to a former pupil, Edward Jenner. "Why think?" he asked. "Why not try the experiment?" Acting on that suggestion, Jenner attacked the scourge of smallpox, an extremely deadly human affliction; victims who recovered were often horribly disfigured. In 1796, Jenner brought out an improved vaccine that was an effective protection against smallpox and steadily cut down its ravages. Subsequently, the principle of vaccination was applied in immunization against cholera, typhoid fever and other diseases.

The title of "father of histology," or the study of tissues, was conferred upon Marie F. Bichat, a French specialist in pathological anatomy. The Italian Spallanzani showed how gastric juices functioned in the process of digestion and proved that the theory of spontaneous generation of germs had no foundation in fact. If bottles were hermetically sealed and their contents previously boiled, microbes could not grow. Diagnosis of sickness became more accurate after the invention of a clinical thermometer and the stethoscope (1816). Treatment of the mentally ill grew more enlightened as the old theory that an insane per-

Karl Linnaeus

son must be possessed of the devil was patiently whittled away. And yet, until well along in the nineteenth century, confinement in cells and savage floggings were considered to have therapeutic value for the demented.

NATURAL HISTORY

It was not until the nineteenth century that natural science was fragmented into highly specialized departments of inquiry. As late as 1750, the sciences of botany, zoology and geology and their many subdivisions were lumped together as "natural history." Yet no logical scheme for the classification of plants and animals had been devised. The need for such a plan had become more urgent by reason of the huge additions to the store of knowledge on flora and fauna resulting from more thorough explorations of the globe.

The Olympian figure in arranging and systematizing "natural history" was an accomplished Swedish savant, Karl Linnaeus. Spoken of as the father of botany, he introduced the custom of using double Latin titles for each clearly different variety of plant and animal, the first name for the genus or family, the second for the species. The red maple, to illustrate, was labeled *Acer rubrum*. Linnaeus was the first to propose that the human race should be designated by the hopeful term *Homo sapiens*.

In the course of his researches Linnaeus, keen observer that he was, noticed that there were similarities in the anatomical structure of man and lower animals. And yet he clung to the time-honored view that all living things had been specially created as explained in the ancient Book of Genesis, though he thought the numbers had grown by reason of intercrossing with other species or through degeneracy caused by climatic changes. His writing stimulated investigation into the origin of species by contemporaries and successors.

It is sometimes said, with pardonable inaccuracy perhaps, that the labors of Linnaeus were carried forward by the French naturalist, the Comte George de Buffon, a wealthy aristocrat. His studies in zoology disclosed structural likenesses between man and anthropoids and his thought wavered between the conventional theory of special creation and the idea of evolution. Buffon was impressed by the fact that breeding had produced new varieties of animals and spoke of the disappearance of species not well adapted to their environment. He hit upon the sound idea that the surface of the earth had taken form gradually, starting perhaps 75,000 years ago.

Though Buffon was fond of bold generalizations, he had no desire to incur ecclesiastical wrath and so declined to express adherence to the evolutionary hypothesis. An attractive literary stylist, gifted for the work of popularization, Buffon swept together the known facts of natural history in a vast encyclopedia running into forty-four volumes. This *Natural History*, lavishly illustrated, quickened interest in the study of nature. Buffon's scientific ideas, however, quickly went out of fashion and nowadays he is of interest as a man of letters more than as a scientific investigator.

The groundwork for a rational geology was laid by the Scotsman, James Hutton. Blessed with an ardent passion to know, a tireless traveler and something of a scientific farmer, Hutton searched for a more adequate explanation of the history of the earth than the traditional biblical theory. He concluded that the surface of the earth, instead of being shaped once for all time, had been undergoing change for a long, long time because of erosion and other commonplace geological occurrences. His treatise, *Theory of the Earth* (1785), though awkward in style, is prized as a classical contribution to the literature of geology. These pathfinders from Linnaeus to Hutton prepared the way for the investigations of Charles Darwin and other men of science in the next century.

PROGRESS IN CHEMISTRY

In the meantime the science of chemistry had been built upon firm and rational foundations. As the branch of learning devoted to the experimental study of the composition of substances, chemistry may be said to have veered away from alchemy and the art of the physician in the late seventeenth century. An Englishman, Robert Boyle, who was imbued with the research enthusiasms of Francis Bacon, insisted upon experimentation to test the validity of hypotheses. He carefully distinguished between compounds and elements, or substances incapable of further analysis, without, however, winning ready acceptance of his definitions.

To the very end of the eighteenth century chemical progress was retarded by the ancient theory that there were only four elements, earth and water, air and fire. All forms and kinds of matter, it was believed, were made of various combinations of these four elements in different proportions. Another false theory, too, the phlogiston principle, acted as an anchor upon chemical learning. According to this theory, all combustible bodies contained a substance known as phlogiston which was released in the process of combustion.

These encumbering concepts collapsed in the face of observations which proved their inaccuracy. Creative investigations with revolutionary implications were carried out by Joseph Priestley and Henry Cavendish in England and by Karl W. Scheele in Sweden, all of whom were adherents, with varying degrees of tenac-

Joseph Priestley

Antoine Lavoisier and Mme. Lavoisier

ity, to the phlogiston fallacy. Their work as well as that of lesser discoverers was brilliantly summarized and elaborated by the French genius, Antoine L. Lavoisier, who at last thoroughly discredited the phlogiston theory.

Priestley, who spent his last years in Pennsylvania, sought relaxation in chemical experiments when not engaged in theological pursuits, for he was a clergyman, a key figure in modern Unitarianism. He found and prepared several gases, notably oxygen and nitrous oxide —the "laughing gas" of the dentist. Proof that the air was a mixture of the gases of oxygen and nitrogen and that water, most important of chemical compounds, was composed of oxygen and hydrogen (or "inflammable air") was presented by Cavendish. In his private life one of the strangest of human beings, Cavendish was a remarkably precise and accurate research man. He pioneered in investigations to determine the density of the earth, reaching surprisingly sound conclusions for the time.

As a discoverer of new substances, Scheele topped his distinguished contemporaries, producing chlorine, glycerin, citric and other acids. By his unusual researches he fairly started organic chemistry on its tumultuous journey. His study of gases anticipated the findings of Priestley and Cavendish at several points. William Nicholson found that water could be decomposed by passing an electric current through it, a discovery applied to many scientific and industrial operations.

Pride of place among eighteenth century chemists belongs, however, to Lavoisier, more eminent as a coordinator of studies of other men perhaps than as an original investigator, though his own experiments were models of painstaking ingenuity. Insisting that the balance must be used in chemical experiments, Lavoisier demonstrated by meticulous weighing that while matter might be altered in form by chemical reactions, matter could neither be created nor destroyed. That concept of the indestructibility of matter is a cornerstone of very modern science. But even this theory is now being questioned.

Lavoisier established the principle that combustion actually produced an increase in weight and thereby he upset the phlogiston notion. He defined chemical elements in the modern manner and correctly distinguished twenty-three of them. Another important innovation for which he was responsible was the labeling of substances in keeping with their chemical composition.

As an author, Lavoisier is best remembered for *An Elementary Treatise on Chemistry* (1789), which brought together and explained existing knowledge of chemistry and the nature of chemical processes. A capable administrator as well as a man of science, Lavoisier improved the methods of manufacturing gunpowder[2] and of agriculture. In the heat of the French Revolution, Lavoisier was executed by the guillotine as an accomplice of royalism, but today scholarship honors him as a founding father of experimental and rational chemistry.

Growth in knowledge of the nature of electrical phenomena was another significant facet of eighteenth century science. Obscure, systematic experimenters proved that electricity could be conducted or could be insulated, and could be accumulated in a condenser called the Leyden jar (1745). In America Benjamin Franklin demonstrated, with a boy's kite, in a famous thunderstorm, that lightning, far from being a manifestation of divine wrath, was electricity acting in accordance with fixed laws.

It was also learned that electricity stimulated the action of the heart and the flow of the blood or could contract muscles. That knowledge was applied to the alleviation of rheumatism and of nervous disorders. Researches of two Italians, Luigi Galvani and Alessandro Volta, ushered in a new era in electrical science leading to the electrical contrivances of the next century. Their contribution to the history of electricity is suggested by the galvanometer, a device to detect or measure electric currents, and the volt, the unit of electromotive force, named for these Italian pioneers.

A plate from Galvani's De Viribus Electricitatis, *1792, showing his experiment with two dissimilar metal rods applied to the muscles of an animal*

REASON AND "ENLIGHTENMENT"

Advances in the physical sciences from Newton onward profoundly affected the eighteenth-century mind in the whole range of thought and

[2] An employee in the factory, E. I. Du Pont, carried his knowledge of powder-making to the United States, starting there a small concern which has grown into the immense Du Pont industrial empire.

knowledge. Scientific investigations, grounded upon experiment and analytical reasoning, had wonderfully pressed back the frontiers of the kingdom of knowledge. Would not the same rational techniques, if applied to religion and ethics, government and law, learning and social customs and economics, yield equally beneficent results for mankind?

Unconventional minds answered that question in the affirmative. Intellectuals were bedazzled in particular by the implications of the Newtonian principle of gravitation which had bound all matter together in harmonious unity. Popular books interpreting the *Principia* appeared, fifty of them in English alone. It seemed to some intellectuals that science had revealed design, order and law in the universe, dismissing mystery and supernatural forces. It seemed that the Deity had endowed man with reason to be used in making him master of his destiny. It seemed that the whole of reality, or very nearly that, was amenable to the human mind. Like the medieval scholastics whom they despised, the rationalists did not arrive at their conclusions inductively, but they nonetheless treated their views as having all the certainty of mathematical axioms.

It was assumed that natural and unchanging laws governed terrestrial affairs and that these laws could be found by the intelligence of man. Once discovered, an enlightened humanity would make beliefs and motivations conform to these laws. Anything and everything incompatible with cold reason would be discarded and society would move forward handsomely. Instead of being merely the name of a man, Newton came to imply an infallible world outlook, in itself an intellectual revolution.

Confidence in progress and the perfectibility of man captivated speculative intellectuals of the early eighteenth century. That faith was well disclosed by Alexander Pope in his *Essay on Man*:

> All Nature is but art, unknown to thee;
> All chance, direction, which thou canst not see;
> All discord, harmony not understood;
> All partial evil, universal good:
> And, spite of pride, in erring reason's spite,
> One truth is clear, whatever is, is right.

The optimism spread that a dawn impended in which it would be bliss to be alive. That "climate of opinion" permeated the Western world but the very headquarters of the "new thought" was Paris. Writers known as *philosophes*, who were really only accomplished publicists, disseminated the rational and critical spirit; and they slyly attacked the status quo in travelogues, romances, plays, pamphlets and books in attractive language. The *philosophes* intended to be read and they wrote accordingly.

Criticism was regarded by the *philosophes* as the proudest hallmark of a free man. No subject was too ancient or too sacred to escape rationalist censure. Rationalists claimed the right for all men to think, speak and write freely. Although not philosophers in the strict sense, the *philosophes* nonetheless proclaimed a philosophical message—a message of enlightenment and emancipation, an optimistic evangel of human progress. They had real zest for the future.[3]

The Age of Reason challenged the Age of Faith. It was an epoch of ferment, intellectual restlessness and acute concern for novelties, an age of rampant skepticism and positive unbelief. Old and prized institutions were ruthlessly attacked, the shams, the irrationalities and inequities of the existing society were laid bare. And some of the *philosophes* offered proposals that would liberate and regenerate society. Their iconoclastic writings were discussed in salons, in public gatherings and clubs. Thus the ideological foundation for the American and the French Revolutions was formulated.

Rationalists—one and all—parted company with the Christian Church and the Christian interpretation of life's meaning. Three definite influences had disturbing consequences for conventional religious doctrines, with the discoveries of science the most corrosive, doubtless, of all. Specifically the Newtonian law of gravitation seemed to depersonalize the Deity, to

[3] Diderot, a leading *philosophe* explained: "There is nothing which costs less to acquire nowadays than the name of philosopher; an obscure and retired life, some outward signs of wisdom, with a little reading, suffice to attach this name to persons who enjoy the honor without meriting it."

make Him a sort of Divine Mechanic who had set the vast machine of the universe in motion and then retired, never again to interfere with the orderly operation of His handiwork. In the second place, some Europeans had become familiar with the religious systems of heathen peoples, of the Chinese and New World aborigines, for example, which raised doubts regarding the validity of the Christian scheme of life. And third, endless disputations among Christian sects on beliefs of the faith, each claiming a monopoly on truth, persuaded some men that all of them must be in error.

Most of the *philosophes* and their disciples are properly called deists. They acknowledged the existence of a Deity, an utterly impersonal First Cause of things, but rejected the revelations and the usages of the Christian creed as irreconcilable with reason. For them the proposition of John Locke that "the works of Nature everywhere sufficiently evidence a Deity" was indisputably sound. A minority of their fellows dogmatically repudiated any theistic belief and so were known as atheists. Both groups were anti-clerical since they condemned ecclestiastical intervention in what they considered secular affairs.

Men of "the Enlightenment," appeared in many countries, but they were most numerous and most vocal in France. Frenchmen, in a real sense, shouldered the White Man's Burden of intellectual progress. In the vanguard of the French apostles of "enlightenment" marched Voltaire, the pseudonym of François Arouet.

VOLTAIRE

Voltaire incarnated the skeptical spirit of the century in its most enthusiastic and destructive mood. Eighty-four years of age at the time of his death, he had long been esteemed or reviled as the uncrowned king of living men of letters. That distinction he owed to his versatility, his sprightliness as a popularizer, his lucid, satirical, charming literary style and his dexterity in manipulating the flexible French language.

Neither an original nor a systematic thinker, Voltaire was marvelously gifted for making abstract ideas intelligible and attractive. Someone has dubbed him an incomparable journalist and nothing more. He was conceited but courageous, selfish and irreverent, yet a firm believer in the innate dignity of man and the authority of reason. To all subjects, whether sacred or secular, he applied identical canons of rationalist criticism. He was a tireless, happy warrior for freedom of thought and tolerance, a fighter against cruelty and oppression.

How then did Voltaire conceive of tolerance? In spite of his deep cynicism, he was persuaded that men were good and kind by nature, but they had been bewitched by revealed religion. Men should be allowed full liberty of expression, dissenting opinions should be tolerated, and as well competing versions of Christianity

François Arouet, called Voltaire. A portrait in youth

and free-thinking. His attitude on tolerance was frozen into a famous epigram: "I disagree heartily with every word you say; but I will defend to the death your right to say it."

Throughout his long and active life, Voltaire militantly flayed practices that violated his standards of humanity and justice—neglect of the indigent, abuse of the criminal and the demented and persecution in the name of religion. "Crush the infamous thing," he cried, and he meant, destroy the spirit and the instruments of fanaticism and of man's inhumanity to man.

A deist, Voltaire deliberately worked to undermine the Catholic Church. He never ceased to mock divine revelations, miracles and the mystical doctrines of the Christian faith. His most withering satire was reserved for monks, whom he regarded as worthless parasites on society. Nonetheless, he acknowledged that there was "a divinity which shapes our ends," and he wrote, "If God did not exist, He would have to be invented." For him, personal morality formed the vital essence of religion.

Voltaire was the son of a prosperous lawyer. For seven years he studied in Jesuit institutions where he first came into contact with deistic notions. His father urged him to enter the legal profession, but he cared not a fig for the law, and chose the more hazardous career of a professional writer. Shrewd to the point of unscrupulousness in financial affairs, he never suffered the pangs of poverty. His talent and industry quickly made him a celebrity—and twice landed him in the Bastille.

In 1726 Voltaire began a three-year period of voluntary exile in England. That was an extremely fruitful experience for he acquainted himself with the thought, thinkers and way of life of the island kingdom. Later on he lived as the guest of Frederick the Great at the Prussian court, and he spent his last decades on the edge of Switzerland.

Not long after his return from England Voltaire published (1734) the polemical *Letters on the English Nation,* which is spoken of as the opening broadside by French men of letters against the prevailing order of society. He portrayed England as a very paradise for merchants, authors and scientists; Newton was lavishly praised and the Quakers admired for their aversion to ceremonialism and war.[4] It was the intention of Voltaire to ridicule France and her ways by extolling the freer atmosphere across the channel—and he succeeded. The French government advertised the *Letters* by branding the book as scandalous and having it publicly burned. Voltaire's prestige as a writer profited.

For the next half-century he found a ready market for his literary output ranging from poetry to history, and running into a library of over ninety volumes. Contemporaries spoke of him as a dramatist equal to Sophocles; nowadays his plays are never acted and seldom even read. Contemporaries lauded him as a poet; but now his poetry gathers dust on library shelves.

But his mordantly satirical tales which Voltaire himself thought of as amusing trifles still attract eager readers. Best of all is *Candide* (1759) in the nature of a travelogue, humorously exposing and ridiculing the inequities of government and lampooning the easy optimism that this was the best of all possible worlds. A wise man, he concluded, would "cultivate his own garden" and let the rest of the world go by. The many-sided personality of Voltaire shines most vividly in the voluminous correspondence, replete with flattery, wit and sarcasm, which he carried on with admirers all across Europe.

Although it is short on historical perspective and long on angry criticism, the *Philosophic Dictionary* faithfully discloses Voltaire's mastery of frivolous and corrosive argument and his violent hatred of ecclesiasticism. Mixed in with reflections on the Deity, destiny, democracy and liberty are articles on kissing, astrology, adultery, nakedness and climate. Many of the statements are in the form of questions. "Why are there more insects than men?" "Why are the rich always respected, courted and admired?" "Why does a little, whitish, evil-smelling secretion form a being which has hard bones, desires and thoughts? And why do these beings persecute each other?" On

[4] Voltaire spoke of emigrating to Pennsylvania there to dwell among the Quakers, but the rough sea voyage deterred him.

democracy, he wrote: "Democracy seems suitable only to a very little country, which must be happily situated. Small though it be, it will make many mistakes, for it will be composed of men."

In his historical writings, which are entertaining but inaccurate, Voltaire emphasized the common folk, not crowned and mitered heads nor military chiefs and aristocracy, as was the habit with historians. He ruled out miraculous forces in the human pageant and assailed existing evils by pointing to happier, more enlightened eras in the past. In the cynicism of old age, however, Voltaire came to think that history contained little sense and much driveling nonsense. In his *Essay on Manners* (1753), probably the most influential of all his works in popularizing the rationalistic approach to man and society, Voltaire attempted to prove that war and religious intolerance had been the main barriers to the advancement of mankind. Remove those evils, and then society would go forward famously.

All in all, Voltaire was the most titanic intellectual energy of the century—always active with his pen, bubbling over with ideas and plans. Congenitally superficial and fluffy, men dacious, tactless, often unbalanced in judgment, he nonetheless possessed an immense capacity for making readers think. Only the unthinking can question his stature. His preachments against religion had application in the French Revolution—English conservatives indeed held him responsible for the coming of the Revolution. And he must be regarded as the intellectual sire of the anti clerical agitators of future generations. To this day Voltaire personifies for the orthodox Christian irreligion and immorality, while admiring disciples place him among the major prophets of enlightenment, a heroic foeman of intolerance and supernaturalism.

RATIONALIST HISTORY

The rationalist approach in the writing of history which was favored by Voltaire attracted other and even more distinguished practitioners. Animated by essentially the same spirit as contemporary workers in science, rationalist historians discarded as untenable the long accepted theory that historical developments merely manifested the will of God. History should be treated as the record of human thought and action and the dynamics of events should be searched for in human motives and in secular, not theological sources.

Historians of the "Age of Reason" did more, for they extended the range of their studies beyond conventional political and religious themes. They infused their writings with a cosmopolitan flavor and, in the main, with the idea of progress. The historical masterpiece of the century, perhaps the most fascinating and polished of all historical compositions, was *The Decline and Fall of the Roman Empire* by Edward Gibbon. The first three volumes of this famous work carry the history of the Empire into the mid-fifth century and the rest illuminate the evolution in the Byzantine East during the Middle Age.

As Gibbon explained, he wished to show "the triumph of barbarism and Christianity" in throwing down the Roman state. Rationalist that he was, he portrayed the emergence and victory of the Christian Church along unconventional lines, which infuriated conservative churchmen. Like other historians before the nineteenth century, Gibbon neglected to investigate economic forces with fullness and later scholarship necessitated considerable revisions in his narrative. Nevertheless, the *Decline* stands as the classic example in the English language of a historical work of rare literary excellence, which the passage of time has supplemented but not superseded.

More skeptical than the skeptics, however, was David Hume, a brilliant and serene son of Scotland, who challenged the smug complacency of confident rationalism. His *Natural History of Religion* set out to explain how religious ideas had arisen from human experience; the operation of supernatural or miraculous forces was rigidly excluded. Hume's crowning work on the *History of England*, though far from being a piece of painstaking and meticulous scholarship, documented his philosophical conviction that history had neither "a plot, a rhythm, nor a predetermined pattern."

It was incumbent upon the historian, he thought, to "recognize in the development of human destinies the play of the contingent and the unforeseen." Hume could not discover the fact of progress "written plain and large on the page of history."

Incredulity and skepticism on the reliability of history rose to such a pitch that one writer concluded that history was no more than a fable upon which men had agreed. Yet the fundamental assumptions of many later secular historians were established in this epoch; they adopted as the goal of their investigations not dogmatic certainty but proof beyond reasonable doubt. Diligent scholars, many of them churchmen, meantime, edited massive collections of original manuscripts which have proved inexhaustible quarries of information for succeeding generations of students.

Cesare, Count Beccaria

MONTESQUIEU AND BECCARIA

Voltaire concerned himself but little with governmental institutions, though he definitely preferred an enlightened monarchy. That preference he shared with a distinguished contemporary, Montesquieu, a learned advocate of changes in the French government and of broader human freedoms. The thought of Montesquieu was deeply colored by his examination of the British "constitution" and British political customs, parts of which he believed should be copied by France.

His enduring fame springs from *The Spirit of the Laws* (1748), which presumed to codify the teachings of experience on governmental institutions. The work teemed with denunciations of the Bourbon despotism and recommended that the authority of the crown should be curtailed by separating the functions of government into executive, legislative and judicial branches. That principle would be applied in eighteenth century American constitutions and in the French charter of 1791.

Montesquieu commanded respect, too, for his *Persian Letters* (1721). Here are portrayed the reflections of a mythical but wideawake pilgrim from Asia who prowled about Europe in order to ascertain what civilized existence actually meant. The French monarchy is castigated in shrill tones and the book roused the thoughtful in the Old World and the New to the shortcomings of royal despotism. A comfortably fixed aristocrat, Montesquieu desired a moderate reformation which would give France an enlightened parliamentary system. He studiously kept aloof from radical extremists whom he regarded as dangerous, hare-brained crackpots. For Montesquieu any suggestion of revolution was revolting.

The case for humanization in the methods of handling crime and punishment was persuasively pleaded by a Milanese noble, Count Beccaria. The aim of justice, he reasoned, should be to cut down crime, not vengeance upon a wrongdoer. He denounced the savageries of torture, cruel and vindictive punishments, the imposition of heavy penalties for slight crimes and loathsome prison conditions. Other

Denis Diderot, a portrait by Fragonard

reformers rallied to his support and the worst abuses in criminal law and procedure gradually went out of fashion.

DIDEROT AND THE ENCYCLOPEDISTS

Rationalist ideas were stridently voiced by a band of French writers, called the Encyclopedists, who prepared a vast compendium of knowledge—the *Encyclopedia*. Organizer and editor of this monumental enterprise was Denis Diderot, a militant and uncompromising partisan of the "Enlightenment." It was the intention of Diderot and most of his collaborators not only to condense existing knowledge into crisp pellets, but to awaken readers to the necessity of radical changes, which would sweep away the relics of feudalism, an antiquated theology and royal despotism.

Volumes of the *Encyclopedia* started to appear in 1751 and poured rapidly from the press despite stiff opposition from government and church authorities. Many contributors were jailed for their ideas or rather for their temerity in putting them into print. They had their reward, however, in the applause of friends and in the confidence that they were winning converts to causes dear to their hearts. It is questionable whether the *Encyclopedia* was in fact much read, though it was subscribed to by a surprising list of aristocrats, churchmen and bourgeoisie.

Called by Voltaire, "a sacred repository of all the arts and all the sciences," the *Encyclopedia* dealt with upwards of 60,000 topics and contained a wealth of fine illustrations. Special attention was devoted to the utilitarian arts and crafts which formerly men of learning had scorned as beneath their dignity. The editor wanted these articles so exact and complete that if Europe was destroyed by a natural cataclysm and only a single set of the *Encyclopedia* was saved, the arts and sciences could be reestablished without impairment in the New World. Contributors denounced slavery, demanded unfettered freedom of expression and schooling for all children. Compassion for humanity rang out on page after page.

Articles were assigned to authors in keeping with their special interests or recognized competence. The introduction to the work, for instance, which reviewed the history of science, was prepared by D'Alembert, a learned mathematician. From the blunt pen of Diderot flowed an article on the Bible, which, among other things, sketched the basic problems of biblical scholarship, while Voltaire wrote on a broad range of topics and Rousseau did the piece on music.

Several contributors revealed in their articles that they were dogmatic adherents of a creed that explained all existence in terms of purely physical processes. Spoken of as materialism, this pattern of thought was crudely deterministic holding that the human will was absolutely controlled by environmental conditions. Freedom of individual choice, in other words, was dismissed as a delusion. Allied with materialism was atheism to be woven into the complex texture of Western thought. Materialism and atheism in the future, not least the revolutionary theories of Karl Marx, would draw inspiration and ideas from French writers of the "Enlightenment." It must, however, be emphasized that deism, not atheism, was more representative of the outlook of the *philosophes*.

Nowadays an encyclopedia means an assemblage of facts, set forth with balance, economy and sobriety. It is a settling source of information, while the French work of the eighteenth century was unsettling—a vehicle of propaganda, not without evidences of erudition, to be sure, but parading the convictions and the theories of belligerently unconventional minds.

A plate from the Encyclopedia, *showing a tool-making shop at top, and below the component parts of a turning machine.*

THE NEW ECONOMICS

While some men were untangling the mysteries of nature or speculating on religion, government and social justice, others were preoccupied with ways and means of increasing national income—the stomach side of history. Their reasoning, too, was touched by the prevalent magic of nature and natural law. They too proclaimed principles which they considered as valid and as immutable as the law of gravitation itself.

As has previously been indicated, the doctrines of mercantilism dominated thinking on economics into the eighteenth century. But the flaws in that creed had already impressed some thinkers; they would soon be dramatically exposed by the American Revolution. Vigorous criticism of mercantilism appeared first in France, the country in which Colbert and his successors had most systematically applied governmental planning of economic activity. In the spirit of the age critics asked whether existing laws on taxation, tariff and subsidy policies, state regulation of commerce and manufacturing were reasonable. A school of French intellectuals, the Physiocrats, concluded that mercantilist practices stifled initiative and efficiency and so were harmful to national well-being.

Chief theoretician of the group was François Quesnay, physician at the royal court. As he read the "natural" laws of economics, agriculture formed the most important source of a nation's wealth; to raise the prosperity of a country, the productivity of the soil would have to be increased. Taxes should be levied solely on income derived from the land and, indirect taxes, as on the trade in grain, should be abolished. Private ownership of property was an absolute right, rooted in natural law. Interference by government in the processes of consumption and production should be kept at a minimum. This principle was spoken of as "laissez faire," the state should keep "hands off." The economic activity of the individual should be determined, not by public authority, but by his personal inclinations. The French statesman Turgot stood on the edge of the physiocratic group and as a minister undertook to apply the "liberal" principles.

Adam Smith, a canny Scotsman, was the foremost expositor of economic liberalism in Great Britain where freedom of enterprise was already being practiced to a considerable extent. Smith presented his own ideas and borrowings from Frenchmen in a comprehensive volume, *The Wealth of Nations.* This book, which came off the press in 1776, has been called a declaration of independence for individual economic enterprise. Smith wrote in an interesting style and fortified his reasoning with an arsenal of facts.

Stressing the importance of commerce and industry, Smith argued that the wealth of a nation simply equalled the collective wealth of the individual citizens. Each man knew how best to enrich himself and the state should not interfere with the process of competition. The surest way to increase efficiency and wealth in every walk of life was to let the best man win. The government should simply act as a silent policeman; it should protect property, enforce contracts and improve means of transportation, all beneficial to business. The state, he felt, might properly own industries engaged in producing military equipment, but that exception apart, individual enterprise should be unfettered.

The maxim of buying in the cheapest market, moreover, and selling in the dearest, which every merchant pursued in his personal dealings, should be applied to international trade. Tariffs should not be imposed for the purpose of protecting domestic producers nor should bounties be granted to home concerns to help them in competition with foreigners.

Smith advocated freedom for colonial economic enterprise too, rejecting state action to restrain or direct the trade and industry of dependencies. This section of *The Wealth of Nations* must have been finished before the quarrel between the British government and English America had reached serious proportions, for the book is silent on that subject. Smith's masterpiece served as the standard source book on economic liberalism; future economists started their speculations from his writings.

JEAN JACQUES ROUSSEAU

In the intellectual firmament of the late eighteenth century Voltaire, the rationalist, was eclipsed by Rousseau, the romanticist. Swiss-born, Rousseau vaulted to sudden fame in France at the age of thirty-seven. In a prize-winning essay he argued paradoxically and with eloquence, that primitive man had lived more happily than cultivated, sophisticated Frenchmen. That was so, he claimed, because the noble savage lived close to nature while men of the eighteenth century were debauched by the artificialities and conventions of civilization.

"Man was born free and everywhere he is in chains," Rousseau wrote. He could escape from prison by going back to the simplicity of the "Golden Age" when learning and literature were unknown and ignorance was bliss. Man was naturally good but the corruptions of civilization had tainted his finer self.

The highly imaginative outlook of Rousseau was reflected in his favorite prayer:

> Almighty God, deliver us from the sciences and the pernicious arts of our fathers! Grant us ignorance, innocence, and poverty once more, as the only things which can bring happiness and which are of value in Thine Eyes.

Jean Jacques Rousseau

His teachings harmonized with the mood of many a "little man" and of well-to-do persons who had grown weary of the icy approach of the rationalists to problems of living and death.

Rousseau's thinking reflected his curious and questing personality and his perverse career, full of emotional vicissitudes. His early home environment was most unhappy; the reading of romantic novels and an ardent love of nature encouraged incurably fanciful notions within him. An introspective thinker he never learned the lessons of intellectual discipline and orderliness and poverty plagued him constantly. At sixteen he became a rover, wandering aimlessly about, and eventually drifting to Paris.

In time Rousseau gravitated into the orbit of Diderot and his rationalist cronies. But finding their philosophy and ethics not to his tastes, he broke with them and struck out on his own. He was truly a child of the "Enlightenment," but not at all a friend of rationalism. He preferred to trust the heart, not the head; instead of responding to the dictates of abstract reason man should be guided, he contended, by his instincts, his emotions, his inborn feelings. Like the rationalists, Rousseau was passionately interested in the happiness of mankind, but whereas they were dedicated primarily to destruction, Rousseau was more a builder. And as a literary stylist, persuasive and epigrammatic, he was at least the peer of his rivals.

Rousseau published his views in three famous books: *La Nouvelle Héloise, Émile* and the *Social Contract* (1762), the last an exposition of his political theories. *La Nouvelle Héloise* is a series of letters, teeming with eloquent sentimentalism and dreary pathos and preaching that only by returning to a simple state of living could mankind find salvation. The content of an ideal education and religion are discussed in *Émile*. Starting from the assumption that a child was inherently good, Rousseau insisted that education should allow a pupil full freedom so that his native capacities might flower without restraint. Adolescent minds ought not to be stuffed with the opinions and attitudes of the older generation; disciplined instruction was in fact wicked and degrading. And the maturing of a child's physical faculties should not be sacrificed to book learning. Rousseau decried instruction in religion before a youth had reached the age of eighteen. In the matter of religion he took his stand with the "natural" cult of the deists; his version, though, possessed a warmth conspicuously lacking in Voltaire, for example.

No other secular book has shaken modern society more violently than the brief *Social Contract*, though some time elapsed after its publication before it attracted a wide reading; Rousseau's other major works, in contrast, pushed quickly onto the "best seller lists." Few works on political philosophy have roused more controversy or nourished such diverse patterns of thinking. Believers in individual liberty, advocates of anarchism, spokesmen of political democracy, champions of authoritarianism—all alike have drawn arguments from the *Social Contract*. Little enough of the content originated with Rousseau. He borrowed generously from John Locke, infusing the ideas with vivid color and attuning them to the dominant French temper of the time. The *Social Contract* boldly proclaimed the moral and legal equality of all men, the sovereignty of the people in public affairs and the supremacy of the "general will."

Rousseau claimed that the original state had resulted from an agreement, a social contract, in which individuals had voluntarily united to protect their persons and their possessions. Public power belonged of right not to a despotic monarchy, but instead to those who were governed and since that was so, the governed were privileged to overthrow their government. When, however, a state had been set up which conformed to the "general will," the new government must wield unlimited authority in political and religious affairs. Passages in the book sanctioned, in other words, violent revolution, upheld political democracy, or justified arbitrary measures by public leaders. Therein lies the secret, if secret it is, of the importance of the *Social Contract* for world civilization.

Rousseau possessed personal qualities which charmed those who were able to penetrate his reserve and uncouthness. Yet he was faithless as a husband, neglectful as a parent, and customarily repaid favors with ingratitude. Throughout his mature life he was haunted by an acute sense of persecution. His mind, never very robust, cracked and he was a mental invalid in his last years.

Nevertheless, this extraordinary character occupies a secure niche in the intellectual history of the eighteenth century and his writings are still a living force. The cult of the natural which he propagated led to a powerful reaction against the frigidity and austerity of rationalism. His political doctrines were soon put to the test by leaders in the French Revolution, and they furnished a literary basis for the fervent nationalism of the nineteenth century. He helped, moreover, to divert creative literature and religious sentiments into warmly emotional channels, while his exhortations on schooling found fertile lodgment in programs of educational reformers.

RAYNAL'S "HISTOIRE"

An extremely popular tract for the times, colored by the sentiments of Rousseau, bore the pretentious title: *A Philosophical and Political History of European Trading Posts and Commerce in the Two Indies* (1770). Composed chiefly by the Abbé Raynal, and more fiction than history, it set forth the convictions, the aspirations and the sophistries of the "Enlightenment." It was cleverly designed to convert, to awaken men to what was wrong in France, and to spur them to action to set matters aright.

The way of the noble savage or the Chinese sage was pointed to as preferable to the decadent civilization of Europe. The New World of America, which one day surely would surpass Europe, was extolled as the habitation of men who had recaptured the "Golden Age." With rejoicing went, however, a counsel of experience: "People of North America . . . dread the influence of gold, which, with luxury, introduced corruption of manners and contempt of the laws. Dread too unequal a distribution of riches, which means a small number of wealthy citizens and a multitude of men plunged in misery; from whence arises the insolence of the former and the degradation of the latter. . . ."

The *Histoire* was published in at least twenty authorized editions and many more pirated ones. Readers were fascinated by glowing accounts of men living in fabulous bliss and obeying strange religious principles. The democratic flavor of the *Histoire* appealed strongly to discontented and restless French spirits.

TRENDS IN GERMAN EUROPE

The revolt against the tyranny of pure reason identified with Rousseau was reinforced by interesting and significant currents in German thought. A religious revival called Pietism, the idealistic philosophy of Immanuel Kant, and a romanticist upheaval in literature, challenged the prestige and acceptability of rationalism.

Pietism reflected the recurrent mysticism and the endless search for sincerity in the religious mind of Germany. As a practical force it was a

Immanuel Kant

revulsion against the ritualism and theological dogmatism of the Lutheran faith. Originating in seventeenth century Holland, Pietism spread into central Europe and found congenial soil in the new Prussian University of Halle. Indifferent to dogma, Pietism, like Quakerism, which had its background in Pietism, interpreted religion as a matter of the heart more than of the head.

A sense of intimate kinship with the Deity, the efficacy of sudden conversion, fervent preaching and performance of deeds of piety were traits of Pietism. Adherents were moved to revive the faith and the works of primitive Christianity; worldly amusements were frowned upon as inimical to spiritual health. Under Pietist auspices schools and charitable institutions were founded and missionaries were despatched overseas to convert heathen populations. By mid-eighteenth century Pietism had softened the frigidity of Lutheranism and increased moral earnestness. It influenced the musical compositions of Bach and had a connection with the Wesleyan movement in Great Britain.

Immanuel Kant is one of the most respected of systematic thinkers, the founder of the German school of idealist philosophy. He gave an immense stimulus to European thought in general. Here was profundity and solemnity in contrast to the gay wit and superficiality of the French *philosophes.* A partisan of rationalism at first, Kant's thinking underwent modification due to the influence of Rousseau.

Inquiries which he made into the nature and limitations of knowledge were incorporated in *The Critique of Pure Reason* (1781). Fundamental religious concepts such as the existence of the Deity, the immortality of the soul, freedom of will and the compulsions of morality could not be rationally demonstrated, Kant explained. But those ideas nonetheless possessed value for the individual; he would do well, therefore, to accept them on faith and live accordingly. In the lecture hall at the University of Königsberg, Kant taught that liberty and equality were basic principles of ethics and politics.

It was the moral duty of every citizen, Kant argued, to enlist in the maintenance of peace among the nations and help to bring that golden ideal to realization. Toward the end of his career he put forth his creed in *Perpetual Peace* proposing a universal organization to settle international quarrels; the actual constitution of this body should be drawn up by statesmen who were thoroughly familiar with the dynamics of power and the lusts of states. Kant's program for international peace contained ideas that were implemented in the international organizations that appeared after the world wars of the twentieth century.

German literature was violently churned up by the rebellion of the emotions against the grim tyranny of the intellect which Rousseau had unleashed. Writers dwelt upon the imaginative and sentimental elements in human personality and concerned themselves with commonplace things in life. The closest counterpart to Rousseau in Germany was the versatile Johann G. Herder, who had studied with Kant. A believer in the back-to-nature cult, Herder prized originality and proclaimed that creative intellects were a law unto themselves.

In his view, the peasants of Slavic countries most nearly approached Rousseau's vision of an idyllic and pacific society. He reminded his age of the primitive beauty of folk songs and laboriously collected the popular melodies of many lands. By stimulating an active interest in the German past and in the peculiarities of German culture, Herder kindled enthusiasm for nationalism among his own countrymen.

The early writings of Johann Wolfgang Goethe reflected the romantic emotionalism of Herder, his former teacher. Among German authors Goethe stands supreme, comparable to Dante in Italian or Shakespeare in English. His leadership commenced before the French Revolution and outlasted that upheaval. He established his reputation by a vividly romantic novel, *The Sufferings of Young Werther* (1774). This sentimental piece tells of a disillusioned lover whose passions were too strong for his spirit to withstand. Werther boldly defied traditional conventions of religion and morality, but, unable to come to terms with reality, he found release by taking his own life.

In part the tale reflected Goethe's own feelings, and it captured with fidelity the dreamy mood of many an adolescent romanticist of the time. Unsympathetic critics condemned the book as an apology for suicide, and perilous for morality and religion. This minor classic was translated into several languages, extensively imitated and widely read; Napoleon Bonaparte, for instance, confessed that he read it seven times, crying as he did so, and British intellectual circles were gripped with "Werther fever."

About the same time, Goethe wrote the first version of his celebrated masterpiece, *Faust*, a revealing portrayal of the restless romantic temper. Doctor Faust studied and inquired into all manner of subjects, but he felt that he neither knew anything nor was anything. He lamented:

> I have studied, alas, Philosophy,
> And to my cost Theology,
> And here I stand, with all my lore,
> Medicine, Jurisprudence too,
> With ardent labor, through and through,
> Poor fool, no wiser than before.

The purpose of living had eluded Faust. So he turned to supernatural mysteries and to dabbling in the black arts in the hope of discovering the meaning of existence.

Like German literature, poetry in Great Britain responded to the romantic cult of Rousseau, delight in homely commonplaces and enthusiasm for the picturesque beauties of nature. The "Elegy Written in a Country Churchyard" by Thomas Gray was a fine specimen of the romantic mood—sincere, simple and intensely emotional. Similar were the lyrics of the Scottish national bard, Robert Burns, Writing in the native dialect, he melodiously crystallized his hard personal life, reflections on rural Scotland and, later on, he decried the limitations upon human freedom and proclaimed a warm democratic faith. Burns excelled in poetic idealizations of humble things ("Cotter's Saturday Night"), and in evoking primitive sentiments, as in "Auld Lang Syne." Gray and Burns opened the way for British romantic poetry of the next century.

THE FINE ARTS

Something of the richness of the eighteenth century in the realm of music has already been suggested. Italian genius had struck out along fresh lines and German musicians followed along carrying the technique of composition to unprecedented heights, and imparting to the century the quality of a golden age in music. Royal courts and a discriminating, cosmopolitan aristocracy by their patronage enabled musical art to flourish; by the middle of the century Vienna had become the acknowledged capital of "the language of the emotions."

Johann Sebastian Bach set new standards in harmony, performance and luxuriance of melody. Born into a talented musical family, Bach excelled in almost every musical form except opera, and he was an accomplished organist as well. His compositions, which have been collected in more than sixty volumes, range from large cantatas and church music without or with orchestra, to secular pieces for voice. Permeated with deep religious seriousness, these compositions are noted for freshness of style and intensity of expression. His masterpiece,

Johann Sebastian Bach

many musicians would agree, is the *Well-Tempered Clavichord*. Outside of Germany, Bach's talent was not appreciated while he lived, but in the following century his music influenced many distinguished composers.

Operatic productions of enduring popularity were written at a rapid pace by Christopher Gluck. Settling in Vienna, Gluck composed under the patronage of Empress Maria Theresa and gave lessons in music to her children. He departed from the beaten path in opera, infusing his best works with rare emotional and dramatic power; that quality was fully exhibited in the perennially favored *Orpheus*.

Musical art was brought to classic perfection in Vienna by Joseph Haydn and Wolfgang A. Mozart. Haydn wrote without ceasing, masses, quartets, sonatas, symphonies and dramatic pieces, the last seldom heard nowadays. The darling of the Austrian patrician class, Haydn insinuated his abiding love of nature into his music and made fruitful use of primitive folk melodies. Simplicity, serenity and clarity are conspicuous traits of his compositions, as one might expect in the son of a humble Croatian peasant. Haydn also composed the stirring Austrian national anthem (1797) in the midst of warfare with Revolutionary France.

Mozart, the friend and in a measure the disciple of Haydn, occupies a unique niche in the history of music. A genius of the first magnitude, he benefited immensely from foreign travel and study. Up to a point, the grace, elegance and charm of Mozart reflected the musical currents of the age in which he lived. He chose to concentrate on the composition of music to the exclusion of almost everything else and the kingdom of culture gained thereby.

Skillful in all varieties of composition and master of a majestic style, Mozart was at his best doubtless in opera—*The Marriage of Figaro* and *Don Giovanni*, for example. He raised opera with spoken dialogue to an unequalled height. "What else is genius," Goethe inquired, "but the power that produces deeds worthy to stand in the presence of God and Nature . . .? To this class belong all Mozart's creations." His music glistens and sparkles; tender emotions blend harmoniously with deeply tragic feeling. An astonishing insight into the nature of man pervades the art of Mozart and partly explains his lasting popularity and far-reaching influence upon professional musicians of future generations.

As Germans carried tastes and standards in music to new levels, so Frenchmen excelled in eighteenth-century painting and sculpture. Here, too, the patronage of the leisured nobility benefited the realm of culture. Taking Rubens for his model, Antoine Watteau broke away from the stiff formalism of his French predecessors. His canvases and portraits re-

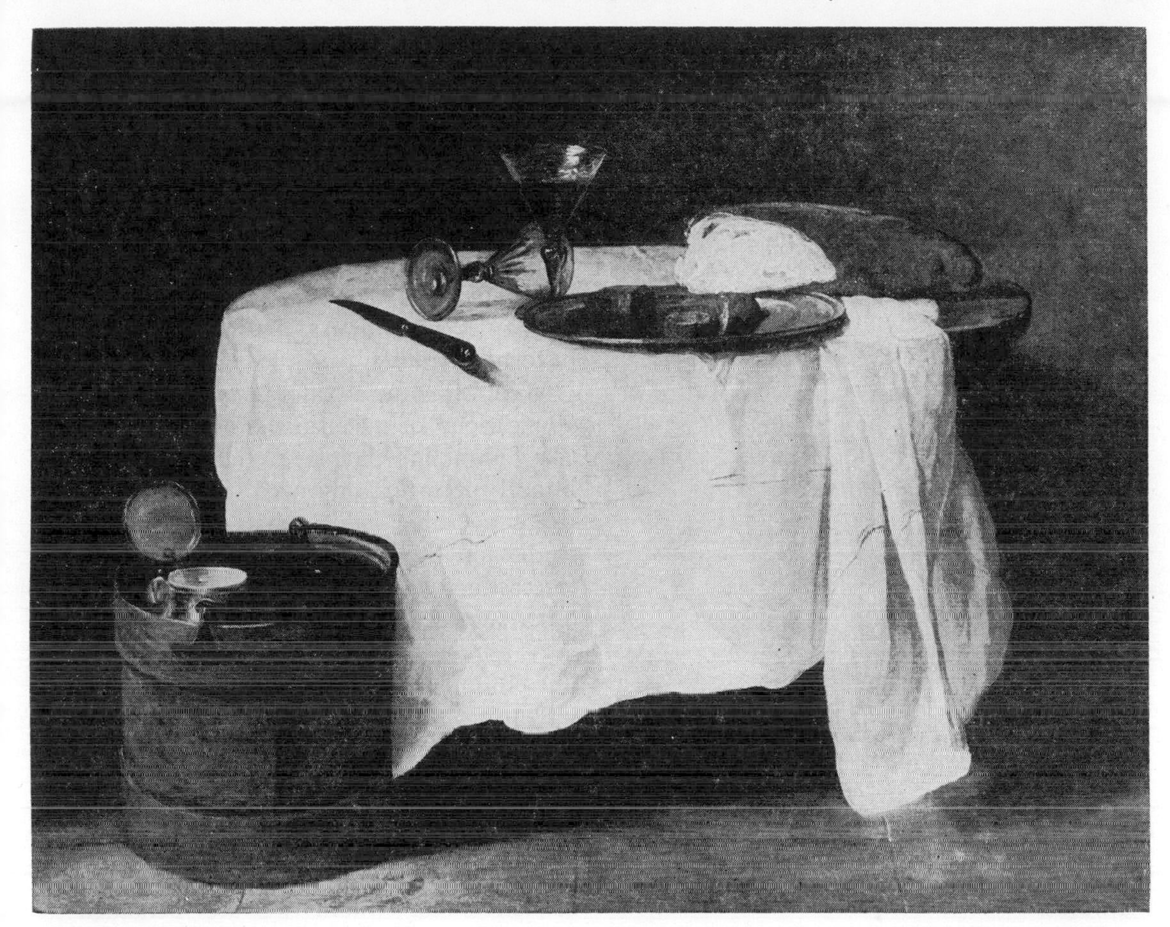

The White Tablecloth, by Jean Chardin

produced the artificiality and gaiety of aristocratic society. Fond of decorative design and lush coloring, Watteau touched the peak of his artistry in "Embarkment for Cythera."

His disciple and imitator, François Boucher, catered to the refined passions of the nobility at the Court of Louis XV, which he served as official painter. He is best known, perhaps, for decorative mythological pieces, delicately sensuous in style, such as "The Dog's Education." Elegant grace and rich coloring typified his interpretations of feminine beauty. Friendly with Madame de Pompadour, mistress of the king, Boucher painted several notable portraits of that sultry siren.

Equally adept at translating the tastes of the profligate French aristocracy onto canvas and more given to accenting sensuality was Jean H. Fragonard. "The Sleeping Bacchante" and "The Fair-Haired Boy" are popular specimens of his craftsmanship. Another favorite in court circles was Jean M. Nattier, who specialized in portraits, frivolous ladies of Paris preferred, though he also painted a valuable picture of Peter the Great.

Most talented, no doubt, of the lot was Jean S. Chardin, who responded to the Rousseauan cult of the natural. He translated onto canvas the simple commonplaces of daily living as in "Le Bénédicité": a mother serving a meal, pauses to help her child with an unfamiliar word in the blessing. Jean B. Greuze also belonged to the back-to-nature school. His pictures, for example, "The Broken Pitcher," were calculated to appeal to aspiring middle class folk, whose outlook and sentiments Greuze

Benjamin Franklin

well expressed. There is an air of youthful vigor and heartiness and touches of melodrama in his works.

Among sculptors Jean A. Houdon stands apart. Connoisseurs of the plastic arts regard the busts of contemporary leaders in thought and politics which he carved as the finest creations in a century or two. Representations of Voltaire, for which Houdon is probably best known, portrayed the man—the lean, sly face and brightly gleaming eyes—with almost photographic fidelity. The teacher of Houdon, Jean B. Pigalle, created statues and tomb ornamentation to satisfy the craving of the well-born and the wealthy.

BENJAMIN FRANKLIN

In its curiosity about nature and allegiance to reason, the mind of the eighteenth century was neatly summed up in the interests—and the limitations—of Benjamin Franklin, the first American to win an international reputation. Although he was eminent as an editor and a public servant, and wrote on music and befriended authors and painters, it is only Franklin the man of science and the *philosophe* that is of present concern. His interest in science was quickened during a youthful visit to England when he expressed a wish to meet the great Newton. His reputation as a scientist rested principally on his demonstration of the identity of lightning and electricity. But his keen and restless mind was forever busy with mechanics and physics, mathematics, "natural history," chemistry and medicine.

With his name are associated many practical applications of scientific knowledge, such as the "Franklin" fireplace, the lightning rod, bifocal spectacles, improved street lighting and the convertible ladder chair. He engaged in studies on the course of the Gulf Stream, in forecasting weather conditions and in many other subjects.

As a man of the "Enlightenment", Franklin was profoundly affected by the liberal and utilitarian spirit of his adopted city of Philadelphia. With sparkling wit and shrewd common sense he revealed his philosophical convictions in *Poor Richard's Almanack* and in his *Autobiography*, an unfinished classic. David Hume spoke of this self-made genius as "the first great man of letters for whom we are beholden to America."

Few of the standard ideas of the Age of Reason are missing from Franklin's pages. He tolerantly accepted the world without illusions. He shunned "superstition" and mystery, passionately espoused the cause of freedom and preached the virtues of prudence, benevolence and reason. Cheerfully optimistic about posterity, he devoted himself to long-range plans for social betterment. His religious position was that of a conservative deist. And Franklin was a cosmopolitan who could write, "God grant that not only the love of Liberty but a thorough knowledge of the Rights of Man may pervade all the Nations of the Earth so that a philosopher may set his foot anywhere and say, 'This is my country.' "

Frenchmen of the "Enlightenment" esteemed Franklin nearly as much as they admired Voltaire. It appeared that this American, witty and wise, serene and simple, possessed the attributes with which men were imagined to have been endowed in the never-never Golden Age of the past. Fully aware of the political value of the image that he created, Franklin exploited his personality to win friends for his young country. When the foremost genius of eighteenth-century America passed away, the French National Assembly proclaimed a period of mourning out of respect for "the sage whom two worlds claim as their own, the man for whom the history of sciences and the history of empires contend with each other. . . ."

The attitudes and outlook of the "enlightened" intellectuals which Franklin so well represented were not generally shared in Western society. The great mass of men continued to walk the well-beaten paths of their fathers unaffected by the novelties of the age. Most men were basically conservative, allergic to the new, clinging to the past, to the familiar and to ingrained habits with primitive tenacity. It was, however, the inquiring, unconventional minds who lighted the trail into the future and that is why they deserve attention out of all proportion to their numbers.

FOR FURTHER STUDY

PRESERVED SMITH, *A History of Modern Culture* (Vol. II, New York, 1934) PAPERBACK

HERBERT BUTTERFIELD, *The Origins of Modern Science, 1300–1800* (New York, 1951) PAPERBACK

JOHN W. N. SULLIVAN, *Isaac Newton* (New York, 1938)

CARL L. BECKER, *The Heavenly City of the Eighteenth Century Philosophers* (new ed., New Haven, 1955) PAPERBACK

DANIEL MORNET, *French Thought in the Eighteenth Century* (Eng. trans., New York, 1929)

ERNEST CASSIRER, *Philosophy of the Enlightenment* (Eng. trans., Princeton, 1952) PAPERBACK

JOHN B. BURY, *The Idea of Progress* (new ed., New York, 1960) PAPERBACK

JOHN MORLEY, *Diderot and the Encyclopaedists* (new ed., 2 vols., London, 1923)

ALEXANDER L. LINDSAY, *Kant* (new ed., New York, 1946)

CARL C. VAN DOREN, *Benjamin Franklin* (new ed., New York, 1956)

PAUL HAZARD, *European Thought in the Eighteenth Century* (New Haven, 1954)

ALFRED R. HALL, *The Scientific Revolution* (London, 1954) PAPERBACK

FRANK E. MANUEL, *The Age of Reason* (Ithaca, 1951) PAPERBACK

GEORGE R. HAVENS, *The Age of Ideas* (New York, 1955) PAPERBACK

ARTHUR M. WILSON, *Diderot* (New York, 1957)

VERNER W. CRANE, *Benjamin Franklin and a Rising People* (Boston, 1954)

A List of Significant Dates

WESTERN EUROPE		CENTRAL AND EASTERN EUROPE		OVERSEAS	
1651	English Navigation Act	**1640**	Frederick William, the Great Elector	**1637**	Japan excludes foreigners
1652	Anglo-Dutch Naval War	**1667**	Russia acquires most of Ukraine	**1644**	Manchu dynasty in China
1660	Stuart Restoration	**1673**	Sobieski King of Poland	**1654**	Portuguese oust Dutch from Brazil
1661	Louis XIV King-in-fact	**1683**	Turks defeated at Vienna	**1664**	English supplant Dutch in North America
1665	Colbert, Controller-General	**1689**	Peter I Tsar	**1682**	LaSalle claims Louisiana Territory
1667	Louis XIV invades Holland	**1699**	Treaty of Carlowitz	**1682**	Pennsylvania founded
1685	Revocation of Edict of Nantes	**1709**	Battle of Poltava	**1699**	English factory in Canton
1688	The "Glorious Revolution"	**1721**	Treaty of Nystadt	**1720**	Texas under Spanish rule
1715	Death of Louis XIV	**1733**	War of the Polish Succession	**1732**	Founding of Georgia
1721	Walpole Prime Minister of England	**1740**	Frederick II King of Prussia	**1760**	French Power in India destroyed
1760	Accession George III	**1740**	Maria Theresa Empress	**1763**	French retire from North America
		1755	University of Moscow founded		
		1762	Catherine II Tsarina		

CULTURAL AFFAIRS		GENERAL	
1651	*Leviathan* (Hobbes)	**1648**	Peace of Westphalia
1652	Raskolniki Schism	**1687**	War of the League of Augsburg
1656	*Provincial Letters* (Pascal)	**1702**	War of the Spanish Succession
1662	Royal Society of London	**1713**	Peace of Utrecht
1666	French Academy of Science	**1740**	War of the Austrian Succession
1681	*Universal History* (Bossuet)	**1748**	Treaty of Aix-la-Chapelle
1687	*Principia* (Newton)	**1756**	Seven Years' War
1690	*Treatises on Government* (Locke)	**1763**	Treaty of Paris
1717	*Well-Tempered Clavichord* (Bach)		
1721	Holy Synod—Russia		
1734	*Letters on the English* (Voltaire)		
1738	Beginning of Methodism		
1741	"Messiah" (Handel)		
1748	*The Spirit of the Laws* (Montesquieu)		
1751	French *Encyclopedia*		
1762	*The Social Contract* (Rousseau)		

PART II

THE FRENCH REVOLUTION AND NAPOLEON

CHAPTER IX

THE ROAD TO REVOLUTION

FRANCE IN THE EIGHTEENTH CENTURY

FRANCE in the eighteenth century was the leading nation of Europe. Her large standing army, her excellent diplomatic service, her bureaucratic officialdom, her economic policies, her elaborate and immoral court, her ideas, manners and language were admired and imitated by other countries. Although upset by wars and recurrent famines, French standards of comfort moved modestly upward in the eighteenth century as is revealed in one way by the growth in population from about eighteen to twenty-six millions. "In spite of the abuses in administration," Frederick the Great wrote, "France is the most powerful state in Europe."

Unconventional French writers set in motion a rising tide of active discontent with prevailing institutions and customs. The growing French middle class, wealthy, intelligent, self-assertive, clamored for a share in public affairs and demanded that the special immunities and privileges of clergy and aristocracy should be taken away. And the social structure of eighteenth-century France typified reasonably well that of Continental Europe as a whole.

It has been said that the history of France "from the death of Louis XIV to 1788 is the history of the approach of the Revolution." There is much solid truth in that judgment, but it is very easy to fall into the error of portraying a period of history in the light of what happened afterward. It is misleading, actually, to interpret French developments of the eighteenth century as pointing unerringly toward the revolutionary explosion of 1789. Few men, if indeed any, foresaw an upheaval of the kind that in fact occurred—one of the most stirring and pregnant events of all recorded history.

But an analysis of the structure of French society, the real nature of the Old Regime, discloses more than mere hints on why the Revolution came to pass.

Here are the three Estates personified in a costume plate prescribing the dress to be worn by each at the assembly of the Estates General. Left to right, *the Clergy, the Nobility, the People.*

CLERGY AND CHURCH

The social order of Continental Europe was anchored firmly on the assumption of human inequality. By reason of birth or calling, it was believed, men belonged to precise social castes in keeping with the will and the wish of the Almighty. Broadly speaking, there were two social categories: the privileged and the rest of humanity. The privileged element, in turn, was divided into the churchmen, or First Estate, and the aristocracy, the Second Estate. Considerable differences existed among the members of these groups in education, breeding, income and outlook.

The sacred nature of their vocation, coupled with long-standing tradition, placed the Christian clergy at the very top of the French social pyramid. Counting all categories, bishops and abbots, monks and nuns, parish priests and assistants, this class exceeded 130,000 on the eve of the Revolution. The higher clergy, prelates and abbots, were recruited largely from the titled aristocracy and shared the general outlook of that class; not a few of them were impregnated with the spirit of rationalism and took their ecclesiastical responsibilities lightly. Occupying luxurious palaces and recipients of fat incomes, the leading ecclesiastics belonged to the royal entourage. Many a bishop knew little about his diocese and landed estates except that they were the sources of his income.

Another story must, however, be related about the parish priests who in the main were of humble origins, as was true, also, of most monks.[1] Living close to their parishioners, attentive to duties and morally decent, the priests

[1] Rather more than a thousand monastic institutions for men and women existed in France. Rarely did they have more than a handful of inmates: they were not conspicuous for spiritual zeal.

were generally respected and beloved by those to whom they ministered. This was more especially the case in the rural areas. Incomes of priests were extremely modest, often they lived in want, and the sumptuous worldly way of life of their superiors generated bitter indignation. In the first flush of the Revolution the lower clergy sided decisively with the unprivileged mass of the French population.

Across the centuries, extensive properties had accumulated in the hands of churchmen. To them, or more accurately to the Catholic Church herself, belonged more than a tenth of the acreage of the kingdom as well as valuable properties in the cities and towns. In addition to revenue from these sources, the clergy collected a tithe from the faithful. Nominally a tenth of one's income, the actual amount of the tithe varied from a twelfth to a twentieth in keeping with local custom, resistance to paying the tithe mounted in the eighteenth century, producing an enormous crop of lawsuits. Church properties and churchmen were exempt from practically all direct taxes, though periodically financial grants were made to the royal treasury.

Aside from maintaining the clergy, high and low, and church buildings, ecclesiastical revenues financed educational institutions and charitable enterprises. From time immemorial churchmen held a monopoly on learning and schools; until their expulsion in 1764 Jesuit fathers controlled secondary education and some higher institutions, though universities, definitely stagnant in the eighteenth century, were under royal direction. Hospitals, orphanages, care of the insane and relief for the indigent were other social responsibilities of the clergy. Churchmen also possessed authority to censor publications and to prohibit the circulation of literature which they disliked, though that right fell into disuse in the 1760's. Certain types of legal cases had to be tried in church courts.

Theoretically all the inhabitants of France belonged to the Catholic Church and adhered to the doctrines which had been fashioned through centuries of experience. But in fact a stubborn Huguenot minority existed and an increasing number of Frenchmen entered the ranks of the freethinkers under the influence of the slings and arrows of Voltaire and other skeptical authors. Ecclesiastical waters were roiled up by controversies between Jansenists and Jesuits, until the latter were suppressed amidst the hearty applause of their clerical enemies and the *philosophes* alike.

On the general state of the Church in France on the eve of the Revolution the English historian, Hilaire Belloc, himself a Roman Catholic, has written:

> "Within memory of all men living, the Church had become more and more official, the masses of the great towns had wholly lost touch with it; the intelligence of the country was in the main drawn to the Deist or even the purely sceptical propaganda, the powerful Huguenot body was ready prepared for an alliance with any foe of Catholicism, and in the eyes of the impoverished town population—notably in Paris, which had long abandoned the practice of religion—the human organization of the church, the hierarchy, the priesthood, and the few but very wealthy religious orders which still lingered on in dwindling numbers, were but a portion of the privileged world which the populace hated and was prepared to destroy." [2]

CROWN AND ARISTOCRACY

The king of France, like his fellow monarchs, took precedence over all his subjects. Ruler by the sanction of the Almighty, the object of prayers by the clergy for his health and salvation, the king was accountable for his stewardship only to God. No constitution other than tradition, no national assembly defined or infringed upon his authority. All public power, executive, legislative and judicial reposed in his hands. The king ruled as well as reigned.

In the royal name laws were published, public moneys collected and disbursed and officials

[2] Hilaire Belloc, *The French Revolution* (New York, 1911), p. 235.

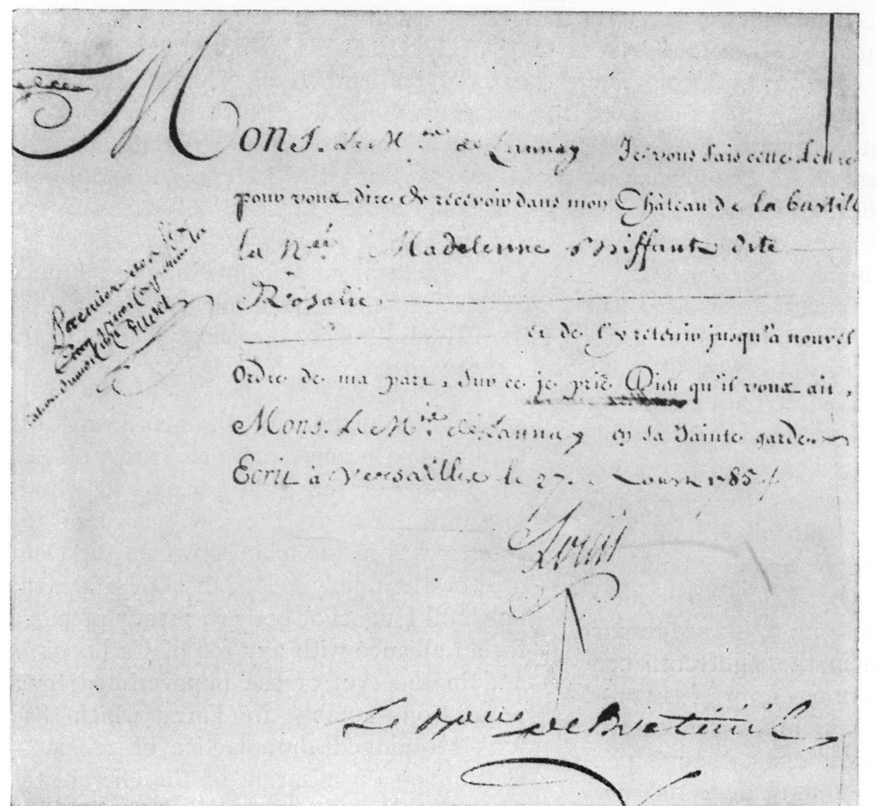

Mons. le M.is de Launay Je vous fais cette lettre pour vous dire de recevoir dans mon Château de la Bastille la N.lle Madeleine [illegible] dite Rosalie, et de l'y retenir jusqu'à nouvel Ordre de ma part, sur ce je prie Dieu qu'il vous ait, Mons. le M.is de Launay en sa sainte garde. Ecrit à Versailles le 27. [illegible] 1785.

Louis

Le Baron de Breteuil

Specimen of a "Lettre de Cachet" or royal warrant for imprisonment without due process of law

appointed. The king was responsible, moreover, for diplomatic strategy and foreign policies and he was commander-in-chief of the fighting services. He possessed power to commit any man to a state prison—such as the huge, glowering Bastille in Paris—for the rest of his days without explanation or trial. Invested with immense grandeur and surrounded by pomp and pageantry, the king was looked upon as a benevolent, fatherly protector, infallible too—or so at least Frenchmen were taught and doubtless the vast majority believed. Hoary and hallowed tradition, the Christian Church and her clergy, the privileged aristocracy, the officialdom and the standing army—these were the pillars upon which the Bourbon monarchy rested.

In reality the prestige of a French monarch depended to no inconsiderable extent upon his personal qualities and character, or at any rate, upon the image which the populace had of his personality. In reality, too, public policies were determined by ministers and top-ranking bureaucrats who had access to the royal ear. The more alert of these men were not unaffected by the growing volume of criticism of the conduct of state business and of the prevailing institutions of government themselves.

The French aristocracy was composed of about 400,000 people who owned approximately a fifth of the soil of the kingdom. This estate was divided into an older element, whose ancestors had historically belonged to this caste, and men ennobled for public services or by reason of marriage or of an office they filled. About a thousand families, the élite of the élite, comprised the court aristocracy. They derived their incomes principally from great landed estates, whose management was entrusted to stewards. Properties inherited by the Marquis de Lafayette, to illustrate, yielded an income equivalent to something like $150,000 a year. Certain grandees received donations from the royal treasury or held sinecures in

State or Church which paid handsomely. Even so, many an aristocrat was obliged to place mortgages on his land in order to meet debts.

The nobility of France had no direct responsibility for state affairs. In that respect the French aristocracy stood apart from the aristocracies of other countries. On the Continent nobles had been drawn into some form of public service, while in Britain they actually managed the government. And yet, although deprived of independent political authority, the French patrician class was more frequently than not the actual master of the kingdom. King and ministers repeatedly danced to the will or the whim of the more influential aristocrats.

France, very definitely, was an aristocratically ordered society. Whether at Versailles or in spacious rural chateaux, courtiers and courtesans lived a life of refined luxury, marked by conspicuous consumption in houses and furnishings, in clothes, carriages and stables, profligate frivolities and expensive entertainments. With their decorative swords, plumed hats, powdered wigs, silk stockings and suavity of manners, these proud folk formed a caste apart, a slice of Western humanity that has vanished beyond recall. The grandees had their special tastes in art and literature—some were generous patrons of the arts and sciences—and their own standards of personal behavior. Among the aristocracy, "vice lost half its evil by losing all its grossness," the Englishman, Edmund Burke, remarked.

Small wonder that the exclusive nobility regarded theirs as the best possible of all worlds. Conservative standpatters, in their blindness and sloth, they declined to admit that anything was really out of joint and they were prepared to resist stubbornly any changes likely to impair their privileged position.

The bulk of the hereditary aristocracy was wholly excluded from court circles and lived on provincial estates. Some impoverished nobles eked out an existence scarcely superior to that of well-to-do peasants. Arrogance matched their poverty. They envied the upper aristocracy, despised the pushing, ever wealthier bourgeoisie but disdained to engage in business or a

This sample of aristocratic frivolity was described as the "new English headdress".

profession. Some of them became inoculated with the reformist sentiments that were abroad in the land and dreamed of brighter, better days in the future. Other squirearchs, however, were as adamantly opposed to significant change as the great lords and ladies.

Newly ennobled aristocrats—the "nobility of the robe"—were as a rule rich and proud. Many of them functioned as administrative or judicial officials; members of the *parlements*, courts of law primarily, came from this element as did many of the *intendants*, the chief administrators in the provinces. Time tended to blur the distinctions between the new nobility and the older aristocracy.

As a class, nobles were exempt from most varieties of taxation and received privileged treatment in criminal trials. From the peasants they exacted rentals and other dues, which, though not large in amount, were thoroughly hated by those who paid them. Nobles maintained local courts in which extortionate fees were charged and they jealously guarded the privilege of the profitable sport of hunting. Over the Continent as a whole the aristocracy comprised a kind of international fraternity. But nobles to the east of the Rhine and south of the Pyrenees, inferior though they were to the French in polish and culture, possessed authority over the peasants which their "brothers" in France had lost.

THE THIRD ESTATE

More than twenty-four million Frenchmen, bourgeoisie, artisans, town laborers and countryfolk, were grouped in the unprivileged "Third" estate. The bourgeoisie, or propertied middle classes, had grown in response to the expansion of trade and industry and improvement in means of transportation, until it equalled the aristocracy in sheer numbers. Not at all homogeneous, this group embraced financiers, merchants, manufacturers and shipowners, shopkeepers, members of the liberal professions of law and medicine, writers and journalists and skilled craftsmen. Prosperous middle class families owned about a sixth of the land of the kingdom.

French trade multiplied fourfold in the course of the eighteenth century and the bourgeoisie benefited greatly. Some large fortunes were piled up by businessmen and by moneylenders who extended loans to the straitened government, or cashed in on advances to the nobility. In this category, too, were financiers who purchased the right of gathering the indirect taxes in sections of the kingdom and pocketed the excess that was collected. Manufacturing of course was carried on principally under guild roofs, but some enterprising individuals had accumulated wealth from the domestic or putting-out type of production. By 1789 a few rich capitalists were operating large-scale textile factories and iron mills. The professional classes, lawyers most of all, had increased in numbers and in prosperity.

Plutocratic bourgeoisie in Paris and the larger provincial communities enjoyed a scale of living rivaling the aristocracy and some of them generously patronized authors and artists. While professing to despise the "upper classes," many an opulent middle class man actually envied them, built a palatial mansion and in other ways aped his social betters. By marriage or the purchase of a state office, some bourgeoisie wormed their way into the social élite.

By and large, however, the bourgeoisie hotly resented their inferior social status and their exclusion from public business. They longed for an order of society in which money, not birth, would be the controlling consideration. They desired greater scope for personal initiative and enterprise, the elimination of state interference with the free play of economic forces. They were keenly interested in attaining a fuller measure of happiness on this earth.

Ambitious, hard-working, self-assured, the French bourgeoisie greedily devoured the publications of the *philosophes* which so engagingly expressed what the middle classes thought. Books forbidden by the censorship were "bootlegged" about with remarkable abandon, and their contents were discussed in homes, societies, clubs and lodges. Men of the middle classes came confidently to believe that the future belonged to them. The French Revolution would be a bourgeois movement in the main; and the minds and emotions of the middle classes were prepared for significant changes before they made them the work of their hands.

Paris and a dozen other substantial cities contained a propertyless working class. There were guildsmen, for instance, who expected to rise to master rank, shop and factory employees, unskilled day laborers and peasants driven from the land by harsh conditions or piecing out their incomes by seasonal employment. No organizations or clear feeling of class consciousness united these wage workers. Of the Paris population, which exceeded 500,000, approximately half belonged to wage-earning families. Wholly untaught, poorly fed, poorly housed, poorly clothed, working long hours for small pay, this miserable element readily responded to ideological fashions and one-word arguments. Cruel want goaded lowly Parisians to street riots on several occasions in the eighteenth century, though they were in fact less unruly than their counterparts in London.

THE PEASANTRY

Nine out of ten Frenchmen depended upon the land for their daily bread. Probably somewhere between two-fifths and one-half of the land of the kingdom belonged to peasants, in the sense that they could not be dispossessed and could bequeath holdings to heirs. For a good deal of the land which they worked, peasants owed nominal rentals to nobles in the neighborhood. Most of the rustics operated only small farms, sufficient merely to supply the necessities of their personal families, if indeed that; a few cultivators may fairly be described as capitalistic farmers. Still other peasants cultivated land on shares or hired out as day laborers. Underemployment was a chronic evil in rural France. When crop yields were short, many poor peasants were reduced to beggary or actually starved, and insufficiency of food was commonplace.

Acute distress in the countryside fanned discontent and encouraged vagabondage and thievery. Writing from Paris in 1785, Thomas Jefferson reported: "Of the twenty [sic] millions of people supposed to be in France, I am of the opinion there are nineteen millions more wretched, more accursed in every circumstance of human existence than the most conspicuously wretched individual of the United States."

Like their prototypes in any age or clime the French peasantry of the eighteenth century were coarse and cunning, noted for credulity, quarrelsomeness, suspicion of outsiders and willingness to plod along. In the most backward districts, lay and clerical estates were cultivated by serfs, who totalled a million at most. Traditional rights of the serfs and their persons were protected by royal courts of law.

Antiquated farming techniques persisted in France, helping to degrade levels of living. The law of the land, as well as inclination, bound the peasants to time-tested routines and to excessive concentration on grain production. Due to the old-fashioned custom of fallowing, somewhere between a third and a half of the French soil lay idle at all times, it has been soberly estimated. A large growth of rural population in the eighteenth century worsened the material lot of the French peasantry. Farm animals were scarce, and manure, consequently, was in limited supply, a handicap to more intensive cultivation. French agriculture failed to satisfy the food requirements of the growing urban population.

Apart from rentals to landlords, the peasants had to make payments for the use of the manor grain-mill and wine press. They deeply resented regulations which reserved the snaring of game to the nobility, and made it a crime to kill animals that invaded their growing crops. And many deliberately tried to evade their obligation to the church, the tithe. Far more burdensome than the dues owed to lords or to the Lord were the taxes and other obligations paid to the rapacious Bourbon government. The basic direct tax was the *taille* levied on real property or, in places on crops, and varying considerably in amount in different sections of the kingdom. Assessments were increased if a cottage was fixed up or fields kept in good condition, so calculating peasants tended to neglect their properties. Payment of this *taille* was a mark of inferiority for the upper classes were exempt.

Other direct taxes were the *twentieth,* which sometimes ran as high as a sixth of one's income and a poll tax paid by the head of every household. In effect, a tax was the *corvée,* which compelled peasants to perform unremunerated labor to keep roadways in trim or to mend bridges and canals. They might be called upon, too, for carts to move troops or to provide lodgings for soldiers. Lucky they were if they escaped enrollment in the royal army.

Piled upon these direct taxes, was an array of concealed levies, and the greatly hated *gabelle* or salt impost. Every household had to buy a minimum quantity of salt, needed to preserve meat and fish and to protect livestock

In this satirical engraving of 1789, the taille, *the* impôts, *and the* corvées *make up the stone which presses out the life of the common people. The clergy and the nobility are assisting the process by standing on the stone.*

against disease, as well as for ordinary seasoning. The price of the salt varied greatly, and penalties for smuggling from provinces where the cost was low extended to life and limb. Excises were also laid on alcohol, tobacco, soap and other articles of mass consumption. And customs duties had to be paid on goods imported from abroad—no special burden for most peasants—and on commodities passing through towns and provinces. Shipments of wine from the south of France to Paris paid forty fees on the way. Armies of collectors were employed to enforce the tax laws.

Counting everything, at least three-fifths, probably more, of the income of the poor man was drained off by clergy, nobility and state, so that the peasants though mostly freemen were economically enchained. It was the Bourbon government that was the insatiable Leviathan and the rustics hated and cursed it with primitive fervor. Nothing so feeds revolutionary ardor as a deep sense of grievance.

And yet the French peasants were better off than the sordid and degraded soil workers in other countries of Europe, for the latter were shackled by burdens of personal servitude as in the medieval centuries. It was permissible, for instance, for the lord of Hesse to sell the services of his young men to the British king for warfare against the revolting American colonies.

This sweeping survey throws into bold relief the actualities, the inequalities, the archaicisms of Old World society in the eighteenth century. And it must be emphasized that the lot of the non-privileged in France was superior to that anywhere else in Europe. Because there was more wealth, more enlightenment in France, Frenchmen were more dynamically discontented with the status quo, more ready for drastic changes.

DECLINE OF ROYAL PRESTIGE

Louis XIV had raised the principle of divine right monarchy to the summit of perfection, however much the physical fibre of France had been impaired by misguided ambitions at home and abroad. His successor, Louis XV, who presided over the national destinies until 1774, was a man of different mold, though equally persuaded that he was the Lord's Anointed. Authoritarian government to succeed requires a dynamic, vivid and resourceful master at the helm. Louis XV failed to measure up. No question of the native intelligence of the

Louis XV,
King of France

man, nor of his dignified even handsome appearance. He would have made an ideal monarch for a theatrical production. But he did not relish the role of royal dictator and he performed badly at it. Resembling a routine bureaucrat without personal force, he was incapable of taking the long view and only spasmodic in application to public business.

As king, Louis XV showed little confidence in expert advisers, choosing rather to heed the counsel of dazzling female beauties who shared his bed. Grossly immoral in private life, he nonetheless publicly professed warm devotion to the state religion, and brooded morbidly over the punishment awaiting him in the world beyond.

Early in the reign, Cardinal Fleury, once tutor to the king, served as captain on the bridge. A staid, solid and competent statesman, he set energetically to work on the immense task of repairing the ravages which the wars of Louis XIV had wrought. In no small measure, the economy of France was bettered, but involvement in fresh wars nullified the good that had been accomplished. After the passing of Fleury the king announced that he would himself steer the ship of state. But self-indulgence soon had him in its enervating grip. He discovered a queen of hearts in every attractive woman. An hour a day seemed sufficient to devote to public responsibilities, which left plenty of time for the diversions of hunting and gambling—and the ladies.

For a generation Louis XV's favorite mistress, Madame de Pompadour, uttered the decisive word on state policies. Despite her physical charms and undoubted intellectual ability—perhaps because of these traits—she was detested by aristocratic courtiers who could not forget her bourgeois lineage. Ministers of state and generals came and went as this benevolent female despot willed, but her influence upon the government was seldom beneficial. Madame du Barry succeeded Pompadour in the royal affections and in the direction of state affairs. To speak charitably of her, it might be said that she was nothing more than a disreputable and ravishing adventuress, without competence to act as counselor to the crown. Political and moral paralysis at court, ominous deficits in state finance and the shadow of military defeats cast a chill upon the French nation.

Spirited indictments of the shaky Bourbon administration by the *philosophes* and recurrent popular outbreaks boded ill for the future. "After me the deluge," Louis XV is said to have jested. Perhaps he guessed that the gathering storm would soon break with fury upon the discredited Bourbon regime. At death, the body of Louis XV was removed from Paris under cover of darkness. Bystanders who saw the coffin pass shouted: "Tiaout! Tiaout!"—the cry with which royal huntsmen were accustomed to throw a broken stag to the hungry hounds.

The most immediate danger threatening France was the peril of national bankruptcy. Decade after decade governmental outlays had exceeded income by good round figures. Constant recourse to loans to cover deficits had pushed the national debt to dizzy heights and interest on the debt consumed a high proportion of state income.

Three main reasons explain the sorry financial predicament. To the huge legacy of debt which the wars of Louis XIV had passed on were added the expenditures in prosecuting the wars of the reign of Louis XV, notably the War of the Austrian Succession and the Seven Years' War. Even in peace time, the maintenance of the fighting services devoured enormous sums. Parenthetically, these international conflicts, far from raising the prestige of the House of Bourbon had distinctly lowered it; instead of territorial gains, vast possessions overseas, in America and in India, had been wrested away by Britain, which infuriated patriotic Frenchmen.

Colossal and prodigal extravagance at the court, in the second place, ate deeply into public funds. It was expensive to maintain luxurious palaces, to stage grand parties, to erect new buildings and to supply spending money to royal favorites. And last of all, public finance was grossly mismanaged. No regular system of handling funds existed, so that venal officials fastened on to part of the revenues intended for the treasury and took a slice of outbound appropriations. Louis XV would not economize and the privileged courtiers would not shoulder a fair share of the financial burden of government. Consequently, the monarchy was compelled to float fresh loans or to increase taxes.

The latter expedient aroused militant resistance from the *parlements*. Although fundamentally supreme courts of law, these bodies, notably that of Paris, performed political functions as well. No royal edict, for instance, was valid unless and until it was formally registered by the *Parlement* of Paris. The power to register was the power to refuse.[3] Quarreling between crown and *parlement* was endemic, for *parlement* disputed the royal right to lay taxes without its concurrence or to banish judges who defied the monarchical will. Repeatedly the *Parlement* vetoed a royal decree and was dismissed by the king, only to be restored because of popular pressure. At last in 1771 the *Parlement* of Paris was superseded by a new royal court and the provincial *parlements* were similarly eliminated. The long agonizing con-

[3] Aside from being the only direct check on the prerogative of the crown, the *parlement* protected abuses and hindered reform.

test heightened detestation of the crown and furnished ink for the pens of the *philosophes*.

By the time Louis XV died, the flood of literary criticism, appealing now to reason, now to emotion, had seriously sapped faith in the status quo. French society, as interpreted by the *philosophes*, was tied down to the ground like Gulliver by a myriad of tentacles and strings. But their publications had loosed the bonds; they had supplied future leaders against the monarchy with formulas and phrases and encouraged a passionate optimism in better days to come. Not least of their accomplishments, unconventional French authors had fostered reformist attitudes which touched foreign countries as well as their own. And they had kindled idealisms which would inspire disciples to heroic resolution.

BENEVOLENT DESPOTISM

Benevolent despotism is not an unpretty term. It implied, in the latter half of the eighteenth century, that kings and princes, influenced by French writings and by British ways and manners, would govern in keeping with principles of right reason. Certain European rulers not only read the books of the intellectuals of France but fraternized with them on terms of easy familiarity. An unmatched princely concern for the welfare of subjects followed. Notions of economic progress, of equality before the law and of administrative improvements captivated "philosophers" seated on thrones. And yet "enlightenment" never penetrated into one transcendently important area of government—foreign affairs. Exponents of benevolence in domestic matters unhesitatingly indulged in ruthless aggrandizement in international policy, as the partitions of Poland sufficiently showed.

That piece of brigandage in fact illustrated the supreme aim of benevolent princes. They wished fundamentally to strengthen the state as a military instrument; if, as a by-product, subjects benefited in a material or psychological sense so much the better. Beyond that, whatever was attempted was done from above without fostering initiative on the part of the governed. A supreme flaw in any variety of benevolent authoritarianism is that the schoolmaster does all the lessons for his pupils, to recall a simile coined by John Stuart Mill. Citizens might in truth be uplifted, but the uplifters showed neither respect nor affection for the objects of their solicitude.

More than that, the custom of hereditary succession to thrones carried no assurance that one progressively inclined ruler would be followed by a man of like temper. Frederick II of Prussia glibly dismissed contemporary princes as "illustrious imbeciles," and Thomas Jefferson thought "there is not a crowned head of Europe whose talents or merits would entitle him to be elected a vestryman by the people of any parish in America."

Those judgments, however, range wide of the mark. Rulers such as Joseph II of Austria, Catherine II of Russia and Frederick II himself were endowed with active and sensitive minds. All were indefatigable workers, devoted to public duty and many a prince in smaller countries displayed somewhat similar qualities. They sponsored changes which bridged the gulf between eighteenth-century absolutism and the trend toward representative government of the nineteenth.

The beau ideal of the enlightened autocrats was Frederick II, or the Great, tagged thus because of his military exploits. Calling himself the first servant of the state this exemplar of Spartanism methodically drove himself and his officialdom to heal the wounds caused by the Seven Years' War and to prepare for the next conflict. Frederick neatly explained his conception of duty in a letter of 1770 addressed to Voltaire: "My principal occupation is to combat ignorance and prejudice in the territories of which the accident of birth has made me the ruler, to enlighten minds, to refine manners, to make people as happy as human nature and my means allow."

Praiseworthy objectives indeed, but how was the philosophy actually applied? Himself indifferent in matters of religion, Frederick II tolerated all manner of religious sects. "In my kingdom," he proclaimed, "everyone can go to heaven in his own fashion." The gates of Prussia were flung open to the Jesuits after the

Joseph II of Austria

suppression of their order by the Pope, mediæval discriminations against the small Jewish minority were relaxed and these people were encouraged to merge with the Christian population.

On the economic front, virgin plowlands were opened to settlement by the drainage of marshes and the reclamation of wasteland, and the state fostered modest innovations in farming. Transportation facilities were improved by the digging of canals and deepening of harbors; taxes on goods moved inside the kingdom were eliminated. Where industry was concerned, Frederick II showed himself a narrow mercantilist, for tariffs were ordained to protect home producers, while mines, mills and foundries were fostered by state subventions and the monopolistic guilds were strengthened. These policies, which handicapped initiative and chilled individual enterprise, firmly established paternalism as a hallmark of the Prussian state.

A royal project for universal schooling fell far short of its goal, although standards were raised and schooling facilities were increased. Architecture, literature and science profited from the patronage of the king. And the Prussian legal structure was thoroughly overhauled, laws were codified and the iniquity of torture abolished except in cases of alleged treason and murder. The king insisted on efficient, honest and expert administration of justice and he had his way. On the other hand, training of subjects in the arts of government was wholly ignored and serfdom went untouched.

Of Frederick the Great, Voltaire remarked: "He is an exceptional man, very attractive at a distance." For his virtues—and his faults—"Old Fritz" in time was chosen as patron saint of Prussia and later of Germany. A cult grew up around the man, half legendary, half solidly grounded. Whenever in the future Germans experienced heavy hardships they invoked the memory of the glory and grandeur of the state when Frederick II wielded the scepter—and they drew inspiration from that.

More colorful and less successful than Frederick, whom he adopted as his hero, was Joseph II of Austria. Having drunk deeply at the wells of "enlightenment," this learned, serious, impulsive, fussy monarch undertook to transform his polyglot patrimony into an ideal empire. In pursuit of that ambition he rode roughshod over prejudices and privileges and raised up a pack of enemies. Undeterred, this doctrinaire and dogmatic son of the Age of Reason declared: "The father of a family who holds the welfare of his children at heart must not allow himself to be turned from a salutary course because of ill-judged complaints."

Reason dictated to the "revolutionary emperor" that his personal authority must be unlimited and his disparate peoples unified in spirit and in fact. Germans, Czechs, Hungarians (mostly Magyars), Poles, Italians, Belgians—all would be poured into a rigid rationalistic strait jacket. Accordingly, decrees were published making German the official tongue of the realm and creating uniform administrative services, without at all disturbing the cumbersome Hapsburg bureaucracy. The Hungarian diet was stripped of its ancient prerogatives and other agencies of local government were re-tailored.

As an expression of his humanity, Joseph II improved the codes of law. Penalties for wrongdoing were softened and torture was proscribed; all subjects were declared equal before the judge and tax collector, and censorship of publications was temporarily eased. More radical, the burdens of serfdom were lifted from the backs of the country people. In other phases of economic activity the reforms of Joseph II intimately paralleled the measures of Frederick II. Imperial game preserves were broken up and the spacious Prater on the edge of Vienna was converted into a playground for the public.

Drastic religious innovations by the "revolutionary emperor" provoked angry outcries. Full tolerance for all creeds was proclaimed, and Jews were freed from many hateful discriminations; they were ordered to take family names—hitherto they had been known merely as Jew Isaac, Jew Sarah and so on. Though styling himself the guardian of the Catholic Church, Joseph II struck savagely at papal authority. He wished to sever in fact the international connections of Catholicism entirely, and to reduce the Church in his own dominions to a pliant tool of the state. Clergymen were deprived of the tithe, they were ordered to study in seminaries under state auspices and to take an oath of loyalty to the emperor. Church courts were abolished and marriage was defined as a civil contract outside the jurisdiction of the Church. Christian holy days were cut down, public manifestations of religious piety and ornamentation in houses of worship were subjected to state regulation. One of every three monasteries and nunneries, institutions which Joseph II passionately despised, was bolted and barred.

It was the Emperor's professed ambition to rule over a literate population, and accordingly, universal and compulsory education was decreed. That measure was only feebly executed, but attendance in schools increased and the teaching function was withdrawn from churchmen.

No statesman, in all probability, could have weathered the storm unloosed by these far-ranging political, social and religious innovations. Wide sections of the population, injured vested interests taking the lead, demonstrated beyond any doubt that they preferred traditional ways and "unenlightened" institutions. Belgium revolted. Magyar oligarchs were on the verge of revolt. Churchmen were blatantly hostile. Economic changes depressed industrial establishments. The imperial treasury was emptied and the state debt soared. Conceivably, matters might have fallen out otherwise if Joseph II had been supported by a large and "enlightened" bourgeoisie such as existed in Bourbon France.

The "revolutionary emperor" went to his grave in 1790 with the House of Hapsburg tumbling down about him. His brother and successor, Leopold II, who had acquired a reputation for enlightenment as ruler of Italian Tuscany, promptly reversed imperial policies; appeasing concessions were granted to Church and national minorities. The career of Joseph II vividly demonstrated the perils which beset a capricious, autocratically minded "philosopher on the throne."

Catherine II of Russia also responded to the currents of enlightenment, tepidly to be sure. She engaged in correspondence with French intellectuals, read their books and paid them to advertise her liberal intentions. At one point she brought forth a project to modernize the Russian law codes and convoked an assembly of her peoples to discuss the proposal and to air grievances. Over two hundred meetings were held but the idea of reform never moved beyond the planning stage. Catherine improved medical and charitable institutions, it is true, and even toyed with a plan for public schooling. Yet, except for religious toleration, her liberalism was only skin-deep; instead of bettering the lot of the rural millions, she riveted serfdom upon Russia more firmly than before. Of the American Revolution and British constitutional government she strongly disapproved.

At the opposite end of the Continent, Spain experienced modest renovation under the direction of the industrious Charles III and a set of forward-looking ministers. Since her sixteenth-century heyday of eminence, Spain had slumped dismally, lived in a coma of dogmatism, outside the pale of the West, save for diplomatic involvements. Behind the lofty barrier of the Pyrenees, symbol of intellectual aloofness, the country had been ruled by indolent and fanatical monarchs, reinforced by a large and influential clergy, who owned a fifth of the acreage of the kingdom.

Late in the eighteenth century, the "iron curtain" was raised because of zeal for foreign culture and by economic and social innovations matching the other "enlightened" monarchies. Madrid, for example, was spruced up and Spanish industry was promoted by typical mercantilist expedients; restrictions, however, on trade with Spanish America were canceled. Codes of law were humanized, clerical exemption from taxes ceased and curbs were imposed upon the Court of the Inquisition. These reforms elicited heated criticisms from the privileged classes, and the successor of Charles III slipped back into familiar grooves.

Other European countries, Portugal, the Scandinavian nations and Italian principalities also witnessed spasms of reform. Enlightenment was in the air. In terms of world history, the ill-starred gestures at benevolent despotism in France command the greatest consideration.

BENEVOLENT DESPOTISM IN FRANCE

We are told that King Louis XVI and Queen Marie Antoinette, on learning of the passing of Louis XV, exclaimed "O God! Guide us, protect us; we are too young to reign." He was twenty, she nineteen. They had been married four years earlier as boy and girl, to seal the diplomatic alliance between France and Austria, homeland of the queen. The new monarch meant well and sincerely wished his subjects to be happy. He practiced the everyday Christian virtues, but as an actor on the royal stage he was not convincing. Fat, clumsy, unkempt in appearance, he seemed more a yokel than a scion of the royal House of Bourbon. His Majesty lacked majesty.

Not stupid—he enjoyed history and drama—Louis XVI came to power ignorant of France and the needs of the time. He much preferred outdoor sports or fiddling with keys and locks to grappling with tangled problems of statecraft. Mediocre and irresolute, he allowed vital state papers to go unread and blissfully dozed off in ministerial conferences where important decisions were being made. Talking to him was like trying to kindle soggy wood. An inept judge of the qualities of the men who advised him, he often followed the counsel of the frivolous queen. Plainly the stock of the Bourbon monarchy was about played out, had run to seed.

Beautiful, vivacious, charming Marie Antoinette looked like a queen to the day of her death. But her head was as light as her heart was gay. Improperly educated and mentally indolent she read next to nothing. This pleasure-loving child of Vienna acquired extravagant habits in clothes, jewels and cards; it was believed that her heavy losses at the gaming table were paid out of the royal treasury. The ugly epithet of Madame *Déficit* was pinned on to her. Vulgar jests and bawdy songs about the private life of the queen blackened her reputation; rumor had it that Louis XVI was not the father of her children.

Marie Antoinette labored under another cloud, for she was a princess of Austria, a country which Frenchmen had been taught to hate through generations of warfare. It was easy to believe that she would sell her adopted France down the river in time of grave crisis. After frittering valuable years away, Marie Antoinette experienced a change of heart, put childish things aside and devoted herself to pressing questions of state. Her adoring husband imprudently allowed the queen remarkably free range; almost invariably her interventions in public affairs turned out disastrously, and she caused the discharge of competent ministers in favor of incapable sycophants.

On the long calendar of reasons for the downfall of the old regime in France, the character

Marie Antoinette, Queen of France

of the royal pair and the dwindling prestige of the House of Bourbon stand high.

REFORMER TURGOT

For all his limitations, Louis XVI started his reign auspiciously by restoring the *Parlement* of Paris, suppressed in 1771, and selecting a corps of able ministers. Chief of them was Anne Robert Jacques Turgot, who was put in charge of the national economy as controller-general. As *intendant* in one of the poorer provinces, he had increased production and built up a reputation as a gifted and conscientious public servant, an administrator worthy of the best traditions of his country. *Philosophes* and economic reformers applauded his appointment to the ministry for he was one of their very own. Turgot courageously intended to transform the French kingdom into an "enlightened" monarchy, starting with a frontal assault upon urgent fiscal problems. France would be made prosperous by the stimulation of agriculture and commerce. To that end, the grain trade was freed from internal tolls, the monopolistic privileges of the guilds were withdrawn and the *corvée* was canceled—landlords were ordered to keep roads and bridges in repair.

Turgot also proposed revisions in the tax laws, so that the broadest financial backs would bear a reasonable proportion of state expenses. On the other side of the ledger, he chopped down royal expenditures and the large doles allotted to favored courtiers. Accompanying these measures were formal published statements on the evils they were designated to correct. In that fashion, knowledge about the flaws in French society was more widely diffused. Turgot's gallant efforts at political education received well-merited praise from his admirers, but their joy was short-lived.

Like Joseph II of Austria, Turgot moved too fast and too far. Vested interests whose pocketbooks were adversely affected or threatened by the innovations clamored loudly for the dismissal of the minister. The *Parlement* of Paris

Turgot

refused to register some of the ordinances that were presented and that proved Turgot's undoing. Louis XVI meekly bowed and in 1776 forced the minister to walk the plank; the hated *corvée* and the prerogatives of the guilds were forthwith revived. With his removal from the public stage France was deprived of the one statesman whose insight and foresight might have staved off the upheaval of 1789.

FINANCIAL PERPLEXITIES

Presently the crown entrusted the management of finances to a rich Geneva banker, Jacques Necker, respected as a shrewd financier. Sharing the general outlook of Turgot he nonetheless proceeded more tactfully. By petty economies and borrowings from foreign capitalists he gradually brought the budget into balance, which gratified all sections of French society. Unhappily however for financial stability, the Bourbon monarchy at that juncture allied itself with the revolting colonists in English America. Large military expenditures, equal to more than three years of French national revenues, disastrously upset the financial applecart.

Necker decided upon an unprecedented maneuver. He prepared and had published in 1781 a detailed analysis of the current financial plight and the prospects ahead. It was disclosed that income would cover ordinary expenditures, but fresh sources of funds would have to be tapped to meet war debts. The financial wizard recommended that donations to aristocrats from the public coffers should be pared down and, more unpalatable, that all citizens should be made equal before the tax gatherer. In a few weeks over 100,000 copies of this document had passed into circulation.

It was Turgot all over again. And as the crowning stroke, Necker proposed, as Turgot had done, that assemblies for the expression of the will of the governed should be created in each province. That proposal was too much for crown and courtiers and Necker was compelled to quit the ministry. Another milestone on the road to revolution had been passed.

The impact of the American Revolution upon France was not confined to the disruptive effects upon national finance. French arms had handsomely avenged earlier defeats by Great Britain, which buoyed up the prestige of the monarchy, though only momentarily. The triumph of liberty and natural rights in the New World, the unprecedented circulation of corrosive doctrines of republicanism and revolution, the flood of revolutionary anti-British propaganda which poured over France during the war excited the spirits of change-minded Frenchmen. The gallant Lafayette, lionized upon his return from America, appeared to be the finest personification of liberty and freedom.

Other French officers and soldiers who had fought in the trans-Atlantic struggle brought home stories about the freer and fuller life in the New World, and reports on experiments in kingless government that had been established. Might not equal resolution, some Frenchmen inquired, produce equally desirable changes in France? The achievements of the rebellious Yankees, beyond any doubt, helped to prepare the doom of the Bourbon autocracy.

In the meantime the unenviable task of trying to solve the financial problem had fallen to Charles de Calonne, nominee of Marie Antoinette. He borrowed on a lavish scale as long as lenders could be found, then resorted to monetary juggling acts, but the deficits persisted. Any suggestion of altering the tax laws was vetoed in advance by the *Parlement* of Paris. Calonne appreciated that France was slithering over the abyss into bankruptcy. Bluntly and without equivocation he presented the naked truth to the weakling who wore the crown. France, he declared, "is a kingdom where the richest class is the most lightly taxed, where privilege has upset all equilibrium . . . necessarily therefore it is a most imperfect kingdom, very full of abuses and in its present condition impossible to govern." Calonne prepared a schedule of changes on fiscal policies, which included a plan for taxing the landed properties of the privileged.

THE END OF THE ROAD

On Calonne's recommendation Louis XVI convoked in 1787 an assembly of leading aristocrats and churchmen to consult on taxation of their classes. For those dignitaries the finance minister laid bare the bleak fiscal situation, cleverly arguing that the remedy lay in getting monies from the exempted. The privileged nobles turned savagely upon Calonne, charging him with maladministration and venality and they succeeded in hounding him from office. The nobles stubbornly refused to contribute to the state and proudly refused to surrender their privileged status, their financial exemptions. Spurning moderate reform, they invited immoderate revolution. As the writer Chateaubriand put it, "The patricians began the Revolution, the plebeians finished it."

Furious controversy, meanwhile, had broken loose between the crown and the *Parlement* of Paris, the inveterate critic of the monarchy. By actively opposing payment of taxes and proclaiming that the French representative assembly, the Estates General, should be summoned, the judges attained the stature of popular heroes. Here indeed was a French version of the "no taxation without representation" doctrine.

Believing that they would be able to manipulate the Estates General, privileged nobles joined in the clamor for the calling of that body. Some of them even went so far as to incite rebellion among peasants and townspeople. Violent disturbances occurred in Brittany, while Paris and the larger towns witnessed grave street disorders. Pressure for the Estates General mounted in intensity and volume. Moneyman Necker accepted the office of finance minister again, on the condition that the Estates General would be resurrected. A royal order, accordingly, summoned the Estates

On May 5, 1789, the Estates General opened its sessions at Versailles.

General to convene in 1789. That decision amounted to an admission that the crown could no longer manage French affairs by itself. Initiative in questions of state quickly passed from the myopic aristocracy to the enthusiastic and aggressive middle classes.

Not since 1614 had a French national assembly, representing the three social categories, come together. Questions were raised about the organization and the competence of the body. For instance, how many deputies should each estate be assigned? Spokesmen of the Third Estate demanded that their class should have representation equal to the noble and clerical estates combined, and Louis XVI glumly conceded the point. Should deputies sit in separate houses, each group having one vote, or should the deputies assemble as a whole and make decisions by majority vote? That issue had not been answered when the Estates General convened.

So far as the suffrage right of the clergy was concerned, it was decided that parish priests should vote in elections for deputies of the clerical estate. Two out of three of the clerical deputies subsequently chosen were ordinary parish priests, familiar with the grievances and the desires of the Third Estate. Every taxpayer was eligible to vote for the Third Estate, which meant that the great mass of the countryfolk could participate. An indirect system of election was adopted, with the result that the bourgeoisie gained control; over half the deputies of the Third Estate were lawyers, with a sprinkling of nobles and churchmen.

Each deputy appeared at the meeting of the Estates General armed with written instructions, or *cahiers*, containing specific grievances of his class and district and recommendations for reform. All manner of changes were called for, abolition of royal absolutism topping the list. Loyalty to the crown, on the other hand, was expressed in affectionate phrases and evidences of republican sentiments were conspicuously absent. As a rule the *cahiers* asked for a written constitution, basic civil liberties, a French legislature that would have jurisdiction over public funds and a considerable degree of local home-rule.

Cahiers of the nobles called for the preservation of most of the special rights of that caste, but they expressed differing views on the subject of equality in taxation. Instructions to deputies of the Third Estate called vigorously for liberty, equality and the division of governmental power into separate executive, legislative and judicial departments. They demanded the suppression of the tithe and vestiges of serfdom. Foreshadowed in the bourgeois *cahiers* were later manifestations and attributes of militant French nationalism.

Popular emotions, meantime, were cut to the raw by distressing material wretchedness and rising excitement. Many urban workmen were thrown out of jobs in consequence of a commercial treaty with Britain which became operative in 1788, admitting large quantities of manufactured products, or because employers, rendered uneasy by the political ferment, shut up their shops. Aggravating the hardships, freaks of nature severely damaged grain crops in 1788 and the succeeding winter was the most bitter within memory of living men. Thousands of families were condemned to beggary or resorted to brigandage to obtain food and fuel. Droves of impoverished countryfolk crowded into the slums of Paris to swell the ranks of the restless, the embittered and the desperate.

Upon hapless, nervously excited Parisians, pugnacious preachers of a "new order" for France, hypnotized by their own lyrical phrases, set to work with energy and success. The worm-eaten edifice of the Old Regime, of the Bourbon autocracy, was tottering; it was about to crash and all Europe would echo to the explosion.

AS OF MAY, 1789

Glancing back over the course of France in the eighteenth century, to go no earlier, it is possible to understand how the country had reached the zero hour in the spring of 1789. Groups of contemporaries each had their own pet formula to account for the revolutionary temper of the time and each interpretation contained glimpses of truth.

Admirers of the *philosophes* ascribed the

malaise to the refusal of the crown to pursue "enlightened" principles. Judges in *Parlement* pointed to the arbitrary whims of the king, while employers were sure the business depression was the greatest source of evil. Conservatives blamed the explosive writings of unconventional authors; ministers of state stressed the incorrigible obtuseness of the upper nobility; spokesmen of the peasants dwelt upon the vestigial remains of feudalism and unfair taxation.

Varied abuses and conditions, in other words, had set the stage for far-reaching change. Profound and widespread resentment against things as they were had accumulated because of social inequalities, unequal taxation, restrictions on business, arbitrary and inefficient government, wretched standards of living and religious intolerance.

Many Frenchmen, especially of the middle classes, had been made acutely conscious of the diseases in their society by brilliant and critically-minded authors. They had pleaded for change in the name of reason or emotion, some of them insisting that Britain and America had nobler institutions and a happier way of life. Talk of the absurdity of the divine right of kings to rule, talk of natural rights, of liberty and equality, talk of constitutionalism, democracy and republicanism had been heard in France for many years. The time to translate words into deeds had arrived.

Friends of the status quo in France were more disunited and weaker in 1789 than in earlier periods of grave crisis. The aristocracy had stiffly and successfully resisted ministerial proposals for moderate reform instead of obediently acceding to the wishes of the king. The erratic mediocrity on the throne lacked the personal authority to bend unruly nobles to his will.

Nor could the crown rely with confidence upon the armed forces to uphold the established order, for some of the soldiers were imbued with yearnings for reform. Dissension existed, too, in clerical ranks between humble parish priests and their ecclesiastical superiors. The inability of the government to overcome the desperate financial difficulties by traditional devices provided the immediate occasion for sweeping changes.

For all its shortcomings and imbecilities France of the eighteenth century exhibited much that was admirable—the manner of living, that is, which prevailed before the revolutionary onrush of industrialism. In a vein of deep nostalgia, Talleyrand, a leading figure of the French Revolution, wrote: "He who has not lived in the years near to 1789 does not know how sweet life can be."

FOR FURTHER STUDY

ALBERT SOREL, *Europe under the Old Regime* (partial Eng. trans., Los Angeles, 1947)

ALEXIS C. DE TOCQUEVILLE, *The Old Regime and the Revolution* (Eng. trans., new ed., New York, 1955) PAPERBACK

HENRI E. SÉE, *Economic and Social Conditions in France during the Eighteenth Century* (Eng. trans., New York, 1927)

LEO GERSHOY, *From Despotism to Revolution, 1763–1789* (New York, 1944) PAPERBACK

FRANZ FUNCK-BRENTANO, *The Old Regime in France* (Eng. trans., New York, 1929)

EDWARD J. LOWELL, *The Eve of the French Revolution* (Boston, 1892)

SAUL K. PADOVER, *The Revolutionary Emperor, Joseph II of Austria* (New York, 1934)

GLADYS S. THOMSON, *Catherine the Great and the Expansion of Russia* (New York, 1950)

DOUGLAS DAKIN, *Turgot and the Ancien Regime in France* (London, 1939)

LOUIS S. MERCIER, *The Waiting City, Paris, 1782–88* (2nd ed., Philadelphia, 1933).

MATTHEW S. ANDERSON, *Europe in the Eighteenth Century* (New York, 1962)

ALBERT GOODWIN, ed., *The European Nobility of the Eighteenth Century* (London, 1953)

ELINOR G. BARBER, *The Bourgeoisie in Eighteenth Century France* (Princeton, 1955)

CHAPTER X

REVOLUTIONARY FRANCE

Symbols and mottoes of the Revolution

A DECADE OF REVOLUTIONS

IN THE decade that opened in 1789 France experienced a succession of as convulsive and depth-shaking tempests as ever beat upon a nation. When broad and deep innovations are actually effected in institutions and in attitudes, as was the case in France in these years, then the change constitutes an authentic revolution. As after the more far-reaching Russian Revolution of the twentieth century, so following the French upheaval of the eighteenth, world civilization was never quite the same. Forces emanating from France circled the globe, conquering time and space. "Even today in the middle of the twentieth century," concludes a distinguished American specialist on the French Revolution, "despite all that has happened in the lifetime of men not yet old, and even here in America or in any other part of the world in which the countries of Europe no longer enjoy their former commanding position, it is still possible to say that the French Revolution at the end of the eighteenth century was the great turning point of modern civilization." [1]

Ordinary Frenchmen, not to speak of French intellectuals, still discuss the events of the revolutionary decade with asperity, emotional fervor and conviction. Political "parties" and much else in contemporary France reflect, in a measure, the swirling currents of the late eighteenth century. It was a full century after 1789 before the dust had settled and historical scholarship had reached something like a consensus on what had actually happened.

As so often with major historical developments, differences in interpretation persist. Controversy, for instance, over the character and conduct of Mirabeau, Robespierre and Danton, to mention no other prominent revolutionary worthies, still rumbles on. Certain historians have condemned the Revolution for the atrocities that attended it and the woolly aspira-

[1] R. R. Palmer, Preface p. v, of *The Coming of the French Revolution* by Georges Lefebvre (Princeton, 1947).

tions of leading spokesmen. Other writers pronounced the end result praiseworthy, condoning the physical excesses as the inescapable accompaniment of building a better order; still others have discovered France's finest hour in the short-lived dictatorship of Robespierre (1794).

The very complexity of revolutionary France, the moving and dramatic episodes blending the heroic and the tragic, romantic only in retrospect and at a safe distance, have invited and sustained contradictory judgments. From one angle of approach the decade may be thought of as having a first phase lasting to 1792 when the teachings of Voltaire and Montesquieu were in the ascendant and changes were introduced that have endured. In 1792 the period of Rousseau began, characterized by a sharp break with traditions and a "war of all people on all sovereigns," which led into the dictatorship of Napoleon and the wider diffusion of "French ideas" across Europe.

The generous aspirations and benign spirit of the Rights of Man in the first stage contrast strongly with the frenzy of a nation in arms as the way to national salvation and European regeneration in the second part. In the first phase public power was shared by the monarch with elected representatives of the nation; from the autumn of 1792 to 1799 France was a republic, and more or less a democracy.

Whatever the approach, the creed of 1789 was incorporated in the immortal slogan of Liberty, Equality and Fraternity. These terms, alas, did not carry precisely the same connotations throughout the revolutionary decade; they were variously interpreted at different times. Ideas are ever tantalizingly elusive and to them almost always a certain ambiguity is attached. Fundamentally, however, the spirit of 1789 reflected middle class ideals and aspirations. Liberty carried the implication that the conduct of the government should be shared by chosen representatives of the nation. It implied basic civil liberties, such as freedom of speech and press, freedom of conscience and opinion, freedom from governmental interference in business and security of property.

The principle of equality asserted that everyone regardless of birth or wealth, sex or race, color or religion was endowed with certain natural rights, such as equality before the law. It accented respect for the human personality, condemned serfdom and special privileges for churchmen and nobility. Holding that all blood was alike ancient, equality insisted that careers should be open to talents.

Fraternity is the most difficult of the revolutionary trinity to clarify. It referred particularly to the bonds of sentiment and conviction uniting members of the French nationality and is cousin to the words nationalism and patriotism. More exactly, a patriot was a "right-thinking" bourgeois who wished Frenchmen to be prosperous and contented through the application of the teachings of the "Enlightenment," and who desired France to be great and respected. At the beginning of the revolutionary epoch, fraternity possessed something of a cosmopolitan quality, untainted by impulsive militant extravagance; the flags of Britain and the United States were gaily hoisted alongside of the French. But an impassioned, mystical nationalism seized the country when it engaged in a holy crusade against domestic enemies and foreign governments; then, only the revolutionary tricolor was flaunted.

FRANCE OBTAINS A PARLIAMENT

At the outset of May, 1789, deputies of the Estates General convened at Versailles in the regal elegance of Louis XIV's grand palace. After hearing Mass and a sermon, the deputies were welcomed by King Louis XVI in an atmosphere of friendliness and mutual good will. The crown expected that the Estates would revise existing tax legislation, impose limitations on free expression in the press, recommend a few minor political reforms and then dissolve. It seemed as though the court had said that the Bourbon government was unable to solve the desperate financial plight and had tossed the problem into the lap of elected representatives of the nation, of the three estates.

Leaders in the Third Estate had opinions of

their own as to what the gathering should in fact accomplish. Not that they were antipathetic to the monarchy or king, for the Third Estate declared in an address to the king, "Sire, your faithful Commons will never forget what they owe their kings; never will they forget that natural alliance of Throne and People against the various aristocracies, the power of which can only be established on the ruins of royal authority and public happiness."

The Third Estate demanded that deputies of the three estates should sit jointly and make decisions by majority vote, not in three separate bodies, each having one vote. If that medieval custom had been applied the Commoners would, of course, have been at the mercy of the Lords and Clergy. The crown hesitated to acquiesce in the demand. Signs of rising discontent multiplied in Paris and the provinces.

On their own responsibility deputies of the Third Estate, reinforced by fragments of the clergy and the aristocracy, after more than a month of maneuver and delay, adopted a set of epochal resolutions. Boldly they announced (June 17) themselves to be a National Assembly and invited deputies of the other estates to sit with them. They declared that only taxes authorized by the assembly were valid and they approved the celebrated "tennis court" oath, pledging "never to separate . . . until the constitution of the kingdom shall be . . . established on secure foundations. . . ." They asserted that representatives of the nation were immune from arrest. As plainly as could be, the self-constituted National Assembly had proclaimed its independence of royal absolutism.

A substantial majority of the deputies from the clergy and a fifth of the representatives of the nobles presently took seats in the National Assembly. That body and only that body, as

The taking of the "Tennis Court" oath

even the weak-willed king came to perceive, could obtain the funds which the government so desperately required. Louis XVI, instead of invoking force to disperse the Assembly, tamely submitted to what had happened, recognized the authority of the National Assembly to legislate for the kingdom and to draw up a constitution. The three estates were instructed to combine in a single united parliament of some 1,200 deputies. Advocates of representative government and of the equality of all classes before the law had scored a resounding victory. It remained to consolidate the triumph in actual pieces of legislation.

Mirabeau

MIRABEAU, STATESMAN

Easily the most influential figure in this phase of revolutionary history was an extraordinary and rebellious scion of the nobility, Count Gabriel H. Mirabeau, sent to Paris as a deputy by the Third Estate. Massive in physique as in personality, his face scarred by smallpox and his leonine head crowned by a great shock of hair, Mirabeau very definitely stood out from the crowd in the National Assembly. Noted for his colorful and scandalous past, talented with pen and tongue, he aspired to make a mark for himself in public life—and he succeeded. For nearly two years he contrived to steer the fierce storm of French political convulsions, as became a man whose obtuse father had ridiculed him as "Sir Hurricane."

The political outlook of Mirabeau was colored by his liking for British institutions which he had observed on the spot. He had written, for instance, that "the king is hired and he who pays has the right to dismiss him who receives payment." And yet he thought that the French kingship should be preserved though subjected to the will of the nation as expressed by elected representatives. Keenly aware of the urgency of far-reaching changes, a sincere advocate of liberty in politics, in economics and in expression, a tireless worker and resourceful parliamentary tactician, Mirabeau fathered practical measures to satisfy the needs of the hour.

Statesman that he was, calm in moments of passionate turbulence, Mirabeau commanded the intense devotion of disciples in the Assembly and the admiration of millions of ordinary Frenchmen. His untimely death from natural causes at the age of forty-two, in April of 1791, robbed France of a persuasive and moderate leader, though it is unlikely that he could have much longer channeled the French tempest in the monarchical stream. He died as he had lived, dramatically, at the zenith of his short span of glory.

STORMING OF THE BASTILLE

While the Estates General was being transformed into the National Assembly, social discipline in Paris had greatly relaxed. Among the underprivileged elements, wageworkers, small shopkeepers and newcomers from the countryside, habitually spoken of as the mob, restlessness had increased. Hungry and unemployed men, in particular, could readily be incited to violence by bourgeois elements for their own ends or by popular demagogues. Disaffection

The assault on the Bastille

among soldiers and the police aggravated the uneasiness in the historic capital.

Sentiments in Paris were angrily enflamed by reports that the king, egged on by aristocratic courtiers, was mobilizing regiments of foreign mercenaries. Would these armed forces be employed to disperse the National Assembly or to overawe agitated and undisciplined Paris? Whatever the purpose, the massing of soldiers on royal order accentuated the rebellious mood in capital and country. Wealthy holders of government bonds, besides, suspected that the crown might repudiate the national debt, a hypothesis that seemed to be confirmed by the replacement of the respected finance minister Necker by an aristocratic sycophant of the crown.

Against that background, the Parisian masses went on the rampage, quite spontaneously. After pillaging buildings containing arms, they assailed the frowning Bastille fortress, symbol of Bourbon tyranny and oppression, and at least potentially a rallying point for operations against malcontents. Without much difficulty, though at the cost of a hundred lives, the attackers captured the Bastille, murdered the commandant and paraded his head and those of other victims on pikes.

That sanguinary episode heralded the beginning of physical violence in the Revolution. The frightened court abandoned all thought of unloosing troops against the new order and terrified aristocrats, among them the brothers and other relatives of the king, betook themselves to foreign parts. For French loyalists, these émigrés were traitors and upon them was saddled the blame, thereafter, for everything that went awry in France. On the other side, the storming of the Bastille inspirited elements sympathetic to enlightened change and a "new deal" for France. The day of the event, July 14, was adopted as the major national holiday of the French people.

To preserve order, middle class groups in Paris took control of local administration and similar action followed in other French towns. A National Guard was created to police Paris, recruiting its personnel from the sober middle classes. Lafayette, a moderate in the National Assembly and greatly esteemed as the intimate confidant of the revolutionary Washington, assumed command of the Guard, which was able temporarily to still lawless passions.

Paris seethed, nonetheless, with nervousness and political excitement. To carry on discussion and propagate agitation, political societies were founded, such as the Jacobins, the Cordeliers and the Girondins. Most important of all was the powerful Jacobin Club, which from headquarters in Paris directed some 400 chapters planted throughout the kingdom. Jacobins came principally from the comfortably situated middle classes and responded to the clarion calls of earnest, dynamic young lawyers.

A veritable cult of Rousseau prevailed in these clubs, and by the Jacobins this dreamy sentimentalist was chosen as patron saint. His *Social Contract* pushed into the best-seller class, being reprinted seven times in 1790–1791 and almost twice as often in the ensuing three years. Agitation for a republican scheme of government, such as Rousseau appeared to recommend, kept increasing. And inflammatory news-sheets, notably Marat's vitriolic "Friend of the People," belabored opponents of far-reaching changes in French life. Monarchical prestige dwindled under criticism, as the National Assembly grappled with the reconstruction of national institutions.

RURAL REVOLT

Events in Paris could scarcely have failed to excite reverberations in the countryside. Even before the assault upon the Bastille peasant outbreaks had taken place, but far more violent escapades filled the last weeks of July. Wide areas of rural France were gripped by a weird psychological fixation, tagged the "Great Fear," which was fanned by alarmist rumors that brigand bands were preparing to ravage villages and that aristocratic conspirators were plotting against the revolutionary order.

Those dreads piled upon wretchedness, hunger for land and hatred of feudal exactions led to spontaneous, unorganized movements against the rural status quo. In some areas the spirit of revolt flamed into a veritable jacquerie marked by pillaging of country seats and even the murder of some nobles. Hoary documents reciting the obligations of peasants to their lords were gleefully put to the torch; old game laws were joyously transgressed. Defiant peasants even fought open battles with improvised police forces; many were slain, more were imprisoned. Rural France in a fortnight of direct action erased the lingering encumbrances of feudalism. It remained for the National Assembly to give legal sanction to what the peasants had done.

Once freed of ancient burdens and soon the recipients of more land, the peasantry in the main were content to return to the quiet, timeless, stereotyped customs of the countryside. Since they were too conservative to forsake farming conventions, Paris and other cities suffered food shortages; for applying crop rotation at least one enterprising cultivator lost his head. Aside from land, the over-arching interest of the peasant was the Church. Embittered by decisions of the National Assembly which cut down the privileges and the prestige of Catholicism, rural France rallied round its spiritual shepherds in an impressive manner.

ACCOMPLISHMENTS OF THE NATIONAL ASSEMBLY

Deputies of the National Assembly, meantime, had initiated deliberations which would run on for two years and bring to pass an immense range of constructive destruction in French government, church and society. Tidings of the riotous excesses in the countryside reached Paris and in an attempt to stem the unrest, the Assembly on the historic night of August 4, 1789, approved a sheaf of acts which formally abolished ancient inequalities.

Noblemen surrendered their authority over the peasants, their hunting privileges, their monopolies on grain mills and wine-presses. Manorial dues were canceled, though the peasant beneficiaries were expected to compensate the nobles at market value for these losses—a proviso that was dropped in 1793. The small serf minority was wholly emancipated. Guild monopolies and the universal obligation to pay a tithe to the Church were abolished. As an eye-witness of the hectic session remarked, "A contagion of sentimental feeling carried the Assembly away." For most practical purposes the social heritage of feudalism had been destroyed; France had taken long strides along the road to social equality.

Next in line, the Assembly enunciated the fundamental political rights which every Frenchman possessed by reason of the fact that he was a Frenchman. In composing this "Declaration of the Rights of Man and the Citizen" the Assembly was influenced by similar professions on the relation of man to society in Great Britain and the United States; Thomas Jefferson, then minister of the United States to France, readily proffered advice. In its completed form of seventeen affirmations, the Declaration was shot through and through with the teachings of Rousseau on equality and popular sovereignty. It enshrined the things which the individual Frenchman wanted and expected from society. Called the death certificate of the old regime, the Declaration was the most authoritative and comprehensive summary of the spirit of 1789.

It asserted, first, that "men are born and remain free and equal in rights." The purpose of government was stated to be "the preservation of the natural and imprescriptible rights of man," itemized as "liberty, property, security, and resistance to oppression." Liberty was defined as "freedom to do all that does not injure others." "The free communication of thoughts and opinions is one of the most precious rights of man." "All citizens," read another clause, "have the right to assist" in making laws. Sovereignty resided in the nation. Safeguards of civil liberty were proclaimed; and religious toleration was assured, though in guarded language so as not to alienate the parish clergy. Property was described as "a sacred and inviolable right" that could not be taken away without due process of law and just indemnification to the owner.

These daring assertions in the Declaration cut across deeply rooted French traditions, and they were to become commonplaces of European society. Sometimes in modified form, this creedal statement appeared as the preamble to constitutions of France and other countries which were adopted in the nineteenth century.

Critics have challenged the Declaration as a bourgeois masterpiece which slurred over or bypassed some really fundamental issues. It concentrated too narrowly on political rights to the neglect of social and economic rights. It was silent on such matters as education and "freedom from want" and therefore was inadequate as society passed from bourgeois individualism into the age of mass industrialism. From another side, the Declaration has been assailed as containing, paradoxically, the seed of totalitarianism in a clause reading, "The principle of all sovereignty resides essentially in the nation; no corporation, no individual can exercise any authority not expressly emanating from it." That clause made nonsense of the principle of the separation of powers expressed elsewhere in the Declaration.

REMOVAL OF GOVERNMENT TO PARIS

Physical hardships among the underprivileged of Paris, in the meantime, had grown harsher. The ranks of the jobless had swollen, food was in short supply while prices soared. Starry-eyed journalists enflamed popular discontents to white heat. And a fresh crop of rumors circulated, for which there were substantial foundations, to the effect that aristocratic France was planning a military coup to restore the old regime.

Supposing that food could somehow be procured from the Court at Versailles, crowds of angry demonstrators, many of them hungry housewives, plodded out to the palace, smashed into the quarters of the royal family and clamored for bread. On the urging of Lafayette, who had arrived on the scene with detachments of the National Guard, the king reluctantly agreed to take up residence in Paris. It was a motley array, loyal nonetheless, that paraded Louis XVI, Marie Antoinette and their son in triumph to the capital and installed them in the old royal residence of the Tuileries. None knew better than the king that he was now the prisoner of Paris and subject to popular intimidation.

Equally, the deliberations of the National Assembly were transferred to a riding school close by the royal apartments. That body could be coerced by the Paris masses and their cold-blooded leaders and thus lost something of its freedom in discussion and decision. Thenceforth government could not afford to disregard, save at its peril, the wishes of the "mob."

Under the gaze of galleries full of excitable spectators, the deputies met urgent financial requirements of the government by declaring the valuable properties of the Church to be state property. Public finances, the immediate occasion for the calling of the Estates General, had staggered from bad to worse. Income from old taxes dwindled to nothing and new levies produced only scanty returns. On motion of Bishop Talleyrand, an unprincipled self-seeking chameleon in ecclesiastical clothes, the Assembly seized church lands; then it issued bonds to obtain sorely needed funds, and later printed paper money (*assignats*) secured by the expropriated land.[2]

By these stratagems the financial requirements of the state were satisfied for the time being, but the temptation to print more and more currency proved irresistible and in the end its value tumbled to zero. As for the church lands they passed very largely into the possession of the peasantry, with the remainder held by middle class men. As compensation for the confiscation of ecclesiastical properties, the state promised to pay modest salaries to the clergy and to maintain the churches. In that way churchmen were made dependent upon the revolutionary order for their living, which was not displeasing to the rank and file of the parish priests, however unpalatable to the higher clergy

The National Assembly, many of whose members were infected with the rationalistic temper of Voltaire, adopted other measures which whittled down the authority and the prerogatives of the Church. Monastic societies, for example, were disbanded and their buildings closed. No longer would the Catholic clergy be treated as a separate caste or estate but like laymen they would be subject to civil laws and state courts. And the old ecclesiastical right to ban distasteful publications was formally taken away. In the summer of 1790, the "Civil Constitution of the Clergy" was enacted into law. Thereby a third of the Catholic bishoprics was suppressed, and clergymen, high and low, would in the future be elected by all citizens regardless of their religious opinions. Papal jurisdiction over French church administration ceased, though Rome would continue to rule on faith and morals.

When the Pope repudiated these innovations and threatened to excommunicate any Catholic who complied with them, the Assembly retaliated by ordering every churchman to take an oath to "the King, the Law, and the Nation." The Pope, in turn, commanded the clergy not to murmur the prescribed oath. Churchmen, plainly, were impaled on the horns of a dilemma and both prongs were sharp. Some of the clergy chose to obey the state, but over half the parish priests and all but seven of the bishops preferred to abide by the higher mandates of the Papacy. Hundreds of clerics emigrated to nearby countries or overseas and state agents struggled to replace recalcitrant clergy with priests who had taken the oath.

The Civil Constitution of the clergy provoked not only schism, but civil war too. Priests loyal to Rome incited their flocks, especially peasants and women, against the new order, even to the point of armed resistance. And Louis XVI, genuinely religious as he was, considered acceptance of the Civil Constitution as an act of gross impiety. The clerical oath was altogether too much for him to stomach; he cast about for ways and means to reverse the revolutionary torrent.

Other laws which reflected the mood of the "Enlightenment" were crowded through the turbulent Assembly. Legal processes, for one thing, were drastically overhauled. Hitherto an accused Frenchman could not engage a lawyer, was ignorant even of the charges against him and was obliged to answer questions put by a judge preparing the case. The case was then handed up to a panel of judges who arrived at

[2] Crownlands and estates of the émigré aristocrats were also expropriated.

a verdict and imposed the penalty, if the accused were found guilty.

The Assembly swept away the old law courts and decreed that judges should be elected. Lawyers might defend an accused man and he was no longer forced to give evidence against himself. For criminal trials the British jury institution was introduced, and the penal code was humanized by eliminating torture and arbitrary imprisonment. Types of crime punishable by death were greatly cut down.

For the sake of uniformity and simplicity the pattern of local government was reconstructed. Instead of the old provinces, France was carved up into *départements*, approximately equal in size. Below that unit elected bodies were set up to look after local affairs without significant control by authorities in Paris. Laissez faire notions of economics inspired the dissolution of the ancient guilds. Citizens were free to enter any craft or profession if they fulfilled state regulations; government inspection of manufacturing processes stopped. At the same time it was declared unlawful to organize combinations of wage earners or of employers.

KING AND CONSTITUTION

Prisoners in the Tuileries, Louis XVI and his queen grew more and more hostile to the course the National Assembly was pursuing. Rumors of the modest role to be assigned the king under the constitution that was being drafted, together with the church laws, spurred Louis XVI to a desperate resolve. He and his family would flee to the northeast, put himself at the head of the French armed forces and foreign troops there, march back to Paris and undo the work of the Assembly.

Mirabeau, most sagacious royal adviser, had earlier urged the king to escape to Normandy and from there exert pressure upon the Assembly and Paris. But in the spring of 1791 Mirabeau died and in June the Bourbon family in disguise made a dash to the east. They reached Varennes within a few miles of Germany before their identity was discovered. They were seized and briskly returned to the Tuileries palace. The king had unmistakably and imprudently identified himself with the émigré traitors and by so doing brought himself to the threshold of the guillotine. The cause of republicanism, which for months had been gathering momentum, was given an immense thrust forward.

Friends of the republican idea arranged a mass demonstration on the Champs de Mars in Paris in July, 1791, to demand the deposition of the untrustworthy king. National Guards, a distinctly bourgeois formation, Lafayette commanding, fired into the crowd, killing several participants. Republican agitators fled abroad or went into hiding, but the "massacre" far from drowning republicanism heightened its popularity, and by the same token further impaired the declining prestige of the monarchy.

Ever since July of 1789 the National Assembly had been known officially as the Constituent Assembly, evidence that its main responsibility was to draw up a constitution for the nation. Discussions on the content of the document paralleled to a remarkable degree the debates in France after the Second World War. In tune with the "enlightened" philosophy, the constitution-makers conceived of their fellowmen as naturally good, requiring only a minimum of political control. Against the strong disapproval of Mirabeau, the Assembly decided that governmental powers should be rigidly separated; no cabinet, for example, would act as intermediary between the crown and the legislature.

The Constitution of 1791 retained the kingship but severely curbed its scope. By exercise of the veto the king might temporarily block laws approved by the legislature but no more. The legislature consisted of a single house of nearly 750 deputies, chosen by adult males who paid taxes equivalent to at least three days' labor. Although the electorate was much broader than in Britain at the time, low-income groups were excluded, which infuriated ardent believers in full manhood suffrage. Only the legislature could initiate laws and it had to assent to any bill before it could become valid. By an absurdly foolish decision the Constituent Assembly forbade the election of any of its members to the new law-making body.

Substantially, the Constitution announced

that France had become a limited monarchy, not much more than a crowned republic. It promised to cater to the wishes of the bourgeoisie whose representatives had drafted the new instrument of government. France has known many patterns of government since 1791, but each of them has been defined in a written constitution in keeping with the revolutionary precedent. After Louis XVI had consented to the Constitution, the Constituent Assembly voted a general amnesty and then disbanded. It seemed as though the Revolution had run its course and that France was ready to go forward in an orderly and disciplined manner. Certain aristocrats who had fled abroad confidently returned to their fatherland.

Actually France in these unsettled times required a strong government and that had been denied her. As has often been the case, one French faction felt that too many and too sweeping innovations had been introduced, while an opposing element was aggrieved because the Revolution had not gone far enough. France, then, as so frequently since, was a house divided against itself. The constructive stage of the Revolution had been crossed; there followed a season of international war and anarchical violence which smoothed the path to the iron rule of Napoleon Bonaparte.

THE LEGISLATIVE ASSEMBLY

The constitutional monarchy set up in 1791 lasted less than a year. The royal court thoroughly detested the parliamentary regime as did the bulk of the aristocracy and most of the clergy. To the legislature was elected a majority of republicans, men unseasoned in practical politics and incapable of coping effectively with grave issues of state.

Factional rivalries ran high in the Legislative Assembly which was divided into Right, Center and Left groupings. These terms, which have been woven into the Western political vocabulary, derived from the fact that deputies sat in a semi-circle facing the chairman, in accordance with their general outlook on public questions. The Right attracted deputies who wished either to return to the pre-revolutionary ways or to see no more changes, friends of the crown,

Danton

and this faction grew progressively weaker. In the Center sat partisans of moderate reform, while a majority of the law-makers lined up on the Left, republicans and democrats, sympathetic to far-reaching changes.[3]

The Left, moreover, comprised two disparate and increasingly antagonistic cliques. Much the larger group was called the Girondins, spokesmen of the provinces, noble idealists and elegant orators, but short on discipline and on leaders capable of leading. The Girondins understood ideas better than they understood human nature.

Competing with them were the deputies of the "Mountain," backed by extremist political clubs and radical newspapers of Paris and lesser cities. Ardent disciples of Jean Jacques Rousseau, these men were the professed and professional champions of the wretched city folk. At their head were two stalwart Jacobins, Georges-Jacques Danton and Maximilien Robespierre,

[3] As rough and ready synonyms, Right may be thought of as conservative, Center as moderate, and Left as radical.

bourgeois lawyers both, spokesmen of the urban masses by choice, domineering, skillful pilots of men. The main strength of Danton, a dramatically convincing orator, lay in the hold he acquired over Parisian slum-dwellers. A big man, simple in his tastes, his heart was of like qualities; audiences lashed to fury by his eloquence indulged in reckless and bloody escapades.

Robespierre, a trim, precise, doctrinaire little fellow, had chosen Rousseau as his personal god and regarded his writings as inspired, inerrant scripture. What Marx later meant to Lenin of Russian revolutionary fame, Rousseau meant to Robespierre. His sympathies were warmly enlisted on the side of the unfortunate and the oppressed; and for his faith he fought like a tiger. With the Jacobin society as his ready instrument, Robespierre dreamed of transforming France into an austerely ideal social and political democracy.

Cleavages within the Assembly on domestic matters were soon dwarfed by issues of foreign relations. War broke out in April, 1792, between France and a continental coalition, which dramatically altered the course of world history. Articulate elements in German Europe had greeted the French events of 1789 with considerable enthusiasm; "freedom fever" seized many cities. German governments, though not at all for the same reasons, applauded changes in France which, it was reasoned, would inescapably weaken the monarchy in power politics—in the interrelated calculations of diplomacy and war.

At the outset of the Revolution, Austria was preoccupied by war with Turkey, upsetting internal tumult and diplomatic maneuvering over the last fragment of Poland. French innovations promised to encourage agitation for kindred changes in central Europe, a prospect that frightened the ruling classes of Austria and Prussia—not to mention smaller German principalities and Catherine II of Russia. Calculating diplomatists, moreover, scented a unique opportunity to pounce upon coveted parcels of French territory and Austrian emperors were apprehensive about Marie Antoinette, their relative.

In August of 1791 the Courts of Austria and Prussia published a celebrated Declaration of Pillnitz, asserting that the welfare of the French king was a matter of concern to all European rulers and hinting at the invocation of armed force if necessary to uphold the authority of the Bourbon crown. Many Frenchmen, already deeply incensed against Austria and Prussia for sheltering refugee aristocrats, interpreted the Pillnitz pronouncement as an insult and a threat. Presently, Austria and Prussia entered into an alliance pointed against France.

Inside France, war fervor, charged with emotions and ideological tensions, had seized nearly every political grouping. At the royal court, it was reasoned that a victorious foreign war would enable the crown to recover its historic prerogatives. Friends of the constitution, on their part, argued that war would consolidate the new France, while bellicose Girondins favored war in the expectation that it would smooth the way to a republic of the sort they wanted. Only a handful of Jacobins resisted the pressure to take up arms. Robespierre prophetically forecast that international war would lead unerringly to the despotism of a triumphant general.

Without waiting for foreign foes to initiate hostilities, the Legislative Assembly plumped for war against Austria by an almost unanimous vote. Thus a titanic struggle started in April of 1792 which, with slight interruptions, would keep Europe and the wider world in unprecedented convulsion for twenty-three years. As one consequence the doctrines of revolutionary France would be widely disseminated across the Old World.

DOWNFALL OF THE MONARCHY

French troops entered upon the contest with dash, thrusting deep into Belgium, only to be promptly hurled back. France in fact was hardly prepared for serious military operations; soldiers were indifferently trained, many veteran officers had emigrated and the court circle treacherously and treasonably disclosed campaign plans to the enemy. To the consternation of French patriots, Austrian and Prussian

The taking of the Tuileries Palace, August, 1792

troops moved across France with Paris as their objective. A manifesto issued by the commanding general, the Duke of Brunswick, implied that the invaders were partisans of the Bourbon House and would inflict fearful punishment upon Paris if the royal family were harmed. Unwittingly that obtuse utterance converted enthusiasm for the Revolution into passion for the French fatherland, and cost Louis XVI his throne.

In August of 1792, Parisian crowds, mobilized by Jacobin zealots, stormed the royal palace and butchered protective guardsmen, sacrificing a thousand lives in the operation. Straightaway the king was suspended, which foreshadowed the end of the experiment in constitutional monarchy. Louis XVI and his family were cast into a medieval dungeon. To manage French public affairs, a new legislature would be chosen by manhood suffrage.

Actual authority in Paris had passed to the municipal government—the Commune—now dominated by Jacobins. It was presently learned that the foreign invader had seized the key fortress of Verdun, which opened the way to Paris. Would royalists in the capital stage an insurrection to aid the foreigners in taking Paris? Perhaps. To forestall that possibility, the Commune filled jails with royalist sympathizers and suspects and then turned them over to drumhead courts for summary trial. First and last, upwards of 1,200 victims were killed in cold blood by fanatical Parisians. That terrible September purge caused a revulsion of feeling abroad, shattered the optimistic faith that the French were traveling the right road to the heavenly city on this earth.

French armies meanwhile had reversed the ignominious record of the first chapter of the war. In September, at Valmy, in the rough Argonne forest region where American doughboys gave a good account of themselves in the First World War, the French halted the slow-moving tide of veteran Teutonic soldiers. The enemy retreated, the French following up the success by conquering Belgium, and pushing into the Left Bank of the Rhine in Germany; General Charles-Francois Dumouriez, in supreme command of French war energies, was acclaimed as a national hero. It soon became evident that the new France, like Bourbon France before it, was striving to make the Rhine the boundary of the country.

The war took on the character of a holy crusade to diffuse revolutionary principles. Propagandist decrees promised neighboring peoples that they could rely upon French assistance if they rebelled against established authority and fought to recover their natural liberties. Revolutionary France, like Soviet Russia later, insinuated into international relations the principle of aggressive state policy linked to a universal missionary enthusiasm.

THE FIRST FRENCH REPUBLIC

In the meantime France had elected deputies to the National Convention, the third assembly chosen in four years. It would draw up a new charter of government. All adult males were eligible to vote but only a small percentage bothered to do so, and republicans in large proportions were swept into office. Promptly the Bourbon monarchy was abolished and a French Republic proclaimed. The newly

Execution of Louis XVI

composed *Marseillaise,* most lyrical of all national anthems, became the battle-hymn of the Republic.

The feud between the moderate Girondins and the extremist, sternly disciplined Jacobins mounted in asperity. They clashed over the conduct of foreign policy—the waging of the war, relations with Britain and other neutral countries. They quarreled over measures to regulate the national economy, and over the disposition of the suspended king. From one angle the fierce rivalry reflected the difference in general outlook between the masses of Paris and the citizens of the rest of France; from another viewpoint, the distinction between physical force and sweet reasonableness in deciding state problems.

The fate of the king was quickly determined. Accused of a long list of crimes, such as plotting against the nation, payment of money to émigré aristocrats and speculating in grain, Louis XVI was haled before the Convention and tried. Convicted of treason, the king was sentenced to death by a very small majority, and in January of 1793, his head was lopped off by a guillotine erected on the magnificent Place de la Concorde, as it is now known. The execution of Louis XVI horrified royalist and conservative Europe; rulers and statesmen everywhere fancied that their own necks were in jeopardy.

BRITAIN AND FRANCE

Already at war with Austria and Prussia, Republican France threw down the gauntlet to Britain which picked it up with ready alacrity. At the start of the French upheaval, British opinion had rather generally applauded what was being attempted. It appeared that France was undergoing a wholesome house-cleaning, was being renovated indeed on the British pattern, which tickled national pride. For many British intellectuals, moreover, it seemed that nature and reason were winning a deserved triumph in France over ancient wrong and injustice, and they were thrilled with lyrical joy. Hard-headed British statesmen joined in the applause, calculating that the Revolution would impair the military potential of France, which a few years before had emerged on the victor's side—in the War of the American Revolution.

Conservative Britons, on the other hand, were scandalized by French ecclesiastical policies and revolutionary confiscations of property. Physical barbarities in France were inflated by jittery British imaginations far beyond the realities. Vague loathing of the Revolution was crystallized into firm conviction by the militant publications of Edmund Burke. Most influential of his flaming tracts for the time was the brilliantly written *Reflections on the Revolution in France.* It came off the press in the autumn of 1790, months before events across the channel had turned violently destructive. Everywhere among conservatives the *Reflections* was an instant success; Louis XVI translated the pamphlet for his private edification. With uncanny accuracy Burke predicted the sequence of French happenings, winning for himself the prestige of an oracle.

No mere blind opponent of change and not at all an intransigent standpatter, Burke had earlier espoused the aspirations of the rebels in English America. He was the eloquent enemy of despotism whatever its inspiration and wherever it appeared. His mind, instructed by history, distrusted swift and sweeping change; his understanding of human nature led him to reject the naively optimistic faith of the "Enlightenment" in reason and the perfectibility of man. He ridiculed the abstraction that men were innately good and therefore naturally reasonable and competent to build a social and political structure in which all would be peaceful and blissfully happy.

By appealing to the received values of Christian civilization, Burke skillfully combatted the appeal of French novelties. Sympathetic though he was to ideals of freedom, he argued the transcendant importance of respect for history and authority in the affairs of men. He grossly underestimated the popular grievances, the fundamental faults in French society, which had fired the revolutionary innovations.

Certain observers of the twentieth century have discerned in the authoritarian regimes of Fascism, Nazism and Communism something

Edmund Burke's protest against the course of the French Revolution was directed to the intellects of Englishmen; but the man on the London street was persuaded by "Anti-Jacobin" cartoons like this one, in which the spirit of Liberty aims death at King, Lords and Commons.

of the same kind of peril which Burke perceived in the France of the time. Fearful lest revolutionary radicalism might leap over the Channel and touch off social upheaval, Burke launched out on his intellectual crusade. The writings of this leading British exponent of enlightened conservatism have been of perennial interest to students of government and political philosophy.

Admirers of revolutionary France promptly issued counterblasts to Burke. Thomas Paine, for instance, of American revolutionary fame, penned the *Rights of Man*. It was a document replete with democratic and republican enthusiasm, which was read by tens of thousands. The torrent of French events, however, brought victory in the ideological warfare to Burke and his fellows. Alarmed by the theories and practices of revolutionary France, and afraid of violence at home, British governing classes supported measures to stifle pro-French sentiments and silence their advocates. In the name of national security, an old-fashioned witch hunt was directed against British radicals and Jacobin "fellow travelers." The prized British tradition of free speech was placed in cold storage.

Prime minister at the moment was William Pitt the Younger, a proud Tory, who had no desire to go to war to check the diffusion of French principles. Indeed, he confidently told the House of Commons in 1792 that there "unquestionably never was a time in the history of this country when from the situation in Europe we might more reasonably expect fifteen years of peace." Yet within a year Pitt was by way of becoming one of Britain's very greatest war leaders, the organizer of a military effort that would last for a full generation.

The pledge of the French Republicans to assist other peoples in overthrowing their governments, the shocking execution of Louis XVI and the threat of Republican armies to Holland swept the British government to the verge of armed conflict. Britain had no intention of letting the Dutch coast, with the implicit menace to her maritime commerce and her very stomach, fall under French occupation. France on crusade imperiled the equilibrium of power in Europe, threatened the safety of the island kingdom as earlier Bourbon France had done. "Britain will never see with indifference," asserted Pitt, "that France shall make herself, either directly or indirectly, the sovereign of the Low Countries, or general arbiter of the rights and liberties of Europe." In February of 1793 France caused no surprise by declaring war upon Britain.

Presently an impressive league of nations was arrayed against the French Republic: Britain, Austria and Prussia, Holland, Spain and Portugal, Sardinia and Sweden, a coalition more formidable than ever Louis XIV had fought. French arms suffered disaster upon disaster, which seemed to spell the certain doom of the revolutionary order. Belgium succumbed to the enemy and the once popular General Dumouriez, alienated by the execution of Louis XVI, turned traitor and deserted. Foreign armies everywhere forced the French troops back and Austria and Prussia let it be known that they intended to partition France.

British seapower blockaded naval stations and commercial ports and lent help and encouragement to French malcontents who had risen against the Paris regime. For civil war had been added to international war when royalists and peasants in western France, incited by their clergy, and dissidents in southern cities rebelled. If France were to be saved from conquest and spoliation resolute leadership and decisive action were necessary. Both were supplied by Jacobins who took charge of French destinies, setting up a revolutionary dictatorship.

A YEAR OF TERROR AND EXPERIMENT

For fourteen months France was ruled by a ruthless and relentless oligarchy of Jacobins, organized as a Committee of Public Safety. At no time were there more than a dozen members, young, spirited, largely of petty bourgeois origins and mostly lawyers by profession. All were intoxicated with the optimistic philosophy of the "Enlightenment." They glowed with intense emotional zeal, and cherished visions of economic leveling and universal suffrage. Almost all were strangers one to the other until a short time before; now they were the all-powerful directors of the most cultivated and most dynamic nation of the world. A cabinet in a sense, the Committee was responsible to a majority in the National Convention. Danton carried the greatest weight at the beginning, Robespierre later.

Here was a rigorously totalitarian regime bent upon thoroughly inspiriting and unifying the nation and waging victorious war against a powerful array of foreign armies. The Committee resorted to dread terror in order to frighten domestic opponents into submission or to erase them forever.

In Paris the instrument of Jacobin terrorism was a notorious revolutionary tribunal, which summarily tried and summarily guillotined individuals who were openly at odds with the Jacobin junta or who were supected of disloyalty. Queen Marie Antoinette, royalists, profiteers, corrupt officials, spokesmen of the moderate and sensitive Girondins, perished on the scaffold in the never forgotten year of terror. Perhaps 20,000 in all were sacrificed, some of them utterly innocent of offenses against the state. Into disaffected French provinces and cities fanatical Jacobin agents on mission were dispatched to crush the spirit of rebellion. They slaughtered and slew without mercy; in Lyons, as an example, about 4,000 were killed in mass butcheries. Ruthless terror coerced France into submission to the Jacobin dictatorship.

Most Frenchmen of course were quite untouched by the gusts of terrorism. They proceeded on their daily rounds much as usual,

Marie Antoinette's last portrait, sketched by J. L. David from a window overlooking the Rue St. Honoré as the one-time Queen was carried by on a tumbril to her death.

safe if they held aloof from politics. What troubled them most was the growing economic predicament traceable to years of commotion, war and creeping inflation of the currency. Wretchedness arising out of hunger gave some measure of sanction to the horrible treatment of traitors and profiteers.

Before the "paroxysm of collective madness" had run its full course, the ruling Jacobins fell to quarreling among themselves. Danton and his associates, contending that too much civilian blood was being spilled, counseled sanity and moderation. That stand infuriated Robespierre, master now of the omnipotent Committee, who engineered the removal of Dantonists by violence. The guillotine devoured her own children. "Liberty cannot be secured," cried the primly doctrinaire Robespierre, "unless criminals lose their heads." His supremacy lasted but a little while.

In the early summer of 1794, the Terror carried off a ghastly toll of victims. No man prominent in public affairs felt secure, not even Robespierre. And with reason, for fearful or repentant terrorists conspired to do unto him what he had done unto others. Arrested in July, Robespierre and his henchmen were hustled under the guillotine without benefit of trial. After that the cruel rule of intimidation petered out. A wave of terror against terrorists exterminated the remnants of the Jacobin high command. The "first modern dictatorship," that is to say, was drowned in blood. Thereafter conservatives in Europe and America were wont to apply the term *Jacobin* to any and every political agitation of which they disapproved; as an epithet, "Jacobin" became the equivalent of "Red" in the twentieth century.

While the Terror raged, enthusiastic French armies had not only expelled Allied troops from the homeland but had driven furiously into enemy territory. Organization of the war effort was entrusted by the Committee of Public Safety to Lazare-Nicolas Carnot, a professional officer in the engineers and a skillful administrator and strategist. Under a momentous decree of August, 1793, the entire French nation, in keeping with the principle of equality, was mobilized for the herculean struggle.

That decree read in part: "Young men shall go forth to battle; married men shall forge weapons and transport munitions; women shall make tents and clothing, and shall serve in hospitals; children will make lint from old linen; and old men shall be brought to public places to arouse the courage of soldiers and preach the hatred of kings and the unity of the Republic." Thus the concept of total war entered into the pageant of history. Previously wars had been fought as "the sport of kings," controlled by certain rules of humanity and some moderation. Now the quantity theory of war replaced the more humane and limited quality principles of war. Fighting became the desperately serious business of whole nations, taught to hate and despise the enemy, and conducted with gloves off.

Raw French conscripts were brigaded with trustworthy contingents of the royal army to form a fighting force of nearly a million, assembled in fourteen armies. Techniques of training were devised for the quick integration of fresh recruits with veterans, and conventional methods of attack were discarded. Remarkable capacity for military leadership was uncovered among non-commissioned officers of the old Bourbon army. Service of supply was transformed, the French troops living as much as possible off the country. In that way they were able to move faster than opposing armies whose speed was regulated by lumbering baggage trains. Sheer weight of numbers, youthful

The master of the Terror found himself mastered by his own creature. Here we see Robespierre, his jaw shattered by a pistol-shot, under questioning in the rooms of the Committee of Public Safety. That same day he was guillotined.

dash and intense patriotic ardor afforded the French soldiers inestimable advantages over the enemy.

On the other side, the Allied coalition was handicapped by reliance on orthodox military techniques and tormented by political dissensions. Austria and Prussia disputed over the division of France before the country had been conquered, and they were at odds over the perennial Polish problem. French troops carried all before them. And by the spring of 1794 France was no longer in mortal peril of conquest. On into Belgium and Holland and western Germany French armies rolled. British successes on the blue water were small compensation for coalition defeats on land.

Early in 1795 the Allied league disintegrated. Prussia signed a peace treaty, conceding French sovereignty over the Left Bank of the Rhine. Belgium was annexed to France and Holland was soon converted into a French satellite as the Batavian Republic. Spain and smaller German states withdrew from the contest, leaving Britain and Austria to carry on alone.

Throughout the year of terror and victorious war the National Convention was technically the supreme authority in France. That body or the radical municipal government of Paris sponsored several unusual innovations, mostly short-lived. To provision the fighting services and to placate the desperate poor of Paris an adventure in planned economy was undertaken. One of its features was an attempt to dictate prices of foodstuffs, other articles of consumption and wages.

At one point Christianity was proscribed. The Worship of Reason was proclaimed as the national faith; a lady of dubious morals was seated on the altar of Notre Dame and venerated as the Goddess of Reason. This atheistic cult annoyed Robespierre, who presently replaced it with a pattern of deism based upon belief in a Supreme Being and the immortality of the soul. This innovation formed part of the dictator's scheme to convert France into a spartan Republic of Virtue in conformity with his reading of the *Social Contract*.

To commemorate the new age of history, a new calendar was devised, with 1792, when the Republic was proclaimed, as Year I. Days and months were assigned appropriate republican titles, and republican holidays replaced Christian holy days. Projects for universal elementary education were sketched, beginnings were made in the codification of the laws of the land, administrative reconstruction and a decimal and metric system of weights and measures were introduced, later to be copied in other Continental countries.

Amidst all the tumult and convulsions, the Convention did not forget that it had initially been summoned to prepare a constitution for the Republic. That assignment was completed in 1795, the charter bearing the name of "Constitution of the Year III." It was prefaced by a declaration of the rights of man and a statement of the responsibilities of a citizen. Executive authority was lodged in a Directory of five, chosen by the legislature. This latter branch of government contained two houses, deputies being indirectly elected by men who met certain property qualifications. On a broad view, the Constitution of the Year III satisfied the wishes and interests of the resurgent middle classes.

It was prescribed that two-thirds of the lawmakers should be selected from the Convention. That arrangement offended French royalists who desired an entirely fresh set of faces in the places of authority. An armed outbreak against the Convention was organized in Paris, but it was easily crushed by loyal troops, some of them commanded by a little known captain of artillery, Napoleon Bonaparte. The Constitution of the Year III became the law of France. It was assumed, as in 1791, that France would settle down to an orderly routine. But the fates swiftly shattered rosy imaginings.

THE DIRECTORY

For four years, the government of the Directory held sway in France. From the beginning it was plagued by a heavy legacy of problems and smoldering popular discontent. Drastic policies, such as the repudiation of the mountain of paper money that had accumulated, fostered economic improvement, it is true, but betterment came too slowly to satisfy general expectations. Moreover, directors wrangled incessantly with one another and the executive and legislative branches quarreled constantly—all of which redounded to the advantage of the ambitious Bonaparte, waiting in the wings.

Royalists and radicals alternated in disrupting the peace of mind of the Directory. Of special note was a secret conspiracy, discovered in 1796, which holds a unique place in the history and legends of economic collectivism. Chief character in the plot was a radical journalist "Gracchus" Babeuf, who sketched out a simple version of communism and attracted a band of disciples to his standards. With all the talk in the air about equality, it was entirely natural that a cry for equality in income should arise. A manifesto of the plotters called for "another revolution . . . far greater" and aiming at "the common good or the community of good." It was planned that reliable members of the conspiracy should worm their way into key government positions as the prelude to the seizure of power by force. Opponents would be ruthlessly exterminated in a manner reminiscent of 1793–1794 and then an authentic egalitarian society would be created.

"Gracchus" Babeuf

Police spies, however, uncovered the conspiracy. Babeuf and his lieutenants were arrested and had a chance to publicize their beliefs and aims at their trial. Babeuf was executed, thus providing collectivism with an early martyr. This episode partly explains the preference of modern French trade unionism for direct action to achieve its purposes. Babeuf's speculations, moreover, influenced the shape of future collectivist thinking. Nicholas Lenin, for instance, the foremost leader of Bolshevik Russia, while an exile in Switzerland, carefully digested the ideas and strategy of Babeuf.

The Directory had inherited a war with Austria and Britain. France desired peace but the price of peace would have been the renunciation of Belgium and western Germany and that price the Directory would not pay. On the contrary Carnot, organizer of the victory in 1793–1794 and now a Director, planned to conquer Vienna and knock Austria out of the war. One French army would drive upon the Hapsburg capital across southern Germany, while a second would proceed thither by way of Italy. As a reward for his help in saving the Convention, Napoleon Bonaparte was designated as Commander of the Army of Italy.

The career and character of Napoleon will be analyzed in the next chapter. At this point only the glittering military exploits which enabled him to forge to the front in France within three dramatic years must be recounted. Bonaparte's soldiers in 1796 crashed swiftly across the Alps into Italy and ensconced themselves in Milan. Employing unconventional and hazardous tactics and by superb manipulation of resources and slick use of propaganda, the French routed five larger (and lethargic) Austrian armies. Italians welcomed the French as liberators from the detested Hapsburgs. Famous Italian art treasures were shipped to Paris, as trophies of victory, while French soldiers looted and pillaged to their heart's content in violation of the code of war. Austria, at war with France since 1792, sued for peace, leaving Britain standing by herself.

By the Treaty of Campo Formio (1797),

largely the personal handiwork of Bonaparte, Austria acknowledged the Rhine to be the French frontier. It relinquished sovereignty over Belgium and Milan, and recognized an "independent" state in northern Italy called the Cisalpine Republic.[4] As compensation for territorial losses Austria was awarded most of the ancient, but decayed, Republic of Venice.

Victory and peace raised Bonaparte's stock immensely. Overnight almost, the General had become the most talked about man of Europe, the darling of the French soldiers and the admiration of many French civilians. Already he was dreaming of setting himself up as dictator of France, backed by his legions. But he did not think the political situation was quite ripe for the overthrow of the Directory. Yet it would never do to hang around Paris allowing his military laurels to accumulate dust. How now could the tenacious British foe be humbled?

So complete was the superiority of Britain at sea that the island kingdom itself was impregnable to attack. Bonaparte decided, therefore, to strike at Britain indirectly, to seize Egypt, cut off trade and eventually drive on to the riches of India. Melodramatically enough, he prophesied that his sharp sword would recover for France the place in the colonial world which the Bourbon monarchy had lost.

In May of 1798, a small contingent of French troops under Bonaparte landed safely in Egypt. They whipped the Turks in a spectacular battle beneath the impassive Pyramids. But the French fleet was utterly destroyed by the British, Admiral Nelson commanding, which cut the French forces off from the homeland. On into Syria the French army plunged only to suffer a decisive check at Acre. Having learned by chance that political currents in France were running heavily against the Directory, Bonaparte shamelessly deserted his soldiers, and hastened back to Paris.

BONAPARTE TAKES OVER

Only cheering news of French military successes in the Near East, not the decisive reversals, had preceded the General and he was rapturously welcomed as a conquering hero. To many a Frenchman he seemed the indispensable man who could bring tranquility to the distraught domestic scene. And the maker of the Treaty of Campo Formio was praised as a diplomatic virtuoso who could win for France an honorable peace from a new European coalition.

At the end of 1799 British diplomacy had cemented another—the second—league of nations against France. Austria came in hoping to retrieve her fallen fortunes, Turkey joined up since her Egyptian province had just been assailed by Bonaparte, and, most interesting of all, Imperial Russia entered the lists. The impulsive tyrannical tsar, Paul I, hated revolutionary France with pathological hatred, and he was frightened by Bonapartist operations in the Near East and by reports that the Directory was intriguing to resurrect partitioned Poland. He was piqued, too, by Napoleon's occupation of Malta en route to Egypt, for Paul I had been named grand master of the Knights of Malta. Patriotic France, on its part, was furious because Russia afforded asylum to thousands of French royalists.

Anticipating war, the Directory in 1798 had replenished French armies by enacting the first general law of conscription. Every man between twenty and twenty-five years was subjected to military service. Even so the French forces were decidedly smaller than the armies of the enemy coalition. Austrian and Russian troops hurled the French out of the Italian peninsula, and drove deep into Switzerland; in western Germany, too, French soldiers were obliged to fall back. Preparations were set in motion for an Allied invasion of France itself; the rough, bluff Russian commander, Suvorov, whose soldiers had displayed almost superhuman qualities of endurance and stolidity, bluntly announced that Paris was his goal. These events robbed the discredited Directory of what little standing it still possessed.

The projected coalition drive into France never came to pass and that for two central reasons. First, the jealous Allied governments fell to bickering among themselves. Second, French troops commanded by General Mas-

[4] Shortly, the Directory established a galaxy of satellite republics in the Italian peninsula.

séna soundly thrashed the Russians in Switzerland and the battered remnant trekked off to Muscovy. France was already out of danger when Bonaparte arrived from Egypt, though Austria, of course, had yet to be disposed of. Before that task was undertaken, the Directory had been tossed into the discard and Bonaparte had vaulted into control of French politics.

One of the Directors, the nimble Abbé Sieyès, a much respected political pamphleteer, had puzzled out a patent formula for eliminating the Directory and equipping France with a strong government. Bonaparte teamed up with him, concealing, however, his dictatorial designs. Soldiers in Paris were placed under command of the popular and picturesque General, who presently summoned the legislature to turn power over to him. When the law makers indignantly balked, Bonaparte staged a military putsch, in November, 1799, ordering troops to disperse the dissenters. A rump legislature then did the General's bidding. Another constitution was drafted assigning the executive authority to a First Consul, Bonaparte, and two subordinate consuls; an imposing array of legislative bodies was created but they were purely ornamental and decorative.

"Citizens," proclaimed the exultant First Consul, "Citizens, the Revolution is true to the principles from which it sprang; it is now at an end." The French state was in fact the ambitious and legend-encrusted General, and the hypnotized electorate of France approved the new scheme of things by an almost unanimous vote. Edmund Burke was right. Maximilien Robespierre was right. What had started off in 1789 as a movement to create a constitutional regime attuned to principles of liberty and equality had in a decade been smothered in the iron dictatorship of an upstart general.

But that was only part of the story and, weighed in the scales of history, not the most important part. To a Rip Van Winkle, roused from a ten-year sleep, the appearance of France in 1799 would have been well-nigh incredible, so ramified and far-reaching had been the changes in the interval. Revolutionary France had, above all else, consecrated the emancipation and the enthronement of the individual toward which Europe had been slowly groping for three centuries.

Besides that, Frenchmen of 1799 had secured civil and judicial rights, freedom of conscience and freedom of economic enterprise such as had only been dreamed of in 1789. Landed estates of the privileged had very largely passed into the ownership of the peasantry and promising beginnings in public education had been initiated. Noblemen and churchmen had been deprived of special privileges and all Frenchmen stood as equals before the judge and the tax gatherer. Serfdom and torture had disappeared. Transforming innovations inside France, ideals proclaimed by French partisans of a finer society for mankind were gradually permeating the nations and peoples of Europe, as Rip might appropriately have noted.

THE UNITED STATES AND REVOLUTIONARY FRANCE

Russia and the United States, which were to be the leading Great Powers at the beginning of the atomic age, were both sucked into the maelstrom of revolutionary France. The Muscovite empire, as has been explained, engaged in brief war with the Directory, while the United States, not only renounced the diplomatic alliance with France, dating from 1778, but fought an undeclared naval war with the great European republic. The commotion of the French revolutionary epoch impinged significantly upon affairs in the young trans-Atlantic republic.

Opinion in the United States responded with lively enthusiasm to the French innovations of the first period of the Revolution. France, it seemed, was being reconstructed on principles which had lately been so gloriously vindicated in the New World and that merited national applause. But as the Revolution ran into violent weather, a division of mind appeared, which was sharpened when Britain and France went to war. Broadly regarded, comfortably fixed Americans recoiled in horror over the physical excesses in France and adopted a pro-British attitude, while citizens sympathetic to "French ideas" sided frankly and passionately with the revolutionaries. Facsimiles of Jacobin clubs were organized, whose members imitated the manners of their French prototypes. They demanded that the United States should side with France against Britain.

To a considerable extent and in a manner that is highly instructive, the coming of a general war in Europe cast up problems and perplexities for the United States paralleling those which arose with the European conflicts of the twentieth century. Although technically, at any rate, the United States was allied by treaty to France, President Washington in 1793 proclaimed neutrality for his country. The nation was summoned by the sedate Chief Executive "to adopt and pursue a conduct friendly and impartial towards the belligerent powers" and urged "to avoid all acts and proceedings whatsoever, which may in any manner" infringe upon neutrality and impartiality. That statement of policy, which set an important precedent, provoked much learned and popular criticism but it stuck.

Subsequently, in his oft-quoted "Farewell Address," published in 1796 at a moment of acute friction with France, Washington adjured his countrymen to avoid embroilments in the quarrels and torments of the Old World. "Our detached and distant situation," he thought, "invites and enables us to pursue a different course . . . 'Tis our true policy to steer clear of permanent alliances with any portion of the foreign world." These admonitions of a founding father formed a vital part of the doctrine that the United States should keep aloof from the strife and struggles for power of the Old World, if that were possible.

Warfare abroad presented lucrative opportunities to shipping and exporting interests in the United States which were avidly seized upon. A large share of European commerce by sea passed to Yankee concerns. But that business caused grave disputes with Britain and France over neutral rights on the blue water. British naval vessels not only intercepted American cargoes bound for French ports, but arrested sailors at work on ships flying the Stars and Stripes, who were allegedly subjects of the British crown. A series of incidents provoked furious anger and preparations to fight Britain were seriously undertaken. Passions cooled down, however, when Britain promised to relax her maritime practices and American shipping experienced dizzy prosperity.

French interference with vessels owned in the United States, while injurious to material interests and wounding to national pride, had, up to this point, been less frequent than the British. But insulting indignities under the Directory generated an intense war spirit in America; the alliance of 1778 with France was terminated, other treaties were canceled and the fighting services were readied for combat. France tossed fuel on the mounting flames by refusing to recognize the minister of the United States.

In the midst of the controversy extravagant fears raced through conservative American minds. It was suspected that the revolutionary government of France would corrupt American citizens, converting some of them into allies against their own country. The hysteria of the hour resembled that which prevailed in Britain against "French ideas" and the dread of "Russian ideas" after the First and Second World Wars. With small sense of proportion, worried American law-makers placed measures on the statute book authorizing the deportation of trouble-making aliens and imposing curbs on free expression of opinion. Those laws churned up acrid partisan animosities which endangered for a time the very continuance of the Republic.

Determined to bring France to book and stop the seizure of American ships, the United States in 1798 started an undeclared naval war, which lasted more than two years. Upwards of eighty armed French ships which meddled with United States vessels were either seized or sunk. A decided shift in French policy, however, attended the accession of Napoleon to power. The First Consul desired to avoid driving the United States into the open arms of his British foe.

An olive branch which the Consulate held out was eagerly grasped by policymakers in Washington, and in the autumn of 1800 France promised that goods hauled in neutral ships would not be subject to seizure, recognized the termination of the treaty of alliance and resumed conventional diplomatic intercourse. Bonaparte dismissed the recent sea skirmishes as merely a family quarrel. And the installation of Jefferson in the White House in 1801 seemed to betoken an era of good feeling in Franco-American relations, for the new President was known to be a warm and admiring friend of France and the ideas of 1789.

FOR FURTHER STUDY

JAMES M. THOMPSON, *The French Revolution* (Oxford, 1943)

GEORGES LEFEBVRE, *The Coming of the French Revolution* (Eng. trans., Princeton, 1947) PAPERBACK

CRANE BRINTON, *A Decade of Revolution, 1789–1799* (New York, 1935) PAPERBACK

ALBERT MATHIEZ, *The French Revolution* (Eng. ed., New York, 1928)

JOHN H. STEWART, *A Documentary Survey of the French Revolution, 1789–1799* (New York, 1951)

LOUIS BARTHOU, *Mirabeau* (New York, 1913)

LOUIS R. GOTTSCHALK, *Jean Paul Marat: a Study in Radicalism* (New York, 1927)

JAMES M. THOMPSON, *Robespierre and the French Revolution* (New York, 1952) PAPERBACK

ROSS J. S. HOFFMAN and PAUL LEVACK, *Burke's Politics* (New York, 1949)

ROBERT R. PALMER, *Twelve Who Ruled* (Princeton 1941)

GAETANO SALVEMINI, *The French Revolution* (Eng. trans., New York, 1962) PAPERBACK

LEO GERSHOY, *The Era of the French Revolution* (New York, 1957) PAPERBACK

PAUL H. BEIK, *The French Revolution seen from the Right* (Philadelphia, 1956)

GEORGE RUDÉ, *The Crowd in the French Revolution* (New York, 1959)

CHAPTER XI

NAPOLEON AND VIENNA

STRANGER THAN FICTION

THE fascination of Napoleon is a historical phenomenon. His career and personality have been the subject of more literature, hostile, idolatrous or disinterested than any other figure of modern times. The dazzling reputation of the "man from Corsica" has intoxicated the imagination of South American dictators, of North American "Napoleons of industry" and of frank imitators like Mussolini and Hitler.

Upon entering Paris in the Second World War, Hitler ordered that the remains of Napoleon at the *Invalides* should be hoisted to the ground floor and Nazi troopers should pay homage. That indefatigable propagandist of women's rights, Susan B. Anthony, when visiting the tomb of Napoleon remarked, "A very great genius. Who knows but if he had lived in another age he might not have been our champion"—a miscalculation surely, for although Napoleon liked the ladies he was no feminist. These two examples, chosen at random, illustrate the adoration which the enigmatic little superman has evoked.

In a real sense, Napoleon was the child and heir of revolutionary France, and up to a point the consolidator and executor of its purposes. He set France aright and turned Europe upside down. Until the advent of Hitler, no other epoch of European history had been so completely overshadowed by a single personality as that of Napoleon.

His restless ambitions despatched armies hither and yon across the Continent, carrying not alone cannon and destruction but also the seeds of 1789—and planting them. The harvest was the reformation of some ancient customs and institutions in neighboring countries and the emergence of ardent national feelings which would go far to shape coming events.

Not only Europe, but the whole world reverberated to the

The young Napoleon, the man of the first campaigns in Italy, said of himself: "I am the Revolution on horseback."

designs of Bonaparte. Into his giddy orbit Africa, Asia and the Americas were drawn; never before had the destinies of the great globe itself depended so decisively upon the fortunes of one mortal. The glittering record of the man has been crystallized by a competent judge in this language:

"No name represents so completely and conspicuously dominion, splendor, and catastrophe. He raised himself by the use, and ruined himself by the abuse, of superhuman faculties. He was wrecked by the extravagance of his own genius." [1]

[1] Lord Rosebery, *Napoleon, the Last Phase* (New York, 1901), p. 277.

Undoubtedly the allure of Napoleon stems in part from the way in which he raised himself from inconsequential origins to become master of France and then overlord of Europe. Bonaparte was born in 1769 on the dwarf isle of Corsica, which France had just purchased from the Republic of Genoa. The unruliness and anarchical tastes of the Corsicans earned for the island the sobriquet of the "Ireland of the Mediterranean." The Bonaparte family, of Italian Tuscan antecedents, shared the general Corsican reputation for combativeness and turbulence.

At the age of ten Bonaparte enrolled at an aristocratic military academy in France where he spent five unhappy years, taunted by his fellows as a Corsican and a social nobody. As a scholar he was neither gifted nor industrious, though smart enough to be commissioned a second lieutenant of artillery at the age of sixteen. In his leisure hours he pored over writings of the *philosophes*, becoming enamoured of Rousseau, whom in maturity he reviled as a madman.

In the summer of 1789 Bonaparte drifted back to Corsica to assist the natives in breaking away from French rule. It was a dream that failed, so the young officer returned to France arriving when the Jacobin dictatorship was struggling homerically against domestic and foreign foes. He prepared a plan of attack which compelled (1793) the Anglo-Spanish enemy to abandon the siege of the naval base at Toulon. Chummy with Robespierre and his henchmen, Napoleon managed by a stroke of luck to escape the doom that befell them.

A series of incidents carried Bonaparte to prominence in the fluid sea of French revolutionary politics. As a commander he helped to rescue the National Convention from the fury of dissident Parisians in 1795; and he married Josephine Beauharnais, widow of a republican general, and herself influential with weight-carrying politicians. Given command of the army of Italy he quickly crowded into top place in the affairs of France, as has already been recounted.

"Nothing has been simpler than my elevation," the First Consul candidly acknowledged. "It is owing to the peculiarities of the time." A great war enabled him to win military promotion rapidly and the ineffectiveness of the Directory presented him with a capital opportunity to seize political power. Gambling for high stakes, he had won.

It was the personal qualities of Bonaparte which determined that he, rather than any one of half a dozen other outstanding French commanders, should take rank with the really decisive figures of Western history. Understanding of Napoleon has been made easier for the twentieth century because of experience with a crop of new dictators. Parallelisms between Napoleon and Hitler, for instance, are plentiful, and, when kept within the bounds of fact, instructive. Both upstarts, they thought and behaved very much alike and both were corrupted by the exercise of arbitrary and absolute power.

In physical appearance Napoleon was an unprepossessing little fellow, only a trifle over five feet tall. His head, like his chest, was abnormally large, his hair untidy, his cheeks hollow, his deep-set grey eyes cold and piercing; in everyday manners he was unpolished and abrupt. Until corpulence stole upon him late in life he was rather thin and sallow.

Among other traits, the Corsican had an extraordinarily rugged, an iron constitution. In the prime of his career he seldom complained of fatigue; on one occasion he directed fighting for five consecutive days without so much as removing his boots. At times he slaved away eighteen hours at a stretch, passing judgment on a variety of public problems; no Louis XVI this. And, full of that boundless self-confidence essential in any man who intends to lead or wield power, he was obsessed with the conviction that he was in truth a man of destiny.

He possessed, furthermore, personal attributes that are indispensable for large achievement in military affairs, the realm in which he excelled. Not only could he conceive and conduct complicated plans of campaign, but, using the techniques of others, he displayed rare ability as a strategist. Principles of mountain warfare, for example, which had been devised by Bourcet, an accomplished French staff officer of an earlier generation, Bonaparte applied with stunning success in the Italian campaign of 1796. He was adept at arousing and holding the admiration, not to say the affection, of his soldiers. Grenadiers complained, "The Emperor makes war with our legs," but year after year they fought, bled and died at his bidding.

And Bonaparte had a statesman's perception of what France needed and showed resourcefulness and intelligence in managing domestic and foreign business. Crass egotist that he was, he cared less for France and the French actually than for his own reputation and fame, but he understood as well as any man how to please crowds. His promises of unexampled grandeur for the French nation were long made good by the troops; Frenchmen gloated over maps depicting how much of the Continent had passed under the sword of the Emperor. They applauded the efficient manner in which home affairs were conducted and the rehabilitation of France was carried out.

Many beneficent social reforms of the Revolution and the egalitarian principle in taxation and legal matters were preserved. Peasants retained the land which they had secured and unemployed city dwellers were set to work on public works projects, for which they blessed the miracle man. Paris was littered with massive monuments, billboards in stone and bronze, to advertise military victories and to fire the patriotic emotions of the plain masses.

Yet for the ordinary human personality Napoleon had no more respect than he had for the freedom of man or the homely virtue of truth. "I grew up upon the field of battle," he said revealingly, "and a man such as I am cares little for the life of a million men." Rarely, very rarely, did he admit that he had erred; for the prolonged, exhausting warfare with which his name must always be identified, he blamed his foreign adversaries, first, last and above all, Great Britain.

WAR AND PEACE

Napoleon's initial military venture as First Consul was a contest with Austria over the destiny of Italy and the Germanies. Austrian armies were besieging Genoa, as the prelude to an invasion of France. Bonaparte with superb generalship marched troops across the Alps and down into northern Italy a second time. The rival forces clashed at Marengo (June, 1800), near Genoa, the Austrians repulsing Napoleon in the first phase of the battle; then reinforcements under General Desaix rushed up and brought victory to the French standards. Desaix was killed in the fighting and Napoleon characteristically claimed personal credit for a battle which decided the fate of Italy.

Nevertheless, Austria was as yet unready to toss in the sponge. Another French army, General Moreau in command, overwhelmed Austrian armies at Hohenlinden in Bavaria (December, 1800) and then the authorities in Vienna submitted once more to the verdict of the battlefield.[2] In February, 1801, Austria signed the Treaty of Lunéville, which confirmed many of the clauses of Campo Formio, and extended the area of French lordship in Italy. Beyond that, the Rhine was recognized as the French frontier, with the proviso that German secular princes who were ousted from the Left Bank should be appropriately compensated with properties elsewhere in Germany.

Very nearly a hundred princely and ecclesiastical states along the Rhine were merged with France. That shift in sovereignty was not entirely distasteful to the Germans involved, for many innovations of Revolutionary France were applied. Archaic feudal and church burdens were lifted, equality and civil liberties were proclaimed and landed properties were parceled out among the peasants. Secular princes who lost land on the Left Bank were indemnified with small territories to the east of the Rhine. And Bonaparte enlarged the middle-sized German principalities, Baden, Württemberg and Bavaria; vassals of their French benefactor, they served as counterweights to Austria and Prussia. By contributing to the consolidation of the German states, Napoleon unintentionally helped to bring about the eventual union of Germany in the Empire of Bismarck.

Napoleon meantime had made peace with Paul I of Russia. The Tsar, irritated by British blockading tactics, proceeded to organize a Baltic League of Neutrals to oppose the despotic mistress on the sea. But a British fleet destroyed the Danish navy and reopened the Baltic to shipping. Paul I was murdered in a palace coup, whereupon the anti-British coalition split asunder. France then stood squarely face to face with British seapower—an elephant confronting a whale, neither able to wage effective war on the other. Policymakers in both countries were prepared to quit fighting, the British the more so in the hope that the commerce of the island kingdom might recuperate.

[2] The accomplishments of Moreau made him a potential competitor of Bonaparte, so he was driven into exile—all the way to Morristown, New Jersey.

At Amiens in March of 1802, a treaty of peace, or more accurately a surface truce, was negotiated by representatives of Britain and France. Britain renounced her overseas conquests, except for the islands of Ceylon and Trinidad, and promised to restore Malta to independent status under certain conditions. Tacitly, at any rate, Britain acknowledged French supremacy in Europe, but the important issue of the ban on the shipment of British goods to French-ruled areas was left unresolved.

The reputation of Napoleon as an astute diplomatist was significantly enhanced by the Amiens settlement. The French electorate expressed (1802) gratitude by voting him First Consul for life. And the British public likewise rejoiced over the return of peace after a full decade of conflict; the name of Bonaparte evoked rapturous cheers on the streets of London, but the British government gazed uneasily at the immense power that Bonapartist France held in its grip.

BONAPARTE AS RULER OF FRANCE

Step by step Bonaparte reinforced his legal position--and prestige—as dictator of France and reconstructed the country in keeping either with his own predilections or the imperatives of the Revolution. In a plebiscite, as noted above, Frenchmen almost unanimously approved him as First Consul for life, which gave him virtually unlimited authority. Reports of plots to remove the dictator, some genuine, others fabricated, impelled Bonaparte to take the title of Emperor.

Napoleon imagined that a Bourbon prince, the Duke d'Enghien, was implicated in a royalist conspiracy, engineered by British agents. Although the Duke was living on German soil he was arrested, tried most unfairly on trumped-up charges and put to death. That judicial murder shattered the dreams of French royalists and shocked the frayed sensibilities of Europe. For the sake of prestige Napoleon in 1804 had himself proclaimed Emperor, revised the Constitution appropriately and staged colorful ceremonies of coronation, the Pope, Pius VII, taking part. The eagle, symbol of ancient Rome, was adopted as the trademark of the new empire, whose master fancied himself a modern Caesar and strutted about wearing a laurel wreath. In truth the authority of Napoleon was more complete and unchallenged than that of the Bourbon kings had been.

Straightway the venerable title of marshal of France was resurrected and conferred upon a score of commanders of distinction. Already Napoleon had created (1802) the celebrated Legion of Honor, most prized of national medallions, which was bestowed upon Frenchmen, soldiers and civilians both, but mostly soldiers, who performed work of especial merit. Wearers of the medal, not unnaturally, felt obligated to render devoted service to the Napoleonic regime.

Associated with the Emperor in the responsibilities of administration was a Council of State composed of technical experts. And several legislative assemblies were created but they were merely ornamental, the members simply uttering "amen" to Napoleon's exhortations. Men of diverse political outlooks were appointed to governmental posts, but anything even remotely suggestive of a political party was ruled out.

Management of local government was concentrated in Paris. Over each *département* Napoleon set a prefect responsible to himself alone and obliged to execute orders sent down from Paris and to rally citizens to the purposes of the Emperor. Prefects in turn appointed mayors in villages and communes, thus wiping out every vestige of local initiative in public business. This tightly centralized administration completed the national unity of France and lasted through all governmental vicissitudes until the Second World War.

An important and busy agency of the Napoleonic dictatorship was the state police. It was headed part of the time by Joseph Fouché, a perfidious political chameleon, who was ready to serve any master if he could thereby advance his own selfish interests. An elaborate espionage service, worthy of a twentieth-century totalitarianism, ferreted out enemies of Napoleon and restricted the liberty of the individual to the minimum. The long arm of police authority ex-

Napoleon crowning himself Emperor, 1804

tended to conquered lands and foreign countries. Newspapers were severely reduced in number and their contents were scrupulously censored. On the other side, Napoleon saw to it that the press published news and views favorable to his regime, not excluding "inspired" articles.

Every empire must have a court of course, and Napoleon's aspired to outshine the Bourbon predecessor. Famous old palaces teemed with crowds of parvenu lords and ladies who had risen on the wings of the new Caesar and who bore decorative titles glamorous beyond all precedent. After the issuance of an amnesty, refugee French aristocrats, or some of them, drifted back to France where they rubbed shoulders with the new Bonapartist nobility.

THE NAPOLEONIC CODES

After his downfall, while a prisoner on St. Helena, Bonaparte contended that the legal accomplishments of his reign, not the triumphs on the battlefield, constituted his strongest claim to the praise of posterity. Codification of French law in all its variety was imperatively needed, for to the tangled legal maze inherited from the old regime had been added the immense volume of enactments since 1789. Gaps in the body of the law and contradictions alike existed.

Preliminary work on codification had been undertaken by the National Convention and the job was finished while Napoleon ruled. Most important was the Civil Code, dealing with the rights of Frenchmen in their relations with one another. The task of codification was carried on principally by legal experts, the "fifty least stupid men in France"; the personal contribution of Napoleon was more colorful than valuable. Yet the Code bears the Emperor's name and most mortals would consider that a suitable monument, judged solely by its importance, to quiet the naggings of pride and ambition.

In a measure the *Code Napoléon* upheld the egalitarian ideal of Revolutionary France. For example, it prescribed that half the landed property of a deceased peasant must pass in equal shares to all his children, a rule which has helped to keep France a country of small peasant proprietors. On the other hand, women were discriminated against; a wife could not testify in a courtroom or dispose of property without the explicit consent of her husband. Equally, a father could consign a son to jail and keep him there as long as he cared to pay for food and lodging. The Code, moreover, was slanted in favor of employers against wage-workers, who were denied, for instance, the right of collective bargaining.

A new criminal code reflected in a limited way the humanizing doctrines of the "Enlightenment," and a commercial code defined the rules for business transactions. Methods of procedure in the courtroom were likewise modified to the advantage of an accused person. French legal manners and methods, it may be noted, have had worldwide influence. They were applied in sections of Europe occupied by French armies and were drawn upon by Greece, Rumania, the Latin American countries and subsequently by Japan when framing standards of justice and judicial processes.

Economic conditions in France, which were in a sorry plight under the Directory, improved remarkably during the first phase of Napoleon's rule. State policies, blending paternalism with the concepts of mercantilism, aided Frenchmen in attaining a broad measure of prosperity. Peasants benefited from reasonable taxation policies, the draining of marshes and the absence of state interference with farming, except as necessary to supply food for Paris and other cities. Wage earners, moreover, enjoyed steady employment and tolerable standards of living. Tariff measures, which shut out British goods, encouraged the growth of textile industries, though the output of iron products increased very little.

A national Bank of France was founded to promote trade and industry and to manage the public debt. At long last a sound system of coinage was devised for France. Taxes were equitably assessed, and though heavy, were less burdensome no doubt than before the Revolution; indirect taxation, which had been given up in the Revolutionary period, was revived piecemeal and in time provoked considerable resentment against the Emperor.

Collection of taxes was efficient, and officials were carefully watched to prevent misappropriation of money such as had bedeviled Bourbon France. Conquered populations were fleeced to furnish funds for the French government and war machine; down to 1812 every campaign paid dividends, which, coupled with the taxes gathered in France, kept the national budget in balance. After that, the Empire was financed chiefly by paper money backed only by popular confidence in Napoleon.

Means of transportation were improved by rebuilding old roads or laying down excellent new ones. The web of French canals was doubled in mileage, and commercial harbors were enlarged. Frenchmen, on the whole, prospered during the first decade of Napoleonic rule, and prosperity, along with the thrilling glories of the army, fortified the authoritarian regime.

THE CONCORDAT

And so did an understanding with the Catholic Church. Friction between the state and the church, which commanded the loyalty of at least half of France, had raged ever since the adoption of anti-clerical legislation by the National Assembly. Bonaparte clearly perceived the value of appeasing disaffected Catholics and of harnessing clerical resources to his political chariot. His inspiration was genuinely conservative and strictly secular, for he had no profound Christian convictions, being at best a deist of sorts. "I do not see in religion," he remarked, "the mystery of the Incarnation, but the mystery of the social order. Religion attaches to heaven an idea of equality which prevents the rich man from being murdered by the poor."

Conversations with the Vatican produced a Concordat, or treaty, of 1801 which regulated the relations of the Church with the French government for more than a century. Catholicism was officially recognized as the religion of the great majority, but toleration for other creeds was assured. Salaries of clergymen, who were obliged to take an oath of fidelity to the state, would be paid out of the public treasury. The Church, on its side, renounced all claims to properties that had been taken away during the Revolution. Appointment of bishops would be a state responsibility as in Bourbon France. The formal treaty, whose execution rested with Bonaparte alone, was supplemented by a set of "organic articles," subordinating the French Church more thoroughly to the French state.

Upon the signing of the Concordat, drum and trumpet heralded the momentous event in every district of Paris and Notre Dame echoed to a solemn *Te Deum*. Owing their security to the Emperor, the clergy dutifully cooperated with his regime for a time. They sang the praises of Napoleon, and a revised catechism prescribed prayers for the master, military service and payment of taxes as a sacred duty; failure to fulfill these obligations would render a Christian "worthy of eternal damnation."

Before long, however, the Emperor clashed acrimoniously with the Pope, who excommunicated him. Whereupon, the Holy Father was arrested and imprisoned. Rough and callous treatment of the Pope scandalized devout Catholics and seriously impaired their allegiance to the imperial order. Bonaparte ultimately confessed "The Concordat was my worst mistake." He regretted that he had not cut France loose from the Vatican and carried her into the fold of Calvinism.

LEARNING AND THE ARTS

Like the Church, French educational institutions were exploited to buttress the authority of the Emperor. Schooling under public auspices had been debated in the National Convention and a ground plan for universal education had been laid out before Napoleon rose to power. Through state schools children could be taught the cult of *La Patrie*, he thought, reverence for the ruler and unquestioning obedience. French youth, that is, would learn what to think, not how to think. Every commune was ordered to provide a primary school and larger centers of population had to establish secondary schools (*lycées*) as well. But shortages of trained teachers and scantiness of appropriations prevented full execution of the plans and at no time was more than one out of eight children of school age receiving even the rudiments of education.

All institutions of learning, from the lowest to the highest levels, were minutely supervised by bureaucrats in Paris. It was said that the minister of public instruction could tell not only what subject was being taught throughout France at a particular hour, but even the verb being conjugated in every school! French universities were not fully liberated from state control until 1896. Despite their shortcomings, Napoleonic schooling policies nevertheless confirmed the Revolutionary doctrines that elementary education was a responsibility of government and that churchmen should not monopolize instruction.

The life of the mind was as severely regimented in Napoleonic France as in the tyrannical police states of the twentieth century. Men of learning out of conviction or as protective coloring surpassed ordinary folk in fulsome adulation of Napoleon. One eulogistic deifier asserted: "Napoleon stands above human history. He stands above our admiration."

Half as advertisement, half to court popularity, Napoleon patronized culture and the arts. In particular, Paris was beautified; the medieval palace of the Louvre was converted into a famous museum and stocked with works of art, not a few of them pilfered from conquered countries. Towering monuments and proud Roman arches of triumph were strewn about the imperial capital. The foremost artist of the day, Jacques L. David, painted colossal canvases glorifying the deeds of the Emperor. Dramatists, too, turned their talents to the inculcation of patriotism and slavish obedience to Napoleon; and men of science profited somewhat from public subsidies.

NAPOLEON'S EUROPE

Napoleon was more the soldier than the domestic reformer, much more. The peace settlements negotiated with Austria and Britain were soon seen to be the merest pauses between rounds. Master of France, Bonaparte aspired to be master of Europe also, and to that end the dominance of France over the Low Countries, Italy and Switzerland was tightened. Spain was drawn into the Napoleonic orbit by an alliance —all of which excited grave concern in other countries, Britain especially.

The expansion of France, the imbalance of power on the Continent threatened British security and prosperity, while British commercial interests chafed under the handicaps to trade resulting from the Napoleonic tariff policies. On top of that, the "Corsican ogre" was ideologically distasteful to British policymakers and the possessing classes, who pictured him as the incarnation of revolutionary Jacobinism, the heir indeed of Robespierre himself. Determined to retain command of the Mediterranean, Britain refused to pull out of Malta as Napoleon demanded, and that stand precipitated the resumption of hostilities in May, 1803.

In the new war Austria again allied with Britain and Russia also joined up. The new Tsar, Alexander I, who preened himself on his liberalism, bitterly resented the murder of the Duke d'Enghien, and imagined that he was the foreordained savior of Europe from Napoleon's lordship. Promises of British subsidies to arm and supply the allied armies cemented (1805) this coalition, the third, against France. The Emperor failed to appreciate that in doing battle with Britain he was fighting less a "nation of shopkeepers," a commercial kingdom, than a nation of manufacturers and workmen, an industrial state capable of equipping great continental military forces.

Napoleon, like Hitler later, toyed with the idea of invading the British Isles. He kept reminding commanders of the Norman Conquest and that the career of Joan of Arc "proved that there is no miracle which the French genius is incapable of working." For two years, elaborate preparations for a channel crossing were made, only to be abandoned as foolhardy. In 1805, an incomparably superior British fleet, commanded by Admiral Horatio Nelson, annihilated the seapower of Napoleon in the decisive Battle of Trafalgar ruining all hope of striking at Great Britain frontally.

The Emperor, meanwhile, had concentrated his magnificent military resources against Austria and Russia. Sweeping into southern Germany, the French defeated the Austrians at Ulm and then smashed the combined armies of Austria and Russia at Austerlitz in December, 1805. "We are babies in the hands of a giant," Alexander I of Russia moaned, while his fellow sovereign in Austria hastened to make peace with the ever-victorious Bonaparte.

That settlement—the Treaty of Pressburg—transferred Austrian holdings in Italy and on the eastern shore of the Adriatic to France and formally ended the ancient Holy Roman Empire, long since a museum piece. Prussia, which had been standing hesitantly on the side lines, now took up arms against Bonaparte, fearful of

The State Epicures at Dinner. *In this British caricature of 1805, Napoleon and Pitt are shown carving up the world between them; while Pitt puts his fork into the sea, Napoleon carves off all Europe.*

being conquered, and inspired by the martial heritage of Frederick the Great.

But Prussian resistance quickly collapsed in 1806 after her troops were overwhelmed at Jena. Napoleon paraded into Berlin while the Prussian king fled to East Prussia where a Russian army was still in being. With great speed the French drove headlong into East Prussia, Napoleon receiving an enthusiastic welcome from Poles on the way. Austria had been picked off. Prussia had been picked off. It was now Russia's turn. If these three countries had cooperated effectively, a very different story would doubtless have been written, but they had not taken to heart the old adage that "in union there is strength."

Two terrible battles of 1807, at Eylau and Friedland, forced Alexander I to come to terms with the seemingly invincible Corsican. Emperor and Tsar melodramatically conferred on the destiny of the Continent on a raft moored in the River Niemen. Napoleon, at his diplomatic best, wheedled the young Russian ruler into a web of agreements known as the Treaty of Tilsit (July, 1807). That settlement spelled the doom of Prussia and brought Russia into the dazzling Napoleonic league of nations.

Territory owned by Prussia in the west of Germany and her Polish provinces were cut away—in all a loss of a third of the kingdom. Heavy indemnities were exacted, strict limitations were laid upon the army of Prussia and French troops garrisoned the truncated kingdom. It was a harsh, unforgettable treaty, but Prussia, though down, was not out by any means. Many a cosmopolitan German, such as the philosophers Goethe and Hegel, fondly expected that Napoleon would create a new and better world for mankind.

Russia fared far better at the hands of the Emperor than Prussia. Alexander I was permitted in fact to annex Finland, the Turkish province of Bessarabia and lands at the mouth of the Danube. For these concessions the Tsar paid in the currency of a secret alliance with Napoleon, pointed against Britain. That transaction, which reminds one of the historic Nazi-Soviet pact of 1939, committed Russia to fight shoulder to shoulder with France in any war, to cease trading with Britain and to assist in coercing other European countries to seal their harbors to British commerce. Never popular in Russia, and not faithfully carried out, the treaty with Napoleon nonetheless lasted for five years. Tilsit marked indeed not only the zenith of Napoleon's fabulous career of conquest and spoliation, but the apogee of French power in the affairs of Europe.

Napoleon created a Duchy of Warsaw out of most of Prussian Poland and a slice of Austrian Poland. This Polish state, it was reasoned, would serve as a rampart against Russia if needed, and as a reservoir of excellent fighting material. Nominally, the Grand Duchy was assigned to the king of Saxony, but in practice he was the merest marionette who responded to the jerkings of a Napoleonic agent on the spot.

The new Poland was granted a constitution which, among other things, abolished serfdom. Yet the freed peasants were not given any land to cultivate, taxation was onerous and military drains upon manpower exhausting. If anything, peasant Poland was worse off than before. But the Napoleonic era, lighted by epic fighting of Polish troops, has meant much ever since in the book of romantic Polish nationalism.

Off to the west, another Napoleonic satellite had been fashioned in 1806—the German Confederation of the Rhine. Bavaria and a dozen small German states formed the original combination. It was presently joined by Saxony, and the Kingdom of Westphalia, embracing territory in western Germany taken away from Prussia. This Confederation represented another stride along the road to German national consolidation. Under Napoleon, the Confederation was taxed in manpower for the imperial armies, and taxed in money to keep the war machine rolling. Into the Confederation French novelties such as the abolition of serfdom, improved highways and schooling and the *Code Napoléon* were introduced.

As Bonaparte gazed at the European panorama on the morrow of Tilsit he may well have concluded that he was lord of all he surveyed, though his vision, it is true, could not penetrate across the English Channel. Southwards, in the Italian peninsula, states ruled directly or indirectly by the Emperor had been blocked out. Over Spain, Napoleon would soon set his brother Joseph as king and yeasty plans for the subjugation of Portugal were maturing; the tinsel crown of the Netherlands had been placed on the brow of Brother Louis. The Germanies were either reduced to vassalage, or, as in the case of Austria and Prussia, curtailed in strength, and smarting under furious military blows and humiliating peace settlements. Great Russia had definitely lined up with France; nearly all the major ports of the Continent were subject to the Emperor in one way or another. Thinking in terms of a United States of Europe, Napoleon exclaimed: "I have to make of all the peoples of Europe one single people, and of Paris the capital of the world." The Continent was Napoleon's, but—and this was a very stubborn but—Britannia ruled the waves—and sometimes waived the rules.

THE CONTINENTAL SYSTEM

No stratagem which the brain of Bonaparte could devise had succeeded against Great Britain. The defeat at Trafalgar had been a stunning blow and French cruisers and privateers could only nibble away at the merchant marine of the island kingdom. There was yet one weapon which, in theory at any rate, might force Britain to her knees—the weapon of commercial warfare. If the Continent could be hermetically sealed against British shipping, the British business community and workmen whose livelihood depended upon foreign trade might compel the London government to sue for an armistice. French producers, meantime, could profit by supplying the Continent with wares normally purchased from British merchants—political mastery over Europe would be matched, in other words, by commercial predominance.

Napoleon styled this program the Continental System. He started to carry it out with decrees issued from Berlin and Milan in 1806–07. These orders prescribed that Continental nations should not do business with Britain, that British merchants in Europe should be arrested and their goods confiscated and that any vessel which hauled cargoes to the island kingdom would be a lawful prize. London struck back with "Orders in Council" placing the Continent under blockade and threatening to seize ships which entered French-controlled harbors.

At first the Continental policy was not rigorously enforced. Ship captains lured on by the prospect of fat profits smuggled British-owned coffee, sugar, tea and manufactured products onto the Continent by way of the islands of Heligoland and Malta; the French government even issued licenses for the importation of "forbidden" articles. The Emperor himself drank illicit coffee and many of his soldiers wore shoes and uniforms made in Britain. But after 1810 the screws were tightened and effective steps were taken to enforce the embargo; British sales dropped sharply. That development infuriated Continental consumers and traders whose stomachs and wallets suffered.

Bent upon denying the Continent to British

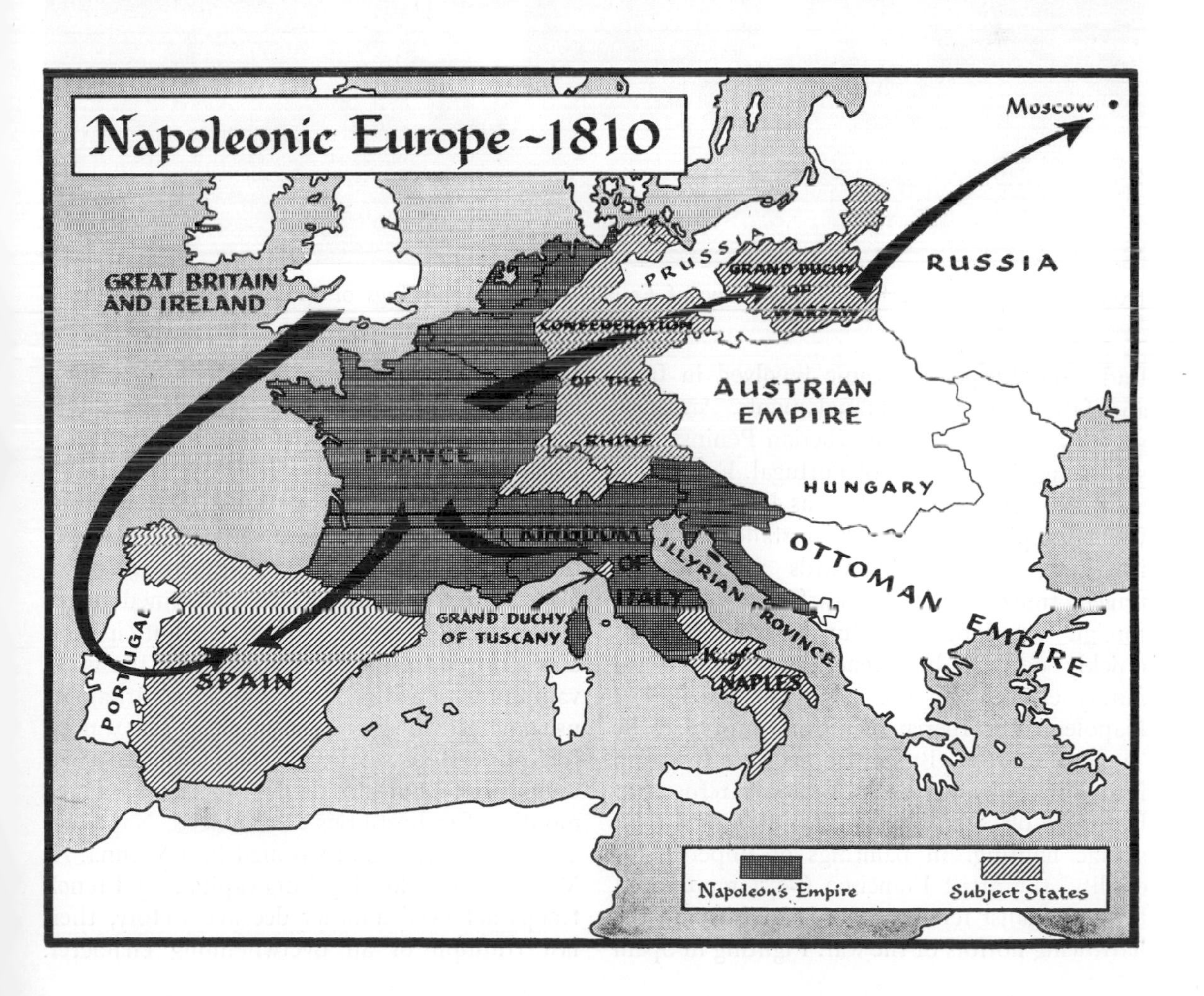

Execution after the Second of May, *one of Francisco Goya's paintings of the war in Spain*

trade, the Emperor became involved in fresh and fateful political entanglements. An army was dispatched across the Iberian Peninsula to stop smuggling by way of Portugal. For a time Spaniards welcomed soldiers as liberators. But when Joseph Bonaparte was installed as Spanish king, patriotic Spaniards rebelled and waged frenzied guerilla warfare against the foreign interlopers. Portugal, however, was quickly overrun by French arms, the royal family escaping to the colony of Brazil. For Napoleon, the Iberian Peninsula proved to be "a running sore." British troops were funneled into Portugal and they stubbornly refused to be driven off. Spanish guerillas intensified their savage fighting. In paintings of imperishable quality, the artist Francisco Goya reproduced the nationalist fervor of the Spaniards and the harrowing horrors of the war. Fighting in Spain and Portugal pinned down half a million French veterans whom the Emperor desperately needed for campaigns in central and eastern Europe.

Emboldened by the Spanish resistance, Austria in 1809 once more flung down the gauntlet to Napoleon. New and resourceful Austrian leadership had reinvigorated the armed forces and aroused popular passions in anticipation of a struggle to liberate Europe from the giant vampire who was the little Corsican. Britain as usual agreed to serve as paymaster. The war effort of Austria was heroic, more spirited than ever before, but decidedly premature. Three months after hostilities commenced, Napoleon and his soldiers again stormed into Vienna. At Wagram near the Hapsburg capital, the French troops achieved another decisive victory, their last triumph of an overwhelming character.

Once more the sovereign of Austria acceded to conditions of peace which Bonaparte presented.

The Treaty of Vienna of 1809 lopped off from Austria territories in the Adriatic region and the Polish province of Galicia. The Hapsburg emperor not only agreed to pay indemnities but even entered into a diplomatic alliance with France. The whole transaction was consolidated by the marriage of Napoleon to a Hapsburg Archduchess, Marie Louise, niece of the ill-starred Queen Marie Antoinette.

The luckless Empress Josephine had not presented Bonaparte with a son, so she was cavalierly discarded. Marie Louise was dumpy, a dull mediocrity in fact, but she was eighteen, a blonde and belonged to the oldest and proudest dynasty of Europe—all of which intrigued the ambitious and amorous Corsican parvenu. The marriage signified that Napoleon had ceased to be the heir of the Revolution and had become the champion of the old monarchical order. To the union a son, called "the Eaglet" was born, which seemed to ensure the perpetuation of the Bonapartist dynasty.

THE UNITED STATES AND EUROPE

Vast and tumultuous events in Europe had important reverberations, meanwhile, in the United States, precisely as had been the case in the French revolutionary decade. Eventually, the British commercial battle with Napoleon led the United States into war with Great Britain. But before that the United States had profited handsomely from the strife of Europe by acquiring the enormous Territory of Louisiana, ranging from the Mississippi to the Rockies.

Napoleon, who had taken Louisiana from Spain, expressed willingness in 1803 to transfer the region to the United States for $15,000,000, a mere bagatelle. With typical arbitrariness, Bonaparte, by making the offer, brushed aside promises he had given to Spain and disregarded prescriptions in the French constitution. He was anxious to enlist the cooperation of the United States against Great Britain. And in any case he knew that Louisiana would fall an easy prey to British seapower. The American government eagerly grasped the Bonapartist offer, borrowing from British bankers to pay the bill. By this gigantic real estate transaction the area of the United States was more than doubled at the bargain price of fifteen dollars per square mile!

Upon the resumption of the Anglo-French war in 1803, shipping interests in the United States prospered by transporting goods to Europe. But both belligerents, each striving to strangle the other commercially, seized American merchantmen and in other ways transgressed American conceptions of the rights of neutrals on the high seas. The British, for instance, boarded vessels flying the Stars and Stripes and removed seamen who were claimed to be subjects of George III. Insults and humiliations inflamed angry war emotions in the United States.

Preferring peace to war, the American government in 1807 tried to coerce the belligerents by prohibiting commerce with Europe. When that experiment floundered, the ban was restricted to direct trade with Britain and France. That compromise did not work either, for confiscations of ships and other displays of arrogance occurred, which outraged American national pride. It was seriously proposed in some circles that the United States should unsheathe the sword against both European belligerents. Diplomatic intercourse with Napoleon was in fact stopped in 1811, and the following year the United States declared war upon Great Britain.

Accumulated animosities due to British highhandedness at sea, coupled with pressure of American "war-hawks," who scented an opportunity to annex Canada and Florida, and very natural suspicions that British agents had incited restless Indians in the west to rebel, goaded the United States into fighting. The verdict for war generated considerable opposition in sections of the country, notably among Anglophiles in New England.

In effect though not in actual fact, the United States became the ally of Napoleon at just the moment that the Emperor had chosen to bend Russia to his imperious will by military force. From the European standpoint the

Anglo-American conflict was emphatically a side-show. After nearly three years of indecisive sparring on land and water, the United States and Great Britain worked out a peace settlement in 1815 which left controversial issues virtually where they had been when hostilities started.

THE RUSSIAN DÉBÂCLE

Back in Europe, in the meantime, the Napoleonic Empire had suffered an irreparable catastrophe. Quarreling between Napoleon and Alexander I reached the point where the Emperor decided that he must force the Tsar to terms by military chastisement. The Tsar, on his side, distrusted French intentions in the Duchy of Warsaw, which might exert a magnetic influence upon the sections of old Poland under Muscovite sovereignty; and he resented Napoleon's veto on Russian expansion toward Constantinople.

To these grievances and suspicions were added Russian apprehensions growing out of the French alliance with Austria and the concentration of Napoleonic armies within striking distance of the tsardom. Russian clergy taught the pious masses that Napoleon was a false Messiah whose destruction was the "will of God," and that the French were not only enemies of the Fatherland but enemies of God Himself.

Napoleon, on the other hand, was enraged by the refusal of the Tsar to enforce the boycott on trade with Britain. Russian commercial interests suffered severely from the loss of business with the "workshop of the world," and they helped to persuade the Tsar of the unwisdom of stringing along with Bonaparte. In December of 1810, ports of Muscovy were thrown wide open to British shipping which provoked a species of "cold war" with Napoleon. In the spring of 1812, the Emperor launched out in a melodramatic invasion of huge Russia.

It was cheerfully assumed by Bonaparte that his Grand Army would score another lightning triumph and that Alexander I, as soon as his capacity to resist had been broken, could be coaxed into a new alliance against Great Britain. In point of fact, the Conqueror of Europe, like Charles XII of Sweden earlier and Hitler later, met his Nemesis in the forests and snowfields of Russia.

For a massive thrust upon Moscow, Napoleon assembled a motley array of about 600,000 soldiers, not more than a third of them French, as many Germans, and the rest conscripted from other vassal countries. Although three times as large as the Russian armies, the invading host was handicapped by lax discipline, desertions and unprecedented problems of supply. Continuous and wearying fighting, moreover, had played its mischief on Napoleon. Old at forty-three, he lacked something of the verve and flexibility of mind displayed in earlier campaigns. And from the beginning to the end the Grand Army was beset by fierce Muscovite guerrilla fighters rising out of the countryside.

The road to Moscow lay through Smolensk, a city to which the Russians retreated, scorching the earth as they pulled back. When Smolensk capitulated to the French, it was put to the torch which infuriated simple Russian peasants everywhere. At the Borodino River, invaders and defenders collided head-on in September, 1812, both sides sustaining prodigious losses. But the French won out and Moscow lay open to easy occupation. Napoleon gleefully established himself in the imperial apartments of the Kremlin, the Muscovite holy of holies. On order of Russian authorities, it appears, fires were started in several sections of Moscow, causing immense destruction.

In spite of the loss of Moscow, Alexander I comforted his mercurial spirit with the thought that space and time were on his side. He stubbornly declined to treat with Napoleon. So the Emperor ordered his forces to evacuate Moscow after a sojourn of five weeks. An epic retreat westward began, one of the unspeakable tragedies of military history. Those grim and cruel Muscovite warriors, Generals November and December, took a heavy toll of the proud Napoleonic legions. So did starvation. And disease. And Cossack horsemen. And the blunt knives of peasant partisans.

When the armies of Bonaparte quit the soil of Russia they had dwindled to a miserable

An episode on the retreat from Russia. The sign reads: "Moscow—325 versts."

rabble of not more than 100,000. His reputation eclipsed almost beyond hope of recovery and the Continental System a forlorn ruin, the Emperor in complete disguise rushed back to France. In Allied countries, Alexander I was toasted as "the Great," the conqueror of the Conqueror of Europe; extravagant notions of Muscovite military power captivated the west of Europe.

THE LIBERATION OF EUROPE

On the heels of the Russian débâcle, Prussia cut loose from Napoleon and lined up in alliance with Russia. It was no longer the Prussia of Jena, however, but a rejuvenated, inspirited Prussia worthy of the best traditions of Frederick the Great. Smarting under the punishment inflicted by Napoleon, an extraordinary set of statesmen, not one of them Prussian-born, curiously, had undertaken to renovate the kingdom along lines suggested by the principles of 1789.

To encourage a deeper sense of political loyalty, Baron vom Stein, a Rhinelander who hated revolution and tyranny alike, secured royal sanction for an ordinance releasing Prussian serfs from bondage and canceling antiquated land customs. Other German states imitated Prussia, though half a century elapsed before serfdom was fully wiped out. To stimulate enthusiasm among the Prussian middle classes, a program of municipal self-government was set in operation. Stein's reforms antagonized Junker aristocrats who reviled him as a Jacobin, and angered Napoleon who eventually forced the king to dismiss this able and enlightened statesman. Prince Karl von Hardenberg, who firmly believed that Prussia "must do from above what the French have done from below," carried forward the work of Stein. Former serfs were assisted in becoming peasant proprietors, though this basic innovation was not much felt in the northern and eastern sections of the kingdom. Guild privileges were canceled, thus removing a large obstacle to the free growth of industry.

Social reforms were accompanied by a sort of moral rearmament, that is, agitation to arouse an ardent patriotism, French-style, in stolid Prussian breasts. Impassioned appeals were addressed to the educated by the philosopher Johann G. Fichte, a pupil of Kant, who eloquently proclaimed that every citizen had a duty to serve the state in every way. A Germany strong in the strength which national consciousness and capacity for war generated could exert a decisive influence, Fichte contended, in the reconstruction of Europe. Patriotic sentiment struck deep root in university circles, particularly in the University of Berlin, founded at this time, and destined to develop into the foremost institution of higher learning in the world. Students dedicated themselves to reassertion of German dignity and to ending French domination.

National spirit among the masses was fostered by pointing to German achievements in the cultivated arts or to the prowess of mighty Germans of the past, Frederick the Great among them. In stirring patriotic poems, Professor Ernst Moritz Arndt summoned fellow Germans to strike off the galling Napoleonic yoke and to work for a united Germany.

Under the direction of General Gerhard von Scharnhorst, the Prussian army was converted into a spirited and effective instrument of war. Scharnhorst understood the connection between the principles of 1789 and the remarkable *esprit* of the French soldiers. The Prussian officers corps was purged of elderly commanders who cherished the outmoded fashions of Frederick II. And, more important, the army itself was drastically remodeled; every able-bodied young man was conscripted for a term of military service.

According to the treaty with Napoleon, Prussia might not maintain an army in excess of 42,000 men. Scharnhorst, however, worked out a scheme whereby conscripts spent a year in rigorous training, patriotic indoctrination included, and then passed into the reserve forces. Reservists might be called to active duty on short notice. This plan, which other countries later copied, enabled Prussia to field an army of over 250,000 in the final campaigns against Napoleon.

Back in France after the ghastly Russian nightmare, Napoleon collected another great army, scraping the bottom of the barrel to do so, and returned to the attack in central Europe. If the French forces could control Saxony and prevent concentration of opponents, a favorable treaty of peace might still be achieved. Arrayed in the enemy ranks were Britain, Russia, Austria and Prussia, the last great partnership organized against Napoleonic France. Division of mind still hampered Allied operations; Austrian policymakers, for instance, suspected that Alexander I wished to assert Russian hegemony over central Europe. They could see little virtue in hopping out of the Napoleonic frying pan only to land in a Muscovite fire. Nonetheless, Allied soldiers were impetuously patriotic, expertly commanded and more numerous and better equipped than the French troops.

After two indecisive French victories in Saxony, the rival armies collided decisively just outside of Leipzig in October of 1813. Called the "Battle of the Nations," that bitter struggle closed in overwhelming French defeat. Napoleon with his shattered legions fell back across the Rhine, pursued by the Allies eager for the kill. The gigantic and servile edifice of the modern Charlemagne which once had extended from the Strait of Gibraltar to the streets of Moscow, cracked and crumbled, though the agony of conflict was not yet over.

Off to the south, British troops in cooperation with Spanish guerrilla partisans had created a "second front." Command of the British forces was assigned to Sir Arthur Wellington, later to win high honors at Waterloo, who led his men from victory to victory. The retreat of the French forces from Spain resembled indeed the withdrawal from Russia, only at a slower pace. Early in 1813 British and Spanish troops advanced into France.

THE DOWNFALL OF NAPOLEON

It had been twenty years since foreign armies had set foot in France. Now they poured in from the south and from the east. The French fought hard in 1814, despite war weariness and civilian apathy, and Napoleon directed operations with something approaching his youthful energy and skill. But the French resistance was in fact as suicidal as that of Nazi Germany in 1945. When Russian and Prussian cavalry forces drove triumphantly into Paris in March, 1814, Napoleon surrendered and was banished an abject prisoner to the tiny isle of Elba off the coast of Italy. Europe at long last was liberated from French lordship and the legitimate Bourbon claimant to the French throne, Louis XVIII, brother of the decapitated Louis XVI, was set up as king by the victorious Allies.

For Bonaparte the stay on Elba was a strange interlude and a short one. Dissension among the Allies over the peace settlements, together with French dissatisfaction over the policies of the restored Bourbon, inspired "Boney," as the British called him, to defy Europe once more. Escaping from Elba, he returned dramatically to Paris, amidst the plaudits of peasants and army veterans at any rate. The Allies evacuated the capital with Louis XVIII concealed in their baggage.

Organizing his last great army, Napoleon marched into Belgium intending to overpower the British and Prussian forces collected there.[3] Fighting centered upon Waterloo, the French scoring minor successes and then going down to irretrievable defeat in June, 1815. Even had the French been successful on the farmlands of Belgium, they could not have won the war, for the resources of the Allied coalition were far greater and *esprit de corps* was very good.

Against his wish and will Napoleon[4] was hauled off to the south Atlantic island of St. Helena, there to find a permanent prison and an impermanent grave. The most glittering of military showmen if not indeed the foremost military genius of all time had passed into history. "Boney" became a ghost with whom English nursemaids threatened unruly charges —a ghost, and for many a Frenchman an imperishable legend. "He was as great as a man can be without morality," a French historian wrote.

Dissatisfaction in France combined with external forces had brought about the crack-up of the Napoleonic Empire. Fateful indiscretions and fatal blunders loosened the Emperor's tyrannical grip upon France and raised up implacable opponents abroad. The "little corporal," that is to say, over-reached himself and became the chief architect of his own ruin. Many Frenchmen turned against him and Europe united to defeat his greedy lust for power.

Inside France, the treatment of Catholic Church and Pope embittered the clergy who branded Napoleon as anti-Christ and incited their flocks against him. And mere laymen had grown weary of the incessant adventures and warfare, which chopped down young French manhood and devoured the national wealth. Not even a Napoleon could keep French war psychology at white heat forever. Some Frenchmen came to doubt whether campaigns were being waged for purposes of national security or to diffuse and safeguard the principles of 1789. It seemed rather that the fighting was being carried on to further the extravagant ambitions of the insatiable Corsican. Increasingly, conscripts refused to respond to the call to the colors.

And yet, resentment in France, great though it became, could hardly alone have brought Napoleon to the earth. Other nations imitated French military techniques and gradually learned the lesson of cooperation for purposes of self-preservation. Economic warfare with

[3] A faction in Britain which had wearied of strife mustered seventy-two votes in the Commons against renewal of the war with Bonaparte.

[4] Napoleon contemplated fleeing to the United States with his brother Joseph who actually did so, but Napoleon soon abandoned the idea.

THE COLCHESTER GAZETTE.

GREAT AND DECISIVE VICTORY OVER THE FRENCH ARMY.

The dreadful conflict has at length commenced, and however much we must lament the sanguinary consequences that have ensued, it is with heartfelt pride we record, that victory has been faithful to our cause, and that additional laurels grace the brows of the allied combatants.

In addition to what we have, in a preceding column, laid before our Readers, we have now the gratification to state, that, after a protracted contest throughout the whole of Saturday the 17th, and Sunday the 18th, the most complete success has crowned the valorous efforts of the allied armies, involving the entire overthrow of Bonaparte's force. The official dispatch, announcing this most glorious and highly important information, was brought by the Hon. Major Percy, Aide-de-Camp to the Duke of Wellington, who arrived at Earl Bathurst's Office between eleven and twelve o'clock on Wednesday night. An Official Bulletin was

An English provincial newspaper reports the battle of Waterloo.

Britain entailed hardships for European consumers, whose governments Napoleon unwisely endeavored to coerce by force.

Besides, Europeans did not care to have their lives run by the French, and recoiled at the idea of a uniform political system; repudiation of uniformity indeed was the one thing in which Europeans were uniform. In the first phase of French domination, elimination of privileges, social abuses and traditional inefficiency was welcomed with gratitude by the masses and with enthusiasm by local philosophers. But later on, liberated peoples rebelled against the Napoleonic strait jacket. Fierce national passions welling up in Germany, in Spain, in Russia, and British bulldog tenacity contributed vitally to breaking the power of the tyrant, first behind the Pyrenees, then on the plains of Russia, at Leipzig, in France and at last on the historic field of Waterloo.

Robert Southey's *Carmen Triumphale*, which appeared in 1813, recounted the tale of Bonaparte's doom in poetic phrasings:

> From Spain the living spark went forth:
> The flame hath caught, the flame hath spread!
> It warms, it fires the furthest North:
> Behold! The awakened Muscovite
> Meets the tyrant in his might;
> The Brandenburg, at freedom's call,
> Rises more glorious from his fall; . . .
> Up Germany! With all thy nations rise
> Land of the virtuous and the wise,
> No longer let that free, that mighty mind
> Endure its shame! She rose as from the dead,
> She broke her chains upon the oppressor's head,
> Glory to God! Deliverance for mankind.

British seapower and matériel of war furnished to continental allies played important roles in the downfall of Napoleon as in the World Wars of the twentieth century. En route to St. Helena, the deposed Emperor confessed to his British captors: "If it had not been for you English, I should have been Emperor of the East, but wherever there is water to float a ship we were sure to find you in the way."

PROBLEMS OF PEACE

Even before Napoleon was finally humbled, Allied statecraft was busy with the exacting tasks of liquidating the Bonapartist adventures, of redrawing the European map and of laying the ghost of revolutionary principles and innovations. Once victory had been achieved, however, the supreme purpose which united the Allies against the common peril lost its effectiveness. "The romance is over," observed a prominent statesman. "We are back in history." As was true after the World Wars of the twentieth century the victor nations fell to quarreling among themselves and the popular enthusiasms of the war years rapidly slumped. At one point controversies among the Allies grew so bitter that it seemed as though arguments across the diplomatic table would be switched to the battlefield.

The peace settlements of 1815 may be thought of as having two parts. First, two treaties with France, one before, the other after the escape of Napoleon from Elba, and second, decisions on other problems that were made at a congress in Vienna. By the final Treaty of Paris, signed in November, 1815, the frontiers of France were thrown back to about the limits of 1789 but practically all the pre-revolutionary French oversea possessions were recovered. It is noteworthy that the triumphant Allies did not wrest Alsace-Lorraine away from France.

As the penalty for rallying behind Napoleon upon his return from Elba, France had to pay a modest indemnity of 700,000,000 francs within five years and to maintain an Allied army of occupation until the debt was liquidated. Stolen works of art had to be restored to their former owners. The terms of peace did not appear to be punitive or unfair, were, indeed, remarkably lenient considering that France had fought and fleeced Europe for nearly a quarter of a century; the honor and integrity of France were preserved. A moderate settlement seemed to British and Russian diplomacy absolutely necessary, if Bourbon King Louis XVIII, who had again been seated on the throne, was to rule with hope of success, and a war of revenge were to be avoided.

THE CONGRESS OF VIENNA

Nearly all the frontiers of central and eastern Europe had to be defined and the sovereigns of many states had to be decided upon. These

Meeting of the Representatives at the Congress of Vienna

Prince Metternich

problems of peace were dealt with at an international congress which convened in the autumn of 1814 at the gay and animated capital of the Hapsburgs on the Danube, and lasted nine months. Never before had so illustrious a galaxy of statesmen assembled for the making of peace, not to mention the veritable swarm of henchmen and lesser dignitaries who gravitated to Vienna.

Leading personage at the Congress was Prince Clemens Metternich, Austrian foreign minister, a relatively young man yet wedded to conservative ideas. What Europe required, he was sure, was stability and repose. Accordingly, princes should be restored to absolute authority and the explosive spirit of nationalism, which was especially dangerous for the polyglot Austrian realm, must be repressed. For the maintenance of peace, the major states of Europe must be brought into balance so that no country would be able to lord over the Continent as France had done. Extremely handsome, extremely pompous and conceited, Metternich considered his personal judgments on international matters as infallible.

Alexander I of Russia attended the Vienna parley in the proud conviction that his Muscovite armies almost single-handed had freed Europe from the odious Corsican tyrant. His sense of eminence and of mission was heightened by tumultuous receptions accorded him and his retinue. While visiting London, for instance, the Tsar was showered with official decorations and crowds forced open the gates of the royal residence to catch a glimpse of the illustrious Muscovite. Even when thirsty Cossacks drank the oil from street lamps, the enthusiasm of Londoners for their Russian guests was not dampened.

Of a mystical turn of mind, Alexander I fancied that God had chosen him to lead society into a brighter and happier era. Avowedly a pacifist, too, he said, "If men were vital Christians, there would be no wars . . . I am sure that the spirit of Christianity is decisive against war." And yet, as the Russian share of the territorial spoils, the Tsar claimed all of Poland, which threatened to upset the European balance and very nearly disrupted the Vienna deliberations.

The interests of Prussia were argued by Prince Hardenberg. His demand for Saxony, whose king had loyally stood by Napoleon, unloosed angry debates at the conference. For Britain the principal spokesman was Foreign Minister Castlereagh, austere, urbane, industrious. An old-school diplomatist, he worked—and successfully—to ensure British security by means of the balance of power, or the "just equilibrium" in his own phrase. More exactly, the Low Countries, Castlereagh insisted, must be protected against French aggression and the power of Russia must not be permitted to expand too greatly. Colonial holdings which had been seized by the British navy should be retained.

Considering the handicaps under which he labored, the slippery and competent Talleyrand, representative of the France of Louis XVIII, outshone his colleagues at Vienna. An apostate priest and political chameleon, his flair for the diplomatic art amounted to genius. He gained admission to the inner councils of the Congress owing to the critical divergence of views among the Allies on the Polish and Saxon problems. Posing as the champion of the principle of legitimacy and the rights of small states, Talleyrand fanned enmities among the victors and managed to do very well for his beloved France.

These five statesmen constituted the real Congress of Vienna. They considered reports of experts and made decisions in secrecy. For the entertainment of the minor diplomatic fry Viennese society presented a round of extravagant and costly festivities, tournaments, operas, military parades, dances, dances and more dances. Vienna danced, but vital business was transacted, though interrupted briefly by the sensational reappearance of Napoleon on the European stage.

Controversies over Poland and over Saxony, as has been suggested, nearly ruined the meeting of the peacemakers. But sane counsels in time prevailed and mutually acceptable compromises were discovered. Looked at in the large, three considerations guided the Vienna verdicts: compensation, which implied that if a state lost territory to which it had claims, it should be appropriately rewarded elsewhere; second, the principle that wherever feasible "legitimate" dynasties should be reinstated on thrones. And finally, that turbulent France should be ringed round with states capable of checking or containing her.

Territorially speaking, how then did the statesmen at Vienna reshape the Old World? Instead of creating a strongly united Germany, as desired by ardent German patriots, the Congress sanctioned a feeble union under the name

The Balance of Power: *a French satire on the Congress of Vienna. Wellington is shown putting English money on the scale to balance the weight of subject peoples handed over in bundles to the sovereigns of Europe.*

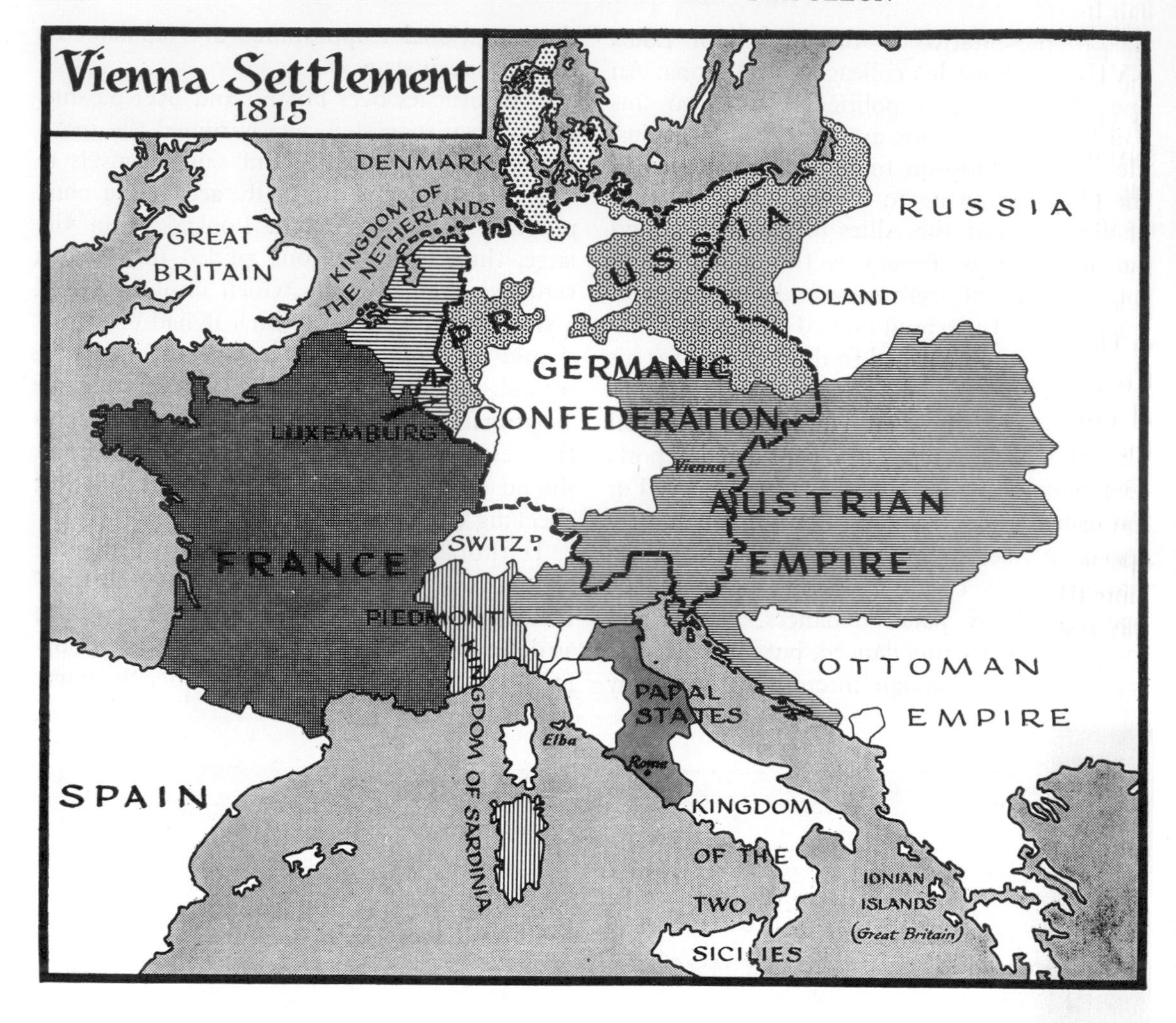

of the German Confederation. Austria, it was stipulated, would hold the presidency and a federal Diet would be organized. Though the German Confederation remained in being for over half a century, it never developed much vigor or influence.

The kingdom of Prussia made splendid gains at the Vienna gathering. Part of her former Polish holdings was surrendered to Russia, it is true, but two-fifths of Saxony and slighter parcels in central Germany were annexed. The principal acquisition, however, was the Rhineland extending northward from Coblenz and embracing the Ruhr Valley. That arrangement placed Prussia, which in 1789 was still tucked away in the northeastern section of Germany, alongside of France. Assuming that France would always be uniquely the disturber of peace, British diplomacy wished that Prussia should control the Rhineland and thus serve as the fortress of Germany. The Prussian authorities went along, albeit reluctantly out of fear that possession of the Rhineland provinces would invite trouble with France. Holding the "Watch on the Rhine," Prussia was almost bound to become the leader of Germany in time.

No country had suffered so frequently and so painfully at the hands of Revolutionary France and Napoleon as Austria. In the Vienna Treaty the Hapsburgs relinquished Belgium, but were richly compensated with lands at the head of the Adriatic Sea (including Dalmatia) and the most productive and intellectually advanced areas of Italy, Venetia and Lombardy. Most of the Polish and Ukrainian inhabited province of Galicia was likewise remanded to Austria. Not more than one in five of the inhabitants of the new Austrian Empire spoke German as his mother-tongue, yet Castlereagh considered Austria the very bulwark of European stability, or as he said, "the great hinge upon which the fate of Europe must ultimately depend."

Italy continued to be, as it had long been, merely a geographical expression. Austria not only controlled Lombardy and Venetia but "legitimate" sovereigns who were Austrian puppets were restored in the principalities of central Italy. The Pope recovered the States of the Church and the legitimate Bourbon monarch was awarded the crown of the Two Sicilies. As a rampart against possible French aggression, the kingdom of Sardinia (Piedmont) in the north-west was allotted the historic Republic of Genoa.

Quite in keeping with the doctrine of legitimacy the old dynasties were reestablished in Spain and Portugal as in France. In accordance with the policy of strengthening countries adjoining France, Belgium was assigned to Holland to form the kingdom of the Netherlands, and Switzerland was slightly enlarged at French expense. Norway was handed over to Sweden as a reward to the ruler, Bernadotte, sometime Napoleonic marshal, who had switched at an opportune moment to the Allied coalition.

The acquisition of Norway compensated Sweden very nicely for the compulsory transfer of Finland to Russia in 1809. The tsardom had also snatched Bessarabia away from Turkey and secured the largest portion of Poland, Warsaw included. Russian Poland, now penetrated like a wedge between the Prussian and Austrian slices of the ancient Polish kingdom.

British territorial winnings were exclusively of a strategic and colonial character. Sovereignty over the former Danish island of Heligoland assured Britain of command of the approaches to the Elbe River, while Malta and the Ionian Islands reinforced the British position in the Mediterranean. The Netherlands ceded valuable Ceylon to Britain and also the Cape of Good Hope, the foundation of the Dominion of South Africa. France and Spain, too, transferred small islands of strategic value to the British Empire.

After distributing lands and crowns, the Allied statesmen consecrated their military triumph by creating machinery to preserve peace in the future, as well as to perpetuate the system established by the treaty settlements. A Quadruple Alliance set up in 1815 was a loose confederation of the victorious Allies intended to be permanent and ultimately universal in function, if not in membership. In some ways the Alliance resembled the international organizations founded after the World Wars of the twentieth century.

Members of the Alliance committed themselves not only to prevent a Bonaparte from returning to the French throne, but also to meet periodically "to consider measures . . . for the peace and prosperity of the nations and for the maintenance of European peace." In keeping with this agreement several conferences were convened in the next decade.[5]

SUMMARY

Apart from presiding over the reconstruction of France, Napoleon I nearly succeeded in uniting Europe under his sword. He claimed that he wished to build a peaceful supernational state. But in point of fact by intensifying national sentiments he effectively blocked the development of such a federation. The intensification of nationalism among European peoples cherishing old and proud traditions was indeed a major legacy of the era of the French Revolution and Napoleon to the later and contemporary world.

Much of the symbolism of nationalism, much of the institutionalism of nationalism

[5] Out of the curious brain of Alexander I issued a peace project known as the Holy Alliance, which is often confused with the Quadruple Alliance. This visionary and informal league obligated monarchs to pursue international policies dictated by the precepts of Christianity; actually, the pact was worth little more than the foolscap on which it was written. Metternich pilloried the Holy Alliance as "a loud-sounding nothing," a hypocritical device of the Tsar to further Russian ambitions.

such as the national flag, the national anthem and the national army originated in this epoch. The French creed of patriotism and the concept of a nation-in-arms pervaded Germans, Italians, Poles and Spaniards. Russians were accustomed to speak of the war with Napoleonic France as the "First Patriotic War"—that with Hitlerian Germany as the "Second Patriotic War." For Great Britain, too, the conflict assumed the quality of a holy national crusade, and Admiral Nelson for more than a century was the best loved name in British ears. Peacemakers at Vienna paid scant attention to the phenomenon of nationalism, which would so largely shape the course of events for succeeding generations.

Other innovations brought to the fore by Revolutionary France were diffused from the Mediterranean to the Baltic by the charioteers, the bureaucrats and the tax-gatherers of Napoleon. These novelties included civil freedoms, religious toleration, civil equality, public schooling, universal military service and popular sovereignty. The statesmen at Vienna declined to come to terms with these dynamic forces. Yet, never again would the divine authority of a ruling family or of a clerical caste and the political inequality of citizens go unchallenged as the foundations of European states.

It must, however, be stressed that the impact of the principles of 1789 varied considerably. To the east of the Rhine and south of the Pyrenees, the institutions and ideas of the old regime were far less disturbed than in the West, lingering on in fact into the twentieth century. Again and again in the future, resistance to French ideas flared up violently, for example, in the Nazi movement of the 1930's; the Nazis substituted the truncheon for liberty, fanatical racialism for equality, German domination for national fraternity.

Last of all, after the final defeat of Napoleon, rewards had been conferred upon the victor countries, the map of Europe had once more been redrawn and machinery to keep the peace had been devised. After more than a generation of agonizing tensions and shattering convulsions which left the nations exhausted, Europe now entered upon nearly a half-century of international tranquility.

FOR FURTHER STUDY

JAMES M. THOMPSON, *Napoleon Bonaparte: His Rise and Fall* (New York, 1952)

HAROLD C. DEUTSCH, *The Genesis of Napoleonic Imperialism* (New York, 1938)

GEOFFREY BRUUN, *Europe and the French Imperium* (New York, 1938)

PETER GEYL, *Napoleon, For and Against* (New Haven, 1949)

ANDREI A. LOBANOV-ROSTOVSKY, *Russia and Europe* (Durham, 1947)

ELI F. HECKSCHER, *The Continental System* (Eng. trans., Oxford, 1922)

EUGEN TARLE, *Napoleon's Invasion of Russia* (New York, 1942)

CONSTANTIN DE GRUNWALD, *Napoleon's Nemesis: The Life of Baron Stein* (Eng. trans., New York, 1936)

ALGERNON CECIL, *Metternich* (New York, 1935)

HAROLD NICOLSON, *The Congress of Vienna* (London, 1946) PAPERBACK

FELIX M. H. MARKHAM, *Napoleon and the Awakening of Europe* (New York, 1954)

ARMAND DE CAULAINCOURT, *With Napoleon in Russia* (New York, 1935) PAPERBACK

JOHN NAYLOR, *Waterloo* (New York, 1960)

A List of Significant Dates

WESTERN EUROPE		CENTRAL AND EASTERN EUROPE		OVERSEAS	
1778	French Alliance with America	**1772**	First Partition of Poland	**1765**	Stamp Act Congress
1783	William Pitt the Younger, Prime Minister	**1773**	Pugachev Revolt	**1768**	Cook's Voyage to Pacific
1788	Eden Treaty Operative	**1780**	Joseph II Emperor of Austria	**1774**	First Continental Congress
1789	French Revolution	**1786**	Death of Frederick II	**1776**	War of the American Revolution
1791	Death of Mirabeau	**1792**	Austria and Prussia fight France	**1786-98**	Wars in India
1793	Execution of Louis XVI	**1795**	Third Partition of Poland	**1781**	Yorktown Surrender
1793	"Reign of Terror"	**1796**	Death of Catherine II	**1783**	Peace of Paris
1795	Directory	**1806**	Confederation of the Rhine	**1789**	Washington President
1799	Napoleon First Consul	**1806**	Battle of Jena	**1791**	Canada Act
1801	Act of Irish Union	**1812**	French Invasion of Russia	**1798**	Bonaparte in Egypt
1801	Napoleon's Concordat	**1813**	Battle of Leipzig	**1803**	Louisiana Purchase
1804	Napoleon Emperor			**1807**	British Slave Trade Illegal
1804	Civil Code			**1808**	Beginning Latin-American Revolts
				1812	Anglo-American War

CULTURAL AFFAIRS		GENERAL	
1764	*Crimes and Punishment* (Beccaria)	**1761**	Bridgewater's Canal
1773	Society of Jesus suppressed	**1764**	Hargreave's Spinning Jenny
1776	*Wealth of Nations* (Smith)	**1769**	Watt's steam engine
1776	*Decline and Fall of the Roman Empire* (Gibbons)	**1783**	Wrought iron (Cort)
1781	*The Critique of Pure Reason* (Kant)	**1785**	Cartwright's power loom
1784	Cavendish explodes oxygen and hydrogen into water	**1793**	First Coalition against France
1786	*The Marriage of Figaro* (Mozart)	**1793**	Whitney's cotton gin
1789	*An Elementary Treatise on Chemistry* (Lavoisier)	**1798**	Second Coalition
1790	*Reflections on the French Revolution* (Burke)	**1805**	Third Coalition
1795	*Theory of the Earth* (Hutton)	**1805**	Battle of Trafalgar
1798	*Essay of the Principle of Population* (Malthus)	**1806**	Continental System
1802	*Genius of Christianity* (Chateaubriand)	**1807**	Peace of Tilsit
1808	"Fifth Symphony" (Beethoven)	**1807**	Fulton's steamboat
		1815	Waterloo
		1815	Congress of Vienna

PART III

THE NINETEENTH CENTURY BEGINS

CHAPTER XII

HISTORY'S GREATEST REVOLUTION

MECHANIZATION TAKES COMMAND

ADDRESSING the Congress of the United States in 1950, President Harry S. Truman remarked: "The scientific and industrial revolution which began two centuries ago has . . . caught up the peoples of the globe in a common destiny. Two world-shattering wars have proved that no corner of the earth can be isolated from the affairs of mankind." The immense transformation which the President had in mind was in fact less sudden than the term revolution may suggest, though it was more far-reaching than any political overturn in history. Besides, the changeover was not merely industrial and technological but affected virtually every facet of human life.

ptain Dick's Puffer," the first locomotive, devised by ard Trevithick (1771–1833) shown here on his business

The term "industrial revolution," coined by French writers in the eighteenth century was popularized in the 1880's by an English scholar, Arnold Toynbee, and may as well be retained. Actually, however, the transformation was not confined to a limited period of time but has gone on continuously in the nature of an evolution. "Innovation bred innovation" and "the ladder of discovery" appeared to have no top. A Utopian drama of the twentieth century, *R. U. R.* (Rossum's Universal Robots), by the Czech playwright Karel Čapek, cleverly captured the spirit and purpose of the age of invention. The robot, or mechanical man, was pictured doing the work of mortals in every respect but one: the robot could do everything but think.

In a narrow sense the industrial revolution implies the vast increase in the output of goods by the use of new forms of power and of machinery capable of large scale production. The making of goods by machine, which is machinofacturing, replaced literal manufacturing, or making goods by hand. The tireless inanimate resources of nature were harnessed to perform work which hitherto had been done by human and

The older type of industry. Spinners at work in an Irish cottage

animal muscle or simple tools. By reason of the machine, men earned their daily bread with less sweat of the brow. This silent, ceaseless revolution, which started in England in the latter half of the eighteenth century, distinguishes the subsequent period of history from all preceding epochs.

A unique economic structure emerged rapidly, irresistibly. Techniques of farming and manufacturing and places of employment changed, food and clothing changed, housing and recreations changed. Methods and institutions of finance and trade changed. Farms and cottages were more and more superseded by factories and cities, rural communities were often converted into urban centers. Men and women "served smoke and fire rather than frost and sun," in Thomas Hardy's apt phrase. Social classes and political groupings underwent drastic modifications.

Applied to transportation the machine accelerated human movement, brought men together in larger groupings, undermining local folkways and dialects. Population increased prodigiously, at a rate without precedent in recorded history, throwing up novel and baffling social problems. Profound changes took place in thinking about the ways of producing and distributing wealth and about human relationships more broadly. As mechanization took fuller and fuller command, other-worldly concerns yielded pride of place to the interests and values of the here and now. The pattern of living became immeasurably more complicated than ever known before.

With the progress of time the impact of the machine circled the globe, bringing wider and deeper changes in some countries, to be sure, than in others, but no nation, not even Paraguay or Saudi Arabia, remained unaffected by the surge of mechanization. Instruments of warfare evolved at an accelerated pace and the physical power and prestige of individual nations were significantly altered.

All in all this surely was history's greatest revolution.

MATERIAL EXISTENCE ABOUT 1750

The real nature of the transformation may be made more vivid by reviewing briefly the general character of material conditions in Western society on the eve of the industrial revolution. Judged by present-day standards social and economic affairs were impressively simple for the masses of men. Down to the mid-eighteenth century economic activity was firmly rooted in the land; the vast majority lived in scattered villages and wrested their livelihood from the earth as serfs, paid laborers, sharecroppers or peasant proprietors. In the unchanging countryside these folk enjoyed the advantages of quiet rural living (except for the interruptions of war on the Continent) to which the human nervous mechanism seems better attuned than to the wearing complexities of urban existence.

Italy, it is true, possessed many large towns, but there too workers on the land predominated. Many European coastal ports were busy hives of trade and exchange and political capitals such as London and Paris already contained large populations. Elsewhere, however, towns were small and unsanitary, generally without public water supplies or facilities for removal of refuse. Livestock roamed the streets of Berlin, for instance, until 1681 when an ordinance prohibited that oddity.

Agricultural methods had changed little for centuries. Ordinarily, arable fields were allowed to lie idle, fallowing every third year and were divided into many small strips. Villagers, commonly, had rights of pasturage and of gathering fuel on the public lands of their communities. The soil was turned up with wretched wooden plows such as Roman farmers had known, and grain, poor in quality, was sown by hand, cut with sickle, scythe, or cradle and threshed with cumbersome flails.

Farm animals were scrawny creatures; a sheep, for instance, was only large enough for a single family meal, and was prized for more for its wool than as meat. Draught animals, oxen more commonly than horses, were incapable of much hard field service. It was customary to keep only a few cattle over the winter, the rest being killed and salted down or smoked in the autumn. Life for the farm woman was continual drudgery, interspersed with child bearing; women and children toiled at field tasks for which they possessed the requisite strength. So preoccupied were rustics with their exacting daily round that they had little leisure time.

Many a farm family employed its energies in the winter months and when the weather was inclement in elementary forms of manufacturing. Middlemen "put out" unfinished goods, especially textiles, to one household for one type of operation, to another for another and so on until the article was completed. George Eliot's *Silas Marner* portrays in a somewhat romanticized way the manner of living under this domestic type of manufacturing.

Equipment was simple and light, though families often had to go into debt to purchase it. Yarn was spun by hand and by hand woven on an old fashioned loom; Penelope, who toiled away at her loom while awaiting the return of Ulysses would have found little that was startling in the cottage of a textile worker at the time that George III ascended the British throne. The product was usually of a coarse grade, uneven, and, of course, time was lost in moving the semi-finished goods from one household to the next. Likely enough the small cottage would be full of dust and dirt because of manufacturing operations.

Remuneration for the work was small. Workers, on the other hand, were their own "bosses," decided when they would work—or go fishing. Child workers frequently were overworked and underfed and there was a good deal of chiseling and cheating on the part of both middlemen and craftsmen. The ebb and flow of business affected domestic artisans but little, though underemployment was a chronic complaint.

In towns and cities manufacturing was carried on in the homes of the workers or in small shops or under guild roofs. Certain areas in Britain as well as Flanders, north Italian cities and Saxony, the most densely settled area of Germany, were noted for textiles, wool, linen, silk for the affluent, but precious little cotton. Many a town lent its name to a special variety of cloth. Muscles furnished much the greater part of the motive power in manufacturing, though in places small mills were driven by the water of streams or the ocean tide or by windmills. Consumers bought such manufactured goods as they required at weekly markets principally or at annual fairs or from wandering pedlars who toted a miscellaneous assortment of gadgets on their backs. International trade, though it had been expanding since the Crusades, was still restricted largely to comforts and luxuries.

In line with mercantilist doctrine each nation strove to make itself and its colonies (if any) self-sufficient, particularly in foodstuffs. Great Britain, for example, shipped away woolen goods and articles of leather and iron, some grain, too, and imported sugar, tea, tobacco, rum, timber and commodities needed in the building of ships. Basic necessities of life had as yet not entered heavily into world commerce.

Wooden sailing vessels were employed to haul goods and men by sea; small affairs these, not much larger than the famous *Mayflower* of 180 tons and accommodating 102 passengers. Ships at sea were at the mercy of winds, so that it was impossible to tell how long a journey would take. When Benjamin Franklin traveled to Europe he was rocked in the cradle of the deep as long as forty-two days. In internal commerce rivers and seas were used to move bulky or heavy goods and passengers as well. Navigation by waterways on the Continent was often hindered by rapids and shallows; customs offices and toll houses dotted the river banks, pushing up costs of transportation.

On land, commodities were transported in awkward, lumbering tumbrils or by packhorses, for roads in the main were unsuited for wheeled vehicles. French roads radiating from Paris were the best in Europe doubtless and yet it required as long to travel from Paris to Rome in the reign of Louis XVI as in the reign of Charlemagne. The stagecoach made its appearance before 1700 which inspired some improvements in road building, but until late in the eighteenth century movement by road was a tedious and exhausting business. Travel was dusty in summer, icy in winter and bogged down by mud in spring and fall; horsemen and animals alike sometimes disappeared in holes even on principal thoroughfares.

Stagecoaches, swung high upon springs, rocked and lurched along like rowboats in choppy water covering at best five miles an hour. Passengers needed patience, a robust physique and courage too, for masked highwaymen, chivalrous and other, lurking in lonely spots, introduced an ugly element of danger; wayside inns were apt to be squalid and overcrowded. Small wonder that travelers prepared their wills before setting off on a long journey and on reaching their destination took to their beds for days to recuperate.

As of 1750 everyday living for the ordinary fellow closely resembled that of several centuries before. Houses contained at most two rooms for living and a bedroom or two, all sparsely furnished; household equipment and furnishings had undergone little revision in a thousand years. If lighted at all, dwellings were lighted by candles or by rude lamps—flat wicks and glass chimneys were eighteenth-century novelties—burning sperm oil; in lieu of matches, flint and steel were the vogue.

Basic foodstuffs originated almost entirely in the immediate neighborhood in which they were consumed. Rye bread was the main staff of life, with potatoes an increasingly popular staple, and meat an event. Home-brewed beer and locally produced wine were consumed in quantities. Most families made their own clothes from wool or flax or engaged itinerant seamstresses to do so; even the garments of the well-to-do were unhygienic and inconvenient. Fuel in the form of wood or coal for cooking and warmth was procured in the locality.

Poverty and illitcracy were general, infant mortality was enormous, diets were monotonous and life was hedged in by the narrow conventions of village and small town. Folk festivals, christenings and weddings brightened the monotonous rustic round. For the most part physical hardships were endured with Oriental patience, Christian fortitude and dense ignorance. The comforting assurances of religion afforded a certain consolation for the drabness of daily existence.

CHANGES IN BRITISH FARMING

The immediate prelude to the trend away from the conditions just sketched must be sought in changes which occurred in British agricultural methods and land holding in the eighteenth century. Influenced by Dutch farmers, British agriculture entered upon a golden era, the pride of the country and the envy of the world, which lasted until the influx of cheap food from the Americas after about 1870. New root crops were planted before the middle of the eighteenth century, notably the humble turnip and grasses such as clover, which derived their nourishment from the air, not the earth. Soil was enriched by the application of various forms of lime and by the adoption of a four-course rotation of wheat, turnips, barley and clover, an innovation which kept fields always in production and reduced the risk of disease.

These changes greatly increased the yield of food and of feedstuffs for livestock in the winter months. Mechanical inventions also improved farming. Jethro Tull devised a drill for sowing seed, which meant a saving of seed and straight rows of growing plants. Crops could be efficiently cultivated to kill weeds and conserve moisture with a horse hoe, which Tull also invented. Plows, too, were somewhat improved and before the century was out primitive reaping and mowing machines were at work; the mechanization of agriculture had fairly begun.

Tull admirably typified the Britons of capacity and enterprise who applied innovations in soil cultivation. Although educated for the law, he switched to farming, learned of better techniques from continental growers, and wrote extensively on his experiments. Another "gentleman farmer," Lord Charles Townshend, eliminated the wasteful custom of fallowing by scientific rotation of crops; his emphasis upon root crops earned him the nickname of "Turnip" Townshend. Even George III took an active interest in agricultural betterment, writing articles on the subject, which he signed simply as "Farmer George."

At the same time the quality of farm animals was raised by better feeding and careful breeding. The pioneer in scientific animal husbandry was Robert Bakewell who bred the large-boned, coarse sheep into a well-fleshed animal which he called the new Leicester; meat on the sheep now counted for more than the wool. Another experimenter developed the great Hereford breed of cattle which thrives equally on the green pastures of Herefordshire or the endless ranges of Texas and Australia. Tougher horses were bred and slowly replaced oxen in western Europe as draught animals. All but three of the twenty breeds of sheep, cattle, horses and pigs which have a world-wide reputation nowadays originated in England. England became and remains the leading exporter of pedigree livestock; when Soviet Russia, for example, set up state flocks of sheep, it purchased breeding rams in Great Britain.

British agricultural experts of the eighteenth century figured out that large acreages could be worked more efficiently than small peasant farms. Consequently a movement to merge holdings got under way somewhat as in the Russian collectivization plan of the 1930's. Enterprising landed gentry, eager for profits, mortgaged their estates at low rates of interest and bought up the land of freeholders. Capitalist farmers also benefited from acts of Parliament which transferred to them common village lands or wasteland covering nearly a fifth part of the acreage of the kingdom. Keen for experimentation, landlords practiced crop rotation, plunged capital into drainage projects and other forms of reclamation which enlarged the plowlands. Big estates blossomed out as veritable "factories" of wheat and meat to satisfy the food demands of the rapidly rising British population.

It was the need for food and more food which inspired the various changes in British farming. Until about 1775 British farms satisfied national requirements but after that grain had normally to be imported, principally from the Baltic area. Many farmers, it is true, clung jealously to traditional ways and only gradually took up with new methods, but over a period of a century the agricultural reformation was so general as to amount to a revolution. Food supplies increased very greatly, fresh meat was available the year around, and the better and more varied diet strengthened resistance to disease and lengthened the life-span of the individual. Progressive cultivators on the Continent copied British farming innovations in time.

Consolidation of landed properties involved the virtual disappearance of the small independent proprietor from the English countryside and therewith much of the cottage manufacturing disappeared. The "little fellow" suffered no little injustice and much hardship, as was true of many Soviet Russian peasants at the time of rural consolidation. The poet Oliver Goldsmith vividly described and mourned the shift in landholding in *The Deserted Village*. Displaced yeomen might, of course, remain in the country and take employment for wages, or they might strike out anew overseas, or they might move into an expanding industrial community and look for jobs in factories and mines.

Associated with the agricultural "revolution" was a prodigious increase in population. Population in England and Wales approximated 5,500,000 in 1700, having shown only modest increase for centuries. By 1750 the population had risen by almost a million and it very greatly expanded in the next fifty years, standing at nearly 9,000,000 in 1801—10,500,000 with Scotland—when the first census was taken. Immigration was not responsible for the increase, for although England exerted a magnetic influence upon the Scotch and the Irish, the exodus from England overseas greatly exceeded the immigration. Rate of births showed no marked rise but the death rate dropped. Men lived longer because of better diet, greater attention to personal hygiene, improved sanitation and medical care. These trends were to persist through the nineteenth century.

WHY BRITAIN PIONEERED IN MACHINOFACTURE

It was in England during the long reign of George III, 1760 to 1820, that machinofacture had its origins and developed amazingly. Just why England should have been the pioneer and pathfinder is difficult to explain fully but a variety of considerations affords much more than a partial answer.

First of all, Britain commanded foreign markets incomparably greater than any other country. Goods consumed by the very numerous but very poor populations of India, Africa and Latin America were principally cheap and simple articles such as cotton textiles which could be turned out by machinery. Aside from foreign demand, consumption in England itself increased in response to the huge growth in population and continental Europe offered an attractive and convenient market. Larger opportunities for sales stimulated improvements in productive techniques which would multiply output.

Britain, which had a rich heritage in manufacturing skill and some measure of division of labor in production, was the mother of inventors to a degree unmatched on the Continent. From Francis Bacon through Newton and beyond, Britons manifested a lively interest in experimentation, in science, pure and applied and they believed strongly that industrial improvements were attainable. It is a stubborn fact that British scientific ingenuity displayed a penchant for the utilitarian and the practical. In the eighteenth century, adept investigators, chemists and physicists, maintained close relations with managers and business promoters, putting their brains to practical application. Scores of individuals, not a few of whom drifted down from Scotland, brought forth inventions or made improvements and the aggregate result was tremendous, revolutionary.

It was in England that a series of inventions revolutionized the manufacture of cloth, and the steam engine was made an efficient tool. It was in England that looms and printing presses were first driven by steam power. Here, too, iron ore was first smelted with coking coal, and the first workable railways were laid down. In fact it was not until the advent of the internal combustion engine late in the nineteenth century that British supremacy in industrial innovations faced serious competition.

Capital at low rates of interest was on hand in Britain to build, equip and operate factories, forges and railways or to open up coal mines. Capital had been accumulated from profits in foreign trade and small-scale industry, or from extensive farming enterprises. Interest on government bonds and funds imported from abroad, especially from Dutch investors, swelled the resources available for industrial undertakings.

Expectation of attractive profits furnished the incentive for investment. If and when enterprises prospered, part of the profits were "plowed back" to expand productive facilities, and that practice seems to have been the principal source of capital to put up new plants and purchase new equipment, or replacements, as industrialism progressed. Profit reinvested in business resembled the wheat seed which a farmer reserved for future production, and in an expanding economy such as the British, there was a constant demand for greater quantities of "wheat seed."

Britain was endowed, next, with good resources of water power, and, more important with time, coal and iron ore were hidden beneath the soil in large quantities and fine quality. By sheer good fortune stocks of iron ore and coking coal lay in close proximity or within a short haul by water. Before very long the economic prosperity of the country came to depend heavily on the output of cheap, plentiful and high-grade coal. Coal and steam furnished fuel and power for large-scale industry; let the coal supply falter and the British industrial machine would quickly come to a standstill.

For the labor force of the new industrial economy there were workers who hitherto had been engaged in handicrafts, families which had been forced out of the countryside, immigrants moving across from Ireland and, later on, veterans from the Napoleonic wars. Overseers of the poor sometimes shunted whole families from the London district to manufacturing centers in the north country. Workers and capital were coordinated by enterprising managers, who were willing to experiment, willing to take risks, flexible and adaptable to change, so essential to survival in a competitive economy.

Atmospheric conditions in northern England were favorable for the manufacture of textiles, cotton especially, and streams contained chemical properties which were admirable for bleaching cloth. The British government, moreover, strong and stable after the "Glorious Revolution" of 1688, fostered the growth of machinofacture by allowing scope for individual initiative in a way that was unapproached on the Continent. Old governmental regulations on industry and restrictive guild monopolies had been abandoned and no tariffs impeded the flow of commerce inside the island kingdom. The government, furthermore, afforded security of property, enforced contracts and protected inventors through patent laws.

Finally, in industrial development, as in political, Britain profited from the security which insularity bestowed. British evolution was not interrupted by marching and marauding armies such as recurrently upset the Continent, rising to crescendo in the wars of revolutionary France and Napoleon. Strife abroad, on the other side, fostered the upbuilding of British machine industry by creating a large demand for the products of textile and armament mills.

Blessed by these diverse circumstances and exempt from any real foreign competition, British industry got a "head start" on other countries. The "nation of shopkeepers" was converted into the "workshop of the world." Machinofacture was far advanced in the island kingdom before it started to transform life and labor abroad, with an exception to be entered in the case of Belgium where capital, coal and old traditions of skilled manufacturing prevailed in a small area.

The Spinning Jenny

RISE OF MACHINE INDUSTRY

Machine industry really started in cloth-making leading on to the mighty British textile industry of the present day. Cotton cloth was not much consumed in Europe before the eighteenth century. Dresses made of calicoes brought to England from India so infuriated woolen handicraftsmen that they stripped the wearers on the streets and Parliament banned the importation of cotton goods. But in time hostile attitudes modified when it was shown that cotton fabrics were cheaper than woolens, and could be turned out in gayer colors and more pleasing patterns. Demand shot up.

Much experimentation was undertaken in the textile industry and a host of labor-saving mechanisms followed. Chance played a role in these discoveries, but in the main they resulted from sustained and systematic experimentation and calculation. Mechanical inventions for spinning and weaving replaced hand tools and the brawn of man and beasts; costs of production tumbled. One contrivance led to another in an impressive and instructive manner; the history of machinery is a record of evolution.

A single improvement in the loom called the flying shuttle, devised (1733) by a clockmaker, John Kay, doubled the output of a weaver, though a generation elapsed before the tool came into general use. In 1767 James Hargreaves patented his "jenny," which enabled a woman to spin eight threads at once and modifications soon raised the rate to eighty. Then Richard Arkwright, an ordinary hair-cutter barely able to read and write, created in 1768 the water frame, a machine which could spin strong cotton thread as well as woolen yarn. This heavy contrivance had to be driven by inanimate power and caused the building of mills and factories. Arkwright prospered famously, becoming the richest and most respected of the early cotton magnates.

But the most decisive of textile inventions doubtless was the spinning "mule" of Samuel Crompton, a mill employee, which went into operation in 1779. Uniting the jenny and the water-frame this machine was capable of turning out all kinds of textiles and making them better and far cheaper than previously. Cloth workers who feared that the Crompton contrivance would rob them of employment resisted its introduction and only gradually was the confidence of the workers assured. Supplies of raw cotton for the dark, satanic mills flowed from the United States after Eli Whitney invented the cotton gin in 1793 which eliminated hand labor in removing seeds from the raw fiber.

Some inventive geniuses, meantime, were seeking mechanical means of driving the new machinery. Wind power while cheap enough could not be relied upon and water power was confined to restricted localities. Thomas Newcomen in 1705 had built a self-acting atmospheric engine, but it was costly to operate and was used principally to pump water out of mines. It was reserved to James Watt, a Scotch instrument maker, to patent in 1769 the first efficient steam engine, consisting of a steam condenser and pump, separate from the engine cylinder.

In making his engine Watt swept together the ideas of many other men, yet he is counted among the master improvers. The beginning of modern history in fact is sometimes dated from the appearance of the Watt steam engine, or *Beelzebub*, as workmen tagged it. Actually, the contrivance was not put into production until Watt teamed up (1774) with Matthew Boulton, a business promoter, and the inventor exercised his patent rights to block improvements in his invention by other minds. As late as 1800 only about five hundred steam engines were at work furnishing motive power to British industry. Since the eighties, steam power had been used, however, to drive spinning machines and looms. Power looms waged ever stiffer competition with hand weavers until the 1830's when the latter were finally crowded aside. Steam power facilitated the rapid expansion of urban factories to the detriment of mills located in the country.

For most of the nineteenth century the steam engine reigned unchallenged and the perfection of the turbine about 1890 temporarily reinforced the supremacy of steam. But by then a more efficient source of energy had been discovered in electricity, which ushered in what is often called the "second industrial revolution."

Power Looms

An early Bessemer furnace

The use of electricity to drive machines became practicable after the development of alternating current generation (1886). Each piece of machinery had its own electric motor which could be switched on or off at will, making operations more economical than with steam power.

Fundamental in the whole dizzy process of industrial expansion was the use of iron and steel in the making of machines for factory and farm—later for transportation equipment—and the use of coal as fuel and in smelting iron ore. In the manufacture of iron, the raw ore must first be smelted in a blast furnace and for that purpose, charcoal, produced by the slow combustion of wood, had traditionally been used. But that method was expensive and the growth of the industry was retarded by the exhaustion of timber resources.

Astute British ironmasters experimented with coke, made from coal, as an alternative to charcoal. About 1709, coke was exploited successfully in the smelting operation, an improvement of the first magnitude, though the application of the new process took place slowly; not until the end of the century had smelting by coke entirely superseded charcoal. It was also discovered (1742) that crucible steel could be fabricated out of iron by liquid melting, an innovation of which little use was made at this time.

In the 1780's wrought iron was produced by stirring or "puddling" semi-molten metal in a furnace, which eliminated impurities of various kinds. The new product was quite malleable and could be readily worked into machines, farm implements, cutlery, weapons and many other articles. The making of cheap and tough iron goods exerted a quickening influence upon nearly every branch of economic activity; by about 1820 machinery made exclusively of iron and steel was being turned out.

In 1856 Henry Bessemer announced a process for converting cast iron into steel cheaply and on a large scale and later it was perfected. This steel was strong, and capable of being forged with the hammer, rolled, or turned on a lathe. The Bessemer discovery was a major event in industry, making possible lighter and cheaper machinery, steel rails and constructional steel skeletons for buildings.

Owing to the importance of coal in the making of iron, heavy industry tended to concentrate in localities where good coking coal was available. Birmingham, in whose vicinity high-grade coal lay in close proximity to easily accessible iron ore, emerged as the capital of the iron industry. It was the most purely nineteenth-century British city. Gradually age-old handicaps to the mining of coal were overcome by technological improvements. Water, for example, was hoisted out of the pits by pumps operated by windmills and later by steam engines. The ever-present danger of explosions due to gas was reduced by better methods of ventilation and by the invention (1815) of the Davy safety lamp. In this ingenious device the light needed by workers underground was shielded from gas by wire gauze.

The output of coal, which multiplied fourfold in the course of the eighteenth century, topping 10,000,000 tons in 1800, increased to 16,000,000 tons by 1829. Expansion of coal-mining stimulated industrial growth generally. Old King Coal had been firmly seated on his throne and at the dawn of the atomic age he had not yet been deposed, for steam, generated by coal, still remained the chief motive force.

Properly impressed by the endless miracles which technology and applied science had performed, the poet Wordsworth wrote in *The Excursion* (1814):

> . . . I exult to see
> An intellectual mastery exercised
> O'er the blind elements; . . . almost a soul
> Imparted—to brute matter. I rejoice,
> Measuring the force of those gigantic powers
> That, by the thinking mind, have been compelled
> To serve the will of feeble-bodied Man.

REVOLUTIONS IN TRANSPORTATION AND COMMUNICATION

British economic prosperity built upon textiles and coal and iron was sustained by cheap and efficient transport probably more than by any other factor. Clever men harnessed the steam engine to transportation facilities, which speeded up communication, widened markets and generally accelerated the progress of industry.

The steam engine was first applied successfully to water transportation by Yankees. John Fitch born in Connecticut, demonstrated on the Delaware River in 1786 the first steamboat worthy of notice. It was a queer and cranky contraption equipped with an axletree which heroically moved a set of oars through the water. Then in 1807, Robert Fulton, sometime a jeweler and portrait painter, in his celebrated *Clermont*, which was outfitted with a Watt engine, dashed from New York to Albany at a speed of five miles an hour. "Fulton's Folly" thus demonstrated that steam-propelled vessels were practicable, at least on the serene bosom of the Hudson River.

Improvements followed so quickly that in 1819 the American ship *Savannah*, driven by a combination of sails and steampower, spanned the Atlantic in twenty-five days. Twenty years later the British *Great Western*, using steam exclusively, negotiated the crossing in fifteen days; in 1854 the time was cut to nine days and in the 1930's to half that—a succession of revolutions. At the middle of the nineteenth

The clippership Lincolnshire

century packets constructed of iron began to replace the wooden ships which had been in vogue since antiquity. Later on, vessels made of iron yielded to steel ships. A perfected screw-propeller was substituted (1854) for the cumbersome paddle-wheel. Ships not only moved more swiftly, but they were built bigger and for greater safety. The British giantess of the 1930's, *Queen Mary,* had space enough in one of her public rooms to stow away a typical steamer of a century earlier, together with the entire fleet with which Columbus undertook his first transatlantic voyage!

In spite of technical advances and greater speed steam merchant vessels did not compete seriously with smart clipper vessels until after the Civil War in the United States. Steamships were obliged to carry so much fuel that little space was available for cargo; and freight rates in consequence were much steeper than on sailing ships. But refinements in marine engines, which brought economies in fuel consumption, and the laying out of coal bunkering bases along the principal sea routes doomed cargo sailing vessels to oblivion. Great merchant fleets were built of iron and steel and mechanically propelled; in the 1890's the steam turbine was installed in ships. But after the First World War coal-burning steamships declined in the face of competition from vessels which used fuel oil and from Diesel-engined motorships.

Long since marvelous progress had been achieved in land transportation. Engineers late in the eighteenth century greatly increased the carrying capacity and comfort of roads by the application of science to building. John MacAdam, who has been called the "Colossus of Roads," engineered methods of constructing turnpikes in the London area especially which are still known by his name. Roads were surfaced with broken stone, scientifically crowned (or arched) and broad enough for two or more conveyances. By 1815 over 20,000 miles of improved highways had been laid down in Britain by private companies which charged tolls, as a rule, for their use. Wagons supplanted pack horses in hauling freight and Royal Mail coaches speeded up communication.

To move bulky and heavy products a web of canals, fed by rivers, was built. The enterprising Duke of Bridgewater promoted (1761) the construction of a canal linking the northern coal fields to the industries of Manchester, which cut costs of transportation in half and inspired considerable imitation. A sort of mania for canals seized the country in the 1790's, so that by the end of the century, England boasted upwards of 3,000 miles of artificial waterways.

The decisive innovation in transportation on land was, of course, the adaptation of the steam engine to locomotion. At first inventors worked at creating locomotives which would operate on highways and streets, but experience taught that stationary tracks were necessary. Early railways were planned to haul coal or serve as mere feeders to canals. It was in 1801 that a Cornish engineer, Richard Trevithick, moved with his "puffing devil" the first load of passengers ever hauled by steam. Costs of operation, unhappily, were so high as to prove fatal.

The title of "father of railways" has been conferred upon George Stephenson, a pit boy in his youth who became a famous mining engineer. A steam locomotive which he built in 1825 pulled a train of cars weighing in all ninety tons from Stockton to Darlington. A man on horseback preceded the engine on the initial trip to keep curious spectators off the tracks; to the amazement of all concerned, not least of the horseman, the train attained a speed of twelve miles an hour, in favorable stretches as much as fifteen.

Four years later Stephenson entered his four-ton *Rocket* in competition with stationary engines from which cables were attached to draw trains. His traveling engine hit forty-four miles an hour, easily outclassing rivals. That demonstration heralded the victory of steam locomotion, and Stephenson at his death had attained world-wide fame and had amassed a great fortune—one of many startling success stories of

The entrance of the railway at Edge Hill, Liverpool, 1831

the era. Railways progressed steadily and soon made it possible for a traveler to go from London to Liverpool in ten hours, instead of a week as was required by stagecoach. Canal and turnpike companies whose vested interests were imperiled attempted to stir up popular hostility against steam railways, but they were voices crying in the wilderness. Lines were rapidly laid down thanks to the availability of capital at reasonable rates, the abundant coal supplies and engineering personnel and laborers who had gained experience in canal construction.

By the mid-century, after an orgy of building in the 1840's, Britain possessed a splendid network of railways, which were consolidated, bit by bit, into four extensive systems. In the beginning railways were primarily used to transport passengers, later parcels, but freight continued to be carried on the cheaper and slower canals until the 1840's. The barge, however, sank under competition, and had to be content to haul heavy and bulky commodities only.

Foreign countries imitated the British pioneer and by 1870 only the Balkan area in Europe was without railway service of some description. Within little more than two generations, in other words, after steam locomotion was put into effective performance most of the Old World was connected with railways of sorts. Transportation was radically transformed. On his hurried flight from Moscow to Paris in 1812, Napoleon with horse and coach had covered about 1,400 miles in slightly more than 300 hours; the railway cut the time to forty-eight hours. Before very long the iron horse had roused somnolent populations all over the globe.

Gradually diminutive wagons were crowded aside by commodious carriages, diners and sleeping cars, which betrayed their stagecoach ancestry. After 1870 steel rails were substituted for wrought iron ones, and that improvement, together with the Westinghouse brake, permitted heavier and faster trains to operate. Powerful locomotives replaced the tiny, original engines, speed shot up and the cost of moving merchandise declined.

Steam transportation held a monopoly until the end of the nineteenth century when electrically or gasoline driven conveyances began to enter into competition. About 1890 electricity was applied in land transportation either on the surface or underground and presently railways were being electrified. More formidable, however, was the challenge of the gasoline engine.

Before the middle of the century cumbersome, smoky "steam carriages," capable of ten miles an hour, had appeared in Europe. And in 1876, a German experimentalist, A. N. Otto, devised an effective internal combustion motor. In the next decade French and German inventors constructed exceedingly light and efficient motors driven by gasoline. French interests manufactured (1891) the first motorcar equipped with clutch, sliding-gear transmission and differential; and in 1895 the Michelin Brothers brought out a demountable pneumatic tire. Far-reaching changes in movement on land rapidly followed, mechanical genius in the United States exploiting the pioneering work in Europe.

Next came the conquest of the air. As early as 1783 the balloon had been shown to be practicable, but it was confined mainly to observation and amusement purposes. Once light and powerful internal combustion engines were available the dirigible balloon became feasible. At the beginning of the twentieth century, a German pioneer, Count Ferdinand von Zeppelin, operated a successful airship, capable of raising an enormous weight.

But the airship was quickly eclipsed by the airplane. The epochal flight of the Wright Brothers in 1903 at Kitty Hawk, North Carolina, is usually considered the first demonstration of the feasibility of a heavier-than-air machine. Six years later a plane crossed the English Channel, but the tremendous potentialities of flight by air were hardly suggested before the First World War. Soon a passenger in a plane could cover more mileage in a few hours than the restless Frederick the Great had traversed in the journeyings of a lifetime. Before long, supersonic flights by air seemed to relegate the horse and buggy era to a remote antiquity. Novel facilities of transportation, in short, caused the great globe itself to shrivel up. Revolutionary innovations had profound implica-

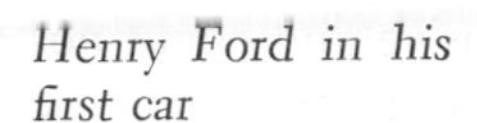
Henry Ford in his first car

tions for many phases of human life, above all, perhaps, for international politics and the conduct of war.

The advent of the internal combustion engine transformed the oil industry beyond all recognition. Just after the middle of the nineteenth century kerosene came into vogue for lighting purposes, as an alternative to the fast diminishing supply of sperm and other oils. Kerosene, distilled from petroleum first obtained in the rough, wooded hills of northwestern Pennsylvania, was soon being shipped abroad. It was peddled from door to door in Germany, replaced tallow lamps in Russia, as well as the native peanut and bean oils of China and lighted the palaces of Indian rajahs. But with the internal combusion motor, oil came to mean power and heat more than light. The automobile ushered in the age of gasoline. Then the airplane, the oil-driven ship, the Diesel engine and home oil-heating enormously increased the demand for oil and impelled an international scramble for oil-bearing lands.

While one contrivance after another abridged distance, new communication facilities radically reduced space. Growing knowledge of the nature and the power of electricity enabled a series of inventors, endowed with creative imagination, to introduce wonder after wonder. The electric telegraph was first practically used in 1844 by an American, S. F. B. Morse, and a generation later (1866) the principle of the telegraph was successfully adapted to submarine cables for transmission of messages between continents; in a few seconds news flashes, business deals and matters of state could be sped along unlimited lengths of wire to the ends of the earth.

At least twenty European and American inventors worked simultaneously to develop a way of transmitting and receiving speech over a wire. Such an instrument, the telephone, conceived in Europe was improved along practical lines by the Scotch-American Alexander Graham Bell as recently as 1876. It was not until the twentieth century, however, that the telephone became a popular means of conversation.[1] Long-distance verbal communication was perfected in an industrial laboratory from which issued scores of other and lesser novelties. Toward the very end of the nineteenth century experiments by the Italian Guglielmo

[1] As of 1880, 54,319 telephones were in service in the United States; in 1960, over 71,000,000.

Marconi presented the world with wireless telegraphy, and not long after the close of the First World War the wireless telephone, or radio, made its début; as nothing else, these instruments of communication converted the globe into a neighborhood. The practicality of television had been proved before the onset of the Second World War.

SPREAD OF MACHINOFACTURE

From its British birthplace machine industry passed to the Continent and eventually girdled the globe. Yet until 1850, or better until 1870, the economy of the European countries more nearly resembled that of Britain in 1750 than in 1850. Continental machinofacture to a very considerable extent represented the leisurely adoption or adaptation of British techniques and processes. Out of fear that foreigners would learn and apply British methods Parliament until 1824 banned the emigration of skilled workers and the exportation of labor-saving machines.

In foreign countries the construction of railways heralded the advent of the age of machinery while in Britain railways appeared after machinofacture had been under way for over half a century. Machine industry developed in an important way in the United States after 1820, in France after 1840, in Germany, Italy and Austria after 1850, in Russia and Japan after 1880.

No country, however, witnessed so thorough a transformation as Great Britain. Germany eventually crowded into second place among the industrial nations of Europe, but the changeover there from shop to factory, from farm to city was never so complete as in the island kingdom. The character and the many-sided implications of machine economy were basically identical in the major countries, but circumstances of time and place produced special effects in each.

MACHINES AND MEN

Among the obvious novelties of the machine age was the replacement of cottage and shop industry by the large mill and factory. By the 1830's the victory of the factory in British economy had been won; manufacturies, or factories for short, had come into being for several reasons. Much of the new machinery, for example, was heavy and expensive and could not be erected in cottage or shop as was the case with the lighter tools of earlier patterns of manufacturing. Machinery driven by power, moreover, had to be located near supplies of energy, streams first, and subsequently in the neighborhood of coalfields. Collected under one roof, workmen could be supervised by technical experts, economies could be effected by greater subdivision of labor and theft of materials could be checked.

Innovations in the administrative side of production formed an important aspect of the general revolution in industry. Wage earners were subjected to a degree of discipline previously unknown, for efficiency in manufacturing required the application of power to all machines simultaneously and management fixed definite hours when workers were to be on the job. Fines were imposed for tardiness, slackness, drunkenness and gambling—and, like other disciplinary measures, were keenly resented by the employed. The clangor of the factory bell grated harshly upon human ears accustomed only to the screech of the owl.

With the factory came greater division in productive methods. In the early phase of the technological revolution many jobs demanded greater skill of workers than previously, but as specialization proceeded apace, workers concentrated more and more on a single monotonous operation. The artistic thrill of creation diminished. Since jobs themselves yielded little inner satisfaction, wage earners toiled for money and by spending surplus money (if any) in their leisure they purchased a good deal of the pleasure they got out of living. Mass production encouraged the mass mind.

Intimate personal associations, furthermore, between man the employer and man the employee were impaired. Technology not only mechanized manufacturing, it tended to dehumanize it. With the progress of time joint-stock or corporate enterprises, in contrast to the small partnership, bulked ever larger in the economy. Administration of the company

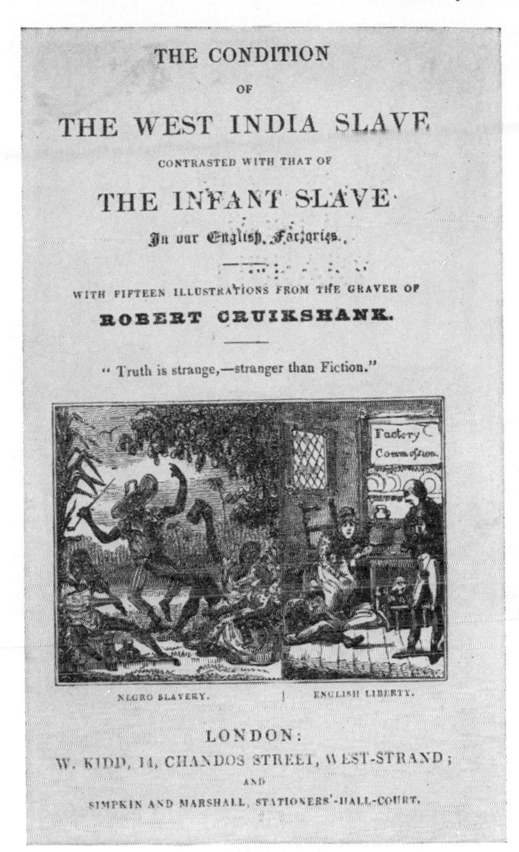

THE CONDITION

OF

THE WEST INDIA SLAVE

CONTRASTED WITH THAT OF

THE INFANT SLAVE

In our English Factories.

WITH FIFTEEN ILLUSTRATIONS FROM THE GRAVER OF

ROBERT CRUIKSHANK.

"Truth is strange,—stranger than Fiction."

LONDON:
W. KIDD, 14, CHANDOS STREET, WEST-STRAND;
AND
SIMPKIN AND MARSHALL, STATIONERS'-HALL-COURT.

The plight of youthful factory hands under the new conditions of industry did not go unnoticed. The title-page and the illustrations shown herewith come from the same book—a comparison of the lot of English children in factories with that of Negro slaves.

English Factory Slaves. Pl. 1. The Morning call. —

English Factory Slaves. Pl. 3 Their daily employment. —

passed to self-perpetuating boards of directors and managers, while owners were holders of shares of stock who usually had slight influence on the behavior of the company. One immediate result was decreased alertness to or interest in the welfare of employees.[2]

[2] Joint-stock companies, which originated in the Renaissance, flourished luxuriantly after the middle of the nineteenth century. Under charters issued by governments, owners were liable to the full extent of their resources for debts which the firm might contract. The institution known as the limited liability company was introduced in Britain in 1855, somewhat earlier in France, and later in Germany; after that joint-stock companies grew enormously.

In the first flush of machine industry the labor and life of the British wage earners, then only a small proportion of the population, was frightful, though whether demonstrably worse than in the pre-technological era is a disputed point among experts. Certainly conditions differed from factory to factory, from industry to industry and from year to year. As was the case with the domestic craftsmen hours of labor for the factory worker were long, ordinarily from dawn to dusk with two brief intervals for meals; few holidays were celebrated. At the start of the nineteenth century, gas was used to illuminate places of employment so that operations

The face of England and Scotland was altered as industry spread out over what once was a green and pleasant land. Here we see a chemical works and a foundry belching smoke from their chimneys. The date of this picture is 1832.

could be carried on at night. Many a mill was dirty, poorly ventilated and without adequate guards to protect "hands" from machinery; more intricate machines brought unprecedented dangers of injury or death.

Women and children made up a considerable proportion of the working force in the early British textile factories. They could offer little effectual protest against harsh conditions of employment. Even before mills popped up in England's green and pleasant land, children of the poor had trod no path of roses; traditionally they had helped in the field or as holders, fetchers and carriers in domestic industry working with the rest of the family. The lot of child laborers in the early factory regime was in all conscience weary and miserable as Dickens made vivid in *David Copperfield*.

These children were set to work in mill or mine as young as seven, and older ones worked twelve to fifteen hours a day six days a week—even more in "rush" seasons. Orphans purchased by employers were legally apprentices, though frequently in fact scarcely distinguishable from slaves; some employers, however, furnished pleasant living places and elementary education. Many child laborers grew up dwarfed and vicious, beaten to make them start for work before the crack of dawn, strapped in the mill if they drowsed on the job, strapped again at night to keep them awake long enough to eat the food they had so bitterly earned.

New industrial and mining districts exhibited as a rule the crudities and roughness of a frontier society. Housing quarters varied considerably, some of them comfortable, some of them ugly tenements or dormitory slums modelled on the factories themselves, overcrowded and unwholesome.[3] Smoke from the factories darkened the sky over rapidly growing communities such as Birmingham and Manchester. While Britain was fighting revolutionary France and Napoleon, construction costs soared and the quality of workers' homes suffered. In Liverpool and Manchester damp, congested cellars were homes for many workers, in particular for men who had come from Ireland.

[3] Slum implies smallness, "a dirty back street or court or alley," as the dictionary tells us.

Individual wages were low, but probably the real incomes of families were higher than those of earlier generations of workers and wages were paid with regularity. Very likely the diet of the wage worker, by 1820, at any rate, had improved in times of good employment. Wheat bread and potatoes were the staple foods and meat was no longer a rarity; when times were hard, however, turnips were often the alternative to starvation. Coal was burned for warmth in homes and in cooking food. Few of the wage workers received even the rudiments of education; popular diversions were often of a degrading character and primitive immorality was common.

Before the coming of machine production industrial workers were familiar with under-employment; in the new age their lives were recurrently demoralized by periods of unemployment. The job of any worker was only as secure as the profits of the concern which employed him. Periodic fluctuations in the tempo of industrial activity cost workers their jobs and condemned families to want and destitution.

As the British economy became more and more dependent upon foreign trade, business at home responded to happenings abroad, a political convulsion, for instance, or the failure of harvests. But other circumstances such as the introduction of a new machine, currency disorders, the crash of a bank, the fraud of speculators, a shift in fashions made for irregularity of employment and dogged the lives of workpeople with dread of starvation.[4]

Why, it may be asked, were the inhuman abuses and stupidities of the early factory regime tolerated? For one thing the economic transformation took place so unobtrusively that years elapsed before men were aware that a "revolution" had in fact transpired and demands were made for corrective remedies. Hardships and abuses, moreover, in mill towns and mills were regarded with insensitive apathy, somewhat resembling the indifference to casualties caused by automobiles in the twentieth century. Certainly in some cases owners and management, hungry for profits, were heartlessly indifferent to the lamentable wretchedness and narrowness in the lives of the wage earners.

In that attitude they were fortified by the prevailing "climate of opinion," by the accepted economic philosophy of the time, which taught that the evils and inequities were unavoidable and inevitable. Every man must look out for himself and the devil take the hindmost. Workers must be free to find their own levels and however dire their straits, public authority should not intervene to help them. Last of all, throughout much of the early phase of machine industry Britain was engaged in war with France which diverted statecraft away from domestic problems.

[4] An industrious German economist in 1895 collected 230 causes of oscillations in industrial activity and more have since been proposed.

GROWTH OF WEALTH, COMMERCE AND POPULATION

In the age of machinofacture, technical knowledge and its practical application advanced enormously, output of goods rose sensationally, wealth multiplied rapidly, commerce expanded greatly and population spurted upward—commonplaces all. More goods resulted in general raising of living levels in industrialized countries, greater physical comfort. The scale of living improved in every direction that can be measured by statistics. Westerners in the mass earned their daily bread with less expenditure of time than ever before; they enjoyed a degree of leisure, which created opportunities to lead a fuller life, such as the world had never known.

Trade between nations and peoples assumed unprecedented proportions. The main task of commerce was no longer the transportation of comforts and luxuries essentially, but rather of basic stuffs to feed man and his machines. Industrialized Europe was robbed of its comparative independence of the rest of the world, so far as the fundamental necessities of material existence were concerned. Improved shipping facilities encouraged specialization in productions; nations and regions exchanged goods almost as conveniently as neighbors had once done. Any grave disturbance in one sector of the globe was likely to cause damaging repercussions in other areas.

As a phase of history's greatest revolution Europe could and did support a larger population, far larger, than ever before. As was the case in England of the eighteenth century, the phenomenal rise in population was due much less to a higher rate of births than to the sharp decline in the death rate. Better health services, more effective control of epidemics and contagious diseases and better nourishment, housing and clothing combined to extend the span of life progressively; of special importance, in this connection, fewer children died in infancy.[5]

Stated statistically, the population of the Old World which stood at about 188,000,000 in 1800, had risen to about 273,000,000 in 1870, to about 452,000,000 by 1914 and 540,000,000 in 1939. It seems probable that more people lived in Europe in 1950 (approximately 593,000,000) than in the entire world in 1650.[6] At the same time that Europe's population raced upward an immense emigration to underpopulated areas overseas took place. People of European origins living outside of Europe increased in the nineteenth century from approximately 5,000,000 to more than 130,000,000. Taking the globe as a whole, the white population tripled and the proportion of whites switched from about a fifth to about a third of the earth's people—one of the most astonishing facts of history.

A highly significant accompaniment of machinofacture was urbanization, so strikingly illustrated in the case of England, but true of other countries in proportion to industrialization. At the time of Waterloo Europe contained only fourteen cities in excess of 100,000, but a century later a tenfold increase had occurred. Giant metropolises such as London, Berlin and Paris expanded at a breath-taking pace and the growth of some new cities—Manchester in England and Essen in Germany, for example—was still more sensational.[7]

Cities historically, from the famed capitals of antiquity in the valleys of the Nile and the Tigris-Euphrates onward, have served as the focal points from which innovations in the human pageant have radiated. It was no less true of the urban agglomerations which burgeoned up in the nineteenth century. Their emergence and expansion involved countless changes and baffling social problems, varying in a hundred and one ways from the sober-paced rustic existence. Clamorous questions of housing and fire protection, lighting and public health, water and sewage systems, transportation, crime and juvenile delinquency, schooling and amusements pressed for answers. In the matter of water supply, for example, interest shifted from the mere quenching of thirst to the pursuit of cleanliness; in the course of the century, residents of great cities came to take pure and abundant water for granted.

THE IMPACT UPON POLITICS

Machinofacture carried in its train other sweeping novelties. Nobles and serfs or peasants, for example, were more or less supplanted as the leading social groupings in industrialized states by the middle classes or bourgeoisie and the workers in mill, mine, or household. The middle classes, far from being a homogeneous social element, embraced industrial magnates, little shopkeepers, professional folk, bank managers, spinsters on small incomes, clerks, independent craftsmen and comfortably fixed farmers.

By reason of its income-getting talents the bourgeoisie, for all its imperfections, contributed vitally to social development. It provided leadership, ingenuity, enterprise, stability, standards of social conduct and patronage for the arts and the sciences.

At the outset of the expanding, mechanized economy a smart and thrifty workman could

[5] According to official records the expectation of life in England increased at the following pace: 1841, forty-one years; 1881, forty-five years; 1921, fifty-seven years; 1940, sixty-three years.

[6] Certain experts believed in 1960 that the upward trend of population in central and western Europe had come to an end and that a decline impended, but in eastern Europe population was constantly increasing.

[7] In round figures the growth was in these dimensions:

	London	*Paris*	*Berlin*
1801	1,114,000	547,000	172,000
1881	4,766,000	2,239,000	1,122,000
1931	8,202,000	2,871,000	4,013,000

hope to push into the employing set and many individuals with technical or commercial abilities actually did so. But the opportunities for a common man to become an uncommon man lessened as the economic organization settled down into ever larger combinations. Generally unenfranchised at the beginning of the machine age the middle classes fought for and achieved a direct share in public affairs; they became the dominant social element in the West and influential elsewhere. The battle of the workers for a place in politics was longer waged and in some countries was not won until the twentieth century.

In the meantime unions of workers had been founded, a trend that was facilitated by the congregation of wage earners in factories and mines, to advance or defend their particular interests. Unions rested on the principle that the individual workman was helpless in the face of the power of the employer; he must, therefore, seek advancement in terms of economic gains and security through concerted action by the members of his group. The growth of unions forced management to modify its methods in dealing with employees. Often adjustments were made only grudgingly and sometimes only after prolonged industrial conflict.

On another plane, machinofacture lent a dynamic impetus to imperial expansion. After about 1875 the quest for rawstuffs, for markets, for places to invest capital provoked furious rivalry to obtain colonies and spheres of interest in the economically underdeveloped areas of the globe.

The mechanization of warfare which attended the industrial age may be illustrated by the example of railways. Actually the changes in military operations due to steam transportation were far more rapid than to the introduction of gunpowder, whose impact was a gradual process extending over several centuries. By 1870 railways had wrought a revolution in the manipulation of armies, facilitated swift victories. The importance of railways in military combat was clearly demonstrated in the War between the States in America and with even greater impressiveness in the Prussian wars of 1866 and 1870.

Before the advent of the railway, military resources had been prodigally wasted by long marches of troops and faulty service of supplies; but those handicaps were now diminished. Professional soldiers devoted particular care to the construction of railways for strategic purposes. By the First World War, the rail network of Germany, for example, had been so perfected that the transfer of divisions back and forth from the French front to the Russian theater was essentially a routine affair. At the beginning of the conflict, German troop trains crossed the principal bridge over the Rhine at intervals of ten minutes for ten solid days!

Equally, the methods of naval warfare underwent drastic renovation. The British Admiralty long and stoutly opposed the building of steam warcraft, "as they considered that the introduction of steam was calculated to strike a fatal blow at the naval supremacy of the Empire." Similar reluctance prevailed over the construction of iron vessels, though the U. S. S. *Michigan*, the first warship made of iron, slid down the ways in 1843. Britain fought the Crimean War (1854–1856) with a fleet composed exclusively of wooden vessels propelled by sails.

But directly thereafter both Britain and France built armored steam warships. The fight between the *Merrimac* and the *Monitor*, ironclads both, during the War between the States, (1862) sounded the knell of wooden men-of-war. Naval architects hastened to lay down stronger and faster battleships leading to the dreadnaughts and the superdreadnaughts of the early twentieth century. These innovations in land and sea fighting equipment were by way of prelude to the fabulous tools of war which the First and Second World Wars called forth.

Another conspicuous consequence of machinofacture was the effect upon the physical power and prestige of the leading European countries. Industrial strength and resources, together with population, very largely determined military power and therewith international standing. As the homeland of machine industry, Britain consolidated the position she held when Napoleon was whisked off to St. Helena. Until the 1880's no nation significantly challenged British ascendancy, but after that Imperial Germany and the United States developed immense economic strength and strode forth as vigorous rivals. Industrial greatness heightened German diplomatic prestige and enabled the country in two world wars to stand against huge combinations of foes.

France, on the other hand, oldest of the Great Powers, remained predominantly a nation of peasants and was incapable of keeping abreast of Britain or Germany in the politics of power. Once mighty Spain, neglectful of industry, was quite outclassed; Austria had to be contented to play second fiddle and Italy sat still farther back in the orchestra. Machine production started to gather momentum in Imperial Russia in the 1880's, but down to the First World War accomplishments were relatively modest. As one result of a program of planned industrial progress in the 1930's the Soviet Union crowded into the very front rank of military nations.

Outside Europe, meanwhile, the United States and to a far lesser degree Japan had undergone swift industrial development which catapulted them into the class of topflight countries.

VARIETIES OF ECONOMIC DOCTRINE

At the outset of the machine age, thinking on economics, the production and distribution of wealth, was dominated by the principles of economic individualism (laissez faire) expounded by Adam Smith. His British disciples, the "classical" economists, or Manchester School, undertook a fuller explanation of competitive private enterprise than their master, and presumed to furnish an unassailable intellectual foundation for prevailing economic conditions and activities. They contemplated in fact an idyllic state of perfect competition between employers, workers and nations, and in advocating unfettered pursuit of self-interest they believed they were promoting the cause of freedom, reason and progress.

Competition, in the thinking of the "classical" economists, was the necessary goad to efficient production, the only way to keep prices down and the quality of goods up. And they assumed that their doctrines possessed the same validity as the truths about the physical universe, natural and immutable. The teachings of these thinkers were translated into legislation and the legislation in turn reinforced individualism and the competitive economy. Laissez faire principles held sway in nineteenth-century Britain and, somewhat refined, still command hosts of followers.

The special ideas of two of the outstanding theorists of the "dismal science," the Reverend Thomas R. Malthus and David Ricardo, wealthy financier, merit short summary. Malthus assigned the poverty and hardships of industrial workers to the operation of an unchanging principle of population. From the beginning of time, he explained in a highly controversial *Essay on the Principle of Population* (1798), the capacity of man to produce offspring surpassed his ability to produce sustenance, chiefly food.

Population tended to multiply in geometric ratio, according to the Malthusian theorem, while supplies of food could be made to increase only in arithmetic progression. In other words, starting with 1 as the unit, population rose at the rate of 1, 2, 4, 8, but food supply could only go up at the rate of 1, 2, 3, 4. Population would tend to double about every twenty-five years, unless checked as it had been in the past by famine, disease and war. Since population could never exceed sustenance, nature would continue to sweep away the excess mouths periodically—by her age-old rough-and-ready correctives.

Inflexible law, Malthus gloomily prophesied, would condemn mankind to perpetual suffering and degradation. He could not foresee that food resources would be immensely enlarged by the opening up of new plowlands beyond the seas and by the application of science and technology to farming. Nor could he foresee that planned parenthood, which he personally ruled out on moral grounds, would be extensively practiced. Nevertheless, his treatise exerted wide and lasting effects upon economic and social thinking.

Influenced by Malthus, Ricardo endeavored

to prove that the real wages of workers must always hover near the minimum necessary to sustain life and perpetuate the species. He thought in terms of a fixed fund of wages which was available for distribution to employees. If wages rose above the subsistence level, more children would be procreated, and the enlarged working force would inevitably press wages down again to the level needed merely to keep men alive. Ricardo held too that the exchange value of a commodity was due solely to the labor expended in producing it. "Classical" economists also taught that workers resembled a commodity, to be purchased just like machines or rawstuffs and equally subject to the inexorable law of supply and demand.

Against the cold, mechanistic reasoning of economic individualism, protesting voices were raised and competing patterns of economic theory were fashioned. Maddened by the evils which unfettered freedom sanctioned, and the arrant dogmatism of its champions, Thomas Carlyle dismissed laissez faire as a "pig philosophy." Thinkers who were concerned with "the greatest good for the greatest number" combined with men of letters and humanitarians in demanding governmental action to remove wrongs. They called for an extension of the voting privilege and the full right of wage-workers to form unions.

Certain of the economic dissenters thought that state regulation of capitalism in the name of the general welfare would solve the problems of the new industrial age. Many regulatory laws were placed upon the statute books of Great Britain. Other reform minded critics contended that policing of capitalism would not overcome iniquities and inequities. As part of the progeny of history's greatest revolution, several varieties of collectivist economic theory appeared, which will be examined later.

FOR FURTHER STUDY

THOMAS S. ASHTON, *The Industrial Revolution, 1760–1830* (New York, 1948)
PAUL J. MANTOUX, *The Industrial Revolution of the Eighteenth Century* (rev. ed., New York, 1929) PAPERBACK
JOHN H. CLAPHAM, *An Economic History of Modern Britain* (3 vols., London, 1927–38)
ROWLAND E. PROTHERO, *English Farming Past and Present* (new ed., London, 1936)
JOHN L. and BARBARA HAMMOND, *The Rise of Modern Industry* (new ed., New York, 1937)
DUNCAN L. BURN, *The Economic History of Steel-Making, 1867–1939* (Cambridge, Eng., 1940)
THOMAS J. MARSHALL, *James Watt* (Boston, 1925)
ST. JOHN C. NIXON, *Invention of the Automobile* (London, 1936)
ADNA F. WEBER, *The Growth of Cities in the Nineteenth Century* (New York, 1899)
CHARLES R. FAY, *Life and Labour in the Nineteenth Century* (Cambridge, Eng., 1920)
GEORGE N. CLARK, *The Idea of the Industrial Revolution* (Glasgow, 1953)
THOMAS S. ASHTON, ed., *An Economic History of England: the Eighteenth Century* (London, 1955)
WILLIAM O. HENDERSON, *The Industrial Revolution on the Continent* (Chicago, 1961)

CHAPTER XIII

GREAT BRITAIN IN THE NINETEENTH CENTURY

WORLD LEADER

MANY readers of these pages will have formed their mental image of Britain from the celluloid products of Hollywood in which castles and aristocrats are much in evidence. But that is a grossly distorted picture, for in the century after Waterloo—and more so since the First World War—Britain has witnessed the steady evolution of popular government, a broader distribution of income, greater equality of opportunity and expanding social welfare services.

As the birthplace and classic land of machine industrialism, Britain in the nineteenth century consolidated her position as

This London street, photographed in 1897, is decorated for Queen Victoria's Diamond Jubilee—the high-water mark of the Victorian era, and almost its end.

the wealthiest and most influential of nations. By reason of machinofacture Britain long resembled a skyscraper in a world of farmhouses. In point of fact, throughout most of the century Britain commanded greater power and higher respect than any single state since the dissolution of the Roman Empire.

Not only was Great Britain foremost in manufacturing but she held leadership in commerce and shipping. Her mercantile marine dominated the seas commercially even as the British navy ruled the waves in a military sense. Supremacy on the oceans kept or helped to keep the globe free of world wars; the British role was not to prevent any war at all, but to prevent a general conflict, which would disrupt lines of trade and engage the economic resources of all peoples.

This nineteenth century, this bourgeois century, was likewise Britain's century. At its outset continental states lay prostrate after a generation of exhausting warfare. Germany and Italy, moreover, were politically disunited, while Russia, though clearly the most powerful land power after the expulsion of Napoleon, had little awareness of her economic potentialities. Outside of Europe the strong nations of the future were either thinly peopled, as in the case of the United States, or slumbering like Japan and China. It was not until the last decades of the century that formidable challengers to British supremacy appeared.

Machine industrialism, in the meantime, enabled England to maintain an enormous population, an important ingredient of national strength, on an area no larger than the State of New York. Whereas in 1801, the United Kingdom contained about ten and a half million people, by mid-century the population had doubled and by 1911 had doubled again, exceeding forty-one millions.[1]

These increasing millions relied primarily upon manufacturing and foreign trade for their bread and butter. Merchantmen brought in industrial raw stuffs (and food) and hauled finished products to the outside world in payment for the imports; exports in the main were intended for mass consumption though some articles were the fine products of expert craftsmanship. Free exchange of goods and freedom of enterprise were the very pillars of the massive British industrial structure. National wealth and international power rested solidly upon world trade; that indeed was the unique formula of the preeminence of the island kingdom among the nations.

The very existence of Britain, not to speak of her prosperity, depended—uniquely again—upon uninterrupted sea transportation. If shipping should cease for only a matter of weeks, economic paralysis would inescapably follow. Consequently, Britain was resolved to maintain a fleet capable of keeping open the channels of commerce under any and all circumstances. The advent of submarine and airplane at the beginning of the twentieth century confronted British naval strategists with unprecedented challenges.

British capital owners piled up large resources from commercial and financial transactions, the earnings of the merchant marine and in other ways. Surplus funds were invested in

[1] It is estimated that about 17,000,000 emigrated from the British Isles (Ireland included) between 1815 and 1914, settling in the United States, Canada, Australia and the other Dominions.

all kinds of enterprises all over the globe, making Britain the world's leading banker as well as the workshop of the world. Britain's strength invited flattering imitation by other countries.

The tide against British supremacy swung slowly at first but relentlessly with the growth of the competitive power of Germany in Europe, of the United States in the New World and later on of Japan in the Orient. The circumstances which made possible Victorian prosperity and greatness and shaped the Victorian mentality vanished beyond recall. After a century of dominance it was not easy for Britain to accept the loss of power gracefully.

Aside from her leadership in industry, commerce and finance, Britain had particular importance in the nineteenth century, as in its predecessor, because of the influence of her governmental institutions and philosophy. British ways together with the French ideas of 1789 were light-houses for progressive political mariners the world over. An impressive list of agitators and unorthodox thinkers of continental origins sought and found in Great Britain a sanctuary of freedom.

THE AFTERMATH OF VICTORY

After the final elimination of Napoleon, victorious Britain was faced with complicated economic perplexities, similar in kind though not in degree to those which arose after the general wars of the twentieth century. The transition from the ordeal of war to conditions of peace was a slow and arduous process, requiring a generation for fulfillment. Agriculture and industry, which had been geared to war production, were confronted with a sudden drop in demand; with the return of peace, manufacturing revived on the Continent, for one thing, cutting down British exports. Veterans released from the armed services clamored for work at a time when employment was contracting and prices were shooting upward.

Overshadowing all else was the huge burden of national debt, colossal by the standards of the day, which the war had saddled upon the country. Napoleon in his island exile consoled himself with the cynical reflection that he had shot "a poisoned dart" into the vitals of the British enemy. State finance was further disarranged by a heavy dose of currency inflation, by lavish gifts to the military leaders of the war such as a magnificent palace for Wellington of Waterloo, and by large outlays for the royal family. Taxes had soared prodigiously and were extremely varied in nature.

Doleful spirits complained against the heavy tax load in language that has a familiar ring. "The dying Englishman," said one contemporary, "pouring his medicine, which has paid seven per cent (tax), into a spoon that has paid fifteen per cent, flings himself upon his chintz bed, which has paid twenty-two per cent, and expires in the arms of an apothecary who has paid a license of a hundred pounds for the privilege of putting him to death. His whole property is then immediately taxed from two to ten per cent, his virtues are handed down to posterity on taxed marble, and he is gathered to his fathers, to be taxed no more."

In the prospectus announcing the first issue (1821) of the famous *Manchester Guardian* readers were informed:

"It may safely be asserted that no former period in the history of our country has been marked by questions of a more important character than those which are now claiming the attention of the public. To anyone who regards for a moment the conflicting views and wishes of the commercial interests—the considerations which may arise out of the existing laws for the regulation of our currency—the present and anticipated pressure of the National Debt and Taxation—this statement will be sufficiently apparent."

That ugly villain the trade cycle worsened the whole economic situation. Violent convulsions entailed widespread uncertainty and distress with manual workers bearing the brunt of the hardships. Wage-earners expressed their grievances by smashing labor-saving machinery, as they had done before, on the principle that fewer machines would mean more employment for human hands; their spirit, if not their precise methods, has been a persistent feature of industrial society.

Mob rioting, strikes and mass demonstrations likewise testified to the wretchedness of the workless or the meagerly paid. On one occasion, near Manchester in 1819, cavalrymen charged a protesting assembly killing eleven and injuring hundreds. Apprehensive of revolution, Parliament adopted drastic legislation to curb popular disorders, flagrantly trampling upon cherished principles of the constitution in so doing. Kindred emotions inspired at the same time the repressive Carlsbad Decrees in central Europe.

The government of the day was still strongly aristocratic and conservative. Parliament was the political master of the kingdom, it is true, but at most not more than 10 per cent of the mature men shared directly in public business. The franchise right for the Commons was reserved to landed proprietors with a scattering of wealthy merchants and industrialists tossed in, and seats in the Commons had not been redistributed for two centuries, so that populous communities which had grown up in response to manufacturing were quite without representation.

A stand-pat mentality, of which the prestige-laden Wellington was a sterling manifestation, ruled in the ministry and the governing class. For the benefit of the wealthy, Parliament increased tariffs to protect growers of grain and by a slim majority repealed the income tax, a wartime expedient. On the other hand, the lawmakers rejected a modest proposal to ban employment of children under fourteen in the hazardous work of sweeping chimneys! Since pauper children were plentiful it seemed of little importance that they died or were maimed or that little chimney sweeps were burned to death.[2] The tragedy of the "climbing boys" was long regarded with insensitive apathy.

Because of his obstinacy against anything that suggested reform, Englishmen began to think of Wellington in terms of this contemporary cartoon: All hat, boot and spur, and very little man.

CLAMOR FOR CHANGE

Agitation for political and social reform came from several quarters. Actively discontented minds, ranging from fanatical extremists to urbane and moderate humanitarians, demanded changes which would remove crudities and injustices and reduce the bleakness in the lives of fellow beings. With tongue and pen, by persuasion and incitement they acquainted men and women with matters that were out of joint, caused them the trouble of thinking about the plight of the weak and poor. Revision of the franchise law, as the necessary prologue to other changes by legislation, stood high on the agenda of the reformers.

Spearhead of the crusade for far-reaching change was a shifting band of thinkers and writers who revered Jeremy Bentham as their oracle, and who formulated the philosophy of

[2] In 1803, nearly 200,000 child paupers were being maintained at public expense in England and Wales, quite apart from street vagrants.

utilitarianism. This creed may be described as teaching that the greatest happiness of the greatest number should be the transcendant aim of personal conduct and of state policy alike. Whatever caused pain was evil, but actions and desires which conduced to the general happiness were good; the Utilitarians, unhappily, never troubled to provide a standard by which that elusive phenomenon, happiness, might be measured.

Utilitarianism ruled out appeal to traditional authority or ancient convention as adequate justification for laws or institutions that had outlived their usefulness. It professed stalwart faith in the capacity of the ordinary man to study evidence and then act in accordance with conclusions. With time the criterion of "happiness" took firm root in the mind of politician and public, and thus the Utilitarian school made a large and lasting contribution to British political and moral thought.

Few existing institutions satisfied the acid test of utility and deserved to be preserved. Evangelical Christianity was intimately allied with the utilitarians in the cause of reform, and so were a handful of Tory humanitarians and an occasional manufacturer, such as Robert Owen, who attributed the distresses of workers to the inequitable distribution of income between profits and wages.

Unconventional journalists and men of letters likewise rebelled against the cult of con-

An English industrial landscape

servatism and current social abuses. A militant and courageous champion of the underprivileged was William Cobbett, who through the columns of his cheap *Political Register* assailed the prevailing order in unbridled language, stirring up primitive passions.[3] To escape imprisonment he took ship for the United States which he thought a very paradise on earth. He returned in 1819 after two years in America to renew his angry agitation for radical social and parliamentary reform.

Romantic poets, such as Shelley and Byron, pleaded for "clothes and fire and food" for all men. And later on, Dickens, angered by the squalor of the industrial towns in contrast to the solid comfort of suburban existence, took up the cudgels against "man's inhumanity to man."

A BUDGET OF REFORMS

Agitation, information, and education all wrought their appointed task—or part of it. The conservative governing classes (or some of them) were shaken out of their lethargy and repose and constructive achievements followed. Wellington, for one, learned that it was harder to fight native ideas of reform than foreign armies.

From the early days of machine industry voluntary combinations of workers had been formed to win, collectively, higher pay or shorter hours which, individually, workmen were too weak to achieve. By the end of the eighteenth century unions had appeared extensively in coalfields, textile plants and seaports. It was feared by the government that these bodies might in fact be tainted with revolutionary Jacobinism and in any case they violated the principle of economic individualism, of every man for himself. Laws were enacted (1799–1800) permitting judges to imprison any unionist up to three months.

That act was not strictly enforced, however, and many new unions were founded, some of which operated quite openly. Trade unionism was a plank in the Utilitarian platform. In 1825 the legality of unions was officially recognized, though severe restrictions were imposed upon the right to strike, the most potent weapon of unionism, and workmen who intimidated or molested others might be severely punished. Unions were organized craft by craft and concentrated on objects of interest to a particular trade; a general coalition of unions (1834) lasted only a short time. But workers were awakened to a consciousness of their power, never thereafter forgotten.

At this time, too, the criminal code was revised along enlightened lines. As of 1800 the criminal law was a jungle of barbarous and irrational ordinances. The state exacted the death penalty for over two hundred misdeeds, many of them petty, such as stealing fish from a pond or forgery. The irrationality of the laws was so blatant that judges and juries frequently refused to convict wrongdoers. A tentative first step of reform was taken in 1808 when an act ordered that pickpockets should be shipped to Australia for seven years instead of being hanged; and in the 1820's scores of antiquated punishments were drastically modified in a humane and enlightened direction. By 1837 punishment by death was limited in fact to the crime of murder.

Simultaneously the famous London police system was created (1829) after long and mounting agitation for more efficient prevention and detection of crime and protection of property. Sponsored by Sir Robert Peel and nicknamed "bobbies," the police rapidly ended the terror of unchecked crime and gained in respect and popularity. The London force indeed set the model and a standard for comparison by other cities of the world. Equally, after prolonged agitation in Ireland had brought that island to the verge of rebellion, old and discriminatory laws against Catholics were removed (1829). Protestant dissenters were also declared legally qualified to stand for Parliament and even to attend the universities.

These innovations whetted the zeal of advocates of changes in the electoral laws and in the distribution of seats in the Commons. The battle against the monopoly of the privileged

[3] In a typical outburst Cobbett wrote, "Of all the mean, all the cowardly reptiles, that ever crawled the face of the earth, the English landowners are the most mean and cowardly."

"Portentous, unexampled, unexplain'd!
——————— What man seeing this,
And having human feelings, does not blush,
And hang his head, to think himself a man?
——————— I cannot rest
A silent witness of the headlong rage,
Or heedless folly, by which thousands die——
Bleed gold for Ministers to sport away."

THESE ARE

THE PEOPLE

all tatter'd and torn,
Who curse the day
wherein they were born,
On account of Taxation
too great to be borne,
And pray for relief,
from night to morn;
Who, in vain, Petition
in every form,
Who, peaceably Meeting
to ask for Reform,
Were sabred by Yeomanry Cavalry,
who,
Were thank'd by THE MAN,
all shaven and shorn,
All cover'd with Orders—
and all forlorn;
THE DANDY OF SIXTY,
who bows with a grace,
And has *taste* in wigs, collars,
cuirasses, and lace;
Who, to tricksters, and fools,
leaves the State and its treasure,
And when Britain's in tears,
sails about at his pleasure;
Who spurn'd from his presence
the Friends of his youth,
And now has not one
who will tell him the truth;
Who took to his counsels, in evil hour,
The Friends to the Reasons of lawless Power,
That back the Public Informer, who
Would put down the *Thing*, that, in spite of new Acts,
And attempts to restrain it, by Soldiers or Tax,
Will *poison* the Vermin, that plunder the Wealth,
That lay in the House, that Jack built.

C

When a body of Manchester workmen assembled with their wives and children to hold a Reform meeting in August, 1819, they were set upon by cavalry and some six hundred were killed or wounded. The reaction of generous Englishmen was sharp and quick. Here is a page of contemporary comment on the "Peterloo Massacre" as it was called.

in Parliament, started late in the eighteenth century, was hushed during the struggles with France, but after that was waged most vigorously. Resistance on the part of the conservatively minded was resourceful. The country was stridently warned of the dire and inevitable consequences of broadening the suffrage. The distinguished historian Macaulay, for instance, argued (1820) that if the demand for universal suffrage were gratified "a few half-naked fishermen would divide with the owls and foxes the ruins of the greatest European cities." Later on, however, the same mind wrote in a celebrated passage, "We smile at these things. It is not impossible that our descendants when they read the history of the opposition offered by cupidity and prejudice to the improvements of the nineteenth century, may smile in their turn."

Demonstrations and riots organized by friends of parliamentary reform were matched by fierce and excited controversies inside Parliament. There was acute danger lest men should seek to achieve by violence that which a hidebound and apprehensive parliamentary majority would not grant by normal processes of law. Revolutionary events in France and Belgium, moreover, lent momentum to the cause and the opposition in the Lords was overcome eventually by the intervention of the crown. The passage of the parliamentary Reform Act in 1832 is part of the story of a British revolution in the first half of the nineteenth century that did not happen—or rather happened peacefully.

Under the provisions of the law the right to vote was extended to a large proportion of the middle classes, tripling the voting population. Seats in the Commons were shifted about so as to give representation to flourishing cities like Birmingham and Manchester and withdrawing M. P.'s from smaller communities. These innovations brought little immediate alteration in the composition of Parliament, for the newly enfranchised returned country gentlemen for the most part; M. P.'s from the manufacturing class were looked upon as sports or oddities.

Beneficiaries of parliamentary reform held that no further extension of the franchise was required. But spokesmen of city wageworkers who had counted on manhood suffrage felt they had been defrauded; not frustrated, however, they carried on a running campaign for votes for industrial workers which won through at long last in 1867.[4]

In the late 1830's, energetic agitation appeared in British working class circles for the implementation of a "People's Charter." It called for manhood suffrage, secret voting, salaries for M. P.'s, so that the individual without a private income might seek election, and lesser concessions. If these reforms were effected, Chartist leaders argued, Parliament would then adopt legislation beneficial to the industrial population. Huge mass meetings, monster processions and a widely circulated press promoted the cause; occasionally clashes between Chartists and officers of the law occurred.

Three petitions, carrying millions of names, many of them fictitious, besought Parliament to enact the Charter. But the ruling classes, alarmed by the mass agitation, rejected the demands, and division of mind in Chartist ranks lamed the campaign. After the third petition, in 1848, Chartism petered out, or better, was absorbed in the broader movement for political democracy. In time the central objectives of Chartism were inscribed on the statute books of Britain.

Enthusiastic humanitarians, such as William Wilberforce, had busied themselves, meanwhile, with the Negro problem. Already a successful crusade had been waged against the lucrative and barbarous traffic in slaves. Ignorant and luckless Negroes had long been purchased by profit-hungry traders along the torrid coasts of tropical Africa and hauled away by the hundreds in the stinking holds of any craft that would float to the lush markets of the New World.

Patient and prolonged education on the iniquity of this wicked business brought its reward, for the slave trade was prohibited by Parliament in 1807—at about the time that parallel legislation was adopted in the United States. British activity at the Congress of Vienna in 1815 secured an international ban on the traffic in slaves which the navy of Britain was called upon to enforce. And in 1833 a bill was passed providing for the gradual emancipation of Negroes in the British colonies, the owners being appropriately compensated by the government.

WORKER WELFARE MEASURES

"What about the white slaves of England?" cried an ardent social reformer in 1830 who was striving to arouse the national conscience to the need for legislation on terms of employment in British factories and mines. "Over a large surface of the industrial community," declared the humanitarian Lord Shaftesbury, "man has been regarded as an animal and that an animal not of the highest order; his loftiest faculties, when not prostrate, are perverted and his lowest exclusively devoted to the manufacture of wealth," in which, he implied at any rate, the workers had only a disproportionate share.

Believers in laissez faire economics were of course dead set against state action to remedy abuses, and manufacturing interests complained that legislation regulating factory employment would prove a boon to foreign competitors. But those protestations were overborne by dictates of humanity and the national welfare and the pressure of the employed. Laws restricting the hours of employment for child workers in cotton mills were placed on the statute books in 1802 and 1819 but never really enforced. That experience demonstrated that until a corps of trained inspectors was created there was little point in prescribing hours of work by law.

[4] A bill of 1835 placed the administration of towns and cities in the hands of the middle classes.

It was in 1833 that the first effective measures on child labor in British textile factories were enacted. No child under nine might lawfully be employed, those from nine to thirteen might not work over nine hours a day, and from thirteen to eighteen the maximum working period might not exceed twelve hours. Of high importance, the law would be enforced by salaried government officials. The obdurate refusal of some employers to obey the law and assist inspectors in their duties quickly led to more stringent regulations.

From mills the advocates of social betterment turned their attention to coal mines. Reports of official investigators revealed perfectly shocking conditions, many of them, to be sure, older than machine industrialism. Children of five, for example, were found opening doors down under the earth; youngsters and women worked like pit-ponies crawling along rough corridors on their hands and knees; women lugged heavy baskets of coal up long ladders to the surface.

Once these and other almost incredible facts were divulged, once ignorance had been dispelled, Parliament enacted (1842) legislation forbidding the employment of females and boys under ten in the mines and setting up a mine inspecting service. Under an act of 1847 the hours for women and children in industry were cut to ten a day which virtually fixed the ten-hour day for men as well, since the work of many men was tied in with the operations of other employees.

Further legislation required management to fence dangerous machinery, to provide proper ventilation in workrooms and to compensate workpeople for injuries on the job. Beginnings in public activity on behalf of the health of the nation date from a Public Health Act of 1848, which authorized local officials to appoint, if they chose, medical officers and to improve sanitation; a generation later the legislation was made mandatory. Measures to protect the welfare of workers flowed thereafter in a steady stream. Illustrative of the broad trend were successive acts raising the miniumum age at which children could be employed in factories: ten years, 1878; eleven years, 1891; twelve years, 1901; fourteen years, 1918. From time to time industrial workers' legislation was systematically codified and glaring gaps were closed.

In the "hungry forties" a group of workingmen themselves initiated consumers' cooperatives to raise standards of comfort. The central object was to cut costs to consumers by eliminating the profit of the middleman in retail trade; consumers themselves furnished the capital and shared in profits in proportion to their purchases. Started at Rochdale in 1844, this institution developed into a giant business with 10,000,000 members (1950) and thousands of stores, resembling in some respects the chain stores and the retail outlets of mail order houses of the United States. With the passage of time the movement branched out, operating scores of factories and workshops, a banking system and even a travel agency; the avowed goal was to supply all kinds of goods and services to consumers. British pioneering in cooperatives was imitated in other countries.

THE VICTORY OF FREE TRADE

By one of those paradoxes with which the pages of British history are strewn, at the very time that unfettered individualism was undergoing modification on the home front, the laissez-faire philosophy was being applied to international commerce. Legal obstacles to the unimpeded exchange of goods were gradually pulled down. Advocates of tariff reduction contended that free trade would promote domestic prosperity by lowering costs of food and forcing efficiency in industry, and would ensure world peace by binding the economies of countries together. The more zealous advocates of free trade in fact discerned in that principle an infallible recipe for the secular ills and aches of mankind.

Preliminary cuts in tariffs were effected in the 1820's and really drastic measures in the forties reduced the number of dutiable commodities by nearly 1,300 items. Since that legislation deprived the government of revenue, state financial requirements were covered by the reimposition (1842) of a tax on the incomes of the well-to-do, seventy years and more before a similar tax was collected in the United States.

The Famine years in Ireland—an eye-witness sketch of a boy and girl grubbing for a rotted potato, and a cartoon from the London magazine Punch *which satirizes official British apathy towards the calamity.*

Spokesmen of aggressive industrial interests, in the meantime, were conducting a furious, uphill struggle to eliminate duties on wheat ("corn" in the British usage), and so lower the price of bread for workpeople. They strummed upon the theme that the government should foster neither agriculture nor manufactures, but should allow them "to flourish or to fade" according to the energies, the skills and resources of the country. Agricultural interests, strongly entrenched in Parliament, both landed proprietors and "little fellows," who stood to lose by the importation of grain, stoutly and stubbornly resisted the free trade gospel.

Tariff protectionism was, however, decisively routed by short crops and a ruinous potato blight in 1845 in Ireland. The mass of the Irish population relied almost wholly upon the humble "spud" for sustenance; blight caused luxuriant green vines to shrivel to a dirty brown overnight and potatoes dug from the earth quickly rotted. Misery in the Emerald Isle was as evil as in Europe at the time of the Black Death; perhaps as many as a million perished in the next few years for want of food or the ravages of epidemics. A huge tide of emigration started rolling to the United States; Ireland in fact was the one country of nineteenth-century Europe in which the pressure of population on food resources was substantially mitigated by emigration.

In the face of the terrible Irish calamity and food shortages in the United Kingdom itself, Parliament finally voted (1846) to rub out the tariffs on grain and admit food without duty. That was a dramatic move heavy with consequences. The Tory Party, then in command of the ministry, and radically divided on the issue of repeal, was torn apart. And the victory over the grain producers certified to the ascendancy of industrialism over agriculture in the national economy. The balance of political power, moreover, shifted from the landed squirearchy to the urban middle classes where it remained just short of a century—to 1945 when the Labour Party, essentially the instrument of the wage earners, rode into control.

The dreadful consequences which it was predicted that free trade in food would have for British agriculture did not become immediately apparent. Actually farming reached the zenith of its prosperity about 1870. But thereafter agriculture languished as grain was brought in from the Middle West of the United States at a lower cost than it could be raised at home and frozen meats were imported from vast ranges overseas. Arable acreage dropped some twenty per cent and rural life, neglected by the state, fell to a very low ebb; the drift of population from soil to city was accelerated. Rising urban demands for milk and meat, however, encouraged the raising of livestock and the national tradition of scientific stock breeding was upheld; it was now, for example, that the "Large White," biggest member of the pig family, started to go to market.

Increasingly Britain relied upon foreign supplies of foodstuffs. As Britain was the world's workshop so the world served as the British granary. With the coming of the First World War and the ensuing U-boat ravages, Britain was confronted with singularly grave problems of feeding her teeming millions.

Repeal of the "corn" laws sealed the fate of the protectionist principle in general. Lingering vestiges of mercantilist doctrine which shielded British shipping from foreign competition were scratched from the books in 1849 and foreign vessels were even allowed to engage in coastwide trade. The national budget of 1860 retained only fifteen dutiable items which yielded an appreciable revenue for the national treasury. From that point to the First World War Britain was practically on a free trade basis.

Lively campaigning was launched in the 1890's for tariffs to protect British factories from stiff competition by Germany and the United States and to save what remained of British agriculture. But the free trade conviction was too deeply embedded in the national consciousness to be overthrown. The British free trade principle, it may be added, had only extremely limited imitation in the world of the nineteenth century.

PARTIES AND POLITICIANS

From a global angle of vision British internal politics carried less significance than economic and social developments and accordingly may be treated more briefly. The subject cannot, however, be wholly overlooked, for British political procedures had world influence, contemporaneously and later.

The heart of British politics beat in the party mechanism, controlling the ministry. Factionalism within the historic parties, Tories and Whigs, wrote an intricate pattern of political divisions and reunions. For a considerable period party organization was embryonic and no ministry could count on an automatic majority; over and over again during the long struggle with Napoleon, for instance, ministers were ignorant of the reception which Parliament would give to vital proposals. It was only after the mid-nineteenth century that it became customary for M. P.'s to follow obediently the program of their particular party—and not always then.

Considerable political reshuffling accompanied the revocation of the "corn" laws, in 1846, which upset both parties, the Tory schism running deeper. It was remarked of the Tory leader, Sir Robert Peel, who piloted the repeal bill through the Commons that he had come upon his Whig adversaries bathing and had mischievously stolen their clothes. The reference was to Peel's change of heart on protectionism. Peel might well have retorted that circumstances alter cases and that a foolish consistency is the hobgoblin of little minds, for in the history of party government it has been a familiar practice of rivals to appropriate political issues from one another.

The very first reason for two parties in a representative government of the British type is that there may be "Ins" and "Outs" and that the two change roles sooner or later. That testimony of history seems heretical to the Utopian cast of mind which insists upon a sharp dividing line between parties, rooted in differences in principles. To the idealogue it appears that British party government is simply a game played between two teams wearing different uniforms and hosiery. He indeed misses the crucial point that unless parties cherished a great deal in common there would be no parliamentary government but civil strife instead; the fundamentals which united the parties transcended the differences that divided them. British parties learned and borrowed from each other, gradually solidifying in the Conservative Party and the Liberal Party.

Benjamin Disraeli

Certainly there were differences between the parties. As the lineal descendant of the Tories, the Conservative Party spoke the mind of the landed gentry and of a section of the new aristocracy of business. It favored protective tariffs, spirited imperial and foreign policies and caution in domestic reform in keeping with time-tested precedents. The Conservative Party was authentically conservative, traditionalist, steeped in that mentality which

> "Makes us rather bear those ills we have
> Than fly to others that we know not of."

The backbone of the Liberal Party was its Whig predecessor, reflecting the outlook and the interests of the middle classes. Liberals were enthusiasts for individual freedom, a competitive economy, free trade and after about 1900 they were more sympathetically inclined toward social welfare legislation than the Conservatives. Liberals were less pugnacious, by and large, in international dealings than their Conservative rivals.

As a habit of mind, the basic assumptions of liberalism were set forth in an *Essay on Liberty* (1859), a work of perennial interest, by the greatest of liberal thinkers, John Stuart Mill, himself a disciple of Utilitarianism. His was a "without tears" approach to the human pageant. Personal liberty should never be infringed, he felt, save as necessary to protect the liberties of others. For Mill freedom of expression was an absolute because only through the competition of ideas could truth emerge. No man, moreover, could be so certain that his view was right as to warrant him in suppressing the opinions of others; Mill declaimed earnestly against "the oppressive yoke of uniformity." There was a certain bloodless quality about the intellect of Mill, for men to him were creatures without strong passions rather like a locomotive. But his preachments on liberty had a broad and lasting influence in Britain, in Europe and the wider world.

The cleavage between Conservative and Liberal was vividly exemplified in the persons of Benjamin Disraeli and William E. Gladstone. Here were the doughtiest warriors, it may be, ever to cross swords in the broad British parliamentary arena. Alternating for a generation in the office of prime minister, they left a deep imprint upon national politics.

Disraeli was in truth something of an upstart, the heir of a Jewish tradition who was

William Ewart Gladstone

brought up as a Christian. In his younger years, he was keenly interested in the wageworkers as he revealed in a novel *Sybil or The Two Nations* (1845), a study in contrasts between rich and poor. Taking to politics he emerged as the spokesman of a band of Tory protectionists who formed the nucleus of the Conservative Party.

As the commanding personality in that party, colorful in language and vests, a nimble debater and masterful tactician, Disraeli accepted domestic change with greater gusto than most of his political bedfellows. He acquired a fine country estate with all the rights and prestige pertaining thereto and had himself raised to the peerage as the Earl of Beaconsfield. Exponent of a "large" foreign policy, he extended the British imperial heritage in several directions and held steady the reputation of his country in the family of nations.

Gladstone, on the other hand, was born to the commercial purple, conventionally educated, a scholar of parts who was as much concerned about orthodox Christian doctrine as about the politics of liberalism. Once upon a time a Tory, he seceded on the free trade issue and stood forth as an earnest liberal reformer, the founder in a real sense of the Liberal Party. Gladstone "might with equal truth be called, and he has in fact been called, a conservative and a revolutionary," writes an admiring biographer, Lord Bryce.

Gladstone sonorously proclaimed the glories of theology and free trade economics, called for a "new deal" in Ireland, or rallied in moral righteousness to the succor of the downtrodden within the Empire (sometimes) and without (sometimes). A man of Churchillian vitality of mind and body he held a seat in the Commons for over sixty years.

VICTORIAN EQUIPOISE

It was a merrier country, this Britain of the two Titans, than post-Waterloo Britain. The ravages of machine industrialism, or the most glaring of them at any rate, had yielded to treatment. For wageworkers a ten hour day was now the custom, their purchasing power was definitely higher in 1850 than in 1825 and

Queen Victoria, the Prince Consort, and the Prince of Wales

Victorian Bow-Front house, with area and basement—a fair sample of middle class comfort

real wages rose by about a third in the third quarter of the century.

Many workpeople were given to overspending on alcohol, and popular tastes sometimes betrayed the coarse inheritance from the past. As late as 1849, for instance, a throng of 100,000, including children, assembled to witness the hanging of two murderers. Special excursion trains hauled spectators to the execution ground where stands were erected for their accommodation. Remarked an eye-witness, "The convicted criminals walked to their fate in decent staidness; the unconvicted mob yelled with vindictive rage, or mere animal excitement. . . ."

It was a flourishing and prosperous Britain; and called Victorian Britain in honor of the queen who took the crown in 1837 and did not lay it down until 1901. Her Majesty symbolized the values and shared the mentality prized by eminent Victorians of the middle classes: prim family life, stern moral rectitude, piety and respectability, aggressive earnestness, fervent patriotism and sublime confidence in the progress of mankind.

Very clearly the middle classes of Britain had risen to the top and they more or less set the standards of behavior for their peers in all countries. It would be false, however, to assume that the Victorian age was one prolonged sunny Sunday afternoon. Domestic affairs, it is true, rested in equipoise from the mid century onward, but in 1867 a fresh tide of change started to roll.

TOWARD A MORE PERFECT DEMOCRACY

Landmarks on the road to fuller democracy were measures which broadened the electorate. Working people, it may be recalled, had been by-passed when the voting privilege was extended in 1832. Well-to-do artisans renewed demands for the suffrage and Gladstone adopted their cause as his own by offering a bill to enfranchise town-dwelling workers. Fearful Conservatives countered with stock dissenting arguments and enough Liberals lined up with them to defeat the proposal. Then Disraeli took over the management of the government and in 1867 secured the passage of a statute similar in tenor to the Gladstone bill.

That "leap in the dark," or "shooting Niagara" as Carlyle called it, inscribed the names of nearly a million industrial wage earners and middle-class men on the voting lists, almost

The "leap in the dark" as the cartoonist of Punch *saw it. Brittania shields her eyes; the rest of the field reins up; but the horse (with Disraeli's face) plunges ahead.*

doubling the electorate. At the same time great industrial cities were allotted more equitable representation in the Commons.

Arguing that all "capable citizens" should be admitted to the franchise, Gladstone had the pleasure in 1884 of carrying through a law which brought the poor and largely uneducated males of the rural working population into the electorate. That gesture, which placed rustics on an equal footing with townsmen, helped to temper the feeling of inferiority which had grown up among the soil people.

Women of course had not been given the ballot, but insistent clamor, growing more militant with the years, demanded equality of political rights and duties.[5] Was it not a grotesque paradox after all that while Queen Victoria was considered eminently qualified to reign over 300,000,000 subjects, members of her sex, half of society, were not regarded as competent to vote for national law-makers? After the First World War and partly in token of the feminine contribution to victory, women over thirty were granted suffrage (1918) and a decade later the voting age was scaled down to twenty-one; eligible women voters outnumbered the males. As the result of a piecemeal process operating across a century universal adult suffrage had been achieved in the "mother of democracies."

As another move in the direction of more popular government the authority of the aristocratic House of Lords was sharply whittled down. A noble lord in Gilbert and Sullivan's *Iolanthe* exclaims, "It so happens that if there is an institution in Great Britain which is not susceptible to any improvement at all, it is the House of Peers." But democratically minded statesmen from Gladstone onward demanded that this relic of the feudal age, the most ancient part of Britain's "unwritten" constitution except for the crown itself, should either be "mended or ended."

The House of Lords was mended in 1911 by a statute which limited its power to reject legislation approved by the Commons. Under this act all money bills became law when adopted merely by the Commons, and other bills became law if passed by the Commons in three successive sessions within two years after introduction. It would be entirely possible consequently for the Commons to abolish the Lords at any time it cared to do so. Another historic change was enacted in 1949 when the delaying power of the Lords was curtailed from two years to one.

After 1911 the Lords was virtually reduced to a learned debating society. It did nothing in particular but did it very well. Active participants in this deliberative rather than policy-making body were largely not hereditary peers but men appointed for conspicuous public service, distinguished former ministers of state, retired diplomatists or civil servants and professional men. Ordinarily only Lords who were familiar through experience or study of the subjects under consideration took part in discussions. Since these "Elder Statesmen" had no need to bother about re-election and had no constituents to impress, they spoke only when they had something worthwhile to say and their judgments often carried great weight in the country.

Lesser reforms with democratizing implications were the abolition of property and religious tests for candidates for the Commons, the introduction of the secret ballot (1872) instead of the traditional oral voting and the appointment and promotion of virtually all civil servants by competitive examinations (1870's). So that men without private incomes might be able to serve in the Commons, provision was made (1911) for payment of salaries to M. P.'s by the government.

By reason therefore of these several innovations, from extension of the suffrage to compensation for M. P.'s, the British government of the twentieth century differed radically from that of Waterloo, and the trend to democracy as a pattern of government was accompanied by a subtler change in spirit, the swing toward democracy as a way of life.

BRITISH SCHOOLING

To the diffusion of the democratic spirit the elementary schools of England made their spe-

[5] Women taxpayers were admitted in 1869 to the municipal franchise.

cial and peculiar contribution. At the outset of the nineteenth century limited education for the masses was furnished by Sunday schools of the Evangelical churches and schools conducted by voluntary societies associated with the Established Church, one of which carried the resounding name of the "National Society for Promoting the Education of the Poor in the Principles of the Church of England." In these schools religious instruction was blended with the fundamentals of secular learning.

It was not until 1833 that the national government accepted responsibility for public education by appropriating an extremely modest sum to aid the voluntary school societies. Small grants were regularly voted thereafter. Schooling for children of poorer families depended on what the local parson or squire would do or induce others to do; at most, as late as 1870, fewer than half the children attended school and illiteracy lay heavily upon the kingdom.

Extension of the franchise to urban workers in 1867 made basic education a matter of urgent national concern. Religious leaders insisted on the preservation of church-connected schools, and the decisive law on education of 1870 conceded the point, but prescribed the establishment of schools in places not already looked after by voluntary societies. Both types of schools received subsidies from the national treasury. In the course of time attendance was made free and compulsory to the age of thirteen (fourteen in 1918, and fifteen in 1947). By 1900 elementary education was available to every child and illiteracy had practically disappeared. Two generations of universal education greatly reduced differences in social habits and tastes between British employers and wage-workers.

Stubborn resistance by churchmen long blocked the development of schooling on the secondary level, but in 1902 county authorities were authorized to build secondary and junior technical schools and rapid expansion followed. As of 1900 only one child in seventy studied in a secondary school, but by 1938 the proportion was nearer one in ten; parents paid slight fees for their children until 1945. Though locally administered, all schools were subject to inspection by national officials.[6]

Institutions of higher learning, parenthetically, responded to the dynamic and prevalent urges of the century. The ancient foundations at Oxford and Cambridge snapped out of their lethargy, curricula were broadened and instruction vitalized. Oxford exerted a considerable influence upon colleges of the United States, especially through Rhodes Scholars. To satisfy the increasing demand for higher training, ten additional universities, all of top quality, were established in London and in such "provincial" cities as Manchester, Liverpool and Birmingham.

GROWTH OF TRADE UNIONS

Few aspects of modern British history are more remarkable than the emergence and growth of the Labour Party. It represented the alliance of Fabian Socialists and other groups with the powerful trade union movement.

Trade unionism, already a force of no little moment, was strengthened in 1851 by the formation of the Amalgamated Society of Engineers, which fused several small societies of workers. Similar mergers ensued in other crafts. These unions developed rather elaborate organizations with restricted membership, weekly dues and salaried officials; national unions met together in 1869 for the first annual Trades Union Congress. Skilled well-paid wage earners, the "labor aristocracy," belonged to these unions.

Men with an urge for leadership and responsibility served as officials, moderate individuals, who much preferred to attain economic objectives by peaceful negotiation with management instead of by strikes. They looked upon the competitive, capitalist economy as a permanent institution, and pushed for the enfranchisement of the workers, winning through in 1867. Organizations of agricultural workers,

[6] Boys of well-to-do families studied in "public" secondary schools which were distinctly private, old-line institutions, such as Eton and Rugby and newer creations like Marlborough and Wellington. Wearers of "old school ties" continued to play a prominent part in the affairs of the kingdom.

which appeared on the horizon in the 1870's, devoted particular attention to helping distressed rustics to emigrate overseas.

Adoption of measures by Parliament which clarified the legal status of unions testified that distrust of combinations of workers had lessened in the governing classes. Certain obstacles to the protection of union treasuries were removed in 1871 and the legality of peaceful picketing in conducting strikes was conceded (1875). Plainly, unions and collective bargaining between management and men had come to stay. The vigor of unions, however, fluctuated in keeping with the tempo of business activity.

Starting late in the 1880's unskilled and irregularly employed workmen were drawn into unions which were organized industry by industry in contrast to the older craft unions—a development broadly corresponding to that in the United States in the 1930's under the C.I.O. Whereas in 1892 British unions contained about 1,500,000 members, enrollment had risen by 1914 to nearly 4,000,000, or something like a fifth of the employed adults. Newer unions tended to be less conservative and more militant than the older ones, less persuaded of the values of the capitalist economy.

Strikes and industrial disturbances frequently occurred, but machinery for conciliation and arbitration of disputes with management was steadily developed. By acts of Parliament unions were exempted in 1906 from damage suits because of strikes and were allowed (1913) to collect funds for political purposes, provided contributions were voluntarily made by members. That legislation suggests the linkage between unions and the Labour Party which by then had been established on firm foundations.

NOVEL PATTERNS OF SOCIAL CHANGE

Economic crises, social distress and unrest marked the 1880's. A study conducted by one investigator revealed that one of every three Londoners lived constantly on the edge of destitution. There was no shortage of answers to the age-old questions of why the many were poor and how poverty and its attendant ills might be eradicated.

Only two of the novel solutions, both hostile to economic individualism in the classic British citadel of capitalism, can here be considered. The collectivist philosophy of Karl Marx (Chap. XVII), who spent most of his life in London and whose thinking was considerably molded by his reading of British history, appealed to a small and evanescent company. Most attractive of the converts surely was a gifted poet and craftsman, William Morris, whose sensitive intellect rebelled against prevailing social inequities.

In *News from Nowhere* (1891), an engaging tract for the times, Morris painted a gleaming vision of what Britain would be like if society were re-ordered along Marxist lines. But the physical violence implicit in Marxism repelled him, as it did almost all British social radicals, and he soon seceded from the movement. The doctrines of Marx had in fact only a negligible influence in the island kingdom, but his writings on human conditions in the British past were "like lifting the lid off hell."

The version of collectivism, of anticapitalist doctrine, which really mattered in Britain was shaped by the Fabian Society of Socialists (1883). Originally a little circle of middle-class intellectuals, full of humanitarian compassion, they adopted as their exemplar the Roman general Fabius Cunctator, who chose to make haste slowly and conquer the enemy by attrition. Fabians proposed to convert Britain to a state-regulated economy by the unhurried method of free consent registered in free elections. Through a process of evolution they would bring about a bureaucratic revolution, placing the economic affairs of the kingdom under the control of the government.

Deeply rooted in the democratic tradition, the Fabian approach has been described as "discussion, argument, reading, research, often confined to small groups of people, are the sound foundations for a nation's advancing freedom and social responsibility." Outstanding among the Fabian pioneers was Sidney Webb, scholar and author, who was chiefly responsible no doubt for making this British variety of collectivism constitutional and respectable and differentiating it from Marxism.

The chosen role of the Fabians was to educate the educated to malignant flaws and faults in British society and to enlist public support for far-reaching changes by parliamentary methods. Fabians were persuasive pamphleteers and lecturers who buttressed their arguments with statistics and other evidence drawn from the experience of Britain. An even-tempered lot, they imputed to those who disagreed with them no sins more original than ignorance, stupidity and avarice.

WORKPEOPLE IN POLITICS

In collusion with trade unionists, the Fabians created the Labour Party. The groundwork for a workers' political organization was laid with

THE

FABIAN PARLIAMENTARY LEAGUE,

34, BOUVERIE STREET, E.C.

FABIAN TRACTS, No. 6.

THE

True Radical Programme.

LONDON:
GEO. STANDRING, 7 & 9, FINSBURY STREET, E.C.
1887

Price One Penny.

A specimen of Fabian pamphleteering

The Socialists. *An etching by William Strang, 1896*

the extension of the suffrage to urban workmen (1867). Although two spokesmen of the miners' union were returned to the Commons in 1874, workers in the main voted at first for middle-class candidates, Liberals mainly.

However, in 1893, a Scottish M. P., Keir Hardie, launched the Independent Labour Party which advocated government ownership of productive property and government distribution of the goods created. Seven years later a small conference representing that party, several collectivist societies and certain trade unions voted to call a congress "to secure the return of an increased number of labour members to the next Parliament." That resolution of 1900 marked the actual birth of the Labour Party, which in 1945 would assume the management of British affairs, backed by an immense majority in the Commons.[7]

In the formative stage the young party was hastened to maturity by hard-headed trade unionists largely, whose devotion to the organization possessed a quality of religious intensity. For many a leader, indeed, the party usurped the place which chapel or church had formerly occupied in his affections. As a militant, crusading educational force, with Fabians acting as coaches, the Labour Party advanced steadily.

[7] Upwards of 200 of the Labour M. P.'s of 1945 belonged to the Fabian Society.

Voting strength and financial resources came from the organized workpeople though some unions skeptically kept aloof. Twenty-nine Labourites were elected to the Commons in 1906 and before 1914 the delegation had grown to forty; in the Scotch intellectual, Ramsay MacDonald, the party possessed an eloquent orator, a skillful organizer and an adroit parliamentary tactician. To secure laws favorable to trade union interests and social welfare legislation, Labour M. P.'s teamed up with Liberals in the Commons.

SOCIAL LEGISLATION

The desirability of governmental action to better the welfare of the masses and to distribute wealth more equitably pervaded broad layers of the British population. That conviction harmonized with the spirit of the times, for on the Continent social reform under state auspices had been gathering momentum since about 1870; an august British minister, indeed, had been heard to remark: "We are all socialists now." That paradox presently became a commonplace in the sense of a universal and ever-present consciousness of social values. Considerations of social expediency, moreover, the impulse of democratic ideals and the flame of Christian ethics, stimulated pressure in Britain for legislation which would narrow the gulf between the "Two Nations," between the luxury of the minority and the insecurity and lowly standards of comfort of the majority.

The Liberal Party, which had identified itself with the cause of social amelioration, triumphed at the general election of 1906. Allied with it were two minority delegations, the Labour Party and the Irish Nationalists, each with its own particular objectives. In the years which followed the area of British legislative activity was considerably extended in utter defiance of the axioms of the "classical" economists. The traditional conception of the State as an impartial umpire in economic affairs gradually gave way to the view that the State should guarantee a certain standard of material welfare for all citizens.

Capably bearing the heat and burden of the day for the "new Liberalism" was David Lloyd George, a humble Welshman, who literally pulled himself up by his bootstraps. After winning a local reputation as an exponent of Welsh nationalism, he attained national prominence by eloquent denunciations of the war against the Boers (1899–1900), as befitted the champion of a small nation. In spirit he remained a Welshman and instinctively sided with revolt against the conventional. As Chancellor of the Exchequer, tenacious, agile, redoubtable, skillful in party leadership and a platform orator in the great British tradition, Lloyd George quickly became the strongest personal force on the stage of British politics.

Consciously or unconsciously the controlling element in Parliament was animated by the lofty resolve penned by William Blake a century earlier:

> I shall not cease from mental fight,
> Nor shall my sword sleep in my hand,
> Till we have built Jerusalem
> In England's green and pleasant land.

From the legislative hopper flowed a stream of laws on social policy, many of which seem the veriest commonplaces nowadays. As a measure of security for the poor in the eventide of life, a modest pension was voted in 1908, which relieved the indigent elderly from being herded into public poorhouses, as had been the fashion for generations. To benefit workmen in periods of illness or incapacity, a compulsory insurance plan was adopted (1911), the premium being shared by workers, employers and the government; an ailing person was assured of hospital and medical care and a small weekly income.

A beginning was made (1911) in obligatory unemployment insurance covering certain types of jobs in which work was seasonable or highly cyclical in nature; and state bureaus were established (1909) to supply information on employment openings. Funds were appropriated (1909) on a small scale to replace slum dwellings with wholesome homes. Older legislation, furthermore, requiring employers in industry and agriculture to compensate workers for accidents was brought up to date (1906) in matters of coverage and care. And the principle of a minimum wage for workpeople was inscribed (1909) in the statutes.

These and lesser laws cost the government money, of course, and that at exactly the time that a furious naval race with Germany was making staggering demands upon the treasury. To hold state finances in balance existing taxes were increased and new ones were added. Income taxes, for example, were upped, on the principle that the broadest backs should bear the heaviest burdens and partly as a means of redressing inequalities of fortune.

Inheritance taxes, too, were raised and levies upon landed properties in city and in country were so devised as to transfer to the government a large part of the rental value of land due to its location, or what is spoken of as the "unearned increment." These measures not only swelled the revenues of the government, but operated to bring about a certain leveling in incomes.

Social and fiscal policies of the "new Liberalism" elicited passionate outcries, prophecies of impending doom from Conservatives. But the electorate upheld the ministry by comfortable majorities and when the House of Lords obdurately vetoed tax proposals its fangs were drawn (p. 300). Throughout the stormy controversies the Irish Nationalists loyally backed the Liberals and now they were given their promised reward.

THE IRISH PUZZLE

Like a thick green thread, the tangled problem of Ireland runs through the tapestry of British history in the nineteenth century. Inherited animosities were sharpened in an age of intensifying nationalism, deepening democracy and growing concern with material betterment. Broadly regarded, Ireland displayed in a relatively mild form those dark, vehement and persistent passions which are familiar on the frontier lands of Europe where national hatreds, the scourge of religious enmities and alien landlords rendered meaningless ordinary notions of compromise and conciliation. When Britons sounded off on repression of minorities on the Continent, foreign statesmen were bound to retort: "Physician, heal thyself."

What then were the fundamentals of the Anglo-Irish antagonism as it unfolded in the nineteenth century? They may be treated under three main headings: economic, principally agrarian, religious and political. An overwhelming proportion of the Irish wrested their livelihood from the soil, and a desperately bleak living it was. Vast tracts of land were owned by insensitive landlords residing in England who cared little about their properties or their tenants so long as rental payments kept rolling in.

In spite of the sharp fall in population which attended the ruinous potato famine in the 1840's, multitudes of Irish peasants scraped along on a bare subsistence ever haunted by the specter of starvation. As was true of soil people anywhere, the Irish wished to own the fields they tilled. Quarreling with landed proprietors over rights of tenancy and rentals was endemic and often flared up in deeds of physical violence and destruction of property.

Gradually, all too gradually to suit militant Irish interests, the land controversy yielded to intelligent treatment. Under the leadership of Gladstone in particular, for whom appeasement of Ireland became a prime preoccupation of statecraft, burning grievances over tenure and rent were somewhat reduced. In the eighties and nineties Parliament passed laws to assist peasants in buying land with loans from the British treasury which would be repaid in installments over half a century. On the eve of the First World War upwards of 7,000,000 acres had been transferred from English landlords to Irish landworkers.

The religious piece in the Irish puzzle thoroughly bedeviled the entire question, proving less amenable to adjustment than the agrarian problem. Far the larger part of the Irish, approximately nine out of ten, belonged to the Roman Catholic Church and were ardently devoted to their faith and clergy. The creeds of Calvin and Wesley claimed most of the Protestant minority with a scattering of Anglicans. Concentrated in the northern counties (known together as Ulster), the Protestants prospered on manufacturing and shipping. Protestants, too, were inflexibly attached to their religion, which so openly set them off from the Catholic majority, and encouraged an attitude of superiority.

It was standard belief among Protestants that if Ireland were allowed to govern itself they would be the victims of discrimination and inequitable taxation at the hands of the Catholic majority. Consequently the Protestants stood intransigently for the maintenance of the political links with England; and they had the unswerving support of many English co-religionists. It was irritating and irksome for non-Anglicans, Catholics and Protestants alike, that they had to pay tithes for the purposes of the official church, the Irish branch of the Church of England. That complaint, however, was silenced in 1869 when Parliament canceled the privileged status of the Anglican Church and abolished tithes.

There yet remain the political aspects of the problem, which were intertwined in fact with the agrarian and religious strands. Of first importance in English thinking was the conviction that the political bond with Ireland was desirable if not indeed indispensable for national security. An independent Ireland in alliance with a foreign foe would be a pistol directly pointed at the English heart, and besides, Irish ports were serviceable for the British fleet. If "John Bull's other island" had been as remote as Australia, say, the Anglo-Irish feud would scarcely have attained much significance. As so often in disputes of this sort, the immutable facts of geography went straight to the heart of the matter.

On the Catholic Irish side, among the politically articulate at any rate, a passionate longing developed for the Emerald Isle to shape its own destinies. The aspiration of "Ireland for the Irish" animated, or rather helped to animate, insurrection after insurrection. While Britain was grappling with Napoleon, for instance, in 1798 Irish patriots, Catholics and Protestants, raised the standard of rebellion. The insurrection was stamped out by English troops with shocking ruthlessness and the decision was then taken to abolish the Irish Parliament which had been revived a generation before.

Resorting to crude and costly bribery English authorities purchased enough Irish votes to secure approval of parliamentary union with Britain (1801); a hundred seats in the Commons were allocated to Ireland. It was a sullen and unstable union, upheld by bayonets, and presently broadened by the inclusion of Ireland in the common tariff system; it lasted until 1922. At first Catholics were not eligible to seek election to the Commons but spirited agitation won that right (1829) and set a precedent for later campaigns. Just when the potato tragedy had cowed and decimated Irish commoners, a small company of Irishmen, bent on gaining independence, took up arms (1848). That outbreak was as futile as its more glamorous predecessor of 1798, and the leaders were shipped away to Tasmania. Another rebellion in 1865, simply repeated the earlier fiascos.

With a view to reconciliation Britain now applied the ecclesiastical and land reforms described above. But inside Ireland a formidable nationalist agitation had taken shape, aiming to achieve self-government by constitutional processes. The central brain and controlling power of the Nationalists came to be Charles Stewart Parnell, one of the most effective of all Irish patriots. English educated and of English ancestry, a Protestant and a landlord, Parnell was fiercely anti-English; he made frequent excursions to the United States in quest of moral support and cash from Irish-Americans.

Nationalists to the number of sixty were returned in 1880 to the Commons, where, spurred on by Parnell, they resorted to all manner of filibustering to prevent the transaction of business. Their price for propriety was Irish self-government; they proposed to plague Pharaoh until he let the people go. Spokesmen of minority groups on the Continent, incidentally, perfected and ingeniously applied the turbulent obstructionist tactics of the Irish Nationalists.

Anarchic outrages in the Emerald Isle coupled with the verbal warfare in London, induced Gladstone to declare himself, boldly and courageously, in favor of Irish home rule. When a definite plan to implement that avowal was presented to Parliament in 1885, an impassioned tumult swept the kingdom; a section of the Liberal Party, calling itself the Unionists, turned savagely upon Gladstone, defeated his proposal and aligned permanently with Conservative opponents of Irish freedom. A second home rule bill, sponsored by Gladstone, managed to get through the Commons (1893), but was killed in the Lords.

In 1912 the Liberal ministry, faithful to pledges to its Irish Nationalist allies, brought forth a third self-government project. It prescribed that a separate parliament with a considerable range of autonomy should be instituted in Dublin, though all legislation would be subject to approval by the crown; Protestant religious interests were carefully safeguarded. Foreign affairs, questions of land ownership and the collection of taxes would be determined by the London Parliament, to which Ireland would send forty-two deputies instead of the traditional one hundred. These proposals, it will be noted, did not divorce Ireland from the United Kingdom.

The home rule scheme unloosed the gravest British crisis in a century. Most Irish political chiefs welcomed the plan with unalloyed jubilation, but an extremist fragment would be satisfied with nothing short of full independence and an Irish republic; for that element Ireland for the Irish meant precisely that and no compromise. This group had been active in reviving the use of the ancient Irish language which made it possible to insult the English without danger of being understood.

Protestant Ulster, on the other hand, instinctively and absolutely opposed self-government and so did Conservative and Unionist opinion in England. The whole acrimonious controversy was embittered by the linkage of the competing Irish factions with the two leading British parties. Nevertheless, the home rule measure was driven through Parliament, royal sanction being given in September of 1914.

Passions in the Emerald Isle itself had risen to the point of explosion. Private armies, first in Ulster and then in the Catholic South, had been whipped into shape and Ireland quivered in the balance as the perils of civil war threatened. Prominent figures in the British military services openly condemned home rule, which raised anxious questions as to whether, if fighting actually started, the plan could in fact be put into operation. The angry feud between military leaders and the Liberal ministry was to have serious consequences in the conduct of the First World War.

An Irish follower of Parnell is evicted from his house.

As matters worked out, the coming of war obliged Parliament to postpone the application of home rule for the duration of hostilities. The physician had gone far along the road of healing, but the patient was still ill and restless.

AS OF 1914

The Britain which plunged defiantly into the First World War differed sharply from the Britain which had deported Napoleon to St. Helena. The marvellously flexible constitution had evolved, statute by statute, in response to the requirements of an ever-changing social environment. Freedom slowly broadened down from precedent to precedent in line with the instinct of continuity so strongly rooted in the British national tradition.

As of 1914, Great Britain was still managed primarily by the middle classes and the aristocracy, though all men (not yet women) shared in declaring public policies and in selecting the representatives to carry out the general will. "Society" still possessed something of its glamorous prestige and many a man excluded from that caste by the accident of birth was eager to crash through its portals.

Wealth-creating resources, mills and mines, finance and shipping had fabulously multiplied. Population had risen enormously and British levels of living surpassed, no doubt, those of any other large European country. The heavy human mortgage from early industrialism had largely been liquidated and large opportunities for constructive and creative achievement lay before the common man of uncommon talent and ambition.

Due to reliance upon uninterrupted foreign commerce the place of Britain in the world of nations was uniquely delicate and peculiarly vulnerable. Beyond all else, the very life of the country depended upon command of the ocean routes and free approach and departure from her ports.

Despite the spate of social legislation, government had not invaded the realm of business enterprise. The rigorous individualism of "classical" economics had been tempered, but fundamentally it was still assumed that individual energy and acumen should earn their rewards, that competitive capitalism would ensure the best development of productive resources and that free competition would protect consumers against excessive prices and inferior qualities of goods. The First World War, however, would bring a sensational if temporary increase in both the range and the intensity of governmental authority over economic activities.

If popular education had failed to march abreast of the finest in Europe, British science and scholarship, British art and literature could claim a place at or near the top. Within "this fortress built by Nature for herself," it was possible to detect a certain mood of complacency and confidence about the future, high pride and dignified tolerance.

But the darkening international horizon had aroused gnawing apprehensions. Britain throughout the century had accumulated fresh colonial and imperial trophies and developed older ones, engaging in plenty of international disputes and minor wars to those ends. Not long after Waterloo it had become fixed British policy to eschew diplomatic entanglements with foreign nations. Proud and mighty Britain stood resplendent in the robes of global arbiter.

But the swift and portentous emergence of Imperial Germany as a powerful nation, bursting with untamed energy, wrought a revolution in British diplomacy as the Victorian age faded to its close. Britain bound herself tightly to Japan, more loosely to France and still more loosely to tsarist Russia. Diplomacy, too, bestirred itself—and fruitfully—to cultivate and to merit the good opinion of the upsurging Yankee giant beyond the Atlantic.

FOR FURTHER STUDY

CHARLES R. FAY, *Great Britain from Adam Smith to the Present Day* (new ed., London, 1950)

GEORGE M. TREVELYAN, *British History in the Nineteenth Century and After* (new ed., New York, 1937)

DAVID THOMSON, *England in the Nineteenth Century* (London, 1950) PAPERBACK

ÉLIE HALÉVY, *A History of the English People* (6 vols., New York, 1924–1947) PAPERBACKS

ASA BRIGGS, *The Age of Improvement* (New York, 1959)

ERNEST L. WOODWARD, *The Age of Reform, 1815–1870* (Oxford, 1938)

ASA BRIGGS, *Victorian People* (London, 1954)

ROBERT C. K. ENSOR, *England, 1870–1914* (Oxford, 1936)

ROBERT B. MCDOWELL, *British Conservatism, 1832–1914* (New York, 1959)

HENRY M. PELLING, *The Origins of the Labour Party* (London, 1954)

ERIC B. STRAUSS, *Irish Nationalism and British Democracy* (New York, 1951)

CHAPTER XIV

RESTORATION AND REVOLUTIONS (1815-1852)

CONSERVATISM AND LIBERALISM

TERMS such as "conservatism," "reaction" and "liberalism," which appear in the following pages, are relative, without ironclad authority or tyrannous meanings. The implications of these words have varied from time to time, from place to place, and consequently have been (and are) used with different emphases by different writers. These terms stand for ideas, fluid ones, and uniformity in meanings is not to be expected. It would be grossly unjust to condemn a man to the stocks for confessing puzzlement on how to use them properly.

The opposite of post-Napoleonic conservatism was the Marquis de Lafayette (above, in 1825) who personified the liberal dream of "liberty and order."

Conservatism in post-Napoleonic Britain, for example, was not precisely the same as in Austria, nor the same in Austria as in Imperial Russia. Historical traditions, together with the extent of the sufferings which the late wars with France had brought, largely determined the character of conservatism in any country. Taking Europe as a whole, throughout the nineteenth century conservatism was the dominant creed. It accented the relevance of the accumulated wisdom of the past in dealing with human affairs. What had worked acceptably in the past should not be tampered with. Conservatism was not, however, blindly averse to change, not totally wedded to stagnation. An aphorism of Edmund Burke, the Nestor of modern conservatism, served as a guiding admonition: "A state without the means of change is without the means of its conservation."

A reactionary, in the context of 1815, may be described as an advocate of the return, without discrimination, to the institutions and customs which prevailed before the onset of the French Revolution. Any change, unless it were backward, elicited the anathemas of unimaginative and fearful reactionaries. As that discerning British observer Sydney Smith said, "There are always worthy and moderately gifted men who bawl out death and ruin upon every valuable change."

Organized Christianity in its most popular expressions furnished strong support to conservatism. Conservatively minded statesmen whose personal interest in Christian theology and ethics might be shallow, nonetheless recognized in the churches a bulwark of stability and order. Primarily concerned with the world beyond this world, professional churchmen were prone to interpret human miseries and limitations in this life as fleeting and comparatively unimportant; it was a British thelogian who wrote: "Religion smooths all inequalities, because it unfolds a prospect which makes all earthy distinctions nothing."

Continental conservatism after Waterloo was gripped by nightmare memories of the French wars and of the terrific military energies which French ideas had nourished. Never before in modern times had Europe been so thoroughly impoverished and exhausted. Conservatives in the main viewed with alarm the grant of constitutions or anything approaching popular participation in government, for they had little or no faith in the political capacities of the ordinary man. They resisted, too, agitations which aimed at achieving unity and independence for politically divided or subject nationalities.

National campaigns necessarily threatened the stability enshrined in the peace settlements arranged after the elimination of Napoleon. It was feared in conservative circles that concessions to the principles of revolutionary France would invite a return of the warfare and the tyranny of the tumultuous epoch of 1789–1815. For peace, order and stability it was thought essential to oppose agitations for freedom and national unity. The dread which French principles generated in the conservative heart was crisply summarized in a piece in the *London Times* on the eve of Waterloo.

> "The revolutionary ideas of France have already made but too great progress," it read, "in the hearts of men in all countries. . . . It is not Bonaparte that at present forms the danger of Europe: he is unmasked. It is the new opinions; it is the disorganization of men's minds; . . . it is the most deadly of all contagions, the contagion of immorality, of false philanthropy, of a perfidious self-styled philosophy; from all which the world requires to be protected. This is the true hydra which must be destroyed, or it will destroy all Europe. . . ." [1]

Liberalism, on the other hand, was solidly grounded upon French revolutionary principles and drew its disciples mainly from the middle classes. Free spirits of the time cherished the sentiment of John Milton, "Give me the liberty to know, to utter and to argue freely according to conscience, above all liberties." The authentic liberal regarded experimentalism in government and social policy sympathetically. He had faith in the common fellow and demanded the maximum freedom for the individual with due regard for the good of society as a whole.

Belief in the authority of individual reason and in the reasonableness of man was a fundamental tenet of the liberal creed. Rational interchange of opinions would surely produce the answer to any problem. "If there be any among us," asserted Thomas Jefferson, "who would wish to dissolve this Union or to change its republican form, let them stand undisturbed as monuments to the safety with which error of opinion may be tolerated where reason is left free to combat it." Since men were reasonable, differences could be (and should be) settled by compromise, not by fighting it out.

More exactly, liberalism in post-Napoleonic Europe called for constitutions which would allow the governed a share in public business and ensure civil rights such as freedom of expression and freedom of worship. Liberalism, as a rule, insisted that the individual must be free to carry on economic activities with the minimum of state control. Out of that tenet arose a major contradiction of liberalism, which implied belief in fundamental equality as well as in freedom. But the freer a society was—and is—the greater the differentiation among its members in talent, in culture, in wealth and in personality.

Intertwined with the liberalism of the time was the conviction that each distinct nationality had the right to be politically united and independent and the right itself to determine its form of government. Quite commonly, lib-

[1] Quoted in H. G. Schenk, *The Aftermath of the Napoleonic Wars* (London, 1947), p. 122.

erals pushed for universal schooling and cherished an optimistic, unquenchable faith in the progress of mankind.

METTERNICH AND PEACE

In the forepart of the nineteenth century, Prince Clemens Metternich, foreign minister of Austria, dominated the European international stage. His leadership at the Congress of Vienna has already been remarked upon. An extremely conceited man, he flattered himself to think that he had been the master-architect in delivering Europe from the yoke of Napoleonic despotism and that upon him rested responsibility for keeping the peace in the future. Despite his obvious awareness of his capacities, Metternich was a highly intelligent man. His charm, courtesy and loyalty to conservative principles grew into a legend of European politics.

Metternich had spent his youth in the Rhineland, studied in universities there and was touched by the French "Enlightenment." Expelled from his homeland by invading French armies, he gravitated to cosmopolitan Vienna, married a prominent countess and rapidly climbed to the top of the Hapsburg diplomatic ladder. Metternich, who came of an aristocratic family, admirably personified the conservatism of the post-Napoleonic age. In outlook and by experience a cosmopolitan, he was familiar with several national cultures and languages and wrote in French by preference. As a conservative, cautious and intelligent, he upheld established rights and vested interests. Occasionally he resorted to reactionary devices, it is true, but in the main he hewed to the conservative line; "stability is not immobility," he once aptly remarked. After the Napoleonic torments, the nations desperately needed tranquillity and, under Metternich's guidance, war-weary Europe enjoyed a rather long span of peace, except for a minor conflict involving Turkey.

The Austrian prince dreaded and fought movements for national unity as prejudicial for the maintenance of peace and dangerous for the greatness and integrity of his adopted Austria of many tongues. Only in a stable Europe could Austria survive and that was Metternich's main preoccupation. Equally he frowned upon the grant of constitutions and representative government before men had training and were prepared to govern themselves. For the ills that afflicted mankind he offered no magic cure.

Too sensible to be logical, too much the cynical skeptic to be an arch-persecutor, Metternich, nonetheless, had no hesitancy in despatching expeditionary armies to reinstate stupid kings on thrones from which they had been expelled by liberal revolutionaries. Evidently he understood that the trend of history was pointed against him, for he confessed that his energies were being expended to "underpin buildings that are mouldering into decay."

A clever and frequently an unscrupulous diplomatist, Metternich desired a united Europe as well as a tranquil Europe, and the tool ready to his hand was the monarchical alliance forged after the elimination of Napoleon. The diplomatists of Britain, Russia, Austria and Prussia conferred from time to time for the purpose of consolidating the peace. At a meeting in Aix-la-Chapelle in 1818, for example, the "Big Four" admitted France into the monarchical partnership on a footing of equality and arranged to pull Allied armies of occupation out of France a mere three years after the close of the Napoleonic wars.

At subsequent parleys, the "Concert of Europe" dispatched troops into Mediterranean areas to suppress revolutionary unrest. Austria and Russia heartily supported intervention to preserve the divine prerogatives of monarchs, and Prussia tagged along. Britain, however, remonstrated, arguing that the alliance had no authority to poke into the domestic affairs of other countries.

So long as there seemed a chance to guide the Continental Powers into wholesome courses, Britain remained in the alliance. But in 1822, when it was proposed to intervene in Spain, the London government cut loose. Collective tyranny seemed as dangerous to liberty in British eyes as the militarism of Napoleon. "Every nation for itself, and God for us all," explained the British foreign minister, as his country decided to revolve in her own orbit. The defection of Britain gravely impaired the

Concert, and France dropped out in a short while. The Concert disintegrated utterly in 1825 when Austria vetoed a Russian scheme to apply military pressure upon the decaying Ottoman Empire. This primitive experiment in international government undoubtedly contributed to the preservation of peace, but it collapsed because the continental autocracies tried to do too much. More than thirty years passed before new life was breathed into the Concert.

RUMBLINGS OF LIBERALISM

The first menacing challenge to the status quo after 1815 issued from Spain. Toward the close of the war against Napoleon Spanish middle-class elements had put into force (1812) a constitution, plagiarized in parts from the French charter of 1791. The Spanish document, which served as a model for liberal spirits in other countries, assigned supreme powers to a representative assembly, chosen on a limited franchise; the king was little more than a decorative figurehead. Payment of tithes to the Church and the hated Inquisition were abolished. Thenceforward into the twentieth century, articulate Spain was divided into friends and enemies of constitutionalism and the principles of 1789.

When King Ferdinand VII, a pretentious mediocrity, regained the throne of Spain in 1814 he restored the Church to her ancient privileges and revoked the constitution, which infuriated the thin layer of middle-class intellectuals in the leading towns and cities. Dissatisfaction was rife in the army, too, which the government unwisely neglected. Sporadic mutinies preceded a major military rising in 1820, with liberals taking a hand, and the king was forced to restore the constitution of 1812.

At a conference of the monarchical alliance held at Verona, Italy, in 1822, the troubles of Spain were thoroughly aired. Britain contended that the dust should be allowed to settle of its own accord in Spain, but the other four powers plumped for intervention. Tsar Alexander I proposed that a Russian army should march into the peninsula and re-establish royal authoritarianism. That offer was rejected by the other allies, for they were deeply suspicious of Muscovite aims and fearful of Russian arms whose strength had been so dramatically demonstrated in the struggles with Napoleon. Instead of Russia, France was authorized by the conservative allies to put the Spanish house in order.

French troops moved in. It was a "crusade on behalf of absolutism." Spaniards who had fought with savage ferocity against Napoleon offered almost no resistance to the Bourbon armies. Ferdinand VII was restored, and reasserted his unqualified authority. In a spasm of ideological witch-hunting, Spanish liberals were rooted out with merciless severity.

Simultaneously with the Spanish insurrection of 1820, a rebellion had broken out in Portugal. The legitimate king, who had been living as an exile in the colony of Brazil, returned home promising to reign as a constitutional monarch. Britain declared that it would protect Portugal against interference from outside, which forestalled whatever chance of French intervention there may have been. Colonial holdings of Spain and Portugal in South America had, in the meantime, pulled away from their masters. Britain stood out against European intervention to recover the lost dominions. In that attitude Britain had the backing of the United States which, in the famous Monroe Doctrine of 1823, warned Europe to keep hands off the New World.[2]

Convulsions in the Spanish peninsula touched off risings in sections of Italy. After the Vienna settlement of 1815, Italy continued to be politically divided as it had long been. An uninspired Bourbon autocrat had been placed over the Two Sicilies (Naples and Sicily), the Pope had regained his extensive temporal possessions, and the more progressive dynasty of Savoy had returned to Piedmont or Sardinia. For the rest, Italy was merely a prolongation of the Austrian Empire; the northern provinces of Lombardy and Venetia belonged wholly to Austria and small principalities in the north were ruled by sprigs of the Austrian House of Hapsburg. Practically regarded, Austria was lord of Italy.

French mastery of the peninsula in the Napo-

[2] These matters are explained in Chapter XXIII.

leonic period had imprinted indelible marks. Ideas of unity and freedom had been extensively circulated, though much less widely accepted; on the other side, French control had not been attended by redistribution of land such as had transpired in France itself. Landlords owned vast acreages which were cultivated by share-croppers or laborers, poor, illiterate, impervious to liberal principles; perhaps as much as 90 per cent of the Italian population wrested a bare existence from the soil. Except in the north, industry was almost entirely of the household type. The small middle class in the peninsula was made up of merchants and financiers, civil servants and professional folk.

Secret political societies of liberal outlook emerged in Italy, of which the *Carbonari* attracted the largest support. It was pledged to the expulsion of Austria and the union of the Italian states on a constitutional foundation. Home and stronghold of the *Carbonari* was Naples, largest of Italian cities. The society appealed primarily to the well-to-do, but it also had an appreciable following in the armed services. Spies and undercover agents waged picturesque conspiracies against the Austrian overlord. The Neapolitan army, no less than the Spanish, was honeycombed with disaffection. In 1820 the soldiers revolted and in conjunction with the *Carbonari* compelled the king to issue a Spanish-style constitution. Metternich feared that unless the flame of insurgency were quenched, it would race madly across the entire peninsula. On his urgings the conservative alliance sanctioned the despatch of Austrian troops against the revolutionaries. Hapsburg white-coats plunged into the kingdom, meeting little resistance.

Straightway the autocratic power of the crown was restored and rebel leaders were savagely dealt with. On the heels of the disturbances in the south, an uprising occurred in Piedmont, but the course of events there duplicated the pattern in Naples. Austrian military strength was more than a match for the feeble forces of Italian liberalism, disjointed as they were.

As in Italy, so in Germany symptoms of liberalism alarmed Metternich and the conservative classes. Visions of German unity which had soared high during the final campaigns against Napoleon had been dashed to the earth by the Vienna settlement; the lifeless German Confederation was from the start a frail and forlorn reed. Some of the smaller German states obtained constitutions, it is true, but the assemblies which were set up were strictly aristocratic bodies and the repeated promises of the Prussian king to grant a constitution were not fulfilled. For German liberals the fruits of the victory over Napoleon were bitter, apples of Sodom turning to dust in the mouth.

German peasants were scarcely more interested in the purposes of liberalism than their counterparts in Italy. Towns and cities were the homes of liberal sentiment, but they were small, the ten largest of them together only slightly bigger than London. More than the cities, perhaps, German universities were nurseries of liberal doctrines and of an intense nationalism whose cutting edge was turned toward the hereditary French enemy.

Free-lance nationalistic agitators blasphemed against France in language that the Nazis might almost have envied. They loved to recite a nationalistic poem, "The German's Fatherland" by Ernst M. Arndt. One verse ran:

> Where is the German's fatherland?
> Name me at length that mighty land!
> 'Where'er resounds the German tongue,
> Where'er its hymns to God are sung,
> Be this the land,
> Brave Germans, this thy fatherland.'

Liberal students organized militantly patriotic societies, such as the *Burschenschaft*, which chartered chapters in sixteen universities. On the emblem of the society was inscribed the revealing legend: "Honor, Liberty, Fatherland." "All the mischief in Germany," the Duke of Wellington testily observed, "seems to have its rise in the universities." German autocrats of the day felt much the same. Student spokesmen gave voice freely to the kind of optimistic aspirations that are the privilege of the young and irresponsible. At a grand student festival at Wartburg in 1817 there was a flood of exuberant rhetoric and then symbols of authority, distasteful books and even a copy of the Code Napoléon, were tossed into a bonfire.

A shiver of apprehension ran down the spine of the German ruling classes. Matters rose to a climax when a fanatically nationalistic student murdered (1819) a minor poet, Kotzebue, who was in the employ of the Russian Tsar. That dastardly outrage furnished Metternich with a pretext to strike hard at manifestations of liberalism and nationalism in intellectual circles. A batch of laws, the notorious Carlsbad Decrees, dissolved student societies, rigidly censored publications and set "curators" to keep professors and learners under surveillance. Even Dante's *Divine Comedy* was put on the black-list on the ground that the divine should not be the subject of comedy! Sermons of liberal clergymen were scrutinized and outspoken nationalistic firebrands were disciplined or silenced.

These draconian measures clearly disclosed that the governing authorities, Metternich coaching them, were seriously frightened by the phantom of revolution. Mild though the Carsbad Decrees were when laid alongside of the laws of twentieth-century totalitarianism, they were sufficient to stifle, or at any rate to drive underground, the friends of German unity and constitutionalism. Freedom of inquiry and expression is the very breath of intellectual life, and deprived of that the German universities degenerated into little more than technical training schools.

RETURN OF THE FRENCH BOURBONS

Upon the removal of Bonaparte the victorious Allies, egged on by a secret royalist society, reinstated the Bourbons in power. Louis XVIII, brother of the guillotined Louis XVI, was proclaimed king. Exhausted and disillusioned after the wasting warfare, France desired peace, order and convalescence. And yet the revolutionary epoch had bequeathed legacies of bitterness and hatred which gravely divided the country; time would soften asperities, but not efface them. Aristocratic society quickly regained something of its old position, managing, for instance, to recover a good share of its landed properties. A conservative wing of the nobility, chastened by experiences, intelligently compromised on its class privileges, but a reactionary clique obstinately clung to outmoded social and political beliefs. This set was in fact more royalist than the king.

Cheek by jowl with the aristocracy stood the forces of clericalism, which were enheartened by the writings of intellectual champions of Catholicism and by the return of Jesuit fathers. Revolutionary principles were an abomination to churchmen, for they had brought fearful hardships to the Roman Church. The hold of the clergy upon the rural masses, over 70 per cent of the French population, had not been materially loosened.

Thrifty, largely illiterate, standpat in everything, not excluding farming methods, the French peasantry proved a mighty bulwark of conservatism. Here and there an enterprising peasant turned to raising new crops, potatoes, sugar beets, turnips, but only large proprietors copied British agricultural innovations in a substantial way. Inarticulate politically for the most part, the peasants were bounded in their interests by their fields, their church and their village. They reacted unsympathetically to the adoption of military conscription in 1818 which bore most heavily, of course, upon rural households.

The French bourgeoisie, substantially larger than in countries to the east, were devoted in large measure to the principles of 1789 which had netted them real benefits. The lower middle classes, however, who were denied the right to vote chafed under the Bourbon restoration and resented the resurgence of clericalism. In this social element the cause of Bonaparte had ardent partisans as was also true with war veterans who had difficulty in adjusting themselves to civilian routines. Among urban workpeople the revolutionary spirit of Jacobin republicanism and the anticlerical heritage of Voltaire were active forces; grinding poverty gripped this class, and ordinarily a sixth of the inhabitants of Paris depended upon charity for bread.

Upon taking the crown Louis XVIII promulgated a constitution which carried a declaration of the rights of man in tribute to the historic document of 1789 and in response to an order of the Allies. Full executive authority was retained by the king, but the law making responsibility was lodged in a legislature of two houses; the king nominated the members of the upper body, while the chamber of deputies was elected by men who met high property qualifications, under 100,000 in all. The land settlements of the Revolution, the Napoleonic Code, the Concordat and the institutions of local government were left untouched.

Reactionary royalists were the most zealous partisans of the Bourbon restoration. Due to their influence ardent admirers of Napoleon were ruthlessly liquidated in an orgy of terrorism and they stubbornly resisted the broadening of the franchise right. By their short-sighted and selfish tactics the extreme royalists discredited the whole conception of reseating the Bourbon on the throne of France. Louis XVIII, who had learned something as an exile, never tried to swing France back to "the good old days."

It was otherwise, however, with his brother, Charles X, who in 1824 succeeded to the crown. A libertine turned saint and equipped with the meager mentality of an intelligent cat, he candidly declared his allegiance to the divine right philosophy and applauded the enactment of legislation beneficial to royalist and ecclesiastical interests.

Charles X dug his own political grave by signing a set of ordinances in July of 1830 which suspended liberty of the press, dissolved the chamber of deputies and revised the electoral laws so as to consolidate the rule of the landed aristocracy. That piece of arrant folly unloosed a quick, successful insurrection in Paris which swept the Bourbon house into the discard.

In the restoration era, France recovered from the worst effects of the Napoleonic wars. State finances were whipped into shape and some advances were achieved in agriculture, industry and means of communication; protective tariffs shielded French manufacturers from British competition. Then too, the standing of France in international society was enhanced by her admission in 1818 to the monarchical alliance, by the military thrust into Spain to restore autocracy and by operations against pirates in Algeria. That last enterprise opened the way to French annexation of Algeria, the cornerstone of the immense French African empire.

The July Revolution of 1830 was the handiwork of the middle classes and wage earners of Paris. Lively support for a republican regime was in evidence, but the establishment of a republic would almost certainly have invited European intervention. Lafayette, moreover, now a factious old gentleman but a highly respected symbol of republicanism, bestowed his blessing upon Louis Philippe, nominee of opulent middle-class politicians, as king. Cousin of the deposed Bourbon and himself a repentant Jacobin, Louis Philippe of the Orléans family, was awarded the crown. The "July" regime represented an obvious compromise between legitimacy and parliamentary government. Called the "citizen king," the new sovereign was in reality the king of the wealthier middle classes. The constitution was retailored so as to reduce the authority of the crown and the voting privilege was extended to about three per cent of the adult males, more than doubling the electorate. That act ruined aristocratic power in French public life—permanently as matters turned out. Inasmuch as the Orléans monarchy was anti-revolutionary no foreign hand was raised against it, but the July Revolution excited reverberations in neighboring countries.

INDEPENDENT BELGIUM

The victory of the Parisian insurgents lighted an explosion in Belgium, beginning in Brussels. At the Vienna Congress Belgium had been linked to Holland as a sentinel on the northern border of France. From the start the partnership had been troubled in spite of the fact that manufactures of Belgium complemented Dutch agriculture and commerce. Differences in religion, in language, in customs and historical traditions caused disruptive and endless bickering.

In 1830 Belgium proclaimed its independence and Britain and France approved. The eastern autocracies were too preoccupied with problems at home to take a hand in the west,

The July Revolution of 1830 was the work of the people of Paris. Up went the tricolor, down went the lilies of the monarchy, and barricades were hastily thrown together in strategic streets.

Louis Philippe recommended that a member of his family should be chosen Belgian king, but Britain icily objected, faithful to the principle of keeping the Low Countries out of the orbit of any strong state. Eventually the crown was conferred upon Leopold of Saxe-Coburg, a dwarf German principality, and an agreeably liberal constitution was adopted.

Holland sullenly declined, until 1839, to acknowledge what had happened. In that year all the major powers signed a treaty guaranteeing the perpetual neutrality of Belgium, an arrangement not violated until the German invasion at the beginning of the First World War. A new state was thus brought into the family of nations, and Belgium and Holland thereafter pursued their separate ways until the formation of the Benelux union after the Second World War.

THE NATIONAL TIDE IN ITALY

Liberal Italian nationalists flared up too after the French revolution of 1830. An outburst in the Papal States, engineered by the Carbonari, spread into adjoining principalities. True to custom, Austrian whitecoats swarmed into the disaffected districts and clamped down upon the rebels. An uprising in Piedmont proved equally futile. Among the participants in these disturbances was an engaging young lawyer of Genoa, Giuseppe Mazzini, one of the really great figures of the age. No other Italian exercised so profound a moral and regenerative influence upon his countrymen as Mazzini. Sick at heart over the methods and the frustrations of the Carbonari, Mazzini organized in 1831 a society of "Young Italy" dedicated to the union of the country on a republican foundation. Nature herself, Mazzini believed, was ranged on the side of national unity. "God has stretched round her, sublime and indisputable boundaries," he cried, pointing to the Alpine mountain rampart and the encircling seas.

And "Italy is the only land," he reminded disciples, "that has twice uttered the great word of unification to the disjointed nations," once from the throne of the imperial Caesars, once from the throne of militant medieval Popes. Mazzini wanted his league of young Italians to merge in a federation of societies of Young Europe as an instrument for the moral reconstruction of the Continent. "We are nations," he declared explaining his concept of nationalism, "—and therefore members one of another in the great human family of which each individual nation is a unit." Dreaming illimitable dreams, he conceived of a "United States of Europe," a voluntary union of free and democratic states. A century and more went by before that vision came within the domain of practical politics.

Under the motto of "God and the People," in both of which Mazzini reposed mystical faith, Young Italy recruited thousands of partisans up and down the peninsula. Young men upon entering the society swore to work without ceasing "to constitute Italy, one, free, independent, republican nation." To attain the goal, propaganda taught, the existing autocracies must be overthrown by physical force. "Ideas grow quickly," said Mazzini, "when watered by the blood of martyrs."

Young Italy planted "seed beneath the snow" from which in the fullness of time a united Italy grew. But the doctrines of violence and republicanism alienated many Italian moderates. They preferred a promising plan of unification presented by a scholarly priest, Vincenzo Gioberti. In a book, *On the Moral and Political Supremacy of the Italians* (1843), Gioberti explained that Italy had enjoyed pre-eminence when the Papacy was all-powerful. That stature could be regained, the ardent ambition to become a Great Power could be realized, if the several states were united in a confederation under the headship of the Pope.

The program of Gioberti appeared to take on a practical quality when, in 1846, a new Pope, Pius IX, known as a friend of unification, stepped into the spacious chair of St. Peter.

King Louis Philippe rides out with his sons. His large family and his keen money-sense recommended him to the wealthier middle classes.

Pius IX started off by freeing political prisoners in the States of the Church, easing the limitations on the press and allowing Rome a civil municipal administration. To tender advice on public policies a Council of State, to which laymen were eligible, was instituted. "We were prepared for anything," Metternich muttered and moaned, "except a liberal Pope." But Pius IX had gone as far as he intended to go. Italian unity under papal auspices would have entailed war with the great Catholic power Austria, a vista repulsive to the Pope. Pius IX, moreover, could scarcely have combined the responsibilities of a national sovereign with worldwide spiritual authority. And, besides, he had no desire to see the Papal States swallowed up in a united nation.

The tide of national aspirations was rising, however, in the peninsula, though in fact neither the republic of Mazzini nor the confederacy of Gioberti provided the eventual answer to the national urge.

TOWARD GERMAN UNITY

Successful revolutions and constitutional innovations in France and Belgium in 1830 awakened echoing responses in western Germany. Several rulers were compelled by popular demonstrations to publish constitutions setting up representative assemblies. Metternich endeavored to quell disturbances by bringing out a stricter version of the Carlsbad Decrees, and police pounced upon citizens suspected of holding dangerously liberal enthusiasms.

Beneath the surface, however, forces sympathetic to national unity were gathering strength. Prussia took the lead in the economic amalgamation of the German states. Controlling the major tradeways of the Rhine and Elbe rivers, Prussia held a commanding position in German commerce. Scores of tariff walls within the sprawling kingdom were pulled down (1818) and a uniform currency replaced the hundred and more monetary systems; duties on imports were kept low and rawstuffs were admitted free.

Prussia then attracted neighboring principalities into a customs-union or *Zollverein*. The process took time and patience for the German princedoms were jealously proud of their independence, but the economic advantages of cooperation were apparent and by 1834 two-thirds of Germany had joined. Eventually uniform coinage, weights and measures were adopted by the *Zollverein*. Austria, inveterate rival of Prussia for leadership in German Europe, was deliberately debarred from the customs-union. Commercial unity, moreover, did not spell political unity, not immediately in any case, for the masters of the smaller German states often sided with Austria in disputes involving Prussia.

German unity, as a German caricaturist saw it—each uniform represents a different kingdom or principality, each face a different Germanic type.

German agriculture, meantime, was advancing in the light of British experience or because of the stimulus imparted by agricultural societies and schools. Scientific rotation of crops was practiced more and more, better implements were introduced, greater intelligence was applied to stock-raising and sugar beets and potatoes were extensively planted. Potatoes quickly became half the life of Germany, it was said, but a blessing only if crops escaped blighting disease.

To about 1840, German peasants produced mainly for their own consumption or for sale locally. Then, with a view to increasing output, many a peasant mortgaged his property to buy livestock, labor-saving tools and the like. Loans and potatoes indeed were spoken of as the props of the rural economy in western Germany. But in the mid-forties hard times befell the peasants as capital was diverted to railways and factories and harvests failed in successive years; emigration to the United States was accelerated, precisely as in the case of the Irish.

Commercial farming flourished on the estates of the large German proprietors and it was these farms which satisfied the food requirements of the growing towns and cities. By 1849 approximately a third of the Germans was classified as urban compared with a fifth at the close of the Napoleonic wars. In the interval the German population had risen from 25,000,000 to 35,000,000, despite the emigration overseas of 1,500,000.

Until after the middle of the century German handicraft and cottage workers were responsible for the larger part of the manufactured goods. But already the waning vitality of the guilds, the importation of British capital and machinery, the large free-trade market of the *Zollverein*, the fast expanding population and the laying down of the first railways betokened a revolution in industrial processes, particularly in the making of cloth. Factory-made clothing invaded the rural areas in the forties with ruinous consequences for homespun textiles.

Heavy industry occupied, as yet, only a minor place in German economy. Although the Krupp concern, which one day would become the largest establishment of Europe, was started in 1819, thirty years later it was employing a mere 140 workers. At that point coal output in Prussia would not have satisfied the annual needs of London alone. Only a gifted prophet could then have foretold the fabulous expansion of the coal and steel industries in the Ruhr valley which the future held.

British teachings of laissez faire dominated German economic thinking until effectively challenged by *The National System of Political Economy*, prepared by Friedrich List. A professional economist and reformer, List argued persuasively that government must intervene to raise levels of living and to build up national political strength. Specifically, he recommended the enactment of protective tariffs to guard young industries from foreign competition; were that done, manufacturing could be brought into balance with agriculture and Germany would become economically self-contained. Industries, List described as "the offspring . . . the supporters and the nurses of science and the arts." At this time, too, novel collectivist doctrines entered Germany from France. German writers circulated ideas intended to undermine the existing social order and they found no little acceptance among poorly paid wageworkers.

A roar of ardent and bellicose emotionalism, inspired by a short-lived dispute with France, arose from the Germanies in 1840. The passionate fervor of the hour found expression in the moving anthem, "The Watch on the Rhine." Prussia was pointed to as the only state with military resources capable of commanding respect for German interests and German honor. And that same year the Prussian kingship was inherited by a reputed liberal, Frederick William IV. The new ruler excited lively hopes among liberal enthusiasts by lifting the ban on political gatherings and lightening the censorship on publications.

But it was soon apparent that the liberalism of Frederick William IV was only skin deep. A staunch adherent of the divine right philosophy, he had no intention whatsoever of giving his subjects a constitution or allowing them civil freedoms. A kingdom, he felt, should be governed in keeping with the laws of God and the personal discretion of the sovereign. The heavy hand of the police-state silenced tongues and pens which were critical of the status quo. To obtain backing for new taxes and loans the Prussian autocrat in 1847 summoned a united diet, composed of representatives from the provincial assemblies. When forward-looking deputies demanded a permanent royal assembly as the price of their approval of royal fiscal proposals, the king indignantly adjourned the deliberations.

As the century moved toward its mid-point, undercurrents of restlessness were evident in many German principalities. Middle-class longings for a unified Germany endowed with free parliamentary institutions, lean years in the countryside and the lowly lot of urban workpeople provoked unrest and commotions. Discontent prevailed most widely in districts adjacent to France where the influence of French principles was more pronounced than farther east.

AUSTRIAN COMPLEXITIES

No country of Europe contained a greater medley of peoples than the Austrian Empire. It was in truth a realm of nationalities, a circumstance that had constant and vital bearing on public policies. If liberal nationalism should triumph, the Austrian Empire would be ripped apart; hence, Metternich's unwearying fight for peace and stability.

The leading nationality of the empire, which may be called Austro-German, spoke the German language and prized German cultural traditions. Mainly concentrated in Vienna and adjacent provinces, Germans also dwelt in towns and cities all across the Empire and in scattered islets in the countryside. Czechs and large blocks of Poles and Italians were also subjects of Austria. In the Hungarian section of the realm, Magyars were the dominant nationality, living alongside of Slovaks, of Serb and Croat members of the Yugoslav family and of Rumanians. The small educated classes of all these nationalities were somewhat familiar with French teachings of liberty, equality and nationalism.

The Austrian government was typically autocratic, though the several provinces and Hungary as well possessed local assemblies of their own. None of them, save the Hungarian, however, had much to do beyond acquiescence in taxation projects prepared in Vienna; small opportunity was allowed in assembly meetings for the give-and-take of criticism and debate. A council of ministers obedient to the Emperor managed public business and an inelastic, hidebound bureaucracy looked after administration. An elaborate police and espionage service, fit almost to be compared with Napoleon's, kept watch and ward over citizens, intimidating men of independent mind. Church, bureaucracy, army, dynastic loyalties and the highest aristocrats, owning enormous acreages cultivated by serfs, held together this strange, polyglot country.

As a minister of state, Metternich naturally carried much weight, but his actual influence on domestic policies has often been exaggerated. He lacked the energy, perseverance and mastery of practical detail required of an administrator and he never claimed to be one. Foreign affairs was his bailiwick and he was not too wide of the mark when he confessed: "I ruled Europe sometimes but I never governed Austria." On more occasions than one he proposed that a constitution and parliament representing the several nationalities should be created and that provincial assemblies should be assigned real powers, but his recommendations went unheeded.

Until his death in 1835, the commanding figure in Austria was Emperor Francis I, hardened reactionary, a devout exemplar of unenlightened despotism. His political outlook was crystallized in his oft-quoted remark: "Peoples? What does that mean? I know only subjects." "Rule and change nothing," he instructed his son. In a lecture to a company of scholars Francis I gave classic utterance to his conservative philosophy: "Keep yourselves to what is old, for that is good; if our ancestors have proved it to be good, why should not we do as they did? . . . I have no need of learned men. I want faithful subjects. . . . He who would serve me must do what I command."

It was the spirit of Francis I, a man horrified

by the physical excesses of revolutionary France and obsessed by memories of the military humiliations inflicted by Napoleon and the dislocations during and after the war—it was the pinched and narrow spirit of the emperor rather than the conservative cosmopolitan Metternich that dictated the course of internal politics in Austria. State officials kept learning and learners under close supervision and prescribed what might be read and studied. It was unlawful for journalists even to print the word "constitution"; only musical genius in fact was permitted free and full expression. State officials attempted to restrain industrial development as inimical to the more easily managed agrarian society.

Nevertheless, the economy of the Austrian Empire underwent changes broadly similar to those taking place in Germany, though on a less imposing scale. Agriculture progressed modestly and machinofacture penetrated into the cities. That novelty brought about the decline of guild and domestic manufacturing and forced the growth of the middle classes and the urban working class. Vienna, in particular, became the center of a varied industrial activity, and of a substantial, cultivated and liberal bourgeoisie.

Serfdom reigned almost universally across the Austrian Empire, the soil people paying in labor, kind or cash to their masters. But many landlords had arrived at the conclusion that this heritage of medievalism should be abolished, mainly because it was economically unprofitable or out of fear that if the countryfolk were not voluntarily emancipated they might resort to violence to tear off their shackles. Progressive magnates tried to increase the productivity of their properties by new crops, land reclamation and agricultural training schools and societies.

What then of the political currents among the national groupings in this complicated realm? As a general rule, middle-class men and a sprinkling of aristocrats clamored for constitutions, representative governments and the liberties which prevailed in the west of Europe. Czech intellectuals, for instance, fostered the use of their mother tongue and composed works of literature and history proudly and romantically extolling the glories of the medieval kingdom of Bohemia. Nationally minded journalists indulged in spirited, if subtle, criticism of the Austrian administration and furious clashes between patriotic Czech liberals and conservative Bohemians repeatedly rocked the meetings of the provincial assembly in Prague.

In Galicia a rather peculiar nationality situation existed, for Polish landed interests lorded over Polish and Ukrainian (Ruthenian) serfs, who lived on a primitive and brutish level. Polish patriots heroically proclaimed the independence of their nation in 1846 and called upon the Ukrainian laborers to fight shoulder to shoulder with them in the battle for freedom.

Instead, the serfs, incited by Hapsburg officials, turned upon their oppressive Polish masters, butchering them in cold blood—a sequence of events prayerfully noted all over Austria, and beyond. It was now (1846) that Austria absorbed the tiny Polish republic of Cracow, the focal point of Polish national plottings, which had been set off as a free state at the Congress of Vienna.

The most unruly, the most assertive nationality was the Magyar, or more accurately the Magyar gentry, for the soil workers were immune to politics and the highest aristocracy was contented with the status quo. By pressure on Vienna, the Magyar ruling class secured the restoration of hallowed medieval privileges, including a national assembly. Magyar men of letters and historians awakened golden memories of the illustrious past and kindled visions of a glorious future.

Members of the gentry class had learned something about the freedoms and institutions of Britain and the United States, not to speak of French principles. Out of all this developed a lively agitation for "home-rule" for Hungary. A lawyer and rural politician, Louis Kossuth, noted for his sonorous eloquence with tongue and pen, assumed leadership of the Magyar national cause; in 1847 his disciples captured control of the national assembly. Passionate in their campaign for broader freedoms for themselves, Magyar patriots deliberately combatted symptoms of national consciousness among smaller nationalities in Hungary. It was the purpose of Magyar zealots, pursued in fair weather and foul, to coerce all inhabitants of Hungary into the Magyar linguistic and cultural mold—a design which infuriated politically articulate Yugoslavs and Rumanians. In time of crisis, the government in Vienna could confidently rely upon the cooperation of these peoples against the overbearing Magyar chauvinists.

After 1835 the conduct of Austrian affairs rested with a regency, in which Metternich was a partner, for the new Emperor Ferdinand I was mentally incompetent. Rigors of the press censorship were somewhat relaxed and greater liberty was allowed in university lecture halls. Those concessions, coupled with squabbling inside the regency and the social consequences of machine industry, encouraged the forces of liberalism and nationalism.

ANOTHER FRENCH REVOLUTION

Revolution had installed Louis Philippe on the French throne in 1830, and revolution drove him away eighteen years later. Eminently respectable in every way, the king tried desperately to ingratiate himself with ordinary Frenchmen, but he failed. In the get-rich-quick atmosphere of the time he leaned upon the plutocratic bourgeoisie, the enfranchised class, to whose interests the state obediently responded. As in Britain, wage earners and peasants were wholly excluded from the suffrage. Ministers managed domestic affairs, but Louis Philippe spoke the decisive word on foreign relations. Despite mild censorship, the French press prospered, and not a little of the writing ridiculed the acts and aims of the bourgeois monarchy.

Plenty of evidence—strikes, street disorders and attempts to kill the king—testified that all was not well in France. Social questions took on new urgency as manufacturing assumed a greater place in French economy. By the end of the reign, workpeople formed a seventh part of the population, with much the larger proportion craftsmen rather than factory employees; then as now, French industry emphasized quality and variety instead of mass output.

As yet only cotton manufacturing, in which many women and children were at work, had entered the factory stage to any significant degree. Technological unemployment followed the installation of labor-saving machines as the night the day. Paris grew as an industrial center and the working population expanded correspondingly. Heavy industry in France was retarded by the scarcity of fuel, though coal was mined in increasing quantities near Belgium and in the southeast. Railway building commenced in the forties, the state furnishing subsidies, but by 1848 only one trunk line was actually in operation; rails, like machinery for factories, were largely purchased in Britain. Protective tariffs reserved the home market to domestic producers.

Wretched poverty, shabbiness and cycles of unemployment were the lot of ordinary French wage earners, and so were drab overcrowded living quarters and chronic shortages of necessities, as in the case of British workers. And the bourgeois monarchy introduced little remedial social legislation. True, an Education Act of 1833 prescribed that every commune should maintain an elementary school; though the law was not faithfully enforced, the number of literates doubled. True also, a Factory Act (1841) prohibited the employment of young children in the larger plants, but again enforcement was quite inadequate. Throughout the reign, collective bargaining thrived, in spite of its illegality, and standards of comfort moved upward slightly.

Restrictions on the suffrage, the sorry fortune of workpeople and the revolutionary principle of equality nourished a bumper crop of novel social philosophies, some bizarre, some ephemeral, but all attracting quotas of partisans in France and abroad. Divergent though these philosophies were in detail, they uniformly considered poverty as the mother and father of evil and repudiated unfettered economic individualism, as taught by French disciples of Adam Smith.

Doctrinaire schemes for social reconstruction were propounded by the Count Henri de Saint-

Plan for a Fourierist "Phalanctery" or ideal cooperative community

Simon and François Fourier. An eccentric aristocrat, Saint-Simon mapped out a plan to convert France into a collectivist economy managed by technical experts. Privileges of every description would be canceled without exception. Saint-Simon argued that the proper study of mankind was no longer man but the masses, and social institutions should be designed to improve the condition of the masses. Industry, production and organization were key themes in the thinking of Saint-Simon. On the basis of Christian ethics, he wished to found a novel and secular religion, "the New Christianity" as he called it. Disciples systematized and propagated the rather vague principles of the master; most distinguished of them was Auguste Comte (p. 356).

Fourier thought in terms of a network of cooperative communities. They would be owned by the residents and would produce everything needed for their physical well-being. Beneficent cooperation would replace the waste, inefficiency and other shortcomings of the prevailing economy. Fourier typified the romanticism of early nineteenth-century speculators on collectivism; naively he set aside an hour a day waiting for a right-minded plutocrat to come forward with the cash to launch his cooperative society. Colonies on the Fourierist pattern were actually established in France and the United States, but their histories were short.

More attractive to harassed French workpeople than these "Utopian" blueprints was a program drafted by Louis Blanc, a resourceful and influential collectivist thinker. In journalistic pieces and a famous book, *The Organization of Labor* (1839), Blanc contended that the government had an obligation to assure employment to all the able-bodied. To that end the state should set up cooperative workshops which would in time crowd private enterprise to the wall. His catchy battle-cry, "We will work and live, or we will fight and die" seemed gospel truth to many French wage earners.

Another theorist, Pierre Joseph Proudhon, a wild, introspective, restless spirit, vigorously flayed the status quo and denounced private

Louis Blanc

property as theft. His thinking turned more diffuse and paradoxical with age so that he has been variously classified as a philosophical anarchist and a forerunner of fascism. Proudhon sensed the perils implicit in a highly centralized government and warmly sympathized with the individual struggling against the authority of the state. Persuaded of the virtues of "joyous poverty," he assailed the materialistic emphasis of much current collectivist thinking. No great school of thought arose out of the ideas of Proudhon, but his writings exerted a considerable influence upon European social radicalism.

Novelists with a flair for words and moods portrayed the sordid and unsavory sides of life in the July Monarchy. And thinking along democratic lines was quickened by a book, *Democracy in America* (1835), remarkable for insight as well as industry, written by Alexis de Tocqueville. This trenchant exposition of the human experiment in the New World reawakened something of the eighteenth-century French interest in America, her institutions, her pattern of living.

Policymakers of the bourgeois monarchy obtusely ignored the signs of the times and the shrill urgings of reformers. Best personification of the regime was François Guizot, prime minister in the forties, who had served an apprenticeship as an historian before entering upon the toil and heat of the political arena. His studies had convinced him that only the wealthy middle class possessed competence to deal with public affairs. The voting right should be reserved, therefore, to the affluent; let other men slough off their lazy and dissolute habits and accumulate cash and then they would be entitled to the franchise. Guizot and his colleagues repulsed demands for universal suffrage, which conjured up in their minds recollections of revolutionary France, anarchic confusion, blood-spilling, wars and the tyrannous Napoleon. Preaching to the converted, Guizot managed very well, but his antiquated political philosophy failed completely to calm the unregenerate.

By 1848 a pack of enemies confronted the bourgeois monarchy. Bourbon partisans, few

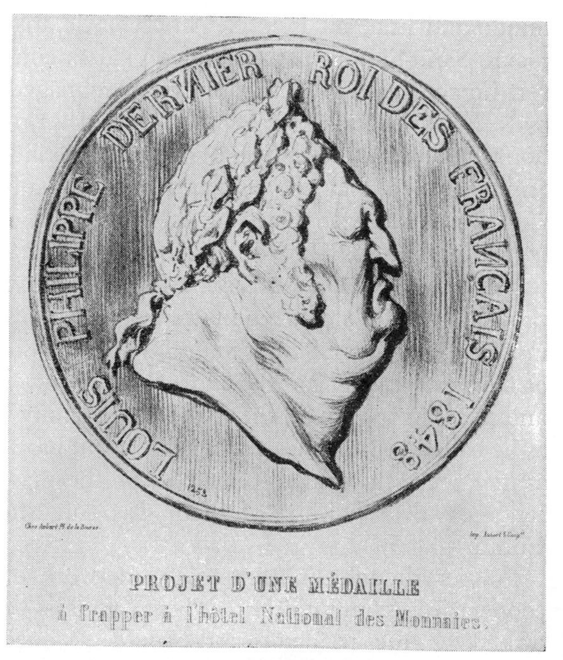

Satirizing at once Louis Philippe's appearance and his reputed love of money, the great French artist Daumier issued this suggestion for a medal commemorating "the last King of the French."

Daumier painted the mood of the 1848 Revolution, as he remembered it, in The Uprising, here shown.

and inconsequential, had never acknowledged the legitimacy of King Louis Philippe. And Bonapartists, cherishing romantic memories of the glories and grandeur of the Napoleonic Empire, desired its revival. In his writings at St. Helena, Napoleon had represented himself as a genuine liberal, the champion of freedom and equality. Eulogistic poets, old grenadiers and vanilla flavored histories richly embroidered the Napoleonic legend; and reverent popular affection for the little Corsican was excited in 1840 when his mortal remains were fetched from St. Helena and deposited in a magnificent tomb in Paris. The nephew of the Emperor, young Louis Napoleon, appropriated the glowing legend, and twice unfurled the standard of revolt against the colorless and uninspiring Louis Philippe.

Abroad, as at home, the record of the bourgeois monarchy contrasted sharply with the glamorous exploits of Napoleon I. French rule over Algeria was consolidated, it is true; but of that colony someone remarked, "Our opera box, but a terribly expensive one." The project of Louis Philippe to seat his nominee on the throne of Belgium failed, and, after boldly backing the governor of Egypt in a dispute with Turkey, he beat an ignominious retreat under international pressure. The British Foreign Office, hectoring critics charged, was leading proud France around by the nose. When, however, the king quarreled with Britain over the choice of husbands for certain Spanish princesses, he was roundly condemned for antagonizing Britain. Not much glory in the July Monarchy; Frenchmen were jaded and bored.

Partisans of social reform and collectivism, partisans of Bonapartism and republicanism, partisans of a broader suffrage harried the bourgeois monarchy on one flank and another. "Hard times" in the mid-forties swelled the volume of discontent and dissent. Short crops pushed up prices of bread and wine, while a severe financial crisis, precipitated by frenzied railway speculation, cost workers their jobs. Hungry men seized upon the anti-capitalist ideology of Louis Blanc as a panacea for their afflictions.

This situation was actively exploited by champions of parliamentary reform. Marshal of the reformers was Adolphe Thiers, sometime a popular historian, who had supported the Revolution of 1830, but had subsequently swung violently against Guizot and the monarchy. The cause of reform was furthered in large and popular banquets, one of which was planned for Paris in February of 1848.

When the government banned this meeting, workpeople and students in the capital raised cries of "Long live reform," and "Long live the Republic." Out came the barricades. Up went red flags. Bonfires cluttered the streets. Troops fired upon paraders which set Paris ablaze. Guizot fled to London. Louis Philippe also fled to London, presently to be joined by discarded celebrities from other continental countries, for the disturbances in Paris exploded combustible materials over much of Europe. France had coughed and Europe sneezed, ran a favorite aphorism of the time.

THE SECOND FRENCH REPUBLIC

Upon the dethronement of Louis Philippe, a republic was proclaimed in Paris and passively accepted by the rest of France. Amidst much talk of the "eternal principles of 1789," liberal middle-class men and anti-capitalist spokesmen, Louis Blanc above all, set about putting the republican house in order. An assembly, largely bourgeois republican in composition, was chosen by manhood suffrage to draft a new constitution. Conditions among Parisian workers, meantime, had taken an evil turn. Political uncertainties deepened the business depression, swelling the army of the workless and placing the living of other Frenchmen in jeopardy. Writers, allowed an intoxicating freedom, said what they pleased in whatever way they liked. Papers, pamphlets and snappy songs clamored for far-ranging social reforms.

In a diluted form, the provisional government applied Blanc's "right to work" philosophy. Idle men in Paris, the number rising eventually to more than 100,000, were given employment at public expense. Much of the work was of an unproductive character and was administered by officials unsympathetic to the principle that the state had a duty to supply employment for men who could not find jobs in private enterprises. Middle-class concern for political freedom collided head-on with the novel and costly principle of security for wage-earners. And in June of 1848 public subsidies for the work projects were abruptly withdrawn. Whereupon infuriated blue-bloused workers of Paris hoisted the red flag, dragged out barricades and took up arms in an outburst of frenzied fury against the bourgeois republic. They were animated by a mystical anti-capitalist spirit, never thereafter absent from France.

The February uprising had consolidated the political position of the middle classes. But when it became apparent that the driving force of the revolution had passed to Parisian workmen and that property, not monarchy, was under attack, the middle-class leadership shifted to the other side of the barricades. Reliable republican soldiers, commanded by a republican general, waged open war upon the insurgent workers. For three days dramatic fighting on an unprecedented scale tormented the world's most sophisticated city; upwards of 5,000 were killed and thousands more were later banished to Algeria. The bloody "June days" underlined the rift between bourgeois democracy and collectivism, left a heritage of apprehension among the propertied classes, deep bitterness among the defeated and a fearsome precedent for the future.

The constituent assembly presently completed a constitution providing for a president and a legislature of one house, both to be elected by all adult males. At the balloting for the presidency three-quarters of the votes were cast for Prince Louis Napoleon Bonaparte, hitherto ridiculed as an absurd light-weight. It was a striking victory for a name rather than the man.

This uncouth adventurer was ambitious, extremely so, and he possessed smooth managers who cleverly enlisted support for their candidate. For middle-class men, young and old, urban and rural, the magic name of Napoleon implied order, discipline, glory, prestige, and on that they pinned their hopes. Monarchists voted for the upstart on the hunch that he would be a mere "caretaker," who would soon give way to a legitimate king. Many workmen were won over by assurances that Louis Napoleon was genuinely interested in the welfare of the commoners; after all, had he not composed an anticapitalist pamphlet on *The Extinction of Poverty*? So the "dark horse" was swept into the presidency by a landslide.

Elections for the national legislature, however, disclosed other and different political attitudes. Bonapartists won only a handful of seats, authentic republicans not many more, while avowed monarchists captured two-thirds. Holding that the press and theater were responsible for the continuing social ferment, the conservative assembly laid heavy restraints upon them. The President, ever with an eye to the main chance, courted the devout and the clerical by approving the despatch of troops to Rome to succor the Pope and by accepting a law restoring Catholic authority in the domain of education.

When the legislature imprudently withdrew the voting right from some 3,000,000 workmen, Louis Napoleon masqueraded as the stalwart champion of manhood suffrage. Confident that the army would rally obediently behind a Napoleon, the ambitious President staged a *coup d'état* in 1851, dismissed the legislature, and had opponents by the thousand imprisoned. On a ratio of fifteen to one in a referendum Frenchmen endorsed what had transpired.

Promptly the constitution was overhauled, giving the President tenure of office for ten years and drastically whittling down the scope of the legislature, which, however, would be chosen by manhood suffrage. Another year and President Bonaparte had blossomed into Emperor Napoleon III. The ex-vagabond toured the Republic in a dashing general's uniform, delivering intimate chats on his great uncle and lavishly promising the pet formula of the professional politician: peace, prosperity and progress.

At the end of 1852 France and the world were blandly informed that the Second Empire had been born. The electorate ratified that coup even more handsomely than its predecessor. Frenchmen clearly preferred the substantial values of order and prosperity to the ideal values of liberty. In the preamble of the imperial constitution France was assured that national energies would no longer be frittered away in "useless interruptions, frivolous questions, or excited rivalries." France once more had a master, democratically endorsed to be sure, an emperor who imposed an authoritarian rule and engaged in extravagant foreign policies. It was Napoleon I over again, only this time as the sturdy republican, Victor Hugo, caustically commented, it was "Napoleon the Little."

1848: ANNUS "MIRABILIS"

The February events of 1848 in Paris loosed a tempest of revolutionary storms in Europe. A new generation, for whom the terrors of war and revolution were things to read about in books, had grown to maturity since Waterloo and was eager for action. Old World thrones everywhere trembled, except in Russia and Britain, the popular mood at the peak of the excitement was expressed by a British poet:

> Nation awakens by nation
> King by king disappears.

The ideals of 1789, aggrieved national feelings, the intellectual ferment of the preceding generation, economic crisis and the inspiring example of France combined to produce a succession of explosions, more particularly in central Europe and in Italy. It appeared as though prized middle-class aspirations of liberalism and national unity would in fact be achieved. While there were sporadic disturbances in rural areas, the most meaningful upheavals occurred in the ever-expanding cities, substantial working class populations playing prominent roles. The abyss between the propertied and the wage earners, the impact of industrialism, the struggle of craftsmen against the irresistible invasion of machinery were brought sharply to the fore.

March of 1848 was the most exciting month, filled with uprisings in Vienna, Berlin, Munich, Milan and Rome. Amidst great popular enthusiasm and high optimism, cowering sovereigns published or promised liberal constitutions. But they quickly recovered their equilibrium and by the middle of 1849, the political scene was nearly the same as at the beginning of the *annus mirabilis*. 1848, in other words, was a year of general disturbance and little decision, a year of exalted expectations and disillusioning frustration.

TUMULT IN AUSTRIA

Furious revolts in Vienna, Bohemia, Hungary and the Italian provinces threatened for a time the very existence of the Austrian monarchy. On the morrow of the Paris revolution, liberal bourgeoisie of Vienna, students and craftsmen too, stridently demanded the resignation of Metternich and a constitution. To these demands, terrified Hapsburg dynastic leaders bowed. At the patriarchal age of seventy-five, Prince Metternich, for forty years the "Rock of Order," the outward personification of an epoch, took off for London in heavy disguise. And a representative assembly was commissioned to draw up a constitution for the realm.

In answer to peasant clamor, and indeed in keeping with the recommendations of many landed aristocrats, the assembly canceled the burdens of serfdom, the major accomplishment of the revolution in Austria. Vienna, in October, 1848, experienced a second upsetting convulsion, which had sharp social and class undertones. Street fighting roared to fierce dimensions, but an imperial army bombarded and occupied the city and drowned the disorders in blood. An iron-souled reactionary, Prince Felix Schwarzenberg, then assumed dictatorial authority surrounding himself with a set of capable colleagues. One of his first acts was to replace imbecilic Emperor Ferdinand by his nephew, Francis Joseph, a stripling of eighteen, who presided over the Hapsburg realm until 1916. An imperial constitution was published later on, but never put into operation; absolutism reigned anew in the valley of the middle Danube.

In Bohemia Czech and German rebels joined hands after the flight of Metternich in extracting liberal concessions from the House of Hapsburg. But they quarreled when Czech nationalists disclosed that they desired home-rule for Bohemia, and were totally opposed to the entry of the province into a united Germany then under consideration. Speaking the mind of Czech nationalism, Francis Palacký, author of a beguilingly romantic history of Bohemia, declared for the preservation of the Austrian Empire and its reconstruction along federal lines on the basis of equality of nationalities.

In June of 1848 a pioneer conference of Slav leaders of Austria and a few foreign Slavs convened in Prague to deliberate on political questions. Instead of demonstrating Slav solidarity, the conference showed that the principle of national self-determination carried awkward implications for democracy and peace. A clique of Czech firebrands engaged in battle royal with German Bohemians, which caused the intervention of an Austrian army and the conquest of the city. That episode marked in truth the beginning of the Hapsburg triumph over the challengers of the status quo.

The tide of revolt in Hungary pursued a more tortuous and sanguinary course. As demanded by the impassioned Magyar nationalist Louis Kossuth, the government in Vienna accorded Hungary virtually full control over its own destinies. Serfs were emancipated and broad freedoms were promised, but the Magyar politicians stubbornly withheld elementary human rights from national minorities in the kingdom. The menace of Magyar chauvinism seemed more dreadful to articulate Rumanians and Yugoslavs than Hapsburg absolutism. Egged on by Vienna, these peoples fought the Magyars, and Austrian troops were thrown into the struggle.

Whereupon Kossuth in 1849 declared Hungary a republic, wholly divorced from the House of Hapsburg. Since Austria lacked sufficient military resources to beat down the Magyar rebels, an appeal for help was addressed to the Russian Emperor, Nicholas I. In the name of monarchical solidarity and fearful lest the flame of rebellion should leap across to his own monolithic autocracy, the "Iron Tsar" complied with alacrity. Muscovite soldiers dealt (1849) the *coup de grace* to the Magyar insurgency.

Austrian authorities then blotted out every vestige of Hungarian home-rule. Kossuth, however, escaped, visiting the United States in 1851 where he was rapturously welcomed. Later,

Louis Kossuth welcomed in New York—a contemporary lithograph

this national hero of the Magyars settled in Italy and resumed agitation for Hungarian independence. It is of interest to know that when a Hungarian republic was created after the Second World War, the sponsors stressed the point that the new regime was the spiritual heir of Kossuth's short-lived adventure of a century earlier.

A FALSE DAWN IN ITALY

Loyalty of the armed services, antagonisms among dissidents, strong-willed administrators and invaluable Russian assistance had rescued Hapsburg absolutism in central Europe and made possible its recovery. A story of like character was written in the Italian peninsula. When the Hapsburg House was tottering along the Danube, partisans of liberty and independence endeavored to break Austrian mastery over Italy and bind the several states in union. The spark of revolt was kindled in the Two Sicilies, the king being forced to grant a progressive constitution. Thereupon it rained constitutions in other Italian principalities, though only the Piedmontese charter, which was framed on orthodox liberal lines, survived the revolutionary tempest.

The Austrian provinces of Lombardy and Venetia rebelled against their overlord and the ancient Venetian republic was formally resurrected. Thinking the time ripe for a war of liberation, the King of Piedmont, Charles Albert, called "the sword of Italy," albeit an exceedingly blunt one and not brandished with decision, marched his soldiers against Austria. Superior Austrian military strength blasted Italian national hopes. Help which Charles Albert expected from other sections of the peninsula never materialized; after his armies had twice been beaten by Hapsburg soldiers, the King willingly relinquished the throne to his son, Victor Emmanuel II.

Under duress Pope Pius IX had given a constitution to the Papal States and then escaped to the Two Sicilies. A Roman Republic was organized with Mazzini as the directing figure, and Giuseppe Garibaldi at his side. Garibaldi, the real man of the year in Italy, had earned his spurs as a guerrilla fighter in South American revolts. Courageous in high degree and an inspiring leader of men, he was a tower of strength to the republican cause. From his place of refuge, the Pope appealed to Catholic Europe for help, to which the France of Louis Napoleon obediently responded. French troops snuffed out the Roman Republic and restored papal authority. The Republic of Venice, stricken with famine and cholera, succumbed to Austrian arms.

1848 proved to be a false dawn for Italian nationhood. Austrian dominance over the peninsula was once more reasserted and the old political order was fast restored. The Mazzinian philosophy of republicanism had been painfully discredited. But, on the other side, national sentiments had been quickened and the moral prestige of Piedmont heightened by reason of its heroic fight for freedom, the retention of its new constitution and the sanctuary afforded thousands of refugees from other parts of unhappy Italy.

Victor Emmanuel II cheered many a weary spirit with the avowal: "I will hold the national tricolor high and firm," and that is precisely what he did. The hostile stand of the Pope on unification infused the national movement with an anticlerical tinge. And, not least in significance, the intervention of Louis Napoleon in Italian politics foreshadowed the decisive boost to the cause of unity which France would deliver a decade later.

AND IN THE GERMANIES

"Our revolutions like our fashions," explained a German liberal of 1848, "we are wont to receive from Paris." Under the impulse of the watchwords "Unity, Freedom and Power," revolutionary uprisings in 1848 rocked the states of western Germany. Rulers acceded to certain propositions of the rebels who next pressed insistently for a national union to take the place of the feeble German Confederation. "Through power to freedom, this is Germany's predestined path," proclaimed the liberal historian Dahlmann, a prominent spokesman of freedom and unity.

In autocratic Prussia, a cloud no bigger than a man's hand suddenly blew up in a violent revolutionary convulsion. Berlin itself witnessed severe barricade warfare. King Frederick William IV, petrified by the angry march of events, professed willingness to see Prussia absorbed in a unified Germany and sanctioned the election of an assembly to prepare a constitution for his kingdom. That body removed the lingering remnants of serfdom, drew up a code of civil liberties and indulged in interminable debates. Toward the end of the year, the success of the Hapsburgs in crushing revolutionary forces in Vienna emboldened the Prussian king to strike back. Soldiers, thrown into the assembly hall, sent the deputies packing. An illiberal constitution, however, was handed down by the crown in 1850 and it remained in operation until the end of World War I.

The constitution contained a standard declaration of the rights of man and the citizen and called for a parliament (Landtag) of two houses. Deputies of the lower chamber would be elected by manhood suffrage, so regulated, however, that a small minority of well-to-do taxpayers would choose two-thirds of the members. The assembly would share in making laws and was clothed with the right to approve or reject the royal budget. Otherwise the legislature could exercise little restraint upon the crown, to which the ministry was responsible.

An earnest drive to unify the German Fatherland had, meantime, come to grief. In May of 1848 a national assembly chosen by manhood suffrage, foregathered at Frankfurt-am-Main, to prepare a plan of national government. A more learned and dignified assembly of constitution-makers had never come together; most of the deputies held university degrees, and many were themselves university professors. Few of the members, however, were versed in public affairs, and the assembly lacked authority to commit the sovereigns of the several states to any program that might be framed. Street fighting more than once interrupted the deliberations at Frankfurt.

Liberal political precepts and the governmental institutions of Britain, France and the United States were examined at Frankfurt from every imaginable angle and debated on an elevated intellectual plane. Ardent nationalists contended that non-German minorities in mixed areas, Czechs, Poles and the duchies of Schleswig-Holstein should be dragooned into the projected German realm; like Magyar chauvinists, many German deputies esteemed selfish national interests above love of liberty.

After prolonged discussions the men at Frankfurt decided upon a monarchical type of government, much to the disappointment of a radical republican minority. A more shattering division of mind arose over the relation of Austria, with its German-speaking nucleus but predominantly non-German population, to the federal union. It was voted ultimately to exclude Austria, which was tantamount to asking the House of Hapsburg to resist the unification plan. The Frankfurt constitution prescribed liberal rights for citizens, promised a legislature of two houses and assigned executive authority to a German emperor.

The crown was offered to Frederick William IV of Prussia who, however, haughtily declined to wear it. He reasoned that acceptance might well incite Austria to war and, as a believer in authoritarian and divine right government, he had no hankering for a crown proffered by a representative assembly. The refusal of the Prussian king to go along with the Frankfurt decisions ruined the unification scheme. Minor republican skirmishings in western Germany which followed were inconsequential, and many a disenchanted liberal set sail for the United States.

The problem of German unity paralleled, in a measure, the problem of uniting western Europe a century later. The ideal of German nationhood attracted appreciable and influential private enthusiasm, very largely among the well-to-do classes, to be exact, but governments adopted a tepid attitude or were downright hostile. Without the hearty support of responsible

"How is your horse behaving?" asks the Prussian of his fellow German rulers in this caricature of 1848. "If he takes the bit in his teeth again, count on me to help you break him."

public authorities, all the generous enthusiasms and all the lofty ideological lectures were bound to prove futile, as indeed they did.

A ray of national hope flickered momentarily when in 1850 the sovereigns of nearly thirty German states banded together with Prussia in a loose federal combination. Austria, excluded from this union, bluntly demanded that the project be abandoned, under peril of war. Nicholas I of Russia offered to serve as mediator, which won him recognition as lord paramount in Germany and almost as master of continental Europe. The Prussian government supinely surrendered, but spirited Prussians did not forget the disgraceful humiliation that had been inflicted. Proudly the House of Hapsburg had reasserted its ascendancy among the German states and the German Confederation, under the management of Austria, resumed its somnolent course.

Out of the revolutionary disturbances, the Germans had netted modest constitutional gains, notably in Prussia, and inconsiderable extensions of popular liberties. But the dream of national consolidation suffered a blow. It is clear in retrospect that the failure to unite Germany at the mid-century on a liberal foundation was an unmitigated calamity. Otto von Bismarck would presently build a united Fatherland, less, however, by processes of rational discussion and tolerant agreement than by diplomatic finesse and physical force.

SUMMARY

A striking fact in the history of the Continent after Waterloo is the absence of international war. Exhausted by the Napoleonic struggles, Europe coveted peace and that it enjoyed. Conservatism, when not reaction, rode in the saddle, stoutly resisting the application of French revolutionary principles. Stability prevailed except during the convulsions of 1820, 1830 and the more momentous upheavals of 1848. Liberalism and nationalism, essentially the interests of intellectuals and the middle classes, pressed hard against the status quo. It seemed to many liberals that constitutions were the open sesame to richer and fuller living.

It was an epoch of growing population and of quickening tempo in material affairs. Agricultural output turned upward, railways and steamships started to transform transportation on the Continent, industrial technology and machine production advanced, though as yet few large factories had appeared. The middle classes increased in numbers and in social and political importance, more so in France than in other countries. The plight of urban wage earners claimed the attention of some thoughtful individuals who devised patterns of social reconstruction.

The currents of the age were thrown into high relief by the tumults and confusions of 1848. Inspired by exalted intentions, these movements excited great expectations only to taper off in disappointment and despair. Defeat of working-class insurgents in Paris, Berlin and Vienna sealed the doom of the revolutions. The extent and comprehensiveness of the initial insurrectionary successes were less remarkable than the speed and the thoroughness of the conservative recovery.

Armies staunchly upheld the established order, peasants manifested few signs of rebellion, insurgent leaders were divided in objectives and ineffective in striving to attain them. The melancholy outcome of the mid-century revolutions dramatically demonstrated that conservatism was stronger than the forces of change. National struggles petered out and authoritarianism, somewhat diluted, regained the ascendant.

And yet the uproar of 1848 left lasting marks upon the face of the Continent. Constitutionalism had scored victories, Prussia and Piedmont conspicuously had obtained legislatures of sorts. National sentiments had been quickened among Germans, Italians, Czechs, Magyars and smaller groupings. The cleavage between wage workers and the propertied elements had been thrown into sharper focus, but it would be straining the evidence to set the revolutions down as proletarian class struggles. Nevertheless, the advent of the industrial wage earners as a conscious and serious political force dates from 1848. Beyond all that, the peasants of the Austrian Empire and unfree rustics in the German states had been released from serfage and many acquired property which strengthened them in their conservatism.

The next epoch—the age of national consolidation—would witness the vindication of the national ideal, though not in precisely the manner advocated by the enthusiastically romantic idealists of the forepart of the century.

FOR FURTHER STUDY

Frederick B. Artz, *Reaction and Revolution, 1814–1832* (New York, 1934)

Peter Viereck, *Conservatism Revisited: the Revolt Against Revolt, 1815–1849* (New York, 1949) paperback

Helene du Coudray, *Metternich* (New Haven, 1936)

Kent R. Greenfield, *Economics and Liberalism in the Risorgimento, 1814–1848* (Baltimore, 1934)

Heinrich von Treitschke, *The History of Germany in the Nineteenth Century* (Eng. ed., 7 vols., New York, 1915–1919)

John P. T. Bury, *France, 1814–1940* (Philadelphia, 1949) paperback

John M. S. Allison, *Thiers and the French Monarchy, 1797–1818* (Boston, 1926)

George F. H. Berkeley, *Italy in the Making, 1815–1846* (3 vols., Cambridge, Eng., 1932–40)

Priscilla Robertson, *Revolutions of 1848: A Social History* (Princeton, 1952) paperback

Raymond Postgate, *1848: Story of a Year* (London, 1955)

Frederick A. Simpson, *The Rise of Louis Napoleon* (new ed., London, 1951)

Guido de Ruggiero, *The History of European Liberalism* (Eng. trans., new ed., London, 1959) paperback

Jacob S. Schapiro, *Liberalism: Its Meaning and History* (New York, 1953) paperback

John P. T. Bury, ed., *The Zenith of European Power, 1830–1870* (Cambridge, England, 1960)

John P. Plamenatz, *The Revolutionary Movement in France* (London, 1952)

Frank E. Manuel, *The New World of Henri St. Simon* (Cambridge, Mass., 1956)

Theodore S. Hamerow, *Restoration, Revolution, Reaction in Germany* (Princeton, 1958)

Leonard Krieger, *The German Idea of Freedom* (Boston, 1957)

Gaetano Salvemini, *Mazzini* (New York, 1957) paperback

R. John Rath, *The Viennese Revolution of 1848* (Austin, Texas, 1957)

Geoffrey Bruun, *Revolution and Reaction* (New York, 1958) paperback

CHAPTER XV

CURRENTS IN WESTERN CULTURE

"THAT BLESSED MOOD"

THE dominant intellectual temper of the period directly after Napoleon is summed up in the term "romantic." It was not at all a novelty, for it was present late in the eighteenth century with Rousseau as its leading representative; now, however, romanticism thoroughly permeated literature and the fine arts all across Europe. Romanticism, someone has said, responded to the "call of the wild." It resented the roar of men and machines. It blended love of nature with love of country, overlapping with patriotic emotions. Artists with pen or brush contributed notably to more than one form of beauty.

In its essence romanticism rebelled against the frigid cult of reason, against formalism and polished precision. It voiced disillusionment over the potentialities and perfectibility of man, optimistically overrated as these hopes had been by the French heralds of "Enlightenment." It catered to a war-weary generation that wished to be entertained rather than instructed. Practitioners of romanticism in all lands exalted freedom, gave expression to the fanciful, the instinctive, the emotions of the heart. They rediscovered the medieval centuries with their knights and ladies, their monks and fairies, and drew inspiration from the unspoiled handiwork of nature.

As well as any other, the English poet William Wordsworth described the romantic outlook as

> That blessed mood
> In which the burthen of the mystery,
> In which the heavy and weary weight
> Of all this unintelligible world
> Is lightened.

Wordsworth, a portrait painted at about the time the Lyrical Ballads were written

ROMANTIC POETRY AND DRAMA

Wordsworth, who in his "thoughtless youth" had rapturously applauded the French Revolution, turned sour and conservative as he meditated on the iron despotism of Napoleon. His writings in that phase of his career ushered in an era of lyric and imaginative poetry unmatched in English literature. "Poetry," wrote Wordsworth, "takes its origin from emotion recollected in tranquillity." He delighted in the glories of nature and in ordinary everyday things, writing of them in delicate and sensitive tones, touched with mysticism. A confessed pantheist, Wordsworth was haunted by a vision of the unity of the universe and the essential harmony between the universe and the soul of man. His diction was simple and forthright, as shown, for instance, in the autobiographical pageant "The Prelude; or Growth of a Poet's Mind" and "Tintern Abbey."

As a literary force and an influence upon contemporaries, Lord Byron easily eclipsed Wordsworth. To aristocratic birth, wealth and a tempestuous gift of poetry, he added in this age of romantic fancies, elements of mystery, of fantastic debauchery and yet a heroic attachment to human freedom. His enthusiasm for the rights of man was as unrestrained as his iconoclastic condemnation of prevailing society. ("Childe Harold's Pilgrimage"). Harshly and satirically Byron castigated the smug middle classes and preached revolt and liberty with malicious glee. The dash and freshness of his language, his dramatic and magnificent descriptions, scarcely less than the themes he dealt with, attracted imitative disciples in Europe. This vivid personality has continued to be a strong cultural link between England and the Continent. Admiring champions esteem him as the leading English man of letters since Shakespeare, no doubt an overvaluation. Not inappropriately, the quixotic Byron perished as a

Lord Byron, sketched by a contemporary in 1823

Goethe during his classic tour in Italy, 1786–1788

crusader on behalf of Greek independence from the Turks.

Equally interested in freedom for Greece, equally contemptuous of orthodox social standards was Percy Bysshe Shelley. A born revolutionary, gifted with a highly fanciful imagination and a man of intense enthusiasms, Shelley pursued a tumultuous career which is reflected in his passionately beautiful verse. ("Prometheus Unbound"; "Ode to the West Wind"). His genius as a craftsman with the English language excused many discreditable indiscretions. Accidental death cut down this prophetic reformer at an early age, but his poetry, little appreciated while he lived, gained steadily in the evaluations of critics.

Johann Wolfgang Goethe, to whom allusion was made earlier, towered above his contemporaries and promoted the whole romantic movement in music as well as in literature. Called the "world's last truly universal man," the accomplishments of this fascinating mind were bewildering in their diversity. Short lyric poems, sparkling aphorisms and the majestic *Faust* made Goethe the foremost literary celebrity of the age. Admirers perched him upon a pedestal from which he has never been dislodged. Under his influence Weimar blossomed as the capital of German literary culture; and he attained a considerable reputation as a public servant and something of a name as a scientist.

Particularly in *Faust*, Goethe taught that personal salvation must be sought in the unending endeavor of the individual to perfect himself, and that everyone had a duty to contribute to community well-being. Take life as it comes, Goethe seemed to say, and live to the full, for the real purpose of life is life itself. Deep love for humanity was matched by qualities of tolerance, generosity and sublime faith in progress. That is not to say, however, that Goethe was a democrat, for he definitely preferred paternalism in government; he approached politics and culture in the spirit of liberal conservatism. And yet he was a "good European," unwilling, for example, to employ his pen in the service of German patriotism during the warfare with Napoleonic France.

Atala and René, *by François René de Chateaubriand (above), stand at the beginning of the romantic movement in French literature.*

Compared with Goethe, contemporary men of letters seem on the small side. Asked to pass judgment on Goethe, G. B. Shaw retorted: "Insects will buzz around the colossus, but not I. I take off my hat and hold my tongue." Time has heightened the prestige of Goethe as an author, as a thinker, and as a man.

Among the many romantic writers who acknowledged the authority of Goethe, Heinrich Heine stands out. His brilliant lyrics glorifying nature on land and water ("Die Lorelei," for example) and witty satires on the contemporary scene won him international esteem. In vivacious verse, Heine lampooned the smug complacency of the German middle classes and worshiped the goddess of freedom, though he succumbed to adulation of Napoleon. Paris, "the New Jerusalem of Liberalism," was his spiritual home and there he lived during the latter part of his life, proclaiming the ideals of liberty in journalistic pieces.

French poets, meantime, had been drawn into the irresistible current of romanticism. Relaxation of the censorship on letters imposed by Napoleon encouraged freedom of literary expression. After the departure of Goethe, Victor Hugo, another almost incredibly versatile author, forged to the front rank of continental men of letters. A lover of nature and of homely things, an intense admirer of Napoleon and France, Hugo conveyed his sentiments in lyrical verse rich in color and unsurpassed in imagery. The sensitive Alfred de Musset, hero of scores of amorous triumphs, sang of tragic love with sentimental artistry; not a distinguished stylist he nonetheless became the darling of Paris salons. Alfred de Vigny, an extreme romanticist in some of his moods, infused his poetry with a flavor of somber pessimism.

Among Italian literary men, devotion to country inspired romantic verse intended to stir men to political activity, as was exhibited in the *Fifth of May* by Alessandro Manzoni, the ultimate in tributes to Napoleon on his death. Poetry in Slavic tongues, not previously of European stature, now claimed international attention. And yet the leading Russian poet, Alexander Pushkin, received little praise outside of his own country before the twentieth century.

Alexander Pushkin made this little sketch of himself.

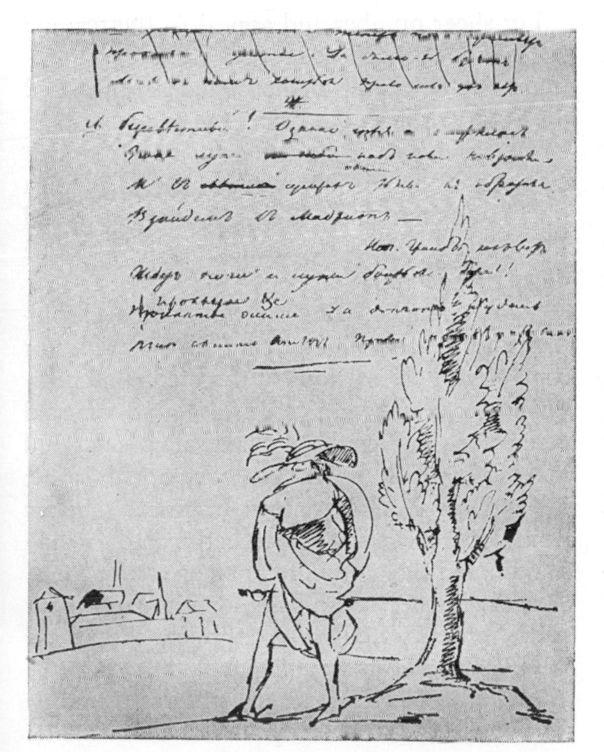

A page of Pushkin's manuscript

An author of prodigious vitality Pushkin composed lyric poetry more or less consciously on the model of Byron. In clever and epigrammatic verse he belligerently reproached everything and everybody not to his taste. He wrote contemptuously of the Muscovite aristocracy for instance, reviled serfdom and applauded political assassination, which may account for his popularity in Soviet Russia. Pushkin had boundless admiration for the ways of the West which he desired his own country to copy. An equestrian statue of Peter the Great, the arch-Westernizer, inspired him to compose one of his finest pieces, "The Bronze Horseman." His lengthy masterpiece, *Eugene Oneygin*, pleaded for freedom and recalled entertaining Russian legends. It reveals a good deal about the inconsequential character of aristocratic existence in the Russia of the era. Ending on a note of harsh frustration, this national epic exerted a profound influence upon later Russian literature. Russian critics are inclined to rank Pushkin high above Byron.

Like Pushkin, the most engaging Polish poet, Adam Mickiewicz, responded to the vogue of Byron. The greatest creation of Polish literature, *Sir Thaddeus*, revived old folk tales, glorious and bloody traditions of heathen Lithuania and the colorful heritage of the Polish nation. It was a trumpet call to articulate Poles to enlist in the work of national resurrection. Another ardently patriotic composition, *The Ancestors*, depicted the evolution of a romantic lover into a sturdy national leader; reverently Mickiewicz asserted the messianic role of Poland, likening his dismembered country to the Christ, who had been crucified for the sins of Europe.

A man of action as well as a literary genius, Mickiewicz took part in rising after rising against hated Russia. Teacher and prophet of his nation, he instilled generations of Poles with the faith that one day their country would resume its place in the family of nations. When Columbia University established a professorship in Polish literature and culture (1948) it was assigned the name of this artistic exemplar of romanticism. Poets in the languages of the smaller European nationalities also prepared the ground for national literatures, writing intensely emotional and patriotic romantic verse.

French playwrights dominated the output of romantic drama, tragedies and historical plays or compositions with contemporary settings. Victor Hugo, for example, broke away from classical French styles in drama; *Hernani*, which is replete with lyricism, sumptuous historical re-creations and democratic social emphases, provoked a regular battle among intellectuals in Paris. Comedy plays extolling bourgeois tastes were a specialty of Eugène Scribe, while Alexandre Dumas the elder wrought highly emotional romances dramatizing the spirit of dissent against social conventions.

The outstanding playwright in the German language was Franz Grillparzer, the idol of Viennese theatergoers. Certain of his dramas vivified stirring episodes in the Austrian past (*King Ottokar*). Though he tried to foster loyalty to the Hapsburg dynasty, Grillparzer nonetheless fell under the frown of the official world. Consequently, he turned to themes beyond the range of controversy, sagas of antiquity and glorifications of nature.

NOVELISTS OF THE PERIOD

For sheer number and appeal to the reading public, novels eclipsed other literary productions. At the outset of the period fiction based on history or legend enjoyed the greatest popularity, giving way in time to novels which endeavored to portray everyday existence with photographic fidelity. It was Walter Scott and the *Waverley Novels* which brought historical fiction into prominence.

Scott ransacked English and Scotch chronicles and folk traditions to find materials for romantic interpretations of the medieval epoch (*Ivanhoe*; *Kenilworth*). He displayed unusual genius for vivifying dusty medieval episodes and making his men and women live and breathe; in so doing he helped turn historical scholars from great events to homelier records which illuminated the entire life of an age and people. Readers in the British Isles, on the Continent and in the United States thrilled over these tales and imitators were legion.

Critics are inclined to place *Notre Dame de Paris* by Hugo at the top of French romantic novels. Richly picturesque in language and highly imaginative, this novel pictured medieval Paris not as it in fact was, but as Hugo wished it might have been. The phenomenally industrious and exuberant Dumas and his aides poured forth an avalanche of beguiling and melodramatic period pieces; *The Three Musketeers* and *The Count of Monte Cristo* have entertained generation after generation.

Manzoni produced the supreme classic of Italian historical romance in *The Betrothed.* It portrayed life in Lombardy when that district was ruled by Spain, and was calculated to impress upon Italians the point that foreign lordship had robbed their country of the birthright of freedom. The manners and customs of picturesque Cossacks were reproduced in the exquisitely written *Taras Bulba* by Nicholas Gogol, himself a native of southern Russia. It is an exceptionally exciting tale of adventure, war and love of country. By the same author is *Dead Souls,* an immense canvas, and a realistic one, on Russian rural society. Gogol graphically sketched the revolting inhumanities of serfdom and the prodigality, meanness and ignorance of the landlords. Spoken of as the Russian "Dickens," Gogol described Russian character as spineless, short on resolution; invariably his male characters are dull, witless fellows, incapable of improvement. *Dead Souls* stimulated agitation for emancipation of the serfs and inspired the better-known realistic Russian novelists of the next half century.

Idealization of the peasantry crowds the choicer pages of the French romancer, George Sand, to use her pseudonym. Partly of peasant stock herself, she understood and lyrically interpreted the moods, the dreads, the problems, and the earthy interests of the countryfolk, as in *François le Champi.* Extremely fond of Rousseau, this rebellious spirit stormed against the bourgeois code of matrimony (*Indiana*), popularized Utopian collectivist doctrines and for a short time preached the cause of republicanism. Her varied and unconventional career and her easy familiarity with leading authors and musicians of the day furnished materials for a whole library of novels, few of which are read any longer. But her views on relations between the sexes and her advocacy of feminism were given wider currency by the next generation of French writers.

Characteristic products of the romantic temper were collections of *Fairy Tales* by the Dane, Hans Christian Andersen and by the Grimm brothers of Germany. Out of the wealth of Teutonic mythology, the Grimms, who were scholars of high standing, selected such favorite legends of childhood as *Rapunzel* and *Snow White and the Seven Dwarfs.*

Realistic fiction was raised to great heights by Honoré de Balzac and Charles Dickens. It was the deliberate purpose of Balzac to expose the very warp and woof of French bourgeois society in the reign of Louis Philippe and to define what was enduring and universal in the relations of man to man. Those aims he accomplished in a career of unique fertility and

Charles Dickens reading to his daughters

amazing productiveness. The *Comédie Humaine,* in nearly a hundred volumes, contains almost 2,000 portraits, and even minor figures in this immense gallery seem real and vital. Balzac deftly illuminated the inner spirit of the French—provincial and Parisian, political and philosophical, military and social. His deviation from subjectivity to frank realism guided and inspired the oncoming generation of French authors. *Père Goriot* and *Eugénie Grandet* alone would have ensured him an enviable niche in the pantheon of world letters.

Dickens too wrote voluminously, though his social data do not always satisfy the test of historical accuracy. And yet, consummate artist that he was, Dickens caught the color and nuances of the period in a way seldom equalled by the social historian. Of humble origin himself and largely self-educated, Dickens displayed warm compassion for the underprivileged, the forgotten. The wretched and destitute in England, the deformed, the shabby, the indebted, the sufferings of the nobodies on the hard road of life found in Dickens an expositor and an ardent champion.

Dickens flayed the inadequacies of the British schooling facilities, the law courts and kindred shortcomings in perceptive and vivid novels, such as *Oliver Twist, Bleak House,* and *Martin Chuzzlewit* (in which he pays his respects and disrespects to the United States). Dickens' novels helped to dispel middle-class ignorance about the lowly and to rally sentiments of pity and fear on behalf of remedial social legislation. Flashes of wit, droll humor, moving pathos, abiding faith in moral principles and superbly etched personalities, many of which became household words, earned Dickens a place of lasting distinction in the English-reading world.

THE AMERICAN CONTRIBUTION

So little of cultural consequence had as yet been produced in the United States that a witty Briton felt constrained (1820) to write: "In the four quarters of the globe, who reads an American book? or goes to an American play? or looks at an American picture or statue?" In the next generation, however, American authors achieved a considerable reading in Europe. At the middle of the century, German publishing houses brought out two extensive sets of works by American writers, one of them running to eighty volumes.

In the prevalent temper of romanticism Washington Irving composed pictures of New World and British life. (*The Sketch Book*). His jovial revivals of Dutch legends and folk lore attracted an appreciative audience at home and abroad. Profiting by the fame of Irving, James Fenimore Cooper, called the "Walter Scott of the New World," won large and lasting success with thrilling and romantic stories of Indian ways and customs. Cooper is the literary grandfather in truth of the dime novel which flourished so luxuriantly later in the century. *The Last of the Mohicans,* in particular, has remained a popular favorite of juvenile readers. *Uncle Tom's Cabin* (1852) by Harriet Beecher Stowe was very widely translated in Europe and sold by the millions. It did much to mold foreign attitudes on the American slavery issue.

For sheer influence upon Europeans, especially upon French men of letters, Edgar Allan Poe surpassed other American writers. Morbid and temperamentally melancholic, he was at his best in the realism of the subconscious, as is seen in his most characteristic piece, *The Fall of the House of Usher.* As the parent of the detective story and the "atmospheric" tale, Poe probed into the mysterious and the pathological (*The Murders in the Rue Morgue, The Gold Bug*).

In intellectual circles as far away as Russia the *Essays* of Ralph Waldo Emerson commanded respectful reading. A rebellious critic of austere conventionalism, Emerson extolled the values inherent in everyday virtues: self-reliance, sobriety, confidence in the future. He also implored authors in the United States to emancipate themselves from the literary traditions and emphases of the Old World. That counsel was scarcely necessary for his protégé, Henry D. Thoreau, an unconventional, obstinate and sensitive spirit, who shared Emerson's broad philosophical outlook. Combining under-

Edgar Allan Poe

standing of nature and reverence for her ways with intense detestation of tyranny, whether over the body or mind of man, Thoreau made his literary mark with *Walden*. This autobiographical piece recounts a fascinating two-year experiment in solitary living which enabled the philosopher-naturalist, seeking the road to freedom, to explore many corners of his inner consciousness and to point up what really mattered on the journey from cradle to grave. In time the writings of Thoreau were extensively translated, influencing the thought and action of the Indian seer, Mahatma Gandhi, and many others.

If Thoreau properly belongs among the optimists, Nathaniel Hawthorne took a dim view of his kind, looking upon them through darkly tinted glasses. A profound searcher of the human conscience and a charming stylist, he raised the novel as a literary art to a high level on this side of the Atlantic. *The Scarlet Letter*, his masterpiece, dramatized the career of an unorthodox Puritan lady, leaving readers with an unforgettable, though lopsided, impression of good and evil in colonial New England. His friend, Herman Melville, rather the pessimist too, concerned himself with tales of the sea, drawing upon his own remarkable adventures on the blue water. Best of all was *Moby Dick*, replete with mystifying symbolism and subtly portraying the everlasting struggle of virtue and vice in the fate of man.

All these creative authors from Emerson to Melville speculated on the eternal mysteries—man, nature, the universe—challenged accepted values of their society and wove their views into their literature. Staunch allegiance to ideals of freedom and equality stamped them as fit sons of the youthful trans-Atlantic democracy. By their pens, they released quality writing in the New World from the confining chains of parochialism and carried for American letters an honorable place in western literature as a whole.

Among the poets, Henry Wadsworth Longfellow, a cosmopolitan who knew Europe at

Ralph Waldo Emerson

first hand, acquired an international reputation. His lyric pieces ("The Psalm of Life") were less prized than his romantic verse, notably *Evangeline* and *Hiawatha*, celebrating the legendary and the historical in the New World environment. Neither original nor deeply thoughtful as a literary artist, Longfellow lost standing with the passage of time, but the clear melodious language of "The Village Blacksmith" and "Excelsior" has become familiar to millions of American school children.

HISTORICAL WRITING

At the outset of the nineteenth century, historians who considered their subject primarily as a department of literature jostled with scholars bent upon establishing history as a realistic, even a scientific, discipline. In particular French, American and Slavic recorders of the doings of men reflected the romantic spirit of the age. Their narratives were replete with colorful detail, picturesque imaginings and philosophical and political sermonizing.

Those traits were admirably exemplified by Jules Michelet, dubbed "the Victor Hugo of history." In addition to a colorful reconstruction of medieval France, Michelet prepared a remarkably popular *History of the Revolution.* It was an eloquent defense of the French revolutionary years, marked by warm affection for France and intense humanitarian and democratic sentiments. Judged by the rigorous standards of scientific—or university—history, the works of Michelet are faulty with errors in fact and distorted emphases, but as literature their appeal has been sustained.

Quite in keeping with the prevalent "climate of opinion," historical writers in the United States indulged in patriotic glorification and passionately proclaimed the virtues of liberty and freedom. George Bancroft, for example, composed a spacious and eulogistic *History of the United States*. Scarcely a work of literary art, it interpreted the evolution of English America and the liberation from Britain as the handiwork of supernatural forces. In his description of the making of the Constitution, Bancroft rose to heights of rhetorical ecstasy. The epic story of French colonialism in North America was lengthily recounted by Francis Parkman. As an artist in words he deserves to be grouped with Michelet himself. The heroism of French explorers and lusty struggles with the British for New World lordship were painted in unforgettably dramatic colors. A literary Bostonian, Parkman did not always understand clearly the position of France in controversial matters.

Distinguished practitioners of the historical calling in Great Britain were Thomas Carlyle and Thomas B. Macaulay, brilliant literary masters both. Carlyle is best remembered for a colorful and friendly portrayal of the great French Revolution. Ordinary fellows appear as the real heroes in these pages, but Carlyle was deeply impressed with the role of the great man in history as he showed in a full length account of Frederick the Great (*A History of Frederick II of Prussia*). Men and events of the late seventeenth century were described, picturesquely and with imaginative force, by Macaulay in a famous *History of England*. Ardently partisan in tone this work nonetheless belongs among the classic masterpieces of historical composition.

Characteristic of Slavic histories written in the romantic spirit was the work of František Palacký, a Czech intellectual of great influence. His elaborate and emotionally gripping *History of Bohemia* dramatized the medieval grandeur and glory of his country and vividly recounted the fierce struggles between Czechs and Germans before Bohemia passed under Austrian lordship in 1526. Like its counterparts by historians of other subject nationalities, the writing of Palacký contributed importantly to the awakening of Czech nationalism. Perusal of the work kindled national sentiments among the rising Czech bourgeoisie and quickened the desire for home-rule. Palacký, typically again, participated actively in the political renaissance as well as in the intellectual revival of his nationality.

Dispassionate and comparatively objective reconstruction of the past had been cultivated, meantime, by German scholarship. The pathfinder in that approach to history was Barthold Niebuhr, who insisted upon searching for and utilizing original historical evidence and criticizing materials in the austere and severe spirit favored by natural scientists. As he demonstrated in a learned *History of Rome* the past could be recreated with a minimum of partiality, philosophical, theological or other, and with a maximum of objectivity. The aim of objective historical scholarship was the nearest thing to truth attainable.

Something of the prestige of Niebuhr derived from the renown of his ablest disciple, Leopold von Ranke, undoubtedly the foremost historian of the century. The responsibility of the professional historian, Ranke asserted, was to recount events as they properly happened, or in his own language, "History has had assigned to it the task of judging the past, of instructing the present for the benefit of ages to come. To such lofty functions [my] work does not aspire. Its aim is merely to show what actually occurred." Somewhat later the British historian Lord Acton phrased the ideal of the historian as detached onlooker this way, "Our account of Waterloo . . . must be one that satisfies French and English, German and Dutch readers alike."

That indeed was a counsel of perfection, for the historian cannot possibly reconstruct the past to suit every taste and seldom or never can he present all the evidence at his disposal. Rather he must select what seems to him important, interesting and worthy of recall. As for impartiality, the pages of Ranke himself are somewhat shadowed by convictions and prepossessions which he cherished. Yet it is undeniable that he tried harder "to stand above the battle" and was more successful in doing so than his contemporaries and many of his successors. Cool detachment remains a necessary quality of anyone who aspires to write history in the Western tradition.

Ranke practiced what he preached in a *History of the Popes*, dealing with the age of the Reformation. More fascinating than fiction, it is a remarkably dispassionate account of a highly controversial epoch, and a model of painstaking and searching analysis of original documents. In an extremely long life of fruitful toil, Ranke also composed valuable studies in German, Austrian, French, English and universal history.

At his seminar in the university of Berlin, the acknowledged founder of modern historiography instilled in students a deep conviction of the importance of history and his ideals of objectivity and independence in the quest for historical truth. The scholarly techniques which he prized were diffused across Germany and thence to seats of learning around the world; significantly Ranke was the first scholar elected to honorary membership in the American Historical Association, founded in 1884, the leading society of professional historians in the United States.

Under the inspiration of Ranke many historical craftsmen searched for new knowledge in old sources of information. They presented their findings and conclusions in definitive essays or monographs. Such studies, instead of large syntheses, came to be regarded as the finest type of historical scholarship. Highly refined and cautious specialism threatened to submerge the general historian, who preferred not to confine himself to a narrow corner of a special subject. Yet only the burrowings of the historical mole could make the bird's eye view accurate and tenable.

History as literature tended to be eclipsed by scientifically ordered and minute monographs. Little professional energy was applied to the search for general "laws in history." Feats of that character seemed to belong in the province of the philosopher, not of the historian. To enrich historical studies, scholarship was lavished on the discovery and publication of authentic original manuscripts. With Baron vom Stein as sponsor, German savants edited the sources of German medieval history, uncovering hitherto inaccessible records. Published as *Monumenta Germaniae historica* (1826–1925), this massive compilation filled 120 stately volumes and set standards for similar publications in other countries and for other historical periods. It would be erroneous, however, to assume that German scholars in preparing the *Monumenta* were animated solely by love for exact historical truth. The enterprise, at any rate originally, was inspired by the enthusiasm generated in the warfare against Napoleon and was designed to further the cause of German national unity.

The lofty ideals of learning proclaimed by Ranke did not long command the allegiance of the more popular historians. All across Europe, and not least in Germany, historical writers dipped their pens into nationalistic ink, allowed fervent national passions and aspirations to color narratives, ignoring evidence which failed to fit into their versions of events —or their dreams for the future.

THE VISUAL ARTS

The realm of the visual arts of the early nineteenth century was immensely broad and varied, with disparate viewpoints and styles. Variety was no doubt a sign of vitality and of the freedom of expression in the age. Partisans of romanticism, who cast aside conservative and retrospective tendencies, battled strenuously with upholders of academic traditions.

Whereas classicists in painting, for example, prided themselves on design and orderliness, romanticists delighted in color, action, borrowed themes from the medieval, the mysterious East, or the unsullied countryside. Affection for nature became the leading artistic trait and landscape painting was the chief creation of the period in art. It is noteworthy that artistic novelties, as with other forms of creative activity, were appreciated at first only by the few; almost all the painters nowadays generally acclaimed as talented were originally misunderstood, neglected, or ridiculed by critics and the public.

Definitely in the tradition of the late Renaissance artists was Eugène Delacroix, a pioneer in French romanticism. Making violent use of

Countryside, *by Jean-Baptiste Camille Corot*

The Glebe Farm with View of Langham Church, *by John Constable*

color and sprawling design, he painted in a spirit of rebellion and endeavored to place on canvas the passions and inner motives of men. The "Entry of the Crusaders into Constantinople," is typical of his thought and work. Amplitude of coloring, gorgeous scenery, spirited Crusaders charging forward on horseback distinguish this characteristically romanticist production. Smoke from homes rises in the background while darkly ominous clouds deck the sky. It adds up to a magnificent picture, vivid, intensely emotional, authentically romantic.

Traditionalism in art had a worthy French exponent in Jean A. Ingres, who relied upon old and proved sources of aesthetic strength. An excellent draughtsman, he designed with solidity yet subtlety. ("The Vow of Louis XIII.") Color served merely to accentuate drawing. Ingres fought manfully against "the romantic horde," but eventually his school was crowded aside. Landscape painting in France passed under the spell of two Britons, John Constable and J. M. W. Turner. Constable glorified the natural beauties of rural England and painted in the open—an innovation. "Hay Wain," portraying a placid rustic scene, reveals how keenly Constable felt the atmosphere of the country; representations of Salisbury Cathedral and the lovely environs are characteristic specimens of his art.

As a technician, Constable painted with heavy strokes and smears or splashes of color, which is the reason he is sometimes called the father of French Impressionism. Turner, too, interpreted the elusive and inexhaustible riches of nature, especially as seen at the beginning and the close of day. He is also famous for paintings of Venice and sea-pictures ("Fighting Téméraire"), featured by dazzling color and light.

French artists of nature congregated near the village of Barbizon, which gave its name to a noted school of painting. True to the romanticist pattern, these artists obtained ideas and inspiration through direct association with the countryside. Best known of them were J. B. C. Corot and Jean F. Millet, the latter, himself of peasant stock, much admired for chaste, expressive studies of peasants ("The Sower"), done in pleasantly fresh tones.

Architecture and sculpture in France reflected the rivalry between classic and romanticist conceptions. While the noble Madeleine Church in Paris, begun as a shrine of martial glory by Napoleon, is the finest example of the Roman revival, romanticist sculptors completed the imposing "Arc de Triomphe." For that monument François Rude created a dramatic piece of sculpture recalling the departure of volunteers for the revolutionary wars. Although the men wear Roman costumes, the intensity of expression and the sense of patriotic emotionalism which the warriors evoke are typically romantic. James Pradier, most popular French sculptor of the generation, carved harmonious, distinctly pert, personifications of Lille and Strasbourg to adorn the Place de la Concorde. And for the sarcophagus of Napoleon he created twelve dignified sentinels in the classical mode.

The great architecture of Great Britain followed Greek or Gothic patterns. The National Gallery on the edge of Trafalgar Square in London, for example, and the majestic colonnade and portico of the British Museum stand as splendid witnesses of the Greek Revival. On the other hand, the Houses of Parliament, more than a generation in the building, reveal the perennial appeal of Gothic to the human spirit. This majestic masterpiece of Sir Charles Barry, best British architect since Wren, was admirably suited to the wonderful site along the Thames. It stimulated general interest in Gothic designs, especially for Roman Catholic churches and for parliamentary buildings in continental capitals.

In German Europe, Berlin and Munich were thriving centers of artistic creativity. Architects excelled in Greek Revival structures as seen in the Royal Theater in Berlin and the Nicolas Church of nearby Potsdam. Sculptors carved a spirited "Quadriga" for the Brandenburg gate and a vigorous equestrian statue of Frederick the Great. Kings of Bavaria proudly embellished their capital with Greek structures, many of which were demolished by bombs in World War II; notable were the Glyptothek and the old Pinacothek, which was stocked with simple German pieces of sculpture. Under royal patronage sculptors carved mediocre busts of Bavarian worthies and a colossal bronze monument of Bavaria. Munich was also the site of the leading German school of romantic painting.

Elsewhere in Europe few works of distinction in the visual arts appeared. No doubt, the finest sculptures of the period were executed by the Dane, Bertel Thorwaldsen, in the great tradition of Greece. Artists in Slavic countries painted enormous historical canvases, clearly derivations from second-rate German painters, and intended to quicken sentiments of patriotism. The choicest Russian painting, a very large tableau, "The Appearance of Christ to the People," by Alexander Ivanov, still attracts throngs of spectators in Moscow. This canvas heralded the beginning of a distinctly Russian school of painting.

ROMANTICISM IN MUSIC

It was in music that romanticism attained its fullest and most perfect expression. It may be said, indeed, that all music, the unique international "language of the emotions," contains traces of romanticism, since it accents freedom of individual expression. Once the monumental figure of Beethoven is passed, musical compositions of the early nineteenth century are noted for the absence of formalism, for uninhibited self-revelation and vivid coloring. Greater perfection in instruments, the piano in particular, afforded artists broader range and flexibility for the display of talents. And, whereas composers had previously depended upon the patronage of church and aristocracy, the principal support in the industrial age came from the cultivated and aspiring middle classes.

The reputation of Vienna as the capital of classical music was heightened by Ludwig van Beethoven. An unusually versatile composer, and gifted for musical architecture on the grand scale, he carried symphonic music to the highest level of perfection ("Eroica"), and wrote many instrumental pieces which have maintained their popularity. His later compositions foreshadowed the coming of romanticist styles. For variety and depth of feeling Beethoven has rarely been equalled and perhaps never surpassed. Not only was he one of the master musical minds but a peculiarly gigantic artist fit to be classed with Dante or Michelangelo.

With the appearance of the works of Carl Maria von Weber, the epoch of romanticist music had fairly opened. Staunch German patriot that he was, Weber incorporated in the opera *Der Freischütz*, the distinguishing traits of the new music: fanciful treatment of folk legends, intense feeling for nature, glorification of country and lavish exploitation of peasant melodies. Lyric songs had supreme expression in a Viennese prodigy, Franz Schubert. Simple in form and design, his exquisite music ("Du bist die Ruh,"; "Rastlose Liebe") is prized for dreamy, youthful sentimentality. An inspiration to many other composers, Schubert died young, like Weber, before his genius had fully flowered.

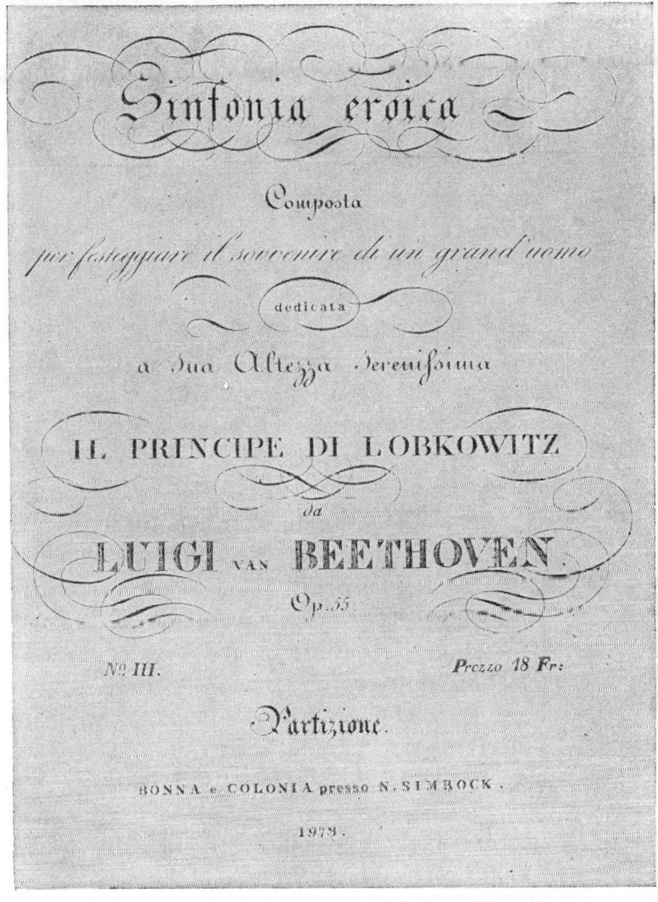

Title-page of the first edition of Beethoven's Eroica, *inspired by the composer's short-lived conception of Napoleon as a liberator of oppressed peoples.*

Better than any other composer doubtless Robert A. Schumann represented romanticism in all its resourceful novelty and inherent defects. Almost every variety of music, except church music, was enriched by him. Charming piano pieces and melodious songs to accompany the lyrics of Heine reveal Schumann at his finest. Romantic opera attracted several eminent composers of Italian nationality with Gioacchino Rossini as leader. Much attached to the spectacular, Rossini doted on melodramatic subjects (*William Tell*), dressing them up with ostentatious tunes calculated to appeal to bourgeois patronage; nowadays he is remembered mostly for an opera, *The Barber of Seville*. Crowning the achievements of Italian operatic composers were the works of Giuseppe Verdi. His early writing was clearly bound up with romantic literature, *Rigoletto* being inspired by a Hugo play.

Thanks to the influence of Italian musicians, *opéra comique* flourished in Paris. Rather akin to vaudeville, this type of production featured merry instrumentation and flippant, amusing text dealing with contemporary manners and morals. Sharp-witted business promoters joined forces with composers with facile pencils to gratify the tastes of the middle classes. "People are enamored of the beautiful, the brilliant, and the pompous," commented one critic, "because their own existence is shabby, obscure, and miserable." Scribe dashed off librettos for the music of Daniel F. Auber—*Masaniello, Gustav III*—and Giacomo Meyerbeer. As the *Huguenots* and *Robert the Devil* illustrate, Meyerbeer linked historical or legendary themes with extremely theatrical music. His technique had considerable imitation, but present-day judges are prone to dismiss his music as frothy and mediocre.

French romantic music reached its pinnacle in the compositions of Hector Berlioz. "The dominant qualities of my music," he confessed, "are passionate expression, internal fire, rhythmic animation and unexpected changes." This heir of Beethoven in a sense embodied the qualities of romanticism in the *Symphonie fantastique*.

Frédéric F. Chopin, Polish born artist of a rare creative power, has been called a romantic poet at the keyboard. Writing only for the piano and making rich use of dance patterns and homely rhythms of his beloved Poland, Chopin contrived to develop greater intimacy between composer and audience than many other musicians. Delicate by nature, Chopin is spoken of as a woman's artist because he was concerned with the simplest and most poignant moods of the human heart. In Paris where romanticism was the rage—it was the era of Hugo, Musset and Delacroix—the talents of Chopin were properly appreciated. Distraught by the fate of Poland he idealized Polish sorrows and wrongs in melancholic music, just as Mickiewicz did in verse. Chopin's compositions brought Polish music an international reputation that has persisted.

Out of Russia, meantime, had come a foretaste of the rich musical genius of that nation. Even as Ivanov had ushered in a national style of painting, so Michael I. Glinka started a Russian school of music. His choicest production, an opera, *A Life for the Tsar*, recaptured the patriotic emotions which had been set rolling by the desperate struggle against Napoleon. Taking his theme from a Polish invasion of Russia in the seventeenth century, Glinka portrayed the career of a romantic hero who fought, bled and died, quite impersonally, for the honor of tsar and country. Popular Muscovite folk tunes were skillfully woven into enchanting melodies. Glinka prepared the way for the great Russian musicians of later generations, whose compositions are calculated to stir the most sluggish spirits.

PATTERNS IN CATHOLICISM

Revival of interest in religion, as faith and hope, was as much a characteristic of the forepart of the nineteenth century as the prevalence of romanticism in letters and the arts.[1] After a long period of warfare and agony, apprehensions and disillusionments, many men sought shelter and solace in the assurances of historical Christianity. The cause of religion profited from nostalgic longing for peace of mind and popular desire to greet the unseen with confidence. Conservative statesmen, on their part, looked upon religious institutions with favor as bulwarks of discipline and stability, reliable allies in the struggle against the volcanic forces unloosed by the French Revolution. On behalf of Roman Catholicism, an array of gifted and earnest French writers combatted rationalism, condemned the Revolution and pleaded the case for the ancient creed of the nation.

Profound affection for the Roman Catholic Church and a lyrical conception of the Middle Ages gripped the mind of François-René de Chateaubriand, leading champion of the moral and intellectual regeneration of French Catholicism. He set forth his convictions most persuasively in the *Genius of Christianity*, a magnificent blend of pugnacity and eloquence; a fine stylist, his writing was refreshing to jaded palates. Chateaubriand extolled "revealed religion," interpreted Catholicism as a consecrated instrument of authority and mercilessly flayed unbelief and secularism.

In his thinking, all worthy advances in civilization were due to the historic Church and he ardently supported the principle of papal authority in religious affairs. Of all creeds Christianity, he asserted, was "the most poetical, most human, most favorable to freedom, art

[1] The course of Orthodox Catholicism in Russia is considered in Chap. XX.

and letters." The beauty of Christianity sufficiently proved its truth. Something of a disciple of Rousseau, Chauteaubriand appealed primarily to the emotions, kindled imagination by glowing rhetoric and awakened intellectual interest in the Middle Ages. Once more it became fashionable to converse about religion in Parisian literary circles and salons.

Catholicism had another doughty French exponent in Joseph de Maistre. He insisted in *The Pope* upon the absolute authority of the Pope over the Christian world, "the one great champion of Christianity against all its enemies." The ills which afflicted society he traced backward to the Protestant irruption and forward to the French Revolution. Catholicism he regarded as the indispensable ally of the Bourbon crown for social and political tranquillity.

The idea of progress proclaimed by skeptical "princes of secular thought," de Maistre derided as silly; it was sheer stupidity, he reasoned, to attempt to improve mankind by laws and constitutions. Only the Catholic faith, prayer and sacrifice would set society on the right path. His enthusiasm instructed the minds of other Catholic intellectuals.

While de Maistre repudiated compromise with novel ideas, the Abbé Félicité de Lamennais recommended that attempts be made to reconcile the principle of religious authority with the secular doctrine of liberty. As he read the signs of the times, unless altar and crown were separated, popular detestation of arbitrary kings would be transferred to the clergy and church; identification of Catholicism with discredited monarchy, in other words, invited religious suicide. Advocacy of liberalism brought Lamennais under condemnation by Rome and he was buried without the rites of the Church, but his writings have been an unfailing source of encouragement to Catholics desirous of bringing their church into harmony with prevailing trends in secular politics. Though it condemned Lamennais and all that he represented, the Papacy, on the other hand, removed from the Index of Forbidden Books the writings of Galileo and some other scientists. The universities of Louvain and Munich, in the meantime, had developed as distinguished homes of Catholic theological learning.

Aside from the activity of intellectuals the vigor of religious orders contributed to the revitalization of Catholicism. The Society of Jesus, restored to papal favor in 1814, busied itself in educational work, founding several new institutions of learning. Jesuits in pulpit, classroom and press asserted the absolute supremacy of the Pope over national churches, or what is called ultramontanism, a doctrine heartily seconded by French Catholic intellectuals. Less well-known societies of men and women engaged in charitable, educational and foreign missionary enterprises. French Catholics especially were zealous propagators of the message of the Church to non-Christian peoples of Africa and Asia.

Treaties or concordats, moreover, were negotiated by the Papacy with several governments. These understandings assured Catholic worship of financial support from state treasuries, defined the rights of clergy and assigned to governments the decisive voice in the selection of bishops. Discriminations against Catholics in Great Britain were whittled away until the kingship was the only public office from which Catholics were legally debarred, but the Catholic religion was still an object of scorn and aversion in Britain. A steady inflow of Irish immigrants and converts from the Church of England led to the establishment of a Catholic episcopacy in England in 1850 (and soon afterward in Scotland), which called forth a burst of printed indignation.

Catholicism did not, however, have clear sailing all the way. Controversy over mixed marriages provoked recurrent quarrels with governments in central Europe. Anticlericalism gathered force among Italian elements which considered the Papacy an obstacle to national unity. And in France and other Catholic countries as well anticlericalism possessed considerable vitality, resisting as best it could the encroachment of churchmen on what were deemed secular affairs. The working class of Paris preserved its reputation for Voltairean free-thinking.

PROTESTANTISM

The creeds of Luther and Calvin also underwent quickening experiences, though perhaps not so far-reaching as Catholicism. Protestantism had an acute and influential theologian in Friederick D. E. Schleiermacher, professor in the Berlin university and a preacher of commanding power. His thinking passed through a tortuous evolution. Once skeptical of the claims of Christianity, his university studies in philosophy and history led him to a distinctly mystical conception of the faith.

Denying that reason was the right road to religious truth, Schleiermacher contended that every individual possessed an instinctive sense of absolute dependence upon a Supreme Being. The central responsibility of religion, he thought, was to bring man into harmony with the Infinite. Christianity best accomplished that purpose, for at the heart of Christianity was Christ himself, the reconciliation of the finite to the eternal. Since his theological outlook bordered upon pantheism, Schleiermacher antagonized many churchmen and his moral tolerance also provoked adverse criticism. Protestant theologians of the century acknowledged, nonetheless, a large obligation to this prophet of feeling, imitated his method of approach, but shied away from his pantheistic emphases.

Thinking in Protestant circles was considerably affected by the application of the techniques of historical inquiry to the Holy Scriptures, the source of theological ideas. According to the standard Protestant view, the contents of the Bible were literally true, the infallible revelation of Christian belief and practice. "The Bible, the Bible alone," declared a seventeenth-century churchman, "is the religion of Protestants." Precisely because their faith rested on literal acceptance of scriptural statements Protestants had a vested interest in orthodox interpretation.

Historically theologians had interpreted the sacred text without regard for either the origins or original meanings. Critically-minded scholars, however, endeavored to determine whether the documents making up the Bible were in fact original, and tried to ascertain the meaning of the contents at the time of writing. Reverently and in the spirit of objective inquiry, investigators scrutinized the basic literature of Christianity in the same way that other historical records were examined. Conclusions which they arrived at were sometimes disturbing, sometimes destructive, to settled Christian assumptions.

Strictly speaking critical study of biblical texts was initiated in the seventeenth century and was carried forward by many investigators, such as Alexander Geddes, a Catholic priest in Scotland. Researches and a translation of the Bible which he edited led him to unconventional opinions. He decided, for instance, that the Pentateuch had been compiled from "the journals of Moses" long after his death. For his publications, which provoked a storm of indignant reproach, Geddes was censured by his church and dismissed from the priesthood as a depraved heretic.

Protestant scholars in the German university of Tübingen made that institution the stronghold of historical study of the Scriptures and of early Christianity. Professor Ferdinand C. Baur based his investigations of primitive Christianity upon the fragmentary evidence that had been preserved. Gifted with acute critical faculties and talented for abstract thought, Baur illuminated the history of Christian beliefs in the formative epoch of the faith. The validity of his findings was somewhat impaired by the undue importance he assigned to the Apostle Paul, but his books had permanent value and greatly stimulated historical probings of the Bible.

David F. Strauss, who studied with Baur, concerned himself especially with the literature of the New Testament. After careful research, he prepared a highly controversial *Life of Jesus*, challenging many fundamental conceptions. The work caused an immense sensation and robbed the author of appointment to a university chair.

The task of interpreting New Testament records on the "historical Jesus" was of course extremely delicate and challenging. Few Christians could even approach the subject apart from countless associations of their childhood and of much of the finest poetry and art of many centuries. Small wonder, then, that Strauss's book met with a violent reception. He asserted that much of the material in the gospel narratives had no standing before the bar of scholarship, dismissing reported miracles, for example, as dubious adaptations from Old Testament records or as natural occurrences inaccurately understood. No really adequate biography of the Christ could be composed, Strauss concluded, because of the scantiness of historically acceptable information.

Late in life Strauss published a popularization of his *Life of Jesus* and presently abandoned the Christian faith for pessimistic materialism. Translated into English, the writings of Strauss unloosed angry polemics in the British Isles, but they encouraged scholarly exploration of the evidences of Christianity. Certain critics, while they agreed with Strauss that a full-length biography of Jesus was out of the question, argued that he must be understood by faith.

Subsequently scholars discovered serious blemishes in the biblical researches of the Tübingen investigators and discarded or refined some of their judgments. A heavy debt was, however, acknowledged to them for defining the problems of classical Christianity and contributing to their solution. The Tübingen school, it must be said, founded historical theology as opposed to the dogmatic emphasis of Christian thought, and in so doing directed religious thinking into fresh channels. Many later theologians, who in the forepart of the nineteenth century would have denounced historical criticism as the spawn of the devil, found that approach nourishing to their conception of Christianity. What had been reviled as blasphemous outrage, in other words, was adopted by some Christians as orthodoxy. Faith fought heresy, but heresy became faith.

Up to a point the outlook of Strauss in his last years was molded by the German thinker, Ludwig A. Feuerbach. In his youth a theological student, Feuerbach repudiated Christianity as out of harmony with the intellectual temper of the times. He embraced atheism, describing belief in a Supreme Being and in immortality as subjective illusions springing from imagination and desire. Coiner of the epigram, "man is what he eats" (*Der Mensch ist was er isst*), Feuerbach ruled out the spiritual in favor of the material. His major book, *The Essence of Christianity,* was extensively translated. Read by Karl Marx and his associates, it helped to shape their materialistic atheism; and it had similar effects upon radically inclined Russian intellectuals.

Outside of the German states European Protestantism displayed little vitality. Efforts to infuse new energy into French Calvinism netted small results and in Holland Calvinism was disestablished (1848) as the state church. Nor did the Church of England seem a vital force in the life of parishioners. Anglican bishops, instead of furnishing vigorous spiritual leadership, applied themselves to scholarship and the preparation of learned treatises. As for the parish clergy, they performed their duties perfunctorily, caring little for ceremonies or theology and less for dogma.

The enthusiasms of evangelical Methodism excited individual Anglicans, it is true, without however making much of an impression upon the Church of England as a whole. Barriers of prejudice and snobbery separated Anglicans from adherents of dissenting Protestant sects. Methodists, Baptists and Presbyterians were generally dreaded as politically radical, uncouth, little lettered and socially unreliable.

But in the 1830's invigorating currents swept across the Anglican communion. Acts of Parliament prohibited clergymen from holding more than one parish and distributed ecclesiastical revenues more equitably. It was proposed in some circles that the Established Church should be detached from the state and that its special privileges should be cut down. The spread of secularism and of unconventional Christian ideas, moreover, challenged traditional Anglican beliefs.

Against that background the Oxford or Tractarian Movement emerged within the Anglican Church. Certain scholars at Oxford began in 1833 to issue "tracts for the times," crisp essays on Christian thought and practice which con-

John Henry Newman, sketched in 1841, the year in which he published Number 90 of Tracts for the Times *and drew the full fire of his fellow-Anglicans.*

tained Catholic interpretations and emphases, commonly regarded as popish. Tractarians asserted, for instance, the divine and supernatural origin of the Church and claimed continuity for Anglicanism with the pre-Reformation Church. If you strip Christianity of revelation and dogma, the Tractarians asked, so that everyone can believe in it, what will remain for anyone to believe in? If Christianity became too broad, they seemed to say, it would fall flat. Far from being mere pedantic ritualists, they counteracted the appeal of rationalism by insisting that it was precisely where reason ended that faith began.

The leading spirit of the Oxford Movement, John Henry Newman, caused a great stir when he entered (1845) the Catholic Church as a priest, carrying a few disciples with him. A persuasive preacher and author, Newman eventually was appointed a Cardinal.[2]

In spite of Newman's change of ecclesiastical allegiance, the Anglo-Catholic movement survived and indeed grew in popularity. Under its influence churchmen manifested greater spiritual zeal, public worship was brightened with music and emphasis was placed upon ceremonial ritualism. Theology hewed close to Catholic principles, repelling typically Protestant points of view. Lay organizations were founded to attract ordinary men and women to the "High Church" position. Friction between Anglo-Catholics and the "Low Church," or the more "Protestant" Anglicans, persisted until after World War I.

Promotion of foreign missions was a significant development in nineteenth-century Protestantism. Inspired by the evangelical enthusiasms of the time Protestant groups energetically set about converting heathen peoples who bowed down to wood and stone "from Greenland's icy mountain to India's coral strand." A powerful impulse was given to the cause of missions in Britain by William Carey, who was instrumental in founding the Baptist Missionary Society (1792), and who carried on pioneer evangelical work in India.

Better known as a propagator of the faith was the Scotsman, David Livingstone, assigned to Africa in 1840 as a representative of the London Missionary Society. After eighteen years of preaching and teaching he entered the service of the British crown doing much to tear the veil from the Dark Continent and to open it to Western influences. Scores of Protestant organizations despatched dedicated men and women to Africa and Asia on errands of conversion. Never before in history had so many peoples been brought into touch with Christian conceptions of the good life.[3] Missionaries

[2] Newman has been honored as the patron of Catholic clubs in colleges and universities of the United States.

[3] Protestant bodies in the United States, of course, played a larger role in missionary enterprise than their co-religionists in the Old World. The initial missionary society in the United States was the American Board of Commissioners for Foreign Missions organized in 1810 by the Congregational Church.

not only planted the seeds of Christianity but contributed, often unintentionally, to the diffusion of Western customs and ideas in general.

In carrying on their labors missionaries were signally aided by translations of the Bible into the tongues of the peoples to whom they ministered. Much the greater number of translations appeared under the imprint of the British and Foreign Bible Society organized (1804) for the exclusive purpose of facilitating wider "circulation of the Holy Scriptures without note or comment." Similar societies patterned on the British parent and financially assisted by it appeared on the Continent, the most active of them in Russia.[4] By the beginning of the twentieth century, the Scriptures were available in over 500 languages or dialects, a ten-fold growth in a hundred years.

Michael Faraday in old age. On the table beside him are grouped a Leyden jar and other instruments symbolic of his achievements in turning electricity to practical account.

SCIENCE IN REVIEW

Building impressively on the work of predecessors, men of science in the forepart of the nineteenth century enlarged understanding of the ways and whims of nature, of the physical and the biological world. Researches were practically applied in the ceaseless changes in industrial technology, in raising agricultural output, or improving the care of the human body. Some investigations, furthermore, altered the time span which had long been considered fixed and immutable, and ideas on the purpose of life and the destiny of the race were subtly influenced.

Fruitful results attended the exploration of the nature of electrical phenomena. French and German workers were rather overshadowed by the Briton, Michael Faraday. Among other things he discovered that the motion of a conductor in a magnetic field could produce an electric current. So the way was prepared for the crucial invention of the dynamo, rudimentary to be sure, to convert mechanical energy into electric power. It then became practicable to use electricity for illumination and as a means of transmitting power over long distances.

Basic to the general expansion of science was the gradual acceptance of the atomic theory, which assumed that everything was made up of tiny, indivisible particles or atoms. Like many another imagined scientific novelty, the atomic conception of the nature of matter was known to Greeks in antiquity. The studies and reasoning of an English chemist, John Dalton, formed the starting point for the fabulous—and explosive—chain of atomic developments. His inquiries into the "ultimate particles of bodies" led him to an understanding of the atomic structure on which the whole universe is built. The idea, moreover, had broader than scientific applications, for the atomic method of analysis invaded the whole realm of learning, until attempts at synthesis were decried as foolish or at any rate gravely unprofessional.

The pathway to German leadership in ap-

[4] The counterpart in the United States of the British society, the American Bible Society dates from 1816.

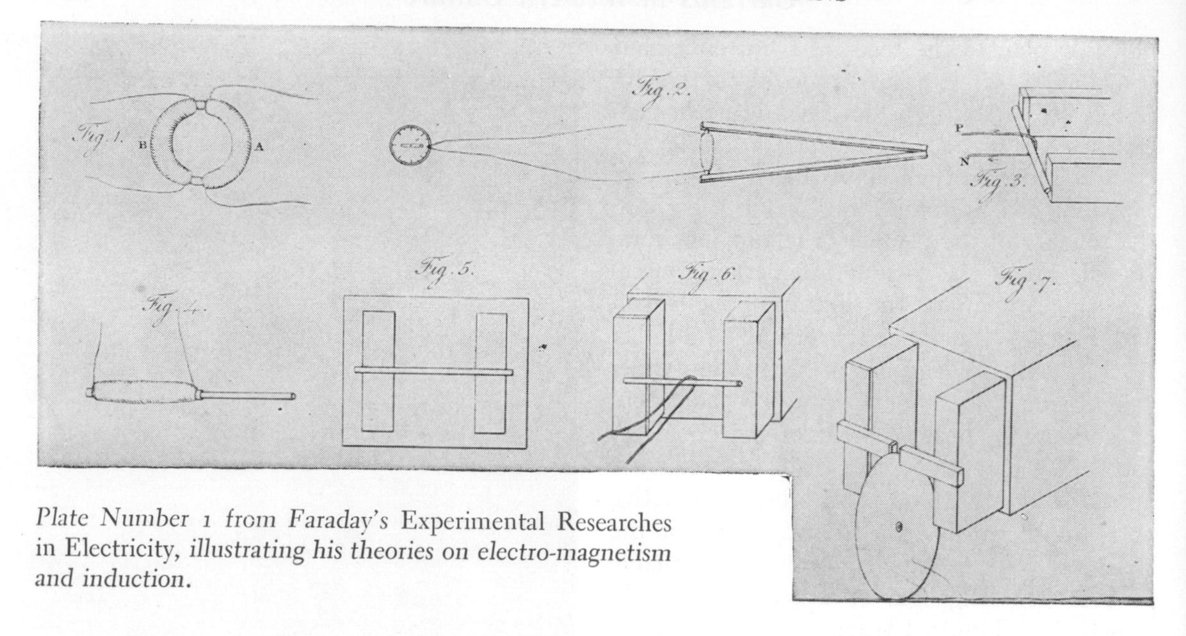

Plate Number 1 from Faraday's Experimental Researches in Electricity, *illustrating his theories on electro-magnetism and induction.*

plied chemistry was opened by Justus von Liebig. After studying in Paris, he laid out a unique laboratory at Giessen, near Frankfurt-am-Main, to train budding chemists. Other centers of learning copied that innovation and slowly the laboratory method of instruction in science was introduced into educational institutions at all levels. Liebig perfected techniques for analyzing organic compounds and enriched chemical knowledge of animal and vegetable matter. His discoveries on the magic of artificial fertilizers, for example, were widely and beneficently applied.

Chemistry joined with physics to give birth to photography. Search for a way to obtain permanent pictures by the prolonged play of sunlight on chemically sensitized plates resulted (1839) in the process coupled with the name of Louis J. Daguerre, French physicist. For moderate pocketbooks, daguerreotypes were a cheap substitute for expensive portraiture by painters.

Popular confidence in the methods of science was reinforced (1846) by the uncanny success of mathematicians in computing the exact location of an unknown planet, subsequently called Neptune. Astronomers identified ten times as many stars as the eighteenth century had known and the fanciful notion that the sun was inhabited was scientifically disproved.

Geology advanced in stature by reason of the studies of the British savant, Charles Lyell. Sweeping accumulated observations together, he published (1830–33) his epochal *Principles of Geology* in three volumes. The central the-

Louis J. Daguerre, a daguerreotype portrait

sis of the book was disclosed in the subtitle, "an attempt to explain the former changes of the earth's surface by reference to causes now in operation." Commonplace geologic activity, in other words, such as frost and rain had long and continuously operated to shape the surface of the earth. Revised editions of this masterpiece incorporated current discoveries in geology, including information picked up by Lyell in the United States. No other work so effectively promoted the progress of geologic science. Lyell was the recipient of extreme adulation from admirers and of caustic abuse from shocked contemporaries who believed that the earth had been specially created once for all time as related in the Hebrew Book of Genesis.

Speculation on organic evolution, meanwhile, had moved hesitantly forward. A remarkably coherent hypothesis was propounded by J. B. Lamarck, which still excites consideration and discussion. This French naturalist attributed observed differences in animals to gradual evolution from simpler forms due to the operation of changing environment upon physical structure. He suggested that new organs acquired by one generation could be and indeed were transmitted to the next.

The very idea of organic evolution set off a furious intellectual controversy, with Georges Cuvier, the most respected French scientist of the age, winning out over Lamarckism. Cuvier himself made fundamental studies of extinct vertebrates and comparative anatomy, yet he could not agree that one species of animal developed from another. To state the situation another way, he clung doggedly to the time-honored explanation of origins contained in Genesis. The future, however, would confirm the validity of the ancient maxim that "truth is the daughter of time"—and, it should be added, of dedicated study.

Not the least interesting facet of scientific learning of the early nineteenth century was the growth of knowledge on early human societies and fascinating archaeological speculations. French savants discovered how to decipher hieroglyphs on ancient Egyptian monuments, and presently excavations were started in Mesopotamia and other points in the Near East. These activities, which illustrate the insatiable curiosity of man about his ancestry, pushed the span of history steadily backward. Previously anyone who spoke of "ancient" civilization was understood as a matter of course to be referring to Greece and Rome; nowadays Greece and Rome seem recent indeed compared with Egypt and Babylonia.

Scholarship proceeded logically into the speculative domain of archaeology. As early as 1819, a Danish pioneer, Christian Thomsen, laid the foundation for prehistory. He suggested a three-age plan of prehistoric archaeology, stone, bronze and iron. Studies on the ethnic origins of men, investigations of the beginnings of social existence thousands of years before writing began, introduced a highly desirable perspective to the story of man on earth. Only slowly, however, did the implications of prehistory enter into the thought stream of the cultivated.

The establishment of the cell theory, putting biology on a solid basis, ranks with the major scientific achievements of the period. It was proved by Theodor Schwann (1839) that animals and plants were composed of many units or cells. Other German and French workers elucidated the nature of protoplasm and so prepared a scientific foundation for pathology, the science of disease. The art of auscultation, or listening to sounds produced in the chest by breathing and the action of the heart, and post-mortem pathology exploded old theories and made medical science more exact. These basic innovations were the achievement of French experimentalists in an era of singular brilliance in French medicine. A distinguished French physiologist, Claude Bernard, explained the vaso-motor systems and increased understanding of digestive processes, while Johannes P. Müller and his pupils in Germany discovered novelties about the blood, hearing, the voice and speech.

Paris became a mecca for surgical as well as medical training. Clinical and anatomical teaching there and the establishment of medical museums contributed fruitfully to advances in the treatment of the ailing. Students from Great Britain and the United States carried home the enthusiasms and the techniques which they learned in Paris. Physicians in the United States and Scotland proved the anaesthetic property of chloroform to deaden or reduce pain in surgery and in obstetrical practice.

Arguing against heavy dosages of drugs, Samuel C. Hahnemann, a German, founded the school of medicine spoken of as homeopathy. He insisted that nature be allowed to effect cures with a minimum use of medicines; aided by disciples he enriched knowledge on the curative properties and limitations of drugs. Though ridiculed by orthodox physicians, the principles of homeopathy spread from Germany outward, flourishing most luxuriantly in the New World.

TWO PHILOSOPHERS

This general survey of the higher living may fittingly be rounded off with some consideration of two systematic thinkers, Georg W. F. Hegel and Auguste Comte. The ideas of these men, the first a German, the other French, attracted respectful consideration while they lived and since.

The thinking of Hegel, it must be confessed, is extremely difficult to follow, likely to be unintelligible to the plain man without a gift for metaphysics. Of particular importance are his ideas on government and history and on the process of thought. By the time he was named to the chair of philosophy at the university of Berlin this austere thinker had turned into an extreme apologist of Prussian discipline and authority, as his famous book on *The Philosophy of Right* discloses. He has properly been tagged "the Aristotle of very modern authoritarianism."

According to Hegel, thinking proceeds by comparison and contrast of opposing ideas leading into a fresh synthesis. A given idea (or thesis), in other words, held the field until it was effectively challenged by its opposite (or antithesis). Out of the debate a third idea (or synthesis) emerged, more in keeping with the facts than the first two. The third idea stood until challenged by its opposite and so on down the corridors of time.

Following that dialectical formula Hegel pondered deeply on the nature of the state, which, he concluded, was "the Divine Idea as it exists on earth." Every state, he taught, was a law unto itself, and must settle disputes with other states by arms when necessary. Hegel was persuaded of the therapeutic value of war, for peace inescapably encouraged softness in a nation. As for the individual, he must submerge his identity in the community, in the state.

Hegel presumed, moreover, to interpret the whole panorama of the past in a grand plan of history (*The Philosophy of History*). History showed him the progressive development of the consciousness of man toward the goal of freedom; and yet, for practical purposes, freedom meant to Hegel an obligation to obey laws, to serve king and state. In every stage of history, it seemed to him, a chosen people predominated which had a supreme idea to confer upon society. That accomplished, the "world people" gave way to another chosen folk. In this evolution human personality played only a minor role; the importance of Alexander the Great and Charlemagne, for instance, arose from their ability to recognize that for which the time was ripe and to bring it to fulfillment, not from their personal qualities.

For the nineteenth century the Germans were the chosen people—a Hegelian notion which inspirited contemporaries eager for a united German nation. Hegel's deification of the state dignified nationalistic impulses in Germany, not excluding Nazi Germany, and chilled cosmopolitan ideals. The insignificance which he assigned to the individual delighted authoritarian men of action. Himself a conservative, the "German Edmund Burke" in a sense, though no mere dogmatic upholder of the status quo, Hegel turned out intellectual ammunition serviceable to political conservatism. But his teachings also encouraged rebels against the prevailing order, conspicuously Karl Marx and unorthodox Russian theorists who discovered that the safest way to propagate "dangerous thoughts" was in the form of commentaries on Hegelian philosophy.

Comte was cast in a different mold from

Hegel, reflecting in his thought the impact of unfolding science and of machinofacture. Comte in fact valued knowledge only as it might be practically applied to improve the material and social welfare of mankind. He regarded the individual as a social product rather than society as the product of individual men. Societies, not individuals, were the proper object of study and generalization. A humorless eccentric personality, Comte fancied himself a Messiah authorized to reconstruct society along "scientific" lines. He believed that there were discoverable laws of society—for which he invented the term "sociology"—as precise and binding as the fundamental axioms of natural science. Morality lay at the heart of his speculations and he bequeathed to posterity the word altruism, which he coined.

There is a good deal of indigestible food for thought in his encyclopedic books, *Positive Philosophy* (six volumes), and *Religion of Humanity*. Each department of knowledge, he asserted, moved through three stages, the theological, the metaphysical and on to the positivist or scientific. In this final stage knowledge would be grounded solely on facts. Sociology indeed had reached that maturity, and, under its direction, human society should be managed by high-minded, competent experts, clothed with authoritarian power. This regime would ensure to man the full benefits of the machine age and would eradicate abuses which had arisen.

Comte plotted, too, a cult of humanity, elaborately ritualistic, in which collective mankind would be venerated instead of the Supreme Being. For the worship of God he substituted the worship of the good. Wishful thinker that he was, Comte serenely imagined that Western Europe would presently unite in a republic of brotherly love, which, in turn, would lead all men everywhere to terrestrial perfection.

Comte's works or abridgments of them were avidly perused by eager minds desirious of social betterment from Russia to Mexico and back again. His teachings reinforced secularist and anticlerical tendencies and the agnosticism of the late nineteenth century. The quest for moral satisfactions through service to mankind owes something to the fertile imagination of Comte. He was a prime sower of the seed of evolutionary progress in which the next generation showed such confident faith.

FOR FURTHER STUDY

Leonard A. Willoughby, *The Romantic Movement in Germany* (Oxford, 1930)

Albert L. Guérard, *French Civilization in the Nineteenth Century* (New York, 1914)

Dmitrii S. Mirsky, *A History of Russian Literature* (new ed., New York, 1934) PAPERBACK

Van Wyck Brooks, *The Flowering of New England* (New York, 1936) PAPERBACK

George P. Gooch, *History and Historians in the Nineteenth Century* (new ed., London, 1952) PAPERBACK

Paul H. Láng, *Music in Western Civilization* (New York, 1941)

Béla Menczer, *Catholic Political Thought, 1789–1848* (London, 1952)

Edward C. Moore, *An Outline of the History of Christian Thought Since Kant* (New York, 1918)

Charles F. Harrold, *John Henry Newman* (New York, 1945)

Kenneth S. Latourette, *History of the Expansion of Christianity*, vol. IV, *The Great Century* (New York, 1941)

Gwilyn O. Griffith, *Interpreters of Man: Hegel to Barth* (London, 1943)

Albert J. George, *The Development of French Romanticism* (Syracuse, 1955)

Philip H. Spencer, *The Politics of Belief in Nineteenth Century France* (London, 1954)

Hans Kohn, *The Mind of Germany* (New York, 1960)

Jacques Barzun, *Berlioz and His Century* (New York, 1956) PAPERBACK

Brian Simon, *Studies in the History of Education* (London, 1960)

CHAPTER XVI

CONSOLIDATION OF THE NATIONS (1853-1871)

THE TEMPER OF THE TIME

THE European generation which reached maturity at the mid-nineteenth century lived through a series of international wars. Out of those struggles a united Italy and a united Germany were forged at the expense of Austria and France, and Russian pressure upon Turkey was checked, though indecisively. Diplomacy exalted rude force uninhibited by moral scruples or sense of responsibility to the European community.

Guided in their operations by state interests and by no other consideration, ethical or material, statesmen were ever ready to appeal to force or fear to settle controversies. Each considerable state exercised pressure of one kind and another upon other states. The conduct of affairs was severely pragmatic, unromantic, deceitful, for which a German journalist coined the term *Realpolitik*—and it stuck. Men remembered the bleak verdict of Thomas Hobbes in *Leviathan* on "the general inclination of mankind," that it is a "perpetuall and restless desire of power after power, that ceaseth only in death."

An assertive and more bellicose nationalism superseded the gentler variety of the forepart of the century. The difference was vividly illustrated in the contrasting personalities of Count Camillo Cavour, hardboiled maker of united Italy, and the idealistic dreamer, Mazzini. International peace societies which had met frequently in the preceding decade passed into eclipse. Outside of Europe, Japan in this period deliberately shed the cloak of the hermit, and North and South fought a desperate war in the United States. These countries, like Germany and Italy, soon claimed rank with the Great Powers.

As instruments of power politics, the military services, rather neglected since Waterloo, were "modernized." Armies were enlarged and supplied with more deadly weapons, while the rapid growth of railways created novel problems and opportunities for military strategists. And the advent of ironclads wrought radical changes upon naval warfare. State administrative services were expanded and made more efficient; duties of civil servants became more exacting.

Humanitarian instincts, on the other hand, alleviated some of the grosser horrors of war. It was prescribed in the Geneva Convention of 1864 that belligerents were obligated to care for wounded soldiers on the battlefield. The international Red Cross was organized to minister to the needs of injured combatants, and requisitioning of the property of citizens in war time declined.

FRANCE UNDER NAPOLEON III

Straining the evidence somewhat, Napoleon III has been described as a precursor of the arbitrary despots of the twentieth century. How he made himself master of France for a full generation has already been explained. Up to about 1860, the Napoleonic star seemed to be leading onward to a glorious destiny. Benevolent despotism was attended by "good times," and it won glittering triumphs in the arena of diplomacy and war. Then the scene shifted. Miscalculations and imprudences in foreign affairs provoked growing opposition in the cities especially, which forced democratic concessions. In 1870 the Second Empire crashed to inglorious destruction.

As Emperor, Napoleon III was very much an enigma—the Sphinx of the Tuileries. A dull man with a rather adolescent mind, he was unsuited for the role of arbitrary ruler which he adopted. Sly, vacillating, well-intentioned but utterly unpredictable, he could be, nevertheless, as ingratiating as any Bourbon grandee. A serious malady, which grew worse with time, impaired his capacity for judicious decision. And yet it is not necessary to accept fully the harsh description of the Emperor by Count Otto von Bismarck, "from afar something, close up nothing, a great misunderstood incompetence."

Napoleon III loved to appear before his subjects on horseback and he built up a gay and brilliant court which would have pleased Napoleon I or even Louis XIV. Social functions—fetes, balls, operas—featured the Emperor, with great waxed moustache and fashionable goatee, accompanied by the Empress Eugénie. This tall, handsome, red-haired Spanish countess was deeply devoted to Catholic interests and dabbled incautiously in politics. To reinforce the Napoleonic myth, to remind Frenchmen of the greatness of the founder of the Bonaparte dynasty, the emperor had vast quantities of the correspondence of Napoleon I published. Letters on the darker sides of the reign were, however, judiciously kept under lock and key. Sensitive to that elusive something called public opinion, Napoleon III instructed officials to report, in detail and frequently, on popular feelings and attitudes. Plebiscites were conducted occasionally, which allowed Frenchmen

Napoleon III, the Empress Eugénie, and the Prince Imperial

to do little more than say "amen" to what had already been decided upon.

France had hoisted Napoleon III to power as an answer to popular apprehensions and in the confidence that he would ensure order, prosperity and glory. He had promised that "the Empire means peace," and that future French conquests would take the form of religious revitalization, economic well-being and colonial development.

Under the constitution of the Second Empire legislative authority belonged to a senate, whose members were picked by the emperor, and a legislative assembly elected by manhood suffrage. Yet the latter was mere window-dressing since candidates were officially selected and state servants manipulated elections. Legislative sessions were secret, discussions stereotyped and sterile, the lawmakers mechanically acquiescing in ministerial proposals.

As for the ministry it was responsible to the crown; Napoleon III himself functioned in fact as prime minister. While he sometimes harkened to the counsel of advisers, he had no hesitancy in undertaking diplomatic commitments on his own responsibility or in inserting passages in public addresses of which ministers were ignorant. Appointments to policymaking posts were the prerogative of the Emperor. He broadened the powers of provincial prefects and relied upon them and the police to manipulate the machinery of local government.

This bureaucratic regime stifled freedom of expression and seriously curbed criticism of public policies. The press, for instance, was controlled by a monotonous round of warnings and fines, though rarely were papers forced to cease publication. Almost to a man, the literary world, staunchly republican, stood against the Napoleonic regime. The veteran and exiled champion of liberalism, Victor Hugo, poured out fierce philippics against the "worm Napoleon." Censors destroyed or banned circulation of books, such as the writings of Voltaire and Diderot, which were deemed undesirable. Professors who strayed beyond the narrow orbit of political orthodoxy were dismissed and universities passed under the surveillance of churchmen. Repudiating the tradition of free expression, the despotism of Napoleon III fancied that France could be ruled as though it were Turkey or Russia.

But it must also be said that the record of the Second Empire was not stained by ruthless purges and arbitrary executions. Compared with the Jacobin or with twentieth-century dictatorships, the rule of Napoleon III seems benevolently enlightened.

Army, bureaucracy, church, agricultural and business classes upheld the Second Empire in its palmy period. Once more it was demonstrated that most Frenchmen were conservatives at heart, not least on account of the basically agrarian character of the country. But the loyalty of churchmen sagged by reason of the course pursued by Napoleon in Italy and because of the curtailment of the ecclesiastical role in popular education. The need for greater attention to public schooling was pointedly revealed in 1859 when a third of the army recruits was unable to read and write and nearly half of all French brides could not so much as sign the marriage register.

Napoleon III and his henchmen could point with pride to the thriving condition of the national economy. Wealth probably increased more rapidly than in any previous period of French history. To cover deficits in the state budget, the government issued large public loans, purchased by little investors and big. Railway mileage increased sixfold, trans-Atlantic steamers were put into service and merchant shipping at Havre was surpassed only by London and Liverpool. French engineers and capital cut (1869) a canal across the Suez Isthmus, though not without stubborn resistance from Britain which feared for her Asiatic trade.

Factories and heavy industries, some of them beneficiaries of government subsidies, kept France second to Britain in manufacturing. Production of iron and coal in Lorraine moved steadily upward and the mills of Alsace turned out more cotton goods than were manufactured in all the German states. To foster commercial prosperity laws on joint stock companies were liberalized and new banking establishments were organized whose operations ranged across Europe.

Second Empire concepts of what constituted beauty of face, figure and fashion tended to the flamboyant. This painting of the Empress Eugenie and some of the ladies of her Court (the Empress is shown fourth from the right) is by F. X. Winterhalter, and is in its artifice and studied grace of pose a very expressive document of the era.

As a means of stimulating foreign commerce the Second Empire veered away from the protectionist dogma which France had followed since the first Napoleon. Paradoxically the authoritarian regime imposed upon the French middle classes liberal economic measures which in Britain were adopted by an enthusiastic middle class Parliament. A commercial treaty of 1860 with Britain lowered tariffs and encouraged a trend toward free trade throughout western Europe. For France as a whole the results were undoubtedly beneficial, though some industries suffered and some workers were displaced by foreign competition. Out of the profits from growing commercial activity, heavy investments were made in foreign countries.

The bourgeoisie benefited most obviously from the "good times," but the government did not entirely neglect the workers. Napoleon III in fact professed to be keenly interested in the extinction of poverty. To that end workmen were encouraged to organize cooperative societies to buy and sell goods. A start was made in insurance programs for workers in case of accident or upon death. The legality of trade unions and the right to strike were recognized; but Napoleon III never succeeded in winning the affections of the workingmen of Paris. Land reclamation schemes were pushed and peasants who profited from the general well being of the empire praised the name of their benefactor.

Public works projects, which glorified the reign and provided employment, claimed the special attention of Napoleon III. Outstanding was the reconstruction of down-town Paris under the skillful supervision of Baron Haussmann, city-planner *par excellence*. The government pulled "down a fourth part of the town," a hidebound curmudgeon lamented. Magnificent boulevards, splendid public buildings, large department stores and houses consolidated the reputation of Paris as the queen city of the world. It was the acknowledged international capital of fashion and culture, of gayety, frivolity and naughtiness; pleasure-seeking foreign plutocrats flocked to Paris in droves. Population increased to 1,800,000 by 1870 or nearly double that of a generation earlier, clear evidence of material prosperity.

AUTOCRACY IN DECLINE

Despite police, propaganda and prosperity, dissident voices were raised against the personal rule of Napoleon III. Elections in 1863 netted gains in Paris and other large cities for partisans of republicanism. The emperor nodded to the temper of the times by allowing a degree of independence in the legislative chamber, which whetted appetites for greater freedom, more democratic concessions.

Ecclesiastical and lay emotions were churned up by disasters in foreign affairs and republican and other elements clamored for an authentic parliamentary government and the restoration of the civil freedoms of the great French Revolution. Spirited barristers cherishing democratic convictions converted courtrooms into pulpits from which they flayed the veiled autocracy and preached republicanism. Manufacturers hurt by low tariffs and wage earners discontented with their lot aligned themselves in the opposition camp.

Seeking to placate the appeasable, the rapidly aging Napoleon III suddenly and discreetly relaxed (1867) press regulations and permitted more freedom in elections and in debate in the imperial legislature. A dangerous and revolutionary press immediately burst out in furious attacks upon the very foundations of the empire. Presently the ministry was made responsible to the elected lawmakers, who were also allowed to initiate proposals for law. The wheel of government, in a word, had turned full circle. A parliamentary regime, responsive to the general will, had come into being and it was overwhelmingly approved (1870) in a national referendum.

But in a matter of months the "new order" had been swept into the discard as a result of the defeat of France in war with Germany. As that conflict approached, however, the forces of republicanism, hostile to Napoleon III though they were, rallied loyally to the defense of French interests. Love of country crowded ideological principles aside.

FRENCH FOREIGN ADVENTURES

"The Empire means peace," Napoleon III promised. Yet in fact the empire meant restless searching for popularity, more empire and war. In the conduct of foreign policy Napoleon III —and final decisions were taken by him—like many another dictator, resembled a bicyclist who had to keep pedaling else he would fall to the earth. The Emperor and his advisers lurched from one diplomatic adventure to another without ever understanding the reasons for failure. They wished to uphold national honor without courting the risk of war; they wished to preserve the peace without making sacrifices.

The very name of Napoleon argued that he would seek fame and glory as indeed he did—in Asia, in Africa, in America, in Europe. The Emperor counted upon successes abroad to bedazzle his subjects and to shore up the dynasty at home. And deep down, this quixotic crusader believed he had a mission to promote the democratic ideal of national self-determination, as the way to international peace. It was the tragedy of the Second Empire that the military resources of the country were unequal to the demands which diplomacy made upon them.

More than once, the Napoleonic Empire interfered in Asiatic affairs. War was waged against China, for instance, in conjunction with Great Britain and expeditions to Indo-China prepared the way for an impressive French colony in that peninsula. France, moreover, reasserted herself as protector of Roman Catholic interests in Syria and picked up island clusters in the South Pacific. Similarly in Africa, French lordship over Algeria, over Senegal on the west coast, and over Madagascar was either consolidated or asserted, and French interests which dug the Suez Canal were active in Egypt.

But the most fantastic Napoleonic adventure overseas had Mexico as its stage. Initially France intervened (1861) with Britain to collect debts owed their nationals by citizens of Mexico, but after Britain withdrew Napoleon III plunged ahead with a grandiose design to create a Latin Catholic empire in the New World. Success in the undertaking would surely have gratified French Catholics, opened up broader commercial opportunities and generally heightened the prestige of the Napoleonic regime. Nearly 40,000 French troops were thrown against savage Mexican guerilla fighters, and an unemployed Austrian Archduke, Maximilian, was proclaimed Emperor of Mexico.

The United States, which was immersed in the War between the States when the French adventure began, protested militantly in the name of the "hands-off" principle of the Monroe Doctrine. And after the surrender of Lee at Appomattox, Washington threatened to expel the French army by physical force. That prospect, criticism at home over the Mexican

An American comment on French ambitions in Mexico, 1862—Brother Jonathan advises Napoleon III to take his poodle off the premises

fantasy, so costly in blood and treasure, and above all perhaps, the menacing turn of events in central Europe forced Napoleon III to abandon the gleaming vision of empire in the New World. After the French evacuation, Maximilian fell before a Mexican firing squad. For the Second Empire the reckless enterprise in America was not only a national disgrace, it was an irretrievable fiasco. Victor Hugo warned his countrymen that the Napoleonic sands had run out.

What then of Napoleonic diplomacy in Europe itself? As early as 1854 the much vaunted professions of peace were cast to the winds as France, aligning with Britain, took up arms against Russia in the Crimean War (p. 485). That bid for imperial glory, that gesture of support for Catholic interests, that effort to avenge the Russian humiliation of Napoleon I, that extravagant expenditure of lives and francs paid only tinsel dividends.

It was heartening of course to French pride that the congress which wrote the treaty of peace convened in Paris. The international standing of France touched heights unexampled since Waterloo and the popularity of the parvenu Emperor rose correspondingly. While the principal business of the meeting was the adjustment of Near Eastern issues, significant understandings on maritime warfare were also agreed upon.[1]

French participation in the Crimean War was not easily forgotten by Russian policy-makers. And tempers were not at all sweetened by Napoleonic sponsorship of the unification of the Balkan state of Rumania (1859). Relations were definitely worsened when Napoleon III spoke incautiously about intervention on behalf of oppressed Poles who rebelled against tsarist rule in 1863. Equally the diplomacy of the Second Empire with reference to the Italian peninsula worked out harmfully. As a youth Napoleon had believed that Italy should be united and as master of France he wanted to play the diplomatic cards so that France would profit from the way in which unification was achieved. In his more romantic moods the Emperor even envisaged a federal union of all Latin nations.

French clericals, on the other hand, were strong partisans of the Papacy, averse to any change in Italy that might impair papal sovereignty over the States of the Church. Napoleon found himself, consequently, on the horns of a dilemma and both prongs were sharp. By furthering the cause of a united Italy he curried favor with French liberalism but by the same token he antagonized the clericals; when he reversed the field and fortified papal authority with French bayonets, churchmen were happy and liberals angrily critical. Out of the Italian transactions France acquired the districts of Savoy and Nice, which tickled national self-esteem but excited suspicions in Britain that the new Bonaparte harbored ambitions of wider territorial aggrandizement.

Napoleonic diplomacy in central Europe culminated in ignominious disaster. In that area the principal aims of France were, first, to prevent either Prussia or Austria from growing so powerful that they might imperil French security, and, second, to push out the frontiers of France in emulation of Napoleon I. Pursuit of those objectives, coupled with the dynamic of German nationalism, eventually tumbled the Second Empire into the dustbin of history.

THE MAKING OF ITALY

After the mid-century revolutions Italy remained a disjointed geographical expression with Austria as firmly entrenched as mistress of the peninsula as ever. Italian partisans of national independence were still radically divided in mind, some preferring a centralized monarchy headed by Piedmont (Sardinia), others desiring a republic, others some form of loose federal union. "Whoever disregards local patriotism in Italy," a knowing voice remarked, "will always build on sand."

In the end it was the Piedmont solution of Italian unity which was actually applied. That small state had emerged from the revolutionary tumult of 1848 with a constitution resting upon enlightened principles and with a new sov-

[1] The use of privateers was outlawed, a blockade of an enemy country had to be effective in order to be binding on other countries and neutral rights on the high seas in wartime were more sharply defined.

ereign, Victor Emmanuel II, vulgar and dissolute, but a patriot willing to follow resolute leadership or to goad it into action. Liberally minded refugees from all over the peninsula flocked to the freer atmosphere of Piedmont; thirsting for unity, patriots often accused slow-moving Piedmont of stolidity.

It was apparent, however, to the more realistic advocates of Italian nationhood that the elimination of Austria required outside aid. The France of Napoleon III seemed the best bet; certainly Piedmont with only 5,000,000 inhabitants could not lead from strength. If she were to be the core round which the Italian states would cluster, recourse to stealthy political intrigue and the stratagems of diplomacy were necessary. By happy coincidence the requirement of the hour was matched by the man, Count Camillo Cavour. Here was a unique personality, fascinating, a diplomatic virtuoso, equipped with wide experience and a sense of history. Stumpy in figure, owlish in face, and always wearing fierce spectacles Cavour looked like an inconsequential research chemist in an out-of-the-way German laboratory.

Studies in Britain had taught him admiring respect for the political institutions and habits of the island kingdom. As a journalist, progressive farmer and industrial promoter Cavour earned a reputation for himself before plunging into politics and rising to the dignity of statesman. His conception of statecraft was distinguished by breadth of vision, no little idealism, realism of approach, flexibility, subtlety and sanity—altogether a rare combination. As became the leader of a small state with large ambitions, Cavour was not always scrupulous in the means he employed to attain his ends. "If we were to do for ourselves what we are doing for Italy," he reminded colleagues, in the language of *Realpolitik*, "we should be great rogues."

At the age of forty-two, Cavour was summoned to the premiership of Piedmont. His energies at first were concentrated on strengthening the state by cutting down ecclesiastical privileges in keeping with his formula of a "free church in a free state," by expanding the fighting services and by fostering economic advancement. Commerce was quickened by removal of internal duties, lowering tariffs on imports and the building of railways, which of course had strategic value too. These innovations raised the stature of Piedmont in the eyes of patriotic bourgeois Italians everywhere. To secure the enactment of laws he desired, Cavour employed no little chicanery and "jockeying" with Piedmontese deputies.

As his supreme goal, Cavour set the independence of Italy from Austrian control and influence. To that end, he wished, in particular, to add the Austrian-held provinces of Lombardy and Venetia to the patrimony of Piedmont. And in time, slowly and with much misgiving, he came to the conclusion that only a united kingdom of Italy would ensure the independence of the peninsula. Under pressure from Victor Emmanuel II, with whom he repeatedly exchanged angry words, and on urgings from Britain and France, Cavour, against his own best judgment, carried Piedmont into the Crimean War. The Italian state had no quarrel whatsoever with Russia, so that the intervention was pure showmanship, a deliberate publicity gesture to advertise the quality of Piedmont and to bring the problem of Italy before the bar of European opinion.

One out of seven of the Piedmontese soldiers perished in the war, no territorial or financial gains accrued to their country, but the Italian question was ventilated at the Paris peace conference. It was sweet music to the ears of Italian patriots to hear the principal British representative upbraid the government of the Papal States as scandalous. Cavour himself described the Italian scene in tones of studied moderation, winning British and French applause—and dark reproaches from the Austrian side. His ambition to acquire for Piedmont one or more of the small duchies in north central Italy was frustrated.

From words Cavour passed to conspiracy and then to deeds. At a secret meeting with friendly Napoleon III in the isolated village of Plombières in the Vosges, the two adventurers struck (1858) a momentous bargain. French armies would fight shoulder to shoulder with

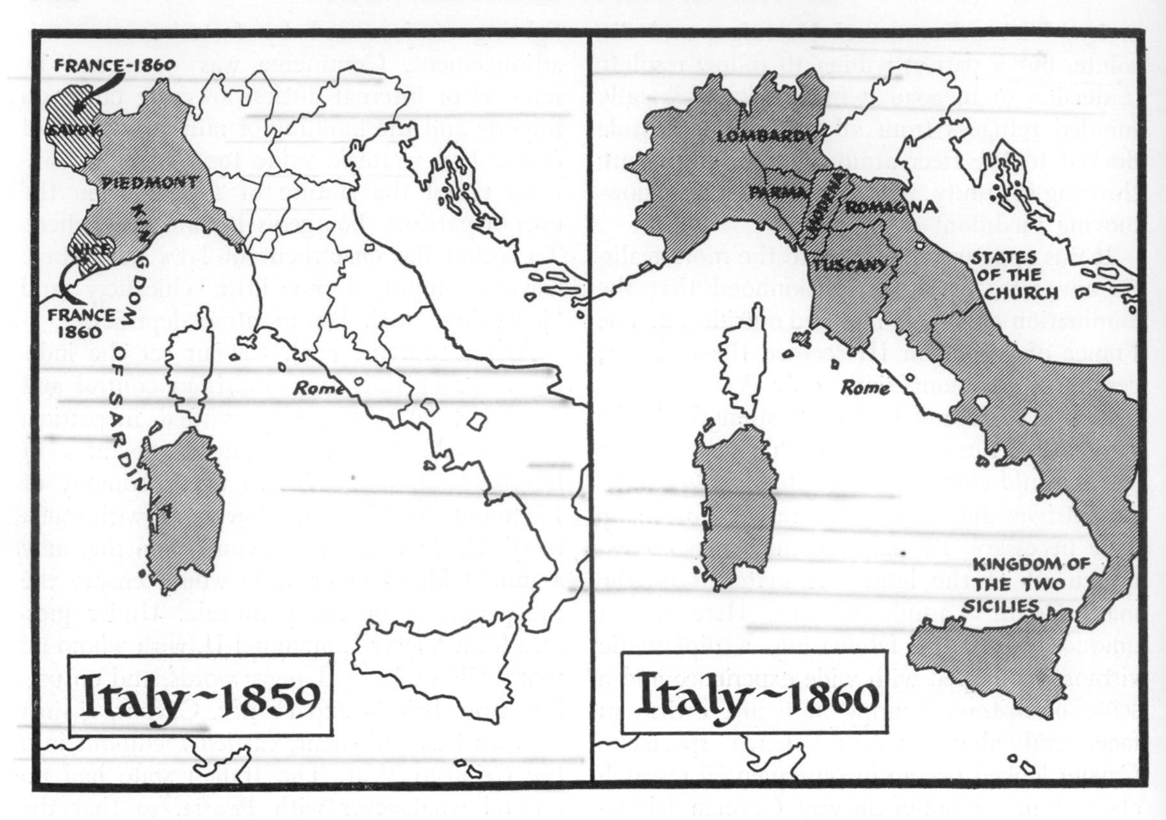
FRANCE-1860
SAVOY
PIEDMONT
KINGDOM OF SARDINIA
NICE
FRANCE 1860
Rome
Italy~1859
LOMBARDY
PARMA
MODENA
ROMAGNA
TUSCANY
STATES OF THE CHURCH
Rome
KINGDOM OF THE TWO SICILIES
Italy~1860

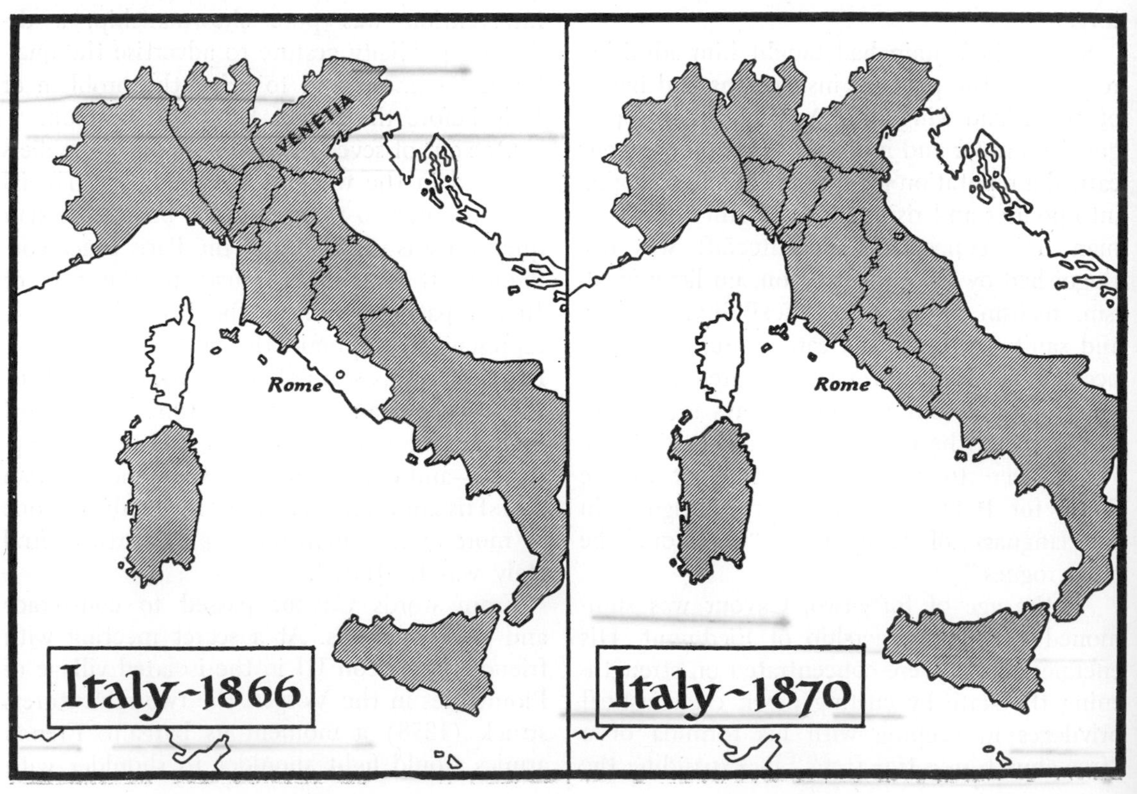
VENETIA
Rome
Italy~1866
Rome
Italy~1870

Piedmont in expelling Austria from Lombardy and Venetia. That accomplished, a kingdom of north Italy would be organized and, with the rest of the peninsula, would form a confederation under the honorary presidency of the Pope. Naively the French emperor supposed that this arrangement would advance the cause of Italian unity while adequately safeguarding papal interests. As compensation for French help, Cavour, in defiance of the Piedmont constitution, promised to cede Savoy and Nice.

Implementation of the Plombières plot rested largely with Cavour, who in 1859 deliberately provoked Austria into a declaration of war. In cruel battles at Magenta and Solferino in Lombardy, French and Piedmontese armies soundly thrashed the Austrian forces. If these successes by the soldiers of Napoleon III were not of the magnitude of the triumphs of Napoleon I in Italy they were nonetheless unmistakable victories. Austria retreated from Lombardy. At that juncture Napoleon III developed a crippling case of moral paralysis. His tender spirit had been wounded by the bloodspilling, unrest was mounting among French Catholics, who feared for papal independence, and Prussian armies were assembling ominously in the Rhineland.

Under these circumstances, the Emperor abruptly broke off the fighting and negotiated the armistice of Villafranca with Austria (July, 1859). By that agreement only Lombardy was released to Piedmont, Austria retaining choice Venetia. The craven defection of Napoleon dealt a heavy blow to Italian dreams. Cavour, a sadder but in some respects a wiser man, blurted out that "the Emperor has dishonored me before my King." In high anger he resigned as prime minister, but presently he concluded that the best way to save face was to keep the lower part of it closed, and he returned to office.

National patriots in north central Italy, meantime, secretly abetted by Piedmont, had driven petty rulers away and seized control of papal Romagna. When application for union with Piedmont was made Cavour approved with alacrity. Napoleon III now claimed his pounds of flesh—Savoy and Nice. More or less artfully managed plebiscites ratified these transactions.

Giuseppe Garibaldi

It was then the turn of southern Italy—the benighted and backward Kingdom of the Two Sicilies. And there the key figure was the legend-encrusted, veteran republican Giuseppe Garibaldi. Politically inastute and contemptuous of diplomatic protocol, this simple sturdy patriot with the brains of an ox and the heart of a lion gathered together about a thousand red-shirted buccaneers to bring the Two Sicilies into the Italian national fold.[2]

When Garibaldi's expedition set off from

[2] A distinguished British historian, G. M. Trevelyan, chose Garibaldi for detailed study as the most poetic and appealing theme of the nineteenth century.

Garibaldi enters Naples—a sketch made in the Strada di Toledo by Thomas Nast

Genoa for the south, the Piedmont authorities turned a blind eye and British naval units benevolently prevented attack by the Neapolitan fleet. The occupation of Sicily and then of the mainland of Naples presented few difficulties, had something of the appearance indeed of a picturesque parade. Garibaldi soon announced his intention of thrusting into the papal domains. That news alarmed Cavour who dreaded lest France should intervene to protect the Pope. First he negotiated an understanding with Napoleon III, guaranteeing Rome to the Vatican, and then he hustled Piedmontese regulars into the eastern States of the Church and annexed the region. Next the royal army advanced into Naples. Patriotically Garibaldi handed over the Kingdom of the Two Sicilies to Victor Emmanuel II and once more popular referenda sealed the work of unity almost unanimously.[3]

[3] In the city of Naples, for example, only thirty-one dissenting votes were registered out of 106,000 eligibles.

Early in 1861, the Kingdom of Italy, with nearly 25,000,000 inhabitants, was formally proclaimed. The administrative and parliamentary institutions and centralized bureaucracy of Piedmont were fitted to the whole country and Victor Emmanuel II was saluted as the king of Italy. Italy of the Italians was not, however, complete, for outside were the Austrian province of Venetia and its environs and about a quarter of the erstwhile States of the Church. Garrisoned by soldiers of Napoleon III, the papal fragment included Rome, and "without Rome Italy is nothing," someone muttered.

Cavour passed away prematurely in 1861, elated by what had been accomplished even though he wondered whether the kingdom would hold together. He had contributed notably to the principles of ministerial responsibility and to parliamentary supremacy in Italy which lasted until the victory of the Fascism of Mussolini. But, on the other side, to the new Italy he bequeathed enduring traditions of devious manipulation in parliamentary affairs and a heritage of *Realpolitik*, of deceit, guile and duplicity in conducting diplomatic transactions. Nonetheless, he stands unchallenged and unchallengeable among the makers of modern Italy.

The heirs of Cavour cleverly exploited international complications to carry forward the task of national consolidation. Venetia was wrested from Austria after the War of 1866 (p. 374), in which Italy was allied with Prussia against the Hapsburg power. The fighting services of Victor Emmanuel suffered humiliating reverses on land and sea, but in defeat there was victory, for Prussia triumphed in the north and rewarded Italy with Venetia. In keeping with custom, a plebiscite confirmed the union.

The last parcel of papal territory joined the Italian Kingdom as a result of the French War of 1870 with the German states. So long as soldiers of France lingered in Rome the prospect of acquiring the area was remote indeed. Italian statesmen, it is true, tried to bargain with the Vatican, proposing that the Pope surrender his territory, in exchange for assurances of unfettered papal freedom and financial compensation, but to no avail. Garibaldi led volunteers in vain forays onto Roman soil, which merely enhanced the popularity of the red-shirted hero as the supreme personification of Italian patriotism and unity. But in 1870 Napoleon III called his troops home to fight the onrushing Germans. Their departure gave the cue to Italy to take over Rome. On September 20, 1870, thereafter celebrated as a national holiday, the walls of the Eternal City were breached and royal troops filed through. In a referendum 133,000 voters cast for union with Italy with only 1,500 opposed. Forthwith Rome was proclaimed the capital of the Italian nation.

At long last the goal of national unity which had animated Italian prophet and poet from Dante onward had been crossed—or very nearly that, for Austria still ruled districts peopled by Italian-speaking folk. But the attainment of physical consolidation left the nation spiritually exhausted, saddled with an unhealthy deficit and confronted by formidable problems. "Now the prose," King Victor Emmanuel warned, "must follow the poetry."

Not least of the problems was the hostile attitude of the Vatican. Pope Pius IX excommunicated the "robber king" and spurned overtures of reconciliation made by the Italian government. He insisted that for full independence he must have temporal authority over at least a parcel of territory. Catholics were instructed

Italian troops attacking through a breach in the walls of Rome near the Villa Bonaparte, September, 1870

not to take part in Italian political affairs and for half a century relations between Vatican and Kingdom remained severely strained.

Beyond that, the Kingdom of Italy had been built by only a fraction of the population, mainly the middle classes. For the masses, who were unenfranchised, the notion of a free government held precious little meaning. And local loyalties had not been much diminished; Italian psychological unity was desperately incomplete. "We have made Italy," observed a senior statesman, "now we must make Italians."

Time and patience would be required to smooth out the sectional divergencies between North and South, between forward-looking Piedmont and Lombardy and the long misgoverned and heavily illiterate Two Sicilies. The development of a sense of national consciousness was no light assignment, "harder than fighting Austria or struggling with Rome," Cavour had sagely prophesied. And there was no commanding personality, no Cavour, no Washington to steer the new ship of state across rough and uncharted waters.

PRUSSIA AND BISMARCK

While the consolidation of Italy moved methodically forward, a similar process unfolded in Germany. Prussia was the Piedmont in the German piece and here again Napoleon III and Austria were deeply—and disastrously—involved. The ideal of German unification on democratic foundations had sustained decisive defeat in the events of 1848–1849. It was only with reluctance that many a German liberal resigned himself to having union brought to pass through the instrumentality of illiberal Prussia.

After groveling abjectly before Austria (p. 332) in the competition for leadership of German Europe, Prussia hastened to strengthen herself in preparation for the next encounter. She commanded of course a serviceable asset in the customs-union or *Zollverein* embracing most of the German states. Prussia had also secured a constitution (1850), which authorized a legislature of two houses, the upper branch aristocratic, the lower popularly elected on an inequitable class basis. In the fifties and sixties the Kingdom was greatly invigorated along economic and military lines.

It is an axiom that the power of a modern state depends in the final analysis upon industrial resources and capacity to fight. After 1850 foundations were solidly laid for the phenomenal material progress which Germany experienced later in the century. The unification of Germany was as much the work of coal and iron as of blood and iron. Production of coal, iron and steel increased swiftly, so that in 1870 the German states were far ahead of France in coal output and at least abreast of France in heavy industry. In the valley of the Ruhr, which developed fast after 1850, Prussia possessed the largest stock of coking coal in Europe.

In that district the growth of the House of Krupp was a crucial fact of the era. Krupp factories turned out all manner of iron products, especially railway equipment, before winning international fame for small arms and heavy guns, such as breach-loading cannon. Apart from its role as official munitions manufacturer for Prussia, the Krupp firm delivered military supplies to neighboring countries. The head of the company, Alfred Krupp, was inducted into the Legion of Honor by Napoleon III and Russia honored him with a knighthood of the Order of Peter the Great. He ranks with the statesman Bismarck and Moltke the soldier as a builder of modern Germany.

In the Germanies as elsewhere on the Continent at the time, transportation facilities were much enlarged. By 1870 a web of some 12,000 miles of German railways was in service and they were of the utmost importance in stimulating the progress of business and to the military strategist. Railway power meant to a continental state what seapower did to Britain. The celebrated German steamship lines, the Hamburg-America and the North German Lloyd, had already started operations, though British ships still hauled the bulk of German foreign trade.

Expansion of Prussian military resources paralleled the growth of economic power. The army was the particular pet and pride of King William I, who became the real ruler in 1857, as it had been for other Hohenzollern sovereigns. Thoroughly the soldier in outlook, simple and obstinate in his habits, cautious in disposition, William I believed implictly that a Higher Power had ordained him to rule. Popular control over public policies was anathema to him. Given that attitude a quarrel between the monarch and progressive spirits in this Prussian land of contrasts was almost certain to arise.

There was no question of the obedience, loyalty and conservatism of the bulk of Junker squirearchs dwelling in the feudal environment of their estates east of the Elbe. By inheritance and training they were a stiff caste, socially arrogant, intellectually narrow, but intensely convinced of their duties to authoritarian king and kingdom. The strength of liberalism, on the other side, lay with middle classes of the expanding Prussian cities and with the peasant proprietors of the Catholic Rhineland, some of whom had been touched by French or British ideas on the nature of good government or by liberal practices in small nearby German states.

As partners in a program to build up the Prussian army, William I enlisted two of the most competent military minds of the modern age: Helmuth von Moltke, chief of the general staff, and Albrecht von Roon. Devoted servants of the crown and ardent nationalists both, the first excelled in planning campaigns, the other in army administration. Together they worked out plans which would nearly double the standing army, equip it with the latest tools of war and raise training to the peak of perfection. To carry out the plans would be very expensive by the standards of the time.

When the army program was presented (1861) to the lower branch of the Prussian legislature, liberal deputies, a majority of all, balked. They insisted that the ministry must be made subservient to the legislature after the manner of Great Britain, called for reformation in the make-up of the upper chamber and refused to vote taxes to implement the military bills. That stand marked the high point in the history of political liberalism in Prussia. Crown and deputies collided head on, bringing the machinery of government to a standstill.

Otto von Bismarck, symbol of German strength

The disgusted monarch in desperation even contemplated abdicating the throne.

On the recommendation of von Roon, however, Otto von Bismarck (1815–1898) was appointed minister president of Prussia. He was reputed to be a strong man, as in fact he was, able and ready to ride ruthlessly over the liberal insurgency. With Bismarck we come face to face with the leading public figure of the nineteenth century, the chief artisan of German national unity, the supreme practitioner of *Realpolitik*, the master mind of European diplomacy for almost three decades.

Born in the year of Waterloo, Bismarck belonged to the old-line Pomeranian aristocracy and displayed in tastes and crudities the standard traits of the Junker caste. Tall, amply proportioned, hewn from granite, he seemed to be a giant out of an ancient Teutonic folk tale, though his voice resembled the high soprano of a schoolgirl. As a university student he had made his mark as an expert swordsman, not in academic studies. For food, sport and books he had a gargantuan appetite, though the rough school of experience taught him more than reading.

Neither art nor music had much attraction for this philistine and his living habits were severely spartan. On a visit to England he relished the spectacle of lords mounted on horseback and the privilege granted him in restaurants of carving and devouring as much meat as he liked. Unlike Cavour, Bismarck cared not a fig for British parliamentary institutions and civil liberties—quite otherwise.

After a stint as a local civil servant and as manager of the family properties Bismarck appeared as a deputy in the Prussian royal assembly. Having tasted the fruit of the tree of political knowledge, he decided that he would eat nothing else. During the political storms of 1848 the Junker squire stood out as a brusque Prussian patriot, thoroughly opposed to the unity of Germany and a fearless and rabid champion of royal authoritarianism. For eight years he represented Prussia in the assembly of the Germanic Confederation. His official reports were instructive masterpieces of their kind and fellow delegates were duly impressed with the native abilities and the tireless industry of the man.

At sessions of the assembly Bismarck quarreled venomously with the Austrian representatives, hurling sharply barbed insults at them. Slowly he came round to the conclusion that Prussia must solve the age-old German political problem. Thenceforth it became the central purpose of his life to assist in making Prussia

"Will the Prussian Hercules be able to lift it?" the peoples of Europe ask in this Daumier cartoon. The weights represent the vast war budget of Prussia.

the dominant factor in Germany first, and after that in Europe. The Prussian patriot, in a phrase, had matured as a German nationalist.

From 1859 to 1861 Bismarck served Prussia as ambassador in St. Petersburg and for a shorter period at the Court of Napoleon III. Those assignments enabled him to form valuable personal estimates of men and conditions. All in all his knowledge of German affairs and of European politics was unrivaled. "Take care of that man," Disraeli warned after hearing Bismarck discourse on the subject of a united Germany, "he means what he says."

Appraising the many-sided personality of this almost superhuman mortal, a learned biographer, Edward Eyck, has written:

> He could be as supple as a courtier, as polite and accomplished as a marquis of the old school, as contemptuous and satirical as Heine, sensitive as a poet, but also hard and brutal as a Renaissance despot, sly as a fox, bold as a lion. Rarely has nature dealt more lavishly with any human being. Yet she denied him the sense of right and justice. So he stands among the giants, a figure not to love and still less to imitate, but to study and despite his limitations, to admire.

Upon assuming the headship of the Prussian ministry of 1862 Bismarck bluntly informed Prussia and the wider world how state business would be carried on. "The great questions of the day," he thundered, "will not be decided by speeches and resolutions of majorities—that was the blunder of 1848 and 1849—but by blood and iron." That pugnacious utterance dispelled any lingering doubts that a strong hand had grasped the Prussian tiller. Liberal deputies angrily flayed the man but his professional hide was tough and he was not one to be trapped in his own rhetoric.

Bismarck thoroughly detested liberalism and everything it implied, and liberals despised him and everything associated with him. Only the king and the Almighty could issue orders to the arrogant, outspoken Junker, and sometimes the king was impotent. Bismarck proceeded to collect the taxes for the army expansion program without legislative concurrence and a mighty machine of war was quickly fashioned. Unfriendly newspapers were muzzled and the civil service was purged of men tainted with liberal heresies.

THE ROAD TO GERMAN UNITY

The mind of Bismarck was restlessly preoccupied with ways and means of consolidating Germany under the aegis of Prussia. First in line, Austria would have to be expelled from the German house and then by hook or crook, by force or cajolery the litter of German states would be politically linked to Prussia. In the prodigious designs which he unrolled the audacious Bismarck, like a clever chess player, was customarily a considerable number of moves ahead of opponents.

The years from 1864 to 1871 witnessed the most stupendous events in European political history between Waterloo and the First World War—the physical expulsion of Austria from German affairs, the conquest of France by Germany in the most momentous of nineteenth-century wars and the dramatic proclamation of the German Empire. Without recourse to arms, it is extremely improbable that Germany, any more than Italy, could have been consolidated.

As a kind of preface to the epochal work of national union, Bismarckian Prussia aided (1863) Imperial Russia in crushing a Polish insurrection. By that gesture Russian friendliness toward Prussia, ever a cardinal point in Bismarckian statecraft, was cemented; in the ensuing wars for German unity, the benevolent neutrality of Russia served Prussia handsomely. The elimination of Austria from German Europe was the end result of an acrimonious controversy over the two small duchies of Schleswig and Holstein, lying to the south of Denmark. Though they had long been governed by the king of Denmark, most of the inhabitants spoke the German language, the rest Danish. It is unnecessary to probe into the tangled intricacies of the Schleswig-Holstein problem, which baffled statesmen then as it has harassed historians since.

When in 1863 the Danish ruler presumed to merge Holstein with his kingdom, nationalism in Prussia and other German states exploded. Bismarck scented an opportunity to pick up territory, and he personally considered his handling of the Schleswig-Holstein business as the choicest specimen of his diplomatic craftsmanship. Armies of Prussia and Austria marched (1864) into the disputed provinces, Denmark gallantly resisting but without success. It was the first of three *Blitzkriege*, short and snappy, in which the "modernized" Prussian army had a chance to prove its mettle.

Help which Denmark expected to receive from outside never materialized. British statesmen talked, but preferred to hold to diplomatic aloofness, to splendid isolation, and thereafter Bismarck almost ignored the island realm in his calculations. "I wasted several years of my life," he confessed, "in the supposition that England was a great nation." Nor did the France of Napoleon move a single soldier to succor Denmark.

Scarcely had Schleswig-Holstein been detached from the Danish crown, than Austria and Prussia fell to quarreling. Nominally the dispute hinged upon the division of the spoils, but the fundamental issue was which of the rivals should be master of central Europe. With dark clouds of war lowering, Bismarck assured himself of Italian support by promises of the Austrian province of Venetia. Most of the smaller German states, on the other side, apprehensive of Prussian domination, rallied round the Hapsburg Empire. Fighting broke out in 1866, a war which the Prussian strategist Moltke pithily described as "long-planned, quietly prepared for and fought not for the acquisition of land or increase of territory, but for an ideal and—for a position of power."

In its larger perspectives the War of 1866 was a conflict within the German household, a brothers' war somewhat akin to the conflict in the United States which had ceased just before the guns cut loose in central Europe. In both cases the more industrialized and probably the more spirited north overwhelmed the southern adversary. To the surprise and consternation of Europe, Prussia vanquished her enemies in a few short weeks. Superior Prussian armament, stronger morale, skillful exploitation of railways, masterly manipulation of manpower quickly brought Austria to her knees. A resounding and decisive drubbing was administered to the Hapsburg forces at Sadowa in Bohemia in July of 1866. By pinning down Austrian resources in the south Italy contributed to the lightning Prussian triumph.

Considering the magnitude of the victory, Prussia imposed decidedly lenient terms of peace upon Austria, treated her more considerately than the North did the South in the United States after 1865. The moribund German Confederation was scrapped, which eliminated the House of Hapsburg from German politics. For Vienna that was a bitter pill but it had to be gulped down. Austria ceded Venetia to Italy, though it had to pay only a token war indemnity. "Not a foot of land," to quote Moltke again, "was exacted from Austria by Prussia, but she had to renounce all part in the hegemony of Germany."

If William I and the generals had had their way the Austrian sacrifices would have been much heavier. But Bismarck, his eye focused cannily on the future, persuaded them to be content with a mild settlement. After Sadowa, Viennese policymakers thirsted for revenge, and yet within a dozen years Bismarck contrived an alliance with Austria which lasted until the end of World War I. The German master handled the diplomatic cards with an astuteness rarely equalled and seldom surpassed.[4]

On the morrow of the War of 1866 most of the small states of northern Germany, Schleswig-Holstein among them, were annexed to Prussia, and the rest, as is indicated below, were drawn into the North German Confederation. Presently the south German powerlets signed secret treaties of alliance with Prussia. Bavaria, for example, had much more in common with Austria than with Prussia, but the flowing tide of German nationalism, propelled by French menaces, proved irresistible. On the principle that "nothing succeeds like success" the thunder of the guns at Sadowa converted many of Bismarck's liberal enemies into submissive admirers. Repenting for past

[4] After the war the Austrian Empire underwent drastic reconstruction as is explained on page 435.

indiscretions, the Prussian legislature now legalized the collection of taxes since 1862. What remained of German liberalism would soon be further whittled down by victory over France and the foundation of the German Empire. Nationalism, it is clear, routed aspirations of political liberalism, depriving Germans of any chance to develop free governmental institutions and liberal tenets of human rights.

In the constitution of the North German Confederation of 1867, embracing Prussia and the independent states of the north, Bismarck, to be sure, permitted a modest concession to the democratic spirit. Deputies of the lower branch of the legislature (*Reichstag*) would be elected by manhood suffrage. All legislation had to be approved by that body, but it had no control whatsoever over the executive. The more powerful upper house (*Bundesrath*), in which laws would be initiated, contained representatives of the member states, a concession to still untamed local prides. Executive authority in the Confederation was monopolized in fact by the king of Prussia and a ministry presided over by Bismarck as Chancellor. Exclusive control over the military and foreign policy was retained by the crown. Four years later this constitution was adapted to the requirements of a broader union—to the German Empire.

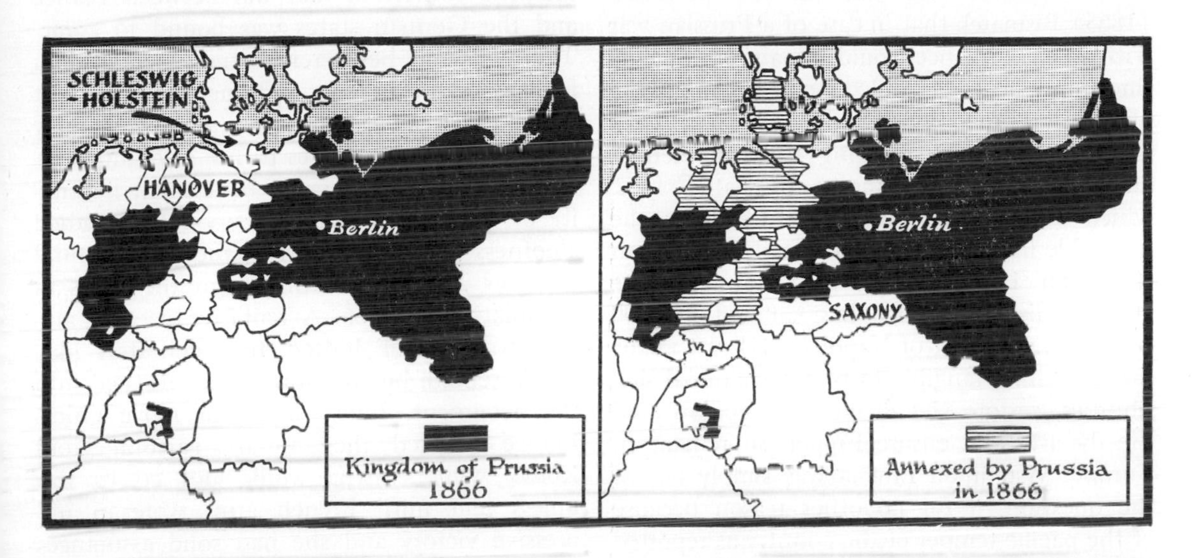

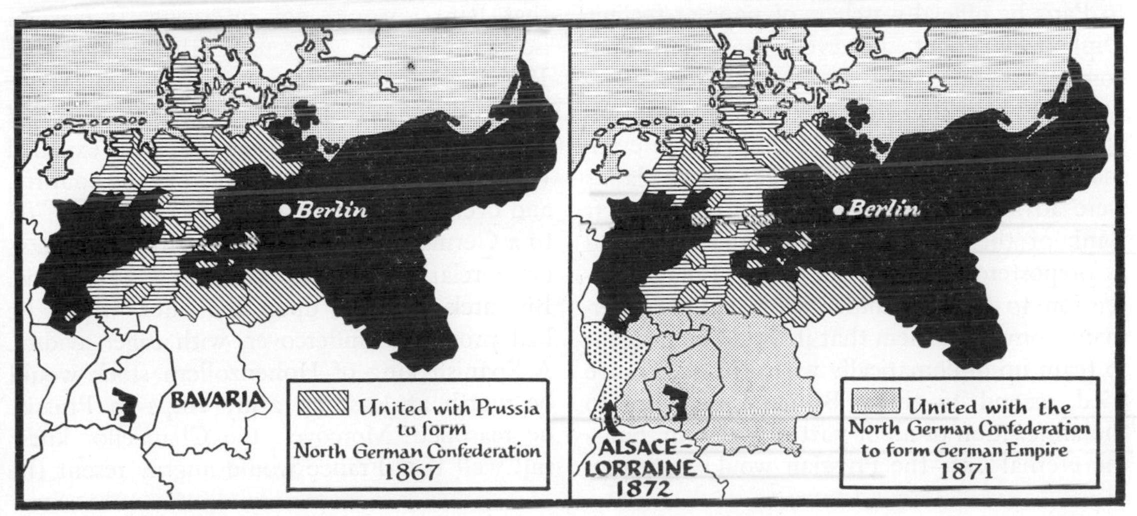

FRANCE AND GERMANY

No neutral capital was more stunned, nor more alarmed by the dramatic sequence of events in central Europe than Paris. Almost overnight political disunity to the east, so advantageous for French security and peace of mind, had vanished. Policymakers in France, the ailing Napoleon III among them, had reasoned that the Prussian-Austrian struggle would be protracted and exhausting for all concerned. France would then step forward as mediator and claim territory on her northeastern frontier, a standing aim of the Second Empire. In line with that reading of the future, Napoleon III had indeed promised (1865) Bismarck that in case of a Prussian war with Austria, France would remain on the side lines; and he even smiled benignly upon the alliance of Prussia with Italy.

Then came the smashing Prussian victory, disillusioning and shocking to articulate France, which already was deeply disturbed by the miserable fiasco in distant Mexico. The veteran statesman Thiers pointed to Sadowa as "the greatest disaster France has suffered for 400 years." The cabinet of Napoleon III cast about for something tangible to placate national sensibilities, restore the dwindling popularity of the dynasty and ensure French supremacy in Europe. War upon Prussia was simply out of the question, if for no other reason because of the pacific temper of the country as reported to Paris by official watchers of popular feeling. Diplomacy might, however, exact territorial compensation.

The French ministry took up three projects of expansion in turn, every one of which eventually landed in the waste-basket. First, claims were advanced to parcels of land on the Left Bank of the Rhine, which Bismarck scorned as preposterous. Disclosure of this French pretension to the governments of southern Germany convinced them that it would be prudent to team up diplomatically with Prussia. France tried, second, to obtain Bismarck's consent to the annexation of all or part of Belgium, but—the eternal but—the Prussian would not commit himself. Revelation of that plan at a propitious moment swung British sentiment against the regime of Napoleon III.

Third, France maneuvered to take over Luxembourg, German-speaking but under the Dutch flag. That design was frustrated by the Great Powers and Luxembourg was defined as a neutral state forever, rather like Belgium. The French quest for compensation, in sum, had accomplished nothing, nothing, that is, except to enflame chauvinistic feelings and to encourage dark suspicions all around. Menacing memories of centuries of Franco-German feuding crowded to the fore.

The course of events had nourished the fatalistic conviction that war between France and the German states was bound to come. The potential belligerents strengthened their fighting establishments and engaged in a hunt for allies. Prussia, as has been indicated, drew the south German states to her side and reckoned confidently upon the benevolent neutrality of Imperial Russia and upon the studied aloofness of Britain. For France the natural ally was Austria, smarting from the Prussian humiliation of 1866. A tentative pact of alliance was in fact drafted, to which Italy likewise assented, but life was never breathed into the document. Italy would not move unless France recalled the military garrison from Rome, while Austria would not go to war unless and until French arms won an impressive victory and she had solid assurances that Russia would not intervene. It was an isolated France, therefore, that fought in 1870.

The direct occasion of the war arose out of Spain. A military insurrection had expelled (1868) the Spanish monarch from the country, and eventually the crown was tendered (1870) to a German prince, Leopold of Hohenzollern, close relative of King William I of Prussia. Bismarck pounced upon the offer, which he had promoted undercover, with eager avidity. A Spanish king of Hohenzollern stock would be worth at least an army corps to Prussia, he reasoned. Moreover, the Chancellor knew full well that France would angrily resent the prospect of a German on the throne of Spain; it was indeed for that very reason that he had energetically pushed the Hohenzollern candidature.

Neither Prince Leopold nor the Prussian king responded sympathetically to the Spanish bid, but they were mere clay in the hard, calculating hands of Bismarck. When Leopold eventually announced that he would accept the crown, a tornado of passionate protest swept Paris; France would be encircled, would become a nut between two jaws of a German nut-cracker. The French ministry let it be known in Berlin that withdrawal of Leopold's candidacy was the price of peace. Bellicose newspapers fanned blazing nationalist emotions on both sides of the Rhine.

Due to the French resistance Leopold on his own account resigned the Spanish crown and King William acquiesced. That decision meant a spectacular diplomatic victory for France and by the same token delivered a body blow to the expectations of Bismarck. Emboldened by success, the decidedly amateurish French cabinet made a suicidal move which played straight into Bismarck's hands. The French ambassador to Prussia was instructed to secure a pledge from William I, who was vacationing at Ems, that the candidacy of Leopold would never again be renewed. King William considered that demand insolent, inasmuch as he had already approved the abandonment of the candidacy. Unwilling to turn the other cheek, he declined to give the declaration which the French ambassador sought and sent him away.

A detailed account of what had transpired at Ems was dispatched by telegram to Bismarck in Berlin—the fateful Ems telegram. Before the arrival of the communication, the Chancellor and the Prussian military chiefs were enveloped in total gloom, for the likelihood of war with France, which would set the coping stone on German consolidation, seemed quite improbable. But the telegram furnished Bismarck with a golden opportunity. Without at all altering the text, Bismarck cut out a great deal and sent the abridged edition to the press. "The telegram and its manner of publication," Bismarck chortled, "will have the effect of a red rag on the Gallic bull." He was right. As interpreted by readers it appeared that the king of Prussia had insulted the French ambassador and the latter in turn had insulted the Hohenzollern monarch.

It was generally felt in France and in Prussia that national honor had been impugned and that war could be the only appropriate answer. On July 19, 1870, Napoleon III issued a declaration of war, assuming thus the onus of formal technical aggressor. The London *Times*, regarded on the Continent as the responsible mouthpiece of the British government, boomed forth:

> The greatest national crime that we have had the pain of recording in these columns since the days of the First French Empire has been consummated. War is declared—an unjust, but premeditated war. The dire calamity which overwhelms Europe with dismay is, it is now too clear, the act of France, of one man in France [Napoleon III]. It is the ultimate result of personal rule. . . . Whatever may on former occasions have been the offences of Prussia, she will in this instance have on her side all that moral support which is seldom denied to those who take up arms in self-defence.

But longer perspective and fuller information on the coming of war in 1870 compel revisions in that contemporary verdict. The struggle was not a malevolent assault launched by an unprovoked brute upon an innocent victim. Policymakers in both Berlin and Paris had played dangerously with fire, confident of success if a conflagration actually broke loose. The articulate public in each country welcomed the appeal to arms, feeling sure of victory.

French nationalism, in other words, collided head on with German nationalism. When an irresistible force strikes an immovable object sparks fly. The burden of responsibility for the coming of war was divided between the statesmen and citizenry on both sides.

THE WAR OF 1870 AND ITS CONSEQUENCES

To a surprising degree the German victory over France in 1870 paralleled the conquest of 1940. In both cases the great German war

The German war-machine struck fiercely and with decision against France. The field armies were crushed, isolated strongholds were invested, and soon Paris herself was besieged. Here we see troops moving up to the lines past the boarded-up Arc de Triomphe.

machine rolled with eerie precision. In both instances France considered its armies and generals as the world's finest, but the fighting was in fact complacently directed by commanders steeped in outmoded traditions of war, who took a dim view of military novelties. Effective French resistance collapsed in six weeks with the decisive battle, on each occasion, centering upon Sedan. Large French forces were cooped up in Metz and other fortresses and Paris capitulated to the enemy—after a desperate siege in 1871.

In both wars a provisional French government was hurriedly organized to negotiate an armistice with the triumphant Germans. A national leader emerged who scorned surrender and preached fighting to the bitter end—Léon Gambetta in 1870, Charles de Gaulle in 1940. Germany imposed severe terms upon the vanquished, a definitive treaty in the first case, only an armistice in 1940. There, however, the analogies cease, for in the second war the collapse of France did not end the fighting.

Napoleon III himself was caught in the humiliating disaster at Sedan. Out of sentimental considerations of prestige, the Emperor had refused to retreat to the walls of Paris and there oppose the German strategy which culminated at Sedan. Report of his capture gave the signal to republican elements in Paris to overthrow the discredited Second Empire and to proclaim a third republic which was not, however, formally constituted until 1875. Few men in France came forward in defense of the fallen Bonaparte; liberals despised him for his personal rule, patriots blamed him for losing the war. Ever since, a large block of French opinion has been invincibly opposed to any politician on horseback.

Before the peace treaty was signed, Paris

was smitten by the bloodiest and most fiercely contested civil struggle of nineteenth-century Europe. Physical hardships which attended the war and the siege, the bitter sting of defeat combined with ideological convictions to produce this nasty episode, spoken of as the Communard Insurrection. Certain Parisians were persuaded that a show of force was necessary to ensure a republican France, while collectivists of several varieties imagined that they could reconstruct the country on their particular patterns.

Defying the provisional French government, the insurgents set up a "Commune" government in Paris with the red flag as emblem. In the spring of 1871 loyalist troops bombarded the capital and then fought ghastly street warfare; far more of Paris was destroyed than had been wrecked by German guns. Both sides indulged in cruel ferocities, the rebels butchering hostages and applying the torch to historic buildings as the end neared. Thousands of insurgents in turn were ruthlessly punished by death or deportation. The effects of the social antagonisms which were then enflamed would not soon die away.

In the book of Marxian Communism, the Paris rising forms a vital and instructive chapter in the history of the class struggle, a characteristic and legendary distortion. All over

Barricades filled the streets of Paris once more, and the bloody Commune ran its course.

Europe, however, conservatives were horrified by events in Paris and governments hastened to repress radical social agitations. Even so the Parisian rebels contributed something to the ultimate victory of the republican cause in France.

When writing the French peace settlement Bismarck departed widely—and most unwisely—from the considerate spirit he had shown in dealing with Austria five years earlier. Either he was unwilling or unable to override the imperious pressures of king and military demigods. Under the Treaty of Frankfurt (May, 1871) France ceded Alsace and Lorraine to Germany; at the time these provinces were passionately French in national sympathy, though predominantly German in speech. By the transfer France tacitly conceded that Germany had become the leading state of Europe. To regain the "lost provinces" became an authentic national ambition for many a Frenchman; that was one of the tangled roots of the First World War.

France, moreover, promised to pay a war indemnity of a billion dollars—a good round sum at the time. Until the debt was liquidated German soldiers would garrison sections of northern France; within three years the last franc was paid and the Germans withdrew. These items of history were not forgotten after the First World War when France rode in the victor's saddle. From the German viewpoint, the transcendant outcome of the war was the consolidation of Germany. The south German states united with the North German Confederation to form the German Empire. In January of 1871 at the Versailles palace of Louis XIV, the dignity of German emperor was conferred upon William I of Prussia and the empire was formally announced to the world.

SUMMARY

So the lush age of national consolidation had reached fulfillment. The France of Napoleon III resembled a skyrocket among nations; it had soared to dizzy heights and then collapsed ingloriously, a dead stick. And yet France came through the ordeal of war and civil war with amazing resilience; the government was reformed on a republican foundation, and the economy of the country was fundamentally sound as the speedy liquidation of the German indemnity testified.

After prolonged travail, dexterous diplomacy and bloody struggles, Italy had taken its seat in the family of nations. Occupation of Rome during the Franco-German war crowned the labors of Mazzini, of Cavour, of Garibaldi and of a multitude of unremembered patriots. But more momentous by far was the piecemeal evolution of Prussia into Germany. Proposing a toast on the evening of the Sedan victory, William I said: "You, Minister of War von Roon, have sharpened our sword; you, General von Moltke, have wielded it; and you, Count von Bismarck, by the policy you have pursued throughout many years, have brought Prussia to the high eminence she enjoys today."

That utterance was the language of sober truth. The prestige of the Junker diplomatist was simply immense and he proceeded to manipulate Germany and to direct Europe. Behind him stood the strongest military machine the world had known for a long time. What Germany had appropriated by force would be protected by force. Part of the German success lay in reliance upon *Realpolitik* and in the superb Prussian army. Europe flattered the victor by imitation. Peace returned to the Old World in 1871, but it was an uneasy peace, a peace dependent upon armed might.

FOR FURTHER STUDY

Robert C. Binkley, *Realism and Nationalism* (New York, 1935)

Albert L. Guérard, *Napoleon III* (Cambridge, 1943)

Philip Guedalla, *The Second Empire* (new ed., New York, 1937)

William R. Thayer, *The Life and Times of Cavour* (2 vols., Boston, 1911)

Bolton King, *The History of Italian Unity* (2 vols., London, 1899)

George M. Trevelyan, *Garibaldi and the Thousand* (new ed., New York, 1920)

Erich Eyck, *Bismarck and the German Empire* (London, 1950)

Lawrence D. Steefel, *The Schleswig-Holstein Question* (Cambridge, Mass., 1932)

Heinrich Friedjung, *The Struggle for Supremacy in Germany* (Eng. ed., London, 1955)

Robert H. Lord, *The Origins of the War of 1870* (Cambridge, Mass., 1924)

James M. Thompson, *Louis Napoleon and the Second Empire* (New York, 1955)

Massimo Salvadori, *Cavour and the Unification of Italy* (New York, 1961) PAPERBACK

Denis M. Smith, *Garibaldi* (New York, 1956)

Eugene N. Anderson, *The Social and Political Conflict in Prussia* (Lincoln, Neb., 1954)

Werner E. Mosse, *The European Powers and the German Question* (Cambridge, Eng., 1958)

Lawrence D. Steefel, *Bismarck, the Hohenzollern Candidacy, and the Origins of the Franco-German War of 1870* (Cambridge, Mass., 1962)

Michael Howard, *The Franco-Prussian War* (New York, 1961)

A List of Significant Dates

WESTERN EUROPE		CENTRAL AND EASTERN EUROPE		OVERSEAS	
1820	Revolt in Spain	**1819**	Founding of Krupp Company	**1819**	Britain acquires Singapore
1829	Catholic Emancipation Act	**1820**	Italian revolts	**1823**	Monroe Doctrine
1830	French Revolution	**1825**	Decembrist rising: Russia	**1825**	Erie Canal
1832	Parliamentary Reform	**1828**	Russo-Turkish War	**1833**	Slavery ends in British Empire
1833	British Factory Act	**1829**	Greek Independence	**1839**	Anglo-Chinese War
1833	State aid to Education: Britain	**1834**	*Zollverein* firmly established	**1839**	Durham Report on Canada
1837	Queen Victoria	**1848**	Francis Joseph Emperor of Austria	**1840**	Livingstone to Africa
1837	Chartist Agitation	**1852**	Cavour Prime Minister of Piedmont	**1845**	Texas in the Union
1839	Separation Belgium and Holland	**1859**	Austro-Sardinian War	**1848**	Treaty of Guadalupe Hidalgo
1844	Rochdale Cooperative Society	**1861**	Emancipation of Russian Serfs	**1853**	Taiping Rebellion
1846	Repeal of the "Corn" Laws	**1861**	Kingdom of Italy	**1854**	Perry Treaty with Japan
1852	Louis Napoleon Emperor	**1862**	Bismarck, Prussian Minister-President	**1858**	Government of India Act
1867	Parliamentary reform	**1864**	Danish War	**1858**	Second Anglo-Chinese War
1869	Irish Church disestablished	**1866**	Austro-Prussian War	**1861**	War between the States
1870	Compulsory education in Britain	**1867**	*Ausgleich*	**1862**	*Merrimac* and *Monitor* (End of wooden men-of-war)
1870	Franco-German War	**1870**	Italy takes Rome	**1867**	Dominion of Canada
		1871	German Empire	**1867**	Purchase of Alaska
				1869	Suez Canal opened

CULTURAL AFFAIRS		GENERAL	
1821	"The Hay Wain" (Constable)	**1822**	Congress of Verona
1823	*Philosophy of History* (Hegel)	**1825**	Steam locomotive
1830	*Principles of Geology* (Lyell)	**1837**	Business Depression
1830	*Eugene Oneygin* (Pushkin)	**1838**	Transatlantic Steamer
1833	The Oxford Movement	**1840**	McCormick's reaper
1836	*The History of the Popes* (Ranke)	**1844**	Telegraph
1848	*A General View of Positivism* (Comte)	**1848**	Year of Revolts
1848	*The Communist Manifesto*	**1853**	Crimean War
1849	*History of England* (Macaulay)	**1856**	Treaty of Paris
1850	"Lohengrin" (Wagner)	**1857**	Business Recession
1857	*Madame Bovary* (Flaubert)	**1864**	Red Cross
1857	"The Gleaners" (Millet)	**1866**	Transatlantic cable
1859	*The Origin of Species* (Darwin)		
1859	*Essay on Liberty* (Mill)		
1863	*Man's Place in Nature* (Huxley)		
1864	The Syllabus of Errors		
1865	*War and Peace* (Tolstoy)		
1867	*Das Kapital* (Marx)		
1869	*The Subjection of Women* (Mill)		
1870	Papal Infallibility		

PART IV

TOWARD A GLOBAL SOCIETY

THE LATER NINETEENTH CENTURY

CHAPTER XVII

DEMOCRACY, NATIONALISM, COLLECTIVISM

SEMANTICS

OCCASIONALLY in the preceding chapters the terms "democracy," "nationalism," "collectivism" and associated words have cropped up. They will appear more often in later chapters, for these verbal tokens hint at great and dynamic forces at work in modern civilization. All are hard to pin down, never static, employed with disconcerting ambiguity, easier to describe than define. Democracy, for instance, suggests one set of fundamental values in Moscow's Kremlin and quite another in the Congress at Washington.[1]

Upon the student of society devolves responsibility to probe below words and seek positive meanings, subject always to revision and refinement. Natural scientists, we are told, seldom dispute about terms, but they handle technical matters with sharp exactness and move in a realm rather remote from mass emotions. Wise old Confucius, asked by a disciple what his first act would be if he were emperor of China, is said to have replied, "I should begin by fixing the meaning of words."

EVOLUTION OF THE DEMOCRATIC IDEAL

Prior to the nineteenth century, absolutism had been the prevalent form of government. In early modern Europe kings and princes ruled by the sanction of the Almighty and were to be strictly obeyed. Bishop Bossuet (pp. 34–5) declared, "Rulers act as ministers of God and his lieutenants on earth. The royal throne is the throne of God Himself. . . . As in God are united all perfection and every virtue, so all the power of all the individuals in a community is united in the person of the prince." The triumph of Parliament in

[1] At the Moscow Conference of 1947, the senior advisers of the United States delegation consumed nearly six hours in hammering out their description of democracy.

seventeenth-century England thoroughly upset the philosophy of divine right. Behind that event stretched, of course, a long tradition of limitation on royal authority running back to Magna Carta and beyond. English political principles spread into Europe and across the Atlantic, forming the ideological framework of 1776 and 1789.

Into the stream of Western political thinking, meanwhile, novel ideas on government had entered. Something had been learned about democracy in the small city states of Greek antiquity. For the ordinary Greek, democracy meant a government in which supreme authority was vested in a general assembly of citizens. Every citizen had a vote, and an equal right to discuss, criticize or offer proposals for law. Unfettered freedom of expression was fundamental in the Greek practice of democracy. Arguments favorable and hostile to democracy in ancient Greece paralleled, to a curious degree, those heard in the modern world.

In the Age of the Renaissance, ancient Greek authors acquainted intellectuals of western Europe with old concepts of democracy.[2] Presently the Protestant upheaval furthered the growth of democratic concepts. Certain extremist sects taught that even as all men were equal in the sight of God so politically they

[2] It appears that the word democracy was first used in England in 1531 in a book by Sir Thomas Elyot, *The Governor*.

LEVIATHAN
Or
THE MATTER, FORME and POWER of A COMMON-WEALTH ECCLESIASTICALL and CIVIL
By THOMAS HOBBES of MALMESBURY
London
Printed for Andrew Crooke
1651

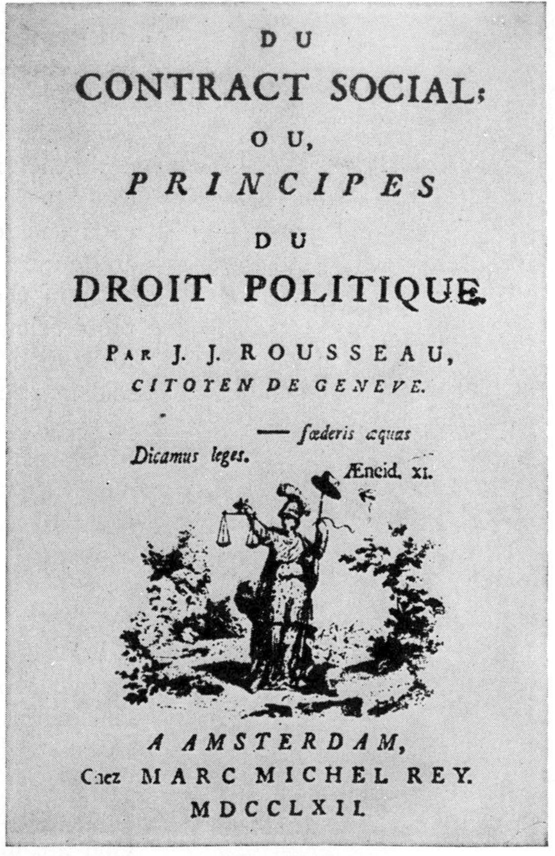

DU
CONTRACT SOCIAL;
OU,
PRINCIPES
DU
DROIT POLITIQUE.
PAR J. J. ROUSSEAU,
CITOYEN DE GENEVE.

— fœderis æquas
Dicamus leges.
Æneid. XI.

A AMSTERDAM,
Chez MARC MICHEL REY.
MDCCLXII.

The giant figure of the monarch, on this emblematic title-page to the 1651 edition of Hobbes's Leviathan, is made up of many tiny individuals and emphasizes the author's contention that men associate only for security and must hope to find it under some form of absolutism. Contrast the fantasy of this Seventeenth Century title-page with the austere setting for the first edition of Rousseau's famous treatise on the Social Contract.

Houses of Parliament, London

should enjoy equality of freedom and self-expression. Church organization in Calvinist Christianity was popularly managed, though the leading Protestant spokesmen themselves had small or no faith in the capacity of ordinary fellows to decide public questions. By reason of the Reformation, furthermore, the Church everywhere was forced into the role of junior partner in relation to the state. And, at a time when the unlimited ecclesiastical authority of the Pope was under challenge, certain Western thinkers asked why and within what limits secular rulers ought to be obeyed. Unconventional answers had much to say about the origins of government in a contract between governor and governed.

An English philosopher, Thomas Hobbes, contended that brute anarchy had reigned in primitive communities. Or, as he imagined the situation, "No place for industry, because the fruit thereof is uncertain; no arts; no letters; no society; and what is worst of all continual fear and danger of violent death and the life of man solitary, brutish, and short." To avert universal destruction, according to Hobbes, men out of self-interest bound themselves to cooperate for security. Thus government, absolutist and authoritarian, had come into being.

Later interpreters of the contract theory, such as John Locke and Rousseau, proposed that the governed were in fact supreme, endowed with natural rights, including the right to expel a distasteful ruler from the throne. Ultimate public power, in other words, belonged to the governed, in itself an argument for limited monarchy or even republicanism. Although the contract theory of the origin of the state and of government had no apparent foundation in historical fact, that was no barrier to its acceptance. The philosophy of natural rights as expressed in the English, American and French Revolutions would not thereafter down. British political institutions—Parliament, cabinet, and parties—were deliberately copied in the nineteenth century by one continental country after the other.

DEMOCRACY IN THE NINETEENTH CENTURY

Outside of France, continental statesmen in the Age of Metternich shuddered at the very suggestion that ordinary fellows should take part in the processes of government. Some of their opponents, on the other hand, sincerely believed that representative government would cure the aches of mankind. The revolutionary convulsions of 1848–1849 imparted an impetus to democratic ideas. After that, principles of democracy moved hesitantly forward and appeared likely to sweep rival philosophies into the discard.

By 1914, on the eve of the First World War, representative government in some form prevailed in every Western country and in sections of Asia too. The proclamation of a democratic republic in China, upon the collapse of the moribund Manchu Empire in 1912, seemed to set the seal upon the victory of political democracy. Actually, however, wide disparities prevailed in the amount of effective public power entrusted to the governed. To the east of the Rhine in Europe and south of the Pyrenees the shadow of self-government had penetrated but not the substance.

In the light of nineteenth-century history the essential hallmarks of political democracy may be pithily summarized. First a constitution, ordinarily a formal written document, prescribed the functions of governmental organs, the choosing of officials, and declared the fundamental liberties and obligations of the individual. Second, some of the governed, adult males in the main, participated in the conduct of public business through the medium of the ballot. Third, enfranchised citizens were eligible to be candidates for elective office. Fourth, to express divergent attitudes on public issues, political parties were organized. Fifth, the electorate periodically chose the representatives it desired in free elections. Sixth, if representatives fell into disfavor they could peacefully be removed by defeat at the polls. And last, while the will of the majority prevailed, dissenters must be allowed full and fair opportunity to make their opinions known.

Marked differences prevailed in the measure of control which the popularly elected legislature exercised over the executive branch of government. In Great Britain, France (of the Third Republic) and Italy the executive, or ministry, could be dismissed by an adverse vote in the legislature, but in the United States the chief executive could not be removed without an intricate process of impeachment. In the major countries of central and eastern Europe the executive was not at all responsible to the legislature; there the tradition of monarchical authority counted far more than the novelty of democracy.

DESIGN OF DEMOCRACY

As it evolved, democracy involved much more than a government of participating citizens. It meant, as in ancient Greece, freedom to criticize public policies and to assemble for political discussion and persuasion. It meant freedom of publication and of other means of communication. It meant legal protection of the individual from arbitrary imprisonment or punishment or abuse by unofficial hoodlums.

The nature of the ideal democracy was skillfully sketched by the British statesman James Bryce. In an ideal democracy, he explained, "the average citizen will give close and constant attention to public affairs, recognizing that this is his interest as well as his duty. He will try to comprehend the main issues of policy, bringing to them an independent and impartial mind, which thinks first not of his own but of the general interest. If . . . parties become inevitable, he will join one and attend its meetings, but will repress the impulses of party spirit. Never failing to come to the polls, he will vote for his party candidate only if satisfied by his capacity and honesty. He will be ready to be . . . put forward as a candidate for the legislature (if satisfied of his own competence), because public service is recognized as a duty. . . . Office will be sought only because it gives opportunities for useful service. Power will be shared by all, and a career open to all alike. . . . There will be no excuse for violence, because the constitution will provide a remedy for every grievance. Equality will produce a sense of human solidarity, will refine manners, and increase brotherly kindness." [3]

In that final observation Bryce touched upon democracy as a faith, as a creed which ordered individual conduct and social relationships. For democracy, in addition to being a pattern of government assuring liberties to citizens, implied a certain mood, an elusive yet vital "way of life."

In this larger sense, democracy affirmed the dignity and worth of every person. It tolerated dissenting opinions and was prepared to seek compromise and accommodation. Out of a sense of fair play, democracy protected the interests of minorities, repudiating oppression and persecution. It insisted upon opportunity for the individual to excel in keeping with his abilities and creative talents. It asserted that men were capable of infinite improvement in character and in their institutions.

For democratic vitality, the record of history seemed to show that several preconditions were necessary. Democracy was, first of all, an evolutionary growth over a rather long span of time and could not quickly be inculcated in a people from without. It prospered best in a material environment providing reasonably decent living standards, some measure of economic security which created confidence in and strengthened the democratic creed, and a considerable degree of social homogeneity. It required, too, comparative safety from external attack. On an overall estimate, the democratic philosophy flourished most luxuriantly in newly developed countries, remote from the power centers of Europe and in which levels of comfort were relatively high.

[3] James Bryce, *Modern Democracies* (2 vols., New York, 1921), I, 48.

CONS AND PROS

Despite the spread of popular government and the democratic faith with each passing generation, searching questions were raised on their values and virtues. More than one discordant voice recalled that Alcibiades, Athenian general and statesman, had lampooned the democracy of his day as "acknowledged madness." It was evident in all truth that the revolutionary democratic experiment, put to work by fallible mortals, had fallen short of the ideal expectations of optimistic apostles.

Certain conservative intellectuals protested that democracy was more a poison than a tonic. They condemned the democratic way either on the score that it weakened authority and so invited social chaos or that it would lead into tyranny by the masses. A politically illiterate electorate, it was said, would expropriate the rich and well-to-do and would prove fatal to freedom of expression, for the masses were unsympathetic to enlightened speculation and scientific innovations.

Popular control of foreign policy, it was argued, was impossible without incurring risks of weakness and vacillation. In the nature of things the public could not have access to all sources of information available to a government. Often ignorant of the facts, and subject to gusts of passion, the public could not intelligently direct international relations. The passions of the populace, moreover, could readily be whipped up by a nationalistic government, leaving decisions on international questions to the fate of the emotions.

At the other extreme, certain collectivist critics bombarded democracy as a capitalist scheme of things calculated to promote and perpetuate the ascendancy of the propertied to the detriment of the propertyless. Representative government, in other words, barred an equitable distribution of income, defeated social justice and reduced talk about liberty and equality to cant.

It was also urged that political democracy did not always install men of first-rate ability and character in elective office. Commonplaceness, favoritism and jobbery were all too prevalent. And popular government, critics alleged, was inefficient, extravagant, or too slow or too timid to grapple appropriately with grave emergencies. It was further asserted that the enfranchised neglected to take their civic responsibilities seriously enough. Many men were so apathetic that they even neglected to vote. Others voted solely in keeping with self-interest or were easily gulled by the catchwords of agitators and honey-dew demagogues. Some cynics indeed dismissed popular government as "the election of the incompetent by the uneducated to legislate for the indifferent."

Finally, a democratic society, it was contended, placed a premium on conventionality. It favored those who kept step with the slowest march of thought and tended to exalt and encourage mediocrity. Suspicious of any kind of superiority, democracy ignored or ridiculed excellence and glorified the commonplace. "Democracy is not favorable to the higher forms of intellectual life," wrote the historian W. E. H. Lecky, a trenchant Victorian critic of democracy, "Democracy levels down quite as much as it levels up." [4]

Admirers of democracy as faith, hope and practice made full and persuasive answer to these and kindred indictments. While conceding and in no sense condoning the failure of democracy to attain heights of perfection, they argued that it yielded preferable practical results to rule by one man or by one class. It provided the most favorable environment for the unfolding of "the whole dignity of man"—and woman. It assured fundamental freedoms to all and gnawed away at privilege.

Ever with its eyes focused on the future, democracy, it was claimed, was more flexible, more dynamically responsive to shifting social conditions and changing social perspectives than more stereotyped governments. By parliamentary methods democracy effected an increasing measure of social well-being without loss of liberty and with a minimum of repression and coercion. In the long run, moreover, democracy was as efficient as alternate forms and the remedy for shortcomings lay within the democratic mechanism itself. A democracy, in other words, mirrored the democrats living in it.

By its very nature democracy, said its champions, enlisted the energies and the devotion of citizens in periods of supreme crisis, whether of peace or war, more effectively than authoritarianism. Men in democracies not only felt an inner compulsion to take the initiative in effort, but displayed greater fortitude, resolution and staying qualities. Acknowledging that the dictator or tyrant held an advantage of initial swiftness, democrats argued that freedom of thought and action encouraged an element of long-range strength not found in the arsenal of despotism. Inherently again, democratic states were more pacific, since popular government required deliberation and consent. In an environment of freedom of speech and discussion it was difficult if not quite impossible for public leaders to plan aggressive war secretly and unchallenged.

Democracy, in sum, was not invalidated by imperfect accomplishment. It rested its case on the claim that it was comparatively better than any alternative scheme. Throughout the late nineteenth century and into the twentieth arguments on democracy, con and pro, rocked back and forth. During the First World War, popular governments, faced with tasks of unexampled magnitude, yielded in greater or lesser degree to oligarchic control. After hostilities ceased, however, democratic ideas and institutions extended their geographical range in Europe and prospered without precedent, but a counter-current of dictatorship presently challenged democracy as never it had been challenged before.

NATIONALITY AND NATIONALISM

Many an influential author of the nineteenth century insisted that even as the individual

[4] W. E. H. Lecky, *Democracy and Liberty* (2 vols.; London, 1896), I, 131.

possessed an inalienable right to freedom, so each distinct nationality had a natural right to separate political existence. Rule of one nationality over another was assailed as a species of slavery. "It is in general a necessary condition of free institutions," declared (1861) John Stuart Mill, "that the boundaries of governments should coincide in the main with those of nationalities." That conviction grew out of and overshadowed the older pattern of value which prized a united humanity above any single national grouping.

It was the great French Revolution which thrust the ideas of nationality and nationalism into the foreground of the Western panorama. Certainly traces of nationalism had existed before that; nationalism, to cite one illustration, contributed heavily to the dissolution of Western Christendom in the era of the Reformation. Yet before 1789 nationalism had a strongly dynastic flavor, exalting ruling kings and princes. After that, nationalism acquired a more popular, a more democratic quality. Linked up with that was the notion that all able-bodied men, not royal mercenaries or professional soldiers, should fight the battles of a nation. Previously, soldiers thought it neither shameful nor a matter for reproach to take service with a foreign state. Revolutionary France applied the nation-in-arms principle, Bonaparte disastrously exploited it, Prussia in time perfected it and other countries flattered Prussia by imitation.

At the Vienna Congress of 1815, nascent national aspirations were swamped by dynastic traditions and appetites. But dreams of unity inspired, or helped to inspire, sporadic risings in Italy and Germany, for instance, in the forepart of the nineteenth century. Champions of nationalism reasoned that human personality could not fully flower nor peace be assured unless Europe and the wider world were partitioned into independent and sovereign nation-states. For German and Italian nationalists the goal of territorial integration was achieved, as has been explained, under the guidance of Bismarck and Cavour.

Thereafter, in Europe at any rate, nationalism was much intensified and made imperious demands upon the individual. It became in fact a religion transcending in authority any major expression of Christianity. Nationalism, moreover, imparted a mighty dynamic to overseas expansion; it encouraged a revival of tariff protectionism or neo-mercantilism and a quest for economic self-sufficiency.

Nationalism likewise nourished domestic intolerance, detestation of the foreign and foreigners and was conducive to international strife. It was one of the largest causes of incessant convulsions in Balkan Europe and in colonial territories; it flourished in any climate, among the Boers of South Africa no less than among the French Canadians of Quebec. It flamed forth in Japan and China. It lay at the root of the First and Second World Wars. Small wonder that with the passage of time many thoughtful Europeans condemned nationalism as the supreme plague, the most insidious and somber enemy of civilization.

On the other side of the ledger, nationalism promoted the higher living, inspiring much that was noble and uplifting in art and music, in literature and scholarship. Baffling confusions and contradictions, it must be said, arise whenever the terms nationality and nationalism are introduced. For they carry different implications at different times for different minds. The nationalism of the liberal humanitarian Mazzini, for example, did not exactly parallel the assertive nationalism of Cavour, nor was the nationalism of Cavour the same as the volcanic, exclusive nationalism of Mussolini.[5]

As a working definition, a nation-state may be thought of as an independent country, containing a single nationality, as in the case of France. A nationality was neatly described by the Italian philosopher-historian Vico as "a natural society of men who by unity of territory, of origin, of customs, and of language, are drawn into a community of life and social conscience." Thought of in that way, a nationality might exist without having a state of its own as was so true of the Poles, for instance,

[5] In the United States nationalism once meant merely strengthening the federal government at the expense of the individual states.

throughout the nineteenth century. No sovereign Polish state existed, yet there was a distinct Polish national personality embracing populations under the rule of Russia, Prussia (Germany) and Austria.

Nationalism in turn may be regarded as the state of mind (and emotion) of members of a nationality which esteemed loyalty to the nationality above every other allegiance. Nationalism easily passed into chauvinism, or impulsive, irrational enthusiasm for national glory, especially of the sort fostered by military exploits. Patriotism differed from nationalism. Patriotism implied devotion to country, pride in it and recognition of duty to it. Patriotism summoned citizens to think independently about their country, to criticize responsibly and if need be to sacrifice for its betterment. Patriotism combined love of one's own country with respect for the liberties and manners of other countries.

FOUNDATIONS OF NATIONALITY

In the conception of nationality proposed by Vico several points were cited which require a bit of elaboration. "Unity of territory" sometimes has helped to make one nationality different from another. Italy, for example, is the home of a definite national grouping partly because the peninsula is geographically separate. But well-marked natural boundaries have not been an indispensable component of nationality, as Poland amply witnesses.

Many a time and oft it has been asserted that community of "race" or blood unity distinguished one nationality from another and invested it with superior mental, moral and physical qualities. The irrationality upon which that superstition rested may be as old as the first organized human societies. Euripides in ancient Greece bragged:

> It is meet
> That Greece should o'er Barbarians bear the sway
> Not that Barbarians lord over Greece;
> Nature hath formed them slaves, the Grecians free.

Apologists of the French aristocracy, parenthetically, were accustomed to defend their privileged status by the argument that their blood differed from that of common fellows in France.

The myth of the superiority of chosen nationalities by reason of "race" was given classic exposition in the sham erudition of Comte J. A. de Gobineau. His best known piece of writing, *Essay on the Inequality of Human Races* (1855), argued that "races" were innately different in talent and capacity to create or absorb. Not much respected while he lived, Gobineau attained renown after his death, especially in Germany where a fanatical cult of "racial" superiority came into being.

Findings of ethnology and biology refute the thesis of "racial" purity as a basis of nationality. Human groupings have long been so intermingled that an ethnic tangle beyond unraveling has resulted. What ethnology teaches, the testimony of history reinforces. Migrations and military occupations have thoroughly mixed up the blood strains of Europe; every nationality is in literal truth a melting pot. The absurdity of the "racial" foundation of nationality should be sufficiently proved by the cases of the United States or Russia. Nevertheless, it must be stressed that persuasive and pernicious theories of "racial" purity have convinced groups that they were in fact bound together by blood ties. That delusion, like many another myth, appealing powerfully as it did to mass romanticism, carried more weight than the actualities.

Almost always, linguistic uniformity differentiated one nationality from another. Speaking the same tongue, a nationality developed a peculiar sense of kinship and unity. Due to the importance of language in leading a folk to feel unique, national agitators in the nineteenth century worked assiduously to achieve linguistic uniformity among men considered as fellow nationals. And yet a common language was not an absolutely essential foundation of nationality. Consider the Swiss, who spoke four languages, but nonetheless acquired a remarkable reputation for national solidarity. Two peoples, furthermore, may share the same language and yet form distinct nationalities as the British and the inhabitants of the United States readily illustrated. Although language, in short, was generally a reliable criterion of nationality it was not invariably so. To what nationality did a given individual *feel* he belonged was the ultimate test.

Perhaps the indispensable element in creating a sense of national oneness has been the cherishing of a particular set of traditions and aspirations. "These constitute a nation (nationality)," wrote the Frenchman Renan, "who, having accomplished great things in the past and wish to accomplish them in the future, believe themselves to be such." And it was conspicuously upon the memory of the political past and military sagas that distinct national personalities were grounded. Beyond that, revival of interest in ancient grandeur and glory quickened desires for national unity and future prestige. Recollection of the eminence of Italy in the Roman and Papal heydays, for instance, and in the Age of Renaissance stimulated national consciousness among Italians.

As a final point, a nationality was bound together by a feeling of cultural uniqueness, set off from other human groupings by ideals and ideologies, customs and costumes, social conventions and folkways, habits of work and play. If religion may be taken as a facet of culture, then religion was sometimes an important force in persuading a group that it constituted a distinct nationality. Thus the Roman Catholic Poles felt themselves different from the Lutheran Prussians and the Orthodox Catholic Russians. If a nationality belonged to a single religious confession the sense of community was likely to be heightened.

DIFFUSION AND MANIFESTATIONS OF NATIONALISM

Intellectuals, especially romantic historians, students of language and men of letters, wrought significantly in building up and inculcating the state of mind called nationalism. Their products were seized upon by the energetic middle classes who through various societies and institutions furthered activities which were calculated to make co-nationals keenly alert to their national heritage and greatness. It would appear that the middle classes responded more fully to nationalistic urges than ordinary fellows. Clergymen were prime promoters of nationalism in countries like Russia, Bulgaria and Ireland. Conversion for clergymen in the Balkans meant winning a person from one nationality to another, whether accomplished by persuasion or force.

Very likely parents and neighbors by word of mouth were the most important influence in shaping the national outlook of most individuals. Significant, too, were elementary schools which children entered when the mind was "wax to receive and marble to retain." Reading books, studies in geography and history which emphasized uniqueness and dramatized exciting and colorful episodes fostered national ardor. Formal class lessons were supplemented and reinforced by singing national anthems, ceremonial festivities on anniversaries of stirring national incidents and on the birthdays of folk heroes. When a boy became a man he by no means put all childish things away.

Where military conscription was the law, the army carried forward the indoctrination of the school. National ideals and prejudices were drilled into troops along with instruction on the manipulation of weapons. And, as literacy spread, the inexpensive press, newspapers and magazine, and the stage and pulpit contributed influentially to the diffusion of national attitudes of mind. Wherever freedom of expression was denied or abridged secret societies were organized to cultivate and inspirit national sentiments.

As has been suggested, nationalism expressed itself in a variety of ways which may be summed up in tabloid form. (1.) Nationalism might inspire a nationality, or its spokesmen at any rate, with a desire to form a nation state. (2.) It might encourage a nationality under alien lordship to push for political independence. (3.) It might lead a national minority to seek inclusion in an existing state of the same nationality. (4.) Nationalism might excite an obsessive mania to acquire territory inhabited by fellow-nationals. (5.) It might foster extravagant pride in national history, language, or cultural attainments and a feeling of superiority over lesser breeds beyond the pale. (6.) It might reveal itself in ardent passion for the safety, the prosperity and the "historic destiny" of one's nationality and nation-state.

To these ends men were prepared to work and fight and bleed and die. Imbued with impassioned nationalism men asked, in language which Macaulay put in the mouth of Horatius:

> And how can man die better
> Than facing fearful odds
> For the ashes of his fathers
> And the temples of his gods?

It would be inaccurate to imagine that nationalism was precisely the same in all European countries either in expression or intensity. History and geography accounted for considerable differences. Nationalism was likely to be more explosive and menacing to peace among nationalities not united in independent states, or recently united, or subject to a foreign power. Nationalism like character was strengthened by adversity. Countries long united, such as Britain and France, needed no drum and trumpet agitations to excite self-esteem or to achieve unity or win independence.

THE NATURE OF CAPITALISM

Democracy challenged authoritarianism. Nationalism challenged cosmopolitanism. Collectivism challenged capitalism, or the individual enterprise scheme of economics. Originating in the Renaissance centuries, capitalism was neither fixed nor static; in the nineteenth century it evolved in an ever-expanding industrialized society. A body of economic theory had been worked out by Adam Smith and other "classical economists" to explain and fortify the institution of private capitalism. Economic theory is what somebody supposes to be the best way in which society can secure and use the material means to live the kind of life men think possible and desirable.

The central institution of capitalism was of course private ownership of the means of production, exchange and distribution. Strictly speaking the owner of any productive property qualified as a capitalist, whether the peasant possessing a small acreage or the large estate proprietor, whether the partner in a small undertaking or the holder of a life insurance policy, since the funds of the company were invested in capitalistic enterprises, whether the individual operated a shop or mill of his own or was the holder of shares in a joint-stock company. Increasingly the impersonal joint-stock corporation occupied a larger and larger place in capitalistic economy.

Men invested savings in an enterprise with the expectation of receiving dividends or interest and in the hope that the value of the investment would appreciate. Capital owners assumed risks and took profits or suffered losses. On the other side, two categories of workers, salaried men and wage earners, were paid wages, but had no share in profits—if any. For the employee the standard incentives were the "carrot" of financial reward or the "stick" of unemployment. Employers and workmen had a common interest in steady employment and "good times." They diverged, however, as to the part of the net income of an enterprise that should be distributed as profits and wages, respectively.

In keeping with laissez faire teachings, employers resented and resisted external interference in their businesses. They alone decided the wages to be paid, for instance. They preferred to negotiate with workmen individually instead of on any plan of collective bargaining. Competition, it was claimed, spurred individuals to greater efficiency, encouraged skills and prevented social stratification. The mainspring of production indeed was held to be the desire of the individual to reap the reward of personal talent, ability and thrift. In the course of the nineteenth century, regulatory legislation by government and the growth of trade unionism sharply modified the "rugged individualism" of earlier capitalism.

Credit was another fundamental feature of the capitalistic regime. Principally through banking houses, individual savings were channeled into industrial and commercial undertakings. Prices were not set by the intrinsic value of an article nor by the cost of its production but rather by what "the traffic would bear" in a more or less competitive market.

VARIETIES OF COLLECTIVISM

Certain thinkers on social problems and prospects concluded that the free enterprise economy must either be drastically mended or ended. Their outlook, up to a point, was shaped by perusal of older writings inveighing against private property and seeking an answer to the perennial question, "Why are the many poor?" [6]

Unconventional social thinking was affected by the drab slums and factories, the human wretchedness and destitution of early machinofacture and by the French revolutionary slogan of equality. The end product of the speculations was compounded of faith in the natural goodness and perfectibility of man, and of detestation for the economic institutions which prevailed.

Anti-capitalist theorists were labeled, or labeled themselves, socialists, or communists, or collectivists, or anarchists—all extremely fluid terms. Novel social philosophies developed in fact a vocabulary peculiarly their own. Collectivism may be regarded as the most general of these terms, covering any and all programs for the reordering of the economic structure in such fashion as to impair or abolish the prevalent capitalism. Stated otherwise, collectivism represented in greater or lesser degree the obverse of economic individualism.

Collectivism, in its many and somewhat bewildering versions, indicted capitalism on four major counts. It condemned capitalism, first, as involving an inequitable distribution of wealth and income between the owners of productive property and the many at work in mill and mine, in factory and field. Capitalism was attacked, in the second place, as politically unwholesome, since it concentrated real power in a minority and made a mockery of the freedom of the majority. Critics argued, third, that competitive capitalism entailed indefensible waste in production, and made for inefficiency by reason of duplication of operations, advertising and in other ways. And finally, anti-capitalist thinkers charged that the planless and chaotic nature of individual enterprise economy invited periodic business depressions, unemployment and resultant human wretchedness.

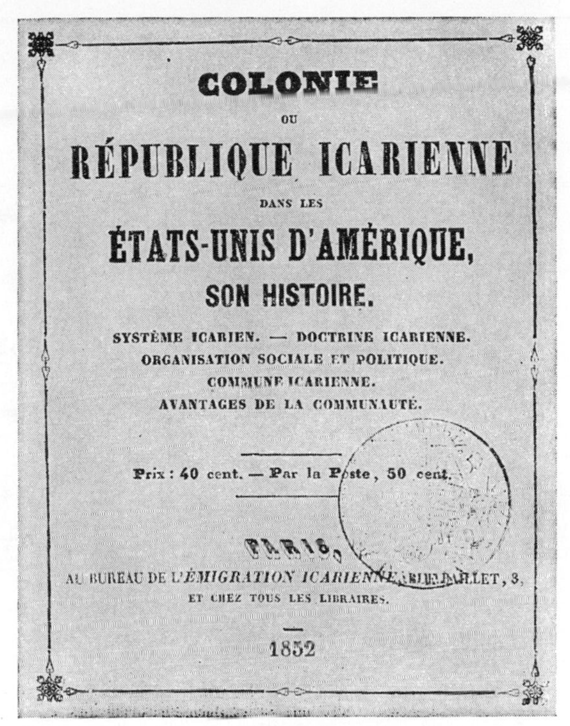
COLONIE
OU
RÉPUBLIQUE ICARIENNE
DANS LES
ÉTATS-UNIS D'AMÉRIQUE,
SON HISTOIRE.
SYSTÈME ICARIEN. — DOCTRINE ICARIENNE.
ORGANISATION SOCIALE ET POLITIQUE.
COMMUNE ICARIENNE.
AVANTAGES DE LA COMMUNAUTÉ.

Prix : 40 cent. — Par la Poste, 50 cent.

PARIS,
AU BUREAU DE L'ÉMIGRATION ICARIENNE, RUE BAILLET, 3,
ET CHEZ TOUS LES LIBRAIRES.

1852

This pamphlet of 1852 reported progress at another communitarian colony, the Icarian experiment at Nauvoo, Illinois.

Early in the nineteenth century an array of communitarian collectivists appeared, who have often been referred to as "Utopian Socialists." Idealistic, middle class men, these theoreticians devised schemes for the reformation of society by means of small colonies or communities. In an ideal environment members would live and work harmoniously on communal terms. Specific blueprints were many. A large-hearted, self-made British cotton magnate, Robert Owen, who coined the term "socialist," drafted a plan for small cooperative commonwealths each self-supporting. On the principle that if the environment was changed, conduct would change, Owen founded a famous "Utopian" colony at New Harmony, Indiana. And somewhat parallel programs were projected by French social theorists (p. 323). "Not a read-

[6] There was considerable interest in the sketch of a communal society entitled *Utopia*, written by Saint Thomas More, an English Catholic of the sixteenth century.

New Harmony, Indiana, sketched in May, 1826, by C. A. Lesueur.

ing man," wrote Emerson in 1840, "but has a draft of a new community in his waistcoat pocket."

About a hunded and fifty communitarian colonies were actually set up, mostly in the backwoods of the United States. All had checkered careers and as a rule short ones. While it was engrossing to philosophize in a drawing room on the perfectibility of man and the nobility of toil on the soil, it was something else to assume membership in an isolated colony and have to spread manure and plant turnips, and worst of all to eat them. Nothing of lasting importance flowed from these interesting adventures in communal living, though some of their ideas and ideals influenced subsequent collectivist thought. As the nineteenth century marched along, other collectivist creeds were propounded, attracted disciples and left their mark upon the age. Directly or indirectly they were affected by Marxist theories, analyzed below.

Late in the century, certain advocates of social reform, moved by vague inward feelings of unrest, sought ways to distribute wealth more equitably and to raise standards of mass comfort within the framework of private capitalism. Especially influential in Germany, they contended that government had a responsibility to ensure decent standards of living for wageworkers and to secure them against the normal hazards of life. Called "state socialists," they pushed for insurance programs to provide assistance in time of accident, sickness and old age and for public ownership of railways and public utilities.

In Christian circles, too, voices were raised in a fervor of righteous moral indignation against the shortcomings of competitive capitalism. "Christian Socialism" was given a patent of respectability among Roman Catholics by the social teachings of Pope Leo XIII. Hailed as the workingman's Pope, he inveighed against the misuse, not the existence of private

Pope Leo XIII

productive property. Through political parties, Catholics promoted social welfare legislation and special banks were organized for wage earners and peasants. Without organizing formal parties many Protestant churchmen wanted to "Christianize the social order" and worked for "the establishment of the Kingdom of God on earth."

Still another challenger of capitalism—and much else—was the creed of anarchism. Protesting against the inequalities and tyranny of wealth, anarchism would destroy the institution of private property, and would utterly extinguish the state, organized religion and established social conventions. While one sect of anarchists advocated pacific methods to attain the declared objectives, a militant faction, and the more important, preached violence and sabotage—"propaganda by deed." Its foremost spokesman, the Russian aristocrat Michael Bakunin, was the most feared revolutionary of his generation. Assassination of prominent political personages was a preferred weapon of terroristic anarchists. Only in Spain did anarchism strike firm root among the masses, though it had adherents in other sections of Latin Europe and in the Slavic East, Russia notably.

In France, anarchist doctrines invaded trade-unions giving rise to syndicalism, which stressed the idea of a general strike as the stimulus to revolutionary action. Syndicalism proposed to destroy the prevailing social order by violence and then parliamentary functions would be performed by trade-unions (for which the French term is *syndicats*). Management and control of industry would be placed in the hands of joint committees of workers and consumers. Spreading into Spain and Italy, syndicalism had passed the peak of its popularity before the First World War, though certain of its tenets were woven into the Fascist fabric of Mussolini.

In the United States syndicalism became the fundamental doctrine of the Industrial Workers of the World, whose adherents indulged in industrial warfare not exceeded in violence anywhere in the world. The British version of syn-

Michael Bakunin

A local newspaper artist sketched this Anarchist demonstration in Chicago in 1886.

dicalism took the name of "guild socialism." This ephemeral flutter of idealism shared with the Fabian Society (p. 302) the basic proposition that the means of production, distribution and exchange should be state owned, but it rejected the principle of bureaucratic management in favor of the syndicalist committee principle. Riven into pacific and revolutionary wings, guild socialism failed to attract anything like the following of "Fabian Socialism," in some respects the most influential of all collectivist philosophies.

THUNDER ON THE LEFT

About three hundred years ago a gentleman named Eustace Peachtree wrote: "Among the notionable dictes of antique Rome was the fancy that when men heard thunder on the left the gods had somewhat of special advertisement to impart. Then did the prudent pause and lay down their affaire to study what omen Jove intended."

For the continent of Europe—and subsequently of Asia—this thunder on the left was heard in the version of collectivism coupled with the name of Karl Marx (1818–1883). Becoming a powerful force among European intellectuals and industrial wageworkers toward the end of the nineteenth century, the fighting faith of Marx, somewhat modified, captured great Russia in 1917. The prestige and accomplishments of Marxist Russia dynamically stimulated the collectivist cause all over the world. After the First World War, and far more so after the Second World War, the specter of Marxian Communism developed into a grim global reality, claiming the allegiance of a third of the human family.

Many Marxist sects have arisen and quarreled with one another. But all venerate the saint of "scientific socialism" as guide and teacher and claim to be his authentic disciples and heirs. The susceptibility of Marxist theories to different interpretations is one of the explanations for the enormous amount of controversy that surrounds the name of Marx. His leonine head with its slightly Fijian mop of hair and luxuriant beard has served as the symbol of Marxism for generations of believers. Marx has a fair chance to be among the winners in the roulette of immortality.

Born in the Rhineland of a well-to-do and cosmopolitan Jewish family, Marx made a very creditable record in his university studies. For a time this congenital dissenter practiced journalism, pondering the while and writing about the social perplexities which the machine age had accentuated. He loved to stick pins into conventional opinions, traditions and persons. Falling afoul of the Prussian police because of outspoken criticism, Marx took off for Paris, plunged into the ferment of social speculations there, then moved on to Brussels and London.

Marxist collectivism may be dated from 1847 when Marx, then twenty-nine, and another restless German radical, Friedrich

Karl Marx

Engels, outlined their social philosophy to a conference of wageworkers in London. Next year the address was expanded into a pamphlet, *The Communist Manifesto*, which became in time the ground plan of a secular religion for hundreds of millions. Marx fancied that the revolutionary convulsions of 1848 were an application of his theories, though in fact they had little relation to them.

Settling in London Marx lingered there, with short interruptions, the rest of his life. His grave in the British capital is a shrine of Communist devotion. Much of the time, Marx and his family lived in squalor and harsh poverty. At one point his only assured income was modest payments for correspondence to the New York *Tribune*; trans-Atlantic readers could hardly have guessed that this unknown journalist would shape human thought and behavior as have few writers in history.

After Engels inherited a small fortune, he generously shared his cash with his life-long friend. Marx himself turned into something of a recluse, studying in that scholar's paradise, the British Museum—thinking, writing, planning. Mazzini, who knew Marx intimately at this period, described him as a "man of acute yet dissolvent genius, domineering in temper, jealous of the influence of others, and with more of anger in his heart, albeit righteous anger, than of love."

THE MARXIST PATTERN

Marx aspired to and professed an incredible omniscience and displayed that dogmatic self-confidence which is often the besetting sin of dissenters. Naturally his thinking was molded by university studies and by what he and Engels learned of human conditions in Britain in the formative stage of machinofacture. As explained by Nicholas Lenin, his most celebrated disciple, Marx "continued and completed the main ideological currents of the nineteenth century belonging to the three most advanced countries of mankind."

From the German philosopher Hegel, Marx inherited the idea that history proceeded on the principle of thesis fighting its antithesis, the conflict creating a new synthesis. His belief in insurrection stemmed from the revolutionary heritage of France, while many of his economic theories represented a reworking of the teachings of British classical economists. All were swept together in a formidable pattern of revolutionary philosophy.

The historical studies of Marx on British factory workers and his philosophical and economic speculations were incorporated in a mammoth performance *Das Kapital* or *Capitalist Production*.[7] Much of this grim-visaged work is a befuddling analysis of the origins and functioning of capitalism. None but the author could honestly and fully explain in detail what the study was about. But along with the *Communist Manifesto, Capitalist Production* forms

[7] The crucial first volume came off the press in 1867 and was translated into Russian in 1872 and into English in 1886. The other two volumes were finished by Engels after the death of Marx and largely from his manuscript.

the canon of sacred writings of Marxian Communism, acceptance of which came to be regarded as the acid test of Marxist orthodoxy.

Spoken of as the "bible of communism," this work has been variously interpreted, and is seldom read because it is unreadable and runs into 2,500 pages. Even so, no writing since Rousseau's *Social Contract* has exerted a comparable impact upon thought and practice. The quintessence of the Marxian challenge to the individual enterprise system may readily be gleaned from the slim, stridently rhetorical *Communist Manifesto*. Stripped to the bone, the Marxian philosophy provided an intellectual justification for the overturn of the existing society by revolutionary violence. Productive property—factories and farms, railways, banks and so forth—would be transferred from private to state ownership and management. Thereafter the economic mechanism in all its complexity and magnitude would be managed by public officials.

More particularly, Marx argued that the value of an article expressed the amount of labor expended in producing it. Since workmen created all value they should be rewarded with all value created. But under the prevailing regime, capitalists paid workers merely enough to live, Marx contended, and pocketed the remainder as profits—"surplus value" in the Marxian vocabulary—and so were guilty of exploitation. Unless a capitalist, Marx said, squeezed maximum profits from his workers he would be driven to the wall by competitors.

Bound up with the "labor theory of value" was a "materialistic" interpretation of history, which presumed to reduce everything to economic terms. According to Marx, it was a matter of unswerving law that economic compulsions and motives dominated society and governed human behavior. No man was other than the creature of his material surroundings, fundamentally of the way in which he acquired his daily bread. The character of laws and government, of morality and religion, of art and literature, everything was determined by economic conditions.

History taught, as Marx depicted it, that the past had witnessed ceaseless struggles for possession of the means of production between conflicting classes.[8] "One fact," he wrote, "is common to all past ages; namely the exploitation of one part of society by another." In the very modern world the antagonists in the class war were the owners of productive property—the bourgeoisie—and the propertyless wage-workers or proletariat.

Owing to the relentless quest of capitalists for greater profits (surplus value), the condition of the employed must grow more and more desperate and degraded, the prophet of the proletariat asserted. And the owning class must grow progressively smaller, for the stronger capitalists would devour the lesser. On the other side, the proletariat would keep getting bigger and bigger, as once independent merchants and peasant proprietors were pressed down into this social category. At an auspicious moment the proletariat, goaded beyond endurance, filled with hatred of the possessing bourgeoisie and thoroughly class conscious, would rebel and sweep away the capitalist regime, lock, stock and barrel. "The knell of capitalist private property sounds. The expropriators are expropriated," Marx proclaimed. "Force is the midwife of every old society pregnant with a new one."

Government would then wholly supplant individual enterprise in economic activity. Competition would cease, for all men would be enveloped in one overarching classless fellowship. Class conflicts, acquisitiveness, exploitation would become simply memories of a dark past. Marx, it is true, had small interest in drafting a detailed blueprint for the post-revolutionary order. At the outset, an authoritarian dictatorship might be necessary, he explained, but eventually the state would wither away in a classless society. The golden age of the prehistoric past would return. Harmony would prevail among men. Paradise would in fact be regained.

For his scheme of things, Marx arrogantly claimed the certitude of science. Inexorable historical law, the march of destiny, would surely

[8] By a class Marx meant a social group whose economic interests were broadly identical.

bring the revolution and a collectivist society to pass. Men were watching the flowing tide of the inevitable, powerless as Canute. And yet Marx summoned workingmen of all countries to unite in a universal coalition to fight against the bourgeoisie. Proletarians had no fatherland, he asserted; they had nothing to lose but their chains; they had a world to win.[9]

THE INTERNATIONALS

Practicing politician as well as a theorist, Marx became the guiding spirit in the First International of collectivists set up in 1864 in London. It contained members of British and continental working class societies and contemplated bringing together similar groups in all countries. Periodically conferences were held, theories debated and policies mapped out. But the organization collapsed, partly because of the Communard insurrection in Paris (p. 379) which led to the suppression of collectivist societies generally, partly because of a furious ideological feud and struggle for power inside the International involving Marx, partisan of the strong state, and the anarchist Bakunin, who wished to see the state destroyed.

A Second International was founded in 1889 by Marxists and moderately minded collectivists of many countries. By and large, this organization stood for a peaceful transition from private to state ownership by parliamentary processes. It held frequent congresses in which common interests were discussed and evils in the prevailing society were roundly flayed. But with the onset of the First World War the Second International disintegrated. After that war the Third International was organized in Moscow and became the foreign missionary society of Soviet Russia.

THE ATTACK UPON COLLECTIVISM

Marxism struck not alone against the existing economy, but against traditions, values and ideas that had gone into the making of Western civilization as a whole. Defenders of the individual enterprise system launched thunderbolts at Marxism as well as at other patterns of collectivism; for them collectivism was like reading one's name on a tombstone. In the assault on Marxism, advocates of capitalism at some points found allies in adherents of other collectivist schemes. Large areas of Marxist theory were attacked as contradictory or as at variance with the facts. Basic Marxist premises, it was charged, instead of possessing the quality of unassailable law, were in fact dogmas requiring faith for acceptance.

The validity of the Marxian teaching on economic value, for example, was flatly denied. Capital helped to create wealth by erecting and equipping factories, railways and so on and made possible payment of wages in advance of the sale of products. From another point of view it was urged that if profits arose from labor alone, as Marx reasoned, and not from machines, then obviously there was no virtue in introducing machinery which would curtail profits.

As for the Marxian interpretation of history, it was derided as distorted, lop-sided, attaching too much weight to economic forces. The causes of large historical developments, it was contended, were so complicated and so thoroughly interlaced that no one set of factors could rationally be singled out as decisive. Human urges, such as love of freedom, love of country, religious enthusiasms, social idealism, none of them material, had been at least as powerful determinants of the course of events as economic appetites. Marx allowed wishful imaginings, it was asserted, to interpret the record of the past. The fatalistic materialism of Marx, furthermore, reduced man to a mere pawn, cutting away purposeful striving or inventiveness.

It was argued, too, that the Marxian postulate of the class struggle was fictional. Populations were not in fact divided into two rigid and hostile classes; rather, middle groups, increasing in number and strength, stood between the wealthy capitalists and the propertyless elements. The class struggle idea assumed

[9] The internationalism of Marx stopped short at the Slavs, Russians among them, whom he long despised with the fervor of an ordinary German bourgeois.

among wageworkers, moreover, a degree of solidarity which they did not in fact display. Workers in different industries within the same country were not united in purpose and action, not to speak of workers in different countries. Nonetheless, the idea of class struggle became a burning conviction with orthodox Marxists, arousing envy, vindictiveness and justifying a proletarian blood bath.

It was further declared that whatever attractions a collectivist economy might have on paper, as a philosophical ideal, those advantages could not be achieved in practice. "The inherent vice of capitalism," Winston Churchill once pungently asserted, "is the unequal sharing of blessings; the inherent virtue of socialism [collectivism] is the equal sharing of miseries." Some anti-collectivists maintained that a governmental bureaucracy could not manage mills, banks, farms, railways, as efficiently and productively as private enterprise. Other critics contended that it was impossible to turn up enough competent administrators to manage a gigantic collectivist machine, and any administration less than first class in intelligence, in devotion to public welfare and in ordinary horse-sense would invite disastrous consequences.

It was also said that in a collectivist commonwealth a small clique might gain mastery over the institutions of government, and degrade other citizens to so many robots, subject to the dictates of the state. Collectivism, it was asserted, could not operate without suppression of free institutions, representative government, liberty of press and speech. Cherished freedoms of the individual, in other words, could not be preserved in a collectivist society.

Another line of attack insisted that the factors involved in creating wealth were so diverse and complex that no more satisfactory method of distributing income could be devised than that which had long prevailed. The regime of individual enterprise while imperfect had nonetheless worked for progress, the general welfare and better standards of comfort. Any scheme to bring about equality in income would surely flounder, for men were innately competitive and sooner or later the brainier, the shrewder, the more energetic would forge ahead of his less well-endowed fellows.

It was reasoned, too, that in a Marxist society the pressure of population upon economic resources would soon grow overwhelming. Under the capitalist system the desire to get restrained the desire to beget. Remove that check and the birth-rate would increase prodigiously carrying destitution and misery in its train. In the thinking of other opponents, collectivism would entail unwholesome changes in the heritage of morality. A good deal of Marxist literature referred disparagingly to the institution of marriage and disputed the individualist tradition of parental responsibility. That emphasis invited obvious attacks, as did Marxist ethics which contained no absolute moral standards, no set codes or fixed rules of conduct.

As Lenin remarked: "We decry all this morality borrowed from concepts exterior to class or even to humanity. We say that it is only a trick to deceive the workingman and the peasant and to occupy his attention to the great profit of property owners and capitalists. Our own morality is entirely subordinated to the interests of the proletariat and the needs of the class struggle." Ruthlessness, deception and terrorism were all justified by Marxian doctrine if they promised to advance the revolutionary cause.

Certain opponents of Marxism based their indictment upon religious grounds. Marx himself was an atheist, who interpreted human purpose and destiny along purely materialist lines. Religion in any form he scoffed at as nothing other than a fairy tale, a species of wishful thinking, which persisted because it served the selfish ends of capitalistic exploiters and kept the masses submissive in the expectation of blissful reward in the world beyond.

Religion is "the sigh of the hard pressed creature," Marx cried, "it is the opium of the people." "The idea of God must be destroyed, it is the keystone of a perverted civilization." Devout churchmen, in consequence, looked upon Marx with the same horror that a pious medieval monk viewed the devil. Christian, Jew and Moslem perceiving in Marxism a deadly foe, combatted it with all the resources at their disposal.

The international flavor of Marxism, finally, drew fire in an age of nationalism. Wageworkers, Marx taught, should repudiate national allegiance in the prouder consciousness of class solidarity. Love of country, instead of being a noble emotion welling up within man, was designated as a tricky fraud propagated by exploiters or their lackeys to perpetuate their privileged position. Particularly, wage workers should resist wars or preparations to fight, since international conflicts were fought merely to enrich competitive capitalistic interests. Nationalists, on their part, flayed Marxism and Marxists as downright traitorous, the virulent enemies of the nation.

THE MARCH OF MARXISM

Regardless of criticisms, Marxism (and competing varieties of collectivism) gathered strength in Europe after 1880. For many discontented men and women, the militant creed of Marx seemed to diagnose expertly the ailments of the age and to offer an infallible recipe. Much of the strength of Marxism lay in its acceptance by intellectuals who believed this system contained insights and validity denied to any other analysis of society. Intellectuals popularized the abstract teachings of the master for industrial wage earners.

Silent allies of the Marxist cause in an era of rapid industrial changes were hunger, destitution, psychological dislocations and insecurity in urban communities. Hope was buoyed up by the assurance that workingmen "have nothing to lose but their chains." Up to a point, the ideology of Marx (and other collectivist patterns) filled the vacuum resulting from the decline of faith in the religious heritage.

Political parties grounded upon the Marxian credo were organized in the countries of continental Europe, attracting millions of followers and fellow travelers. As of 1914, the Marxist delegation was the largest in the popularly elected branch of the legislature of Imperial Germany. Over a hundred avowed Marxists held seats in the French parliament and large and disciplined parties existed in Austria, Italy, Belgium and Sweden. Nineteen disciples of Marx sat in the Imperial Russian legislature.

But among Marxist sects, fierce ideological quarrels, a maze of controversy and heresy hunts had arisen. Marxists were split into two main and antagonistic factions. Far the smaller group, which may be called Communist, international and revolutionary, believed in the conquest of power by physical force when political conditions were ripe. The other major wing of the movement was often spoken of as the evolutionary Marxists, doubtless better called the democratic Socialists. As the name suggested, this school advocated gradual transition to government ownership of productive facilities by peaceful and constitutional procedures. It would attain the declared goals of collectivism on the installment plan.

Spokesmen of democratic Socialism had no hesitancy in calling attention to miscalculations in the oracular prophecies of Marx. It was pointed out that his thought had solidified amidst the wretchedness and hardships of an age of scarcity which was giving way to an era of potential plenty. Orthodox Marxism, in the view of revisionists, was fighting an extinct Satan. Conditions of wageworkers had vastly improved, not grown more miserable. Pressure by trade unions and social welfare legislation had taken the sting out of much of the original Marxian argument against capitalism, while tax policies tended to effect levelling in incomes by due process of law. Leaders of evolutionary Marxism, moreover, whatever their public professions, esteemed the interests of their particular country above the Marxian principle of the international fraternity of toilers with hand and brain.

Though repudiating the Marxian ideology, the British Labour Party exhibited a good deal of the general outlook of democratic Socialists on the Continent. So attached was Britain to ideas of personal freedom that the Labour Party seemed the only feasible instrument to establish a collectivist society.

FOR FURTHER STUDY

ALEXANDER D. LINDSAY, *The Essentials of Democracy* (Philadelphia, 1929)
JAMES BRYCE, *Modern Democracies* (2 vols., New York, 1921)
BENJAMIN E. LIPPINCOTT, *Victorian Critics of Democracy* (Minneapolis, 1938)
CARLTON J. H. HAYES, *Essays on Nationalism* (New York, 1926)
HANS KOHN, *Panslavism: Its History and Ideology* (Notre Dame, 1953) PAPERBACK
JOHN A. HOBSON, *The Evolution of Modern Capitalism* (rev. ed., New York, 1926)
FRIEDRICH A. HAYEK, ed., *Capitalism and the Historians* (Chicago, 1954)
ISAIAH BERLIN, *Karl Marx* (new ed., New York, 1948) PAPERBACK
PETER GAY, *The Dilemma of Democratic Socialism* (New York, 1953) PAPERBACK
OSCAR D. SKELTON, *Socialism: a Critical Analysis* (Boston, 1911)
LOUIS L. SNYDER, *The Meaning of Nationalism* (New Brunswick, 1955)
BOYD C. SHAFER, *Nationalism* (New York, 1955) PAPERBACK
GEORGE D. H. COLE, *A History of Socialist Thought* (4 vols., London, 1953-56)
GEORGE WOODCOCK, *Pierre-Joseph Proudhon* (London, 1956)
JOHN H. JACKSON, *Marx, Proudhon, and European Socialism* (New York, 1957) PAPERBACK
SIDNEY HOOK, *Marx and the Marxists* (New York, 1955) PAPERBACK
ROBERT C. TUCKER, *Philosophy and Myth in Karl Marx* (London, 1961) PAPERBACK

CHAPTER XVIII

SCIENTIFIC DEVELOPMENT AND ITS HUMAN IMPLICATIONS

ON

THE ORIGIN OF SPECIES

BY MEANS OF NATURAL SELECTION,

OR THE

PRESERVATION OF FAVOURED RACES IN THE STRUGGLE FOR LIFE.

By CHARLES DARWIN, M.A.,

LONDON:
JOHN MURRAY, ALBEMARLE STREET.
1859.

ON THE ENLARGEMENT OF KNOWLEDGE

SUSPICIOUS though the historian is of the apparent newness of the new, he is prone to dwell upon novelties and to point up the impact of change upon civilization. Change has been the record of man, and promises so to be in the future. Though varying in intensity from age to age and country to country, change nevertheless is an everlasting phenomenon. Nothing that lives is static.

At times change has been more far-reaching, more dynamic, swifter than at others. Such was the epoch of the Renaissance, for example; such again was the nineteenth century with the development of technology and the machine, with man's heightened mastery over the raw forces of nature, with the explosive might of nationalism and the compulsions of democratic principles, and—not least—with the huge, unexampled increase in scientific knowledge and scholarship. It is easy to appreciate the material products which the magic of science brought forth, the tangibles to satisfy physical wants which affected day-to-day living. Science has been called "ordinary common sense," which will do if it is understood that what seemed common sense to one age may be considered nonsense by a later generation.

Advancing natural knowledge and bold generalizations of science disturbed many an idea which had long gone unchallenged as sublime truth. By the same token these novelties fostered fresh speculations on the whole scheme of life, subtly wrought a revolution in the whole intellectual outlook of some minds on man, his world, his social obligations and his destination. Arguably, the grip which science as the inspiration of intellectual innovations gained upon society may be as great as, or even greater than, the significance of science as the supplier of material goods.

Concerning the velocity and the magnitude of the enlargement of knowledge, a sensitive British scientist has written:

> We look on helpless while our material civilization carries us at a breakneck speed to an end which no man can forsee or even conjecture. And the speed forever increases. The last hundred years [written about 1945] have seen more change than a thousand years of the Roman Empire [sic], more than a hundred thousand years of the stone age. This change has resulted in large part from the applications of physical science which, through the use of steam, electricity and petrol and by way of the industrial arts, now affects almost every moment of our existence. Its use in medicine and surgery may save our lives; its use in warfare may involve us in utter ruination. In its more abstract aspects, it has exerted a powerful influence on our philosophies, our religions, and our general outlook on life.[1]

So mechanistic, so thoroughly this-worldly did the general outlook of the late nineteenth century become, that one historian of the period selected as the title of his book, *A Generation of Materialism*. Withal the dominant mood of the time possessed a strongly optimistic quality. The age was infused with the secular conviction that continuous improvement was as certain as the growth of a tree. And yet many men and women bothered little about the intellectual implications of scientific discoveries. They were too busy making a living, or making love, or having fun to care much about new ideas or old ideas. They adhered to accepted interpretations of man "and what is above, beneath, around, and within" man. For many personalities of prestige, Gladstone, for example, or Bismarck, the revelations of science or learning compelled no modifications in the "eternal verities." Content to greet the unseen with a confidence inspired by Christian orthodoxy, such individuals unconsciously influenced their fellows to hold to age-old beliefs.

The real nature of the intellectual innovations which have been ceaselessly at work since the mid-nineteenth century may be best appreciated by reference to the ideas on man and the world which were almost universally cherished at that point.

[1] Sir James Jeans, *The Growth of Physical Science* (London, 1947), p. 1.

INTELLECTUAL OUTLOOK ABOUT 1850

About 1850 the intellectual outlook of Western society was rooted deeply in the teachings and emphases of traditional Christian theology, in the faith which was "once and for all committed to the saints." Almost all Westerners believed that the earth and all living things had been created by special acts of the Supreme Being some 6,000 years earlier. The word "Westerners" should be heavily underlined because peoples outside the Western heritage, such as Chinese and Hindus, cherished other opinions on these matters.

That Western conception of origins emerged, of course, from the sacred literature of the ancient Hebrews, which in turn may have had antecedents in Mesopotamia. Among the champions of the idea of special creation, few have carried more weight in English-reading communities than John Milton. In his marvelous epic, *Paradise Lost*, it is explained how

> He took a golden compasses, prepared
> In God's eternal store, to circumscribe
> This universe, and all created things . . .
> And said, Thus far extend, thus far thy bounds,
> This be thy just circumference, O world.

A learned biblical scholar, Archbishop James Ussher, a contemporary of Milton, even went so far as to fix the precise time at which man was created—"October 28, 4004 B.C. at nine o'clock in the morning." That calculation was long looked upon as authoritative and still is by some people.

It was further believed that the Deity resembled a man in appearance with head, arms and other physical features, the Eternal Father so vividly painted by Michelangelo on the ceiling of the Sistine Chapel of the Vatican. In popular fancy, He was a benevolent old gentleman, heavily bearded, very like the portrait of Father Time caricatured annually on December 31. It was believed, moreover, that man and each and every form of lower animal had been created separately and was quite unrelated to other types. In the language of the Scriptures, "The Lord God formed man out of dust of the ground and breathed into his nostrils the breath of life; and man became a living soul."

Man and woman had been placed on this earth as sinless beings in a perfect, idyllic setting—a golden environment of bliss and felicity. But the first human pair sinned through eating the fruit of the tree of knowledge, and, as a result, all succeeding generations inherited a congenitally depraved nature. For a Chinese, to strike off one contrast between predominant Eastern and Western concepts, man was inherently good, not evil. A Confucianist scholar would have repulsed as abhorrent the Christian teaching of the innate sinfulness of man.

According to Christian belief, furthermore, the Almighty had sent His Son to this earth, a Man-God, without spot or blemish. By His sacrifice on Calvary's Cross, He had made atonement for the sins of all mankind. By belief in the Lord Jesus it would be possible for any man to assure the salvation of his soul in the world beyond. For those who died virtuous a glorious reward awaited, but for the wicked and sinful, horrible destruction. Consequently the supreme objective of man while on this earth was to ensure his salvation in the future, in keeping with the prescriptions of theology. "Remember man," the Scriptures admonished, "that thou art dust and unto dust thou shalt return." These several beliefs, then, were standard in orthodox Christian circles about the middle of the nineteenth century.

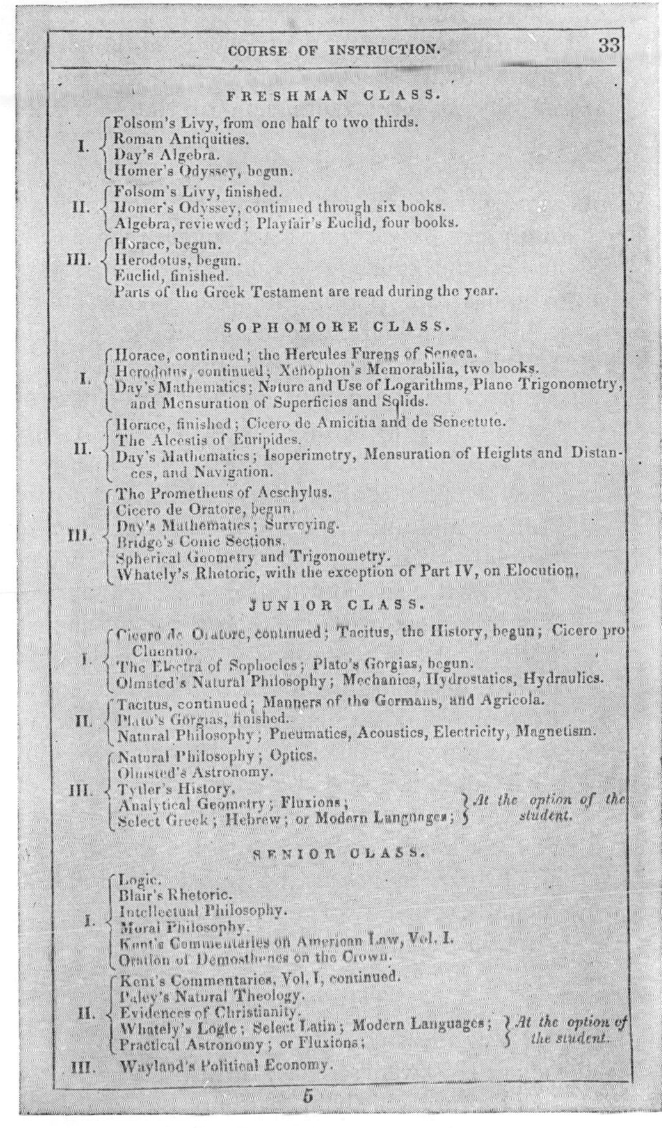

COURSE OF INSTRUCTION. 33

FRESHMAN CLASS.

I. Folsom's Livy, from one half to two thirds.
Roman Antiquities.
Day's Algebra.
Homer's Odyssey, begun.

II. Folsom's Livy, finished.
Homer's Odyssey, continued through six books.
Algebra, reviewed; Playfair's Euclid, four books.

III. Horace, begun.
Herodotus, begun.
Euclid, finished.
Parts of the Greek Testament are read during the year.

SOPHOMORE CLASS.

I. Horace, continued; the Hercules Furens of Seneca.
Herodotus, continued; Xenophon's Memorabilia, two books.
Day's Mathematics; Nature and Use of Logarithms, Plane Trigonometry, and Mensuration of Superficies and Solids.

II. Horace, finished; Cicero de Amicitia and de Senectute.
The Alcestis of Euripides.
Day's Mathematics; Isoperimetry, Mensuration of Heights and Distances, and Navigation.

III. The Prometheus of Aeschylus.
Cicero de Oratore, begun.
Day's Mathematics; Surveying.
Bridge's Conic Sections.
Spherical Geometry and Trigonometry.
Whately's Rhetoric, with the exception of Part IV, on Elocution.

JUNIOR CLASS.

I. Cicero de Oratore, continued; Tacitus, the History, begun; Cicero pro Cluentio.
The Electra of Sophocles; Plato's Gorgias, begun.
Olmsted's Natural Philosophy; Mechanics, Hydrostatics, Hydraulics.

II. Tacitus, continued; Manners of the Germans, and Agricola.
Plato's Gorgias, finished.
Natural Philosophy; Pneumatics, Acoustics, Electricity, Magnetism.

III. Natural Philosophy; Optics.
Olmsted's Astronomy.
Tytler's History.
Analytical Geometry; Fluxions; } *At the option of the*
Select Greek; Hebrew; or Modern Languages; } *student.*

SENIOR CLASS.

I. Logic.
Blair's Rhetoric.
Intellectual Philosophy.
Moral Philosophy.
Kent's Commentaries on American Law, Vol. I.
Oration of Demosthenes on the Crown.

II. Kent's Commentaries, Vol. I, continued.
Paley's Natural Theology.
Evidences of Christianity.
Whately's Logic; Select Latin; Modern Languages; } *At the option of*
Practical Astronomy; or Fluxions; } *the student.*

III. Wayland's Political Economy.

5

This was the complete Yale curriculum in 1846–1847.

HIGHER LEARNING

If it is true that the educated are the farseeing eyes, the sensitive antennae of society, it is important to know what was being taught about the middle of the nineteenth century. The content of learning on the higher planes tells in fact a good deal about the interests and perspectives of the time. To that point colleges in the United States, for instance, were operated fundamentally to promote the spiritual growth of a young and fluid continent. Except for the University of Pennsylvania and Columbia, all institutions of higher learning founded before the American Revolution, were designed to send forth an educated Christian clergy; as late as 1850, indeed, approximately one out of four college graduates had entered the professional service of the Church.

Classical literatures, for sheer quantity, still bulked largest in the curriculum. The writings of Greeks and Romans had by no means lost the prestige attained in the Renaissance centuries. But Christian doctrine, ecclesiastical learning and the inculcation of moral values claimed considerable attention inside the college classroom and without. Scriptural and church history were regarded as immeasurably more important and nourishing than the secular record of man. The disciplines of science still awaited effective admission to the course of study.

Institutions of higher learning, in short, were permeated with a definitely religious atmosphere. Aside from class exercises, ordinarily under the tutelage of churchmen, Scripture readings and prayers, morning and evening, were standard fare. As one student wrote: "Yale College is a little temple, prayer and praise seem to be the delight of the greater part of the students, while those who are still unfeeling are awed into respectful silence."

As the nineteenth century rolled along, many colleges and universities forsook a unified sense of Christian mission for intellectual fragmentation. That deviation in itself reflected the enlarging range of knowledge. Instead of religious authority the accent came to rest upon freedom of investigation. Instead of interest in the salvation of the learner, emphasis was laid upon toughening of character and preparation for social and civic responsibilities. Comparison of the curriculum in a secular college or university at the opening of the atomic age with that of 1850 strikingly reveals the dramatic and fundamental changes which swept over the Western mind in the interval.

THEORIES OF EVOLUTION

Many ideas considered indisputably valid as late as 1850 were seriously disturbed in the next half-century, chiefly by reason of the irresistible tide of science, though not for that cause alone. "Science moves, but slowly, slowly creeping on from point to point," Tennyson sang in *Locksley Hall* in 1842, just about the time when science was preparing to move forward at dazzling speed. Among the most arresting hypotheses in recorded Western history were doctrines of evolution—the slow growth of the earth from a simple, amorphous condition and the descent of existing forms of living things from earlier and lower types.

Geological findings and speculations, notably those of Lyell (p. 354), pushed the age of the earth far beyond the limits of biblical tradition. Despite differences in detail geologists came to agree that the globe was formed by an evolutionary development extending over a long, long time. Geological science talked in terms of millions of years and soberly conjectured that the earth was at least two billion years old. It seems improbable that life existed on the earth for more than a quarter of that time, and mammals may have been present for only about seventy million years. As yet, however, only beginnings have been made in establishing an absolute geologic time scale; suggestive evidence on this problem has resulted from study of radioactive elements that were used in the atomic bombs of the Second World War.

Just as geology quarreled with long accepted assumptions on the age of the earth, so zoological researches brought forth a hypothesis on the natural origin of man, animals and plants. Popularly this theory has been identified with the name of Charles Darwin, though Darwin did not in fact "discover" evolution. Rather the hypothesis was the outcome of speculations and investigation carried on spasmodically for many centuries, and is almost as old as European thought itself.

Like many another "revolutionary" idea, the germ of the evolutionary assumption appears to have originated in the fertile minds of old Greeks. Probably the first writer to deal with the problem was Anaximander, who lived five and a half centuries before the beginning of the Christian era. And Aristotle, ignorant of course of Hebrew teachings on origins, propounded some shrewd guesses on the evolution of organisms. Then, for long centuries the notion of evolution lay dormant save for the chance imaginings of philosophers.

It was late in the eighteenth century that studies of naturalists, such as Linnaeus and Buffon, quickened interest in the possibility of a physical relationship between man and higher members of the monkey family. Thereafter the subject was eagerly canvassed in learned circles; it is significant that Charles Darwin was only one of a galaxy of investigators exploring along similar lines. Darwin, however, overshadowed forerunners and contemporaries and earned the enthusiastic applause of subsequent students.

The wealth of careful observations and arguments with which Darwin fortified his conclusions, not the novelty of his thinking, gave him his exalted reputation. Fittingly, his remains rest in Westminster Abbey only a few paces removed from the grave of Isaac Newton.

DARWIN AND HIS CONTRIBUTION

Born on the same day as Abraham Lincoln, Darwin as a boy was a huge disappointment to his father, a well-to-do country physician. His grandfather, Erasmus Darwin, a naturalist himself, produced another eminent man of science, Francis Galton, founder of the science of eugenics. Dynasties, by the way, seem to occur more frequently in science than in other departments of intellectual endeavor.[2] In his youth Darwin acquired a passion for collecting and talent for precise observation. First he studied medicine and then for the ministry, without distinguishing himself for scholarship.

His experience with science was amateurish and unsystematic before he signed up as a naturalist on the British warship, *Beagle*, which in the 1830's sailed round the globe on scientific explorations. An attack of fever almost prevented Darwin from making the voyage. On that trip he accumulated scientific data which impressed him with the interrelation of all living things; he decided to devote his life to science, and he contracted an affliction which proved permanent. In consequence, he was obliged to live a cloistered existence, an advantage really, for he escaped distractions which consume the time and energy of so many scholars. Patience, industry, modesty and extreme intellectual reticence were marks of the man.

Darwin's thinking, "the whole tone of his mind," as he acknowledged, was profoundly influenced by the geological writings of Lyell. And the clue to his interpretation of the process of organic evolution—the concept of natural selection—flashed upon him after reading Malthus. Malthus, it may be recalled, pounded home the argument that population was inclined to increase faster than food supply and that natural agencies—disease and famine—tended to cut down weaker individuals. Comparable forces, Darwin conjectured, must operate to destroy lower animals and plants. He concluded that living forms best adapted to their environment—the fittest—survived in competition and produced offspring.

Charles Darwin

In the year 1858, a young British investigator, Alfred R. Wallace, sent Darwin an essay setting forth conclusions identical with those Darwin had himself arrived at. Next year Darwin published his famous *The Origin of Species*, with the subtitle, *By Means of Natural Selection, or the Preservation of Favoured Races in the Struggle for Life*. Only 1,250 copies were printed in the first edition.

His book, Darwin commented, was "one long argument," to the effect that existing animals and plants, far from being independently created, had evolved from older forms, by reason of many minute, random variations over extensive stretches of time. His logic may be sketched something like this: Living organisms

[2] The sons of Charles Darwin, Francis and George, maintained the scientific distinction of the family, as did a grandson, Charles, son of George.

Coincident with publication of Darwin's The Descent of Man *appeared this cartoon of him in a series entitled "Men of the Day."*

multiplied in geometric proportions, far more than grew to maturity and gave birth to offspring. Yet the numbers of individuals tended actually to remain more or less stationary. Unceasing competition between individuals and between species caused many to perish before maturity and so kept numbers in check.

What then determined which individuals or species should survive? Slight variations, each good for the individuals, gave them a little edge of superiority, made them better adapted to their environment, better equipped to survive. This theory on the mechanism of evolution by natural selection was Darwin's central thesis. Down through the ages, he seemed to say, nature had been performing the same function as experimental breeders of horses or corn, for instance. Finally, natural selection yielded enough slight, advantageous peculiarities, which, passed along from generation to generation, amounted to a major difference—a new species.

In a kind of supplementary volume, *The Descent of Man* (1871), Darwin wrote one of the most provocative books ever written. It argued that man was an animal and that if organic evolution was a tenable hypothesis, then clearly it applied to humans no less than to lower forms of life. Put in this light, man had evolved as the result of a prolonged process of natural selection.

"Man is descended from some lowly organized form," wrote Darwin, and "cannot any longer" be regarded as "the work of a separate act of creation." He foresaw that these views would "be highly distasteful to many," but he asserted: "We are not here concerned with hopes or fears, only with the truth as far as our reason permits us to discover it. . . ." The *Descent* churned up vastly more angry controversy than the *Origin* because of its unconventional pronouncement on the antecedents of man.

With the passage of time the thinking of Darwin underwent refinement, and in the last revision of the *Descent* he confessed uncertainty on the *cause* of the origin of species. Later investigators discarded much of Darwin's science; learned objections to the theory of natural selection were advanced by the score. That is not to say, however, that much authoritative dissent from the crucial idea of evolution was expressed; rather that scientific disagreement focused on the explanation of differentiation in species.

Exactly how the infinite variety of living things came about remained an unsolved mystery, though year by year pertinent evidence was uncovered. A hypothesis of evolution that did not evolve would be grotesque indeed. For example, a Dutch biologist, Hugo De Vries, proposed in 1901 that on occasion substantial variations instead of minute ones had taken place; mutations he called them. Nature selected these mutations, just like lesser changes, and transmitted them to later generations through the germ plasm.

If man has in fact descended from inferior ancestors, the process required an enormous time. It was suggested that probably more than a million generations had elapsed since the human and anthropoid stems branched off. And the precise line of evolutionary descent remained unknown. Some individuals accepted the hypothesis of evolution not because it could be proved beyond peradventure of doubt, but because the alternative theory of special creation imposed too heavy a strain upon their credulity. Not at all a dogma, the evolutionary concept was rather an assumption, which many men of science came to accept as a working hypothesis without effective rival.

OTHER LINES OF SCIENTIFIC INQUIRY

Driven on by curiosity and the competitive spirit, scientific workers pressed back the boundaries of knowledge on virtually every front. New knowledge, however trivial it might appear, might have consequences not at all trivial. As the reader will appreciate, the smallest, the simplest atom might radically shift the stream of history. Only a very few of the scientific discoveries of the late nineteenth century can be touched upon here and in a crude and elementary fashion at that.

Laced in with studies on physical evolution were geologic and related researches which led to fresh interpretations of the age of man. Lyell, for instance, published *The Antiquity of Man* (1863) which contained evidence of human existence for upwards of 50,000 years. Bones and part of the skull of a manlike creature were found (1856) in the Neanderthal valley near Düsseldorf in the Rhineland. Anthropology, the comparative study of mankind, identified them as the remains of a primitive human intimately related to the anthropoid ape. Vestiges of a hundred other specimens of fossil man, from *Pithecanthropus Erectus* on, were subsequently uncovered.

In another direction, explorers of the heavens radically diminished the significance of the earth in the majestic panorama of the universe. Whereas the older astronomy told of sun and planets, their movements and nature, the newer astronomy endeavored to describe the life history of sun and stars, their birth and death. Improved instruments of investigation revealed flocks of hitherto unknown stars, some of them of incredible magnitude. Bringing together the findings in astronomy, Sir James Jeans offered this illuminating comparison of stars and earth:

"A few stars are known which are hardly bigger than the earth, but the majority are so large that hundreds of thousands of earths could be packed inside and leave room to spare. Here and there," he went on, "we come upon a giant star large enough to contain millions of millions of earths. The total number of stars in the universe is probably something like the total number of grains of sand on all the seashores of the world."

"Such is the littleness of our home in space," Jeans concludes, "when measured up against the total substance of the universe." Small wonder, then, that the author entitled his book *The Mysterious Universe*.[3] The myriads of stars, we are assured, are constantly rushing about and are composed of elements familiar to the chemist.

It has been asserted that the greatest romance of very modern science is physics. Novel hypotheses on light, sound and heat were brought forward only to be discredited and supplanted in time. Investigations confirmed the principle that energy was indestructible. The publication in 1900 of the quantum theory of radiation by the German physicist Max Planck is recognized as the decisive event, revolutionary in its implications, in very modern physics.[4] As the hypothesis unfolded it upset "classical" physics, and led to the conclusion that the laws of nature are not

[3] Sir James Jeans, *The Mysterious Universe* (New York, 1930), p. 1.

[4] Planck discovered, it has been explained, "that a quantity called 'action,' which is mathematically related to the energy or to the momentum of a moving body, always changes by very small steps or 'quanta' of fixed and equal amounts and does not vary continuously as one would expect from ordinary observation."

Louis Pasteur

the clear-cut, unchanging rules they had seemed from Newton until then.

Down to 1895, the atom was thought of as a small indivisible mass, the exact structure of which could not be determined. But in that year the German physicist Wilhelm K. Roentgen discovered the X-ray in his laboratory at Würzburg, one of the few buildings in that city, incidentally, which escaped destruction in a devastating air-raid in the Second World War. Unwittingly he provoked more consternation, perhaps, than a military conqueror. X-rays led to the conception that matter was something composed in part of electrons, which are smaller than atoms. In the end it turned out that electrons are constituents of atoms. The atom itself seems to be a complicated system with a nucleus at the center and electrons revolving around it in a state of intense activity.

The leading scientific adventure of the twentieth century, it may well be, was the investigation of the structure and internal mechanisms of atoms. Probers in the spacious realm of physics begged to point out that all units of matter in the natural universe dance furiously. And what a dizzying dance the wizards in the laboratory led the layman with their atoms and electrons and later, photons and quantums.

Thanks to the X-ray, the living body could be photographed, which simplified the treatment of certain maladies. And by 1880 the germ theory of disease had won scientific acceptance; it traced disease to the multiplication of bacteria or other microscopic organisms in the body. That advance resulted largely from the pioneer researches of Louis Pasteur and Robert Koch. Starting off as a chemist, Pasteur switched to biology and laid the foundations of bacteriology. He demonstrated, among other things, that micro-organisms caused many infectious diseases and that if bacteria were excluded from anything susceptible to fermentation it would not ferment. His name is commemorated in "pasteurized" milk.

Through imaginative researches, Pasteur proved that disease could be fought by inoculation with a small number of germs which produced the disease in a mild form. All in all his discoveries imparted a tremendous stimulus to the study of disease-producing organisms. Frenchmen in a popular poll acclaimed this scientist as the most praiseworthy son of France. Paralleling the labors of Pasteur, Koch hit upon the micro-organism which caused tuberculosis, while other men isolated typhoid, cholera, plague and prepared protections against them.

Applied to surgery the germ theory compelled the use of antiseptics in operations and the sterilization of instruments, dressings and the surgeon's hands. Pathfinder here was a Briton, Joseph Lister. Medical and surgical innovations accounted in considerable measure for the unprecedented increase in the span of human life and the phenomenal growth in Western—later Asiatic—populations. Investigations on heredity proved serviceable in the breeding of animals and plants.

Out of chemical laboratories flowed an endless stream of compounds and synthetic products, such as dyes, drugs and disinfectants. Startling novelties quickly became commonplaces. The discovery of nitrocellulose, for example,

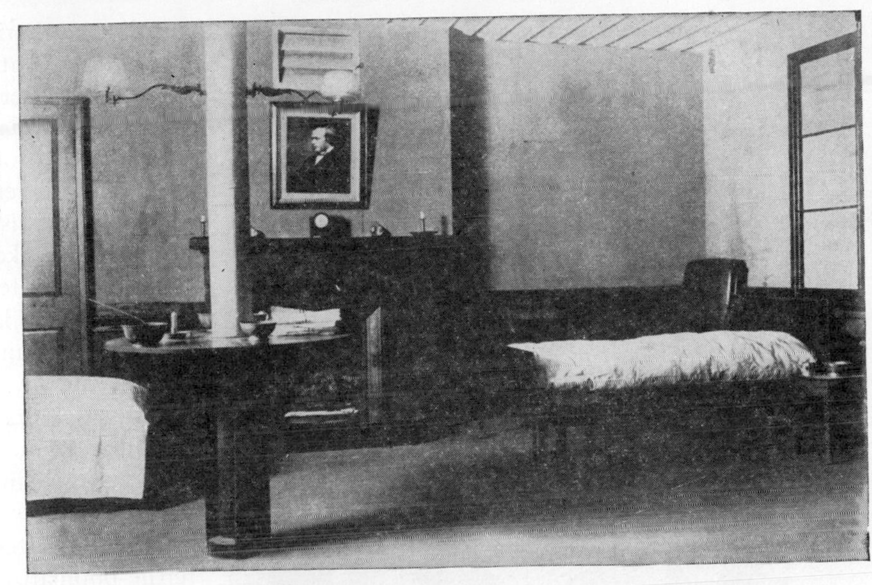

Reconstruction of Lister's ward at the Royal Infirmary, Glasgow, where in 1865 he evolved and put in practice the principles of antiseptic surgery.

pointed the way to the manufacture of such diverse products as high explosives, cameras, motion pictures and artificial silk. Expert chemists, the Russian Dmitri Mendeléyev for one, established the periodic law arranging elements in order of their atomic weights. In the meantime, the study of human behavior, psychology, started to divorce itself from philosophy and to move in the direction of an exact and experimental science.

So ramified and so rapid was the accumulation of scientific data after 1850 that it staggered the normal human intelligence. In a single year the titles of original monographs alone in physical science alone filled seventeen closely printed volumes. It was estimated that 25,000 publications were devoted to reports, which were intelligible only to highly specialized specialists. Many of the newly disclosed data were trifling in character, it is true, filling in details without contributing to advances in theory or interpretation.

Enormous gaps, moreover, still waited to be closed. In medicine, for example, ailments like the common cold, cancer, arthritis, heart failure and the degenerative diseases had not yet been conquered. Science had only the vaguest notion as to what happened to a piece of beefsteak after it was eaten; nor was it yet possible to predict what the weather would be a fortnight later. It would appear that scientific research, for all its accomplishments, had done little more than scratch the surface of the potentialities. Lord Tennyson phrased the situation poetically:

> As we surpass our father's skill
> Our sons will shame our own,
> A thousand things are hidden still
> And not one hundred known.

THE IMPACT OF "DARWINISM"

The onward rush of science carried varied and violent repercussions in its train. Learned circles were shaken up as seldom before, inspiring the poet Matthew Arnold to exclaim:

> But we, brought forth and rear'd in hours
> Of change, alarm, surprise—
> What shelter to grow ripe is ours,
> What leisure to grow wise?

Evolutionary hypotheses required a drastic revision in the conventional time perspective. They suggested, too, that the surface of the earth instead of being fixed once for all time underwent endless change and that the origins of man had to be searched for along naturalistic lines. Such notions, terrifying to many, profoundly affected all areas of thought. The Darwinian assumption, moreover, upheld the general proposition of evolution and growth—the idea that the present is the heir of the past and

Punch *contributed a humorous comment on the Evolutionary Hypothesis.*

the parent of the future. It became fashionable to speak of the evolution of the battleship, or the evolution of ethics, or the evolution of what not.

Thus a major impetus was imparted to the idea of progress, of unending improvement, which penetrated deeply into the general perspective of the time. Darwin himself predicted that "man in the distant future will be a far more perfect creature than he now is . . . after a long-continued slow process." That prophecy clashed head-on with the popular belief that perfection had prevailed in the past, in a paradisical Garden of Eden. In an era when science had achieved ascendancy over the mind of man, even of some ordinary men, practitioners of science were tempted to exploit the awe which their learning invited and to pronounce with seeming authority on subjects not their own. Not infrequently when scientists wandered from their special preserves they tended to dismiss their standards of scholarship and to sound off in tones of arrogance. But science was not in fact omniscience.

Many scientists, it is true, older ones more especially, mocked at the evolutionary doctrine, but others hastened to give wide currency to the hypothesis laying their own sophistication upon it. Certain popularizers of science performed the invaluable role of middlemen between specialists (with their technicalities) and inquiring laymen who wished to get the gist of the thing and its bearing upon the common life.

Britain boasted two extremely effective and fertile popularizers of evolution in Thomas H. Huxley and Herbert Spencer. Nicknamed "Darwin's bulldog," Huxley, a biologist of note, proved a redoubtable controversialist for the evolutionary hypothesis. Master of the barbed epithet, Huxley either pelted adversaries with insults and clichés or waved them aside with pitying contempt as too ignorant to see the

Thomas Henry Huxley

light. He likened the acrimonious debate over the acceptability of evolution to a "new Reformation."

In immensely popular writings such as *Man's Place in Nature* (1863) and *The Struggle for Existence in Human Society* (1880), Huxley asserted that man was nothing more than a transitional being in the evolutionary process. In body and brain, he remarked, man was "more nearly allied to the higher apes than the latter are to the lower." He thought, however, that education and social action, not the survival of the fittest, would promote social progress. No admirer of Christian theology, Huxley derided beliefs which lay beyond the grasp of the senses, inventing the term "agnostic" to describe his own state of mind. As the guide to the good life he preferred experimentation to the admonitions of Christian theology.

Perhaps Spencer was more successful than any other social thinker in rooting the evolutionary concept in English-reading communities. Even before the publication of *Origin of Species,* he had expounded the idea of gradual progress in human and institutional development; Darwinism was manna from heaven for him. As an author, he undertook to unify and explain all scientific achievements and their philosophical implications. Contemporaries said that he possessed the most capacious intellect on record, an Aristotle joined to a Newton. His monumental enterprise, *A Synthetic Philosophy,* occupied ten volumes and required thirty-six years for fulfilment.

It was Spencer's contention that science and theology alike must acknowledge an inscrutable Power behind phenomena, the Unknowable. Concerning this Unknowable, however, science could affirm nothing. Spencer baldly identified the fittest with the best and evolution with progress. "Evolution can only end," he thought, "in the establishment of the greatest perfection and the most complete happiness." Spencer extolled the notion of progress in such naive and optimistic language and with such pseudo-scientific verbiage that he invited attack and discredit. And yet, in the half century before the First World War, Spencerian optimism provided the nearest approach to a philosophy for multitudes of Western men.

The leading herald of the Darwinian theorem and the doctrine of the survival of the fittest in German Europe was a Jena zoologist, Ernst Haeckel. Highly respected for scientific attainments, Haeckel urged that the evolutionary principle held good for thought in general and for religion as well as for natural phenomena. His easy-to-read books, *The Natural History of Creation* (1868) and *The Riddle of the Universe* (English edition, 1901), familiarized thousands with his interpretations of Darwinism. A pantheist by conviction, Haeckel repudiated many standard Christian teachings. To rancorous criticism of his views he scornfully replied in kind. For the general reader, too, was *Force and Matter* (1855) by the German scholar, Ludwig Büchner. It served as the law and the prophets for many a young German and Russian intellectual. Vigorously polemical, this tract ridiculed the supernatural explanation of the universe and popularized aridly materialistic currents of belief. The evidences of science appeared to vindicate the dogmatism of philosophical materialism.

Whereas in Europe independent thinkers, under the shadow of Darwinian science, moved toward a mechanistic interpretation of life, in the United States the thought of William James and others bowed to relativism. Since they subordinated the intellectual to the practical they were labeled pragmatists. Moral and religious ideas, according to pragmatism, evolved in close relation to human experience. Rather than being absolute, ethical standards and religious beliefs were simply provisional. They were to be prized in the measure that they strengthened character and enriched experience. According to the pragmatist philosophy, currently acceptable ideas might be fruitfully revised in the future.

"SOCIAL DARWINISM"

Darwin personally was not much concerned with social applications of his great generalization, but his teaching was exploited by others to account for political and social customs and institutions. Many a writer interpreted, or rather misinterpreted, the science of Darwin to mean that the law of tooth and claw was the law of nature, not only for the animal kingdom but for man himself.

Thus an influential and versatile London publicist, Walter Bagehot, in *Physics and Politics* (1869) described the evolution of political communities, arguing that they too proceeded toward perfection by slight changes. Other writers interpreted the struggle for existence as the supreme dynamic force in international affairs: through the stern ordeal of war, the better nations were chosen while the inferior ones were crowded to the wall. Armed conflict, far from being an affliction of society, would impel social progress, in keeping with the unrepealable law of nature.

"History shows me one way, and one way only, in which a high state of civilization has been produced," declared the British mathematician Karl Pearson in 1900, "namely, the struggle of race with race, and the survival of the physically and mentally fitter race. . . . Mankind as a whole, like the individual man, advances through pain and suffering only. The path of progress is strewn with the wreck of nations; traces are everywhere to be seen of the hecatombs of inferior races, and of victims who found not the narrow way to the greater perfection."

Aggressive partisans of a kindred doctrine appeared in Germany and in distant Russia. Nor was the notion a mere passing fad, for as late as the Second World War, Dr. Robert Ley, head of the Nazi Labor Front, explained: "War is not in contrast to peace, but simply another form of expression of the uninterrupted battle of nations and men. It is an expression of the highest and best in manhood."

In a similar way, the Darwinian assumption was enlisted to support unfettered economic individualism. Proficiency in the amassing of wealth was interpreted as clear evidence of inherent excellence. Allow full freedom of indi-

Pedagogy was transformed by the evolutionary concept. The day of the child-centered school dawned and "learning" was attempted on the playground as well as in the classroom.

vidual enterprise, it was argued, and the fittest would survive in fierce competition, precisely as nature operated selectively in the animal kingdom. The survival of the fittest was the survival of quality. Individual differences seemed to "result simply from the different degrees of success with which men have availed themselves of the chances which were presented to them," declared the Yale sociologist, William Graham Sumner.

On the other side, collectivist advocates of the overthrow of the private enterprise economy discovered in the evolutionary principle confirmation of their particular convictions.[4] Pointing to evidences of mutual aid among ants and bees, some writers argued for a collectivist organization of human society. It seemed to them that animal life was in fact governed by a law that read: "Cooperate or die." The fittest were individuals or species who best practiced working together. They asserted that cooperative influences were biologically more important than competitive and destructive forces, from the lowest form of life to man himself.[5]

Other departments of knowledge were permeated by the evolutionary concept. Historians, as never before, conceived of society as an evergrowing organism which had evolved out of a simple, undifferentiated culture. In the same way, literature on pedagogy teemed with the jargon of "variation," "selection," and "adaptation." Child consciousness was investigated as a process of development. No branch of learning or thought wholly escaped the implications of the cautious, tentative and apologetic reasoning of Darwin.

THE NEW LEARNING AND RELIGIOUS THOUGHT

Above all, no doubt, the impact of the Darwinian assumption upon religious thought had the most profound importance. But before appraising the bearing of the new learning upon religious thinking, two other streams of investigation which shaped the course of religion in the West must be mentioned: critical scrutiny of biblical records and a deeper study of comparative religion—neither of them, of course, novelties.

Representative of the literature in the first category was *Ecce Homo* (1866), a slight essay dealing with the human aspects of Jesus, by John R. Seeley, a Cambridge University don. Written with force and sobriety, the book was extensively circulated and provoked impassioned criticism from Christian spokesmen as destructive of Christianity itself. Far more popular was a beautifully written *Life of Jesus* (1863) by Ernest Renan. Educated as a theologian, Renan switched to skepticism by reason of his studies. Rejecting what he considered miraculous elements in the gospel stories, Renan portrayed the founder of Christianity as "an incomparable Man" and an inspiring moral teacher. While Renan shied away from the supernatural in Christianity, he nonetheless warmly espoused religion as an aesthetic force.

Prominent among British scholars who applied historical criticism to the Old Testament was W. Robertson Smith. His books, *The Prophets of Israel* and *Religion of the Semites*, told of similarities in the beliefs and ritualistic customs of the ancient Hebrews and other groups in the Near East. A succession of Jewish, Dutch and German scholars, notably Professor Julius Wellhausen at Göttingen, enriched the body of critical literature on the Old Testament.

Studies of primitive cults and moral codes and of Buddhism, Hinduism and other Asiatic creeds showed them to contain much that was philosophically impressive and ethically exalted. In a work of immense erudition entitled *Primitive Culture* (first ed. 1871), E. B. Tylor blazed a trail for searchers after the origins of the belief in gods among savages. Personally he found the major clue in the desire of men to establish relations between themselves and unseen powers, conceived of in terms of spirit.

[4] Karl Marx thought so well of Darwin that he considered dedicating *Das Kapital* to him. At the funeral of Marx, Engels declared, "In the same way as Darwin has discovered the law of evolution of organic nature, so Marx has discovered the evolutionary laws of human history."

[5] See, for instance, Ashley Montagu, *On Being Human* (New York, 1950), a clear, short analysis by a prominent anthropologist.

Later appeared the classical work of James G. Frazer, *The Golden Bough* (1890), which eventually expanded into a dozen volumes. An anthropologist, interested in primitive and civilized creeds, rituals and beliefs, Frazer ransacked the world of mythology and folklore in his quest for evidence. Everywhere, magic preceded and was woven into the many varieties of religious experience, he concluded. Certain rites and doctrines of Christianity appeared to him to have parallels in half-buried myth and ritual of primitive cults. *The Golden Bough*, which dazzled a whole generation with its brilliance, is often listed among the most outstanding books of all time.

Slowly some knowledge of comparative religion entered the consciousness of the general intelligent public. Specialists in the subject were intrigued by the fact that the principal religions originated in Asia. All alike taught much the same ethical principles, at points in almost identical language. Ideals inspired Christians and Shintoists to energetic activity, but to passivity in the case of Hinduism or Buddhism. Each creed praised poverty and assured believers that the Almighty would unfailingly provide for the morrow.

All of these religions offered human consolations, some more radiant than others, some more reasonable, others more extreme. Just as it is difficult to imagine that Confucianists, for instance, would fight one another for generations over points of belief, so it is hard to believe that a Joan of Arc could emerge from the Hindu environment. Whatever the practices of disciples, the "world" religions uniformly proclaimed reverence, compassion and brotherly love.

KNOWLEDGE QUARRELS WITH THEOLOGY

Conflict between advancing knowledge and theological beliefs has been perennial in modern history. But in tone and tempo, controversies of the late nineteenth century outdid anything that had gone before. Christianity in particular faced a major intellectual crisis. Exponents of scientific theories, who smugly pretended to have solved the riddle of the universe, battled furiously with no less belligerent advocates of Christian orthodoxy. Men concerned about the things of the mind and spirit, men confronted with plain problems of the individual conscience, were aware of a great unrest.

Scanning the revelations of astronomy, for example, some minds were impressed by the power of the Creator who had fashioned this mysterious universe. Others, however, thought it absurd that man, dwelling on the small speck called the earth, should assume that the universe was created for him.

An epic and hectic battle raged over the evolutionary hypotheses, especially over the theory of the natural origins of man. The explicit challenge to the verbal accuracy of the Scriptures defied much that was traditional and standard in the Christian scheme of things. To assume and assert that humankind had descended from lower animals was repudiated by many theologians as degrading, an insult to human intelligence, the monstrous aberration of a wicked and degraded mentality. Declared one prominent churchman: "These infamous doctrines have their only support in the most abject passions. Their father is pride, their mother impurity, their offspring revolutions. They came from hell and return thither, taking with them the gross creatures who blush not to proclaim them."

Taking a broad view, the response to the intellectual fashions of the time differed in the two great branches of Catholicism and in Protestant quarters. Orthodox Catholicism, the predominant creed of Russia and the Balkans, was little affected, held contentedly to conventional orthodoxy, though radically minded Russians often adopted the new perspectives in a crude and extreme form.

Within the Roman Catholic Church the reaction to the new views tightened theological opinions and the authority of the papacy. Pope Pius IX defiantly thundered against the Darwinian hypothesis as relegating man "to the level of unreasoning brutes." In time, however, the concept of evolution came to be regarded in Catholic circles as of doubtful validity, for in any case man was endowed with an immortal soul, which had no bearing on the origin of his physical body. "The human soul," wrote a Catholic scholar, "could not have been derived through natural evolution from that of the brute, since it is of a spiritual nature; for which reason we must refer its origin to the creative act of God."

The Roman Catholic aversion to contemporary secular tendencies was strongly manifested in several ways. On his own initiative, Pope Pius IX proclaimed (1854) belief in the Immaculate Conception of the Virgin Mary to be a dogma, whose acceptance was necessary for salvation. According to this doctrine the mother of Christ was born, like Him, without taint of original sin. This teaching should not be confused, as is frequently done, with the doctrine of the Virgin Birth of Jesus.[6]

In 1864, when papal temporal power was dangerously jeopardized by the Italian unification movement, the Pope published a *Syllabus of Errors*. In it he reiterated blanket condemnation of eighty prevalent ideas and assumptions which had been denounced in detail in earlier papal utterances. Included in the indictment were pantheism, rationalism, communism, Bible societies and unacceptable opinions concerning the authority of the Church and the Pope. The Pope, it was asserted, neither "can nor should reconcile and align himself with progress, liberalism and modern civilization."

Much that the *Syllabus* condemned was repugnant to all Christians of the time, but certain of the censures were construed by non-Catholics as perilous for the principle of "a free church in a free state." Fervent outcries of alarm resounded in non-Catholic quarters. Defenders of the papacy hastened to protest that misinterpretations had arisen because the "errors" had not been examined in their original context. It was also pointed out that the *Syllabus* elicited little approval beyond the papal court itself.

[6] Four years later this dogma was invigorated by the most celebrated Catholic mystery of the century. A young French girl reported that the Virgin Mary had appeared to her near Lourdes and revealed the location of a hitherto unknown spring possessing curative properties. Lourdes swiftly became the most frequented pilgrimage shrine of Roman Catholic Christianity.

That differences existed in fact between papal declarations and practice was illustrated in concordats or treaties negotiated with the governments of Austria (1855) and Latin American countries. Catholicism, it is true, was defined in these documents as the state religion and churchmen were assigned monopolistic control over education. But there were other clauses. Governments were authorized to nominate the key-men in the Christian hierarchy, the bishops; and clergymen lost the old privilege (except in Ecuador) of trial in ecclesiastical courts.

On the very eve of the loss of temporal power in Rome, Pius IX vigorously asserted papal spiritual ascendancy. For the first time in three centuries leading churchmen met in Council at the Vatican, and added the dogma of the personal infallibility of the Pope to Catholic doctrine. At the conclave, fundamentals of the faith were clarified and the principal shortcomings of the age were enunciated.

Concerning the question of papal infallibility two factions appeared in the Council, the larger assenting to the view that adoption would reinforce the prestige of the Pope. A considerable minority, on the other side, made up of bishops from countries of mixed Christian professions, opposed the dogma as inexpedient or bound to arouse resentment. On the decisive vote, however, the dissenters sank into obscurity and only an occasional negative voice was registered (1870).

According to this doctrine, whenever the Pope speaks *ex cathedra* on matters pertaining to faith or morals he is infallible, cannot err, and his opinion becomes binding on the faithful. Among theologians, differences of opinion have prevailed as to just when the Pope is speaking *ex cathedra;* but in any event all papal pronouncements carry great weight with the tens of millions of Catholics around the world.

These several acts, extending from 1854 to 1870, strengthened loyalties of some Catholics, but alienated others, diverting them into secession or agnosticism. While the great majority of Catholics accepted papal infallibility, sharp dissent sounded in German Europe, more particularly in theological schools. Intellectual leadership in the protest devolved upon Professor Johann J. Döllinger, church historian at Munich, who assailed the infallibility dogma as historically indefensible. In the spirit of French Gallicanism he called for limitations on papal jurisdiction. Excommunicated for his stand, Döllinger was cheered by admiring colleagues who elected him rector of the University of Munich. A small contingent of Catholics actually withdrew from the church, and, calling themselves the "Old Catholics," set up a special organization, without, however, departing from the basic tenets of Catholicism.

In spite of all buffetings, in spite of some desertions, Roman Catholicism continued to bring religious satisfactions to millions. Under Pope Leo XIII the papacy attained to prestige unexampled for centuries. That a man could be at once an eminent scientist and an observant Catholic was well illustrated in the case of Louis Pasteur. Asked how an individual with his scientific interests could retain faith in religion, Pasteur replied, "The more I know, the more nearly does my faith approach that of the Breton peasant. Could I but know it all, my faith would doubtless equal even that of the Breton peasant women."

How then did Protestantism cope with the intellectual acids of modernity? Since the new learning disputed the literal accuracy of the Scriptures, it seriously disturbed those who contended that "the Bible only is the religion of Protestantism." Very many shadings of belief appeared in Protestant churches, which may be thought of as falling into three broad categories.

First, the conservative Fundamentalists, who insisted intransigently upon the verbal inspiration of the Scriptures and the authority of the inherited creed. Against modern perversions they confidently reasserted their allegiance to traditionalism. Revisions in belief were as unwelcome as a cold douche on a bleak day. They were militantly hostile to evolutionary theories. Fervent Fundamentalists even argued that remains of fossil man had been deliberately planted in the earth by the Almighty (or Satan) to test the fidelity of Christians. Fundamentalists also rejected as incredible, secular historical explanations of the origins and diffusion of Christianity. For them the rugged fundamentals of Protestantism expounded by Luther, Calvin, Wesley and their successors were entirely tenable and entirely adequate.

"Modernists," the second category, in various shapes and different degrees, endeavored to adjust Christian thought to the newer perspectives. They struggled, hesitantly for a time, to find a compromise between acquiescence in ancient orthodoxy and the abandonment of almost all that the noblest Christian minds of the past had cherished. Breaking through the bonds of habit, the "modernists," wise in their generation, welcomed whatever was accepted by science. They tried to bring religious teachings into conformity with ordered knowledge of the world.

It seemed plain to the modernists that man had ascended, slowly, tortuously from lowly origins. It seemed plain to them that the Golden Age lay somewhere in the future, not in the remote past. Experimentalism and adventuresomeness in religious thinking appealed strongly to this wing of Protestantism. For some modernists, the presumed transformation from animal to human intelligence and ethical ideals sufficiently warranted the assumption of a Guiding Hand. Some would have endorsed the verdict of Balzac: "Even if God seems to you incomprehensible and inexplicable, confess at least that in all physical phenomena you recognize in Him a consistent and exquisite craftsman."

Less and less concerned with theological issues, modernists placed increasing emphasis on the ethical and social values of Christianity. Opposed to restraints upon the quest for religious truth, modernist clergymen expressed their honest convictions and reserved the right of private judgment to worshipers.

Although modernists differed widely among themselves, the statements which follow may be taken as representative attitudes on some of the crucial features of the Christian heritage. The Bible, first of all, was looked upon as containing inspired literature on the relation of man to the Supreme Being and to his fellows. Its contents should be examined by the same tests of reason and literary value as any other works. Accepting Jesus as an historical personage, modernism held Him to be divine in a way that any individual was potentially divine. His character and teachings merited reverence and emulation. Human nature was interpreted as imperfect but not inherently evil; by a gradual process man had risen to a higher plane, which argued that he could go on improving. The doctrine of eternal punishment for wrongdoing was cast away. Whatever the future might hold in store, the best preparation was to live abundantly in the present.

A third category of Protestants, an exceedingly amorphous group, withdrew entirely from organized Christianity. They chose to work out their beliefs without the ministrations or guidance of clergy. Certain dissenters, it is true, acknowledged that Christianity possessed elements of inspiration superior to those of other great religions. But they eschewed many traditional teachings as unsupported by enough evidence to make them worth bothering about. They were prone to dismiss the certitudes of ancient Christian authority as delusive.

Yet they prized the Christian way of life conceived of as ethics, such as that the strong ought to bear the infirmities of those that are weak, and that it was "a duty to care for him who shall have borne the battle and his widow and orphan"—Christian ethics devoid of Christian dogma. Certain of the men and women who withdrew from the Church looked upon the Gospels as guides to secular idealism and social progress. The Sermon on the Mount, as an example, contained sound advice concerning personal behavior and on how to discover success, tranquillity, peace of mind and soul.

Some former Protestants became quite indifferent to religious realities and lapsed into a state of moral nihilism. Humane but disillusioned they believed in nothing very much, aside from a vague benevolence. A class emerged which was more secular and agnostic than at any other period in Christian history, without faith, with very little hope, only charity. John Stuart Mill, in his *Autobiography*, referred to "this age, in which real belief in any religious doctrine is feeble and precarious, but the opinion of its necessity for moral and social purposes almost universal." The cult of humanism, which called itself religious but substituted faith in man for belief in a Supreme Being, obtained no small popularity. "Glory to Man in the highest! for Man is the master of things," sang the English poet, Algernon C. Swinburne in *The Hymn of Man* (1871).

JUDAISM

To a remarkable degree, Judaism, the seedbed of the Western spiritual traditions, responded to the intellectual currents of the nineteenth century in a manner akin to Protestantism. Previously Jews had stood apart from their Christian neighbors, partly by choice, partly by compulsion. So different were they from the people among whom they lived that they were considered, and indeed considered themselves, as a separate group. They prided themselves on their own day of rest and worship, their own dietary laws, their own literary language, their use of Hebrew in religious services and their special education.

For centuries Jewish children minutely studied the *Talmud*, a discursive commentary of immense bulk on the books of Moses. It emphasized religious forms, ceremonies and pietism. No skepticism challenged obedience to scriptural and ecclesiastical authority. Orthodox Jews cherished, too, the dream of an eventual restoration to Palestine; by them the exile from the ancient homeland was interpreted as temporary punishment for the sins of the forefathers.

By reason of deep-seated and hereditary antipathies, Jews were generally debarred from many kinds of employment and subjected to special taxes in many countries. They were confined to prescribed districts in city and village and were the victims of other forms of discrimination. Beginnings in the emancipation of Jewry were made in the seventeenth century in Holland and England. But the major impulse to liberation came from the French "Enlightenment" and the French revolutionary principles of freedom and equality. Bit by bit, legal discriminations were relaxed and equality of rights

Moses Mendelssohn

was proclaimed, though social ostracism was not easily swept away.[7]

Inside Jewry, meantime, forces were wearing down the walls of isolation. Under the progressive and tolerant leadership of Moses Mendelssohn, late in the eighteenth century, cultivated Jews of Germany embraced modern modes of thought. An expert in philosophical and religious literature, and gifted with rare powers of lucid analysis, Mendelssohn was hailed as "the Jewish Plato." He pleaded with his coreligionists to study secular learning, to employ the German language in their services of worship and in other ways to assimilate themselves to the Gentile environment. Mendelssohn flatly denied the uniqueness of Judaism which encouraged a drift into Christian communions. More than that, he promoted critical examination of the literature and rich inheritance of Judaism. Such studies, coupled with the impact of scientific progress, created fissures within the Jewish fellowship.

Many Jewish leaders, in eastern Europe notably, preferred to follow the conservatism of the fathers in beliefs and ritualistic devotions. What was spoken of as neo-orthodoxy was persuasively expounded by a German-Jewish theologian, Samson R. Hirsch. Never afraid of speaking his mind with conviction and erudition, Hirsch silenced current doubts and ridiculed the assertion that the new learning demanded revision in time-proved fundamentals.

Jewish "modernists," however, forsook portions of the traditional faith and observance. At Hamburg a "reformed" synagogue was organized (1818) with services in German and with instrumental music. The notion of an eventual return to Palestine was abandoned. A few congregations in western Europe and the United States copied the Hamburg reforms, while more extreme "modernists" dropped the conventional Jewish Sabbath, the rite of circumcision and study of the *Talmud*. Holding that opinions rested upon the right of individual judgment, Jewish modernists wished to bring religious beliefs into line with modern learning.

As was true of the Protestant modernists, their Jewish counterparts manifested deeper interest in the social applications of their creed than in theological debates. And in a similar fashion, the larger section of Judaism clung to conservative fundamentalism. That orientation was particularly true in the East of Europe, especially in Russia, which contained (1910) about half the Jews of the world, then estimated at 11,500,000. As was the case with Protestantism, again, scientific discoveries and the force of secularism impelled some Jews to disassociate themselves wholly from the faith of the fathers. In the era of assimilation, traditional differences between Jews and Gentiles gradually decreased or vanished altogether, in spite of many counteracting factors. Jews were perhaps more fully integrated with the general community in Germany than in any other continental country containing a substantial Jewish population.

SUMMING UP

The "century of hope" was distinguished by a prodigious expansion of science and knowledge. Applied science brought forth more and different material products and extended life

[7] For Jews in Imperial Russia, see pp. 461–2.

expectancy, while facile inferences from scientific findings wrought radically upon inherited ideas. Not only did science contribute to fresh interpretations of experience, but it had bearing upon ethics, the study of society and of religion. The concept of evolution, most importantly, thrust into every department of thought and learning.

Intellectual novelties profoundly affected the religious heritage of the West. Not only the several branches of Christianity, but Judaism, too (and Mohammedanism), were sorely troubled and replied divergently to changing climates of opinion. Simultaneously strong secular tendencies captured the whole philosophy of living of some men. The appeal of Marxian collectivism, purely materialistic and antitheistic in outlook, lured many away from old religious moorings. Papal resistance to national consolidation weakened the hold of the Church upon some Italian patriots. Everywhere the imperious claims of nationalism blacked out religious interests, as did materialism and worldly preoccupations in an age of machinofacture, growing comfort and greater leisure.

Altogether the late nineteenth century marked the third stage in the progressive deviation from ancient and medieval religious beliefs and and practices. The earlier phases were of course the Renaissance and the Reformation and the intellectual rationalism associated with the person of Voltaire. Having said that, it must also be said that a majority of men and women clung to the satisfactions and security which religion afforded and from their faith derived values which lie beyond the appraisal of history.

FOR FURTHER STUDY

William C. Dampier, *A History of Science* (new ed., New York, 1958)

Alfred N. Whitehead, *Science and the Modern World* (New York, 1926) paperback

Paul B. Sears, *Charles Darwin* (New York, 1950)

Jacques Barzun, *Darwin, Marx, Wagner* (Boston, 1941) paperback

Paul de Kruif, *Microbe Hunters* (New York, 1926)

Richard Hofstadter, *Social Darwinism in American Thought, 1860–1915* (Philadelphia, 1944) paperback

Karl Pearson, *National Life from the Standpoint of Science* (London, 1901)

John M. Robertson, *A History of Free Thought in the Nineteenth Century* (2 vols., New York, 1931)

Henri de Dorlodot, *Darwinism and Catholic Thought* (Eng. trans., London, 1922)

David Philipson, *Reform Movement in Judaism* (New York, 1931)

Gertrude Himmelfarb, *Darwin and the Darwinian Revolution* (New York, 1959) paperback

Loren C. Eiseley, *Darwin's Century* (New York, 1958)

Stow Persons, ed., *Evolutionary Thought in America* (New Haven, 1950)

CHAPTER XIX

THE ASCENDANCY OF GERMANY

GERMANY MOVES UP

"EUROPE has exchanged a mistress for a master," it was remarked after the French defeat by Germany in 1870. As epigrams go, that one will do. Possessor of the strongest military establishment, Germany, at the end of the century, started to construct a great battle fleet. A colonial "have not" power, she struggled to obtain overseas empire, and in so doing significantly shaped the course of world diplomacy. Nowhere was nationalism more intense or assertive than in the proud, cocky and exuberant young German Empire.

The prevailing trends of the epoch were impressively exhibited in the country of Prince Bismarck and Emperor William II. Militarism, imperialism, the pursuit of power flourished luxuriantly. Machine industry transformed a relatively poor nation into the wealthiest of continental states. German manufacturers, the merchant marine and capital forged vigorously ahead in international competition.

State activity in the economic and social domain was immensely enlarged. At several vital points Imperial Germany pioneered in the ways of the welfare state, tempering the hard realities of very modern cause-and-effect society. Here, too, the workers' political movement achieved unequalled prominence. German educational methods, on the university level more so than in elementary schooling, and the civil service set standards envied and imitated abroad. Foreign experts closely studied the administration of German cities. And the ideas which captured the headlines of the time were expressed to a considerable degree in the German language.

GOVERNMENT IN GERMANY

In one department—and it was crucial—the lusty giant of the Old World lagged behind the spirit of the age. The form and substance of government were permeated with traditionalism. A constitution, it is true, was in force, manhood suffrage prevailed, but the opinion of the few weighed more decisively, as a rule, than the popular will.

The imperial Constitution of 1871 reproduced in its essentials the charter of the North German Confederation. Bismarck, architect of both documents, shaped their contents in keeping with his autocratic philosophy and to fit his own massive personality. Prussia, by far the largest and most populous German state, necessarily predominated in the Empire.

In fact Imperial Germany was a tightly knit federal union of twenty-six states under Prussian headship. To appease regional sentiments and religious differences, Bismarck allowed the individual states considerable home-rule in internal affairs. Local patriotisms, as time moved along, were more and more thoroughly sublimated in German national consciousness.

Supreme executive authority in Germany was lodged in the emperor, who was also king of Prussia. Policy-making federal officials were responsible to him, and he controlled the fighting services and diplomatic policies. If he wished, he could dismiss the upper branch of the legislature, the *Bundesrath*, and with the assent of that house he could dissolve the *Reichstag*, the popularly chosen chamber. Chief officer of the empire was the chancellor, who generally served also as minister president of Prussia. His tenure and that of his ministerial associates depended upon the favor of the monarch. As chancellor until 1890 Bismarck practically supervised the whole range of German public business.

Members of the *Bundesrath*, sixty-one in all, represented the several states of the German union, as with the Senate of the United States. Seats were distributed somewhat in accordance with the importance of the states and delegates were appointed by the rulers of the individual states. All federal legislation had to be approved by the *Bundesrath*, and the Constitution was so drawn that the Prussian delegation—the tool of the Prussian king—could prevent changes in military laws or alterations in the Constitution.

Every adult male was granted the right to vote for *Reichstag* deputies, of which there were three hundred and ninety-seven. This body could not cause the downfall of the executive, although the ministry, if the *Bundesrath* concurred, could send the *Reichstag* home. Deputies could debate public questions and had to consent to laws, but seldom did they propose bills. Organized political parties operated much as in any parliamentary regime. Very definitely a façade as compared with the popularly elected legislatures of Britain and France, the *Reichstag* was nevertheless something more than "a fig-leaf of absolutism," as one enraged critic derided it.

As for Prussia, the structure of government raised in 1850 persisted without alteration. Public power rested solidly in the hands of the king, the aristocracy and the wealthier middle class.

Semi-authoritarianism as exemplified in the imperial Constitution accorded with the predominant tradition of Germany or rather of Prussia, for the south German states were accustomed to more popular government. Democratic enthusiasms in Prussia never recovered from the disasters of 1848 and the iron-handed procedures which Bismarck pursued as minister president in the 1860's. The fact that national unity had been achieved by force further diminished the popularity of the principles of political democracy. Moreover, the upsurge of collectivism, presently to be described, tended to drive the fearful middle classes more completely into the monarchical mold. Not entirely, however, for a small faction in the *Reichstag*, known as the Liberal Party, pleaded for the "development of a truly constitutional life . . . through the legal organization of a responsible Reich ministry . . ."

Bismarck himself had no faith in, only distrust of, democratic government. Firmly believing as he did that he was an instrument of Divine Providence and that strict discipline was essential to stabilize and deepen national unity, this Junker felt no compulsion to promote the ways of democracy. During the full generation that he held the national tiller he neglected to prepare his countrymen to assume real political responsibilities.

Yet another circumstance operated to chill democratic impulses—the factor of geography. Impinging upon Germany were countries she had despoiled and which might seek to pay off old scores, if opportunity favored. The British, for instance, secure in their island stronghold, could indulge in governmental experiments, which Germans could not afford to do. "The German Empire," explained Prince von Bülow, sometime chancellor, "situated in the middle of Europe and insufficiently protected by nature on its frontiers, is, and must remain, a military state; and strong military states have always required monarchical [i.e. authoritarian] guidance."

THE ROLE OF BISMARCK

In the initial phase of the empire the political history of Germany might almost be written as a biography of Bismarck. This Olympian superman thoroughly dominated the political stage. The maker of the Second Reich relied confidently upon the support of William I, whom he had raised to greatness; differences cropped up between them, but invariably the monarch yielded to his "dutiful servant."

Bismarck had enemies aplenty, but no genuine rivals. As vindictive as he was dogmatic, he fought opponents with gloves off. Critics were showered with scurrilous abuse in the manipulated press or attacked frontally if that appeared desirable. The influence of the Chancellor retarded the development of an energetic and independent press which could have been an instrument of democracy. In the last stage of his public career the veteran statesman grew as tyrannical as any grizzly bear.

Bismarck had far greater talent for foreign relations than in handling domestic problems. After the achievement of national unity, he stood forth as a man of peace. But at home, in tussles with the *Reichstag,* he was more than once compelled to retreat. That was supremely annoying, for in his book the *Reichstag* was expected simply to tender advice on legislative proposals that were offered to it. In dealings with the Roman Catholic Church and the workers' political movement, the Chancellor suffered sharp reverses.

In the eyes of Bismarck, the reliability of a large section of the Roman Catholic minority was suspect. Including Poles and Alsatians, Catholics comprised a third of the population of the empire. As a practicing Lutheran, the Chancellor felt that Catholics owed primary allegiance to their Church; distrust mounted with the issuance of the dogma of papal infallibility (1870). He attacked bishops as "functionaries of a foreign sovereign . . . who by virtue of his infallibility is the most absolute monarch on the globe." He imagined that the "black international," goaded on by French clericals, might try to disrupt the young and predominantly Protestant Empire.

Bismarck would have liked the German Catholics to renounce papal jurisdiction and merge with the "Old Catholics" (p. 422). That being out of the question, he decided to solve the Catholic problem by brusque action. At his behest the Prussian government adopted laws subordinating the Roman Church to the authority of the state; education, for example, was handed over to laymen. Clergymen had to be trained in seminaries and in subjects approved by the government. Jesuits were banished and civil marriage was made compulsory. Protesting bishops and priests by the score were thrown into jail; 1,400 parishes were without clergymen.

Churchmen pilloried the Chancellor as the "modern Diocletian," another Attila. Passionate memories of medieval German struggles between state and church revived, as this *Kulturkampf*, this battle of beliefs, was being waged. Millions of Catholics were stirred to fury, feeling that since their patriotism had been impugned, they were less than first-class citizens. Before long Bismarck discovered that Catholic communicants could not be coerced. The Catholic political party, the Center, instead of disintegrating, grew in popularity. Needing the support of that party in the Reichstag, the Chancellor revoked (1879) most of the anti-Catholic legislation, piece by piece. The Jesuits, however, were permanently disbarred and schools remained under lay supervision. The Center Party developed into a powerful force in German politics.

Founders of the German Center Party: Ludwig Windthorst, Bismarck's stoutest opponent, stands second from the left.

The campaign against Catholicism had been broken off partly because Bismarck more deeply distrusted the workers' collectivist movement, "the red international." Under the Socialist label, two deputies had been returned to the first Reichstag and depression in business enhanced the appeal of the collectivist doctrine. Diverse groups amalgamated in 1875 to form the Social Democratic Party, whose objectives were avowedly anti-capitalist and international, though not sufficiently Marxian to please Marx himself. At the polls in 1877, over 500,000 votes were registered for Social Democrats.

Conservatives took alarm. Memories of the destruction and bloodshed which attended the Communard episode in Paris (1871) were still very green. Mistrustful of this class-centered, antimilitarist and international party, Bismarck fully shared the apprehension. The collectivist goal impressed him as a castle in the sky with clouds for its foundations. Adherents should be treated as robbers and thieves, he thundered, or exterminated like rats.

Attempts to kill Emperor William I furnished (1878) pretexts for draconian laws against the "red specter." Socialist clubs and trade unions were outlawed; it was made an offense to hold Socialist meetings or circulate Marxist literature. Violators of the laws and Socialist suspects were imprisoned or hounded from the country. But the repressive tactics succeeded no better with Socialism than with the Catholics. Under persecution, the Marxist movement prospered. Much against Bismarck's wishes, the antisocialist legislation was repealed in 1890; at the next balloting for the Reichstag, Social Democrats polled three times as many votes as in 1877.

For all his hatred of international collectivism, Bismarck was not without solicitude for the industrial wageworkers. Under his guidance indeed, a comprehensive program of state-aided insurance and pensions was enacted in the 1880's which other countries sooner or later

Bismarck's anti-socialist campaign as satirized in Punch

imitated. Workers were assured of modest incomes if victims of accident or sickness and in old age.[1]

While Bismarck in laying these foundations for the social welfare state was mainly motivated by considerations of expediency, and the desire to counteract collectivist doctrines, other reasons underlay the legislation. Hohenzollern Prussia, for example, had an established tradition of state intervention to resolve conflicting interests; never had the philosophy of economic individualism attained the momentum in central Europe that it generated to the west. Intellectuals in university chairs, furthermore, professional economists, taught that the state should intervene to compel more equitable distribution of income and to remedy the more glaring shortcomings of industrial society.

Self-supporting labor in a rural economy, it was pointed out, was giving way more and more to employment in factory or mine. Seldom were workmen able to set aside sufficient funds to provide for themselves if wages should cease for any cause. And medical science, by steadily lengthening the life span, increased the number of men who were too old to earn their daily bread.

Give the industrial workmen a personal stake in the country, it was urged, give them something to conserve, and thus at one stroke banish apprehensions of their loyalty and foster greater efficiency. Enlightened self-interest, that is, supported legislation which would enhance the security of the employed. The humanitarian theme, too, was not absent: lending a helping hand to those in distress would be an application of Christian ethics. Arguments of this order convinced influential bureaucrats, who pressed for the enactment of social security legislation.

The German welfare laws of the 1880's were accompanied by other types of public participation in economic affairs. Railways, telephone and telegraph services were owned and operated by the states, and public authorities also held title to some mines, factories and forests. Governmental units, such as municipalities, owned public utilities, savings banks, carried out housing projects and supplied recreational facilities in the ever-expanding cities.

All in all, these measures raised living levels, nourished a greater sense of security and doubtless improved productive efficiency. To the criticism that security tended to stifle initiative, the answer flew back that freedom from worry about the future heightened morale and stimulated enterprise. Germany was exempt from the more appalling destitution and the more violent industrial warfare of neighboring countries. Although worker discontent was mitigated, democratic Socialism, far from being killed, moved from strength to strength.

ECONOMIC POWER GROWS

Germany, in the meantime, had forged ahead vigorously in manufacturing and commerce, developing a remarkably strong, well-integrated economy. Rapid progress in large-scale production marked the 1890's and by the First World War Germany boasted an imposing industrial structure. By reason of industrial resources, in the final analysis, Germany fought most of the world in the herculean struggle from 1914 to 1918.

The advancement in specific types of production will illustrate the general trend. Output of coal moved up steadily, so that by 1914, 300,000 miners were at work in the Ruhr Valley and thousands more in the Saar Basin and Upper Silesia. Volume of production nearly equaled the British mines and in estimated reserves Germany was much better off. German factories and railways consumed the larger part of the coal. The Lorraine district contained bounteous stores of iron ore, and output was stepped up to meet demands for iron and steel.

In the making of steel and steel products German firms moved ahead in spectacular fashion. Production doubled in the 1880's, Britain was passed in the next decade, and by 1914, Germany was turning out almost as much steel as all other European countries together. Steel was the mainstay of national military potential, and the Ruhr, the principal area of steel-making, symbolized German industrial capacity for war.

[1] Individual German cities operated plans for unemployment assistance.

The Krupp works at Essen

On foundations solidly laid before 1870 the House of Krupp created the largest private industrial concern on record, with 75,000 names on payrolls. Not less astonishing was the record of the steel tycoon, August Thyssen; his small establishment of seventy men (1871) had blossomed by 1914 into a gigantic industrial empire of 50,000 employees. Krupp and Thyssen belonged among the very wealthiest citizens of Germany.

Excelling in the manufacture of synthetic products, German chemical companies set an example for the world. Plants manufacturing electrical goods and optical glass likewise set world standards. Although Germany lagged a long way behind Britain in over-all output of textiles, this branch of industry nonetheless grew substantially as power-driven machinery was increasingly installed. German manufacturers of silk, in which methods of dyeing and finishing are of high importance, outstripped French concerns, formerly the leaders in this patrician fabric.

In the course of the 1890's, German industry shot past agriculture as an employer. As of 1907, nearly two-fifths of the gainfully employed were engaged in industry as compared with about a third working on the land and in forests. By means of scientific farming the supply of foodstuffs was doubled, although productivity per soil-worker was probably less than half that in Great Britain. On the eve of the First World War, Germany relied upon imports for something like a fifth of the food normally consumed.

Paralleling the forward march of industry, the foreign trade of Germany turned sharply upward. Hamburg and Bremen, on the edge of the short North Sea littoral, quickly expanded into prosperous seaports and each was the home of aggressive shipping companies. Competition of the German merchant marine made inroads into traffic which once had been well-nigh a British monopoly. The enterprising Hamburg-America line speedily developed into the largest of all shipping concerns, and eagerly competed with British companies for the swiftest and most luxurious passenger ships afloat.

Year by year, more German capital was invested in foreign countries, both in Europe and beyond. Major German banks established branch offices abroad through which funds were funneled into business undertakings. Prospects of gain generally determined where investments should be made, but the Foreign Office sometimes influenced the flow of capital into countries from which it was anticipated diplomatic advantages would accrue. As of 1914, German foreign lending approached $6,000,000,000, or nearly a fifth of the national wealth, and yet less than French and much less than British investments abroad.

Little mystery, little of the sinister, surrounded the economic prosperity which Imperial Germany achieved. Roughly similar forces operated to produce roughly similar results in the United States at the same time. In drawing comparisons, however, it must be remembered that Germany was no more extensive than Texas. First of all, Germany profited from superior natural resources. Iron ore resources of Lorraine lay in close proximity to the coal of the Ruhr; there were valuable supplies of subterranean wealth, too, in the Saar and Upper Silesian districts. Application of ingenuity (and fertilizers) to the cultivation of the soil yielded handsome returns.

Several considerations of an essentially political character accelerated business progress. The unification of the German states into a single nation brought obvious material advantages, such as uniformity in laws and regulations touching economic operations. By annexing Alsace, Germany acquired a technically advanced textile industry which compelled improvements in factory processes elsewhere in the empire, and annexed Lorraine was the main supplier of iron ore.

Government aided industrial growth by protective tariffs, which were also designed to shield agrarian interests against the competition of the United States and Imperial Russia. It was in 1879 that tariff protectionism was first adopted as national policy and it was held to consistently thereafter; Germany's course influenced other European countries to enact comparable tariff measures. Further, government furnished subsidies to shipping companies, actively fostered cartels, and instructed consuls and other officials in foreign cities to aid exporting houses.

Rapid growth of the German population increased the number of consumers, the working force, and somewhat stimulated industrialization to provide employment. Whereas in 1871, about 38,000,000 lived in the empire, by 1914 the figure stood at nearly 68,000,000, much the largest population in Europe, except for Russia. Rural population showed little change, the phenomenal growth was almost exclusively urban. Down to 1900 a substantial exodus from Germany had taken place annually; in the eighties alone about 1,500,000 emigrated to the United States alone. But in the new century, economic opportunities converted Germany into a magnet for immigrants from eastern Europe.

Not unlike Yankees, Germans acquired a reputation as hard workers, willing to toil intensively, readily adaptable to the ways and requirements of machine production. Spartan notions of discipline, orderliness, thrift and temperance, inculcated in school and army, were fruitfully applied in manufacturing and business. Universal literacy, too, was an undoubted economic asset.

An enterprising German managerial class, moreover, contributed vitally in raising the country to unprecedented prosperity. Courageous and creative, thorough and persistent, men of large executive and administrative abilities pushed industrial growth at a brisk pace. Opulent business magnates often started from scratch; seldom were large fortunes accumulated by speculation, but rather by the exploitation of a technological discovery or an improvement in business organization. Many a prominent German industrialist served an apprenticeship in Britain, carrying British methods home with him. Cheap imitations of wares made in other countries were a German specialty; Japan later copied Germans in this practice. German firms were sharply reproached for indiscriminate copying, design piracy and use of British commercial labels.

Up to a point, the economic expansion of Germany was facilitated by a business organization called the cartel (*Kartell*). A cartel was a league of independent companies engaged in the same kind of production, such as coal or steel, and resembling the monopoly or "trust" of the United States. These combinations fixed selling prices, determined quantity of production and sometimes divided up foreign markets. As a sort of economic planning, a cartel tended to hold prices and employment steady and to eliminate cutthroat competition in the type of production in which it dominated.

As a rule, cartel agreements could be enforced in courts of law. Not until 1923 did the state undertake to regulate cartels and restrain practices which were injurious to consumers. Partly as a result of cartels, German industrial and financial power was concentrated in a relatively small group of citizens. Great German banking houses, furthermore, had their fingers in many a manufacturing pie; finance and industry were interlocked as nowhere else in the west of Europe before the First World War.

At all levels of training Germany maintained excellent technological, trade and commercial schools which sent forth men equipped with the most up-to-date know-how. To an unapproached degree, German firms stressed scientific research having industrial implications; the amazing chemical industry, conspicuously, was reared upon applied science. And German managers squeezed profits out of by-products in a way that invited imitation in other countries. Finally, the national economy benefited from superb transportation facilities. After unification, the web of railways was extended, under state auspices in the main, and rivers were methodically deepened and supplemented by canals. In choosing routes for new railways strategic interests as well as economic advantage entered into decisions. Service was efficient and economical, and rates were often manipulated so as to promote exports to foreign countries.

To push business abroad, German companies used advertising skillfully and improved merchandising technique. "Made in Germany," as a trade-mark, attained international respect. Commercial representatives going abroad learned the language of prospective customers, studied native habits regarding shapes, colors and the like and offered attractive terms of credit. Drummers often negotiated sales in ways which competing agents considered reprehensible. In one way and another, German exports crowded into markets which formerly had been British preserves.

EMPEROR WILLIAM II TAKES OVER

In the year 1888, William II, twenty-nine years old, ascended the thrones of Prussia and Germany. Spirited, impulsive, reckless and tactless in speech, the most consequential Hohenzollern since Frederick II cherished spacious visions of German grandeur and might. Though he displayed many of the traits of a modern man, he believed implicitly in the outmoded divine-right concept of rulers and acted accordingly.

As a young man, William II revered and idolized the venerable Bismarck, the most powerful personage in the world. But as he grew older he became critical of Bismarckian policies both at home and in external affairs. Youth and age collided over the treatment of Social Democrats and other political malcontents, whom William II desired to reconcile by appeasement. And, whereas the Kaiser wished

"Dropping the Pilot"—a classic cartoon comment on the Kaiser's dismissal of Bismarck

Germany to expand as a colonial and naval power, Bismarck argued for concentration on the European scene.

Tempers flared up furiously on both sides. Then, dramatically, William II requested the resignation of the aged Chancellor (1890) and of course received it. His withdrawal was hailed with lively satisfaction in many circles. Feeling that he had been deeply wronged, Bismarck devoted his remaining years to criticizing policies which he thought harmful and to preparing illuminating memoirs on his conduct of statecraft.

From a world viewpoint, William II swiftly eclipsed Bismarck as the personification of Imperial Germany. For a quarter of a century he was the most forceful monarch, the most glamorous actor on the European stage. He thoroughly identified himself with the new industrial and commercial forces and the ever-stronger empire. Considering himself a universal genius—and his knowledge was undoubtedly extensive—he loved to discourse on everything under the sun and theology. Theodore Roosevelt, no mean judge of human nature, assured him in 1910: "In America you would have your ward behind you and would lead your delegation at your party's national convention."

After the brief partnership with Bismarck came to an end, William II acted as German chancellor in fact, though not in name. It was now that Germany set sail upon a "new course," symbolized by an eager quest for additional overseas possessions and the building of a great navy. Seapower was the special pet—and folly—of the Emperor; his thundering speeches on Germany's growing strength and intentions darkened international counsels and helped set the stage for the First World War.

GERMAN SOCIAL FORCES

In spite of the phenomenal upsurge in German industry and commerce, old-line conservative elements retained control of public affairs in the empire and in Prussia. Arrayed in this class were a few hundred aristocratic families, owners of large landed properties, and intimately associated with the political and military policymakers. Favoring the preservation of the status quo, they dreaded proletarian collectivism and fought it, and they obtained legislation on taxes and tariffs beneficial to their own set.

Most German university professors were adherents of the conservative camp, or that at least was true of those who did not consider it undignified for scholarly gentlemen to concern themselves with workaday affairs. University lecture halls were frequented almost wholly by sons of the aristocracy and the plutocracy. And the Protestant clergy in general cherished the political outlook and social perspectives of the upper and governing caste. The wealthier industrialists, financiers and merchants, though not top-flight socially, lined up with the landlords and elicited the unflagging applause of William II.

Ideas of democracy, as a form of government and less so as a way of life, had considerable acceptance among the less affluent middle classes in the larger cities and in Southern Germany. Several of the smaller southern states operated on terms of ministerial responsibility to popularly chosen legislatures. Spokesmen of the progressively minded middle classes pleaded for genuine parliamentary government in Prussia and in the empire.

Once the iron hand of Bismarck had been removed, the Catholic Center Party which recruited its leaders from all social layers, espoused freer, more democratic, ways in public affairs. Alsatian and Polish deputies generally saw eye to eye with the Center and counted upon it to defend minority interests. As a rule, the Center supported worker welfare legislation and spoke out fervently against abusive treatment of natives in the German colonies. The Catholic priesthood was more enlightened socially than Lutheran pastors.

But the principal pressure for democratizing reform came from the Social Democratic Party, which constantly attracted more and more voters. In the election of 1912, the last before the First World War, Socialist candidates for the *Reichstag* polled nearly one out of three votes cast. The Socialist delegation was by all odds the largest in the legislature. After prolonged and intense debate, most of the leaders of the democratic Socialist Party and of the allied trade unions had switched to an evolutionary, or reformist, version of Marxism.[2] Whatever the ideological tenets, the party had become a movement for social and democratic changes. It called for ministerial responsibility, extension of welfare legislation, broader freedom of press and speech, complete secularization of schools and equality for women. With these emphases the party appealed to multitudes who had no sympathy for fundamental Marxist principles.

Representative Social Democrats acidly condemned public policies of which they disapproved. Colonial expansion, the building of a great battle-fleet, aggressive diplomacy and sword-rattling were subjected to severe and unwearied attack. At moments of grave international crisis, Social Democrats staged huge antiwar demonstrations in the great German cities. The German official world, on its part, denounced Socialists as unpatriotic and discriminated against members of the Party. "Treasonable horde" was one of the milder epithets hurled at the Social Democrats by the Emperor. Nevertheless, in the supreme diplomatic crisis of July, 1914, Socialist deputies in the *Reichstag* loyally approved the military credits requested by the imperial authorities. Love of Fatherland and fear of "Muscovite barbarism" blacked out ideals of internationalism and doctrinaire economic determinism.

THE HAPSBURG MONARCHY

Diplomatically allied to Germany after 1879 was the ancient monarchy of the Hapsburgs. That curious state, unique in its history, had recently undergone radical constitutional changes. Reformation was dictated by humiliating defeats and painful losses of territory and prestige in the wars of 1859 and 1866. It was essential above all else that the ruling caste of Hungary, the Magyar gentry, be appeased. Various constitutional projects, providing for a unified parliament for Austria and Hungary, were devised, without winning acceptance by the Magyars.

Finally, in 1867 a famous compromise (*Ausgleich*) was worked out which allowed virtual home-rule to Hungary; and Austria was put on a similar basis. Unity was maintained between the two partners through a common sovereign—emperor in Austria, king in Hungary—and joint ministries to manage foreign affairs, the fighting services and finances for these purposes. Each partner had its own ministry and

[2] Trade unionism was much less developed in Germany than in Britain, for example. About 80 per cent of the organized wage earners belonged to unions aligned with the Socialist Party. Most of the rest were members of Catholic trade unions and were inclined to vote for Centrist candidates for public office.

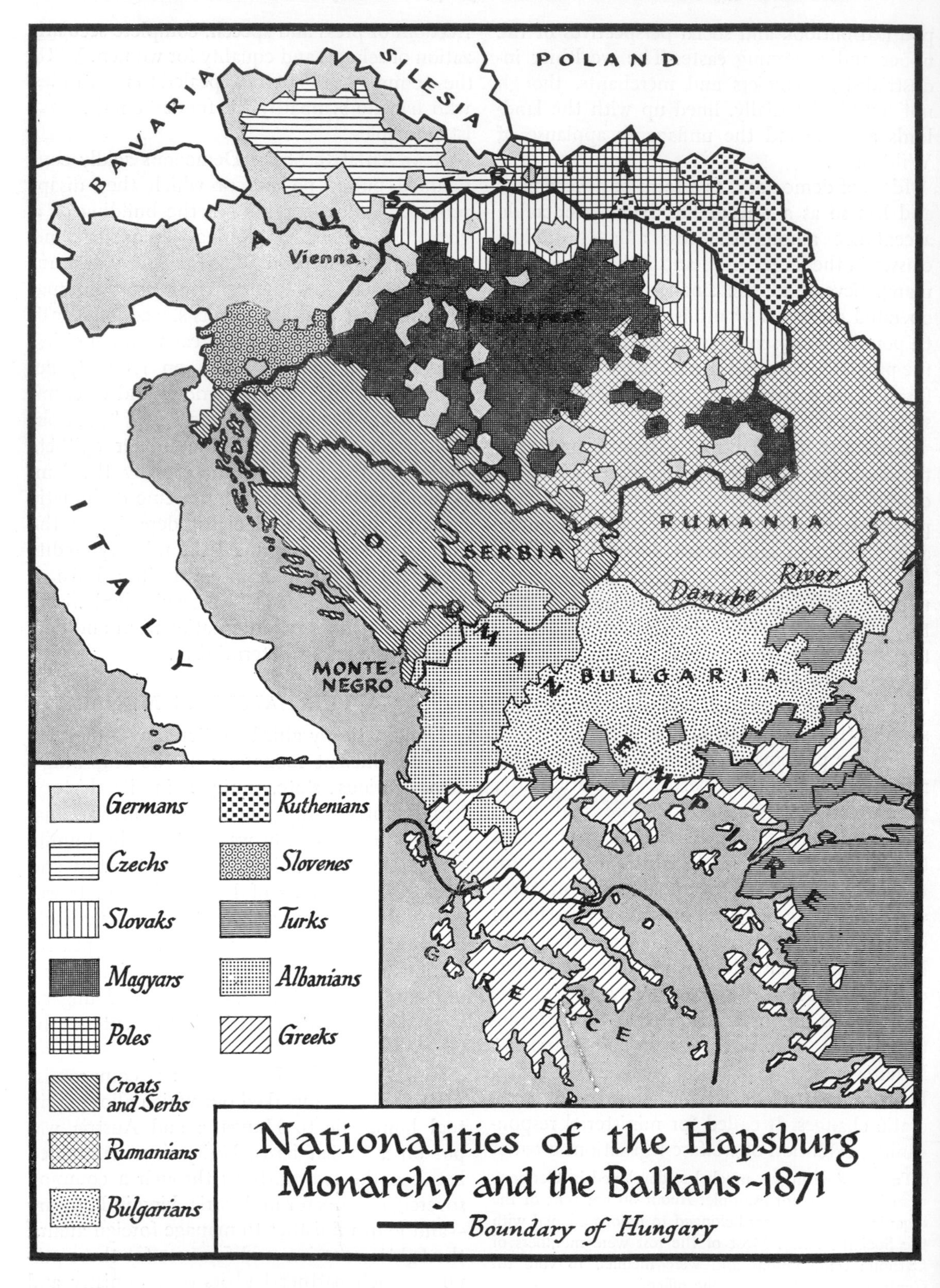

Nationalities of the Hapsburg Monarchy and the Balkans–1871

View of Budapest in the early 1890's

parliament to legislate on home affairs. These arrangements created what was often spoken of as the Dual Monarchy, and they continued in force until the dissolution of the realm at the close of the First World War. In area almost exactly as large as Germany, the population of the Dual Monarchy exceeded 50,000,000 at its peak, with three fifths of all living in Austria.

Masters at last in their own house, the Magyars lorded over subject nationalities as had been their wont for generations. By reason of the franchise laws, the Hungarian parliament contained few representatives of the smaller nationalities, though taken together they outnumbered the Magyars in the population. To the very end, the Magyar governing class successfully frustrated all efforts to impair its monopoly on public power. More than that, Magyar officialdom strove to dragoon the subject minorities into the Magyar nationality. School, army, church (up to a point), and varied and fancy kinds of bribery were instruments of Magyarization. Results of Magyarizing policies were mixed. Slovaks, for example, were rather thoroughly merged with the Magyars, Serbs and Croats (of the Yugoslav family) much less so, and articulate Rumanians remained overwhelmingly separatist, desirous of uniting with the Kingdom of Rumania.

Hungary continued to be preponderantly an agricultural country with vast estates owned by the titled aristocracy, the lesser gentry and Roman Catholic prelates. Yet the government deliberately fostered the growth of machinofacture and shipping by means of subsidies and tax concessions. Budapest blossomed out as one of the loveliest of European capitals, with stately public buildings and spacious mansions of the aristocracy.

As a center of flour-milling—the Minneapolis of the Old World—and focal point of railways, Budapest developed a typical urban social structure—bustling bourgeoisie, somewhat affected by the democratic ideology, and a restless proletariat for whom Marxism seemed the recipe of salvation. Large masses of Hungarian rustics were landless or holders of only small properties. From those elements, as well as from the discontented in Austria, hundreds of thousands emigrated to the United States.

One section of the politically active Magyars never approved the compromise of 1867. What they desired, at bottom, was a fully independent Hungary and for them Louis Kossuth, the revolutionary chieftain of 1848, was mentor and inspiration. Appreciating that separation from Austria lay outside the bounds of practical politics, they worked to obtain an independent Hungarian army and to whittle down economic connections with Austria. Separatist agitation generated considerable momentum in the first years of the twentieth century.

THE EMPIRE OF AUSTRIA

The Austrian half of the Dual Monarchy wrote a rather different record from Hungary. Industrialism flourished in Bohemia, and in Vienna and adjacent areas. Manufacturing was more highly developed in Bohemia than in any other section of the Monarchy. As the Hapsburg capital, the home of high finance and of considerable industry, Vienna expanded rapidly. Extremely cosmopolitan, as in the past, it retained its eminence in music and earned international renown for scholarship, particularly in medicine and psychology (variants included).

Politically, Vienna became and remained a focal point of fierce contentions between the Christian Socialists, a form of political Catholicism, and the Social Democrats. Though venerating Marx, the democratic Socialists pressed for social reforms which would bring immediate benefits. The Christian Socialists, however, controlled the city, converting it into a

The Graben, a fashionable shopping street of Vienna

unique and instructive laboratory of "municipal socialism."

German-speaking folk constituted the leading nationality of Austria, and the reigning dynasty and court were German—Austro-German in speech and sentiment. German-speaking deputies in the parliament were split into many political groupings, much the larger part of them loyal to the Hapsburgs and monarchical integrity. A small and noisy faction, on the other hand, the Pan-Germans, agitated for the union of the provinces of German speech with Imperial Germany.

The Slavic nationalities in Austria enjoyed broader civic freedoms than their counterparts in Hungary. Among the Czechs of Bohemia, as prosperity increased, clamor for home rule grew more intense, causing endless political convulsions, but no formula acceptable at once to Czech nationalists and to the authorities in Vienna could be discovered. Poles in Galicia, however, obtained a large measure of autonomy, which kept them contented and made them the envy of their co-nationals in Russia and Germany. The Ukrainian minority of Galicia turned restive under Polish discrimination and repression.

Of all the nationalities in the realm, the Yugoslavs eventually provoked the greatest anxiety. This element was enlarged in 1908 when the Monarchy formally annexed the provinces of Bosnia-Herzegovina (p. 492). Part Slovene, part Croat, part Serb, the Yugoslav grouping—or rather the politically articulate elements in it—was very much divided in political outlook. Some Yugoslavs wished to unite with the Kingdom of Serbia, others were content with the status quo, while still others favored the creation of a Yugoslav state inside the Hapsburg complex.

This last alternative contemplated a state, embracing the Yugoslavs of Hungary as well as of Austria, which would have the same standing as the Austrian Empire or the Hungarian Kingdom. If carried out, that plan, in other words, would have converted the dualistic into a trialistic realm. It attracted respectable backing in Austria, but was stubbornly opposed by the Magyar masters of Hungary. Even broader schemes to reconstruct the Monarchy as a federal union had their partisans, but the appealing idea of a "United States of Austria" got precisely nowhere. An Italian minority in Austria was divided, like the Yugoslavs, in political attitudes. Some Italians were acquiescent in Austrian rule, while militant secessionists dreamed of union with Italy. Partly to placate national groupings, manhood suffrage for parliamentary elections was introduced (1907) in Austria.

Nonetheless, national commotions, instead of receding, grew more intense, more dangerous for the integrity of the realm. Nationalistic filibustering, on the model of the Irish Nationalists, repeatedly brought parliamentary transactions to a standstill; whereupon the Emperor carried on necessary business by ordinances having the full force of law. Austria belonged among the semi-authoritarian countries of Europe.

WHY THE MONARCHY HELD TOGETHER

Due to national antagonisms inside each half of the Hapsburg Monarchy and between the two partners, it was freely predicted that the realm must inescapably crack up. And yet dissolution came only after four years of gruelling and wasting strife in the First World War. Counteracting the centrifugal pressure of nationalisms were forces operating to keep this state of many nationalities intact.

High on the list of cohesive influences must be placed the popular affection for the Emperor-King, Francis Joseph. Ascending the throne amidst the revolutionary convulsions of 1848, he continued to reign well into the First World War. As Britain adored Queen Victoria, so the Hapsburg Monarchy venerated Francis Joseph, whose private life was studded with tragedies that could not fail to evoke popular sympathy.

Another binding tie were the fighting services, commanded by loyal aristocrats, and enrolling young men of all tongues. Fidelity to monarch and monarchy were inculcated in barracks and on drill-ground. Of similar import was the elaborate bureaucracy, recruited from

Francis Joseph, Emperor-King, photographed on an occasion when he was happiest—a hunting-trip in the Austrian mountains.

the different nationalities, and in the main wedded to the preservation of the realm. Since most of the citizens, moreover, belonged to the Roman Catholic Church, community of religion and the activity of churchmen in teaching loyalty and discipline helped to perpetuate the status quo.

The force of inertia operated, too, to hold together a realm that had existed for centuries. In addition, as a united state, economic interdependence between the several districts had developed and was reinforced by the construction of railways. Exchange of products between the agricultural east and the industrialized west was beneficial to all concerned. A common tariff protected common economic interests, while bankers in Vienna financed enterprises across the whole Monarchy.

Further, the Slav-speaking minorities were never able to arrange a common front against the ascendant Austro-Germans and Magyars. Disunity spelled weakness and invited manipulation by the dominant groupings. Considerations of security, lastly, contributed to cohesion. Leading statesmen dreaded the Russian colossus and Russian machinations among the Slav peoples; in unity there was strength and mayhap safety. Along with that, there was a desire to extend the interests and fortify the prestige of the Monarchy in the Balkans and to combat the covetous aspirations of Italy. After 1879, when the Dual Monarchy allied with Germany, that diplomatic bond was of no little importance in keeping the realm together.

THE KINGDOM OF ITALY

Just as Germany and the Hapsburg Monarchy were allies, so from 1882 onward both were bound up diplomatically with Italy in a celebrated Triple Alliance. Italy was the weakest and least reliable link in the chain of partnership. Only recently unified, the Kingdom was in truth cruelly handicapped in the general race for power and glory.

For one thing the public leaders who served Italy were men without distinction, who lived in the spirit of Dickens' Mr. Micawber. Of glowing ideals there was no shortage, but rarely were they translated into acts of policy. Politicians masquerading as statesmen grossly manipulated elections and managed parliament with unscrupulous opportunism. Ministers holding the portfolio of home secretary controlled administration through prefects and police. Standards of public morality, the sense of duty to the community, fell below the levels of more comfortably situated countries.

The governmental institutions of Italy had not risen out of the national soil, but had been very largely imported from Britain and France. The process of transplantation worked out none too well. Italy possessed the apparatus of a democratic regime—or pieces of it—without either democratic traditions or outlook. The royal ministry, to illustrate, was responsible to the elected Chamber of Deputies. At first deputies were chosen on a narrow franchise; the voting privilege was several times broadened, and in 1912 about 5,500,000 peasants and wage workers were enfranchised, which very nearly tripled the electorate, but manhood suffrage was not adopted until after the First World War. Of local self-government, so essential for healthy national government, there was precious little. Italy, in a word, was not democratic in the larger connotation of the term.

But more than that must be said. The Italian population rose at a prodigious rate. It exceeded 41,000,000 in 1913 as against 25,000,000 two generations earlier—and that in a country where natural resources were scanty. To relieve the acute population pressure, multitudes of Italians sought employment in the uncrowded Americas or in industrial centers of Germany. Illiteracy, an ancient evil in the peninsula, gradually yielded to treatment; by 1914 three out of four Italians could read and write, with the proportion substantially higher in the North than in the southern provinces.

Cutting across all problems which perplexed Italy was the thorny issue of Vatican hostility to the kingdom. Never did the Popes cease demanding the restoration of temporal power as indispensable to the liberty of the head of the international Church. Never did the Popes emerge from the seclusion of the Vatican. On papal instructions, observant Catholics declined to take part in public business, even to the extent of voting. Aloofness lasted until 1905, when the papacy enjoined the faithful to fight Socialists, the dread foes of religion, at the polls and in Parliament. Promptly an earnest Catholic party took its place in the arena of national affairs.

Secular politicians, on their side, feared foreign intervention on behalf of the Pope, which never in fact materialized. The fires of anticlericalism were stoked by ecclesiastical aversion to the Italian state. Silent warfare between partisans of the Vatican and their adversaries constantly troubled the course of national history.

ECONOMIC EVOLUTION

While the question of the Vatican was peculiar to Italy, her social and economic difficulties paralleled those of other countries. Compared with Germany, for instance, these secular problems were aggravated because Italy was desperately poor in mineral wealth and vast areas of the peninsula were not suitable for cultivation.

Subsistence peasant farming prevailed in many sections of the kingdom, but in the south, large estates cultivated by hired laborers were the rule. Enlightened patriarchal landlords were greatly outnumbered by proprietors who bled the land for quick profits. Workers were available in overabundance, while productive land was severely limited. Under-employed, crowded together in squalid towns with four generations in as many rooms in a single house, the south Italian countryfolk eked out a miserable existence.

Food could not be extracted from mountains, but electric power could be—and was—generated from hillside streams. Development of "white coal" as an alternative to the imported black variety promoted industrial expansion. And so did the importation of foreign capital to supplement the meager native resources. Machinofacture was concentrated in the northern cities, historically the centers of manufacturing. Much the greater part of the industrial rawstuffs had to be brought in from outside. A characteristic collectivist movement paralleled the growth of machine-industry. Existing on wretched levels, Italian wageworkers were vulnerable to Socialist oratory and bombast; and crowds of desperate rustics rallied to the collectivist banner. In 1892, a political party, grounded upon Marxist teachings, was organized.

Tormented by schisms and factionalism, Italian Marxism was generally controlled by fervently doctrinaire revolutionaries. And yet, the capacity of outstanding Socialist leaders for selfless devotion to the welfare of the masses has sometimes been likened to the disciples of

St. Francis of Assisi. Strong enough in 1903 to return thirty-three deputies to the royal legislature, the Socialists then, as later, rejected invitations to enter the ministry and cooperate in governing the country. From time to time, hard-pressed workmen fought against poverty and unemployment with widespread strikes and destructive rioting. Anarchism, which caught hold on the extreme left wing of the workers' movement, caused (1900) the assassination of King Humbert I.

BEGINNING THE TWENTIETH CENTURY

The division between North and South, already pronounced before unification, was rendered immensely greater by the spread of industry in the North. Two Italies, so to speak, entered the twentieth century side by side, the one despising the other, the other bitterly resentful. While the North forged ahead, the deep South remained in the grip of a primitive and inefficient agriculture—the Cinderella of the peninsula.

In harmony with the spirit of the time, the Italian government adopted socializing legislation. Frankly imitative of German models, these laws assured workmen some benefits of social security. Railway lines were bought up by the state and city administrations experimented with municipally owned enterprises in the hope of bettering the material lot of the masses. Practically all males, as has been said, were allowed to vote after 1912.

Long since, Italy had come to be reckoned among the "Great Powers." National feeling had deepened since 1871, prodigal outlays had been made to create a strong army and navy and Italy had joined in the universal scramble for empire and overseas dominion. Staunch patriots, moreover, coveted areas under the Hapsburg flag which were peopled by Italian-speaking folk. Called unredeemed Italy—*Italia Irredenta*—these districts included the South Tyrol, Trieste and the countryside near it and stretches of Dalmatia. Technically, of course, Italy was the diplomatic associate of the Hapsburg Monarchy, and of Germany, in the Triple Alliance.

THE THIRD FRENCH REPUBLIC

The obverse of the primacy of Germany after 1871 was the sharp reduction in the international stature of France. Alone among the major states of Europe France, after defeat, adopted a republican pattern of government. Its record was scarcely calculated to win friends for republican institutions.

This third French adventure in republicanism started under quaint circumstances. Partisans of monarchy formed the majority in the National Assembly of 1871, chosen before the war with Germany had officially ended. Devoted friends of the republican philosophy were heavily outnumbered. Three claimants to the throne pressed their suits and the royalist leaders ultimately decided to award the crown to the Count de Chambord, the legitimate Bourbon contender. Blind to political realities, he ruined his prospects by demanding that the lares and penates of the House of Bourbon should be restored along with the monarchy.

Whereupon, Adolphe Thiers, veteran politician, a monarchist at heart and chief executive of the provisional government, cast his weighty influence on the republican side. A Republic, he declared, "divides us least," adding, in words of lasting validity, "The Republic will be conservative or it will not be at all." Followers of Thiers, together with confirmed Republicans, secured the adoption of the "constitution" in 1875 by a small majority.

Under the constitutional laws, the President of France would hold office for seven years. To forestall a repetition of Louis Napoleon's march to power, the President would be chosen by the two branches of the legislature, not by direct popular vote. Little authority was assigned to the President; the real executive would be the ministry, which would exercise authority so long as it commanded a majority in the lower house of the legislature, the Chamber of Deputies. Deputies would be elected by manhood suffrage, while the Senate, or upper house, would be chosen indirectly and under provisions which virtually assured it a conservative complexion. Without substantial modification, this structure of government served France until 1940.

Champions of monarchism regarded the Republic as only temporary. The first President, Marshal MacMahon, threatened indeed to turn the state over to the royalists in 1877, naming one of their leaders as premier, dissolving the deputies and ordering a national election. The Republican elements picked up the gauntlet. At their head stood Léon Gambetta, eloquent, tenacious, the very soul of French patriotism, a convinced republican and democrat, anticlerical. In the dark days of national humiliation, crowned by the loss of Alsace-Lorraine, Gambetta had kept French faith and hope alive with tongue and pen. For his labors in fashioning the Republic he was awarded the sobriquet of "father of the Third Republic."

The coup contemplated by the royalists was defeated in the exciting election of 1877. Identifying leading Roman Catholic churchmen with the purposes of royalism, Gambetta invented the battlecry, "Clericalism, that is the enemy." The Republican victory at the polls had large and lasting effects. Royalism never recovered from the blow, and yet whenever the republican regime got into hot water or was touched by the breath of scandal, the streets of Paris resounded with shouts of "Vive le Roi."

"L'ÉTAT C'EST MOI!!!"

The troubled course of French politics seemed humorous to Englishmen. Here is Sir John Tenniel's comment on Leon Gambetta in 1881, when he was suspected of aiming at a dictatorship.

Legislation was promptly enacted which narrowed the role of churchmen in the affairs of France. Never thereafter did a French president seriously oppose the deputies; it became a tradition in fact that the Chamber should under no condition be dissolved by executive order. Many students of politics, inside France and without, consider that custom a serious weakness in the governmental system of the Republic.

Another feature of French public life much criticized was the endless shifting of ministries. By reason of the many "parties," or rather of undisciplined political groupings in the Chamber of Deputies, ministries depended upon fluctuating coalitions. On the average, cabinets lasted less than nine months, giving the impression of chronic political crisis and instability. That interpretation was, however, somewhat misleading for in spite of frequent ministerial upsets the same small group usually returned to office, basic public policies were pursued with considerable consistency and the body of permanent officials assured administrative continuity. The stability of France was independent of the merry-go-round in the national parliament. But unending ministerial convulsions tended to discredit republican principles.

CHALLENGES TO THE REPUBLIC

Fierce storms beat upon the republican regime before the nineteenth century had run its course, but they were outridden. The strength of republican sentiment, and allegiance to the democratic faith, lay principally with the middle classes; once firmly in the saddle the bourgeoisie were never unhorsed. The prevalent opinion that the reign of Napoleon III had been an unqualified disaster counted favorably for republicanism and against the monarchists. To that was conjoined widespread popular desire for revenge upon the hereditary enemy beyond the Rhine: revenge for the ignominious surrender at Sedan, revenge for the loss of Alsace-Lorraine, revenge for the humiliating parade of German grenadiers down the broad Champs Élysées.

The spirit of revenge loomed large in a challenge to the Republic associated with General Georges Boulanger. In a way the Boulangist effervescence resembled the Hitlerian nightmare later on in Germany; both agitations crowded into the limelight about fifteen years after military humiliation and thrived on the weakness of a young, wobbly Republic installed by that defeat. Both movements were intensely chauvinistic, appealing strongly to young men who had been boys at the time of national disaster.

Boulanger, who had achieved a reputation as a soldier, was a dashing cavalier, a lath painted to look like iron, not unlike Napoleon III. He seized upon an incident along the German frontier (1887) to beat the tom-toms of war, obtain cheap cheers and stir visions of *revanche*. True to the formula of the aspiring dictator, Boulanger broadcast conflicting appeals, complaining of the insufficiently democratic character of the Republic and the feebleness of parliamentary government. "The Republic consolidated, authority restored, liberty guaranteed" served as the Boulangist slogan. He decried professional tub-thumpers in public office and stridently demanded constitutional revision.

Boulanger formally bid for dictatorial power by standing for election in various French constituencies, winning out even in Paris. He attracted to his standards all manner of discontented elements, from royalists, the hard core of his following, to extreme leftist sympathizers. The portrait of this evanescently popular hero even replaced the king of hearts on playing cards!

When democratically-minded Republicans perceived the real objectives of Boulanger, they closed ranks. Rumors circulated that the government intended to arrest the ambitious adventurer, which caused shivers to run down his spine. On April Fools' Day of 1889 he fled with his mistress to the coziness of a Brussels hotel. Unlike Hitler, Boulanger lacked resoluteness and political skill, and France was a country which cared more for liberty and in which democratic common sense was deeply rooted. Celebration of the hundredth anniversary of the beginning of the great French Revolution quickly blotted out the memory of the potential dictator. Republicanism emerged from the encounter stronger in morale and courage, better able to overcome later threats.

The next serious menace to the safety of the Republic—and extremely serious it was—arose out of the notorious Dreyfus affair. In 1894 Captain Alfred Dreyfus was convicted by court-martial of transmitting military secrets to an agent of Germany. As punishment he was exiled to fearsome, tropical Devil's Island, off the coast of French Guiana. Dreyfus protested his innocence and evidence was presently uncovered proving him guiltless. Relatives and friends of the wronged Dreyfus naturally demanded that the judicial error should be rectified. But highly placed military and political authorities, criminally complacent, retorted that the case was closed, to reopen it would impugn the honor of the army. Insidious anti-Jewish prejudices darkly stained the whole episode, for Dreyfus was of the Jewish tradition. Coarse and scurrilous French newspapers had for years been stirring up opinion against Jews.

Over the rights and wrongs in the Dreyfus condemnation, France was split in two as with a sword. On one side were aligned the disparate opponents of republicanism and democracy: military conservatives, royalists and many churchmen. Pitted against them in the wracking controversy were the partisans of Dreyfus—and justice—friends of the Republic and human rights, scholars, writers and anticlerical politicians. At one point sober observers predicted that the acrimonious feud would culminate in civil war. Inflamed French passions were matched by intense excitement in foreign countries.

Fresh revelations, confessions of guilt by individuals who were actually implicated in treasonable trafficking with Germany forced the military chiefs to grant Dreyfus a new trial. In spite of plain evidence of innocence, the court-martial again convicted Dreyfus, though "under extenuating circumstances." The French president promptly pardoned the victim. But supporters of Dreyfus insisted upon complete vindication and reappointment to his military rank. In the van of the protagonists was fiery, irrepressible Georges Clemenceau, one of the few decisive personalities of the Third Republic. Claiming the mantle of Gambetta, he had won notoriety in the Chamber of Deputies as a militant nationalist, a sturdy republican and an implacable enemy of clerical intervention in what he deemed the secular domain.

Clemenceau possessed rare capacity for stirring up hornets' nests. His satirical tongue lashed many a ministry to destruction. The descriptive name of "Tiger" was fastened upon this bonny fighter. Philosopher, orator, journalist, he dedicated his admittedly great talents to obtaining justice for Dreyfus. At long last, in 1906, Dreyfus was fully exonerated, awarded the Legion of Honor medal and restored to the army, in which he served with distinction during the First World War. Clemenceau was handsomely rewarded with the premiership. Justice and humanity had triumphed in France, the country which Thomas Jefferson once acclaimed as every man's second fatherland. Convulsive echoes of *l'affaire Dreyfus* reverberated in the Republic for many a year.

ANTICLERICAL LEGISLATION

As well as vindicating the Republic and the democratic heritage, the Dreyfus affair had other noteworthy consequences. Army leadership, for example, was purged of men known for their strong royalist or clerical leanings. Sweeping legislation soon followed, affecting church schools and the Catholic Church itself. As a matter of fact, the republican campaign against the Church commenced soon after MacMahon's ill-starred flirtation with royalism. Clericalism had then been reviled as the tool and ally of royalism. Zealots appeared on both sides of the controversy. In this most intellectual and most secular of countries, the struggle centered on the training of youth.

Churchmen wished children to be educated as devout adherents of Catholicism. They believed that not only the doctrines of the faith but other subjects as well should be taught in a religious environment by Catholic teachers. Secular education was insufficient and morally wrong. On the other hand, anticlericals assailed church schools as seed-beds of royalism or, as free-thinkers, felt that religion should have no place in the education of children. Ardent republicans desired lay schools in which the inculcation of national patriotism and a republican ideology would supplant religious instruction. Lay teachers would be evangelists of secular values.

An act of 1880 declared elementary education free, compulsory and secular in state schools. At that time these institutions cared for rather more than half of the children attending school. Execution of the law gradually whittled illiteracy down to the vanishing point. Presently priests were conscripted for military service; anticlerical fury then slacked off. And Pope Leo XIII recommended (1892) that practicing Catholics should accept the Republic as permanent and engage in politics in order to repeal distasteful laws and protect the interests of the Church. Obedient to that suggestion, a Catholic political party was formally organized.

It was during the ferment excited by the Dreyfus case that anticlericals revived and broadened their campaign—a "war on religion" in the Catholic view. Charged with teaching hostility to the Republic, all religious orders were placed (1901) under state regulation. Many orders were dissolved, their members scattering to neighboring countries or overseas. Church-connected schools, moreover, were closed wholesale and French diplomatic representation at the Vatican was broken off.

As the climax, the Concordat which Napoleon I had negotiated with the papacy was discarded (1905). That meant, among other things, that the state no longer had a voice in the choice of bishops, nor would the state have responsibility for the salaries of priests and the maintenance of ecclesiastical buildings. These matters would be handled by churchmen and laity as in the United States, for instance. Catholicism became independent in France in a sense untrue before. Protestations over these changes, inside France and from Rome, hardened the hearts of exponents of "a free church in a free state," French style.

ECONOMIC AND SOCIAL AFFAIRS

Disparities in economic potential between France and Germany widened as the years rolled by. Consider population, for example, which registered only a slight increase in France, standing at approximately 40,000,000 by the First World War, while Germany had grown to nearly 68,000,000. Burials in France in some years exceeded births. The relative falling off in French manpower had direct bearing, of course, upon the international influence of the Republic.

Not only was the French population almost stationary, but less than a third of it was classified (1913) as urban. Industrial development, that meant, had not gone forward as in Germany and Britain. Only modestly endowed with mineral resources, France relied upon imports of coal and iron ore in developing heavy industry. Small plants employing only a few workman were still characteristic of French industry. Textile manufacturing prospered and communication facilities were extended, the state gradually purchasing a fifth of the railway trackage.

The Gleaners, *here shown, and many other paintings of peasant life by Jean François Millet stress the French farmer's love for his few acres and the care he lavished on them.*

Tariff legislation protected not only manufacturers from foreign competition, but agriculture also. Farming continued to be the mainstay of the national economy; the millions of peasants operating their small family properties were a stout pillar of conservatism. For them the soil was an object of affection, not a factory, as it was to the farmer in the United States, with his labor-saving machinery. There was not much incentive for efficiency in cultivation, but nonetheless France was self-sufficient to a degree envied by more highly industrialized neighbors.

Blessed with an abundance of excellent harbors and ideally located, France was in an advantageous position for participation in foreign trade. Yet the merchant marine slipped behind relative to the German, and a large share of French exports consisted of luxury wares for the stomach, back or home of opulent foreigners. Catering to tourists and the pleasures and luxuries of Paris were valued as national assets.

Despite the comparatively limited foreign trade, French foreign investments expanded greatly. Only Britain in fact surpassed France as an international lender; by 1914, thrifty, saving Frenchmen had plunged something like $11,000,000,000 into other countries. For the most part, French capital exports passed to European nations instead of to the immense French colonial empire or to the Americas. Imperial Russia, diplomatic ally of the Republic after 1894, borrowed something like $2,500,000,000; and more than 1,600,000 Frenchmen owned Russian securities. The French Foreign Office determined to a considerable extent where investments should be made abroad.

Inside France bourgeois capital owners had to reckon with the growing vigor of wage-worker movements. Trade union organization proceeded along much the same lines as in Great Britain, except for the wider popularity of radical syndicalist doctrines (p. 399). Partisans of this philosophy, like left-wing intellectuals in any generation, were noted for self-righteousness and vainglorious claims to a monopoly of principle. Persuaded that only "direct action" would bring desired results, men of extreme sympathies engaged in sabotage and waged bitter strikes. These activities, however, netted only inconsequential gains.

More moderately inclined wage earners affiliated with the Marxist cause. The history of the Socialist Party, founded in 1879, was a stormy record of competition between revolutionary and evolutionary principles, of divisions and reunions. At length, in 1905, a United Socialist Party gathered together splinter factions and became a powerful force in the politics of the Third Republic. It stood for the transformation of the prevailing economy by legislative processes and in 1914 attracted 1,250,000 votes, capturing a hundred and two seats in the Chamber of Deputies.

Partly in response to Socialist pressure, worker welfare and security legislation was introduced in France, though hardly on as extensive a scale as in more highly industrialized Germany. French Socialists professed pacificism and internationalism, but they rallied to the defense of the homeland in 1914 with as much alacrity as their counterparts across the Rhine. For all the domestic bickerings and confusing political turbulence, which foreign observers were prone to interpret as decadence, there was iron in the French physique and stamina in the *esprit* of France as the ordeal of the First World War demonstrated.

IN RETROSPECT

After the First World War, the French statesman Clemenceau remarked: "It is the glory of our civilization that one is occasionally able to live a normal life." Certainly, many inhabitants of the countries whose history has been sketched here would one day look back upon the epoch 1871 to 1914 as "normal" living. Nostalgically, they recalled the era as a time of comparative stability, prosperity, progress and peace of mind.

Measured by some tests it was indeed an age of notable achievement. Setting the pace for the others, Germany drove restlessly forward in many departments of human activity. Population surged ahead sharply, standards of comfort advanced, better diet and homes, more leisure, a longer life expectancy. Conflict between possessing classes and workers was somewhat mitigated by social welfare measures.

Broadened schooling facilities silently combatted the darkness of illiteracy. Religious institutions were challenged by the incoming tide of secularism. Countries moved progressively toward popular government, with the spirit of democracy more vital in France than in neighboring states. Everywhere the cause of collectivism, principally in revisionist forms of Marxism, pushed ahead vigorously. Love of country, revealing itself in nationalism or even chauvinism, transcended in potency all other values. Under that spell, men of all lands would rise to extraordinary heights of endurance and united effort in the gruelling war which impended.

Did then the era represent the twilight of the middle classes and bourgeois society in the West of Europe? Did it ring down the curtain on a "good old world"? Perhaps. Or did the remembrance of things past only seem good to the old?

Assuredly the era did not mark the end of militant nationalism. The war would bite deeply into settled values and standards, but nationalism would rise to fresh peaks of intensity and recklessness after the holocaust. As for the ascendancy of Germany it would endure, except for a brief interlude, for yet another generation.

FOR FURTHER STUDY

CARLTON J. H. HAYES, *A Generation of Materialism* (New York, 1941)

JOHN H. CLAPHAM, *Economic Development of France and Germany* (new ed., London, 1936)

WILLIAM H. DAWSON, *The German Empire, 1867–1914* (2 vols., London, 1919)

WILLIAM H. DAWSON, *Bismarck and State Socialism* (2nd ed., London, 1891)

GUSTAV STOLPER, *German Economy, 1870–1940* (New York, 1940)

ARTHUR J. MAY, *The Hapsburg Monarchy, 1867–1914* (new ed., Cambridge, Mass., 1960)

BENEDETTO CROCE, *A History of Italy, 1871–1915* (Oxford, 1929)

ARCANGELO W. SALOMONE, *Italian Democracy in the Making . . . 1900–1914* (Philadelphia, 1945)

DENIS W. BROGAN, *France Under the Republic* (New York, 1940)

EDWARD M. EARLE, ed., *Modern France, Problems of the Third and Fourth Republics* (Princeton, 1951)

FRANK H. HINSLEY, ed., *Material Progress and World-Wide Problems* (Cambridge, Eng., 1962)

MARSHALL DILL, JR., *Germany* (Ann Arbor, 1961)

CARL E. SCHORSKE, *German Social Democracy* (Cambridge, Mass., 1955)

J. ALDEN NICHOLS, *Germany after Bismarck*, (Cambridge, Mass., 1958)

DAVID THOMSON, *Democracy in France* (new ed., New York, 1952)

RENÉ ALBRECHT-CARRIÉ, *Italy from Napoleon to Mussolini* (New York, 1960) PAPERBACK

CHAPTER XX

IMPERIAL RUSSIA (1815-1914)

THE COLOSSUS OF THE EAST

"NAPOLEON prophesied, at St. Helena, that all Europe would soon be either Cossack or Republican," wrote a British historian at the middle of the nineteenth century. "The events of the last few years, by weakening and disuniting all her European neighbors have immeasurably augmented the relative superiority of the Muscovite empire over all the other Continental powers."

"With a population exceeding sixty [sic] millions," he continued, "all implicitly obeying the impulse of a single ruling mind; with a territorial area of six millions and a half of square miles; with a standing army eight hundred thousand strong; with powerful fleets on the Baltic and Black Seas; with a skillful host of diplomatic agents planted in every court and among every tribe; with the confidence which unexpected success creates, and the sagacity which long experience fosters, Russia now grasps, with an armed right hand, the tangled thread of European politics, and issues her mandates as the arbitress of the movements of the age." [1]

As this analysis illustrates, worry in the West because of Russia was not a novelty born of the Communist regime. It was true throughout much of the period after the final expulsion of Napoleon from the European stage. Dislike of Russian authoritarianism, apprehension because of the military strength and expansionist appetites of this populous and extensive empire were common in the nineteenth century. Formed as she was of a solid block of territory, Russia reduced other European countries to mere gnomes.

Yet nature imposed heavy shackles upon this eastern colossus. For one thing, the northerly location—the Black Sea lies

[1] Edward S. Creasy, *The Fifteen Decisive Battles of the World* (London, 1851), pp. 289–290.

on about the same latitude as the Great Lakes—handicapped the dwellers on the vast Eurasian plain. Climate is continental in character, with long, bitterly harsh winters, and short, hot summers. And over large areas, the insufficiency of rainfall cuts crop production or forbids it entirely.

Communication and transportation facilities were decidedly inferior to those of the West. Roads were dirt tracks, though well along in the nineteenth century, graveled highways were built between the principal cities, and a considerable network of railways was constructed. Roads were most useful in the winter months when the ground resembled rock and was covered with snow; during the spring thaw, land transport was often brought to a standstill.

Up to a point, a splendid web of rivers compensated for indifferent travel by land. Here, however, there were grave drawbacks, for in the winter months ice clogged the rivers, and the great Volga River emptied into the inland Caspian Sea. Access to the west of Europe was rendered difficult by the shortage of Russian frontage on the sea. The longest expanse of coast fronted on the Black Sea, but to reach the outer world that way vessels had to traverse the Turkish Straits, which Turkey might close if she wished. Equally the route to the West from Baltic ports (partly icebound every year) passed through the Danish Strait; and only a short strip of the Arctic littoral could be navigated. Consequently Russia could rather easily be blockaded by an enemy with superior naval strength. Geography, in short, contributed to Muscovite isolation from influences that were transforming the nations of the West.

It was not until late in the nineteenth century that Russians awoke to the realization—and not fully then—that their country was a treasure house of natural wealth. Abundant and varied resources of minerals lay hidden beneath the Muscovite soil. Inexhaustible forests and alluvial soil in the south had long sustained the Russian millions; yet famine was a periodic peril, bringing destitution and starvation about every three years.

At the outset of the nineteenth century, Imperial Russia seemed more Oriental than European. Patriarchal economic and social institu-

Peasant house, northern Russia

tions, political authoritarianism, and cultural backwardness set the tsardom off from the advancing West. But dynamic forces, flowing mainly from outside, fostered newer ways and attitudes. The ignorant and brutish peasant masses, for example, were released from feudal bondage, industry and commerce pushed ahead, much enlarging the middle classes and the urban industrial working force; facilities for formal education were furnished on a more generous scale. Recurrently the flame of revolt burst forth, the participants holding divergent opinions on ultimate objectives, though in the main they were dedicated to the downfall of the Romanov autocracy.

Alexander the First

AUTOCRACY AND AUTOCRATS

To commemorate the victory over Napoleon, Tsar Alexander I ordered the erection of a towering arch of triumph in St. Petersburg. That monument symbolized the conviction that Russian arms had in point of fact freed Europe from the odious tyranny of Bonaparte. As trophies of war, Russia had annexed a larger slice of Poland, the former capital city of Warsaw included, Finland, Bessarabia and provinces to the south of the Caucasus Mountains. In 1815, the international prestige of Russia stood higher than at any time in history before the Second World War.

Russian merchant, about 1870

As emperor, Alexander I exercised, of course, unfettered authority. "One God in heaven, one tsar on earth," summed up Muscovite political philosophy. Or, as a prominent bureaucrat declared: "the tsar of all Russia is an autocratic and absolute monarch. God Himself commands obedience to the tsar's supreme authority, not only out of fear, but as a matter of conscience." As the Lord's anointed, the tsar was the object of superstitious veneration, and Orthodox churchmen inculcated respect and loyalty to the "little father." Criticism of the deeds or decisions of the emperor was sinful in the eyes of the Church.

Alexander I was a mercurial and rather tragic figure. Youthful associations had bred in him admiration for the teachings of the French "Enlightenment," and he even professed to be a cheerful atheist. Critics of the status quo greeted his accession with romantic enthusiasm. On the throne, he had visions of converting

Russia into a progressive and well-regulated monarchy, and to that end, he created an advisory Council of State, which prepared projects for laws and he gave ministries of state more definite form. Plans to publish a constitution and to abolish serfdom were canvassed, but cast aside; Russia's "peculiar institution" was left untouched, except for the liberation of the serfs in the Baltic provinces, and they were freed without being allotted land on which to earn a livelihood.

By 1820 Alexander I, under the urgings of Metternich of Austria and conservative native counselors, had gradually abandoned the enlightened idealism of his young manhood. Nothing more was heard of refashioning Russia along liberal lines. Lord Byron pilloried the emperor as

> The coxcomb Tsar,
> The autocrat of waltzes and of war,
> With no objection to true liberty
> Except that it would make the nations free.

Upon the death of childless Alexander I in 1825, confusion and uncertainty prevailed over which of his two brothers should inherit the crown. That situation gave the signal for a disorganized, futile attempt to throw down the autocratic regime. Since the outbreak occurred in December, it has passed into history as the "Decembrist Revolt." Involved in the rising were the intelligentsia, which was just taking shape in Russia, young men and women who read big books, thought long thoughts and brooded grimly over what they perceived to be out of joint in their Fatherland. Among the discontented were army officers who had learned of the ways of the West during and after the struggle against Napoleon, as was true of their counterparts in the Second World War.

Secret revolutionary clubs dreamed of making Russia over. Some aggressive progressives envisaged a constitutional monarchy, while others preferred a republic; at least one rebel venerated George Washington as his patron saint. A strongly nationalist tinge colored the plotting, for it was hoped to fuse the diverse national groupings of the Empire into a single Russian people. Utopian in their aspirations, the "Decembrists" were an impractical lot, wanting in realism and short on resolution.

Nevertheless, in December of 1825, conspirators stirred troops stationed in St. Petersburg into mutiny. The younger brother of Alexander, who had become Tsar Nicholas I, quickly suppressed the rising, and the main leaders were either executed or banished to dread Siberia. The stone wall of the autocracy, it was demonstrated, could not be broken through by a few excited foreheads. Thenceforth the Russian intelligentsia played the leading role in agitating and scheming against the autocracy. An aura of romanticism gathered round the Decembrist martyrs; Lenin, the principal architect of the Bolshevik insurrection of 1917, showered praise upon them, and schoolboys in Communist Russia were taught to revere the Decembrists as revolutionary heroes.

Called the "Iron Tsar," Nicholas I enforced what he conceived to be law and order with ruthless tenacity. Fearful of the effect of foreign ideas upon a population unaccustomed to independent thinking, the Tsar, like Stalin a century later, raised an "iron curtain" against the West, and banned as effectively as possible the diffusion of insidious ideas within the empire. Utterance of unorthodox opinions might be penalized with beatings, confinement in an insane asylum, or banishment to Siberia. An army man himself, Nicholas I intended to govern the Russian millions with military discipline.

In devotion to duty as he saw it, Nicholas I was similar to Peter I, attending to public business with meticulous care. His reign witnessed the codification of the laws of the empire and modest improvement in the administration of state finance. When Polish dissenters rebelled, (1830–31) they were smacked down without mercy. When Magyar insurgents in 1849 threatened to break loose from Hapsburg authority, the "gendarme of Europe" intervened and extinguished the rebellion.

PILLARS OF ABSOLUTISM

Upholding the Romanov autocracy, whether before Nicholas I or after him, were four stout pillars: the aristocratic landlords, the bureaucracy, the army and police and the Orthodox Church. The only possible check, indeed, upon the arbitrary will of the tsar was the upper aristocracy. Members of that caste had choked Tsar Paul I, as mad as a hatter, to death (1801); that gruesome incident later emperors could not forget. It was better to make no move likely to infuriate these gentry. Many functions of local government were actually carried on by landlords or their stewards.

"The landlord," a leading bureaucrat explained, "is the most reliable bulwark of the sovereign. No army can replace the vigilance and the influence which the landowner continuously exercises in [on] his estates. If his power is destroyed, the people will become a flood endangering in time even the Tsar himself . . . the landowner is the most faithful, the unsleeping watchdog guarding the state; he is the natural police magistrate."

From the landlord class were recruited top policy-making figures in government and army. Distinctly a privileged élite, this social element, about one per cent of the population, shared with crown and church a virtual monopoly on landholding and the labor services of serf-workers. The wealthier noble families lived prodigally in their city apartments or rustic "nests," attended by small armies of flunkeys. Orchestras in private theaters entertained with the best in music; hospitable on a lavish scale, aristocrats staged immense parties which sometimes ran on for days.

Although the poorer gentry kept to the seclusion of their country estates, they too belonged to the privileged. Crippling mortgages weighed upon many properties. "Great luxury and little morality," a British ambassador reported, "seem to run through every rank. Flattery and servility characterize the inferior class, presumption and pride the higher one. A slight though brilliant varnish covers in both the most illiterate and uninformed minds." The attitude of most landlords toward the rural masses combined ignorance with indifference. Even in language the two social classes were separated, for the landlords preferred French to the peasant vernacular.

The civil bureaucracy was another stout prop of tsarist absolutism. Organized in a hierarchy from policy-making and administrative ministers down to a horde of petty officials, these servants of the state operated the lumbering governmental machinery. Since they were recruited on a haphazard basis of personal patronage, officials owed allegiance to the man responsible for their appointment, as well as corporate loyalty to the emperor. As a class, Russian bureaucrats were haughty and quite callous in dealing with ordinary citizens; poorly paid, they fleeced the public to piece out their slim incomes. Venality and corruption in Imperial Russia touched depths sufficient to bring a flush to the pale cheeks of the Tammany Tiger.

Close to the bureaucracy were the police; the ordinary type to enforce law and discipline, and secret police to ferret out the politically heterodox. Nicholas I instituted (1828) the notorious "Third Section," which was charged with hunting down men believed to be infected with Decembrist or kindred heresies. A network of special agents covered the empire, arresting and imprisoning arbitrarily. These officials also kept St. Petersburg posted on grosser instances of bureaucratic corruption and on the temper of popular opinion.

Police spies deftly wormed their way into suspected clubs or discussion groups and brought members to book. To extort confessions, torture might be applied with flogging, imprisonment, or Siberian exile as punishment. Clergymen and porters in city buildings were often undercover agents of the nefarious police regime. When needed, rough Cossack horsemen were employed to silence mass disturbances or to cow the rebellious among subject nationalities.

If all else failed, the levies of the huge Russian regular army could be thrown against dissenters. Rigorous discipline and cruel punishments prevailed in the military services, which few young men cared to enter voluntarily. Landlords picked the serfs on their properties who were to become soldiers; their fellows commiserated with conscripts as men condemned to death, since service normally lasted a quarter of a century.

THE ORTHODOX CHURCH AND THE SECTARIANS

Beyond all question the Orthodox Church was a mighty bulwark of conservatism and obscurantism. State and Church operated on terms of closest intimacy. The clergy, a special category of officials, spiritual gendarmes, in truth, were responsible for the political guidance of parishioners as well as for performance of ordinary ecclesiastical duties. They taught obedience to the crown, preached contentment with the status quo, reported on political suspects and through schools and censorship fought unconventional ideas. Missionaries of the Orthodox Church brought Siberian nomads into the national religious fold and carried the Christian faith to some pagans of eastern Asia.

Whenever the Russian government desired to rouse mass emotions, it appealed to popular religious instincts. It used to be said that the ringing of the bells on the forty times forty churches of Moscow was sufficient to march Russia into battle. For humble citizens, wars invariably took on the quality of religious crusades against Turkish infidels. Polish or German heretics, or Japanese heathen. Clergymen, carrying icons, accompanied troops in battle, and if victory was won, pious praise was bestowed upon the sacred objects.

Supreme authority over the Orthodox Church was vested in the Holy Synod, presided over by a tsar-appointed layman, with leading prelates as his colleagues. Bishops, who were drawn exclusively from monastic ranks, belonged to the privileged caste. Ordinary priests, poor, sodden and meagerly trained, were scarcely more enlightened than the masses to whom they ministered.

Apart from performing religious functions (likely enough in a mechanical manner), clergymen were called upon to combat drought or epidemic, to bless ripening grain and similar exertions. For exceptional services, fees were exacted which led to endless bickering with parishioners. And there was no little exploitation of popular credulity for priestly profit or prestige. "I have witnessed," a non-Communist Russian has written, "the victimization of . . . simple souls by cunning unscrupulous priests, who sold them all kinds of 'miraculous' gadgets —bottles of 'holy water' alleged to be the genuine tears of the Virgin Mary; 'holy oil' from the skull of a saint . . . alleged to flow therefrom eternally from a miraculous source; feathers from the Holy Ghost . . ." [2]

Varieties of religious experience were almost as diverse in Russia as in the United States. Approximately a third of the subjects of the tsar worshiped outside the official state Church. There were, for instance, the Old Believers professing to be more orthodox than the Orthodox and with a following of possibly 10,000,000 at their peak. Much smaller sects held to rationalist, evangelical, or quaintly mystical doctrines, and a host of weird cults flourished.

Non-Orthodox Russians were generally hostile to the government, sometimes militantly so. They refused to observe laws, or balked at paying taxes or fighting in the imperial legions. These folk plainly demonstrated that some Russians at least were ready to defy authority in a department of life deemed vital. Though subjected to relentless persecution, the sectarian faiths were never stamped out. Similarly abused were minorities of Roman Catholics, Uniates who acknowledge the headship of the Pope but follow the Orthodox liturgy, Protestants and Jews. Moslems in the Asiatic provinces seem not to have been seriously molested.

AN AGE OF REFORM

Ideas sometimes penetrate "iron curtains" and ferment, as was true in the Russia of Nicholas I. Isolated Russian thinkers and writers inside the tsardom or in foreign exile, students and professional men became poignantly conscious of the disparities between their country and the rest of Europe. In such ways as were open to them they called for the advancement of Russian society, for the "modernization" of Russia. Over against the "Westernizers" stood the Slavophiles—together they represented the two main and enduring currents of Russian secular

[2] Vladimir de Korostovetz, "The Religious Factor in Eastern Europe," *Contemporary Review*, CLXVIII (1945), p. 173.

A Russian serf

thought—who were staunchly nationalist, glorying in the unique features of Muscovite civilization and desirous of preserving them. St. Petersburg and Moscow, respectively, symbolized the Western and the native outlook on men and affairs.

A typical Slavophile exulted: "The Russian nation is a new and wonderful phenomenon in the history of mankind. The character of the people differs to such a degree from that of the other Europeans that their neighbors find it impossible to diagnose them." That line of emotion led inescapably to the conclusion that all Slavic-speaking groups would benefit if brought under the Muscovite roof.

Whatever the general cast of mind, many a reflective Russian was convinced that the institution of serfdom must be either mended or ended. This gigantic problem involved over ninety per cent of the Russian population, with upwards of 20,000,000 serfs on estates of landlords, either as soil-workers or as domestic servants, almost as many on crown properties and the balance on church lands. The richest Russian aristocrat lorded over 300,000 serfs, which may be compared with the largest slaveholder in the United States who owned 300 Negroes.

Their lives bounded by the villages in which they were born, the serfs were illiterate and their interests narrow. The way of life of the rustics reflected in fact the unrelieved monotony of the vast, interminable Russian plain. Obedient to Church and Tsar, these "brothers of the ox" took no interest in public affairs. Social conditions varied a great deal, it is true, depending largely on whether the landlord was humane or otherwise. In any case, serfs were obligated to work about half the time for the master, furnishing their own tools and draught animals. The landlord exercised full jurisdiction over his serfs, acting as tax collector, recruiting agent for the army, policeman and judge.

It was permissible for masters to correct laziness or other shortcomings by flogging with the knout, imprisonment, or deportation to Siberia. And there were plenty of instances of inhumane cruelty. If mutiny broke loose in a village, police or soldiers were thrown in to restore order. Sale of serfs, however, was legally abolished in 1808, yet it was not uncommon for a landlord to swap a whole hamlet for a troupe of actors or to exchange serfs for some good hounds.

No serf could lawfully withdraw from his village without the landlord's consent. A few serfs worked in mills or as traders; one unusually enterprising fellow got control of an entire village. The sole ways for serfs to escape bondage were by flight, which appealed only to the hardier, or by manumission on the part of the landlord either as an act of piety or in return for payments by the freed man. In exchange for labor services the serf occupied a cottage, and harvested the produce from a garden patch and from strips of the community farm lands. Strips were periodically redistributed among the households of the community in accordance with the number of mouths or the number of males.

About the middle of the nineteenth century, pressure for the abolition of serfdom mounted in volume and intensity. Even Nicholas I set

Exiles to Siberia at the crossing of the Yenisei River, 1886

committees to study the problem and encouraged landlords to free their workers. The novelist Ivan Turgenev, in *Sportsman's Sketches*, which was published in the same year as *Uncle Tom's Cabin*, dramatically pointed up the evils of the institution of serfdom; both books were read widely in Russian circles that mattered. The idea spread that serfdom transgressed natural human rights, was morally outrageous, and fostered intellectual apathy.

Weightier than that, doubtless, certain influential landlords were persuaded that farming by serfs was unprofitable and that their private interests as well as the national economy would benefit from emancipation. Precisely that logic had counted heavily in the liberation of serfs in the Hapsburg Monarchy in 1848, a reform not unnoticed in Russia. Rising disorders in the countryside caused apprehension lest a general insurrection might break out if the country people were not set free. Tsar Alexander II remarked: "Better to abolish serfdom from above than to wait until it begins to abolish itself from below."

The decisive push toward emancipation was given by the sorry showing of Russia in the Crimean War. The iron regime of the "Iron Tsar" was weighed in the most severe of balances and found wanting. Agitation for drastic overhauling of national institutions was much intensified. Alexander II, a wise and benevolent personality, on the whole, and capable of long views, became emperor in 1855, and he acted promptly. He stands second only to Peter I as a reformer of Imperial Russia. By uprooting the iniquity of serfdom, he earned the title of "Tsar Liberator."

First in line, the serfs on state properties were freed by a series of imperial decrees. Then in 1861, just a few weeks before an attack on Fort Sumter unloosed a terrible war in the United States, a war which was to eliminate Negro slavery, an edict published by Alexander II peacefully emancipated the millions of Russian private serfs from servitude. Under the provisions of the law peasants became free citizens. However, instead of assigning farmlands to individual households, properties were transferred to village communities as a whole. The customs of allotting strips of land to each household (some of them worked as many as 150) and of periodical redistribution were perpetuated. For land which they lost, noble proprietors were compensated in state bonds; these

Siberian exiles slept on the wooden shelves shown in this sketch of the distribution cell at Tomsk.

bonds were to be liquidated by annuities (or redemption fees) payable by the villages for nearly half a century. Domestic serfs were not assigned any land, and upon them the emerging factory towns exerted a magnetic attraction.

Such were the fundamentals of emancipation, but their application entailed all manner of complexities, and a full generation elapsed before readjustments were completed. Peasant beneficiaries in general complained angrily over the land settlements. It was small consolation to the liberated to be told—if told they were—that they had received better economic terms than serfs in other countries (or the Negroes in the United States) at the time of emancipation.

Whatever else liberation may have meant, it did not bring economic contentment. On the principle that land belonged of right to those who tilled it, peasants bitterly resented the obligation to pay redemption fees, and in many cases the land handed out was inadequate; maybe half the rural families were condemned to bare subsistence or less than that in recurrent famine years. Physical comforts had been better for many households under the regime of servility.

Discontent flared up in rapine and rioting which the arm of the law repressed, but the grievances simmered on. In the 1880's the government, it is true, reduced the burden of direct taxes on the peasantry, but for many rural households the struggle to exist grew more intense. For that evil situation there were two special reasons. Population in rural Russia soared prodigiously, touching 80,000,000 in 1905 as against fewer than 50,000,000 in 1860. And, in the second place, methods of peasant farming remained inefficient. Output of crops failed to match up with the increased number of stomachs. Some rustics took employment in the cities for all or part of the year, or trekked off to the virgin soil of Siberia.[3]

[3] Before a peasant quit his home-village, he had to obtain permission from local authorities, usually on the understanding that part of his earnings would be sent to the village to help in meeting redemption fees and taxes.

As for the landlords, emancipation cut down the real incomes of many and debts accumulated. Much of the compensation which accrued to them for the loss of serf labor services was applied to the cancellation of old mortgages. Nonetheless, after emancipation rather more than half the land of European Russia still belonged to the landlords. Some owners engaged peasants to cultivate their fields paying them wages or in shares of crops. The more energetic, progressive landlords introduced up-to-date farming methods and on their estates was grown most of the grain that was shipped abroad to pay for Russian imports. Others preferred to sell all or part of their farmlands; by 1905 possibly half the landlord acreages had passed into the ownership of either city capitalists or peasants, and by 1916 the proportion thus disposed of equaled about three-fifths.

By reason of lease or purchase of land, a class of well-to-do peasants gradually emerged, *kulaks* they were called. All in all, emancipation was an enormous economic and social upheaval and there were profound psychological implications as well. Yet this was only the largest and most enduring change in the age of reform.

Institutions of local government were radically revised to meet needs thrown up by the ending of landlord authority over serfs. Village assemblies, animated by democratic principles, looked after strictly local affairs. More of an innovation in 1864 were county councils, elected by peasants and gentry and empowered to levy taxes and employ their own officials. Activities of these bodies touched transportation, public health, education and practical aid to the peasantry.[4] Vigorous and forward-looking, the county councils provided jobs for a new race of civil servants and afforded experience in self-government on a local level, which would be preparation for participation in a national legislature. In time, however, the county councils fell under the numbing rule of the central bureaucracy.

The Russian judicial system, hitherto a synonym for bare-faced corruption and rank injustice, was fundamentally reformed in the light of British and French practices. Alexander II declared his intention to create "fast, just, and merciful courts, equal for all" and beyond the range of administrative surveillance. Steps were taken, accordingly, to better the quality of judges, lawyers might plead on behalf of clients and the jury institution was introduced, this last a daring innovation. Courts, moreover, were made independent of the police and public administrators; judges could no longer be removed by the whim of a bureaucrat. Elected justices of the peace instead of police ruled on petty misdemeanors. Taken together the judicial experiments represented an interesting application of the spirit of humanitarianism. Executive and legislative departments of government remained in the tight grip of despotism, but the judicial branch passed under more or less popular control.

Supervision of the press by state officials was substantially relaxed in the age of reform. Newspapers and journals might discuss public questions, with greater latitude allowed in dealing with foreign policies than home affairs. Equally, restrictions on learning in secondary schools and higher institutions were lightened; attendance in universities expanded to 10,000, a five-fold increase. And, for the first time, the central government displayed active interest in popular education, furnishing subsidies to church-connected schools as was the custom in England. Many more children, however, attended schools financed by county councils, so that by 1893, about 3,000,000 were receiving the rudiments of education.

Lastly, the Russian military establishment was drastically reconstructed on the Prussian-German model. The Crimean humiliation, which touched off the spate of reforms, had painfully revealed the necessity of army reform. The obligation to serve in the military forces was now made universal, the length of service was pared down and troops were treated more humanely and were better weaponed. In the future, as in the past, the army would be the strong right arm of the monolithic autocracy. On paper at any rate, the varied changes of the age of reform bade fair to bring Russia

[4] Comparable councils were established in the larger towns and cities.

abreast of the more progressive nations of the West.

REVOLUTIONARY FERMENT

The innovations of the "Tsar-Liberator" had not gone far enough to suit left-wing intellectuals. And to add to their sorrows, the pendulum of government presently, and characteristically, swung back to retrogression. In their studies in secondary schools, technical institutes and universities these folk had learned of Western political, social and economic theories. Increasingly, sons—fewer daughters—of middle-class families gravitated into the thin stream of revolutionary discontent. A class of professional revolutionaries emerged, whose members devoted themselves to intellectual speculations, secret conspiracy and propaganda.

From reading foreign books and brooding on the Russian scene the intelligentsia of the 1860's and 1870's—or the radical wing—came to the conclusion that desperate surgical operations were needed to cut out diseased organs. This set, which was called "nihilist" in derision, could find little in Russian society that was worthy of preservation. Making science their idol, the nihilists took up with shallow philosophies of materialism and non-theistic beliefs. The prevailing political regime and the landlords must go, they insisted, and semi-Asiatic Russia must be converted into a nation of self-governing peasant communes. Nihilists prided themselves on unconventionality in dress, manners and speech. They were terribly serious, terribly in earnest. Their strongest weapon, as of any revolutionaries, was the conviction that their way alone was the right way.

To insinuate their aspirations into the peasant millions certain of the youthful visionaries, called *Narodniki*, moved into villages and took employment as teachers, nurses, physicians, or manual workers. As opportunity afforded they tried to penetrate the dark forest of the peasant mind, to convert the rustics to their beliefs, to fire them with revolutionary zeal. But the illiterate masses refused to be uplifted and often handed eager young evangelists over to the police for consignment to dungeon or Siberia.

Infuriated by mass apathy or hostility, some of the *Narodniki*, who were imbued with anarchistic notions, turned to terroristic conspiracies. Others of them, denying the efficacy of terrorism, drifted into the budding Marxist movement. The most famous victim of anarchistic violence was Tsar Alexander II himself. Scarcely a liberal in any fundamental sense, and quite chary of the foaming steeds of reform, he had nonetheless sponsored far-reaching innovations. Though his ardor for change cooled, he deliberated seriously on the desirability of creating a national consultative assembly. Fanatical anarchists followed the Tsar about like hounds after a stag, repeatedly tried to slay him, and in March of 1881 finally trapped him and tore him to shreds.

That crime cancelled whatever likelihood there may have been that Russia would receive some kind of a parliament. With unsurpassed ferocity, government agents smashed conspiratorial clubs or drove their followers underground. The autocracy, that is, treated the political disease as though it were a pimple when in fact it was cancer.

PLIGHT OF THE MINORITIES

Alexander III, who succeeded his murdered father, greatly admired the tyrannical Nicholas I and intended to govern in his spirit. The new Tsar was no parlor aristocrat, no fancy playboy, but a physical giant and an intellectual pygmy with the general interests of a peasant. He was a centenarian in his outlook—one hundred per cent Russian, credulously believing in the greatness, the goodness, the uniqueness of his Fatherland.

Professor Konstantine P. Pobedonoscev, sometime tutor of the Tsar and now his fatherly counselor, whispered that salvation demanded strict observance of the Muscovite trinity of nationalism, autocracy and Orthodoxy. As Procurator of the Holy Synod, this champion of Slavophilism was in an ideal position to practice what he preached. Under the banner of one Russia, one Faith, one Law, one Tongue, one Tsar, the ponderous governmental machine swung brutally against the disparate minorities of the realm. This "nation of nations" would be dragooned into sterile uniformity.

Russian police excavate a mine dug by the Nihilists in a St. Petersburg street.

Convicted Nihilists at start of their journey to Siberia, 1887

The assassination of Alexander II

The hand of tyranny descended with unprecedented violence upon the Jewish element in the population. Well over half the Jews of the world were subjects of the tsar, living mostly in the districts acquired from Poland. Except for a favored few, Jews were obliged to reside in a strictly defined Pale of Settlement of Russian Poland, and almost all lived in cities; Warsaw contained the largest Jewish population. Jews resembled in fact human islands set in the midst of a sea of ignorant and poor Slavs. In the main Jews led a separate existence cherishing customs and costumes, a language and a religion peculiar to themselves. Few of them were engaged in farming; mostly they were traders, petty middlemen, or craftworkers. Financial astuteness was bred in the hard school of the ghetto, but probably a fifth of the Russian Jews were paupers, eking out a miserable and uncertain existence in cramped urban quarters.

Aside from confining Jews to the Pale, Russian laws debarred them from the civil service, prevented them from rising higher than the rank of corporal in the army, and set quotas or wholly excluded them from institutions of learning. Special taxes, moreover, were assessed upon Jews. Through the artifices of bribery, it is true, Jews often evaded discriminatory legislation. Before the 1880's physical abuse of Jewry was sporadic.

Then, because some Jews were affiliated with revolutionary clubs, the whole Jewish community fell under condemnation as malignant conspirators. Pent-up prejudices against Jewry blazed forth in beatings, plunder and murder; and the official world afforded little or no protection to victims of fanaticism. Pobedonoscev is credited with the assertion that a third of the Jews would have to change their religion, another third would have to emigrate and the rest would have to be killed. Persecution of Jewry made Russia the by-word for barbarism and inhumanity in the civilized world. Somewhat later the bizarre and vicious myth was circulated that Jewish leaders were plotting to enslave the world under a dictatorship and that Russia would be the theater in which the first act in the global conspiracy would be played. Belief in that silly monstrosity fanned the flames of hatred against Jewry afresh.

Oppression and persecution tended to strengthen Jewish solidarity on the principle that "Common sorrow unites men more closely than common joy." Articulate Jews responded in a variety of ways to endless fear, abuse and pogroms. Some chose to collaborate with Russian moderates who desired to replace the autocracy by a progressive regime. Others could see no solution except in the destruction of the Romanov dynasty and of capitalistic economy and the inauguration of a thoroughgoing collectivist society. For still others emigration seemed the best bet. A decided stimulus was imparted to the vision of recovering the ancient Zionist homeland in Palestine, and a mass exodus to the United States, with its material opportunities and freedoms, was set flowing. Emigrants carried their burning hatred of the tsarist autocracy with them.

Treatment of the Jew in Russia more or less accurately mirrored the official attitude toward other minorities. Consider, for instance, the Poles with their distinctive language and literature, their national traditions of which the Roman Catholic faith formed an important part, and their feeling of cultural superiority to their Russian overlords. In 1815 a remarkable degree of home-rule had been granted to the Polish provinces by Alexander I, but rights were gradually whittled down and then virtually canceled after risings by spirited Polish nationalists in 1830 and 1863. Property of rebellious Poles was seized and leaders were deported to Siberia or fled into foreign exile.

As aspects of the Russification policy, restrictions were laid upon Polish intellectual institutions, the use of the national language and Catholic worship. Clergy were often fined or imprisoned, yet Catholicism stood firm as the great rallying center of Polish faith and hope. Barriers were raised against the admission of Poles to the higher posts in the Russian bureaucracy and the army. Discrimination and oppression of the Poles embittered Slavs beyond the borders of Russia.

In the meantime, the Polish areas had responded to the coming of machine industry. Population in the historic capital, Warsaw, doubled in a generation. Polish mills became the largest textile producers in the Empire, and a limitless market stretching away to the Pacific lay open to them. Under the impact of changing circumstances, certain Polish leaders reasoned that political energies should be concentrated on seeking home-rule within Russia. But others, unregenerate, clung to the hope that partitioned Poland could be reunited and resume its place as an independent member of the family of nations.

Smaller national groupings, Finns, Esths and Letts in the Baltic provinces, the best educated and most progressive peoples in the Empire, Lithuanians, the Armenians off to the south, were likewise subjected to oppressive Russification. Finland, which had long enjoyed autonomy, was deprived of its special rights. Public officials everywhere drove hard against national linguistic, literary and religious traditions; yet in each area Russification stimulated a national renaissance, intensified longings for freedom and increased the unsleeping enemies of the autocracy. The Ukrainians, however, were a separate case, for whatever sense of distinctive national spirit existed among them was rather effectually smothered.

COMING OF MACHINOFACTURE

Alexander III's ardent national feeling not only led him to applaud the coercion of minorities, but also to promote the industrialization of the country. Given time, Russia might escape from dependence upon Western manufacturers and might create employment as well for the swelling population. Previously, manufacturing in Russia had been very largely of the household or domestic type; handicraft industry supplied such everyday articles as knives, locks, tools, garments and objects made of wood. It was not until the end of the century that Russian domestic industry commenced to feel the competition of mass production factories. Down to about 1870, only mills making military goods had anything more than local significance.

It was in the 1860's, simultaneously with the serf-emancipation, that the mechanism of capitalistic economy started to expand in an important manner. Growth of private banks, joint-stock companies and activity on the stock exchange were symptoms of changing times. Readjustments in the countryside released an abundance of unskilled manpower for employment in machine-industry.

Russia, like the United States, depended heavily upon foreign capital for industrial expansion. Funds flowed in from German, British, Belgian, but above all, from French sources. In some cases entire plants were imported from abroad, and foreign companies, American included, were invited to set up branch factories with assurances of government subsidies or public contracts. Perhaps as much as two-fifths of the capital invested in Russian industry before 1914 originated in foreign countries; Lenin once commented sardonically that Russia was a colony of alien capitalists. More than that, Russian engineers and professors were dispatched abroad to learn foreign manufacturing techniques. And experts with industrial "know-how" were brought in from Britain, and by thousands from Germany.

Resistance in high places retarded for years the laying down of railways, but after 1860 there was a feverish burst of construction. The principal cities and ports of European Russia were linked up by railroads. As the central feature of a second wave of construction, in the 1890's, a line was thrown across the Siberian vastness to the Pacific. When completed (1905), the Trans-Siberian Railroad covered nearly 6,000 miles, a distance from New York to San Francisco and back again. Migration from European Russia into Siberia increased greatly and trade grew with the building of this railway.

That gigantic undertaking stands as a really impressive monument to Count Sergius Witte, holder of several ministerial portfolios and an expert on railways. As energetic as he was arrogant, Witte was more responsible than any other man for the growth of Russian industry. A firm believer in protectionism, he watched the national tariff wall rise to heights comparable with American tariffs. Witte accumulated reserves of gold and then put (1897) the currency on a gold basis, which assured greater stability in business transactions and gave foreign investors more confidence in the Russian economy. Half to increase public revenues, half to combat the national curse of drunkenness, Witte established a state monopoly on vodka and other intoxicating beverages. With him at the helm, the tradition of state paternalism in economic affairs deepened, and an embryonic species of planned economy developed.

Machinofacture was concentrated in half a dozen areas. As the capital of the Empire and a principal port as well as a manufacturing center, St. Petersburg had passed the 2,000,000 mark by 1914. Textiles and heavy machinery were the leading productions, with the Putilov company, which specialized in armaments and railway equipment, as the largest firm in the empire; at its peak Putilov employed 20,000 workers. Giant factories were indeed a feature of Russian industrialism; they involved big capital investments, particularly since living quarters often had to be provided for workmen. Moscow, which had been swiftly rebuilt after the Napoleonic occupation and fire, contained the highest proportion of wage workers in Russia. Population expanded fivefold between 1860 and 1914, when it touched nearly 2,000,000. Moscow was the focal point of railways and the principal center of textile manufactures; about a quarter of all Russian industrial workers was employed in this city and nearby communities.

The largest district of steel production was the Donetz area, centering upon Kharkov; iron ore and coal were there available in close proximity. About a fifth of the Russian pig iron output was produced in the Urals. Baku on the Caspian Sea was the turbulent capital of the oil country, while Kiev and Odessa, and Warsaw and Lodz in the Polish provinces were other manufacturing communities of major importance. Cities took on something of the appearance of Western industrial communities, whereas rural Russia remained very largely in the grip of semi-Asiatic agriculture.

Hand in hand with industrial growth, Russian

A Cossack

foreign trade moved upward. Certain industries such as cotton mills came to rely heavily upon imported rawstuffs, which would be largely cut off in the event of war and blockade. By 1914 nearly half of all goods imported into Russia came from Germany. Grain held first place in exports—something like a seventh of the cereal yield was normally sold abroad—followed by timber, dairy products and rare minerals.

In the familiar pattern, machinofacture in Russia was accompanied by the growth of the middle classes and the industrial workers. Professional classes as well as business men prospered, without however attaining anything like the size or public significance of their counterparts in western Europe. The bourgeoisie were recruited from old merchant families or pushed up out of obscurity (or serfdom) as was true of the managerial and moneyed classes in Western countries. Many of them took an active part in public affairs, usually on the side of progressive reform, and some blossomed out as patrons of culture.

Fully accurate statistics on Russian industrial workers are impossible to obtain, but by 1914 they comprised rather more than five per cent of the population. Approximately 3,000,000 were employed in factories and mills (a third of them women and children), another million in mining, and about 800,000 on railways. In addition, peasants streamed into the cities for seasonal employment, returning to their villages in the spring and summer months. Not until about 1890 did a distinctly urban class-outlook begin to pervade the industrial wage earners.

Conditions under which the proletariat worked and lived were reminiscent of the situation in Britain in the first flush of machinofacture. Hours of employment were long, wages low, discipline rigid if not brutal and the working environment generally unwholesome. A government inspectorate service, belatedly created, was utterly inadequate. Living conditions were sordid as a rule. Housing facilities in

A Russian peasant woman, mid-Nineteenth Century

swiftly industrialized cities failed to keep pace with the working force so that it was said an individual had hardly more space than in a coffin; clothing like housing absorbed an abnormally high proportion of wages. Food, on the other hand (and the diet was that of the peasantry), was relatively cheap. Ill-housed, ill-clothed, ill-treated by management and almost wholly untaught, a large percentage of the Russian wage earners grovelled in misery and destitution.

As early as the 1880's, industrial workers over wide areas engaged in strikes with a view to forcing improvements in their wretched lot. Then as later, cries of "Down with the autocracy" mingled with demands for better standards of living. Then as later, strikes were broken by police and Cossacks. In the stormy year of 1905, virtually every Russian wage earner walked off the job in a paralyzing general strike. After that, some betterment in workers' conditions was effected. Trade unions, previously forbidden, were declared lawful, but their sphere of operations was confined strictly to economic matters and to a locality. Never were more than 1,250,000 men drawn into unions, indifferently organized unions at that. Beginnings were made in social welfare legislation imitative of Germany, but the laws were never faithfully executed. Unconcealed discontent, which revolutionaries could channel to their purposes, prevailed in large layers of the still small proletariat of Russia.

NEWER REVOLUTIONARY CURRENTS

Out of the disparate fragments of Russian radical thought of the 1870's emerged two newer and more dynamic revolutionary patterns. One type, grounded on international Marxist theory, evolved into the Social Democratic Party and eventually into the Communist Party, master of Russia after the November Revolution of 1917. Its origins deserve, therefore, fuller exposition than the significance of the party in the history of Imperial Russia alone would warrant. The second sect was a purely Russian phenomenon, coming to be known as the Social Revolutionary Party.

Founder of Russian Marxism was Georgi V. Plekhanov. Once affiliated with the *Narodniki*, he pulled out because he thought terroristic violence stupid and futile. Transferring his allegiance to Marxism, he translated the *Communist Manifesto* into Russian and founded (1883) the first Marxist circle. As a thinker, bold, independent and disciplined, Plekhanov ranks at the top of the Russian expositors of Marx. A prolific and engaging writer on the Marxian vision of a golden tomorrow, he became the venerated teacher of the Russian Communists.

Even before the conversion of Plekhanov, Marxist doctrines had found their way into the tsardom. Marx himself corresponded with blindly fanatical Russian disciples, and in 1872 *Das Kapital* was translated into the Russian language. The imperial censorship tolerated the circulation of the book, for it was reasoned that so massive and forbidding a work could not possibly contain political dynamite; books infinitely more innocuous were strictly forbidden.

Marx himself, it may be recalled, had proved to his own satisfaction that capitalist economy would collapse where it was ripest, remote from overwhelmingly agrarian Russia. He felt that big, industrially immature, uncivilized, despotic Russia would serve as the spearhead of a crusade against collectivism once it had triumphed in the advanced West. Later in life, it is true, his distrust of Russia somewhat declined. He started indeed to learn the Russian language and to study Russian social conditions; conceivably the tsardom might carry within it the germs of revolution on the Marxist pattern.

Marxist propaganda was diffused in ways familiar to underground Russia. Literature was printed and distributed on the quiet; meetings were held in an atmosphere of secrecy and stealth. A network of cells grew up in the leading cities, admission being extended only to men and women who met stern tests of integrity and reliability. Among discontented Jews a special branch of Marxism, spoken of as the *Bund*, was organized (1897).

The first general congress of the Russian Social Democratic Party convened in 1898. Formal organization was effected at that meet-

Пролетарія всѣхъ странъ, соединяйтесь!

ИСКРА

„Изъ искры возгорится пламя!"... Отвѣтъ декабристовъ Пушкину.

Центральный Органъ Россійской Соціальдемократической Рабочей Партіи.

№ 53. 25-го ноября 1903 г. Годъ III.

Извѣщеніе

о второмъ очередномъ съѣздѣ Россійской Соціальдемократической Рабочей Партіи.

Недавно состоялся второй очередной съѣздъ Россійской Соціальдемократической Рабочей Партіи. Послѣ пятилѣтняго промежутка, протекшаго со времени перваго съѣзда, мы, россійскіе соціальдемократы, имѣемъ наконецъ фактически возстановленную и единую организованную партію. Сплоченный въ рабочую партію, нашъ пролетаріатъ удеся-

...туировались и приступили къ своей дѣятельности на основаніи организаціоннаго устава Партіи.

Товарищи! Передъ нами стоитъ теперь громадная задача провести въ жизнь тѣ рѣшенія, которыя приняты вторымъ съѣздомъ, превратить на дѣлѣ нашу Партію въ то, чѣмъ она должна стать по мысли съѣзда, — въ принципіально-выдержанную, организаціонно-сплоченную коллективную силу, способную руководить всѣми проявленіями классовой борьбы всего пролетаріата всей Россіи и вести его на рѣшительную борьбу за свободу всего народа и за освобожденіе труда отъ всѣхъ видовъ гнета и эксплуатаціи.

Товарищи! Мы прекрасно сознаемъ всѣ гигантскія трудности этой задачи. Но мы знаемъ твердо, что она можетъ быть осуществлена и будетъ осуществлена — за это руча-

...не могло быть и рѣчи о заполненіи партійной оболочки реальнымъ содержаніемъ.

Но между тѣмъ, какъ подъ напоромъ жизни и усиленнымъ воздѣйствіемъ литературной пропаганды петербургскіе, московскіе, одесскіе и др. экономисты превращались на дѣлѣ въ *россійскихъ соціальдемократовъ*, росли и множились элементы дѣйствительнаго *организаціоннаго* единства, способные создать и поддержать техническій аппаратъ партійной организаціи. Соціальдемократическій „кустарь" вытѣснялся профессіональнымъ революціонеромъ, получавшимъ свое политическое воспитаніе на все усложнявшейся работѣ передовыхъ организацій, въ атмосферѣ революціоннаго подъема, характеризующаго послѣдніе годы.

Идейная борьба 1900-1902 годовъ создала для громаднаго большинства дѣйствующихъ товарищей идейное единство. Съ того момента, какъ эта цѣль была достигнута, насущнѣйшей задачей дня стало положить начало *оформленному* существованію такой организаціи, которая была бы способна осуществить это

Masthead of Lenin's newspaper Iskra *(The Spark)*

ing, and resolutions on policy that were adopted were pure, unadulterated Marx. In attendance were intellectuals almost exclusively, some of them learned authorities on Marxist theory. The most outstanding personalities were Russians, though there was a sprinkling from the minorities, notably from internationally-minded Jews. Many of the participants in the congress were pounced upon by tsarist police.

Absent from the congress was Nicholas Lenin, at the time an exile in Siberia. Born into a well-to-do family, this architect of Bolshevism was educated as a lawyer. But, becoming a convert to the Marxian gospel, he devoted himself to the cause as organizer and writer. For him Marxism implied not merely sound economic theory and correct analysis of society, but the herald of a new civilization from top to bottom. An austere little man, with many of the instincts of a scholar, Lenin relished nothing so much as intellectual combat and turning out Marxist hand-grenades in the form of pamphlets. Shipped to Siberia for revolutionary agitation, Lenin emigrated to Switzerland upon his release. There he was instrumental in founding and editing a Marxist newspaper, *Iskra*, "The Spark," whose masthead carried the watchword "From a Spark Comes Flame." By devious means the paper was smuggled into Russia to further the work of propaganda—or education. In their Swiss sanctuary, Russian revolutionaries, Marxist and other, debated, wrote, planned and plotted.

Square and strongly built, though rather undersized, Lenin had a distinctly Mongolian appearance, even to the slit of his eyes. Nervous and abrupt in manner, resolute in speech and action, his thought was at once incisive and lucid. As an interpreter of Marx, he never renounced or disputed anything the revolutionary master had written. On the other hand, he added interpretations, he "Russified" the original doctrines in order to fit them to the peculiar situation of Russia.

Lenin argued, for example, that the bourgeois stage of society could be and must be skipped over in the Russian march to Marxian collectivism. He insisted, too, that the Russian Marxist party must be a small, uncompromising, thoroughly disciplined, centrally controlled band of professional revolutionaries, which would direct the urban masses in the revolutionary seizure of power.[5] That emphasis, in fact, was the principal contribution of this shrewd tactician to Marxist procedure. It represented a distinct novelty in Russian conspiratorial activity, which hitherto had been notoriously haphazard and fluid. On the fundamental tenet that Marxists and non-Marxists could not

[5] The first issue of *Iskra* was dedicated to training "people who will devote to the revolution not only their spare evenings, but the whole of their lives."

coöperate for the common good, that rather an irreconcilable hostility existed between them, Lenin was as doctrinaire and dogmatic as Marx himself.

Almost from the beginning Russian Marxism was riven by acrimonious polemics over the methods and tactics to bring revolution to pass. Given the immaturity of machinofacture and the preponderantly agrarian character of Russian economy, given the weakness of class consciousness among industrial wage earners, one school of Marxists was willing to string along with bourgeois progressives in effecting changes inside Russia. Their position, in other words, was essentially the same as the evolutionary Marxists of Germany: revolution by evolution, conversion by persuasion.

Not so the strait-laced Marxists for whom Lenin became acknowledged spokesman. They shared Lenin's convictions, and believed in compulsion and violence to achieve revolution. "Give us an organization of revolutionaries," Lenin cried, "and we will turn Russia upside down." Controversial bickerings led to an open rupture in the Social Democratic Party at a second Congress convened in 1903 in London. More than two-score Russian Marxist exiles attended the meeting, all intellectuals, save for three or four manual workers. On a decisive vote concerning party tactics a majority of the delegates lined up with Lenin, and to this wing of the movement was attached the Russian name for majority, Bolshevik. The defeated faction, sympathetic to opportunistic procedures, became known as the Mensheviks, or minority; the veteran Plekhanov leaned toward the Menshevik position without actually endorsing it.

In 1912 the Bolshevik group wholly separated itself from the Mensheviks. Highly-disciplined as it was, Bolshevism commanded most of the Social Democrats in the two biggest Russian cities, St. Petersburg and Moscow, and in the Ural industrial district, while the strength of the Mensheviks lay primarily in southern Russia. Neither of them, to be sure, represented anything more than a cloud the size of a man's hand. Both relied upon the proceeds from raids and robbery to finance their activities.

Tough-textured individuals grew up with the Marxist movement, played hide-and-seek with tsarist police, lived in a fever of intrigue and fear. After the revolutionary seizure of power in 1917 these hardened men assumed the direction of the machinery of government, the secret police, collectivist economic institutions and the Communist fighting services. The psychology and the conspiratorial methods of the prerevolutionary era were not sloughed off.

Just as the Social Democrats originated in the non-terrorist branch of the *Narodniki*, so the Social Revolutionaries claimed descent from the terrorist element. And, whereas the prime concern of the Social Democrats was the city workers, the Social Revolutionary Party pinned its faith upon the peasantry. This movement assumed permanent form in 1898 but, like other indigenous expressions of Russian radicalism, it was not well-organized, nor were the objectives clear cut. Social Revolutionaries wished to destroy the autocracy, of course, and talked of an agrarian collectivist paradise resting upon the peasant villages. Its scope, unlike international Marxism, was confined to Russia alone.

Thousands of idealistic young intellectuals identified themselves with the Social Revolutionary cause. For methods they relied upon acts of individual terrorism, courageously striking down hated tsarist bureaucrats; that and propaganda among the peasants, calculated to incite them to rioting and destruction. A savage feud was waged with Marxists, who derided their competitors as visionary romantics, perilous for the "true" aims and techniques of revolution.

Russian revolutionary groups, under whatever name, carried on their operations in the greatest possible secrecy. It would have been in the interests of the tsardom, a safeguard indeed against violence and extremism, if the discontented had been allowed to express their grievances openly. Radical notions are less dangerous to things as they are when expressed rather than repressed. "With radical ideas," remarked Mr. Justice Oliver Wendell Holmes, in words of universal wisdom, "as with . . . champagnes, the best way to let them get flat is to let them get exposed to the air." Repression of unconventional ideas by self-appointed guardians of opinion has often encouraged revolution, which is precisely what happened in Imperial Russia.

THE REVOLUTION OF 1905

The last tsar of all the Russias, Nicholas II, took the crown in 1894, abdicated in 1917, and with his family was executed by the Bolsheviks in 1918. On becoming emperor he proclaimed his intention of maintaining the autocracy without modification. Nicholas II was charming, dignified and, no doubt, desired to govern wisely, but he was destitute of the qualities of mind and will required of an authoritarian autocrat. He prayed, more than once, that some magical incantation would wipe out the whole brood of his critics and enemies.

Nicholas II was neither the real ruler of Russia, though final decisions rested with him, nor was he a mere figurehead. Shy and easily befuddled, he ordinarily acted upon the advice of ministers or of members of the court camarilla [advisers] who had his ear. Disasters and defeats which rained down upon him were stoically accepted as the "will of God", and he abdicated the throne in the spirit of a bird released from his cage.

Often likened to the ill-starred Louis XVI of France, Nicholas II had no taste for ceremonies or crowds. He much preferred the seclusion of the family circle surrounded by the Empress Alexandra and their five children. Though raised at the sober court of Queen Victoria and of German stock, the Empress turned to mysticism in the Russian environment. She wished desperately that her only son should

Nicholas II and his family

wield autocratic power; in time she became the worst of all the counselors of her flabby husband. Her evil genius in turn was a sinister "holy man," Gregory Rasputin, ignorant, a lustful connoisseur of feminine beauty, immune to moral scruples, but an exceptionally clever politician. To the Empress, alas, Rasputin seemed to be an oracle of all wisdom, secular and divine. He possessed an uncanny power to help the heir-apparent who was a "bleeder" (hemophiliac). This malevolent creature personified "the dark forces," the adventurers and nonentities, who exercised influence at the court of Nicholas II in the closing years of the reign.

Gregory Rasputin

Barely had Nicholas II seated himself on the throne before his political tribulations began. Application of "Russification" policies in Finland set that province on fire, culminating in the murder of the chief local dignitary, the Governor-General. Mob attacks upon Jews, in which officials in high places connived and police did little to curb, discredited the tsardom afresh in the eyes of the civilized world. Outbreaks in industrial communities, student demonstrations and widespread rioting by unhappy peasants multiplied the national troubles. Bold Social Revolutionaries removed unpopular officials by violence in broad daylight.

In this tormented time the voice of Russian liberalism rang out with clarity and conviction, conspicuously in the county councils. Not at all revolutionary, but desirous of far-reaching changes, progressive bourgeoisie and even a few aristocrats pleaded for a constitution and an elected national parliament. They spoke up for ordinary civil liberties, the elimination of the hateful secret police, arbitrary imprisonment, mistreatment of minorities and kindred abuses. But the ears of Nicholas II and his closest advisers were sealed.

Matters took a radical turn after Russia became involved in war with Japan in 1904. Military defeats at the hands of the despised little Orientals, shameless corruption and incompetence on the part of commanders, disorganization of economic life, quickened and enheartened the advocates of political reform. Disorders on the home front started with outbreaks of workmen in the Baku oil fields and before the echoes had died away St. Petersburg witnessed in January of 1905 the terrible spectacle of "Bloody Sunday." Unarmed wage-workers paraded to the Winter Palace bearing a petition for the Tsar, requesting civil freedoms, better educational facilities, the right to organize trade unions and other concessions. Imperial troops mowed down the procession, killing some 500 and wounding 3,000 more.

That sadistic outrage touched off a wave of strikes and riots. Revolution crackled across Russia. Spearheads of revolt in the cities were striking workmen and *soviets*, or factory councils, which popped up spontaneously to give voice to working class demands; the biggest soviet appeared in St. Petersburg. Factory employees clashed with police, and peasants indulged in destructive outbreaks, raids and lootings such as Russia had not seen in more than a century; contingents in the imperial navy mutinied. Liberals intensified their clamor for a constitution, and minorities demanded recognition of natural rights and the removal of legal disabilities. Insurgency reached flood tide in October, 1905, when almost everybody in the Russian cities balked at doing anything. A general strike tightly tied up industry and communications.

It seemed as though the Romanov autocracy must certainly crack asunder. That, however, did not come to pass because the army never wavered in its fidelity to the crown, because Parisian bankers loaned the imperial regime desperately needed funds, and because Nicholas II published the appeasing October Manifesto. That document was drafted by Count Witte, whom Nicholas II despised but found indispensable. It promised that a legislature (duma) with real law-making powers would be created and assured civil liberties, including religious freedom to all and sundry. The Tsar put his signature on the Manifesto with great misgivings, confiding to his mother, "You cannot imagine what torments I went through first. . . . It is not days but years we have lived through, so great have been the torments, the doubts, the struggles."

The October promises and dismissal of detested officials placated moderate dissenters and the government beat down extremists with severity. Sharp street fighting raged in the textile districts of Moscow, Lenin and his Bolsheviks taking part. The rising was crushed with artillery fire by troops released from the Japanese war, and Lenin set off on his foreign travels again; outbreaks in other cities were similarly extinguished. Punitive expeditions were dispatched to areas of rural disaffection, though troubles in the country continued into 1906. Savage Cossacks came, punished and departed. Gangs of vicious ruffians, a Russian version of the Ku Klux Klan, slaughtered enemies of the dynasty without mercy, Jews being singled out for especial vengeance.

The worst of the revolutionary convulsions had passed—and with what results? First of all, many a Russian hitherto disinterested in public affairs had been shaken out of his lethargy. Second, the way was opened for a representative government of sorts. Third, minority groups were promised the elementary rights of men. But it was soon apparent that the imperial ministry would not be responsible to the elected legislature. And Nicholas II poured water into the wine of optimistic progressives by announcing that the old and government-controlled Council of State would have coequal power with the duma. The Tsar, moreover, might veto any legislative measure and he retained unfettered control over foreign policy and the fighting services.

Another consequence of the Revolution of 1905 deserves mention: the effect of the failure upon the thinking of Lenin. Previously, Marxists had paid scant attention to the peasant masses, except for the landless soil-people. But in the revolutionary storm, rustics had demonstrated impressive potentialities as revolutionaries. "The peasants want land," Lenin said, "I will promise it to them. I will simply say—go and take it, it is yours." Concerning other social groups, Lenin remarked, "To the workmen I will promise ownership of factories. To the ambitious I will promise good jobs according to their professional capacities and ambitions . . . The army is dangerous," he concluded, "but a first-class international war will help us to round the corner."

A DECADE OF EXPERIMENTATION

Almost every adult male was eligible to share in election of deputies to the first Russian duma. That body of nearly five hundred convened in the spring of 1906. Loosely organized political parties were arranged on the conventional pattern of Right, Center and Left, with unclassifiable groups representing national and religious minorities. Deputies of the Right divided into a reactionary group no more progressive than barnacles, and a genuinely conservative faction.

The largest and best balanced party, the Constitutional Democrats or Kadets, formed the Center. This party was essentially the mouthpiece of middle-class liberalism and more immediately concerned with enhancing the authority of the legislature at the expense of the executive than in basic social and economic legislation. Its real leader, Professor Paul Miliukov, a historian and publicist of distinction, who had traveled and lectured extensively in Great Britain and the United States, wished the duma to be as influential in the government of Russia as the House of Commons in Britain. Parties of the Left represented diverse shadings of radicalism, but there were no Social Revolutionary or Social Democratic deputies, for both sects had boycotted the elections. The processes of peaceful parliamentary reform held little attraction for apostles of revolutionary action.

The Russian experiment in limited popular government worked out none too well. Only proposals on inconsequential matters were passed into law by the first duma. But there was a torrent of turbulent oratory and insistent demands that the legislature be granted control over the ministry, after the manner of Great Britain. So fully had Nicholas II and his ministers recovered from the terrors of 1905 that they ordered the dissolution of the duma after two and a half months of existence.

Thoroughtly embittered, a large minority of the deputies, Kadets taking the lead, protested the action of the crown in the historic Viborg Manifesto. It demanded a responsible ministry, far-reaching agrarian reforms, and summoned the nation to refuse to pay taxes or appear for military duty. The response to the appeal was negative, disillusioning, and many of the protesting deputies were apprehended by the police and imprisoned. In the balloting for a second duma, the mood of the voters turned strongly leftward. Substantial delegations of the extreme revolutionary parties were returned and sessions were more tumultuous than before. Once more the deputies were sent home, but this time the dissolution evoked little outward dissent.

At that critical juncture the commanding place in Russian affairs was taken by Peter A. Stolypin, described as "a tall stiff man with a dead-white face and a dead-black beard." Coming into prominence as a tough and resourceful provincial bureaucrat, he had pushed to the front among the counselors of Nicholas II. That he possessed unusual abilities and unsurpassed understanding of national problems even his sharpest critics acknowledged. And he was not at all a mere marionette of the crown.

Of Stolypin's passionate affection for Russia and his courage, there could be no question. He seems sincerely to have wished to raise the level of existence for the masses and to transform Russia into a parliamentary monarchy in time. No doctrinaire, his general outlook is best described as enlightened conservatism. He piloted the Russian ship of state until 1911 when a revolutionary fanatic murdered him. His administration of affairs was noteworthy on three counts. First, articulate dissenters were hammered into silence by one device or another and shackles were imposed upon institutions of higher learning and the county councils. The democratic character of the duma, second, was severely modified; and third, radical innovations were inaugurated in peasant land-tenure. The last two items require fuller comment.

Upon the dismissal of the second duma, the franchise law was revised in defiance of the Tsar's solemn promises. The voting strength of large landlords and of the wealthy city element was much increased, while that of the poorer classes and of national minorities was whittled down sharply. As the crown desired, deputies in the third and fourth dumas were predominantly men of substance, conservative or reactionary in outlook. However, that is not to say they were do-nothing assemblies. Among the laws that were enacted were measures of social security for industrial workers and extension of schooling facilities; by 1914 probably half the children of school age were receiving instruction, though the school term was short. Deputies discussed the conduct of imperial diplomacy with vigor and patriotic zeal and the bolder ones denounced the wily Rasputin and his malign influence upon public business.

The fourth and last duma carried on deliberations, with interruptions, from 1912 until the March Revolution of 1917 which toppled

Nicholas II from the throne. In the final stage, a majority of the deputies organized themselves as the "progressive bloc" and stridently reiterated the demand for an authentic parliamentary regime. Despite wide and disconcerting detours, the course of Russian politics after 1905 ran in the general direction of popular government.

In the meantime, rural Russia was undergoing important changes. Premier Stolypin contemplated appeasing the peasantry and correcting the one-sided emphasis on industrial growth by radical agrarian reforms. Contentment in the countryside, he was convinced, would have to precede the development of authentic parliamentary institutions. And he argued that the formation of a large class of independent peasant landholders was indispensable for rural tranquillity. Given time, peasant proprietors would shrug off their collectivist heritage, likely enough, and become as steady and as conservative as the peasantry of France or Germany.

To that end, Stolypin proposed to parcel out the lands of the village communities among individual households.[6] A peasant family, furthermore, would have its land in a consolidated piece instead of scattered strips as previously. "The government," Stolypin explained, "has placed its wager, not on the needy and the drunken, but on the sturdy and the strong—on the sturdy individual proprietor who is called upon to play a part in the reconstruction of our tsardom on strong monarchical foundations."

Legislation to implement Stolypin's plans was enacted. The laws had of course to be supplemented by many administrative decisions on the spot, and shortly after the beginning of the First World War, the application of the land reforms was suspended. By then perhaps 2,000,000 peasant householders had become independent farmers and slightly more than 2,000,000 others were on the way to becoming landowners. Besides, before the Stolypin reforms about 2,800,000 peasants owned the land they worked. In other words, by 1914, approximately two-fifths of the households were either farm owners or on the verge of becoming owners; many holdings, to be sure, were of the dwarf variety, though to cultivate the larger farms, peasants hired less fortunate neighbors.

[6] The government in 1906 canceled village obligations to pay redemption fees for land received at the time of serf emancipation.

In many villages, however, the Stolypin legislation was never put into force. The coming of the First World War prevented that. Consequently large masses of rustics kept toiling away on communal land, much more often than not for merely subsistence returns. Poorer peasants envied and hated their fellows who were more economically comfortable and secure; only by the spoliation of the landlords and of well-to-do peasants could land hunger be appeased. And that is exactly what came to pass in 1917–18.

AS OF 1914

Imperial Russia underwent far-reaching changes between 1815 and 1914. By the First World War, the Muscovite realm which Napoleon I had invaded seemed remote indeed. No matter what tsarist obscurantism might do, ideas and institutions from the West had leaped over the Russian wall. The crucial event, of course, was the emancipation of the rural millions. Powerful forces were thus unleashed which carried Russia to the highest material and cultural levels in all her history.

Many peasants had become landowners, though more of them were still chained to their village communities. Rural Russia had an ancient tradition of poverty and hardship, accepted fatalistically, yet the attitude of stoical indifference to the world beyond one's wooden village was slowly disintegrating. Hospitable, easy-going, inefficient, primitively virile, the ordinary Russian peasant seemed more like a strong, grown-up child than a man.

Instead of the individualism of the West, the mind of Russia, especially of the peasant mass, was deeply tinged with collectivism. According to peasant philosophy, for instance, land belonged of right to those who worked it, not to those who legally owned it. Possibly 100,000,000 in all, the peasantry held more than 400,000,000 acres of land in 1914 in contrast to the 100,000,000 acres owned by the landlord class of about 1,000,000. The social conscience of the large landowners, conservative troglodytes in the main, was only feebly awakened. The richest grandees continued to charm and bedazzle French watering places as had long been their wont.

Industrialism in all its aspects and implications had advanced impressively in half a century. Somnolent hamlets had been transformed within a generation or two into busy cities. Railways spanned the semi-Asiatic empire from the Baltic to the Pacific and from the Arctic to the Black Sea, and Siberia had been opened to systematic settlement. State participation in economic activities ran much deeper than in the leading countries of the West. The middle classes had grown in response to machine industry and so had the industrial wage earners, though both were small compared to the rustic population.

Proletarian class consciousness, encouraged by lowly living conditions, was unmistakably on the rise. For a brief time after the tumult of 1905, quiet prevailed, but, from 1910 on, waves of disturbance again rolled over cities and mining areas. In July of 1914, a general strike was proclaimed, 200,000 workmen downing their tools in St. Petersburg alone. Barricades were thrown up in streets as angry workmen, some of them egged on by Bolshevik agitators, fought brutal Cossack columns. More than his country cousin, the Russian city-worker was a creature of moods, capable of violent action, living not by bread alone but by catchwords.

Broad cultural and educational progress had been registered in Russia since the mid-nineteenth century. Artists had created a rich national literature and music. Two members of the small Russian cultivated class had won coveted Nobel Prizes and Russian universities, hampered though they were by imperial regulations, had attained international respect.

Popular education, starting in the 1860's, had substantially reduced the dark illiteracy of the past. As of 1914, about half of the Russian youth was literate, a higher proportion in the cities than in the villages, more among males than females, more in Europe than among the "colonial peoples" of Asiatic Russia. The Russia of 1914 was not a nation of unlettered savages, as is sometimes imagined.

In the political sphere, a strong breath of freedom began to blow with the Revolution of 1905 and the establishment of an elected duma. That innovation somewhat impaired the historic absolutism, which rested more on inertia, moribund tradition and military power than on popular affection. The philosophy of the divine right of rulers to rule, the idea that the tsar was father to his people, still dominated the stage. And yet for all its shortcomings by Western standards, the young duma nonetheless furnished an open forum for debate and contained a complete rainbow of political colorings; in the fourth duma, for example, there were nineteen Marxists, six of them Bolshevik left-wingers.

Qualified freedom of the press prevailed, allowing some opportunity for treating political issues and problems of social welfare. True, police often clamped down on opposition papers, including *Pravda,* the mouthpiece of the revolutionary Bolsheviks, but it managed to reappear under a very thin alias. Safeguards against arbitrary arrest and imprisonment for "dangerous views" or political agitation were extremely slender, but there was effective trial by jury and a class of independent lawyers. In 1913, for instance, a Jew named Beiliss was haled before a jury on charges of ritual murder. Crown officials tried desperately to obtain a conviction; and yet twelve jurors, seven of them ordinary peasants, acquitted Beiliss.

Measured by French or British standards, Russians in 1914 enjoyed little political liberty, but judged by the Muscovite despotism of 1850 (or 1950) there was considerable freedom. The trend was toward popular government and more respect for the dignity of man. Many and stubborn obstacles stood in the way, but the general direction was democratic.

In another place the predatory and fatal course of tsarist diplomacy is sketched. It is sufficient to note that in 1914 Russia collided head on with the Hapsburg Monarchy and its partner, Germany. Imperial counsellors, military and civilian, persuaded Nicholas II that general mobilization of the immense Russian armies would put a stop to demonstrations of workmen in the great cities. Some authorities thought that foreign war was necessary to avert a recurrence of the domestic convulsions of 1905, while other policy-makers viewed the impending conflict as a war to uphold dynastic prestige.

In any case, once the tocsin of battle had sounded, Russia was gripped in an almost universal enthusiasm of national patriotism. Pan-Slav emotionalism invested the conflict with the appearance of a crusade. Even some Marxists, such as the veteran Plekhanov, applauded the war as a struggle for national defense.

Not so, however, the little Bolshevik splinter. Competitive struggles for markets and the machinations of sinister capitalists had caused the war, according to the Bolshevik interpretation. Open critics of the war policy were seized at once by the tsarist police. Lenin, in the safety of his Swiss exile, argued that the war would be the locomotive of social change, would smooth the way to the epochal revolution foretold by the oracular Marx. And Lenin was right. The First World War taxed the resources of Imperial Russia beyond the limits of endurance, making possible, though not "inevitable," the world-shaking Bolshevik Revolution of November, 1917.

FOR FURTHER STUDY

DONALD MACKENZIE WALLACE, *Russia* (last ed., New York, 1912)

ANATOLE LEROY-BEAULIEU, *The Empire of the Tsars and the Russians* (Eng. trans., 3 vols., New York, 1902–1905)

MAURICE PALÉOLOGUE, *The Enigmatic Czar, Alexander I* (London, 1938)

RICHARD HARE, *Pioneers in Russian Social Thought* (New York, 1951)

JOHN S. CURTISS, *Church and State in Russia* (New York, 1940)

HUGH SETON-WATSON, *The Decline of Imperial Russia, 1855–1914* (London, 1952) PAPERBACK

CONSTANTIN DE GRUNWALD, *Tsar Nicholas I* (London, 1954)

STEPHEN GRAHAM, *Tsar of Freedom, Alexander II* (New Haven, 1935)

GEROID T. ROBINSON, *Rural Russia Under the Old Regime* (New York, 1932)

THOMAS G. MASARYK, *The Spirit of Russia* (Eng. trans., 2 vols., 2nd Ed., New York, 1955

JAMES MAVOR, *An Economic History of Russia* (new ed., 2 vols., London, 1925)

DAVID SHUB, *Lenin, a Biography* (New York, 1948)

BERNARD PARES, *The Fall of the Russian Monarchy* (New York, 1939) PAPERBACK

BERNARD PARES, *Russia* (New York, 1949) PAPERBACK

AVRAHM YARMOLINSKY, *Road to Revolution* (New York, 1959) PAPERBACK

MIKHAIL ZETLIN, *The Decembrists* (London, 1958)

SIDNEY MONAS, *The Third Section* (Cambridge, Mass., 1961)

WERNER E. MOSSE, *Alexander II and the Modernization of Russia* (New York, 1958) PAPERBACK

HENRI TROYAT, *Daily Life in Russia under the Last Tsar* (London, 1961)

RICHARD D. CHARQUES, *The Twilight of Imperial Russia* (New York, 1959)

CHAPTER XXI

THE NEAR AND MIDDLE EAST

THE OTTOMAN REALM

AT THE outset of the nineteenth century Eastern Europe—Russia and the Balkan peninsula—lay beyond the orbit of Western civilization, little touched by the powerful forces and higher values which lifted the West out of medieval ways and institutions. Overwhelmingly and primitively agrarian in economy, the East was authoritarian in the philosophy and practice of government. Predominantly Orthodox Christian in religion, the masses were sunk in ignorance and lethargy.

By common usage the term Near East refers to the territory of the Ottoman Empire as of 1815. That realm embraced the Balkans, Asia Minor, Arab provinces to the south, east Mediterranean islands and the sweep of northern Africa almost to the line of Morocco. The real heart of the Empire was European Turkey, the Balkans and the historic citadel of Constantinople. In 1815, the population of this region was a modest 8,000,000; in area it was slightly smaller than Texas, but by 1914 Turkey in Europe was no more extensive than Maryland. Much history, very much, was written in bringing that revolution in the map to pass.

Statesmen and publicists were accustomed to speak of the "Near Eastern Question" by which they meant the problem and the destiny of Turkey, more particularly of its European provinces. No area of the globe more frequently challenged the wisdom and patience of European statecraft or more persistently vexed the spirit of diplomatists than the Near East. The problem was likened to a volcano by Stratford Canning, most celebrated of all British diplomatic professionals, which "has intervals of rest but its outbreaks are frequent, their occasions uncertain, and their effects destructive."

The Balkans acquired an evil reputation for violence, warfare, comic-opera episodes and virulent chauvinism. It was once fashionable to label graft and corruption, brigandage and political assassination as Balkan. In the end, the First World War arose directly out of this troubled and tormented region.

The "Middle East," on the other hand, is the title given to a broad tract of Asia, lying between the Russian Empire and British India and containing the states of Persia (Iran), Afghanistan and Tibet. It should also be said that after the First World War the "Middle East" often referred to the lands extending from Egypt to India. In the present exposition, however, the older connotation of the term will be followed.

Comprising many tongues and traditions the sprawling Ottoman realm lacked fundamental elements of cohesion, stability and solidarity. History had built the empire; history would destroy it. The Turks themselves who lived principally in Constantinople and its environs and in Anatolia, diverged from Europeans in all the essential ingredients of nationality. Their language was distinctive and their history was studded with tales of the conquest and plunder of inferior peoples.

Social habits, such as polygamy, the veiling of women and Friday as the day of rest, also marked the Turks off from other national groupings. They boasted of "racial purity," which gave them an edge on mongrel Christians, though in point of fact Turkish "blood" was quite mixed. In religion they followed the creed of Mohammed, and between the covers of the sacred Koran and commentaries on it, Turkish men of learning discovered whatever intellectual nourishment they required. An agricultural folk very largely, the Turks allowed Armenians, Greeks and Jews to monopolize such trade, shipping and handicraft industry as existed.

Throughout the nineteenth century the Ottoman Empire was a theocratic absolutism presided over by the sultan. As spiritual head of the far-flung Islamic world, he exerted some influence upon Moslems everywhere, and he possessed the right to summon them to a holy war, a *jihad*. Now and then a competent personality turned up as sultan, but more commonly wielders of the Ottoman scepter preferred the enticements of the harem to the exacting and heavy tasks of government.

Actual administration was handled by provincial governors, who in fact were self-centered adventurers, alternately the servants and the usurpers of the sultan's authority. So long as they kept tax revenues flowing to Constantinople, questions were seldom raised. Undercover police and espionage agents pieced out the network of despotism. Bribery, corruption and slovenly maladministration characterized the operators of the Ottoman political machine. Until suppressed in 1826, the *Janissaries* were powerful in state affairs. Recruited mainly from the Christian populations, this military corps degenerated in martial prowess and attained an evil notoriety as cruel and undisciplined plunderers. An army composed exclusively of Moslems replaced it.

It is wide of the mark to imagine that Turkish rule was unmitigated despotism, ruthlessly enforced. Massacres occurred repeatedly, it is true, caused by jealousy, fanaticism or suspicions of political disloyalty. No doubt the worst aspect of Turkish administration was heartless and discriminatory taxation. And Christian believers, who were regarded as little superior to livestock, seldom obtained fair treatment in courts of law. Yet no sustained effort was made to dragoon non-Moslems into Islam. Each religious society enjoyed cultural autonomy and control of its own schools (such as they were) and charities. Nor were young men of subject populations obliged to serve in the Ottoman army.

Tales of physical abuse of Christians in the nineteenth century periodically churned up storms of popular indignation in Christian Europe. Demands were raised for effective action to compel reforms. By contrast, after the coming of the First World War, barbarities, expulsions and butcheries, the globe around, became so commonplace that only the grossest indignities stirred the social conscience of men.

Representatives of the Great Powers often complained about Turkish injustice and cruelty. Time and again sultans blithely promised administrative reforms, but pledges invariably turned into scraps of paper as soon as international pressure was relaxed. No Great Power pursued a consistently humane course; considerations of national self-interest, the sacrifice of principle to expediency, often led foreign offices to condone the iniquities of the Turk.

THE SUBJECT PEOPLES

Within the Ottoman borders lived a variegated array of conquered peoples who awakened to national consciousness in the nineteenth century. Liberation became the consuming purpose of Balkan nationalities, or at any rate of the politically articulate. Two nationalities, the Serbs and the Rumanians, claimed territory in the Hapsburg Monarchy occupied by their kinsmen.

Entering the Balkan Peninsula meant stepping into an ethnographical museum. National groupings were so hopelessly intermixed in certain districts, such as Macedonia, that no agency, human or divine, could fix boundary lines in a way that would be fully acceptable to all concerned. It is absurd to dogmatize about the nationality of people who spoke Bulgarian in the family circle, but Greek in the market place or coffee house. Ottoman officials classified subjects according to religion and let it go at that.

Insatiable, clashing territorial rivalries among the Christian nationalities helped to keep the cauldron boiling in Balkania. And once the nations gained freedom they had no scruples against seeking to assimilate minorities within their borders by force. The idea of accommodation or mutual tolerance was alien to the Balkan temperament. National competitions and appetites begat fierce antagonisms, antagonisms begat primitive hatreds, hatreds begat poisonous wars.

Leading the parade of the subjects of Turkey were the Greeks. At the dawn of the nineteenth century, national feeling even among them was extremely feeble. Heirs of brilliant traditions, half blessing and half curse, the Greeks who longed for independence comprised only a small fraction of all. Yet for sanguine spirits the "Great Greek Idea" seemed within the realm of the practicable. That gleaming vision contemplated nothing less than the resurrection of the medieval Byzantine Empire with Constantinople as the capital. Apart from the Balkan mainland, Greeks lived in Aegean islands, in Crete, in Cyprus and in sections of Asia Minor.

More than other Balkan peoples, the Greeks were a seafaring folk, though most of them wrested a slim living from the inhospitable soil. Beyond most countries, Greece was endowed with seas, skies and scenery, but harsh mountains covered most of the land. Under sufferance of the sultan, Greeks occupied the commanding position in the Orthodox Church

Church and square of Alexander Nevski, Sofia, Bulgaria

Public building and park in Bucharest, Rumania, about 1900

of the Balkans. Illiteracy prevailed generally, even among the clergy, the driving force of Greek patriotism. Religious hostility toward the Moslem overlord was uncompromising.

More subservient to the Turk than the Greeks were the Bulgars, a nation of small peasant proprietors. Among them, national aspirations of a substantial character developed only after the mid-century. By reason of their toughness and aggressive instincts, the Bulgars earned the name of "the Prussians of the Balkans." Rumanians resented being lumped with other Balkan nationalities. Their language had something of a Latin foundation and they claimed descent from Roman legionaries who stormed into the region early in the Christian era. Yet because they inhabited the "Danubian Principalities," and for centuries had been subject to the Turks, they may fairly be reckoned as a Balkan people.

Whether the Serbs form a separate nationality or belong in fact to the larger grouping of Yugoslavs, embracing Slovenes and Croats, has been much discussed. On balance, the latter interpretation is preferable. But whereas the Serbs owed allegiance to Turkey, Croats and Slovenes dwelt mostly under the Hapsburg flag. Serb patriots wished, first, to escape the Ottoman chains, and then to have their country serve as the nucleus round which all Yugoslavs would coalesce politically. Serbia, that is, would be the core of Yugoslavia even as Piedmont had been the center of a united Italy.

Montenegrins, relatives of the Serbs, proudly boasted that their mountain fastnesses and pleasant valleys had never been wholly subdued by the Turks. A small area was formally granted home-rule in 1799 by the sultan. Montenegro, or at any rate its spunky princes, entertained grandiose dreams of expansion. Unlike other Balkan nationalities, the Albanians were mainly Moslem in religion. Possessing a language, traditions and customs peculiar to themselves, these fierce and lawless folk grew conscious of their uniqueness toward the end of the nineteenth century. Pseudo-scholars contended that their Albanian fellows were not only the best of the Balkan nationalities, but, indeed, the oldest. Mixed in with the urban populations of the Balkans were colonies of Jews, many of them descendants of Israelites who had fled from Spain.

The human situation in the rest of Turkey underscored the polyglot character of the realm. Aside from the Turks of Anatolia there were Armenians and Arabs strung out in a maze of tribal communities. Adherents of a peculiar version of Christianity, with their own saints and martyrs, the Armenians never wholly forgot their independent existence before the Turkish subjugation. They had a language of their own and a slender body of literature; smart traders, they wandered into business centers all across the Empire. In the final quarter of the nineteenth century a typical agitation for a free Armenia, instigated primarily by the clergy, turned the Armenians from passive loyalty into open resistance.[1] Political unrest coupled with economic jealousies invited savage Turkish repression. Massacres of Armenians, like the Jewish pogroms in Russia, shocked the civilized world.

The Arab peoples shared memories of an illustrious history, a common language and in the main followed the Prophet. But there was next to no sense of political unity among them. Individual sheiks, however, here and there wished to be free from Turkish lordship and World War I presented them, at last, with an opportunity to gratify their ambitions. Across Africa from Egypt to the west, other Arab stocks responded in greater or lesser degree to the national impulse, which augured ill for the preservation of the Ottoman realm.

GREAT POWER INTERESTS AND RIVALRIES

Continuously, and with growing force as the nineteenth century ran its course, the Great Powers of Europe interfered in the affairs of the Near East, which was traversed by valuable mercantile and military thoroughfares. This intervention very greatly aggravated the confusions and turmoil in the Near East, bedeviled international relations and provoked wars and rumors of wars. Without attempting to define the policies of each of the major countries with full precision, it is nonetheless possible to state their general interests in capsule form.

The desire in Imperial Russia for aggrandizement at the expense of the Turkish Empire had deep roots and broad inspirations. The Russian policy toward Turkey in the nineteenth century had something in common with the attitude toward Poland in the eighteenth, but there were distinguishing features. The ambition to possess Constantinople and the Turkish Straits ran far into the Muscovite past. The Straits, commanding Russian communications with the Mediterranean, constituted "the keys to Russia's backdoor," in the apt phrase of Bismarck.

Controversy over the passage of ships through the Straits was perennial. An international convention of 1841 sealed these waters to warships, unless Turkey itself should be at war. Commerce-carriers, on the other hand, might freely move through, though Turkey if it saw fit might bar the gates. That arrangement irked the Court of St. Petersburg, especially because shipments of grain, flax and oil by way of the Straits increased steadily. The security of the southern Ukraine and of the Caucasus provinces, too, might be threatened by foreign war craft if Turkey allowed them passage through the Straits. If a strong power had commanded the approaches to the Gulf of Mexico, the United States would have been handicapped much as Russia was.

Articulate Russia wished to convert Constantinople into a Muscovite city. It was popular to refer to the Turkish capital as the "Third Rome," the spiritual headquarters of Russian Orthodoxy. Seeking to win that glittering prize, the diplomacy of Russia (and on occasion her arms) was ceaselessly busy. But the other Great Powers would not tamely acquiesce in the establishment of the tsardom on the Bosphorus,

[1] A fragment of the Armenians were citizens of Russia.

Their repugnance was crisply epitomized in a remark of Napoleon I to Tsar Alexander I, "Constantinople? Never! It is the mastery of the world."

As another interest, Russia arrogated to herself the role of protectress of the Balkan Christians. Allegedly these peoples were Slavic in "blood," as certainly they were Slavic in language; and they were adherents of Orthodox Catholicism. To the Russian masses, it seemed an elemental duty to help their Christian fellows to break loose from the Moslem "infidel." By appealing to this authentic national emotion, the Court of St. Petersburg could easily enflame the martial spirit.

Impassioned Pan-Slavic evangelists periodically proclaimed the desirability of uniting all Slavs under the scepter of the tsar which, inescapably, excited mistrust and apprehension in other countries. And many times Muscovite soldiers marched into the Near East ostensibly to free the Christian populations. Late in the nineteenth century, Russian expansionist energies switched from the Balkans to the Orient, but when Japan bested Russia in the war of 1904–05, the weight of Muscovite diplomacy reverted to the Near East with redoubled intensity—and fatally.

For generations, Austria was the constant rival of Russia in the Balkans. Early in the nineteenth century, competition relaxed somewhat as a kind of monarchical trade-union started to function. But distrust and enmity revived after the Crimean War, and, though interrupted by short interludes of cooperation, persisted into the First World War. One of the largest roots of that conflict, in fact, was Austro-Russian antagonism, centering upon the Balkans.

For political and strategic reasons Austria desired to extend her sovereign authority in the Balkans. Defensively, the Hapsburg Monarchy worked to prevent the emergence of a power situation in the peninsula which would be perilous to her own integrity. Then too, Balkan markets and the execution of railway projects under the auspices of Austrian capital gave the monarchy substantial economic interests in the region. On idealistic grounds, moreover, the government in Vienna posed as the champion of the tiny Roman Catholic minority in the Balkans. After 1878, it was the Austrian cue to keep the Ottoman Empire intact as long as it was physically possible.

Throughout most of the nineteenth century Britain, not Austria, was the most formidable opponent of Russian aspirations in the Near East. Britain had considerable and growing commercial and financial interests in the area and a very large interest in the eastern Mediterranean as part of the trade route to India and the East. Commerce expanded with the opening of the Suez Canal in 1869, and, to defend the Canal, Britain established (1882) a protectorate over Egypt and constructed a naval base along the coast.

British publicists were accustomed to speak of the Mediterranean as the "lifeline" of the Empire. But in point of fact never more than a fifth of all British commerce was borne over the Middle Sea, and an alternative, though longer, pathway to the East was available, of course, round southern Africa. To guard the Mediterranean route Britain developed a chain of garrisons from the crouching lion of Gibraltar at the western portal, the synonym for strength and stability, straight across to Egypt. Malta, securely anchored in the mid-Mediterranean, resembled a huge battleship, while Cyprus where Britain obtained a special position (1878) had large potentialities as a naval station. The Mediterranean was very nearly converted into a British lake dominated by British seapower.

Until almost the end of the century Britain regarded a strong Turkey as the indispensable bastion against Russian advance to the south. Ottoman integrity seemed necessary, moreover, to preserve the equilibrium of Europe. In pursuit of those principles Britain repeatedly came close to fighting Russia and once actually did so. Rarely did apprehensive pundits in Britain or elsewhere accurately evaluate the bearing of internal stresses upon the military potential of the Slav giant.

Ideological detestation of Russia, it must be added, contributed to the antagonism. Liberal minded Britons conceived of Russia as the land of the knout and the pogrom, the unsleeping hangman of European freedom. The autocratic Court of St. Petersburg, on its side, despised Britain; Nicholas I declared, for example, that the king by acquiescing in the parliamentary reform act of 1832 "had thrown his crown in the gutter." Besides, British selfishness, it was protested, denied Russia free access to outlets on the open seas.

In the domestic affairs of Turkey, British influence was cast on the side of administrative reforms which would lessen the burdens of the subject peoples and bolster up the country. Passionate popular outcries of righteous indignation because of Turkish infamies frequently disturbed British dealings with the Ottoman official world. About 1890, leading British policymakers came to doubt whether the pro-Turkish orientation was the wisest of all possible courses in the Near East. By backing Turkey, Britain had placed "its money on the wrong horse," an influential diplomatist blurted out.

Perhaps the free Balkan nations would prove more reliable and effective obstacles than Turkey to the advance of any Great Power into the Near East. Any Great Power—for Germany had now become a graver challenger to Britain's interests than Russia. Britain disliked the German intrusion no less keenly than earlier it had resented the Muscovite threat. Anglo-Russian relations took a turn for the better as Anglo-German relations deteriorated.

During the Bismarckian era, the direct interests of Imperial Germany in the Near East were strictly limited. Indirectly, however, Germany became heavily implicated as a result of a diplomatic alliance with Austria (1879). Bismarck wished to allay Austro-Russian rivalry by having the Balkan Peninsula divided into a western Austrian sphere of influence and an eastern Russian zone. That speculation never came to fruition, but the Iron Chancellor, by extraordinary displays of diplomatic dexterity, kept Austria and Russia from going to war—into which Germany inescapably would have been drawn.

After the withdrawal of Bismarck from the Foreign Office in 1890, German interests in the Near East leaped forward. Turkey served as a kind of happy hunting ground for German merchants. And German capitalists arranged with the Ottoman government to construct the celebrated Bagdad railway which would run from a point opposite Constantinople by way of Bagdad to the Persian Gulf. If and when completed, the line would open up Asia Minor to commerce and trade. "Mesopotamia," exulted a jubilant German publicist, "Mesopotamia can provide all Germany with wheat and cotton."

But the Bagdad road would also extend the long arm of German strategic operations. Potentially, at any rate, it represented a threat to British and Russian interests, stirring up shrill criticisms in both countries. In the meantime, Emperor William II had been assiduously courting the good will of the Turkish governing classes. In a grandiloquent address at Jerusalem in 1898, he promised Moslems everywhere —300,000,000 of them—that they could rely upon the German ruler as their friend—a gesture duly and nervously noted in Britain, Russia and France, each of whose imperial holdings contained fanatical Moslem populations.

Regimes in Turkey changed but German influence suffered no change, was cemented in fact by the despatch of military missions to drill Turkish armies. That friendship paid large dividends in the form of economic concessions and diplomatic sympathy. In the First World War Turkey cast its sword on the German side of the balances.

The Kingdom of Italy, after unification had been achieved, took a hand in Near Eastern affairs. Imperially minded Italians asserted that the Adriatic Sea must again become an Italian lake, as it had been in the heyday of the Republic of Venice. Enterprising financial houses opened up trade with the western Balkans and brought forward plans for railways in Montenegro and Albania. It seemed to Austria that Italy was encroaching upon her special preserve and discordant wranglings ensued. Avaricious Italian eyes, moreover, were cast upon Turkish tributary provinces in northern Africa. Italy contrived to pick off Tripoli or

Libya (1912), but her aspirations to Tunisia were frustrated by French imperialism.

As for France, once the worst effects of the Napoleonic wars had spent themselves, she resumed her traditional activity in the Near East. Ever since the Crusades, France had looked after Roman Catholic interests in the eastern Mediterranean, and early in the sixteenth century she had established friendly ties with the Ottoman Empire—the first of the major Christian states to do so. Napoleon's campaign into Egypt excited French concern for that Turkish province which persisted throughout the century. French imperialists hoisted the flag of their country over Algeria (1830) and over Tunisia (1881).

And French capital flowed into a generous assortment of Near Eastern projects. Short railways were built, for instance, in Syria, a region which France looked upon with especial favor; construction of the Suez Canal was a French venture, and cash was invested in banking houses, railways and government bonds of Turkey and the Balkan Christian states. By allying with Russia (1894), France became entangled in the Near Eastern question in somewhat the same fashion as did Germany by her alliance with Austria.

A word on the small nineteenth-century interests of the United States in the Near East will be in order. The chief interest was missionary work directed initially to the conversion of Moslems, but later more heavily weighted to raising the standards of the Christian natives. Schools and colleges, such as Robert College (1840) in Constantinople, were the main agencies of the missionaries. Commerce with the Near East was confined to a few specialties.

Americans shared in the general sympathy for the Armenians which Turkish atrocities aroused across the Christian world. Pressure groups, more than once, begged the United States government to intervene on behalf of the Greeks struggling to free themselves from the Turks. But the official policy was consistently "hands off." Scarcely a sign before 1914 hinted at the important role which the United States would undertake in the Near East after the First World War.

THE DAWN OF BALKAN FREEDOM

It was the Serbs who blazed the trail to freedom for their Balkan neighbors. Marshaled by Karageorge, a magnetic though illiterate peddler of pigs, Serb peasants in 1804 fell upon the arrogant and rapacious *Janissaries* in the area. From small beginnings, the Serbian insurgency cycled into a general campaign to lift the Ottoman yoke. Russia despatched some help to the rebels, then withdrew, and the revolt collapsed.

But in 1813, another rising, organized this time by Milan Obrenovitch, a swineherd too, forced the sultan to grant autonomy (1817) to a small Serbian district along the Danube. Obrenovitch took over as chief of state,[2] and presently these arrangements were internationally ratified. Only a small fraction of the Serb-speaking folk lived in the new creation, but at least a start toward national independence had been made.

By an appeal to arms, the Serbs, or some of them, had escaped the chains of Ottoman slavery. Might not a similar show of daring produce a comparable outcome for the Greeks? Some Greeks, passionately devoted to the country's past and the country's future, felt so. The ageless tradition of Greece, warm folk memories woven into national ballads, and the clergy of the Orthodox Church inspired a sporadic "resistance movement" in picturesque Greek mountains. A more formal revolutionary conspiracy was hatched by a secret society *Hetairia Philiké* (The Friendly Society), which may have enrolled 200,000 patriots.

A war for independence began in 1821, the first phase ending disastrously for the Greek cause. Distracted by fierce factional discords, the revolutionaries nonetheless kept the fight going and won considerable victories; a free and parliamentary republic was proclaimed. By way of reply, the sultan shipped fanatical soldiers of Egypt into Greece; both sides indulged

[2] Thenceforth rivalry between the Karageorge and the Obrenovitch dynasties for leadership in Serbia kept the country in almost constant turmoil.

in shameless atrocities. Word circulated in European capitals that the Turks intended to blot out the entire Greek population.

A wave of humanitarian sympathy for the Greek rebels surged across Western Europe. In an era when educated men still thrilled over the ancient classics, affection for the Greeks was intense. And for pious Christians the Greek struggle appeared as an insurrection against hated and despised Moslem "infidels." Lord Byron sang of

> Fair Greece, sad relic of departed worth!
> Immortal, though no more; though fallen, great!

By sacrificing his life in the cause of Greece, Byron stirred the conscience of Europe. Philhellenic sentiments overcame the hesitations and caution of diplomacy. Acting as a unit, Russia, Britain and France summoned the sultan to stop the savage hostilities. When he refused, a joint naval expedition disposed (1827) of the Turkish fleet and Muscovite troops advanced toward Constantinople. Wisdom being of valor the better portion, the sultan then gave way and accepted in 1829 the Treaty of Adrianople.

That settlement provided for the independence of a small Greek state, and autonomy for the little Serbia. Ottoman provinces on the eastern Danube were virtually set free, though placed under the tutelage of Russia. Russia acquired no territory in Europe, but was assigned small parcels along the eastern rim of the Black Sea. Solid assurances were given that unarmed vessels might freely use the Turkish Straits, an arrangement never infringed thereafter, except when the Ottoman Empire was at war.

Under international auspices, Greece was launched on her independent career as a constitutional monarchy. As first king, the Powers in 1832 chose Prince Otto of Bavaria, slightly demented, unversed in politics, but regal in architecture. He brought along with him a bevy of Bavarian bureaucrats, who crowded native Greeks out of public offices. That folly could not fail to foment divisive factionalism in Greek politics. But at any rate the country was released from Turkish bondage; the prime task of the future would be to acquire Ottoman areas inhabited by Greek-feeling folk.

RUSSIA DRIVES FOR CONSTANTINOPLE

By contributing to the establishment of the Greek kingdom, the Russian titan had enhanced his international stature. But little positive headway had been made toward Constantinople and the Straits. Dame Fortune soon smiled benignly upon the Court of St. Petersburg. Mehmet Ali, grasping governor (or pasha) of Egypt, not only rebelled, but paraded troops through Asia Minor en route to the Ottoman capital. The terrifying military weakness of Turkey was patent to all and sundry.

Invited by the sultan, Tsar Nicholas I deployed soldiers near Constantinople and checked the Egyptian onslaught. An Ottoman dignitary, no lover of Muscovite benevolence, murmured, "A drowning man clings to a serpent." Out of gratitude, the Turks in 1833 placed their country under Russian military guardianship and denied transit of the Straits to men-of-war of all countries, except Russia.[3] Never before had Muscovite influence at the Porte soared to such heights. Britain, with France echoing, raised loud and fervent protests.

In 1839, Mehmet Ali went to war again. France supported his pretensions, while Britain—and Russia also—championed the interests of the sultan. Black clouds of war hung low over Europe until France, amidst much blustering, abandoned its protégé. Mehmet Ali contented himself with hereditary family rights to the governorship of Egypt. It was at this time (1841) that the understanding referred to above, closing the Straits to *all* foreign warships, was written into international usage. For Russia that decision represented a grievous setback.

Muscovite statecraft, meantime, was deluded into thinking that Turkey was "the sick man of Europe," on the threshold of the grave indeed. Would not dangerous complications be

[3] The pact carried the unlovely Turkish name of Unkiar Skelessi, the palace in which it was signed.

Another of Punch's *famous cartoons satirizes the attitude of France and England with respect to the "Sick Man of Europe"—the Turkish Empire.*

avoided if his last will and testament were drawn up by the most interested powers? Nicholas I thought so and in 1844 recommended to Great Britain that the two governments should act as attorneys—or rather as surgeons—in parceling out the Ottoman estates. That proposal London spurned, fearful lest the grand prize of Constantinople might somehow fall into the Muscovite lap.

But a rebuff was not necessarily a defeat. Controversy arose over the question—the trivial question—of the management of certain sacred shrines in Jerusalem associated with the career of the Christ. Louis Napoleon, avid for the applause of Catholic France, vigorously asserted old pretensions of Roman Catholicism to the Holy Places, while Russia insisted upon guardianship by Orthodox divines. When the sultan sanctioned the French claim, Nicholas I exploded. He disliked Napoleon anyway as a commonplace adventurer who had pulled himself by his bootstraps into top place in France.

A second time, Russia recommended to Britain that Turkey should be sliced up by a gentleman's agreement. Again Britain repulsed the suggestion. Then Nicholas I called upon Turkey to grant Russia an exclusive protectorate over Orthodox Catholics throughout the length and breadth of the realm. Acceptance would have reduced Turkey to a mere Muscovite vassal; on counsel of Britain and France, the Porte brushed the demand aside.

Once more Nicholas I erupted and this time ordered his armies to roll into Turkey across the Danubian Principalities. Pan-Slav zealots waxed jubilant. The prospect of winning a "window on the Mediterranean" brightened. "A strange superstition," the minister of the United States in St. Petersburg reported, "prevails among the Russians, that they are predestined to conquer the world, and the prayers of the priests in the church are mingled with requests to hasten and consummate this 'divine mission,' while appeals to the soldiery founded on this idea of fatality and its glorious rewards are seldom made in vain. To a feeling of this sort has been attributed that remarkable patience and endurance which distinguish the Russian soldier in the midst of the greatest privations." [4]

Napoleon III gingerly picked up the gauntlet thrown down by the Tsar. Victorious foreign war would bring glory to his parvenu dynasty and name; by defeating Russia, moreover, the emperor might pay off old family scores and consolidate his position with the powerful clerical elements. Despite the obvious possibility that Muscovite armies might plunge into Constantinople and beyond, the cabinet of Britain —prosperous, comfortable, unmilitary, Victorian Britain—vacillated. But eventually Britain joined Napoleon III in declaring war upon Russia.

From the pen of an obscure journalist came the fundamental logic behind the British resistance to Muscovite designs. "The vital interests of England," he argued, "should render

[4] Quoted in W. B. Smith, *My Three Years in Moscow* (Philadelphia, 1949), p. 304.

Great Britain the earnest and unyielding opponent of the Russian projects of annexations and aggrandizement . . . as sure as conquest follows conquest, and annexation follows annexation . . . [it must lead to] the ultimate realization of a Slavonic empire. The arrest of the Russian scheme of annexation is a matter of the highest moment. In this instance, the interests of revolutionary democracy and of England go hand in hand." That remarkable piece appeared in the New York *Tribune*, and was written by—Karl Marx.[5]

Serious fighting started in 1854. Russia confronted Turkey, Great Britain and France, with the Sardinia of Cavour edging in toward the end. Prussia and Austria lingered on the side-lines; rank ingratitude on the part of Austria, the Russians felt, since only a few years before tsarist legions had quenched the Magyar rebellion for the Hapsburg dynasty. Never would the men on the Neva forget nor forgive the perfidious Austrian neutrality.

Most of the fighting took place in Russia's backyard, in the Crimean peninsula which gave its name to the war. This conflict, the first of magnitude since the elimination of Napoleon I, was the last of the pre-scientific wars. Supplies for Russian troops were hauled over indifferent roads by primitive ox-carts. Care of Allied soldiers, more of them victims of disease than of Muscovite steel, was abysmally inefficient. Florence Nightingale—"the angel with the lamp"—won imperishable fame by drastic reforms in sanitation and military hospitals. Her superhuman exertions in the Crimea and her subsequent career as philanthropist and social reformer effectively promoted the cause of women's rights.

Warriors on both sides of the battle lines fought with tenacity and valor, to be recounted in patriotic verse and prose. No question of the martial qualities of the Russian soldiers, who were still serfs of course. They resisted the foreign invader with the same stubborn bravery displayed by their grandfathers against Napoleon I and their descendants against the Germany of William II and Adolf Hitler. The ideological complexion of the Russian regime counted for naught with soldiers of the line.

"Russia has two generals who never fail—January and February," said the Tsar. Soon afterwards he died of pneumonia, and Punch made the most of the occasion.

Overborne by superior odds, though not decisively whipped, Russia in 1855 broke off the fighting. Alexander II, successor to Nicholas I, came to terms with the West and then bestirred himself to reconstruct his empire within. So far as the Near East was concerned the outcome of the war was written into the Treaty of Paris of 1856.

The Russian dream of mastery over Turkey was dealt a lethal blow—temporarily at any rate. Claims to interfere in Ottoman affairs

[5] Apprehensive lest Russia should reach out for the ice-free coast of northern Norway, then governed by Sweden, Britain promised assistance to Sweden, if suspicions should turn into reality.

This sketch by an artist-correspondent of the Illustrated London News introduced Europe to Florence Nightingale—the "Lady with the Lamp" in the wards at Scutari.

A primitive but effective piece of picture-reporting—the correspondent of the Illustrated London News portrays himself going over the field of Inkerman after the battle. It was here that the medical services broke down and the fighting men had to carry their own wounded off the battlefield.

were abandoned, the semi-protectorate over the Danubian Provinces was given up and to them the tsar ceded the province of Bessarabia. Russia, furthermore, might not have men-of-war or erect naval stations on the Black Sea. For a generation, while the unification of Germany and Italy proceeded, the Muscovite colossus withdrew from the center of the diplomatic arena. At a favorable moment in 1871, however, Russia arbitrarily cancelled the Paris prohibitions on naval power in the Black Sea.

Something more must be noted about the Paris peace. The Powers undertook to restore "the sick man" to physical health and political sanity. He was formally admitted to the family of Europe, on the understanding that definite reforms would be initiated in the treatment of subject peoples. But no betterment was actually effected. Subsequent Turkish promises of reform were never translated into deeds. Oppressed Balkan peoples grew more restive and isolated explosions occurred. In a surprise move Sultan Abdul Hamid II, newly come to power, issued a constitution in 1876 and convoked an imperial parliament. But as soon as international pressure slackened, the parliament was abruptly adjourned and the constitution was put in cold storage, where it remained for thirty years.

RUSSIA TRIES AGAIN

While Italy and Germany were being welded into united states, the Near Eastern question simmered. But in the late 1870's, the Balkans boiled over anew. Mutterings of rebellion in the provinces of Bosnia-Herzegovina [6] preceded open insurrection in 1875 against Ottoman tyranny. This area, which became the "Alsace-Lorraine" of the Balkans, was peopled mainly by Yugoslavs. Their cousins in Serbia flew to arms against Turkey, which hammered them down rather easily.

Imperial Russia, having recuperated from the Crimean disaster, sympathized warmly with the little Christian and Slav brothers struggling for liberation from the Moslem Turk. Indignation rose to war heat in 1876 when irregular Ottoman soldiers barbarously beat down a rising of Bulgars, who were animated by the "Spirit of 1776." Bulgarian towns and villages were erased and populations slaughtered wholesale by sadistic bands of Turks. The sonorous eloquence of Gladstone kindled British moral fervor against the unspeakable Turk.

Diplomatists held conferences, discussed proposals and counter-proposals to straighten out the Ottoman Empire. But at every turn, Turkish dignitaries blocked efforts at reform. Not content to argue out infamies on a legalistic basis, Russia in 1877 resorted to armed force. Publicly it was asserted that Russia was fighting on behalf of oppressed Christian minorities, but foreign statesmen scented a fresh Muscovite thrust toward the Ottoman capital.

Turkish troops put up a spirited resistance, but in time the weight of Russian men and metal proved too heavy. The Muscovites pressed hard upon the gates of Constantinople, and the Straits appeared to be within their grasp. Russia was playing the game for high stakes and playing it not without skill. Britain was determined, however, to deny the prize to the Muscovites, and demonstrated her resolution by the despatch of a battle fleet to the Straits zone.

Nevertheless, Russian diplomacy coaxed battered Turkey into a preliminary peace (San Stefano). Boiled down, this treaty would give the tsar a virtual protectorate over the Balkans; featured was a "Big Bulgarian" state, which would simply be a Russian puppet. That prospect elicited belligerent outcries from Great Britain and Austria. London music halls resounded with the strains of "We don't want to fight, but by jingo if we do, we've got the ships, we've got the men, we've got the money, too." Jingoistic fervor on the streets was matched by British preparations in the eastern Mediterranean to fight, and by stern diplomatic warnings to St. Petersburg.

British firmness persuaded the Russians to tear up the preliminary pact with Turkey. Problems of the Near East would be attacked by the pen instead of the sword. Secret deals on Balkan territory were negotiated among the most inter-

[6] The term Bosnia will be used hereafter for both provinces.

ested Powers before the assembling of an international congress at Berlin in 1878. The choice of Berlin as the meeting place underlined, by the way, the stature which Germany had attained in European politics. Calling himself an "honest broker," Prince Bismarck presided over the deliberations, which at times were exceedingly stormy.

The eventual Treaty of Berlin of 1878 laid the ground lines in the Near East for the next thirty years. The estate of the "sick man" suffered heavy amputations. Bulgaria was set up as an autonomous state, with its southern frontier at the Balkan mountains; the section of "Big Bulgaria" directly to the south, called Eastern Rumelia, was made a separate principality under the suzerainty of the sultan—the remainder of "Big Bulgaria," Macedonia, was remanded to full Ottoman control.

Turkey acknowledged, moreover, the unfettered independence of Serbia, Montenegro and Rumania and ceded substantial territories to each. A little later the frontier of Greece was extended northward at Ottoman expense.[7] Rumania, parenthetically, comprised the Danubian Principalities, mentioned above, which had secured autonomy in 1856, and had installed (1866) a German Hohenzollern as ruler. By the Berlin Treaty, Rumania was obliged to cede Bessarabia to Russia, and acquired the sterile Turkish province of Dobrudja.

In addition to Bessarabia the tsardom picked up small pieces of Turkish Armenia. These souvenirs of victory seemed slight rewards for Russian military efforts, the expenditures of blood and treasure; Constantinople and the Straits were almost as far away as before the war. Muscovite spirits were further embittered by the fact that Austria was authorized to occupy and administer Bosnia, the region in which the recent trouble had originated.

The British delegation withdrew from the Berlin parley with the island of Cyprus in its pocket. In exchange for effective control there, Britain promised to protect Turkey in Asia. Prime Minister Disraeli saluted Cyprus as "the key to western Asia"; it might indeed have been developed as an important link in British Mediterranean defenses, though little in fact was done. For Disraeli the Berlin Treaty appeared to bring "peace with honor." Assuredly a general European conflict had been averted and the Russo-Turkish war had been ended. But the Russian Court, thwarted and frustrated, interpreted the Berlin settlements as peace with dishonor, a humiliating disgrace. Ardent Pan-Slavs and Muscovite generals never referred to the Berlin Congress without spitting blasphemy.

None of the Balkan Christian countries, moreover, was pleased with its territorial allotments. Reiterated Ottoman promises of a "new deal" for minorities had no more significance than cigarette smoke. The years ahead saw considerable revisions in the Treaty of Berlin.

AFTER THE BERLIN TREATY

All the Balkan free nations had peasant economies, which yielded little more than a subsistence living for the masses. All were limited monarchies presided over by ruling houses brought in from abroad, with the important exception of Serbia which boasted a native dynasty, or rather two of them. All were intensely nationalist, or in any case the middle-class leadership was, and keenly desirous of expanding territorially. All possessed branches of the Orthodox Church, vital instruments in the propagation of nationalism.

Bulgarian history was replete with stormy episodes. At the outset of its autonomous existence, Bulgaria was virtually a satellite of Russia, hailed as the national liberator. But Muscovite dominance was soon broken and in 1885, on the heels of a bloodless revolution, eastern Rumelia was incorporated with Bulgaria. After considerable diplomatic sparring, the Great Powers sanctioned the merger. Little Serbia, on the other hand, resisted to the point of war, but Bulgaria triumphed quickly. The conflict sharpened the old feud between these rivals.

Among the areas coveted by the Greeks was Crete, the scene of endemic rebellion against Turkey. In 1897, Greece provoked a war with Turkey by boldly proclaiming the annexation

[7] Great Britain in 1863 transferred the Ionian islands to Greece. At about the same time a Danish dynasty replaced the Bavarian royal family.

of the island. Badly whipped, Greece was obliged to indemnify the sultan; yet, thanks to the intervention of the Great Powers, Crete was granted autonomy under a prince belonging to the Greek royal family.

Greece, and Bulgaria and Serbia also, cherished aspirations in the Turkish province of Macedonia, ranging northward from the Aegean. Nationalities in this district were and still are inextricably intermingled. Consequently national claims overlapped and conflicted, and each pretender schemed to obtain for itself the maximum share of the area. Before 1912 proposals for an amicable bargain on the distribution of Macedonian territory invariably ran into sand.

All three countries claimed Salonica, "the pearl of the Aegean," by divine right of nationality. Competing companies of guerilla fighters, egged on by intriguing Turks, kept Macedonia in chaotic turmoil; butcheries and rapine thoroughly distracted the everyday life of civilians. The situation was worsened, if anything, by the threadbare international device of asking Turks to reform administrative procedures.

Slightly before the Macedonian controversy crowded into the international limelight, the press of the world horrified readers with stories of Turkish atrocities in Armenia. A Turkish spokesman blandly declared that the way to get rid of the Armenian problem was to get rid of the Armenians. Savageries reached a brutal climax in 1896, when hundreds of Armenians were slaughtered in Constantinople in the broad light of day. Diplomatic protests elicited fair words from the Porte, never implemented, however, by measures of reform.

By this time Imperial Germany had supplanted Great Britain as the strongest influence with the Ottoman government. And the cabinet in Berlin refused to push energetically for more humane treatment of minority peoples, whether in Armenia or in Macedonia. It was in this period, too, that German engineers began constructing the railway toward Bagdad and German officers toned up the Ottoman army. Befriended by Berlin, the Porte turned aside renewed Russian demands for passage of Muscovite warships through the Straits. Great Britain, now the unchallenged lord of the Mediterranean, firmly established in Egypt, and nauseated by Turkish abuse of minorities, abandoned the traditional policy of upholding the integrity of the Ottoman realm.

THE MIDDLE EASTERN SCENE

Anglo-Russian rivalries in the Near East, meantime, had somewhat moderated, half because of mutual distrust of Germany, half because adjustments were effected in the Middle East. The Middle East, it may be repeated, embraced the territory lying between Asiatic Russia and India, that is, Persia (Iran), Afghanistan and Tibet. Throughout the nineteenth century, the two imperialisms expanded their positions in Asia, striving to capture markets, limited enough though they were, striving to protect colonies already in hand or to disseminate their particular way of living. "Let her [Russia] go eastward," Prince Bismarck had counselled, "there she is a civilizing force."

Russian imperialism applied a rhythmic pattern in central Asia: penetration, conquest, annexation. By the eve of the Crimean War, the tsardom had appropriated a rectangular zone down to the Aral Sea and Lake Balkhash. Military or diplomatic pressure upon enfeebled Persia netted slight territorial and commercial concessions. As viewed in Britain, Russia was making ready to pounce upon India; to which St. Petersburg retorted that avaricious Britain was seeking to monopolize the business of central Asia. At the mid-century British troops marched into Kashmir to prevent Russia from seizing that area.

After the Crimean defeat, Russians resumed the advance into the no-man's lands of central Asia. Picturesque principalities, or khanates, inhabited by exotic, nomadic, Moslem tribesmen and petty merchants, were toppled over one by one. A new Russian dominion of western Turkestan, capital Tashkent, appeared on the map. Colonists moved into the conquered territories, and then railways knit the regions to Europe. The empire of the tsar now stood cheek by jowl with Persia and Afghanistan. No outsider knew where the Muscovites intended to stop, but everyone knew that appetite grows with eating. As ramparts against possible thrusts upon India, Britain absorbed Baluchistan (1876) and five years later proclaimed a protectorate over mountainous Afghanistan.

On two occasions, in 1885 and again in 1895, Russian maneuvers along the fringes of Afghanistan provoked acute tension with Britain, which very nearly broke into war. Persia, likewise, was the theater of keen competition between Russian and British diplomatic agents, financiers, merchants and railway projects.

At the beginning of the twentieth century Anglo-Russian rivalries touched a level of asperity unknown for a generation. The Muscovite slogan appeared to be "Full steam ahead." It looked as though Tibet, technically a Chinese province, huge, inhospitable, forbidding, might fall into the clutches of "the bear that walks like a man," as Kipling put it. But the British thwarted that prospect by extorting a treaty from Tibet, which acknowledged the diplomatic authority of Great Britain and forbade any rights whatsoever to a third party.

Over in Persia, Russian agents edged into the good graces of the Shah to whom funds were generously supplied. From him the Russians tried to obtain permission to lay out a coaling station on the Persian Gulf, which might conceivably expand into a naval base. The British Foreign Office let it be known that it would not allow any Great Power to plant itself along the Gulf; a kind of Monroe Doctrine for the area was in fact announced. Adding to the British interest in Persia, a British subject secured a concession to search for oil; the great Anglo-Persian (later the Anglo-Iranian) oil company was organized (1909), and a large bloc of the stock was purchased by the British government.

The exigencies of international politics, in the meantime, especially the growing might of Germany, had induced Britain and Russia to bury the hatchet in the Middle East, albeit not too deeply. Policy-makers in St. Petersburg, anxious for British help in getting the Turkish Straits opened to Russian warcraft, were prepared to make real concessions in the Middle East.

The upshot of negotiations was a famous Anglo-Russian entente, or understanding, of 1907. Both parties promised to keep hands off Tibet, and the British protectorate over Afghanistan was confirmed, on the understanding that the principality would not be occupied nor annexed. But the real core of the convention, and the most reprehensible feature of it, related to Persia. That land which boasted one of the oldest civilizations in the world, was

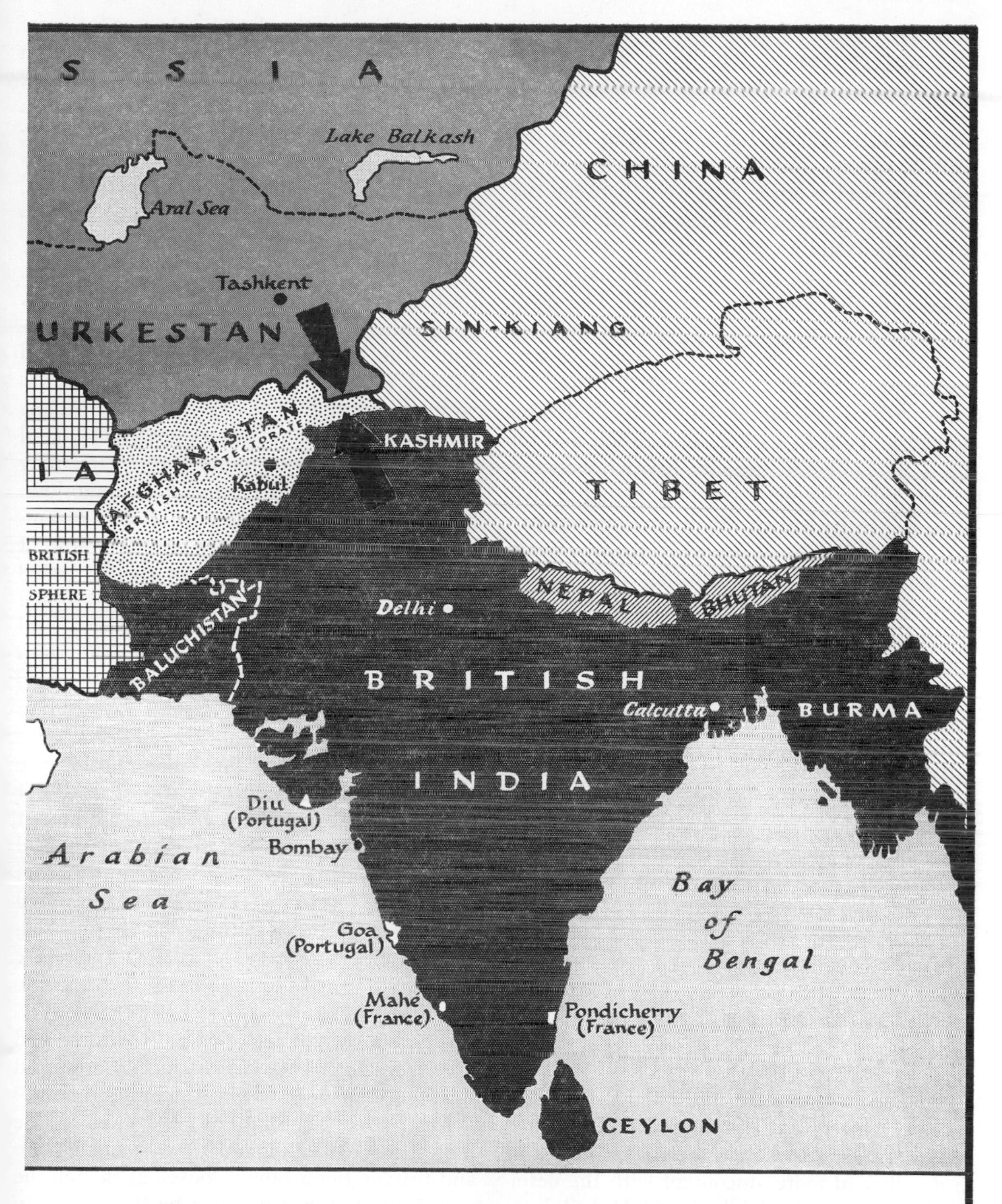

The Middle East *and* India
1913

formally recognized as an independent country but was partitioned into three zones. The northern and most populous district was earmarked as a Muscovite preserve; a zone in the south, abutting upon India, was defined as the British sphere, and the central area was declared neutral, a fence, as it were, between the other two. The wishes of Persia and the Persians were nonchalantly overlooked.

Persia, however, had been somewhat inoculated with the virus of nationalism. The small educated minority, intensely proud of national traditions, hotly resented the Anglo-Russian transaction. The Shah, who prided himself on being "the Pivot of the Universe," had been forced in 1906 to issue a constitution and set up a parliamentary regime. Friction between crown and parliament soon culminated in civil war. Russia backed the Shah, sending military aid and offering sanctuary when the insurgents deposed him. Through Russian intrigue, an American currency expert, brought into Persia to put finances in order, was unceremoniously ejected. And Muscovite agents converted northwestern Persia into a virtual province of the tsar. They wanted, besides, to lay a railway across the country, with valuable economic privileges on both sides of the track.

Britain bristled over the aggressive moves of Russia, and old passions flared up afresh. Yet, unwilling to alienate her newly-found partner, Britain tempered her complaints, though adamantly opposed to the railway scheme. Welcome though the bargain of 1907 was for Anglo-Russian reconciliation, it by no means smoothed out rivalries, and to Persia it had brought not peace but a sword.

THE BALKAN POWDER BARREL

In Balkan Europe, in the interval, a revolution organized by reform-minded Turks had unloosed a melancholy cataract of events. For a decade and more, discontent with the despicable tyranny of Abdul Hamid II had been incubating. "Young Turk" zealots, responding to the impact of Western ideas and practices, decided that the realm of their fathers must be renovated and rejuvenated.

For Turkish reformers the shining symbol of a better day was the short-lived constitution of 1876. They wished to have the constitution restored, improve the army and administration, effect social betterment, rationalize the religion of Islam and detach it from the state. Young intellectuals, professional men and army officers rallied round the banner of reform. The army, in particular, was honeycombed with revolutionary sentiments.

Early in July, 1908, the flag of rebellion was hoisted, the military forces lining up with the insurgents. Under duress Abdul Hamid restored the constitution and when he proved disloyal to the new order of things he was cavalierly ousted. The Young Turk victors assumed full control of government. Very grand it all seemed, for they promised parliamentary rule and enlightened treatment of minorities. It appeared as though the new masters of Turkey would exert the tonic effect of a flow of fresh air into a stuffy room. But realities belied appearances, for the Young Turks attempted to Turkify subject peoples with energy and efficiency. That course fanned old enmities into angry flame. Balkan Christian politicians decided to solve the Near Eastern question to their own liking.

It must be said that the Young Turks were forced to travel a rough international road. For one thing, Austria announced in the autumn of 1908 that Bosnia, legally Turkish property, had been annexed. Under Austrian administration since 1878, Bosnia had experienced unwonted prosperity and order. Annexation transgressed, of course, the Treaty of Berlin, and since Yugoslavs formed the largest part of the population of Bosnia, it was much coveted by Serbia. Serbia, whose relations with Austria had been chronically bad, raised a mighty howl and threatened to fight to prevent annexation.

Russia, the big Slav brother, joined in the protest as did her diplomatic partners, France and Britain. For a time it looked as though the rancorous controversy might be thrown on to the battlefield. But Germany supported her Austrian ally to the hilt, causing Russia to back down and acquiesce in the Bosnian annexation. Sullenly the Serbs followed the Muscovite lead and even promised to live on good

Shevket Pasha, principal military figure of the Young Turks (center foreground), enters Pera at the head of his troops.

neighborly terms with Austria. Turkey had no alternative save to string along.

Before the Bosnian business had been settled, the Young Turks suffered another setback; the prince of Bulgaria declared the independence of his country and assumed the title of tsar. On top of that, Greece annexed Crete, nativist risings broke out in Albania and Macedonia and Italy impudently pounced upon Libya (Tripoli). That last spoliation Turkey resisted with arms but to no avail. A peace treaty of 1912 awarded sovereignty over Libya to Italy and sanctioned Italian garrisons on the Dodecanese Islands in the Aegean.

The Young Turks had quickly come to terms with Italy, for a graver storm was brewing in the Balkans. A wonder of wonders had come to pass: inveterate enemies, Greece, Bulgaria, Serbia and Montenegro, had arranged in 1912 a league of Balkan nations under the patronage of Imperial Russia. In secret treaties these nations planned, up to a point, to partition European Turkey, if war should come and the ancient oppressor should be defeated.

War actually started in the fall of 1912. With one accord the Balkan allies fought Turkey, and to their surprise—and the astonishment of the world—whipped her readily. Serb troops crashed across to the Adriatic Sea; Bulgars, bearing the brunt of the fighting, advanced to within walking range of Constantinople. Badly pummeled, Turkey begged for peace. The Concert of Europe, the Great Powers, insisted that settlements should be negotiated at a general conference in London.

Tackling problems of immense delicacy, the European powers contrived to maintain peace among themselves, although quarreling between Austria and Russia came close to the breaking point. The peacemakers, alas, were

King Ferdinand of Bulgaria and staff officers at start of the Balkan War, 1912.

unable to work out territorial arrangements acceptable to all the Balkan belligerents. Serbia, for instance, claimed a portion of Albania with frontage on the Adriatic. That pretension was vetoed by Austria, gingerly seconded by Italy; Albania, it was decided should become a free and independent state.

Denied access to the Adriatic, Serbia demanded more of Macedonia than had been assigned to her in pre-war treaties. Salonica, the major Aegean port, was another bone of contention. Greek soldiers had captured the city, but Bulgaria stridently contended that it belonged of right to her. In 1913, old passions, unrelenting jealousies provoked a second Balkan war, a savage dog-eat-dog business. Never was there a more instructive spectacle of human stupidity and folly. Bulgaria battled against Greece, Serbia and Montenegro. And Rumania, unwilling to see Bulgaria grow too powerful, entered the fray, as did Turkey, down but not out.

Within a month Bulgaria was beaten to the earth. A peace treaty, which turned out to be little more than a truce, was fashioned at Bucharest. The organization of an independent Albania was reaffirmed; Serbia and Montenegro achieved handsome territorial gains, mainly in Macedonia, which whetted appetites for another meal—with Austria this time acting as host. Rumania was rewarded with a strip of Bulgarian soil on the Black Sea.

Greece retained the prize of Salonica, as well as lands running off to the east, and full sovereignty over Crete. Bulgaria picked up a few crumbs of comfort, a section of Macedonia and a short stretch of the Aegean littoral, far less than Bulgarian nationalists held to be legitimately theirs. Turkey, however, emerged from the devastating rough-and-tumble still

An unnamed Serbian village after a skirmish, 1912

possessor of Constantinople and a narrow zone to the west.

Mere enumeration of the real estate shuffling gives only a faint impression of the turbulent psychology, of the vindictive feelings in the Balkan powder barrel at the end of the wars. Nationalist furies did not easily cool; fears and dark rumors of new wars abounded. And events in the Near East had dangerous reverberations on the larger European diplomatic stage.

Agents of Russia and Austria tried to organize competitive Balkan partnerships, under their direction. Inter-Slavic bonds were drawn tighter than ever before with Serbia as the special pet of the Muscovite colossus. While the primary aim of Austria was to hold spunky Serbia in leash, as necessary for the preservation of the Monarchy, the supreme Russian objective was to push along in the old ambition at the Turkish Straits. Policymakers in St. Petersburg earnestly discussed the Straits issue anew, deciding that Russia must have them, though Constantinople itself might remain with Turkey. Proposals to seize the Straits by physical force were, however, vetoed by Muscovite military authorities in the highest echelon.

IN RETROSPECT

Over a century of time the once formidable Ottoman Empire had shrunk to a mere fragment. Most of the European territory fell away and so did the east Mediterranean islands. Britain controlled Egypt and Cyprus, Italy held Libya, France had Tunisia and Algeria. Only in Asia was Ottoman power solidly based and even there restless Armenians, a restless Greek minority and restless Arab sheiks caused sleepless nights in Turkish official circles. Internal dead-rot, which the Young Turks at the end struggled to overcome, and foreign interference had cost Turkey dearly.

Out of the loins of the Ottoman Empire had emerged, one by one, ancient nations, proud, spirited, avaricious. It was an impressive procession: Greece, Serbia, Montenegro, Rumania, Bulgaria, with Albania tagging along uncertainly at the rear. Not one of these Balkan nations was satisfied in 1913 with her frontiers; each of them coveted land under another flag or flags. Mutual animosities and burning chauvinism made the Balkan peninsula the most dangerous of the danger zones of Europe.

Add to the decadence of Turkey, the pugnacity of the Christian nationalities and the jealous ambitions of the Great Powers and it becomes apparent why the adjectives complicated or intricate invariably accompanied the term "the Near East." Russia and Britain waged a long duel over the region, with words mostly, with steel once. France and Italy sought to further their particular ambitions, and, more importantly, so did Imperial Germany. It was, however, the life-or-death contest between Russia and Austria which turned out most disastrously for Western civilization. Over the Bosnia annexation and again during the first Balkan war, these ramshackle eastern empires nearly came to blows. In 1914 an armed clash began.

Sanguinary developments in the Balkans along with violent antagonisms elsewhere led many a European to the fatalistic conviction that a general war was bound to come. Prophets of doom were not deceived, for it was precisely in the turbulent Balkans that the lamps first went out in 1914.

FOR FURTHER STUDY

WILLIAM MILLER, *The Ottoman Empire and its Successors* (3rd rev. ed., Cambridge, Eng., 1927)

WILBUR W. WHITE, *The Process of Change in the Ottoman Empire* (Chicago, 1937)

WILLIAM MILLER, *A History of the Greek People* (New York, 1922)

ROBERT W. SETON-WATSON, *History of the Roumanian People* (Cambridge, Eng., 1930)

HAROLD W. V. TEMPERLEY, *History of Serbia* (London, 1917)

WILLIAM N. MEDLICOTT, *The Congress of Berlin and After* (London, 1938)

EDWIN PEARS, *The Life of Abdul Hamid* (London, 1917)

HENRY N. BRAILSFORD, *Macedonia, its Races and Their Future* (London, 1906)

HANS R. MADOL, *Ferdinand of Bulgaria* (London, 1933)

BERNADOTTE E. SCHMITT, *The Annexation of Bosnia* (Cambridge, Eng., 1937)

GEORGE YOUNG, *Nationalism and War in the Near East* (New York, 1915)

LEFTEN S. STAVRIANOS, *The Balkans since 1453* (New York, 1958)

CHARLES JELAVICH, *Tsarist Russia and Balkan Nationalism* (Berkeley, 1958)

ERNEST E. RAMSAUR, JR., *The Young Turks* (Princeton, 1956)

WILFRED C. SMITH, *Islam in Modern History* (New York, 1959) PAPERBACK

CHAPTER XXII

EUROPEAN EXPANSION OVERSEAS

THE IMPERIAL IMPULSE

JUDGED in perspective, the expansion of Europe overseas after about 1875 ranks among the decisive trends of very modern times. Not that the imperial impulse was new, for at that point perhaps half the world had already been touched by western ways. Now with restless energy Europeans carried their business practices and political institutions, their educational systems, their religious creeds, their science and industry to the farthest ends of the earth. "Darkest Africa" was somewhat illuminated by the bright light of white civilization. The "changeless East" experienced changes without precedent.

To this latest epoch an Austrian historian has attached the name "The Age of Imperialism." And the word "imperialism" has been loosely used to cover a highly complicated process. It implied, for instance, political mastery over economically backward territories, control over strategic waterways, the carving out of spheres of influence and the like, contracts and loans to lay down roads and railways or to facilitate the opening up of resources of soil and mine. Obviously, too, a certain distinction must be drawn between overseas possessions which attracted large settlement by Europeans and colonies populated by native peoples.

As a working definition imperialism may be thought of as the promotion and protection of vital national interests, or those considered vital, in economically immature areas, by all the available agencies of the national government, if need be by force or the threat of force. Conceived of in that way, imperialism in its application was restricted to extra-European regions which were backward in a material sense.

During most of the nineteenth century the colonial flame burned but fitfully. The record of the Americas seemed to teach that colonial dependencies were more liabilities than

Lord John Russell rating the British colonies by size—a satirical reference to official ignorance of colonial problems.

assets; like children, they required expensive care until they were mature, and then they drifted away from the maternal roof. The prevalent economic theory, the vigorous current of free trade, taught too that motherlands should not seek to monopolize colonial business; everyone rather should trade where it seemed most advantageous. As early as 1812, the British statesman Castlereagh asserted that "Great Britain has derived more commercial advantage from North America since the separation than she did when that country was . . . part of her colonial system."

Disinterest in empire reached its maximum in Britain in the 1860's. Certain advocates of "Little Englandism" even recommended that the ties with Canada should be severed. Countries on the continent, moreover, were so thoroughly preoccupied with recovery from the wars of the French Revolution and Napoleon, or so immersed in the task of nation-building, that little energy availed for overseas operations. Imperial Russia, it is true, pressed her dominion deeper into central Asia, and several countries cast about for special privileges in Far Eastern countries.

WHY IMPERIALISM REVIVED

The resurgence of colonial activity must always be associated with the name of the British imperial statesman Benjamin Disraeli. Empire could ask for no more eloquent and colorful evangelist. As prime minister, late in the 1870's Disraeli secured effective British control over the Suez Canal and Cyprus and had Queen Victoria serenaded as Empress of India. Those events ushered in the new epoch of imperialism.

Germany and Italy, unified now, but "have not" colonial powers, energetically struggled for places in the colonial sun commensurate with their standing in the European community. France, or rather some Frenchmen, envisaged in imperial dominions compensation for defeat in 1870 and the loss of Alsace-Lorraine. France would demonstrate to the world that she was still a first-class nation by conquering an empire in Africa. And Russia resumed her onward march in Asia. Only recently it had been discovered that malarial fever, the deadliest enemy of man, could be efficiently combatted by quinine, a discovery which greatly facilitated expansion into Africa. As the century neared its close Japan and the United States entered into the furious scramble for empire.

It was the lure of material things which imparted the principal dynamic to very modern imperialism. Overseas holdings might furnish rawstuffs, not otherwise available, to feed the white man and his machines. The coming of the bicycle and the automobile, for instance, stimulated the search for rubber (first in tropical Africa, and then in and off southeastern Asia), for oil at several points in Asia and Latin America and for tin in southern Asia and Bolivia. Colonial specialties such as coffee, tea, cocoa, sugar and tobacco, formerly choice luxuries, had become comforts if not indeed necessities.

Imperialism, furthermore, would lead to an increase of trade, open up markets in which to dispose of "road-rails, pig-lead, . . . iron-ware, and cheap tin-trays," and a thousand other gadgets of the white man's factories. Imports and exports would mean profits for European enterprisers and employment for workers in time of peace and would ensure greater national security in the event of war.

Besides, moneylenders of a speculative turn of mind could plunge surplus funds into plantations, railways, government loans and the like in economically backward areas. Risks of investment ran higher than at home, but prospects of gain were also more exciting. Surplus human initiative, too, displayed on the playing fields of Eton or in the technical institutes of Berlin, Paris, or St. Petersburg, might find spectacular opportunities in imperial possessions.

The idea of planting excess population in untenanted areas of the earth appealed persuasively in Germany, Italy and Japan. Instead of moving off to the Americas, intending Italian emigrants, it was argued, must have outlets nearer home which would avoid the rigors of an Atlantic crossing and the terrors of the English language. And the quest for empire was fostered by pervasive nationalism, the desire for prestige to satisfy national pride. Without impressive colonial holdings, a Great Power was not quite great, it was not a world power.

Occasionally, a parcel of territory was picked up in order to protect an older possession or to frustrate a rival. Military experts, moreover, pointed to the advantage of having strategically located naval bases or coaling stations. French army leaders pushed for the acquisition of colonies which would be converted into recruiting grounds for soldiers; black troops would counterbalance the German superiority in manpower.

In several instances colonies were founded as results of the activities of adventuresome explorers. Of them, the most spectacular surely was Henry M. Stanley whose jungle wanderings covered much of central Africa. To rare hardihood in exploration, Stanley linked unusual talent as a propagandist of African potentialities in business and in souls.

The compulsions of religion, ever an important inspiration of European expansion, operated with peculiar force in the nineteenth century. Proceeding on the assumption that "the day of the Lord" must speedily dawn, missionaries carried the Gospel into every nook and cranny of the globe. They did more, for they trained converts to read the Scriptures and then turned to educating the whole man. Brighter pupils passed on to centers of learning in the West, becoming apostles of Western ways among their fellows upon their return.

Medical missionaries raised standards of native health. Other Christian agents devoted

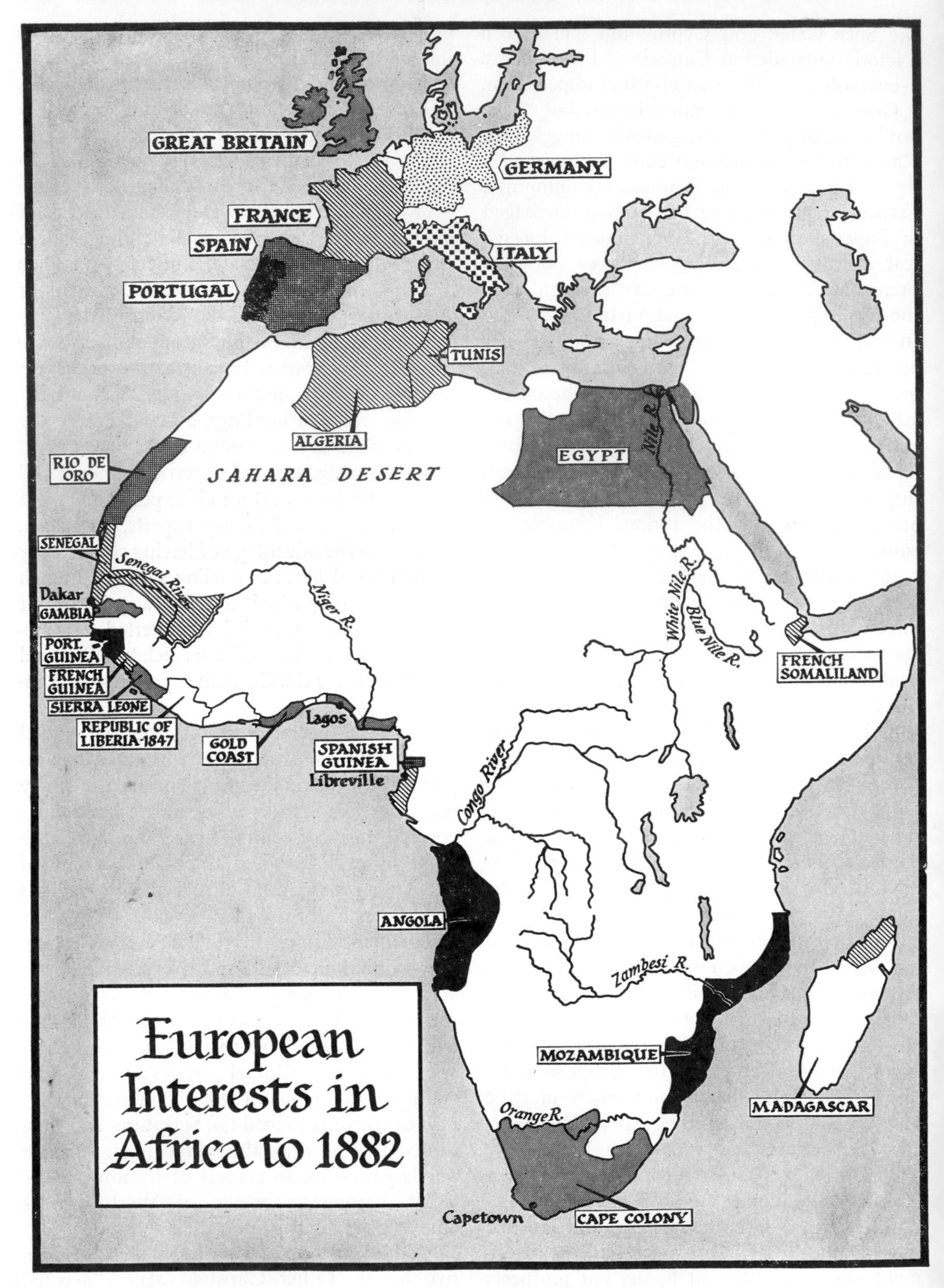
European Interests in Africa to 1882
GREAT BRITAIN
GERMANY
FRANCE
SPAIN
ITALY
PORTUGAL
TUNIS
ALGERIA
EGYPT
Nile R.
RIO DE ORO
SAHARA DESERT
SENEGAL
Senegal River
Dakar
GAMBIA
Niger R.
White Nile R.
Blue Nile R.
PORT. GUINEA
FRENCH GUINEA
SIERRA LEONE
REPUBLIC OF LIBERIA-1847
GOLD COAST
Lagos
SPANISH GUINEA
Libreville
FRENCH SOMALILAND
Congo River
ANGOLA
Zambesi R.
MOZAMBIQUE
MADAGASCAR
Orange R.
Capetown
CAPE COLONY

themselves to the service of natives by trying to make two blades of grass grow where one grew before, on the principle that no man was likely to be concerned with his soul if his mind were absorbed by the hunger of his stomach. Because of activity in exposing abuses of natives by white men, "the interfering missionary" often stirred up the resentment of government and trading interests. Christian evangelists encouraged native appetites for the material goods of the West. And on more occasions than one governments intervened to protect missionary interests, being rewarded for their pains with promising strategic or economic concessions. Merchants sometimes followed trails blazed by missionaries and after merchants, marines. The Western claim to be builders of Christian civilization in colonial possessions involved a good deal in the way of Christian practice, which was often woefully lacking. The rule of gold frequently obscured the Golden Rule.

Closely related to religious zeal as a dynamic of imperialism was the urge of humanitarianism. "Imperialism means philanthropy—plus five per cent," laconically observed Cecil Rhodes, the prince of British empire-builders. A stern moral obligation, it appeared, rested upon the white man to confer upon "lesser breeds without the law," the blessings, the benefits, the more abundant life of the West. Barbarous native customs—slavery, cannibalism, polygamy—would have to be rooted out; recurrent and disrupting tribal warfare and comic opera revolutions would have to be stopped.

The White Man, indeed, like Atlas of old time, felt a duty to carry the great globe itself on his shoulders, had to uplift and civilize the stagnant and benighted blacks, browns and yellows of the earth. Easily the most persuasive singer of the moral imperatives of imperialism was Rudyard Kipling, whose "the White Man's Burden" was the classic piece on the subject in any language. Ere long Japanese imperialists came up with the Nipponese Man's Burden.

PARTITION OF AFRICA—BRITAIN'S SHARE

Although Africa is the second largest of continents, it is the poorest and most backward of all. With her torrid climate, her diseases, her pests and impenetrable jungles, central Africa frankly declared war on all invaders. Yet in the 1880's European avarice hoped for considerable and quick wealth from the region. As time disclosed, the chief value of Africa lay in the top six inches of soil and the people living thereon.

At the start of the lush age of imperialism Africa was an unknown continent save for the fringes. Britain possessed the southern tip and small outposts on the west coast where slaves had once been collected for export and Portugal held colonies on both coasts toward the south. The French flag floated over Algeria, and

A Boer ox-cart—the vehicle of the great trek

Cecil Rhodes, with Lords Abercorn (left) and Grey (right)

Frenchmen competed with Britons for ascendancy in Egypt.

In short order, Great Britain annexed territory which gave her an almost continuous chain of empire from the Cape to Cairo. Britain had supplanted Holland as sovereign of Cape Colony during the Napoleonic wars. The Dutch population, called Boers, irritated by the influx of British immigrants, trekked north and east, founding the republics of Transvaal and the Orange Free State. For a time Britain annexed the Transvaal, but later (1881) granted it independence, under the British flag, an accommodation that pleased neither party. Quarreling was intensified with the migration of Britons into the Transvaal following the discovery of gold and diamonds in 1885. The Transvaal Republic, headed by cantankerous President Paul Kruger, denied the newcomers (*Uitlanders*) ordinary political rights, taxed them heavily and discriminated against them in other ways.

Into the South African story at that page entered Cecil Rhodes, the wealthiest and most respected man on the continent. His far-sighted vision had obtained extensive tracts for the British crown—part of it called Rhodesia. He dreamed of a great and grand confederacy of South Africa. Though prime minister of Cape Colony, Rhodes connived in a plot to remove the Transvaal Republic by armed force. But the conspiracy dismally collapsed (1896), and Rhodes was forced from office. Defender of Transvaal integrity and interests against British encroachment was a brilliant young Boer lawyer, Jan Christiaan Smuts, fresh from academic triumphs at Cambridge. By a curious quirk of history, this daring and successful Boer cavalry general became in fact the chief executor of Rhodes' grandiose designs for southern Africa.

Friction between Britain and tough old Kruger over the rights and wrongs of the *Uitlanders* led up to the Boer war which dragged on for three years (1899–1902). British miscalculations and military ineptitude stood in striking contrast to the gallant guerilla fighting of the Boer farmers. A prominent British critic charged his country with "methods of barbarism" in conducting the war, a phrase which struck and stuck.

In 1902 the Boers ceased firing and a treaty was drawn up recognizing British authority, promising the Boers home rule and unfettered use of the Dutch language in school and court. Compensation would be paid by Britain for farmsteads ruined in the fighting. That intelligent, not to say generous, settlement contributed greatly to assuaging the wounds of the war.

Certain Boer leaders collaborated in the creation (1910) of the Union of South Africa, a self-governing member of the British family of nations. Smuts ("Slim Jannie") more than any other was the architect of the Union; he developed rapidly into a highly influential Commonwealth and world statesman, one of the unmistakably great figures of civilized society in his era. Among unreconstructed Boers, on the other hand, the spirit of independence smoldered, causing no little concern during the First World War and after.

Constantly plaguing the Union were grave racial discords. Native Negroes greatly outnumbered the white residents and Hindus were imported from India to work plantations and mines. The bitter racial ferment and the disruption of Negro folkways by white innovations caused endless trouble. These matters have been described in *Cry, the Beloved Country*, a modern novel of unusual poignancy and poetic beauty by Alan Paton.

At the opposite extremity of Africa, Britain planted itself firmly in Egypt. Nominally a Turkish province, this country became an arena of sharp competition between French and British financial interests, which invested in varied enterprises. The opening of the Suez Canal in 1869 greatly heightened the importance of Egypt in international affairs. The wastrel governor—or Khedive—sold his block of canal shares to Britain in 1875 and the following year Britain and France took over the management of the disorderly Egyptian public finances.

Patriots, who rebelled against foreign supervision of their country, were crushed by British troops, France holding aloof. Then agents of Britain assumed exclusive management of Egyptian affairs. Finances were straightened out, agriculture was somewhat improved and commerce and industry expanded. Never in all its lengthy and colorful history had Egypt known greater physical well-being, though the masses lived in dire poverty. Nevertheless, Egyptian nationalists keenly resented the alien administration and guidance. The yeast of nationalism fermented in Egypt as elsewhere.

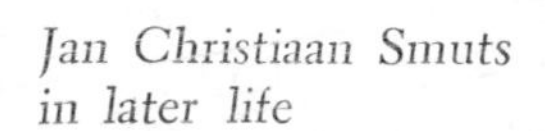
Jan Christiaan Smuts in later life

For its existence Egypt depended—and depends—upon a steady supply of water in the Nile, whose sources lie outside the limits of the country. To control the tributaries in the immense Sudan territory, scarlet-tunicked soldiers of Queen Victoria fought their way into that area against fanatical opposition. Under British rule, the Sudanese enjoyed unparalleled personal safety and prosperity.

While Britain moved into the Sudan from the north, a French contingent thrust in from the west, jealously claiming part of the region for the Third Republic. At Fashoda, on the Blue Nile (as yellow as the Blue Danube) the expanding imperialisms met (1898) face to face. Controversy over ownership reached such asperity that an Anglo-French war impended. Happily an amicable accommodation was worked out in 1904, France conceding British ascendancy in northeastern Africa in exchange for Britain's blessing upon French ambitions in the northwest. Shortly after the beginning of the First World War Britain proclaimed a formal protectorate over Egypt and the Sudan.

Aside from South Africa and Egypt, Britain appropriated British East Africa (Kenya), Uganda, a section of Somaliland and the island of Zanzibar. On the western side of the continent, the boundaries of the colony of Nigeria were pushed out and smaller colonies were tied into the British imperial economy.

FRENCH AFRICA

From the standpoint of square mileage, the French dominions in Africa, extending from the Congo to the Mediterranean, surpassed all the other empires. Before the days of expansive imperialism, France had annexed Algeria, which was governed as a part of France itself. To the east lay Tunisia, whose untamed tribesmen habitually trespassed across the ill-defined Algerian frontier.

In the name of colonial defense, French troops invaded and subjugated (1881) Tunisia and it was declared a protectorate of France. That success infuriated Italy, which coveted the province, lying as it did close to Sicily and the home of thousands of Italian settlers. By way of answer Italy joined (1882) Germany and Austria in the Triple Alliance, and never ceased to protest the French occupation.

Morocco, or the major share of it, passed under the French flag after stormy encounters with Germany. Twice, in 1905 and in 1911, the destiny of Morocco, which was imagined to be rich in minerals, very nearly touched off a general European war. Grudgingly France in 1912 bought out German pretensions with a slice of the Congo colony. That done, France proclaimed a protectorate over Morocco, except for the Mediterranean littoral which was assigned to decadent Spain.

Southwards, meantime, French imperialists had laid hold of the Sahara, largest desert on the globe, and sustaining only a sparse population in favored oases. Senegalese tribesmen plodded eastward from their native haunts raising the tricolor as they proceeded, and Frenchmen also seized upon a slice of Somaliland and the large island of Madagascar (1895). France was keenly interested in the Congo Basin, too, whose potential wealth had been lavishly advertised by Stanley and other explorers. Merchants under many flags participated in the small Congo foreign trade, but no country exercised political authority. Portugal, it is true, dusted off old paper claims, but France and the Belgian King Leopold II, a quaint blend of the humanitarian and the soulless exploiter, wished to be proprietor of the area. Britain, Germany, and Holland feared the Congo might be converted into a commercial monopoly of one or another of the contestants.

To decide the status of the region a West African Conference was convoked in Berlin (1884–85) and out of the deliberations came a series of interesting understandings. The principle was laid down that traders of all nations might freely do business along the Congo (and the Niger). Suppression of slavery was proclaimed as an international ideal and intention. No nation might stake out a new dominion without appropriate warnings to other countries and if disputes arose they should be submitted to arbitration. Given the intensity of the imperialistic mood at the time, the West African Conference was a masterly achievement.

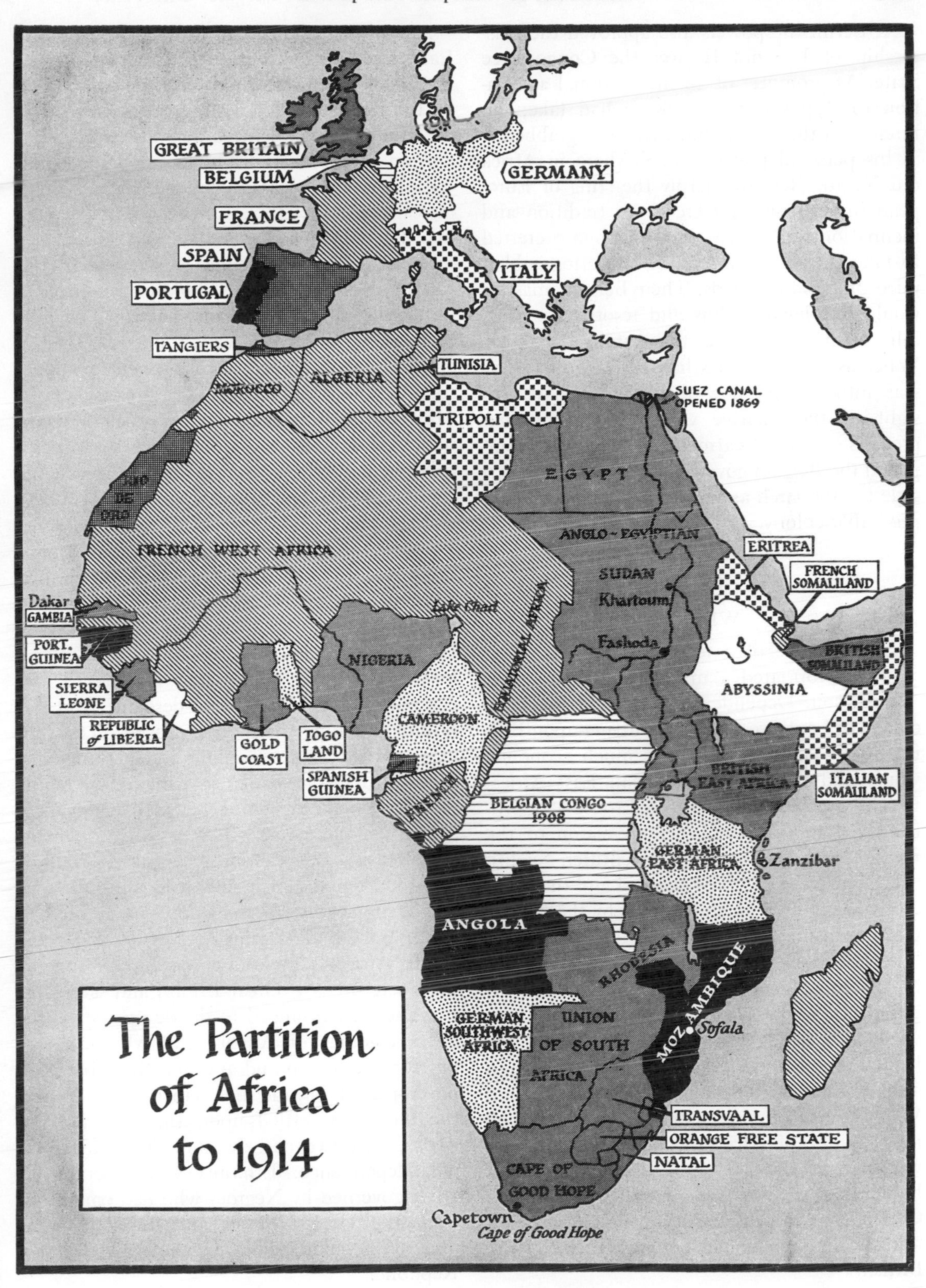

The Partition of Africa to 1914

At Berlin the powers also approved the trusteeship of Leopold II over the Congo Free State. As promoter of an international association to stop slavery, the King had taken an interest in the region and then slyly grabbed it as his personal possession. Nowhere in Africa did Negroes feel so sharply the sting of European imperialism and greed. By tradition and inclination the natives of the Congo preferred to take their ease instead of collecting rubber juice or building roads. Their Belgian masters would not have it thus and resorted to gross inhumanities to force the natives to work. Whereas once Negroes had been hauled overseas into slavery, now they were enslaved in sight of their native villages. Humanitarian protests over the treatment of the natives compelled the Belgian government in 1908 to supersede the monarch as sovereign of this huge and profitable colony.

GERMAN AND ITALIAN WINNINGS

In the space of a few years Imperial Germany appropriated a million square miles of African soil. Dependencies included the large colony of Southwest Africa, abutting upon British South Africa, and not of much economic value, and the superior German East Africa, which lay athwart the projected route of a British Cape to Cairo railway. By reason of the meanderings of a free-lance adventurer, Nachtigal, Germany acquired Togoland and the Kameruns, which was much enlarged by the French Congo cession of 1912.

Although these holdings were inferior to the better French or British colonies, Germans busied themselves with the development of what they had. At the same time, Germany looked round for more territory, and if German arms had been victorious in the First World War Germany undoubtedly would have forced the transfer of African colonies. In dealings with natives, the German record was not much better than the Belgian—or the French in the Congo—but in other respects the German administration compared favorably with the British.

Another late-comer to the colonial game, Italy, fared less well in Africa than the other top-flight countries. From a foothold gained on the Red Sea, Italian empire-builders carved out the colony of Eritrea and also annexed a portion of Somaliland. On the map these possessions looked pleasant enough, but as pieces of real estate they were scarcely worth developing. Their main value in fact was as avenues into Ethiopia (Abyssinia) over which the Kingdom of Italy in 1889 boldly announced a protectorate. Native chiefs balked, however, and native troops, who were trained by French officers and equipped with French weapons, soundly thrashed an Italian army at Aduwa (1896)—the only instance in which a white nation was decisively humiliated by African tribesmen. Partly to avenge that disaster, Mussolini in 1935 embarked upon the conquest of Ethiopia.

Good fortune smiled upon Italian aspirations in the Turkish province of Libya (Tripoli). After a starkly imperialistic war in which Turkey was overwhelmed (1911–12), Libya was handed over to Italy. The colony looked impressive but except for the narrow coastland, it was barren and desolate. And the task of subduing the natives proved excessively expensive for the struggling Italian kingdom. Not less than Germany, the partition of Africa left Italy with a strong sense of grievance; glaring at her across the blue Mediterranean were British Egypt (not to speak of Malta) and the French North African possessions.

The pioneer states in European expansion, Spain and Portugal, kept hold of dependencies on the African mainland and island clusters off the western coast. Great Britain and Germany twice secretly arranged to divide up the Portuguese colonies of Angola and Mozambique, but for one reason and another, these bargains never passed beyond the paper stage. When the dust had settled upon the scramble for Africa, only two parcels retained a semblance of independence: Ethiopia and Liberia, the latter governed by Negroes who had emigrated from the United States and in effect were under the guardianship of the trans-Atlantic Republic.

IMPERIALISM IN EASTERN ASIA

Asia was radically different from Africa and the course of Western imperialism was forced into rather different channels. Climate, for one thing, was more beneficent, the population vastly greater and wealthier. While the Oriental masses were overwhelmingly poor peasants, imbued with a deep sense of family loyalty, there were also developed trading, professional, administrative and fighting classes.

Whereas in Africa the white man confronted savage tribesmen, Asiatics for the most part had strong and ancient cultural traditions. Highly intelligent, the Asiatics possessed elaborate philosophical and religious systems, a heritage of art and architecture, tasteful craftsmanship and literatures. These possessions nurtured a feeling of pride unknown to primitive African Negroes. Something approaching organized governments, furthermore, prevailed in Asia, with authority vested in a few hands, but with considerable traditions of local self-government. Western ascendancy in the Orient turned out to be only temporary in contrast to the more permanent dominance over Africa.

WESTERN PENETRATION INTO CHINA

China is the classic land of imperialism. Long before the nineteenth century Europeans had ventured into China as missionaries, merchants and mariners. In the sixteenth century, Portuguese traders seeking tea and silk had opened up business relations, leasing the island of Macao, not far from Canton, as a base for commercial operations. English and Dutch ships presently engaged in trade, which by Chinese regulations was confined to the city of Canton.

The Chinese authorities much preferred that their country should remain isolated. Symbolical was the Great Wall which had been raised as an "iron curtain." Here was an ancient civilization, rich and mature, though deficient in science and technology, whose manners and morals had spread extensively across eastern Asia. Chinese economy was essentially self-sufficient, resting upon agriculture; desperately poor peasants by endless and dogged toil dragged a bare existence out of "the good earth." Ingenious handicrafts satisfied the simple wants of the soil-people and furnished comforts and luxuries for well-off and cultivated city-dwellers. Facilities of transportation by land and water were surprisingly well provided. Religious rites centered in the

Of all the arts which were fostered by the civilization of old China, the West is most familiar with fine Chinese porcelain, which called forth supreme efforts of both artist and craftsman. This vase was made under the Ming Dynasty, A.D. *1368–1644.*

Cells for examination of Chinese Civil Service candidates, about 1900

family circle with the accent on reverence for ancestors and veneration of graven images.

By Chinese standards, a gentleman was a cultured scholar and civil servant who earned his place through familiarity with the writings of the great sage Confucius. Appointment and promotion depended on achievement in searching examinations. Government was a rather free and easy affair, the authority of the central power, with headquarters in Peking, being distinctly limited. Philosophy exalted pacifism and passivity, discouraged individual initiative and sense of social responsibility.

In her long history China had several times succumbed to foreign invasion. But invariably the newcomers had been absorbed into the national mass; "China is a sea," ran a homely proverb, "which salts all waters which flow into it." In 1644, Manchu conquerors from the north had made themselves masters of China. The Manchus compelled natives to wear pigtails as symbols of servitude, and were never loved. Concessions and privileges which Manchu officials eventually granted to Westerners intensified popular resentment against the alien overlords.

The Manchus strictly forbade the diffusion of the Christian religion and surrounded Western trading operations at Canton with all manner of restrictions. Foreign merchants—barbarians in Chinese eyes—might not reside in Canton, for instance; they were subjected to a variety of variable fees and their lives and fortunes were ever in jeopardy. Attempts by British diplomacy to establish Western-style relations were superciliously rejected by the Manchu court. Accumulated animosities burst into flame when Chinese authorities decided in 1839 to prevent foreigners from shipping morale-sapping opium into the country.

That decision led directly to the first Anglo-Chinese war (1839–42), which the British, of course, won easily. As the fruits of victory, Britain, in the Treaty of Nanking, obtained the then barren island of Hong Kong,[1] an indemnity to cover the cost of the war, and fixed tariff and other charges. Canton, Shanghai and three other Chinese ports were opened to foreign residence and trade. Other nations, the United States for one, promptly arranged similar treaties, which carried two additional privileges. First, foreigners accused of wrongdoing were exempted from Chinese jurisdiction and would be tried in courts presided over by foreign consuls (the right of extraterritoriality). And second, missionaries were permitted to propagate the gospel within prescribed areas.

In the "treaty ports," of which Shanghai on the great Yangtze Kiang River attained largest importance, foreigners blocked out "concession areas" in which Westerners lived and carried on business. These districts were administered by foreigners without reference to Chinese officials. Trade in tea and silk increased modestly, as did missionary enterprise, but native dislike and distrust of "outside barbarians" persisted. Conservative, blissfully contented China showed precious little inclination to borrow the ways and institutions of the West.

[1] Hong Kong was soon flourishing on a great entrepôt trade; it became a unique oasis of security and order in the troubled East.

The Shanghai waterfront, about 1850

Starting in 1853 and running on for over a decade, China was torn by a devastating civil war known as the Taiping Rebellion. In part at least the insurgents were resentful of privileges extended by the Manchu court to Western nations. Loyalist armies crushed the rebellion, but the episode marked the beginning of the movement which eventually destroyed the Manchu dynasty.

Controversies and bickerings produced a second Anglo-Chinese war (1858–60), with France fighting alongside of Britain. As consequences of that struggle additional cities were opened to foreigners and lesser privileges were conceded. At this period foreigners did not try to stake out dependencies or spheres of influence in China. The principle of free trade, of equality of opportunity for traders of all countries was still in the ascendant in Western thought. British interests handled twice as much of the Chinese foreign trade as all other merchants combined.

JAPAN AWAKENS

Before the middle of the nineteenth century Japan was more hermetically sealed against foreign influences than China. Contacts between Japan and Western traders and missionaries in earlier centuries had not proved beneficial, so by decree foreigners were forbidden to enter Japan and Japanese were forbidden to go out. For two hundred years Japan kept herself to herself, ignorant of the outside world except for meager information which filtered in through Dutch merchants who were allowed to carry on a strictly limited commerce. Vainly did Russia and other countries try to persuade Japan to cast off the hermit's cloak.

What European overtures were unable to accomplish was achieved by the United States

Commodore Matthew C. Perry meets the Mikado's representatives at Yokohama.

in the person of Commodore Matthew C. Perry. Advancing upon Japan with a flotilla of warships in 1853, Perry requested a treaty of commerce and amity. After a lively debate, the Japanese leaders, aware that their country could not resist the eloquence of Western guns, acquiesced and a treaty was negotiated with the United States. Perry had succeeded in opening up the Pandora's box of Nippon. Other countries hastened to make arrangements with Japan which allowed merchants and missionaries to ply their respective professions, fixed tariff charges and prescribed extraterritoriality. Spirited Japanese firebrands who resisted the intrusion of the West were silenced with cold steel.

In many respects "the Land of the Cherry Blossom" diverged from the slumbering Chinese giant. All told the Japanese islands were small, not much more extensive than California, and the population could not have been more than a tenth that of China. Japan was almost as mountainous and infertile as Scotland; five out of six acres were too rugged for cultivation, the rest supplied the masses with an extremely simple livelihood. Japan had imported parts of her civilization from China, but the dominant religious creed, Shinto, was purely indigenous. It prescribed worship of the emperor as a sacred being, inculcated unquestioning obedience to him and venerated natural features of the homeland. Religion and nationalism, in other words, were intimately intertwined, and that was a signal asset for Japanese solidarity.

At the time of the Perry mission the emperor, though the supreme religious figurehead, was a political zero. Actual power was wielded by a hereditary deputy, or shogun, who was aided by a feudal bureaucracy. The prominent social categories included the court aristocracy, landowning barons and the fighting caste or *samurai*. The ideal man in Japan was the soldier who lived by the knightly code (*Bushido*), which exalted courage, discipline, loyalty, honor and physical fitness as the great virtues. From feudal clansmen and their warrior-retainers came the leadership which rather rapidly transformed Japan and claimed for her a place among the Great Powers of the earth. Unlike China, Japan developed a vigorous, competent and Westernized administrative class.

It was the proud boast of the Japanese that their islands had been invaded by ideas, but never by men. By highly selective imitation of the West, Japan would prevent foreign domination and then would beat the West at its own imperial game. Japan proved incomparably the smartest pupil of the West and in the long run she was not exactly a joy to her teachers.

An important step toward the "modernization" of Japan was taken in 1867, when the shogunate was abolished and the emperor was restored in theory to full political authority. "Knowledge and learning," the emperor proclaimed, "shall be sought for all over the world . . ." and he meant it. Emperor Mutsuhito, a philosopher on the throne, presided over the making of modern Japan until his death in 1912. Presently the archaic feudal regime and the institution of serfdom were scrapped (1871), making for a strongly centralized state, though the patriarchal attitude of the "great" toward the "small" did not disappear forthwith.

In creating a Western-style army Japan took Germany and its conscription principle as model, while the Japanese navy was patterned upon the British. Primary education was made compulsory and bright young men were sent abroad to learn the customs and the secrets of the West. Schools, conscript army and Shinto shrines were employed to teach implicit obedience, to foster a fervent national spirit and in general to train up a regimented and disciplined population. Courts and law codes on Western principles were introduced and once they were in effective operation foreign nations were obliged to renounce the right of extraterritoriality. For about a generation a craze for

Black-coated Samurai accompanying a young nobleman, the Lord Kaga—a Japanese print of the Seventeenth Century.

Western ideas and things seized Japan—foreign clothes, manners, pictures, education and religion.

Imitating Western precedents, Japan in 1889 adopted a constitution, similar to that of Prussia, which curtailed modestly the absolute authority of the emperor. A parliament was organized, the lower house being chosen by limited manhood suffrage and containing political parties. In practice, however, the conservative bureaucracy of clansmen and *samurai* governed the realm.

The economy of Japan quickly responded to Western ways. Railways and factories, a banking system and merchant marine all betrayed borrowings from the West. Having the most advanced industrial techniques in Asia, Japan claimed the title of the workshop of the Orient, the Britain of the Far East. Machinofacture, while it supplied employment for the swiftly rising population, was handicapped by shortages of rawstuffs. Japan had no iron, little coal and that of inferior grade, no oil, nor cotton nor rubber. Imperialism, perhaps, would yield raw materials, food and markets.

At the very moment that Western audiences were roaring over the operetta *The Mikado* (1885), which fostered the utterly false impression that Japan was a pleasantly innocuous Pacific kingdom, the masters of that country were preparing to respond to the imperial urge on the Asiatic continent. Already the aggressive newcomer to the family of nations had taken possession of islands in the vicinity of the homeland. Imported silk hats, steam engines and translations of standard Western authors could not be trusted as evidence of fundamental change in the Japanese outlook. Rather a thin veneer of Westernism had been laid over the ancient and bizarre Japanese folk mentality.

SPOLIATION OF CHINA (1894–1900)

The eyes of Japan fastened covetously on the decrepit kingdom of Korea, which was under the nominal sovereignty of China. Failing to break the Chinese hold by pacific means, Japan resorted to the sword (1894–95). Superior firepower promptly brought China to her knees. Korea was declared wholly independent, which laid it open to Japanese penetration, and China ceded the island of Formosa to the victor. A part of southern Manchuria, including Port Arthur, was also assigned to Japan, but Russia intervened, and, backed by France and Germany, compelled the Nipponese to drop that morsel. Deeply aggrieved by the Muscovite interference, Japan pushed along with the perfection of her fighting services.

The easy Japanese triumph unleashed a furious scramble by Western powers for areas of control in China. Great Britain acquired a strip on the mainland opposite Hong Kong, now a flourishing commercial community, secured a lease on the strategically located harbor of Wei-hai-wei and claimed a sphere of influence in the populous Yangtze Valley. As atonement for the murder of two missionaries, Germany extorted from China a sphere of interest in Shantung province and a lease on the port of Tsingtao. France took over the port of Kwangchowan and enlarged her established position in southern China. Russia gained a leasehold at Port Arthur, from which the Japs had just been ousted, and fastened her claws upon Manchuria. Under pressure the Manchu court signed contracts with representatives of half a dozen countries for the construction of railways, which had unmistakable imperialistic implications.

Small wonder that observers prophesied that China would be broken up on the model of Africa. That, however, did not come to pass and for three main reasons. Chinese, incensed by the foreign depredations, broke loose in the murderous Boxer fanaticism. The United States, which had just become ruler of the Philippines, sponsored the principle of the "open door." That doctrine prescribed equality of trading opportunities for all countries everywhere in China and upheld the territorial integrity of the Manchu Empire. To the "open door" principle the interested powers gave lip acquiescence, nothing more. But most important of all, Japan resisted the predatory ambitions of Russia with words first and then with steel. For an understanding of the Russo-Jap-

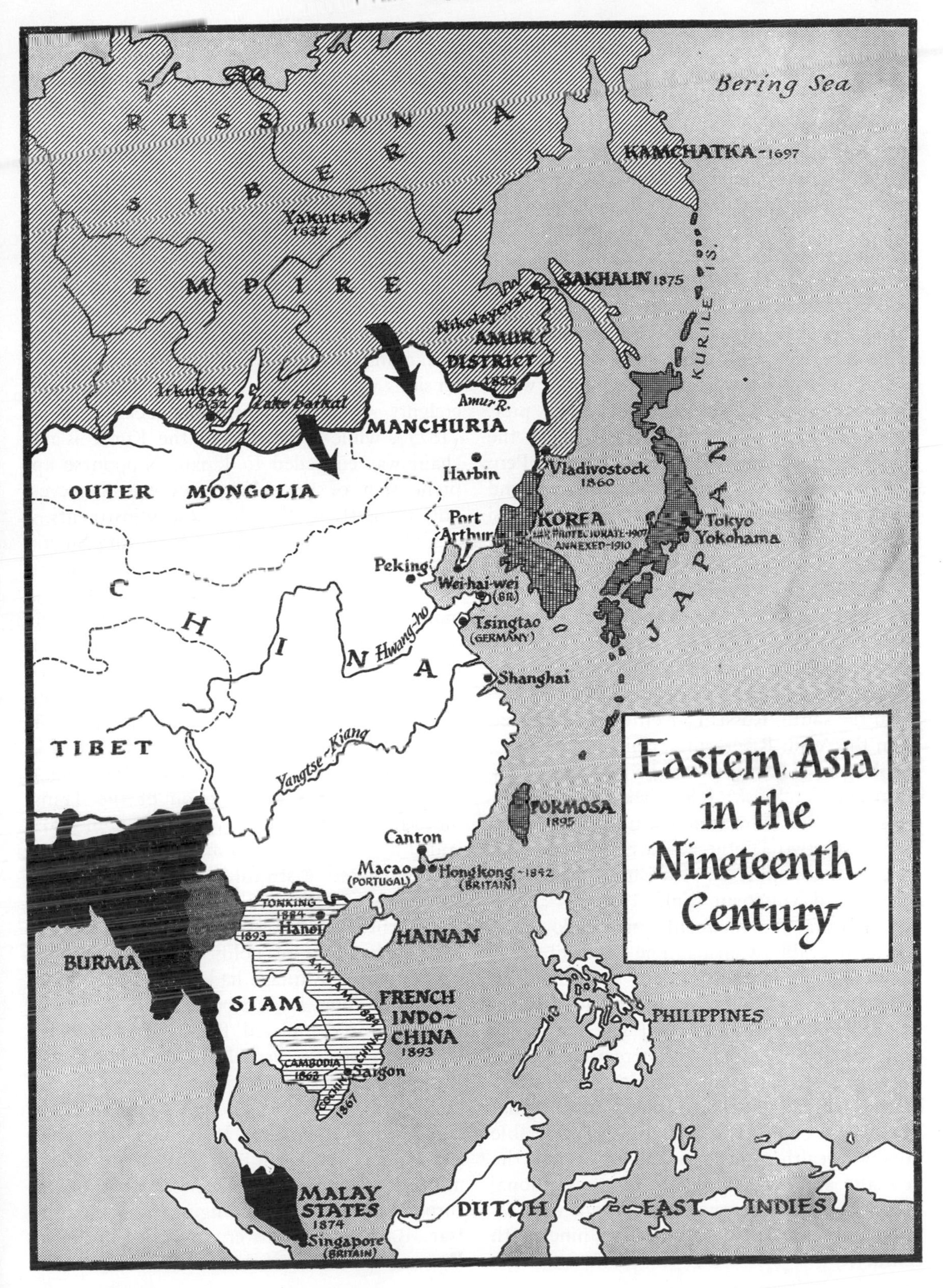
Bering Sea
RUSSIA
SIBERIA
EMPIRE
KAMCHATKA-1697
Yakutsk 1632
SAKHALIN 1875
KURILE IS.
Nikolayevsk
AMUR DISTRICT 1858
Irkutsk 1652
Lake Baikal
Amur R.
MANCHURIA
Harbin
Vladivostock 1860
OUTER MONGOLIA
KOREA
PROTECTORATE-1907
ANNEXED-1910
Port Arthur
Tokyo
Yokohama
JAPAN
Peking
Wei-hai-wei (BR.)
CHINA
Hwang-ho
Tsingtao (GERMANY)
Shanghai
TIBET
Yangtse-Kiang
FORMOSA 1895
Eastern Asia in the Nineteenth Century
Canton
Macao (PORTUGAL)
Hongkong-1842 (BRITAIN)
TONKING 1884
Hanoi
1893
HAINAN
BURMA
SIAM
ANNAM-1884
FRENCH INDO-CHINA 1893
PHILIPPINES
CAMBODIA 1863
Saigon
COCHIN CHINA 1867
MALAY STATES 1874
Singapore (BRITAIN)
DUTCH EAST INDIES

anese War it is necessary to remark upon earlier Muscovite activities in eastern Asia.

RUSSIA PUSHES EAST

On a broad view the march of Russia eastward to the Pacific paralleled the later advance of the United States westward to the great ocean. It was an epic Muscovite story of exploration, conquest and tardy exploitation. Previously Asiatic marauders had thrust into Europe, but toward the end of the sixteenth century Muscovite buccaneers reversed the process, hacking their way beyond the Urals across Siberia toward the rising sun.

This period was precisely the time when European man, fiercest of all beasts of prey, was beginning to make himself lord of the planet. Spanish conquerors of Mexico and Peru had counterparts in the Russian brigands and freebooters who subjected little, unorganized tribes of Siberia to the rule of the tsar. A veritable ocean of land, double the extent of the United States and very thinly peopled, was quickly added to the dominions of Russia. After the Pacific had been reached, the flag of Muscovy was carried triumphantly across to Alaska.

To the south, Russian adventurers blundered upon the Amur River valley, claimed by China. Fighting of a desultory sort persisted until the Treaty of Nerchinsk (1689) debarred the Russians from the Amur region; a rule which stood for nearly two centuries. Russians, however, developed a small trade with China, tea becoming a prized Muscovite comfort.

In natural environment and endowment Siberia resembles Canada. The word Siberia is likely to raise in the mind of the reader an image of a frigid, sprawling wasteland, a gigantic refrigerator. But in actual fact, large sections are fit for habitation. There are extensive tracts of good farmlands, limitless forests, furbearing animals (which excited the original Muscovite cupidity), fish and considerable mineral wealth. Siberia, in short, is not the desolate and barren region of conventional fancy, though extensive occupation was delayed until the last quarter of the nineteenth century.

About the middle of that century, Russian interest in eastern Asia revived, after languishing for generations. Ambitious imperialists marched anew to the Amur and China was forced (1858) to cede the north bank to Russia. Next, the Maritime Province (*Primorsk*) was wrested away (1860) from China. That region contained a fine bay on which the commercial and naval port of Vladivostok was built; it grew from a cluster of log cabins into a major city, somewhat like Hong Kong. The harbor, alas, froze over two months or more of the year. Advancing Russia frightened awakening Japan, but clashing territorial pretensions were pacifically adjusted. Russian sovereignty over Sakhalin was acknowledged (1875), while ownership of the Kurile island chain was conceded to Japan. Nipponese apprehension of the Muscovites was, however, only modestly soothed by these adjustments.

Until late in the nineteenth century Siberia served Imperial Russia primarily as a prison for convicts and political criminals. Perhaps as many as a million dissenters were sentenced at one time and another to the east; Joseph Stalin, for instance, was thrice shipped thither. Voluntary emigration was exceedingly small before the emancipation of the serfs. Thereafter, in several cases entire villages moved from Russia across the Urals, though substantial migrations awaited the construction of the Trans-Siberian railway, which was finished in 1905. Aided by the government approximately 5,000,000 emigrated eastward in the twenty years before 1914, vastly more than in the preceding three centuries of Russian control.

Considerations of political strategy as well as economic advantage had dictated the building of the long Trans-Siberian railway. Before the job was completed Russia arranged with China to run a branch road—the Chinese Eastern—across Manchuria to Vladivostok, and to drop a line down through southern Manchuria to Port Arthur. It seemed that huge Manchuria, fertile in soil and blessed with mineral resources, would inescapably be incorporated into the far-ranging empire of the tsar. Railways, moreover, promised to make Russia the master of eastern Asia. Japan was greatly alarmed and fears for the security of the island kingdom itself were intensified by Russian machinations in Korea, which the Nipponese had already marked out as their very own prey.

JAPAN CHALLENGES RUSSIA

First the court at Tokyo tried to check the predatory Muscovite expansion by diplomatic negotiation. But when diplomacy failed Japan unhesitatingly withdrew the sword from the scabbard. The United States and Britain equally disliked the prospect of Russian dominion over Chinese Manchuria. As has been indicated, the United States imagined it had accomplished something in the way of staving off the spoliation of China through its "open door" diplomacy. The British response to Muscovite aggressiveness took the more positive form of an alliance (1902) with Japan pointed against Russia. In effect the London cabinet promised that if Japan fought Russia, Britain would prevent a third power from aiding the tsar. That assurance encouraged Japanese self-confidence and bellicosity.

Early in 1904 Japan struck a thunderbolt blow at Russian Port Arthur, suddenly and dramatically, as later at Pearl Harbor. It appeared that the war which ensued would be an unequal struggle between the toy kingdom of the Mikado and an empire that stretched half-way round the globe. Actually it was a contest between the most European of Oriental nations and the most Oriental of European countries—a reenactment of the classic drama in which the youthful David unloosed his deadly sling at Goliath. On land and sea the Japanese covered themselves with glory and the tsardom, rocked by internal tumult, had grudgingly to confess defeat in the Treaty of Portsmouth of 1905.

Russia relinquished to Japan her railway and harbor privileges in southern Manchuria, ceded the southern half of the island of Sakhalin and promised to keep hands off Korea. Five years later "The Land of the Morning Calm" dropped into the Nipponese imperial basket. The Japanese victory and the peace startled the Western world. Russia ceased to be a major counter in the imperialistic rivalries of eastern Asia, even though it retained special privileges in northern Manchuria. Britain renewed and revised the alliance with Japan; in the new edition, each party was bound to aid the other in the event of an attack upon its Asiatic holdings, British India included.

Japan had forged into the class of first-rate powers. That point was carefully noted in the United States, which had already been involved in acrimonious exchanges with Japan over Nipponese emigrants in California. Apprehensive Americans suspected that Nippon might pounce upon the newly-gained Philippine archipelago. It was evident that the pleasant and prolonged Japanese-American honeymoon dating from the Perry treaty of 1854 had drawn to an end.

As the West suffered a rude shock by the demonstrated strength of Japan, so the East

Two of the Russian cruisers sunk by the Japanese in their raid on Port Arthur

Suppression of the Boxer Uprising—United States Marines off U.S.S. Newark enter Tientsin, China, 1900.

was profoundly impressed. Nipponese arms had shown that the white man, as represented by Russia in any case, was not invincible, but could be brought to bay if Asia learned and applied the military techniques of the West. A wave of anti-imperialist and nationalist emotion swept Asia from the Philippines to Turkey. As was not fully appreciated until nearly half a century later, the Japanese victory over Imperial Russia unloosed a revolt of Asiatics against the West, of which Soviet Russia, paradoxically, became the spearhead.

CHINA IN FERMENT

Inside China, small reformist elements had turned vigorously against Western domination. Mass spleen was directed especially against Christian missionaries and native converts by fanatical secret societies. At the end of the century, these clubs—of which the Boxers gave their name to the episode—engineered bloody butcheries of white men and Christian Chinese in the northern provinces. The tottering Manchu court abetted and applauded the murderous doings.

An international expeditionary force, containing American, Japanese and European elements, moved into China and put down the disorders without ruth. As penalties for the outrages, China was obliged in 1901 to permit foreign soldiers to garrison Peking, and to pay an excessively heavy indemnity. A portion of the reparations which accrued to the United States was eventually applied to the education of Chinese.

The Boxer fiasco, Western infringements upon Chinese sovereignty and the Japanese victory over Russia quickened national sentiments in China. Or that at least was true of Chinese who had drunk at the wells of Western learning. Missionaries had not only won converts and helped to undermine confidence in Confucianist conservatism, but they had taught ideals of liberty, equality and representative government. Chinese who studied in foreign countries returned home imbued with a patriotic passion to reconstruct China in the light of what they had learned and seen.

At the same time the invasion of Western industrialism was disturbing static economic traditions in the Chinese "treaty ports" and their environs. Growing foreign trade and shipping, the laying down of railways and telegraph lines, more and more commercial and banking establishments and factories and mines challenged the ancient somnolence of the Celestial Empire.

Early in the twentieth century, the Manchu court published a perfect flood of reformist decrees. Various customs of the country and aspects of administration were thereby changed—on paper. But militant reformers complained that the Manchu regime could not be mended, it must be ended. Secret revolutionary and republican societies cropped up in many a Chinese community, being especially numerous and vocal in the South. Acknowledged head of the republican agitation was Dr. Sun Yat-sen, who one day would be toasted as the "Father of the Chinese Republic." Educated in a Hong Kong medical school, and an extensive

The Dowager Empress of China, Tzu Hsi, and members of her Court

traveler in the United States and England, Sun absorbed to the full Western political and social principles. As a young man he naively supposed that the ways of the West could readily be transplanted to populous, lethargic China.

In the autumn of 1911 a successful republican revolt swept over major Chinese cities. The detested Manchu autocracy was cast into the discard and a democratic republic was installed in its stead. The intoxicating wine of the West had been poured into old Chinese bottles with explosive consequences. A ruinous schism developed among the politically articulate Chinese. The southern faction of Dr. Sun was committed to a constitutional regime, while its northern opponent was staunchly monarchical and militarist at heart.

After a short period of cheerfulness, China slipped on to the treadmill of uncertainty and confusion, which would go round for generations. The rival groupings took up arms; war lords seized control of provincial governments; brigandage and anarchy ran rife. Chaos in China invited Japan to sink her talons deeper into the flesh of the Oriental giant.

Huge borderlands, meanwhile, which were under titular Chinese sovereignty, had fallen away. Outer Mongolia gravitated into the orbit of Imperial Russia. Spacious Tibet, though nominally independent, passed largely under the influence of Britain and the French appropriated, parcel by parcel, the densely peopled region of Indo-China. That dependency, along with special rights in southern China, and minor trophies of eighteenth-century French enterprise in India, gave the Third Republic an active interest in Asiatic affairs.

BRITAIN IN INDIA

Growing nationalism and political unrest pervaded the educated classes of India to a greater degree than China. Fervent wails of protest against British imperial authority betokened the eventual collapse of the rule of the "Raj." But throughout the nineteenth century India stood out as "the fairest jewel in Britain's colonial crown." Protection of India constituted indeed a controlling factor in British diplomacy, most notably in dealings with the Russia of the tsars.

Since Britain held a monopoly in India there

was no competition for place and pelf as in Africa or China. For a long period this vast area was the private preserve of the British East India Company, which waxed fat on trade. It maintained its own administrative bureaucracy and its own army for employment against native rulers or unruly natives. Mismanagement, corruption and resentment over the existence of "a state within a state" brought on changes in India. Political authority was withdrawn from the Company in 1784 and other rights were eaten away bit by bit. Indian troops or sepoys were engaged in bringing additional territories under British authority.

In 1858, the British crown wholly supplanted the East India Company and a generation later, amidst Oriental pomp and circumstance, Queen Victoria was proclaimed Empress of India. She reigned over an immense array of Indian peoples and cultures varying "as much as Esquimaux from the Spaniards, or the Irishman from the Turk." The eclipse of the East India Company followed a bloody rebellion of sepoys and other Indians, worthy to rank with the later Boxer risings in China. Rebels resented the invasion of Western ways and manners or feared forcible conversion to Christianity. British citizens were massacred in 1857 in northern cities and property was destroyed. Soldiers crushed the insurgents with merciless severity, as Indian Nationalists were later wont to emphasize.

By the political reformation of 1858, India—or most of it—was placed under the authority of a British Viceroy, an absolute monarch really, though legally responsible to the government in London. Scores of native princes continued to preside over their domains, which covered a third of the peninsula, but they were subject to British supervision. Officials brought out from the United Kingdom occupied the more important administrative posts. Like many a later civil servant, Lord Macaulay, eminent essayist and historian, took service in India in the 1830's, for what he frankly termed financial reasons. In five years, he confided to his sister, he ought to return home with £30,000 to his account, which presumably he did.

THE BRITISH IMPACT

The supreme concerns of Britain in India were commerce and the investment of capital. Altruism was undoubtedly operative, but material interests were of over-riding importance. In exchange for cotton textiles, hardware and other manufactures, British ships carried away industrial raw materials, foodstuffs, cotton, rice, tobacco, jute and the like. Rightly or wrongly, Britons contended that business transactions benefited buyer and seller alike. British capital was plunged into banks, railways and factories, which generally netted handsome dividends.

Under British rule, improvements were effected in native agriculture, carried on in thousands of villages. Huge irrigation projects, for instance, greatly extended the area of productive soil and better roads as well as railways facilitated the movement of crops. As a nation of shopkeepers, the British understood that to keep shop there must be security of person and property, enforceable contracts and so on, and those things they gave to India generally. The maintenance of law and order, better medical care and hygiene were reflected in the startling growth of population, despite periodic famines and occasional riots.

The army of India, though officered by Britons, was largely recruited from natives. Taxes were levied with relative fairness and honesty, rates rising, naturally enough, as public services were extended. Hallowed native customs and native creeds went untouched as long as they did not too grossly offend British moral sensibilities or interfere with business; the inhumane practice of burning widows (*suttee*), for example, was prohibited. Teachings of Christian missionaries on the brotherhood of man tended to weaken the hateful caste system.

Something more than beginnings were made in furnishing educational facilities reaching up to universities. The English language was taught, which created a common bond among educated Indians in a country of wide linguistic divergencies. Macaulay while in India fought and won the language battle in favor of English; it was his contention that British dominion over India could only be justified if the natives were taught everything the British knew from parliamentary government to railways. As Macaulay foresaw, the inescapable corollary of that policy was the self-destruction of British authority.

At Indian universities or at Oxford and Cambridge, young Indians learned of the ideas of Shakespeare and Milton, of Newton and Darwin, of Hampden and Gladstone. Principles of liberty and self-government were just so much political dynamite in India. From the Western-educated classes came spokesmen for political rights and responsibilities and agitators for Indian independence.

To channel political aspirations, the Indian National Congress was founded in 1885. It was predominantly a Hindu organization, speaking in some sense the wishes of two out of three Indians. Annual meetings were occasions for demanding, with rhetoric and invective, an Indian parliament and the appointment of Indians to policy-making governmental positions. The corrosive materialism of the West and British exploitation were denounced as destructive of Indian welfare. Congress leaders considered British rule and enterprise as temporary phenomena, whose termination could be hastened by effective pressure. Starry-eyed romantics fondly believed that the departure of the "Raj" would bring a new earth and a new heaven to India.

As a counterweight, up to a point, of the National Congress, an All-Moslem League was created (1906). It claimed to speak for that quarter of the Indian millions who obeyed the precepts of Mohammed. In answer to agitation, British officials admitted more and more educated Indians to the civil service, but outbreaks against British rule were frequent. An apprehensive Viceroy, Lord Curzon, banned singing of "Onward, Christian Soldiers," thinking it undesirable for Indians to hear: "Crowns and thrones may perish. Kingdoms rise and wane." A decided impetus was imparted to the Hindu nationalist agitation by the First World War.

Long since, British control had been asserted over Burma and the collection of colonies called Malaya, a large supplier of tin and rubber to the world. Chinese immigrants swarmed into Malaya attracted by the freedom from fear and want which British administration helped to establish. The Kingdom of Siam, wedged uneasily between British Burma and French Indo-China, contrived to preserve its independence. But it also was drawn into the commercial stream of the West.

EMPIRES IN THE PACIFIC

Islands and archipelagoes in the Pacific vastness passed under the flag of one or another white imperialism, or of Japan. Only with the fighting of the Second World War did Westerners wake up to the immensity of the Pacific. Vast though continental United States is, when compared with the wide open spaces of the Pacific it looks like another Belgium; 1,355 New York States could be plunked down in the Pacific without entirely covering its surface. Peppering this ocean of magnificent distances are groups of islands, mostly tiny.

Islands which are mere dots on even large-scale maps were gobbled up by imperial powers. Flags sometimes were hoisted simply as romantic gestures, but more often Pacific islands contained economic attractions, strategic advantages or opportunities for Christian evangelization. Tropical isles, known previously only to God, blossomed into outposts of Western civilization.

Commercially, the most valuable of the Pacific empires was the Dutch East Indies. As extensive as the United States east of the Mississippi, this possession was inhabited by extremely fecund peoples; mostly Moslems in religion, the natives spoke many languages and dialects. Earlier it has been explained how this archipelago became the property of the Dutch East India Company. In 1798 the Dutch government took over the rule of the colony, and the record of little Holland as a colonial administrator surpassed, on balance, that of any other imperial power. Scientific experimentation coupled with the skill of the peasants gave the Dutch East Indies the most diversified and advanced agriculture in the Pacific tropics.

This archipelago was a rich storehouse of goods. Among its products were rice, pepper, sugar, coffee, tea, tobacco, quinine and industrial rawstuffs such as rubber, fibers, tin and oil. Dutch capital operated large plantations, but most of the land belonged to native cultivators. The prosperity of the Netherlands was intimately bound up with rising trade with the Indies.

Throughout most of the nineteenth century, docile natives were compelled to toil on public projects, but more enlightened and humane policies were later introduced. Slavery was legally abolished in the Dutch Indies five years before similar action was taken in the United States. Dutch-operated schools trained a native intelligentsia, which, like its counterpart in India, pushed for freedom and independence. The Japanese defeat of Russia in 1905 infused new energy into the agitation, but before the First World War independence sentiments were largely restricted to the small European-educated minority.

THE BRITISH DOMINIONS

Australia and New Zealand were "discovered" by the United States as a by-product of the Second World War. These flourishing Commonwealths are virtually projections of Britain itself in the South Seas; British ownership stemmed from discovery by Captain James Cook. Only small sections of Australia, which is as big as the United States, are suitable for close agricultural settlement; the interior is desert and wasteland. Population is concentrated to a remarkable degree in coastal cities, especially in the southeast. By 1914, about 5,000,000 whites, almost all of British stock, resided in Australia, on levels of living equal to the best in the world.

Britain first used Australia as a place to ship convicts, but the penal character of the island lasted only a short while. It was the opportunities for sheep-raising that originally attracted free emigrants from the British Isles. The merino sheep has been called indeed "the ancestor of Australian prosperity"; upwards of 100,000,000 sheep roved the plains and hillsides. Production of wool and mutton, which were readily marketed in Britain, half-way round the globe, developed into the largest single industry. Gold, discovered in 1851, lured thousands to Australia in quest of quick and easy riches; but many of the newcomers soon turned to building up prosperous ranches and farms. Mineral deposits, varied and widely distributed, would one day nourish substantial industries. The foreign trade of Australia was closely knit to the British economy, to the common gain of colonists and motherland.

Without much difficulty the scattered and primitive aboriginal peoples were rounded up in interior reservations. Whole tribes, however, were destroyed through disease, alcohol and warfare. Fearful lest the island might be inundated by the teeming millions of Asia, Australia adopted laws to debar colored races and to keep Australia white. With time, six separate colonies, each self-governing, were blocked out. Discussions for a united state came to fruition in 1901 with the establishment of a federal Commonwealth having a parliamentary type of government. Parochial jealousies were obliterated within a generation by the prouder consciousness of Australian solidarity. Except for a governor-general from Britain, instead of a president, government in Australia resembled that of the United States. The legal bonds of the Commonwealth to Britain were as flimsy as cobwebs, but cultural and ideological affinities and commercial ties were as strong as steel. Australia relied, of course, upon the long arm of the British navy to protect it against foreign aggression.

That was true also of the sister Dominion of New Zealand, lying 1,200 miles to the east and about the size of New York and Pennsylvania. The history of this colony generally paralleled that of Australia. Whalers and other adventurous pioneers drifted to the islands early in the nineteenth century and group settlement began in the 1840's with the introduction of sheep. Land-hungry whites pressed hard upon the interesting native Maoris, who fought energetically to defend themselves. Racial strife was tempered when the Maoris accepted Christianity; in the twentieth century they multiplied twice as fast as the whites, creating new problems. Dense forests, tough fern growth and rugged mountains presented very great difficulties for agriculture, but sheep-raising and dairying proved profitable.

New Zealand and Australia attracted world attention altogether out of proportion to their populations because of experimentation in social security and democratic control. The watchword was "A decent life for all." Governments pioneered in social welfare legislation, operated communication services and owned mines. Australia gave the world the secret ballot, and the Dominions "down under" admitted women to the suffrage responsibility a generation before Britain itself did.

In addition to the self-governing Dominions, Britain acquired dozens of Pacific islands such as the Gilberts and the Fiji cluster and sections of Borneo and New Guinea. French dependencies in the Pacific were limited to the southern area. On the basis of early explorations France annexed tiny oases of noble savages (not really so noble) such as Tahiti. New Caledonia served as penal colony, naval station and a supplier of nickel.

OTHER IMPERIALISMS

Imperial Germany, exuberant novice in the Pacific, claimed sovereignty over groups of islands which other nations had passed by. It picked up a slice of New Guinea and the Marshall Islands and bought the Spanish Caroline and Mariana strings which the United States neglected to take from Spain after the War of 1898. By arrangement with the United States, Germany in 1899 came into possession of the largest Samoan island and acquired the Solomon archipelago through a comparable deal with Britain. Altogether the German empire in the Pacific ranged over 2,500 miles of open ocean, north and south of the equator—literally bushels of insular pin-points. These possessions afforded opportunities for missionary zeal and extremely modest commercial outlets, but several of the isles had potentialities for naval purposes, and all of them looked lovely on maps—big German maps.

Spain, under whose flag navigators had first plowed the unknown Pacific, lost all of her holdings. The United States was the major legatee. After the Spanish-American war the Stars and Stripes replaced the tattered banner of Spain in the Philippines and Guam (in the Mariana group). At the same time the United States annexed Hawaii, and earlier it had appropriated Midway, Wake and smaller islands. Part of Samoa, too, was drawn into the Pacific realm of the United States, with Alaska and the Aleutian chain, purchased from Russia in 1867, as the northern frontier.

Very swiftly the United States had become owner of the economically promising clusters of the Philippines and Hawaii, and of four of the most desirable harbors in the Pacific. Spanning the great ocean, a chain of American-owned islands linked California to China. Only the British and Dutch holdings in the Pacific outclassed those of the lusty New World titan. After the emergence of Japan as a strong naval power, strategic ports belonging to the United States were converted into fleet bases to protect the Americas.

BALANCE SHEETS OF IMPERIALISM

Only the doctrinaire can sum up the complex consequences of modern imperialism with a few neat and facile strokes. Finite human beings are aware that good is seldom unmixed with evil and wrong is rarely done without traces of right. To arrive at sensible judgments on modern imperialism, two balance sheets must be cast up—one for the imperial countries themselves, the other for the peoples who felt the imprint of the imperial impulse.

By 1914 nearly 20,000,000 square miles of extra-European territory owed allegiance to European states. In the interval since 1875, Britain added some 2,000,000 square miles to her already enormous colonial heritage. Here was the greatest empire the world had ever known, comprising a quarter of the earth's surface and population. This globe-girdling "super-power" combination embraced every type of state and people from the most primitive to the most civilized.

On the accession of Edward VII in 1901, the world was reminded that "His Majesty rules over one continent, a hundred peninsulas, five hundred promontories, a thousand lakes, two thousand rivers, and ten thousand islands. . . The Empire to which Victoria acceded in 1837 covered a sixth of the land of the world; that of King Edward covers nearly a quarter. The Union Jack has unfolded itself . . . over two acres of new territory every time the clock has ticked since 1800."

In point of fact France of the Third Republic, in creating the second great French colonial empire, accumulated more acreage after 1875 than Britain. In size France overseas exceeded France in Europe by twenty times and contained about 60,000,000 inhabitants. The flag of Imperial Germany was hoisted over more than 1,000,000 square miles after 1871 and Imperial Russia annexed nearly as much. The Italian empire exceeded 860,000 square miles, while the Belgian Congo was ninety times larger than the homeland. The Netherlands and Portugal held on to large colonial inheritances, but the Spanish empire dwindled to insignificant dimensions. Japan pounced upon sizable dependencies and the United States between 1898 and 1914 annexed colonial territory faster than any of the European empires.

Were colonies then paying propositions as of 1914? It may be asserted with confidence that dependencies yielded their imperial owners only slightly more commerce than would otherwise have been obtained. Trade tended to follow the price level, not the flag. Profits from colonial traffic fell below the costs of administering and protecting the holdings. On the other side, individual firms and investors benefited and many workmen were employed in producing goods for colonial consumption.

Imperialism did not bring substantial advantages in access to raw materials in time of peace. And in wartime, as the First World War amply illustrated, everything depended upon control of lines of communication to sources of colonial rawstuffs. If the economic case for imperialism rested on dubious factual foundations, the ready retort was that a colony resembled a business undertaking—it could not be expected to earn profits until it was operated on a sound commercial basis by administrators with know-how. Spokesmen of imperialism ever pinned their faith on the future.

The argument for colonies as outlets for surplus population required revision in the light of experience. Few Europeans actually emigrated to territories over which their motherland held sovereign control; vastly more Germans, for instance, preferred Canada to German Africa. New York State meant home for fifty times as many Italians as the Italian empire in Africa. Emigrants moved, in other words, to places where opportunities to earn a livelihood were most attractive, or where political or religious freedom prevailed, not where colonial enthusiasts would have liked them to go. More than that, emigration afforded no fundamental answer to population pressure; in fact, emigration as a solution of the problem of surplus population worked only in the isolated and special case of Ireland.

But there was another side to the picture. Account must be taken of the kind of emigrants and the purposes for which they went. If colonies provided a livelihood for only a limited number of industrial wage earners and peasants, they did furnish opportunities for business and professional men and some artisans.

From the standpoint of Christian conversion, imperialism netted only slight results that are statistically measurable. Allegiance to traditional creeds severely handicapped the progress of evangelization in Asia. Perhaps half of one per cent of the inhabitants of China embraced Christianity, and about one per cent in India; in Africa the proportion stood a notch higher. Worship of ancestors formed the vital essence of religion for most African tribesmen, but widespread belief in a Higher God eased the task of Christian conversion. Over against that advantage must be set the competition of Mohammedanism with its simpler theology and less exacting moral standards. As of 1914, black, brown and yellow mission fields were still waiting for the Christian harvest.

What then of the effects of the relentless Western invasion upon native peoples? Afri-

A type of the civilizations the Europeans found in their colonial areas—a bush kraal *in South Africa, about 1820*

cans and Asiatics experienced the rough edge of all the white man's arts from gunpowder through gin to diplomacy. Some natives resented the disturbance of conventional habits and customs, loss of land, forced labor, and the color bar and superiority attitude of the white men. Growth of color feeling was a significant accompaniment of modern imperialism. It is almost a universal rule that people tend to look down upon men of darker pigmentation than themselves; whites regard themselves superciliously as superior to men of other colors; browns turn up their noses at Negroes; light-complected Indians fancy themselves better than their darker-skinned countrymen. All of which may be due to the elemental habit of associating whiteness with purity, darkness with evil and to thinking of the day as lovelier than the night.

"Even the morally best and the idealists," Albert Schweitzer, one of the most respected Christian thinkers of the twentieth century, once wrote from Africa, "find it difficult out here to be what they wish to be. The Negro is a child, and with children nothing can be done without the use of authority. The child of nature does not know what responsibility is . . . They give just as much return of labour as the others [whites] can force out of them."

Spirited natives, at any rate, retaliated against wrongs and discriminations by assaults upon Western intruders. Outbreaks were invariably crushed, ruthlessly sometimes. As a British satirist explained:

> Whatever happens, we have got
> The Gatling gun and they have not.

After Japan had demonstrated her military prowess, sons of Nippon were treated with more consideration by the white nations. And missionaries or secular reformers reminded the age of the moral commitment of the strong to the weak, prodding the white conscience to mitigate abuses in handling the colored masses.

While the pace of the Western impact was rapid it was uneven. It was not unusual to find in the same colony the twentieth century alongside of the eighteenth, the thirteenth or even the Stone Age. Yet almost everywhere that Western imperialism penetrated, native populations bounded upward. Indeed the supreme fact about the inhabitants of Asia and Africa was the staggering rate of increase. Consider Java which witnessed something like a ninefold increase in a century; Egypt, after two generations of British control fed, albeit precariously, twice as many mouths as previously.

Native populations soared for several reasons. Orderly administration and due process of law replaced anarchy and violence; medical science and sanitation cut down mortality while improved communications counteracted short crops. And schools lightened mental darkness and unchained minds from barbarities committed in the name of religion. The ways of the West, in short, interfered with nature's traditional correctives of excessive population: war, famine and disease. The expanding millions frustrated projects for social betterment; human fertility outran the fertility of the soil.

By 1914 a class of Westernized intellectuals had emerged in areas under imperial rule. Some of them passively acquiesced in the lordship of the West, while others, embittered by the squalor and wretchedness around them, blamed the West and turned revolutionary. The explosive force of nationalism, besides, had penetrated to backward peoples, and some national leaders eventually harkened to the siren voice of Communist Russia. Having sown the wind in colonial areas, the West would presently reap the whirlwind.

Yet another point must be posted on the ledger: competition overseas generated dangerous tensions among the European contestants, not to overlook the trail of blood left by imperialistic wars. Fuel was heaped on smoldering enmities on the Rhine and the Bosphorus, in the Mediterranean and the North Sea by rivalries over Africa, the river valleys of the Congo and Mesopotamia and the markets of the Orient. International incidents multiplied, diplomatic crises recurred more frequently. The British statesman Lord Salisbury alluded to Africa as a continent "created to be a plague to foreign offices." Disputes, envies, unfulfilled ambitions arising out of the struggle for empire helped to set the stage for the First World War.

FOR FURTHER STUDY

MARY E. TOWNSEND and C. H. PEAKE, *European Colonial Expansion* (Chicago, 1941)

WILLIAM L. LANGER, *The Diplomacy of Imperialism* (new ed., New York, 1950)

HALFORD L. HOSKINS, *European Imperialism in Africa* (New York, 1930)

BASIL WILLIAMS, *Cecil Rhodes* (new ed., London, 1938)

JOHN T. PRATT, *The Expansion of Europe into the Far East* (London, 1947)

GEORGE C. ALLEN and A. C. DONNITHORNE, *Western Enterprise in Far Eastern Development* (New York, 1954)

EDWIN O. REISCHAUER, *Japan, Past and Present* (New York, 1946)

W. W. LOCKWOOD, *The Economic Development of Japan* (Princeton, 1954)

DAVID J. DALLIN, *The Rise of Russia in Asia* (New Haven, 1949)

LYON SHARMAN, *Sun Yat-sen* (New York, 1934)

DAVID C. SOMERVELL, *The British Empire* (London, 1948)

GROVER CLARK, *The Balance Sheets of Imperialism* (New York, 1936)

ARTHUR P. NEWTON, *The Imperial Idea and its Critics* (London, 1959)

KAVALAM M. PANNIKAR, *Asia and Western Dominance* (new ed., New York, 1959)

RONALD ROBINSON, ed., *Africa and the Victorians* (New York, 1961)

REGINALD COUPLAND, *Britain and India* (London, 1941)

SSU-YÜ TENG and JOHN K. FAIRBANK, *China's Response to the West* (Cambridge, Mass., 1954)

HUGH BORTON, *Japan's Modern Century* (New York, 1955)

CHAPTER XXIII

GROWTH OF THE AMERICAS

EUROPE AND LATIN AMERICA

CIVILIZED existence in Latin America was molded by three forces operating inextricably upon one another. The transplantation of Spanish and Portuguese manners and institutions, the response of Central and South American peoples to the European bequests and the post-colonial impact of the Old World and the United States. The outreach of nineteenth-century imperialism increasingly affected the course of events in this section of the globe as in Africa, Asia and the Pacific.

Considerable and undeveloped economic resources in Latin America appealed irresistibly to imperial appetites. Soil suitable for agricultural production, notably of tropical specialties and for cattle raising, immense woodlands and rich and varied mineral deposits lured outside interests to the South American countries. As gold and silver had attracted foreigners in the sea-roving sixteenth century, so did supplies of base metals in the industrial age. Chile, it was learned, contained rich copper reserves; Bolivia, tin and wolfram, the source of tungsten; Peru, zinc, lead and vanadium; Brazil, iron and manganese, the Guianas, bauxite.[1]

South America possessed very little coal and that of inferior quality, but abundant stocks of petroleum and hydro-electric potentialities compensated for that deficiency. Since native capital and know-how were lacking, the opening up of the natural wealth depended upon foreign enterprise and investment. Owing to natural obstacles and shortage of funds, communications were of the primitive sort. In the heady Latin climate, revolutions and *coups d'etat* were familiar phenomena. Chronic instability invited foreign intervention though not, to be sure, on the scale of Africa or Asia.

[1] A veritable mountain of iron ore was discovered in 1950 in Venezuela.

Looked at broadly, the physical environment of Latin America resembles that of Africa. Over half the area is tropical or sub-tropical, unappealing to permanent settlement by Europeans. Yet climate in the southern sections is salubrious and there hundreds of thousands of immigrants from the Latin countries of Europe took up new homes; many Germans, too, invested their lives and fortunes in southern Brazil, Argentina and Chile. Small companies of Chinese and Japanese added to the richly mingled blood of Latin America.

In the colonial era Spanish and Portuguese administrators and churchmen had brought the Indian aborigines and Negro slaves imported from Africa into the Roman Catholic communion and the general orbit of Western civilization. Cultural bonds with Latin Europe resting upon community of language and tradition outlived political control. For such prosperity as it enjoyed, Latin America relied in large measure upon foreign trade, the exportation of primary products. Broadly speaking, areas which raised tropical agricultural goods like fruit, coffee and sugar, and in which industrial rawstuffs were mined carried on their principal commerce with the United States. But non-tropical food producers such as the Argentine and Uruguay, developed trade with Europe, mainly with Britain, with Germany and the Latin countries edging in.

Capital investments tended to follow trading connections. As the world's leading banker Britain invested heavily in South American enterprises, such as nitrate mines in Chile, railways and meat packing establishments in Argentina. Early in the nineteenth century, propaganda literature in Britain lavishly advertised the financial rewards awaiting the export of funds to Latin America; the youthful Disraeli, for instance, devoted three flamboyant pamphlets to opportunities available in mining. By 1914, approximately $5,000,000,000 of British capital had been placed in Latin America for investment in government bonds and railways principally, but also in some 500 other undertakings. Argentina had become in a real sense a partner in the world-wide British commercial realm.

Despite cultural and economic links with foreign nations, the Latin American countries, once they had broken loose from their European political masters, contrived to retain their independence. They developed into a score of more or less distinct national individualities.

HOW LATIN AMERICA WON INDEPENDENCE

Convulsive forces unleashed in the era of the French Revolution and Napoleon excited revolts in Latin America. Two schools of political opinion appeared among the articulate in the Spanish Empire. The opulent social élite, owners of large estates, leading churchmen, bureaucrats and men of Spanish descent were generally content with the rule of Spain. Standing against these conservative elements were the partisans of political independence. The thinking and emotions of intellectuals had been enflamed by the French "Enlightenment" and the Yankee success in casting off the British yoke. Economic hardships and social discontent stoked the fires of unrest and rebellion. Spanish mercantilism, for example, tried to restrict colonial commerce to business men in the motherland; merchants from other countries, who traded in Spanish America, were treated as pirates. Pocketbooks of colonials suffered because of Spanish commercial regulations.

Moreover, to support the Spanish colonial bureaucracy, unenlightened and oppressive, heavy taxes were levied. The toiling masses, Indians, Africans in Brazil and Cuba and mulattoes were ground close to the starvation level, victims of grasping landlords and churchmen and of social discriminations. It was not, however, this large and amorphous class of "common men" which ignited revolutions. That role was assumed by educated Creoles, native-born men of Spanish ancestry, who wanted freedom, the elimination of the Spanish tyranny and who desired public and ecclesiastical offices.

The struggle for emancipation in Latin America dragged on longer than in English America. Spanish officials repressed minor risings of the late eighteenth century, but the tide of insurgency gathered unequalled vigor after the soldiers of Napoleon stormed into Spain (1807).

Armed outbreaks in the south (Argentina, Chile and a section of Peru), directed by the rather timid and hesitant General José de San Martin, shattered Spanish authority. Creeping disillusion converted San Martin from republican principles to monarchism; he is honored as the hero of the emergence of the southern Latin American states into nationhood.

Heart and brain of the rebellions to the north was the more dynamic General Simon Bolívar, surnamed the Liberator. A wealthy Creole, who had read extensively in the literature of the "Enlightenment" and had traveled widely in Europe, Bolívar came to think of independence and republicanism as inseparable. He was distinctly conscious of the social wretchedness of the masses, which he ascribed to Spanish rule.

After several small and futile revolts, Bolívar enlisted under the revolutionary banner hundreds of British and other veterans released from the Napoleonic wars. Loans from British sources aided the insurgent forces, inspiring Byron to write:

> Every loan
> Is not merely a speculative hit,
> But seats a nation or upsets a throne.

Bolívar lived to see Venezuela, Colombia, Ecuador, all of Peru and Bolivia (commemorating his name) freed from Spain and established as independent republics. He rightly feared that the anarchy which prevailed in the infant states would inescapably lead to despotism. His dream of a union of the republics to present a united front in a dangerous world was frustrated. Political turbulence in the liberated colonies filled his last days with bitter despair and disillusionment. "Those who have served the cause of the Revolution," Bolívar mournfully lamented, "have plowed the sand." Nevertheless, he stamped the imprint of his republican ideals from Mexico to Peru and the birthday, July 24th, of the most loved name in northern Latin America is celebrated as a holiday. Time has treated his faults with affectionate indulgence.

The severance of political ties with Europe followed special paths in Mexico and in Brazil. In Mexico (New Spain) where loyalist sentiments ran deeper than in South America, independence came about in 1821 by reason of the collaboration of conservatives and Creole dissidents. Governmental institutions similar

This sketch of the battle of Carabobo, Venezuela (June 24, 1821), was drawn by one of the volunteers fighting in Bolivar's forces. The Liberator's victory at Carabobo was decisive in the struggle to free northern South America.

to those of the United States were adopted (1824). The little states of Central America imitated the example of their Mexican neighbor.

Brazil, far the largest and most populous of the Latin colonies, belonged not to Spain, but to Portugal. When Napoleon's troops marched (1807) into Portugal, the royal court betook itself to Brazil. There were no anti-European outbursts as in the Spanish colonies. In 1821 the king resumed the throne in Portugal, appointing his son, Pedro, as viceroy of Brazil. Pressure for separation from Europe led, in the next year, to the proclamation of an independent empire of Brazil, with Pedro as sovereign; a constitution prescribed a parliamentary form of government. That arrangement prevailed until 1889, when, on the heels of a short, almost bloodless insurrection, Brazil entered the constellation of New World republics.

After the flood of revolution had subsided, twenty independent states had taken their places in Latin America.[2] Only small fragments of the erstwhile European empires in Latin America remained. Spain retained her grip upon Cuba and Puerto Rico.[3] France owned small islands in the West Indies. Guiana on the northeast coast of South America was ruled by Britain, Holland and France; and Britain commanded an island chain ranging from Bermuda through West Indian archipelagoes to the Falkland Islands, deep in the South Atlantic. The Union Jack also fluttered over a small colony—Honduras—in Central America.

INDEPENDENCE ASSURED

Independence had been achieved, but could it be preserved? There were some indications that the conservative monarchies of Continental Europe, which thoroughly detested revolutions anyway, might intervene to overthrow the republican governments and restore Spanish lordship. The broad expanse of the Atlantic, however, presented a major obstacle to the carrying out of such a policy. And even more formidable, then and later, was the opposition of Great Britain and the United States.

British statecraft had greeted the New World insurgencies with a hallelujah chorus. Mercantilist restrictions on commerce having been thrown down, Latin America afforded additional opportunities for British trade and investment. The London government let it be known in European capitals that it would frown upon any attempt to reestablish the authority of Spain. On more varied grounds, the United States desired that the Latin states should remain free and independent. The South American revolts had evoked transports of applause in the Northern Republic, which had so recently cut the umbilical cord to the British motherland. Adoption of republican forms of government by the new nations heightened popular sympathy and official respect in the United States.

American commercial instincts, moreover, were aroused. And, above all else, the security of the United States was enhanced by the overthrow of European authority in the lands to the south. Latin American freedom, that is, accorded with the interests of the United States, and, in 1822, diplomatic recognition was extended to several of the former Spanish possessions.

All that was preliminary to the issuance of the Monroe Doctrine (1823), which became a key principle of the foreign policy of the United States. The London government recommended that the two nations should publish a joint declaration against European intervention in Latin America. But the authorities in Washington preferred a more general statement which would convey a warning not only to the monarchies of western Europe but also to Russia, whose aggressive agents were advancing on the Pacific Coast. And as the cocky Secretary of State, John Q. Adams, remarked, the United States had no desire to appear "as a cock-boat in the wake of the British man-of-war."

Unilaterally then, the government of the United States announced to all and sundry that intervention in Latin America would be in-

[2] The French colony of San Domingo had in fact set the pace, tearing itself away from political ties with Europe in 1804.

[3] Florida was reluctantly transferred in 1819 to the United States.

Back of the Monroe Doctrine was thrown what force the United States could muster. It was small but effective. Here we see a squadron including the North Carolina, *ship-of-the-line, the* Constitution *and the* Brandywine, *frigates, the* Erie *and the* Ontario, *sloops-of-war, leaving Port Mahon in Minorca shortly after the President's declaration of our policy.*

terpreted as "the manifestation of an unfriendly disposition toward the United States." Neither conquest nor colonization of any independent New World territory would be permitted in the future; existing colonies would not, however, be disturbed. Substantially the Washington government declared to Europe, "Your citizens may come to the New World Republics with valises or briefcases, but guns must be left at home."

Given the military weakness of the United States at the time, the Monroe pronouncement contained elements of the bold not to say the heroic. For many years to come, however, the principle sheltered behind the shield of the British navy. Whatever inclination may have existed in monarchical Europe to interfere in Latin America—and at no time was it strong—disappeared. Britain in 1824 accorded full recognition to the Latin republics. "Spanish America is free," proclaimed the British Foreign Minister, "and if we do not mismanage our matters sadly, she is English." He was half right.

ADVENTURES IN REPUBLICANISM

Latin American countries of the nineteenth century were not persuasive advertisements of the advantages and benefits of republicanism. On paper, governments resembled the United States, but in practice they were quite otherwise. Bullets, not ballots, frequently decided controversial questions, and censorship proverbially muzzled the opposition press.

Without experience in self rule, the young republics could not readily shake off the heritage of long-standing authoritarian convictions. Parties defeated at the polls, instead of accepting the verdict, appealed to arms; military contingents raised and deposed dictators, who, nonetheless, commonly styled themselves "constitutional presidents." Repression of violence was frequently invoked as an excuse to suppress civil liberties. Moderation seldom blended with patriotism in the conduct of Latin American politics.

In certain of the Latin countries there was greater political stability and discipline, it is true, than in others. The general contrast between the larger republics and the small primitive states was rather striking. Argentina and Chile fared better than the rest with Colombia and Peru following along. But even in them civil fighting was recurrent. Bolivia, whose geography favored insurgents, witnessed no fewer than sixty revolutions and the assassination of six presidents in the seventy-four years after 1824. Constant, bloody violence entailed destruction of life and property, dislocated economic activity and caused trouble with foreign governments, whenever the interests of their nationals were damaged. Public funds which might have been advantageously devoted to public health and schooling were consumed in internal warfare. Illiteracy ranged especially high in the rural areas.

Passionate feuds over boundaries, moreover, churned up Latin American affairs. Boundaries of colonial territories had never been neatly defined or had been traced on the basis of information later discovered to be inaccurate. Sometimes, though not often, disputes over frontiers culminated in open war.

Endless controversies marked the relations of the Latin republics and the Catholic Church, a stronghold of conservatism. As the official creed in all the countries, Catholicism was exempt from payment of taxes, operated courts of its own and dominated educational institutions. Anticlericals, coming chiefly from the small but enlarging middle classes, clamored for the abolition of ecclesiastical privileges, seizure of the landed properties of the Church and for state-directed schooling.

To complicate matters further, acute social and economic cleavages divided the Creole governing classes from the peasant masses. Racially, too, the population was extremely diverse; as of 1914, there were about 30,000,000 whites, 25,000,000 Indians and Negroes and 45,000,000 of mixed ancestry. In general the primitive Indians and Africans, hewers of wood and drawers of water, struggled along on wretched Oriental standards of subsistence. Mass misery repeatedly exploded in revolutions.

Political discord, suspicions and uncertainties imposed heavy handicaps upon social and economic progress. National economies rested uniformly upon agriculture, carried on for the most part on a subsistence level. Where foreign influences penetrated, goods for the world market—grain, coffee, fruit, cattle—were raised. Due to intensive specialization in productions for export, the Latin American economies were highly susceptible to fluctuations in the world price of a single or a few commodities.

Internal trade and maintenance of order were handicapped by the inadequacy of transportation facilities. Roads were as a rule poor and railways few. Great dependence, consequently, was placed upon sea transportation, most of the vessels engaged in the traffic being foreign owned. To 1914 manufacturing for the most part was in the handicraft stage or consisted of primitive processing of raw materials, though large cities such as Buenos Aires, Rio de Janeiro, and Mexico City had already been invaded by the machine. Exploitation of mineral resources, including petroleum, was largely in the hands of foreign interests.

Until well after the middle of the nineteenth century, the external connections of the Latin countries, whether economic or cultural, were predominantly with the countries of western Europe. Thereafter the impact of the United States was felt with increasing force, which aroused considerable alarm lest the northern behemoth should establish dominance over the proudly independent Latin states. These developments will be explained later (Chapter XXVIII).

PHYSICAL EXPANSION OF THE UNITED STATES

If continental United States were superimposed upon Europe it would stretch from London to the Urals and from Sweden to the African shore. England and Wales are no bigger than Illinois; France could be fitted nicely into Montana and Idaho, the Germany of 1914 into Texas, Italy into California; only

Russia among European countries compares with the United States in extent.

From the Mississippi, the boundary of the original United States, the nation spread irresistibly westward until the Pacific called a halt to expansion. Parcel by parcel, thinly populated border regions were annexed, peacefully in all but one instance, though not without sharp diplomatic encounters with the imperial powers of Western Europe. As districts were settled and knit to the older area by transportation facilities, they were granted political equality with the original states of the Union.

The most important single fact in the growth of the United States was the purchase and then the peopling of the immense Louisiana Territory. Vast in space and at first with undefined boundaries, the Territory extended from the mouth of the Mississippi northward and westward to the formidable Rockies. Except for a French settlement in and around New Orleans and a scattering of land-hungry pioneers from the States, the area was inhabited only by wandering tribes of Indians. By a stroke of bold and imaginative statecraft the United States in 1803 bought the Louisiana Territory from Napoleonic France for a song.

After no little astute diplomacy and the assumption of American claims on Spain up to $5,000,000, the Stars and Stripes in 1819 supplanted the flag of Spain in the peninsula of Florida. Texas, a province of Mexico, stood next on the agenda. Impelled by the desire for fresh land and visions of "manifest destiny," a thin trickle of settlers had flowed into Texas from the United States. Chafing under the Mexican administration, which certainly left much to be desired, the immigrants rebelled in 1836, proclaimed the independence of Texas and begged for admission to the Northern Union.

Hesitantly and partly at least out of fear that the huge Lone Star Republic of magnificent potentialities might gravitate into the British

Mexicans raided San Antonio in 1842; the Texans attempted a reprisal against the Mexican town of Mier. The Texan expedition is seen here descending the Rio Grande.

On May 8, 1846, hostilities began against Mexico with a cannon duel at Palo Alto (above)—a few miles north of the Rio Grande in what is now part of the state of Texas.

imperial orbit, the Congress of the United States voted in 1845 to welcome the state into the Union. Mexico, which had never acknowledged the independence of Texas, retorted by withdrawing her diplomatic representative from Washington. Besides, it was suspected in Mexico, and with reason, that the United States coveted other territories under the Mexican flag. Bellicose nationalism in the Mexican governing class collided with an urge to expansion that had become dominant in the Northern colossus. Ever since Mexico broke away from Spain the country had been in a state of chronic turbulence; property of citizens of the United States had suffered injury, for which compensation by Mexico was not forthcoming.

To embitter the antagonism, it was claimed by the United States that the left bank of the Rio Grande River belonged by right to Texas, a claim which Mexico disputed. Overtures by Washington to settle differences peacefully and to purchase territory ranging off to the Pacific were repulsed by Mexican authorities. Then in 1846 an armed force of the United States, sent to occupy the strip between the Rio Grande and the Nueces Rivers, clashed with Mexican troops and several soldiers of the United States were killed. That sanguinary incident furnished the Congress of the United States with persuasive grounds for declaring war upon Mexico. If the course pursued by Washington was less than pretty, it was, to be sure, paralleled in the dealings of strong European powers with smaller neighbors.

Over the protestations of a vocal, dissenting minority, the United States in its first large-scale foreign adventure fought Mexico. The war was won at small cost and quickly. As spoils of victory, in a peace settlement of 1848, the United States acquired legal sovereignty not alone over Texas, but over a veritable empire running off to California and California itself. A token money payment to Mexico sealed the transaction. Presently a small fragment on the south was bought (1853) from Mexico—the Gadsden Purchase—but agitation for the annexation of the remainder of the Latin Republic was turned aside.

Meantime an acrimonious dispute with Britain over the Oregon country had been amicably resolved. British commercial interests had pushed from Canada into the northern section of Oregon, while several thousand citizens of the United States, trappers and traders chiefly, had drifted into the southern tier. Imperially minded Yankees claimed for their country the Pacific coast up to the border of Russian Alaska. That extravagant pretension was, however, repelled by the cabinet in London. After considerable bellicose talk, the United States prudently accepted (1846) a compromise, splitting the Northwest Coast at the Forty-ninth Parallel, but giving all Vancouver Island to Britain.

In less than half a century, then, while the imperial urge in Europe lay rather dormant, the domain of the United States had been pushed to its continental maximum. Here was a large, unbroken country shaped like a rectangle, except for outthrusting salients in New England, Florida and southern Texas, and the indentation of Ontario peninsula, north of Lake Erie. Immense size and compactness conferred upon the United States the inestimable military advantage of great depth.

WHY THE UNITED STATES ATTAINED GREAT POWER STATURE

Not until Europe had fully appraised the contribution of the United States in the First World War was the trans-Atlantic Republic popularly admitted to the exclusive circle of Great Powers. But progress toward that stature had been abundantly indicated in the nineteenth century, with gathering momentum after the War between the States. The salient elements in the meteoric rise of the United States admit of no debate.

Breadth of the land base, while impressive, was of secondary significance; Australia or Brazil is as large as the United States, Canada even bigger, but none of them belongs in the Great Power category. It must, however, be noted that circumstances of geography, two broad ocean moats conspicuously, relieved the United States of the nineteenth century from serious threat of foreign invasion. Brawn, brains and resources, which European countries felt obliged to expend on military preparedness could be applied to more productive purposes in the New World Republic.

First of all, the United States profited from the unexcelled gifts of nature. The varied and beneficent climate has been conducive to human well-being and energy. Fertile soil was available in lush abundance; nine out of ten acres in the Republic produced some kind of economic wealth and a trifle more than half of the land surface was suitable for cultivation. That beneficence yielded a splendid variety and quantity of crops, livestock and forest products.

Treasures of the soil were matched by extensive and marvelously balanced subterreanean resources upon which a highly industrialized society could be built. Mineral fuel was available in the form of bountiful, almost inexhaustible stocks of coal, supplemented by supplies of oil, natural gas and waterpower. Most of the metals required in machine-industry were mined within the borders of the country. Output of iron ore, for example, enabled the United States to surpass all other nations in steel production by a wide margin. This natural wealth stirred admiration, not untinged with envy, in European capitals. Withal the United States was not wholly self-sufficient, for it depended upon foreign supplies of tropical and semi-tropical foodstuffs and certain industrial raw materials such as jute and silk, rubber and tin, platinum and manganese.

In the second place, the population of the United States has grown prodigiously because of natural increase and a steady influx from Europe. At the first census in 1790, the population was just under 4,000,000, it topped 31,000,000 in 1860, 63,000,000 in 1890, 92,000,000 in 1910, and by 1960 passed 186,000,000, or greater than the United Kingdom, France and Germany put together. Most significant doubtless was the occupation of the Mississippi Valley, which contained about 36,500,000 people in 1910 as against a mere 130,000 in 1790.

The number of immigrants from Europe in the course of the nineteenth century exceeded 38,000,000. Sentiments chiseled on the base of the Statue of Liberty were addressed to the Old World:

> Give me your tired, your poor,
> Your huddled masses yearning to breathe free,
> The wretched refuse of your teeming shore,
> Send these, the homeless, tempest-tossed, to me. . . .

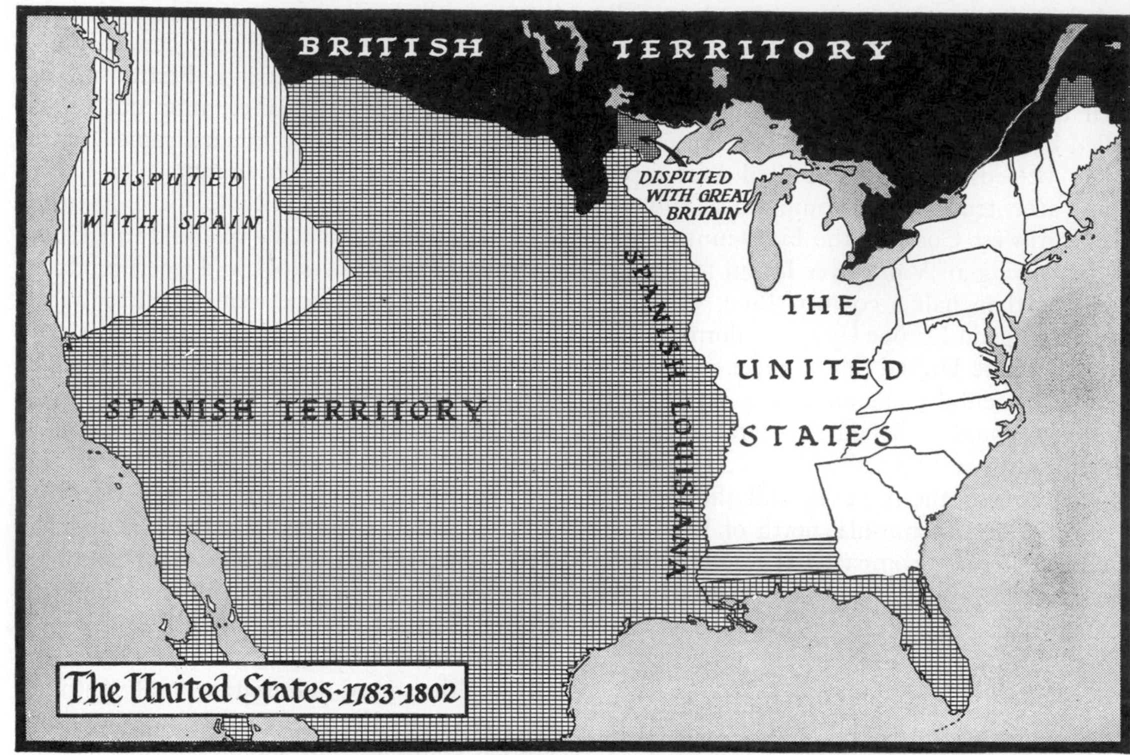

The United States-1783-1802

The Growth of the Continental

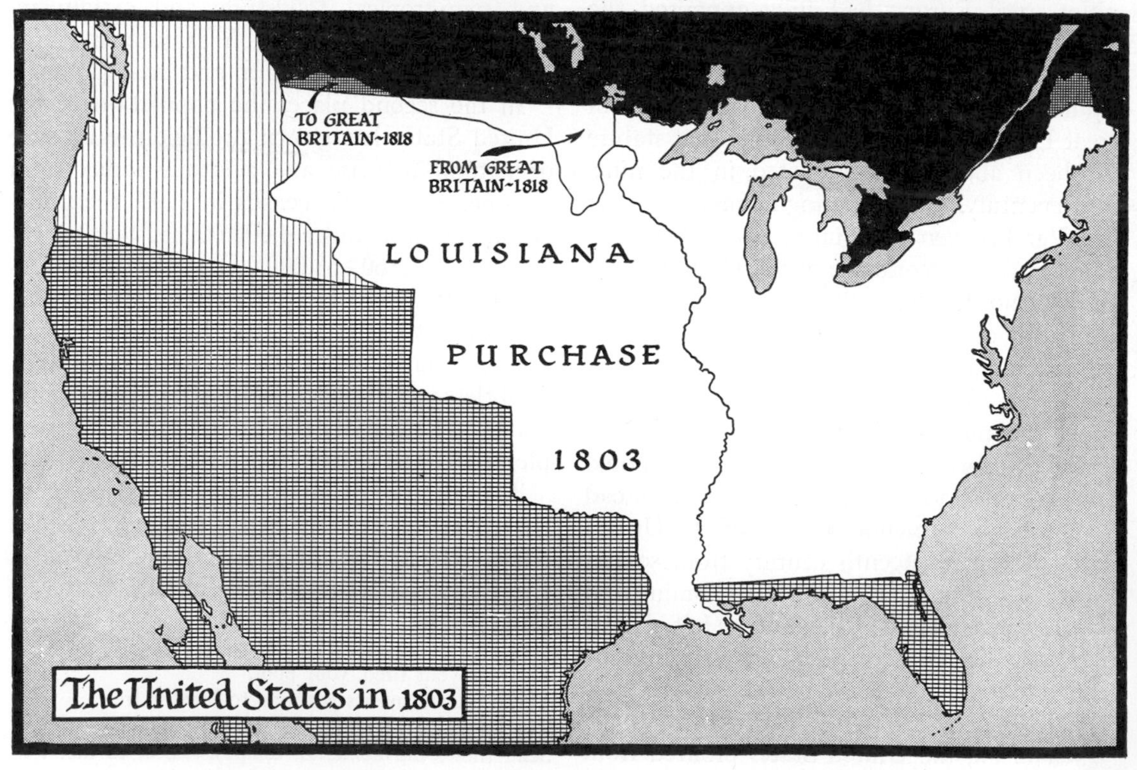

The United States in 1803

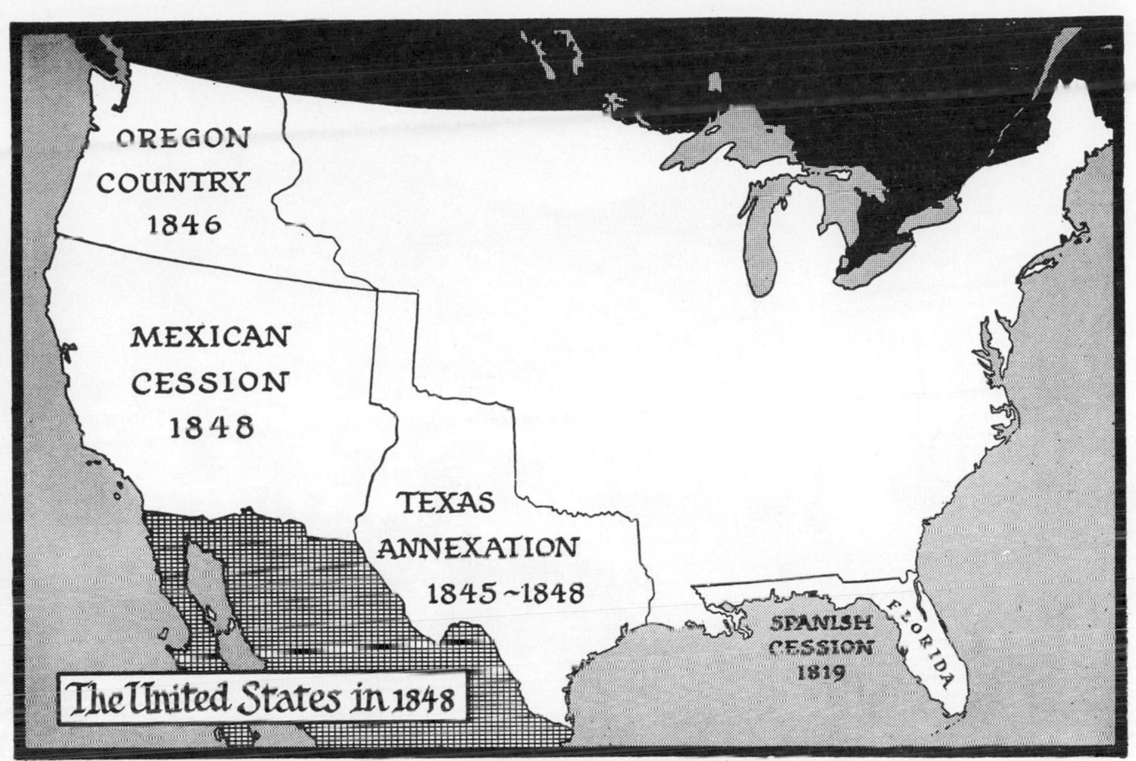

United States, 1783~1853

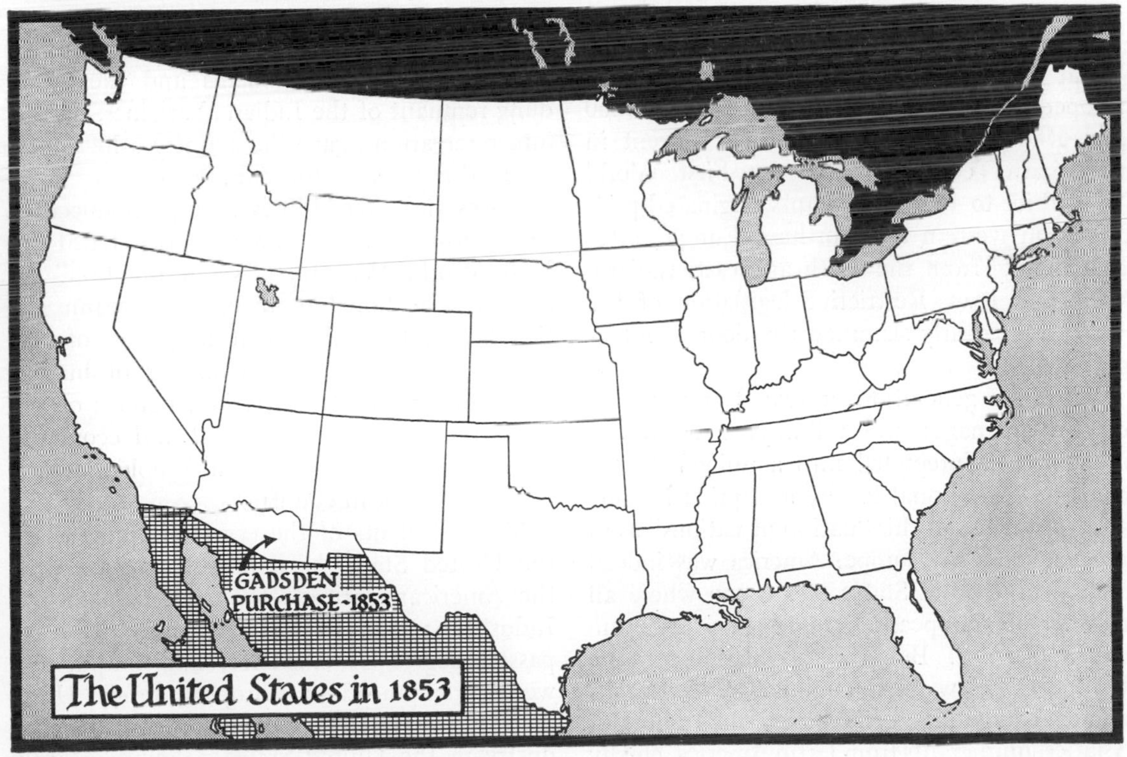

Iron ore furnace on the site of the future city of Marquette, Michigan, 1849

What started as a stream after Waterloo developed into a river between 1840 and 1860 and attained the dimensions of a torrent in the quarter century before the First World War. Prior to 1890 immigrants originated principally in western and northern Europe; after that mainly from the south and east, Italians, Slavs and Jews. Restrictive legislation of the 1920's very nearly slammed the door of immigration shut.

Within a generation or two, Europeans of diverse languages and folkways were almost miraculously integrated into a unified American whole. National loyalty and pride became at least as keen in this "nation of nations" as in the countries of Europe. America was indeed a kind of United States of Europe where all manner of Europeans lived together and generally liked it. But the population of the United States was not confined to Europeans alone. A large bloc of Negroes, small knots of Asiatics, immigrants from Latin America, chiefly Mexicans, French Canadians and the dwindling remnant of the Indian aborigines, herded into reservations, gave the country a highly diversified human complexion.

Biases along racial lines were pronounced in the South and on the Pacific coast. Until the First World War the "Negro question" remained a sectional problem, but became national with the subsequent migration of Negroes to northern cities. Conflicts of human adjustment within the spacious borders of the United States threw up social and economic perplexities akin to the minority problems which plagued European countries.

Many students of the economic progress of the United States have been impressed with the American aptitude for machine industry. Industrial processes were carried to an unsurpassed degree of efficiency, and output per worker ran ahead of European levels. Unrestrained by inherited ways of doing things, industry in the United States sighed constantly for new worlds to conquer. Ever-expanding technological knowledge was reflected in more efficient tools and better operating methods.

Russian and Polish immigrants being vaccinated at Quarantine, New York, 1881

NEW WORLD DYNAMIC

Inventions, applied science, faith in technical progress distinguished the dynamic New World society. An infectious zest for bigger and better things inspired an endless stream of innovations and experiment. "Hard times" might indeed halt the tempo of expansion briefly, then it moved forward more sensationally than before. The vitality of youth, dash and restlessness were accompanied by unquenchable optimism. As a perceptive European observer remarked, the citizen of the United States knows "there will be a tomorrow. And he believes in tomorrow."

Freedom of economic enterprise and political stability—aided by constitutional elasticity—assisted the United States in marching forward. Conditions of existence on a virgin continent reinforced the proud colonial traditions of ingenuity, self-reliance and resourcefulness. Doctrines of economic individualism and personal push required no elaborate philosophical exposition in the United States, needed no learned school of "classical economists."

Experience itself and the popular theological teaching that the individual was a free moral agent buttressed the creed of individualism. In time that faith was carried over from a rural and agricultural economy to a heavily urban and industrialized society. America was a land (like other newly opened countries) where careers were open to talents, where the ordinary fellow had a better chance to escape from the treadmill of scarcity and the thraldom of insecurity. A premium was placed upon adventuresomeness, which was particularly conducive to the growth of competitive enterprise. Faith in the values and virtues of unfettered economic individualism—with little concern for its faults and shortcomings—had deeper acceptance in the United States than in major European countries.

As another point, the United States drew generously upon the economic innovations and the reservoirs of capital in Europe. Improvements in agricultural and manufacturing processes, for example, in which Britain pioneered, were borrowed by the United States. Researches of German scientists laid the foundation for some American chemical industries. Direct investments by Europeans in American undertakings and credits extended to importers also assisted substantially in the unfolding of the United States. For more than a century, the trans-Atlantic Republic was a debtor, on balance, to Europe. Interest and principal on loans from abroad were long satisfied by exports of food and raw materials.

Yankee ingenuity contrived improvements in European bequests, it is true, but to a considerable degree, the United States relied upon the technological experiences, the inventions and the capital of the Old World. In the fullness of time, America experienced the thrill which accrues to the pupil who outruns his master: Europe copied the industrial methods of the United States and obtained desperately needed "know-how" and capital from the New World titan.

NATIONAL ECONOMY TO 1860

For more than a century, cultivation of the soil was the predominant occupation in the United States. As late as 1860 five out of six inhabitants were listed as rural. Land-hungry pioneers plodded steadily westward, blocking out farms in the virgin earth of the Mississippi Basin. According to the thesis of a distinct school of United States historians "the ever retreating frontier of free land is the key to American development."

Methods of farming in America tended to be slovenly, skilless, wasteful and that tradition was encouraged by the difficulty of transporting crops in excess of local consumption. Northern and western farmers—or at least those living at a distance from waterways—were chained to a simple, subsistence type of agriculture. In the Southland, on the other hand, along seacoast and rivers, commercial farming on plantations flourished. Tobacco, "that bewitching vegetable," raw cotton and other specialties found ready markets in Europe.

Eli Whitney in 1793 brought forth a famous machine that cleaned as much cotton in a day as ten slaves. That contrivance made cotton-raising lucrative, riveting Negro bondage upon the South. The cotton crop jumped from 500,000 pounds in 1793 to 90,000,000 pounds by 1810. Exports of cotton, which were negligible before the Whitney invention, soared beyond a million bales by 1850. King Cotton was solidly seated on his southern throne.

Model of Whitney's original cotton gin

Ingenious Yankees contributed significantly to the invention or improvement of farm equipment. A few decades indeed witnessed more valuable innovations in agricultural tools than many centuries had seen. In particular, labor-saving implements marvelously speeded up the processes of plowing and of reaping grain and grass. At the start of the nineteenth century fields were generally turned up with a clumsy wooden "bull" plow; though a solid cast iron plowshare had already been made, farmers feared that it would poison the soil or shied away at the price.

By the 1830's, however, tradition and superstition had been overcome and factories turning out efficient iron plows found ready purchasers for their wares. In 1837, John Deere of Illinois brought forth a light-weight steel plow, easily cleaned and well-suited to the needs of heavy prairie land. At first, mills in Prussia supplied part of the steel; but very soon, relatively cheap and strong plows wholly made in America set the standard for the world.

For some minds the skillful mower, cutting wheat or clover with scythe or "cradle," represents the poetry of motion. But in fact it was slow, exhausting work. That branch of farming was revolutionized by the machine reaper, devised principally by Cyrus H. McCormick. His first machines appeared on the market in 1840 and within a generation reapers were being extensively used on the grain-growing prairies and on some large estates in Europe. Subsequently the binder was added to the reaper and together they enabled a single farm worker to do what had required a dozen men. Machinery helped to make the United States a granary of Europe, but the machine did not remedy wasteful methods of cultivation.

In the meantime, labor-saving machines were transforming the manufacture of goods. Machinofacture in the United States may be said to date from 1789 when an English mechanic smuggled in the jealously guarded secrets of

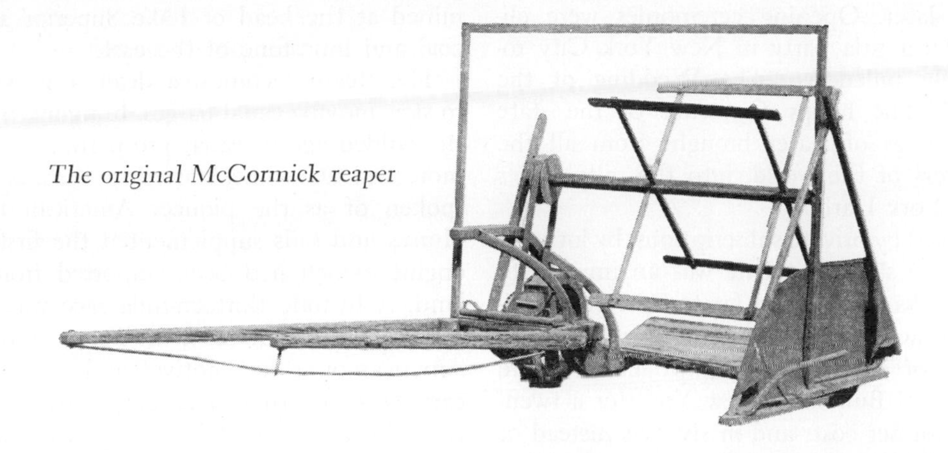

The original McCormick reaper

British textile factory machinery. During the Napoleonic era, when all manufactured wares were difficult to procure from Britain, small mills and factories popped up like mushrooms. In this germinating stage, Britain was drawn upon for technological knowledge and machinery.

Yet Yankee minds were not idle. It seemed to Ralph Waldo Emerson that Americans had "the power and habit of invention in their brain." Eli Whitney not only devised the cotton gin but fathered the idea of interchangeable parts. That principle, indispensable for mass production, he applied most fully while executing a government order for muskets during the War of 1812. Europeans referred to interchangeable parts as "the American system of manufacturing."

Robert Fulton made the steamboat a practical proposition, Charles Goodyear hit upon a way (1839) of vulcanizing rubber, Morse made the telegraph workable, and in 1849 Elias Howe lightened the chores of the housewife and stimulated the making of clothes in factories by his sewing machine. Industrial inventions spilled out indeed at such tempo that the Commissioner of Patents wrote in 1843: "The advancement of the arts from year to year taxes our credulity," and he lugubriously predicted "the arrival of that period when human improvement must end."

As in Britain, trade unions arose in the United States late in the eighteenth century, but had very rough sledding in their early days with employers, press and pulpit stubbornly resistant to organized pressure for higher pay, shorter hours or better conditions of employment. Boston master carpenters, for instance, vetoed (1830) demands of craftsmen for a ten hour day on the score that it would open "a wide door for idleness and vice" and that unionism was "an evil of foreign growth." Court decisions flatly condemned trade union practices as conspiratorial.

TRANSPORTATION FACILITIES

If machine industry was to prosper on the grand scale, if agriculture in the trans-Appalachian region was to become commercialized, inexpensive and faster means of communication were required. Beginning in the 1790's journeys by land became less rough and taxing with the construction of turnpikes, on Macadam engineering principles. Freight rates dropped, though not sufficiently to make haulage of bulky commodities feasible, and hard roads were confined to seaboard regions.

The appearance of canals ushered in a new era of cheap transportation. Most profitable of the early canals was the Erie, the original Thruway of New York State, running from Lake Erie at Buffalo to Albany on the Hudson River. Finished in 1825, this waterway tied the immense Great Lakes region to the wharves of New York City. It was the largest construction undertaking in the Americas to that time and the building, all done by hand, was no less exacting than the Panama Canal job nearly a century later. Opening ceremonies were climaxed by a gala party in New York City romantically billed as "The Wedding of the Waters." The happy Governor of the state emptied kegs of water brought from all the large rivers of the world, into the salty waves of New York Harbor.

Financed by private subscriptions, by lotteries and by the state, the Erie was an immediate success, tolls bringing in fat ten per cent dividends annually. Bustling cities like Rochester rose out of forest and swamps. Goods were hauled from Buffalo to New York for a twentieth of former costs and in six days instead of twenty. Canals were hurriedly dug in other areas, and with rivers and the Great Lakes they moved most of the internal trade to about 1860. As busy ribbons of commerce these inland waterways enjoyed only brief glory, but the Great Lakes continued to serve the nation in the transport of wheat, and in bringing together at steel-making centers the iron ore mined at the head of Lake Superior and the coal and limestone of the east.[4]

The steam locomotive dealt a heavy blow to slow-moving canal barges, bringing to a close the golden age of canal prosperity. The Baltimore and Ohio line, started in 1828, is usually spoken of as the pioneer American railway. Horses and sails supplemented the first steam engine, which had been imported from England. A historic thirteen-mile race was run in 1830 near Baltimore with *Tom Thumb*, an American-built locomotive, and a horse and carriage competing. The horse nosed out the Iron Horse. But the following year a prize winning American engine pulled a fifteen ton weight at fifteen miles an hour.

There ensued a feverish orgy of railway build-

[4] The Soo Canal, lifeline of American heavy industry, connecting Lake Superior with Lake Huron, has been called "the most important mile in America." Traffic exceeded in 1955 the combined tonnage of the Panama, Suez and Kiel Canals.

Junction of the Erie Canal with the Hudson River at Albany, New York, a contemporary engraving

The Baltimore and Ohio locomotive Tom Thumb lost this race against a fast horse on August 28, 1830.

ing; wood with all its hazards served as fuel until about 1848. The fifties witnessed furious competition for Middle Western traffic; Chicago, the principal objective of these rivalries, commenced to boom and bloom with St. Louis, another major beneficiary. In spite of the multiplicity of railway companies, a standard gauge for tracks was first adopted in the 1860's. Certain of the early railways as well as most of the canals were public enterprises, but experimentation with government ownership and operation was soon abandoned as uneconomical.

By 1860 some 30,000 miles of track had been laid down and railways had outstripped waterways as haulers of goods. Farming in the Middle West had entered the commercial stage and manufacturing had captured an important place in the economy of the area. Nearly half the population of the Republic now resided west of the Appalachians.

It was agreed almost from the beginning of the independent existence of America that tariffs should not hamper the flow of goods between the several states. That decision opened to native business a market ultimately spanning the continent. Only this enormous home market could have provided the opportunity for the sensational achievements of mass production in the twentieth century.[5]

[5] After the First World War, charges by states on motor trucks hauling goods across state lines were tantamount to tariffs.

But the free trade principle was not applied to foreign productions. It was in 1816 that tariffs were adopted to shield industries which had been established during the Napoleonic wars. Protection saved small factories and mills from extinction—but they did not always remain infants. Yet, ever since, except for short intervals, the United States has clung doggedly to the dogma of tariff protectionism.

AS OF 1860

Down to 1860 then the United States was preponderantly an agricultural country, not rich as compared to Britain, for example, though the population exceeded that of the British Isles.

Cities had matured in the East, where waterpower to drive factories was at hand, and beyond the Appalachian Mountains. The agricultural South, on the other hand, contained few cities. New York had already outstripped Berlin and Rome in population, though it was still far behind London and Paris. Thomas Jefferson, who was thoroughly familiar with Paris, dreaded the emergence of huge communities in the New World. "I view the great cities," he said, "as pestilential to the morals, the health, and the liberties of man." But neither the Sage of Monticello (nor anyone else) could have checked the urbanization that accompanied industrialism.

Economic growth and territorial expansion

"Coronation of Jenny the First—Queen of the Americans" was Punch's *original caption to this cartoon on Jenny Lind's tour in the United States. The faces and attitudes ascribed to us reflect current European notions of our crudeness in the 1850's.*

exerted quickening influences upon the national spirit of the United States. There were echoes of just that in the productions of the American mind. In his most influential literary piece, *The American Scholar*, Emerson adjured (1837) his generation: "We have listened too long to the courtly muses of Europe . . ." For the future he promised, "We will walk on our own feet; we will work with our own hands; we will speak with our own minds."

Less exalted was the exuberance of a Southern gentleman in conversation with an English traveler. The latter had remarked that Providence evidently intended Great Britain and the United States to civilize the globe: "Two nations?" broke in the American, "Guess there's only one, stranger; goin' to annex that island of yourn one of them fine days; don't know how little Vic will like that, but got to do it, and no mistake about that." [6]

[6] Allan Nevins, ed. *American Social History as recorded by British Travellers* (New York, 1923), p. 293.

By 1860 visitors from Europe had written a voluminous literature on the trans-Atlantic Republic, part of it perceptive, some of it ill-informed, part of it flattering, some of it derogatory, little enough of it balanced and dispassionate. Alert Europeans were aware that agricultural machinery from the United States had carried off blue ribbons at the London International Exhibition of 1851 and that American sewing machines, rubber articles, locks and revolvers—as well as such oddities as crackers, rocking chairs and mint juleps—had excited interest and admiration. It was known, too, that a Yankee yacht, the *America*, had outsailed the British best and that the clipper ship *Rainbow* had victoriously challenged the "onrushing tyranny" of steampower.

On another level, the United States had been exporting ideological intangibles to Europe—ideas of personal freedom and popular government, ideas of constitutionalism, ideas of the rights of women and the wrongs of slavery. Withal, many a European still conceived of the

United States solely in terms of the Atlantic seaboard, firmly anchored in the culture and mores of the Old World. Likely enough, the West was assigned to Indians, bison and fur-bearing animals, and the South, to picturesque landlords with their cheroots and slaves.

To ordinary Europeans the United States of 1860 may well have seemed a confused hodge-podge of wooden houses, crude manners, pigs cavorting noisily in the streets, gunmen with glistening barrels lurking at any city corner and out beyond a limitless star-spangled wilderness.[7]

As of 1860, America implied to many a European a place in which food and raw materials were procured, manufactured articles disposed of, surplus cash invested and emigrants absorbed—a sort of dependency, still, of the Old World. Few would have foretold that in the remaining decades of the century the United States would crowd into a place alongside of the top-flight powers.

Not many foreigners were as perspicacious as Edward Creasy who at the mid-century alluded to "the mighty commonwealth of the Western Continent which now commands the admiration of mankind. That homage is sometimes reluctantly given, and is sometimes accompanied with suspicion and ill-will. But none can refuse it. All the physical essentials for national strength are undeniably to be found in the geographical position and amplitude of territory which the United States possess: in their almost inexhaustible tracts of fertile but hitherto untouched soil, in their stately forests, in their mountain chains and rivers, their beds of coal, and stores of metallic wealth, in their extensive sea-board . . . and in their already numerous and rapidly-increasing population. . . . No one can look on this fearless energy, the sturdy determination, the aptitude for local self-government, the versatile alacrity, and the unresting spirit of enterprise which characterize the Anglo-American [sic], without feeling that here he beholds the true elements of progressive might."[8]

FROM APPOMATTOX TO ARMAGEDDON

On the broad scroll of the nineteenth century the War between the States in America (1861–1865) and the wars between the German states ran parallel in time and in purpose—national unity. But the agonizing ordeal in the New World had larger meaning than that. It left the Southland socially disrupted, impoverished, prostrate, a generation of young men cut down on the battlefield or physically and mentally maimed. Bitterness lingered. The war liberated some 4,000,000 slaves, but neglected to provide them with land as had been the happier lot of the Russian serfs upon emancipation. And the war released dynamic industrial elements which swiftly transformed the United States in a manner unequalled in history.

Military requirements resembled a forced draft under northern industry. Great meat-packing concerns were organized and the output of iron mills increased sharply, speeded along by the construction of two railways which bound the Mississippi Valley to the Pacific coast.

Expansion of industry in the North after 1865 proceeded at a fabulous pace, carrying the United States to first place among manufacturing nations by the 1890's; it had ranked only fourth in 1860. Whereas production of pig iron was in 1865 only a fifth that of Britain, Britain was passed in 1887 and by 1900, American output equalled that of Britain and Germany together. Steel production touched nearly 12,000,000 tons in 1899, a ninefold increase over 1880. Between 1899 and 1914 overall industrial output in the United States doubled, exceeding Britain, Germany and France combined. As another sign of the age, ten times as

[7] As late as 1893, the firm of Karl Baedeker of Leipzig, king of guidebook publishers, in the first edition of *Baedekers United States* felt obliged to explain: "Throughout the country traveling is now as safe as in the most civilized parts of Europe and the carrying of arms is unnecessary." But the book added paternally, "When ladies are of the party it is best to frequent only the best hotels. . . . Restaurants which solicit the patronage of gents should be avoided."

[8] Edward Creasy, *The Fifteen Decisive Battles of the World* (London, 1851), p. 323.

Running eastward in 1869 to the famous ceremony of driving the "last spike" of the transcontinental railway system, a Central Pacific Special is shown here passing a westward-faring train of prairie schooners.

many American patents were granted in the last third of the century as in the first two-thirds.

It was an era of imaginative economic empire-builders who cultivated a domineering Napoleonic manner. Bold, resourceful business organizers appreciated the advantages of centralized control and administrative links with banking houses much as prevailed in Germany. They fastened their grip on every instrument of production from day laborer to politician and they frequently exploited natural resources with reckless prodigality. Many a business "tycoon," furthermore, was not averse to violence if that seemed necessary to attain his ends; many a prominent capitalist exhibited small vision beyond the orbit of his personal power.

Business organization changed radically as large corporations, concentrating industrial and financial resources, more and more overshadowed the individual proprietor or smaller partnership of an earlier period. Gigantic leagues of capital, spoken of under the general name of "trusts," appeared in many branches of industrial activity. Standard Oil set the pace and pattern for immense concentrations of business, gathering unto itself by 1879 about 90 per cent of the refineries and pipelines in the Republic.

Operating on a large scale and efficiently, these enterprises effected economies in production and distribution. By and large, they supplied commodities of superior quality at lower prices. But, on the other side, they tended to create monopolies yielding excessive earnings and forcing smaller competitors to the wall. Crowning the trend was the formation of "holding companies," corporate institutions owning the shares of stock and other securities of several firms; the giant of them all and typical in structure was the United States Steel Corporation (or "Steel Trust") founded in 1901. This combination merged ten iron and steel companies, commanding nearly 70 per cent of raw steel capacity, and later other firms were annexed to the empire. By 1910 approximately three-quarters of all manufactured goods were being turned out by large corporations.

In and of itself industrial bigness was not socially reprehensible, but when greed for gain overrode common sense, defied the general welfare and corrupted political morality that was something else. "We nearly transferred complete political power to those who controlled corporate wealth," President W. H. Taft one day observed, "and we were in danger of a plutocracy."

Long since popular pressure had arisen for government action to defeat the monopolistic implications of business concentrations, to ensure values to consumers at highly competitive prices. Which is to say that the prevalent economic doctrine of laissez faire, enjoining that the government should keep hands off business, had been weighed in the balances and found wanting. Around 1890 state after state passed legislation to regulate industrial combinations and to eradicate other iniquities of corporate business. But those laws were not faithfully enforced.

In 1890, the federal government adopted the fundamental Sherman Act, pointed against "trusts." Drafted in a hurry, the law contained many gaps and at first was rendered ineffective because of court interpretations. Subsequently, refinements were introduced in the regulations affecting business combinations and prosecution of violators was pressed with greater resolution. Courts of law ordered the dissolution of some quasi-monopolies into individual and competing firms, as was the case, for instance, with the Standard Oil Company of New Jersey (1911).

By supplementing and closing loopholes in existing statutes, the Clayton Act of 1914 substantially extended public authority over corporate enterprise. Not to smash "big business" and so sacrifice the advantages of large volume, the avowed objective of the Clayton legislation was to enforce free and fair competitive trade. The last word on "trusts," however, had by no means yet been written.

RAILS AND MOTORS

Construction of railways was pushed with such zeal and zest after Appomattox that by 1910 the United States had 240,000 miles of trackage, as much as all the countries of Europe. The automatic coupler (1863) and the Westinghouse air-brake (1869) came into common use in the 1880's making rail travel swifter and safer and requiring more steel in the manufacture of cars. Carrying capacity of cars was enlarged and gradually all-steel cars became the vogue; in 1867 the luxurious Pullman car was placed in service. As in Europe, extension of railways accelerated industrial growth generally.

Land and other concessions were handed out to railway companies by the federal government with lavish generosity. The Northern Pacific road, for example, was the recipient of about 12,000,000 acres, an area equal to New York and Massachusetts. Instead of being servants, railway concerns threatened to become masters. Congress stepped in, it is true, with the Interstate Commerce Act of 1887, which prescribed that railway charges should be reasonable and should be determined by a federal commission. But court decisions impaired the force of the law, leaving companies virtually free to fix rates as they pleased. Two decades of controversy ensued, ending when laws empowered (1906) the commission to veto unreasonable or discriminatory charges and to set maximum rates (1910).

Before the regulation of railways had been adequately achieved, motor vehicles had appeared as sturdy competitors in transportation. Beginnings were crude indeed, usually reflections of European pioneering, but evolution was steady: the steam motor (1875), the electric motor (1891), and then in 1892, the brothers Duryea, Charles and Frank, startled Springfield, Massachusetts, with a gasoline engine featuring electric ignition and a spray carburetor. For convenience and cost the gasoline car excelled competing machines.

The way was open for the amazing performance of Henry Ford. Ford appreciated that automobiles were expensive because there were so few of them and that there were so few of them because they were so expensive. The central tenet of Ford's faith was that low cost production through maximum division of labor would yield benefits for the consumer. As no one before him, the Wizard of Detroit demonstrated, for all the world to see, the tremendous potentialities of the machine-belt and assembly line. By 1916, 3,500,000 cars, open jobs, to be

One-cylinder, four horsepower Duryea automobile, 1893

sure, were on the road. The motor car had become an established feature of American living. Prices of cars had tumbled to a level which put them within reach of millions—with untold consequences for the life of the Republic.

Ever more efficient, power-driven machinery spoke tirelessly and raucously the language of the age—the language of mass production. Investment of capital per worker ranged much higher than in Europe, bringing the advantages of greater division of labor. Output per factory worker just about doubled between 1865 and 1899 and doubled again in the next thirty years. Overall production multiplied much faster than the population. Between 1860 and 1919 production of manufactured articles in the United States increased about thirty times—a sensational record which caused all the world to gasp.

Mass production entailed greater standardization in goods. Articles identical in appearance were manufactured in large quantities to be sold at low prices. The Model T Ford may be cited as Exhibit A in that connection—buyers could choose any color so long as they chose black.

INDUSTRIAL WAGE WORKERS

By about 1910 the balance of population in the United States had shifted from country to city. Nevertheless, America offered a pleasing variety of living across its vast expanse. Urban and suburban Massachusetts differed from rural Vermont, highly diversified Illinois from agricultural Mississippi. Precisely as in western Europe, the shift from farm to factory was accompanied by great disparities in income and style of living between opulent capital owner and wage worker.

And yet the history of the industrial workers in the United States by no means exactly duplicated the record of the Old World. So long as free land was available in the West, employers were obliged to offer attractive terms in order to hold workmen. Opportunities for personal improvement in a young country of gigantic resources and a splendid future, relatively high standards of comfort, the deeply ingrained spirit of individualism, the diversity of language and customs among immigrant workers—all accounted for the differences between wage workers on the two sides of the Atlantic.

About 1875 grave worker discontent manifested itself. Demands were raised for a larger share of the industrial income, more leisure and better conditions of employment. Many a worker was irked by the many and varied regulations laid down by the employer. Illustrative were the rules of the Cambria Iron and Steel Works of 1874. It was prescribed that "Persons detected in stealing coal will be charged the price of a load of coal for every lump so stolen and persons taking wood, fencing, mine timber, or other timber, will be charged the price of a cord of wood for each and every stick so taken." Brawling on company premises, another rule warned, would be corrected "by a fine of not less than five dollars nor more than ten dollars [fully a week's wages] or the discharge of the offender."

Owners and managers responded violently and negatively to worker demands. No one would tell them how to run their establishments, no one. Robust individualism had enabled them to prosper, grow rotund around the equator, had it not? Every man should look out for himself, adherence to that philosophy had brought wealth to the nation and would do even better in the future. Above all, government must not intervene in economic matters, save to act as policeman. Some companies attempted to protect themselves against labor troubles by the employment of spies and private police. Blacklists and allied devices were invoked by employers against troublemaking workmen.

Serious industrial strife of national dimensions broke out in 1877 among railway men who had suffered wage cuts and nursed other grievances. From coast to coast strikes were attended by rioting and destruction of railway property. The intervention of state and federal troops restored order at the cost of lives on both sides; strikers drifted back to their jobs without gaining their objectives. Those con-

Destruction in the railroad yards at Pittsburgh, a product of the 1877 strikes

troversies heralded three decades of recurrent and bitter strife between men and management; as a rule, aggrieved workpeople called for higher wages and a shortened workday. Disturbances affecting many branches of industry were marked by mob turbulence and regular battles with guardians of the law in which blood was shed. Only Imperial Russia among European countries, it seems fair to say, witnessed worse industrial disputes than the United States.

During the early phase of unrest, existing craft unions were built up and new unions were organized to defend or advance the interests of the wage earners. For the most part, they were local associations without any central direction. The first permanent union on a national basis was founded in 1881 and baptized as the American Federation of Labor five years later. It grew steadily, reaching a membership of over 4,000,000 by 1920, very largely skilled craftsmen, the aristocracy of labor. Few unions existed outside of national organizations and only one legitimate union operated in a given craft—both points in which the trade union structure of the United States differed from the pattern in Britain, for example. Successive acts of Congress strengthened unions that had been formed among railway workers.

Leaders of American unions, like their prototypes in Great Britain, were conservative, preferring peaceful bargaining with management to spectacular industrial warfare. When Labor Day was proclaimed as a national holiday in 1894 less than one industrial worker in ten belonged to a union. But unionization grew at a modest pace regardless of attacks under conspiracy laws and court injunctions. Eventually the Clayton Act of 1914 banned the issuance of injunctions to prevent peaceful quitting of work, peaceful persuasion or peaceful picketing.

Despite occasional setbacks due to temporary recessions in business, the trend of real wages advanced rapidly, doubling about every thirty to forty years, faster than had ever before happened in history. Hours of employment declined, chances for advancement were good and working conditions generally improved, though worker welfare legislation lagged behind the measures of the major countries of Europe. To promote the interests of wage workers, a Department of Labor was added in 1913 to the national cabinet.

ANTICAPITALISM

The history of anticapitalist political movements in the United states contrasted sharply with the swing of events in Great Britain and on the European Continent. In the late nineteenth century collectivist parties, Marxist on the Continent, expanded in all the industrialized countries of Europe. Anticapitalist literature circulated and anticapitalist parties were formed in the United States, it is true, mainly among German immigrants, and there were outcroppings of anarchism; President William McKinley was murdered in 1901 by an adherent of that radical doctrine.

Advocates of collectivism in any of its varieties were reviled on every side as "un-American revolutionaries," who deserved to be struck down. Nonetheless, a Socialist Party on evolutionary Marxist foundations came into being in 1898. The party polled its highest proportion of votes in the presidential election of 1912—a trifle more than six per cent. The principal domestic importance indeed of the anticapitalist ideology lay in the impulse to social legislation it exerted upon the country at large.

More militant than the Socialist Party were the Industrial Workers of the World (I. W. W.) who first attracted attention in 1905. Pledged to direct action to overthrow the individual enterprise system, the I. W. W. resembled syndicalism in France and Italy. This movement appealed primarily to casual farm workers and lumbermen and at its peak may have had 100,000 adherents. Doings of the "wobblies" excited no little alarm, and members were sometimes victims of prejudiced and vindictive courts. The I. W. W. opposed intervention in the First World War on the ground that it was a "capitalists' war," and that proved its undoing; the wobblies quietly declined and soon wobbled off the national stage.

Most of the strength of the I. W. W. had lain with immigrant workers, and yet the overwhelming majority of the newcomers were no more sympathetic to novel European social philosophies than the native born. Wages seemed fabulously high in comparison with the small rewards in Europe and opportunities for advancement were excellent in a swiftly expanding labor force. Astonishment may well have reigned in the Norwegian home which was informed in a letter from an immigrant, ". . . I can tell you that here we do not live frugally, but one has eggs and egg pancakes and canned fish and fresh fish, and fruit of all kinds, so it is different from you who have to sit and suck herring bones." As a German scholar explained, in accounting for the limited appeal of European collectivist ideologies in America: "On the shoals of roast beef and apple pie all socialistic Utopias founder."

Political reformism in the United States did not take naturally to action along anticapitalist lines. It was much more likely to manifest itself in campaigns to accomplish a specific objective such as curbing monopolies or the inflation of the currency or the introduction of an income tax.

As a means of increasing federal revenue and to level off some of the glaring inequalities in the distribution of wealth, an income tax was placed on the statute books in 1894—half a century after comparable legislation in Great Britain. The constitutionality of the law was debated before the Supreme Court. An eloquent legal opponent of the tax warned that "the communistic march must be stopped"; "Property," he cried, "demands immediate and unconditional security in its right." By majority vote the justices of the Supreme Court tossed the income tax into the waste basket. But in 1913 a constitutional amendment went into operation granting the federal government unfettered authority to tax incomes. The Republic did not collapse, nor individual initiative fall into torpor.

PROGRESS IN AGRICULTURE

Agriculture, like manufacturing, experienced profound changes in the half century after Appomattox. For one thing, individual farms increased from 2,000,000 to nearly 7,000,000, thanks in part to the Homestead Act of 1862 and other laws. These measures were designed to promote independent landowning in the immense area to the west of the alluvial Mississippi Valley which had already been occupied. It was prescribed in the Homestead Act that any citizen or newcomer who intended to become a citizen might secure 160 acres of government land by paying a nominal sum and living on the property for a minimum of five years.

Although some arable land was parceled out under the Homestead Act, the larger proportion of the soil covered by the law (and amendments) was adapted to cattle-raising rather than cultivation. Subsequent pieces of legislation made available for occupation vast acreages of Indian land and public property that had been set aside to finance institutions of learning. By reason of these laws tens of millions of acres quickly passed to adventuresome settlers. By the 1890's the era of attractive cheap land, literally dirt cheap land, had virtually closed. The spatial frontier in the United States, that is to say, had entered into history.

Output of farm products, meanwhile, had skyrocketed. Exports of wheat, for example, jumped from about 17,000,000 bushels in 1860 to over 200,000,000 by 1900. Cattle-raising expanded in this heyday of the romantic cowboys. Refrigeration facilities in land and water transport increased overseas sales. Landed proprietors and peasants in Europe growled about the fierce competition of the western prairies. Responsive Continental governments raised protective tariffs or imitated Britain in shutting out meat from the United States which, allegedly, was infected with disease. Not only did the opening up of the Middle West cause farming in Britain to languish, but it stimulated cooperative societies and encouraged imitation of American agricultural methods at places on the Continent.

The enormous increase in American farm productions was not due solely to the extension of plowlands. Reckless exploitation of the

On September 16, 1893, the so-called Cherokee Strip, the northern part of Indian Territory, was opened for settlement. We show here the scene at noon when the cavalry drew back from the border and the last great land-rush began.

soil was gradually superseded by more intelligent techniques of cultivation, and an endless crop of bigger and better machines was harvested. The steam engine, for instance, was employed in plowing, only to be replaced at the turn of the century by the gasoline or kerosene tractor. Equipped with a tractor, the plowman no longer plodded his weary way. And machinery raised the social prestige of the farmer in the eyes of the "city-feller," who had come to look upon the countryman as a bumpkin. Agriculture, more and more, turned into a capitalistic business, financed almost exclusively out of American resources.

And farming switched to more scientific methods. A Department of Agriculture was authorized in 1862 to distribute information on agricultural techniques and to perform other services of significance to growers. Publicly financed colleges offered technical instruction and conducted experiments on seeds, insecticides, fertilizers and stockbreeding.

Before the nineteenth century was over the farmer in the United States who produced for foreign markets was faced by competition from newly-opened frontier countries, Canada, Australia and Argentina. Agrarian communities, consequently, became keenly concerned about lower transportation costs and marketing economics. Noisy discontent over eastern financial and railway lordship flared up in the Granger clamor of the 1880's and the Populist ferment of the next decade.

The oracular William Jennings Bryan, ardent oratorical partisan of agricultural interests, swept millions into hysteria during the presidential campaign of 1896 with his battle cry that humanity should not be "crucified upon a cross of gold." "Better times," however, presently blunted the agrarian agitation, yet political militancy in the quarter century before the First World War was more strident in rural America than in industrialized communities.

GROWTH OF FOREIGN BUSINESS

The remarkable economic expansion of the United States after Appomattox was attended by meaningful shifts in foreign business. Sales of goods abroad were eight times as valuable on the eve of the First World War as at 1860. The United States had in fact developed into the foremost international trader, first in the value of exports, second only to Britain as an importer. Effervescent patriots loudly trumpeted that huge American corporations were girding for the commercial conquest of the globe. European interests recoiled in alarm before the competitive challenge of the New World; the American peril industrial took its place alongside of the American peril agricultural.[9]

The character of American exports, moreover, had altered percentagewise. Although food and rawstuffs still retained pride of place, the proportion of manufactured articles shifted from a fifth in the early seventies to almost half by the First World War. Yankee agricultural equipment, cash registers and sewing machines crowded into all the markets of the world. Nevertheless, the United States exported only a small part of its manufactured goods as compared with Britain or Germany.[10] Europe of course continued to be the destination of much the larger share—better than three-quarters—of exports. Yet trade with Latin America, the Orient and the British Dominions had increased and was still going up.

Almost a third of the foreign commerce of the United States was carried on with Great Britain, which bought nearly half of all the exports as compared with a fifth sold to Germany, for instance. With the British realm as a whole, the United States transacted half of its foreign business, shipping three-fifths of its exports to the United Kingdom and the Dominions. These commercial associations were not without political implications.

Curiously enough, in terms of the general economic progress, the ocean-going merchant marine of the United States failed to keep abreast of the expanding volume of foreign trade. In the generation before 1860 fast American clipper ships hauled about two-thirds of the overseas commerce of the country. Decline set in with the War between the States, and at 1910 less than a tenth of the exports was being carried by vessels flying the Stars and Stripes.

Even at that, a surprisingly high proportion of the American ships were sailing vessels, built of wood. British concerns, the maritime leaders, had long since switched to steamships of iron and steel, and imitative Germany followed in the wake of Britain. The chief reason for the lowly condition of the American merchant navy was that foreign companies carried goods at rates with which American enterprise did not care to compete. Shortly after the beginning of the First World War, the government of the United States embarked upon a gigantic program of cargo ship construction.

At the end of the nineteenth century financial interests in the United States started to invest abroad in a major way and colonial possessions were accumulated. Irrevocably, the New World giant had become an integral segment of an interdependent global economy, but few Americans perceived or understood the implications of what had come to pass.

BRITISH NORTH AMERICA

The United States and Canada cherish as many interests and values in common as any two nations of the globe. As heirs of European traditions, both responded in similar ways to the dynamic impulses of the nineteenth century, the one freed from British authority, the other under the British flag. The institutions and practices of popular government expanded,

[9] Henry Cabot Lodge confided to his bosom friend Theodore Roosevelt, ". . . there is a fundamental danger which arises from our rapid growth economically. We are putting a terrible pressure on Europe, and this situation may produce war at any time. The economic forces will not be the ostensible cause of trouble, but they will be the real cause. . . ." Lodge to Roosevelt, March 30, 1901, in *Correspondence of Theodore Roosevelt and Henry Cabot Lodge* (2 vols.; New York, 1925), I. 487.

[10] At the beginning of the twentieth century suggested percentages were United States four, Germany twelve, Britain, twenty-five.

national consciousness matured, machine industry developed, enterprise and dash flourished. European immigrants helped to convert western prairies into huge granaries or in the operation of factories and mines.

Sharp boundary and other quarrels cropped up between the two countries, but, save for the War of 1812, controversies were peacefully adjusted. After about 1870 the expansionist urge of the United States ceased to be a threat to Canadian security; building of frontier fortifications stopped in 1872, and at about the same time the last British regular troops were withdrawn from the interior of Canada. Four thousand miles of undefended boundary symbolized the fraternity of the two nations, a shining lesson for Europe and Asia to take to heart.

Dissimilarities, however, prevailed. For one thing, nature had bestowed her bounty upon Canada with a less lavish hand. Although Canada occupied over half the surface of North America, geography imposed severe restrictions upon the areas of settlement, so that the Canadian population never exceeded 10 per cent of its southern neighbor. Only miners, trappers and nomadic Indians prowled the immense sub-Arctic northlands. And yet Canada was by no means "the acres of snow" of Voltaire's disdainful cynicism; on her soil and in the minerals beneath, there lay rich potentialities for good living.

The original Canadian settlers, it may be recalled, were French in language and customs, and attached to the Catholic faith.[11] The French heritage persisted though affection for France itself dwindled to the vanishing point. As part of the British imperial web, the political evolution of Canada, from crown colony to nationhood, pursued distinctive lines.

[11] Quebec remains of course distinctively French, and church and state live on terms of closest intimacy. French peasant crafts and folk literature are features of the indigenous culture. Woman suffrage was not introduced in Quebec until 1944, a generation later than in the other provinces.

Interior of a farmhouse in French Canada, about 1848

At the time of the American Revolution, Canada which had fallen to Britain only a decade before, sheltered a population of merely 65,000, nearly all of French stock. British officials treated local customs and folkways tenderly and Canada dutifully supported the crown during the Revolution. Some 40,000 residents of English America, preferring to live under the British flag, abandoned their worldly possessions and started life anew in what are now Ontario and the Atlantic maritime provinces. Thousands of immigrants from the British Isles presently joined these pioneering United Empire Loyalists (U. E. L.'s).

The lesson in imperial administration taught Britain by the American Revolution was modestly—very modestly—applied in Canada. By parliamentary act of 1791 the territory was partitioned into two colonies: Lower Canada (Quebec), French in complexion, and Upper Canada (Ontario), mostly British, in which Toronto became the major community. As had been true in English America, the Canadian colonies were governed by a powerful crown governor in collaboration with an elected assembly; the governor was clothed with authority to issue ordinances and to veto laws enacted by the legislature. Canada sided faithfully with Britain in the War of 1812, repulsing then, as it repulsed later, attempts by the United States to effect a merger.

Antipathies, however, developed between royal governors and legislatures in Canada as they had earlier in English America. It was much the same pre-1775 story of pull-devil-pull-baker between imperial authority and the turbulent spirit of colonial self-determination. The French elements were especially irked because so many of the desirable government jobs were filled by English-speaking Canadians. Tension in Quebec rose to the point of insurrection in 1837, and Ontario was the scene of a revolt. Both risings were quashed, however, without much loss of life or property damage.

At that juncture Lord Durham ("Radical Jack") was despatched to Canada to investigate grievances on the spot and to make remedial recommendations. His report of 1839 stands as a major milestone on the British imperial road, for he proposed that the two colonies should be united and, more important, that they should be granted responsible government. These proposals were promptly (1840) implemented. The new regime represented a clean break with the past and the beginning of a unique experiment in self-rule.

The crown-appointed governor-general took orders from London on questions concerning the Empire as a whole—trade, defense and international relations. But everything relating to Canadian internal affairs belonged in the jurisdiction of a ministry responsible to an elected Parliament. In the event that ministerial policies displeased a majority of the lawmakers, the ministry could be dismissed, exactly as in Britain itself. That arrangement, which proved an instant success, has prevailed in Canada ever since, and was subsequently applied in other white-inhabited sections of the British realm.

It was assumed by Durham that the line of demarcation between "imperial" and "local colonial" affairs would last indefinitely. He was wrong, for he had unwittingly sponsored something that was dynamic. Bit by bit, the Canadian government whittled down the powers originally reserved to London. In the 1850's when Canada imposed tariffs on iron and steel goods, the British ministry mildly tut-tutted, but it was informed, civilly though firmly, that this was the business of Canada alone.

THE DOMINION OF CANADA

As the next phase in the unfolding of government, the Dominion of Canada was established in 1867. Pleas of "Little Englanders" in Britain that Canada, now the home of 2,500,000, should be given unfettered independence were brushed aside. Under the Act of 1867 a royal governor-general presided in a titular way over a federal union embracing the provinces from Ontario eastward, except Newfoundland. Through the governor-general, London continued to manage foreign affairs and Dominion defense.

The federal Parliament comprised a Senate, whose members were appointed for life, and a democratically chosen House of Commons.

Each province retained a local government of its own with a responsible ministry as in the central government. Eventually ten provinces—Quebec and Ontario had been separated—formed the Dominion circle, Newfoundland with Labrador, never a particularly bright jewel in the British Crown, though important in air strategy, entering last of all in 1949.

Spreading westward, the Dominion admitted Manitoba (1870) and British Columbia (1871) to the confederation. The Canadian Pacific railway, running from coast to coast and opened to traffic in 1885, bound the Dominion together and carried settlers to the almost unoccupied mid-western plains. Alberta and Saskatchewan, in 1905, took their seats around the Dominion table.

Cordiality between Canada and the United States, in the meantime, had grown famously and commercial and cultural ties had richly increased. Capital passed from the United States northward in rising volume; the time would come (1948) when a third of all private United States capital shipped abroad was invested in Canadian enterprises, over $5,200,000,000. On the other side, Canadian emigrants, French-speaking and English, struck off for greener pastures to the south. Somewhat paradoxically, a counter-current of land-hungry farmers from the United States trekked into the west of Canada. With its great, ever-expanding market, Canada developed into the largest single customer of the United States, though the bulk of Canadian exports were shipped to Britain and western Europe.

Upon the outbreak of the First World War, Canada demonstrated the depth of its attachment to Britain by taking part in the grim struggle as soon as hostilities started. By signing the Versailles Treaty in 1919, the Dominion announced to the world that it had attained national stature with a consciousness distinctly its own.

ADDING MATTERS UP

Down to the end of the eighteenth century, the Americas, north and south, formed outposts of great European empires. But a wide gulf yawned between the founding fathers of the United States and the First World War. In the intervening century, the lush epoch of nationalism, national individualities prospered in the Western Hemisphere. And other molding currents of Western civilization in the period stamped themselves upon men and mores in the New World—the trend toward democracy in terms of government and as secular creed, the wider recognition of the rights and dignity of man, the expansionist urge, the onrushing, transforming might of machinofacture and the relentless quest for higher standards of material comfort.

The relative impact of these forces obviously varied as between most of North America and the Latin Republics to the south. Detectable differences, moreover, existed inside both the United States and Canada; regionalism, that is to say, nurtured diversities comparable in a way to the differences between the individual countries of Europe or of Latin America.

Into the Western Hemisphere flowed a ceaseless tide of immigrants from Europe. Newcomers left behind a world which they identified with restrictions, struggles for bare existence, ignorance and social stratification. Down through the century rang a prophetic utterance of the German philosopher Hegel. America, he wrote, is "the land of the future, where in the ages that lie before us, the burden of the world's history shall reveal itself. . . . It is the land of desire for all those who are weary of the historical lumber-room of old Europe."

Out of the mélange of peoples and cultures emerged American types somewhat distinguishable from their European relatives. Life in the Americas diverged from Old World norms in the larger economic opportunities, fluidity of classes, restlessness, invincible optimism, respect for industrial experimentation and quantity production.

In spite of the enormous heritage from Europe and the continuing human and other bequests, European institutions and manners underwent a process of Americanization. The outcome might be illustrated in many ways; the record of Christianity in North America will serve as an example.

The fantastic multiplicity of sects was a hallmark of North American Christianity. Nimble statisticians in time were able to count approximately two hundred and fifty denominational fragments, based upon divergent theological emphases, differing social outlooks or the national origins of communicants. As another contrast with the tradition of Europe, churches were divorced from government.[12] Separation of church and state was dictated partly by the conviction that such an arrangement was right and proper, partly because competing denominations would not permit any one of their set to obtain special privileges from government.

[12] That condition did not obtain in Latin America or in Quebec, and even in sections of New England separation of church and state was not achieved until the 1830's.

Christianity in the New World differed, again, from the European parent because of the subordination of the intellectual aspects of the faith to the concerns of social welfare. Professional churchmen who dedicated themselves to theological puzzlements were conspicuously rare in North America. Standard perplexities of Christian thought, such as the nature of God or the existence of evil, for instance, engaged little speculation. Salvation in the New World would be purchased less by doctrine and dogma than by deeds.

Churches in North America were inclined to stress humanitarianism and good works. They fought vice, disseminated the gospel among the heathen of Asia and Africa, furnished help to the indigent and the unfortunate and established schools, colleges and hospitals. As social

The tranquil state of the American mind at the close of the Nineteenth Century is reflected in this picture of a contemporary New England village street.

service centers, churches enlisted popular enthusiasm to an extent unapproached in Europe at large. In time, it is true, New World secular emphases attracted imitation across the ocean, the trend being accelerated by the First World War.

As is suggested in the next chapter, cultural interactions between the two sides of the Atlantic were diverse and altogether healthy. But even in this department of life exchanges and borrowings tended to adapt themseves to the environmental surroundings of America.

A final point by way of summary deserves to be made. The century of the growth of the Americas was a century of unusual international tranquility. No general war rocked the globe between 1815 and 1914. Relatively remote from the discontents, the rivalries and the blood feuds of Europe, the Americas could work out patterns of living in their own sweet way and in comparative security. It would need the obstinacy of an ostrich to deny that the history of the Americas from 1914 onward taught that the past was simply prelude. During and after the First World War, the New World as a whole, particularly the United States, advanced, as never before, into the spacious and exacting arena of world history.

FOR FURTHER STUDY

CHARLES A. and MARY R. BEARD, *The Rise of American Civilization* (4 vols., New York, 1927–1942)

MARY W. WILLIAMS, *The People and Politics of Latin America* (new ed., New York, 1955)

JOHN B. TREND, *Bolívar and the Independence of Spanish America* (New York, 1948)

FREDERICK J. TURNER, *The Frontier in American History* (new ed., New York, 1948) PAPERBACK

MARCUS L. HANSEN, *The Atlantic Migration* (Cambridge, Mass., 1940) PAPERBACK

OSCAR HANDLIN, *The Uprooted: The Epic Story of the Great Migrations that made the American People* (Boston, 1951) PAPERBACK

HALVDAN KOHT, *The American Spirit in Europe* (Philadelphia, 1949)

ARTHUR C. BINING, *The Rise of American Economic Life* (New York, new ed., 1955)

ARTHUR M. SCHLESINGER, *The Rise of the City* (New York, 1933)

HAROLD U. FALKNER, *The Quest for Social Justice* (New York, 1931)

EDGAR MCINNIS, *Canada* (new ed., Toronto, 1958)

MASON WADE, *The French Canadians* (New York, 1955)

FRANK THISTLETHWAITE, *The Great Experiment* (Cambridge, Eng., 1955) PAPERBACK

THOMAS D. CLARK, *Frontier America* (New York, 1959)

LOUIS B. WRIGHT, *Culture on the Moving Frontier* (New York, 1956) PAPERBACK

HARVEY WISH, *Society and Thought in America* (2 vols., New York, 1950–52)

EDWARD C. KIRKLAND, *Dream and Thought in the Business Community* (Ithaca, 1956)

GEORGE MOWRY, *The Era of Theodore Roosevelt* (new ed., New York, 1960) PAPERBACK

ARTHUR S. LINK, *Woodrow Wilson and the Progressive Era* (New York, 1954) PAPERBACK

CLARENCE E. HARING, *Empire in Brazil* (Cambridge, Mass., 1958)

DONALD G. CREIGHTON, Story of Canada (Boston, 1960)

CHAPTER XXIV

A PANORAMA OF WESTERN CULTURE (1850-1914)

ACCENT ON REALISM

EXCEPT here and there in the Asiatic civilizations of India and China, the West of the late nineteenth century faced no rival in any phase of humane culture. And the predominant accent of the time was realistic, often blatantly so. Men of letters in particular attempted to penetrate beneath the surface of men and their institutions and to reproduce their findings with camera-like fidelity. To the more extravagant expressions of realism, sordid, coarse, pessimistic and reflecting the methods of science, the term "naturalism" was attached.

As John Ruskin sagely observed, "we can but consider art in relation to the inner spirit of the age in which it exists." Culture in general mirrored the overarching trends and tendencies of the age: the onward advance of machine technology; the dominion of the scientific spirit; the triumph of nationalism, which affected letters and the arts as well as politics and economics; advancing cosmopolitanism, as innovations in one country leaped over national frontiers and across the Atlantic and back again; intense controversies over social and religious theories; the increase in social consciousness shown, for instance, in the attention paid by cultural workers to social legislation, to the industrial worker and the humble peasant.

Not new, of course, realism rather indicated a new emphasis, and the older romantic style, looser and more imaginative, was not displaced. Versatile celebrities frequently exhibited both tendencies in their productions. Increasing literacy and more leisure broadened the human base for the appreciation of the things of the mind and the spirit. New libraries and museums, for example, brought larger opportunities for cultural enrichment. The ever-expanding press often carried literary pieces as well as popular versions of the latest developments in science. Middle-class men and sometimes governments furnished the financial backing for authors and artists, which once had come primarily from aristocratic patrons.

The temptation is strong to recall many reputable worthies of the period, for it was singularly rich in cultural and intellectual talents. But a parade of names makes dusty reading, hardly more palatable than a telephone directory. Attention in this survey will be focused, therefore, upon a few representative figures in the major departments of the higher living.

THE ART OF THE NOVEL

Of all literary forms the novel attained the widest popularity and story-tellers in the French language were most characteristic and accomplished. The greatest novelist in France was Gustave Flaubert whose literary principles and approach to the human pageant attracted universal admiration and considerable imitation. A desperately serious man, little given to humor, Flaubert devoted meticulous care to style and diction.

Émile Zola, a portrait by Édouard Manet

His *Madame Bovary* is acclaimed as the foremost fictional work of the century, an artistic masterpiece. It is a faithful portrayal, satirical and searing, of bourgeois mediocrity and morality—the story of a sentimental woman, married to a physician, who had commonplace love escapades with commonplace fellows in a commonplace community of Normandy. For its impious treatment of Christianity and indifference to moral customs, the novel was condemned by the French censorship, a verdict which the courts declined to uphold. Flaubert loved to flay and startle the bourgeoisie, yet he displayed bourgeois common sense in ample measure. His vivid pen set the style for a whole school.

Foremost apprentice of Flaubert was Guy de Maupassant, a hard-boiled realist, who regarded living as "an ugly business." He had a rare talent for exposing the drabness of peasant life and describing crude sexual adventures (*Bel Ami*), which did not hurt sales. A master of the realistic short story, Maupassant composed unconventional, thoroughly unpleasant tales, which make the flesh fairly creep. Though born in a château he died in a madhouse.

More journalist than literary artist, Émile Zola accumulated a fortune and acquired the dignity of founder of naturalism through his novels concerning a French family in the reign of Napoleon III. A prolific writer, his pages graphically reflect the pessimism and melancholy which gripped French letters after the defeat by Germany in 1870. A multitude of characters crowd his novels, men and women are remorselessly pictured as brutes, bestial, obscene, ugly and dull (*Germinal*). Middle class morality is savagely and dogmatically satirized in *L'Assommoir*, no doubt the most Zolaesque of his productions. Zola bravely championed the cause of Dreyfus (p. 444) winning renown for his courage and tenacity.

Ivan Turgenev, about 1881

Another literary swordsman for Dreyfus was Anatole France, pen name of Anatole Thibault, the most generally esteemed writer of the Third Republic. An urbane skeptic, a pagan in more than an artistic sense, he etched the problems of his period in prose of crystalline brilliance; but neither his mind nor pen was at all prosaic. His allegiance to freedom bordered upon anarchy. In an ironical and caustic spirit, worthy of Voltaire, France unveiled shame and hypocrisies in church and society. As the conclusion to *Penguin Island*, a sterling specimen of his art, revolution sweeps away the prevailing society and prepares the way for social reconstruction. A national institution while he lived, like Shaw or Wells in Britain, France was avidly read the world over.

As never before or since, creative Russian literature attracted universal interest; until about 1860 the works of Russian authors were scarcely known in the West. Flowering genius gave the literary world three remarkable realistic novelists: Ivan Turgenev, Feodor Dostoievsky and Leo Tolstoy. Concerned to remedy the miseries of their native land, these writers took the place of press, parliament and pulpit at home, and marvelously interpreted Russia and the Russians to outsiders. Never idle tellers of tales, these authors were without exception and consistently preachers of long, impassioned sermons. Among Western novelists they deepened interest in the psychology of the subconscious and abnormal, and encouraged speculation on the religious and the metaphysical.

Turgenev, the first Russian writer to be much read abroad, established his reputation with *A Sportsman's Sketches*. It was a propagandistic tract for the times portraying the iniquity of serfdom and it helped to achieve the break-up of that odious institution. A superb stylist, one of the finest in the history of the novel, Turgenev excelled in descriptions of the lyric beauties of the Muscovite countryside. His extraordinary and heart-breaking *Fathers and Sons* presented the aimless nihilist hero Bazarov, a caricature of the outlook of a

Tolstoy, about 1876

whole generation of young intellectual idealists. Here and elsewhere Turgenev revealed himself a Westernizer, the most un-Russian of Russian novelists, but imbued with an ardent passion for freedom. His central characters readily sacrifice everything to love, but something always goes wrong—an approach that is typically Russian.

The novels of Dostoievsky are extremely helpful in understanding Russian character. Consequently there has been persistent and growing interest in his fiction and in the man, for he was a highly autobiographical novelist. His personal life was full of horrible experiences, but he somehow outrode every obstacle which fate and his own folly placed in his path. Dostoievsky specialized in abnormal, depressed and unbalanced characters. Grim, overwhelming naturalness pervades his novels, lightened now and then by religious mysticism and infrequent gems of wit. His writings have been scrupulously studied by all manner of intellectual workers from psychiatrists through moral philosophers to students of medical pathology.

Fatalistic submission to the inescapable and to suffering as the prerequisites to growth are recurrent themes in Dostoievsky's tales. Through suffering, he explained, every variety and degree of wrong-doing could be expiated. *The Brothers Karamazov* is a novel calculated to trouble the reader with nightmare dreams. *Crime and Punishment*, embodying the mature philosophy of Dostoievsky, teems with the agonies and brutalities of urban living and compassion for the unfortunate and the oppressed.

A violently expressed jingoism, rising into melodramatic Pan-Slavism, taints many of Dostoievsky's pages. "The future of Europe," he was confident, "belongs to Russia." Muscovite might, he believed, lay in the peasant millions and their attachment to Orthodox Christianity and Romanov tsar. He passionately proclaimed that Mother Russia had a messianic mission to merge her peculiar civilization and the rest of world society in a fresh synthesis. His aversion to the bourgeois West, his glorification of war and prophetic utterances concerning social revolution assured him a sympathetic reading in Soviet Russia.

Tolstoy also identified the authentic Russia with the simple people of the soil. Eminent as a novelist and a moralist and cherishing a thoroughly individualistic interpretation of the Christian creed, Tolstoy at the end of his days was the uncrowned king of Russian letters. His novels were translated into virtually every written language. Rebelling against the artificialities of civilized living, the strident clangor of the machine age, and manifestations of man's inhumanity to man, he pleaded for a return to nature and he himself lived much like the peasants on his estates. His general philosophy blended anarchism and pacifism with anti-individualism, and in spirit at least he became the greatest of the Russian nihilists. Nonresistance to evil, chastity, and sentimental compassion for mankind ranked at the head of the Tolstoyan pattern of virtues.

Like fellow Russian authors, Tolstoy informed the West on the peculiarities of the Russian way of life. *Anna Karenina*, for instance, is a decidedly realistic exposé of the aristocratic class to which the novelist belonged. His masterpiece, *War and Peace*, is perhaps the finest specimen of all historical fiction. An immense tableau, it recounts the struggle against Napoleon, discloses a good deal about serf-owning society and about Tolstoy's all-embracing philosophy. Extravagantly colored scenes, graphic realism and praise for the common soldier have intrigued generations of readers. Although written with lucidity and force, there is too much of a muchness to *War and Peace*, for it runs into 1,800 pages.

FICTION IN ENGLISH

Compared with French and Russian novels the imaginative fiction of other peoples appears somewhat pale in quality and meager in vitality. And yet for sheer bulk the British novelist, Anthony Trollope, deserved high marks; annually for a generation he ground out several romances (*Barchester Towers; Dr. Thorne*). Trollope skilfully portrayed the customs and people of the Victorian era, when men had faith in God and in themselves, and he was a

Anthony Trollope

goad to welfare legislation; but his novels are uneven in quality and they never quite attained first rank. More faithful to human realities was George Eliot (Mary Ann Evans), most popular of British lady novelists. As *Silas Marner* amply revealed, she instinctively understood the interests of ordinary folk, possessed remarkable talent for appraisal of motives and had rich natural gifts for sheer story-telling.

Intellectually more akin to the realistic Frenchmen was Thomas Hardy. His sardonically pessimistic view of existence caused him to paint the human pageant in harsh, uncompromising language. Only peasants, quaint in speech and homely in interests, seemed to him to derive much pleasure from living, and that because they were less than civilized. Violent tragedies stud the novels of Hardy. For many the charm of Hardy lies in the transparent sincerity of his prose. His descriptions of the natural beauties of southern England are classics, even though he chose to describe nature as sinister and unfriendly to man. Cruelty and compassion are cleverly intertwined and Christianity is subjected to cutting satire, for Hardy gloried in being a pagan. His most prized novel, *Tess of the D'Urbervilles*, reveals his qualities as a literary stylist. In an historical saga on generous lines, *The Dynasts*, Hardy lavished praise on the ordinary British soldier battling manfully against Napoleon, somewhat as Tolstoy had done for the Muscovites in *War and Peace*.

In muscular romances, hearty short stories and verse, Rudyard Kipling chanted the glories of British overseas expansion. He brought India with its heat and vermin, its diversities of caste and creed into the homes of Britain. Imperialism as defined by Kipling was a holy crusade to confer the blessings of British administration and habits upon backward peoples, "half devil and half child." In the Mowgli stories he invented boldly imaginative and charming tales which promise to live.

Kipling suffered a considerable eclipse with the emergence of H. G. Wells, who employed romances to teach scientific lessons and social collectivism. Once intelligence and science were enthroned, once men of competence and good-will were seated in the places of authority, then poverty and attendant evils would be conquered and mankind would advance into an era of unprecedented felicity, the many-

George Eliot (Mary Ann Evans)

Mark Twain (Samuel L. Clemens) in old age

sided Wells taught. Venerated as a contemporary prophet and seer, Wells' imaginative flights, always engrossing, quickened the conscience and thought of two continents and three generations.

Fiction in the United States came into its own with the sagas of Mark Twain (Samuel L. Clemens). Genuinely American, a projection indeed of the frontier yet familiar with other sections of the country, Twain acquainted foreign audiences with the robust individualism, the addiction to moral uplift and the salty humor of the New World. A picturesque narrative of adventure and vagabondage in the Middle West, *Huckleberry Finn* (1884), was extensively translated, even into such a language as Croatian. "Huck," as was so true of his creator, was a "noble savage" in revolt against polite manners and social conventions.

Under the influence of Old World realism, William Dean Howells who turned out more than a hundred volumes, indulged in pungent criticism of "the gilded age" of unrestrained American capitalism. To him the roaring industrialism and the crop of triumphant millionaires were morally revolting. His best and best known novel, *The Rise of Silas Lapham*, laid bare the crass and the lurid in the career of an opulent business magnate; it lacked, however, the subtleties and propaganda power of first-rate literature, though it broke a path for later specialists in social criticism.

A flood of stories of permanent interest assailed the prevalent standards of business ethics, condemning the affluent and pleading the cause of social reform. Representative were the writings of Jack London and Upton Sinclair, collectivists both. London probably attracted wider reading in Europe (*The Call of the Wild*) than any other American author. Sinclair's gruesome, hair-raising description of life and labor in the Chicago stockyards, *The Jungle* (1906), a product of the muckraking era, deserved to be shelved alongside of the grimmer French productions.

A rising artist in German fiction was Thomas Mann. An elaborate account of the emergence and collapse of a family of German commercial patricians, *Buddenbrooks* (1903), foreshadowed still finer novels to come after 1914.

THE WORLD OF DRAMA

It was a curious fact that several of the leading, path-breaking dramatists came from the thinly-peopled Scandinavian countries. The Norwegian genius, Henrik Ibsen, radically altered the content of plays and invigorated the technique of stage presentation. He specialized in the social or problem drama, dealing satirically with everyday middle-class experiences (*The Pillars of Society*). Seldom did Ibsen vouchsafe basic solutions for the problems he raised, though retribution usually followed commission of wrong. Anarchic and gloomy in temperament, this intellectual idealist rebelled against authority and convention of all sorts. In *A Doll's House* he appealed vigorously for full rights for women. As is disclosed in the romantic drama, *Peer Gynt*, Ibsen held his fellow beings in low esteem. Superb as a craftsman of drama, he has had a large class of imitative disciples.

In front of the National Theater of Oslo

stand statues of Ibsen and his fellow countryman, Björnstjerne Björnson, an Ibsenite, but warmer and more humorous than his master. While Björnson raised ugly social issues, he usually offered solutions for them. A staunch humanitarian, he protested vehemently against callous abuse of minorities. His novel, *Arne*, portrayed Norwegian peasant manners in charming fashion and with conviction.

The foremost Swedish man of letters, August Strindberg, at his best as a playwright, ranged over a variety of literary forms. He rivaled Ibsen in unveiling the mean and deceitful, and produced some extremely disagreeable and coarse examples of realism (*The Father*). His personal career was a tortured ordeal and nearly everything he wrote had an autobiographical tinge (*The Dance of Death*). Student life at Upsala University was crudely satirized in his finest novel, *The Red Room*. Of his gift for dramatic expression, as of his monstrous egotism, there could be no question, but Strindberg died as unloved as he was unlovable.

Out of Russia came the "slice-of-life" dramas and short stories of Anton Chekov. He portrayed his country and countrymen with sanity, fidelity and extraordinary psychological insight. There is much that is dark and foreboding in the works of Chekov, much pathos and tragic gloom and characters behave in flabby and irritating ways, but passages of broad comedy brighten plots. In *The Cherry Orchard*, Russian social types of many kinds parade across the stage; feckless squires are shown futilely floundering about after the liberation of the serfs.

Grandson of serfs, Chekov warmly sympathized with the underdog, though he refrained from picturing the peasants with the sugary sentimentalism of Tolstoy. Into the mouth of one of his characters, he put (1900) these grimly prophetic lines: "The time has come, an avalanche is moving down upon us, a mighty, wholesome storm is brewing . . . is already near and soon will sweep away from our society its idleness, indifference, prejudice against work, and foul ennui. I shall work, and in some twenty-five or thirty years everyone, everyone will work too."

The greatest of British playwrights, G. B. Shaw, once published a book *The Quintessence of Ibsenism* and proceeded to walk in the footsteps of the Norse innovator. Mordantly critical of social irrationalities and imbecilitics, as he saw them, Shaw lashed out against the seven deadly sins of respectability and capitalistic economy. Everything in which he did not believe was jauntily dismissed as superstition, and yet he was as full of superstitions as an everyday peasant. Teaming up with the Fabian collectivists, he became their literary high priest.

Shaw exploited the theater as a pulpit for the propagation of social criticism and anticapitalism. Unique and eccentric, witty and pugnacious, he was an intellectual gadfly in a changing world, a major influence upon thought

Eleonora Duse in 1923 at her final New York performance of Ibsen's The Lady from the Sea

George Bernard Shaw

and opinion for three generations. Prefaces to his plays resembled sermons independent of the dramas themselves. Although unappreciated at first, Shaw's productions presently lifted him to an undisputed place among the masters of stagecraft (*Man and Superman; Androcles and the Lion*). All in all Shaw restored animation and vitality to the languid British theater and effectively fostered faith in collectivism. Ever the irreverant iconoclast, he vied with Anatole France for the gaily-colored mantle of Voltaire.

An accomplished German follower of Ibsen was the versatile Gerhard Hauptmann. Sensing the dramatic potentialities in the fast-changing economy of Germany, he captured the temper of the times with stark realism. *The Weavers,* possibly his finest production, depressingly depicts the response of handicraftsmen to the invasion of the machine. Unfortunate victims of the new currents in industry are sketched with life-like authenticity. Inferior to Hauptmann in talent though always interesting and frequently caustic was Hermann Sudermann (*Dame Care*). Much praised in France though little honored in his native Italy was Gabriele D'Annunzio. Very much the swashbuckler, and quite rhetorical, D'Annunzio poured forth a large mass of patriotic and social plays (*Fire; The Triumph of Death*).

THE MUSE OF POETRY

A wealth of talent in poetry, late in the nineteenth century, expressed prevailing cares and joys, doubts and aspirations. Wearer of the laurel of official British poet for two generations, Alfred Tennyson had attained distinction before the mid-century. Along with folk legends and history, Tennyson looked for inspirational themes in the problems of the earnest Victorians. Hesitantly, in an age of onrushing scientific novelties, he affirmed faith in accepted fundamentals (*In Memoriam*). Full of praise for British royal virtues, an ardent patriot ("The Charge of the Light Brigade") and a herald of irresistible progress, Tennyson captivated traditionalist spirits. He excelled too in lyrics, such as the exquisite "Crossing the Bar."

Incorrigible optimism pervaded much of the verse of Robert Browning though, quite frankly, a good deal of his poetry was obscure or at any rate extremely puzzling. He rather stood aloof from the janglings of the time in the social sphere and in politics, preferring religious subjects or stories in lyrical verse ("Saul"; "Rabbi Ben Ezra"). Stridently aggressive and unconventional was the poetry of Algernon C. Swinburne, a sort of reincarnation of Shelley. Detestation of monarchy and shrill skepticism matched the ardor for republicanism and freedom of this congenital image-breaker ("Garden of Proserpine").

Poetry in France was noted for diversity both in content and form. Of lasting influence were the writings of Charles Baudelaire, a partisan of romanticism just when realism was coming into fashion. An ardent admirer of Edgar Allan Poe, whose writings he beautifully translated, Baudelaire chose themes for his verse which were quite revolting and horrible. His own life was a bed of thorns and he liked to shock more fortunate members of society. Baudelaire prided himself on the stylistic elegance of his compositions ("Fleurs du Mal"). But in grace of

Baudelaire, a portrait by Deroy

workmanship he was excelled by Paul Verlaine. Acclaimed as the most talented poet of the period, Verlaine early in his career penned simple, pessimistic verse, tinged with bohemianism; in maturity he switched to mystical, religious melodies. Another disciple of Baudelaire, Stéphane Mallarmé, carried "symbolism," which spurned romanticism and realism alike, to a brilliant height.

The French symbolist sect defied accepted standards, reveled in experimentation and endeavored to probe accurately into the psychological depths of the human heart and spirit. For this group skilfully polished style, a wealth of metaphor and simile or highly symbolical diction counted heavily. Beautiful in form, the deliberately enigmatic pieces of Mallarmé puzzled even his own pupils. Philosophers of poetry as well as literary artists, the symbolists explained in elegant language what the poet's intellectual obligation really was. From its French breeding-ground symbolism penetrated across Europe.

When symbolism sputtered out, French poetry inclined to return to the style and language of classicism. Representative of this trend was Charles Péguy, a pessimistic analyst of his generation, who felt, however, that a revival of faith and piety would remedy current disillusions. Not pleasing as a stylist, Péguy relied upon artistic grace and simplicity to attract readers, and his influence extended beyond the frontiers of France. His final contribution, "Eve," beautifully described death on the battlefield, the fate of the poet himself, who perished in the First World War.

New World idealism reached literary circles of Europe through the poetry of Walt Whitman, especially his masterpiece, *Leaves of Grass.* Emerson referred to it as "a nondescript monster, which yet had terrible eyes and buffalo strength, and was indisputably American." Assertive, lacking rhyme and oddly arranged, the

Paul Verlaine, a portrait by Carrière

writings of Whitman bespoke confidence in the future, staunch individualism, love of country and primitive faith in freedom and the democratic way. Translated into many languages, the poetry of Whitman elicited warm appreciations by leading European critics.

THE TIDE OF HISTORY

Much of the most distinguished writing on history of the late nineteenth century appeared in the form of chaste monographs in which a small topic was exhaustively explored. But some historical craftsmen composed large syntheses of general interest and enduring value. The stress which Marx placed upon economic forces, coupled with the predominantly materialistic spirit of the period, tended to cool interest in purely political narratives and to set historians to grubbing for economic facts and influences.

Another German scholar, Theodor Mommsen, ranked with Ranke as the leading historian of the century. An expert on ancient Rome, he prepared specialized studies on Roman law and an extensive *History of Rome*. Admirably written and full of interesting and little known detail, the *History* promptly took its place among the masterpieces of the historian's art. To a wealth of original information, Mommsen joined a judicial temper in appraising events and personalities. Instead of confining himself to politics—the *History* stopped with the death of Julius Caesar—Mommsen illuminated early Roman civilization in general.

Mommsen summed up his creed and the limitations imposed upon historical craftsmanship in language of lasting interest. "To get rid of all presuppositions," he declared, "is the ideal aim of all scholarly research, which every conscientious man strives to achieve, but which no one achieves or can achieve. Every man brings with him from his home religious, political and social convictions; and although it is our sacred duty to seek to understand views contrary to our own and if possible to do them justice, this is a divine attribute which no mortal will dare to claim."

Less dispassionate than Mommsen, but his superior in quantity of writing, was Heinrich von Sybel. Best known of his histories was an elaborate *Founding of the German Empire*, replete with flaming nationalism, intense enthusiasm for Bismarck, and largely based upon evidence drawn from the Prussian state archives. Partisan prejudices also mar somewhat a large study of the French Revolution which von Sybel undertook, but a history of the Crusades attained praiseworthy detachment as befitted a pupil of Ranke. Later scholars dissented from many of the judgments of von Sybel on the Crusades, but they marveled at the range of his learning and the sweep of his pen.

By the test of popularity beyond academic circles, Heinrich von Treitschke outstripped all other historians of his generation. His fascinating and spirited *History of Germany in the Nineteenth Century* exerted considerable influence in official and policy making circles of Imperial Germany. This "Bismarck of the chair," who freely acknowledged that his blood was too hot for a historian, scorned impartiality in presentation; both in his books and his crowded lecture hall at Berlin he preached with evangelical fervor on the history of Prussia and the glorious destiny of the German nation. "I write for Germans," he bluntly explained, "the narrator of German history should feel and create in the hearts of his readers delight in the Fatherland." His purpose was less to discover and proclaim truth than to advance one of those perversions of systematic thought called ideologies.

And Treitschke hated as ardently as he loved. His detestation of Britain and representative government, anything indeed savoring of liberalism, developed into a consuming passion; he unloosed his siege guns upon Jews as destructive of the good life in Germany. He dogmatically asserted that "the state is power," which encouraged worship of the state and deification of force and war. Small wonder that Treitschke was claimed by the Nazis as one of their intellectual forerunners.

Counterpart of Mommsen in British historical circles was Samuel R. Gardiner, who devoted a full life to the intensely controversial history of England in the seventeenth century. Rational, reliable, though not particularly readable, the work of Gardiner reveals a mind which operated without prejudice or sentiment. Of the same generation was W. E. H. Lecky whose interests ranged widely over the moral development of Europe, the rationalist tradition and studies of high quality on the eighteenth century. Lecky enlivened his learned pages with personal philosophical insights and enthusiasms. Parting company with political affairs, John R. Green composed *A Short History of the English People*. This comprehensive social history brought together in pictures full of vitality and color aspects of popular living which previously had been treated independently or neglected. Permanently valuable as literature, Green's narrative falls short at times on accuracy and balance of emphasis.

Among historical writers in the United States, John B. McMaster resembled Green somewhat. Relying heavily upon newspapers and other periodical material he compiled a spacious *History of the People of the United States*. Free of partisanship and rich in everyday details, this monument of scholarly industry often overlooked the larger currents which shaped the course of affairs in the New World. Equal to the best productions of Europe was a *History of the United States* by Edward Channing. Written with great skill and learning and generally objective, this work belongs among the classics of historical composition. Of almost equal stature was a long *History of the United States of America during the Administrations of Jefferson and Madison* by Henry Adams. A literary artist, Adams wrote with verve and superb sweep and enriched diplomatic analyses with materials from European archives. He is also remembered as the author of a penetrating study of the Middle Age (*Mont Saint Michel and Chartres*), one of the ablest contributions to European history by a trans-Atlantic scholar.

Significant innovations in historical learning were spread abroad by James Harvey Robinson, in particular. He was concerned with instructing the intelligent general reader rather than the specialist. Taking as his special province the unfolding of the Western mind, Robinson insisted that the arts of peace had been grossly neglected by historical craftsmen in their search for truth in the realms of politics, diplomacy and war. History is or ought to be encyclopedic, the sovereign corrective of all highly specialized learning.

Influenced by the outlook and concerns of the English Fabians, Robinson dwelt upon the importance of everyday matters, the existence and interests of the ordinary fellow and the onward march of science. Knowledge of the past, he contended, should foster sensible action to overcome the ailments of contemporary society and lead humanity to a more perfect welfare. Robinson's "New History," which in fact was quite old, enlisted a considerable discipleship in the United States, both in principle and in practice.

From the host of French historians Hippolyte A. Taine may be singled out for particular comment. Professedly an exponent of detached objectivity, he was in reality mastered by a pessimistic and schematic personal philosophy. In his major effort, *The Origins of Contemporary France*, Taine offered an explanation of the dismal collapse of France in the War of 1870. The great French Revolution was examined in microscopic detail and the Jacobin dictators were flayed as selfish visionaries. Realistic French literary folk drew inspiration and nourishment from the writings of Taine.

GERMAN ADVENTURERS IN IDEAS

In the domain of pure thought the outstanding personalities of the second part of the nineteenth century were two Germans: Arthur Schopenhauer and Friedrich W. Nietzsche. Prince of the philosophers of gloomy despair and dank pessimism, Schopenhauer presumed to demonstrate that this world was the worst of all possible worlds (*The World as Will and Representation*). For him life was "something which better were not; a sort of delusion, knowledge of which should remove us from it."

Suffering and sorrow were inescapable penalties of mere living. The forces that make for order and discipline in society were so feeble, thought this grim sage, that they were barely sufficient to keep citizens from cutting one another's throats. Schopenhauer expressed the hope that some day a wise man would bore a hole into the earth and sink enough powder into it to blow the entire planet to smithereens. Only through quietism and absorption in art could man possibly find deliverance from the irrational tyranny of the world.

By conventional Western standards Nietzsche was a strange mortal. Writer on philosophy and ethics, he once esteemed Schopenhauer as master, but found his formula of deliverance through art unsatisfying. Nietzsche rested his faith in science as redeemer and applied a crudely personal twist to the Darwinian hypothesis. His mature years were tortured with pain and anguish, and in the last decade of life his mind was totally beclouded.

Up to a point the writings of Nietzsche reflected his physical weakness and loneliness. This introspective professor of classical studies —an innocuous vocation, it might be supposed —identified his own incurable malady with the disease which he thought afflicted European culture and threatened to destroy it. Militant and passionate, he set forth his views in a small library of books, notably *Thus Spake Zarathustra* and *The Will to Power*. As a rule he preferred to write in aphorisms, colorful, burning, persuasive. In part his basic ideas were a product of the eternally recurrent German search for the absolute good. He had glowing confidence in the capacity of the "best men" to transcend their present selves and become "supermen." "There are higher and lower men," he explained, "a single individual may in certain circumstances justify whole millennia of existence."

Christianity and the French Revolution he satirized as expressions of the slave morality, intended to benefit the weak and the downtrodden. Since Christian ethics exalted altruism, pity, humility and humanity, it was a standing obstacle to the development of the higher master type of men. Equally anathema to him were democratic principles of equality of peoples and love of peace.

A master caste of supermen, according to Nietzsche, must be raised up who would cut loose from traditional morality and pursue a creed of the strong. The supreme traits of the great man were desire for change, willingness to live dangerously, passion for dominion, he thought. Power and the struggle for power—a philosophy of force—were the ultimate values. Concerning war he wrote, "War and courage have done more great things than love of thy neighbor." Ruthlessly the inferior must be trampled down and even denied the right to reproduce—a Nietzschean inference from the science of Darwin.

Nietzsche speculated, moreover, on a united Europe freed from the plague of nationalism.[1] "Nationalism and race hatred," he condemned, "on account of which the nations of Europe today are . . . secluded from one another, as by quarantine." Though a German, he despised Germans, especially Prussians, as submissive and contemptible. Nietzsche wished to be a Pole, envied the lucidity of the French mind and passionately loved Italy. Napoleon, half French, half Italian, he praised as a great superman.

Nietzsche dead proved vastly more potent than Nietzsche alive. Like Marx before him, he directly challenged the values and aspirations which lay at the heart of the Western conception of the good life. And yet, he stands with Treitschke as a prime molder of the very modern German spirit. A London bookseller in the First World War advertised his stock of war literature under the title, the "Euro-Nietzschean War."

Counted among the pupils of Nietzsche was Houston Stewart Chamberlain. A renegade Briton, Chamberlain held with Nietzsche that a higher type of humanity could and must be produced. That order of supermen Chamberlain called the Aryan. "Physically and spiritually," he cried, "the Aryans stand out among all men; hence they are by right lords of the earth." Not "racial" purity, but similarity of character and habits of thought distinguished Aryans from inferior folks. While he lauded the Germans, Chamberlain denied them the eminence of the "master race"; rather they were a people who could be properly manipulated by a new

[1] Sometimes he referred to the ideal human type of the future as a "good European," sometimes as a "superman."

race of leaders (*Foundations of the Nineteenth Century*).

It may be noted here that Adolf Hitler formed a "mutual admiration" society with Chamberlain. The Nazi fanatic had earlier pored over the flaming pages of Nietzsche, adopting those of his doctrines which he liked and could understand—the will to power and the idea of breeding a master caste, for instance. Ere long Hitler came to conceive of himself as a superman. The effect of Nietzsche upon Hitler was profound, perhaps the most decisive of all intellectual influences. Mussolini, too, must be reckoned among the disciples of Nietzsche. He boasted that reading the works of the German philosopher had converted him to the necessity of dictatorship and the virtue of living dangerously. But the Italian never puzzled out ways of applying the teachings of Nietzsche as did the harsher Nazi "superman," Hitler, who ruthlessly translated ideas into actions.

SOME OTHER PHILOSOPHIES

Revolt against coldly mechanical interpretations of the world had an inspired French champion in Henri Bergson. He denied the preeminence of reason and underscored the importance of the instinctive, the validity of intuition (*Creative Evolution*). His thought turned many Frenchmen away from the clogging emphases of naturalistic realism, and some of them passed into Roman Catholic mysticism. Intellectual leader of Italy for half a century, Benedetto Croce fashioned a gigantic philosophical structure. Although he rejected the discipline and dogma of the Roman Church he had no sympathy with scientific rationalism. Or, more positively, Croce argued for a cosmopolitan and democratic approach to human problems. Absolute idealism had a brilliant advocate in the United States, Josiah Royce. Placing great stress on social and ethical values, Royce expounded his ideal of life in *Philosophy of Loyalty*. Christianity for him implied loyalty to the community of the common man.

These practitioners of the higher philosophy moved, of course, in realms in which only metaphysically-minded intellectuals felt at home and comfortable. Popular outlooks on living had a much simpler quality. For many men the interpretation of life's purpose offered by one or another religious body proved adequate and satisfying. Some disillusioned individuals sought satisfactions in the haunting verse of the ancient Persian stargazer, Omar Kháyyám. His *Rubáiyat*, translated into English, enjoyed considerable popularity late in the nineteenth century in the English-reading world.

It sketched a philosophy compounded of hedonism and fatalism, appealing to individuals who had grown bored with the debate between religion and science, the conflict between faith and doubt. Skeptically pagan, the *Rubáiyat* explained that human existence was an incomprehensible mystery. No one knew, or could know, whence man came, nor whither he went. Therefore, man should enjoy the present, eat, drink and be merry for tomorrow he would be gone.

Confidence in the secular progress of mankind, unsurpassed by any previous epoch of history, was widely prevalent. The dynamic of evolution, it appeared, was inexorably forcing society forward. "Progress is not an accident but a necessity," Herbert Spencer proclaimed. "Always toward perfection is the mighty movement—toward a complete development and a more unmixed good." Many a man was gripped with the belief in "getting ahead," moving toward full freedom and perfect mastery over his own destiny.

The world was generally thought of as safe and sane and "on the up and up." All was right with the world—or soon would be. Peering into the future, many men were inclined to applaud the lead of Tennyson who "saw the vision of the world, and all the wonders that would be." Optimistically they anticipated the dawning of the day when

> . . . the war-drum throbbed no longer
> and the battle-flags were furled
> In the Parliament of Man, the Federation
> of the World.

The world would, to be sure, go on spinning "down the ringing grooves of change." Everyone was expected to face that reality without flinching. What the Victorian poet laureate could not foresee was that the world might spin so fast that it would end in a calamitous smash-up. The rosy popular optimism of the late nineteenth century came in for some extremely rough treatment during the First World War and its aftermath.

THE STATE OF RELIGION

The impact of intellectual and secular forces upon the Western religious heritage has already been reviewed (Chap. XVIII). It remains to pick up some loose threads and summarize certain aspects of religious history, more particularly of Roman Catholicism.

At the age of sixty-eight Pope Leo XIII was elected (1878) to the papal chair which he occupied for a quarter of a century. Keenly alert to the living issues of the day, a scholar and a diplomatist, he was the ablest pontiff since the Middle Age. His classic utterances on contemporary social and political problems set lasting standards for Catholicism. In 1891 he issued a famous encyclical, *Rerum Novarum*, defining the rights and duties of wage earners and employers, which brought him the title of "the workingman's Pope."

While the right of private ownership of property was approved and a collectivist economy condemned as a deadly plague, Leo XIII pleaded for restraints upon economic competition to remedy misery and destitution. The state should enact social legislation and workers should form unions to advance or protect their interests. Only the application of Christian ethical idealism, the Pope contended, could overcome the social abuses attendant upon industrialization; men of wealth had grave social responsibilities toward the less fortunate. Political parties were organized in several countries to implement papal social teachings and to safeguard ecclesiastical interests.

Leo XIII zealously promoted learning and theological scholarship. Under his guidance, interest in the philosophical system of St. Thomas Aquinas was richly invigorated. By means of "neo-Thomism" the Pope endeavored to bring rationalism and progress into harmony with, and to the support of, the Church. The archives of the Vatican, furthermore, were opened to qualified scholars and church institutions of learning, high and low, were expanded. Coming up from the rank of parish priest, Pope Pius X carried forward the general policies of the illustrious Leo. Catholic laymen were instructed to work for social reform, church law was codified and theological deviations were sternly combatted.

Several national governments, late in the century, clashed acrimoniously with the Vatican. Leo XIII carefully outlined the official attitude of the papacy toward secular states, asserting that any type of government which promoted the general welfare would be acceptable. On the other hand, he insisted that Roman Catholicism must be the established religion in countries having a Catholic population. Beyond that, if and whenever a government sanctioned anything repugnant "to the divine or the natural law," the faithful should resist. Love of country and struggles for national independence were given papal approval. "The natural law," Leo XIII declared, "enjoins us to love devotedly and to defend the country in which we... were brought up."

Some antagonisms with secular authority were conciliated, as in the case of the "Kulturkampf" in Germany. On the other hand, despite occasional rumors of impending settlement, the angry Roman Question persisted, and the Church sustained heavy reverses in clashes with the French national state. Leo XIII summoned (1892) French Catholics to rally to the Republic and to work for the repeal of laws which offended religious convictions, but French royalist elements responded unsympathetically. Anticlericals struck hard at ecclesiastical interests, closing church schools, dispersing monastic orders and cutting off all links between State and Church.

Elsewhere the Catholic monopoly over education if not ended was at least curtailed, and the State replaced the Church as the final authority in questions of marriage and divorce. Spain, in contrast, remained an exception to the general rule. There the Church commanded great wealth and power, and secular education made little headway. But anticlericalism was a growing force in Spanish intellectual circles and among industrial workers.

Of large meaning for world Catholicism was the rapid growth of communicants in the United States, aided by the constant stream of immigration. Catholics in the United States exceeded 16,000,000 by 1914; they displayed great zeal in building parish schools and colleges, promoting foreign missions and furnishing funds for general Catholic purposes. The social emphases of Pope Leo XIII found sympathetic reception in the United States, and for a short time, "Americanism," which stressed social welfare rather than theological doctrine, became a fad in Catholic Europe, in France especially.

While the Vatican regarded the invasion of "Americanism" with mixed emotions, it declared war to the death upon "modernism." Partisans of modernism wished to reinterpret Catholic teachings in conformity with contemporary secular scholarship, more particularly with historical inquiries into the literature of the Bible. Active in France and Italy, modernism attracted the support of some younger priests and small followings of laymen.

Pope Pius X branded (1907) modernism as "a synthesis of all heresies," repudiating, in particular, sixty-five propositions which departed from Catholic interpretations and directives handed down through the centuries. In effect the Pope flatly rejected the contention that secular learning necessitated alterations in Catholic tradition. Abbé Alfred F. Loisy, the outstanding exponent of modernism, was excommunicated and his writings were posted on the Index of Forbidden Books. The diffusion of modernism was effectively checked.

The Orthodox Eastern Church was lamed by jealousies and warring factions. Sixteen separate and quarrelsome Orthodox bodies acknowledged the primacy of the Patriarch in Constantinople, but his role was purely titular. Orthodox sectarians in the Balkans came to hate one another even more passionately than they despised the Moslem Turk. As a religious institution the Orthodox Church was a lifeless, wooden formalism, exerting only negligible influence upon the rank and file of communicants. Clergymen, short on education, exhibited small capacity for spiritual leadership.

A report by a team of international investigators described Balkan Orthodoxy with reasonable accuracy. "The Church does not systematically teach either morals or religion; its bishops and priests are the employees of the State and are the propagandists of nationality. Conversion with them means a change from one nationality to another, whether accomplished by persuasion or force. Religious conviction or faith have nothing to do with it." [2] The Russian Orthodox Church continued to be an invaluable ally of the tsarist regime, as it had been for centuries. After the Revolution of 1905, limited freedom of worship was extended to non-Orthodox creeds. The novels of Tolstoy and, more so, the growing appeal of radical social ideologies encouraged secession from the official national religion.

European Protestantism moved toward the "social gospel," or applied Christianity as some adherents called it. Concern for theological fundamentals slacked off as Protestants came to grips with everyday human welfare. Symptomatic was the organization (1865) of the British Salvation Army, which, by means of open-air evangelism, appealed to the unchurched and the unfortunate. To help the poor and needy, social service institutions were founded. The Salvation Army was soon carried to the Continent and to the United States. Protestant organizations such as the Young Men's Christian Association (1844) and the Young Women's Christian Association (1877) cut across denominational lines. Cooperation in foreign mission fields was foreshadowed in a world missionary conference of 1910.

Within Judaism, toward the end of the nineteenth century, a notable renaissance of Zionism occurred. Wherever they had wandered, devout Jews preserved the hope of ultimate restoration to the ancient home in Palestine.[3] If

[2] *Report of International Commission to Inquire into the Causes and Conduct of the Balkan Wars* (New York, 1914), pp. 271–272.

[3] In their ears sounded the ancient vow of their scattered people:

> If I forget thee, O Jerusalem
> May my right hand forget its cunning;
> May my tongue cleave to the roof of my mouth,
> If I remember thee not, O Zion!

that dream were fulfilled Jewry would be freed from discrimination and oppression and the faith of the fathers would escape the corrupting corrosions of secularism, it was contended. Portentous waves of anti-Jewish agitation which rolled across Russia, France and other countries immensely stimulated the Zionist revival.

Unprecedented energy was infused into the Zionist cause by Theodor Herzl, a sensitive and practical-minded journalist of Vienna, who urged the establishment of an autonomous Jewish commonwealth in the Turkish province of Palestine. He and like-minded Jews founded an international organization to promote Zionism, but the Turkish government could not be won over. As early as 1882, however, Jews from Russia and Rumania staked out agricultural colonies in Palestine and they were reinforced by later companies of settlers. Seeds were thus sown which would mature during and after the First World War.

Despite the activities of religious bodies it is probably accurate to say that apathy and agnosticism were more prevalent in Europe in the half century before 1914 than at any other time in modern history. Church attendance in Berlin throws some light on the general religious situation in western Europe. Church accommodations in the German capital were sufficient for only two per cent of the population; on one Sunday early in 1914, only 35,000 Berliners worshiped in Protestant churches out of a potential congregation of well beyond a million.

What may be termed the religion of progress captivated many an educated and cultivated European. For such individuals organized religion was not a living issue, but had ceased to have meaning, like alchemy or witchcraft. The idea of progress, as has been suggested above, assumed that society, impelled by science and reason, was proceeding automatically to the millennium. The pursuit of happiness in this world and a sense of ethical duty to posterity shouldered aside concern about the unknowable individual future. The fruits of secular learning challenged biblical or ecclesiastical authority. Aspirations of liberty, equality and human brotherhood confronted the Trinity of the Christian tradition.

THE FINE ARTS: ARCHITECTURE

As the nineteenth century moved along the architectural scene grew bewilderingly chaotic,

Cathedral of St. Isaac, St. Petersburg

Westminster Cathedral, London

responding to the needs and tastes of an industrialized and urbanized civilization. Great cities bulging with people and commerce presented architect and engineer with novel problems and opportunities. Never before of course had so many edifices with pretensions of beauty been erected: governmental and ecclesiastical, educational and industrial, residential and recreational. Separate "schools" of architecture conformed somewhat to national traditions, but there was considerable interchange of patterns between countries.

As the leading artistic nation, France frequently set the pace in architectural style and decoration. Paris strengthened its reputation as the most beautiful of cities; international exhibitions in the French capital invariably invigorated architecture and pictorial decoration. Students of architecture from all the world drifted to the renowned École des Beaux Arts to put the finishing touches on their training. Perhaps the central personality in architectural thought of the nineteenth century was Eugène E. Viollet-le-duc. Versatile and a titan for work, he reconstructed many medieval Gothic structures—Notre Dame in Paris, for instance, and as a writer on medieval architecture and allied arts he had no peer.

Architectural monuments of various kinds and for various purposes were raised in the

The first skyscraper—Home Insurance Building, Chicago

great cities of central Europe. The *Ringstrasse* of Vienna, flanked by a Gothic city hall, a parliament building on classic lines, museums, theaters and university buildings, rivaled the magnificent boulevards of Paris. The principal new edifices of Berlin, a huge Reichstag building and a cathedral, symbolized the young German Empire, heavy, without grace, or notable distinction.

The masterpiece of architecture in Russia was the majestic Cathedral of St. Isaac in St. Petersburg, breath-taking without and within. Russian designers sometimes reverted to distinctive native traditions as in the Cathedral of the Redeemer and Merchants' Row fronting on the Red Square in Moscow. Never had Russian architecture been so busy as in the decade after the Revolution of 1905. Palatial residences and apartment blocks in the principal cities were erected for wealthy landlords; new industrial and commercial structures testified to the acceleration in business activity.

British interest in Gothic architectural styles slacked off late in the nineteenth century, except for ecclesiastical structures. A dignified and stately Gothic cathedral at Liverpool, started early in the twentieth century, witnessed to the perennial appeal of Gothic. The Byzantine pattern was faithfully copied in the striking Roman Catholic Cathedral of Westminster in London. British designers (and their patrons) came increasingly to value sculpture and the other decorative arts in planning buildings. But as a whole, London appeared rather drab and utilitarian compared with the glittering French capital.

Architecture in the United States displayed in some respects more enterprise and originality than in Old World countries. During the first part of the nineteenth century the chaste classical heritage of Greece and Rome was in the ascendant. Then for a time Gothic and Renaissance models held the field (St. Patrick's Cathedral in New York and the Boston Public Library), only to give way under the inspiration of Henry H. Richardson, to Romanesque and Byzantine imitations. In home architecture, unpretentious and picturesque country houses exhibited novelty in conception and planning.

But the supreme contribution of the New World was the "skyscraper" in bustling cities, made possible by the fast elevator, fireproofing and changes in materials of construction, particularly steel girders. The desire for greater efficiency in transacting business operations, the high cost of urban land and the American taste for bigness combined to give vogue to the multi-story building. In the pioneering stage of the tall building, walls supported the weight of the upper floors, so that greater height required thicker masonry at the bottom. Important innovations were introduced in constructing the first "skyscraper," the Home Insurance Building in Chicago (1888), structural steel-framing carried the weight. This ten-story structure was believed to be about as high as construction could safely go. But Louis H. Sullivan and his pupils sent their buildings climbing ever higher into the sky. European architects imitated the skyscraper of the United States in a few instances, though on a less imposing scale.

TRENDS IN PAINTING

French schools of painting sustained the great European tradition and Paris was as fully the artistic capital as Florence had been in the Renaissance. Aspiring painters the globe over were drawn to old Paris whose heart was young and gay, as by a magnet. Creative energies and achievement in art ran as riotous a course as in poetry. Highly independent spirits experimented in forms which might mystify the layman, but seemed to testify that the artists were faithful to their inner visions. Instead of competing with photography, as yet scarcely more than a novelty, painters represented romantic moods and images on canvas; "good likenesses" of things seen passed out of style.

The "impressionist" school gloried in light and color in singularly imaginative compositions. Camille Pissarro, the dean of this art form, excelled in Parisian street scenes and slices of rural France. Many young men whom he inspired attained high distinction in the visual arts. Most distinguished of the impressionists was Édouard Manet; a nude by him known as "Olympia" is considered by some connoisseurs as the starting point of "modern" art. He also painted brightly-colored commonplaces, a bull fight, a horse race or the bar at the Folies Bergère. Only after a terrific struggle with conventional artists was the work of Manet admitted to be art.

One set of painters, known as the "post-impressionists" (or "expressionists"), cultivated "an eye in fine frenzy rolling" and allowed the hand to re-create the quaint twists of the brain. Of that company, Paul Gauguin deserted the sophistication of Paris for distant Tahiti and painted the primitive islanders in primitive styles. The Dutchman Vincent Van Gogh, an intensely individualistic spirit, created a fresh new world of painting, turbulent, frequently illogical, but usually understandable ("Iris"; "Saint Remy"). As became a former missionary to coal miners, Van Gogh produced several plain but expressive pieces on industrial workers. His more popular paintings ("Portrait of the Artist," for example) were reproduced wholesale and a Van Gogh exhibition at the

The Bar of the Folies Bergère, *painted by Édouard Manet*

Metropolitan Museum in New York broke all records (1950) for interest in a one-man showing there.

A major artist of great influence was Paul Cézanne, whose painting evolved through several stages. Cutting down on detail, Cézanne gave his creations a remarkable sense of space and he was more chary of color than was the current vogue. "Women with a Coffee Pot" reveals the serenity and sincerity of Cézanne's art; he also painted notable landscapes of southern French scenes ("Landscape with Bridge"). His work marked the culmination of French painting of the nineteenth century and served as the point of departure for more bizarre and restless techniques.

Though born in the United States, James A. McNeill Whistler spent most of his creative career in Europe. Alone among American painters he won international acclaim for both portraits and landscapes, though only after an uphill battle against angry critics who denied his productions classification as art. Influenced by Japanese styles and French impressionism, his best known picture, called "Whistler's Mother," was eventually purchased by the French government. Harmonious in line and color, this canvas conveyed delicate emotions with impressive simplicity. Another expatriate from the United States, John Singer Sargent achieved fame as a fashionable portraitist ("Theodore Roosevelt"). He also painted the prized mural decorations in Boston Public Library, illustrating the evolution of religion.

A tempestuous wave of "futurism" rolled out of Italy whose practitioners defiantly broke away from artistic norms. Without reproducing outward appearances "futurists," condemning all that had gone before, wished to capture the energy of the rushing world of machines and the sensation of movement and conflict. "Dynamism of a Footballer" by Umberto Boccioni, the dominating personality of futurism, is vivacious and analytical. Hailed by many critics as the most brilliant of living painters, the Spaniard Ignacio Zuloaga stimulated a rebirth of the rich artistic traditions of his country. Exotic treatments of Spanish human types, landscapes and nudes by Zuloaga were much sought after by art collectors in Europe and the United States.

Painting in the British Isles pursued distinctly national lines. More sober, less experimental than Continental painters, British artists of distinction were preachers or teachers with the brush. Holman Hunt, an intensely religious man, was best known for allegorical religious paintings ("The Light of the World"), which achieved lasting appreciation. Harmoniously colored portraits of contemporary celebrities and historical canvases of note were painted by G. F. Watts. Accomplished as a worker in water colors, Edward Burne-Jones exerted considerable influence upon decorative design, especially stained glass, for buildings. He belonged to an interesting set of British artists, spoken of as the pre-Raphaelite brotherhood. This group encouraged the revival of skilled craftsmanship in the lesser arts which the tyranny of the machine threatened to destroy.

Russian talent in painting was best expressed by Vassili Verestchagin and Ilya Repin, both of whom sat at the feet of French masters. Belonging to the landowning class, Verestchagin

The Card Players, *by Paul Cézanne, in the collection of Mr. Stephen C. Clark, Museum of Modern Art, New York*

The White Girl, *painted by James McNeill Whistler*

revealed his skill in painting episodes from Russian wars of the nineteenth century. He developed a great moral repugnance to war and by depicting war with horrible realism endeavored to further the cause of peace. Tsarist censorship banished some of his canvases to the closet. Repin, too, showed the full range of his capacity in historical and mythological themes ("The Reply of the Cossacks to Sultan Mohammed IV"). His paintings possessed a national flavor and were gorgeously colored. Repin's finest portraits, as of Count Leo Tolstoy, belong among the masterpieces of Russian art.

THE WORLD OF SCULPTURE

In the department of sculpture Frenchmen, again, took top honors. Not since Michelangelo had any artist with the chisel equaled Auguste Rodin. Endowed with a prodigious and fertile mind, Rodin rebelled against artificiality and worked under the inspiration of realism. His ability for portraying anguish and terror was splendidly illustrated in "The Gate of Hell." But the best-loved piece by Rodin is "The Thinker": an elemental mortal sits meditating with such intensity that his toes literally dig into the earth. Placed in front of the Pantheon in Paris, this splendid monument fittingly symbolizes French genius in arts and letters. A learned and refined contemporary, Jules Dalou, infused democratic enthusiasms and faith in the masses into "The Triumph of the Republic."

The Belgian sculptor Constantin Meunier carved remarkably realistic and original figures of industrial workers at their jobs in mine and factory. Meunier had taken lessons in French studios as had the foremost sculptor in the United States, Augustus Saint-Gaudens. Best known doubtless of his creations is a statue of Lincoln in Chicago, clearly in the mood of interpretative realism. His exquisite Adams memorial in a Washington cemetery, wonderfully evocative of the mood and mystery of death, has been praised as the most finished work of sculpture produced in the United States.

Like the United States the British Isles could not boast of a truly national school of sculpture, but the highly personal pieces of Alfred Stevens, of which the statue of Wellington in St. Paul's in London is typical, reflected the influence of French technique. National sculpture in Russia was initiated by Marc Antokolsky, who carved figures of Russian worthies and of the philosopher Spinoza. German and Viennese artists turned out large quantities of sculptures, the pieces of Max Klinger, in particular, attracting international applause ("Beethoven").

The Adams Memorial, Rock Creek Cemetery, Washington, D.C. This superb sculpture by Augustus Saint-Gaudens, profound in its expression of resignation and compassion, has been called "the finest thing in America."

THE MUSICAL SCENE

Creative music was probably the most active and fruitful of the fine arts and German composers continued to merit first place in international esteem. Towering above all others, was Richard Wagner, the most interesting mentality, it may be, in the entire history of the art. His was a mind touched by the bleak pessimism of Schopenhauer, and as a ferocious egotist, he was completely fascinated by himself. In the composition of grandiose and romantic operas Wagner stands supreme. "The Master" he was called. For subject matter he drew upon an extraordinary range of material, but principally upon German folk mythology. *Die Meistersinger*, for example, lauds the ancient glories of the Germans and expresses confidence in future greatness. The luxuriance of Wagner's music, its strenuous energy and the inexhaustible inventive faculties of the composer elicited the admiration of contemporaries and successors in two continents.

Wagner vividly outlined his approach to music in his description of *Tristan and Isolde*: "Endless yearning, longing, the bliss and the wretchedness of love; world power, fame, honor, chivalry, loyalty and friendship all blown away like an insubstantial dream; one thing alone left living—longing, longing unquenchable, a yearning, a hunger, a languishing forever renewing itself; one sole redemption—death, surcease, a sleep without awakening."

The influence of Wagner ranged far beyond operatic dramas. His romanticism stimulated rabid political nationalism and Pan-Germanism especially in Munich, Bavaria, whose king generously patronized the composer. It was precisely there that the National Socialist fanaticism of Adolf Hitler had its beginnings. "Whoever wants to understand Nazi Germany," Hitler once said, "must know Wagner." The dreamy, fiery mysticism of the musician entered Hitler's receptive spirit. The Führer identified himself with the knight in shining armor of *Siegfried*, who had been summoned to slay menacing dragons.[4]

The title of heir of Wagner was conferred upon Richard Strauss. *Der Rosenkavalier* is a charming operatic classic which brought the Viennese waltz to its climax. Strauss called Vienna home as did Johannes Brahms, the closest rival to Wagner for preeminence as a composer, but, unlike him, devoted to the classical legacy of Beethoven. Disciples of Wagner criticized the compositions of Brahms as the work of an old-fashioned fuddy-duddy. But he was a great creative artist, who wrote many types of musical literature in which he made lavish use of folk melodies. His gift for emotional intensity and mastery of form was fully displayed in the *German Requiem*. As a classicist, Brahms upheld the fertile musical traditions of Vienna.

From one angle the most interesting feature of musical writing in the late nineteenth century was the emergence of an internationally respected Russian school, represented by Nicholas Rimsky-Korsakoff and Peter I. Tschaikowsky. These composers, whose work gave Russian music a place in the great art of the world, were amateurs really, moving into the profession of music from government service. They energetically exploited Muscovite folk-tunes and often chose subject matter from the tumultuous history of their country.

[4] Significantly the fortifications in western Germany, constructed under Nazi auspices, were called the Siegfried Line.

Rimsky-Korsakoff achieved world acclaim with his symphonies, the first Russian to compose in that form. But at home his operatic dramas (*The Golden Cock*), full of vitality and vividly colored, received the weightiest applause. As conductor of the orchestra in St. Petersburg, this many-sided genius vigorously promoted national musical studies. Tschaikowsky likewise drifted to the capital, though his early reputation was made as director of the newly established Moscow conservatory. An opera, *Eugen Oneygin*, based on Pushkin's poetic masterpiece, songs and symphonies (*Sixth or Pathetic*), established Tschaikowsky among the leading composers of the time. Though his music is unrestrained to the point of boisterousness, it has maintained its popular appeal. The composer undertook concert tours to the West, the United States included.

Operatic drama in France found a master of originality and high quality in Charles F. Gounod. His greatest composition, *Faust*, inspired by Goethe, was tremendously successful from the first and never lost its popularity. Pieces for church presentation (*The Redemption*), consolidated the position of Gounod as the most influential French musician of his generation. His real successor was Claude Debussy, often referred to as the father of French "modernism," who tried to stir the mind as well as the emotions of music lovers. Producer of many works of various types his chief title to fame was a lyrical drama, *Pelléas et Mélisande*.

British music, which had depended mainly upon importations from the Continent, entered a new phase with the compositions of Arthur S. Sullivan. To exceptional mastery of the composer's art, Sullivan added extraordinary versatility. Much appreciated for sacred music, such as "The Lost Chord" and the moving "Onward, Christian Soldiers," his talent flowered most fully in opera (*The Golden Legend*). But for popular entertainment his charming light operas (*H. M. S. Pinafore, Mikado*), with humorous librettos by W. S. Gilbert, belong in a class by themselves.

Edward Elgar, who was knighted, as was Sullivan, for his musical contributions, made a name for himself with an oratorio, *The Dream of Gerontius*, and a stirring marchpiece, "Pomp and Circumstance." Music in the United States moved into a creative era with the orchestral and other pieces of Edward A. MacDowell, who reflected the influence of studies in France and Germany. The possibilities in native folk music were hinted at in his *Indian Suite*. John Philip Sousa attained worldwide celebrity for heart-tingling march music ("The Stars and Stripes Forever"). The natural talent in the United States for vocal music was demonstrated by a long list of eminent men and women soloists.[5]

[5] Composers of international stature appeared in several of the smaller European nationalities. Many of them made excellent use of the folk-tunes of their homelands. Worthy of mention were Franz Liszt, claimed by Magyars and Germans; the Czechs, Bedrich Smetana, and Antonin Dvórak, who composed for a time in the United States; the Norwegian, Eduard Grieg, writer of the music for Ibsen's *Peer Gynt*; the Finn, Jean Sibelius, whose thunderous tone-poem "Finlandia" is the product of a genius. Very popular were operas by Italian masters such as Giuseppe Verdi, and Giacomo Puccini (*Madame Butterfly*).

SUMMARY

By many tests, the nineteenth century must be appraised as the most productive of centuries, and the second half, arguably, excelled the first. Scanning the record it is not difficult to understand the claim that this century vindicated the philosophy of progress, though, likely enough, progress would be conceived in terms of the extraordinary sweep of science and technology or, maybe, in terms of the fabulous increase in population.

The late nineteenth century was in truth a kind of second Renaissance in the things of the mind and spirit, the flowering of world culture. Separating the gold from the dross, the all-around accomplishment may be recalled by the mere names of the cultural giants. Strung out in alphabetic order they were: Brahms, Cézanne, Channing, Flaubert, France, Ibsen, Leo XIII, Mommsen, Nietzsche, Rodin, Shaw, Tennyson, Tolstoy, Verlaine, Wagner, Wells, Whitman.

The whole structure of culture, the heritage of human effort and strivings over the centuries, was crystallized in a predominantly middle class civilization. This social element was vigorous, comfortable, educated, tolerant, respectful of law, secure and it looked into the future with an optimism that verged on the fantastic. And yet there were strong overtones of social restlessness, not least because the basic necessities of life cost so dearly, although comforts and luxuries were more generally available.

It had been a prosperous and enlightened half century, and a peaceful one. Cultural treasures had accumulated at a pace worthy of the unconquerable mind of man and they promised to make him:

> For aye removed
> From the developed brute, a god though in the germ.

FOR FURTHER STUDY

JAMES T. MERZ, *A History of European Thought in the Nineteenth Century* (2nd ed., 4 vols., Edinburgh, 1912–1928)

BENEDETTO CROCE, *European Literature in the Nineteenth Century* (New York, 1924)

GILBERT K. CHESTERTON, *The Victorian Age in Literature* (new ed., New York, 1946)

VAN WYCK BROOKS, *The Confident Years: 1855–1915* (New York, 1952)

GEORGE P. GOOCH, *History and Historians in the Nineteenth Century* (new ed., London, 1952) PAPERBACK

JOHN H. RANDALL, *The Making of the Modern Mind* (new ed., New York, 1940)

HUGH A. REYBURN, *Nietzsche* (London, 1948)

RENÉ FÜLOP-MILLER, *Leo XIII and Our Times* (New York, 1937)

ERNEST TROELTSCH, *The Social Teaching of the Christian Churches* (Eng. trans., new ed., 2 vols., London, 1960) PAPERBACKS

ISRAEL COHEN, *Jewish Life in Modern Times* (new ed., New York, 1929)

GERMAIN BAZIN, ed., *A History of Modern Painting* (Eng. trans., New York, 1951)

ERNEST NEWMAN, *The Wagner Operas* (New York, 1949)

NIKOLAUS L. B. PEVSNER, *Outline of European Architecture* (London, 1960) PAPERBACK

ANDREAS DORPALEN, *Heinrich von Treitschke* (New Haven, 1957)

A List of Significant Dates

WESTERN EUROPE		CENTRAL AND EASTERN EUROPE		OVERSEAS	
1871(5)	Third French Republic	**1873**	*Kulturkampf*	**1875**	British control Suez
1883	Fabian Society	**1877**	Russo-Turkish War	**1877**	Victoria Empress of India
1884-5	Britain: Extension of Franchise	**1878**	Treaty of Berlin	**1881**	French Protectorate over Tunisia
1886	First Home Rule Bill	**1879**	Protectionism in Germany	**1884-5**	West African Conference (Berlin)
1894	Dreyfus Case	**1881**	Assassination Tsar Alexander II	**1885**	Indian National Congress
1897	Victoria's Diamond Jubilee	**1884**	German Social Legislation	**1885**	Trans-Canadian Railway
1900	Birth of Labour Party	**1888**	William II German Emperor	**1889**	Brazil, a Republic
1904-5	Separation Church and French State	**1890**	Bismarck Resigns	**1894**	Sino-Japanese War
1909	British Social Legislation	**1894**	Tsar Nicholas II	**1898**	Spanish-American War
1911	House of Lords Reformed	**1897**	First German Naval Bill	**1899**	Boer War
1914	Adoption of Home Rule	**1898**	Russian Social Democratic Party	**1901**	Commonwealth of Australia
1916	Easter Rebellion: Ireland	**1903**	Beginning of Bolshevik Party	**1901**	United States Steel Trust
		1905	Russian Revolution	**1904**	Russo-Japanese War
		1906	Duma in Russia	**1910**	Japanese Annexation of Korea
		1908	Young Turk Revolution	**1910**	Union of South Africa
		1912	Manhood Suffrage: Italy	**1911**	Chinese Revolution
		1912-13	Balkan Wars	**1914**	Panama Canal Completed
		1917	March and Bolshevik Revolutions		

CULTURAL AFFAIRS

1872 "Mother" (Whistler)

1877 *The Pillars of Society* (Ibsen)

1878 Pope Leo XIII

1881 *The Brothers Karamazov* (Dostoievsky)

1883 *Thus Spake Zarathustra* (Nietzsche)

1885 *The Rise of Silas Lapham* (Howells)

1885 *Germinal* (Zola)

1890 *The Golden Bough* (Frazer)

1890 "Women with Coffee Pot" (Cézanne)

1890 *The Influence of Seapower Upon History* (Mahan)

1893 *Evolution and Ethics* (Huxley)

1899 "The White Man's Burden" (Kipling)

1903 *The Lower Depths* (Gorki)

1904 "The Thinker" (Rodin)

1908 *Penguin Island* (France)

1912 *Androcles and the Lion* (Shaw)

1910 "Firebird" (Stravinsky)

GENERAL

1873 Business Depression

1876 Internal combustion engine

1876 Telephone

1879 Austro-German Alliance

1879 Edison electric lamp

1882 Triple Alliance

1884 Steam turbine

1888 Chicago skyscraper

1894 Franco-Russian Alliance

1895 X-rays

1897 First Zionist Conference

1899 Hague Conference

1901 Transatlantic wireless

1902 Anglo-Japanese Alliance

1903 Wright aeroplane

1904 Anglo-French Entente

1905 Einstein: theory of relativity

1905 Moroccan Crisis

1907 Triple Entente

1908 Bosnian Crisis

1911 Turco-Italian War

1914 First World War

1917 Entry of the United States

1919 Paris Peace Treaties

1919 Third International

PART V

THE WORLD IN FERMENT

CHAPTER XXV

THE FIRST WORLD WAR

THE SMOLDERING VOLCANO

A SOLID, realistic understanding of the origins of the First World War is of the utmost importance for the student of contemporary society. That struggle and the Second World War have doubtless shaped the character of present-day society more than anything else. A period of history came to an end in 1914, in so far as anything in history ever ends. Western Europe ceased to be the active center of the world; gunfire shattered the traditional sense of stability and confidence. As wars have run, the First World War was relatively short, but terribly destructive and exhausting. Who in 1914 could have imagined that a mere thirty years later the once powerful and prosperous countries of Western Europe would depend upon aid from the United States to stave off economic chaos, or that they would be utterly incapable of protecting themselves against attack?

For two generations before 1914, Europe had been free of wars, except in the Balkan peninsula. No general conflict had occurred in fact since the banishment of Napoleon. In an era of comparative concord, the ideal of perpetual peace had attained unprecedented popularity, though the idea of an appeal to the sword was definitely less repugnant than after the First World War.

Officer's dress helmet, Imperial German army, 1914

The economic interdependence of the nations had grown apace. Expanding exchange of goods, international business leagues to fix prices and parcel out markets, and international fairs in the leading cities of the world knitted material bonds between countries. International congresses touching virtually every facet of human interest convened periodically. Meetings of the Inter-Parliamentary Union, for instance, founded in 1889, reflected need for exchange of views by law-makers from all countries in which democratic constitutions were in force. Religious bodies cherished international ties, as did Marxist collectivism, which dogmatically ascribed armed conflicts between countries to competition for markets or raw materials. A congress to celebrate the founding of the First International was scheduled to meet at Vienna in the summer of 1914, but the outbreak of war cancelled the plans.

Since 1843 international societies dedicated to the cause of peace had met at irregular intervals. In the early twentieth century praiseworthy recognition for individual contributions to the preservation of peace was made in the Nobel Peace Prizes, and Andrew Carnegie generously endowed an organization to promote the abolition of war. Learned scholars and humanistic novelists taught that wars were as futile as they were unnecessary. For example, *War Now Possible?* (1899), written by Jean de Bloch, developed the theme that war in the industrial age must invite mutual destruction; the victor would emerge from the struggle as impoverished as the vanquished. A philosopher in the United States, William James, eloquently pleaded for a *Moral Equivalent of War* (1910).

It was urged in some circles that disputes between nations could be peacefully resolved if armies and armaments were restricted and quarrels were submitted to arbitration. Accordingly, two important conferences were assembled at The Hague (1899, 1907) attended by representatives of twenty-six and forty-four nations respectively. No understanding to curb armaments could be worked out, but bans were laid on certain types of weapons. And a permanent court of arbitration at The Hague was created to which parties in a quarrel might have recourse, though there was no obligation to do so. Several disputes were in fact amicably adjusted by the Hague Court, setting useful precedents for the future. Preliminary steps, moreover, to define and codify "international law" were taken. Seeds were planted, in short, which one day would grow into the League of Nations and later into the more mature United Nations.

In addition, a series of bilateral international pacts pledged signatories to seek accommodation of differences by arbitration. The record of the United States and Great Britain in arbitrating quarrels stood as a shining example to the world. These two nations got along for a century without war, and it certainly was not for want of materials for quarrels. The years after 1815 were especially critical and that was notably true again during the War between the States. More than once peace was saved by moderation and the good sense of statesmen. Many other disputes between nations yielded to arbitration, but never questions of fundamental importance about which governments and peoples cared deeply. Physical force remained the final arbiter in international affairs. Declared the American naval philosopher, A. T. Mahan, "The nation will have the strongest arguments which has the strongest organized force." Europe lived on the edge of a smoldering volcano; and in 1914 it erupted.

RESPONSIBILITY FOR THE WAR

On one side of the battleline in the First World War were arrayed the Central Powers: Germany, Austria,[1] Turkey and Bulgaria. Against that bloc stood the Allies (or Entente), embracing Britain, France, Russia, Japan, Italy, Serbia, the United States and others, more than thirty countries altogether.

The question of responsibility for the coming of war has long been debated by passionate partisans and sober scholars alike. Historians may well argue the matter until Doomsday—or at any rate until the day before Doomsday. There is reasonably full agreement, however, on the point that responsibility for the war was shared by the major countries of Europe and Serbia. A goodly company of scholars has traced the fundamental sources of the struggle to certain dynamic interests and impersonal forces operating in modern civilization.

The information upon which the historian relies in his appraisal of causes comes from three principal sources. First there are the official archives of the several governments. Each country preserved in its secret vaults copies of the documents dispatched and received by its foreign office, together with official commentaries. These papers disclose a great deal about the reasoning and the acts of policy makers.

[1] When Austria is used in the following pages, the Hapsburg Monarchy of Austria-Hungary is implied.

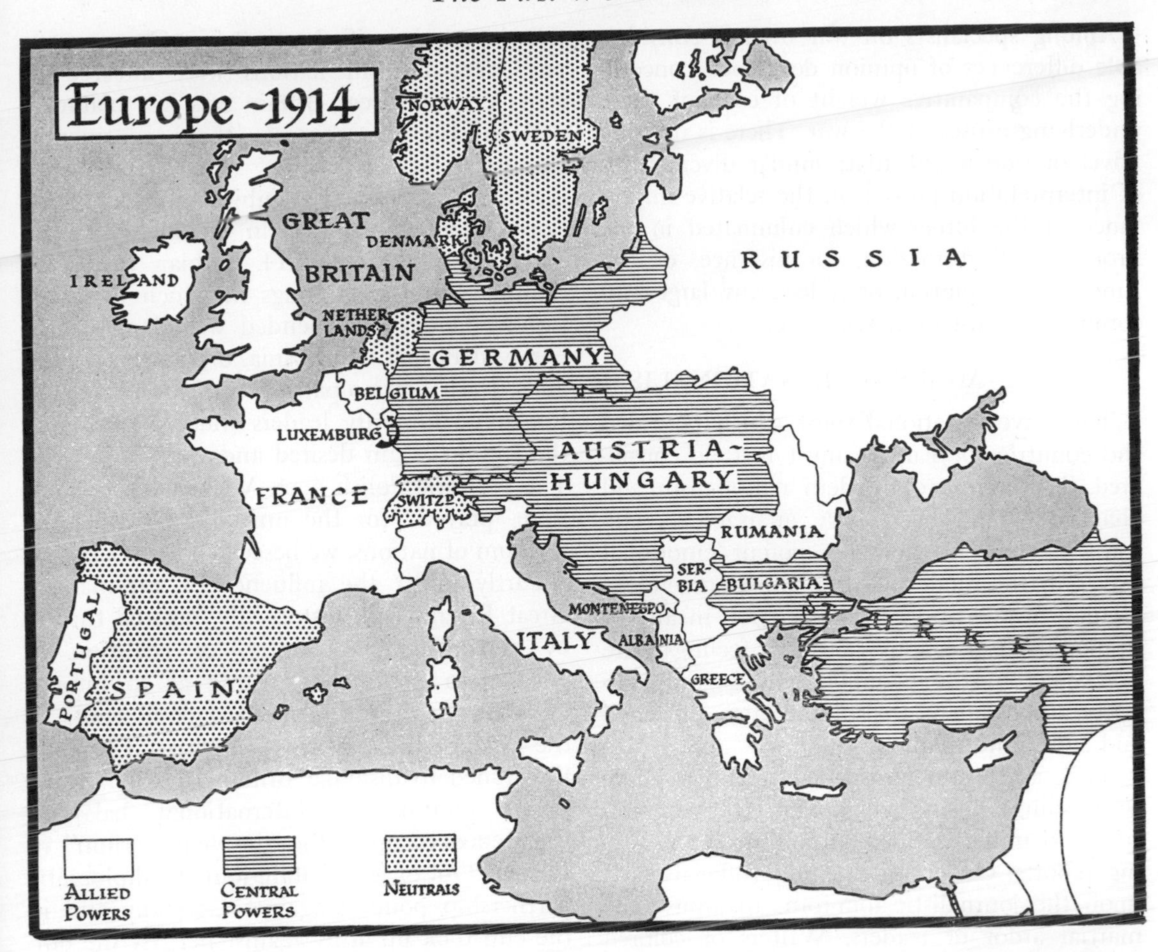

Ordinarily this highly secret and fascinating literature has not been available for scholarly study until long after the events occurred. But the Bolshevik government of Russia began to publish the diplomatic records of the tsarist government in 1917, intending to prove the predatory objectives of the tsardom and its Western allies. After the war the new governments of Germany and Austria imitated the Bolshevik example, and later on so did Britain and France. All in all, thousands upon thousands of diplomatic documents saw the light of day, more than for any previous period of history. While these records do not tell all, no acceptable historical reconstruction can be prepared without them.

In the second place, many European public leaders entered the witness box with reminiscences, diaries, private papers or autobiographies. These revelations have been modestly supplemented by interviews of scholarly investigators with prominent statesmen and military chiefs. And third, a wealth of information in newspapers and magazines swells the enormous mass of evidence in many languages. Drawing upon and sifting these voluminous materials, literally thousands of articles and books have endeavored to illuminate the coming of the First World War.

Adding matters up, it becomes clear that three or four distinguishable forces combined to make the conflict of 1914 possible: excessive and aggressive nationalism, imperialism and economic rivalries and commercial jealousies, and competition in fighting forces. These three elements gave rise to a fourth factor; that is, the competing partnerships into which the leading nations of the Old World twisted themselves after the Franco-German War of 1870.

Among specialists on war origins, considerable differences of opinion developed concerning the comparative weight of each of these underlying causes of the war. There is nothing novel or odd about that; similar divergencies of interpretation prevail on the relative importance of the forces which culminated in the Protestant Reformation, for instance, or the American Revolution or indeed any large and complicated historical sequence.

AGGRESSIVE NATIONALISM

The fervent national spirit which pervaded the countries of Europe must first be considered. The nature of modern nationalism and chauvinism has been fully analyzed heretofore. They were the most potent emotional drives in the modern world, the transcendent secular creed, stronger than religion in any of its popular expressions. National feelings were quickened in the common schools and conscript armies, inculcated by the press, preached and sung unto men.

Time and again newspapers inflamed jingoistic feelings, falsified the doings of other countries and minimized the importance of pacifying reports. On occasion, public officials beat upon the journalistic tom-toms to arouse the martial ardor of readers. Writers of colored and poisonous history, too, contributed to the intensification of national biases. Addressing the American Historical Association in 1916, Professor H. Morse Stephens remarked: "The historian...feeds the spirit of national intolerance today as his predecessors fed the flames of religious intolerance in days gone by. Woe unto us! if we cannot see, written in blood, in the dying civilization of Europe, the dreadful result of exaggerated nationalism as set forth in the patriotic histories of some of the most eloquent historians of the nineteenth century."

So, in one way and another, Europeans came to believe that their own government was never wrong in its dealings with other countries. They came to believe in the moral, material and military superiority of their own nation, and the inferiority of other peoples. Assertions of superiority were most strident and provocative in newly-unified countries, Germany in particular, but all nations were affected in some degree. Great Britain was less blatantly nationalistic, in general, than continental countries.

Among spokesmen of subject minorities, national passions increased in vehemence in the half century before 1914. Serbian cafes, for example, rang with songs in which praise of bygone heroes was blended with laments for enslaved Bosnia. "O Bosnia, orphan before the gods, Hast thou no patriots in thy land today?" For some minority leaders war alone seemed the way to attain desired and valid objectives. The patriotic Polish poet, Mickiewicz, to illustrate, prayed "for the universal war, for the freedom of nations, we beseech Thee, O Lord."

Partly under the influence of nationalism, Great Britain had, historically, resisted threats by a continental country, or coalition of powers, to become so strong as to imperil the security of the island kingdom itself. In the twentieth century, Imperial Germany threatened to dislodge Britain from her traditional position as international balancer, threatened to upset the "just equilibrium" of Europe. Out of fear Britain joined a diplomatic partnership pointed against Germany and in the end took up arms against her. At the outset of the war Prime Minister Herbert Asquith explained that Britain was fighting "to withstand as we believe in the best interests not only of our Empire, but of civilization at large, the arrogant claim of a single Power to dominate the development of the destinies of Europe."

Among Germans, assertive, blustering nationalism demanded a larger place in the European and the world sun. Well educated, hard working, a nation of vigorous and disciplined warriors, many Germans felt capable of mastering Europe and itched to do so. Slighting allusions were made about "degenerate Britain, corrupt France, barbarous Russia." Persuaded of the incomparable excellence of their country, German nationalists came to believe that they were encircled by jealous and predatory neighbors.

French national pride smarted under the

memory of the loss of prestige which France had suffered at the hands of Germany in 1870–1871. The ceded provinces of Alsace-Lorraine were the flaming symbols of French humiliation. For some influential Frenchmen, the recovery of the lost provinces (and of French primacy in Europe) transcended all other secular aspirations.

In Russian circles there was much talk, responsible and otherwise, about a national mission to advance or protect Pan-Slav interests. Expansionist dreams extended into every district of Europe that was peopled by Slavs. Coupled with that was the long-standing Muscovite ambition to acquire Constantinople and the Turkish Strait. And nationalism, or something akin to nationalism, impelled statesmen of Austria to strive to hold together that realm of many national elements.

In the southern sections of Europe, nationalism fostered aspirations prejudicial to peace. Italian patrioteers ardently desired to annex Austrian provinces (including the port of Trieste) that were inhabited by Italian-speaking folk, and to achieve mastery over the Adriatic. Hot, explosive chauvinism ruled in the Balkan states, being greatly stimulated by wars in 1912 and 1913. Serb, Bulgar, Rumanian and Greek nationalists cherished lavish visions of territorial expansion. Nationalistically imbued Turks wished to rehabilitate the fallen fortunes of their ancient Ottoman fatherland.

Nationalism, moreover, nourished the furious drive for overseas empire which contributed to the oncoming of war. It supported the universal demand for ever stronger fighting establishments to ensure national safety, and thus intensified popular apprehensions and suspicions abroad. Nationalism, indeed, so interpenetrated the Europe of the twentieth century, in mind and emotions, that it crops up in every aspect of the background of the war.

IMPERIALISM AND ECONOMIC RIVALRIES

Imperialism, too, helped to make conflict possible in 1914. It was not at all a novel phenomenon. Rivalry for overseas areas and their trade has provoked international jealousies and bitterness ever since the beginning of the modern age. Recall the recurrent Anglo-Dutch wars of the seventeenth century or the prolonged Anglo-French duel of the eighteenth over North America and India. Germany and Italy, entering the colonial race late, proved energetic competitors and in neither case were their ambitions appeased.

Rivalries over empire heightened tensions and hatreds among nations with conflicting interests in Europe. Old enmities along the Rhine, on the North Sea and the Mediterranean were aggravated by newer disputes over South Africa, over China, over Morocco and over Mesopotamia. It is hard to blame any one of the contestants more than another for the animosities and crises which the struggle for empire generated. But Germany, definitely a "have-not" colonial power, was assuredly rougher and less feline in her tactics. "Before we blame Germany," writes the British historian, Harold Nicolson, "we must first blame our own Elizabethans. The spirit was exactly the same: the Germans, however, . . . behaved less blatantly; and were less successful."

It is sometimes argued that economic competition, with which the struggle for colonies was indissolubly intertwined, was the principal cause of the grisly catastrophe of 1914. The economic interpretation of war has in fact a long history; in the old Vedic language of India, for instance, the word for war is equivalent to the "desire for cows." As applied to the First World War the theory insists that nations were rushed into battle by the moneyed classes, that the war was the "inevitable" outcome of the clashing interests of commercial and financial groups from different countries. Exporters, bankers, shipping companies and "merchants of death" spurred on diplomatists, so the argument runs, bamboozled legislative bodies and whipped up bellicose hysteria in the masses by means of artful propaganda.

The favorite German explanation of the coming of the war was that British capitalists wished to destroy the Fatherland, an enterprising and successful rival in world trade and shipping. But that facile theory fails to hold up, when tested by the facts. Far the greater part of the business community in all countries dreaded a major war, which, at the very least, would have upsetting consequences upon the economy. The crude economic interpretation of the First World War is a popular oversimplification. It makes a molehill out of a mountain. Commercial rivalry engendered international ill-will and friction, undeniably, but that factor was only one among others in bringing on the conflict.

MILITARISM AND ARMAMENT COMPETITION

Competition in fighting services and glorification of war envenomed the European atmosphere and helped greatly to make the First World War possible. For purposes of military preparedness governments appropriated what then seemed perfectly colossal sums—"a staggering burden." The philosophy of preparedness was made up of several persuasive themes. It was everywhere argued that strong armaments were indispensable for national safety and to preserve the peace. That reasoning reflected the old Roman proverb "Si vis pacem, para bellum"—"If you want peace, prepare for war." Superior military strength, that is, would deter an enemy power from attacking.

The influence of a nation in time of international controversy, moreover, was directly proportional to its capacity for war. The foreign office of any country was only the façade of its fighting services. A British poet epitomized (1896) the idea in verse:

> Let lawyers and statesmen addle
> Their pates over points of law,
> If sound be our sword and saddle
> And gun-gear
> Who cares one straw?

The case for preparedness rested also on the belief that war was "inevitable" by reason of the very nature of human nature. The record of history was invoked to buttress the argument. Down through the centuries, the pages of the past were strewn with wars. Long ago in ancient Israel, the Psalmist had lamented: "And the way of peace they have not known." Every state was, potentially at any rate, a war-making institution, proclaimed as such by the fighting animals chosen as national symbols: the lion, the bear and the eagle. The lamb appeared only on the standards of the Christian Church.

Some advocates of preparedness bestirred themselves to prove that investments in armaments would pay handsome dividends. Witness the gains which accrued to Prussia by defeating France in 1870, or the Japanese prizes from the victory over Russia in 1905. In the light of history it was elementary wisdom to assume that other wars would come and elementary prudence to prepare against the testing time.

Logic of that order was reinforced by sociological interpretations of biological science. The Darwinian theorem of the survival of the fittest, it was contended, applied equally to nations as to species of animals. The race was always to the strong. In the fierce ordeal of war, the better nation would crowd the inferior aside. The survival of the fittest was the survival of quality. "If it were not for war," proclaimed the German general Bernhardi, "we should probably find that inferior races would overcome healthy, youthful ones by their wealth and numbers." "It is the competition of life," explained Professor W. G. Sumner of Yale, "which makes war, and that is why war has always existed and always will."

Bound up with convictions of that sort was the doctrine that warfare yielded desirable values for a nation. Dozens of illustrations of this belief might easily be culled from the literature of modern Europe. Thundered the German Treitschke, "God will see to it that war always recurs as a drastic medicine for the human race." A British general, Lord Roberts, put the matter this way: "War is salutary, necessary, and the only national tonic that can be prescribed . . . Peace begets overcivilization and overcivilization degeneracy. Then comes a war . . . a country revives . . . and rises like the phoenix."

Acting on the logic of preparedness, countries of continental Europe built up armies on the Prussian model. Young men were obligated to take military training for two years or more. After that, conscripts passed into the reserve forces, appearing periodically for "refresher courses," and subject to call at any time until late middle age. Such training, it was urged, was necessary for national security and was also beneficial for the conscripts; it smartened up the slovenly, goaded on the lazy and improved the health of the physically deficient.

Large conscript armies increased the responsibilities and the importance of professional soldiers, general staff and lower officers. That august caste in some European countries exercised more political influence when diplomatic crises arose than civilian authorities. It was a powerful element in Russia, Germany and Austria, less influential in France, and still less in Britain. In the crucial emergency of 1914 Russian military chiefs persuaded the inconsequential Tsar Nicholas II to summon his immense reserve forces to the colors. Germany followed suit, declared war and the struggle was on.

Great Britain maintained only a small army, raised by voluntary enlistment, and employed principally as police garrisons in the Empire. For security and the protection and promotion of national and imperial interests, Britain relied upon its celebrated navy. Generation after generation, Britain had ruled the kingdom of Neptune with its storms and fogs and mysteries. There was no inclination whatsoever to relinquish the shield and scepter. Rather it was the avowed British intention to have a fleet equal in fighting strength to the next two strongest naval powers.

After 1898 Germany started to emulate the land of Nelson on the blue water by building a formidable battlefleet. Emperor William II regarded the navy as his very special pet and he was intensely proud of it. Popular support for fleet expansion was usually enlisted by pointing to Britain as the potential enemy. Alarmed by the growth of German seapower, Britain exerted herself to keep a comfortable margin of superiority. The naval rivalry which ensued disastrously envenomed Anglo-German relations. British overtures to halt the costly race by mutual agreement limiting naval armaments ran into sand. In the dank soil of naval competition, ill-will and suspicion thrived.

Great and enlarging fighting establishments on land and sea, equipped with ever more deadly weapons, generated hatred, suspicions and perpetual dread on every hand. Europeans

Units of the expanding German navy (the Moltke, *the* Stettin *and the* Bremen*) on a 1912 courtesy call in United States waters*

everywhere lived under the everlasting threat of a sudden and possibly an overwhelmingly decisive attack. Primitive fears, thus stimulated, were in themselves conducive to war, which, paradoxically, armaments were intended to prevent.

THE WEB OF DIPLOMATIC PARTNERSHIP

In the midst of the First World War, Woodrow Wilson shrewdly observed: "No single outstanding fact caused the war; really the graver blame rested upon the whole European system, a concatenation of alliances and treaties, a complicated network of intrigue and espionage which unerringly caught the entire family in its meshes." It is the considered judgment of many experts that this "concatenation of alliances and treaties" formed the largest of the tangled roots of the war. International anarchy reigned in a Europe that was divided into two powerful diplomatic combinations. If individual members of the opposing partnerships took up arms, their friends would almost inescapably be drawn into the struggle.

The arrangement of these partnerships was the work of diplomacy. After the war it became fashionable to reproach diplomacy as a black and sinister art, conducted by men of incredible incompetence or infinite cunning. The inference was that wiser, more enlightened and less secretive handling of international relations would have staved off the conflict. Diplomacy has been defined as "the application of intelligence and tact to the conduct of official relations between governments of independent states." In nature and in technique intergovernmental negotiations resembled the dealings between business firms or even individuals. Across the centuries, a code of customs had grown up for the conduct of relations, but, as in chess, more depended on the character of the players than upon the rules of the game. Benjamin Franklin once proposed as the formula for an ideal diplomatist: "Sleepless tact, unmovable calmness, and a patience that no folly, no provocation, no blunders can shake."

Much the greater part of the "old diplomacy" was carried on in secret, which was conducive to deceit, chicanery, espionage and often increased tension and mistrust in potentially enemy countries. Secret treaties, secretly arrived at, were the order of the day. Final decisions on diplomatic policy rested with a few individuals in any country. "How few are the persons in every state in whose hands lie the issues of war and peace!" wrote Lord Bryce, the British diplomatist, in an analysis of the coming of war in 1914. "In some of the now belligerent countries the final and vital decisions were taken by four or five persons only, in others by six or seven only. Even in Britain decision rested practically with less than twenty-five." [2]

The conduct of diplomacy was entrusted to professionals, as a rule, who made a career of international affairs—experts in the dangerous and fascinating arena of power politics. Ideally, the foreign minister was a veteran statesman with an imaginative grasp of policy, capable of seeing foreign relations in large perspective and of thinking in terms of the next generation. The permanent officials in each foreign office, the real specialists, handled day-to-day transactions, assessed national interests and potentialities and scrupulously analyzed every controversy that arose.

Diplomatic representatives stationed abroad, ambassadors and ministers, resembled mouthpieces of the home office after the telegraph and the telephone made quick communication possible. These agents carried on transactions with the foreign office to which they were assigned and reported on what they learned of thought and opinion. Responsible diplomatic posts were seldom casually awarded as political consolation prizes. On an overall estimate, European diplomatists before 1914 were high-minded gentlemen, much more concerned with peaceful adjustment of quarrels than with stirring up trouble. There were exceptions, of course, and standards of diplomatic behavior in Balkan capitals were notoriously below average levels.

[2] James Bryce, *Some Historical Reflections on War, Past and Present* (1916), p. 8.

HOW THE PARTNERSHIPS ORIGINATED

For a generation after 1871, Prince Bismarck, the autocratic director of German diplomacy, dominated the diplomatic stage. Having brought about the consolidation of Germany, this audacious and resourceful statesman regarded his country as satiated. His masterly maneuvers aided greatly in preserving peace, except for localized Balkan wars. With the great German army behind him, Bismarck moved upon the diplomatic board with notable skill and success. Feeling that France would seek revenge, if the international scene seemed favorable, Bismarck worked to keep the Third Republic in diplomatic isolation. He wished, more exactly, to maintain friendship with Austria and Russia, and to prevent a coalition of either of these monarchies with France. Germany dreaded a major war on two fronts in much the same way that the United States, later on, feared a two-ocean conflict.

When clashing ambitions in the Balkans obliged Bismarck to choose between Austria and Russia, he chose Austria, without, however, wholly alienating Russia. A secret Austro-German treaty of 1879 brought into being a defensive alliance directed against the tsardom. That first link in the German diplomatic partnership was renewed periodically and was in force in 1914. In 1882, Italy, at odds with France and anxious to bolster her position among the nations, united with Germany and Austria in a Triple Alliance. After that the cabinets of the three countries cooperated on international issues until the first years of the new century; then the loyalty of Italy cooled. Satellite states were attracted to the Triplice, Rumania being the most important.

The withdrawal of Bismarck from the German Foreign Office in 1890 closed an epoch in diplomatic history. Despite the alliance with Austria, Bismarck had contrived to remain on tolerable terms with Russia. But in 1894 his haunting nightmare—a Franco-Russian alliance—became a reality; the Old World was divided into two opposing camps. The great wing powers of Europe pledged themselves to make war on Germany, if either were attacked by Germany. Like the Austro-German pact, the Franco-Russian treaty possessed a strictly defensive character. France, now recovered from the worst effects of the War of 1870, ceased to be a pariah nation, and could engage in a more vigorous international policy.

Great Britain, in the meantime, had pursued a course of aloofness. But in the 1890's, certain British leaders came to doubt whether isolation was the wisest of possible policies. Recurrent friction with Russia, France and Germany caused growing uneasiness in London. Consequently overtures for an alliance with Germany were quietly initiated. But the price demanded by Berlin was too high. So Britain turned to its Oriental counterpart, Japan, with which a treaty pointed against Russian expansion was negotiated (1902).

Presently, in view of assertive German naval and colonial activities and the danger of Teutonic dominance in Europe, British diplomacy was given a revolutionary turn. First, the island kingdom ranged herself alongside of France, an ancient foe and a modern rival for empire. By a friendly understanding, or *entente cordiale*, of 1904, Anglo-French colonial controversies were ironed out, and that adjustment smoothed the way for diplomatic collaboration. Secret military and naval understandings tightened the bonds between the Channel neighbors.

Meanwhile, in 1907, an Anglo-Russian entente was arranged. The formal agreement allayed jealous rivalries in the Middle East somewhat. Beyond that, the British settlement with Russia, like the bargain with France, led to limited cooperation of the two states in the field of diplomacy in general. Inescapably Britain became entangled in the aspirations and quarrels of her political associates. It was customary for the European press to speak of the Triple Entente—France, Russia and Britain. On the edge of this partnership stood Japan by reason of the British alliance and of less formal engagements with France and Russia.

While the Entente combination was in the making, Italian allegiance to the Triple Alliance weakened. That defection left Germany and Austria confronting the ring of Entente powers. Repeatedly in the decade before 1914, the solidarity of the rival blocs was severely tested. Any of the crises might have exploded into war. As well as poisoning the international atmosphere, each crisis inspired expansion of armaments. The balance between peace and war was delicately and perilously poised.

VARIATIONS ON A THEME

Sharp disputes over the status of Morocco, an independent principality in northwestern Africa, twice threatened to precipitate a general conflict. With the blessing of her friends, France was making ready to annex Morocco. Germany saw—or thought it saw—an opportunity to tear apart the Anglo-French *rapprochement* and perhaps to increase her overseas holdings. In 1905, the German Foreign Office threw down the gauntlet to France by declaring that Morocco must continue to be an independent country.

To dispel the danger of an international conflict, a conference of the powers on the Moroccan question was assembled. The friends of France, Great Britain among them, supported French pretensions at the conference, while only Austria stood by Germany. France obtained a controlling position in Morocco, though the independence of the kingdom was formally reasserted. The German design of driving a wedge between France and Great Britain was frustrated.

France kept nibbling away at the integrity of Morocco and in 1911 Germany delivered a second frontal challenge. A German gunboat steamed into Agadir on the Moroccan coast, avowedly to protect the interests of German nationals, but really as a warning that France should not absorb Morocco unless suitable compensation were given to Germany. Again Britain lined up solidly behind France and a general war seemed imminent. Happily, a compromise (displeasing to all concerned) was worked out, authorizing France to lord over most of Morocco and transferring portions of the French Congo to Germany.[3]

[3] Spain obtained a protectorate over the Mediterranean littoral of Morocco.

More menacing to peace than Morocco were Austro-Russian controversies over the perennially explosive Balkans. Austria had annexed Bosnia in 1908. That act provoked an extremely acute international crisis involving the two diplomatic partnerships. Serbia protested vehemently against the annexation and Russia strongly supported her little Slav brother. France and Britain aligned themselves with Russia, albeit moderately. But Germany let it be known that if Russia and Austria fought, the German armies would march shoulder to shoulder with Austria. Ill-prepared for war, Russia backed down and sullenly acquiesced in the annexation of Bosnia; infuriated Serb nationalists hated Austria more passionately than ever. In the Bosnian crisis the Austro-German bloc had scored handsomely over the Entente, but at the cost of gravely heightening international tensions.

More than once during the Balkan wars of 1912–13, Austria and Russia nearly came to blows. But British and German diplomacy contrived to find amicable adjustments of disputes. Once more Russian prestige suffered reverses. Once more the expansionist dreams of Serbia fell short of fulfillment. Nor was Austria happy over the outcome, for her protégé, Bulgaria, had been worsted, while Serbia had grown in stature and pugnacity. For all practical purposes, Serbia had become the ally, if not the pawn, of Imperial Russia.

The Balkan struggles, moreover, left their mark upon the broader European scene. France and Britain drew closer to their Russian companion; and yet the London ministry would not accede to Russian overtures to convert the Triple Entente into a conventional military alliance. On the other side, Italy moved closer to her Triplice allies, after a period of dubious loyalty. On every hand preparations to fight were accelerated. Gloomy forebodings deepened, the pernicious obsession that a general European struggle could not be avoided won new converts. Primitive popular passions had risen to white heat, a point not always adequately appreciated by unemotional students of the origins of the First World War.

Police seize Gavrilo Princip, murderer of Archduke Francis Ferdinand at Sarajevo.

HOW WAR CAME

The final variation on the theme of approaching conflict was written, not inappropriately, in the Balkans. "I shall not live to see the Great War," Bismarck had long since prophesied, "but you will see it and it will start in the East." On June 28, 1914, the heir to the Austrian throne, Archduke Francis Ferdinand, and his wife were assassinated by a juvenile Serb nationalist on the streets of Sarajevo, the capital of Bosnia. Whether without that dastardly outrage, Europe would have gone to war in 1914 will never be known.

The Sarajevo crime brought to a climax the deadly Austro-Serbian antagonism that had been flaming for years. Austria was determined to preserve the integrity of the monarchy, while the Serbs wished to acquire Austrian provinces containing Yugoslavs. The murder plot had been prepared in the Serbian capital, Belgrade, and the assailant of the Archduke and the tools of death had been brought to Sarajevo from Serbia. Although the Serbian ministry possessed knowledge of what was planned, it took no effective steps to prevent the carrying out of the conspiracy. All of this, it must be emphasized, was not known during the crisis of 1914.

Charging Serbia with responsibility for the crime, Austria prepared to inflict military punishment. Before proceeding decisively, Austria obtained unconditional assurances of support from the German ally. Berlin policy makers signed that "blank cheque" on the assumption, or rather on the fantastic hope, that fighting could be restricted to Austria and Serbia. The Germans were ready, however, to run the risk of a general conflagration. Four weeks after the Sarajevo tragedy, the thunderbolt struck: Austria dispatched a very stiff ultimatum to Serbia. It demanded that Austrian representatives should be allowed to ferret out the traces of the crime that reached into Serbia and they should be permitted to take part in punishing Serbian citizens who were implicated in the conspiracy. Serbia was also called upon to suppress anti-Austrian agitations and societies. Only forty-eight hours were allowed Belgrade for a reply.

The Austrian ultimatum was designed to be rejected. Serbia acquiesced in considerable measure to the demands, but Austria dismissed the answer as unsatisfactory. Heedless of moderating counsels from Germany, Austria, on July 28, declared war upon Serbia. The fat was in the fire. The chances of preserving the peace of Europe by diplomacy were substantially diminished.

The angry Austro-Serb quarrel, meantime, had flared into another trial of strength between the two diplomatic coalitions. More self-confident than at any time since the Japanese war, Russia made it plain that Serbia would not be left in the lurch as in previous disputes. As for France, it stiffened the Muscovite backbone by assurances that the alliance of 1894 would be loyally fulfilled.

With war clouds lowering by the hour, Great Britain recommended diplomatic action to solve the crisis peacefully, or, failing that, to limit the area of conflict. Those proposals were coldly received in continental chancelleries. Notwithstanding appeals from abroad, the British ministry hesitated to say what Britain would do in the event of a European war. The Foreign Secretary, Sir Edward Grey, kept repeating that the cabinet could promise nothing which it was not certain it could carry out. On the other hand, the British fleet was posted at battle stations and rather naive German efforts to purchase British neutrality were brushed aside.

By way of reply to the Austrian declaration of war upon Serbia, the Russian government ordered full mobilization of its immense reserve forces; general mobilization, instead of concentration against Austria only, was insisted upon by tsarist military chiefs on technical grounds. The fateful Russian decision had much to do with transforming a war in the Balkans into a general European conflagration. "Russia's mobilization," the American ambassador in Germany wired, "makes war inevitable." Germany called its reservists to the colors and forthwith declared war upon Russia. Military strategists, afraid that the enemy would gain an advantage in initiating operations and eager to set long-matured plans of campaign in motion, crowded diplomatists aside.

As soon as Russia and Germany unsheathed their swords, French intervention became inescapable. The way to victory, German military planners calculated, was to strike down France quickly and then concentrate against the slow-moving tsarist armies. When France declined to reveal its military intentions, Germany launched a war declaration against her and sent troops hurtling into Belgium en route to the Third Republic. That act violated a treaty guaranteeing the perpetual neutrality of the little Low Country which Germany (Prussia) had signed. Military necessity, the Berlin government told the world, forced this transgression of a solemn international engagement.

In the meanwhile, Italy proclaimed her neutrality. But Great Britain, after much anxious vacillation and weighing of alternatives, entered the lists against the Central Powers. A decision in the cabinet to take up arms preceded the actual German invasion of neutralized Belgium; the invasion convinced many a hesitant Briton of the moral rightness as well as the strategic necessity of going to war.

In a matter of days, then, very hectic and exciting days, the spark lit in Sarajevo had flamed across Europe like a prairie fire. Underneath lay a large accumulation of combustible materials—national ambitions and antipathies, national rivalries and hatreds, greeds and envies, aspirations and apprehensions. In the supreme crisis, the network of diplomatic partnerships had counted decisively.

No one country, no one social class, no single dynamic force in very modern civilization was exclusively responsible for the outbreak of war. The First World War was neither deliberately provoked nor premeditated. Rather Europe stumbled and staggered into the abyss.

BROADENING OF THE CONFLICT

After the tocsin had sounded, each belligerent group drew allies to its side. In the autumn of 1914, the Turkish Empire, already secretly bound to Germany, openly teamed up with the Central Powers. Dread that Russia would exploit the war to realize the age-old ambition to possess the Straits, and dislike of British

The Cloth Hall at Ypres, survivor of five centuries of wars, was an early casualty of the German drive through Belgium.

control of Egypt, together with the wish to recover lost prestige inspired the Turkish decision for war. A year later, Bulgaria, still smarting under the humiliation of the War of 1913, and seeking revenge and territory in Macedonia, lined up with Germany and Austria.

The Entente combination, or the Allies, was reinforced by the intervention of Japan, Italy, several Balkan nations, and above all of the United States, which tipped the scales to eventual victory. Quite in keeping with her treaty with Britain, Japan was ready to intervene as soon as warfare started in Europe. But Britain prevailed upon the Nipponese authorities to remain neutral, though only for a few weeks. The adversity of Europe presented Japan with a golden opportunity for easy expansion in the Orient. When Germany refused to relinquish its interests in Chinese Shantung, Tokyo declared war and promptly despatched troops into the coveted province.

Similar calculations of national interest induced Italy to cut loose from the Triplice, and, in May of 1915, to move into the Entente camp. As the reward for intervention, Italy was secretly promised impressive territorial advantages, mostly at the expense of Austria, the ancient Italian foe. Hostility in Rumania to Austria, which contained millions of Rumanians, was widespread. On the model of Italy, Rumania renounced her alliance with the Central Powers and joined the Entente in August, 1916; assurances of lavish acquisitions of Austrian territory were given to Rumania in secret. Greece likewise ranged herself alongside of the Allies in 1917, having been promised coveted Turkish lands.

The intervention of the United States was the outcome of diverse and interlaced strands of reason and emotion. When the fighting began in Europe, America assumed the role of an onlooker, more or less detached. But the German treatment of Belgium and the use of horror weapons such as poison gas, roused angry passions across the Atlantic. Allied publicity activities in the United States, featuring stories of German atrocities, heightened hatreds. Even before 1914, antipathy toward Germany had been generated by suspicious operations in Latin America and bellicose utterances of German public leaders.

On the other side, cultural and institutional affinities predisposed many Americans to the cause of the Allies. War orders, moreover, pulled the United States out of a business slump and set a wave of prosperity rolling across the trans-Atlantic Republic. Steel output, to take one illustration, which stood at 23,500,000 tons in 1914 (about half of plant capacity), rose sharply in 1915, and in 1916 approached 43,000,000 tons. Borrowing by the Allies paid for about two-sevenths of the goods that were

French poilus moving up through a ruined town, 1917

MAY 1, 1915.

SPRING AND SUMMER RESORTS. Atlantic City.

SPRING AND SUMMER RESORTS. Atlantic City.

Always Delightful, but Particularly Attractive During the Late Spring and Early Summer

Atlantic City

America's Famous All-Year Resort

The refreshing salt air, blown in gentle zephyrs off the ocean, the warm sunshine and unlimited opportunities for outdoor recreation and pleasure, have spread Atlantic City's fame as an all-year health and pleasure resort over the entire American Continent.

The leading hotels are noted for the excellence of their accommodations and service.

THE LEADING HOUSES

will furnish full information, rates, etc.

Marlborough-Blenheim

The Holmhurst
The Shelburne
Hotel Chelsea

Seaside House
Galen Hall
Hotel Strand

Hotel Dennis
Hotel St. Charles
The Pennhurst

Only three hours from New York City by through trains via Central R. R. of N. J. or Penna. R. R.

Adirondacks.
THE NEW
Whiteface Inn
DESIRABLE SOCIAL ENVIRONMENT ON BEAUTIFUL LAKE PLACID ADIRONDACKS, NEW YORK
Cottages and camps for rent.
WILLIAM PERCIVAL, Manager.

SARANAC INN
Upper Saranac Lake. Camps to rent.
Harrington Mills, Manager.
Until June 1. The Grafton, Washington, D. C.

Connecticut.

The Edgewood
"New York's Ideal Suburban Hotel"
AT GREENWICH, CONN.
Opens Saturday, May 29.
Fine auto run of 28 miles from town.
Booking Office at
The Vanderbilt, Park Av. and 34th st.
IN CHARGE OF MR. A. D. CUSHING.
The ALFRED S. AMER CO., Owners & Props.

New York.
A Summer Resort of the Best Class.
NEAREST MOUNTAIN RESORT TO N. Y.
MIZZEN TOP
Hotel and Cottages.
ON CREST OF QUAKER HILL,
SOUTHERN BERKSHIRES, PAWLING, N. Y.
OPENS JUNE 17
90 minutes from N. Y. city; 1,200 feet elevation.
PICTURESQUE NINE HOLE GOLF COURSE,
SURROUNDINGS; ORCHES-
BILLIARDS, BOWLING, &C.

Hotel STRAND
ATLANTIC CITY, N.J.
THE LATEST FIREPROOF HOTEL
American plan. Always open. Capacity 300. On beach directly, between the two great Ocean Piers. Sea water in all baths. Orchestra. Garage. Illustrated literature. Ownership management.

HOTEL CHELSEA
Occupying entire block of ocean front, in the fashionable Chelsea section; 300 bed chambers with private baths (fresh and sea water). High class orchestra, cafe, grill, &c. French chefs. Golf privileges. Autos meet trains. Booklet. Open all year. J. B. THOMPSON & CO.

ROYAL PALACE
HOTEL AND COTTAGES.
on the Beach, ATLANTIC CITY, N.J
"A RESORT IN ITSELF."
Near all Piers and Amusements.
CAPACITY 600.
Bookings for Summer may now be made.

GALEN HALL
HOTEL AND SANATORIUM.
ATLANTIC CITY, N. J.
Always open. Always ready. Always busy. Cannot be excelled for comfort or table and service. A delightful place for spring. Tonic and curative baths, with trained attendants.
F. L. YOUNG, General Manager.

OCEAN STEAMSHIPS.

CUNARD

EUROPE VIA LIVERPOOL
LUSITANIA
Fastest and Largest Steamer now in Atlantic Service Sails
SATURDAY, MAY 1, 10 A. M.
Transylvania, Fri., May 7, 5 P.M.
Orduna, - - Tues., May 18, 10 A.M.
Tuscania, - - Fri., May 21, 5 P.M.
LUSITANIA, Sat., May 29, 10 A.M.
Transylvania, Fri., June 4, 5 P.M.

Gibraltar–Genoa–Naples–Piraeus
S.S. Carpathia, Thur., May 13, Noon

ROUND THE WORLD TOURS
Through bookings to all principal Ports of the World.
Company's Office, 21-24 State St., N. Y.

NOTICE!

TRAVELLERS intending to embark on the Atlantic voyage are reminded that a state of war exists between Germany and her allies and Great Britain and her allies; that the zone of war includes the waters adjacent to the British Isles; that, in accordance with formal notice given by the Imperial German Government, vessels flying the flag of Great Britain, or of any of her allies, are liable to destruction in those waters and that travellers sailing in the war zone on ships of Great Britain or her allies do so at their own risk.

IMPERIAL GERMAN EMBASSY

WASHINGTON, D. C., APRIL 22, 1915.

American Line
AMERICAN STEAMER

The pair of advertisements at the right of this illustration speak for themselves.

purchased. Consciously or otherwise, the United States acquired a substantial financial stake in Allied victory. Sabotage operations of Central Power agents to hamper the manufacture and shipment of goods to the Allies sharpened animosities.

As the war dragged on, two other important considerations played upon the American mind. It came to be feared in some circles that victory for the Central Powers would have perilous implications for the democratic institutions and the physical security of the United States in the future. And second, the idea gained acceptance that the United States had moral obligations to set Europe and the wider world aright and to throw its weight behind plans to ensure lasting peace. That line of thought operated with peculiar force upon President Woodrow Wilson, who pitched his eventual appeal to fight upon lofty principles of morality and humanitarian duty.

All these and lesser considerations helped to make war between America and Germany possible. But it was unrestricted German submarine warfare, directly challenging the interests and the honor of the United States, that elicited the decision for war on April 6, 1917. Several Latin American nations and China, too, torn though it was by civil strife, followed the United States into the herculean struggle.

THE COURSE OF HOSTILITIES

At the outset of the war, the great German military machine rolled with expected precision across Belgium and deep into France. "Thirty-five days since mobilization," Emperor William II exulted, "...and the advance guards of our cavalry stand fifty kilometers [thirty miles] from Paris." And yet the German plan of crushing France in six weeks was wholly disappointed. A military deadlock developed, an agonizing struggle of attrition, both belligerents digging trenches from Switzerland to the North Sea. Time and again, costly but fruitless frontal assaults were unloosed in the hope of breaking the gigantic stalemate. Until 1918 battle-lines in the West held firm; then mobile tactics were resumed, the Germans thrusting close to Paris again, only to crack when the Allies, reinforced by American armies, unleashed a titanic and decisive counter offensive.

On the eastern front, the tides of battle pursued a more fluid course. In the beginning, the tsarist "steam-roller" advanced more rapidly than the Central Powers had anticipated. But in 1915 the situation changed radically as German and Austrian troops hurled the enemy eastward, exacting heavy tolls in life and prisoners. That same year the Allies undertook an ill-managed, unsuccessful assault upon the Turkish Straits intending to open a supply route over the Black Sea to Russia.

Economic and social conditions inside the tsardom deteriorated from bad to intolerable; the morale and fighting capacity of Russia crumbled ominously. In March of 1917, revolutionary elements swept away the discredited Romanov dynasty and in November the radical Bolsheviks seized power. Their leaders pulled Russia out of the war, signing an ignominious treaty of peace with the Central Powers.[4]

At about the same time that Russia caved in, Rumania capitulated to the Central Powers. On the other side, British occupation of Bagdad and Palestine in 1917 heralded the defeat of Turkey. Along with Bulgaria, the Ottoman power collapsed in the early autumn of 1918. On the Italian front, Italy and Austria, with some German support, waged a see-saw contest. At one point in 1917 it looked as though Italy might be knocked out of the war, but Allied reinforcements swung the pendulum in the opposite direction. In October, 1918, the venerable Hapsburg Monarchy broke into a litter of national fragments.

On the blue water, British superiority in seapower counted heavily for the Allied cause. Only one major engagement with the German fleet was fought—off Jutland in 1916. Both contestants claimed victory, but the salient fact was that the German battlefleet never again ventured to seek a decision. The British navy imposed a tight blockade upon Germany, remorselessly denying her essential imports, and

[4] The chain of events culminating in the Bolshevik triumph is explained in Chap. XXVI.

Trench warfare, 1916

thus hastening the exhaustion of the Central Powers. As a counterpoise to British mastery on the surface of the sea, Germany endeavored to strangle Britain and win a quick victory with the submarine.

By issuing orders to U-boats to sink cargo carriers without warning, the Germans promoted the submarine to a major weapon of attack and introduced new and unknown factors into seapower. The submarine achieved some remarkable successes; in the spring of 1917 sinkings were so great that it seemed as though Britain might be starved into submission. But scientists, shipbuilders and seamen applied countermeasures which first checked the losses and then slowly but surely gained the ascendancy over the U-boat. By appealing to the submarine Germany not only failed to win the war, but ensured her own defeat by provoking America to belligerency. At sea, as on land and in diplomacy, the iron dice rolled against the Central Powers.

Factories and technicians fought the First World War along with the armed services and strategists. Industrial production as well as moral fortitude determined the outcome of the gruelling struggle. Machines wrought with revolutionary force upon the science of warfare. The internal combustion engine, for example, made it possible to strike an enemy not only on land but also from beneath the sea or above the land. Yet airpower was prized chiefly for reconnaissance, as a weapon of destruction it did little more than cause psychological scars.

For ground forces the principal weapons were cannon and machine gun. Firepower was progressively increased for the purpose of breaking the trench siege in the West. But the real answer to that problem appeared in the fall of 1916, in the form of a self-propelled war chariot

A British tank, 1917

of steel, known by the odd name of tank. Resembling a battleship operating on land, this British invention greatly enhanced the mobility and striking power of armies.

PRELIMINARIES OF PEACE

In November, 1918, the German commanders, sensing that political upheaval impended at home and wishing to save their beaten armies, applied to the Allies for an armistice. The upshot of ensuing negotiations was a formal agreement to the effect that a peace treaty would be arranged in keeping with terms outlined by President Wilson in wartime addresses. Wilson had called for the destruction of German military power, the re-drawing of the European map on the democratic basis of the self-determination of peoples, and the organization of an international league to keep the peace. Allied policy makers inserted a clause in the pre-armistice agreement obligating Germany to pay reparations to cover "the damages done to civilians and their property on land, on sea and in the air." The military conditions of the armistice made it impossible for Germany to resume fighting. Germany's allies surrendered unconditionally.

In January of 1919, delegates of the victor nations, thirty-two in all, congregated in Paris to prepare treaties of peace. All the world was represented except enemy and neutral countries and Russia, gone Bolshevik. Final verdicts on larger issues were delivered by the "Big Three": President Wilson, the British Prime Minister,

David Lloyd George, and the Premier of France, Georges Clemenceau.

Up to a point, the tasks and methods of the Paris Conference resembled the work of the Congress of Vienna at the end of the Napoleonic struggles. But there were several important and instructive differences. In the interval the material fabric of the West had undergone drastic transformation, throwing up complex problems of economic readjustment undreamed of a century earlier. Nationalism, in the second place, whetted appetites for territorial gains and fanned vindictive, popular passions; fear, anger and resentment against the enemy ran

The signing of the Treaty of Versailles, a painting by Sir William Orpen

high in Allied countries while treaties were being arranged. And then, the peacemakers of Paris were subjected to political and newspaper pressures such as the aristocratic statesmen of 1815 had not experienced. A war-ravaged world blandly expected that peace settlements would be so constructed as to assure future tranquillity. Lastly, Allied decisions at Paris were influenced by the Bolshevik specter of Moscow and apprehension lest the Red flood should surge westward.

Bitter wranglings and threats of a break-up studded the deliberations at Paris. On one occasion Clemenceau, for instance, denounced Wilson as a pro-German and indignantly withdrew from the deliberations. But by one concession and another, clashing viewpoints were somehow reconciled and a draft treaty was drawn up and handed to the Germans. They protested at length and with asperity that the document departed from the pre-armistice agreement, since it did not conform to the Wilsonian principles of peace. They assailed both the spirit of the treaty and particular clauses. Certain alterations were admitted by the peacemakers and then the Germans were obliged to sign, the ceremony taking place in June, 1919, at the grand chateau of Louis XIV at Versailles.

A British cartoonist, Will Dyson, drew a cartoon of the victor statesmen coming out of the palace after the signing of the treaty. Clemenceau is poking his bald, condor-like head to one side; the caption is a remark attributed to the Frenchman at the time, "Curious, I seem to hear a child crying." In the cartoon a child is crying, a French child, and by an uncanny prevision, Dyson, in 1919, labeled the boy, "Class of 1940."

THE TREATY OF VERSAILLES

Under the terms of the treaty, Germany lost about 10 per cent of her territory and population in Europe. Alsace-Lorraine was retroceded to France and the industrial Saar Valley was detached temporarily from Germany. By plebiscite, small German areas passed to Denmark and Belgium. Extensive tracts of eastern Germany, largely Polish-inhabited, were transferred to the Republic of Poland. One section of resurrected Poland—"the Polish Corridor"—separated Germany proper from the province of East Prussia. Danzig, lying at the mouth of the Vistula River, was set up as an independent state. These areas were to be the direct source of the renewal of war in 1939.

Outside of Europe, Germany lost all her prewar interests. Colonial possessions were parceled out among the Allies as mandated areas. Victor statesmen proceeded on the principle that overseas holdings had value, in spite of the indictments of imperialism that had been served up by humanitarians, economic collectivists and other critics of empire. Armament clauses in the treaty were intended to draw the fangs of German militarism forever. The army was restricted to 100,000 volunteers, and was forbidden to have planes or tanks. Fortifications in the Rhineland were razed, and Allied troops garrisoned the area. The size of the German navy was severely limited and submarines were prohibited.

Lastly, Germany was obligated to compensate the Allies for the property destroyed in the war and for pensions to Allied soldiers and sailors. The full bill on reparations would be presented in two years; in the meantime, Germany should pay an installment of $5,000,000,000. An accompanying clause implied that the whole responsibility for the war rested upon Germany and her allies.

Many a competent judge, not to speak of utopian idealists, flayed the Versailles Treaty, especially the reparations provisions, as unwise, unworkable and dangerously vindictive. Arch-critics, inside Germany and without, labeled the document a Carthaginian peace. That appraisal was, however, a gross perversion of fact, for Carthage vanished, while Germany within less than a generation had again become a formidable Great Power. Nonetheless, the Versailles Treaty proved to be one of the most persuasive weapons in the armory of Hitler's Nazis. The verdict of history parallels the analysis offered by Colonel E. M. House, confidant of Wilson. "Looking at the Conference in retrospect," House said, "there is much to approve and much to regret. It is easy to say what should have been done but more difficult to have found a way of doing it . . ."

THE LEAGUE OF NATIONS

The Covenant of the League of Nations, of which Wilson was the principal architect and champion, made up the first section of the Versailles Treaty. Its purposes were "to achieve international peace and security, establish open, just, and honorable relations between nations, and establish firmly the understandings of international law." Instead of each nation seeking to ensure its safety by means of armaments and alliances, the security of every country was declared to be the responsibility of all nations. Each League member bound itself to submit disputes for pacific settlement. If, however, any nation resorted to war, the League powers would apply economic penalties and perhaps military force as well against the troublemaker. League members were committed to seek limitation of armaments. Agencies of the League, moreover, would supervise certain interests of international importance such as protection of minorities and of populations in mandated areas. Special League bureaus would work to raise standards of labor and health around the globe and combat social evils such as traffic in opium and in women.

As the instrument of international government, the Covenant provided, first of all, for an assembly, a sort of world forum which might deliberate but could not legislate. Each member country would have one vote. Second, a council, which contained representatives of the strongest countries and of a few other nations to be periodically elected. Rather similar to an international cabinet, the council was invested with authority to take action in time of a quarrel between nations. A staff of civil servants—the secretariat—would make itself generally useful in carrying on the work of the League. As heir of the pre-war Hague Court, the Covenant provided for a "World Court,"

Woodrow Wilson pleading for United States support of the League of Nations, 1919

to adjust international quarrels by judicial processes.

For many a lover of peace and the orderly settlement of international disputes, the League of Nations stood at the very top of war gains. Apparently the First World War had indeed been "the war to end war." It was widely supposed that the United States would be the mainstay of this novel adventure in "world government." But that was not to be. The Treaty of Versailles was subjected to thorough and impassioned discussion in the United States. In the end, foes of the document bested its supporters.

Some critics attacked the Treaty as too harsh on the late enemy—others as too lenient. The transfer to Japan of the former German privileges in the Chinese province of Shantung attracted heavy fire, but the hottest attack was leveled against the League Covenant which was stigmatized as robbing the United States of sovereign attributes without compensating advantages. Rancors of partisan politics embittered the great debate. Wilson obstinately declined to accept any substantial alteration in the Treaty, and in so doing contributed to the Senate's refusal to ratify the document. A separate peace was arranged with Germany in 1921.

SETTLEMENTS WITH THE ALLIES OF GERMANY

Once the Versailles Treaty had been completed, Allied diplomatists turned to settlements with the other defeated countries. Already the old Hapsburg Monarchy had disintegrated and its dynasty, which had been a factor in European affairs for six centuries, had been cast into the discard. Separate treaties were presented to the Austrian and the Hungarian partners in the broken monarchy. Austria was restricted to a little state of German-speaking people, and forbidden to unite with Germany. Hungary, too, was reduced to small dimensions. Both states were allowed only small armies and agreed to pay substantial reparations. Segments of the former Monarchy passed to Rumania, Yugoslavia (pre-war Serbia), Italy and the new republics of Czechoslovakia and Poland. As a general rule, territory was allocated in harmony with the principle of self-determination. There were deviations, however, from this ideal, which time made more glaring and more productive of controversies and dangerous tensions.

For allying with Germany, Bulgaria was penalized by losing her frontage on the Aegean Sea to Greece and by ceding small parcels of land to Yugoslavia. The original peace settlement with Turkey was torn to shreds by militant Turkish nationalists, and a definitive treaty, more acceptable to Turkish sensibilities, was written at Lausanne in 1923. It formally destroyed the venerable Turkish Empire. The new Turkey embraced the section in Asia Minor peopled by Turkish-feeling folk and in Europe Constantinople (Istanbul) and its environs. Arab provinces of Turkey were entrusted to Great Britain or to France as mandated territories, while an independent state in Arabia was launched on a destiny of its own.

DARKNESS AND LIGHT

Peace treaties having been arranged, the world could contemplate the immediate and tangible consequences of the great holocaust. On the human side, the scythe of Mars had cut down millions in the freshness of young manhood while other millions of civilians had perished. It has been soberly estimated that the loss in population traceable to the war approached 50,000,000; mortality in Russia alone may have run as high as 16,000,000. Any estimate of financial costs must contain a large admixture of guesswork. An overall figure of $337,000,000,000 was proposed shortly after the war, but that calculation took no account, of course, of the continuing outlays for the wounded and war veterans, nor of financial losses arising out of the impact of the war and the peace treaties upon the complex economic mechanism of Europe.

As another result, the application of the doctrine of national self-determination dismembered the German, the Austrian, the Turkish and the Russian monarchies. Several new or resurrected states appeared on the map and other older, small states were enlarged; patriots in these countries ranked the First

Territorial Changes in Europe after World War I

World War among the brightest and most glorious chapters in history. The reappearance of Poland in the sunlight of history, for instance, due to the sudden and surprising eclipse of the three partitioning powers—Russia, Austria and Germany—seemed to Polish nationalists a decent reward for the agonies of the war.

After the war, a wave of democratic republicanism swept across central and eastern Europe up to the threshold of Russia. Fundamental civil liberties were proclaimed for all and women were granted the suffrage on the same terms as men. And among colonial populations, or at least among their nationalistically minded minorities, the First World War fostered national enthusiasms and quickened desires to be rid of white overlordship.

As another pregnant outcome of the war, the authority of the state in economic affairs was extended. To meet wartime needs, governmental controls were generally imposed upon instruments of production, restricting the area of private enterprise. Wartime experiments and experiences fostered ideas of peacetime collectivism and the welfare state.

Not susceptible of measurement were the advances in technology and science made while the fighting raged. Noteworthy improvements were registered in medical care and sanitation, for example, and in turning out substitute products. Under the stimulus of war conditions, rubber substitutes were developed, "sugar" was squeezed out of sawdust and "wool" was extracted from milk and other proteins. Progress during the war in aeronautics, last of all, was readily applied to civilian purposes.

FOR FURTHER STUDY

RAYMOND J. SONTAG, *European Diplomatic History, 1871–1932* (New York, 1933)

LUIGI ALBERTINI, *Origins of the War of 1914* (Eng. trans., 3 vols., New York, 1952–57)

SIDNEY B. FAY, *The Origins of the World War* (new ed., New York, 1948)

BERNADOTTE E. SCHMITT, *The Coming of the War* (2 vols., New York, 1930)

GEORGE P. GOOCH, *Before the War* (2 vols., New York, 1936–1938)

ROSS J. S. HOFFMAN, *Great Britain and the German Trade Rivalry* (Philadelphia, 1933)

ALFRED VAGTS, *History of Militarism* (New York, 1937)

CHARLES SEYMOUR, *American Diplomacy during the World War* (Baltimore, 1934)

CHARLES C. TANSILL, *America Goes to War* (Boston, 1938)

CHARLES R. M. F. CRUTTWELL, *A History of the Great War, 1914–1918* (Oxford, 1934)

PAUL BIRDSALL, *Versailles Twenty Years After* (New York, 1941)

HAROLD NICOLSON, *Peace-making, 1919* (new ed., New York, 1946)

DAVID THOMSON, ed., *The Era of Violence, 1898–1945* (Cambridge, Eng., 1959)

THEODORE ROPP, *War in the Modern World* (new ed., New York, 1962) PAPERBACK

CYRIL FALLS, *The Great War* (New York, 1961) PAPERBACK

BARBARA W. TUCHMAN, *The Guns of August* (New York, 1962)

ARTHUR S. LINK, *Wilson the Diplomatist* (Baltimore, 1957)

CHAPTER XXVI

REVOLUTIONARY RUSSIA (1917-1939)

THE ROAR OF THE AVALANCHE

IN THE calendar of master events of the twentieth century, nothing, it may be, surpasses the Bolshevik Revolution of 1917 and its sequel. And yet it is highly improbable that an upheaval of that dimension would have overtaken Russia without the First World War. The tsardom entered the contest with dash and enthusiasm. Armies thrust onto German and Austrian soil with unexpected rapidity, throwing the military timetable of the Central Powers askew.

Not long after the fighting started, Russia arranged a binding alliance with Britain and France. None would make peace independently nor even entertain peace proposals except in concert with its allies. Allied diplomatists at once began to discuss the division of war spoils. Russian claims mounted when Turkey became a belligerent, and the Western Allies promised Russia control over Constantinople and the Strait. That glittering prize, the realization of an old ambition, stood at the very top of tsarist war aims.

But the tide of battle presently turned against Russia. Fierce onslaughts by the Central Powers forced the Muscovites to pull back, suffering terrible losses as they did so. Repeatedly the Russians launched offensive gestures, which were a boon to the hard-pressed Western Allies, but disastrous for tsarist power and morale. Russian Poland fell to the enemy in 1915, cutting away important grainlands and industrial resources. Appalling shortages of guns and ammunition developed. Factories inside Russia were incapable of meeting the prodigious demands for military equipment, the supply services faltered, and the Allies—as well as munitions plants in the United States—delivered only trickles of assistance. In desperation Russian church bells were melted into guns, but that expedient could not begin to satisfy the need for cannon and rifles. Russian losses of men killed, maimed and captured outran anything on record, and floods of refugees streamed from battle areas eastward into Russia.

The heroism and the stolid endurance of the Russian troops were unquestioned but the generals, more often than not, were incompetent, very independent, and lacking in resourcefulness. High officers had secured their places more out of favoritism than by ability. Fighting left heavy gaps in the ranks of experienced junior and non-commissioned officers. As the great retreat swept along, Tsar Nicholas II took the supreme command for himself and thus more thoroughly associated the dynasty with the odium of military disaster.

The Russian ship of state, meanwhile, drifted helplessly toward the rapids. Never tightly integrated, the state apparatus could not meet the exceptional wartime requirements. Pro-German intrigue in high places, partly real and partly fancied, and defeatist propaganda gnawed away at public morale. Dark forces surrounding the imperial household evoked fervent criticism from patriots; the personification of evil, Rasputin, was assassinated in December of 1916, but too late to save the dynasty. Instead of rallying the Duma fully to the war cause, the ministry quarreled constantly with that body, and Nicholas II rebuffed pleas for a responsible ministry to the very end.

Inside Russia the roar of the avalanche grew ever more ominous. Colossal physical losses darkened hundreds of thousands of homes and huts; enthusiasm for the war sagged, while hearts were gripped with the prospect that the fighting might drag on indefinitely and entail still heavier sacrifices. War-bred discontent intensified hatred with prevailing conditions among the peasant millions. It was in the great cities, however, that human misery was deepest and the spirit of unrest most inflamed. Economic activity was badly crippled and dislocated; food was in short supply; fuel was in short supply; prices soared; factories ran out of raw materials; transportation facilities were unable to discharge their functions. Articulate critics of the government—conservatives, progressives and radicals—all were ready for far-reaching changes.

A DEMOCRATIC INTERLUDE

Quite spontaneously in mid-March, 1917, hungry and bedeviled workers in Petrograd (St. Petersburg), many of them women, roamed the streets shouting for food, the abolition of the monarchy and withdrawal from the war. The anti-monarchical fever penetrated into student circles. Tsarist police—Pharaohs they were tagged—charged riotous mobs and entangled themselves in bloody street brawls. But Cossacks and guard regiments mutinied and joined forces with civilian protestants. Law and order in the capital disappeared.

Under these circumstances a group of deputies in the Duma persuaded Nicholas II to abdicate. The end of the Romanov dynasty was a singularly undramatic business; the ex-tsar seems to have been delighted to be relieved of his onerous responsibilities. For eight months, until the Bolshevik seizure of power, public authority was lodged in a Provisional Government made up of Duma men; it was republican, and the most democratic regime Russia had ever experienced.

Freedom of press and speech and other civil liberties were proclaimed, political prisoners were amnestied, and minorities were assured the right of self-determination. To prepare a constitution, an assembly would be chosen by universal adult suffrage. Efforts to restore public order were nullified by food riots and strikes which convulsed the cities, while land-hungry peasants slaughtered estate-owners and appropriated their properties. Spokesmen of national minorities demanded separate political existence for their peoples. The spirit of revolt spread remorselessly.

Most imprudently the Provisional Government tried to keep the war against the Central Powers going, when the popular mood cared only for a cessation of hostilities. By insisting upon an orderly adjustment of land problems, the new regime lost caste among the poorer peasants. Intending to strengthen the prestige of the new order, the government of the United States, which joyously welcomed the overthrow of tsarism, despatched a special diplomatic mission to the young government and granted it loans. While Russian regiments disintegrated, troops of Germany pushed relentlessly onward. Many a *mooshik* soldier trekked disconsolately off to his home village.

By mid-summer, Alexander Kerensky, hitherto an obscure left-wing deputy, had risen to the top in the Provisional Government. An eloquent orator, as audiences in the United States would later discover, Kerensky was lacking in qualities of statesmanship, and the cataract of events soon swept him into the discard. In July radical Bolsheviks launched a premature bid for control, which quickly fizzled out. Later, an old-line general, Kornilov, politically a child, madly attempted to establish a military dictatorship. That Napoleonic fantasy set the stage for a climactic uprising by the Bolsheviks, which destroyed the brief interlude of democracy in Russia.

BOLSHEVISM TAKES CHARGE

Throughout its chequered career, the Provisional Government faced a formidable competitor in the soviets or councils that spontaneously appeared in factories, military contingents and villages. The most important soviets, which were patterned on similar bodies that emerged during the revolutionary storm of 1905, were located in Petrograd and in Moscow. Arrogating to itself the functions of a government, the Petrograd soviet published decrees, one of which instructed the armed forces to form soviets, retain their military equipment and return home. That order impaired army *esprit*, already low, and accelerated the collapse of resistance to the Central Powers.

By one stratagem and another, control over the great urban soviets was captured by the Bolsheviki under the direction of their peerless leader, Nicholas Lenin. His earlier career and his refinements of the Marxist creed have previously been outlined (pp. 466–7). An exile in Switzerland during the war, he believed that the forces of social upheaval which the conflict had released in Russia must be turned to the purposes of revolution. Communism on the pattern of Marx must first be imposed upon Russia, whence it would leap over into other countries. For all his confidence in ultimate revolution, Lenin, as late as January, 1917, doubted whether he would live to witness the event. Then came the March uprising.

With the connivance of German military chiefs, who intended to exploit them to knock Russia completely out of the war, Lenin and about twenty other exiled Bolsheviks reached Petrograd in April, 1917. A multitude of cheering workmen greeted Lenin—this "German plague bacillus" in the colorful phrase of Winston Churchill—with delirious enthusiasm. His patient, single-minded leadership of the Bolshevik wing of the Social Democrats now paid handsome personal dividends. He could rely upon a small company of tried and proved disciples who were ready to kill and to die for the Communist cause. In the next seven years Lenin made himself the most potent figure of his time, if greatness is measured by one's power over the fate of millions.

Presently another fanatical revolutionary and fugitive, Leon Trotsky, returned to Russia from New York City where he had been living and writing for an anticapitalist Russian language paper. Son of a prosperous Jewish family, residing near Odessa, Trotsky had taken up with Marxism as a youth and had been a leading figure in the St. Petersburg soviet of 1905. His old prestige and remarkable gifts as an orator enabled him to forge to the front in Bolshevik circles, though he did not always see eye to eye with Lenin on doctrine and tactics. From his Siberian prison, another whole-souled, hard-as-nails Marxist, Joseph Stalin, came back to Petrograd and gradually pushed into a commanding position in the party.

Bolshevik hot-gospellers strummed upon familiar Marxist themes. They kept appealing to workmen to prepare for rebellion since they had nothing to lose but their chains. Under the new Bolshevik dispensation, a happy society would flower, resting upon equality, without rich or poor. Lenin and his colleagues stridently demanded that all public power should be entrusted to the Soviets, in which the Bolsheviks had entrenched themselves, and promised the bewildered Russian masses the things which they most ardently craved: peace, land and bread. Hard-pressed industrial workers

Incident of the street fighting, Petrograd, 1917

naively envisaged the coming of the millennium, with no strings attached.

At Petrograd and other leading cities the Bolsheviks organized Red Guards, recruited from soldiers, sailors and workmen. The fanatical and ruthless force in Petrograd did not exceed 20,000. On November 7, 1917, the Bolshevik high command—a handful of intellectual Marxists, agitators, soap-box orators, underground operators inexperienced in government—decided that the pear was ripe. "The government is wavering," Lenin cried. "It must be given the finishing blow at all costs." Circulating the fiction that tsarist sympathizers were plotting to restore the monarchy, the Red Guards seized snowbound Petrograd without serious difficulty. The remnants of the Provisional Government were dramatically toppled over, and the Bolsheviks planted themselves upon the empty throne of the tsars. Similar successes crowned similar revolts in other cities within a few world-shaking days. The Bolshevik conquest of power was carried out "like a piece of music played from notes." And yet foreign "experts" on Russia kept asserting that Bolshevism was simply a passing storm which would soon be blown away.

"We shall now occupy ourselves in Russia," Lenin proclaimed, "in building up a proletarian socialist [collectivist] state." On the approval of an all-Russian Congress of Soviets, the Bolsheviks appointed a Council of Peoples' Commissars to govern the country. Thus the methods and organization of a purposeful and ruthless conspiracy were applied to the management of the largest of European states. Lenin took the presidency of the Council, Trotsky was put in charge of foreign affairs and Stalin was commissar of nationalities. Avowedly it was a dictatorship of the proletariat, but in reality it was a dictatorship imposed upon the proletariat and everyone else—and that by revolutionaries ostensibly dedicated to the loftiest aspirations of mankind.

A MARXIAN EXPERIMENT

Russia was immediately launched upon a momentous experiment, for it was the first country to be based deliberately upon the Marxist analysis of society. A sheaf of decrees abolished private property in land, turned control of mines and factories over to the workers and pledged freedom to minority groups. A declaration of the Rights of Toiling and Exploited Peoples proclaimed as fundamental the suppression of "all exploitation of man by man, to abolish forever the divisions of society into classes, and to bring about the socialist [collectivist] organization of society in all countries." Lenin and other Bolshevik worthies after him condemned the celebrated French Declaration of 1789, since it was silent on economic and social rights.

Other radical measures dropped hurriedly from the hopper of the Red usurpers. Obligations owed by Russia to foreign moneylenders were repudiated—a bill of $13,000,000,000 was later presented to the Soviet government by foreign powers. Diplomatic archives of the tsar were ransacked and the selfish wartime bargains between Russia and the Western Allies were exposed to an incredulous world. A venomous assault was unloosed upon religious organizations and flagrant deviations from conventional morals went unchecked. Small wonder that the cumulative impact of the Bolshevik Revolution roused animosity and hatred in the outer world, and stirred up violent "Red scares."

The Red flag was adopted as the official banner of the November Revolution and on it were stencilled a hammer and sickle symbolizing the solidarity of industrial workers and peasants. The Communists, as the Bolsheviks now called themselves, selected Moscow as their capital with the historic Kremlin as the headquarters of the administration.

Communism had vaulted into the saddle, but it was not yet firmly seated. As promised by the Provisional Government, elections for a constitutional assembly were held; that was the only opportunity Russia ever had of expressing itself freely in a democratic election with competing parties and universal, direct and secret voting. Communist candidates captured less than a quarter of the votes, mostly in the industrial centers, their arch-rivals, the Social Revolutionaries, outscoring them nearly two to one. That challenge to Bolshevik ascendancy was, however, surmounted by the simple expedient of dispersing the assembly in January of 1918 by physical force. The left-wing section of Social Revolutionaries then collaborated with the Communists, while others were imprisoned or laid away in their graves. At this point the Communist Party (always carefully limited in numbers) counted only 115,000 adherents, and many doubted whether the new regime could survive. Communism in Russia was neither predetermined nor inevitable.

PEACE AND WAR

The restoration of peace lay close to the heart of Lenin, who seems to have believed that a general uprising would break out as soon as the European masses were offered a peace without annexations or indemnities. But failing to persuade the Allies to seek peace on this basis, the Communist chiefs turned to an independent settlement with the Central Powers. The conditions which the Germans offered were hard and humiliating, and the debate over their acceptance opened the first serious rift in the Communist leadership.

Trotsky proposed that the terms be rejected and that Communist energies be concentrated on promoting world revolution. But Lenin scorned those counsels, feeling quite rightly that the Communist regime was incapable of challenging the West of Europe at that time. He carried the day, Stalin seconding him; the division of mind thus revealed runs through later Soviet history. By the Treaty of Brest-Litovsk (March, 1918) Russia lost the Polish and Baltic provinces and the fat Ukraine, but the pact was nullified by the German Armistice in November. Russia, however, had ceased to be a belligerent at all.

Enemies of the Communists, friends of tsarism or of bourgeois democracy, lumped together as the "Whites," bitterly resented the Brest-Litovsk peace and indeed everything associated with the November Revolution. Armies of "Whites" were assembled to drive the "Reds" from the seats of authority, and a struggle for power dragged on in desultory fashion to the autumn of 1920. Out of mixed motives, partly strategic, partly political and ideological, the Allied governments aided and abetted the "White" elements. Indignation in the West over the Bolshevik dealings with Germany and the desire to create a second front in the East were mated with detestation of the Communist tyranny and a desire to check the spread of the revolutionary menace. It was, of course, the freely declared intention of the Communists to win the world to their side by physical force.

Contingents of Allied and American troops were thrown onto Russian soil, something Communist hierarchs never forgave nor forgot. They pointed everlastingly to this intervention as proof that non-Communist countries wished to overthrow the Communist regime. As a matter of fact, by their timely defeat of Germany, the Allies and the United States saved Russia from dismemberment—a vital point which Soviet propaganda studiously ignored.

Soldiers of Poland also pressed into Russia occupying Kiev. But Red armies expelled the Poles and carried the torch of revolution to the gates of Warsaw before suffering decisive reverses. A peace settlement, which was signed at Riga in 1921, awarded Poland less territory than national leaders claimed but more than the Kremlin felt belonged of right to Poland.

For a time the "White" armies threatened to overthrow the Communists, who fought on half a dozen fronts simultaneously. Hastily organized Red troops, marshaled by Trotsky, "the architect of the Red army," and commanded in places by former imperial officers, gave a good account of themselves. Guerilla fighters rendered valuable assistance as did appealing Communist propaganda. Another effective Red resource was the Cheka, or secret police, directed by men who were thoroughly familiar with the methods of their tsarist forerunners. Aristocrats, middle-class men, some churchmen and peasants, anyone suspected or known to be hostile to the Revolution, the tsar and his family among them, were summarily liquidated by the terrorists. Desperate men that they were, Lenin and his associates stopped at nothing to consolidate the power that accident almost had thrust into their hands. Some estimates place the number of victims claimed by the dreaded Cheka as high as a million.

The Counter-revolutionaries were lamed by indecision, dissension and shortage of matériel. It would doubtless have been possible for the Allied-"White" combination to defeat the Bolsheviks who at the outset controlled only a small area of Russia. But war-weariness caused the Allies to evacuate their troops and, soon after the conclusion of the Polish war, the "White" forces gave up the struggle.

Russia was in sorry disarray when the strain of civil warfare ceased. Experiments in collectivist economy had panned out disastrously. Famine and disease stalked wide areas of the country. Refugees of the "White" persuasion streamed by thousands into foreign countries, and minority nationalities on the fringe of Russia seized the chance to assert their independence. The Baltic states—Finland, Estonia, Latvia and Lithuania—were recognized as free countries by the Kremlin, but it steadfastly refused to validate Rumanian occupation of the province of Bessarabia. On the other hand, the Communists cancelled the special privileges that the tsardom had accumulated in backward countries, from Turkey through Persia (Iran) to China, except for the railway traversing Manchuria.

THE SOVIET GOVERNMENT: THEORY AND PRACTICE

"The first step in the revolution by the working class," the *Communist Manifesto* of 1848 explained, "is to raise the proletariat to the position of the ruling class and to establish democracy." Russian Communists claimed that their plan of government harmonized with that Marxian prescription and was a much higher type of democracy than had previously been known, since it promised equality in scale of living. It was further contended that the November Revolution meant a striking advance in the age-old struggle of humanity for freedom. The basic and unchanging tenets of Communism included class consciousness, class hatred, class warfare and world revolution.

As conceived by Lenin and other theorists, the Soviet state was a self-perpetuating institution that would provide security and equality for its citizens. The state derived its ultimate authority from the Revolution, and existed apart from and above the individuals residing in it. The permanence and expansion of the state were sacred responsibilities for those entrusted with its physical powers. Citizens belonged to this "non-consent" state, not the state to the citizens. As soon as world revolution had destroyed capitalist rivals, then the U.S.S.R. would develop into a "stateless" society.

Whatever the theory, whatever the blueprint for the future, the Soviet government in day-to-day action and performance was strictly authoritarian and totalitarian. Compared with it, the tsarist despotism was limited in scope, for it did not presume to control the whole of life. When Communist authors and orators lauded the "Soviet democracy" they had in mind radically different concepts from those which had evolved in Western society. "When I use a word it means just what I want it to mean, neither more nor less," says Humpty-Dumpty in *Through the Looking Glass*—and Communism agreed, for it used a language peculiar to itself and baffling to those who attached a conventional meaning to words.

The framework of the Communist government was outlined in a constitution of 1923. The Soviet state, the Union of Socialist Soviet Republics (U.S.S.R.), was a federal union embracing several republics, territories and regions and autonomous areas. Public authority was in actual practice centralized in Moscow; outside of cultural affairs and to a slight extent economic matters, local governments never acquired much significance.

The Constitution granted the franchise to all workers over eighteen. Individuals who had been closely identified with tsarism, well-to-do folk and clergymen were denied the voting privilege. Each village or industrial plant chose a soviet or council, and through a complicated ladder of soviets, the Communist system led up to an All-Union Congress of Soviets (1500). Selection of representatives was so contrived as to give urban communities far greater weight than rural Russia. In practice the All-Union Congress had little else to do than choose a central executive committee (450), to which the Council of Commissars (17–19), or ministry, was nominally responsible.[1]

Constitutionalism in Soviet Russia has never been other than window dressing. All public questions began—and begin—with the Communist Party. Proudly hailed as the militant vanguard, the party contained (1939) just under 2,500,000, counting candidates, or possibly 4 per cent of the adult population. Almost everyone who was anyone in the U.S.S.R. belonged to the party.

Admission to the party followed stiff training and demonstration of faith by works. Periodic "housecleanings" eliminated members who were less than total in their allegiance to the party and its leadership; in a wide-ranging purge of 1933, for example, about a third of the members was expelled. Strictly disciplined, the party was minutely and hierarchically organized from local "cells" up to the All-Union Congress which met only infrequently. A central executive committee with several sub-committees, exercised control between party congresses. The secretary-general who managed the party machinery, stood close to the seat of authority. But the real core of power was an inner steering committee of the party, the political bureau, or *Politburo*. That body of nine to fourteen men, the authentic and dictatorial masters of Russia, meeting in the Kremlin, decided primary questions of home and foreign policies, issues of war or peace.

Upholding the government and the Communist Party were the secret police, the army and an elaborate, ever-expanding program of mass indoctrination under state auspices. Under changing titles, the secret police, which Stalin lauded as "the indefatigable guardian of the

[1] Ministries in the U.S.S.R. increased prodigiously after 1930, so that by 1947, fifty-nine were operating; thereafter the number was scaled down.

С. С. С. Р.
Народный Комиссариат Внутренних Дел
ГЛАВНОЕ УПРАВЛЕНИЕ ЛАГЕРЯМИ
УПРАВЛЕНИЕ УХТО-ПЕЧОРСКОГО ИСПРАВИТЕЛЬНО ТРУДОВОГО ЛАГЕРЯ
УЧРАСПРЕДОТДЕЛ
6 Июня 1938 г.
№ 6354339
Адрес: г. Чибью Коми Области
Для телеграмм: Чибью УХТПЕЧЛАГ Н. К. В. Д

ФОРМА

СПРАВКА

Дана гр. Пироговой Михаил Поликарповне рождения 1904 г.
уроженцу Ст. Тацинская Морозовского Района Азово-Черноморского Края
осужденному Жительнице г. Ростов на Дону.
Особым Совещанием НКВД 19. Января 1936 г.
по ст. ст. СОЗ сроком УК к заключению в ИТЛ
на три года
ОНА ПИРОГОВА

с зачетом рабочих дней из УХТО-ПЕЧОРСКОГО ИСПР. ТРУДОВ. лагеря освобождена 8 Июня 1938 г.
На проезд выдано требование по Ф. № 5 за № до ст.

Местожительство служить не может. При этом не освобождается.
Начальник УХТПЕЧЛАГ'а НКВД — /ТКАЧЕНКО/
Начальник Учетно-распредотдела — /РЫКОВ/

ПАСПОРТ ВЫДАН 1938

Document certifying expiration of a term in a slave-labor camp, Uchto-Petchorsk region, Russia, 1938

Revolution," attained such strength that it was an open question whether it was subordinate to or actually stronger than the party itself. Police seized "enemies of the Soviet regime," an elastic phrase, or even mere grumblers, allowed them to rot in prisons, arbitrarily imposed the death penalty or sentenced them to corrective labor camps.

With time the forced labor corps developed into a major factor in solving the chronic shortages of workers in certain places of employment. Prisoners were set to work in building roads and railways, on lumbering and mining operations and in industries. In some camps at least, food was distributed to prisoners—and they ran into millions—in accordance with their efficiency on the job. Politically active Soviet citizens, high and low, lived in constant dread of a "knock on the door at night," a bullet in the neck or a living death in a labor camp.

The Soviet army, which grew steadily in effectiveness and in numbers, comprised another invaluable prop of the Communist tyranny. Soldiers benefited by better living standards than ordinary citizens and learned trades to be pursued upon their discharge. Press, radios with loud speakers installed in every square and clubhouse, in factories and in villages,[2] movies, theaters and schools were harnessed to the Soviet chariot, proclaiming in season and out the glories and achievements of the Communist regime, the evils of capitalist society, the heroic qualities of Communist leaders, or the proper attitude to be adopted toward foreign countries. As in other totalitarian states, the tone of propaganda could be, and was, switched up and down, to bold or cautious, to fierce or sweet, to suit the mood of the ruling oligarchy. The Soviet tyranny was "tyranny over the mind of man," to borrow the language of Thomas Jefferson.

[2] Lenin once defined the radio as "a journal that needs no paper and knows no distance."

Stalin (right) and Lenin in 1922

LENIN AND STALIN

Chief of the Communist showplaces in Moscow is a red-black mausoleum, just outside the somber brick walls of the Kremlin, containing the embalmed body of Nicholas Lenin. Pilgrims from all across the U.S.S.R. undertake journeys of respect and veneration to this holy shrine, and the prowess of Lenin has been woven into the folk legends of his country. Unquestionably this master-architect of the Soviet Union was one of the very crucial personalities of the twentieth century, the decisive voice in Russia until his death in 1924. His passing was mourned by admirers in every country of the world—a unique distinction to that time.

A philosopher as well as a man of action, Lenin was accustomed to think wholly in terms of the class struggle and an egalitarian society, as became a follower of Marx. Supremely self-confident, gifted with shrewd common sense and an adroit tactician, he paid careful attention to details of planning and administration. For all his devotion to doctrine, he nevertheless displayed a quality of flexibility and distrusted overly schematic blueprints for the future. Austere in his private life, Lenin could be perfectly ruthless in crushing dissent. "Sentimentality," he explained, "is no less a crime than cowardice in war." But party leaders who disagreed with him were assured of a considerate hearing and humane treatment. He seems to have preferred collective leadership to personal dominance, and he favored the principle of national self-determination.

Upon the death of Lenin, it was widely assumed in Russian circles that counted that his personal authority would pass to the popular and magnetic Trotsky. But Trotsky was challenged, defeated and then eclipsed by Joseph Stalin, who had literally pulled himself into the ruling hierarchy by his bootstraps. Born in 1879 in the Transcaucasian province of Georgia of humble parents who were descendants of serfs, Stalin had a most remarkable career. From birth he was handicapped by a warped arm, which, among other things, kept him out of the Imperial army. At the age of fifteen, he enrolled in a theological seminary, but he was expelled because he read scientific and revolutionary books.

Blossoming out as a tough-textured revolutionary conspirator, Stalin teamed up with Lenin and adopted his version of the Marxist pattern of society. Short, swarthy, taciturn, cunning, resentful of established authority, Stalin won respect in Bolshevik circles for fearlessness, perseverance and reliability. As a professional revolutionary, operating under a dozen aliases, he robbed and stole to obtain funds for party purposes and carried on revolutionary agitation among industrial workers. To an extraordinary memory and unusual capacity to concentrate, Stalin added a wide range of knowledge and grasp of detail. "That wonderful Georgian," as Lenin called him, was arrested time and again and banished to Siberia, only to return with his hatred of tsarism hardened by his prison experiences.

In 1912 Stalin was appointed to the central committee of the Bolshevik party and helped in editing *Pravda*, the party newspaper. Exiled again to Siberia, he shared the amnesty extended by the Provisional Government after the March Revolution. Not long after his return he contrived to get a place on the crucial *Politburo*, and was made commissar of nationalities, a minor office, in the original Bolshevik ministry. A superb machine politician, he was named secretary-general of the party in 1922 and in that capacity was able to install personal followers in strategic positions in party and in state.

In the epic duel with the intellectually brilliant Trotsky, Stalin, "backstairs" operator that he was, profited from the support of key-men in the party. Up to a point, the two protagonists and their cronies diverged on the timing of world revolution, which both regarded as a necessity. Trotsky, however, felt that world revolution should have first place on the Soviet agenda, while Stalin argued for concentration on building up Russia as a model of collectivist society, which would invite imitation. It was Trotsky's opinion, too, that full-bodied Communism must be imposed upon Russia as rapidly as possible, while Stalin preferred to support the Leninist New Economic Policy.

Trotsky lost out, was expelled from the party, and later on was exiled from Russia. Soviet writers have either ignored, minimized or distorted the services which he rendered the revolutionary regime in its first years, a role second only to that of Lenin himself. Trotsky perished (1940) in distant Mexico, the victim of an assassin who drove a pickax into his skull.

Many a foreign pundit falsely construed the defeat of Trotsky as meaning the abandonment of the idea of world revolution. Stalin reigned supreme, an uncrowned tsar, yet more despotic than any Romanov. Pictured to the Soviet public as an infallible and omniscient leader, "the Father of the Peoples of the Soviet Union," Stalin had the distinction of being deified while he was still living. Russians showed once more an almost superstitious reverence for absolute authority. Possibly the Stalin legend, elaborated in his lifetime with resources of invention unknown to Napoleon, may equal or surpass the Napoleonic legend.

Unlike Lenin, whom he constantly and lavishly praised, Stalin never hesitated to strike down party folk who disagreed with him, even his oldest and closest friends. He tossed the principle of economic equality overboard, fostered a cult of the leader and established a personal dictatorship.

Insistence upon Stalinist orthodoxy, the distortions of propaganda and secrecy and the denial of reasonable facilities for travel to foreign observers enveloped the Russia of Stalin with a fog of legend and myth. After about 1930 it became increasingly difficult for an outsider to obtain satisfactory information on what was going on. The monolithic character of the dictatorship ruled out candid and open discussion of many public problems. During the Second World War an almost impenetrable black-out prevailed in the Soviet Union. Consequently writing about Russia has been deeply colored by conjecture and opinion.

"WAR COMMUNISM"

Once the Communists had established their authority, their consuming passion was to make Russia economically powerful under a regime of state collectivism. The means to the end varied, for neither Marx nor Lenin prepared a detailed program. Three distinct phases in Soviet economic evolution may be detected: an adventure in full Communism, which yielded in 1921 to modified state control over economic affairs, and that in turn was superseded, beginning in 1928, by breath-taking programs of planned economic advance.

The experiment in full Communist methods of production and distribution was launched under melancholy conditions. Participation in the European war had radically upset Russian economic activity, then came the Revolutions of 1917 and the devastating civil struggles. The guiding principle of "war Communism" was "From each according to his ability, to each according to his need." All instruments of production were taken over by the government; committees of workers and party members managed factories and mines, which caused—or helped to cause—further declines in productivity. By 1920 industrial output had fallen to a fifth of the prewar level. Simultaneously the Communists printed vast quantities of paper money to finance the civil war, which led into runaway inflation, the collapse of the currency and disruption of the entire economy.

Predominantly a peasant country, Russia could weather the fierce convulsions that beset her with rather less suffering than would have been the case in the highly industrialized nations of the West. Farm production in 1920 was about half of the 1913 yields. For that drop the seizure of large estates by land-hungry rustics was partly responsible. Besides, peasants would not turn over their surplus products to the state to supply the needs of the city workers, whose loyalty was essential if the Bolsheviks were to retain power. When the Communist authorities attempted to requisition grain with armed gangs from the cities, the peasants retorted by reducing acreages. A vicious cycle spiraled: the factories could not turn out wares that the peasant millions wanted, and the peasants would not grow the food required by the city populations.

A severe system of urban rationing was instituted which failed, however, to meet the needs for human sustenance, and emigration from the cities to the countryside reached large dimensions. It was Communism clearly enough, equality in living standards to a greater degree than Russia would see in the future—and equality in misery. For a time the old Russian proverb that "The man who walks and the man who rides on horseback are not comrades" lost its validity. Doctrinaire Marxists rejoiced over the turn of events, but the realistic Lenin, who had never liked the idea of immediate collectivism, perceived that compromise with dogma was imperative. He had to deal with situations, not theories.

A revolt among disillusioned sailors in the Baltic Fleet at Kronstadt near Petrograd, the most serious internal threat to the regime since the Revolution, was drowned in a ten-day blood bath. But that rising convinced Lenin of the urgency of abandoning "war Communism." That judgment was reinforced by a terrible famine, the worst Europe had seen in three centuries, and attended by decimating typhus and plague. The death toll, which exceeded 4,000,000, would have been even more staggering if help from outside had not been forthcoming.

That prince of Communist authors, Maxim Gorky, issued in July of 1921 a piteous appeal for foreign assistance. "I ask all honest European and American people for prompt aid to the Russian people. Give bread and medicine." The response was instant and generous. Nearly a million tons of food as well as quantities of clothing and medicines were shipped from the United States alone; at the height of its operations the American Relief Administration was feeding over 10,000,000 Russians. Costing in excess of $65,000,000, this relief was furnished by the United States government and by private American charities—and forgotten by the beneficiaries.

Child victims of Russian famine

THE NEW ECONOMIC POLICY (N.E.P.)

Already Lenin had ordered relaxation of "pure" Communism, allowing considerable scope to personal initiative and private profit. Under the new economic policy, which was Lenin's last major act, it was lawful to engage in retail or wholesale trade or operate small factories for private gain. Profit-seeking foreign capitalists were invited into Russia, the hope being that they would teach industrial know-how and raise productivity. The state retained control of transportation, banks, foreign trade and most of the mines and large factories, whose output was sold to private tradesmen. A new variety of currency became standard in 1924, new rubles being exchanged for old on a ratio of one for 50,000,000.

Above all, the peasants were authorized to sell their products freely. In lieu of requisitioning, they paid taxes to the government. Thanks to these concessions a class of better-off-than-average farmers, *kulaks* they were called, reappeared. As "prosperity" returned to the countryside, taxes were stepped up, and again peasants fought back by planting less or hiding their products; in 1927, requisitioning was revived.

Partial restoration of capitalism helped the Soviet Union to recover from the economic malady at an astonishingly swift pace. By 1928 industrial production was running ahead of 1913 records, and farm crops were almost up to pre-war standards. Even so, in a country of nearly 150,000,000 inhabitants, mills turned out only about 4,000,000 tons of steel and something like 30,000,000 pairs of shoes annually. Prices were relatively stable and the state budget was brought into balance. Very probably, urban living levels in 1928 were the highest that Soviet Russia has ever known, and differences in income were slight, though town and country had witnessed the emergence of a new middle class, the "Nepmen."

In announcing the N.E.P., Lenin confessed to "having suffered a heavy defeat. We have begun a strategic retreat," but he added, "We will construct everything anew, only on a more lasting basis." Events verified the prophecy. By 1928 state agencies in competition with private merchants handled about four-fifths of the internal trade, and economic recuperation was so well advanced that it seemed practicable to apply the collectivist ideology more fully. A five-year program for the coordination and expansion of industry and agriculture was inaugurated. Announcement of the plan was accompanied by a detailed exposition of Russian economic geography, location of raw materials and the sites where industries would be constructed.

THE FIVE-YEAR PLANS

Building upon the remnants of the Imperial Russian industrial structure and bountiful supplies of raw materials, machine industry expanded more rapidly in the U.S.S.R. in the decade or so after 1928 than in any other country in history. An elaborate array of state committees prepared plans and directives for the advance; production targets and major decisions were set by top authorities in Moscow. It was the avowed intention of Soviet policy makers to demonstrate that a publicly owned and a centrally planned and controlled economy was superior in productivity to free, competitive enterprise. The Soviet Union would outstrip the United States.

As the short range objective, the economic plans were calculated to strengthen capacity for war against potential foreign enemies. Stalin kept repeating that Russia had been whipped in the past because of industrial backwardness. That must not happen again. Special attention was devoted to developing the industrial resources of the Urals and western Siberia, areas less vulnerable militarily than other centers of production. The more distant goal of planning was to raise the lowly conditions of living among the Soviet millions.

Two Five-Year Plans were carried out between 1928 and the involvement of Russia in the Second World War, and a third plan was scheduled for fulfillment in 1943, but had to be laid aside with the onset of war. In each instance the accent rested heavily on capital equipment, not on goods for consumers. Large-scale factories, huge blast furnaces, large tractor plants were erected; great hydro-electric stations were built, mining operations were greatly accelerated and railways and other means of communication were considerably extended. According to the official reports, the output in nearly every type of production exceeded the plans, though the quality of goods seems not to have come up to expectations. Nevertheless, the Soviet plans set an enormous vogue for social planning in other countries.

In assessing Soviet industrial progress, students are wholly dependent upon published governmental facts and figures. Statistics in any country have proverbial shortcomings; rarely are they complete or fully accurate, and interpretation of Soviet statistics was somewhat beclouded by the use of terms carrying special connotations in Russia. That is not to say, however, that Soviet figures were deliberately juggled; reliable statistics were obviously of the greatest importance to state planning boards. Reports disclosing failure to attain targets occasionally reached the outside world.

Assuming, then, reasonable reliability in Soviet statistics, the growth in industrial strength can only be described as sensational. Output of steel, for example, increased between 1929 and 1939 from four to eighteen million tons, of coal from thirty to one hundred and seventy million tons, of electric power from five to fifty billion kilowatt hours. Industrial workers increased by somewhere between ten and fifteen millions, and the urban population grew by nearly 30,000,000. On an overall estimate, industrial production in 1939 exceeded the levels of 1913 by at least four times, possibly considerably more, and stood at one-third of the output of the United States.

The gigantic expansion was accomplished without foreign loans, though relatively small sums were obtained from abroad by selling art treasures to foreigners. The plans were financed either by heavy taxation, the proceeds from the sale of state bonds, or through huge increases in the currency. For the ordinary Russian the industrial program involved severe sacrifices not only in comforts but, at periods, in necessities also. The U.S.S.R., it has been said, was "starved into industrialization."

Owing to currency inflation during the first Five-Year Plan, workers experienced sharp losses in buying power. Pay envelopes were fatter, it is true, but prices moved up faster. Rigid rationing was clamped on in 1929 and persisted throughout the "Iron Age," as this period has appropriately been labeled. Food, which consisted principally of bread, potatoes and cabbage, rarely meat, was in short supply, and clothing scarce. The swarming of workers to cities intensified the appalling housing congestion in spite of immense new construction; at the very best, families had only two or three rooms in an apartment and shared kitchen and bath facilities with others.

By 1935 the situation had been brought under some degree of stability, and rationing was discontinued. For three years—the Golden Age doubtless of Soviet planning—prices held firm, living standards improved, without, however, regaining the levels of 1928. Then another wave of inflation swept the country, in response to intensified preparations for war. Real incomes sagged and fell still lower when Russia became fully involved (1941) in the Second World War. Misery and impoverishment reminiscent of the years of "war Communism" returned. Violent oscillations in the purchasing ability of workmen, while exciting, must have been confusing and nerve-wracking.

It must be added that urban workers received substantial social benefits. Rentals for dwelling places were low and the state provided medical care and schooling free, as well as inexpensive recreational opportunities. Nevertheless, living standards, though high compared with Asia, remained substantially below Western levels.

COMMUNIST CONSOLIDATION

To shore up morale, propaganda agencies kept reminding workers that they actually owned the factories and everything else. Harsh conditions now were the inescapable price that had to be paid for richer living in the future. And, besides, workers were taught that they were in fact better off than their counterparts in capitalistic countries—but Russian soldiers who marched into the West during the Second World War were astounded to discover industrial workmen enjoying "bourgeois" comforts. Sometimes the Soviet authorities ascribed consumer shortages to the menace of foreign enemies, and the necessity of concentrating industrial resources on the production of military equipment. Or blame for shortages was attributed to the incapacity or stupidity of individual bureaucrats.

Accompanying and buttressing the expansion of industry were other significant changes in the Soviet economic scene. The ideal of equality in income, for instance, was thrown overboard. In a speech of 1931, "New Conditions and New Tasks," Stalin openly repudiated equality in wages in favor of the principle "From each according to his ability," to "each according to his work."

To raise the shockingly low productivity of workers, competition was stressed—piece-work and "payment by result." Each factory and mine contained a contingent of "speed-king" workers, who set the pace for their fellows, and were remunerated appropriately. Highly efficient and skilled workers received as much as ten times and more wages than the ordinary employee. When rationing was in force, individuals with ready cash could buy meat and butter, for instance, at special stores, paying exorbitant prices. Surplus funds might be plunged into state bonds, the purchase of which seems to have been almost compulsory. Bonuses for superior performance might take the form of money, or a pair of shoes, or strips of cloth, or coal, or more pleasant living quarters. Good shoes, as the present writer observed in the Russia of 1939, were the unmistakable mark of men of distinction. Awards of merit badges and press publicity were further incentives to efficiency.

Trade unions, too, were responsible for raising worker productivity, as well as combatting the high labor turnover and furnishing technical training. Membership in unions increased fabulously, but they were not at all independent organizations with loyalties of their own to force betterment in conditions of employment. Officers were drawn principally from party members of some standing and the unions themselves were cogs in the gigantic machinery of collectivism. As the result of various stimuli, from high pay to pressure by the union, output per man-hour may have risen as much as 80 per cent.

In any form of industrial society, whether planned or unplanned, the managerial and technical personnel is of crucial significance. This class gained in importance and numbers as Soviet industrialism progressed. As in Imperial Russia, thousands of technical experts and consultants were invited in from Germany and the United States to acquaint natives with the latest processes in widely distributed industrial undertakings. Students in the higher technical schools exceeded 600,000 in 1939, better than three times as many as a decade earlier.

The authority and responsibility of the Soviet managerial class became at least as great as in capitalistic countries. Managers had considerable latitude in hiring and firing employees and in tightening up discipline in mill and mine. Plant managers were well paid, socially esteemed, beneficiaries of special privileges and more and more of them were Communist Party members. The general manager of a steel plant in Magnitogorsk, to illustrate, lived in a brick dwelling containing ten rooms, a billiard and a music room and a comfortable study. Surrounding the home were a small deer park and a spacious garden, all shielded by a high wall and protected by guardsmen. Such "tycoons" employed household servants, and might spend their evenings at the theater or ballet, week-ends in the country and vacations at state resorts. The luckier ones also had motorcars.

Aside from superior workmen and managers, there were other recipients of high incomes in the U.S.S.R. Among the most lavishly remunerated were artists with words, music, or palette, entertainers and scholars. The secret police also belonged to the elite, as did officials in government, army and party, though not the party rank and file. A veritable army of officials was engaged in the paper work of the planned economy. Very like their prototypes in other countries, Soviet bureaucrats were notorious for their lack of initiative and their reluctance to assume responsibility; they were accustomed to wait until decisions had been taken higher up. Procrastination might be the thief of time, but it might also lengthen one's life-span.

Beyond doubt, differentiation in incomes fostered class feeling in Soviet Russia and provoked dissatisfaction among the unfavored. That has been called the "Achilles heel" of the Soviet Union; but the future would have to disclose whether social stratification and perpetuation of classes would last. In any case, careers were open to talents in Soviet Russia to a degree unexampled in the history of the country.

THE REVOLUTION IN AGRICULTURE

Despite the great industrial expansion, two Russians out of three in 1939 still depended upon the soil for their livelihood. After the March Revolution (1917) the pre-war trend toward individual proprietorships proceeded apace making Russia essentially a country of peasant owners—upwards of 20,000,000 of them. Quarreling between the government and the better-off peasants was a recurrent theme in Soviet history. With a view to integrating agriculture in the planned economy, eliminating private ownership of property and enlarging farm output, the Kremlin in 1929 inaugurated a headlong collectivization of the land. Instead of individual holdings, farms would be consolidated into large properties, wasteful practices such as the "strip" system would disappear and cultivation with labor-saving machinery would be advantageous. Stalin declared that the relatively well-to-do peasants (*kulaks*) must be extinguished; for that class collectivization meant a violent and painful psychological wrench.

Physical force was ruthlessly applied to coerce balky peasants into collectives and then to keep them in. Victims sullenly protested by reducing the areas sown, hiding grain or slaughtering their livestock; flocks and herds had not recovered from excessive killing by

Laborers on a Russian collective farm

1940, which meant less of certain foods for the cities—milk, butter and meat—less leather and wool for clothing. Stalin's slogan of a cow for every rural family fell short of fulfillment.

Soldiers and state agents moved into districts where disaffection was rife, provoking virtual civil war. Huts were ransacked to find concealed grain to supply the cities or for export. Executions and widespread starvation cut down better than 4,000,000 rustics in the grim winter of 1932–1933. If the Soviet Union had become involved in foreign war at this critical time, the whole Stalinist fabric might have collapsed. But resistance to collectivization was broken, the program was driven forward and by 1939 private farms had practically disappeared. Apart from the collectives, Soviet authorities organized gigantic state farms, which were operated as nearly as possible on factory methods of production.

On the collective farms, each household had a garden plot (*usadba*) of its own and each might own livestock for family use. Administration was lodged in a managing committee nominally chosen by the peasants, but in practice appointed by Communist agencies. Gradually, machinery was made available, so that by 1940 over 550,000 tractors were at work, in spite of the fact that many tractor factories had by then been converted to production of tanks. Machine tractor stations serviced fifty or more collectives, and the personnel was closely supervised by party agents. Tractor drivers and officials on the collectives developed into a separate and favored rural class, the successors, in a sense, of the liquidated *kulaks*. As in industry, certain collectives were picked as "pacesetters" to stimulate increased output by neighbors. Each collective had its own school and nursery and a primitive medical center.

As another aspect of the revolution in the countryside, agricultural experts applied scientific techniques to farming: better seed, greater use of artificial fertilizers, rotation of crops and improved methods of stock breeding. By one device or another state agencies got hold of the surpluses raised on the collectives. Yet the battle with stiff-necked peasants who tried to evade the obligations to deliver grain was not entirely successful; it was impossible to determine in what measure the peasantry had been reconciled to collectivism, though resentment against "social discipline" remained a serious problem.

By 1939 a smaller number of soil workers was tilling more ground than in 1929 and harvests were approximately a fifth greater. Whether increased output was keeping pace with the fast growing population was a matter of conjecture; something like 170,000,000 were living in Russia in 1939 as compared with 140,000,000 in 1913. On the eve of the Second World War the Soviet Union had approximately the same amount of crop acreage as the United States, but the latter raised about 50 per cent greater harvests; it was estimated that one farmer in the United States produced as much as six in the U.S.S.R. The disparities were partly due to differences in equipment and in methods, but also because vast areas of Russian soil were not favored with sufficient rainfall or were handicapped by climatic conditions. Odessa on the Black Sea lies on the same latitude as Duluth, Minnesota, and Aroostook county in Maine.

THE SOVIET "WORLD OUTLOOK"

From a world viewpoint revolutionary Russia had universal significance not alone for the experimentation in monopolistic state control of economic activities but because it struck violently at traditional social institutions and religious values. It was the avowed aim of the Soviet policy makers to rear up a new type of person in a Marxist type of society.

Bolshevism hated the official Orthodox Church with pathological fervor. The Church seemed to be nothing more than a corrupt and intriguing tool of the tsarist order, a bulwark of superstition and the sleepless enemy of enlightenment. On principle, Communists detested and despised all religions in keeping with the remark of Marx that "religion is the opium of the people"—a dictum which was liberally placarded about Russian cities and villages. Man himself, it was explained, possessed unlimited capacity to interpret and reg-

A Russian "anti-religious museum," formerly a Moscow convent. The signs advertise a state lottery.

ulate both nature and society. Instead of anticipating a heaven beyond the grave, Russians should build a happy and joyous society on this earth. Avowal of atheism was a prerequisite for admission into the Communist Party.

Communism offered an alternative to religious traditions. It possessed a sacred scripture in the writings of Marx and Lenin. Portraits of these worthies were substituted for religious icons and the tomb of Lenin became a place of reverent worship. Communism possessed a hierarchy in the Communist Party and in place of a theology it had the doctrines of materialistic Marxism. The Communist faith was simple, direct, confident and it inspired action. It explained not only the past and the present but forecast the future; inevitably the world must ripen toward Communism. To deviate from this "integrated outlook" or even to question it openly, invited the penalty of excommunication which might involve exile or death.

The Communist offensive against organized religion fluctuated from time to time. In the first flush of the Revolution the economic and political strength of the Orthodox Church was irreparably shattered, many church edifices were converted to secular purposes or made over into anti-religious museums and many clergymen were imprisoned or put to the sword. Propaganda against religion was widely diffused through the schools and mass communication media. Later on, pressures were relaxed, then renewed, and relaxed again during the Second World War, when all the energies of the country were enlisted in the military effort.

"Religion is like a nail," a leading Bolshevik remarked in 1928, "the harder you hit it the deeper it goes into the wood," which was another way of saying that the campaign against religion was by no means wholly successful. Atheism appealed more powerfully to youths than to elders and to the cities far more than to the villages. Official estimates of 1937 indicated that a third of the city dwellers and two-thirds of the peasants were still believers in religion.

Communism propagated its own norms of right and wrong which were destructive of the ethical concepts of civilized tradition. The exclusive test of right behavior was—and is—the degree to which conduct contributed to the cause of Communist revolution. Conventional moral customs were lightly dismissed as products of an antiquated and malevolent form of economic organization. Loyal Communists were expected to "reject every attempt to impose any moral dogma as an eternal, ultimate and forever immutable law," in the language of Engels, the colleague of Marx. Lenin crisply stated the official Communist position, writing, "Morality is what serves to destroy the old exploiting society. We do not believe in an eternal morality."

SOCIAL INNOVATIONS

The institutions of marriage and the family underwent modifications in Soviet Russia. Extremist theories on the emancipation of women flourished at the outset of the revolutionary era. Family bonds were loosened, there was much sexual irregularity and divorce could readily be procured by either party. But decrees tightening family relations and parental responsibility were published in the 1930s. A higher fee had now to be paid for divorce, and the price was raised again in 1944. At that time the Kremlin announced a "positive" population policy to make up the losses suffered in the Second World War. Children of unmarried mothers would be maintained at state expense and allowances for large families were raised so as to make motherhood a lucrative vocation. After the Second World War babies appeared at the rate of about 5,000,000 annually as compared with 3,000,000 in the preceding decade.

In keeping with the doctrine of equality between the sexes, women were granted the franchise on the same terms as men and were drawn into remunerative employment. As workers, women would be financially independent and would, of course, swell the labor force. Crèches, or day nurseries, were installed in factories and collective farms, and kindergartens were provided for children of employed mothers. Women, even teen-age girls, operated mechanized farm equipment and were trained as agricultural experts. Sex equality was strikingly demonstrated in the Second World War, when Soviet women fought as snipers, guerillas and as plane pilots.

Perhaps the most effective agency for the inculation of the Communist "world-outlook" was the Soviet school. Adult mentalities could not easily be remolded, teaching old dogs new tricks is always tricky, so the Bolshevik revolutionaries laid the accent on youth on the principle that as the twig is bent so will the tree incline. School attendance was made compulsory with the leaving age higher in the city than in the village. Illiteracy dropped from about a half to a fifth of the population, the most notable progress taking place among women and Asiatic peoples; and the Communist ideology was firmly embedded in the consciousness of youth. School children learned the glories of a collectivist economy, the evils of conventional religion and capitalism and the infallibility of the masters in the Kremlin, Stalin first and last.

In the thirties nationalist indoctrination, something utterly repugnant to Lenin, entered the curriculum of schools. Stress was laid upon the continuity of Russia as revealed in history and literature and upon affection for "Mother Russia," emphases not altogether pleasing to the non-Russian nationalities. Toning down on the Marxist theorem of history as an unending class struggle, teachers instructed their pupils that Russian tsars had been glorious patriots and valiant fighters against national enemies. Stalin was wont to remark during the Second World War that the Russian soldiers were fighting less for the Soviet Union than for Mother Russia. Communist attitudes planted in the schools were reinforced in youth associations of various kinds and in the conscript army for the boys.

Learning at more mature levels emphasized the practical, not the cultural side of life. Every Russian city boy, it is fair to say, aspired to be an engineer. The government furnished stipends to students and those earning superior marks were rewarded with special perquisites. As early as 1924, universities and other advanced institutions of learning were transformed into Marxist institutes in which every department of study from art to zoology was taught as an expression of the Communist interpretation of existence. Only youths of working class or peasant antecedents were eligible for admission Rigid control of books and a pervasive censorship suffocated the life of the mind and spirit.

Intellectual freedom had no place whatsoever in the Soviet dictatorship. In the name of a mighty impersonal plan the Soviet regime was prepared to apply any device to coerce the body and twist the mind. Writers, painters and composers worked under instructions from party officials and in strict conformity with official policies and principles which stifled originality and deadened imaginative expression. "Art must serve propaganda," cried Lenin. Even cartoons in *Krokodil*, a droll and influential comic paper, were directed to "the socialization of the emotions," or to the wickedness of the capitalist West. Freedom of the press meant freedom to praise the Stalinist paradise and its superhuman leader. An invisible shield, an "Iron Curtain" kept Russians from learning of the actualities in the world outside.

Novelists dilated upon material themes—mills and mines, factories and collective farming—always subject to gimlet-eyed censors; and movies and the theater fulfilled their duty by parading the qualities of the new Soviet man, exposing survivals of the horrid bourgeois past, or rousing mistrust and hatred of "imperialist beasts" and "war-mongers" in capitalist countries. Artists, servants of the party, too, endeavored to make intelligible to the masses their historic destiny in harmony with Marxist dogmas, or declaimed against drunkenness, laxness, thievery, and other evils—among which they included religion!

THE CONSTITUTION OF 1936

In the thirties Soviet Russia definitely moved out of the Leninist into the Stalinist era of its evolution. The speed-up in industry, the differentiation in incomes, the pressure to render family life more stable, the creeds of nationalism and Pan-Slavism, the shift in foreign policies, described below, and the hardening of the personal rule of Stalin were open manifestations of the changing pattern of events. And in 1936 the publication of a new constitution seemed to argue a trend toward democratic principles and personal freedoms in the Western manner.

This constitution, which bore the name of Stalin, promised the fundamental civil and religious liberties of Western tradition with reservations. It asserted that private property in the form of personal belongings or savings and the right of inheritance would be protected. The Stalinist formula of greater rewards for greater services was underlined and everyone was assured of the right to work, to rest and to leisure, and of social security. Military service was prescribed as a universal duty, and the franchise right, which would be exercised in secret, was conferred upon everyone over eighteen.

The highest organ of state power—legislative, executive and judicial—was (and is) the Supreme Soviet, whose normal life-span would be four years. It was a body of two co-equal chambers: the Council of the Union, made up of one deputy for every 300,000 in the population, and the Council of Nationalities, whose members were chosen by each territorial division. The Supreme Soviet selected two executive bodies which were nominally responsible to it. First, the Presidium of some forty members, which exercised the authority of the Supreme Soviet when it was not in session, and its leading dignitary was the president of the Soviet Union. Second, the Council of People's Commissars, consisting principally of the heads of the ministries of the U.S.S.R.; the chief of the cabinet may be called the prime minister, a post Stalin assumed in 1941. Amendments to the constitution required concurrence by two-thirds vote in the Supreme Soviet.

Such then was the substance of the Constitution of 1936, but what of the actual operation of government? The Supreme Soviet sat for only a short while, usually less than a week, twice a year, and perfunctorily ratified proposals. Although the constitution assigned to the Supreme Soviet the exclusive prerogative of legislation, it neither debated nor opposed, but rather approved unanimously and without hesitation whatever measures the Council of Commissars presented. Much the greater part of the laws took the form of decrees, decisions and ordinances issued by the Presidium or by the Council of Commissars. Voices of deputies were raised only to hail the name of Stalin whenever it was mentioned, which was often. Etiquette prescribed that speeches in the Supreme Soviet should begin and end with eulogies of the All Wise One, offered sometimes in verse form. The Supreme Soviet, in short, resembled a puppet show dancing as the Kremlin pulled the strings.

Elections for the Supreme Soviet revealed the real nature of the Communist "democracy." Polling was an occasion for expression of popular fidelity to the Soviet scheme of society, a demonstration of loyalty to the new dispensation. Voters doubtless felt that they were taking an active part in public affairs. At the first balloting, in 1937, 96.8 per cent of the eligibles turned out, and the figure soared to 99.7 in 1946—a record hard to beat. Perhaps the principal value of the Supreme Soviet lay in the fact that through the deputies the rulers in the Kremlin were kept informed on popular sentiments in the far-flung realm.

It meant something to occupy a seat in the Supreme Soviet. Deputies formed an elite ranging from the ambidextrous milkmaid to the august Red Army general. Unquestioned loyalty was required of all deputies though they were not necessarily Communist Party members; about a quarter indeed did not belong to the party. As a rule, only one candidate "ran" in a constituency and he was carefully picked after a spirited nomination campaign from names proposed by the local branch of the Communist Party, by trade unions, or youth associations.

The Constitution of 1936 in no wise impaired the monopolistic role of the Communist Party. For all practical purposes the *Politburo* of the party remained omnipotent and the voice of Stalin was decisive in the *Politburo*. The Soviet tyranny, which carried in itself no seed of self-reformation, was not a passing phase of Russian political evolution but a permanent and self-intensifying condition.

THE GREAT PURGE

Wholesale purges in the late 1930's revealed anew the autocratic nature of Stalin's authority. Secret police apprehended thousands of individuals prominent in government, army, or party on charges of treasonable plotting with Nazi Germany and Japan or sabotage. The technique of the political trials which followed accorded with the basic conception of law as explained in 1924 by Krylenko, then Public Prosecutor. "Every court," he stated, "has the task of defending the interests of a given governing class and is distinguished from other means of defence only by its specific form and nothing more."

Incredible admissions of guilt were uttered at the trials, in which the leading prosecutor was Andrei Y. Vishinsky, an eminent legal expert, best known as the Soviet spokesman in the United Nations after the Second World War. Many culprits confessed, partly to save their families or friends from abuse, or knowing that confession would make no difference in the punishment, or after the application of torture by secret police—blinding light in the cell day and night, hunger, cold, terror, enforced sleeplessness, absolute silence, except during interrogation hour after hour.

Beyond any doubt the great purge was inspired more by personal antipathies and Trotskyite or other heresies than by treason. There is evidence, however, other than that taken at the Moscow trials, that a military conspiracy against Stalin was hatched in 1936. In any event

Andrei Vishinsky (second from right) as a judge at the Russian "purge trials"

nearly all the living founding-fathers of the Communist regime, large numbers of party leaders, Commissars and members of the General Staff were swept away by Stalin's iron broom, imprisoned, or banished. Thus the strength of Stalin was confirmed in blood and the mind of the masses was impressed with foreign dangers to the Soviet Commonwealth.

OUTLINES OF FOREIGN POLICY

Soviet foreign policy was steered along new tacks in the thirties. Up to a point, Communist Russia inherited the aims and interests of tsarist Russia. Equally with other nations, it was intent on preserving its political independence and territorial integrity, relying principally on its own armed power for that purpose. But Communist Russia cherished another objective, namely, the dissemination of Marxist principles in foreign countries and the promotion of world-wide Marxist revolution. Tactics varied in keeping with the international situation or with conditions inside Russia, but the long-range commitment to the downfall of capitalistic society was immutable. "It is inconceivable," Stalin wrote, "that the Soviet Republic should continue to exist for a long period side by side with imperialistic [i.e. non-Communist] states. Ultimately one or the other must conquer. Meanwhile a number of terrible clashes between the Soviet Republic and the bourgeois states are inevitable."

The ready agent of world revolution was the Comintern or Communist (Third) International founded in 1919 by Lenin at Moscow. Many a Bolshevik at the time thought that a general revolution was essential to the success of Marxist theory and that it was as certain as the Second Coming seemed to early Christians. Attending the conference which launched the organization were delegates from thirty countries, an array really of generals without armies. From the beginning, the dominant force in the Communist International was the moral authority of the Russian Revolution and the physical strength of Soviet Russia.

According to the first manifesto of the movement, the "Third International is the International of open mass action, the International of deeds." It "will support the plundered colonial peoples in their fight against Imperialism, in order to hasten the final collapse of the imperialistic world system." Freely it was avowed that the Comintern would "struggle by all available means, including armed force, for the overthrow of the international bourgeoisie and the creation of an international Soviet Republic as the transition state to the complete abolition of the State." A Soviet poet limned the dominant sentiments of the hour:

> We for the woe of all bourgeois
> Will light a fire throughout the world,
> A fire throughout the world in blood
> The blessing of the Lord be upon us.

The first Comintern congress assembled when Europe to the west of Russia was in the throes of economic and political turmoil and confusion at the end of the First World War. Revolutions were brewing or had already exploded in Bavaria, Hungary and Italy, and Poland and Germany were believed to be on the verge of taking the road to Moscow. But countervailing forces set in, such as the passionate desire for peace and order after the cessation of hostilities, which wholly upset the calculations of the Communists. No country, unless an exception be made in the case of Outer Mongolia, imitated the Russian example in the era between World Wars.

Nevertheless, the Third International kept up its operations, always under the central direction of Moscow, and congresses convened periodically. Representatives from as many as fifty-nine national Communist parties participated in deliberations. A detailed blueprint for revolution in colonial areas was drawn up; Asia and the Comintern would unite against capitalism and imperialism. Assistance was in fact rendered to the Chinese Nationalists in the mid-twenties as they fought to unite their country. But when victory was in sight the Nationalists broke with their allies, sent Comintern agents packing and separated themselves from the Chinese Communists.

At a congress of the Third International in 1928 it was proclaimed that Communist parties must fight against middle-of-the way and democratic Socialist groups. Implementation of that decision contributed to the weakening of democratic governments in Europe, in Germany above all else. Appreciating too late the damage that had been done, the Comintern in 1935 instructed individual Communist parties to align themselves with other political elements that were resisting Rightist authoritarianisms. The very existence of the Comintern and its dedication to international revolution excited mistrust, ill-will, waves of hysteria and fear in foreign countries. National Communist parties obsequiously followed instructions from Moscow, making the Third International almost exclusively an instrument of Russian foreign policy.

In spite of distrust, Soviet Russia was gradually admitted into the community of nations. One by one foreign countries extended diplomatic recognition to the Red regime and negotiated commercial treaties with it, the United States holding back until 1933. Pacts of nonaggression were eagerly arranged with countries along the borders of the U.S.S.R. The Kremlin sent representatives to various international meetings convened under League of Nations auspices, without entering fully into the work of the League; indeed, Bolshevik leaders flayed the League in vitriolic language as a capitalistic institution inimical to the security and well-being of the Communst Commonwealth.

But imperialistic expansion by Japan and the enthronement of the Nazis in Germany (1933) caused the Kremlin policy makers to ask for membership in the League. The request was granted, Russia being given a permanent seat on the Council—tacit recognition that she belonged in the Great Power class. But in the late thirties, Soviet ardor for the League and collaboration with the Western powers cooled, and after the Munich conference of 1938 Russia reverted to a policy of isolation. Preparations for war were pushed with fresh energy and patriotic enthusiasms were whipped up among the masses.

In August of 1939 the Kremlin, to the amazement of the world, negotiated a bargain with Nazi Germany, which helped to precipitate the Second World War. That conflict afforded boundless possibilities for the diffusion of Communism and for the expansion of the Soviet Empire. Stalin, every whit as ambitious as Peter the Great, tightly held the Russian reins in his fists.

FOR FURTHER STUDY

HUGH SETON-WATSON, *From Lenin to Khrushchev* (new ed., New York, 1960) PAPERBACK

SIDNEY and BEATRICE WEBB, *Soviet Communism: a New Civilization* (2 vols., New York, 1936)

MICHAEL T. FLORINSKY, *The End of the Russian Empire* (New Haven, 1931) PAPERBACK

WILLIAM H. CHAMBERLAIN, *The Russian Revolution* (new ed., 2 vols., New York, 1952)

BERTRAM D. WOLFE, *Three Who Made a Revolution* (New York, 1948) PAPERBACK

MERLE FAINSOD, *How Russia Is Ruled* (Cambridge, Mass., 1953)

FREDERICK L. SCHUMAN, *Soviet Politics at Home and Abroad* (New York, 1946)

ISAAC DEUTSCHER, *Stalin* (New York, 1949) PAPERBACK

HARRY SCHWARTZ, *Russia's Soviet Economy* (new ed., New York, 1954)

JOHN MAYNARD, *The Russian Peasant and Other Studies* (London, 1942) PAPERBACK

JOHN S. CURTISS, *The Russian Church and the Soviet State* (Boston, 1953)

FRANZ BORKENAU, *The Communist International* (London, 1938)

JOHN N. HAZARD, *Law and Social Change in the U.S.S.R.* (London, 1953)

JOHN S. CURTISS, *The Russian Revolutions of 1917* (New York, 1957) PAPERBACK

EDWARD H. CARR, *A History of Soviet Russia* (6 vols., New York, 1950–59. Other volumes to follow)

GEORG VON RAUCH, *History of Soviet Russia* (new ed., 1957) PAPERBACK

JOHN MAYNARD, *Russia in Flux* (New York, 1948) PAPERBACK

RICHARD PIPES, *The Formation of the Soviet Union* (Cambridge, Mass., 1960)

ISAAC DEUTSCHER, *Trotsky* (2 vols., New York, 1954, 1959)

JOHN S. RESHETAR, *A Concise History of the Communist Party* (New York, 1960) PAPERBACK

ROBERT V. DANIELS, *The Conscience of the Revolution* (Cambridge, Mass., 1960)

FREDERICH C. BARGHOORN, *Soviet Russian Nationalism* (New York, 1956)

GEORGE S. COUNTS and NUCIA P. LODGE, *The Challenge of Soviet Education* (New York, 1957)

RALPH T. FISHER, *Pattern for Soviet Youth* (New York, 1959)

BASIL H. LIDDELL HART, ed., *The Red Army* (New York, 1956)

CHAPTER XXVII

DEMOCRACIES AND DICTATORSHIPS (1919-1939)

MAJOR TRENDS

IN A very real sense the West of Europe never recovered from the effects of the First World War. The physical and spiritual tragedies of the conflict, the economic dislocations and intergovernmental financial obligations, the flame of truculent and selfish nationalism, the discontents arising out of the peace treaties and, not least, the haunting specter of Communist Russia rendered impossible a return to "the good old days" of 1913. And yet, appalling though the plight of Europe was in 1919, the general situation was less harsh and confounding than after the Second World War.

The epoch between World Wars in Europe, the Twenty Years' Truce, may be thought of as having four parts. First, 1919–1924, a time of insecurity, dizzy swings in the trade cycle and acute economic paralysis in the central part of the Continent. Bewilderment, exhaustion and hunger prevailed, millions being dependent for the essentials of existence upon the largesse of the United States, either in the form of government assistance or private charity. Currencies danced a weird inflationary dance before collapsing utterly in several countries, and radically shaking up social classes and distorting political attitudes. France and Poland in particular shouldered onerous burdens of rehabilitating areas that had been destroyed or grievously damaged during the war. Under circumstances somewhat peculiar to itself, Italy gravitated into the authoritarian regime called Fascism.

In the second inter-war stage, beginning in 1925, Western Europe experienced four years of material recovery which was attended by growing political stability. Production of goods increased, monetary systems were stabilized, the volume of international trade snapped back to pre-war levels, living standards improved, the upsurge in Germany bordering on the sensational. Controversies over intergovernmental debts, bequeathed by the war, yielded to intelligent and constructive treatment. It was an Indian summer of comparative prosperity and plenty. Cheerfulness in the economic realm was matched by unmistakable symptoms of betterment in international politics. Solid foundations, seemingly, were being laid for lasting prosperity, progress and peace. These fond and very human anticipations were shattered in the decade that followed.

The third chapter in the "Long Armistice," the era of the Great Depression, opened with a financial landslide on Wall Street in the autumn of 1929. Rapidly the grim hurricane of business recession raced round the globe, disturbing the peace of mind of everyone who was at all affected by international commerce. Prices, production and profits tumbled at terrifying speed, the gold standard collapsed and trade between nations dried up. Mass unemployment soared to unheard of heights and governments resorted to novel experiments to cure the malady. Paced by the United States, country after country sought its own salvation by jacking up tariff rates and kindred mercantilist expedients.

Political deterioration, internal and international, accompanied the economic malaise. Hitler rode into power in Germany, setting up a dictatorship that helped to undermine democratic governments in other nations of central and eastern Europe. To men who were weary of want and wretchedness, dictatorships held out glittering but specious hopes. Condemning freedom as an outmoded relic, dictators promised an economic square deal, social discipline and "something better" than democracy. By the middle of 1933 the economic fates seemed to be relenting and in several countries business activity, and therewith employment, picked up remarkably. But dictatorships, instead of fading away, consolidated their control.

With the invasion of African Abyssinia by Fascist Italy in the autumn of 1935, the curtain lifted on the final and most fateful act in the world drama. Stride by stride Europe proceeded along the familiar road to general war, reaching journey's end in September of 1939. In the interval, technological changes and enlarged productivity had probably raised standards of living above the levels of 1913. Governmental policies were guided by the principle that the state could never again permit citizens to be victimized by earthquakes in business.

THE SWEEP OF POPULAR GOVERNMENT

During the First World War, representative governments had to grapple with problems of unexampled magnitude and complexity. That necessity led to sharp deviations from established democratic practices. For the sake of planned efficiency, for the winning of the war, the executive branch of government assumed dictatorial authority; and compromise was made with cherished civil liberties. Even so, legislators and the press aired grievances, offered suggestions and even engaged in criticism of military policies.

After the victory, the triumphant democracies reinstated pre-war political customs and procedures—in every instance, except Belgium, without important changes. Success of the democracies in the gruelling ordeal of battle appeared to vindicate the advantages of government by consent. Application of the democratic dogma of self-determination in the treaties of peace produced a lush array of new or enlarged states, carved out of old monarchies. When governments raised memorial monuments after the First World War, they intended to express national gratitude to an "Unknown Soldier," not to advertise a conquering generalissimo as had been the way with Napoleon I. That switch in itself testified to the new recognition of the worth and dignity of the ordinary fellow.

All across Europe up to the line of Russia, democratic patterns of government were adopted, usually with an elected chief executive which made them republics. Outside of the Old World, Japan nodded modestly to the prevailing democratic fashion, and democratizing concessions were extended to the British

Armistice Day services at the Cenotaph, Whitehall, London, erected in honor of the British dead in the First World War

Dominions, to India and other overseas dependencies.

Written constitutions were adopted by the new governments of Europe, the defeated nations included. In drafting these documents, French and British practices were generously drawn upon, some items were borrowed from the United States and other sections were devised by constitution makers in each country. As a general proposition, the executive head of the new states was a president, whose powers were severely limited as in France. Without exception, real executive authority was lodged in a prime minister (or comparable official) and his cabinet.

Responsibility for making laws was usually assigned to a bicameral legislature, the lower house invariably having more power than the upper chamber. The latter might impede or postpone the adoption of legislation, but in no country could it override or permanently thwart the wishes of the popularly elected lower house. The lower house, moreover, determined the tenure of a ministry, which had to resign if defeated on an important proposal. It was possible for an electorate to change the constitution by peaceful processes if it wished to do so.

Franchise rights were conferred upon all adults in new states and old, except for France and Italy, which denied the vote to women. That discrimination was dictated largely by the belief that, if women were enfranchised, they would be sympathetic to clerical interests. Due to the appearance of a multiplicity of political parties, reflecting a veritable rainbow of attitudes on public issues, the proportional representation principle was incorporated in the new constitutions. Each party would be represented in the legislature in keeping with the number of votes it polled.

The multi-party system, no one party having a majority, meant that as in France a ministry depended for its tenure upon a coalition of parties. Withdrawal of support that deprived a ministry of its majority obliged the ministry to resign. As matters worked out, the multi-party arrangement proved less responsible, less efficient than the essentially two-party governments of Great Britain and the United States; and the system of proportional representation turned out to be a grave-digger of political democracy in central and eastern Europe.

In imitation of established precedents, elaborate bills of rights were enshrined in the new constitutions. Citizens were guaranteed civil liberties, such as freedom of speech, press and assembly, the right to hold public meeetings and freedom of religious worship, though in some cases these rights were hedged round with restricting limitations. Minorities, as a rule, were given special constitutional guarantees concerning the use of their language and schooling facilities.

Clauses in the constitutions, lastly, authorized governments to extend their scope in the economic domain. In the course of the war, governments everywhere had imposed controls upon industry and agriculture, fuel and clothing, transportation and communications. Private property had been conscripted, in a manner of speaking, as well as men for the fighting services. Besides, workers had been involuntarily shunted from place to place in order to meet manpower needs in the war effort. And the treaties of peace had sanctioned infringements on the principle of private property by confiscating possessions and commercial rights belonging to nationals of the defeated countries. These precedents, together with the concept of distributive justice, led the makers of the constitutions to provide for greater state authority in economic affairs. Articles relating to the redistribution of large landed estates, for example, to publicly owned mines and to state aid for the unemployed were written into the new constitutions.

In the enthusiasm of the post-war period, then, Europe to the west of Russia seemed to have been made safe for democracy, or at any rate about as much was achieved as parchment could accomplish. Doubts were expressed, it is true, as to whether voters without experience in the exacting art of self-government would be capable of working parliamentary institutions with reasonable effectiveness. Much would depend upon the measure of economic well-being that the new states achieved and upon the discretion and the wisdom of the political leadership in the new states.

It appeared plain, furthermore, that the cluster of small, sovereign countries in central and eastern Europe contained within themselves elements of grave risk. It was all very well to argue that little states in the past had contributed richly to human culture or that small countries might serve as proving grounds for social experiments. But they were unable to protect themselves militarily and their tariff, transportation and currency policies jeopardized or thwarted economic progress. Several plans to organize federations of little countries of eastern Europe cropped up between World Wars, but none of them was put into operation.

THE NEW GERMANY

Of all the adventures in republican democracy, the experiment in Germany carried the greatest importance. Despite the war and the peace Germany was still the most powerful country of Europe, and her economy was intimately interlaced with that of neighboring countries. As Germany went, so, likely enough, would go the other states lying between the Danube and Russia. Germany emerged from the war, weary, cynical, disillusioned. High hopes of military victory had persisted into the summer of 1918 only to collapse abysmally in the autumn. In the very moment of defeat, revolutions swept away the German Empire and Emperor; rulers of petty German states abdicated; and for a time democratic Socialists, representing the industrial workers, took charge of public affairs. The revolutionary storm subsided before control could pass to wilder elements.

For a time it looked as though Germany might possibly take the road to Moscow. Thinking that the triumph of Communism was imminent, Lenin wrote, "The crisis in Germany . . . will infallibly end with the transference of political power into the hands of the proletariat." Actually, the rank and file of German workingmen, rejecting every form of dictatorship, stood four-square behind the democratic Socialists. Armed forces marshaled by the provisional democratic Socialist regime crushed Communist (Spartacist) revolts, without crushing the Communist movement.

In spite of bitter internal antagonisms, the spirit of German national unity prevailed. The disparate parts of the country were kept within a single state, a great achievement indeed, arguing the innate strength of the national ideal. The middle classes survived the vicissitudes of economic confusion and the peasants and working classes exhibited anew their ingrained habit of hard work.

The unity of Germany was confirmed in the Weimar Constitution of 1919.[1] As before the war, Germany in the future would be a federal union, though the several states were allowed less power than previously. Proposals to divide up Prussia, covering about 60 per cent of the country, were discussed, but they were tossed aside. The president of Germany was assigned more authority than his French counterpart, especially in emergency situations, but a chancellor and his cabinet were made the principal executive instrument.

Similarly, although the Weimar Constitution provided for an upper house, real legislative authority was vested in the Reichstag, the lower house. It controlled the ministry and had to approve, of course, all proposals for law. Deputies would be elected by adult suffrage and on the principle of proportional representation. Certain clauses in the Constitution pointed toward the development of a social welfare state and the liberties of citizens were guaranteed in an exemplary bill of rights. Although the spirit of compromise shaped much of the content of the Weimar document, it nonetheless faithfully reflected prevailing ideas of government by consent.

THE WEIMAR REPUBLIC

From the beginning, the Weimar democracy was beset by tangled and desperate problems. Self-rule and democratic ways were innovations, in large measure, outside the range of the German tradition. It was true, of course, that the Socialist Party, which was committed to democratic and moderate Marxist principles, had emerged before the war as the largest single political grouping. That party and the Center or Catholic Party constituted the principal bulwarks of the Weimar Republic and they were reinforced by small bourgeois factions of democratic outlook. Uneasy coalitions of these three groups managed the public affairs of Germany until 1933 when the Nazis took command.

Opposed to the forces of democracy were conservative or frankly reactionary elements. These included the Junker aristocracy, the professional military caste, many wealthy bourgeoisie, the top layers of the bureaucracy and ordinary citizens who were influenced by these groups. Also hostile to the Weimar Republic, though on different grounds, were the Communists, whose popularity fluctuated in response to economic conditions.

The Weimar Republic carried two other heavy handicaps. In a very real sense the demo-

[1] The Constitution took its name from the pleasant community, redolent with memories of Goethe, in which it was drafted.

German banknote of the inflation period—one billion marks

cratic regime had been imposed upon Germany as a penalty of military defeat, and it had accepted the Versailles Treaty, many of whose terms were hateful to almost every section of the German population. More than that, educational institutions, which should have become vital instruments for teaching democratic ideals, were not radically overhauled. Many a schoolmaster and more university professors held to conventional, conservative and chauvinistic convictions.

It must also be said that self-government was inaugurated in Germany in a time of intense economic confusion and distress. Weimar Germany inherited from the war a heavy legacy of debt, and, although productive property had not been damaged by shot and shell, industrial plants had deteriorated under the imperative demands of the war. By the Versailles Treaty, furthermore, Germany had lost territories containing valuable resources, such as the iron mines of Lorraine, the great merchant marine had been taken away as reparations and Germany was committed to pay large sums in further reparations.

Only in part did Germany meet her reparations obligations, and in 1923 a Franco-Belgian army occupied the crucial Ruhr Valley, on a collection mission. To finance passive resistance in the Ruhr, the German government issued enormous quantities of paper money. Since the end of the war mismanagement of public finance and other errors had caused the German currency to slip in value, and now runaway inflation set in. At the peak of the currency frenzy, it took the equivalent of $50,000,000 to buy a newspaper! Society was churned up from top to bottom, some groups bettering their economic status, but the solid middle classes and workers suffered severe losses. Extremist political parties, Right and Left, made capital out of the desperate economic chaos.

In the late 1920's, however, Germany recovered remarkably. A "new deal" in reparations, the Dawes Plan helped to restore confidence and spur initiative, and a stable currency was created. Industrial activity was stimulated by arrangements among companies (cartels) which reduced competition, and by technological innovations. A stream of suggestions for industrial efficiency flowed in from the United States, and Henry Ford became a sort of patron saint for many a German manufacturer and engineer. Books by the dozen on Ford were published—such as *Ford or Marx, and the Practical Solution of the Social Question*—while the *Autobiography* of the Wizard of Detroit attracted some 300,000 German purchasers.

Capital, too, in substantial quantities passed from the United States to Germany, aiding in the equipment of plants with more up-to-date, labor-saving machinery. German foreign trade and shipping bounded upward and the number of unemployed shrank sharply. For large sections of the population, standards of comfort approached or even surpassed pre-war levels. Political stability accompanied economic improvement. It appeared indeed that the Weimar Republic was gaining in popularity and steadiness—until the Great Depression.

THE BRITISH WAY

While the new German democracy was taking root, the veteran democracy of Britain encountered and somehow outrode terrific gales. As the world's greatest trader, in terms of imports and exports combined, British prosperity was linked at every turn with global conditions. British purchases furnished employment for farmers, miners and industrial workers in all corners of the earth. By deranging the world economy, the war bequeathed to Britain special short-term problems pending the restoration of "normalcy." Competition of foreign industries that had mushroomed during the war cut down sales in old markets, and turmoil in Germany and in eastern Europe likewise depressed the exports of the United Kingdom.

For her very existence Great Britain required heavy imports of industrial rawstuffs and food—meat from the Dominions and Argentina, wheat from Canada and the United States, dairy produce and fresh vegetables from the Continent and a thousand other articles. Imports were paid for partly by the proceeds from British investments all over the globe, and

Unemployed Englishmen looking for work, 1924

partly by banking and shipping services for foreign interests. German U-boats had cut deeply into merchant marine tonnage, but those losses were largely covered by ships turned over by Germany as reparations. The principal way of paying for imports was by selling industrial products abroad. Consequently, contraction of international trade wrought ominously upon British welfare.

Employment rolls directly reflected the ups and downs in post-war trade. A huge mass of workless men became a permanent feature of the British scene; in 1921, for instance, one out of five employables lacked a job. Government furnished the bare necessities of existence to the unemployed by means of doles, since the unemployment insurance funds were unable to cope with the needs. Industrial strife, provoked by disputes over wages, rose to a climax in 1926 when a general strike temporarily paralyzed the country. Parliament soon outlawed (1927) the general strike, a ban that stood on the statute books until 1946.

It seemed clear to influential members of the Conservative Party that the enactment of protective tariffs was essential for the restoration of "good times." Reluctantly, in the years of the war, the British government had imposed protective tariffs on a few classes of goods and that practice was moderately extended in the twenties. Full-bodied protection, however, a radical shift indeed, was postponed until 1932 when Britain was in the throes of the Great Depression. New or expanded measures of social welfare, especially in regard to housing, unemployment and pensions for the aged, were inscribed on the statute books. And in 1928 the suffrage was extended to women on the same terms as men; women eligible to vote then exceeded the men.

As with industry, so British farming, employing over a million, felt the impact of the war and changing global conditions. World output of grain increased without a corresponding growth in demand. Beginning in 1924, the British government paid subsidies for some kinds of home-raised crops, the list being steadily broadened after that. New grasses of finer quality and scientific breeding of livestock preserved the British reputation as the "stud farm of the world." In spite of highly intensive methods of cultivation on small farms, Britain relied upon imports for two-thirds of the food for humans and for a third of the food for farm animals—a serious disadvantage in the event that war returned to the world.

Politics responded to the ebb and flow of material affairs. After the Armistice in 1918 a coalition ticket made up of the Conservative Party, a section of the Liberal Party and a few Labourites swept the field in a general election. The Prime Minister, David Lloyd George, dominated the political stage for nearly four years; if he was not "the man who won the war," he had helped materially to bring victory to pass by his tenacity and unquenchable enthusiasm. In subsequent general elections, the salient developments were the consistent strength of the Conservative Party, the disintegration of the historic Liberal Party and the gathering popularity of the Labour Party.

On two occasions, in 1924 and again in 1929, the Labour Party organized ministries and assumed the management of national and imperial affairs. The broad objectives of Labour were authoritatively stated by Clement R. Attlee, who in 1945 became Labour Prime Minister, in *The Labour Party in Perspective* (1937).

> "The aim of the Labour Party," Attlee wrote, "is the establishment of the Cooperative Commonwealth. Its object expressed in the Party constitution is to 'secure for the workers by hand or brain the full fruits of their industry and the most equitable distribution thereof that may be possible, upon the basis of common ownership of the means of production, distribution, and exchange and the best obtainable system of popular administration and control of each industry or service.'" Concerning land he said, "Land will be owned by the community, not by private industry!"

While in control of the government in the twenties the Labour Party was not able to implement its collectivist doctrines, for one reason because it depended upon the parliamentary support of the small contingent of Liberal M. P.'s in the Commons. Application of Labour principles had to await a surprising electoral victory after the Second World War.

COMMONWEALTH AND EMPIRE

Participation of the British Dominions in the First World War quickened feelings of self-confidence and heightened their international prestige. As a concession to local sentiments, Canada, Australia, New Zealand and South Africa were allotted seats in the Assembly of the League of Nations. And then in the historic Statute of Westminister of 1931 each Dominion was constitutionally defined as a sovereign and separate state. The principle that no law of the British Parliament should apply to any Dominion without the latter's consent, which had prevailed for some years, was spelled out in specific and legal language.

Only the Crown stood as the symbol of the free association of members of the Commonwealth, but economic, cultural and vague though potent psychological bonds linked the Dominions to the United Kingdom in mind and spirit. The common British ties were a way of life and shared ideals, qualities of fairness and tolerance in both private and public affairs, the observance of engagements and agreements for defense and to promote trade. Each Dominion pursued its own course, often subtly guided by authorities in London. Though lacking the centralized power of an old-fashioned empire, the British Commonwealth nonetheless exerted far-reaching influence upon world affairs. Tariff legislation, for example, designed to foster Dominion industries was enacted, but trade preferences were given to the United Kingdom. Continuing a pre-war policy the great Dominions in the Pacific debarred immigrants from the fecund lands of Asia; in Australia the "white policy" took on the quality of a religion, causing no little trouble with Japan, which proudly resented the exclusion of her sons and daughters.

To the list of Dominions, an Irish Free State was added in 1922. Due to the outbreak of war, the plan to grant Ireland home-rule had been put on the shelf, but Irish nationalism kept clamoring for the natural right of freedom. Militant nationalists, headed by Eamon de Valera, swung into the *Sinn Fein* (Ourselves Alone) Party, which would be content with nothing short of full independence for an all-Ireland republic. Thinking the time propitious to strike for freedom, Irish extremists rebelled on Easter day of 1916. But British troops beat down the insurgency and the ringleaders were put behind iron bars. Open warfare of a savage guerilla type tormented the Emerald Isle after the end of the First World War.

Happily, however, moderate leaders in both Ireland and England got their heads together and worked out a compromise solution. The agreement established (1922) the Irish Free State covering the whole island except for the northern and predominantly Protestant counties of Ulster. Put on the same constitutional basis as Canada, the Irish state would have its own parliament sitting in Dublin, and a responsible ministry; a governor-general would personify the link with the British Commonwealth.

Accepted by Irish moderates, this arrangement was repudiated by the De Valera faction, which resented the separate status of Ulster, and once more appealed to arms. In time, however, De Valera concluded that the national goal could best be achieved by orderly parliamentary processes; and in 1932 his followers elected a majority of the law-makers. A series of acts then severed the constitutional connection with Great Britain, the office of governor-general being abolished in 1936. Presently the Free State was rebaptized as Eire and proclaimed a free and separate republic. That the Dublin government was in fact independent was demonstrated in the Second World War when it stayed neutral throughout the struggle. Ulster, on the other hand, formed an organic part of the United Kingdom, as the Irish nationalists bitterly lamented.

The dependent portions of the British realm, the colonial empire in the exact sense, underwent notable changes between World Wars. Within that empire were embraced over fifty parcels of territory extending from the West Indies across Africa into the Pacific and containing peoples of many languages, religions, colors and levels of culture and intelligence. From these possessions the United Kingdom

Street barricade near the Four Courts during the 1916 Dublin insurrection

procured foodstuffs and industrial raw materials in exchange for manufactured wares. British officials aided the indigenous populations by building up transport services, fighting disease and destructive parasites, broadening educational opportunities and circulating information on more efficient agricultural methods. Discovery of the drug antricyde, for instance, made possible the immunization of cattle against the deadly African tsetse fly.

Extension of self-rule to the natives was a gradual affair bound up with the development of economic resources and the spread of literacy. Speaking generally, dependencies were presided over by British governors, responsible to London, and in some colonies they were flanked by executive and legislative councils in which natives had a voice. Much stress was placed upon "indirect rule" in the African colonies, which meant using indigenous institutions to train populations for greater political responsibility. In the more mature colonies responsible self-government flourished.

The record in Tanganyika illustrates prevailing trends in British colonial administration. Belonging to Germany before the First World War, this mandated territory was half again as large as Texas and inhabited by about 5,250,000 people. German-owned estates were acquired by British and Indian interests mainly, though some of the lands were distributed among native African farmers. Slavery and forced labor were outlawed and workers were encouraged to form unions to defend their interests. Research institutes busied themselves with raising agricultural production and finding remedies for sleeping sickness and other tropical maladies. Mineral resources (gold and diamonds) were exploited and the railway facilities somewhat enlarged. Sisal, cotton and coffee were the principal exports of Tanganyika and about a third of all foreign business was transacted with the United Kingdom, though the rule of commercial equality for traders of all countries was preserved.

British administrators strengthened existing tribal organizations, transferring control over local affairs to local authorities. As African officials and native law courts gained experience they were assigned more and more responsibility. Over-all supervision of administration was lodged (1926) in a legislative council composed of Britons largely but with some African members.

Hospital and tribal dispensaries were extended and schools, operated by missionaries or the government, endeavored to improve the character and the efficiency of the natives and to train administrative and technical leaders. By 1938, Africans made up three quarters of the administrative officials. As the case of Tanganyika bore witness, management of British dependencies after the First World War was more enlightened, more humanitarian than in the nineteenth century.

UNEASY FRANCE

Informed Frenchmen surveying their country and her prospects on the morrow of the First World War might well be forgiven a feeling of pessimism and despair. The hereditary foe beyond the Rhine had been defeated, it is true, Alsace-Lorraine had been reclaimed and interesting additions had been made to the overseas dependencies. But the ledger contained another and a darker side. Fighting had cut down 1,400,000 men, not to overlook the tens of thousands of wounded—a human toll which thereafter was never absent from French calculations on war or peace. Choice northern provinces, the major industrial centers, had been wrecked, upwards of 750,000 buildings needed repair or reconstruction, mines and highways had been knocked out and wide stretches of farmland had to be cleaned up before agriculture could be resumed. Reconstruction, as well as the costs of the war, would entail heavy financial outlays, which French optimists imagined would be paid by Germany. During the war, taxes had not been substantially increased and there was no inclination to impose heavier taxes after the victory; also, the collection of taxes in France was notoriously lax.

The French parliamentary democracy traveled much the same road that it had known before the war. Many "parties" existed, deputies were not amenable to party discipline, ministries were dependent upon unstable blocs of political groupings and the average tenure of cabinets ranged well under one year. Cabinet reshuffling was the accepted French way both of political bargaining and of resolving differences among the ruling parties, and French opinion regarded the frequent changes in the ministry with comparative equanimity.

Chronic budgetary deficits and monetary troubles upset one ministry after another. When Germany failed to produce the expected reparations, French soldiers occupied (1923) the Ruhr Valley. That adventure netted little for the reparations account, not immediately at any rate, though doubtless the French experienced a psychological lift at the writhing of Germany. Although the French currency did not slide into worthlessness as did the German mark, it nonetheless tumbled sharply in value with unhappy consequences for most purses.

To right the desperate situation, Raymond Poincaré was installed (1926) in the premiership. A smart lawyer and astute financier, he had been more responsible than any other politician for the strong line against Germany that had culminated in the Ruhr occupation. But he personified confidence and reinforced it, and with him at the helm taxes were raised, the state budget was balanced and the franc pegged at a fifth of its pre-war value. Costs of industrial production declined, which encouraged foreign purchases of French products, while tourists crowded into France, attracted by the cheapness of living.

For several years France rode on the crest of good times. Out of the taxpayers largely, came the funds that restored the war-devastated areas. More generally agrarian than her great neighbors, France was less affected by the wild oscillations in foreign trade after the war. Certain industries expanded into larger establishments, and that trend was accompanied by an increase in organized workers, but the greater part of French manufacturing was still carried on in small shops and factories. Devaluation of the currency in 1926 to a fifth of what it had been infuriated the large class of thrifty and saving Frenchmen who had invested in government or corporation bonds. At that, they were better off than French investors—perhaps as many as 1,600,000—who had purchased Russian securities before the war, all of which were repudiated by the Communist government.

THE SMALLER DEMOCRACIES

Belgium and Holland, the Scandinavian countries and Switzerland held aloft the democratic banner and profited from democratic freedoms. Monarchies all, except republican Switzerland, the theory and practice of the democratic way of living was deeply rooted. Broad social and economic equality prevailed and standards of living were generally good. Sweden in many ways paced the world in social experimentation, attracting particular attention because of public housing projects and programs of economic cooperation.

Belgium was a special case among the smaller Western democracies. Fought over and occupied by German troops during the war, Belgium was awarded compensation in the form of small parcels of German territory, an extension of its Congo colony (as a mandate) and reparations. While the war was on German agents fanned national sentiments among the Flemings in Belgium as Germans did again in the Second World War. The Flemings spoke a language akin to Dutch and were warmly attached to conservative and Catholic principles. With time they exceeded in numbers the French-speaking Walloon element, which in general was more comfortably fixed economically. Strong in the northern provinces and in rural Belgium, the Flemish cause captured the universities of Louvain and Ghent. Extremists desired political union with Holland, but linguistic and administrative concessions appeased moderate Flemings and kept Belgium intact. Brussels was declared bilingual—street signs, for instance, were in Flemish and Walloon—and the king symbolized the unity of the two tongues in one nation.

Nowhere did democratic freedoms rest on more stable foundations than in Switzerland. Back in 1291 mountaineers and peasants in this little land of the Alps entered into a perpetual pact to safeguard their heritage of local self-government. For many generations the Swiss, who numbered around 4,000,000 and spoke four different languages, had worked in harmonious cooperation—the admiration and envy of less favored nations. The Swiss tradition of absolute neutrality fitted the country to perform many important international services. As the headquarters of the International Red Cross and of the League of Nations, Geneva acquired unique distinction among the cities of the world.

THE ADVENT OF FASCISM

The institutions and ideology of democracy had shallower roots in Italy than in the other free governments of the West. Scarcity of mineral resources and other industrial raw materials, moreover, widespread illiteracy, an anachronistic agriculture in the South and a rapidly growing population denied to Italians in general the standards of comfort that prevailed in France, for example.

At the close of the war Italy was gripped by an economic and psychological crisis of very serious proportions. The nation had entered the conflict deeply divided, with large sections of opinion apathetic or downright hostile, and military reverses had impaired national morale. Expectations of territorial gains and of social betterment after the war fell short of fulfillment. For many an Italian the toll of 600,000 dead, a zone of ruins along the Austrian frontier, the gyrations of the currency, considerable unemployment and mounting budget deficits argued that the war had not only been fought in vain, but had been an unmitigated calamity.

Veteran politicians presumed to conduct public business as usual. Vacillation and corruption in the government persisted while strikes and open fighting in city and countryside increased. The parliamentary machine creaked and groaned. Leaders of the democratic Socialist Party, the largest in the Chamber, not only declined to work with bourgeois parties, but stubbornly refused to form a ministry

Fascist leaders make a triumphant entry into Rome, October, 1922. From left to right, Grandi, De Bono, Mussolini

of their own. By encouraging violence and disregard for the Constitution, the Socialists contributed materially to the eventual victory of Fascism. Popular unrest reached its peak in 1920, then symptoms of convalescence appeared as the worst effects of the war wore off, and by the autumn of 1922 the crisis was virtually over.

Alongside of the pre-war political groupings, three new parties appeared, each with its own remedies for national health and salvation. From conservative and Catholic circles issued (1919) an energetic Christian Democratic Party (*Partito Popolare*), which appealed particularly to the well-to-do and to impoverished peasants of the South. The radical wing of the democratic Socialist Party organized a Communist Party preaching class warfare, revolution and a dictatorship on the Russian model. For a time Communism had considerable popularity among urban workers of the north, who occupied factories and in other directions interfered with private property rights; in some districts, wretched peasants living on the knife-edge of starvation, seized the land that they worked. Reaching its height late in 1920, the Communist fever receded thereafter, but the bogey of Bolshevism supplied an effective battle-cry to partisans of a Rightist form of authoritarianism.

The third new party, founded at Milan in 1919, took the name of Fascist, a word derived from the Latin *fasces*, meaning a bundle of rods, and recalling the aphorism that in union there is strength. Offering Italians a program half revolutionary and half nationalistic at the start, Fascism gradually attracted the frightened, the disinherited and the ambitious in every province and city. The gathering strength of the party was traceable to its tight discipline, support given by high military authorities and business interests that desired to disrupt working class organizations, strong-armed treatment of opponents by black-shirted thugs and the histrionic qualities of the leader, Benito Mussolini, *il Duce*.

Mussolini typifies the men of lower middle-class origins who attained dictatorial authority in the epoch between World Wars. His life story is rather dull, for he was a poor creature, who brashly aspired to be something tremendous. His ambition was shaped by the old Italian adage, "Better a bull for two years than an ox for a hundred"—and his ascendancy lasted twenty years! Once a revolutionary Marxist agitator, a radical journalist and a wounded veteran of the war, Mussolini dreamed Napoleonic dreams.

The Fascist chief and his henchmen promised great things for Italy if they were installed in power—honest and efficient government, solution of economic ills, discipline, national glory and prestige. As Plato long ago remarked, the tyrant makes his entry on the stage as a liberator. In the month of October, 1922, Fascist legions marched upon Rome, and the king, instead of manfully resisting the revolutionary bid for power, supinely accepted Mussolini as prime minister.

Step by step Fascist mastery over Italy was consolidated. The democratic opposition, friends of freedom and parliamentary institutions were bewildered, hopelessly divided, and the more outspoken of them were clapped into jail or exiled. A courageous democratic Socialist deputy, Giacomo Matteotti, who eloquently attacked anti-democratic acts and police brutalities, was taken for a ride, literally, and assassinated by Fascist thugs. Whether Mussolini was directly implicated in the murder, as seems probable, was never proved. In any case, the shameless crime unloosed an uproar that momentarily threatened to unseat the Fascist chief. Not only did he outride the storm, but in January of 1925 he formally proclaimed himself as dictator. Brute force had triumphed, setting an evil example for the authoritarian-minded in other countries.

THE NATURE OF FASCISM

Fascism was undisguised tyranny, offering almost nothing that was original. Tagging democracy as a "putrescent corpse," Mussolini imitated despotisms from time immemorial by suppressing civil freedoms, exalting the State, extending the economic authority of government, glorifying war and whipping up chauvinistic passions. His totalitarian regime rested upon force and violence, applied by the Fascist Party. A massive bureaucracy (civil and military) constituted the ruling oligarchy and was the principal beneficiary of the "new order."

In the Fascist scheme of things the State was everything, the individual citizen was nothing. Public institutions and private societies, school and press were harnessed to the twin task of inculcating Fascist loyalties and nationalistic fervor. Fascism endeavored to persuade men that all was for the best and that Italy, sheltered from the democratic decay of the West (and the Red ruin of Russia), was somehow

"Children of the Wolf"—members of a Fascist children's organization

in the vanguard of humanity. Under threat of severe punishment Italians were obliged to conform to Fascist orthodoxy and condemned to a life of perpetual enthusiasm. The principle of legislative deliberations persisted, it is true, but lawmakers were mere puppets; actual power was concentrated in *il Duce*, who was adored by the mesmerized as a sacred, infallible leader. Statistically, Italy became overwhelmingly Fascist, but in the testing time of the Second World War, the proportion that was willing to suffer greatly in order to further the aims of Mussolini turned out to be small.

On the economic front, the Fascist authoritarianism outlawed strikes and lockouts, and dragooned employers and workmen into confederations or "corporations." These bodies were charged with peaceful adjustment of industrial disputes and eventually were authorized to nominate candidates for parliament. The interests of the employing class were definitely favored as against wage-earners, but more and more the state assumed control, when not outright ownership, of industrial undertakings. Mussolini boasted of stabilization of the currency, advantageous settlements of war debts with Britain and the United States and the enforcement of discipline in the cities and in the provinces.

And he contrived to reach an accommodation with the Vatican which adjusted the quarrel between State and Church that had persisted since 1870. The way to a settlement had been prepared before Fascism took command of Italian affairs. It was arranged (1929) that the Pope should exercise sovereignty over Vatican City and should be given financial compensation to liquidate outstanding claims against the Italian government. Religious marriage was recognized as valid and Catholic teaching was restored in the schools. Unquestionably the reconciliation with the Vatican enhanced the standing of Mussolini, but friction soon developed with the Church over the control and education of Italian youth. Bent upon creating an unqualified totalitarian state, Mussolini would brook no rival.

Fascism, which proved to be contagious, like a disease of children, is the common term for very modern tyrannies of the non-Communist type. Two other Latin countries—Spain (1923) and Portugal (1926)—cast democratic institutions overboard in favor of military dictatorships, imitative of the Italian, though free of nationalistic braggadoccio in an intense form. Both countries pursued the restrictive practices of the totalitarian state—shackles upon civil liberties, secret police, strict censorship and a ban on strikes. Parliaments existed only in name, full of what the Portuguese called "amenistas," or yes men. For sheer longevity the Portuguese dictatorship has outlasted all the others.

THE GREAT DEPRESSION

The trend from democracy to dictatorship was given a decided boost by the Great Depression, the great divide in the interval between World Wars. Fascist authoritarianism, which many democratic observers were inclined to dismiss as an ephemeral aberration, was in fact greatly strengthened and extended. Confidence in democratic methods was challenged as it had not been challenged in peacetime before.

Writing under the cloud of the Great Depression, Winston Churchill declared:

> The Parliaments of every country have shown themselves quite incompetent to deal with the economic problems which dominate the affairs of every nation of the world. . . . Great nations are no longer led by their ablest men or by those who know most about their immediate affairs. . . . Democratic governments drift along the line of least resistance, taking short views, paying their way with sops and doles and smoothing their path with pleasant-sounding platitudes.[2]

Happily, the vigor and flexibility with which veteran democracies fought the depression defied these melancholy reflections.

Many learned studies have attempted to account for the Great Depression, the most severe economic upheaval of modern history. Some scholars have attached especial weight to the business cycle of boom and depression, pointing out that the title "the Great Depression" had previously been reserved for the pe-

[2] Winston Churchill, *Thoughts and Adventures* (London, 1932), p. 278.

riod 1873–1896. Other investigators have been impressed with the unresolved problems from the First World War and the peace treaties, such as dislocations in trade and currency, the greater competition of the United States and Japan, intergovernmental financial obligations —reparations and inter-Allied debts—or the excessive production of agricultural goods and industrial raw materials.

Certain students have stressed the relevance of technological unemployment, resulting from labor-saving machines and greater efficiency in other aspects of manufacturing, or the cessation of lending to foreign countries by financial interests of the United States. Some economic thinkers discovered the main cause of the slump in the lack of coordination between savings and investment. Marxist interpretations attributed the Great Depression to inherent flaws in relatively free private enterprise, contrasting the absence of unemployment under the Soviet planned economy with the millions of jobless outside of Russia.

No one could doubt that the Great Depression underlined, vividly and painfully, the economic interdependence of nations. Nor could it be doubted that the crash of stock values in the United States in the autumn of 1929 unloosed the avalanche, though the magnitude of the crisis was not immediately apparent. Within two years prices collapsed, factories and mines closed, agricultural surpluses accumulated, bankruptcies multiplied, foreign trade slumped, foreign lending dried up, harbors stood lifeless. Unemployment and general impoverishment gripped the world. Nation after nation was shaken by acute social convulsions and many witnessed radical alterations in governmental institutions.

The malady was deepened and prolonged by the disruption in 1931 of the international financial mechanism. Starting with the closing of the major bank of Austria, the financial panic spread across Germany and then engulfed Britain, directly because foreigners withdrew their funds from the London money market. Britain was pushed off the gold standard and since the pound sterling was the sheet anchor of many another currency, other countries followed the British example. International exchange of goods was further curtailed.

Every country relied mainly upon national measures to combat the Great Depression. Protective tariffs, fixed quotas on imports and currency manipulation were the favorite devices of harassed governments. By enacting the Hawley-Smoot tariff of 1930, the highest in the history of the country, the United States inspired similar legislation in two-score countries. Even Great Britain, as has been noted, succumbed to the protectionist heresy, laying duties on goods hitherto imported free and granting preferential rates to commodities from the British imperial realm. These measures aiming at national self-sufficiency, or "autarchy" as it was called, broadened the authority of the state and reduced trade between the nations.

Proposals for international cooperation to alleviate the crisis were not entirely wanting. In fact, on the initiative of the United States, it was agreed in 1931 that payments on all intergovernmental debts should be postponed for a year—the Hoover moratorium. And in 1932 German reparations were greatly scaled down; actually reparations transfers had stopped in 1931, and presently payments on Allied debts to the United States ceased. An international conference met at London in 1933 for the purpose of stabilizing currencies and scaling down tariffs. But whatever chance there may have been of positive accomplishment was nullified chiefly by the unwillingness of the United States to stabilize the dollar in relation to foreign currencies.

THE RISE OF NATIONAL SOCIALISM

Nowhere were the political and social consequences of the Great Depression so fatefully malignant as in Germany. One ministry after another tried to overcome unemployment and associated ills but without success. At last, in January of 1933, Adolf Hitler was installed as Chancellor; in a general election which followed his National Socialist (or Nazi) Party captured 44 per cent of the votes and, in combination with the Nationalists, commanded a majority of the deputies in the Reichstag.

Adolf Hitler, a non-military portrait

The Nazis were the German version of Fascism and when Hitler first appeared in the headlines he was often styled the "Bavarian Mussolini." The son of an inconsequential Austrian family, Hitler had moved to Munich, Bavaria, in 1912, and fought in the German Army, sustaining wounds. After the war he joined a new and quite unimportant German National Socialist Party, quickly pushing into the leadership. Bavaria at the time was the rendezvous of the most determined enemies of the Weimar democracy. Physically tough, and endowed with boundless energy, Hitler possessed an extraordinary capacity for enflaming the minds and enlisting the allegiance of other frustrated men. Already he was obsessed with a vindictive mania toward Marxist collectivists, Jews, internationalism and the democratic way. The Fascist *coup d'etat* in Italy confirmed him in the conviction that democracy was doomed.

While French soldiers were astride the Ruhr Valley and runaway inflation was convulsing Germany, Hitler and a band of associates launched (1923) an insurrection in Munich. But troops that were loyal to the Weimar Republic speedily crushed the rising. Arrested and imprisoned, Hitler set to work preparing his autobiographical *Mein Kampf*. A muddy and diffuse volume, it proclaimed the objectives of National Socialism, and served as the holy book of the Nazi cause, selling in millions of copies. Far from being an inspired statesman, Hitler resembled a patriotic parrot, ready to settle every problem by the repetition of empty phrases. Cynical, incredibly egotistical, strong-willed and vindictive, he succeeded in imposing his personality upon the men and women who gathered around him.

As an alternative to the wobbly Weimar democracy, Hitler demanded an authoritarian regime, directed by an all-powerful Führer, and upheld by a single, fearless and dedicated party. He preached German racial superiority, the gospel of the *Herrenvolk*, reviving ancient Nordic tribal superstitions. Jews he bracketed with Communists as the scourges of the German nation, and he vowed to destroy both. Popular suffering and national humiliations were attributed to these two groups who, by reason of their international ties, must inescapably be disloyal to the Fatherland. Hitler glibly offered a set of infallible recipes for national rejuvenation, saying a good deal about economic innovations that would improve the welfare of the butcher, the baker and the candle-stick maker.

In the domain of international policy, Hitler totally repudiated the Treaty of Versailles. Payment of reparations—tribute, in his vocabulary—should stop, and ceded German provinces should be recovered. All German-speaking folk, this ex-Austro-German thundered, must be gathered into a single state, which would require more land (*Lebensraum*) for its superior and energetic population. Military conscription must be revived and the German fighting services expanded into a first-class force. Fierce pugnacity and flaming chauvinism were standard features of the Hitlerian fanaticism.

Masters of demagogic propaganda, the Nazis shrewdly exploited the mood of barren despair that the Great Depression laid upon Germany. Crowd emotionalism, dominated by hate, anger and fear infected even Germans of a normally sober and rational temper. The fervor and contagion of a religious revival suffused Nazi campaigning. The movement was financed by party collections or by subsidies from wealthy industrialists such as the steel magnate, Fritz Thyssen, who desired an upsurge of nationalism to counteract the lure of Communism. (Eventually Thyssen fell out with the Nazis, who confiscated his great steel empire.)

Nazi deputies gained 107 seats in the Reichstag at an election in 1930, as compared with a dozen previously held. Thereafter National Socialism scored almost uninterrupted successes at the polls, drawing support from all layers of the German community. In the spring of 1933, as has been indicated, Hitler and his fellows won control of Germany.

THE NAZI DICTATORSHIP

Promptly upon their enthronement the Nazis imposed their will upon the German nation and attacked the job of national rehabilitation with gusto. The Reichstag obediently suspended the Weimar Constitution and voted dictatorial authority to Hitler; after that the Reichstag was no more than a political sounding board. All political parties save the Nazi were outlawed, and political power was concentrated in Berlin at the expense of the several states. Calling their regime the Third Reich, the Nazis substituted the old imperial flag for the Weimar banner.

Within top Nazi circles, controversy broke out over the implementation of the social ideals of the movement and the role of the Brown Shirts. Asserting that a plot had been hatched against him, Hitler in June, 1934, ordered the execution of dozens of alleged conspirators without benefit of trial. In justification of this sadistic blood purge, Hitler said, "If anyone faces me with the reproach that we should have used the regular courts for trial, I have only one answer: in that hour I was responsible for the fate of the German nation, and therefore I myself was the German people's supreme tribunal."

Not until death removed (1934) Paul von Hindenburg, venerable and popular commander in the First World War and President of the Republic since 1925, did the Nazis feel fully secure. Hitler consolidated the dictatorship by merging in his person the presidency and the chancellorship. Sharp feuds, however, persisted in the higher echelons of the Party and several senior military chiefs looked upon the Nazis with a fishy eye.

As one facet of the Hitlerian order—and it was characteristic—civil liberties were cancelled. Agencies of information and indoctrination, educational institutions, press, movies and radio were lashed to the Nazi chariot. A superb propaganda service mesmerized a divided, confused and partly terrorized nation and generated faith and hope by preaching a narrow and domineering chauvinism. The myth of an infallible Führer, who had a messianic assignment to execute, and stock Nazi attitudes were planted in the German emotions. Belief in Hitler replaced, or at any rate seriously competed with, the Christian heritage.

Herdsmen of the mind were particularly zealous and particularly successful among the youth of Germany. Schools and an organization for boys and girls (*Hitler Jugend*) were effective instruments of Nazi indoctrination. Institutions of learning, elementary and advanced, were purged of teachers whose devotion to Hitlerian doctrines was suspect or who were "racially" undesirable. Eminent scholars, with some exceptions, dedicated their abilities to the promotion of the cult of the superman and other Nazi dogmas, forging sharp ideological weapons for the cause.

How Nazidom conceived of learning was depressingly revealed in an address delivered in 1937 at the famous University of Göttingen. "We renounce international science. We renounce the international republic of learning. We renounce research for its own sake. We teach and learn medicine, not to increase the number of microbes, but to keep the German people strong and healthy. We teach and learn history, not to say how things actually happened but to instruct the German people from the past. We teach and learn the sciences, not to discover abstract laws, but to sharpen the implements of the German people in competition with other peoples." Concepts of that

Inmates of a Nazi concentration camp at Nordhausen

sort driven into plastic minds year after year could not easily nor quickly be rooted out.

Men and women who had the temerity to dissent from Hitlerian theories and practices were hunted down by the nefarious secret police, the *Gestapo*. Non-conformists and "undesirables" were fought with the same diabolical efficiency with which Communist Russia crushed bourgeoisie and kulaks. Hundreds were hounded into loathsome concentration camps or put to death. The bullying Nazi fist descended with malevolent might upon the Jews. Not only were they denied ordinary rights of citizens, but they were ousted from business and the learned professions and subjected to fines and inhumanities. Repeatedly Jews were victims of gross physical outrages, a foretaste of the barbarities of the Second World War when an estimated 6,000,000 sons and daughters of Israel were destroyed by sadistic Nazi butchers. Foreign protests over the abuse of minorities were dismissed by the Nazis as meddlesome interference in the purely domestic concerns of the Third Reich.

True to the spirit of totalitarianism, the Nazis undertook to regiment the Christian churches. Protestant communions were forced to unite and placed under the administration of a Hitlerian puppet, and an attempt was made to bind Catholicism to the purposes of the state. Yet Christian leaders proved the most courageous and outspoken critics of the Nazi

Leviathan. The plucky resistance of churchmen stood in shining contrast to the general acquiescence of university scholars.

Indoctrination and repression do not alone account for the gathering popularity of the Hitlerian dictatorship. Of fundamental significance was the phenomenal improvement in living levels. Economic resilience has been a striking trait of very modern Germany. Like a weighted toy figure, scarcely had Germany been knocked down than it sat bolt upright again—that was the record after the First World War, after the currency débâcle of 1923 and after the Great Depression.

Recovery after 1933 was partly due to world-wide currents which affected Germany favorably, and partly to policies set in train by the Nazis. Public works projects, the dismissal of women from industry and a vigorous trade offensive in southeastern Europe and Latin America furnished considerable employment. Far more important, however, were gigantic rearmament programs which the Nazis carried out; and the revival of conscription (1935) removed hundreds of thousands from the labor market. By 1939 shortages of skilled workmen had appeared, and Germany was a roaring industrial furnace. The conquest of unemployment immensely fortified the tyrannous regime of Hitler. And glittering triumphs in diplomacy were propaganda assets of the utmost value.

Something more must be said about the economic policies of National Socialism. Trade unions were dissolved and wage earners—employers, too—were virtually forced into a state-controlled *Labor Front,* which was responsible for the adjustment of industrial disputes. Piece by piece, the state extended its authority over business enterprises. Although capitalists retained ownership of their properties, they were regulated by public officials. A bit of rural whimsy hit off one distinction between Soviet Communism and National Socialism this way: "If you have six cows, Communism takes the lot, but National Socialism obliges you to keep the cows and appropriates the milk." Avowing keen interest in the welfare of the farmers, the Nazis issued laws to protect propertied peasants, but promises to partition large landed estates were never fulfilled.

AUTHORITARIANISM SPREADS

As early as 1926, police regimes had been set up in Poland and Lithuania and three years later Yugoslavia also became a dictatorship. The victory of the Nazis in Germany and the buffetings of the Great Depression impelled other nations in central and eastern Europe to travel the Fascist road. There was more than a kernel of truth in the judgment later expressed by President Franklin D. Roosevelt, "Democracy has disappeared in several great nations," he said, "and not because the people of those nations dislike democracy, but because they have grown tired of unemployment and insecurity, of seeing their children hungry while they sat helpless in the face of government confusion and government weakness. . . . Finally, in desperation, they chose to sacrifice liberty in the hope of getting something to eat."

Except for Czechoslovakia and Finland, governments in central and eastern Europe had proved generally inefficient, corrupt, unprogressive; only on paper were they democracies. Unaccustomed to the ways of government by consent, the peoples of these countries passed under the rule of dictators who promised order and material well-being and who had the backing of the civilian and military bureaucracy, of the small well-to-do class and the churchmen. The parade marched past in the following order: 1934, Estonia, Latvia, Austria and Bulgaria; 1936, Greece; 1938, Rumania. Hungary and Albania had never been other than authoritarian states in spirit and performance. Only Czechoslovakia and Finland held firmly to the democratic faith and works.

Apart from Czechoslovakia and Austria, which were industrially mature, the countries of eastern Europe were overwhelmingly agrarian and faced with essentially the same rural problems. Huge tracts of land prior to 1918 belonged to large landed proprietors and a semi-feudal atmosphere prevailed. Between World Wars a "Green Revolution," the distribution of big estates among the peasants, was almost completed in Czechoslovakia and the Baltic

Republics, carried a long way in Yugoslavia and Rumania, but the process was only started in Poland and hardly begun in Hungary. In these last countries, the landowners remained politically strong, and each contained a large class of landless agricultural workers.

Taking central and eastern Europe as a whole, variations in climate, soil, crops and farming traditions caused differences in rustic living standards. And yet rural overpopulation was an almost universal phenomenon; population growth was three times as fast in Poland and the Balkans as in the west of Europe. Perhaps a quarter of the rural workers could have left the land, without causing any material decline in production. Certain overcrowded districts suffered severely from malnutrition, in spite of supplementary work by peasants as laborers or in cottage industries and emigrant remittances from the United States. As a rule, peasants concentrated on raising cereals; some hand-planted terraces of wheat were only ten square yards in extent! Small patches of land and runty sheep and goats, whose milk was converted into cheese and whose wool was spun on the distaff, provided about the only income for many households.

Methods of farming were primitive, the whole family toiling from dawn to dusk. Without much incentive, fatalistic, ignorant, the mass of the peasants was resigned to its cramped and insecure lot. It was appreciated in informed circles, more clearly with the onset of the Great Depression, that industrialization was the remedy for rural wretchedness. But the capital required would have to come from abroad and foreign financial interests were reluctant to assume the risks involved.

Most of the eastern countries contained national and religious minorities, sources of grave internal and international tensions. Within Poland, for example, lived millions of Ukrainians and other stocks having relatives in Soviet Russia, while upwards of 750,000 citizens of German speech were scattered about the western provinces. Restless and unruly, these minorities frequently provoked controversies with Poland's great neighbors and contributed, eventually, to the oncoming of the Second World War. Czechoslovakia likewise was constantly involved in diplomatic complications because of her minorities. Of these the most important were 3,000,000 Sudeten Germans upon whom the Nazis exerted a magnetic attraction. Friction between Serb and Croatian politicians created special and divisive perplexities in Yugoslavia.

SPAIN GOES FASCIST

On the other side of Europe, Spain after a short interlude of republican democracy succumbed to a Fascist tyranny of the most repressive type. In the twenties a military dictatorship had taken over and the King, Alfonso XIII, imprudently identified himself with it, thus signing the death-warrant of his dynasty. At municipal elections in 1931, resentment against authoritarianism and monarchy, which a slump in business intensified, was expressed in unmistakable language. Friends of republicanism swept the polls in what amounted to a solemn referendum. Properly reading the signs of the time, Alfonso XIII abdicated the throne; it was in truth a "bloodless revolution," for a Republic was proclaimed and was soon equipped with a democratic constitution.

As portrayed in romantic novels and travel literature, Spain is a country of bullfights, of brilliant shawls and costumes, of senoritas chatting with suitors through barred windows, a mellow land bathed in perpetual sunshine. But that image is, of course, a superficial caricature. The large mass of Spaniards were dour peasants, many of whom worked for meager wages on large estates belonging to landlords, crown and church. Ordinarily inarticulate politically, the Spanish peasantry was capable of fanatical violence if emotions were deeply stirred.

The small middle classes had grown in response to industrialism as had the propertyless workers in Madrid, Barcelona and the mining districts of the northwest. Catalans, residing in and about Barcelona, and Basques on the flank of the Pyrenees claimed to be distinctive nationalities and as such stridently demanded home-rule. Political currents and cross-currents in modern Spain were diverse, extremely confusing and not susceptible to crisp exposition.

Sympathetic to republicanism, with varying degrees of ardor, were middle-class democrats, the home-rule elements and a bewildering array of collectivists: democratic Socialists, strong in Madrid, Anarcho-Syndicalists, strong in Barcelona and sections of rural Spain and small Communist cliques of several shades.

Republican politicians construed the revolution of 1931 as a mandate to clip the wings of the traditional ruling class composed of landlords, churchmen and professional soldiers. Accordingly, many high-ranking officers were dismissed from the army, the privileges of the parasitic aristocracy were withdrawn and large estates, some of them extending over thousands of acres, were nationalized without compensation. Other measures deprived the Church of landed properties, an important step in curtailing the influence of the clergy. Churchmen conducted or controlled nearly all the schools which were now taken over by the Republic; civil marriage and divorce were legalized.

Much of the legislation relating to land and church was not faithfully enforced. But the laws, nonetheless, embittered the interests that were adversely affected. On the other hand, Leftist elements were aggrieved because economic and social reforms had not reached far enough or were indifferently applied. Spain seethed with disorders and risings fomented both by the Right and the Left. As had often happened in the past, Spanish military men plotted to destroy the prevailing government. Heading the conspiracy was General Francisco Franco, who raised the standard of rebellion in July of 1936. To his side rallied the conservative and reactionary forces, calling themselves the Nationalists. Partisans of the Republic, the Loyalists, picked up the gage of battle and for nearly three years Spain reeled under as ruinous a struggle as modern history records. Both sides committed ferociously cruel deeds, not soon forgotten.

Though technically a civil war, the Spanish conflict possessed a distinctly international cast. Fascist Italy and Nazi Germany decisively aided the Nationalists, while Communist Russia sent modest help to the Loyalists. British and French diplomacy barely contrived to prevent the war from turning into a general European catastrophe. Quarreling inside the Loyalist household injured the Republican cause, as the Fascists closed in for the kill. By early 1939 Franco was master of a prostrate Spain in which hundreds of thousands of families mourned their war dead.

The Nationalists signalized their victory by setting up a Fascist tyranny. As an ideology, Fascism had scored a resounding success. Absolute authority was lodged in Franco, saluted as the *Caudillo*, who had at his back the militant Phalanx Party (*Falange Española*). Enemies of the conqueror, if they failed to escape abroad, were vindictively slaughtered or imprisoned, and what remained of the Republican reforms was undone. Landlords recovered their boundless horizons and the Church resumed her traditional prerogatives, though the Vatican steadfastly declined to negotiate a concordat with Franco to replace the treaty denounced by the Republic in 1931.

Spain was thrown into a harsh strait jacket, imposed by a leech-like bureaucracy and a huge standing army, which fought isolated guerilla resistance into 1948. The strongest bulwarks indeed of Franco's regime were the pampered military forces and popular dread lest the horrors and impoverishment of civil war should return.

THE WESTERN DEMOCRACIES

How then did Great Britain and France fare in this time of acute social distress and spreading authoritarianism? As a great commercial nation, Britain suffered severely because of the contraction in world trade and of international turmoil. Unemployment rose to about 2,750,000 laying a heavy additional burden upon the national treasury; in the middle of the slump Britain forsook the gold standard. The Labour Party, which had taken over the management of affairs in 1929, was disrupted by the economic panic. Prime Minister Ramsay MacDonald argued for retrenchment, which antagonized most of the Labour M. P.'s. So MacDonald dissolved the ministry and entered a national coalition, comprising Conservatives and a scattering of Liberals and Labourites. At a national election in 1931, this ill-assorted combination was upheld by a very large majority.

Drastic measures were adopted to put the British house in order. Expenditures were reduced by paring down salaries of civil servants and grants to the jobless; taxation was stiffened and the budget was brought into balance. It was now, too, that Britain joined the procession of tariff protectionists. By positive action, such as housing projects, government greased the wheels of industry. State authority over business enterprise was broadened, though most industries remained under private control.

British attitudes on economic problems, and not only British, were profoundly influenced by the searching and learned writings of John Maynard Keynes, the most influential economist of the age, and one of the great economists of all time. Thoroughly familiar with the mysteries of high finance, his thinking was colored by the huge volume of chronic unemployment which existed. Certain basic principles of conservative economics Keynes dismissed as antiquated; the gold standard, for one thing, he ridiculed as a "barbaric relic," which should be replaced by carefully managed national monetary systems. He insisted, too, upon high taxation in boom times to offset deficit financing when economic activity was in a depressed condition.

To cure the depression and overcome unemployment Keynes advocated liberal public spending. Government should "prime the pump" of business by appropriations for social services and public works, financed if necessary by borrowing. That teaching forms, no doubt, the major contribution of Keynes to political action. It was his contention that new investment in capital goods created the additional savings necessary to finance investment.

Seeking to clarify the causes of unemployment, Keynes probed into the economic and monetary structure of modern industrial society. The results of the investigation were incorporated in *The General Theory of Employment, Interest and Money* (1936), his most influential book, even if badly arranged and hard for the layman to understand. Although the teachings of Keynes, which pursued by new means the old objective of human freedom, were unpalatable to conventional economists, they attracted wide acceptance and exerted distinct influence upon practical decisions in Great Britain, the United States and other democratic countries.

Distress and misery reigned in districts of the United Kingdom that depended upon foreign markets—in areas of textile production, coal mining and shipbuilding. Where employment was spotty and hope absent, social decay set in. Many a business leader pressed for greater diversification in production. "We must have many eggs in many baskets," it was said and said again. Comparatively new industries serving the home market were actually established and prospered—rayon, electrical devices, motor cars and planes. These novel types of production and the application of more brains to manufacturing and merchandising processes testified that British industrial ingenuity had not atrophied. Late in the thirties, large-scale rearmament, dictated by the darkening international sky, set British factories humming, though a hard core of unemployment persisted in the export industries.

Meanwhile, a parliamentary election in 1935 reproduced the broad pattern of 1931. The Conservative Party dominated the Commons, though Labour tripled its representation. It was a Conservative ministry, presided over by Neville Chamberlain after 1937, which shaped British diplomacy during the nerve-wracking perplexities that led up to the Second World War. A lunatic fringe in Britain professed Fascist doctrines, and Communism had a solitary representative in the Commons, but these totalitarian creeds were invincibly repelled by the British public and press. The ordeals of the interwar epoch seemed to have deepened, if anything, British faith in the democratic process.

FRANCE

The performance of the French democracy was decidedly less impressive than the British. Cabinets were formed and collapsed with disconcerting swiftness and proposals to end this comedy failed to kindle sufficient enthusiasm

Demonstration of the French proto-Fascist group, the Croix de Feu, *Paris, 1936. The man wearing deocrations in the center foreground is its leader, Col. de la Roque.*

to bring about reform. Social and ideological cleavages, not to speak of the everlasting clerical issue, caused almost endless tumult in politics. Due to its nicely balanced economy, France staved off the creeping malady of the Great Depression until her neighbors had started to recuperate. Business recession, damaging to city dweller and peasant alike, smote the country just when the accession of the Nazis excited anxieties over French security and when minds were fearful of an internal conspiracy to subvert the free institutions of the Republic.

A spate of authoritarian organizations flayed parliamentary and business institutions in print and in noisy street demonstrations. Partisans of royalism, known as the *Action Française*, waged a scurrilous campaign against the republican democracy, accusing it of all the crimes on the calendar. Proto-fascist leagues, appealing to despondent youth and inspired by the example of Italy and Germany, mouthed the doctrines and praised the practices of Mussolini; what *il Duce* had done could be imitated by Frenchmen. Typical of these societies was the *Croix de Feu* (Cross of Fire), which enrolled war veterans primarily in a large and disciplined agitation. Its spokesmen called for tax reduction, state regulation of business, a more ardent patriotism, and they violently denounced parliamentary deputies, lumped together indiscriminately as thieves.

With political passions running high, a notorious scandal—the Stavisky affair—disclosed that certain public officials were implicated in shameless financial transactions. Lurid tales of racketeering and treachery by Republican politicans were enough to fire a major explosion. In February, 1934, anti-parliamentary crowds assembled in the spacious Place de la Concorde in Paris, only a few paces from the Palais Bourbon where the Chamber of Deputies was in session. Disorderly rioters threatened to storm the building and scatter the deputies to their homes. When police intervened to disperse the mob, stones were thrown and police were hurled into the Seine; then machine-guns came into play. For the first time in this century blood was shed in Paris; over twenty demonstrators were killed and many more were wounded. But the challenge to the integrity of the Republic was frustrated.

Alarmed by the militancy and the menace of Fascist leagues, the Left in French politics, the Radical Socialists (who were in fact a middle-of-the-way group), the democratic Socialists and the Communists, combined in a Popular Front. That bloc captured a majority of the deputies in a national election of 1936; the Communist delegation increased six-fold, winning seventy-two seats, which frightened moderates and conservatives. A Popular Front ministry pushed emergency legislation through the Chamber to meet an emergency situation; it was the conviction of Premier Leon Blum, a democratic Socialist, that social reforms were the only alternative to bloody revolution. Anti-democratic organizations were outlawed though not entirely broken up, and laws beneficial to the peasants were matched by legislation desired by industrial workers. A forty-hour work-week was introduced, collective bargaining was made compulsory, social security benefits were extended and factories making armaments were partly nationalized.

Opponents charged that these and lesser acts of the Popular Front upset the national economy and hampered armament production (which was inaccurate) at precisely the time that the Hitlerian menace loomed ever more ominous. The Popular Front fell apart and political recriminations mounted in volume and venom. As the Second World War drew near, social discord and ideological contentions critically impaired the national morale of France.

IN MINIATURE

The European generation which lived from the Versailles Peace to the Nazi invasion of Poland in 1939 experienced immense political vicissitudes and economic fluctuations. After 1918 the principles and practices of government by consent enjoyed unexampled popularity. From the Rhine to Russia short-lived democracies took their places alongside of the historic democracies of the West.

A galaxy of independent states appeared in the center and east of the Continent, based essentially on the shibboleth of self-determination and reversing the nineteenth century trend (except in the Balkans) toward political consolidation. Sharp national jealousies and competitive tariff, currency and railway policies in the new countries augured ill for the common welfare.

The triumphant democratic creed exalted the worth and supremacy of the individual. It looked upon the state as a servant, simply a mechanism for the convenience and comfort of the citizens. Inherent rights entitled every man to freedom and equality with every other man. On principle, the democratic ideal was committed to the protection of human interests in all countries whether or not they were capable of self-government.

Commencing in Italy with the victory of Fascism, an *alias* like Communism for government by coercion, a tide toward despotism set in. Representative government, after brave experiments, was stifled or withered away in almost every country where it had not gained a firm footing before the twentieth century. Totalitarian tyrannies, which drew strength from the propagation of persuasive myths, subordinated the individual to the interest of the State. Fanatical and vulgar leaders, commanding enthusiastic followings, imposed their wills upon reluctant or inarticulate majorities. These autocrats made their forerunners in the age of Metternich, for instance, seem tame by comparison. Totalitarianism offered, it is true, the advantage of simplicity; no compulsion rested upon the individual to think. There was every reason, indeed, why he should not think.

The "Twenty Years' Truce" was an epoch of economic dislocations and sharpening social tensions. After relatively "good times" in the late twenties, Europe was ravaged by the tornado of the Great Depression. The economic mechanism, it became clear, could no longer be trusted to look after itself, but had rather to be controlled by positive state action. In the topsy-turvydom of crisis behavior, governments sought salvation for their peoples in self-sufficiency, or autarchy. Only inadequately was it appreciated that a selfish national course aggravated the universal chaos. International co-operation for economic stability was indispensable for the general welfare and peace. And yet it is quite possible that levels of comfort in 1939 were higher than in 1914. The economic malaise, however, fed the cause of dictatorship, most importantly in disenchanted Germany.

Only for purposes of clarity can the course of domestic history be studied in isolation from international affairs. As is explained in a later chapter, it seemed in the late twenties that Europe and the wider world were traveling the road to international harmony. A cheerful, if restrained, optimism welled up. But discontents and hatreds, fears and suspicions had not been conjured away. When brutal and aggressive dictators tried to impose their wills upon foreign nations, they shattered the vision of collective security and Europe slithered into the Second World War.

FOR FURTHER STUDY

QUINCY HOWE, *The World between Wars* (New York, 1953)

ARTHUR J. MAY, *Europe and Two World Wars* (New York, 1947)

HAROLD NICOLSON, *King George the Fifth* (New York, 1953)

SAMUEL W. HALPERIN, *Germany Tried Democracy* (New York, 1946)

EDWARD M. EARLE, ed., *Modern France* (Princeton, 1951)

HERMAN FINER, *Mussolini's Italy* (New York, 1935)

H. W. ARNDT, *The Economic Lessons of the Nineteen Thirties* (New York, 1944)

ALAN BULLOCK, *Hitler* (new ed., New York, 1960) PAPERBACK

JOHN W. WHEELER-BENNETT, *Nemesis of Power* (New York, 1954)

HANS ROTHFELS, *German Opposition to Hitler* (Chicago, 1948)

HUGH SETON-WATSON, *Eastern Europe between the Wars* (Cambridge, Eng., 1945)

GERALD BRENAN, *The Spanish Labyrinth* (new ed., Cambridge, Eng., 1950) PAPERBACK

DAVID T. CATTELL, *Communism and the Spanish Civil War* (Berkeley, California, 1955)

ROY F. HARROD, *The Life of John Maynard Keynes* (New York, 1951)

CHARLES L. MOWAT, *Britain between the Wars* (Chicago, 1955)

ERICH EYCK, *A History of the Weimar Republic* (Eng. trans., Cambridge, Mass., 1962)

KLEMENS VON KLEMPERER, *Germany's New Conservatism* (Princeton, 1957)

ROBERT G. L. WAITE, *Vanguard of Nazism* (Cambridge, Mass., 1952)

THOMAS L. JARMAN, *The Rise and Fall of Nazi Germany* (London, 1955) PAPERBACK

DOROTHY M. PICKLES, *The French Political Scene* (New York, 1939)

CHARLES F. DELZELL, *Mussolini's Enemies* (Princeton, 1961)

S. HARRISON THOMSON, *Czechoslovakia in European History* (new ed., Princeton, 1953)

BERNADOTTE E. SCHMITT, ed., *Poland* (Berkeley, 1945)

STANLEY G. PAYNE, *Falange: a History of Spanish Fascism* (Stanford, 1961)

HUGH THOMAS, *The Spanish Civil War* (New York, 1961) PAPERBACK

CHAPTER XXVIII

THE UNITED STATES COMES OF AGE

ECONOMIC EXPANSION ABROAD

AS A belligerent in the First World War the United States dispatched upwards of 2,000,000 soldiers to the battlegrounds of Europe. Their presence abroad testified—dramatically testified—that the United States had come of age as an international power. The march of the New World Republic to global stature and its enlarging role in world affairs resulted from expanding foreign economic interests and growing physical strength, along with its distinctive pattern of democracy and its concern for human freedom.

At the outset of the modern epoch shipments of gold and silver from the Americas produced creeping inflation in Europe which helped to disrupt medieval economic institutions and affected many other aspects of living. Later on, cargoes of potatoes, tobacco, other soil products and industrial rawstuffs wrought radically upon the European economy. After 1860 the opening up of the Middle Western prairies, coupled with cheapened oceanic transportation, frightened Old World farming interests and they pressed for tariffs to stave off the deluge. Between 1870 and 1900 American shipments abroad actually tripled in value.

Down to 1890 exports from the United States consisted principally of farm and mineral commodities. But by then the United States had matured industrially and thereafter manufactured articles—farm implements, typewriters and dynamos, for instance—formed an ever higher percentage of exports. By 1914 about half of the foreign sales of the United States was industrial products. "American factories are making more than the American people can use," explained Senator Albert J. Beveridge of Indiana. "American soil is producing more than they can consume. Fate has written our policy for us, the trade of the world must and shall be ours."

Capital investments overseas accompanied the growth of foreign commerce. Until 1914 the United States was a debtor country, borrowing in the money markets of Europe to construct railways or to finance manufacturing and mining enterprises. As late as the First World War, European capitalists owned nearly $5,000,000,000 of fixed investments in the United States. Financial houses in the United States, meantime, had been shipping funds abroad. Plantations, mines and railways in Mexico, Cuba and Canada attracted investments from the United States. Small loans were floated for Swiss cities, and for Japan, during the Russo-Japanese War, and capital was plunged into undertakings in China or applied to the construction of branch factories in Imperial Russia and other countries. As of 1914 foreign investments approached $3,500,000,000, and betokened the coming of age of the United States in terms of international finance.

During most of the nineteenth century the United States hewed rather consistently to a policy of tariff protectionism for industry. Between 1861 and 1913 rates moved steadily upward except for two very modest and short-lived reductions. So long as the United States imported capital, protectionism worked tolerably well, but the policy had taken such deep root that it was not easily modified when the country became a creditor nation on balance.

PILLARS OF FOREIGN POLICY

Although American foreign policy has been a subject of controversy, often acrimonious, ever since the founding of the Republic, several guiding concepts evolved. Three underlying considerations shaped the attitude of the United States toward the outside world. Geographical position, first, which afforded the country a "precious advantage" over other major powers. Second, the fabulous growth in territory throughout her history and the expansion of physical strength after 1865. And, finally, national interests expressed in terms of foreign trade and security. Security ranked really at the top. It was Alexander Hamilton who wrote, "Safety from external danger is the most powerful dictator of national conduct." Strictly speaking, security implied that the territorial integrity and political independence of the United States were not in danger of external attack. In practice, however, security was inescapably a relative condition, affected by shifts in power relations among foreign countries and by technical innovations having military implications.

What then were the pillars of diplomacy resting upon these foundations? Four larger ones may be singled out. (1) Aloofness from the combinations and collisions of European high politics. Reinforcing the counsel of President Washington on this point, Thomas Jefferson recommended in 1801 that the United States should seek honest friendship with all nations but "entangling alliances with none." (2) "Freedom of the seas" or the right under all circumstances to engage in lawful maritime trade with any country. In time of war commerce with a belligerent in contraband goods (an elastic term) should cease, but legitimate business should be protected, if need be by armed force. (3) The Monroe Doctrine, with which is associated the concept of Pan-Americanism, and, perhaps as a corollary, control over the Panama Canal and its Caribbean and Pacific approaches, should be included. (4) The idea of the "Open Door" or equality of treatment in commercial dealings for nationals of the United States in foreign countries, particularly China, though not there alone.[1] Supplementing that, the desire for a balanced equilibrium of power among the countries of eastern Asia was eventually appended.

Apart from these fundamentals two other strong ideas operated. First, a preference for arbitration, for give-and-take in the settlement of quarrels with foreign countries. As early as 1794 a batch of disputes with Great Britain was amicably adjusted by a joint arbitral commission. Indeed, except for the antagonisms which brought on the War of 1812, all differences with Britain, some of them extremely delicate boundary and fishing-rights issues,

[1] In Dutch and British colonies, for example, the United States sought the identical commercial concessions granted to any other nation.

were resolved by arbitration or some other diplomatic procedure.

Similarly the United States warmly supported the Hague Tribunal, created in 1899, for the pacific settlement of international disputes. That court possessed no power to enforce its verdicts and the same limitation applied to the Bryan "cooling off" treaties negotiated with thirty-five countries just before the First World War. These pacts, which were hopefully intended to substitute arbitration for war, proved to be still-born, but they attested the allegiance of the United States to the constructive principle of settling quarrels without resort to violence.

Last of all, the United States manifested lively and sustained care for democratic and republican strivings everywhere. It applauded independence for the Latin-American Republics and rejoiced whenever oppressed "underdogs" rebelled and seemed likely to remake themselves in the image of the United States. Nationalities struggling to be free, from the Irish to the Koreans, could confidently count upon popular sympathy in the New World democracy. Abroad as at home, the United States was looked upon as the natural foe of despotism and autocracy, the natural champion of human freedoms. "Not by aggression," declared a nineteenth-century American, "but by the naked fact of existence we are an eternal danger and an unsleeping threat to every government that founds itself on anything but the will of the governed."

THE MONROE DOCTRINE

No facet of international policy was more deeply embedded in the consciousness of the United States than the Monroe Doctrine. Mary Baker Eddy, founder of Christian Science, expressed a widely-cherished conviction when she said, "I believe strictly in our Constitution, in the laws of God and the Monroe Doctrine." The origins of this well-beloved principle, which declared the independence of the Americas, have already been treated (p. 528). More than a generation passed before the doctrine attained the dignity of an article of national faith. But after 1850 the implications brought on several sharp diplomatic encounters with European nations.

Great Britain, for instance, wished to monopolize any canal that might be cut through Central America. Diplomatic maneuverings in the area generated warlike howls of protest in the United States; but cooling counsels prevailed and in 1850 a treaty—the Clayton-Bulwer—was negotiated, prescribing that neither Britain nor the United States should have exclusive rights to dig an interoceanic waterway. When in the 1860's the France of Napoleon III presumed to convert Mexico into a satrapy and Spain deliberately tried to reassert authority over Santo Domingo, diplomatic pressure by the United States helped to frustrate the plans. Thereafter no European country really threatened the political independence of a Latin-American Republic.

But the Monroe principle acquired (1895) added popularity in connection with an Anglo-Venezuelan dispute over the frontier of British Guiana. Appealed to by Venezuela, the United States brusquely asked Britain to arbitrate the quarrel, threatening to invoke force if necessary. "Today the United States," it was pungently asserted, "is practically sovereign on this continent, and its fiat is law . . ." Jingoistic newspapers on both sides of the Atlantic fanned traditional animosities by their dangerously bellicose language. Yet the British government, confronted by a grave contention with Germany over South Africa, had no intention of unsheathing the sword. Rather it agreed to impartial settlement of the controversy and an arbitral commission ruled that most of the British claims on the territory in dispute were valid. The prestige of the Monroe Doctrine profited; seemingly the United States had effectively twisted the lion's tail.

WAR WITH SPAIN—1898

Before the Venezuelan imbroglio had been ironed out, the fate of Cuba crowded to the fore in an ugly manner. Subjects of Spain, Cubans were more or less imbued with aspirations for independence and government by consent. A war for Cuban freedom, stimulated in part by "hard times" resulting from a United

Wreck of the Spanish cruiser Reina Mercedes—*one of the casualties of the naval engagement off Santiago, Cuba*

States sugar tariff, began in 1895 and was waged on the Spanish side with primitive ferocity. Yankee interests in sugar plantations and other enterprises suffered severely.

Assertive nationalism in the United States, best personified by the impulsive Theodore Roosevelt, demanded that Spain should be booted out of the New World bag and baggage. Fellow feeling in the United States for the Cuban insurgents resembled in fact Russian attachment to the little Slav brothers in the Balkans. Popular indignation against the Spanish monarchy was whipped up by two sensation-seeking newspapers in New York City battling for circulation and echoed in the provincial press. Mass emotions boiled over when the warship *Maine* exploded mysteriously in Havana harbor, carrying over 250 seamen to a watery grave. The Spanish authorities were charged with responsibility for the gruesome tragedy.

Pacific gestures by the Madrid government, hinting at autonomy for Cuba, were ineptly handled by the State Department. In 1898 an enflamed Congress stampeded the country into war, though financial groups with investments in Cuba resisted the appeal to arms. For one reason and another, Continental Europe favored the Spanish cause, while Great Britain, impelled by considerations of European politics, sympathized with the Yankees and thus helped to diminish the old antagonism between the two countries.

The quick triumph over Spain, essentially a naval achievement, marked the début of the United States into the society of Great Powers. As fruits of victory, Cuba was released from Spanish lordship; and the United States annexed Puerto Rico, and in the western Pacific the Philippine archipelago, Guam and many islets. Voices of responsible criticism were raised against acquiring colonial possessions, but they were overborne by a robust and expansive nationalism. Whether for weal or woe, the virus of European imperialism had entered the blood of the New World Republic, albeit in a somewhat diluted form.

YANKEE IMPERIALISM

Manifestations of the imperial mood multiplied. For practical purposes the Caribbean was converted into a sea of the northern Republic, a sphere of interest. Cuba was granted independence in 1902, it is true, but strings were attached transferring land for a naval station and authorizing the United States to step in to uphold law and order. When disorders occurred in 1906, troops were landed and they lingered on for three years and there were other interventions later.

As one aspect of expansionism in the Caribbean area, the United States obtained the Panama Canal Zone, writing an embarrassing story in the process. An interoceanic waterway, it was pointed out, would enable battleships of the United States to shuttle quickly from ocean to ocean and would bring commercial advantages as well. First, a treaty was negotiated in 1901 with Great Britain, which had icily rebuffed earlier overtures, superseding the agreement of 1850 and permitting the United States to construct the canal on its own. After the legislature of Colombia threw cold water on a treaty ceding a canal zone to the United States, the Province of Panama rebelled.

With the connivance of Washington, Theodore Roosevelt in the White House, Panama (1903) declared its independence of Colombia and became a satellite of the United States. It is extremely doubtful whether the secession of

The Panama Canal under construction. Lower gates of Miraflores locks as they looked on July 5, 1913

Panama would have succeeded if United States war vessels had not appeared in near-by waters. A strip for a canal was ceded to the Northern Republic in perpetuity; subsequently (1921) the United States compensated Colombia to the tune of $25,000,000 for the canal zone. The canal was opened to shipping in 1914, though the finishing touches required six years more. Publicists referred to Panama as the "life-line" of the United States much as Britain looked upon Suez.

Venezuela, meantime, had pushed into the international spotlight a second time. Warships of Britain, Germany and Italy, on a debt collecting mission, staged demonstrations in 1902 off Venezuela, which roused lively fears in the United States that territory would be occupied. The behavior of the German force was especially disturbing, though it is reasonably certain that the Germans nurtured no territorial designs. Arbitration presently settled the dispute.

The United States desired orderly and friendly regimes in the Caribbean area and wanted constitutional governments, not dictatorships, throughout Latin America. In the confident tones of the schoolmaster, President Woodrow Wilson is reported to have said (1913), "I am going to teach the South American Republics to elect good men." Well before that, in 1904, Theodore Roosevelt had proclaimed the right and duty of the United States to intervene in the Latin states if disorders occurred or if they neglected to pay their foreign debts. Roosevelt wished to avoid a repetition of the Venezuela Affair of 1902. "The frontiers of the United States virtually extend to Tierra del Fuego," declared a member of the Roosevelt Cabinet with goatish complacency.

To conquer evil, evil, it seemed, had to be committed. In the somber guise of a sheriff the Northern Republic presumed to collect debts owed to foreigners by Latin countries and to protect the lives and properties of foreign nationals. To put down disturbances, Marines marched into Santo Domingo (1905, 1916), Nicaragua (1912) and Haiti (1915); natives danced to the tune called by the occupying troops. And in 1917 the United States bought the strategically attractive Danish West Indies, called poetically the Virgin Islands.

Dealings with Mexico were particularly tumultuous and vexing. Starting in 1910 and lasting for thirty-six years, Mexico experienced a dizzy round of revolutions and counter-revolutions, in which social and political considerations were intertwined. Chronic friction between the United States and the southern neighbor resembled the standing quarrel of Austria and Serbia in Europe. Revolutionary disturbances took American lives, imperilled Yankee investments, which exceeded $1,000,000,000 and wounded the Yankee sense of honor. Pressure upon Washington for armed intervention was long and loud. When a patient course of "watchful waiting" and even mobilization of troops on the frontier failed to elicit the desired response from the Mexican government, forces of the United States in 1914 occupied the port of Vera Cruz. Then diplomacy intervened and straightened out the tangle, which had threatened to develop into open war.

Belligerent passions flared up again after a gang of Mexican raiders ravaged (1916) the town of Columbus in New Mexico, killing seventeen citizens. Military detachments dispatched into Mexico were unable to apprehend the raiders and the Yankee mind was presently diverted from problems to the south by involvement in war with Germany.

The advancing shadow of *Yanqui* imperialism excited resentment, distrust and alarm in Latin-American circles. Books by the score and hundreds of press articles, from Mexico to the Argentine, fulminated against the United States as the aggressive and greedy "Colossus of the North." A distinguished Mexican jurist, for instance, rebuked "the ambitions of a powerful people who pretend to exercise their hegemony over a group of weak peoples, giving to their domination the insincere appearances of unselfishness and benevolence."

Whatever the altruistic professions of Washington, many an articulate Latin regarded the United States as simply a hungry wolf in a sheep's clothing. Only Brazil of the major

Ruins of Columbus, New Mexico, after Villa's Mexican raiders came

South American countries followed the United States into the First World War, though all the Caribbean states entered except El Salvador.

Substantial support, in the meanwhile, had grown up for cooperation of the New World Republics in matters of common concern, even for a customs-union. On four occasions before the First World War, Pan-American conferences were assembled, the first at Washington in 1889, and a broad range of subjects was discussed. Not much of value was accomplished by these parleys, though a Pan-American Union was created with headquarters in Washington. Differences in language, cultural patterns, social customs and political habits, as well as Yankee imperialism, militated against hemispheric collaboration. Out of a pharisaical sense of superiority, moreover, ordinary Yankees tended to look southward with a vague feeling of condescension. It was assumed that peoples below the United States in latitude were below them in dignity and qualities of greatness. Time, happily, would temper national snobbery and alter cultural perspectives.

EXPANSION IN THE PACIFIC

While the growth of the Yankee position in Latin America proceeded, interests in the Pacific and eastern Asia expanded notably. Commerce with China, which began immediately after the American Revolution, was placed on a formal treaty basis in 1844. Merchants profitably engaged in tea, silk and pepper business with the Celestial Empire and with southeastern Asia; and missionaries were at work winning souls.

At the mid-century, just after the extension of continental United States to the Pacific seaboard, Yankee expansionists envisaged glittering potentialities in the lands along the great ocean. William H. Seward in 1852 assured his Senatorial colleagues, "The Pacific, its shores and its islands, and the vast regions beyond will become the chief theater of events in the world's great hereafter." Presently the big black ships of Commodore Matthew C. Perry appeared in Japan and induced (1854) the Nipponese authorities to cast off the hermit's cloak. Privileges of coaling and other rights granted to Perry were soon broadened into regular, Western-style commercial and diplomatic relations. No European country exerted a greater influence than the United States upon Japan as it strode out of obscurity toward leadership in the Orient.

By purchase from Russia, the United States picked up (1867) huge Alaska and the long Aleutian appendage, stepping stones across the north Pacific. For this "sucked orange of the

Tsar," Washington paid a penny an acre. The importance of the dependency lay (and lies) primarily in its location; as the northernmost outpost of the United States and the area nearest to Russia, Alaska serves as a defensive shield for North America—or a route for a possible enemy advance, such as Japan threatened in the Second World War. Alaska came to occupy a crucial place in the global strategy of the New World. The rich natural resources of this "last frontier" of the United States remained virtually untouched until well into the twentieth century.

It was in the spacious McKinley era that the Stars and Stripes were at last hoisted over Hawaii, nearly 2,500 miles from California. More than half a century earlier Yankee mariners, merchants and missionaries had started to transform the islands into a sort of Pacific New England. In 1884 the native government conceded to the United States the privilege of constructing a naval station at Pearl Harbor, though projects to incorporate Hawaii in the United States ran onto the rocks.

In the 1890's, however, manifest destiny moved in unmysterious ways her wonders to perform. American sugar planters and others, abetted by officials and marines of the United States, cast aside the native Hawaiian government, and, after no little pulling and hauling, the United States annexed the islands in 1898. A racial melting pot, containing whites, Orientals and happy-go-lucky natives, Hawaii was nevertheless singularly free of intolerance and racial discord, partly, at any rate, because of general prosperity. Pearl Harbor was built into a mighty bastion to defend the ever-enlarging interests of the United States in and along the Pacific Ocean.

Among those interests were the Philippines and other possessions acquired from Spain. Before American rule over the Philippines became a reality, a Filipino insurrection had to be beaten down—and a costly and depressing business it was. By planting the flag in the western Pacific the United States undertook novel and challenging political and strategic responsibilities and tacitly announced that it intended to participate in the power politics of eastern Asia. Though pleasantly endowed with agricultural and mineral wealth and inhabited by a people quick to learn and eager to improve their welfare, the Philippines failed to attract the capital investments needed for progress. Financiers hesitated to enter a region from which the United States might withdraw, something frequently promised to the natives. In fact extensive home-rule rights were authorized in 1916, foreshadowing the independence of the Filipinos thirty years later. A major American fleet base was constructed in the archipelago.

Rounding out the Pacific empire, the United States took over choice portions of Samoa. As early as 1878, the American flag had been raised over Pago Pago, known as the finest harbor in the south Pacific. British and German interests competed with the United States in idyllic Samoa, making it a storm center of international rivalry. But in 1899, Britain pulled out, and Germany and the United States agreed to partition the isles, Tutuila on which Pago Pago was situated passing to the United States. Congress withheld official recognition of ownership for thirty years. Midway Island was appropriated in 1859, Wake in 1898, and the United States also asserted sovereignty over smaller island pinpoints in the Pacific vastness.

ACTIVITIES IN EASTERN ASIA

Toward the close of the nineteenth century, it looked as though European imperialisms might carve up populous and somnolent China. At that time Washington brought forward (1899, 1900) the "Open Door" formula for China, which implied, first, that businessmen of all countries should have equal opportunities, and, second, that the territorial integrity and political independence of the Manchu Empire should not be further impaired. Commercial and altruistic motives alike underlay this piece of American diplomacy. If China were broken up, existing American trade would have been frozen out and haunting visions of a vast commerce in the future would have been shattered. Then too, many a Yankee, touched by missionary emphases, felt that helpless, hapless China ought to be protected from the covetous appetites of Europe.

Great Powers with stakes in the Celestial Empire were requested to subscribe to the "Open Door." Most of them did so, though not Imperial Russia, and even the assenters held their tongues in their cheeks; it was not indeed until 1922 that the "Open Door" was spelled out in a concrete manner. Nonetheless, once the "Open Door" was formalized by the United States, it remained the key to American dealings in the Orient, both with the eastern nations themselves and with Western powers having interests in eastern Asia. The growing preoccupation of the United States with the Far East was again indicated in 1900 when 2,500 "leathernecks" shared in beating down the Boxer insurgency.

American business commitments in China increased slowly, but weightier by far was the investment of American religious and emotional capital. Missionaries, educators and sunshine-spreaders on a global scale fostered widespread compassion in the United States for the Chinese millions; and it was wishfully imagined that China could be molded, and in truth was being molded, in the American image. Upon the proclamation of the Chinese Republic in 1912, a Secretary of State, no less, was heard to remark, "Now that the Chinese people are practicing our form of democracy they will, within a quarter of a century, solve all of their difficulties." Old China hands thought otherwise, and the future vindicated their gloomy calculations. American concern for Chinese sensibilities was not strong enough to prevent legislation excluding yellow laborers from the shores of the United States.

Expansion in the Pacific area brought the United States face to face with ambitious and pugnacious Japan. Until 1905 an almost incredible cordiality linked the two nations together; the years since the Perry mission were rather like a lengthy honeymoon. It was reasoned in Washington that the American interest would best be served if a condition of "balanced antagonism" prevailed between Japan and Imperial Russia in eastern Asia. When, however, the Land of the Rising Sun whipped Russia in 1905, relations with the United States took a turn for the worse. Japan had demonstrated her prowess as a seapower, and suspicions and mistrust cropped up. Proud Nipponese blamed peace-maker Theodore Roosevelt for the failure of their country to extract a war indemnity from St. Petersburg. But much more irritating were discriminatory treatment and physical abuse of Japanese nationals who had emigrated to California. Vigorous protests by Tokyo provoked serious war scares.

Pickwickian fat boys of yellow journalism made white flesh creep with the calamities that would ensue if barriers were not raised against Japanese immigration. They would treat assertive Japan in the same fashion as impotent China. Responding to the "Yellow Peril" physical clamor, the State Department in 1907 skillfully negotiated a "gentlemen's agreement" with Tokyo, obligating Japan to keep its laborers out of the United States. Not content with that, California enacted (1913) laws restricting alien ownership of land to men who were eligible to citizenship. That measure, which was pointed straight against the Nipponese, was interpreted by spirited Japan as an intolerable insult.

Adding to the tension, the United States resisted imperialistic Japanese operations in China and was apprehensive of a possible Nipponese descent upon the Philippines. On the other hand, the absorption of Korea by Japan (1910) received the blessing of the State Department. As witness of the capacity of the United States to fight, a formidable American battle-fleet called at Japan in 1908, while on a dramatic round-the-globe cruise. This great "White Fleet" was the proudest and mightiest armada the Pacific had ever borne.

NAVAL EXPANSION

The upbuilding of American seapower typified in one way the advent of the United States to Great Power standing. If, as some naval historians teach, the United States in 1865 led the world in naval strength, the fleet thereafter was allowed to degenerate into innocuous unimportance. Rearmament commenced in the early eighties with the laying down of three steel cruisers, and when the conflict with Spain broke, the navy had regained international proportions. Fleet expansion will always be associated with Theodore Roosevelt, whose irresistible enthusiasm and tireless energy made the United States "navy conscious," precisely as Emperor William II was doing in Germany at the same period. The "Rough Rider" had a powerful and persuasive ally in Captain (later Rear Admiral) Alfred T. Mahan, the high-priest of seapower. Having written classical, if rambling, treatises on the influence of seapower upon history, Mahan counselled his countrymen on the present and future importance of naval strength and of fleet bases in distant regions, as essential for national greatness. Japanese naval power furnished a potent argument for enlargement of the fleet of the United States.

As President, Roosevelt watched, radiantly happy, while naval appropriations doubled. Upon his retirement from the White House, the American navy was surpassed only by the British, whereas it had ranked a mere fifth when he became President. Later, more powerful battleships, imitative of European dreadnaughts, were designed, and the United States was on the way to having, as Woodrow Wilson said (1916), "incomparably the most adequate navy in the world." As the same time Japan expanded her seapower, and competition in naval armaments aggravated tensions between the two major Pacific countries.

"ISOLATIONISM" WOBBLES

Until the very end of the nineteenth century, the United States heeded the admonitions of Washington and Jefferson to keep clear of political involvements with the world outside of the Americas. That tradition was threatened during the War between the States, when Napoleon III professed willingness to intervene in the civil struggle whenever Britain was ready to cooperate. But that moment never arrived. British shipmasters, it is true, built commerce raiders for the Confederacy, which gnawed away at Northern shipping. After the war, upon representations from Washington, Britain submitted the grievances over the raiders to arbitration, and damages in the amount of $15,000,000 were awarded (1871) to the United States.

After 1865 the United States kept more completely aloof from world politics than had been true in the forepart of the century—down to the War with Spain, that is. Nevertheless, the principle of isolation was not pursued in an absolute sense. Delegates of the United States attended international parleys of a technical character, for instance, and the Republic signed over a dozen pacts relating to patent rights, submarine cables and similar matters. Washington, moreover, joined the European nations in 1880 in insisting upon elementary rights for foreigners in Morocco, and took part in the Hague Peace Conferences (1899, 1907). As the century approached its end, the isolationist heritage was tossed aside so far as the Far East was concerned. Territorial gains in the western Pacific, the enunciation of the "Open Door," cooperation in the Boxer expedition and the activity of Roosevelt in the settlement of the Russo-Japanese War were visible marks of departure from established convention.

In the Old World, too, Roosevelt deviated from rigid adherence to the "hands off" formula. During the Moroccan crisis of 1905, he worked undercover to bring about a pacific accommodation between France and Germany. His contribution enhanced the diplomatic stature of the United States, though it was not at all decisive as Roosevelt liked to think; his was almost a case of chanticleer loudly crowing over the sunrise he had caused. When Morocco was again (1911) the direct cause of a terrifying European war scare, Washington studiously kept silent. On an over-all view, Rooseveltian diplomacy pointed toward a shifting attitude in the world relationships of the United States. As the "Rough Rider" read the signs of the times, "We have no choice, we people of the United States as to whether or not we shall play a great part in the world. That has been determined for us by fate, by the march of events. We have to play that part. All that we can decide is whether we shall play it well or ill."

And yet the United States displayed little interest in or understanding of the international anarchy in Europe which marked the decade before the First World War. With complete candor Woodrow Wilson asserted in December of 1913, "Many happy manifestations multiply about us of a growing cordiality . . . foreshadowing an era of settled peace and good will." Eight months after that optimistic utterance, the United States was shocked and stunned to learn that Europe was convulsed in a great and destructive war. Neutrality was immediately proclaimed. For nearly three years the trans-Atlantic Republic prayed that the bitter cup from which the Old World was drinking might be turned from its lips. But under circumstances previously reviewed, the United States in 1917 entered the titanic struggle.

That decision signified that the role of the United States in relation to the outer world had undergone an immense and fateful change. Temporarily the great Republic had cut adrift from aloofness, and had donned the robes of global leadership. But by spurning the Treaty of Versailles and the League Covenant embedded in it, the United States tacitly declared its desire to revert to the old policy of the free hand. The brief ascendancy of the United States in world politics resembled a rocket; it suddenly soared sky-high, dazzling the eyes of all beholders for a short spell, and then it fell lifeless, leaving the nations in semi-darkness. It was impossible, however, to ignore the stark and unpalatable truth that the United States was entangled, in fact, in every large issue of world affairs.

DIPLOMACY IN THE TWENTIES

So powerful was the post-war tide of nationalism, so strong the prejudice against the League of Nations, that the State Department for a time would not so much as acknowledge communications from that source. Bit by bit, however, that frigid posture moderated in favor of limited cooperation with the League. First, informal American observers were attached to League bodies and, after 1924, official representatives sat on committees dealing with economic and armament problems. A special corps of diplomatic agents was stationed at Geneva, the League headquarters. Thus far the United States would go, and no farther. It was not a pretty spectacle.

Pressure for entry into the League while vocal and energetic was ineffective. Among practical politicians, sentiment sympathetic to League membership dwindled with the years. Equally, the United States held aloof from the World Court, the lineal descendant of the pre-war Hague Tribunal. Several times the White House recommended joining the Court, but the Senate would not concur, for, although the Court was in reality a free agent, it had certain organic connections with the League. Individual Americans, on the other hand, served as judges in the Court and hundreds entered the employ of League agencies. As evidence of the increased importance of world affairs, and of the necessity for more efficient management of foreign policy, the Foreign Service of the United States underwent considerable reorganization in 1924. Not only were the consular and diplomatic branches amalgamated, but promotion of personnel in the service would be determined in the future by demonstrated merit. That rule did not apply to the highest diplomatic posts abroad, though it became standard practice to appoint to those positions individuals who had chosen the diplomatic service as their career.

Other symptoms of heightened attention to international affairs were much fuller treatment of world news by press (and radio) than before the war, and the organization of scores of societies, educational and propagandistic, learned or popular, to foster better understanding of world politics. Courses devoted to international affairs crowded into college and university curricula, and growing numbers of young men and women studied abroad in the summer months or for longer periods.

The United States in 1921 initiated a notable meeting in the interest of international tranquility. The five leading naval powers, and other nations having large stakes in the Orient,

Japanese delegates on the steps of the Capitol after the Washington Conference, 1921

except for distrusted Soviet Russia, were invited to Washington to work out plans to clear the murky political atmosphere over the Pacific and to reduce demands upon public treasuries for naval purposes. Particularly important were the steps taken to ease American-Japanese diplomatic tension and naval rivalry, which had picked up momentum after the war, and to aid tormented China in preserving national integrity.

Out of the Washington parley emerged several elaborate international engagements. Limitations were imposed upon capital warships and aircraft carriers of the major seapowers; tonnage of the United States and Great Britain would be equal, Japan would have 60 per cent of the strength of either of these countries and France and Italy each slightly more than half the fighting capacity of Nippon. As a special concession to Japan, the United States and Great Britain promised not to build new fleet bases or improve existing stations within proximity to Nippon.

It was agreed, furthermore, in a celebrated Nine-Power Treaty, that the nations would obey the "Open Door" in China; specifically and positively the powers, Japan among them, pledged themselves to the guiding American principles in China, equality of commercial opportunity and preservation of the territorial integrity of the country. Since the United States and the British Dominions in the Pacific took strong exception to the prolongation of the Anglo-Japanese Alliance, dating from 1902, that treaty was superseded by a Four Power Pact. Thereby the United States, Britain, Japan and France pledged themselves to respect the colonial possessions of each other in the Pacific and to refer any future quarrels to peaceful adjustment. It was a grandiose pronouncement which had precious little practical importance, save as it provided decent burial for the Anglo-Japanese Alliance. The whole Pacific settlement depended, really, upon the willingness of Japan to abide by her plighted word.

Sharply criticized by the naval-minded in all countries as conceding too much for too little in return, the fleet limitation understanding, nonetheless, quieted unhealthy international suspicions and lightened the burdens on taxpayers. A precedent, moreover, was established which might be applied to other types of armament. Indeed, at a London Conference (1930) the "Big Three" naval countries agreed to restrict lesser classes of warships; Japan obtained higher proportionate tonnage than in capital vessels. These naval bargains, which remained in force until 1936, confirmed the supremacy of Japan in eastern Asia.

Millions of Americans sincerely believed that the First World War had been in truth a war to end wars and that international strife was over and done with. They welcomed, consequently, a Pact of Paris (or Kellogg-Briand Pact) of 1928 which committed the nations not to resort to war as an instrument of national policy. The Pact, however, possessed only vague moral value, for no machinery was created to enforce the pledge and an appeal to arms for the sake of defense was not outlawed; any war could be interpreted as defensive.

FOREIGN ECONOMIC POLICIES

The post-war opinion in the United States was more favorable, if anything, to nationalist policies in economics than in politics. Indifferent to the implications of the fact that the United States had become a great creditor nation, the Congress in 1922 jacked up tariff rates to unprecedented levels. Few commodities, other than specialties and tropical goods, could be advantageously imported. And the notorious Hawley-Smoot Act of 1930 carried protection to skyscraper heights.

In spite of the difficulties of payment which tariff legislation imposed, the United States expected countries that had contracted loans during and after the war to "come across." The United States Treasury held claims upon some twenty nations for about $11,500,000,000. American economic experts argued that cancellation of these obligations would benefit the economy of the United States over the long pull, but their counsel was brushed aside as an academic vagary. Foreign governments had borrowed the money and they must pay up. Starting in 1923 funding treaties on war debts were negotiated which took into account the ability of the debtors to pay and scaled down interest charges. The Allies expected war reparations from Germany to cover their remittances to the United States. Reparations and war debts were in fact Siamese twins, a relationship which Washington declined to concede. None is so blind as he who will not see. Financial geniuses from the United States twice served at conferences that revised German reparations downward, but the American government itself had nothing officially to do with these transactions.

After the war, sales of American products abroad topped all records, soaring to new highs in the boom years of the late twenties. And, as had not been true for generations, a large proportion of the exports was hauled in American bottoms, for the post-war cargo fleet approached 15,000,000 tons. Up to a point, foreign sales were financed by American private lending on a prodigious scale; as of 1930 the stake overseas, counting both private and governmental loans, exceeded $29,000,000,000. When capital stopped flowing abroad from the United States, economic maladjustments, hitherto concealed, took charge. As the Great Depression tragically advertised, the United States had attained the dominant place in global economy.

Radical innovations on immigration to the United States also reflected the nationalist mood after the war. Upwards of 800,000 newcomers entered "the land of promise" in 1921, not so many as in certain pre-war years, but a host nevertheless. It was argued that unless limitations were imposed, millions would pour in from impoverished, war-weary Europe, flooding the labor market and aggravating the task of social assimilation. A torrent of anti-foreignism, moreover, set rolling doubtless by the frustrated idealism arising out of the war, culminated in the shameless Ku Klux Klan fanaticism.

As early as 1917, a literacy test was required

of immigrants, and Orientals, apart from the Japanese and the Filipinos, were totally excluded. A novel "quota" principle appeared in a law of 1921 which restricted immigration of each nationality to 3 per cent of that group resident in the United States as of 1910. That tentative measure was supplanted by an act of 1924 cutting the percentage to two and fixing 1890 as the test year. Northern and northwestern Europe benefited by that arrangement; on the other hand, only about 5,800 Italians, for instance, might enter in any year. By damming up the emigrant flow, the United States encouraged unrest in Europe and nourished agitation for colonial expansion.

One clause in the act of 1924 was designed to appease Japanophobes in the Pacific coast states. It denied admission to aliens ineligible to citizenship, which meant, actually, the Japanese. If the quota rule on immigration had been applied, as the State Department strongly recommended, only about 146 Japanese would have come in annually; that number, no matter how prolific, would not possibly have endangered white supremacy in California.

Whether so intended or not, the exclusion clause argued that Nippon had not faithfully observed the "gentlemen's agreement" of 1907, an entirely groundless insinuation. Exclusion was a criminally complacent insult to a cocky and morbidly proud nation, and it was never forgotten.[2] Resentment against the United States rose to new heights, and down to the attack upon Pearl Harbor relations with the New World Republic meant for the ordinary Japanese discriminatory exclusion primarily.

DOMESTIC TIDES

From Versailles to Pearl Harbor life inside the United States was gaudy and chaotic. After

[2] Japanese feelings had been severely rasped by the failure to write a racial equality statement into the preamble of the League Covenant; blame for that was popularly pinned upon Woodrow Wilson.

Part of a General Motors assembly plant in 1922

a sharp business recession in 1920–21 the country entered upon a boom which roared along until 1929. Industrial output per man-hour rose steadily due to improved manufacturing techniques, heavier investments in equipment, greater efficiency of workers and smarter managerial methods. Mechanical energy performed miracles of mass production that were reflected in lower costs—and sometimes in lower prices. For most American workmen, real wages, or what money wages could buy, moved upward, and that broadly determined how well they were able to live. Luxuries became comforts, comforts became necessities as the general popularity of the automobile sufficiently illustrated. Hours of work declined allowing more leisure, and improving health lengthened life expectancy.

Public educational facilities expanded at an impressive pace. The school-leaving age was raised and attendance in high school and college bounded upward. No large nation since history began had known the comforts and conveniences that the United States enjoyed in the late twenties, and they would not be duplicated until after the Second World War. In the billowing wave of prosperity it was easy for President Herbert Hoover to say that America was on the verge of eliminating poverty and want.

The wealth of the nation, as later its woe, overflowed national frontiers. The American business spirit spread overseas along with American technological triumphs. Winds from across the Atlantic blew into Europe American ideas, methods, gadgets, Coca-Cola, safety razors, vacuum cleaners and buying on the installment plan. Hollywood celluloid products, "the shock troops of American culture," acquainted the world with slices of American life—love, home and Cinderella—and roused either admiration or envy for the New World standards of comfort.

Golden prosperity, it must be said, did not reach into all American homes. Changes in manufacturing methods deprived some workers of jobs, textile and coal production suffered in slack seasons and the disparities between town and countryside widened. Foreign markets for farm commodities, especially for wheat and cotton, fell away, and, adding to rural problems, Mother Earth yielded bumper harvests. Cries ascended to heaven—and to Congress—for farm relief. Plainly the ascendancy of Amer-

The Prohibition Law in action— a speakeasy interior, circa 1927

Bread line, New York, 1931

ican agriculture running back to the colonial epoch had passed. Despite increasing urbanization, over a quarter of the American population still followed the slow and sure ways of the older rural United States. That element exerted a large influence upon the country as a whole, through a powerful agricultural lobby in Washington, and in manners and morals and in the steady rejuvenation of the cities by fresh young blood from the farmlands. Small towns in rural America, moreover, were strongholds of nineteenth-century conceptions of economic individualism.

Much of the most sophisticated literature of the period lampooned or severely criticized contemporary society. Bottomless cynicism was fostered by flagrant evasion of legislation, which came into force in 1919, prohibiting the sale of alcoholic beverages; until abandoned in 1933 Prohibition nourished high-powered lawlessness, lucrative racketeering and gang wars by "bootleggers." The *American Mercury*, a journal edited by Henry L. Mencken, and the novels of F. Scott Fitzgerald, such as *The Great Gatsby*, interpreted the lusty and seamy social mores of the "Jazz Age."

The most provocative author of the time was no doubt Sinclair Lewis, the first American to carry off Nobel laurels for literature. His stream of novels (*Main Street; Babbitt; Arrowsmith; Dodsworth*) depicted, with a wealth of picturesque detail, the vapid narrowness of small town existence, provincial prides and prejudices, religious vagaries and the morals of scientific research. Of Lewis—"Red" to his cronies—a frank critic wrote that he was better at "caricature than at character." He gave foreign readers as crudely distorted impressions of the United States as moving pictures did.

THE GREAT DEPRESSION

Interest in critical literature was dwarfed, however, by interest in the boisterous Stock Market. Intoxicating stories of easy money and overnight fortunes without effort cast a rosy hue over the public imagination. Wonderful expectations of buying a low-priced stock and then reaping a hundred for it lured unwary amateurs with surplus funds—veteran professionals, too—into the profit parade. But in the autumn of 1929, the gilded bubble suddenly exploded, blowing away $30,000,000,000 of fictitious values in two months. The gravity of the crisis was not sensed immediately, yet before long it was evident that this was not just another panic, such as was familiar in United States history.

The hurricane which swept Wall Street unloosed the Great Depression, entailing hardships and despair the globe around. Confidence in the capitalist system suffered a profound shock, and heretical voices shouted that long hallowed "axioms" of economics were not suitable for the complexities and strains of industrial society. In this hour of social jeopardy panaceas flourished, and Soviet collectivism competed, as never before, with the individualist philosophy of America for the allegiance of the Western world.

From 1929 to 1933 the United States staggered under the relentless punches of the Great Depression. Prices deflated rapidly, foreign trade tumbled by two-thirds in three years, farm incomes dropped as huge agricultural surpluses piled up and rotted, and expenditures for industrial equipment fell off sharply. At the lowest point of the "hard times," 13,000,000 could find no employment. National income in 1933 was only half that of 1929. Business failures, mortgage foreclosures, rioting in rural areas, the closing of banks and soaring government deficits bore witness to the creeping economic paralysis and loss of national confidence.

Hesitantly and reluctantly the federal government launched public projects to provide employment, took crop surpluses off the market and rallied to the rescue of banks and railways. As a "temporary" substitute for private banks whose lending functions had been paralyzed, the government created in 1932 the Reconstruction Finance Corporation to shore up distressed banks, to keep railroads out of receivership and to furnish credit to farmers. These measures foreshadowed the unexampled activity of the federal government in the economic sphere which began in 1933.

THE NEW DEAL

With President F. D. Roosevelt as captain on the bridge, America sailed across a sea of economic experimentation called the "New Deal." Whereas Great Britain under the impact of depression switched to the Right in politics, the swing in the United States was Leftward. Social innovators, tagged the President's "brain trust," and more or less under the influence of the theories of J. M. Keynes, mobilized the resources and authority of the national government to fight the depression and to give "the forgotten man" security and a chance to better his fortunes. Critics of Rooseveltian policies, thinking in terms of conventional economics, contended that state intervention in economic activity would hinder recovery, create a bureaucratic octopus and push the national debt to unbearable heights. Natural economic forces, it was argued, if left to themselves would operate powerfully toward the restoration of equilibrium. But the opponents of the "New Deal" could not win a majority of the electorate to their convictions.

The New Deal in its diversity and magnitude amounted to a revolution. It applied to statecraft the philosophy of pragmatism. It assumed that society was plastic, susceptible to experimentation and it justified specific acts by their expediency or their results. On the principle that society owed a job to everyone who could work, a series of measures attacked the grim mountain of unemployment frontally. Funds poured from the national treasury for a variety of public works enterprises or to provide at least sustenance for the workless. Millions of the idle were engaged to build roads, drain swamps, pretty up parks, clear squalid slums and construct housing and school facilities.

Manufacturing industry was somewhat stimulated by the suspension of anti-monopoly laws, and the adoption of codes to curtail unfair competition in each type of production or by emergency loans from Washington. Banks were required to qualify for clean bills of health before resuming operations and the currency was manipulated in order to inflate prices, lighten debt burdens and invigorate foreign trade. Looking toward freer international commerce, legislation of 1934 encouraged larger imports by a selective reduction of tariffs, in return for concessions on American goods by other countries. Nauseating practices that had disfigured the sale of stocks in the fevered twenties were fought with regulatory acts.

GROWTH OF UNIONS

Unionization of industrial workers was promoted by laws in 1935 that obligated management to bargain collectively, stipulated that a majority of the workers in any establishment might speak for the entire group and banned "company" unions. By this legislation, the government converted unions from private associations of workers into semi-public institutions. A number of new unions, known eventually as the Congress of Industrial Organizations (C. I. O.), split off from the American Federation of Labor (A. F. of L.). Holding that the organization of workers by crafts, the A. F. of L. principle, was inappropriate for mass production plants, the C. I. O. created vertical unions in industries. It recruited the bulk of its members in the coal mining, automobile and steel industries. The C. I. O. soon boasted as many members as the well-established A. F. of L. and outmatched it in enthusiasm and militancy. By 1940 about 8,000,000 workers belonged to unions, nearly a four fold growth since 1933. Organized labor had become a major force in American affairs and its leaders commanded immense power.

More or less in imitation of time-tested European precedents, social security laws were written (1935) into the statute books. Under a system of contributory pensions many classes of workers were assured of retirement benefits at the age of sixty-five, and compulsory unemployment insurance laws guaranteed an income of about half their normal earnings to the jobless. Public assistance was authorized for aged unemployables, for the blind and for widows with dependent children. Minimum wage rates were prescribed, child labor banned and the interests of working women more adequately safeguarded.

THE CASE OF AGRICULTURE

After more than a decade of agitation for effective measures to lift agriculture out of the doldrums, Congress in 1933 passed the Agriculture Adjustment Act. The original measure and revised versions represented one of the most striking pieces of social engineering ever applied in a capitalistic community; they called for the active cooperation of millions of farmers. In essence, the farm program was intended to establish "parity," or a fair relationship between the prices received by the grower and the cost of the things he had to buy, and to regulate agricultural production in keeping with demand. At the outset, marketing quotas were set for a few key crops such as cotton, wheat and corn, but the list was subsequently broadened until half of all farm products were covered. Farmers who agreed to curtail output would be generously compensated by the government, and the government would also buy up surpluses and withhold them from the market.

Whatever its defects, the agricultural laws relieved the plight of farmers who operated on a commercial scale. In time the upswing of "sheltered" prices tended to interfere with sales of farm commodities to foreign countries. And the fundamental idea of restricted production irritated Americans who believed that a high level of output and low unit cost were indispensable for economic health.

In the thirties, cooperative societies for the purchase of goods required by farmers and for the sale of agricultural products expanded notably. And the shift from animal power to machinery in working the land proceeded without abatement, being much accelerated during the Second World War. More tractors, mechanical corn-pickers, cotton-pickers and milkers, and two-row tobacco planters upheld the primacy of the United States in labor-saving farm implements. It was said that a farmer of 1945, equipped with machinery, produced as much as thirty farmers of 1830 with hand tools. Revolutionary contrivances displaced thousands of farm laborers, particularly Negroes in the South, many of whom drifted to Northern cities in search of employment.

Primarily for the benefit of the rural population in the Tennessee Valley, an area more than double the size of Texas, the Tennessee Valley Authority was created in 1933 under government auspices. It was empowered to develop the hydro-electric resources of the region, to promote industrial development and control floods—a gigantic adventure in public planning, suggestive of Soviet projects. Plans for rural electrification, a godsend on the isolated farm, were pressed forward.

A BALANCE SHEET

Balancing matters up, the New Deal, together with the operation of undercover economic processes, restored confidence in the prostrate economy with surprising speed, and alleviated the burning discontent of the poor. Business indices of the late thirties marched up and down, it is true, but by 1939 national production had reached a new high record. And yet an estimated 10,000,000 still lacked regular jobs. Presently armament contracts from Europe and, more importantly, orders to accommodate the enormous defense requirements of the United States itself, set industrial wheels humming.

To finance New Deal measures, taxes on large incomes were raised and borrowing increased the national debt by nearly $20,000,000,000. It was believed that a substantial part of the debt would be cancelled by repayment of grants extended to various enterprises. As never before it was recognized that great inequalities of fortune and the concentration of financial power were sources of instability and weakness in America. In consequence, tax rates in the higher income brackets were steeply increased and basic social services were either given free or subsidized by the government. More than that, the United States was committed to the principle that a high level of national income and employment was essential and must be maintained at all costs, compatible with the preservation of fundamental individual freedoms. As another result, the authority of the federal government was considerably enlarged, and so, for good or ill, was the authority of the executive branch of the government.

During the Great Depression the American economy had been shown to be flexible enough to undergo far-reaching changes without unloosing serious disorders. Looked at in broad perspective, it was astonishing that the cruelest depression in American history had not diverted more men to the anticapitalist ideologies so popular across the Atlantic. Marxism in any of its varieties remained fundamentally a hot-house product of American metropolitan centers; at the presidential election of 1936 barely one voter in every two hundred, taking the nation as a whole, cast a ballot for either the democratic Socialist or the Communist candidate.

Even the unemployed in the United States were not persuaded that they lived in a stratified society or that class warfare was the best weapon to overcome their afflictions. It could be said without smugness that living levels of Americans on relief compared favorably with current standards of the employed skilled artisan in the Old World.

Communism won over some left-wing intellectuals, who had no inconsiderable importance in the hey-day of the New Deal, and captured a few trade unions. At its peak Communist Party membership reached 130,000, though many sympathizers with the doctrines of Moscow refused to align themselves openly with the party. Only two avowed Communists were elected to public office, both of them to the city council in New York.

Another anticapitalist group, the American Labor Party, appeared on the horizon in the midst of the depression. But its appeal was confined almost entirely to New York State and it showed no sign of repeating the spectacular growth of the British Labour Party. It was as plain as a pikestaff that the American spirit was still predominantly individualistic, and it seemed equally clear that the economic problems of the country would be resolved within the existing institutions of democracy.

THE GOOD NEIGHBOR

The Great Depression touched off violent political disturbances in Latin America. In many of the countries, government was overturned by revolutions, and "authoritative democracies," more or less thinly disguised police regimes, took command. Carefully avoiding previous procedures, the United States did not intervene to safeguard life and property. Marines moved into and out of Nicaragua, it is true, but in 1933, they were finally evacuated; and in 1934, troops were called home from Haiti, the last of the Latin Republics to be garrisoned by the arms of the United States. Beyond that, the United States renounced its special privileges in Cuba, except for the naval station, and financial controls in Santo Domingo and Haiti were abandoned (1941).

These acts harmonized with the policy of the Good Neighbor which President Roosevelt phrased in 1933 as "the neighbor who respects his obligations and respects the sanctity of his agreements in and with a world of neighbors." Hinted at before the First World War, this approach in United States diplomacy had been applied in the twenties in dealings with revolutionary Mexico; the "retreat from imperialism" south of the border had unmistakably begun. Old wounds had been reopened when Mexico nationalized oil lands and other properties owned by foreigners and laid restrictions upon the Catholic Church, her clergy and schools.

So acute did tensions become that in 1927 talk of war with Mexico was heard. That year a special United States ambassador, Dwight Morrow, poured oil on the troubled Mexican waters. Through his intelligent and conciliatory gestures a compromise was worked out which quieted the confused and acrimonious quarrel over property rights and a temporary accommodation was effected in the delicate Church issues. Later on, arrangements were made for Mexico to purchase the oil fields—a plan acceptable to Washington, if displeasing to financial interests in the United States.

At successive Pan-American conferences, meanwhile, very real progress toward hemispheric solidarity was being achieved. Gradually these gatherings ceased to be "congresses of mice presided over by a cat," as South American publicists, distrustful of the United States, had once tagged them. Under spirited pressure from the Latin Republics, Washington announced in 1933 that it would not interfere militarily on its own initiative in the countries to the south. In the future the maintenance of law and order would be the collective responsibility of all the American Republics. That interpretation of the Good Neighbor concept was highly gratifying to Latin *amour propre*.

In 1936 the American Republics pledged themselves to mutual consultation in the event that the safety of the New World was threatened from outside. And, crowning the trend toward hemispheric solidarity, it was agreed in 1940 that any attempt by a non-American power upon any American Republic would be equivalent to an attack upon all. Although Canada lay outside the circle of Republics, it was given assurances in 1938 that if its integrity should be challenged, the United States would not stand idly by. Naturally enough, the United States retained leadership in New World politics, but its role was that of first among equals, no longer the wielder of "the Big Stick."

Pursuit of the Good Neighbor philosophy caused resentment and suspicion of "the Northern Colossus'" to taper off in the Latin states. Commerce expanded with growing good will, so that in 1939 a third of the foreign trade of the South American countries was transacted with the United States. Yankee salesmen discovered that business benefited if they knew the language of the people with whom they traded and offered products appealing to customer tastes. New York financial houses replaced European money markets as the principal source of capital for Latin America. In spite of staggering defaults during the Great Depression, United States investments approached $3,000,000,000 as of 1940. Cultural bonds between North and South were laced tighter by a broad program of intellectual and artistic interchange, fuller press coverage and increasing study of the history and languages of Latin America in the United States.

As the Second World War approached, Washington was disturbed by evidence of Fascist influences in several of the Latin American states. Naturalized Italians and Germans carried considerable weight in the larger countries. Germans served as advisers of presidents and German-trained military men dabbled in politics. A ceaseless volume of praise for authoritarian doctrines flowed across from Franco's Spain. Nevertheless, the Latin countries spontaneously followed the Northern Republic into the Second World War, Chile and Argentina, the declared rival of the United States for leadership in Latin America, lagging behind the others. Supplies of oil and strategic minerals were shipped to the United States for war industry and military missions from the United States aided Latin Republics in building up their fighting services. Brazil placed airfields at the disposal of the United States and actually despatched an expeditionary force to the battlefront in Italy.

TROUBLES IN THE ORIENT

While the United States was quietly putting the "Big Stick" in the spacious closet of history, Japan was brandishing a similar instrument over eastern Asia. Under circumstances discussed in the next chapter, Nipponese troops charged into Chinese Manchuria in the autumn of 1931. It was evident that Japan intended to detach the region from Chinese sovereignty.

The United States instantly assumed leadership of the opposition to Japanese brigandage. Repeatedly and sharply Tokyo was reminded that it was infringing upon the "Open Door" and transgressing other international engagements. Spokesmen of Japan artfully justified the Manchurian operations by pointing to the United States precedents in Latin America, such as the Panama incident and the many armed interventions in Mexico and Caribbean countries. Engrossed as it was with the depression, the United States was not disposed to grasp the nettle firmly, to apply force to bring the law-breaker to book. Washington cooperated, however, with the League of Nations in exerting moral pressure upon Japan; and the United States issued (1932) the Stimson Doctrine, notifying Tokyo that it would not recognize the validity of any territorial change brought about in defiance of international usage. But Japan plunged ahead in the conquest.

With an ineptitude that amounted almost to genius, Japan asserted in 1934 that she had an exclusive mandate for the preservation of "peace and order in eastern Asia." Nations that were assisting Nationalist China to develop her economic and military resources were sternly upbraided. To those declarations and their implications, Washington dissented vigorously. Japan countered with protests over measures which hampered exports to the United States, where business interests had grown apprehensive of cheap Nipponese manufactures.

It was at this time that the United States passed (1934) legislation promising the Philippines independence after a period of transition. That act was construed to mean that the United States intended to pull completely out of the Orient. To the traditional arguments against retention of the archipelago, two others had been added: certain farm organizations and sugar growers in the United States wished to be rid of Filipino competition, and exclusionists wanted immigration of Filipinos restricted. Although independence of the islands was voted, the United States still felt responsible for the security of the Asiatic ward. The decision to set the Philippines free invigorated agitations for independence in other white empires of the East.

Another link in the growing chain of American-Japanese antagonism was forged in 1936 when Japan cancelled the Treaties of Washington and London restricting naval tonnage. As the price of the prolongation of the limitation pacts, Japan had demanded equality with the United States in all classes of warships. To that Washington retorted—London seconding—that existing treaty ratios afforded Nippon equality of security, which was all that could reasonably be expected. With the lapsing of limitation agreements, a typical race in naval armaments ensued. Stories circulated in the United States that Japan was constructing giant, heavily weaponed battleships and was developing major fleet bases and submarine lairs in the Pacific mandated islands, which was true.

American naval appropriations of 1938 soared to $1,000,000,000, foreshadowing the creation of a two-ocean navy. Fleet facilities in the Philippines were somewhat improved, but

Survivors from U.S.S. Panay *landing medical supplies after the bombing*

Congress declined to appropriate funds to reconstruct the dilapidated naval station on Guam. Relations between the two great Pacific powers took a definite turn for the worse when Japan launched full-scale war against China in the summer of 1937. President Roosevelt pleaded that international law-breakers should be quarantined—he had one eye cocked on Europe—but the Congressional response was unsympathetic.

In prosecuting campaigns against China, Japan flagrantly trampled upon the rights and interests of the United States. The American gunboat *Panay* was sunk by Nipponese airmen, a deliberate act of war. Yet Washington contented itself with stiff protests, accepted profuse Japanese apologies and a financial indemnity. Personal indignities were inflicted upon American nationals in China and arbitrary Japanese regulations interfered with commercial transactions. The Chinese door was being slammed shut just like the Manchurian. American investments in excess of $200,000,000, about a sixteenth of all foreign capital in China, were imperiled as were philanthropic and missionary establishments. Atrocities upon Chinese civilians and indiscriminate Japanese air bombardments of cities enflamed humanitarian passions in the United States. First and last, the State Department filed over two hundred separate protests in Tokyo on depredations and treaty violations.

As a mark of friendship for embattled China, the United States in 1938 furnished small credits for planes, trucks and other military supplies. Next, the commercial treaty with Japan was abrogated. On the other hand, American companies sold oil and scrap iron to Nippon and contingents of marines were evacuated from Chinese districts seized by Japan.

The course of events in the Orient increased the predictions of an "inevitable" conflict between the United States and Japan, which had been current for two generations. Nippon had embarked upon a relentless drive for economic self-sufficiency and for political domination over eastern Asia at least. The United States stood forth as the principal, almost the solitary antagonist of unbridled Japanese expansion. Washington desired China to be independent, strong, friendly, and it desired a power balance in the Orient. Unless Japan or the United States drastically modified its attitudes, a clash of arms could scarcely be avoided.

CLOUDS OVER EUROPE

Growing tension with Japan had a part in leading the United States to establish diplomatic relations with Soviet Russia. Ever since the Bolshevik Revolution the two titans had proceeded officially as though the other did not exist. Not only was the United States repelled by Red totalitarianism, the maltreatment of dissenters, doubts as to the stability of the Communist regime and persecution of religion, but it had financial claims upon Moscow, amounting to about $650,000,000, for loans to pre-Bolshevik Russia and for confiscated properties of American citizens. Poisonous Communist propaganda in behalf of world-wide revolution and alleged "dumping" of Soviet goods produced by forced labor fed the fires of distrust and hatred. It was argued that the United States should have no official contacts with a country that would like to tear the American house to pieces and that forced people to work against their will.

On the other side, spokesmen of the Soviet Union kept declaiming against the intervention of small contingents of American troops in northern Russia and Siberia after the Bolshevik seizure of power. Kremlin statisticians with sharp pencils drew up a formidable bill of damages against the United States for the intervention. According to Moscow, moreover, the United States constituted a vital link in the menacing "capitalist encirclement" of the Communist Commonwealth.

Despite the refusal of the United States to recognize Russia, American firms carried on more business with the Soviet Union than had been transacted in the day of the tsars. In 1930 American sales to Russia had shown a gain, in contrast to the decline in exports to thirty-seven other countries. But then shipments contracted sharply, though it was obvious that Russia offered an enormous potential market for American products. Diplomatic recognition, sanguine spirits reasoned, would facilitate sales.

By 1933, at any rate, it was plain for all to see that the Communist regime was a going concern, not likely to collapse as had once been confidently predicted. Except for the United States, the Great Powers had all entered into ordinary diplomatic intercourse with Moscow, though some of them had subsequently broken off relations. A Russia friendly to the United States would be a diplomatic asset, it was contended, in view of the pugnacity of Japan and the assertiveness of the Fascist dictatorships in Europe. Those lines of argument, commercial and diplomatic, finally weighted the balance in the direction of recognition. Foes of recognition, however, clung to the opinion that to deal with Soviet Russia was a sin against the light, an invitation to Communist infiltration.

On the initiative of President Roosevelt, conversations with the Kremlin were undertaken and in November, 1933, an understanding was worked out. In return for recognition, Moscow promised that Americans in Russia might worship freely and that Communist activities in the United States would be stopped; no settlement was reached on financial claims and counterclaims. Thereafter, envoys were exchanged between the two countries, commerce with the Soviet Union increased somewhat, but the pledge to restrain revolutionary propaganda in the United States was not faithfully executed.

Japan on the rampage was alarming, but the welter of hates and fears in Europe excited

Franklin D. Roosevelt as President

much greater and increasing alarm in the United States. While the dicatorship of Mussolini rasped democratic sensibilities, Nazi Germany was far more loathsome. Abuse of Jews and dissenters, the denial of liberties and freedoms and the horrors of the concentration camp generated hostility and hatred. Anxieties about the future multiplied as the dictatorships —brown and black—exhausted the resources of legal violence by diplomatic *coups*.

Yet there was another side to the American picture. A fresh wave of disillusionment about the First World War and its aftermath had raced across the Republic. Pacifistic literature and movies, works of historical exposition, popular and scholarly, and Senatorial investigations of the antecedents of the entry of the United States into war in 1917 pointed to the conclusion that participation had been a piece of arrant folly. Public counsels were darkened by a cloud of accusations ascribing involvement to insidious British propaganda or to the soulless machinations of profit-seeking munitions merchants and banking houses or to an unneutral President who naively thought the war might conceivably be turned to constructive ends. Ominous war-breeding developments abroad, moreover, shattered the widely cherished illusion that the United States in 1917 had fought a war to end war. And, to swell the chorus of disillusionment, European countries, except Finland, suspended payments on war debts.

A shrewd British observer of the American scene summed up one facet of the dominant mood in this way:

"We Americans went into the last war to save democracy. We pulled you out of a hole and we received very grudging thanks. At Versailles and after Versailles you trampled on democratic ideals. Now, largely through your own fault, you are in trouble again and you want our help. Well, we've learnt our lesson." [3]

Neutrality laws which were enacted in 1935–1937 reflected the prevailing mood of America. Advocates of this legislation reasoned that measures to prevent certain things that figured in the background of intervention in 1917 would keep the country clear of future conflict in Europe. Yet history never quite repeats itself, though historians repeat one another. According to the Neutrality Acts, whenever the President declared that an actual state of war ex-

[3] R. H. B. Lockhart, *Comes the Reckoning* (London, 1947), p. 25.

isted, it would be unlawful to export munitions or extend credits to any belligerent; other cargoes might be shipped to a warring country only if they were paid for in advance and hauled away in foreign vessels; and no American might travel on a ship flying a belligerent flag. These laws applied to civil wars as well as to struggles between countries.

As Europe moved toward the Second World War, President Roosevelt time and again published apocalyptic warnings of woe to come. He earnestly pleaded with foreign governments, especially with the dictator states, to settle disputes around a council table. At the same time the Administration facilitated undercover purchases of airplanes by Britain and France and pushed steadily for the enlargement of American fighting services. Neutrality laws or not, one could not be certain that if war came to Europe the United States would find it politic to remain aloof, or would indeed be able to do so.

When the fighting actually started the President, after recalling the efforts of the United States to preserve peace, said, "Some day . . . we can be of even greater help to crippled humanity . . . the influence of America should be consistent in seeking for humanity a final peace which will eliminate, as far as it is possible to do so, the continued use of force between nations. . . . I hope," he went on with inimitable buoyancy, "the United States will keep out of this war. I believe that it will. And I give you assurance and reassurance that every effort of your government will be directed toward that end."

IN SUM

Roosevelt spoke to a nation of some 130,000,000, a country very different from the America of a hundred and fifty years earlier. Instead of a young Republic of about 4,000,000 along the Atlantic seaboard, the United States now stretched from sea to shining sea with dependencies in the Atlantic and Pacific, though the Philippines were on the way to self-rule. Commercial and financial relationships with foreign peoples and powers had grown large and diverse.

The New World giant possessed the mightiest military potential in the world, resting upon immense productive capacities. The principal responsibility for keeping international order, which Britain had shouldered with no inconsiderable success in the nineteenth century, had passed to the United States. And for peace of mind in America, a peaceful globe had become a prerequisite.

On the anvil of experience fundamental principles in dealing with foreign states had been hammered out. The "Shield of the Republic" reflected both national interests and national needs. The interest above all other interests was security, a goal unattainable in any absolute sense. Shifting tides of power politics and changes in the tools of war determined the degree of security which the United States enjoyed at any particular time.

Pan-American solidarity and continentalism engaged more universal support in the United States than general international collaboration, though flashes of the latter were not wanting. Foreign struggles for freedom and democracy enlisted American sympathies against tyranny in any guise. Arbitral procedures had adjusted most controversies with foreign nations, though wars had been fought with Britain (1812), Mexico (1846), Spain (1898), Germany and Austria (1917), a bit of a war with France (1799) and skirmishes with Russia (1919), not to overlook many military interventions in Latin America and the Boxer action in China.

The 1930's were a singularly rugged decade in the history of the United States. Before victory in a campaign against blighting depression had been won, the Republic was faced by the grim peril of shooting wars in the Orient and in Europe. The role of the State in economic matters had expanded notably, paralleling the broad trend in the Old World though at a slower, more halting pace.

Withal the United States had attained adulthood. It was by way of assuming a place in international affairs that involved more in terms of responsibilities than of privileges. Only reluctantly, with doubts, hesitations and inconsistencies would a world role be undertaken, and yet not without courage and energy.

FOR FURTHER STUDY

SAMUEL F. BEMIS, *The United States as a World Power* (New York, 1950)
FREDERICK L. ALLEN, *The Big Change, America Transforms Itself, 1900–1950* (New York, 1952) PAPERBACK
DEXTER PERKINS, *The American Approach to Foreign Policy* (new ed., Cambridge, Mass., 1962)
JULIUS W. PRATT, *America's Colonial Experiment* (New York, 1950)
ALFRED W. GRISWOLD, *The Far Eastern Policy of the United States* (New York, 1938)
JAMES W. ANGELL, *Financial Foreign Policy of the United States* (New York, 1933)
BROADUS MITCHELL, *The Depression Decade* (New York, 1947)
DENIS W. BROGAN, *The Era of Franklin D. Roosevelt* (New Haven, 1950)
ALLAN NEVINS, *The United States in a Chaotic World* (New Haven, 1950)
JOHN K. FAIRBANK, *The United States and China* (Cambridge, Mass., 1948) PAPERBACK
CHARLES C. TANSILL, *Backdoor to War* (Chicago, 1952)
FOSTER R. DULLES, *America's Rise to World Power* (New York, 1955) PAPERBACK
GABRIEL A. ALMOND, *The American People and Foreign Policy* (New York, 1960) PAPERBACK
ARTHUR M. SCHLESINGER, JR., *The Crisis of the Old Order* (Boston, 1957)
HARRIS G. WARREN, *Herbert Hoover and the Great Depression* (New York, 1959)
JOHN K. GALBRAITH, *The Great Crash* (Boston, 1955) PAPERBACK
JAMES M. BURNS, *Roosevelt: The Lion and the Fox* (New York, 1956)
DAVID LAWRENCE, *Stumbling into Socialism* (New York, 1935)
DONALD F. DRUMMOND, *The Passing of American Neutrality* (Ann Arbor, 1956)
JACQUES MARITAIN, *Reflections on America* (New York, 1958)

CHAPTER XXIX

ASIA IN GLOBAL PERSPECTIVE

THE TROUBLED EAST

NATIVE unrest in Asia before 1914 foreshadowed the eventual crumbling of the Western colonial regime and the end of the dominion of the white man. Japanese success in the war with Russia in 1905 quickened national prides from China to Egypt. The First World War, attended as it was by idealistic statements by Allied leaders on the rights of small nations and democratic themes, fostered hopes of freedom and independence among politically conscious subject peoples of Asia.

From one end of Asia to the other, the wretched conditions under which the masses lived fed discontent and revolutionary passions. In particular the illiterate and fecund peasants, the key social class of Asia, existed in terrible misery. Their abysmal poverty was—and still is—the common denominator of Asiatic countries; even when harvests were good, millions of stomachs knew lean months. Chronic undernourishment or starvation had long prevailed and had been endured with stoical resignation as the unavoidable bludgeoning of fate. The prospect of death because of food shortage undoubtedly meant more to Asiatics than dislike of political oppression.

In a fundamental sense, the poverty and distress of Asia were consequences of the huge and growing populations crowding desperately upon the resources of tillable land. Improved communication facilities and Western medical science, together with a greater measure of public order, interfered with the traditional corrective factors of overpopulation —famine, disease and war. While numbers increased greatly, methods of farming showed little or no change, remaining primitive and inefficient for the most part. Existing on lowly levels and in blissful ignorance, Asiatics, especially in the eastern and southern areas, displayed little sense of responsibility either to their offspring or to society. The idea of family limitation collided with ancient moral conventions and rooted habits of unrestrained reproduction. Multiplication of babies frustrated the concept of good government as the greatest happiness for the greatest number.

Old-established economic customs, moreover, aggravated the social evils arising from overpopulation. Many peasants, for instance, hired all or part of their land from local proprietors who exacted exorbitant rentals, or they toiled away for pittances on plantations or other enterprises owned by capitalistic interests. Whenever "hard times" befell the peasant, whether because of short harvests, or illness, or some other cause, he was obliged to borrow from an unscrupulous village moneylender, offering his future crops as security. As a rule, loans carried extortionate interest charges and often placed the borrower in the avaricious grip of the usurer for years. Over large sections of Asia, furthermore, tax burdens laid upon the peasantry were excessive and often inequitably levied; the common custom of graft on the part of rapacious officials drained away another portion of the meager peasant income. Asiatic soil-workers, in a sentence, were victims of oppression by the small well-to do classes allied with the governing bureaucracies.

The impact of the West, pervasive and varied in expression, encouraged a spirit of revolt in Asia. For one thing, the importation of Western learning fostered instability and restlessness among politically conscious minorities, especially among the professional and intellectual classes that had been trained as a native bureaucracy to meet the need of Western rulers. Instruction in schools and colleges operated by Christian missionaries or by native governments disturbed long-accepted religious and moral convictions and challenged established standards of moral values. Social practices such as the subjection of women and the subservience of children to fathers were loosened by knowledge of the freer ways of the West. Equally, knowledge of better social conditions in the West persuaded backward peoples that their misery was not inevitable, and could be swiftly remedied. Asiatics who studied in Europe or in the United States frequently became rabid agitators for drastic changes in their homelands.

Western revolutionary doctrines of 1776 and 1789 excited self-conscious national emotions in Asia. Awakening love of country inspired demands for full national independence, liberation from Western controls and the cancellation of special rights and privileges that had accumulated in the nineteenth century. Cries arose for the withdrawal of foreign troops and administrative officials and the abandonment of foreign property rights. Likewise from the West came ideas of political democracy, concepts of constitutionalism and parliamentary government, which clashed with the Asiatic heritage of despotism or of oligarchic rule. Upon static Asia the political principles and practices of the West wrought with explosive force. Tennyson had sung

> Let the East and the West without a breath
> Mix their dim lights like life and death
> To broaden into boundless day.

But the realization of that vision lay in the remote future, if indeed it would be achieved at all.

Moreover, Western economic institutions—machine industry and modern means of communication—upset stereotyped living and thinking habits of Asiatics. That form of Western influence was most pronounced in Japan, of course, but it was also felt from Korea through India to Saudi Arabia—and with growing force. Somnolent agrarian and handicraft societies were shaken up; the customs and outlook of Asiatics who drifted into industrial employment underwent subtle changes.

Last but not least, the aggressive West taught Asia that security and international respect depended ultimately upon military potential. Japan had energetically applied that lesson with results which encouraged imitation in other parts of the "changeless" Orient. Clearly then, the West was responsible, up to a point, for the tensions and revolutionary ferment in the East. Even as Sindbad had invited the Old Man to climb on his back and thus created a desperate predicament for himself, so troubled

Asia was partly the contriving of Europe and the United States. In the end, however, Sindbad got the Old Man drunk, broke his hold and so rid himself of the onerous burden.

In the interval between World Wars a novel factor entered the revolutionary stream of Asia: the ideology and pattern of living of Soviet Russia. Bolshevik doctrines and institutions offered a program that was more attractive to some Asiatics, a veritable panacea for the amelioration of social and economic perplexities, than the ways and creed of Western capitalistic democracy. In particular, Communism posed as the champion of the hard-pressed peasantry in the bitter struggle with greedy landlords and parasitic usurers. Linking the principle of international revolution with the national aspirations of industrially backward peoples, Soviet agents, specially trained for the purpose, skilfully played upon the plastic mind of Asia. Converts to Communism combined evangelical fervor with intense energy arising out of uncritical and dogmatic convictions. As opportunity afforded, Communists endeavored to capture the hearts and loyalties of the Asiatic millions and to rally mass degradation to the purposes of world-wide revolution.

Yet another ingredient figured in the troubles of Asia: the unabashed imperialism of Japan. While China was the principal objective of Nipponese appetites, eastern Asia entire, India along with other areas, fell within the range of the military clique which seized control of the policies of Japan. Appealing to the sword, ambitious Nippon tried to create in fact a Great East Asian Co-Prosperity Sphere, as the imperialistic vision was euphemistically styled.

THE NEW CHINA

At the close of the First World War, as at its beginning, China was in a special sense the sick man of the Orient—wracked by banditry, warlordism and political disunity. A flock of local "strong men" commanding military levies of their own competed for power with two Chinese governments each claiming to be the legitimate authority. The corrupt militarist regime at Peking was officially recognized by foreign governments, but the republican administration at Canton possessed more vitality as well as plenty of plans for national regeneration.

All the articulate elements of China assailed the Versailles Treaty for awarding Shantung to Japan. It was cold comfort to know that special German and Austrian rights in China had been cancelled. Disillusioned intellectuals, with students taking the lead, organized an effective boycott against Japanese products. In the future, the student class, profiting from the traditional prestige of men of learning in China, exerted considerable influence upon the course of public affairs.

As one manifestation of revolutionary nationalism, Chinese intellectuals repudiated the classical literary heritage and promoted a "New Thought" or plain language enthusiasm. Language was simplified and literature was given severely utilitarian emphases, calculated to appeal to ordinary Chinese. Iconoclastic scholars cast aside the legendary in the national tradition, dealing thus a heavy blow at the basic ethic, the teachings of Confucius.

Building on his immense reputation, Doctor Sun Yat-sen took leadership of the republican forces at Canton. The instrument ready to his purposes was the Nationalist (Kuomintang) Party, which had recently undergone a housecleaning. For the guidance of disciples, Sun Yat-sen prepared in 1924 a blueprint of Three Principles on Chinese rehabilitation, which bristled with over-simplifications. Above all else, Sun Yat-sen pleaded for national unification as the prerequisite to gaining a place of equality, respect and freedom in the family of nations. The second principle was constitutional democracy, which Sun Yat-sen, chastened by rough experience, described as a long-term objective. China, in the meantime, must pass through a season of "political tutelage," a period of governmental experimentation, to which Sun Yat-sen meticulously avoided setting a time limit.

His third principle—social welfare—summoned the China that was to be to combat mass misery and to enable every citizen to better his level of living. Government should exercise strict surveillance over private capital and should distribute large landed properties among the toiling peasants. Ever since their enunciation the Three Principles have served as the law and the prophets for all Chinese political factions. Like other sacred texts, however, they were susceptible to varied interpretations. At his death in 1925, Sun Yat-sen was canonized as the patron saint of revolutionary China and his teachings have been constantly propagated through press, school and army.

For help in translating ideals into realities, Sun Yat-sen turned to Soviet Russia, without adopting Marxist doctrine as the way to Chinese salvation. Already Moscow had courted the good will of China by renouncing the special rights acquired by Imperial Russia except for the Chinese Eastern Railway, spanning Manchuria. Fluid China exerted a peculiar attraction upon Moscow, since the prospects of Communist expansion in Europe at the time were dim. "The road to Paris," Lenin laconically explained, "lies through Peking and Calcutta."

In 1923, Soviet Russia and Nationalist China arranged a partnership. Communist political advisers, specialists in propaganda and military experts descended upon Canton; heading the contingent was Michael Borodin, a wizard in the strategy of politics, who had lived for a time in Chicago. An army of better than a million men was whipped into shape and properly indoctrinated, while picked Chinese Nationalists pursued advanced studies in Moscow.

Sun Yat-sen and his wife in the early 1920's

Under the guidance of Russian agents, the Nationalist Party structure was reformed in 1924 on the Soviet pattern. It was decided that if and when the Nationalists succeeded in unifying the country, China should be ruled by a party dictatorship manipulated by a small executive committee. In the same year, the little Chinese Communist Party, which had been founded four years earlier and which was in liaison with the Third International, struck up an alliance with the Nationalists. By boring from within, the Communist fragment and its Soviet sponsors might be able to take charge of the destiny of China.

When Sun Yat-sen died, the mantle of Nationalist leadership fell upon his disciple, Chiang Kai-shek, thirty-eight years of age. Son of a wine merchant, Chiang had chosen the army as his career and had studied military science in both Japan and Soviet Russia. One of the most controversial figures of the twentieth century, Chiang could be as ruthless as he was courageous and as autocratic as he was conservative. A whole-souled patriot, whose antipathy to foreign influences increased with the years, Chiang had considerable talent for inspiring faith and hope among his soldiers. He married the sister of Sun Yat-sen's wife, Mei-ling Soong, who came of a wealthy and aggressive financial family. Educated at Wellesley College, Madame Chiang was an invaluable aide in Nationalist dealings with the English-speaking world.

Chiang Kai-shek (right foreground) and General Chang Hsueh Liang at Nanking, 1930

Nationalist armies exploded out of Canton in 1926, Generalissimo Chiang commanding. Judiciously mixing patriotic hullabaloo with bribery and cold steel, the Nationalists swept triumphantly northward against the warlords. Great Shanghai and Nanking capitulated in 1927; the following year Peking (renamed Peiping) was taken, and even the warlord of Manchuria hoisted the flag of Nationalist China. Seemingly a new China had been created, though in several districts, of which Manchuria was one, the allegiance of local potentates to the central government was nominal only.

In the meantime, moreover, the right-wing Nationalists had collided head-on with the Communists and less extreme left-wing elements. Fundamentally, the cleavage arose out of ideological differences, the Communists being desirous of remaking China in the image of Soviet Russia. The dominant Nationalist set, on the other hand, was extremely conservative, if not indeed reactionary, resembling a cyclops with only a single eye and that in the back of the head. Feuding rose to a climax when the Communists set up a capital in the industrial city of Hankow and by assaults upon foreigners tried to discredit the Nationalist cause in world opinion. Chiang not only smashed the Hankow adventure, but in 1927 expelled Communists from the Nationalist Party and ordered the wily Borodin and his fellows back to Moscow. Amidst angry recriminations the "marriage of convenience" between Nationalist and Communist ended in sudden divorce.

Thereafter the Nationalists waged war to the knife against the Chinese Reds. In 1934 Communists zealots sought refuge in the northwestern province of Shensi, remote, wild and primitive. A Chinese Peoples' Soviet Republic was proclaimed (1936), which was an ever-pricking thorn for the Nationalist regime. Heading the Communists was a shrewd intellectual of tough-textured peasant stock, Mao Tse-tung. After the Second World War, this veteran and doctrinaire Marxist emerged as the commanding personality of China. The Communist Republic organized an army trained for guerilla fighting, and it applied a rough-and-ready version of economic collectivism, striking hard at landlordism and "bureaucratic capitalism"; as a general rule, the share of the harvest taken by the landlord as rent was cut in half. Mao preached a clean sweep of the old Chinese culture and economy. He and his henchmen believed passionately in what they were trying to accomplish, and they were convincing to many.

Administration in Red China was reputedly honest and efficient, which naturally impressed Western observers favorably. Compulsory indoctrination in the Communist philosophy buttressed the revolutionary order and from headquarters at Yenan issued obsequious paeans of praise for Stalin and Soviet policies. Yet it would be an error to set Mao down as simply a stooge of Moscow; ardent devotion to China and Chinese welfare ranked high among his attributes.

THE NATIONALIST DICTATORSHIP

The Nationalists in the meantime had picked Nanking as capital and had assumed the management of Chinese affairs. Despite outrages upon foreign citizens and properties as the Nationalists marched to victory, foreign governments in 1928 recognized the Nanking regime as the legitimate government. Backed by the army, Generalissimo Chiang undertook the responsibilities of president and prime minister. Instead of a parliament, political authority was lodged in the Nationalist Party and its all-powerful Central Executive Committee. Senior party officials filled the policy making posts in administration; though called "democratic centralism," the government was in fact a military oligarchy. The problem of training a corps of competent and honest administrators was never solved.

Personal rivalries, primarily, provoked incessant controversies and revolts within the Party, with Chiang playing the role of umpire. The more outspoken dissenters were crushed or silenced by terrorism and an elaborate bureaucracy, reinforced by secret police and censors, endeavored to control thought. Though the Nationalist regime started off with no little dash and enterprise it rather easily succumbed to unashamed graft, nepotism and inefficiency, traditional shortcomings of government in China.

Beginning in 1934, under the guise of a "New Life Movement," Chiang fathered a revival of the Confucian cult, which Nationalist spokesmen had previously ridiculed. Unity of the country, Chiang evidently hoped, would be bolstered by ancient sacrosanctities, which generations of Chinese students and public leaders, though not the masses, considered outmoded and a drag on progress. "One's daily activities," Chiang proclaimed, "should be guided by the famous virtues, courage, justice, integrity and constructiveness." Western journalists reported that regulations to implement the New Life Movement paralleled the "blue laws" of colonial New England. Many a Chinese intellectual, disenchanted by the dictatorial temper of the Nationalist government, or alienated by the Confucian revival or the unwillingness of the administration to apply far-reaching social and economic reforms, drifted leftward, some of them ending up in the Communist camp.

Regardless of the conservatism which prevailed in Nanking, significant social changes moved across the country. Conventional family ties and marital customs switched toward Western fashions, and women and young people, in the cities at any rate, revelled in a new freedom. The rate of literacy among males increased to a third of all, though the education of women and peasants suffered neglect. State universities outstripped missionary institutions in the quality of instruction offered and in research; all schools operated under the close surveillance of Nationalist officials. Industrialism proceeded at a steady pace in cities such as Shanghai, Tientsin and Hankow. In consequence the urban working class and the middle classes increased, though neither was anything more than a small drop in the huge Chinese bucket.

Large masses of Chinese peasants groaned under burdens of high rentals, heavy taxes and usurious charges for loans. According to Nationalist figures, half the tillable soil of China belonged to a tenth of the population—landlords and well-to-do farmers; normally half the crop raised on a piece of rented land passed to the owner. There was much discussion in Nationalist circles about amelioration of the lot of the depressed peasantry, but not much of a positive character was accomplished. Country people plodded along in harmony with an old folk melody:

> When the sun rises, I toil,
> When the sun sets, I rest,
> I dig wells for water
> I till the fields for food.

Chinese peasants

Yet some improvements in the national economy were made under the Chiang dictatorship. Railway trackage, for instance, was nearly doubled and many good roads were constructed. Order of a sort was established in fiscal policies which enlisted the confidence of financial interests, and state loans of unprecedented size were floated on the home market.

Reforms in the national currency undermined local media of exchange, and holders of precious metals were obliged to turn them over to the national treasury for use in purchasing goods abroad. Duties on commodities crossing provincial frontiers, which handicapped exchange and financed war lords, were abolished. Delegations of technical specialists from the League of Nations, the United States and Great Britain tendered advice to Nationalist China on economic and social problems.

As befitted a military dictatorship, and as seemed indispensable indeed for internal order and external security, the Nationalist government devoted particular care to the armed forces. By Chinese standards, the troops which Chiang led to victory in 1926–1928 ranked high in martial spirit and patriotic ardor. Western military teams were invited to China to improve the national capacity for war. German experts trained the land forces, Britons were advisors on naval matters, and beginning in 1933, instructors and planes from the United States built up Chinese airpower.

By 1937, Chiang had probably 2,000,000 men under arms, though the soldiers were neither well-equipped nor well-disciplined. Together with the large new officer caste, the Nationalist army was an important instrument in upholding the dictatorship, but in the testing time of war it was no match for the legions of pugnacious Japan.

The unequal treaties which Chinese patriots so bitterly resented, and to which Chiang ascribed responsibility for the ills of the country, were gradually whittled away. With the United States taking the lead in 1928, foreign powers relinquished control over Chinese tariff policy. But the right of extraterritoriality, which protected foreigners against the injustices of Chinese legal processes, was a harder nut to crack. Chinese civil and criminal law was remodelled in keeping with Western practices, it is true, but courtroom procedure failed to measure up to Western conceptions of justice; judges, for instance, often bowed to the will or whim of bureaucratic administrators. Small Western countries gave up the extraterritorial privileges, but the United States and Great Britain declined to yield until 1943.

Most of the foreign-administered concession areas in great Chinese cities were reclaimed by the Nationalist government, though foreign troops lingered on in some places and foreign gunboats patrolled certain rivers and harbors. If Sun Yet-sen's goal of unfettered national independence had not been fully attained, impressive progress, nonetheless, had been made.

INDIA MOVES TOWARD FREEDOM

Due to the presence of British administrators and British direction of the armed services, India was far more tranquil than China. Yet the self-same revolutionary currents, especially the dynamic of nationalism, operated in both countries. Patriotic emotions were quickened by the participation of better than 1,000,000 Indians in the First World War, and by British promises of more self-government upon the return of peace.

Unprecedented emotional fervor was infused into Hindu nationalism by Mahatma Gandhi, one of the most intriguing and venerated personalities of the twentieth century. During his lifetime more than 2,000 books were written about this most remarkable of all Hindus, whom entranced co-religionists looked upon as an incarnation of the divine. For the world at large, Gandhi with his toothless grin and scanty loin-cloth personified India militant. Born into high-brow society, Gandhi completed his formal education as a lawyer in England, and for a generation resided in South Africa championing the interests of his countrymen who had settled there. Returning to India during the First World War, he plunged into the Hindu nationalist agitation. A profoundly religious man, Gandhi had pondered long over Hindu and Christian sacred literature. He was fond of quoting the Christian verse

> I loved to choose and see my path;
> But now lead Thou me on . . .

Believing in the fundamental unity of all religions, he once said, "I am a Christian and a Hindu and a Muslim and a Jew." It was religion no doubt that led him into a life dedi-

Mohandas K. Gandhi (second from right) and some of his followers in 1938

cated to the service of India. He strove unceasingly to reconcile creed and deed.

As a devout Hindu, protection of the sacred cow seemed to Gandhi a loftier responsibility than the winning of self-rule. "I am a reformer through and through," he declared, "but my zeal never leads me to the rejection of the essential things in Hinduism." His personality and electrifying eloquence warmed the spirit of millions of hypnotized followers. He energetically espoused the cause of the miserable "Untouchables," which was one reason for his assassination in 1948.

As weapons in his campaign against the rule of the British Raj, Gandhi relied upon peaceful civil resistance and boycotts of British products and educational and political institutions. By precept and example he trained disciples not to cooperate with the British in any way. And yet, time and again, he applied the brake to the disobedience movement as soon as it provoked violence. A brilliant showman, Gandhi was often imprisoned for his agitation, but that only heightened his prestige and popularity as is the way with martyrs. Always an austere ascetic, like Lenin, his diet was meager even when he was not fasting, and in the later years he chose to live in a mud hut in an abysmally squalid village.

Propagation of doctrines of freedom and self-rule was organized by the Hindu-dominated National Congress. Within that body widely divergent opinions prevailed as to how India should be administered once independence was won. And though he was the acknowledged leader of the Congress, Gandhi could not always manage the members. On instructions from Moscow, the small band of Indian Communists, with headquarters in Bombay, affiliated with the Congress, but their plans to capture control were frustrated.

In the 1930's, Pandit (meaning wise man) Jawaharlal Nehru, a lieutenant of Gandhi, but less pacific in his views and impatient with the slow-moving precision of British statecraft, advanced into a place of Indian leadership. Educated at Cambridge University, a lawyer by profession and gifted with a singularly pungent pen and tongue, Nehru dedicated himself exclusively to the national cause. A man of unquestioned integrity, when he took a stand it was out of deep moral conviction. For seditious political utterances, he became well acquainted with the inside of British jails. Nehru was keenly interested in social questions and envisaged a planned and classless society for the India of the future. When Dominion status was granted in 1947, he became the first prime minister of India, the political and spiritual spokesman of more than 330,000,000 people.

Whereas Hindus comprised about two out of three of the inhabitants of the Indian sub-continent, Moslems formed a large minority of about 90,000,000. Organized in the Moslem League, the adherents of Mohammed, or at least their political representatives, repulsed the idea of an autonomous India under Hindu domination. In time Moslem politicians demanded a separate country of their own which they referred to as Pakistan. Bloody and destructive clashes between Moslems and Hindus were recurrent phenomena in Indian affairs. Several hundred princely states, of which perhaps a dozen mattered, presided over by local potentates under British guidance, added to the political perplexities of the sub-continent.

Intruding into every phase of the Indian problem was the formidable and incessant growth in population. On an area half as extensive as the United States, three times as many people as in America lived a crowded existence. In spite of the high death rate—nearly half the children died before their fifteenth birthday—the population mounted at an ominous rate; in the interval between World Wars, the net gain exceeded 80,000,000. Unless this endless increase in mouths were somehow restricted, the outlook for India would be grim indeed.

Social inequalities of Himalayan dimensions, moreover, persisted in the sub-continent. The opulence and grandeur of the wealthy contrasted sharply with the chronic underfeeding or actual starvation and disease of the illiterate multitudes; a famine in Bengal in 1943, as an example, carried off 5,000,000 people. Even in good years, India had to import food-grains, principally rice from the Indo-Chinese peninsula. Industrialism, which many a patriot regarded as the cure-all for social afflictions, progressed significantly between World Wars, but the masses, living in thousands of villages, still wrung their livelihood from the soil.

Mounting nationalist pressures and revolutionary agitation compelled the British government to retreat step by step in India. In handling the Indian question, British statecraft unquestionably committed many blunders, but the hard lessons earlier learned in North America were applied on the installment plan. An Act of 1919, for instance, authorized selected Indians to choose most of the representatives in a bicameral federal legislature, and granted each Indian province an elected law-making body of its own. Those concessions failed to appease Gandhi and his followers. The British Viceroy still retained jurisdiction in foreign affairs and defense, and partial jurisdiction over finance; voting qualifications restricted the franchise to a small minority and the multitude of princely states lay outside the range of the central government.

When Great Britain relinquished control over tariff policy, the Indian government enacted high protective duties, causing imports from Britain to slump sharply; sales of cotton piece goods, for instance, dropped to a tenth of what they had been. Year after year, the proportion of Britons in the Indian administrative and military services declined, natives moving into vacated posts. The increasing employment of Indians in public offices was in conformity with the British ideal of partnership in colonial administration.

After a series of man-to-man discussions in London, shared in by nearly all shades of British and Indian political thought, the scope of Indian self-rule was broadened in 1935. In addition to a considerable extension of the suffrage privilege, greater powers were assigned to the central government; but the resistance of the native princes nullified this understanding. On the other hand, full autonomy was given to the provinces in purely local matters, a concession that was immediately put into operation. Hindu Nationalists captured seven of the eleven provincial assemblies. Yet the law of 1935 fell short of satisfying Hindu and Moslem politicians who wished unqualified liberty in the political domain. Incessant clamor for independence, which was stepped up during the Second World War, foreshadowed the establishment of the free states of India and Pakistan in the summer of 1947.

THE INDO-CHINESE PENINSULA

In broad outlines, the history and problems of the small countries in the Indo-Chinese Peninsula duplicated the record of the larger Asiatic states. In response to the nationalist battlecry of "Burma for the Burmese," Great Britain detached Burma from India in 1935 and granted it embryonic representative institutions, which stimulated demands for the total removal of alien authority. Culturally and commercially Burma was intimately tied to India. Immigrants from India (and China) occupied a controlling position in trade and gained an evil reputation as usurious moneylenders. British authority had to repress fanatical mob furies directed against these grasping newcomers. And Burma contained a special and troublesome minority element, the Karens, inhabiting the northern hill country.

Japanese expansionists turned covetous eyes upon Burma because of its resources of oil, rice and timber and as a springboard for the possible conquest of India. During the Second World War Nipponese troops, aided by Burmese malcontents who served as spies and saboteurs, overran Burma and gravely endangered the security of India.

The French colony of Indo-China likewise passed under the sharp Japanese sword. Native hostility to a bureaucratic government administered by Frenchmen inspired the educated minority to push for self-rule. The more radical elements aligned with native Communists, ever a thorn in the flesh of the French administration and affiliated with the Third International. Between World Wars commercial dealings with France expanded and from Indo-China French cultural influences radiated throughout the East. French engineers built strategic air fields and started to construct a large naval base near Saigon, the capital.

The politically articulate in the adjoining kingdom of Siam (Thailand) set up an agitation for a share in government. As the result of an insurrection in 1932, oligarchic rule superseded royal authoritarianism. Aversion to foreigners prevailed, especially hostility to Chinese immigrants who flocked in in substantial numbers. Since two-thirds of the land was owned by peasant proprietors, rural Siam enjoyed a unique measure of stability.

At the southern extremity of the peninsula lay the British possession of Malaya. Comprising ten small Moslem principalities, the colony was only about the size of New York State and was governed by British officials. Administrators worked to develop patriotic sentiments among the Malays and the large Chinese and Indian immigrant groups, but the docile Malays responded negatively, preferring to hold aloof from the Chinese. If Malay nationalism existed at all it was certainly very faint; benefiting from the security which British rule assured, the Malays did not press for self-government. Eventually the Chinese became as numerous as Malays, and they were more industrious and skilful in amassing wealth. Thousands of tough Chinese families, however, "squatted" on public land, eking out a bare and dreary subsistence—to be a source of serious trouble after the Second World War.

British enterprise and capital, coupled with Chinese labor, drastically altered the face of Malaya. Foreign interests laid out rubber plantations covering over 3,000,000 acres and exploited rich tin mines. Over a third of the world production of rubber and tin originated in this colony with United States firms as the largest customers. Native levels of living were probably the highest in eastern Asia and British officials warred effectively upon disease and ignorance.

Linked to the mainland by a causeway was the small British island of Singapore. The commercial port on the island ranked among the first ten of the world in tonnage and much of the business was handled by Chinese immigrants, some of them very wealthy and actively interested in the course of events back home. One corner of the island was occupied by a great British naval station completed in 1938, and spoken of as the keystone of the British imperial arch in Asia, the Oriental Gibraltar. The easy Japanese conquest of this base in 1942 was one of the most depressing episodes for the Allies in the Second World War.

TURKEY FACES WEST

After the First World War, Turkey, now much reduced in area, experienced far-reaching changes. Stung by military defeat in the war and by a peace treaty which assigned territory in Anatolia to Greece, patriotic Turks marshaled their forces to right what they considered intolerable wrongs. Helped a little by France, Turkish nationalists, after a grim struggle, drove Greek troops off the mainland and then negotiated another peace settlement with the Allies—the Treaty of Lausanne (1923). As fixed in the Treaty, the new Turkey covered Constantinople (Istanbul) and its environs in Europe and Anatolia in Asia; the Arab provinces to the south were cut away. Arrangements were made for the exchange of Turks residing in Greece for Greeks in Turkey; much suffering attended the transfer of these populations, but the transaction brought to a close an angry feud that had long plagued both peoples. Except for an unruly Kurdish minority, Turkey now contained only Turks.

After a dozen years of wracking warfare Turkey settled down to an era of peace and progressive administration. The Nationalist leader, Mustapha Kemal Atatürk, who had earned a considerable reputation as a professional soldier, assumed the direction of government. In 1923, a republic with Kemal as president formally replaced the ancient sultanate, and Turkey was launched upon a social program intended to sweep away the Ottoman and Islamic heritage.

On paper the Kemalist regime was a constitutional democracy with a parliamentary assembly, but in practice it was a military dictatorship. Only the Republican People's Party had legal standing before 1946; as founder of this party Kemal dominated it as he dominated the country, and most of the other public leaders were former army chiefs. Restrictions were laid upon publication, political critics were imprisoned and workers were forbidden to form trade unions. As a mark of the new era, Ankara, deep in the heart of Anatolia, supplanted Constantinople as the Turkish capital; it quickly blossomed into a Western-type city with spacious streets and modern buildings.

Once the dictatorship had been consolidated, government fostered industrial expansion and improved communications, aided by Soviet Russia and Great Britain. Nationalization of concerns owned by foreigners and state-sponsored public corporations reflected the influence of Soviet collectivism. Yet slowly, a Turkish trading and industrialized class emerged and became a power in the country. Model farms were established to teach the peasants more efficient agricultural methods, but the immediate results were not impressive. Western law codes were introduced and surprising reforms were effected in the status of women. The veil, symbolizing subjection, gradually disappeared in city and large town, plural marriage was officially frowned upon, women attended institutions of advanced study, entered the learned professions, and in 1934 they were admitted to suffrage rights on equal terms with men.

The spirit of secularism which pervaded the Kemalist regime led to the adoption of laws that disturbed deep and tender Turkish loyalties. Not only was the Mohammedan caliphate abolished in 1924, but Islam ceased to be the established religion. Sunday was declared the day of rest, instead of Friday, and the wearing of the Moslem fez went out of fashion. Worship in the mosque was carried on in the Turkish language, and Latin characters replaced Arabic in a simplified alphabet. Literacy increased materially. Moslem schools were secularized and laws required compulsory attendance on schools, though they were not faithfully enforced. Special care was devoted in the schools to instilling a strong spirit of nationhood through the study of Turkish history and geography; institutions of learning operated by foreigners were obliged to follow the national "line." Night schools afforded opportunities for oldsters to learn to read and write.

Kemal prided himself on being an enlightened despot, but, unlike his autocratic conterparts in Europe, he harbored no plans of territorial expansion. Turkey, once the terror of Europe, took on a lamb-like appearance. On the whole, the former "sick man of Europe" recuperated remarkably in the era between World Wars.

TRENDS IN IRAN

The Turkish renaissance and nationalist urges affected thinking and policy in neighboring Persia or Iran. That country did not, however, immediately escape being a pawn in power politics. Soviet Russia renounced all special privileges in Persia, it is true, yet Moscow kept an eye cocked on the country, which lay close to the Caucusus underbelly of Russia, possessed valuable mineral deposits and commanded the approach to the Indian ocean. A clause in a Soviet-Iranian treaty of 1921 permitted Moscow to send troops into the country if a third power threatened its integrity or used it as a base for military moves pointed against Russia.

The political pendulum which for generations had oscillated between Russia and Britain soon swung to the side of London. Britain was concerned not only to preserve Iran as a rampart against Soviet pressure southward but also to protect the profitable properties of the Anglo-Iranian Oil Company, of which the British government was the chief shareholder. This company, which obtained a long-term concession for a seventh of Iran, became the largest industry by far in the country and the largest oil producer outside of the Americas. A string of wells extended across the country for two hundred miles and the world's biggest refinery nestled on the island of Abadan. The company was a monument to British enterprise, technical skill and risk capital. Royalties paid for the oil furnished funds for public purposes.[1]

An Iranian counterpart of Kemal, Riza Pahlevi, who became Shah in 1925, abetted the cause of reform and modernization. Distrustful of tradition, he espoused passionate nationalism and believed in the infallible virtue of material progress. Nomad tribesmen and the Moslem religion were subjected to state authority, new roads were built and a railway was laid down by foreign engineers from the Persian Gulf to the Caspian Sea. Beginnings were made in public schooling and in the emancipation of women, without much disturbing the folkways of the peasant masses, squalid, disease-ridden and ignorant. Foreigners brought in to tone up public administration could not overcome the Iranian preference for corruption and inefficiency. Landed proprietors, who dominated the national parliament, displayed almost no sense of social responsibility. Fevered nationalism, however, generated agitation to rid the country of external controls and pressures, causing British political influence to recede.

THE ARAB WORLD

Arab-inhabited lands in southwestern Asia, formerly Ottoman provinces, attained global significance after the First World War. These countries of the Middle East possessed vital strategic and commercial importance—the Bridge of Asia—and beneath the soil immense deposits of petroleum were uncovered. Within a single generation the Aladdin's lamp of oil converted poor and desolate regions into an area of fabulous wealth. An American expert reported in 1944, "The center of gravity of world oil production is shifting from the Gulf-Caribbean area to the Middle East and is likely to continue to shift until it is firmly established in that area." Then too, the Middle East is the center and heart of Mohammedanism, whose followers stretched from the Atlantic in Morocco through northern India and as far away as the Philippines, over 300,000,000 in all.

[1] Rights granted to American interests to search for oil were given up, but a joint Soviet-Iranian firm held on to a concession for a small area near Teheran, the capital.

Under this barren desert lay future wealth for Saudi Arabia—oil deposits whose exploitation would change an immemorial way of life.

The First World War unexpectedly caused an awakening among the easy-going Arabs, moreover, and the establishment of a Jewish sanctuary in Palestine heightened the international importance of this corner of the globe. In the medieval centuries, Arabs had written an enviable record as conquerors, scholars and scientists, but they had fallen behind under the dead-hand of the Turk, and in an age of machinery.

During the war what had hitherto been an Arab cultural renaissance developed into a considerable political agitation, pointed toward independence from alien rule. Anxious to enlist the maximum Arab support in the campaigns against Turkey, the British held out the hope of political freedom after the war. Except for occasional pockets of Christians, the Arabs were Mohammedans and that religious bond, along with a common language, historical memories and aspirations for the future and belief in descent from a common racial stock, set them off from Europeans. In 1945 the Arab revival took political form in a loosely organized league of Arab nations, to cooperate on economic and social issues and to ensure independence. The intrusion of industrialism, especially in connection with oil operations, disturbed a society that was still largely in the tribal stage. Fast-moving motorcars, replacing ungainly camels, symbolized the change that was coming over the Arab world.

Military successes in the war enabled Britain to acquire a sphere of interest in most of the Arab lands with France trailing along in second place. Britain was assigned temporary mandates over Iraq, Palestine and Trans-Jordan, held sovereign control over Egypt and served as tutor for states in the Arabian peninsula, except Saudi Arabia.

From the beginning, politically active Iraqis resisted British authority and desired to be free. Under British guidance King Feisal, imported from Arabia, was installed (1921) as monarch and a constitution of the Western type was adopted. Native police and administrators were trained and efforts were made to modernize agricultural methods. Exploitation of oil fields by a syndicate of British, French and American companies furnished employment for natives and royalties for the Iraqi government. And fabled Baghdad prospered as a nodal point of international aviation services. In keeping with oft-reiterated pledges, the

British government used its good offices to secure the admission of Iraq into the League of Nations in 1932 and Britain then relinquished supervision over the country, though retaining military rights.

THE PALESTINE MANDATE

By taking a mandate over Palestine Great Britain stored up plenty of trouble for the future. Administration of this region was destined to incur violent vituperation from foreign critics of Britain, cause grave moral disquiet at home and antagonize both Arabs and Jews. Arabs, principally Moslems but also some Christians, constituted the bulk of the 650,000 inhabitants, though there were about 85,000 Jews as well. And in the famous Balfour Declaration of 1917, Britain had promised to facilitate the establishment of a national home for Jews in Palestine without prejudicing the civil and religious rights of the Arab residents. The ancient Zionist dream of "the return to Palestine" seemed on the way to fulfillment, as indeed it was. Lord Byron's poignant verse on the homelessness of the Jews

> The white dove hath her nest, the fox his cave,
> Mankind their country, Israel but the grave,

would lose its validity.

Starting in modest fashion in the twenties, Zionist immigration reached large dimensions with the upsurge of Nazi savagery and anti-Jewish agitations in eastern Europe. Over 400,000 Jews of every description, from very poor to accomplished professional men, streamed into Palestine, despite strident Arab demands that the doors should be closed to any more newcomers. It was feared by the Arabs that they would be swamped by the "ingathering of exiles" in this region of limited resources and that they would lose the chance of political independence.

Great Britain brought forward several plans for partition and proposals for self-rule in Palestine, all of which were rejected by the bitterly antagonistic nationalities. Aided by generous philanthropic support from the United States in particular, enthusiastic Zionist pioneers wrought material miracles in the mandate. Areas that hitherto had been technically stagnant or barren slowly moved into agricultural and industrial production; some Arabs, too, bettered their living standards. Yet outbreaks of violence and bloodshed, culminating in a sustained "Arab Revolt" in 1937–1939, kept Palestine in a state of tension and turmoil. In 1939, Britain cut down Zionist immigration to a paltry quota, which, as matters worked out, was tantamount to issuing a death warrant for Jews at the mercy of sadistic Nazis.

Jewish immigrants were excluded from Trans-Jordan, an arid stretch of mountain and uncharted desert with a scanty population of Bedouin and peasants. British civil servants assisted in fashioning a patriarchal monarchy, which proceeded leisurely along the road to independence. In 1946, Trans-Jordan was given its freedom, Britain retaining responsibilities for the security of the country.

OTHER ARAB STATES

Down in the Arabian Peninsula the picturesque and independent state of Saudi Arabia was pieced together. An ambitious and shrewd Moslem chieftain, Ibn Saud, stormed out of the interior with his troops and conquered the Red Sea littoral containing the Holy Cities of Islam. Contracts were presently (1933) negotiated with American companies permitting them to prospect for oil. After many disappointing experiences huge stocks of oil were discovered and exploitation began; royalties, which rose to dizzy levels after the Second World War, flowed into the treasury of the patriarchal autocrat.

Writers had been accustomed to divide Arabia into *Arabia Felix*, the busy western coastal district, and *Arabia Deserta*, the barren wasteland to the east, but oil turned sand into gold. Mushroom oil towns and the coming of Western agricultural, medical and other experts radically disturbed customary folkways; shirts and trousers, for instance, replaced the old *abbah*, though the conventional head shawl, or *gutrah*, was not discarded. Saudi Arabia suddenly zoomed into a world phenomenon.

Of all the Arab countries, Egypt was the most

advanced and boasted the oldest political tradition. The city of Cairo had long been the foremost Arab cultural and intellectual center. Egyptian nationalists, who were divided into several factions, chafed under the British protectorate, proclaimed at the beginning of the First World War. The Wafd Party, the most militant and most powerful body of organized native opinion, enrolled many intellectuals imbued with love of country and ready to demonstrate against British lordship on the slightest provocation. When genteel tactics of persuasion failed to achieve national objectives, extremists unhesitantly resorted to terrorism and assassination of British officials.

Gradually British supervision was relaxed and Egypt obtained in 1922 a substantial measure of independence with a constitution and parliament of its own. Not content with political freedom, Wafdists pressed for the evacuation of British troops protecting the vital Suez Canal Zone, and they imposed regulations upon foreign business and educational enterprises. Britain insisted, however, upon policing the Canal area and upon joint Anglo-Egyptian administration of the Sudan, containing the headwaters of the Nile.

The social situation in Egypt typified conditions in the Arab world generally. A small ruling class dominated the political stage and owned most of the productive soil. Better than 80 per cent of the Egyptian peasants or fellaheen rented the land they worked or were sharecroppers, converting the riches of the soil into the profits of the landowner. A dense population was crowded into narrow belts of soil along the Nile, so that fellaheen had only small parcels of ground, and squalor, dreariness and illiteracy prevailed. Millions of Egyptians inhabited crude mud villages, the huts providing shelter for families and domestic animals alike. On the other hand, facilities for schooling were somewhat extended and the women, like their Turkish sisters, were no longer heavily veiled and sequestered in keeping with Moslem convention.

Mandates over Syria and the Lebanon were awarded to France. If anything, the French had more trouble than the British with Arab nationalists. French troops repressed uprisings in Damascus and at other points with an iron hand, yet the tide of nationalism was too strong to be contained. In 1936, the French mandated territories were promised independence, but the coming of the Second World War postponed the implementation of the pledge. Nationalist agitations, meantime, had taken on increasing vigor among Arabs in the French colonies of North Africa; in Tunisia, evidences of fellow-feeling with the Arabs of the Middle East were especially pronounced.

NATIONALISM IN THE PACIFIC

On the morrow of the First World War, organized pressure in the Philippines for independence became more violent and insistent. The politically articulate in the colony, whose ways of living first Spain and then the United States had deliberately and drastically remodelled, were convinced that the archipelago could capably manage its own affairs. Under the Stars and Stripes, Filipinos had been educated in the habits of democracy and had been trained in administrative responsibilities in anticipation of self-rule.

Magic terms like "liberty" and "freedom" had struck deep root in the Filipino consciousness. In a classic expression of Oriental nationalism, Manuel L. Quezon, the leading spokesman of his countrymen, declared, "I would rather live under a government run like hell by the Filipinos than one run like heaven by Americans." That the islanders had profited from the ties with the United States is not open to dispute. Western medicine and sanitation, for instance, overcame small-pox and cholera; schools at various levels were in operation, highways, bridges and harbors were constructed and foreign trade expanded. Many a Filipino lived better than his parents, population figures moved upward and, as an exception to the general rule of the Orient, there was room for a substantially larger number of people in the Philippines.

Prosperity of the islanders depended greatly upon commercial connections with the United States with which most foreign business was transacted. Of first importance were sales of sugar, which supplied the livelihood of some 2,000,000 Filipinos and better than 60 per cent of public revenues; the raising and processing of coconuts for oil and copra, another industry bound tightly to the American market, gave work and bread to over 3,000,000 more. Although the archipelago contained valuable stocks of minerals—the iron ore reserves are the most extensive in the Orient—deficiencies in fuel and shortage of capital hindered industrial growth. As elsewhere in Asia wide disparities in income separated tenant farmers from absentee landlords on the big *haciendas*, holdovers from the Spanish era. No attempt was made to level off differences by taxation, and bitter feuds raged between the proprietors and hapless soil workers.

Under circumstances earlier recounted, the Congress of the United States decided to grant independence to the Philippines, which would come into force fully in 1946. The native legislature adopted a democratic constitution, Quezon being chosen as first president of the Commonwealth. So extensive was the authority he gathered into his hands that an admirer observed that he wielded "more power than Mussolini"; for the rest, government passed into the effective control of the small landowning and commercial minority.

Nationalistic indoctrination through the schools was gingered up and a native dialect, Tagalog, replaced English as the preferred language of the Commonwealth. With General Douglas MacArthur, ex-Chief of Staff of the United States Army, as supervisor, the native military forces were strengthened. Still the sovereign authority in the Philippines, the United States bore responsibility for protecting the Oriental ward against attack from outside.

It was assertive Japan, of course, that might challenge the security of the Philippines. Hemming in the Commonwealth from the northeast and east were three island clusters, the Marshalls, the Marianas and the Carolines, once German possessions, which Japanese marines had seized in the First World War and which had been mandated to Japan in the Treaty of Versailles. Defying the terms of the mandate, Japan fortified key islands in preparation for further expansion. If to these holdings the Philippines were united, Japan would command a strategic screen to the continent of Asia. Besides, the Philippines produced raw materials which Japan could use and offered an outlet for surplus population; upwards of 20,000 Japanese had already settled in the Commonwealth.

The triumph of nationalism in the Philippines heartened partisans of freedom in the Netherlands East Indies. In 1918 the Dutch government promised "to raise the population to such a level that it will be capable of attending to its own affairs and ruling its own country." A legislative People's Council had been instituted (1916), half of whose members were natives, but decrees issued by the Dutch governor-general had full force of law. That arrangement rasped the spirits of the Western-educated minority of Indonesians; nor were they appeased by the steady increase of natives in the civil administration and on local governing councils.

In 1927, the National Indonesian Party, which brought together several patriotic clubs and study circles, was formally organized. An extremely self-determined man, a Javanese engineer, Soekarno, became the leading spirit in the nationalist cause—and in 1949 the first president of the United States of Indonesia. Dutch officials drove the National Party underground, and broke up a small Communist Party, yet they could not stifle the passion for freedom. In 1937 native representatives on the People's Council unanimously requested dominion status for Indonesia.

The Dutch administration accomplished much for the benefit of the inhabitants in this Asiatic empire. Epidemics were largely subjected to science, and population rapidly increased. Elementary schools, a skilfully planned network of highways, more efficient farming, irrigation projects, cooperative societies and light industries testified to the foresight and intelligence of the Dutch administration. While Europeans and Chinese operated large and lucrative plantations, much the greater part of the soil belonged to native cultivators.

From Japan a growing volume of propaganda fanned native antipathy toward the

"Dutch oppressors." And Nipponese immigrants and goods moved into the archipelago until checked by restrictive legislation. Apprehensive of Japanese conquest, the Dutch authorities reinforced the defenses of the islands. This rich storehouse of supplies—oil, rubber, tin and tropical products—would be a welcome asset in the Japanese "co-prosperity" dream of the future.

THE JAPANESE SCENE

Japan emerged from the First World War with heightened prestige, as was shown in one way by the assignment of a permanent seat on the Council of the League of Nations. She collected islands in the Pacific as mandated territory and was awarded former German rights in Shantung. But those rights were relinquished during the Washington Conference of 1921–22, and at that gathering, Japan also promised to be a "good neighbor" of China, gave up her alliance with Great Britain and agreed to limitations on naval tonnage. Extremely sensitive Nippon reacted militantly, as has been noted, when the United States in 1924 debarred Japanese as permanent residents.

In the aftermath of the war, in which Japan had been associated with the victorious democracies of the West, a promising swing toward government by consent developed, and the political influence of the military hierarchy declined. A commoner in fact was named prime minister in 1918 and seven years later the franchise responsibility was extended to all adult males. The Japanese diet or parliament and political parties acquired a larger voice in making public decisions. On the other hand, corruption at the polls and the venality of some deputies tended to discredit the democratic creed.

The Great Depression, falling prices and sharp declines in commerce, wrought balefully upon Japan. The trend away from military ascendancy was reversed, a policy of conciliation with China was jettisoned and popular unrest and disaffection increased ominously.

Statecraft in Japan was constantly plagued by the appalling and ever present dilemma of a rapidly expanding population. In some years the relentless flood of babies added a million mouths; population multiplied by two and a half times in a century, exceeding 73,000,000 by 1940, and that in a country with very limited arable soil and natural resources. Part of the overflow spilled into the colonial possessions or into other regions, but emigration to white-inhabited countries of the Pacific was blocked by exclusionist legislation. Unless peaceful means of solving the fundamental food problem could be found, Japan threatened to explode.

Population congestion, together with the physical and moral ravages of the Great Depression, aggravated distress and restlessness in the Japanese countryside. On the average, the Japanese farmer worked less than a fifth as much land as a grower in Belgium, for example, the most densely peopled European country. Almost half the Japanese were tenant farmers, subject to high rentals, while the peasant proprietors as a class were burdened with debt. Plodding and hard-working, the Japanese countryfolk were noted for patriotism and obedience to authority. Rural hardships critically affected the outlook of the spirited military caste, for army officers and conscript soldiers came principally from the country.

A striking feature of Nipponese economy in the 1930's was the sensational advance in manufacturing and foreign trade. By 1933, exports of inexpensive cotton cloth had outstripped British sales, causing a decline in Lancashire industry, never forgotten; the Toyoda automatic weaver surpassed all rivals in efficiency. Output of rayon and nylon rose steeply, the latter a classic example of a new fabric that developed from a laboratory experiment into a major industry in less than a generation. Exports of gadgets, toys and food delicacies likewise shot up, and Japanese shipping crowded into third place among the merchant navies of the world, a formidable competitor in international maritime trade.

Heavy industries, which would raise the national capacity for war, expanded under the fostering beneficence of the state. Steel production, for example, approached 4,500,000 tons in 1936 and that figure was destined to double in the course of the Pacific war; new chemical plants turned out explosives, as well as cheap dyes and fertilizers. Although Japan had to import virtually all industrial raw materials, except coal, it developed quickly into "the workshop of the Orient." Large-scale manufacturing was concentrated in a small, highly vulnerable area, embracing Tokyo, Osaka and Nagoya, the first two of which ranked among the ten biggest cities on the globe. As never before, Japanese wares invaded the markets of the world to the alarm of Western competitors. The "gallant little Japs" of the First World War were now reviled as "yellow monkeys." Nation after nation laid discriminatory tariffs and quotas on Japanese products.

Of high importance in the Japanese success as a commercial competitor was the low pay of workers—"rice wages." But that was not the whole story by any means. Efficiency in productivity in large establishments matched and sometimes excelled European standards. Alongside of a multitude of small enterprises, gigantic business combinations appeared. Spoken of as the *zaibatsu*, these big concerns dominated the industrial scene; the famous House of Mitsui employed hundreds of thousands of workmen in various undertakings. Government directly promoted the expansion of business by generous subsidies and by depreciation of the currency, which lowered the price of Japanese goods in foreign markets. After the manner of the fascist regimes of Europe, the authority of the state in economic activities increased greatly in the late 1930's, as Japan entered upon a war economy.

Bellicose military clansmen of Japan set up indeed a collective dictatorship. Imbued with the mentality of the feudal past, this clique cherished grandiose visions of imperial expansion and preached that Japan had a sacred mission to execute in eastern Asia. Partisans of conquest and empire polished up the old and absurd doctrine that the Japanese were unique among men, a divine race headed by a divine dynasty that was predestined to rule the globe. Though he was the titular head of the state, Emperor Hirohito actually resembled

A Japanese industrial plant

Hirohito, Emperor of Japan, in traditional robes of ceremony

an idol adored as a sacred being and commanding immense popular esteem. Political moderates who dissented from the ideology or policies of the militarists were often cut down by violence; in a fanatical outbreak of February, 1936, two senior statesmen and a general were murdered in cold blood. Civilian government atrophied, and upon the dissolution of political parties in 1940 the Japanese experiment in government by consent came completely to an end.

Popular passions were enflamed by rabble-rousing condemnations of the West and of Western ways. For her own welfare, Japan must eliminate private enterprise as well as parliamentary institutions, it was said, cultivate the Spartan spirit and revitalize the archaic traditions and standards of value of Old Japan. To an unprecedented extent, the military services, the national Shinto religion, the press and educational institutions and fanatical secret societies were harnessed to the cult of chauvinism and imperialism.

Much sentimental gush was diffused on the theme of "Asia for the Asiatics," which in reality meant "Asia for Japan." Unloosing a barrage of vituperative propaganda against the white world, Nipponese zealots summoned Asiatic colonial peoples to rebel and combine with Japan in an "Eastern Asia Co-Prosperity Sphere," which would net material advantages for all and sundry. Prominent Japanese generals and admirals endorsed (1941) a typically jingoistic manifesto which asserted, "500,000,000 people in Annam, Cochin China, the East Indies, the Malay Peninsula, Burma, India and the Philippines are now groaning under injustice . . . The emancipation of these people is essential for the construction of the 'New Order in Asia.'"

ADVENTURES IN IMPERIALISM

Against the darksome background of social discontent, the dominance of the officers' corps, hatred of the West and unbridled chauvinism, Japan embarked upon imperialistic adventures which in time spelled her ruin in the blazing infernos of Tokyo, Hiroshima and Nagasaki. In the twenties, it is true, Japan pursued a policy of peaceful penetration in China, as desired by powerful business interests. But when the Nationalists succeeded in effecting a semblance of unity in China, Japan feared lest her large railway and commercial investments in Manchuria might be lost. In September of 1931, while the country was quaking under the Great Depression, Nipponese military chiefs, without the foreknowledge of the civilian authorities, ordered troops to seize all of Manchuria.

If that politically unstable region were brought under the rule of Japan, it could furnish rawstuffs, markets for manufactured goods and a place of settlement for land-hungry Nipponese. Manchuria, moreover, would serve as a bastion against Soviet Russia in the Far East. History afforded plenty of examples of comparable spoliations by Western imperialisms; and the masters in Tokyo turned a deaf ear to the fashionable Western argument that a new era had dawned in international affairs which ruled out crude brigandage as ethically repellent. For Westerners who still thought of Japan as a land of kimonos and cherry blossoms alone, the assault upon Manchuria was a disillusioning but instructive lesson in power politics.

Meeting only feeble resistance, the Japanese war machine rolled quickly across the plains of Manchuria. An "independent" state of Manchukuo was proclaimed in 1932 with the last Manchu ruler of China, Henry Pu-yi, as puppet emperor. To coerce China into acquiescence and to break an effective Chinese boycott upon Japanese products, Nipponese troops stormed into the great metropolis of Shanghai.

Foreign countries with Oriental interests scowled and scolded Japan, but none was willing to apply military force to stop the aggressor.[2] China appealed to the League of Nations for protection and redress. After a prolonged and exhaustive investigation of the Manchurian Question, a League agency, the Lytton Commission, presented its findings and recommendations. It denied that Japan had acted purely in self-defense and frankly charged her with infringing the integrity of China in violation of international engagements such as the Nine Power Treaty of 1922.

Pleading for a judicial compromise that would safeguard the special interests of Japan in Manchuria without impairing Chinese sovereignty, the League instructed Japan to evacuate its soldiers. Tokyo refused. Then the League formally condemned Japan, which retorted by resigning from the international organization. Nothing further was done and the principle of collective international security never recovered from the body blow administered by the Nipponese war lords.

When Japanese troops threatened to conquer Peiping, China accepted (1933) a truce, dictated by Tokyo, demilitarizing a zone south of the Great Wall. That ignominious surrender

[2] For a discussion of the policies of the United States in reference to Manchuria and subsequent Japanese operations against China, see pp. 716, 728.

together with the loss of Manchuria seriously undermined the prestige of the Nationalist regime of Chiang Kai-shek. A popular poet hit off the Japanese technique of imperialism in these terms:

> How courteous is the Japanese;
> He always says, "Excuse me, please,"
> He climbs into his neighbor's garden
> And smiles and says, "I beg your pardon";
> He bows and grins a friendly grin
> And calls his hungry family in;
> He grins and bows a friendly bow,
> "So sorry, this my garden now." [3]

Nominally a free state, Manchukuo was in fact a mere dependency of Nippon. Japanese officials managed the administration, stabilized the currency and maintained an unusual degree of security for life and property. As the price of law and order and efficient government, civilians in Manchuria paid in heavier taxation and oppression by Nipponese bullies. The door of Manchuria was slammed shut against Western commercial enterprise. Chinese immigration which had been underway for twenty-five years was resumed and a few Japanese pioneers staked out new homes. Studied efforts were made to create a distinct Manchukuoan sense of nationalism. Japan invested large quantities of capital in varied undertakings and in time the agricultural surpluses of this area and of Korea made the Japanese Empire practically self-sufficient in food. Natural resources were exploited in building up steel, chemical and armament industries, and power in the form of oil, coal and hydroelectric energy was tapped. Industrial productivity in Manchukuo exceeded the output of China.

For commercial and strategic purposes, highways suitable for motor transport were laid down and many new railways were constructed. Service on the older South Manchurian line compared favorably with the best in Europe, and in 1935, after much haggling, Manchukuo bought out the Soviet interest in the Chinese Eastern Railway.

That transaction temporarily eased Russo-Japanese tensions which had run high since the occupation of Manchuria. These traditional rivals in the Far East quarreled over fishing rights in Siberian waters and Tokyo accused Moscow of promoting Communism in Asia, while the men in the Kremlin feared that Japanese soldiers might strike into Siberia again as they had done right after the Bolshevik Revolution. Stalin kept reiterating, "Not one inch of foreign territory do we want, but of our country not one verst will we yield to any one."

Minor border affrays preceded an undeclared war in 1938, when Soviet troops attacked a Japanese frontier guard at the point where Manchukuo, Siberia and Korea met. Thrust back at first, the Japanese returned in force, compelling the Russians to withdraw into Siberia. Both sides mobilized major bodies of troops, but a cease-fire was arranged, and the military garrisons along the frontier were reduced. In other words, after the Japanese had clearly demonstrated their willingness to fight to the end, the Russians had pulled in their horns, and Japan was not again attacked until the last days of the Second World War.

JAPAN FIGHTS CHINA AGAIN

Success in the Manchurian affair whetted the appetites of Nipponese imperialists for still larger gains. Tokyo upbraided Western countries and the League for despatching technical experts to China and blandly informed the world that Japan possessed peculiar duties and rights on the Asiatic mainland. It was a veiled warning to the West not to meddle in Chinese affairs—a pronouncement to which foreign capitals took strong exception. As another symptom of intensifying chauvinism, Japan, in 1936, renounced the international treaties laying restrictions upon seapower.

Bit by bit, Japanese agents stealthily fastened the grip of Nippon upon China north of the Yellow River. That district held the largest coal reserves in Asia, considerable resources in metals and had potentialities for cotton culture, which might relieve Japan of dependence upon imports from the United States and India. Infiltration of Japanese advance agents into northern China evoked a fresh wave of anti-Japanese

[3] From *I'm A Stranger Here Myself*, by Ogden Nash. Copyright, 1938 by Ogden Nash, and used by permission of Little, Brown and Co.

agitation among Chinese students and other articulate elements. Confronted by the danger of complete conquest by Japan, the Nationalist government ceased fighting the Communists, and in 1936 the two factions arranged a united front against the aggressive interloper.

Bent upon controlling North China, the Japanese military party seized upon a skirmish between Chinese and Japanese soldiers in July of 1937 as a pretext to renew armed aggression. Again the fat was in the Oriental fire and it blazed more furiously than ever—until the catastrophic defeat of Japan in 1945. From the standpoint of world politics, the moment chosen in Tokyo to precipitate hostilities was highly propitious. Britain and France were desperately preoccupied with European perils; Soviet Russia was engaged in a monster purge of Communist dissidents; and neutrality sentiment was at crescendo in the United States. More than that, Japan had signed an anti-Comintern pact with Nazi Germany, pointed against the Soviet Union, and Mussolini soon attached his signature to the document. As a by-product, German and Italian military experts serving with the armies of Nationalist China were called home.

Instead of passively submitting to a repetition of the Manchurian amputation, China sturdily resisted Japanese aggression. But the odds were overwhelming. Spirited Nipponese troops quickly overran the most densely populated and wealthiest section of China, the area of the great cities and seaports from Peiping to Canton. Aerial bombardment wrought havoc in crowded urban communities and country districts were ravaged and depopulated. The invader wantonly trampled upon the rights and interests of Western governments in China.

Japanese bombers roared down on the cities of China, leaving vast destruction behind them. Here is a scene in the north railroad station at Shanghai after an attack.

A Chinese appeal to the now impotent League of Nations yielded no tangible results, apart from moral condemnation of Japan.

Driven westward, the Chinese Nationalist government set up headquarters in remote Chungking and struggled to create new military, industrial and commercial centers. Here was a valiant and resourceful gesture at survival, nourished by the hope that a powerful Western country would take a hand in the unequal Oriental contest. Counsels of weaker spirits to sue for peace were unhesitatingly brushed aside by Generalissimo Chiang Kai-shek. Nationalist and Communist guerilla bands and armed peasants gnawed away at the Japanese forces with glum determination, yet each Chinese faction eyed the other with mistrust and suspicion.

From the outside world, limited assistance flowed to Free China. British Hong Kong served as a funnel for supplies, modest shipments of war materials moved in from the United States and slow-gaited camels hauled goods from Soviet Siberia across the ancient silk road of Chinese Turkestan. But these supplies were utterly insufficient to enable China to wage effective campaigns against the invader, and the Japanese steadily tightened the noose of the blockade.

In December of 1941, the Sino-Japanese conflict merged in the Great Pacific War.

LOOKING BACKWARD

From a global viewpoint, Asia attained unparalleled importance in the era between World Wars. Fresh currents of change, or old forces accentuated, surged over the largest and most populous of continents. Diverse influences from the West, doctrinal and material, compounded with unhappy internal conditions and native discontents, nourished the revolt of Asia. Then too, the infiltration of the theories of Moscow and the aggression of Japan churned up Oriental waters.

China managed to achieve a semblance of unity and rid itself of most of the old, unequal treaties, but irreconcilable antagonisms between Nationalists and Communists were not allayed. Nipponese imperialism ate ravenously into the Chinese patrimony. On the other hand, India, statute by statute, proceeded along the path of self-rule. In the Moslem lands to the west, in southeastern Asia, in the Dutch East Indies and in the Philippines, the dynamic of nationalism was performing its customary work. As awakened peoples prepared to take their places among the independent countries of the world, the great white empires of Asia steadily disintegrated.

In contrast to all that, Japan enlarged her imperial dominions gaining mandated islands in the central Pacific, acquiring Manchuria and sealing off the most desirable districts of China proper. Shameless militarists ruled Japan; their ambitions accelerated the industrial evolution of the country and posed a menacing challenge to other countries with interests in eastern Asia and the Pacific. The coming of war in Europe in 1939 exactly suited the book of greedy Nipponese imperialists.

FOR FURTHER STUDY

CLAUDE A. BUSS, *War and Diplomacy in Eastern Asia* (New York, 1941)

GEOFFREY F. HUDSON, *The Far East in World Politics* (Oxford, 1937)

HARLEY F. MACNAIR, ed., *China* (Berkeley, 1946)

DAVID J. DALLIN, *Soviet Russia and the Far East* (New Haven, 1948)

LOUIS FISCHER, *The Life of Mahatma Gandhi* (New York, 1950)

JOHN S. FURNIVALL, *Progress and Welfare in Southeast Asia* (New York, 1941)

ELEANOR BISBEE, *The New Turks* (Philadelphia, 1951)

GEORGE LENCZOWSKI, *The Middle East in World Affairs* (new ed., Ithaca, 1956)

GEORGE ANTONIUS, *The Arab Awakening* (new ed., Philadelphia, 1946)

JACOB C. HUREWITZ, *The Struggle for Palestine* (New York, 1950)

SYDNEY N. FISHER, ed., *Social Forces in the Middle East* (Ithaca, 1955)

TATSUJI TAKEUCHI, *War and Diplomacy in the Japanese Empire* (New York, 1935)

GEORGE M. BECKMANN, *The Modernization of China and Japan* (New York, 1962)

BERNARD LEWIS, *The Arabs in History* (new ed., London, 1958) PAPERBACK

SYDNEY N. FISHER, *The Middle East* (New York, 1959)

CHAPTER XXX

THE SECOND WORLD WAR

SOURCES OF CONFLICT

THE Second World War engaged and devastated more of the globe than any other conflict of history. In the ferocity and fanaticism that the struggle generated, the mind is thrown back to the destructive "religious" wars of the sixteenth century. For the first time, casualties among civilians, whether by bombing, starvation, reprisals or by deliberate mass-murder, enormously exceeded the combatant losses. World civilization, the whole structure of society, was churned up without precedent, and the cessation of hostilities failed to confer peace and stability upon a distraught globe.

Stated crisply, the calendar of major events reads as follows: the European phase of the war began in September 1939 when the mobile might of Nazi Germany rolled across the plains of Poland, a country that Britain and France had repeatedly promised to defend. Most of Europe was promptly involved in mortal combat. In June of 1941, Soviet Russia became a belligerent, when Nazi armies attacked. Since 1937, Japan had been waging ruthless war against China, and on December 7, 1941, Nippon launched a deadly assault upon the American fleet base at Pearl Harbor. Thus the conflict in Europe and the conflict in Asia merged into a single global struggle with the United States in the very vortex.

The sources of the Second World War, like the roots of a great tree, ran deep into the historical soil. Although there were certain differences, to an instructive extent the broad forces and compelling tendencies that made a general war possible in 1914 set the stage for the renewal of strife in 1939.

Toward the end of the 1920's, Europe had recovered from the worst physical ravages of the First World War. And yet the memories of the horrors, the sufferings and the fears of the war years could not be expected to disappear in a decade, nor did they. The League of Nations, as an institution for resolving international antagonisms and keeping the peace, appeared to be growing in stature and prestige. There were plausible grounds, that is, for cautious, conservative optimism concerning the international future. But the Great Depression turned the tide in the reverse direction, and it became painfully evident that the causes of tension, fear and hatred had not been exorcised. As the thirties ran their fateful course, forces that had been conducive to armed combat in the past assumed ever more dangerous proportions.

THE FACTOR OF NATIONALISM

Clashing national ambitions and rivalries, the familiar phenomenon of aggressive nationalism, belong at the head of the column. As both sober statesman and wild-eyed agitator appreciated, nationalism was the uniquely effective and compelling political force. Universal in its appeal, this secular religion diverted Chinese, for example, from their traditional skepticism, enflamed meek-eyed Arabs and pierced through the Marxian international principle in the Russia of Stalin. Under the inspiration of nationalism, peoples of the Western world had endured vast and bloody sacrifices and more would yet be endured.

Between World Wars, nationalistic indoctrination was furthered by the conventional agencies of school, conscript army and popular press and advanced to fresh levels of perfection thanks to technically improved movies and to a novelty of mass-persuasion, the radio. National prides and romantic passions were most enflamed in the new or enlarged European countries that appeared after the First World War and in countries which nursed burning memories of the Paris peace settlements. Blustering, bombastic nationalism became most intense in Germany and Italy after they had fallen under the rule of the arrogant dictators, Hitler and Mussolini.

Acute problems of minorities constantly vexed the European scene. In some districts, minority groups belonged to nationalities that had been on top before 1914, but the peace treaties had transferred them to countries which they considered inferior and toward which they displayed snobbish contempt. That psychology prevailed among many Germans in Czechoslovakia and Poland and many Magyars in the Czech Republic and in Rumania.

Minority antagonisms were not resolved, could not indeed be resolved, in the breathing space between World Wars. Special treaties assuring political, educational and religious rights to minorities were not fully and faithfully executed. When spokesmen of minorities cried out against real or fancied injustices, fellow-nationals across the border echoed the grievances in flaming accents. When zealots in a minority group preached secessionist themes, governmental authorities resorted to repression, which, inescapably, accentuated animosities. As before 1914, Europe was cursed with an array of national "danger zones."

The supreme challenge to European tranquility issued from Germany, Nazi Germany. For one thing, the Treaty of Versailles fostered chauvinism, as had been true of the German peace imposed upon France in 1871. Clauses in the treaty that were construed to mean that Germany and her allies were solely responsible for the coming of war in 1914, clauses depriving Germany of colonies, laying severe limitations upon armaments, cutting away Danzig, transferring Germans to Polish sovereignty and imposing a huge reparations bill—these provisions of the peace treaty humiliated and embittered a proud and great nation.

It was fallacious, however, to tag the Versailles Treaty as a "Carthaginian" peace, as sometimes was done. Carthage vanished, while Germany recovered—and that quickly. Execution of the treaty intensified resentment in German hearts. That was notoriously the case with the carrying out of the reparations claims; but even after the corpse of reparations was tossed into the grave in 1932, Nazi spell-binders enflamed popular passions over the exaction of "tribute."

The Nazis generated an infectious national enthusiasm with promises that they would rid the land of "undesirables," break "the chains of Versailles" and knit together all European areas of German speech in a Greater Germany. Once in power, the Nazis struck ruthlessly against Jews, Communists and brave men and women who declared their democratic faith against fanatical, scornful might. Nazi persecutions and abuse roused fervent humanitarian outcries in the democracies of the West.

THE NAZI AVALANCHE

The announced goals of National Socialism in the international domain were achieved with astonishing, intoxicating ease. By reason of a plebiscite in 1935 the Saar Valley, abutting upon the Rhineland, rejoined Germany. In the same year military conscription was revived and German airpower and seapower were built up, as though the Versailles Treaty had prescribed no limitations at all.

The following year the fabled Rhineland, defenseless since the Armistice of 1918, and from which Allied armies of occupation had been recalled in 1930 as a gesture of hope and faith, was garrisoned by German troops. If France had mobilized and threatened to march into the Rhineland, the German forces would certainly have been evacuated and the Nazi regime might then and there have tumbled into ruin. But France and Britain, though protesting verbally, tacitly acquiesced in this breach

Viennese crowds welcomed the entry of the Nazis in March, 1938.

of international engagements, as in other bold Nazi adventures.

The reoccupation of the Rhineland was heavy with consequences. Hitler's bluff had brilliantly succeeded and many German patriots thought the achievement worthy of a crown of gold. Along the French boundary German engineers started to construct elaborate fortifications spoken of as the West Wall or Siegfried Line. Shielded against French invasion, the Nazi gangsters could pursue a relatively free course in the east of Europe up to the frontier of the Soviet Union. Thereafter the Hitlerian hammer blows descended with accelerating rhythm.

As the next act in the swiftly unfolding Nazi melodrama, German forces swarmed into German-speaking Austria in March of 1938, and that country was annexed to the Third Reich. The Austrian acquisition, the first territorial breach in the Paris peace settlements, brought important material and human resources to Germany and imperiled the independence of other small countries in eastern Europe. Again the British and French governments raised their voices in protest, but they declined to invoke force.

Emboldened by the success in Austria, Hitler demanded in the autumn of 1938 that the western section of Czechoslovakia should be immediately handed over. This region, called the Sudetenland, was inhabited predominantly by German-speaking folk, so that, as in the case of Austria, annexation could be defended on the Wilsonian principle of self-determination. Probably, though not certainly, most of the politically articulate in the Sudetenland and in Austria wished to become citizens of the Greater Germany.

However that may have been, the truculent arrogance of Hitler on the Sudeten Question threatened to precipitate a general European war. France was diplomatically committed to protect Czechoslovakia, and if France took up arms, Soviet Russia was bound by treaty to rally to the aid of the Czechs. If war came Britain almost certainly would have been drawn into the struggle.

Instead of fighting, the British cabinet, under the direction of Prime Minister Neville Chamberlain, chose to resolve the Sudeten controversy by diplomacy. Horrified by the consequences that war would entail, and aware of British military weakness and widespread sentiments of pacifism, Chamberlain proved to be naively credulous in dealings with the Nazi dictator. Crowning the negotiations was a "parley at the summit" held at Munich in September, 1938. Britain and France compliantly consented to German sovereignty over the Sudetenland, an imprudent piece of prudence as the future would reveal. Hitler had scored another audacious coup simply by rattling the sword and thus he heightened his popularity among the German masses.

If few men in the West were happy over the spoliation of Czechoslovakia, there was, nevertheless, joy in the knowledge that the peace of Europe had been saved. Chamberlain in particular gilded the future until it glowed bright with visions of lasting peace. Soviet Russia, on the other hand, which had no representative at the Munich gathering—Nazi hostility if nothing else forbade that—was embittered and estranged. As seen in the Kremlin, the West was deliberately encouraging Hitler to become the "strangler" of the Soviet Union. Under duress the Czechs ceded strips of territory to Poland and Hungary.

Assertions by Hitler that Germany was now content turned out to be no more trustworthy than a dicer's oath. In March of 1939, Nazi troops stormed into the remainder of Czechoslovakia, and Lithuania was obliged to hand over the Memelland high up on the Baltic. So far the Nazis had things their own way. Without involvement in war, they got what they wanted and were able to rely on popular rallying to defense of the gains.

The radical reordering of the political geography of central Europe convinced many a "doubting Thomas" in the Western democracies that Nazi ambitions aimed at domination over the Continent. That prospect roused dread in Britain lest the balance of power would be tilted against the island kingdom by a potentially hostile state. Up to this point Anglo-French statecraft had been shaped on the assumption that concessions to the dictators was

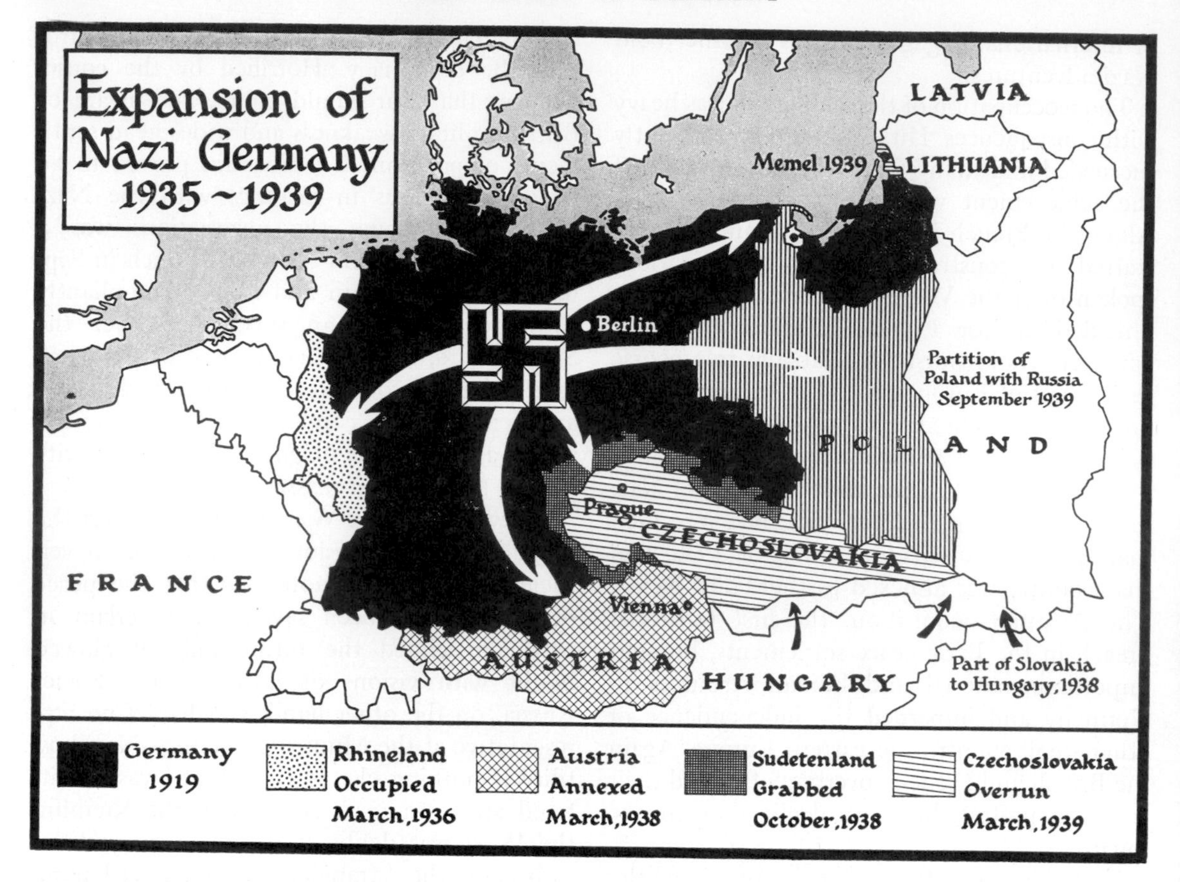

the price of peace—"appeasement" the policy was called.[1]

In the Western democracies, aversion to another war was general and deep-rooted. Nightmare memories of bloodbaths in the First World War, the feeling that a new struggle would annihilate civilization, and so was unthinkable, and wishful thinking fostered official and popular pacifism. Anyone who asserted that war was possible incurred condemnation as a "war-monger." Somehow or other, it was felt, a permanent live-and-let-live arrangement must be worked out between the democracies and militant Germany. That mood, coupled with military unpreparedness, underlay the diplomacy of "appeasement," which, alas, had not appeased, but had rather encouraged the aggressor to trample under foot one country after another.

By the late spring of 1939, the British national mind—and the French—manifested greater solidarity and resolution than at any time since 1914. It was generally agreed that Britain must proclaim, as in fact she did proclaim, "No further aggression." Now that Czechoslovakia had been gobbled down where would the ravenous Nazi appetite turn next? To Poland? Surely. So the Chamberlain ministry headed a movement to unite the states of Europe against the lawlessness of extreme nationalism. First of all, Britain combined with France in a formal pledge to protect Poland, and similar assurances were soon extended to Rumania and Greece. The promise to Greece was published after Fascist Italy had pounced upon the adjoining Kingdom of Albania on Good Friday of 1939.

Few Britons contested the wisdom and desirability of these unprecedented engagements.

[1] In time the word "appeasement" acquired an evil, not to say a sinister, connotation; it came to imply craven concessions to an opponent, and when so used, endangered negotiation, accommodation and compromise so essential in diplomatic bargaining.

If Germany overran Poland, the smaller states of eastern Europe would probably topple like so many nine-pins. France would be the next victim of the Nazi avalanche and then the British Commonwealth and Empire. It was a maxim of British diplomacy that any power or coalition which became undisputed master of the European mainland could become master of the British Isles themselves.

One Briton crystallized his thinking this way: "Our safety, our continued existence as a Great Power, depend on preventing any one nation from dominating Europe—especially from dominating the Low Countries. . . . To give Hitler all he asks is madness. Soon he would strangle our trade without which Britain cannot live. Perhaps without open war he could reduce us to nothing—an island of misery and revolution. . . ."

Another Briton stressed ideological considerations. British "self-interest and calculation," he observed, "should not be our motives for standing against naked force. We should take our stand because we believe that freedom and democracy are right and that dictatorship, oppression and torture are evil." Thinking on these things, the British heart was "garrisoned by faith which casts out fear."

IMPERIALISM AND ECONOMIC DISTRACTIONS

Quest for colonies and paralyzing economic troubles contributed vitally to the oncoming of the Second World War. International jealousies and hostility were generated by the disparity in ownership of wealth-producing overseas dependencies. The colonial "have" powers included small countries—Britain, Holland, Belgium and Portugal—with extensive holdings. On the other side of the fence stood the "have-nots"; Italy and Japan controlled only small and relatively unproductive empires, while Germany and Poland had none at all. Colonial agitators demanded that their countries must acquire overseas possessions befitting their stature as Great Powers and necessary for national economic health.

Resentful over the lost colonies in Africa, Nazi spokesmen agitated for their return and put in claims to other segments of the Dark Continent. These unsatisfied aspirations helped to prepare the German mind for another armed contest with Britain and France. As in Nazi Germany, so in Fascist Italy the imperial impulse ran strong. Publicists loudly complained that Italy had not been allotted a fair share of the African territory redistributed after the First World War. Il Duce arrogantly boasted indeed that he intended to re-create the old Roman Empire. Imperial avarice was first focused upon Abyssinia (Ethiopia), never a possession of the Roman Empire, but an acquisition that would round out the existing Italian empire in eastern Africa.

Clashes of Abyssinians and Italians along the border of Italian Somaliland provoked fears of full-scale war. The League of Nations, to which Abyssinia belonged, proffered recommendations for peaceful accommodation, but Mussolini in 1935 chose to settle matters in the traditions of aggressive imperialism. For the information of any who cared to listen, the dictator shouted:

"The essential arguments . . . are two: the vital needs of the Italian people and their security in East Africa. Put in military terms, the Italo-Abyssinian problem is simple and logical. It admits but one solution—with Geneva, without Geneva, against Geneva."

In the autumn of 1935, Fascist armies advanced upon Abyssinia. Whereupon the League applied partial sanctions against Italy, forbidding the purchase of Italian products, the extension of loans and the sale of certain goods to Italy. But oil, so essential to the Fascist military machine and to Italian industry, was not banned; Mussolini privately observed that if oil sanctions were imposed, the Abyssinian adventure would collapse in a week. Feeling that if oil were shut off, Italy would fight and be joined by Germany, France successfully opposed an embargo. Equally out of fear of war, Britain did not close the Suez Canal to Italian shipping.

Fascist legions conducted the campaign against poorly-weaponed Abyssinia ruthlessly. The bombing of the unprotected town of Dessie in December of 1935 began a gradual de-

On the night of May 9, 1936, the people of Rome celebrated "victory" over Abyssinia.

terioration of civilization, leading on to the dropping of an atom bomb upon Hiroshima ten years later. Abyssinia was quickly forced to her knees and in May, 1936, was annexed to the Italian Empire. The sanctionist measures of the League were exasperating without being effective. Having triumphantly defied the League, Italy resigned from that organization and presently teamed up with Germany in an Axis partnership. The Fascist victory blatantly exposed the weaknesses in the League and dealt an irreparable blow to its authority.

The outcome of the Abyssinian enterprise, moreover, exhilarated Italian nationalism and stimulated agitation for possession of French properties, Corsica, Savoy and Nice, Tunisia and colonies in west Africa. And it was belligerently asserted that Fascism must supplant Britain in Malta and Gibraltar and thus take command of the Mediterranean.

On the far side of the globe, Imperial Japan had seized Manchuria over the protestations of the League and the United States. Then, in the manner of eating an artichoke, Nippon picked off provinces in northern China and in 1937 embarked upon an undeclared war of naked imperialism. Polish spokesmen raised claims to colonies, half as outlets for the redundant population, half to fortify Poland's pretensions to Great Power standing. But the Polish agitations implied no danger to international peace.

Throughout the twenties the twin problem of German reparations and the war-debts owed to the United States weighed desperately upon the neck of the Old World. When Germany fell behind on prescribed payments, Franco-Belgian armies occupied (1923) the Ruhr Valley, the industrial heart of Germany. That operation netted little for the reparations account, but it had disastrous consequences for the German economy and nourished the spirit of revenge.

After that, the Dawes Plan of 1924 removed the reparations question from politics to the sphere of economics. Aided by loans sold to investors in the United States and elsewhere, Germany met her obligations on time. Creditors of Germany transmitted part of the reparations they received to the treasury of the United States to liquidate war debts. Up to a point, these international financial transactions were responsible for the Great Depression, which brought in its train the collapse of reparations. Germany paid nothing after 1931 and in the next year reparations were cancelled for all practical purposes; Allied transfers to America on war-debts soon ceased. Not much had been obtained in fact to repair the damages wrought in the First World War, though Nazi propagandists had effectively exploited the reparations issue in winning Germans to their movement.

The Great Depression looms large in the background of the Second World War. It was attended by wholesale unemployment, popular distress and mass misery, Germany suffering most severely of all. Other highly industrialized countries were badly wounded, it is true, but they had economic reserves to draw upon that Germany lacked. It was in the midst of the economic tornado that the Nazis accumulated sufficient backing to take over the management of affairs, precisely as the militarists seized authority in Japan.

Inability of governments to grapple effectively with immense economic and social problems stimulated bellicose passions. By resorting to higher tariffs, quotas and other barriers to trade, governments endeavored to stabilize their economies, but these practices depressed levels of living and undermined the foundations of world trade and world peace. And not least of the consequences of the Great Depression, perhaps most momentous of all, economic perplexities so absorbed the energies of the Western democracies as to facilitate the march of the dictators from one diplomatic triumph to another.

ARMAMENTS AND POPULAR FEARS

Apprehensions provoked by growing and terrifying military machines helped to make the Second World War possible. After 1918 the fighting services of Germany were pared down to the levels fixed in the Versailles Treaty and armaments were reduced in the victor countries. Conferences at Washington (1922) and at London (1930) set limits upon the naval strength of the leading seapowers. Fearful that the hereditary German foe would seek revenge for 1918, France maintained the largest and finest army in Europe and French security was reinforced by the construction of the famous Maginot Line of fortifications along the border facing Germany.

Apart from such sense of safety as was afforded by the League and by alliances with the smaller and newer countries of eastern Europe, France was protected by the Rhineland security pact of 1925—one of a set of understandings arranged at Locarno, Switzerland. That accord recognized the existing Franco-German boundary as permanent and reaffirmed the demilitarization of the German Rhineland. Britain and Italy promised, in effect, to uphold these engagements. As a sequel to Locarno, Germany was welcomed into the League of Nations. It had not, of course, renounced claims to Polish or Czech territory, and Hitler in 1936 arbitrarily tore up the Locarno engagements.

League agencies, in the meantime, had prepared for an international conference to restrict the size and equipment of armies. In 1932, with the world in the grip of depression and popular demands for economy intense, the "disarmament" meeting assembled at Geneva. German insistence upon equality with France in armaments and armed forces threw the conference into a deadlock. There was considerable juggling of words, but words could not obscure the unbridgeable gap that separated the Germans and the French on essential points. Nothing tangible resulted from the Geneva deliberations; after Hitler withdrew the German delegates, discussions possessed little more than academic interest. In 1936 the naval limitation treaties lapsed, and rivalry in seapower ensued.

As the international situation steadily deteriorated through the machinations of the dictators and diplomatic crises recurred, armament construction, reminiscent of the competition before 1914, gathered momentum. It was Nazi Germany that flashed the signal for the race in Europe and Japan performed similarly in the Orient. Restrictions upon German military strength inscribed in the Versailles Treaty were tossed aside item by item, the Western democracies making no attempt to stop infractions. In a remarkably short time the Third Reich was converted into a gigantic arsenal of war and equipped with the most powerful military juggernaut the world had yet known. Nazi strategic planners concentrated on creating forces that could strike swiftly with the accent on mobile armaments and airpower. Overwhelming superiority in the air (the *Luftwaffe*) imparted peculiar and impressive weight to Hitlerian diplomacy.

Brash propaganda glorifying violence, in opposition to the opinion that war was either a crime or a disease, accompanied the revival of German armed might. "In constant struggle," cried Hitler, "mankind has become great—in eternal peace it [mankind] must perish." Mussolini parroted the Nazi dictator. "War is to man as maternity is to woman," he proclaimed. "I do not believe in perpetual peace. Not only that; I consider peace devitalizing and a negation of the fundamental virtues of man, which only through bloody struggles are revealed in the full light of the sun."

In response to the growing capacity of the dictatorships for war, Great Britain hesitantly and reluctantly embarked upon rearmament. Expansion began in 1935 but the pace of the program was much too slow to satisfy an anxious Conservative minority for which Winston Churchill acted as spokesman. He kept hammering away at the desperate need for catching up to Germany, and for his zeal he was castigated by critics as a contemporary Cassandra. Really big defense appropriations were voted in 1937, which provided, among other equipment, the airplanes that saved Britain three years later. Yet rearmament had not proceeded far enough to encourage British diplomacy to withstand the Nazi dictator at the Munich conference. Up to the eleventh hour, defense preparations and "psychological rearmament" were pertinaciously resisted by the Labour Party, committed as it was to humanitarian idealism.[2]

British military experts initiated staff conversations with their French opposite numbers looking to coordination of all resources in the event of war. But France, upset by fierce political factionalism, lagged behind in military preparedness, though the army was still reputed to be the best in Europe. The French General Staff not only misunderstood the nature of the Nazi regime, but was obsessed by outdated military ideas. War planes and mobile equipment were especially neglected, and many a Frenchman fancied that the Maginot Line allowed him to cultivate his garden without serious danger of an invasion from the East. That fond, very human illusion was shattered to fragments in 1940.

As of 1938, about 8,500,000 soldiers were under arms and nearly 50,000,000 trained reservists were available for duty on short notice. Since 1918 weapons of war had undergone considerable refinement. Major technical advances had been achieved in aircraft and the nations were warned of the havoc that big bombers could cause; stories circulated about secret weapons—a devastating new explosive or destructive gases—capable of wiping out entire cities.

Upbuilding of armaments both mirrored and intensified international tensions and suspicions. Everywhere the growing fighting services accentuated mass uneasiness and dread, until many Europeans felt that a fearful end was preferable to endless fear.

THE DETERIORATION OF THE LEAGUE

In a park of the Palais des Nations at Geneva stands a monument which appropriately symbolized the League of Nations: a golden astro-

[2] As late as April 27, 1939, Labour M. P.'s voted against compulsory military service.

labe dedicated to President Wilson. The planets and the signs of the zodiac are pictured huddled together like the many and diverse members of the League. Here was an embryonic organization for permanent world order and stability to which it was hoped society would proceed.

Born of the harsh experiences of the First World War, the League was dedicated to a regime of collective security. It bespoke the long-cherished dream of a new approach in the settlement of international controversies and of a more rational and safer globe. If the necessity arose, the Covenant provided for a boycott and blockade to paralyze a war maker without bloodshed.

And yet conceptions of the League varied considerably. As envisaged by humanitarian idealists, who thought in terms of "a new heaven and a new earth wherein dwelleth righteousness," the League would be the impartial preserver of world law and order. It was assumed that if a country appealed to force to attain its ambitions, collective international pressure would bring the Covenant-breaker to book. The integrity and independence of each country, that is, were the common responsibility of all nations. But there was another side to the coin. Old-school statesmen, who were wedded to the traditions of power diplomacy, looked upon the League primarily as a partnership to uphold the settlements enshrined in the Paris peace treaties.

Under League auspices much useful and little advertised work of international significance was accomplished. Officials of the League supervised the administration of the Danzig Free State and mandated territories, promoted public health and social welfare projects, fostered intellectual cooperation, struggled to safeguard the rights of minorities, rehabilitated small countries that were in desperate financial straits and drafted plans for the limitation of armaments. Subtly but surely, the League fostered the growth of an international spirit.

In the domain of politics, the League amicably resolved over fifty disputes between nations. These quarrels, it is true, were of a minor character, but the League prevented a real war between Greece and Bulgaria in 1926 that might have touched off a general Balkan conflagration. When confronted by large political controversies, the League faltered, and in the thirties staggered from defeat to defeat in tussles with major powers, bent upon change.

The deterioration of the League, still very young of course, commenced with the Japanese gamble in Manchuria. That setback for the ideal of collective security encouraged other challenges later. Japan resigned from the League and Germany imitated that precedent when Nazi armament demands were denied. Counterbalancing the German defection, Soviet Russia joined up in 1934. Yet the League failed to prevent Italian conquest of Abyssinia in 1936, could not halt renewed Nipponese aggression upon China and was impotent in crises provoked by Hitler in Europe.

WHY THE LEAGUE FAILED

To account for the inability of the League to achieve its high purposes several explanations are in order. It is open to doubt, first of all, whether the world was ready for this particular experiment in collective security. For reasonable success, the League required the sustained backing of hundreds of millions of men and women imbued with an international outlook. Lacking that support the League was almost certain to prove a disappointment, an illusion. As events demonstrated, popular and official allegiance to national interests transcended international concerns and considerations.

Close to the mark were the judgments of a warm Norwegian partisan of the League, who wrote, "As to Europe . . . it was not mentally well prepared to accept and practise the idea of an effective League of Nations. . . The 'practical' politicians . . . did not believe in the efficiency of a League for the security of their countries. They accepted it only half-heartedly . . ." [3]

From the beginning the League was handicapped by the abstention of the United States, whence the most impelling pressure for its creation had come. Without the great trans-Atlantic Republic, the League had the appear-

[3] Halvdan Koht, *The American Spirit in Europe* (1949), p. 261.

ance of a conventional coalition to preserve the status quo. Without the United States the League lacked something in faith and courage as well as in prestige and physical strength. And yet the aloofness of the United States did not fatally undermine the collective experiment. Down to 1936, at any rate, Britain and France were fully capable of stopping German rearmament and restraining Nazi designs of aggrandizement. "The League of Nations," remarked Winston Churchill in 1946, "could have managed to save the peace even without the United States . . . it would have been sufficient simply . . . to prevent the rearmament of Germany."

Great Britain and France declined to honor the commitment, prescribed in the Covenant, to resist acts of aggression on principle wherever they might arise. Blind to the logic that a threat to the security of any country was implicitly a threat to themselves, these governments were not prepared to risk lives and material resources for disorderly and distant Manchuria, for half-barbarous Abyssinia, or even for Czechoslovakia with its restless minorities. The paramount duty, moreover, of upholding international law and peace was beclouded by the prevalent pacifism in the democracies. That attitude precluded the application of stern punitive measures against aggression which might greatly have altered the stream of history. Since the League as such commanded no fighting services, it was helpless to prevent nations from resorting to force in settling disputes. Britain and France, not parties to disputes, were unwilling to display a team spirit, a sense of solidarity in full measure. Moral suasion was not enough to restrain lawbreakers.

Last of all, though first perhaps in importance, the dictators brought about changes to suit themselves by force or the threat of force, as though no international organization for mutual security existed. Field-Marshal Jan C. Smuts, a maker of the Covenant, uttered a memorable epitaph on the League in 1942. "Our ideas," he said, "twenty-two years ago were much too vague and crude, and, at the same time, much too ambitious, with the result that when they came to be tested by hard experience, they proved wanting and their failure helped to contribute to . . . the Second World War."

COALITIONS AND ALLIANCES

Diplomatic alignments must be reckoned among the factors that had bearing on the coming of war. Arrayed in one camp were the satisfied countries, led by Britain and France, and spoken of as the Allies. Partners since 1904, Britain and France on several occasions in the twenties came to the parting of the ways, but the resurgence of a strong and aggressive Germany impelled them to team up again. In keeping with the novel doctrine that the Rhine River had become the frontier of British defense, the London government in 1938 entered into a formal political and military alliance with the Channel neighbor. Rumania and Yugoslavia were already allied to France, leastwise nominally, and so was Poland, which looked upon the Third Republic as the guardian angel. Greece and Turkey also gravitated into the Anglo-French bloc. As explained earlier, the Western democracies promised in 1939 to assist Poland, Rumania or Greece if their independence should be clearly imperilled.

Lined up against this combination were the aggressive and discontented dictatorships. In 1936 a "marriage of convenience," called the Axis, was effected between Germany and Italy and the following year they joined in an ideological alliance to combat Communism; the original edition of this "anti-Comintern" pact had been signed in 1936 by Germany and Japan.

Alone, neither Germany nor Italy felt strong enough to achieve their ambitions, but standing together they might be able to do so. They worked hand in glove with the Spanish rebel chieftain, Francisco Franco, in the ferocious civil war of the late thirties, shipping in armaments and troops to man them. Soviet Russia dispatched limited quantities of military supplies to the Loyalist or Republican government, while British and French diplomacy maneuvered to confine the bloodletting to Spain. In that purpose the Western democracies succeeded, but at the cost of deepening the conviction of the dictators that they were too craven to fight in order to stop aggression. Hitler and his lieutenants reasoned that if the West would not risk war for the vital western Mediterranean, it surely would not fight to save eastern Europe from spoliation. After the Loyalists had been crushed, Franco aligned himself diplomatically with the Axis, though the economic rewards which Germans and Italians expected to reap never materialized.

The Axis mates applauded the territorial expansion of each other, and in the spring of 1939 Hitler and Mussolini negotiated a regular military alliance. In the Axis orbit were Hungary and Bulgaria, both eager to rectify what they regarded as intolerable national wrongs in the settlements after the First World War. And Japan drew close to the Axis, foreshadowing a Three Power Treaty of September, 1940, that converted the Axis into a Triangle.

THE SOVIET SPHINX

What then of Soviet Russia, the most populous of European countries and by the late thirties militarily powerful? A matter of days before the Second World War opened, the Eurasian giant stepped into the Nazi circle with eyes wide open. That alignment, startling to all the world, heralded a total reorientation in the policy of the Kremlin.

Soviet diplomacy has often been tagged sphinx-like, enigmatic, which is fair enough so far as immediate aims were concerned. Maintenance of the security and independence of the Communist Commonwealth in an unsympathetic world of power politics dictated flexible, opportunistic tactics, a course of expediency. Occasionally Stalin expatiated on the theme of "peaceful coexistence" with capitalism, and indicated that the Kremlin was anxious to reach a *modus vivendi* with countries having different social and political institutions.

And yet the long-range objective of the Soviets in world affairs remained unchanged: the victory of world revolution under the aegis of Moscow. That basic tenet imparted to Communist diplomacy a coherency and a stability not matched in other countries. Obedience to the Marxist-Leninist dogma that the predestined outcome of class war would be the violent overthrow of non-Communist states excluded anything beyond surface cordiality with capitalist countries. Hatred for capitalists as a class, suspicion that the governing classes of the West formed a homogeneous whole intent on aggressive war to preserve their wealth, were never entirely absent from Soviet diplomatic calculations.

As an instrument of policy the Kremlin commanded the loyalty of Communists in foreign countries affiliated with the Third International, or *Comintern*. Agents of Moscow, as busy as sandpipers, endeavored to promote the cause of the world proletarian revolution from China to Chile. Yet whatever hopes the Communists may have nurtured of conquering Europe by the sword were frustrated in the summer of 1920. Polish armies, with modest assistance from the West, stopped a furious Soviet drive at the very threshold of Warsaw and then hurled the Red army back. Lenin's assumption that the Polish masses would rebel against their government turned out to be wrong, as he publicly admitted. In 1921, the boundary between Poland and the Soviet Union was drawn in a way that left populations claimed as co-nationals by Russia on the Polish side of the frontier.

After the Communists had firmly established their authority, Soviet statecraft tried to persuade the world that Russia was dedicated to social idealism and peace. But the safety of Russia, it was asserted, was endangered by the avaricious ogre of capitalism; the virtuous maiden of melodrama, so to speak, was constantly imperilled by designing villains. The dispatch of foreign military contingents to Russia after the November Revolution was everlastingly pointed to as proof positive of the predatory intentions of the non-Marxist powers.

Until 1933 the Soviet Union pursued the path of diplomatic isolation, except for Germany, another pariah, which seemed to offer the best chance among the larger countries for a Communist revolution. "All things teach us," Lenin instructed his henchmen, "to look upon

Europe in 1939
NORWAY
Oslo
NORTHERN IRELAND
GREAT BRITAIN
DENMARK
Copenhagen
EIRE
London
NETHERLANDS
The Hague
Berlin
Brussels
BELGIUM
LUXEMBURG
Paris
SAAR
FRANCE
Berne
SWITZERLAND
PORTUGAL
Lisbon
Madrid
SPAIN
CORSICA
Rome
SARDINIA
TANGIER
Gibraltar
MOROCCO (Spain)
SICILY
MOROCCO (France)
ALGERIA
TUNISIA

FINLAND
Helsinki
Leningrad
Stockholm
Tallinn
ESTONIA
Moscow
LATVIA
Riga
SOVIET
MEMELLAND
1939
LITHUANIA
Kaunas
DANZIG
Smolensk
N Y
UNION
Warsaw
POLAND
1939
Kiev
Kharkov
Rostov
ECHOSLOVAKIA
Budapest
HUNGARY
RUMANIA
Belgrade
Bucharest
IGOSLAVIA
BULGARIA
Sofia
Tirane
ALBANIA
Ankara
TURKEY
GREECE
Athens
DODECANESE IS.
(Italy)
CYPRUS

Germany as our most trustworthy ally. She wants revenge; we want revolution. . . . Time will show whether a German hegemony or a Communist Federation will rise from the ruins of Europe." In 1922, Russia signed a treaty of friendship and trade with Germany—the Treaty of Rapallo. Coming out of a clear sky, this understanding alarmed France in particular, which suspected that an assault upon the Versailles peace settlement was being hatched. Thanks to this treaty, Russia broke through the wall of exclusion, while Germany, in addition to commercial benefits, obtained facilities on Soviet soil to experiment in armaments.

Yet the proletarian insurrection in Germany on which the Kremlin pinned its hope failed to come off. Communist faith in the victorious sweep of proletarian revolution over Europe consequently receded, and it declined further as the Soviet Union became preoccupied with domestic problems and projects. Peace and stability were absolute essentials during the first phase of planned industrialization as were decent relations with the West in order to obtain needed machinery and expert technicians. Accordingly, Moscow entered into ordinary diplomatic and commercial intercourse with other European countries and arranged non-aggression treaties with her small neighbors.

Not long after the enthronement of the Nazis in 1933, Soviet foreign policy switched radically. Hitler's venomous denunciations of Communism and his plans for acquiring "living space," *Lebensraum*, at the expense of Russia as blueprinted in *Mein Kampf*, excited grave anxieties in the Kremlin; German technicians and engineers at work in Russia were dismissed and connections between the Soviet and German armies were dissolved. At the same time the bellicose imperialism of Japan menaced the security of Soviet Siberia. Elementary prudence, in a word, dictated that the Soviet Union should draw near to the despised capitalist countries of the West.

On the initiative of Washington, diplomatic relations with the United States, in abeyance since the Bolshevik Revolution, were established. And, more important, Russia in 1934 secured admittance into the League of Nations, which hitherto had been vehemently assailed as an instrument of capitalist enemies dangerous for the Soviet Commonwealth. At Geneva, Russian spokesmen pleaded eloquently for "disarmament," expressed allegiance to the League principle of collective security and called for resistance to "fascist" aggressors. Special treaties of mutual assistance were signed with France and Czechoslovakia, the latter being conditional upon French fulfillment of its obligation to aid the Czechs, if they were victims of aggression.

But the rapid deterioration of the League institution and the transactions at Munich in 1938, which the Kremlin interpreted as the high-water mark of Western hypocrisy, brought another distinct reorientation in Soviet diplomacy. Would Russia have fought if war had resulted from the contentions over the Sudetenland? Not unlikely, it appears, but whether Soviet cooperation with the West would have been whole-souled and decisive may well be doubted. In any event, on the morrow of Munich, angry, humiliated and deeply suspicious, Moscow crawled back into the hermit's shell. *Pravda* observed, "The Soviet Union views with equanimity the question as to which imperialist robber gives orders . . . in one or another vassal state, for it sees no difference between German and English robbers."

STALIN TEAMS UP WITH HITLER

Throughout the spring and summer of 1939, Stalin enjoyed the exhilarating experience of being wooed by two suitors, the democratic West and Nazi Germany. Hitler held out the more flattering inducements, the more alluring prospects for the future, and to Germany Russia became engaged—to the great discomfiture of the more scrupulous rival. In August of 1939, Russia and Germany signed commercial and non-aggression pacts. That much was published, but a secret understanding partitioned Poland between the two conspirators, assigned Lithuania to the Nazi sphere and placed the other Baltic Republics under Soviet influence.

If Germany and the Western democracies now went to war, the Soviet Union might be able to exploit the situation by appropriating territories that she coveted. And if the non-Marxist countries, potential opponents of the Communist Commonwealth, should deplete themselves in a war of attrition, the Kremlin would be presented with a marvellous opportunity to expand, to sweep "bourgeois civilization from the face of the earth." That indeed was the paramount concern of Soviet world policy. "Wars are a necessary prerequisite for our success," Lenin had explained. "They bring economic chaos and economic chaos brings extremism, and we Bolsheviks are extremists."

WAR COMES

By reason of the bargains with the Kremlin, the German sense of security was greatly enhanced. The danger of serious fighting on two fronts in case of war was dispelled. Poland, whose eastern provinces Russia coveted while Germany desired the western districts, came next on the agenda of Nazi aggression.

After Nazi troops had seized the remnant of Czechoslovakia in March, 1939, German pressure upon Poland, which had been rising in tempo, was intensified. Ruffian with a brain that he was, Hitler demanded that the Free State of Danzig should forthwith be incorporated in the Third Reich and that Poland should award Germany a thoroughfare across to the province of East Prussia. It was charged that the Poles, emboldened by Anglo-French friendship, were deliberately exterminating the German-speaking minority in Poland; border incidents enflamed emotions and hatreds in both countries.

Poland had no intention of surrendering to Nazi avarice. The destruction of Czechoslovakia poignantly demonstrated the folly and futility of trying to satisfy the Nazi appetite by concessions. After no little dialectic shadow-boxing, Hitler thrust aside mediation proposals, launched an ultimatum at Warsaw and on September 1, 1939, the heavy weight of the big Nazi battalions crashed across the Polish border. Before the month was over Soviet troops moved in force into eastern Poland.

Britain and France promptly withdrew their swords from the scabbards in fulfillment of pledges to Poland, and the British Dominions, except for Eire (the Irish Free State), followed the lead of the mother country. The other European countries, Italy and Russia included, and the United States, too, proclaimed their neutrality.

Learned historical experts have long debated the controversial question of immediate responsibility for the First World War. Truth, it is well known, is relative and is often alloyed by an admixture of error, but no scholarly war of words is likely to arise over the coming of the Second World War. Direct responsibility for the outbreak rests squarely upon the demonic head of one man, the Nazi Chancellor, Adolf Hitler. He and his closest counsellors appealed to the sword, confident of German superiority, certain that because Germans were more intelligent, more industrious and more disciplined than other peoples, they could overcome and rule them. The war was the climactic act in the monstrous Hitlerian drama, confirming the aphorism that "all power tends to corrupt and absolute power corrupts absolutely."

THE CONFLICT SPREADS: ITALY AND THE BALKANS

Although the ally of Germany, Fascist Italy lingered on the sidelines in the initial phase of the war to the surprise of many observers. However much Mussolini may have wished to fight, preparations for combat were incomplete. The Western democracies renewed their efforts to drive a wedge into the Axis, but neither cajolery, nor promises, nor economic pressure could persuade Mussolini to break with the Nazi partner. In June of 1940, as France reeled in defeat, Il Duce saw—or thought he saw—a chance to make cheap gains. Accordingly, war was declared upon France and Britain, and Blackshirted soldiers advanced a short distance onto French soil before the negotiation of an armistice. Visions of aggrandizement at the expense of France swam before Fascist eyes.

As the next move, in October, 1940, Mussolini carried the fighting into the Balkans, attacking Greece by way of the Albanian satellite. Instead of a quick victory, however, the Fascist troops suffered humiliating reverses at the hands of spirited Greeks. Whereupon Nazi Germany, afraid that British forces would occupy the area, intervened in the Balkan cockpit. Hungary and Bulgaria were more firmly yoked to the German chariot of war and Rumania became the merest puppet. These countries served as staging areas for a Nazi plunge southward in the Balkans.

Rather than surrender to Hitlerian lordship, an anti-German military faction in Yugoslavia defiantly seized the government and made ready to resist domination. The New York *Times* likened the *coup d'etat* to "a lightning flash illuminating a dark landscape." But the Nazi Juggernaut would not be denied. In April, 1941, armored columns and warplanes raced across Yugoslavia and down into Greece conquering Crete as well. Britain rendered limited help to the Greeks, but within a month the Nazis were lords of the Balkans and the spectacular triumph was sealed by a new treaty of friendship and neutrality with uneasy Turkey.

THE INVOLVEMENT OF SOVIET RUSSIA

On June 22, 1941, the great Nazi war machine smashed savagely against Russia, an act which drastically altered the whole war panorama. The Eastern struggle became a mortal duel between military giants. Ample warnings of an impending German invasion had been despatched to the Kremlin by Great Britain, but Stalin was inclined to discount them.

After the making of the August, 1939, pact, Soviet policy was dominated by the determination to keep out of the war, while the non-Communist countries of western Europe ripped one another to shreds. Pursuing that line, the Kremlin courted the favor of the Nazis by shipping large quantities of grain, oil and cotton, permitting Japanese goods to be transported across the Soviet Union for Germany and by even offering to purchase supplies for Germany in third countries and thus circumvent the British blockade.

Yet at the same time, Soviet armaments were hurriedly built up and other preparations were made to fight. Russia also utilized the golden chance to push out its frontiers. Eastern Poland was garrisoned in September of 1939 and the small Baltic Republics were absorbed piecemeal. When Finland manfully declined to acquiesce in Soviet demands, Red armies attacked the country. After stiff fighting, Finland was crushed and obliged to surrender territory to Russia, though retaining its independence. The difficulties which the Soviets encountered in whipping Finland persuaded foreigners, not least the Nazis, that Russia had been overrated as a military power. Presently Rumania handed over Bessarabia and northern Bucovina to the Soviet Union. At most points the Russian boundaries of 1914 had been recovered and even crossed in some areas.

Upon the collapse of France in the spring of 1940, the Nazis maneuvered to bind the Eurasian giant more actively to German purposes. To discuss the whole range of relations, Foreign Minister Molotov journeyed to Berlin in November, 1940. The Nazis proposed that the Soviet Union might appropriate Iran (Persia) and India, but they would not accede to Soviet aspirations in the Balkans and the Turkish Straits. Consequently the Kremlin refused to enter into new understandings. Hitler stopped talking and started girding for battle. He issued (December 18, 1940) a fateful directive ordering that:

"The German armed forces must be prepared to crush Soviet Russia in a quick campaign even before the conclusion of the war against England. . . . Preparations . . . are to be completed by May 15, 1941."

Nazi pressure into the Balkans, which the masters of the Kremlin considered their own special preserve, provoked anger and consternation in Moscow. More troops were mobilized along the western frontiers, but the strong preference to remain neutral persisted. As evidences of that, a pact of neutrality was concluded (April, 1941) with Japan, and supplies were faithfully delivered to Germany, even though Nazi payments in machinery had fallen behind schedule.

Operations in the Balkans, especially against Yugoslavia, upset the Nazi military schedule, decisively delaying the time when the Nazis struck against Russia. Hitler and his top henchmen argued that victory over the Soviet Union would yield sorely needed raw materials and *Lebensraum*, and could be achieved quickly and gloriously. Only the rapid defeat of Russia, Hitler seems to have reasoned, would bring Britain to terms and keep the United States out of the war. When the German invasion started in June 1941, Great Britain promised all possible assistance to Russia on the principle, as Prime Minister Churchill put it, that "if Hitler invaded hell I should make at least a favorable reference to the devil in the House of Commons."

ENTRY OF THE UNITED STATES

The United States became a belligerent under different circumstances from Russia. This "grand climacteric" followed immediately upon a treacherous Japanese descent upon Pearl Harbor of December 7, 1941. Whether without that raid or something comparable to it, the United States would have become a full-fledged belligerent belongs in the misty realm of speculation, not of history. Aversion to war in the United States, the desire for peace at almost any price had been concretely demonstrated in the "Neutrality Acts" of the late thirties. "We are not isolationists," President Roosevelt asserted in 1936, "except in so far as we seek to isolate ourselves completely from war."

Upon the outbreak of the conflict in Europe, the United States faced one of the most momentous problems it had ever had to decide. American public life proceeded on the assumption that all issues—war and peace included—were susceptible to rational discussion, if not always to harmonious solution. Detestation of the dictatorships and their doings were well-nigh universal. The national mind was torn between dread of the repercussions that an Axis victory would have upon the Western Hemisphere and the hope of avoiding involvement in war. A great dilemma, that is, confronted the Republic, stirring up an acrid and divisive controversy. While the President kept repeating that the United States was not going to war, he was firmly convinced that the country must pursue a course calculated to ensure the survival of the enemies of the Axis.

The watchword was "all measures short of war." In the implementation of that policy the United States departed from the traditions of neutrality, in ways that pointed toward intervention in a military sense. As a first and fundamental step, the embargo on the sale of war matériel was repealed in November, 1939; that action promised to benefit Britain and France. After the spectacular Axis conquest of western Europe in 1940, it was feared that Britain might also collapse, and that Axis attacks upon the New World would ensue.

Law after law reflected the growing conviction that the interests and values of the United States were in desperate jeopardy. Huge appropriations were voted to enlarge the fighting services, conscription was adopted for the first time in peacetime, industries were geared to defense production and the bonds of hemispheric solidarity with Latin America and Canada were drawn tighter. Fifty destroyers were transferred to Britain in exchange for military bases from Newfoundland to Trinidad, a transaction that morally bound the United States to the British cause.

Both aspirants for the Presidency in 1940, the Democrat, Roosevelt, and the Republican, Wendell Willkie, argued that the United States should keep out of war, but should furnish supplies to the foes of the Axis. Soon after the election, the epochal Lend-Lease law was enacted (March, 1941), assuring large-scale assistance to anti-Axis countries without cash payments; shipments eventually topped $50,-000,000,000. To protect vessels hauling supplies to Europe from "the arsenal of democracy," naval patrols were authorized. When Nazi submarines actually torpedoed ships flying the Stars and Stripes, an undeclared sea war began.

In Congress and country, a strong but diminishing volume of reason and emotion opposed serious breaches of neutrality on the score that the United States would become involved in a shooting war. With the outbreak of the German-Russian conflict, it was urged in some quarters that the two totalitarian tyrannies should be allowed to fight it out by themselves and that, if the United States intervened at all, it should do so only when necessary to save the one threatened with destruction.

While American eyes were very largely glued upon Europe, relations with Japan continued to deteriorate. Japan, of course, was still fighting China, bent upon dominating that country, but the United States desired an independent China and consistently championed the Chinese Nationalists. As during the First World War, Europe's adversity was Japan's opportunity; plans for the "Greater East Asia" were driven forward. Only the United States stood as an obstacle in the Nipponese path of conquest. As a counterweight to possible American intervention in the Orient, the Tokyo militarists concluded a famous Three Power Treaty with Germany and Italy in September of 1940. Each signatory promised to fight any country—the United States was clearly indicated—that went to war with any one of the three. Beyond that, Japan signed the neutrality pact with the Soviet Union, noted above, which seemed to insure Nippon against attack by the Eurasian titan.

Pearl Harbor after the Japanese came

Companies in the United States kept selling scrap iron and oil to Nippon, until an executive order in the summer of 1941 stopped that traffic. Without supplies of oil the Japanese economy must surely have been paralyzed, and that prospect seems to have inspired the final decision to fight. At the same time, Japanese marines moved into the defenseless French colony of Indo-China and maneuvered suspiciously in the area of the Dutch East Indies. The State Department dispatched repeated protests to Tokyo and diplomatists of the two countries deliberated in Washington on the prevailing antagonisms. That was a wearying and futile business, for neither side would budge from its position concerning China, so no accommodation was or could be reached.

Conversations ended abruptly on December 7, 1941, when Nipponese airmen unloosed their deadly bombs upon Pearl Harbor. The great American fleet stationed there was hopelessly crippled and American casualties exceeded 3,600. The response in the United States to this unparalleled disaster was instant and instructive; with only one dissenting voice, the Congress declared war upon Japan. "Within the hour," as Churchill had promised, Britain too was at war with Japan.

As they were pledged by treaty to do, Germany and Italy promptly declared war on the United States. If they had not done so, it is doubtful whether the military resources of the United States could have been concentrated on Europe as they were. One by one the Latin American states entered the contest, leaving in all the world only a few neutrals, such as Spain, Switzerland, Turkey, Eire and Sweden. More completely than ever before, the spreading conflagration had engulfed the whole globe.

ASCENDANCY OF THE TRIANGLE

From the beginning of the war until well into 1942, the tide of battle ran heavily in favor of the Triangle—Germany, Italy, Japan. In the first month, Nazi lightning tactics, together with Soviet invasion from the East, crushed Poland completely. The conquerors divided the Polish spoils and ruthlessly disposed of elements in the population that might foment trouble. Jews in particular suffered under the sadistic Nazi jackboot; tens of thousands, then hundreds of thousands, were scientifically slaughtered.

In the western theater the fighting was so tepid that observers called the war unreal, a "phoney." Zest for combat was conspicuously absent. Frenchmen complacently assumed that the massive Maginot fortifications would keep the enemy from their fields and hearths. At a leisurely pace British and French military resources were mobilized. It was the calm before the storm. In April, 1940, the Nazi typhoon swept westward with unprecedented violence. Denmark was occupied, all the key-points in Norway were captured in a single day and the Low Countries were rapidly overpowered by fast-moving Nazi ground and air contingents. Worst of all, reputedly strong France proved to be only a brilliant façade, collapsing in a trifle more than a month. Mussolini seized the opportunity to bring the stiletto into play.

The sinister shadow of the Nazi swastika extended from the Pyrenees to the Vistula. All the world was shocked and awed by the rapidity of the German advance. Small wonder that the jubilant Nazis came to believe that the *Wehrmacht* was invincible.

On June 22, 1940, an improvised French government signed an armistice with Hitler (later one with Mussolini), subjecting the country to alien domination. Part of France was organized on authoritarian principles in the image of the Nazi conqueror, though under the administration of Frenchmen with headquarters in Vichy. This collaborationist regime, which possessed little freedom of action, bequeathed a frightful legacy of bitterness and strife to France at the end of the war. Fleecing the French population to the limit, the Germans procured the "butter" which they had been denied in order to make the guns that they carried.

Foreigners with the perspective of frogs pronounced eloquent elegies of doom upon Europe's oldest Great Power. Yet in reality France though down was not out. Stunned into silence and docility at first, the spirit of France quickly reasserted itself. A gallant resistance, part Communist and part nationalist,

The German Luftwaffe put forth all its power in order, as Hitler said, to "punish" London. The destruction was great but the strategic value of the raids was small.

expert in espionage and sabotage, and paralleled by similar movements in other countries conquered by the dictators, contributed to the ultimate destruction of the Axis.

France having dropped out of the war, Britain and the Empire kept solitary vigil on the ramparts of European freedom. British troops that had been committed to the war on the continent had retreated to the sands of French Dunkirk, whence they were fetched home by a marvel of improvisation. Only the narrow ribbon of the Channel saved Britain from the dismal fate of France. Amidst the spring disasters, Winston Churchill supplanted Neville Chamberlain as British Prime Minister, and he enlisted all the political parties in a coalition ministry. Taking the helm at a moment of supreme national peril, Churchill developed into perhaps the greatest war leader in the long and colorful history of the British Isles. His inspired and inspiring speeches, replete with imperishable phrases, belong among the masterpieces of English prose.

> He above the rest
> In shape and gesture proudly eminent
> Stood like a tower.

Britannia, of course, still ruled the waves and imposed a blockade in the classical tradition on the Continent. And the Royal Navy vigorously combatted Nazi U-boats which, in the summer of 1940, took their heaviest toll of the war in terms of the tonnage sunk per submarine. And surface units of the Fascist fleet were severely battered. In one of the epic chapters of the war, the Royal Air Force repelled the fierce assaults of the *Luftwaffe* upon the cities of the island kingdom. Help flowing from the United States enheartened the embattled Britons; factories hummed with armament production; farmers bent to the growing of 70 per cent of the food that was consumed in the island. Hitler debated a landing in Britain but decided that an attempt would be sheer folly. Failure of the Nazis to seal Britain off was doubtless Hitler's greatest military defeat. So long as the island kingdom survived, no conqueror could rest secure as the master of Europe. Neither Nazi bombers nor guided missiles could break the will of Britain nor seriously interrupt industrial output.

THE INVASION OF RUSSIA

After overrunning the Balkans in the spring of 1941, the *Wehrmacht*, with limited cooperation from satellite states, slashed deep into the Soviet Union, killing and burning as they advanced. "Our nostrils were filled," a young Nazi sergeant recorded, "with the stench of burning villages." The speed of the drive seemed to confirm the fashionable prophecy that Russia would quickly be knocked out. Eleven weeks after the campaign began, the official Nazi press proclaimed in banner headlines, "The Great Hour has Struck; the War in the East is Over."

At that point it appeared that Russia was indeed on the verge of disaster. Leningrad was invested as the prelude to a horrible and long-drawn-out siege, and the invader had pushed far into the Ukraine. As the vanguard of the *Wehrmacht* rolled to within walking distance of Moscow, hysteria gripped the community; rioting and looting broke loose, industrial establishments and government offices were hurriedly evacuated. Peasant resistance to the Communist dictatorship flared up in places and soldiers deserted to the enemy in considerable numbers, proving that the Communists had not consolidated themselves with all elements of the country. With singular obtuseness, Hitler vetoed proposals to exploit to the full the popular disaffection with the Stalinist regime.

Yet Russia did not fold up. The very immensity of the country was a military asset of incalculable value, and so was that proverbially loyal ally, "General Winter." Bitterly cold weather and terrific snowstorms—the most terrible winter for a century—wrought havoc upon the invaders. Only inadequate preparations had been made by the Germans for the ordeal of a Muscovite winter so that soldiers froze miserably, as once Napoleon's had done, on bare and windswept plains. Prominent generals recommended pulling back from Russia, a suggestion which Hitler, concerned partly for his political prestige, angrily repudiated.

Piteous Soviet appeals were addressed to London for a "Second Front" in the West of Europe to relieve the suffocating Nazi pressure. But sorely-beset Britain was capable only of shipping military supplies for use against the common enemy. Bleeding the foe at every opportunity, sturdy Russian warriors fought desperately for Mother Russia—scarcely for the economic interpretation of history or any other Marxist-Leninist dogma. When the weather

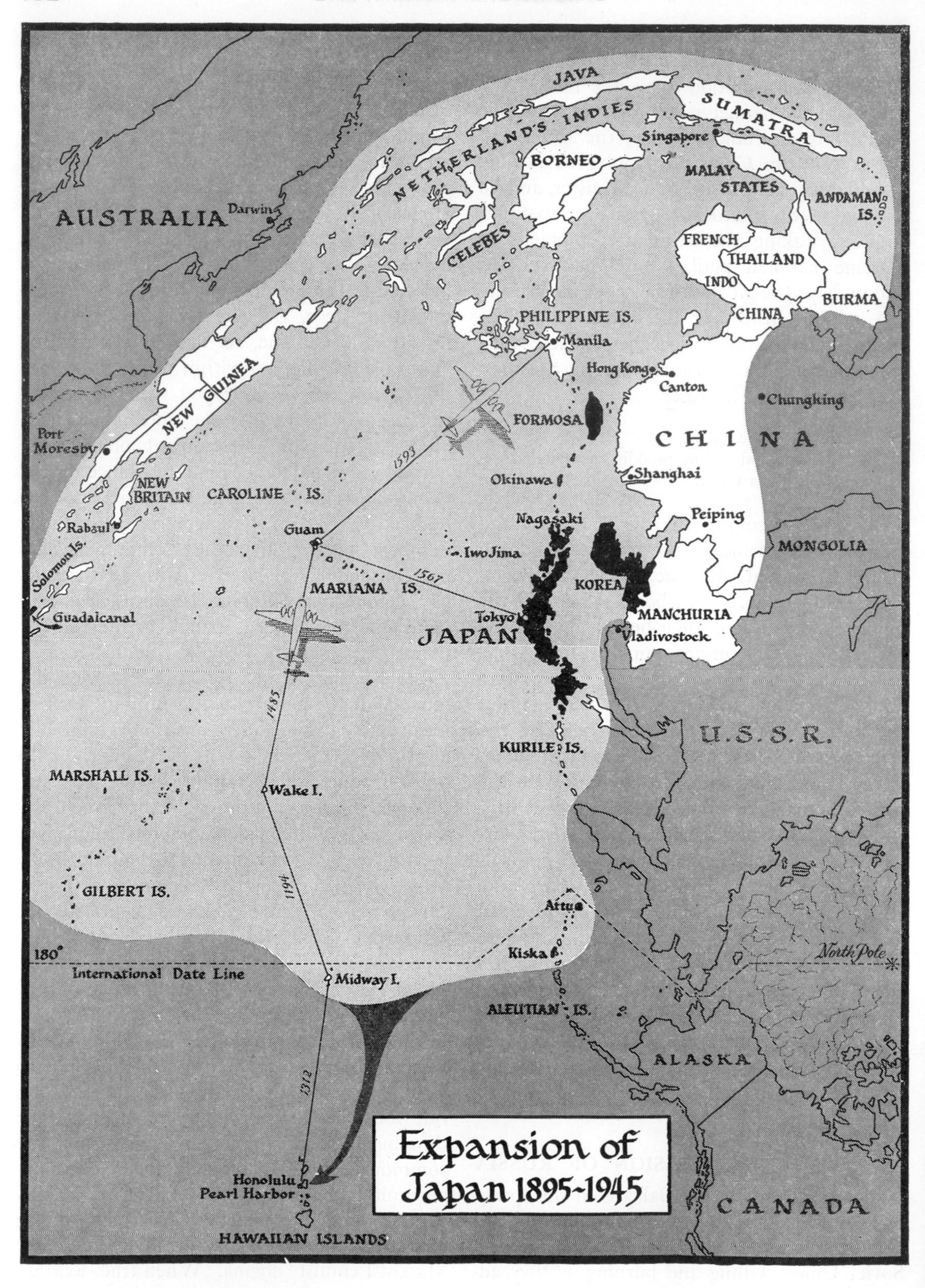

Expansion of Japan 1895-1945

relented in 1942, Nazi armored columns charged into the foothills of the Caucasus and to within sight of the Volga River.

THE JAPANESE ADVANCE

If anything, the Japanese onslaught in the months after Pearl Harbor surpassed the sensational German thrust into Russia. It was a story of almost unrelieved disaster for the Allied cause. With stunning swiftness and a fervor truly impassioned, Nipponese buccaneers boldly seized the states in southeastern Asia, the Philippines, the Dutch East Indies and other islands in the Pacific. Jungle fighting in these areas invested the Japanese with something of the reputation of supermen, and not soon would the Western nations recover from the loss of "face" resulting from their defeats. Early in 1942 the conquest of great India seemed within the range of the practicable, and Nipponese seaforces pushed perilously close to Australia, separated only by narrow seas from the island fringe of Asia. Never before had a foreign power directly threatened to in vade Australia, a continent that has never known war on its soil.

Conquered areas were dragooned into the Japanese "co-prosperity sphere" and native passions were enflamed by stock propaganda against predatory white imperialists. As explained to receptive native peoples, the war was a racial struggle with brown and yellow pitted against white, an utter absurdity of course since the Chinese fought on the "white" side. By smashing the colonial regimes of Western powers and by making their own rule extremely unpopular, the Nipponese promoted unprecedented anti-imperialist sentiments among conquered Asiatics.

THE TRIUMPH OF THE ALLIES

For the Allies, the summer of 1942 stood out as the most critical stage of the conflict. Several lean months lay ahead but by year's end the Triangle had clearly started on the path to surrender. American arms had fought and won great sea battles in the Coral Sea and at Midway. These major strategic victories, achieved by numerically inferior American forces, checked the hitherto invincible Japanese and closed their short-lived superiority in the broad Pacific. Amphibious operations, moreover, had been carried to a triumphant conclusion at Guadalcanal in the Solomons, deep in the South Pacific.

The Red Army, meanwhile, not only overwhelmed the *Wehrmacht* in the decisive battle of Stalingrad on the Volga, but unleashed a powerful counter-offensive. And, after two years of see-sawing in the desert sand and rock of northern Africa, the British, at El Alamein, frustrated an Axis drive into Egypt. That epic battle, in the judgment of Winston Churchill, marked the turning of "the Hinge of Fate." Ultimate victory in the grim, global struggle, though nearly three years away, was assured by the close of 1942.

Italy was the first of the enemy powers to cave in. In November, 1942, while British divisions chased the Axis along the rim of Africa, British and American armies were poured into French Morocco and Algeria. North Africa was cleansed of enemy forces in May, and presently operations were extended to the "soft underbelly" of Italy. Restive Italians exploded; many soldiers had never had any stomach for the war; jealousies engendered friction between Fascist politicians and military commanders; urban workers, resentful of Nazi penetration into their country and much more Communist than Fascist in conviction, broke out in turbulent demonstrations.

So fast did disillusionment and despair spread that in July, 1943, Mussolini was unhorsed. The flimsy Fascist edifice swiftly disintegrated and soon an armistice with the Allies was accepted. Mussolini proclaimed a neo-Fascist Republic, it is true, but it lacked public support and danced obediently to tunes called by the Germans. Arduous campaigning up the rugged peninsula earned the Allies their eventual reward in the surrender of the Germans (May, 1945). Caught by truculent partisans, Mussolini, the loathsome evangelist of Fascism, was butchered like a fat ox.

It was much more difficult and costly to win the decision over Germany. Ceaseless aerial attacks pounded large sections of the

On Guadalcanal

great German cities into wreckage and rubble. For want of planes, it was impossible for the *Luftwaffe,* which had written a spectacular record in the first phase of the war, to perform the many tasks assigned to it. Reconnaisance for U-boat operations, for one thing, faltered disastrously. Allied blockading forces held Fortress Europe in a python-like embrace and navies destroyed German surface ships or drove them into hiding.

Nazi naval energies were then concentrated on undersea warfare. Equipped with the novel Schnorkel breathing tube, a German invention that removed the necessity of having to come to the surface to charge batteries, U-boats could cruise remarkably long distances beneath the water. Sallying forth in packs, they torpedoed so much shipping that Allied leaders feared that transportation across the Atlantic would be disastrously crippled. As in the First World War, months elapsed before British and Allied sea and aircraft were able to counteract the U-boat efficiently. In the spring of 1943 the anti-submarine offensive was thrown into high gear, and before the year was over the "Battle of the Atlantic" had been virtually won.

After the victory at Stalingrad, the Soviet armies started to roll irresistibly westward. From that point on, though not before, Lend-Lease supplies, especially mobile equipment, were of fundamental importance in the Soviet successes. As well as hurling the Nazis from the Fatherland, the Russians crashed into the Balkans and, with the cooperation of native partisans, cracked Axis control there. Then the Red armies hammered up the Danube Valley by way of Hungary into Austria.

To the north Soviet troops fought into Poland. As they approached Warsaw, a secretly organized Polish Home Army went into action against the German forces in the city (August, 1944). Warsaw witnessed possibly the most savage fighting in the entire war, and much of the city was obliterated as though a fantastic plow had passed over it. On into eastern Germany the Russians marched, chopping the Nazis to pieces as they advanced.

THE DEFEAT OF GERMANY

Devastating blows, in the meantime, had been descending upon the Hitlerian Reich from the other side. In the basic strategy of the Western Allies, Europe took precedence over the Pacific area. Colossal masses of American men and equipment were dispatched to the British Isles, and the fabulous industrial resources of the New World, once they had been fully geared to war production, told and told decisively in the theaters of western Europe. As indications of the magnitude of the American military efforts, factories produced nearly 300,000 military airplanes and shipyards turned out upwards of 37,000,000 tons

Beachhead scene—D Day

of non-combat vessels. All told, ships of the United States hauled better than 200,000,000 tons of cargo and transported nearly 10,000,000 troops overseas in the course of the struggle.

Detailed preparations were matured for a crucial cross-Channel assault upon the vaunted Nazi Atlantic Wall in France. Partly in response to Soviet pleading for a "second front," British and Canadian elements raided French Dieppe in August, 1942. That bold enterprise was a tragedy of errors, though lessons were learned which were of material value two years later. The Dieppe raid did not at all satisfy the Kremlin, which never ceased to complain that the Western Allies were not carrying a fair share of the military load. "The Red army," Stalin blurted out angrily, "has borne the whole brunt of the war." A plan that Churchill favored of opening a direct route to Russia across Norway was never put to the test. Supreme command of Allied operations in the West was entrusted to General Dwight D. Eisenhower, only a Colonel when the war opened, but at its end the most admired and respected soldier of his generation.

On June 6, 1944, one of the most stirring dramas of military history started to unfold. Allied armies, shuttled over from Britain, pierced Fortress Europe by landing on the choppy beaches of Normandy. Terrific bombing of military installations in France preceded the invasion, and the time, location and extent of the landings took the German Supreme Command by surprise.

Bloody struggles ensued, but the once invincible Nazi legions could no longer hold their ground. Their defenses crumbled and Allied troops dashed pell-mell into Paris and into the Low Countries. On August 25, the glorious cathedral of Notre Dame looked upon a moving celebration of deliverance, one of the most impressive pageants in her seven centuries of existence. Weird weapons from the Nazi armory—flying bombs and giant rockets—that had torn gaping holes in English cities were throttled. From the Riviera coast on the Mediterranean, other Allied divisions fought northward practically completing the liberation of France.

Instead of the purple bulletins of impending victory which formerly had been dished out, German soldiers and civilians were stridently warned of the dire fate that would befall them if the enemies conquered. Among the rank and file of the armies, confidence in the Nazi leadership stood unshaken to the end. Certain high-ranking officers appreciated that victory was out of the question, but, loyal to their military oath, they proffered expert advice in the hope of averting total disaster.

On the verge of defeat, the opposition to Hitler, hitherto spotty and insignificant, plucked up courage. Anti-Nazi Germans executed in July, 1944, a long prepared plot to remove the Führer by violence, but the scheme fell short by a matter of inches. With adversity breathing hot upon the Fatherland, the *Wehrmacht* in "dark December" of 1944 launched a bloody counter-offensive in eastern Belgium—the Battle of the Bulge. This last desperate toss of the iron dice, the wildest gamble of the whole war, caught the Allied commanders off guard. But after the initial shocks had been blunted, the armies of the United States, from top to bottom, responded admirably, and the terrifying thrust in the Ardennes was quickly repelled.

Presently Allied troops plunged up to the Rhine at several points and then over it. Gripped though their country was by galloping paralysis, the Germans put up a gallant if suicidal resistance. Round the clock bombing shattered German railways and canals. Power plants and heavy industries were crippled by insufficiency of coal, and supplies of oil dropped precipitately. West and East, the Allied noose tightened round the doomed Reich. On April 25, American and Soviet vanguards clasped hands on the banks of the Elbe, slicing Germany in two. On the other side of the globe that same day, a conference opened in San Francisco to draft the Charter of the United Nations; it was widely believed that these two events symbolized a radical alteration in the history of the world. Russian soldiers deliriously hacked their way into bomb-blasted Berlin; Cossacks bivouacked in the parks of the German capital.

Berlin, like Hamburg, Nuremberg and many other German cities, was left a mass of ruins.

Having pulled the temple of Germany and of Europe down in ruins, Hitler perished miserably in a Berlin garden. He hoped, doubtless, to create a weird myth for the Germans of the future. Certain top Nazis emulated their malevolent master by committing suicide, while others were apprehended and held for trial as war criminals. On May 7, 1945, an improvised German government surrendered ignominiously and unconditionally to the Allies.

THE COLLAPSE OF JAPAN

These epochal developments caused loud reverberations in the distant Pacific. It was now the turn of Japan, though the route from Guadalcanal to Tokyo was circuitous and bloody. The Great Pacific War was essentially an American enterprise against tough and fanatical Japan. "Hopping" up the island ladder of the Pacific and cutting across lanes of communication that led from conquered Asiatic countries to Japan, the American forces performed prodigies of skill and endurance. Reconquest of the Philippines and adjacent islands carried the fury of war to the very threshold of the Japanese homeland. Sanguinary conflicts on Okinawa cost the lives of the rival commanding generals, 110,000 Nipponese and 12,500 American fighting men. In three months of frenzied *Kamikaze* attacks upon American shipping, the enemy sacrificed no fewer than 7,800 aircraft.

British armies, in the meanwhile, operating in southeast Asia, combatted Jap and jungle, administering the most crushing reverses on land in Nipponese history. In spite of war weariness and the ravages of runaway inflation, the Chinese kept guerilla warfare going against the enemy. The pre-war feud between Nationalists and Communists was ominously resumed.

American war planes swept the Japanese sky almost clean of enemy fighters and unloosed prodigious bomb tonnages upon the fragile cities of the Mikado. Vast areas were laid waste, public utilities were paralyzed, armament production slumped and so did national morale. Annihilation of the battle fleet, heavy losses in commerce carriers and a tightening blockade robbed Japan, an insular power utterly dependent on uninterrupted maritime communications, of all hope of holding out. As General MacArthur subsequently reported ". . . when Japan surrendered, they had at least 3,000,000 of as fine ground troops as I have ever known," but "they didn't have the materials to fight with . . ."

When the Tokyo government hesitated to accept an Allied ultimatum for immediate surrender, an atomic bomb was unloosed over Hiroshima on August 6, 1945, and another wrecked the industrial city of Nagasaki. These explosions, which ushered in a new era in human affairs, were culminating though scarcely decisive events, for Japan in any case must soon have capitulated. Thenceforth the menace of atomic warfare haunted and chilled the hearts of men the globe around.

An official British report tersely described the effects of the atomic bombs.

> On August 6th, 1945, shortly after 8 A.M., an American Super-Fortress flying at 30,000 feet, dropped a single atomic bomb over the Japanese mercantile city of Hiroshima. The bomb exploded over the city-centre. Three days later, on August 9th, just after 11 A.M., a Super-Fortress, flying at the same height, which had found its primary target cloud-obscured, dropped a second atomic bomb over the city's factory area. In Hiroshima more than four square miles of city were destroyed and 80,000 people were killed. In the smaller city of Nagasaki about one and half square miles were destroyed and nearly 40,000 people were killed. The causes of destruction and death differed in many points from those which had acted in the conventional raids of the past. It was clear that bombing had changed its character and its scale beyond recognition.[4]

Soviet Russia, meantime, had entered the war against Japan and hurled armies into Manchuria. Later the Russians arrogantly and fantastically boasted about beating Japan after the United States and Britain had struggled in vain for four years. Actually the Russian intervention had very limited bearing on the Japanese collapse, but the crude Soviet propaganda carried conviction to the Asiatic masses.

Japanese military chiefs wished the fight to go on, but they were overruled by Emperor Hirohito who, months before, had seen the handwriting on the wall. On September 2, 1945, formal surrender was made to General Douglas MacArthur, Supreme Allied Commander, the personification and chief architect of the Allied triumph in the Pacific. It was implicitly understood that the Emperor would remain as the titular sovereign of the frightfully damaged "Land of the Cherry Blossom."

So the most destructive epoch of fighting in human annals had run its course. Brooding upon the sufferings, the horrors, the agonies of body, mind and spirit, the prolonged martyrdom of humanity since the Nazi columns struck at Poland, men recalled the observation of the Greek tragedian Sophocles, "Many are the marvels and nothing is more marvellous than man."

[4] From F. S. Taylor, *A Short History of Science and Scientific Thought*, by permission of Messrs. W. W. Norton and Company, Inc., New York, and Messrs. William Heinemann, Ltd., London. Copyright 1949.

FOR FURTHER STUDY

DWIGHT LEE, *Ten Years: the World on the Way to War* (Boston, 1942)

LEWIS B. NAMIER, *Diplomatic Prelude, 1938–9* (New York, 1948)

JOHN W. WHEELER-BENNETT, *Munich: Prologue to Tragedy* (New York, 1948)

FRANCIS P. WALTERS, *A History of the League of Nations* (2 vols., London, 1951)

ARNOLD WOLFERS, *Britain and France Between Two Wars* (New York, 1940)

ELIZABETH WISKEMANN, *Rome-Berlin Axis* (New York, 1949)

MAX BELOFF, *The Foreign Policy of Soviet Russia* (2 vols., New York, 1947–1949)

HERBERT C. O'NEILL, *Short History of the Second World War* (New York, 1950)

WILLIAM H. MCNEILL, *America, Britain and Russia* (New York, 1953)

CHESTER WILMOT, *The Struggle for Europe* (New York, 1952)

CHARLES A. BEARD, *President Roosevelt and the Coming of the War, 1941* (New Haven, 1948)

WILLIAM L. LANGER and S. F. GLEASON, *The Undeclared War* (New York, 1954)

WINSTON S. CHURCHILL, *The Second World War* (6 vols., New York, 1948–1953) PAPERBACKS

DWIGHT D. EISENHOWER, *Crusade in Europe* (New York, 1948) PAPERBACK

ARNOLD and VERONICA M. TOYNBEE, eds., *Hitler's Europe* (London, 1954)

CHARLES DE GAULLE, *The Call to Honour* (London, 1955)

GORDON A. CRAIG and FELIX GILBERT, *The Diplomats* (Princeton, 1953)

PHILIP A. REYNOLDS, *British Foreign Policy in the Inter-war Years* (London, 1954)

HERBERT FEIS, *Churchill, Roosevelt, Stalin* (Princeton, 1957)

CYRIL B. FALLS, *The Second World War* (new ed., London, 1950)

ELIOT JANEWAY, *The Struggle for Survival* (New Haven, 1951)

ALEXANDER DALLIN, *German Rule in Russia* (New York, 1957)

HEINZ SCHRÖTER, *Stalingrad* (New York, 1958) PAPERBACK

PETER FLEMING, *Operation Sea Lion* (New York, 1957) PAPERBACK

CORNELIUS RYAN, *The Longest Day* (New York, 1959) PAPERBACK

GERHARD RITTER, *The German Resistance* (Eng. trans., London, 1959)

RONALD W. CLARK, *The Birth of the Bomb* (London, 1961)

ROBERT J. C. BUTOW, *Japan's Decision to Surrender* (Stanford, 1954)

CHAPTER XXXI

MIND AND SPIRIT OF THE TWENTIETH CENTURY

BY WAY OF PREFACE

"THESE divisions are purely arbitrary," the youthful hero in "The Mikado" reminds us. And yet as larger historical perspectives come our way, it seems evident that 1914 marked a line of demarcation in the stream of Western civilization. Two wars fought on a planetary scale, the lowering threat of a third, the Great Depression, widespread social upheavals, the awakening of "backward peoples," unexampled progress in science and technology, the tyranny and tortures of totalitarianism—all these phenomena dyed indelibly the tapestry of culture after 1914.

Hardly a strand of human endeavor or thought escaped modification by these diverse and complex currents. At many points the change was so far-reaching as to be properly called revolutionary. Half a century at least must elapse before the actual dimensions of the period after 1914 can be judiciously measured. Here only a selective, comprehensive survey of the trends and accomplishments in the life of the mind and spirit can be attempted.

The century which ended in 1914, it may be recalled, witnessed such extraordinary advances that it was widely considered the most enlightened and prosperous of all centuries. The growing authority of science and the scientific method undergirded a philosophy of secularism and utilitarianism. Pragmatic progress nourished a glad confidence, complacent cocksureness and optimistic visions of human perfectibility. Obedience to law, care for truth, humanitarianism, concern for the dignity of man, civil liberties, including freedom of inquiry and expression, had won noteworthy victories.

Various titles have been proposed for the latest era of Western culture, such as "The Age of Speed," or "The Age of the Film," or "The Age of Women." Except perhaps in the domains of the fine arts and of philosophic thought, the intellectual attainments compare favorably with any other period of history that might be chosen. And yet Jeremiah-like prophets of gloom and doom felt sure that European leadership in the Western pattern of culture had passed; for them, the Old World appeared to be tired, disillusioned, spiritually exhausted and in decay. In the works of the most discussed writers, a chronic mood of foreboding, a sense of fatality and uncertainty prevailed concerning the shape of things to come. For many, stoicism seemed the most satisfying refuge in a bewildering and indifferent universe.

Certainly the Victorian faith in automatic human advancement was tempered by haunting fears of the possible collapse of civilization, the pride and the justification of Western man. The "principle of uncertainty," known to atomic physics, possessed symbolic relevance for the whole range of human affairs. The social influence of religion continued to decline and older standards of right and wrong underwent modification, most profoundly, beyond doubt, in countries that fell victim to ideological fanaticisms. Harold Nicolson, a thoughtful British man of letters, in a biography of Tennyson, remarked that his generation had "grown up with few illusions left to shatter. We are resigned in advance to whatever misfortunes the future has in store for us; we have lost our faith in individual endeavour; we are losing our interest in posterity."

But as faith declined, standards of comfort moved upward throughout the Western world after 1914. Not only was more wealth available, but also greater capacity for creating wealth. The principle of the welfare state attained more and more importance as governments deliberately committed themselves to ensuring a minimum level of physical well-being for all citizens. Technological discoveries substantially diminished the amount of heavy manual drudgery involved in earning one's daily bread, and employment of children declined.

As well as more mass comfort, society in the West enjoyed greater leisure, which afforded opportunity to lead a fuller, more rewarding life. Facilities for formal schooling were more widely diffused and illiteracy declined. Diet was varied beyond anything ever known, at the same time that medical discoveries and better sanitation alleviated pain, mastered certain plagues and diseases and lengthened the span of life expectancy in spectacular fashion. From time immemorial down to 1800, the average length of life probably did not exceed twenty-five years, but in the 1960's, longevity in the more advanced Western countries reached seventy years. In these lands the proportion of the aged and aging rose sharply, intensifying problems of health care and maintenance in general.

A perplexing, not to say alarming, phenomenon of the post-Hiroshima era was the rapid and accelerating multiplication of the human family. Increasing by around thirty million a year, population in the early 1960's soared to three billion, and if current growth trends persisted, the total would be double that figure by the year 2000. The population explosion was most pronounced in the underdeveloped countries of Asia, Latin America, and Africa, owing principally to a dramatic, swift decline in death rates, especially among infants and children.

Social and biological information to control the tide of births was only modestly diffused in the poorer countries. Poverty and misery, disease and illiteracy prevailed over huge areas in these overwhelmingly agrarian societies, and sober estimates placed the undernourished of the earth at anywhere from a third to a half of the total population. These sorry conditions invited social unrest, political extremism and revolutionary violence.

As the rising rate of divorce indicated, marital relations had become less stable. That phenomenon was connected with the greater independence of women due to broader educational opportunities and greater employment outside the home. Not at all unique in Western society, the "emancipation of women" came with a rush in the Soviet Union, in the cities of Moslem countries and in China. Under conditions of urban living and shifting social standards, families in the West tended to be smaller than in the nineteenth century.

Immediately after the Bolshevik Revolution, family ties in Soviet Russia were quite loose. But in time the Kremlin frowned upon unchastity and successive laws tightened divorce regulations and home bonds in general. Nevertheless, the official press called attention now and then to "bourgeois survivals in the family, manifested in sexual dissoluteness, and in a flippant attitude toward marriage." Legislation in Eire laid an absolute ban on the dissolution of marriage.

SCIENCE RACES ON

In his presidential address of 1951 before the British Association for the Advancement of Science, the Duke of Edinburgh observed:

"The changes brought about in the lives of men and women in the last hundred years have been greater and more rapid than during any other period in history, and these changes have been almost entirely due to the work of scientists and technologists all over the world. They have not only affected the way of living of all civilized people but have also vastly increased our knowledge about ourselves, the earth we live on and the universe around us. I cannot emphasize too much that the sum total of scientific knowledge and technological progress is an international achievement to which every civilized country has made some contribution."

Without dissenting from the core of truth in that statement, it must be said that contribuions to science varied greatly from country to country. No test on this point is more objective than the bestowal of Nobel Prizes, the highest tribute to which a scientist may aspire, conferred with strict impartiality. Since the inception of this honor in 1901 Western Europe and the United States carried off nine out of ten of all the prizes. German scientists, the largest single national group, won almost as many awards as the next two countries, Great Britain and the United States, together.

After the enthronement of the Nazis, however, the great reputation of Germany in science declined and during the Second World War, German science achieved nothing fundamental whether in submarine research, radar bombing, or nuclear physics. On the other hand, the United States advanced remarkably; after 1931, scientists in the United States were awarded more Nobel Prizes than those of any other country. Up to a point, the United States profited from the welcome extended to scientists and other intellectual workers who were victims of tyranny in the Old World, and the other side of the medal was the diffusion of American technical knowledge to other lands. As in international stature, so in science the United States moved to the front rank and that two-sided progress was clearly interrelated. France belongs among the "Big Four" in Nobel honors.

During the twilight of Tsarist history, two Russian scientists earned the coveted Nobel prize, but forty years of Communist rule elapsed before Soviet scientists were awarded this honor. In quick succession four Russian physicists became Nobel laureates, symbolizing the tremendous upsweep of their country in the realm of science. Attaching primary importance to technology, the Soviet authorities lavished huge appropriations upon technical institutes and scientific research.

As early as 1948, Soviet science succeeded in releasing nuclear energy, and the following year an atomic bomb was manufactured. An H-bomb followed along shortly, and in 1957 the Russians not only produced an intercontinental ballistic missile, but fired two rocket-powered satellites, or Sputniks, into orbit around the earth. This sensational accomplishment proved that Soviet rocket engines were the most powerful in existence by a considerable margin. Hardly had the world awakened to the significance of the first Sputniks than three Soviet cosmonauts in turn carried out spectacular voyages into space and returned safely. All this was preliminary to dreams of landing a man on the moon. Crowning Soviet primacy in space technology, the feats of the cosmonauts were rightly hailed as major triumphs in the ageless quest to conquer the natural environment and as heralding the dawn of interplanetary travel.

Soviet adventures into space, it must be said, diverted scarce engineering and technical talent from basic research and from investigations to advance human well-being. Only the Soviet Union and the United States, which also had a moon-landing project, commanded the resources to finance the complex equipment that space research and travel demanded. Benefiting from shorter flights by his American colleagues and from the brains of thousands of scientists and engineers, Major L. Gordon Cooper, Jr., in 1963, thrilled mankind with a thirty-four hour space voyage. That dramatic feat ended the first round of preliminaries for moon landings. Fierce rivalry in these areas of explorations, in "the race for space," developed between the two superpowers.

THE AGE OF SCIENCE

So many-sided and swift was the pace of scientific discovery after 1914 that the title "The Age of Science" might appropriately be applied to the period. Men of science coveted "the supreme delight," as Thomas H. Huxley had earlier said, "of extending the realm of law and order ever farther towards the unattainable goals of the infinitely great and the infinitely small, between which our little race of life is run."

Flexible, open to fresh ideas and tolerant, science in the West was largely made over in the twentieth century. Many a division of science referred to this latest period as its "golden age," both in fundamental research and in industrial or social applications. Since many problems could only be solved by minutely accurate measurements, the instruments and apparatus of the laboratory were constantly refined.

So enormous was the prestige acquired by science, that "progress" was commonly understood to refer to scientific and technological changes alone. Science implied, as never before, truth and power. Equally unprecedented was the anxiety caused by skepticism of social capacity to control the creations of science. It seemed to some observers, indeed, that science had prepared a death sentence for civilized society. Rather naive proposals were put forth for governmental restraint upon scientific research. Were that done, solutions of problems cast up by expanding populations, dwindling stocks of minerals, timber and water supplies might well be missed. If technology could not wholly satisfy social needs, it could contribute fruitfully, at any rate, to that end.

As new horizons opened up, public interest in both pure science and in technology was sharpened. Governments manifested growing concern in research and provided funds for investigations and expensive equipment which, in an older day, would have been privately financed. In both World Wars, scientific talent was diverted to immediately practical ends deemed essential for national survival. Brilliant applications of earlier discoveries resulted, but the extension of the frontiers of knowledge suffered.

Science, it was more keenly appreciated, bore destructive as well as beneficent fruits; atomic energy, for example, promised golden gains for peace time, though it was first employed in mass slaughter of Japanese civilians. More than other intellectual workers, no doubt, practitioners of science needed to cultivate bilingual qualities, speaking in one language in professional circles, and in another to enable interested laymen to assimilate the findings of research. Certain eminent scientists, gifted for popularization, tried to dispel the idea that their specialties belonged in the realm of magical mystery beyond the comprehension of the liberally educated layman.

Yet another trend among scientists must be remarked upon. While some investigators—perhaps most—disclaimed responsibility for the uses or abuses made of their discoveries, another group manifested a lively sense of social obligation. It rejected the advice of Candide to go on cultivating its garden, heedless of social implications. As evidence of this trend, a "Society for Social Responsibility" in science was founded in 1949 in the United States. The twofold purpose of the organization was to oppose encroachments of governmental officials upon the scientific domain and to assert the personal ethical responsibility of research workers for the projects they undertook.

ATOMIC ENERGY

No episode in twentieth-century science quite approached in drama or importance the

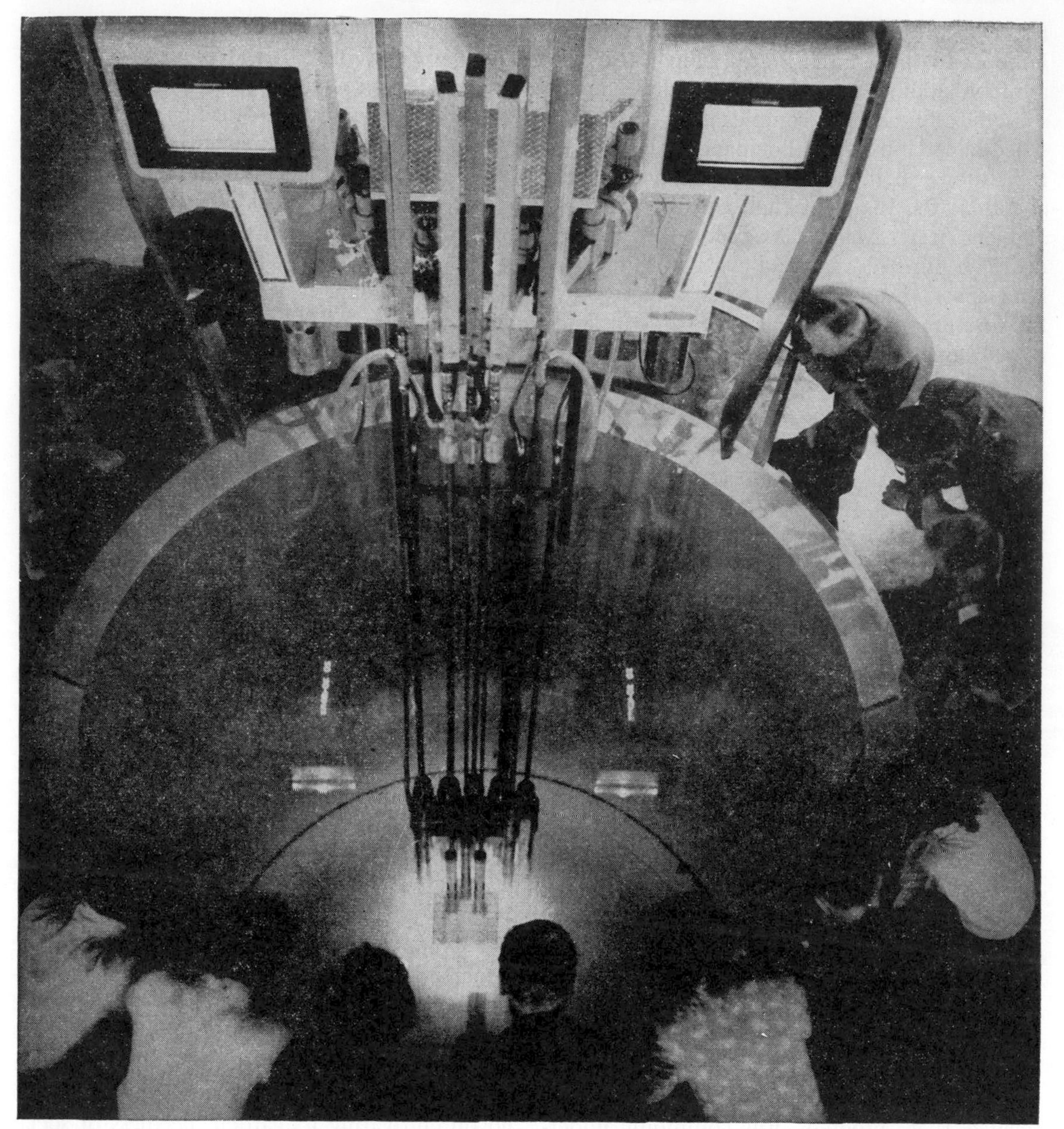

Testing a "swimming-pool" type of research reactor, designed and built at the Oak Ridge, Tennessee, National Laboratory. This reactor was one of the United States' technical exhibits at the United Nations Conference on peaceful uses of atomic energy, Geneva, Switzerland, August, 1955.

release of atomic energy and the manufacture of an effective atomic bomb. The fundamental discovery that atomic energy could be tapped meant infinitely more, of course, than the production of the atomic bomb itself. Building upon previous researches, laboratory workers upset the theory of atomic permanence by proving that particles, named electrons, spun round the nucleus of the atom. In 1920, a British physicist, Lord Ernest Rutherford, who has been tagged "the Newton of the atom," succeeded in changing one chemical element, nitrogen, into another, oxygen, by bombardment with swiftly moving atoms of helium. And in 1931 scientific wizards constructed the cyclotron, a powerful machine to smash the atom. Two German refugees, Otto Hahn and Lise Meitner, working with Professor Niels Bohr in Denmark, found in 1938 that the uranium atom could be split practically in two, thus releasing tremendous energy.

This discovery of nuclear fission, or breaking apart of atoms, touched off a race between Nazi and Western scientists to manufacture an atomic bomb. To carry on researches, the government of the United States set up the "Manhattan Project" in 1942, and the technical brains of Europe were enlisted in the exciting enterprise. For the undertaking the United States furnished the necessary natural resources, university laboratories and industrial "know-how" at an overall cost of $2 billion. Three years of furious work produced the bombs that shattered Hiroshima and Nagasaki. The German rivals, it was discovered after the war, had only arrived at the point the West had reached in 1940, that is, before large-scale efforts on the atomic bomb had begun. German atomic operations were concentrated in Strasbourg in Lorraine; Allied aerial attacks prevented the Nazis from diverting the necessary industrial facilities to research and they would not employ anti-Nazi physicists or Jews in the work.

This skeleton survey only dimly suggests the vast amount of scientific skill, experiment and, above all, thought that was invested in the release of atomic energy. The record has been vividly and succinctly recounted by the eminent physicist Karl T. Compton:

". . . We see the sudden merging of the results of many lines of investigation which had previously proceeded almost independently: fifty years of research on radioactivity; twenty years' development of high-voltage machines; the equivalence of mass and energy announced by Einstein as early as 1905 as part of his theory of relativity; several decades of cosmic rays; fifty years' development of electronics; the whole modern art of chemical separation; the science of radiology, whose impetus had come from medical applications of X-rays and the rays from radium; the most modern refinements of metallurgy, of chemistry, of electrical engineering. And the practical consummation of the atomic energy objectives has called upon the highest skills in engineering design and instrumentation. It is truly an exciting picture."[1]

Continuing technological advances yielded an enormous increase in the destructive power of nuclear weapons. On the heels of the atomic and hydrogen bombs came ballistic rocket missiles that could be hurled hundreds of miles. Bombs were devised capable of destroying by heat alone everything within a radius of twenty to thirty miles below the point of burst.

At the end of the 1950's the United States launched an atomic powered merchant ship, the *Savannah*, while the Soviets put into operation the similarly powered icebreaker *Lenin*. Submarines operated by nuclear power could remain submerged for as long as three months. Their presence underwater could not be detected, while missiles they carried could attack surface ships rather easily.

It was believed that in a few years atomic power would generate electricity at prices competitive with conventional oil and coal fuels. Medical research envisaged atomic energy as an ally in conquering certain diseases. Meantime, research workers sought methods of protection against the poisonous effects upon human beings of fallout let loose by nuclear bombs and testing. (Radioactive debris from nuclear explosions affected bone tissues and blood cells and could cause bone cancer or leukemia.)

CHANGES IN TRANSPORTATION

Research in other areas of physics yielded an endless succession of wonders and improvements. Motor transport, for instance, little used in the First World War, had become indispensable by the Second World War. In the interval, improvements had continuously been

[1] Reprinted with permission from John E. Burchard, editor, *Mid-Century: The Social Implications of Scientific Progress*, John Wiley and Sons, Inc., and the Technology Press of M.I.T. Copyright 1950.

Freeway, Los Angles, California

made; the balloon tire of the 1920's, as an illustration, meant greater comfort and safety, and tire mileage ran up to thirty thousand, a seven fold increase. By the 1960's better than 62,000,000 motor vehicles were operating on the highways of the United States, or double the number of twenty-five years earlier. A new profession of "traffic engineering" had arisen to plan towns and highways to meet growing needs. Freight traffic on American railways slumped in competition with trucks and passenger rail travel suffered an even sharper decline because of the popularity of the automobile.

Transportation by air advanced with breathtaking strides due to refinements in shape, reduction in weight and greater efficiency in power plant. Air travel was hardly taken seriously before 1909 when a French pioneer, Louis Bleriot, crossed the English Channel in a flimsy machine at an average speed of forty-five miles an hour. Considerable progress in plane designing was effected during the First World War, and in 1919 a plane spanned the Atlantic for the first time. The solo flight of Charles A. Lindbergh from New York to Paris (1927) dramatized the possibilities of transport by air. In the late 1930's, American and British companies inaugurated scheduled passenger travel around the globe; interrupted by the war, air traffic in larger and faster planes expanded quickly after fighting ceased. Meantime, in 1941, the jet-powered plane appeared, and presently supersonic airliners went into service.

Grand Coulee Dam

Another significant innovation in transportation was the use of the Diesel engine on highway and railway. Having relatively high thermal efficiency and consuming heavy oil fuel, the Diesel engine was cheaper to operate and less dependent on water supplies than the steam engine. Electrification of railways was a universal phenomenon of the period and new underground lines, capable of handling large crowds, were opened in such widely separated cities as Moscow and Chicago. Inside factories and mines spectacular improvement was achieved in mechanical transportation. It appears that the first moving assembly line was installed in a Ford plant in 1913; by the mid-century huge factories operated like a unified gigantic machine converting materials, skills and energy into an unending flow of products.

OTHER APPLICATIONS OF PHYSICS

Consumption of electrical energy moved up rapidly. Taking the Western world as a whole, the output of electricity doubled every seven years, with the pace even faster in the United States where electric equipment for the home increased greatly—radios, refrigerators, "deep freezes," dishwashers and so on. Greater efficiency in internal illumination was achieved in the 1930's with the fluorescent lamp. Along with greater consumption went continual growth in the size of hydroelectric power plants; the largest were built in the United States (Tennessee Valley and the Grand Coulee) and in the Soviet Union (Dnieprostroi) and huge irrigation projects were operated in connection with each of them.

Labor-saving machines poured out in an incessant stream, such as automatic machinery to perform routine tasks in office and factory, or new tools of research. Among them were uncanny computers, operated by electronic rather than mechanical means and capable not only of working out involved mathematical problems but of detecting and correcting errors; these automatic machines made calculations rapidly and accurately that would require years of mathematical effort. A wide range of instruments for precision measurement appeared. Parts of a machine could be fitted to one ten-thousandth of an inch, which may be compared with fittings of an eighteenth-century Watt engine to within "the thickness of an old shilling."

Of high importance in the Second World War was radar, named thus from the initial letters of radio-detection-and-ranging. A British-devised instrument, it was invaluable in detecting the approach of enemy planes, in offensive operations against hostile warcraft and in identifying coastlines in foul weather. When the war was over, radar was perfected for water and air navigation. Installed in Liverpool harbor (1948), radar speeded up handling of ships and ensured greater safety especially in fog; and it was serviceable in controlling traffic at airports.[2]

New or improved processes in steel-making and better products kept pace with growing mechanization. Of special significance were high-speed continuous sheet mills, electrification and automatic control of operations and stainless and heat resistant steels. Ever-increasing demands for steel rapidly depleted high-grade deposits of iron ore in the Lake Superior area, and American corporations started bringing ores in from foreign sources—Venezuela, the wilderness of Labrador and the jungles of Liberia—which were reported to be of the finest quality. Steelmen also devised methods to employ taconite from inferior grades of ore.

THE USES OF CHEMISTRY

It was the proud boast of a chemist that "chemistry is the basis of everything and nothing escapes it." Certainly the new products of rubber, wood and plastics that appeared in the period under review went far to justify that claim. The making of rubber synthetically, which began in Germany during the First World War, progressed steadily, and in 1955 a manufacturing house was turning out over forty thousand rubber articles. The manufacture of paint became a science, and the development of high octane fuels raised the thermal efficiency of internal combustion motors. Nylon, which made its debut in the mid-1930's, may be considered by women as the most important discovery of the age. Combining remarkable strength with elastic properties, this new fabric had many uses as in glider tow ropes and parachutes; a rival, terylene, was perfected after 1945. For research purposes, chemicals of exceedingly high purity were prepared.

When the British blockade in the First World War cut Germany off from Chilean nitrogen, chemists contrived to manufacture nitric acid from the air. Chemical technology was profitably applied to the preservation of food. Improved refrigeration increased the storage life of food in the home or transported over long distances. Quick freezing processes enabled food to retain color and flavor better than by conventional canning. Methods of dehydration were applied to preserve eggs, milk, meat and other commodities. Fascinating experimental programs were underway to convert salt water into fresh water.

An armory of new insecticides such as D.D.T. appeared to destroy pests that attacked growing or stored crops, and other chemical wonders killed weeds. Search for industrial uses of farm crops gave rise to a new branch of technology called chemurgy. And chemistry contributed generally to amazing advances in medical science.

MEDICAL ADVANCES

It is probably accurate to say that medicine, surgery and dentistry made greater gains after 1914 than in any comparable span of history. Refinements in the apparatus of research, new methods of treating ailments and novel pharmaceutical preparations wrought powerfully

[2] Novel forms of mass communication, incorporating the findings of physics, are discussed on pp. 766–770.

upon the social fabric. A new era in drugs opened in 1935 with the appearance of sulfanilamide which was followed quickly by other antibiotic preparations to combat bacterial infection, such as streptomycin, aureomycin and antrycide. It was also learned that delicate chemical agents called hormones, secreted by ductless glands, seemed to regulate vital processes. Insulin to correct diabetes was first successfully used in 1921, and cortisone, which brought relief to sufferers from certain types of rheumatoid arthritis, in 1949.

Called the "wonder" drug, penicillin ceased to be a laboratory curiosity in 1941 and was produced commercially; it proved invaluable in the treatment of wound infections, venereal disease and other ailments. A novel form of penicillin called penbritin proved (1961) most effective in fighting bacteria. French and American research scientists discovered vaccines helpful in combating certain types of polio.

During the Second World War prophylactic vaccines against plague and some types of influenza were applied effectively. The death rate in armies from disease was cut to a mere fraction of what it had been in the First World War.

The importance of proper nutrition came to be more fully appreciated during the two World Wars, together with a greater realization of the value of vitamins to supplement food. Major advances in the technique of blood transfusion were achieved in the Second World War, a great boon to battlefield casualties. "Six thousand units of blood plasma went ashore at Tarawa," reported an American surgeon. "At least half the wounded owe their lives to plasma."

Sleeping sickness, leprosy, and tropical diseases were treated effectively by new methods. High honors were heaped upon investigators who unlocked hitherto unknown secrets of heredity. Researchers pushed energetically to find remedies for the common cold, cancer, circulatory maladies, and diseases peculiar to the aged.

Surgery moved steadily forward, much of peacetime importance being learned by treatment of casualties in the two wars. Almost unbelievable operations were performed on the living heart and knowledge of anaesthetics was considerably enlarged.

It was learned that certain types of deafness could be treated by surgery and that the human kidney could be successfully transplanted; even more amazing, medical science created an artificial kidney. Among noteworthy improvements in the tools of surgery was an electronic pump, capable of blowing fresh air into lungs and sucking out used air.

More scientific procedures in obstetrical practice sharply reduced mortality in childbirth. Dentistry advanced more nearly to the status of a science after 1914 than in all previous history. Study of nutritional factors in tooth decay, public health dentistry and the use of plastics in dentures were developments of the first importance. Insurance programs for hospital care and sickness grew rapidly, on a voluntary basis in the United States, though compulsory in Europe.

Medical and surgical progress, as noted before, contributed richly to the prolongation of life expectancy. At the same time agricultural experimentation enlarged the food supply; rust disease on wheat, for instance, was nearly conquered, new types of barley, which thrived under either extreme moisture or drought, were grown, and the yield of corn per acre moved sharply ahead. Fertilizer, seed and livestock feed were improved, while more efficient machinery enabled the farmer to raise more with less effort. Novel drugs reduced pestilences that attacked sheep, hogs and cattle. These discoveries and related ones tempered alarmist views on the danger of food shortage so far as Western nations were concerned.

THE USES OF METEOROLOGY

Better techniques of weather forecasting had value for agriculture, and it appeared that science would soon be able to summon rain at will. In the United States, clouds were seeded with iodide crystals to cause them to release their water. Meteorological knowledge was extended by the employment of aircraft at very high altitudes on scientific explorations; the advent of jet-propelled planes, which must fly at considerable heights for economical operation, led to further research in temperature and winds. Along with meteorological study, investigation of conditions and living forms in the deep waters of the sea lessened human insecurity because of the elements of nature.

THE ROLE OF PSYCHOLOGY

In the years after 1914, psychology, which seeks to understand and explain human behavior, became extremely fashionable. Ceasing to be an affair of philosophical speculation and anecdote, it moved in the direction of an analytical and objective science. The language of psychology was not at all standardized and tended to bewilder the layman. And a variety of specialisms or schools clamored for attention.

Psychological inquiries proceeded along two main lines. The first, which studied what went on in one's own mind, offered data that could neither be checked nor accurately recorded and so had little standing in the court of science. More empirical was the careful examination of the actual behavior of human beings and animals. Controlled experimentation and laboratory observations resulted in the accumulation of substantial bodies of statistical evidence with which efforts were made to formulate general principles or laws.

The findings of psychological investigation were applied practically in many directions. They influenced methods of formal education, were useful in industry in remedying physical and mental strain and were resorted to by the military services in tests, for example, to measure aptitudes and personality traits. Psychology was also invoked in polls of public opinion (which had their ups and downs) and in handling problems of mental health.

Doctor Sigmund Freud, a savant of Vienna, pioneered in the use of psychology as a tool to treat mental ills. Making explorations into the dark underworld of the subconscious, Freud concluded that human conduct was shaped by powerful irrational forces which might cause disorders of the mind if inhibited.[3] He and his disciples devised psychoanalysis, a methodical therapy to root out neuroses. It presumed to dredge fears and frustrations based on sex, religion and other half-hidden things out of the subconscious mind. But the procedure was expensive, time-consuming and of marginal curative value. Nevertheless, the catchwords of Freudianism—repressions, complexes and neuroses—penetrated deeply into the imaginative literature and art of the age.

Psychological study, by and large, tended to dispute the idea that men could choose freely and were responsible for the choices they made. Moral invalids who committed unsocial acts, that is, might be mentally ill—a hypothesis that reinforced determinism and deprived society of one of its most powerful sanctions for securing good social behavior. Psychology, often in popular and dubious forms, may well have exerted a very profound influence upon the broad masses.

More respectable than psychoanalysis in scientific circles was psychosomatic medicine, "a ministry of the mind." It ascribed peptic ulcers, sexual aberrations and coronary heart disease, for example, to emotional tensions beyond the control of the conscious will. By "shock treatment" and other techniques, the attempt was made to reduce the number of "nervous wrecks." The appearance of a *Journal of Psychosomatic Medicine* in 1939 indicated that this new branch of the medical art had attained scientific standing.

Leading medical schools established departments of psychiatry, and psychiatric divisions were set up in the better hospitals. A flood of new drugs, which affect human behavior, contributed to the unparalleled advance in understanding and treating mental illness.

THE FINE ARTS

Just as the West of Europe was responsible for all advances in material progress, comfort and hygiene, before the emergence of the United States, so that area contributed more to the stock of world culture than the rest of the globe combined. In the era after 1914 workers in the fine arts responded to the uncertain and changing moods of the time, ever seeking new modes of expression. Creations of a highly individualistic sort resulted, many of them per-

[3] Freud's major contribution to learned literature, *The Interpretation of Dreams,* contains his central theories.

House at Lincoln, Massachusetts, designed by Walter Gropius and Marcel Breuer

The New York headquarters of the United Nations

verse, bizarre or chaotic. For many a layman artistic productions stood in constant need of intellectual vindication. As the bourgeoisie in the nineteenth century had largely supplanted the aristocracy as patrons of the arts, so after 1914 governments more and more furnished subsidies to artists; during the Great Depression even the government of the United States financed cultural and literary projects.

In authoritarian countries, the State required cultural workers to follow orthodox ideological lines. After the Bolshevik Revolution, advanced types of abstract art were created, but in the 1930's public officials disapproved of such productions as aesthetic folderol. Artists—men of letters, too—were instructed to glorify Communist experiments and to spur working people to greater productivity. Somewhat similarly, in Nazi Germany advanced styles in art were banned as "degenerate" and "Jewish"; Hitler, an amateur artist himself, ordered that only "Nordic art" should be cultivated. In the name of the "Aryanization" of culture, paintings were removed from galleries and many artists were expelled—to the enrichment of the United States, whither many emigrated.

ARCHITECTURE

Styles in architecture were diverse, in materials and designs, but the accent of the age was functional. Prominent exponents of functionalism, such as the Frenchman Charles LeCorbusier and the German Walter Gropius, who eventually joined the Harvard faculty, had many disciples and imitators. All over the world an immense amount of construction was undertaken. State and municipal governments in Europe from Liverpool through Vienna to Moscow erected efficient low-cost dwellings, usually in the form of large apartment blocks. Public housing in the United States lagged behind, though some splendid architectural monuments were built. The skyscraping Empire State Building and Rockefeller Center in New York and "the Cathedral of Learning" of the University of Pittsburgh reflected a keener taste for artistic magnificence, as well as spaciousness and economy.

Of the same class was the permanent home of the United Nations rising thirty-nine stories with its gigantic assembly hall; this building was genuinely international, for the constructional and decorative materials were imported from nearly all the countries of the globe. The chaste marble Jefferson rotunda took its place along the Potomac with the massive pile of the Pentagon Building.

These structures merely symbolized the immense amount of construction in post-war America. On an unexampled scale, churches, university and school, office and public buildings, and airports rose all across the Republic. Frank Lloyd Wright, perhaps the most influential architect of his time, won warm praise and stirred up angry controversy with his Guggenheim Museum in New York City. There, too, Finnish-born Eero Saarinen endeavored to translate into concrete and steel the marvel of air travel in the Trans World Airlines terminal building at Idlewild, and he also designed the dramatic Dulles International Airport near Washington, the first airport in the United States built expressly for jet planes. His massive American Embassy in London, with a screaming eagle as centerpiece, provoked no little hostile criticism.

Cities from the Atlantic to the Pacific engaged in exciting urban renewal programs, topped by Manhattan's Lincoln Square Project. A blighted slum area was cleared away to provide space for perhaps the finest cluster of cultural structures in existence. The Lincoln Center for the Performing Arts brought together artistic enterprises previously scattered, and on the drawing boards were facilities for the Philharmonic Orchestra, for opera and drama, and a library.

Domestic architecture in the United States switched to smaller homes, equipped with ingenious labor-saving contrivances, in which diverse mass-produced materials were used. About fifteen million new homes were built in suburban communities; "ranch houses," shopping centers, and motels dotted suburbs and countryside.

An outburst of construction in Latin America, not matched since the erection of churches in the colonial era, gave cities a distinctly up-

Coventry Cathedral rebuilt

to-date and enterprising appearance. Brazil outpaced her neighbors by laying out an entirely new capital, Brasilia, in what had been rough wilderness, some six hundred miles distant from the former capital, Rio de Janeiro. On a vast area, chosen with meticulous care, imaginative architects constructed public buildings, modernistic in design, and cultural and residential quarters for a planned population of half a million. An artificial lake bordered the city, which was served by an intricate pattern of highways at several levels. It was expected that factories would later be built and that Brasilia would become the starting point for the development of the surrounding countryside. Similar in character, though on much less grandiose proportions, was the new capital of Australia at Canberra. The Palais de Chaillot in Paris, classic in symmetry and dimensions, reasserted the French fondness for decorative architecture.

With remarkable swiftness, war-damaged cities of Western Europe were restored in a generation of time. In some places, battered

Card Player, *by Pablo Picasso, in the collection of the Museum of Modern Art, New York*

structures were rebuilt on pre-war lines, as in the case of the famous Opera House of Vienna or the historic heart of Warsaw. Elsewhere, architects applied bold, modernistic designs. Of that tendency, a striking example was the simple yet exquisite Coventry Cathedral in England, erected alongside of the shell of an ancient sanctuary which had been destroyed by Nazi air raids.

Architecture in public projects in authoritarian countries was intended to glorify the state. The devotion of Stalin to the gigantic and the massive was advertised in the Palace of Soviets in Moscow and in the sprawling new university complex on the edge of that city. Warsaw, which emerged like the phoenix from the ashes of war, was dominated by a colossal Palace of Science and Culture, a gift of Stalin, and a painful, daily reminder to citizens of the lordship of Communist Russia. Grandiose plans of Hitler to beautify Berlin never came to fruition; instead, after the war, fine office and public structures and pleasing residential blocks in the western sector replaced wartime devastation. All across Europe, prefabricated buildings, especially apartment blocks, shops and schools, were rapidly constructed. Intelligent planning of cities, whether in Rotterdam or Dresden or Warsaw, to cope with the faster tempo of very modern living, was a hallmark of Europe's latest age.

PAINTING AND SCULPTURE

In the realm of painting a noteworthy trend was widening popular interest, evident from increased museum attendance, sales of paintings and enrollment in art schools. Enthusiastic novices pursued "art for art's sake," painting purely for diversion and pleasure. During the Second World War, artistic masterpieces in the great galleries of Europe were evacuated to places of safety; after the war representative selections from the Viennese and Munich collections toured British and American cities, attracting throngs of spectators. Wealthy business magnates, such as the mysterious oil man C. S. Gulbenkian and Andrew Mellon, the American capitalist, accumulated famous works of art; the Mellon holdings were turned over in 1941 to the National Art Gallery in Washington.

Among professional painters, fashions were extremely fluid, not to say chaotic: romantic and primitive realism, impressionism and expressionism, surrealism and other styles. As in the preceding period, impressionists placed upon canvas an "impression" of what they saw, rather than outward appearance. A painter who "expressed" his feelings and thought about what he saw was tagged an expressionist or a surrealist. The leading exemplar of this set, Salvadore Dali, emphasized meticulous draughtsmanship and precision of detail in his compositions.

As in the late nineteenth century, masters in France continued to make special contributions to painting, and young artists from foreign countries congregated in Paris in pursuit of instruction and inspiration. Art critics showered

By the Window, *painted by Henri Matisse*

applause upon the Spanish-born Picasso, who chose Paris as his home; he exerted a pervasive and subtle impact upon the art principles of the period. An admirer of vitality and with a humorous eye for the absurd, Picasso adopted many styles and chose varied themes. At one point he tried to interpret the mood of an object or episode in geometrical patterns, as in "Guernica," depicting the ruin of a Basque town by Nazi bombers in the course of the Spanish civil war.

The most formidable rival of Picasso was Henri Matisse, who painted a notable array of pictures—and created some little known sculptures, too—primitive in spirit and gracefully simple in form. As was true of Picasso, Matisse's restless intellect kept searching for new theories in technique. While a friend of "impressionism," he explained: "There is an inherent truth which must be disengaged from the outward appearance of the object to be represented . . . Exactitude is not truth."

A set of imaginative Mexican artists, led by Diego Rivera, brought into sharp focus the colorful heritage of the Indian past or portrayed the liberation of underprivileged peasants of Mexico from oppression and squalor. The commonplaces of daily existence and quiet rural scenes engaged the brush of the most respected painters of the United States. International acclaim was bestowed upon the works of Grant Wood, such as the gently

American Gothic, *painted by Grant Wood*

satirical "Daughters of the American Revolution"; three stern-visaged matrons (of Boston, perhaps) mechanically sip their afternoon tea. During the Great Depression, subsidies by the federal government to art workers made possible the adornment of public buildings.

As in the other fine arts, so in sculpture restlessness and unconventionality prevailed, and along with that a search for new media including glass and plastics. A French genius, Aristide Maillol, carved small pieces, simple and serene, making him a worthy claimant to Rodin's mantle. Jacob Epstein, who was born in New York, achieved universal fame by massive figure studies, largely inspired by biblical personalities; "Adam" and "Lazarus" are representative specimens of his splendid talent.

Popular at one point in the United States were smooth sculptures by Ivan Méstrovitch, once a simple Croatian peasant. In his homeland he was passionately admired for luminous, often grossly distorted figures of Yugoslav saints and heroes. The American taste for the grandiose was strikingly exhibited in huge, stone faces of four Presidents, carved by Gutzon Borglum in the Black Hills of South Dakota, and unveiled in 1939. War memorials and decoration for buildings offered unusual opportunities for sculptors of lesser genius.

MUSIC

By the tests of variety, richness and creators of competence, music fared well in the family of fine arts. In the judgment of some critics, the United States forged into top musical rank. Whether that estimate was valid or not, it was certainly true that the writing of music advanced impressively in the New World, being helped by talented refugees from Europe. Among them was Arnold Schoenberg, acclaimed both as a musical thinker and teacher. Described as "the king of the cacophonists," Schoenberg was keenly and continuously interested in new forms and he won many disciples. Paul Hindemith, an émigré also, blended modernistic and traditional styles in composition, but, in the main, his music represented a reaction against clever and delicate refinement. Native-born composers, including Aaron Copland, Howard Hanson and Roger Sessions, carried artistic musical creativity to levels unprecedented in the United States.

Igor Stravinsky, a Russian by birth, profoundly influenced two generations of musicians in France. Frankly a rebel, Stravinsky early in his career sought to infuse his compositions with sprightly realism, only to turn more sober as time gained upon him. For his *Bolero* Maurice Ravel won exceptional praise as did Ottorino Respighi, composer of *The Fountains of Rome*. Claiming Ravel as his master, the Englishman Ralph Vaughan Williams created principally on the modernist pattern. His symphonies and an opera (*Hugh the Drover*), the symphonies of Alan Rawsthorne and the operas of Benjamin Britten—*The Rape of Lucretia*, and *A Midsummer Night's Dream*, for instance—enriched the musical treasures of the British Isles.

No musician commanded more general respect, it may be, than the Finnish master, Jan

Sibelius; his *Finlandia,* written earlier, now became familiar to concert-goers throughout the Western world. Like the distinguished Hungarian composer, Bela Bartók, Sibelius made full use of homely folk melodies. In his long and fruitful career, Richard Strauss, who had rare gifts for clever orchestration, tried to sustain the reputation of Vienna as a musical capital; a charming operatic classic, *Der Rosenkavalier,* was best known of his works internationally. Among Russian composers, top honors belong to Dimitri Shostakovich and Sergei Prokofieff; it appears that temperamentally neither of these artists were conformists to Soviet orthodoxy, but pressure obliged them to satisfy party requirements of "socialist realism." Shostakovich stirringly described Russia fighting the Second World War in his *Seventh Symphony.*

Musical comedies were lifted to a superior plane of integration and technical finish, with Americans as conspicuous innovators. *Of Thee I Sing,* by George Gershwin, a searing satire on the Great Depression, met with widespread approval. New standards were set in musical comedy by *Oklahoma!,* distinguished by clever tunes, improved ensemble and the use of ballet and pantomime.

Based upon G. B. Shaw's *Pygmalion,* the gay songs and enchanting dance numbers of *My Fair Lady* delighted New York audiences nightly for more than six years and earned hearty applause in European show houses, not least in the Red Army Central Theater of

from the New York production of Oklahoma

Moscow. Searching for novelties, composers exploited rhythms and tone combinations from primitive Negro and Slav music. "Jazz," which someone called "the folk music of the machine age," originated in the United States and swept across frontiers and oceans. This art form was the unique musical contribution of the New World to the Old. Encouraged, possibly, by the appearance of catchy, colorful melodies, ballroom dancing attained unprecedented popularity; American soldiers introduced the frenzied "jitterbug" and rumba to all the world. Later, the exotic "twist" was exported from the United States to dance floors of Europe. Increasingly popular were large musical festivals, running a week or longer, staged in such communities as Vienna and Salzburg, Edinburgh and Venice, Warsaw and Bayreuth, Lenox, Massachusetts, and Los Angeles.

Many a serious-minded critic viewed with disapproval the democratization of musical taste. Certain it was that the interest of the general public was quickened by an array of mechanical contrivances, the "juke-box" among them. The radio brought music at all levels into ordinary homes and into factories to counteract the tedium of routine work. Phonograph records were much improved, the long-playing record carrying five times more entertainment than earlier types. As never before, grants from public treasuries financed popular concerts and musical festivals.

Heightened appreciation of the ballet marked the period after 1914. Anna Pavlova and Margot Fonteyn ranked with the most graceful and sensitive dancers of all time; in America, Martha Graham earned general acclaim. Accomplished dancers were matched by great choreographers, George Balanchine, Agnes de Mille and Leonide Massine. Renowned troupes, the Monte Carlo Ballet Russe and Sadler's Wells, delighted audiences on both sides of the Atlantic, and the world famous Bolshoi Theater in Moscow and the Leningrad Kirov Ballet presented classical favorites and newer ballets.

LITERATURE

Rising literacy and greater leisure inspired a substantial increase in the production of books —indispensable tools of a civilized and progressive society. Probably not more than one book in a thousand would survive the winnowing flame of time and outlive the century.

British publishers alone issued (1960) nearly eighteen thousand new titles (their America rivals were not far behind), and about eighteen hundred publishing houses from all across the globe displayed their productions at the annual book fair in Frankfurt. With the marketing in the 1950's of inexpensive "paperbacks," a veritable revolution swept over the publishing industry. Serious as well as tawdry new works and reprints appealed to large audiences which hitherto had purchased few if any books. Approximately a quarter of the world's output of books came off Soviet presses, and it was not unusual for fiction by popular Russian authors to sell in millions of copies, and for volumes of verse in hundreds of thousands.

Works of fiction, ever an elastic category of literature, were printed in overwhelming profusion to meet an eager demand. In subject matter, in feeling for fundamental values and as chronicles of the prevailing intellectual climate, the novels of the period were as diverse as human nature and the interests of man. The present survey can only recall the very cream of the novelists—authors who exerted an international influence or who were recipients of the Nobel literary prize.

Somewhat arbitrarily, the paramount themes of imaginative prose may be listed this way: disillusion and despondency resulting from the global wars and the revolutionary impact of applied science; stern condemnation of the shortcomings of capitalistic civilization; revolt against conventional moral customs with which were associated introspective analyses of character along psychological lines; the narrowness, misery and desperation of proletarian and peasant existence, faith in some variety of collectivism to redeem mankind; revulsion in the West against the Communist doctrine, its arrant dogmatism and intellectual rigidity, on the part of erstwhile fellow-travelers; and, not least, the eclipse of the age of reason as evidenced by ruthless persecution, the cunningly

Marcel Proust, *a portrait by Jacques Blanche*

contrived horrors of concentration camps and related bestialities.

Now and then, a fictional work exploring the religious interpretation of life or reviving a historical episode forged into the best-selling class. Not much imaginative literature in total itarian countries, where publication was exclusively a state monopoly, commanded more than a local reception; novelists in those countries were obliged to exalt the fanatic dogmas of authoritarianism or to spur readers to more heroic efforts for the advancement of the Leviathan state. Fiction in the Soviet Union painted the official picture of the joyous Soviet life of constructive endeavor, however remote the product might be from the grim realities.

Among the outstanding French novelists, Romain Rolland, a pacifist with a leftist social outlook, won praise for the epic series, *Jean-Christophe.* Marcel Proust's *Remembrance of Things Past* and *The Thibaults* by Martin du Gard, both in many volumes, artistically portrayed the mingled strands and stresses of French well-to-do society of the time. The stylistically attractive novels of André Gide, such as *The Counterfeiters,* combined keen insight into human nature with resourcefulness in searching for truth. An arch-rebel and renegade Communist, this enigmatic literary patriarch denied the existence of God and obdurately combatted religion. On the other side, François Mauriac, the leading Catholic novelist, demonstrated that a mind of first-rate quality and a devotion to religious convictions were not at all incompatible. Little known in the English-reading world before 1945, this gifted writer made a profound impression with *A Woman of the Pharisees,* in which he explored relentlessly the nature of human nature; in 1952, the Nobel Prize was bestowed upon him.

The peer of Mauriac in literary brilliance was Albert Camus, who was killed in a tragic motor accident at the height of his creative powers. Aside from deeply searching works of fiction, Camus tossed off essays and journalistic pieces, moral, political, and philosophic. "What interests me," he exclaimed, "is to find out how we should behave."

John Galsworthy

All manner of tyranny and capital punishment he reviled as inhumane behavior; the preservation of freedom and the alleviation of human suffering Camus regarded as the valid goals of existence. His qualities of intelligence, of simplicity and decency shine out in *The Plague,* a gripping novel of the ordeals of disease and death and of resistance to primitive barbarism. The scene is laid in Algeria where Camus was born and grew to maturity. Concerned that the Moslem population there should have a fair deal, he pleaded for reforms and for a working partnership between French Algerians and the Arabs—but in vain. Offering no panaceas to vanquish the ills and aches of humanity, the moral confusions and intellectual convulsions of his time, Camus seems to have believed that mankind could be made better, though scarcely good. In *The Fall* he mercilessly assailed creeds and philosophies that exploited human anxiety and pushed society toward nuclear destruction.

In *The World Of William Clissold,* and other panoramic writings, H. G. Wells fortified his reputation as a resolute and challenging exponent of the application of reason to the solution of human problems. Praised as "the greatest public teacher of his time," Wells kept reiterating that poverty, disease and war could be conquered if only intelligence and scientific knowledge were freely applied. Yet toward the end of his long literary career, grave doubts crowded upon him as he peered into the future; man, he now reluctantly believed, would die off as had other extinct species that could not adjust themselves to their environment.

With artistic realism, John Galsworthy in *The Forsyte Saga* described the disintegration and decay of the British middle classes. An agile Irish craftsman, James Joyce, fathered "a stream-of-consciousness" cult, full of the flavor of uninhibited individualism and iconoclastic disdain for moral conventions (*Ulysses; Finnegan's Wake*). Of a very different sort was George Orwell's *1984,* a sensational tract for the times, presenting a grimly pessimistic vision of a totalitarian future.

The best American storytellers incorporated a wealth of experience and entertainment in their novels, excelling in minute depictions of the surface of life. In contrast to movie scenarios, some of the best novels written in the United States reflected cynical and pessimistic moods. Nobel laurels were carried off by William Faulkner, who portrayed simple, elemental characters of the Deep South with superior stylistic artistry in *Light in August* and *The Sound and the Fury;* by Pearl Buck whose *The Good Earth* poignantly described the miserable way of life of the Chinese peasantry; and by John Steinbeck, who was chosen in 1962 principally because of the realistic and imaginative *The Winter of Our Discontent,* depicting an upright shopkeeper battling against temptation and the waywardness of a cynical son. It is reasonable to suppose, though, that Steinbeck will be longer remembered for *The Grapes of Wrath,* an angry, yet compassionate picture of the plight of migrant American farm workers in the New Deal years.

Equally replete with warm human sympathies and understanding of the crude realities among the disinherited, *An American Tragedy* by Theodore Dreiser attracted an international audience. So did colorful, leanly written tales by Ernest Hemingway, condemning war and

Ernest Hemingway

Albert Camus

tyranny—*A Farewell to Arms; For Whom the Bell Tolls.* His disciplined and emotionally suggestive style and allusive vocabulary set standards for imaginative literature.*The Old Man and the Sea* consolidated his international reputation and earned him a place among the Nobel laureates.

The foremost novelist in the German language was Thomas Mann, who became an American citizen. Author of *The Magic Mountain,* a major achievement of unusual symbolic quality, he also wrote an epic "Joseph" series and *The Tables of the Law,* an artistic dramatization of the life story of Moses. While living in the United States, Mann composed *Doctor Faustus,* a scorching indictment in the form of an allegory of totalitarian bestiality in dealing with the things of the mind, appraised by many authorities as his most notable piece of fiction. Ranked by some critics alongside of Mann was another Nobel prize winner Hermann Hesse. Although little read in English translations, his finest novels (*Demian; Steppenwolf*) commanded very large audiences among the intelligentsia and ordinary folk in Continental Europe. Nazi barbarities were brilliantly condemned in Franz Werfel's *Jacobowsky and the Colonel;* and Franz Kafka, a prolific creative writer, sponsored an international literary cult with *The Castle* and *The Trial,* characterized by unrealistic allegories, dream symbolism and pessimism. Two Italian authors attained world renown: Alberto Moravia, expert in reproducing detailed and passionate portraits of ordinary folk and of the youth of Milan, and Ignazio Silone, an accomplished political novelist, who exposed the iniquities of Fascism with righteous anger (*Fontamara*).

FICTION IN THE SOVIET UNION

A lush crop of novels appeared in Soviet Russia, some of them invaluable for insights into the mentality of the land of the Hammer and the Sickle or for reconstructions of society under the Communist dispensation. Writers understood that it was their bounden duty to stimulate workmen to greater production, to foster patriotism, to educate fellow citizens "to defend the historical gains of socialism," and to fortify spirits amidst the ordeals of war and the privations of peace. Nikita Khrushchev admonished Soviet men of letters that they must be the "long-range artillery . . . to clear the way for the infantry" in the unceasing ideological contest with the free nations.

Woe betide the author who turned out anything that Kremlin authorities might damn as cosmopolitanism or suggestive of dissidence or smacking of Western bourgeois tastes. "Socialist realism," the right of the Communist Party to dictate intellectual creativity, was the official principle for workers in words or in the fine arts. "We writers are called upon," explained E. Popovkin, "to expose our ideological enemies and their pernicious morality . . . We should always remember the basic principles of our literature, its party spirit, its militancy, and spirit of attack. . . ."

The later productions of Maxim Gorky, confidant of veteran Bolshevik leaders, and most glorified of Soviet authors, possessed unmistakable artistic merit. His virile and refreshingly adult novels vividly recaptured the realities of Russian existence down to the Bolshevik *coup d' état—My Universities* (autobiographical) and *The Life of Klim Sangin.*

The pendulum of Communist party supervision over Russian writers and artists swayed to and fro. While the Second World War was being fought, considerable leniency prevailed, only to be followed by a harsh and rigid enforcement of official orthodoxy. After the death of Stalin in 1953, a thaw set in, controls were relaxed, creative freedom enjoyed praiseworthy scope. But, when certain authors broke out in literature of protest against the dictatorial state apparatus, the authorities inaugurated a fresh, vigorous drive for conformity.

In the early 1960's a clear division existed among Soviet writers and other intellectuals. Whereas one set urged the right of freer expression, brought out works critical of the Stalinist regime, and fought against Stalinist conformities, a second school, tagged neo-Stalinist, insisted that literature should be designed solely to advance Communist party interests. Varying shades of opinion prevailed in each camp, though both professed unswerving allegiance to the Soviet state and its propaganda apparatus.

Through all vicissitudes, Ilya Ehrenburg, prolific novelist and journalist, somehow contrived to survive and to retain his position as a Soviet literary oracle. Best known doubtless for *The Fall of Paris* and *The Storm*, he also defined the post-Stalinist relaxation in *The Thaw*, and a sequel, *The Spring*. They depict the way of life in a provincial town remote from Moscow, family ambitions and jealousies, wounded pride, and unrequited love. Though some highly placed bureaucrats are severely treated, the novels end in a mood of genial optimism.

A skeptic and a considerable cosmopolitan, Ehrenburg was gifted with barbed satirical talent. For defiance of the official line in the closing years of Stalin's autocracy, he brought down on his head the wrath of the foes of cosmopolitanism. Before long, he boldly called for more enlightened treatment of literature and the arts. Since his writings ranged the gamut from unabashed Stalinist propagandism to sturdy championship of intellectual freedom, he was often reproached as a cynical opportunist. That accusation Ehrenburg passionately, though unconvincingly, repudiated.

While the short-lived thaw was on, a young novelist Vladimir Dudintsev brought out the iconoclastic *Not By Bread Alone*, which enjoyed an enormous sale and aroused acrid controversy. It was slow paced and hardly a distinguished specimen of creative artistry. The novel decried the imposition of shackles upon individuals and subtly flayed the Stalinist tyranny by assaults upon the self-seeking bureaucracy and the Soviet managerial class. The hero of this realistic tale is a highly individualistic spirit, albeit a devout Communist. A lonely inventor, he questioned the collective approach to problems, and for his boldness suffered persecution at the hands of officialdom. Banished to Siberia, he nonetheless managed temporarily to triumph over his enemies; yet in the end they remained firmly entrenched in power.

Stormy literary petrel that he was, Dudintsev summoned his fellow "privilegentsia" (as someone tagged Soviet intellectual workers) to dedicate their talents to truth and freedom, regardless of consequences. For his temerity, the author was publicly reviled for fostering pessim-

Boris Pasternak

ism among readers and for promoting "low spirits."

More temerity followed in the publications of the staunchly nonconformist Boris L. Pasternak. Greatly respected in Soviet circles for elegant lyric poetry and excellent translations of Shakespeare, this immortal of Russian letters first attracted international attention by *Doctor Zhivago*. A historical novel, the canvas is crowded with characters after the manner of Count Leo Tolstoy. Zhivago is presented as a member of the cultivated intelligentsia of the pre-revolutionary era, who thoroughly despised the regime of the tsars. Becoming an expert diagnostician, as well as a poet and a philosopher, he served as a medical officer in the First World War and later as a physician in Red Moscow. Disillusioned by the chaotic Bolshevik order of society, he took refuge for a time in the East, but subsequently settled down in the Communist capital, a patriotic lover of Mother Russia.

While the best part of the novel relates to the age before the Bolshevik seizure of power, the first phase of the Communist era is treated critically, casual references are made to vile concentration camps, and Marxism is dismissed as superficial and crassly utilitarian. On the Stalinist epoch, Pasternak wrote, "people had to be cured, by every means of terrorism, of the habit of thinking and judging for themselves and...to assert the opposite of what their eyes told them."

Seemingly, Pasternak wished for a collectivist pattern of society, but one in which bourgeois values were honored. Earlier, though perhaps never so courageously as in *Doctor Zhivago*, he had pleaded for artistic independence, earning for himself the epithet of "decadent aesthete." Now Soviet hack writers excoriated him as a "Judas," as a traitor to Mother Russia and her people. The ferocious agitation against *Doctor Zhivago* and its creator touched new peaks when Pasternak in 1958 was awarded the Nobel Prize, both for his achievements in poetry and in prose. Under duress he declined the Nobel distinction and withdrew into seclusion. After his death (1960) the savage vendetta was extended to his intimate friends.

T. S. Eliot

Many a Soviet intellectual implicitly supported Pasternak by preserving total silence.

Never published in the Soviet Union, *Doctor Zhivago* circulated abroad in dozens of languages. The outrageous treatment of the sensitive, free-thinking author stirred up worldwide but, of course, ineffectual protest.

POETRY

The finest poetry of the years after 1914 reflected the discontents and urges of the age or revealed thoughtful meditation on values lying beyond the range of experience. Artists in verse were inclined to avoid stereotyped rhythms. Pundits and public found much to admire in the poetry of Thomas S. Eliot, an American by birth, an Englishman by preference. As *The Waste Land* discloses, Eliot experienced a period of bitter, barren despair inspired by sordid materialism; then he indulged in a kind of nostalgic mysticism ("Four Quartets"). A much admired poetic drama, *Murder in the Cathedral*, attempted to recreate the intellectual wrestlings of the English martyr Thomas à Becket. His finest creation doubtless is *The Cocktail Party*, a drama in verse form. Therein contemporary civilization is interpreted as perverse, dreary and bleak; men are weak and depraved creatures, plodding along in dull

William Butler Yeats

conformity, though not without a sense of social duty.

Among the Irish born, William Butler Yeats, who carried off Nobel honors, belonged in a class apart. Poet, enthusiast for Irish culture, promoter of the arts and letters, Yeats skillfully fostered the nationalist cause in Ireland. In his more mature phase, he distilled the charm of ancient Irish legend and folklore into interpretative lyrics—"The Cutting of an Agate"; "The Winding Stair"—acclaimed as about the best verse of the time in the English language. Alfred Noyes chanted the achievements of scientists in "The Torch-Bearers" and composed stirring ballads such as "The Highwayman." The social enthusiasms of the 1930's were set in poetic form by Wystan H. Auden ("Autumn Journey"). During a sojourn in the United States his philosophical outlook shifted and became more conventional, though sometimes sharply cynical or obscure to the point of exasperation ("The Age of Anxiety"). Wales gave poetry a richly individualistic genius in the person of Dylan Thomas, whose special forte lay in imaginative pieces on elemental themes of universal concern—birth, growth and death, the harshness of nature ("In Country Sleep"; "This Side of Truth"). Likened to Keats by some critics, Thomas died at thirty-nine, his promise as a leading poet of his generation only half fulfilled.

Two exquisite French poets, Paul Valéry and Paul Claudel, stressed intellectual and aesthetic impulses. Claudel, a devout Catholic, dwelt upon the sympathies and viewpoints of his particular creed. "We are wretched ones," he lamented in "Shadows," "and Satan sifts us in his sieve." Distinguished verse in the German language was written by Carl F. G. Spitteler, Hermann Hesse and Rainer Maria Rilke—the last, a charmingly melodic craftsman, was most admired for noble "Elegies."

Vital and original poetry by Americans brought readers face to face with the temperaments of the New World, often in a caustic manner. Best known were Edgar Lee Masters (*Spoon River Anthology*, a collection of epitaphs on small-town personalities), Carl Sand-

Robert Frost

burg, with his oratorically staccato "Chicago Poems" and the more tranquil New England rhythms of Robert Frost—"New Hampshire." Frost's talent for verse was quickened by associations with English writers during a lengthy stay abroad. Probably the most beloved American poet of the time, four times winner of the Pulitzer prize and "required reading" in certain European universities, he infused warmly sympathetic portrayals of plain Yankees and their manner of living with a sincere and forthright personal philosophy ("Death of the Hired Man," "Build Soil—a Political Pastoral"). In his later years Frost was hailed as the "poet laureate" of America. Two years before his death in 1963, at the age of eighty-eight, he crowned his career by participating in the inaugural ceremonics for President John F. Kennedy. Ezra Pound, a poet's poet, produced *New Cantos,* bitterly critical in tone and revolutionary in form. Having lived in Italy as a young man, Pound returned there in maturity to sing the praises of the Fascist regime of Mussolini. He is a controversial figure.

Soviet poets escaped the sterner pressures imposed upon writers of fiction to promote the Communist faith and hope. Vladimir Mayakovsky, perhaps the best representative of them, needed no official prodding, for he was a prerevolutionary Bolshevik, and after the Communist seizure of power merited esteem for his staunchly propagandistic verse ("Left, March"), written in the dialect of the common man. Once idolized by aspiring lyricists, he lost caste in time with the ruling class, and in a mood of despair perished by his own hand. Round a statue raised to the memory of Mayakovsky in Moscow, youthful poets gathered to read their verse to anyone who cared to listen.

DRAMA

Playwrights produced some of the most important and influential literature of the time. Themes responded to the changing social order and moral standards and in other ways paralleled trends among the novelists. In drama as in fiction, authors in the United States attained unexampled international significance. The most popular of them, Eugene O'Neill, soaked himself in psychoanalytic literature; fame and fortune accrued from such productions as *Strange Interlude, Mourning Becomes Electra,* and the less lavishly welcomed *The Iceman Cometh.* Tennessee Williams' *A Street Car Named Desire* and *The Night of the Iguana,* and *Our Town* by Thornton Wilder attracted appreciative attention in Europe.

Sprightly plays flowed in orderly succession from the pen of Noel Coward, no doubt the foremost English theatrical craftsman (*Cavalcade; Peace in Our Time*). Singularly original and important was Christopher Fry's *The Lady's Not for Burning,* which sympathetic reviewers appraised as the finest poetic drama since Shakespeare. Rebelling against drawing room comedy displaying bourgeois appetites, certain younger British playwrights in the late 1950's turned to starkly realistic portrayals of wageworkers and their victimization. Representative was John Osborne (*Look Back in Anger*), who united the grubbier aspects of class hatred with detestation of established British institutions; subsequently, in *Luther,* he struck out on a new trail, dramatizing medieval folk superstitions and the emotional hysteria that enchained the great Christian reformer.

From the pen of Eugene Ionesco came a breezy and thought-provoking satire on the herd mind, *Rhinoceros;* individuals drawn from all social levels transform themselves into a company of rhinoceroses, except for an unsophisticated little clerk, who sturdily insists upon remaining human! An accomplished Irish playwright, Sean O'Casey, resorted to loosely articulated verse in his finest production, *The Plough and the Stars.* It is a beautiful fusion of farce with tragedy, and the last act, which portrays the Irish Rising of Easter Week, 1916, has been acclaimed as the best single act in twentieth-century dramatic expression.

Leadership in the French theater belonged to Édouard Bourdet (*The Weaker Sex*) and Jean Anouilh. Before the Second World War, during the Nazi occupation and after, Anouilh turned out many plays, some of them frothy comedies, others solid and serious dramas describing the endless struggle of ordinary men against insolence and inhumanity (*Ring Around the Moon; Antigone; Becket*). Nobel honors were bestowed upon Luigi Pirandello, an Italian, whose *Six Characters in Search of an Author* illustrated his decidedly intellectual approach to the tragedies and perplexities of existence.

Though it is uncertain whether the influential, Bavarian-born playwright Bertolt Brecht was affiliated with the Communist Party, his starkly realistic dramas surely reflected Marxist ideas. Fleeing Germany when the Nazis assumed power, he became a wanderer in northern Europe and the United States. He settled down finally in the Soviet sector of Berlin, where the Communist authorities exploited his international fame for propaganda purposes abroad. A versatile lyricist, as well as a dramatist, Brecht scored a major success with *The Three Penny Opera;* and in *Mother Courage,* a play centered on the Thirty Years' War, he protested in unbridled yet simple language against social unfairness. His famous *The Caucausian Chalk Circle,* imaginatively merging comedy and social drama, with many aphorisms full of Brechtian irony, teaches humans how to transcend suffering. Awarded the Stalin Peace Prize, Brecht nonetheless was an undisciplined cosmopolitan who balked at following official Communist lines.

MASS COMMUNICATION

Apprehension that the legitimate stage would be wholly eclipsed by moving pictures turned out to be groundless. Yet until the advent of television no art equalled the movies in universal appeal, and for the leisure hours of millions they furnished the principal form of entertainment. The perfection of talking pictures in the late 1920's and colored films in the next decade enhanced the popularity of the screen. The immature crudities of the pioneer period before 1914 passed quickly into history as a race of slick scenario writers emerged and successful plays and novels were screened. A large proportion of the films were flat and banal with stereotyped plots of romance and adventure, lust and violence, wild West and jungle thrills. But amidst the torrent of pictures some works of artistic quality were turned out as diverse as *Hamlet,* starring Sir Laurence Olivier, and *Snow White and the Seven Dwarfs.*

As a rule the dream factories of Hollywood set the pace in movie productions, however much the output was lampooned by native and foreign critics. From the screen, moviegoers the world over derived fantastic impressions of the wealth and luxury of the United States, impressions which the well-fed and superbly equipped American troops in the Second World War did nothing to diminish. Until the Nazis came to power the German film industry probably ranked next to the United States. Britain, France, Italy and Russia boasted directors and performers of distinction, who produced films of superior artistic and technical merit, though many of the most accomplished film personalities of Europe were lured to Hollywood.

Beginning in the mid-1930's, "documentaries," as rivals to the older newsreels, quickly advanced in importance. Facts were wantonly twisted in historical films to furnish entertainment. In totalitarian states, where mere diversion was officially frowned upon, historical pictures along with newsreels were exploited for propagandistic purposes. Hitler set up a film trust and shaped it into a party weapon; the output was frequently weak in entertainment value, but loaded with ideological propaganda.

By the late 1950's, audiences in movie houses had dwindled sharply because of the formidable competition of television. To meet this challenge, film-makers introduced rather more maturity in subject matter and treatment and presented spectacular, costly, and big pictures, such as *Ben Hur, King of Kings,* a popularization of Christian history, and *Cleopatra.* Some producers kept their firms afloat by turning out films for transmission by television.

Earlier, the "movies" had been confronted by another challenger, radio. Pioneer experimentation by an Italian inventor, Guglielmo Marconi, made possible the flashing of the first radio message in 1901, but for a generation

Radio room aboard S.S. Minnehaha, *1904. Note spark-coil transmitter and receiver employing a coherer.*

"wireless" was considered merely a supplement to telegraphy. The first regular radio broadcasts started in the United States in 1920, and two years later the British Broadcasting Company (B.B.C.) was set up; thereafter the popularity of the radio increased sensationally. Whereas in the United States broadcasting was undertaken by private companies, dependent upon advertising revenues, it was very largely a government monopoly in other countries.

The radio was a boon to the illiterate of the earth (who are more numerous than the literate) and to those who found the spoken word easier to follow or more convincing than the printed page. Fishermen in the North Sea could keep in touch with the Liverpool market for herring, the voice of political leaders or the strains of symphony orchestras could be heard in any home. Evolution in broadcasting technique and in types of programs proceeded apace. In America, the scales were heavily weighted in favor of dance music, variety shows and somewhat lurid serial dramas known as "soap operas." With the 1930's more and more time was devoted to newscasts and commentaries; and as a device for insinuating news and views into foreign countries, radio had no peer. In 1946, B. B. C. pioneered in a "Third Programme" which presented classical literature and music and even systematic historical surveys for the serious "high-brow" minority, but the listening audience proved to be disappointingly small. In a world of quantity, the "Third Programme" upheld the ideal of quality; as one friend of the experiment observed, "Eternal vigilance is the price of culture."

Radio possessed a special advantage over television, for it could penetrate across the frontiers of the East and West political power blocs. So broadcasting became a serviceable weapon in the constant competition for the hearts and minds of men. From the West, the B.B.C. and "The Voice of America," conspicuously, transmitted solid information to and nourished hope in the Communist-dominated lands of Eastern Europe. On the other side, the Soviet and Red Chinese broadcasting services conducted propaganda in underdeveloped countries with greater intensity than their Western rivals.

In the early 1960's, some eighty countries boasted television facilities, a few of them capable of sending out images in color. Described as the "ultimate form of radio," this marvel in its first stages was a British specialty, the B.B.C. televising a program as early as 1930. Development proceeded at a leisurely pace, however, until after the Second World War, and then the advance surged forward with a rush, so that in a few years nine out of ten American homes, it was estimated, were equipped with television sets.

Television eclipsed the movie as a form of entertainment. At the outset it resembled a kind of magic lantern presenting demonstrations of cooking and ballet dancing, but offerings quickly broadened into enlightenment as well as light entertainment. Not since the pop-

A second stage of advance in radio—broadcasting studio of KDKA, Pittsburgh, in 1922.

A modern broadcasting studio in action

ularization of the automobile, probably, had any invention changed American ways of living and thinking so vitally. As an ally of popular government and in education, television possessed immense potentialities, though anxieties were roused lest children brought up on "video" would have less taste for reading and reflection.

Critics in the United States also attacked offerings as a "vast wasteland" and called for more creative experimentation, more substantial fare at prime viewing hours; partly in response to such demands, stations presenting educational television were established in many sections of the Republic. Countries in Western Europe organized an international television network, Eurovision, with the central control in Brussels.

When Pope John XXIII was borne through crowds assembled in St. Peter's Square at the opening of an Ecumenical Council in Rome in 1962, the brilliant pageantry and splendor of the procession were promptly conveyed to television screens in American households. That demonstration dramatically revealed that a new chapter in intercontinental communication had opened, made possible by a radio-relay, orbiting satellite, called Telstar. An American achievement, essentially, Telstar was described as "a miniature communications laboratory in space," and although technicians regarded it as experimental, with Telstar the New World captured leadership in important, practical aspects of the conquest of space.

In the general area of communications, exchanges between the Western nations and the Communist East expanded considerably in the late 1950's. Travel restrictions in the Soviet bloc were eased, and a variety of cultural and intellectual relationships was facilitated by intergovernmental agreements. These contacts embraced exchanges of musical, theatrical and dance groups, of students and scientific workers and of artists, as well as conferences and exhibits. Strictly non-political Western publications were allowed a limited distribution in the Soviet Union, and a Soviet government magazine was admitted to the West. On the other hand, Western newspapers and books were banned from Soviet Russia and the Soviets interfered with radio transmission from the West. Communications, in short, were not free and easy, yet they were better than none, and visiting groups were handsomely received on both sides of the Iron Curtain.

Notwithstanding the newer forms of mass communication, the output of reading material for all and sundry rolled steadily upward. The press gave the permanence of print to fleeting facts and opinions on topics ranging from politics to science, cooking to the fine arts, sporting events to economics—not to forget the popular themes of crime and sex. Mass circulation magazines in the United States carried short stories written according to formula and easily digestible articles suited to middle-class tastes. Newspapers continued, of course, to be the most popular member of the press family. In authoritarian countries, state officials deliberately colored or minutely censored what the public might read. For the free world the United States led the way in methods of journalism and in mass production, though not always in the quality of the fare that was offered.

Consolidation of newspapers in "chains" heightened the potential power of press proprietors, while rising costs made it extremely difficult to launch new papers; the number of American papers per million of the population was cut nearly in half between 1920 and 1949. Standards of press accuracy and reliability improved in the democratic world and the speed of operation of the international newsgathering agencies, such as the Associated Press and Reuters, was much accelerated. The telegraphing of photographs, mainly for newspapers, began in the 1920's.

CURRENTS IN PHILOSOPHY

Surveying in 1949 the stupendous achievements of contemporary man, Winston Churchill observed with characteristic zest and felicity:

> This vast expansion was unhappily not accompanied by any noticeable advance in the stature of man, either in his mental faculties or his moral character. His brain got no better, but buzzed the more. The scale of events around him assumed gigantic proportions while he remained about the same size.

Be that as it may, man possessed a super-brain, his measureless and priceless asset, which enabled him to penetrate deeply into the mysteries of matter and mind. More wonderful than atomic fission, for example, were the eyes, hands and brains that brought this miracle to pass. "Thought is great and swift and free," Bertrand Russell, the *doyen* of British philosophers, proclaimed, "the light of the world, and the chief glory of man."

Philosophic thinkers in the West, varied in their approach and temperament, burnished up old concepts of thought or fashioned fresh patterns. However much opposed in shades of opinion, all alike searched for ultimate principles, for unity and order in the external world affecting human destinies, and came to grips with fundamental problems of living, loving and dying that have engaged mankind since the dawn of human thought.

A sense of great urgency was imparted to philosophic enterprise in the West by the challenge of Communism. The propagation of the Soviet ideology forced a reassessment of the basic ideas and values of Western society, just as Soviet practice compelled modifications in Western social and economic practices. The fighting faith of Marxian materialism ridiculed other schemes of philosophy as tarred with the bourgeois brush, naive, decadent and false. Somewhat altered, this creed exerted an incalculable influence, of course, upon human activity in the Soviet Union and the broadening Communist world.

As with other patterns of materialism, the Marxist version nonchalantly dismissed the higher urges of the spirit, accepting nothing beyond the range of the senses. Marxism re-

Arnold J. Toynbee

pudiated belief in spirit for belief in matter. An officially approved Soviet work on philosophy portrayed the history of philosophy as "the birth, emergence and development of the scientific materialistic world outlook and its laws. Since materialism has grown and developed in the struggles with idealistic movements," it was explained, "the history of philosophy is also the history of the struggle between materialism and idealism." Atheistic materialism was not a monopoly of the Soviets, to be sure, but the Kremlin possessed power to put theory into performance.

SPENGLER AND TOYNBEE

Among the intellectual landmarks of the time were weighty, schematic syntheses of history prepared by the German Oswald Spengler and by Professor Arnold J. Toynbee of England. Both of these social thinkers endeavored to extract meaning and form out of the total panorama of recorded history. As interpreted by them, the past had witnessed a series of civilizations, which had moved through definite stages of growth, grandeur and disintegration, as with animal organisms.

Spengler in *The Decline of the West* wholly discarded the idea of continuous human progress that had been so fashionable before 1914. Although the work had been planned and partly written before the war, the first volume was not published until 1917 and two more followed in 1922; the book quickly raced through a hundred German editions and had considerable reading in translations. Hitherto an obscure high school teacher, Spengler, who was much indebted to Nietzsche, suddenly became an international celebrity. With force, learning and imagination he argued that cultured societies had gone through a life-and-death rhythm of development and that the West had sharply declined in the nineteenth century. His vision of the impending doom of Western civilization, on the model of the Roman Empire, excited passionate debate and encouraged spineless fatalism in the epoch between world wars. At the mid-century some observers believed the catastrophic prophecies of the "Jeremiah of Munich" had actually come true.

Lighter of touch, shrewder, more guarded in language and less grim than Spengler, Toynbee, nonetheless, agreed that historic cultures had followed discernible life cycles. Collapse had eventually come, much as one falls asleep without being quite aware of what is happening. The course of events, he argued, had repeatedly come to a crossroads, when choices could be made leading either to the death of a civilization or to its preservation and survival. Toynbee was of the opinion that the West had touched its cultural peak in the thirteenth century, and was now in a state of acute crisis, though he declined to predict whether the melancholy fate of old Rome would be duplicated.

These themes Toynbee exposed in a spacious, multi-volumed *A Study of History* (D. C. Somervell smoothly condensed the work [1947, 1957] into two books). Toynbee's masterpiece was engagingly written, contained stimulating philosophic insights and focused attention on the basic significance of religion in history. It was his considered judgment that social decay ran parallel with the decline of religious influence. For its originality and impressive erudition, *A Study of History* belongs among the most distinguished of historico-philosophical expositions.

MORE FORMAL PHILOSOPHERS

Were professional philosophers being duped by reliance on reason and the apparent certitudes of science? Professor Henri Bergson of the Sorbonne argued the question in the affirmative in *Creative Evolution* and other speculative writings. Taking as his watchword, "We cannot sacrifice experience to the requirements of any system," he protested that dogmatic faith in rational thought fell short of wholeness. The intuitive faculty of man, that is, helped him to appreciate reality from within and consequently possessed relevance and importance. Appealing to a kind of mystical illumination, Bergson disputed the claims of mechanical determinism and materialism. He sponsored a faith that stamped itself upon literature and persuaded some intellectuals to embrace the scholastic synthesis of Roman Catholicism.

Much influenced by Bergson was a distinguished Anglo-American thinker, Alfred N. Whitehead, who regarded philosophy as a thrilling "Adventure in Ideas," remote from the ivory tower. "Philosophy begins in wonder," he wrote, "and, at the end, when philosophic thought has done its best, the wonder remains." No blueprint of philosophy, he felt, could be finished and final due to "weakness of insight" and "deficiencies in language." Whitehead held the sanguine opinion that insecurity and divine discontent supplied the necessary stimulus for social betterment.

The Nestor of philosophic thought in the United States was John Dewey, often belabored as a pagan materialist. Drawing upon the pragmatism of William James, Dewey fashioned a philosophy with direct bearing upon urgent needs of contemporary society. As he saw matters, philosophy implied experimentation in the spirit of the scientist, trying alternatives, casting aside what would not work and applying what would, regardless of how upsetting to tradition and custom. Which is to say that practicality was the touchstone of validity—a proposition congenial to the dominant temper of the United States. In *The Quest for Certainty,* Dewey put forward his own position by contrasting it with older patterns of philosophy. Writers of realistic fiction, such as Sinclair Lewis and Theodore Dreiser, reflected in a measure the pragmatism of Dewey.

By taking thought, Dewey seemed to say, man should be able to adapt himself to his social environment or alter it along desirable lines. Instead of being stereotyped and unchanging, human nature responded in fact to environmental surroundings; a democratic community offered the best chance of maximum fulfillment for the individual, provided he was animated by a sense of social responsibility. As has been noted, Dewey was concerned to apply the doctrine of whatever-works-is-useful to everyday social issues and to formal education. Beyond philosophic circles, his influence was most extensive upon methods in public schooling in the United States and abroad. The school, he declared, must train pupils to be mutually helpful in the adult society to which they would presently belong.

Close to the native American "liberal" or "naturalist" philosophy espoused by Dewey was a British group called the neo-realists. In this set belonged Bertrand Russell, the most lucid if not the most profound intelligence among very modern philosophers. Clarity, wit, flashes of sardonic humor and felicity of expression made his writings a joy to the layman (*Wisdom of the West*). Obsessed with the discoveries of science, Russell identified philosophy with scientific method and "common sense." Ultimate reality, if it could at all be attained, must be ascertained and verified by the processes of the laboratory. He and his followers were not only unsympathetic to the distilled wisdom of the past, but they deeply distrusted emotions, intuitions and "universals." Their repudiation of the supernatural fostered disbelief in the God of the Christian tradition.

An extremely tolerant man, Russell was always ready to compromise and experiment, and he cherished a generally hopeful opinion of the world of tomorrow. Nevertheless, he could write, "One of the painful things about our time is that those who feel certainty are stupid and those with any imagination and understanding are filled with doubt and indecision." Since beliefs could never be more than approximations of truth, in the opinion of Russell, they should only be adopted tentatively. As a voluminous and versatile author and for his untiring championship of freedom of inquiry, Russell was awarded the Nobel Prize in literature in 1950. His advocacy of unpopular causes, such as pacifism and a ban on atomic tests, frequently brought him into collision with the public authorities. Nevertheless, he continued to crusade vigorously into his ninetieth year.

The dean of Italian philosophers, Benedetto Croce, revolted against a rationally mechanical conception of life in the manner of Bergson, and defended an idealist interpretation of the good life. Sturdily, though ineffectively, he resisted the authoritarianism of Fascism, thus enhancing his reputation in the free world. The philosopher George Santayana spent his last years at a Roman Catholic retreat near Rome, though he was born in Spain, reared in the United States, and taught at Harvard for many years. The net outcome of his reflections, as displayed in his greatest contributions, *The Life of Reason* and *The Realms of Being*, recalled the skeptical, pantheistic abstractions of Baruch Spinoza. The world impressed him as an insoluble predicament to be meditated upon sympathetically but with detachment. The aesthetic pleasures of mind and spirit yielded a meed of sanity and contentment to the individual. On his eighty-eighth birthday in 1951, Santayana confessed that answers to the problems of the world were more elusive than half a century earlier.

EXISTENTIALISM

On the morrow of the Second World War, a fresh wave of philosophic pessimism called existentialism excited no little commotion, especially in France and in university circles of western Germany. Existentialism has been described as a philosophy in which "life is seen to be a vain race for death and all [that] the self-consciousness of the individual can achieve is reduced to anticipating this idea and overcoming anxiety by the sense of its ineluctable necessity." The fountainhead of this somber school of thought was a lonely Danish thinker of a century earlier, Sören A. Kierkegaard. Previously not much studied outside of his own little country, he exerted a growing impact upon contemporary philosophic discussion.

An adroit logician, he preferred reliance upon imagination to reliance upon reason. Though familiar with esteemed Christian mystics, Kierkegaard had little or no acquaintance with other religious cultures or with natural science and secular history. He upheld freedom in thought and action, but argued that knowledge and faith belonged in separate compartments or categories. The individual must commit himself to the imperious claims of the Absolute; only the assurance of divine grace and forgiveness made the riddle of existence bearable. Holding that religion was a matter of personal discretion, Kierkegaard parted company with the state church of Denmark.

As elaborated after 1945, existentialism, which has been derided as "an encounter with nothingness," fed the stream of "anti-intellectualism." The ideas of the leading French exponent, Jean-Paul Sartre, are found in *Existentialism and Humanism*. Actual personal experience, he insisted, led unerringly to the conclusion that existence is an absurdity. Since man came from nothingness, to nothingness must he return. Meanwhile, man being born to trouble as the sparks fly upward, he could only await his unmerited fate. Sartre, who turned atheist, professed a philosophy of despair, a devastating philosophy of nihilism.

Existentialism had an influential German advocate in the person of Professor Karl Jaspers of Basel University—*Way to Wisdom* is regarded as the best introduction to his beliefs. An introspective thinker, Jaspers was profoundly impressed with the limitations that surround all thought and are conducive to skepticism. In *The Future of Mankind*, Jaspers reasoned that politicians were incapable of solving the problem of survival in the face of nuclear armaments. Fully understanding the feeling of despair and helplessness that engulfed his generation, he placed reliance upon reason and creative freedom to transform somehow man and his world.

RELIGIOUS THOUGHT

No iron curtain separates philosophic from religious thought. Stated otherwise, theology, the exploration and character of the Divine Reality (however conceived), may be considered as a division of philosophy. Perhaps the foremost Roman Catholic philosopher-theologian of the period was Jacques Maritain, who had sat at the feet of Bergson, and who lectured at Paris, Princeton and other universities. An incisive and significant thinker, he acquired full command of the intellectual resources of Thomas Aquinas and asserted belief in the supernatural with piety, subtlety and assurance. Rationalism, Maritain assailed as leading inescapably to atheistic humanism. He applied the principles of Aquinas to political and cultural problems, affirming the dignity and rights of man and attacking totalitarianism with the weapons of democracy (*Religion and Culture; Freedom in the Modern World*).

For Protestant Europe, the most formidable theologian was Karl Barth, a rebellious prophet of neo-orthodoxy or biblical Christianity. His "theology of crisis," which passed through progressive stages, was colored by his kinship with Kierkegaard and more so by the conviction that the First World War had shattered the facile optimism of inevitable man-made progress toward a golden age of physical and mental well-being. Ugly, stubborn facts, that is to say, had shattered the popular, almost utopian conception of the goodness of human nature and had demonstrated the inability of mortal man, unaided, to build a "heavenly city" on earth.

Breaking with "modernist" Protestant tendencies, Barth argued for dependence upon God as revealed in the Scriptures. In time, Barth came to conceive of the Deity as a stern and righteous Judge, "The Wholly Different One," the God indeed of Calvin. Not only was man impotent in and of himself, but he was guilty of greed and false pride, wickedness and sin—a concept that had almost lost its meaning; he must repent and make atonement as the preliminary to salvation (*The Word of God and the Word of Man*). The Church, moreover, must be given a new sense of direction, must dedicate itself to a new renaissance based upon an intellectual expression of faith; it must not allow itself to be diverted into a genial humanism by dabbling in secular sociology, economics and psychology.

Reinhold Niebuhr

The doctrines of Barth generated considerable enthusiasm (and much hostile criticism) in German Protestant circles and spread to other lands. An American theologian, Reinhold Niebuhr, in *The Nature and Destiny of Man*, for example, energetically set forth the frosty teachings of Barth, with certain refinements. "The conflicts and catastrophies of our era," Niebuhr lamented, "have been the more terrible because we had no philosophy by which we could anticipate them, or understand them when they were upon us." Niebuhr and those who shared his general position devoted far more attention to Christian responsibility for the betterment of secular society than their European master. Both Barth and Niebuhr lashed out against the ruthless practices and philosophies of totalitarian dictatorships.

One of the most fascinating and versatile personalities of the time was another Protestant thinker, the Alsatian-born Albert Schweitzer.

Albert Schweitzer with leper children at his hospital in Gabon, French Equatorial Africa

Becoming a medical missionary in French Equatorial Africa, this saint and sage found time to compose influential books interpreting the Christian view of the good life in terms of mystical experience (*The Mysticism of Paul; Christianity and the Religions of the World*). As a torchbearer of light and reason, Schweitzer contended that every living thing deserved reverence (*The Philosophy of Civilization*). He also made himself an expert on Bach and Goethe and was an accomplished musician.

"Liberal" Protestantism steadily reviewed its thinking in the light of current scientific and intellectual tendencies. A devout and reflective British historian of science expressed his religious outlook in this language: "True religion...is founded on the impregnable rock of direct experience. Some may be colour-blind, but others see the bright hues of sunrise. Some may have no religious sense, but others live and move and have their being in the transcendent glory of God . . . It is not necessary, indeed it is impossible, to define what is meant by God; those who know Him will want no definition."[4]

THE PULSE OF RELIGION

On the institutional side, the salient fact about organized religion in Western society after 1914 was the persistence of trends that had cropped up late in the nineteenth century. The Christian faith, that is to say, decreased in importance as an active force in shaping the ideas and behavior of men and in the conduct of public policies. For that decline there were several reasons: the corrosive impact of science, secular philosophy, and the expansion of historical horizons as the sequel to archaeological and anthropological findings; preoccupation with everyday concerns and social reform which encouraged "secular-mindedness"; the increased respectability of religious indifference, as a by-product of greater tolerance; and, a novel consideration, disillusionment, anxiety and skepticism engendered by the shocking cruelties and destructiveness of two global wars and the threat of a third. As Thucydides long ago observed, war is "a violent schoolmaster."

[4] William C. Dampier, *A History of Science* (4th ed., Cambridge, England, 1949), p. 495.

As suggestive evidence of the trend of the time, clergymen in the Church of England declined by about a quarter, while active membership in the Church, as indicated by Easter communicants, experienced a comparable falling off. Too much, of course, should not be read into these figures, for it was estimated that thirteen million listened to broadcasts on religion presented by the B.B.C. In the 1960's, moreover, nearly two out of every three Americans belonged to churches, a higher proportion both absolutely and relatively than at any other time in national history. Due possibly to tensions engendered by perpetual world crises in the age of nuclear science, church membership in the 1950's increased faster in the United States than the general population. Regular attendance at public worship, however, fell far short of the claimed membership; and the same generalization applied to Christian communions in free Europe. More books on religious themes rolled from the press than ever before, and Christianity was probably more adequately defended by scholarly literature than previously. In 1961, on the 350th anniversary of the printing of the King James' Version of the Bible, English savants brought out a fresh translation of the New Testament from which archaic language was removed. In the first year after it was published, 3,500,000 copies were bought.

ROMAN CATHOLICISM

The tight intellectual framework of Roman Catholicism and its unique organization stood that branch of Christianity in good stead in an era of worry, confusion and religious apathy. To Catholic doctrine was added in 1950, the dogma of the bodily assumption of the Blessed Virgin Mary to heaven—the only papal definition of that sort in nearly a century. Pope Pius XI arranged new treaties (called concordats) with countries containing large Catholic constituencies, notably Fascist Italy and Nazi Germany. The pact of 1929 with Italy restored the Pope to sovereign authority over a tiny state in the heart of Rome embracing the Vatican and St. Peter's Cathedral. Before long, however, the Pope was protesting angrily against Fascist encroachment upon the educational prerogatives of the Church and against pagan veneration of Mussolini's state. Similarly, Hitler and his henchmen were sharply reminded that the individual was endowed with rights transcending the Nazi dictatorship. Courageous Catholic prelates spoke out boldly against Nazi persecution of Jewry.

From Mexico to Russia, conflicts raged between the Catholic Church and the State, reminiscent of earlier battles with Bismarck and Napoleon I, to go no farther back in history. The Vatican carried on unrelenting warfare against godless Communism as "full of errors and illusions" and destructive of religion, social order and the dignity of man. With their claim to be the Vicars of Christ, Popes through pastoral letters and encyclicals or by radio, addressed the nations on vital matters of public and private interest. In the name of social justice, the Vatican appealed for fair treatment of workpeople and promoted the activities of Catholic trade unions; the sanctity of marriage obligations was repeatedly reasserted, along with the responsibility of parents, in association with church and government, for the education of their children. Pope Pius XII, who as Cardinal Pacelli had attempted to bring about peace negotiations in the middle of the First World War, tried to prevent the renewal of hostilities in 1939.

Political parties committed to Catholic social principles and to the protection of church interests gathered strength in continental European countries. After the Second World War, Catholic parties in free Europe were vital agencies in sustaining the Western tradition of freedom and in combatting Communism. The National Catholic Welfare Council in the United States furthered the cause of social betterment. The enhanced international prestige of the papacy was shown by the larger number of diplomatic missions accredited to Vatican City, though the United States maintained only an unofficial personal representative of the President. During the Second World War, Stalin scoffed at Pope Pius XII because he had no armed divisions at his command, but as an international moral force the Pope exerted an immeasurable influence upon the vast fellowship of Roman Catholics, estimated at more than 300,000,000.

Pope John XXIII

Upon the death of Pius XII in 1958, the College of Cardinals elected as the 262nd successor of St. Peter an elderly Italian churchman of humble parentage who adopted the name of John XXIII. An amiable, wise and gifted spiritual leader, he had established a name for himself as apostolic nuncio in several European capitals, Paris especially. Papal encyclicals restated the economic and social teachings of Catholicism, and urgently called upon the richer nations to help poorer countries, recently declared independent. To give broader geographical distribution to the College of Cardinals, a native African, a Filipino, and a Japanese were appointed to that august body for the first time; the number of Cardinals reached eighty-five, the largest in history.

Progress toward integration of Christian bodies was the principal theme of the pontificate of John XXIII. Not only was a Vatican Committee for Promoting Christian Unity named, but the Pope appealed for cooperation between his church and the remnants of Orthodox Eastern Catholicism. When the spiritual head of the Church of England, the Archbishop of Canterbury, conferred with the Pope —a thing unheard of since the Reformation— it was presumed that conversation touched on the subject of Christian reunion. For the first time since 1869, an Ecumenical or General Conference was convoked (1962) to deliberate on proposals concerning church procedures and institutions. Some three thousand prelates of the Church, representing fifty-five countries, attended, though Protestants were present merely as interested observers.

In 1963, the world mourned the death of the brilliant and progressive papal leader, and the College of Cardinals reconvened to appoint another Italian churchman, Giovanni Battista, Cardinal Montini, who took the name of Paul VI.

PROTESTANTISM

"Liberal" or "modernist" Protestant leaders, in the United States more so than in Europe, endeavored to present Christian ideas and ideals in the shifting thought forms of the age. And they were actively concerned with social applications of the Christian teachings of the excellence of the humblest mortal and the equality of all, as children of God. In their interpretation, faith should be demonstrated not alone in the perfection of one's character but in altruistic service to society. Humanitarian compassion and moral indignation over prevailing social ills infused Protestant "modernism" with crusading zeal. Fired with an ardent sense of obligation to their fellows, militant exponents of the "social gospel" pressed for remedial measures, better urban housing, medical care and other improvements in social conditions. They displayed, too, keen interest in international politics, rallied to the support of the League of Nations and the United Nations, and spoke out against war as an unchristian and stupid method of dealing with disputes between nations. Many, who at one time adopted the pacifist position, changed their minds under the conviction that war was a lesser evil than the danger of totalitarian domination.

It was evident, in the years after 1914, that Protestant sectarianism was on the wane. Persuaded of the oneness of Protestantism in essentials, despite the history of separation and competition, several significant mergers were effected among Protestant groups. Three denominations in Canada, for instance, organized a United Church, and in the United States several Lutheran bodies were consolidated, as were the principal expressions of Methodism.

Talks were initiated for the union of the Church of England and the English Methodists, and the former made gestures for full intercommunion with most branches of Orthodox Catholicism. Under Nazi pressure, the Lutheran and Reformed Churches of Germany were combined as the Evangelical Church. Following the Hitlerian downfall, prominent Protestant pastors acknowledged the guilt of their country for the barbarities perpetrated by the Nazi sadists, and they strove, though with limited results, to maintain organic bonds between Protestantism in West Germany and in the Soviet Zone.

Over and above national consolidations were signs of the coming together of Protestant denominations on a world scale, in harmony with an ancient aphorism, "the real is one; sages speak of it variously." To consider points of unity and to foster a spirit of solidarity, interchurch conferences were periodically assembled. With delegates from the United States taking the initiative, a permanent World Council of Churches was created (1948) to advance interfaith objectives. At New Delhi, India, in 1961 a conference organized by the World Council attracted representatives from some two hundred churches along with five unofficial observers from the Vatican. Resolutions proclaimed the deepening sense of Christian unity, roundly condemned racial discrimination, and called for unfettered religious liberty.

RELIGION UNDER COMMUNISM

Many a watcher of the times interpreted the movement toward Christian unity as a response to the challenge of the materialistic and atheistic creed of Communism. Profession of atheism was a prerequisite to admission into the Communist Party. A massive campaign against the Orthodox Church in the Soviet Union was waged by anti-religious propaganda in school, youth organizations and army, and by anti-religious museums and societies. As time moved on, attendance on public worship was largely restricted to women and oldsters. When the Kremlin authorities decided that the historic Church had been sufficiently weakened, pressures were relaxed and, administratively, Orthodoxy was as firmly bound to the state as in the empire of the tsars.

Jew as well as Moslem suffered severely in consequence of the aversion of Communism to organized religion in any shape. A large proportion of the estimated 3,000,000 Soviet citizens of the Jewish tradition fell away from the faith of their fathers. In the early phase of Soviet history, Jews, like other minorities, were allowed to maintain their peculiar educational and cultural institutions, and an area in eastern Siberia was even set aside for Jewish colonization. In the 1950's, however, Kremlin policy shifted; Yiddish schools, theaters, and publications were banned, and officialdom struck hard against Jews suspected of "cosmopolitanism" or of sympathy with the Zionist cause. For about 600,000 Jews in Moscow only three synagogues were open and they were denied chapels for prayer and religious instruction.

It was impossible to evaluate the impact of anti-religious activity upon Mohammedanism in Soviet Asia. It was evident, though, that secularism had fostered religious indifference among Moslem intellectuals there and in the Middle East. The broad masses of Islam, however, seemed immune to anti-religious currents. In the Turkey of the 1950's, an Islamic revival actually took place, witnessed by the erection of hundreds of new mosques, by the strengthening of religious teaching in schools, and by a revival of interest in the traditional pilgrimage to Mecca.

After the Second World War, waves of anti-religion swept over the countries of Eastern Europe that passed beneath the Hammer and the Sickle. Using the techniques and apparatus earlier applied in the Soviet Union, Communist regimes combatted the religious heritage vigorously. Spirited clergymen, Protestants in the Soviet Zone of Germany, and Catholics in Poland, Hungary, and Yugoslavia felt the bullying fist of Communist authority; many were imprisoned or placed under strict police surveillance for alleged "conspiracy against the state," and much church property was confiscated.

In Communist Poland, for instance, where

perhaps three-fourths of the population were devoutly loyal to the Christian heritage, the Catholic leadership struggled in vain to establish a durable *modus vivendi* with the Communist ruling clique. Despite repression and persecution, churchgoing remained very popular in Poland, and faith and hope were buoyed up by the watchword of eloquent and fearless Stefan Cardinal Wyszyński, "the spirit of man is an eternal rebel—rebelling against all slavery and falsehood." Though the Vatican recognized that atheistic Communism was the greatest menace to the Church since the Lutheran revolt, if not indeed of all time, it had to move warily lest it expose believers in Eastern Europe to avoidable risks of physical abuse.

Wherever Communism penetrated beyond Europe, a drive against religion followed. The Castro regime in Cuba denounced "Fascist priests" ministering to the poor, and foreign religious workers were expelled from the island. On the heels of the Communist triumph in China (1949), state officials maliciously propagated old prejudices against Christianity and imposed heavy restraints upon missionaries on the charge that they were simply accomplices of predatory Western imperialism. Nine out of ten churches in teeming Shanghai were seized by the government.

THE LARGE PICTURE

This survey suggests the scope and richness of Western strivings since the onset of the First World War. Considering the wealth of creativity, from scientific investigations through the refined, civilizing arts to philosophic and religious thought, it is plain that Western man was not absorbed exclusively in the secularities of war, politics, and economics. Research and speculation on the higher planes were robust, diversified, instructive, though a balanced appraisal of accomplishments must await the perspective of time.

Clearly enough, certain advances in the sphere of science threatened the very continuance of Western civilization. Likewise, the prevalence of Communism aggravated challenges to the intellectual and religious values in the heritage of the West.

Nonetheless, in spite of the bleakness of brute facts, there was ground for a tempered, manly confidence which yet dared to hope. Familiarity with the past should serve not only as an antidote for dark pessimism concerning the present, but also to equip one to face the ordeals of storm and stress in the future.

FOR FURTHER STUDY

Eric Fischer, *The Passing of the European Age* (Cambridge, 1943)

Henry S. Commager, *The American Mind* (New York, 1950) paperback

Frank S. Taylor, *A Short History of Science and Scientific Thought* (New York, 1949)

Martin Mann, *Peacetime Use of Atomic Energy* (New York, 1961)

André Maurois, *The Life of Sir Alexander Fleming* (Eng. trans., New York, 1959)

Fritz Wittels, *Freud and His Time* (new ed., New York, 1958) paperback

George E. K. Smith, *The New Architecture of Europe* (Cleveland, 1961) paperback

Thomas Craven, *Modern Art* (new ed., New York, 1940)

Raymond Escholier, *Matisse* (New York, 1960)

Marion Bauer, *Twentieth Century Music* (new ed., New York, 1947)

Henri Peyre, *The Contemporary French Novel* (New York, 1955)

Willard Thorp, *American Writing in the Twentieth Century* (Cambridge, Mass., 1960)

John Cruickshank, *Albert Camus* (New York, 1959) paperback

Helen Muchnic, *From Gorky to Pasternak* (New York, 1961)

H. Stuart Hughes, *Consciousness and Society* (New York, 1958) paperback

Walter Kaufmann, ed., *Existentialism* (New York, 1956) paperback

Stephen Neill, *Twentieth Century Christianity* (London, 1961)

Aloysius R. Caponigri, ed., *Modern Catholic Thinkers* (New York, 1960)

John S. Curtiss, *The Russian Church and the Soviet State* (Boston, 1953)

Norman Bentwich, *Jews in Our Time* (London, 1960) paperback

CHAPTER XXXII

AFTERMATH OF THE WAR

COUNTING THE COST

THE total defeat of the Axis including Japan vindicated arithmetic, among other things. Superior Allied productive resources and spirited manpower had vanquished the common enemies. Whether that fundamental and instructive lesson had been learned by any other government which entertained aggressive intentions, only the future could tell.

At war's end, Europe and Asia were distraught physically and psychologically as perhaps never before in their long and checkered past. Shot and shell, immense losses of troops and civilians alike, the vast displacement of persons either dragooned into Nazi labor camps or roughly expelled from their ancestral homes, the dislocation of economic mechanisms, the exhaustion of factory equipment and farmlands, battered and wrecked transport facilities, obscure Russian villages and famous German and Japanese cities terribly broken, the diffusion of the Communist heresy, and the concealed but nonetheless very real psychological tragedies—these varied elements combined to create wholesale misery and a mood of dark despair.

In language applicable to Europe in general, the official British history on civilian aspects of the war soberly concluded:

> Perhaps more lasting harm was wrought to the minds and hearts of men, women and children than to their bodies. The disturbances to family life, the separation of mothers and fathers from their children, of husbands from their wives, of pupils from their schools, of people from their recreation, of society from the pursuits of peace—all these indignities of war have left wounds which will take time to heal and infinite patience to understand.[1]

Europeans—from the British factory manager to the peasant on an Ukrainian collective farm—had to adjust their daily lives to a changed environment. Informed estimates, conveying some idea of the human cost of the terrible

[1] Richard M. Titmuss, *Problems of Social Policy* (London, 1950), p. 538.

Wesel, Germany, devastated by large-scale bombing attacks

ordeal, set the military dead or missing at about fifteen million, while the civilian sacrifice in lives stood substantially higher. In particular, Nazi savagery had singled out Jews and Slavs for deliberate extermination so that the death toll of these peoples approached twelve million.

By reason of the war, too, over seventy million men, women, and children were uprooted from their old homes, and later events unloosed fresh streams of refugees in Europe, Asia, and Africa. So huge and so ghastly was the legacy of crimes and horrors that the conscience of all but the most sensitive was blunted. Small wonder that many men, victims of cynicism and disillusionment, concluded that the refined and humane values of the Western heritage were nothing other than a snare and a delusion.

Somewhat paraxodically, human intelligence and industrial technology were responsible for the magnitude of the wartime devastation. Fast and ruinously they had destroyed, and yet, no less certainly, brains, ingenuity and muscle could rapidly repair the worst material ravages of the holocaust—and in fact did so, though more swiftly in Western than in Eastern Europe. Invisible wounds to mind, heart, and spirit, on the other hand, could not so easily be healed.

While the fighting proceeded, leading Allied statesmen and their expert advisers prepared to deal with postwar perplexities and to build a safer, saner and more secure international society. Through normal diplomatic channels and at conferences between the "Big Three" the postwar treatment of enemy lands and peoples and of liberated countries was framed in outline.

PEACEMAKING

In contrast to the procedure following the First World War, no general conference of victor nations was convened after 1945 to arrange peace terms with the vanquished. No meeting of that sort had been contemplated by the Allies during the war, and the open rift that quickly developed between the free nations and the Soviet-dominated bloc—between West and East—rendered a general peace conference out of the question. Instead, after much pulling and tugging, treaties were hammered out in 1947 for Italy and four smaller Axis nations. The Western powers ratified a separate peace with Japan in 1952, which the Soviet Union, years later accepted. A treaty with Austria was signed in 1955, but the victor powers could not agree upon a definitive settlement with Germany.

Each of the peace treaties of 1947 required the former enemy states to pay reparations, severely limit their armed forces and ensure fundamental civil liberties to their citizens. With a single exception, the treaties prescribed transfers of territory. Under the settlement with Italy, Albania and Abyssinia (Ethiopia) were set free and the African colonies were handed over to the Big Four for final disposition. Eventually, the former colony of Libya was established (1952) as an independent monarchy, a verdict that quickened nationalist passions in neighboring colonial dependencies. Somaliland was entrusted to Italian trusteeship until 1960 when it too became free and Eritrea was merged with Abyssinia.

The Italian peace treaty awarded the Dodecanese Islands to Greece and assigned small parcels of strategically valuable land to France. By the treaty Yugoslavia obtained from Italy most of the province of Venezia Giulia, the seaports of Fiume (Rijeka) and Zara (Zadar) and several Adriatic islands. It was not possible, however, to settle the status of the key port of Trieste and its environs until 1954, when Italy was allowed to retain the city, while Yugoslavia annexed most of the surrounding area. Even before that the Western allies had cancelled (1951) restrictions on Italian armaments.

Territorial arrangements with the lesser Axis satellites—Finland, Hungary, Rumania and Bulgaria—may be crisply summarized. Finland formally transferred the northern district of Petsamo to Soviet Russia, giving her a running frontier with Norway. Likewise, Russia took over southern Karelia and was granted a naval station commanding the Gulf of Finland, which was given up in 1955. Hungary restored most of Transylvania to Rumania, which in turn ceded Bessarabia and Bukovina to Russia and a strip (southern Dobrudja) to Bulgaria. Bulgaria escaped territorial amputations.

THE TREATMENT OF GERMANY

Although no peace treaty was signed with Germany, the lands that had been conquered by the Nazi sword were returned to their rightful owners, and much territory that had belonged to Germany before the Hitlerian expansion was cut away. The Baltic province of East Prussia, for instance, was partitioned between the Soviet Union and Poland, which likewise assumed the administration of the section of pre-war Germany lying to the east of the Oder-Neisse rivers and embracing the industrial and agricultural resources of Silesia. The erstwhile Danzig Free State passed under the Polish flag. These territories were intended to compensate Poland for the compulsory cession of her pre-war eastern provinces to the Soviet Union.

German folk who had lived in the areas taken over by Poland and Russia either perished or fled into what remained of Germany, there to be joined by families of German extraction expelled from Czechoslovakia and other countries of Eastern Europe. All told, more than nine million German refugees sought sanctuary in "rump" Germany.

Certain top Nazi personalities imitated Hitler by committing suicide. Others, charged with being war criminals, were rounded up and tried under Allied auspices at Nuremberg. Several were punished by death or given prison sentences of varying length, and a few were acquitted. Less prominent Nazi officials in the upper echelons were tried in courts presided over by German judges, and efforts were undertaken to root Nazi ideas out of the German mind, with mixed results. All instruments of war were taken away and many factories that had been engaged in armament-making were dismantled in whole or part.

In keeping with wartime understandings arrived at by woefully haphazard methods, Germany was carved into four zones of military occupation. The Soviet eastern zone normally raised a surplus of food, contained important industrial establishments, and completely encircled the capital of Berlin, a position that gave the Russians command of the roads, railways, and air routes leading into the city. Berlin itself was divided into four administrative districts, the Soviets holding the eastern district and Britain, the United States and France the western and more populous area. The British zone of Germany included the huge Ruhr industrial complex, while American forces occupied the southern, more scenic section of the country, and France was assigned a district along the Rhine. The Saar Valley, highly prized for its mills and mineral wealth, gravitated into the French economic orbit until it was finally reclaimed by Germany by agreement with France in 1956.

Despite the division of Germany into zones, the Allies proclaimed their intention to preserve the economic unity of the country. Once an "ideological conversion" had been wrought, the Germans would be permitted to take their place "among the free and peaceful peoples of the world," it was asserted.

The Brandenburg Gate, Berlin—where East German and West German part company

Based upon faulty calculations, the German arrangements did not long endure. Not only did the Soviet authorities impose a ban upon economic unity but, step by step, Eastern Germany was converted into a satrapy of the Kremlin—a Soviet satellite. Yet, if, as seems fairly certain, Stalin wished in 1945 to incorporate all of demoralized Germany in the Communist empire, that grandiose dream was frustrated.

By 1949, it had become apparent that the Kremlin would not consent to the reunion of Germany; wherefore, the Western Allies proceeded to merge their zones and approved the establishment of a West German Federal Republic with its capital in the Rhineland university town of Bonn. Again and again thereafter, the Western governments called for the reunification of Germany, divided against the will of the Germans themselves, through free elections under United Nations supervision. But the Soviet Union flatly rejected these overtures. While Soviet Germany recovered slowly under a totalitarian regime, the West German Federal Republic experienced an astonishing renaissance, as is explained farther along.

AUSTRIA

Like Germany, Austria was split into four zones of occupation with Vienna, the capital, similarly divided into sectors by the occupying powers. Unlike Germany, however, the little Austrian republic was permitted a unified government which managed a large share of domestic affairs. The Russians, however, held valuable oil fields, refineries and over two hundred factories, and until 1955 stubbornly refused to sign a treaty restoring full sovereignty to Austria. In that year, in a surprise move, the Kremlin agreed to a settlement. Thereby Austria became master in its own house and foreign troops were withdrawn, though heavy reparations had to be paid to the Soviet Union. Austria adopted a status of neutrality and promised not to permit foreign military bases on its soil or to enter into a military alliance with any power. Political union (*Anschluss*) with Germany was expressly forbidden.

A NEW JAPAN

Japan in defeat fared better in some respects than her European allies. Territorial possessions beyond the home islands, it is true, were taken away. The colony of Korea was declared independent with Russian troops temporarily in control of the northern half and soldiers of the United States garrisoning the south. China regained Manchuria, and the Soviet Union took possession of southern Sakhalin and the Kurile island chain stretching away from the north end of Japan. The future of Formosa (Taiwan) awaited final definition, while clusters of islands close to Nippon and the former Japanese mandated holdings in the Pacific were entrusted to the United States.

The occupation of Japan and the implementation of a program of demilitarization and of reconstruction were essentially American enterprises. General Douglas MacArthur, the Supreme Commander, guided the work of rehabilitation, winning for himself extraordinary authority and esteem. Japanese war-making resources were broken up, war criminals were punished, violently chauvinistic secret societies were disbanded, great financial combines (*Zaibatsu*) were somewhat weakened, and Shinto declined as a patriotic cult.

On the positive side, a hurricane of Western ways and institutions swept into the land of the Mikado—a constitution, for example, providing for parliamentary and responsible government, women's suffrage, habeas corpus, independent trade unions, and fundamental civil liberties. Once the Japanese had tasted real freedom, the American authorities reasoned, they would not lightly allow freedom to be taken away.

Yet deep-rooted Nipponese habits and emotional responses could not be radically and quickly transformed by edict of foreign conquerors, however well intentioned. Only time could reveal whether the democratic creed had taken firm root in the soil of Japan. In the name of social equity and stability, a third of the cultivatable land passed from large proprietors to more than three million peasant families. Industry recovered swiftly and exports expanded at a brisk pace, though trade with China was severely limited.

With the United States taking the lead, a definitive Japanese treaty of peace was quietly fashioned and went into force in 1952. All in all, the treaty terms were magnanimous, a settlement of reconciliation designed to convert a former enemy into an ally in the gathering struggle with aggressive Communism. Potentially, Japan could develop into a powerful bastion in the Orient against Sino-Soviet imperialism, and that is precisely what the political leadership of the free world wished. Until 1956 the Kremlin, which had no part in the treaty-making, declined to acquiesce in the settlements, remained technically at war with Japan.

In the meantime, Japan had entered upon a golden era of economic, social and educational advance. Large amounts of aid came from the United States; trade with America boomed, making the economy heavily dependent upon business conditions in the trans-Pacific Republic. Plants expanded rapidly and, in terms of percentage, levels of industrial production outstripped the Soviet Union. So passionate was the Japanese instinct for a share in the rising prosperity that securities of companies were huckstered in such improbable places as subway stations and amusement parks! Exports forged ahead at a spectacular pace, so that Japan was able to pay reparations to countries which her forces had damaged in the late war and also to aid developing countries in southern Asia.

Reportedly the average length of life jumped by an incredible twelve years in a decade, and population increased by a million annually. Japan demonstrated how a country poor in natural resources and food could make headway in eliminating dire poverty by the magic of machinofacture.

The young adventure in democratic political institutions, on the other hand, was distracted by factionalism and by disciplined, fanatical, leftist elements which organized strikes and wild mob demonstrations. Communism, however, as a political party, attracted precious little support.

THE UNITED NATIONS

As the successor of the ill-starred League of Nations, the Allied powers amidst the furies of war prepared plans for another experiment in international cooperation—the United Nations (U.N.). Victories on the battlefield, it was widely assumed, would be followed by common victories for peace, progress and prosperity. "A world organization to control lawlessness," remarked the British diplomatist, Sir Alexander Cadogan, "is as essential as traffic regulations to control our modern traffic." The finishing touches were put upon the constitution or Charter of the U.N. in the spring of 1945 at a conference in San Francisco—thus implementing afresh an international ideal cherished over the centuries by isolated thinkers and men of good will. Fifty-one governments promptly ratified the Charter and fifty-nine more came in later.

Built upon the experience with the League of Nations, the U.N. embraced six principal branches and over thirty subsidiary agencies or committees. The major elements were a General Assembly, a Security Council, an Economic and Social Council, a Trusteeship Council, a Secretariat, and an International Court of Justice.

The General Assembly may be thought of as the common parliament of all the member nations. Under the Charter, members were committed to promote "international cooperation in the political field [and in] the economic, social, cultural, educational and health fields"; and to aid "in the realization of human rights and fundamental freedoms for all." Normally the Assembly would meet once a year, though a session might be called at any time either by the Security Council or by a majority of the U.N. states. Each country would cast one vote in the Assembly.

The Security Council resembled an international executive committee, functioning continuously. It contained representatives of the "Big Five"—the United States, Britain, the U.S.S.R., France and China—each holding a seat permanently, and six other countries chosen for two-year terms by the Assembly. To the Security Council was assigned responsibility to investigate quarrels between nations or any situation that might lead to international friction and to propose pacific accommodations. In case of a persistent threat to peace, the Council

The Eighteenth Session of the United Nations Assembly, October 4, 1963

might summon U.N. members to apply diplomatic and economic sanctions against the offending country; if necessary, collective military action might be ordered.

Advisory to the Security Council were a Military Staff Committee and a special Atomic Energy Commission authorized in 1946. The Military Staff Committee, made up of the Chiefs of Staff of the "Big Five," would command armed contingents put at the disposal of the Council by member nations. (No forces have ever been assigned to the Council.) Composed of delegates from the eleven states in the Security Council and from Canada, the Atomic Energy Commission was empowered to deal with international questions bearing upon atomic energy.

Responsibility for carrying out the social and economic objectives of the Charter was entrusted to the Economic and Social Council. Included in the declared purposes were improvement of standards of living and health, betterment of conditions of employment around the globe, and international cooperation in educational and cultural affairs. The Assembly would periodically pick eighteen countries to appoint representatives to the Council.

AGENCIES OF THE UNITED NATIONS

Among the specialized agencies, which operated autonomously, was an Educational, Scientific and Cultural Organization (UNESCO), the center of liaison for intellectual cooperation and research in scientific and social areas. The Food and Agricultural Organization

(FAO) had charge of raising levels of nutrition and bettering the lot of rural populations. A legacy from the League of Nations, the International Labor Organization (ILO), sought to improve social conditions of industrial workers of the world. In the realm of finance, an International Bank would provide loans for reconstruction and development projects which were normally unattractive to private foreign capital. An International Refugee Organization (IRO), which assumed the burden of a wartime relief organization referred to as UNRRA, would care for refugees and displaced persons seeking new homes.

The Trusteeship Council supervised the administration of three classes of dependent lands: pre-war mandated areas, certain colonial territories detached from enemy countries after the Second World War, and any other parcels that might voluntarily be turned over to the jurisdiction of the Council. This body operated under the general authority of the Assembly, except that any territory designated as a "strategic area" passed to the control of the Security Council.

Each government holding a trust territory was pledged to promote the welfare of the area, not excluding measures looking to eventual self-government or independence. Annual reports on the trusteeships would be transmitted to Council officials, who were privileged to inspect trust areas if they cared to do so. The Big Five held seats in this Council along with delegates from other countries holding trusteeships; still others might be named by the Assembly.

The Secretary General of the U.N. was the executive director of the permanent Secretariat, which assisted in the diversified activities of the whole organization. Not only would he act as secretary at meetings of the Assembly and of the three most important Councils, but he might bring before the Security Council any issue that he felt constituted a danger to peace. Elected by the Assembly, on recommendation of the Security Council, the first incumbent of this vital and delicate office was Trygve Lie, a colorful, broad-minded and affable son of Norway.

The International Court of Justice would arbitrate international controversies submitted to it and act as counsel to the U.N. on legal matters. It had no power to force governments to accept its jurisdiction. Fifteen judges would be chosen by the Assembly and the Security Council, and cases would be heard at the Hague Peace Palace, the home of the original tribunal for disputes between nations.

THE PROMISE OF THE UNITED NATIONS

Altogether the institutionalism of the U.N. was quite elaborate, the end product of a lengthy process of experience and experiment. Checks and balances were provided, as in the Constitution of the United States, though there was no supreme court to rule on jurisdictional disputes. It was plain that the "Big Five" would determine the performance of the U.N. Their power would be exercised principally in the Security Council. A negative vote, or veto, by the representative of any of the Big Five countries could tie the hands of the Security Council on any important decision. It was assumed, however, that the veto would be used sparingly as a measure of last resort to avoid war between the leading powers.

Amendments to the Charter would come into force only after approval by two-thirds of the Assembly and ratification by a similar proportion of member states, including all of the Big Five. For admission to the U.N., a state required approval by a majority of the Security Council (all permanent members approving or abstaining) and by two-thirds of the Assembly.

The ability of the United Nations to serve as an effective instrument of security and peace would depend in reality upon the policies pursued by the Soviet Union, the United States and Britain. Of itself the U.N. commanded no more authority to preserve peace, no more power, than the leading members chose to give it. Well before the U.N. was installed in 1952 in its resplendent home in New York City, the expectations of the more optimistic partisans of the infant institution had been belied.

Controversies between the U.S.S.R. and the other large powers gravely hampered the work of the Security Council and led to an enhancement of the responsibility of the Assembly. An Assembly resolution of 1950 prescribed that, if and when the Security Council failed to act unanimously in case of a threat to international peace, the Assembly itself could adopt recommendations for collective action, including the application of armed force, to keep the peace.

THE SOVIET COLOSSUS

When the fighting stopped in 1945, European Russia presented a melancholy panorama defying crisp description. War fatalities and physical destruction were greater there than in all the other Allied countries put together. About ten million soldiers had either been killed or maimed and nearly twenty million civilians had perished by starvation, disease, or enemy action. Undernourishment and wartime strains had impaired the health of additional millions, many of whom subsequently died prematurely.

Rival armies, moreover, had chewed up an area comparable to the United States east of the Mississippi River—towns and villages broken, industrial plants ruined, farming equipment gone, transportation facilities wrecked. It was said that twenty-five million Russians had no roofs over their heads. Small wonder that the Kremlin intended to exact vengeance of the German despoilers! Memories of the agonies and horrors of the war and the tremendous decline in the bare necessities of life would not quickly be erased from the mind of the Soviet masses.

For national rehabilitation and for literally phenomenal economic advances and innovations which followed, the Soviet Union obtained reparations in goods and machinery from late enemy countries and made exactions upon satellite states in Eastern Europe. A modest amount of technological and agricultural "know-how," along with some machinery, was imported from the West. Far more important, however, were the resources and energies of Soviet Russia herself, the rapid increase in scientists, engineers, and technicians generally, less inefficiency in production, and heavy capital investment in factories, mines, and transportation. Economic objectives were blueprinted in a series of five-year plans, which, in 1956, were replaced by a seven-year plan.

INDUSTRY AND SOCIETY IN THE U.S.S.R.

Quite probably by 1950 the material damages wrought by the war had been made good. In the 1950's, the Soviet Union with giant strides crowded into second place among the industrial nations of the globe, with steel, heavy engineering products, and chemicals setting the pace and each having relevance for the military capabilities of the country. Overall economic output probably doubled in the decade, and industrial production did somewhat better than that. Improved performance on the job and more and faster machinery raised output per workman. Farm yields moved up about 50 per cent and standards of living advanced from subsistence levels.

Ordinary Russians benefited only modestly from the striking economic growth, for pledges of vastly larger supplies of consumer goods failed of fulfillment and steep turnover (sales) taxes on goods persisted. Allocation of much scientific and technological talent and of a large part of manufacturing resources to armament production, to atomic science, and to probing into outer space postponed the advent of the promised age of plenty. "We have mastered the Sputniks," remarked (1959) a writer in the Communist newspaper *Pravda.* "We have made an atomic icebreaker. We have built the greatest atomic power stations in the world. Let us take the trouble to produce a pillow properly, or pliers for drawing nails."

Beyond that, growth statistics tended to obscure the urgency of producing more goods of the kind and quality desired when they were wanted and at minimum cost. In defiance of orthodox doctrine, a few economists cautiously proposed that production would improve if workmen shared in the earnings of the factory in which they were employed.

Growing at the rate of 1.5 per cent annually, population exceeded 215,000,000 in the 1960's. The labor force would increase at a slow pace in the early 1960's, owing to a sharp decline in births during the war, but it would mount rapidly late in the decade. Women probably made up a trifle more than half of the working population.

It was evident that Soviet industry, starting from relatively low levels, was moving ahead much faster than the more mature economy of the United States. The narrowing margin of American superiority in output caused alarm in some Western quarters. Communist spokesmen gleefully contrasted Soviet dynamism with the comparative sluggishness in the trans-Atlantic Republic. Moreover, Russian accomplishments made a profound impression upon leaders of developing, industrially immature countries in Asia, Africa, and Latin America who were concerned about improving standards of living for their populations. Spectacular Soviet achievements converted some of these men to the Communist creed—or helped to do so.

If living conditions of the urban wageworkers moved only modestly upwards, hesitant steps were taken to lessen differentials in wages. Hours of work dropped to around forty a week or even less on strenuous jobs. "Fringe" benefits in the shape of longer holidays with pay, health and educational services and the like were broadened. Trade unions, a pillar of the Communist apparatus, embracing nearly all wageworkers, participated in the management of welfare, educational and cultural institutions. Unions also represented workmen in transactions with factory management on wages and working conditions, but disputes never exploded in strikes.

Shortage of materials and of skilled artisans and concentration on the building of industrial facilities ruled out significant progress in reducing the traditional housing congestion. Many small flats were constructed, it is true—2,400,000 of them in 1960 alone—but the urban population had tripled since 1930. Targets in the building industries were not reached; demand outran supply. A goal of a room per person was set for 1975. In the meantime, private construction of dwellings, with government subsidies, accounted for about a third of the new housing in city and town and for practically all buildings erected in collective farm communities.

SOVIET AGRICULTURE AND THE "NEW CLASS"

Though farm yields regained pre-war levels by the early 1950's, agriculture remained a perennial perplexity for Soviet policymakers. A variety of schemes was invoked to enlarge output. Collective farms, for example, were merged into larger combinations for greater efficiency and to diminish lingering vestiges of the property instinct among the peasants. Taxes on farm products were lightened, compulsory deliveries of agricultural products were reduced, higher prices were paid, and additional monetary rewards were given to farm managers for additional effort.

Collective farms, moreover, were allowed to purchase and own tractors and other heavy farm equipment, and larger supplies of fertilizers were made available. Out in Soviet Asia, virgin lands were plowed and planted, which, because of the vagaries of nature, meant a risky gamble. Inadequacy of transport and storage facilities and incompetent management, which fell short of production goals, plagued rural Russia throughout the post-war era. Though there were ups and downs from year to year, the raising of grain and corn and cotton showed substantial gains. Strenuous efforts were applied to boost the output of meat and dairy products; yet both remained in the category of luxuries.

It proved easier to achieve dazzling flights into space than to accomplish substantial betterment in the variety and quality of food supplies. Approximately half of the Soviet population worked to produce an unpretentious diet for the swelling metropolises. In the United States, by contrast, a superabundance of soil products was grown by somewhat less than a tenth of the population. Soviet conditions of rural living, while better than before the war, lagged behind the cities.

War-damaged railways and roads were repaired, new lines were laid down, and substantial additions were made to rolling stock. Besides, the web of air services was considerably enlarged and subway systems were completed in Leningrad and in Kiev. Yet transport, like agriculture, never tallied with planners' blueprints.

In response to the growth of machine industry and of broader opportunities for higher education, a larger class of comfortably fixed families emerged in Soviet society. Foreign writers called attention to the *embourgeoisment* of this social category because of higher levels of consumption, an easier and pleasanter life, and the impact of ideas of moderation and tolerance learned from the West. This set was composed of scientists and writers, engineers and plant managers, professional and Communist party folk who were definitely better off than ordinary fellows. Many of them lived in roomy apartments and possessed little wooden summer houses, or *dachas*, in the neighborhood of the great cities, with gardens, privacy and other amenities, once derided as marks of bourgeois decadence.

Whether this social element, some of whose members lacked the revolutionary élan of the older generation of Communists and manifested less devotion to or confidence in the self-appointed rulers in the Kremlin, exerted significant influence upon larger issues of state policy was a matter of debate among foreign specialists on the Soviet Union. From time to time outcroppings of intellectual discontent appeared in university student circles and among the "priviligentsia."

Soviet foreign trade represented only a small part of the national production and was carried on mainly with the satellite countries. Yet commerce grew with the developing countries of Asia and Africa, with an eye to the political potentialities of transactions. "We value trade least for economic reasons," proclaimed Premier Nikita Khrushchev, "and most for political reasons." Trade manipulation could also be a subtle weapon in the competition with the West, serviceable in disrupting vulnerable markets of the free nations.

PARTY AND GOVERNMENT

While the titanic struggle with the Nazis raged and directly afterward, standards for admission to the Communist Party were relaxed and membership raced past eight million, say, one out of every sixteen adults. On paper, the party ruled the Soviet state, and a small Central Committee ruled the Party. Periodically, party congresses of about seventeen hundred delegates, noted for their disciplined enthusiasm, convened to hear and approve the decisions of the chief policymaking body of the party, the Politburo, or its successor the Presidium, and to choose the personnel of the Central Committee.

Toward the end of the 1940's party discipline was tightened up, army marshals and other wartime heroes in the party were deliberately kept out of the political limelight, and restraints were laid upon intellectuals in the name of Stalinist orthodoxy. It appeared that the millions of Russians who had fought in central Europe or who had served in the occupation forces there and had seen higher standards of comfort and civil freedoms provoked no trouble upon returning home.

Under inspiration from the Kremlin, a veritable cult of the tyrannous Stalin blossomed in literature and history, in art and music. He was lauded as infallible and omniscient, the hero of heroes in the grim and ghastly contest with the Nazis. Nearly every Soviet community boasted a monument to Stalin, and his picture decorated schools and apartments, walls of factories, offices, and collective farm buildings. An exuberant author bracketed the aging Georgian dictator with Socrates as the outstanding personalities of human history! And the Eastern Orthodox Church, which gained somewhat in popularity amidst the worries and horrors of the war, was more tightly bound to the Kremlin chariot.

In the sphere of government, Stalin operated as the unchallenged and unchallengeable boss, surrounded by a little band of obsequious puppets. Like any Oriental despot, his will or whim became the law of the land and, indeed, of the captive countries of eastern Europe which had fallen under the sway of Moscow. The Marshal personally supervised the fighting services, the ultimate source of his power, and vigilant secret police ferreted out malcontents,

Premier Chou En-lai, Premier G. M. Malenkov, Marshal C. Voroshilov, L. Kaganovich, Marshal Bulganin and V. M. Molotov following the coffin of J. V. Stalin through Red Square.

driving them into vile labor camps, the cold silence of Siberia or before firing squads.

THE STALINIST TYRANNY ENDS

In 1953, Stalin, 73 years old, died, and with glittering fanfare his body was placed alongside that of Nicholas Lenin in the chaste mausoleum on the edge of Moscow's Red Square. A disillusioned Communist, who knew the late dictator intimately, wrote of him:

> Every crime was possible to Stalin, for there was not one he had not committed. Whatever standards we use to take his measure, in any event—let us hope for all time to come—to him will fall the glory of being the greatest criminal in history. For in him was joined the criminal senselessness of a Caligula with the refinement of a Borgia and the brutality of a Tsar Ivan the Terrible.[2]

The general tenor of this damning appraisal was endorsed presently at the highest echelon of Soviet authority.

The principal henchmen of Stalin arranged a collective High Command and inaugurated a period of change and readjustment in many phases of Soviet affairs. But shortly, intense factionalism flared up among Stalin's heirs, a fierce struggle for supremacy such as had taken place upon the passing of Lenin thirty years before. By a piecemeal process, accompanied by a succession of dramatic "palace revolutions," an ex-shepherd named Nikita Khrushchev, fought his way to first place in the Soviet hierarchy.

Rivals, one by one, were relegated to posts of obscurity or, as in the case of Lavrenti P. Beria, chief of the secret police, shot as traitors. Denounced as criminals and leaders of an "anti-party" clique, Vyacheslav Molotov, veteran Bolshevik, and other hard-nosed Stalinists were swept from the center of the public stage. By 1958 Khrushchev had firmly established his ascendancy in the party leadership, though he did not command the complete and unqualified authority that Stalin had wielded. Signs indicated that certain policies he espoused came under challenge within the top ranks of the party and the armed services.

[2] Milovan Djilas, *Conversations with Stalin* (New York, 1962), p. 187.

THE THIRD RED TSAR

Born in 1894 in a humble peasant hut just north of the Ukraine, Khrushchev had little or no formal education, and eked out a livelihood in his youth as a tender of sheep and a worker in coal mines and steel mills. Joining the Communist Party at the age of 24, he plodded his way up the organizational ladder, working in Moscow and the Ukraine, and in 1938 he gained a seat in the powerful Politburo. For his services in the Second World War, from which he emerged as a lieutenant-general, Khrushchev was showered with coveted decorations. Back in party harness again, he reinforced his reputation for toughness by heartlessly driving Ukrainian peasants to greater productivity, by promoting innovations in farm programs and, subsequently, by toning up party efficiency in crucial Moscow.

Upon the death of Stalin he fastened on to the potent office of first secretary of the Communist Party, which made him the controller over all influential party posts, supreme manager of the party apparatus, and director of day-to-day party affairs. If there is a secret

N. S. Khrushchev, Chairman of the Council of Ministers of the USSR in his office at the Kremlin

in his meteoric progress, it lay in his command of the party officialdom, just as Stalin had commanded before him.

On principle, Communist doctrine denies that personality can affect the stream of history, and yet in practice the Communist system allowed as much scope to imperious leaders as ever Hitler or Mussolini had exercised.

Within five years Khrushchev, the first authentic proletarian to reach the pinnacle of the Kremlin, had become, in addition to the chief party secretary, Chairman of the U.S.S.R. Council of Ministers (Premier). He was also commander-in-chief of the worldwide Communist organization and a theoretician of Communism, who fancied himself the equal of Karl Marx and Nicholas Lenin themselves, and quite as realistic as the first "Red Tsar."

As robust as an ox, an ebullient orator, and endowed with natural capacity for leadership, Khrushchev demonstrated remarkable facility for intrigue and guile and for outwitting colleagues and competitors. Self-made sophisticate that he was, he tended to look upon Communist "eggheads" with bucolic contempt. Short, corpulent with a roundish bald head and untidy features, he was a perfect delight to cartoonists—foreign ones. Now the colorful extrovert, switching easily from jovial good fellowship to childish tantrums, now the impulsive explosive demagogue, now the tough and cunning politician, he seemed to understand the popular Russian longings for more material things and for assured peace.

Around him the autocrat gathered a circle of protégés, headed by his principal subordinates in the party secretariat, Frol R. Koslov, regarded as the heir-apparent, and Mikhail A. Suslov, the runner-up. Government machinery operated smoothly even during extended absences of Khrushchev in search of rejuvenation or on tours of inspection or on journeys abroad, such as a historic coast-to-coast trip across the United States in 1959, which made him more widely known in America than any other Russian in history.

OSCILLATIONS IN STATE POLICY

Both before Khrushchev had effectively consolidated his authority and after, internal controls underwent modest relaxation, and many grim and nasty features of Stalinism were put aside. Curbs were imposed upon the loathsome secret police and the censors; during a time of "thaw" creative artists and scientists breathed and wrote, composed and experimented more freely perhaps than at any time since the Bolshevik *coup d' état*. Education at all levels, and especially in science and technology, was pressed forward at an unexampled pace. Indoctrination in the fundamentals of the Communist creed was intensified in the schoolroom, in the university lecture hall, as well as in youth organizations and in the military services. As one agency to win friends and influence people in Africa, Asia, and South America, a Friendship University was established in Moscow. Students, tourists, and cultural groups from abroad were allowed to enter the Soviet Union in unprecedented numbers, and corresponding Soviet elements made their way into foreign lands.

Holding out visions of living standards equal to those of America, Khrushchev pushed hard on the industrial and agricultural sectors of Soviet life with varying results, as has already been indicated. Authorities now relied more on persuasion than on coercion to enlist fuller cooperation of the citizenry in economic and social affairs. To combat grave crimes, however, the death penalty, which had been in abeyance for a short period after the war, was progressively extended to embezzlers of state property, to prisoners who terrorized fellow inmates and also to saboteurs and traitors.

On the home front, too, Khrushchev cut down Marshal Stalin to something approaching mortal size. The late autocrat was savagely excoriated for multiplied inhumanities and terrible crimes, especially during the Great Purge of the 1930's, the idolatrous cult of personality was repudiated, and it was proclaimed that more than one path could lead to an ideal Communist society. Presently places bearing the name of the dead tyrant were altered, historic Stalingrad, as an example, becoming Volgograd.

Paradoxically, Khrushchev was almost as

deeply implicated as Stalin himself in the cruel sadism of the late 1930's while the Communist regime devoured its own children. When terrorism had reached its zenith in 1938, Khrushchev had publicly lauded "our beloved comrade," Stalin, as "the towering genius of all humanity, the teacher and guide who is leading us victoriously to Communism."

As climax and crown of the iconoclastic treatment of Stalin, his corpse was removed from the Lenin tomb, many victims of his brutality were rehabilitated, and a monument was erected to their memory. The anti-Stalinist campaign damaged the Communist image at home and abroad; Khrushchev tagged a contingent of highly placed, unregenerate Stalinists as "anti-party" and, as has been indicated, degraded many of them. The position of case-hardened Stalinists in the captive countries of Eastern Europe was severely shaken, when not wholly undermined. On the other hand, the Red Chinese High Command not only flatly declined to have any share in "destalinization," but flayed its sponsors as heretical "revisionists." Disillusioned, thoughtful Russians, who had been taught to venerate the dead Marshal as an infallible deity, might well ask—privately, to be sure—whether his successor was not of like stuff. Speculations of this sort might eat into the authoritarian system like a malignant disease.

In the area of foreign affairs, Khrushchev oscillated even more sharply than in domestic policies, as will be seen more fully farther along. It was no secret that he confidently believed that Communism represented the wave of the future and that he expected it to dominate the great globe itself in the fullness of time. It was no secret that he regarded the political leaders of the free world, Americans first and last, as uncompromisingly and menacingly hostile to the Communist Commonwealth. Yet he appreciated—or seems to have appreciated—the self-defeating, suicidal consequences of a war waged with ever more lethal thermonuclear weapons.

Wherefore, he preached a version of "peaceful coexistence," which in his thought merely implied a brief stage of transition. During this period, economic and ideological weapons would assiduously be employed against the West, culminating in the worldwide triumph of the Communist way of life. "We'll bury you," cried Khrushchev to the free nations and then explained that he meant interment under an economic avalanche. He argued that the fruits of victory could be plucked without shooting, that the superior rate of Soviet industrial growth assured the eventual triumph of Communism, and that Communism was winning through in undeveloped countries. Said he, "The working class of each country will be proud to fulfill this historic mission."

To a book, containing a selection of his utterances on international affairs, was given the title *For Victory in Peaceful Competition with Capitalism* (1958). This avowal of moderation, compared to Stalin's headlong expansion, caused consternation among the Stalinist faithful all over the globe.

THE SOVIET EMPIRE

By reason of the Second World War and the eclipse of the Axis countries and of Japan as military powers, the Soviet Union was able to push out her frontiers and to draw the states of Eastern Europe under her domination.

The Soviet empire in Asia was likewise strengthened and enlarged. Outer Mongolia was more tightly bound to Russia than ever before and, as mentioned, southern Sakhalin and the strategically useful Kurile island chain were wrested away from Japan. More than that, the Soviets acquired a powerful, though temporary, position in Chinese Manchuria and aided, abetted, and heartily applauded the triumph of the Communist forces in China. They also garrisoned northern Korea with Russian troops. Across southern Asia, emissaries of the Kremlin fanned the flames of native nationalisms, dramatized the unfairness and iniquities of Western colonialism and invoked the apparatus of subversion to lure newly independent republics into the Communist camp.

Military conquests and cooperation of small parties of native Communists had enabled the Soviet empire to spread deep into central and southern Europe. Communist rule was imposed by physical force. Moreover, parcels of pre-war Finnish, Rumanian, Polish, Czechoslovak, and German territory, and the former Baltic Republics were annexed outright to the U.S.S.R. And the Kremlin converted the countries of Eastern Europe—Poland and Czechoslovakia, Rumania and Hungary, Bulgaria, Albania and Yugoslavia—together with the Soviet zone of Germany—into captive satellite nations. "Will the Slavonic streams all come and lose themselves in the Russian Ocean?" Alexander Pushkin, best loved poet of imperial Russia, had once asked. The question had now been answered affirmatively.

Soviet ambitions, however, to master Turkey and Greece were thwarted. Yet, for practical purposes, the writ of the Kremlin ran from the western extremity of Soviet Germany to the Pacific, from Albania to the Bering Straits. In a very famous speech of 1947, Winston Churchill warned, "From Stettin in the Baltic to Trieste in the Adriatic an iron curtain has descended across the Continent."

THE COMMUNIST BLOC

Within the Communist camp of Eastern Europe dwelt 110,000,000 people, or half as many as in the Soviet Union itself. Having established control, the Kremlin showed no inclination to abandon it, for the satellite countries were valuable assets. Strategically, they constituted a bulwark against the West, strengthening the security of Soviet Russia in the event of a conventional type of war. They possessed economic potentialities, large reservoirs of military manpower, and they had prestige value—their inclusion in the Communist camp fortified the philosophy that Communism was triumphantly marching toward the goal of worldwide dominion. It is permissible to imagine, however, that if free and fair elections were permitted in the satellites, large majorities would vote for national independence and freedom.

Several general stages in the evolution of the captive countries under Communism may be detected. Directly after the war, ministries, containing some non-Communists, were organized. Then, until the death of Stalin, rigid Communist dictatorships, styled Peoples' Democracies, prevailed, along with ruthless exploitation under the direction of devoted sycophants of the Red autocrat in the Kremlin.

Rebelling against dictation from Moscow, Marshal Josip B. Tito in 1948 angrily withdrew Yugoslavia from the bloc, launched the country on his own version of national Communism, and eagerly accepted material and military aid from the West. For a time the Soviets carried on unrelenting political propaganda and economic warfare against Yugoslavia; later, Khrushchev displayed a curious tenderness toward the apostate. Yet Tito professed a "neutralist" posture and stood forth as a spokesman of the unaligned countries of the globe. Counterparts of the Yugoslav Marshal, spoken of as Tito deviationists, popped up in neighboring lands.

Following the departure of Stalin in 1953, authoritarian controls in the satellites were somewhat lightened and the destalinization process in Moscow weakened the Stalinist cliques. These currents, along with rising grievances over living and working conditions and over Soviet domination, nourished widespread restlessness. Even earlier, discontent had exploded (1953) in the Soviet sector of Berlin and in other East German cities; Soviet guns and tanks promptly quelled the rioting. Yet clear evidence demonstrated dissatisfaction over the "worker's paradise" among East Germans, for by 1961 three million had fled over the border to Western Germany. That revealing exodus was effectively throttled in 1961 when an infamous wall was erected between East and West Berlin.

In the meantime, popular disorders in Poland (p. 836) brought about (1956) significant changes in domestic policies. The Poles gained more freedom than any other satellite people. Numbering thirty million spirited patriots, and cherishing deep religious and cultural attachments to the West, the Poles could not be so easily pushed around as their captive neighbors. The Hungarians, for instance, who in the autumn of 1956 (p. 836), animated by a spirit of "give me liberty or give me death," rebelled against Communist authority. Soviet armor

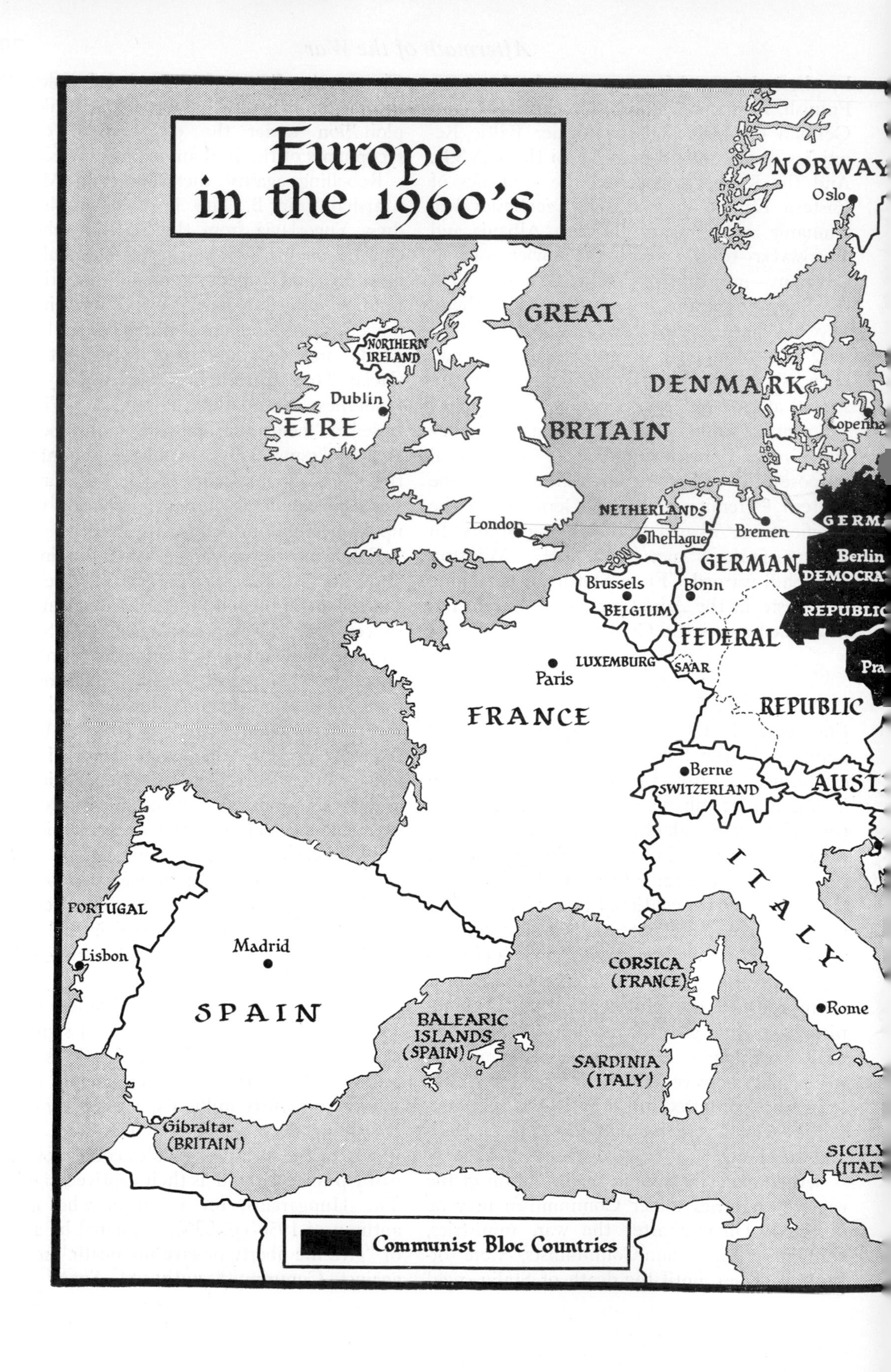

Europe in the 1960's
NORWAY
Oslo
GREAT
NORTHERN IRELAND
DENMARK
Dublin
EIRE
BRITAIN
NETHERLANDS
London
The Hague
Bremen
GERMAN
Berlin
DEMOCRA
Brussels
Bonn
BELGIUM
REPUBLIC
FEDERAL
LUXEMBURG
SAAR
Paris
FRANCE
REPUBLIC
Berne
SWITZERLAND
AUST
ITALY
PORTUGAL
Lisbon
Madrid
SPAIN
CORSICA (FRANCE)
Rome
BALEARIC ISLANDS (SPAIN)
SARDINIA (ITALY)
Gibraltar (BRITAIN)
Communist Bloc Countries

FINLAND
Helsinki
Leningrad
Stockholm
ESTONIA
LATVIA
LITHUANIA
Absorbed as Soviet Republics
Moscow
SOVIET UNION
OLAND
Warsaw
Kiev
ECHOSLOVAKIA
Absorbed as Soviet Republic
MOLDAVIA
Budapest
HUNGARY
RUMANIA
Bucharest
Belgrade
IGOSLAVIA
BULGARIA
Sofia
ALBANIA
Tirana
Ankara
TURKEY
GREECE
Athens
Dodecanese Is. (Greece)

crushed the insurrection in wholesale slaughter. Communism was proved to be weaker than was widely believed abroad.

After the Hungarian revolution, governments in the major satellites acquired a freer hand on internal questions, though they unswervingly followed foreign policies set in Moscow. All were plagued by chronic economic shortages, personality strife in top party ranks, and discords over Communist dogma.

The poorest and smallest of the Communist states, Albania, was expelled (1961) from the bloc when the national leadership denounced the "peaceful coexistence" doctrine proclaimed by Khrushchev and demanded a tough, unyielding line in dealings with the free world. When Albania allied itself with Red China, which also condemned Khrushchev's "revisionism," it was plainly evident that the monolithic type of world Communist dictatorship and of international Communism had been disrupted —at least temporarily.

INSIDE THE SATELLITES

Speaking generally, the Soviet pattern of government prevailed in the captive countries. Small ruling classes drew support from native Communist parties, ramified bureaucracies, terroristic secret police and armies, backed up, if need be, by ever-present Soviet troops. Institutions of learning at all levels increased rapidly, inculcated the Communist faith, and carried on a running atheistic campaign against organized religion.

Five- or Seven-Year Plans set targets in industrial production with the emphasis on heavy producers' goods at the expense of consumers' wares. Urban populations increased markedly and housing congestion was a universal headache. Save for Poland, peasants were coerced into one or another variety of collective farm. All the captive lands lived under a shortage economy, though conditions of life and labor took a turn for the better as time moved along.

Given the pride of historic nations and their cultural heritage, given the widespread discontent with the totalitarian, foreign-imposed, anti-religious regimes, some Western analysts regarded the Soviet satellites as a vulnerable Achilles heel of Communism. It was argued that if an armed struggle between East and West came about, the unhappy satellites possessed the potential to deal telling blows against Russian domination.

CHINA GOES COMMUNIST

Upon the defeat of Japan in 1945, the Nationalist government of Chiang Kai-shek faced a wealth of interrelated problems, some born of the war, others rooted in China's tormented past. And the Chinese Communists resumed their bid to rule this vast, populous, and thoroughly confused country. Disciplined, enthusiastic, spurred on by the creed of Marx and Lenin, the Communists, led by a peasant genius, Mao Tse-tung, profited by the backing of the Kremlin. Had not the oracular Lenin himself declared that "the road to Paris lies through Peking and Calcutta"? The Communists cleverly identified their movement with Chinese nationalism and with mass yearnings for a better and longer life.

In spite of military aid furnished to the Nationalists by the United States, which aroused burning and lasting resentment in Red breasts, Communist armies marched at breakneck speed from success to success in the civil war. In 1949, the shattered remnants of the Nationalist forces withdrew to the offshore island of Formosa (Taiwan), Chiang claiming that his regime was still the legitimate government of China. It was so recognized by the United States, and a representative from Formosa occupied the permanent sea of China on the Security Council of the United Nations. American warcraft served as a shield against possible attack by the Chinese Reds, in keeping with a pledge by Washington to protect Formosa against Communist absorption.

On the mainland, the victorious Communists set up a "People's Republic," signalizing the most stunning triumph for the Marxist faith since the Leninist Revolution in Russia. A treaty of friendship and mutual defense with the Soviet Union testified (1950) to the solidarity of the two big Communist states. From Soviet Russia technical experts, industrial equipment, and military hardware flowed to

Mao Tse-tung (right), Chou En lai (left), and Chu Teh—rulers of Red China

China, though this assistance was not large compared with the immensity of China's needs.

CHINESE HOME AND FOREIGN POLICIES

In harmony with Marxist ideology and more or less in the light of Soviet experience, the Peking Communists drove forward in the task of national reconstruction. Public authority reposed in the hands of a thin phalanx of men at the summit of the Communist hierarchy, quartered in ancient Peking, with Mao wielding supreme power. Though the Party was bedeviled by internal friction and by repeated purges, it contrived to establish national unity, orderliness, and probity in administration, all absent from China for long generations. Programs of planned economic advance were applied, and from these resulted a sharp rise, from a low base, in the output of steel and of heavy industry as a whole.

Much to the unfeigned disapproval of many peasants, farmland was collectivized to a considerable degree; yet, agriculture remained a weak sector of the national economy. An exploding population, which may have surpassed 700,000,000 in the 1960's, intensified traditional pressures upon food resources, and a string of natural calamities worsened the grim privation. A drive for family limitation, quiescent for years, was revived—frank recognition that births could not be allowed to go unchecked. Chinese migration, meantime, had not only swept to the borders of Soviet Asia but in places had crossed over them.

As a facet of a "Great Leap Forward" in 1958–59, Chinese by the millions were herded into swarming communes—"anthills" one critic tagged them—for purposes of mass work and mass living. But muddled mismanagement upset plans and gravely dimmed the more extravagant visions of swift material progress. Red chiefs of state openly confessed that the creation of an "earthly paradise," once reckoned in terms of a few decades, would take much longer. Under a newly announced plan, growth of heavy industry was slowed down, and top priority was assigned to a basic program to mechanize agriculture. It was plain that the cherished dream of overtaking Great Britain, industrially, by the 1970's had been placed in cold storage.

Militant China, meantime, had turned into a major international power factor, disturbing alike to the free world and to the Soviet Union. Red armies overran Tibet, once a tributary of imperial China, and thrust down into districts claimed by India as rightfully hers. They participated, too, in civil wars in Korea (1950) and in Indochina. Emissaries of Red China stealthily carried on subversive activities in southern Asia, where their labors were often assisted by Chinese settlers of long standing. Chinese deeds of violence and fierce and truculent propaganda campaigns against America, "the demon of the imperialists" and "the paper tiger" in Red phraseology, strengthened the resolve of Washington to keep the Peking government out of the United Nations. Opposing that stand, advocates of Peking's admission to the U.N. contended that Chinese military adventurism might be curbed if it were admitted to the world organization and subjected to the thinking and disciplines of that body.

As will later be explained, a fascinating drama unfolded in the 1960's in the relations between Peking and Moscow, the Chinese claiming to be more faithful to Communist teachings than the Kremlin.

FOR FURTHER STUDY

LUCIUS D. CLAY, *Decision in Germany* (New York, 1950)

WALT W. ROSTOW, et. al., *Dynamics of Soviet Society* (New York, 1954) PAPERBACK

HARRY SCHWARTZ, *The Red Phoenix* (New York, 1961) PAPERBACK

KONRAD KELLEN, *Khrushchev* (New York, 1961)

HUGH SETON-WATSON, *The East European Revolution* (London, 1950) PAPERBACK

SEYMOUR FREIDEN, *The Forgotten People* (New York, 1962)

MILOVAN DJILAS, *The New Class* (New York, 1957) PAPERBACK

ROBERT L. WOLFF, *The Balkans in Our Time* (Cambridge, Mass., 1956)

DAVID N. ROWE, *Modern China,* (New York, 1959) PAPERBACK

CHARLES P. FITZGERALD, *Floodtide in China* (London, 1958)

CHAPTER XXXIII

THE FREE WORLD SINCE 1945

RESILIENCE OF THE WEST

WHEN the Second World War came to its agonizing close, the economic and political panorama of Western Europe, home and heart of the Western heritage, had been drastically disrupted. A chorus of Jeremiahs, pessimistic publicists vying with sober students of society, loudly bewailed the collapse of the West. Yet in less than a generation of time, prophets of gloom and doom had been proved alarmists only.

Western Europe demonstrated unexpected qualities of resilience, handsome testimony to its fundamental strength. Within its orbit lived nearly 300,000,000 people, heirs of splendid traditions in manufacturing and technology, in industrial potential and in craftsmanship and farming. They were accustomed, also, to high standards in education and in culture, and in the main, they were devoted to the survival and the future of the Western way of life, its free values, its free institutions, its aspirations, as they had thus far evolved. Historically, the Western European nations had enjoyed better levels of well-being than the southern ones, and that distinction persisted. Mediterranean countries, heavily dependent upon agricultural economies, fared best in areas where machinofacture had matured, conspicuously in the northern reaches of Italy.

Large and continuing infusions of help from the United States, coupled with European brains and brawn, largely accounted for the amazing revival. In exact truth, there was "fire in the ashes," left smouldering after the harrowing ordeal of war. While there were interruptions, pauses for consolidation and adjustment, the universal economic trend was upward, and by the 1960's most segments of Western European society experienced a prosperity without precedent. Full employment contrasted with the chronic joblessness in the aftermath of the First World War, which then bore so vitally upon political restlessness and ultimately nourished authoritarianism. Famous cities, from England's Coventry to Bavarian Munich, battered almost beyond recognition by bomb and shell, rose majestically from rubble and ruins.

Government action broadened out in welfare state programs with more adequate provision for old age and unemployment, health care, subsidized housing, rent control, allowances for children and much else. Affluence blurred traditional social differences due to disparities in income. As social inequality lessened, educational opportunities in keeping with ability increased, though family financial status still had much to do with the amount and quality of schooling a child obtained. These trends invigorated general faith in the future, effectively parried the siren appeal of Communism, which had attained ominous dimensions in France and Italy, and, in time, diminished the popularity of collectivism by parliamentary processes.

So intimately was the material life of Western Europe tied in with the United States that the economic weather across the Atlantic—whether sunshine or cloud—had profound reverberations abroad. And American products and consumer habits penetrated ever more widely—motorcars and refrigerators, prepared and frozen foods, fruit juices and soft drinks, household appliances and purchasing on the installment plan. Manufacturers learned that mass-produced consumers' goods, formerly considered luxuries, could become comforts if not in fact necessities.

Performance in the realm of government and politics pursued a less neat and sharply definable pattern. Very generally, though, political stability—and apathy—marched hand in glove with material prosperity. Within mixed economic systems—partly government-operated, more individual enterprise—wages and take-home pay moved up faster than prices. Conservatively oriented parties upheld ministries that preferred to administer society more than to reform it by fundamental legislative action; technological innovations could be relied upon to bring changes, subtly but inexorably, to pass.

LABOUR REFORMS BRITAIN

After the Second World War and indeed for a quarter century before that, it was clear that Britain had fallen from the lofty eminence it had occupied in the nineteenth century. Yet, with its partners in the far-flung Commonwealth, whose hard core members were Canada, Australia, and New Zealand, the United Kingdom commanded a potentially strong international and commercial position in the world. In proportion as good fortune smiled upon the island kingdom, her influence in global affairs grew, and, in considerable measure, Britain retained her traditional posture as a lighthouse for political mariners on the Continent and in North America. Besides, British scientific brains kept an uninterrupted stream of novel ideas flowing from research laboratories.

Directly after the unconditional surrender of Germany, the British electorate entrusted the management of public affairs to the Labour Party, whose principal support came from the trade unions. For the first time in history, Labour held a clear majority in the House of Commons and a resounding one, which enabled the ministry to disregard an extremist "Keep Left" faction.

For six years, the Labour Party veteran Clement R. Attlee filled the chair of prime minister. A modest, unemotional man, he was short on personal magnetism, yet capable of vigorous self-assertion. He welded most of the disparate elements of Labour into an effective, parliamentary aggregation. Judged by the changes effected in domestic affairs, Attlee ranked among the foremost British peacetime first ministers. In foreign affairs, the bestowal of independence upon the Indian subcontinent, after three centuries of British rule, would alone have given special distinction to the Labour administration. Defying deep-rooted traditions of the party, Attlee secured enactment of peacetime conscription and large-scale building up of armaments.

In line with the formula of "fair shares for all," the Attlee cabinet perpetuated both the wartime control over economic activity and the hard austerity of wartime consumption. Certain sectors of the economy passed under government ownership—the venerable Bank of England, transportation facilities, and the coal and steel industries. Yet by far the larger part of the economic mechanism remained in private possession. On foundations haphazardly laid by earlier generations, a comprehensive network of protective social services was erected. Crowning the measures dictated by the philosophy of a "welfare state" was a National Health Service law of 1948, which assured all citizens of medical and dental care at minimum or no direct cost to themselves. In time, a large majority of the British public, as of the medical profession itself, appeared to be reasonably well satisfied with the operation of this piece of legislation.

Tax laws drastically redistributed incomes in what amounted to a peaceful revolution. To pay for essential imports, the Attlee ministry promoted a highly successful drive to enlarge the volume of exports. Although Britian's position as the special workshop of the world declined, her ancient reputation in agriculture recovered, and the acreage under the plow expanded substantially.

Sir Winston Churchill en route to the Abbey to witness the Queen's coronation, 1953

THE REIGN OF CONSERVATISM

At a national election in 1951, Labour came out in second place and thereafter it continued to be the opposition party. The greatest British public personality of the century, perhaps of any century, Winston Churchill, resumed the prime ministership, though his Conservative majority was too slight to permit much boldness in domestic policies. What were regarded as extravagances in publicly supplied social services were pruned away; yet welfare expenditures kept rising, due especially to assistance provided for the ever larger number of elderly men and women. Piece by piece, government controls over the economy were either eased or abandoned, and state ownership of steel mills and inland transport came to an end.

At the coronation of Queen Elizabeth II (1953) buoyant spirits, encouraged by booming business activity, spoke of the dawning splendor of a second Elizabethan Age. During the ensuing decade, while periods of recession and slackening employment occurred, notably in Scotland and northern Ireland, the United Kingdom approached the status of an affluent society. Living standards of all social elements improved, with the position of the well-to-do advancing relatively more than the rest.

Even so, wage earners with steady employment and income, decent housing and healthy families, possibly a television set and a car, seemed to care less than formerly about inequality of income—or at any rate that interpretation may fairly be made from national election returns. Spokesmen of the Conservative Party contended that major moves toward greater equality would dull the incentive to put forth maximum effort and so would seriously retard economic growth. Their opponents countered that various ways of tax-avoidance—gifts, managerial pension plans, deductions for motorcars and the like—inequitably favored the comfortably fixed.

Full of honors and old in years, Winston Churchill retired as prime minister in 1955 in favor of his chosen disciple, Anthony Eden. After a national election, Eden assumed office with a considerably larger Conservative representation in the House of Commons supporting him. But Eden's tenure was rudely abbreviated by the Suez affair (page 838), which convulsed the party and brought on his resignation. Another devoted follower of Sir Winston, Harold Macmillan took the reins, restored Conservative unity, and in a national election of 1959, with prosperity riding high, gained additional seats in the House of Commons.

Stung by a series of electoral setbacks, the Labour chiefs, aware that their party had declined in zest and vitality, reëxamined the programs they had been espousing. A left wing faction, composed mainly of natural rebels and gadflies, urged that Labour should push for more public ownership and for drastic limitations on nuclear armament, without, however, convincing a majority of party leaders of the wisdom of these proposals.

In the meanwhile, the once powerful Liberal Party, after wandering long years in the wilderness and the victim of the unwillingness of the big parties to approve proportional representation for the House of Commons, scored modest gains in elections. Proudly claiming that theirs was the voice of the middle way, without obligation to any vested interests, Liberal enthusiasts confidently proclaimed that they would soon capture enough parliamentary seats to hold a balance of power, as had twice been true in the 1920's.

CONTROVERSY OVER THE COMMON MARKET

A momentous decision, with far-reaching economic and political, social and cultural implications, confronted the United Kingdom in the 1960's. Should the country join the European Economic Community, or Common Market, that had grown up on the Continent? (p. 859) Among the special problems involved in the decision was the meaning for the overseas members of the Commonwealth, whose exports, due to preferential tariffs, were marketed in the island kingdom.

As it had evolved, the British Commonwealth was an association of peculiar value, yet hardly susceptible to clean definition. It was scarcely more a political and economic league than it was a geographical unit. And, as had been often demonstrated, each partner was bent upon looking after its own particular interests. Grudgingly, the ministries of the overseas Commonwealth nations acknowledged that Britain must decide the Common Market issue herself.

While Liberals came out enthusiastically for the "European Idea" as a whole, the two major parties were divided on entry into the Common Market.

With mingled hope and anxiety, Britons of all party allegiances (or none) appreciated that the island kingdom had reached a great watershed of her history. After fierce intraparty struggles, the leading lights of Labour announced their opposition to membership in the Common Market and demanded that no irrevocable decision should be taken before a national referendum in the form of a general election had been conducted.

Peering into the uncertain future, opponents of affiliation with the Common Market contended that entry would doom the Commonwealth, intensify antagonisms with Soviet Russia, and entail an intolerable surrender of national sovereignty. Certain molders of public opinion predicted that if Britain integrated herself politically with Western Europe, West Germany would emerge as the decisive counter in the combination; they envisaged, too, special difficulties in the area of social welfare legislation and instability in whatever form of supranational government might be devised.

To each hostile argument partisans of entry made full and appropriate answer, emphasizing that the country must not allow itself to indulge in the besetting sin of insularity. Unless Britain teamed up with the Continent, they reasoned, the national economy would suffer a relative, if not indeed an absolute, decline. For these minds, adaptability to changing circumstances largely explained why Britain, historically, had commanded immense power and prestige, instead of being a mere offshore island.

Many an independently minded Briton preferred to form his opinion concerning the Common Market after the precise terms of entry had been worked out. Despite considerable dissent among its followers, the Macmillan ministry seemed intent on joining the Common Market with the maximum possible speed.

THE FRENCH REPUBLIC

"Confident business men putting up new plant, paying out bonuses and sharing profits with employees; blue-collar and white-collar workers driving to factories and offices in cars; farmers using tractor-pulled machinery on their land and electric razors on their faces; TV aerials over city and village roofs; many urbanites moving to suburban greenbelt apartments ...stores, cinemas, restaurants, sports stadiums full of customers"[1]; longer and more expensive vacations.

This graphic sketch of French economic and social well-being in the 1960's contrasts sharply with the fatigued and disillusioned France of 1945. Property destruction and economic dislocation exceeded the losses from the First World War. Memories of the catastrophic defeat in 1940 and of long, dreary years under the Nazi jackboot were green and poignant. Popular affection for the men and women who had courageously resisted the German occupiers matched burning hatred of Frenchmen who had collaborated with the Nazi enemy. The more prominent collaborators were promptly punished.

A constitution of the Fourth Republic, set in operation in 1946, differed little from its pre-war predecessor, though women were now admitted to the franchise. Ministries, dependent on shifting coalitions of deputies in the National Assembly, pursued one another in and out of office as if through revolving doors. The conduct of public business, as between the World Wars, suffered from ministerial instability and indecisiveness. The real novelty in French politics was a powerful Communist Party, backed by a quarter of the electorate, and the willing tool of Moscow. It was unquestionably the most dangerous Soviet political weapon in Western Europe.

[1] *France Actuelle,* Oct. 15, 1962, p. 1.

Providence has richly endowed France, and Frenchmen have a merited reputation for thrift, industriousness, and intelligence. Yet agriculture and industry were relatively backward, and economic worries arising out of budget deficits, taxation inequities, or fluctuations in the currency would not go down. A respected French statesman described (1953) his country as "the sick man of Europe," wanting in civic spirit and needing reforms more urgently than in 1789.

On the favorable side, employment was steady and industrial production picked up rapidly. Directed by Jean Monnet, a wizard in such matters, far-sighted economic programs quickly modernized half a dozen key industries, and free and flexible planning was gradually extended over wider sectors of the economy. Comprehensive systems of social security and of health services carried France far along the road of the welfare state. American help, and business arrangements with neighboring countries, culminating in the Common Market, imparted in time an enormous stimulus to French economic activity.

Slowdowns in the rate of expansion occurred, it is true, but in general business boomed. In the 1950's, the volume of goods and services produced went up four and a half per cent annually on the average, and the prosperity penetrated to all social groups. France ranked second to the United States among leading countries in motorcars per thousand inhabitants, and traffic jams in Paris became routine affairs. During the decade the population of France, which had grown little in the preceding century, shot up by nearly five million. Job opportunities lured perhaps a quarter of the rural families into cities; in the 1960's approximately 8,500,000 people lived in the Paris area, or almost a fifth of the entire French population.

In the sphere of politics, the story of France ran a tumultuous course. The plague of cabinet instability could not be overcome, and quarreling vested interests immobilized the parliamentary machine. Because of unending ministerial crises and ineffective premiers, civil servants largely managed public administration.

Humiliating setbacks in the colony of Indochina robbed the Fourth Republic of moral prestige, and fighting in Algeria (p. 853) brought it tumbling to the ground. When army officers and troop contingents in Algeria threatened a *coup d'état* in 1958, France was faced with the real possibility of civil war. Then, a strong man, General Charles De Gaulle, came out of retirement, took over the direction of public affairs, and the Fourth Republic passed into limbo.

THE ASCENDANCY OF DE GAULLE

On the authority of the National Assembly, De Gaulle had a Constitution of the Fifth Republic prepared. And it was approved by an overwhelming proportion of the electorate. Tailored to suit the stature of De Gaulle, the new Constitution invested very broad authority in the Presidency, an office to which the General was presently elected.

Disdainfully dismissing French politics before his advent to power as "those sterile games of the past," De Gaulle waged a systematic drive to weaken the traditional principle of parliamentary supremacy. Whatever the form, France became in fact essentially a presidential regime.

A De Gaulle proposal for a constitutional revision whereby the president in the future would be chosen by direct, universal suffrage carried (1962) in a national referendum, though only by a slender margin. Directly thereafter, however, in a general election deputies pledged to support the General captured a majority of the seats in the National Assembly. No single political grouping had possessed such

President of France, Charles De Gaulle

strength in France since the introduction of government by discussion and consent in 1871. For woe or weal, the continuance of the De Gaulle system was assured.

A towering figure, physically and politically, De Gaulle could be majestic and he could be exasperating. By profession a soldier, he had commanded French fighting forces abroad during the war, but his bid for political leadership of France was frustrated until 1958. So immense was the authority that he gathered into his hands that extreme opponents pointed ruefully to "Charles the State" and moderate critics tagged his rule "enlightened Bonapartism."

Highly sensitive, something of a prima donna, his patriotism was of an intense character. He wished France to regain her historic place among the great powers of the earth (p. 860). It was indisputably true that France had a distinctive mission in the world, but in arts and letters, in science and scholarship, far more than in the exalted Gaullist vision of the politics of power.

WEST GERMANY RECOVERS

So swift and many-sided was the recovery of Western Germany that the casual traveler might have forgotten that the men and wealth of the area had recently been squandered for the vainglory of the Hitlerian nightmare. Establishment of a sound currency in 1948 paved the way for an astonishing economic upsurge. Trade compacts with neighbors, leading on to participation in the Common Market, encouraged a fantastic boom atmosphere. A "social market economy," fostered by the government, contributed importantly to the unparalleled prosperity. This program combined a high degree of free enterprise with a high degree of state responsibility for social well-being.

Ruined cities and dismantled or damaged factories were methodically rehabilitated, new merchant fleets were built, and exports spurted forward on a prodigious scale. By the 1960's the famous steel House of Krupp was employing 110,000 workmen, and turning out $1,200,000-

Typical of Germany's rapid economic recovery was the rebuilding of her bombed cities and reconstruction of damaged industrial centers. This scene is in Hamburg in 1950.

000 worth of goods annually. Over five million units of the popular *Volkswagen* automobile had been manufactured; the stock of this formerly state-owned company was sold to private investors, many of them individuals with only small savings. Someone was heard to remark that every West German was by way of becoming a capitalist!

As one consequence of the spectacular economic miracle, West Germany experienced a shortage of manpower, and workmen were brought in from Italy and from as far away as Spain and Greece. Rates of industrial growth slacked off in the early 1960's, however, and the country appeared to be traveling across an economic plateau.

Standards of comfort, whose features duplicated those of France, moved progressively upward, the hard-driving business and professional elements coming off best. Yet real income of wageworkers advanced so fast and so far that the historic proletariat of Germany commenced to disintegrate. Relations between management and men were exceptionally tranquil, partly because representatives of workmen participated on managerial boards of many firms, as prescribed by law. Nowhere in Europe were industrial workers more contented than in Germany.

That situation persuaded (1959) the Social Democratic Party, traditional champion of the industrial workers, to revise its doctrines. Collectivist economic principles were downgraded and parliamentary democracy lauded. Basic Marxist tenets, such as class war and government ownership of the means of production, were cast aside, and the Communist version of the Marxist faith was excoriated as a gross betrayal. Social Democracy now preached maximum competition in comparatively private enterprise and careful government planning and regulation of economic activity. Instead of the classical Marxist teaching of internationalism, the party proclaimed that every citizen had an obligation for national defense. Instead of the traditional hostility to churches, the party expressed a wish for "partnership" with organized religion.

From one angle of vision, the reformation in ideology was cleverly designed, in an era of "good times," to attract more voters to the Social Democratic banner. Since German Social Democrats for generations had held a unique place of respect in the Marxist movement, the new emphases exerted no inconsiderable influence upon collectivist thinking everywhere.

To be sure, all was not beer and skittles in Western Germany. Millions of refugees, many with burning memories of harsh expulsion from their ancestral homes, had somehow to be absorbed into national life. Until the raising of the hateful Berlin Wall (1961), tens of thousands escaped annually from the Soviet Zone, seeking jobs and freedom in the golden West. To feed the swelling population, more food than ever before had to be imported. Despite an enormous amount of construction—570,000 dwellings were completed in 1960 alone—housing remained an acute perplexity.

THE ERA OF ADENAUER

Unlike France before the ascendancy of De Gaulle, the government of Western Germany was strong and stable. The Bonn Constitution of 1949 provided for a republican system, democratic in design and intent, assuring fundamental civil liberties to all citizens. Real executive authority was assigned to a ministry, presided over by a chancellor, and responsible to a Bundestag elected by universal adult suffrage.

As first chancellor of the new German adventure in government by discussion and consent, Doctor Konrad Adenauer won international acclaim as the ablest German statesman since Bismarck. A veteran politician, Adenauer had served as mayor of Cologne until the Nazis forced him into retirement. After the collapse of the Third Reich, he assumed leadership of the Christian Democratic Party, recruited mainly from Roman Catholics, but containing a large admixture of middle-class Protestants.

This party scored sweeping successes at federal elections in 1953 and 1957. In the latter year the Christian Democrats won an absolute majority of the seats in the parliament. Minor parties, among them the Communist which had never attracted more than a thin fraction

Chancellor Konrad Adenauer in Washington, D. C., November, 1962

of voters since the war, were practically wiped out. Prosperity and the "European idea" had triumphed, for the Christian Democrats had campaigned on the issue of cooperation of Federal Germany with the West.

The election of 1961, however, cost the Adenauer party its parliamentary majority, and necessitated a ministerial coalition with the Free Democrats, a mixed bag of anticollectivists who advocated more flexibility in diplomatic maneuvers. Retained in the chancellorship, the tough-textured, seemingly indestructible Adenauer largely determined domestic policies and worked with almost a free hand in foreign affairs. His allegiance to the ideal of reunion between West and East (Soviet) Germany appeared to be undiminished.

At the polls in 1961, the principal opposition to Adenauer, the Social Democratic Party, which had consistently elected a third of the Bundestag deputies, picked up a score of seats. General German well-being and a colorless leadership had seriously handicapped the Social Democrats in their appeal to the electorate. As has been outlined earlier, the platform of the party underwent drastic revision in 1959, and the personable and dynamic mayor of West Berlin, Willy Brandt, forged to the front rank of the party, becoming its candidate for the office of federal chancellor. He promised to double living standards in a single generation by economic growth and increased productivity, and he stoutly condemned "all tendencies to bureaucratic arrogance and authoritarianism." An uncompromising foe of Communism, Brandt pledged his party "to change a lot of emphases" in foreign policy without diverging from the broad course charted by Adenauer.

By injecting fresh dynamism and resolution into the opposition party, Brandt contributed signally to a healthier German democracy. Popular government had struck unexpectedly deep roots, but political apathy was nonetheless all too common. The dominance of Adenauer and his domineering personality had retarded the development of an assertive, independently oriented parliamentary body. And sporadic outcroppings of the Nazi mentality and the presence of ex-Nazis in government positions made it evident that the Hitlerian heresies had not entirely disappeared; on occasion, public pressure forced officials, who had been Nazis, to resign from their posts.

Barring an upsetting economic cyclone or widespread dissatisfaction with the Western power bloc in its transactions with the Kremlin, the omens favored a steady evolution of Federal Germany along the road to a more effective democracy.

REPUBLICAN ITALY

The legacy of Fascism lay upon Italy like a black shroud. After carrying the country to unexampled heights in the politics of power and empire, the superficial regime of Mussolini had collapsed ignominiously. Popular disillusionment fed demoralization. Wartime property destruction in the peninsula was extensive, though happily very few of the precious treasures of Italian architecture and art had been destroyed.

By reason of a plebiscite conducted in 1946 the fabric of government was radically altered. A parliamentary republic on democratic principles was set up, and a succession of coalition ministries, supported by conservative and middle-of-the-way deputies, managed public business. The guiding spirit and premier, Alcide de Gasperi, steered the new republic through its first years, and warmly championed ideas of solidarity among the free countries of Europe. He stood close to Vatican circles, which disquieted many an Italian, resentful of growing Church influence in affairs of state.

Ministerial stability ended abruptly in 1953, when the Christian Democratic Party of De Gasperi lost seats in a national election. Thereafter cabinet crises became annual events. Consistently, the Christian Democrats controlled a plurality of the lawmakers, but the party was sadly divided into one faction averse to anything more than modest social and economic changes and a second group which insistently clamored for far-reaching reforms. Too commonly, the sense of social responsibility in affluent Italian families was feeble and frail; evasion of taxes was a flagrant evil.

Communism thrived in an atmosphere of widespread social wretchedness. Capably led and elaborately organized, the Communist Party appealed with the slogan, "What have you to lose?" or, alternatively, "Communism means peace." This gospel carried conviction to millions of Italians who never knew the comfort of a bedsheet nor the hygiene of a toothbrush! A large volume of unemployment, or underemployment in rural areas, nourished the cause of Communism.

Having captured the bulk of the trade unions, mischief-making Communist chiefs ordered upsetting strikes. With its allies, the left-wing Socialists, the Communist Party consistently attracted better than a third of the voters—many of whom, to be sure, desired nothing more revolutionary than tolerable living conditions. Despite unheard of prosperity in northern Italy and secessions from Communism because of Kremlin revelations of Stalinist barbarities, and the heartless suppression of the Hungarian insurrection (1956), the party managed to do better than hold its own in national and local elections. Yet the danger that Italy might be engulfed in revolution and chaos, which seemed acute in the immediate aftermath of the war, lessened with the passage of time.

Italy was the last populous country of the West to become an important industrial power. Native skills and muscle combined with economic assistance from the United States rapidly repaired war destruction and enlarged productive capacities. Manufacturing, which moved ahead slowly in the early 1950's, leaped forward after the establishment of the Common Market. By 1960, the rate of growth in industrial output probably exceeded that of any other Western country.

Hundreds of thousands of workmen were

employed in a vast state-owned economic empire inherited largely from the Fascist regime and managed, in general, imaginatively and profitably. Dynamism was injected into many government enterprises by Enrico Mattei, an extraordinary business manager with a knack for intelligent planning and for exploiting widespread anti-capitalist sentiments. Prodded by moderate collectivists, the government took over (1962) the huge Italian electricity industry.

Steel and engineering, textile and chemical industries registered amazing advances in output. Year by year, newly discovered national resources of natural gas and oil imported from Russia and the Middle East replaced less efficient coal as basic fuels. Whereas in 1950 only one Italian family in seventy owned a car, ten years later the ratio had risen to one in twenty.

Yet this *miracolo economico* was mainly confined to the efficient north, while the traditionally neglected and stagnant south (*mezzogiorno*) experienced only modest betterment. True enough, the building of units of state-owned industries and public works started to transform the economy of what once had been the kingdom of the Two Sicilies. Nevertheless, this region continued to be predominantly agricultural, handicapped by a high percentage of illiteracy, a meagre diet, and crowded living in substandard dwellings.

Under an act of 1950 many peasant households obtained land expropriated from large estates; but farms were small, underemployment was chronic, and many young soil workers drifted off to northern cities or moved away to Germany to escape desperate poverty. Until machine industry was more fully developed, southern Italy would remain a depressed area, a prey to social and political restlessness. Over the peninsula as a whole, the agrarian sector of the national economy markedly declined in importance.

THE SMALLER COUNTRIES

Upon the withdrawal of Nazi armies of occupation, the small nations of northwestern Europe restored their parliamentary monarchies. Ravages of the war era were quickly repaired. Belgium, the Netherlands, and Luxembourg, called collectively the Benelux Union, adopted common tariff laws (1948), then joined the Common Market and reaped rich benefits therefrom, though growth rates were less dazzling than in the larger member states. The Benelux countries also entered NATO (p. 828), and so did Denmark and Norway.

Sweden, however, which had preserved a precarious neutrality during the war, preferred to gamble on neutrality thereafter. On many counts, a trailblazer in the "welfare state" idea, Sweden almost managed to wipe out poverty and enjoyed perhaps the most comfortable living pattern on earth. Finland, like Sweden, walked the tightrope of neutrality, aware that independence required avoidance of offense to the Soviet colossus, with which it had eight hundred miles of common frontier and important economic links.

First the Netherlands, Belgium later, lost their overseas dependencies, which entailed heavy dislocations in national economies. Deep-rooted and mutual hostility between the Fleming element in Belgium and the smaller Walloon population occasionally burst into flame, with disturbing consequences for industry and trade.

Republican Portugal was welcomed into the Western Alliance and managed to hold onto her ancient African possessions. An authoritarian government, presided over by a former university professor of economics, Oliveira Salazar, narrowly restricted civil liberties, and depended upon the army and the security police for survival. Half of the Portuguese lived by subsistence farming, and the lowly lot of the masses improved very little. Apparently the Communists formed the strongest opposition to the dictatorship, but even that amounted to little.

On the diplomatic front, Portugal maintained close ties with the Spain of General Francisco Franco, which, though denied admission to NATO, was drawn close to it by reason of a "dollars for bases deal" with the United States (p. 829).

Whole-souled democrats reproached Washington for the help rendered the Franco regime, for it was a crude dictatorship upheld by army and police. In spite of recurrent strikes and a restive mood in Barcelona, chief city of proud, sensitive Catalonia, the *Caudillo* kept a firm grip on the political tiller. Memories of the horrors of the civil war in the 1930's, though dimmed by time, effectively restrained dissident forces from frontally challenging Franco. It was widely supposed that upon his death the Bourbon monarchy, which had been swept aside in 1931, would be reinstated, without or with normal parliamentary institutions.

THE BOOMING UNITED STATES

The colossal requirements of the armed services during the war, the assistance furnished to allies and to friendly countries after hostilities ceased, the satisfaction of pent-up wants of consumers—these demands and lesser ones immensely accelerated industry in the United States and led on to new levels of material comfort. Not only was the pre-war ogre of unemployment mastered, but millions of men and women released from the fighting services were readily absorbed into the labor force, and a large share of the manufacturing plant switched over to peacetime production without provoking a serious decline in business such as had followed previous wars.

In spite of short recessions at about four-year intervals attended by no little joblessness, output of factory and farm, employment, wages and earnings climbed steadily on statisticians' charts. Huge investments were made in capital equipment: new plant and machinery and research centers. Builders used ever-larger quantities of steel in construction; manufacturers continuously sought, and found, new uses for their products. One ingenious firm, on the hunt for novelties, brought out a stainless steel gown!

Productivity of workers advanced to record levels with the progress of automation and increased efficiency in manufacturing. These trends had another side, for they cost many men and women their jobs and retraining of displaced workmen grew into a grave national problem. Broadening social security legislation, reinforced for many wage-earners by welfare programs of trade unions and of business firms, strengthened safeguards against ordinary hazards of life. More and more women entered employment until they comprised about a third of the total work force.

Average family incomes improved. From 1947 to 1961 the overall increase, before taxes were subtracted, amounted to around seventy per cent in terms of current dollars, or of thirty per cent making allowances for the reduced purchasing power of dollars. Whereas in 1947 family personal incomes stood at about $184 billion, they had soared to $397 billion in 1961. Households with incomes in excess of $15,000 multiplied nearly fivefold, putting roughly one family out of sixteen in that category. These arresting statistics did not mean, however, that poverty had been conquered; nearly seven million households, about twelve per cent of all, lived on incomes of less than $1,000 a year.

Too much of the income of affluent families, certain analysts lamented, was spent for private purposes and not enough for general well-being in the form of public health and educational services, housing, and so forth. On an overall estimate, trade union leadership pressed management less for higher wages than for more satisfactory pension benefits, more paid vacations, and more medical care.

The rate of industrial growth lagged behind the Soviet Union and the more mature nations of Western Europe and Japan. Intensifying competition of foreign firms, in motorcars and steel mill products, for instance, offered special challenges to American managers. "We can and we must demonstrate through sustained economic growth," warned (1960) Undersecretary of State Douglas Dillon, "that freedom works—that it, better than Communism, can mobilize human energies and bring about equitable sharing of the fruits of labor. We can and must bury the Soviet myth that our system is decadent, while Communism is the 'wave of the future.' "

Agriculture in the United States failed to write so fabulous a record as manufacturing. Yet more use of machinery, better fertilizer and seeds, and more effective insecticides impressively raised output per acre. Bulging surpluses of certain farm commodities were taken off the market by the Federal government under price support or subsidy programs; but alas, no formula proved effective for reducing agricultural production to the level of national and export requirements.

In the meanwhile, the percentage of the population engaged in farming dwindled to less than a tenth of the whole. Because of the declining rural population and the phenomenal pace of urbanization, laws were enacted, sometimes on order of the Supreme Court, to redistribute seats in state legislative bodies. These alterations promised to have far-reaching effects upon the political future of America.

ECONOMIC AND SOCIAL TRENDS

Government expenditures at all levels, Federal, state and local, increased swiftly. From the beginning of Lend Lease in 1941 through 1962, the material and military aid pouring from the bountiful American cornucopia to its allies and friends abroad approximated $145 billion. Stupendous outlays for national defense and for the security of the free world, piled on top of ordinary government expenses and interest on the national debt, outran the revenues collected. The Federal debt moved beyond the unimaginable figure of $315 billion and promised to soar even higher.

At the same time, population in the United States expanded at a rapid rate. Better nutrition, better housing, better working environment, better sanitation and medical care, more time for recreation spelled better physical well-being. While families tended to grow larger, life expectancy lengthened, significantly enlarging the number of elderly folk, so that in 1964 the population approached 190,000,000. That traditional hallmark of American society, social mobility, persisted. Metropolitan areas with their swirling freeways and coiling cloverleafs expanded in breath-taking style, heightening demands for homes, cars, schools, public utilities, and the like. Gigantic slum clearance and exciting urban renewal projects distinguished the post-Hiroshima era.

Into the cities of the northern states flowed a rising tide of Negroes from the South, where they were joined by an influx of tens of thousands from the Puerto Rico dependency or from Mexico. The general status of the colored population, a tenth of the national total, improved notably—an evolution little understood or appreciated in foreign countries, especially in the Communist lands. Participation of colored athletes in amateur and professional sports contributed subtly to easing prejudice and discrimination.

Becoming an important political factor in teeming Northern cities, Negroes applied their strength to gaining civil rights, pointing toward racial equality. New York State pioneered (1945) in a Fair Employment Practices Act extending from jobs through the use of restaurants to housing. Successful "sit-in" campaigns in the South were organized by students to open restaurants and other public places to Negroes. The moderating influence of time, together with court decisions, enabled an enlarging proportion of southern Negroes to vote and even to take part in the crucial primary elections of the Democratic Party.

To all intents and purposes, racial integration became a reality in the armed forces and in the District of Columbia. Colored government workers increased remarkably, many filling responsible supervisory and technical positions. Token admissions to qualified Negroes were granted by Southern universities, and in 1954 the Supreme Court wrote future history when it declared that laws on racial segregation in public schools were unconstitutional. In the name of equality in educational opportunities, the Federal government intervened decisively on behalf of Negroes in Arkansas (1957) and in Mississippi (1962).

Despite the progress that had been registered, spokesmen of the colored population called for more governmental vigor to end discrimination, more representation in the policy-making echelon of political parties, and the clearing away of racial barriers in certain trade unions, which allowed colored members to take only lower paid jobs and kept them from influential positions in the unions themselves.

President Kennedy and former President Dwight Eisenhower discuss the Cuban crisis of 1961

POLITICS AND FOREIGN POLICY

Economic and social trends in the United States followed their courses with comparative indifference to the party complexion of the Federal leadership. The Democratic Party, after being entrusted for twenty years with the executive branch of the government, gave way (1953) to the Republicans with popular General Dwight D. Eisenhower as standard bearer. During all but two of his eight years in the White House, Eisenhower, lacking Republican majorities in House and Senate, relied upon cooperation by representatives of both parties in securing the passage of legislation. By a large majority in the Electoral College, though with only a razor-thin margin in popular votes, the young Democratic Senator from Massachusetts, John F. Kennedy, captured the Presidency in 1960, the first Roman Catholic to hold this office.

Throughout the post-war era, bipartisanship generally prevailed in the conduct of American world policies, especially when decisions of transcendent significance were under consideration. For all the power and wealth of the United States, it was keenly understood that the coming of the atomic bomb had opened an era of insecurity and anxiety. As the principal shield of the free nations, the United States confronted the might and the menace of the Soviet bloc.

Beliefs confidently entertained while the Second World War was being fought and won had turned out to be illusions: the assumption that a safe and sane international order would quickly be achieved; the assumption that Soviet Russia would cooperate to that end; the assumption that the United States for a long time to come would hold a monopoly on nuclear weapons capable of massive annihilation; the assumption that China, whose protection had involved the United States in the Second World War, would manifest a friendly, cordial disposition; and, not least, the assumption that the United Nations would succeed, in some mystical fashion, in resolving disputes between the nations and in eliminating the scourge of war.

Not only were these visions and aspirations rudely frustrated, but the grim challenge of international Communism, oscillating in intensity, dictated revolutionary departures in the basic principles of American foreign policy. The particulars of this epochal change will be considered in the next chapter.

CANADA

Closely linked to the United States by bonds of economy, culture and mutual defense, as well as of geography, Canada shared richly in the post-Hiroshima economic expansion. Newly found mineral treasures, uranium and iron ore, and oil in the western provinces, together with higher output from farm and factory, enhanced the stature of the Dominion in global affairs. Helped by fast-rising capital investments from the United States, hundreds of new concerns, large and medium-sized, appeared on Canadian soil. Roughly two-thirds of the foreign commerce of Canada was carried on with the United States.

All occupational groups, except the farmers, benefited from unprecedented good times. The opening in 1959 of the 2,300 mile St. Lawrence Seaway nourished hopes of a great growth in ocean transport and substantially enlarged hydroelectric power resources. By then, however, Canadian economic expansion had tapered off and the Dominion had passed into a period of readjustment featured by a large volume of unemployment. The possibility that Britain would tie up with the Common Market raised fresh perplexities for Canada.

The Dominion joined NATO, dispatching units of her armed forces to Europe, and it worked out unified programs of continental air defense with the United States. A vocal segment of Canadian political opinion expressed alarm over the extent of the military and economic dependence upon the southern neighbor. With the union of Newfoundland (1949), the Dominion household was rounded out, and population exceeded eighteen million, thanks in no small part to recent immigration. Controversies over tax questions and the provision of schooling and health facilities provoked storms in the relations between the Federal government and the provinces, Quebec above all.

LATIN AMERICA

Taking into account traditional differences of culture and language, institutions and history, it was hardly to be expected that the sort of Siamese-twin relationship between the United States and Canada would be precisely duplicated in the Latin Republics. Inter-American "good neighborliness" had grown during the Second World War, which had driven home the stern lesson that hemispheric defense was a mutual responsibility. So well did delegates of the United States and of South America work together in the U.N. that the Kremlin derided the Latin states as mere marionettes of Washington.

Proposals for fuller solidarity in hemispheric defense led to a Treaty of Reciprocal Assistance drawn up at Rio de Janeiro (1947), often called the Rio pact. It prescribed that an armed attack upon any American country would mean war with all the inter-American powers. In the wake of that covenant, came the foundation (1948) of the Organization of American States (OAS), a regional coalition within the framework of the United Nations. If and when political eruptions broke loose, the Organization would deliberate, and presumably act. At an Inter-American Conference of 1954, it was declared that "the domination or control of the political institutions of any American state by the international Communist movement... would call for consultation and appropriate action...." That declaration, from which only little Guatemala dissented, underscored a changing orientation in Washington.

As much as ever before, Washington was determined to prevent any foreign power from obtaining political control in any section of the New World. Yet this principle would be implemented, preferably not by the United States proceeding alone, but in conjunction with the sister Latin republics. Instead of dictation by the United States, a spirit of mutual comradeship, the treaties seemed to say, would govern hemispheric affairs. When Cuba under the direction of Fidel Castro (p. 853) turned into a Communist spearhead and Soviet arsenal, endangering the safety of the New World, the governments of South America reluctantly, but nonetheless definitely and unanimously, backed the policy of Washington. Denunciation by Castro of landowners, capitalists, and "dollar imperialism" made an impact upon many Latin youths and the poorer segments of society—an impact not susceptible of exact evaluation.

Not only in Cuba but across Latin America as a whole, Communist movements were organized on the familiar pattern—an executive committee, cells of believers, and associated "front organizations" of sympathetic students and others. Supported by Washington, the government of Guatemala thwarted (1954) an attempt by Communists to stage a *coup d' état*. The appeal of Communism in the Latin countries stemmed principally, beyond any doubt, from unhealthy economic and social conditions and illiteracy. While child-rich peasants existed on an unprogressive agriculture, a wealthy few and military élites took their ease and manipulated the machinery of government. Besides, old-fashioned distrust of the United States persisted in some hearts and now and again flared into violence.

Throughout the 1950's, the United States concentrated on aiding free Europe and Japan to the relative neglect of the Latin countries. Private American capital, however, was invested heavily in the states south of the border, and brisk commercial relations netted gains for all concerned. Once free Europe was back on its feet, it was high time for Washington to see what could be done to help South America to help itself.

In 1961 President John F. Kennedy unveiled a statesmanlike Alliance for Progress, designed to check revolutionary discontent in the Latin lands and to diminish instabilities and confusion in governments. In return for massive economic assistance and development loans, extending over ten years, the Latin governments promised to carry out a peaceful revolution by breaking up large landed properties, redistribution of family incomes, and provision of schools and health care.

Pessimistic critics insisted that the benefits from the Alliance program would be counteracted, if not actually cancelled, by the exploding South American population. In the twentieth century, population had doubled, going beyond two hundred million in the 1960's. And, if the rate of increase persisted, it was estimated that the population would spurt to almost six hundred million by the year 2000.

Nevertheless, the United States began to implement its part of the Alliance bargain, though evidence was scanty that the Latin beneficiaries, apart from Colombia and Venezuela, had taken significant action to reach the covenanted social goals. Not only did well-to-do, politically influential families show no inclination to share their wealth, they adopted a negative attitude toward social reform. The absence of workable governments in three of the biggest countries—Brazil, Argentina, and Peru—lamed the Alliance for Progress in its infancy. However, the Kennedy Administration continued pressure to make the programs effective, and in 1963 it endorsed the formation of a "Committee for Inter-American Development" with executive powers to allocate aid in proportion to the individual Latin country's efforts at self-help.

FOR FURTHER STUDY

THEODORE H. WHITE, *Fire in the Ashes* (New York, 1953)

CRANE BRINTON, *The Temper of Western Europe* (Cambridge, Mass., 1953)

CLEMENT R. ATTLEE, *As it Happened* (London, 1954)

DON TAYLOR, *The Years of Challenge* (New York, 1960)

EDGAR S. FURNISS, JR., *France* (New York, 1960) PAPERBACK

HENRY C. WALLICH, *Mainsprings of the German Revival* (New Haven, 1955)

ARNOLD J. HEIDENHEIMER, *Adenauer and the CDU* (Hague, 1960)

MURIEL GRINDROD, *The Rebuilding of Italy* (New York, 1955)

RICHARD HISCOCKS, *The Rebirth of Austria* (New York, 1953)

ERIC F. GOLDMAN, *The Crucial Decade and After* (New York, 1960) PAPERBACK

JOHN K. GALBRAITH, *The Affluent Society* (Boston, 1958)

LEWIS HANKE, *South America* (New York, 1959) PAPERBACK

Among the better sources of information on current history are:

Annual Register (London)

The Economist (London weekly)

Far Eastern Economic Review (Hong Kong weekly)

Current History (Philadelphia monthly)

Survey of International Affairs (London annual)

The United States in World Affairs (New York annual)

Foreign Affairs (New York quarterly)

The Year Book of World Affairs (London)

CHAPTER XXXIV

A GENERATION OF PERPETUAL CRISIS

WESTERN COLONIALISM FADES AWAY

REVOLUTIONARY transformations in Asia and Africa, holding two-thirds of the human family, formed a striking feature of history after 1945. The empires of European powers, parts of them centuries old, rapidly became remembrances of things past, except in the case of Portugal, which kept a tenuous hold on its African possessions.

About forty new states took their places on the map. They differed in their historical links with Europe and in their political and economic circumstances, though some things they shared in common. Uniformly, the winning of independence was engineered by bands of native intellectuals, whose outlook was largely shaped by European ideas and ways of living. While internationalism was gathering momentum in Europe, a primitive variety of nationalism, stressing hatred of alien rule and insistence upon equality among the countries of the globe, welled up in the colored continents. Many a revolutionary leader nursed deep mistrust, not to say fear, of the West carried over from the colonial era.

All the emancipated countries were economically backward, short on industry and transport, and needing assistance from outside to build up their economies and administrations. Varied bonds with the West persisted—languages among the educated, schools and colleges, traditions of government, and commercial relationships.

Once independence had been gained, the creation of stable governments required competence in statecraft and in administration on the part of the native leaders. In many countries dictatorships of intellectuals and of military élites took command, and, since frontiers were often mere accidents of history, and ill-defined, national leaderships were confronted with acute difficulties. Even more vital were postures in international affairs. Without much trouble new Asian and African nations obtained admission to the United

Nations, which afforded them a potentially valuable place in world affairs. A few of them aligned with the free countries of the West, while others passed into the Communist orbit, and a third and larger set chose a path of neutrality, aloof alike from the West and the East power blocs.

Not only did the Soviet Union retain colonial possessions in Asia inherited from the empire of the tsars, but it added to them. In a real sense, Russian dominance over the countries of Eastern Europe constituted a fresh version of old-fashioned imperialism. The Communist system penetrated with varying depth into Afro-Asian nations. For many a native intellectual the Marxian way of life seemed perfectly valid and the swift industrial advance of Soviet Russia worthy of imitation, though others found the Marxist pattern repulsive and the sorry Soviet record in agriculture something to avoid. Populous mainland China, as has previously been explained, became a Communist state, furnished military aid to Communists in neighboring lands, and exerted an incalculable impact upon intellectuals in former European colonies. The Peking regime pursued a militantly expansionist course of its own, occupying Tibet and thrusting into territory claimed by India.

Vigorously the Kremlin denounced Western colonial rule, which made a favorable impression upon many leaders of the emerging nations. They possessed only limited knowledge of realities of life and labor in the U.S.S.R. and seemed to have little dread of Communist subversion. While rejoicing over the disintegration of the white empires, Moscow sought to extend its way of life among unstable and plastic new governments.

In such ways as were open, the free world responded to this facet of the Soviet challenge. It sought to kindle in the developing countries a resolute determination to preserve their independence. Western help was extended to combat poverty, disease, and illiteracy. More than once, rivalries between East and West in former colonies threatened to get out of hand and precipitate an international conflict.

THE END OF BRITISH TUTELAGE IN INDIA

On August 15, 1947 the flag of the British Raj came down all over the Indian subcontinent, the climax of prolonged agitation for independence. The termination of British tutelage was accomplished by mutual agreement and attended by reciprocal expressions of good will. Two sovereign states, Pakistan and the Indian Union, were carved out, and both retained membership in the British Commonwealth. Partition of the subcontinent had been decided upon in order to keep peace between Hindu and Moslem, but the record in fact worked out somewhat differently.

Made up of two sections, separated by over seven hundred miles of Indian territory, and inhabited for the most part by Moslems, Pakistan became the largest of Islamic states. The Indian Union, peopled mainly by Hindus, covered the rest of the former British dependency, with the principality of Kashmir, essentially a Moslem region, an arena of rivalry and of sporadic rioting and bloodshed between India and Pakistan. At the time of partition, a nagging feud injurious to the security and the political and economic health of both countries started, and it persisted. Shameless massacres, never forgotten, attended the emigration of millions of Moslems from India to Pakistan and of Hindus to India. Fierce passions and suspicions cooled down momentarily in 1948 when a Hindu firebrand murdered Mahatma Gandhi, revered evangelist of Indian independence.

Heirs of British parliamentary traditions, both nations adopted Western patterns of government. An intimate of Gandhi and a lifelong apostle of "India for the Indians," Pandit Jawaharlal Nehru dominated the Indian state and acquired unique distinction on the world stage. As a student at Harrow and at famous Trinity College, Cambridge, he had learned English ways of life; yet, for all his admiration of the English, he bitterly resented living under an alien yoke.

As prime minister, Nehru nimbly walked the tightrope of "neutralism" in the secular

Lord Mountbatten announces British withdrawal from India

struggle between the free nations and Soviet totalitarianism; he won recognition as the foremost spokesman of the nations of the world unaligned with either West or East. Pockets of Communism in India caused him little concern. He welcomed economic assistance and military supplies from the Soviet Union and from the United States with equal cordiality; in 1962 when Red Chinese armies drove onto Indian soil, his piteous appeal to America and Great Britain for rapid shipment of badly needed armaments was immediately answered.

Borrowing the Soviet principle of state planning, India was launched upon a gigantic program of industrial and agrarian improvement, pointed in the direction of a collectivist system of society. To implement the plans, India was dependent upon help in material form from outside and in training managerial and technical men. Assistance in large amounts flowed from America principally for social welfare ends, while the Soviet Union aided on a much smaller scale with a steel mill, an oil refinery, and the like.

Output of Indian factories and farms touched record highs, though serious doubts arose whether improvement was keeping pace with the exploding population. According to the national census of 1961, life expectancy in India had risen impressively in the preceding decade, and population had spurted ahead by almost twenty-two per cent, reaching 438,000,000. That piece of history disclosed that government promotion of family limitation had not achieved its objective. How could India remain prosperous and free while becoming ever more populous?

Like India, Pakistan embarked upon ambitious projects for economic progress with foreign aid. Its population moved upward even faster than that of India. Apprehensive of Soviet expansionism, the government of Pakistan identified itself with the Western alliance network.

SOUTHEAST ASIA

An array of national groupings, almost all under Western rule, existed in the southeastern reaches of Asia. Everywhere nationalism captured spirited bands of intellectuals, who led successful revolts against foreign overlordship. As sources of rubber, tin, oil and surplus rice, these lands possessed peculiar international importance, and all yearned to develop machinofacture and to raise farm production.

On an average, Japanese rice planters produced four times as much per acre as their counterparts in the southeastern Asiatic nations. Most of them wobbled uncertainly between the free ways of the West and Soviet totalitarianism. Communist agents and small, fanatical Communist parties, imbued with the collectivist conception of the good life, stirred up endless trouble; the West fought back with economic aid and educational activity.

Faithful to promise, the United States granted independence to the Philippines (1946), though retaining military rights in the archipelago. It was often charged by the Kremlin that the United States was tarred with the

Prime Minister Jawaharlal Nehru addressing the Indian army

colonial brush because of its alliance with European countries that once held overseas possessions. Answering that allegation, a Philippine delegate to the United Nations, Francis A. Delgado, declared (1960), "The Americans are no saints, but...as imperialists they proved to be inept...; they allowed us too many liberties...." Due to intimacy with America, material progress and political stability fared rather better than in neighboring lands. Yet the Philippines, like other capital-poor nations, suffered from uneven economic development, and corruption and other political immoralities interfered with good government.

The freeing of the Philippines and the withdrawal of Britain from the Indian subcontinent shook the moral foundations of imperial rule the globe around. In fast order Ceylon, Burma, and Malaya cut loose from their British moorings and set sail on the rough seas of national independence. After years of civil war, the Netherlands relinquished sovereignty over the Dutch East Indies, rich in natural wealth and much of it densely populated, to a Republic of Indonesia. Professing neutralism in world politics and desirous of industrial growth, the new state received equipment and arms alike from Soviet Russia and the West.

In the French colony of Indochina, natives in the northern area, directed by Moscow-oriented nationalists, contrived to break the control of France—a topic discussed farther along.

ASIA'S WEST

The western side of Asia shared with China and the central zone of Europe the unenviable distinction of being a border region between the Soviet bloc and the free nations. Often called the Middle East, this corner of the globe, apart from its strategic importance, attained fresh significance after the Second World War because of the immense oil resources it contained.

Western and southern Europe depended increasingly upon oil from the Middle East, estimated at about two-thirds of the world's known reserves. Foreign capital, principally American and British, developed oil production, paying fabulous royalties into the treasuries of native

Village huts in Morocco

governments and potentates. Political convulsions frequently interrupted the flow of oil to foreign consumers, and the possibility of Soviet encroachment upon oil fields kept the West constantly on the alert.

Alongside a few wealthy families in the Middle East lived poverty stricken Arab masses, eking a meagre subsistence from the soil or in towns and cities. Ordinary Arabs could still be stirred to the depths by their Mohammedan religion.

The Middle East, from Iran (Persia) to Egypt, embraced several Arab nationalities, heirs of proud cultural and historical traditions, sharing a common language, and following the creed of Mohammed. Knots of intellectuals in Arab lands fostered strident nationalisms and conducted successful campaigns to eliminate the political authority of Great Britain and France.[1] Native governments were not strong, and were frequently overthrown by wildly chauvinistic military élites.

In foreign policies, almost all the Arab states preferred not to commit themselves to either power bloc in the cold war, though at times certain of them leaned in a pro-Soviet direction. However, Iran, fronting on Soviet Russia, chose to protect itself against external threats by entering a Western security pact. In addition to the ceaseless activities of Communist emissaries and sympathizers, Moscow missed no chance to fish in the troubled political waters of the Middle East.

Though European political authority ceased, Western influences by no means disappeared from the countries of the Middle East. On more occasions than one, Western armed forces were landed in the Arab nations to preserve order and peace. The most glaring example of military action occurred in 1956, when Anglo-French troops converged upon the Suez Canal zone of Egypt. Master of Egypt at the time was Colonel Gamal Abdel Nasser, an assertive, ambitious nationalist, easily intoxicated by his own rhetoric. Nasser had pushed his way to the top soon after an army *coup d'état*. Popular pride was touched by his success in arranging for the withdrawal of British soldiers from the Suez area and for the independence of the adjoining Sudan.

[1] A lacework of small states along the coasts of the Arabian peninsula remained under the protection of Great Britain.

Pledged to build up the Egyptian economy, Nasser brought forth a gigantic project for a dam at Aswan on the Nile, which required foreign assistance. But promises of help from Washington were withdrawn when the arrogant Colonel coquetted with the Soviet power bloc and promoted anti-Western agitation in Arab lands. Nasser retorted by seizing the properties of the Suez Canal Company (p. 838).

Rebellious Arabs found inspiration and sanctuary in Egypt, and for a short period Syria joined Egypt in a United Arab Republic. Guided by British agents, a loose league of Arab nations had been organized (1944), and sensitive intellectuals cherished yeasty dreams of a vast Arab empire, to which aspiring politicians paid lip service. Yet cooperation among the Arabs seldom passed beyond indignant hatred for the Jewish Republic of Israel.

ISRAEL

In 1948, the arduous Zionist struggle to obtain an independent state for homeless or abused Jews came to fruition with the creation of the Republic of Israel. No longer willing to carry the thankless burden of a mandate over Palestine, Britain had transferred the problem to the United Nations, which authorized the partition of the region into two states, one Jewish, one Arab. Straightway, the Arab League unsheathed the sword against Israel, but its armies met total defeat at the hands of the well-armed, competently commanded, and infectiously enthusiastic Israeli troops.

Better than 800,000 Palestinian Arabs became refugees by reason of the partition and the war. Many of them settled, as wards of a U.N. relief agency, in the Arab kingdom of Jordan, which annexed the portion of Palestine not incorporated in Israel. A barbed wire frontier divided the revered holy city of Jerusalem. Smarting under a keen sense of unfairness and wrong, the Arab nations refused even to recognize the existence of Israel, refused to come to terms with reality. So little had Israel in common with the Arab peoples that no scheme of integration was feasible, though Israel offered compensation to the refugees and agreed to allow a limited number to return to their old homes. Frontier clashes were endemic and grew worse after Nasser assumed the headship of Egypt.

Fresh waves of immigration in the first decade of independence added a million to the population of Israel. Aided by financial assistance from the United States, by the boundless generosity of Zionists everywhere, and by funds from the Bonn Republic, in partial retribution for the monstrous wickedness of the Nazis, the Israeli created a remarkably diversified and up-to-date economy. Organized on parliamentary and democratic foundations, Israel might well have served as a model, politically and economically, for the Arab states to copy. But, alas, the fierce Arab-Israeli feud persisted.

Allenby Road in Tel Aviv, Israel

TURKEY

At an uneven pace, Turkey strode along the road of Westernization, the improvement in agriculture being particularly impressive, though levels were in no sense high. Apparently population increased faster than crop yields. Loans and grants from the United States helped in the construction of factories, many of them poorly managed, and in the laying down of a network of roads and new port facilities. Armaments made up a much larger part of American aid to Turkey than economic assistance. By the early 1960's Washington had financed the Turkish Republic to the tune of more than $3 billion.

In politics, as in economics, the Turks preferred the democratic system of the West—or so at least it seemed on the surface. After a free and fair election in 1950, the Republican (Kemalist) Party, which had managed Turkish affairs between World Wars, peacefully handed authority over to the Democrats, who had captured a majority of the seats in parliament. The ascendancy of the Democrats lasted a full decade and was marked by special concessions to the Moslem faith, no little corruption, press muzzling, and arbitrary imprisonment of outspoken critics and partisans of reform. Matters came to a head in 1960 when rioting students and a military junta overthrew the Democratic ministry. Several prominent Democrats were executed, and, though a representative regime was presently revived, it was scarcely more than a façade for army rule.

Fearful of Soviet Russia, Turkey aligned itself solidly with the Western power bloc, joining NATO and a security pact called CENTO (p. 831), as well as the United Nations. During the Korean War of 1950–53, contingents of Turkish troops in the U.N. armies confirmed the traditional reputation of their countrymen for valor and hardihood.

Western and Turkish military planners alike thought of Turkey as a bastion of free world security against the Soviet Union. With equipment and training provided by the United States, Turkey maintained a larger standing army than any country of Western Europe. American forces operated a radar screen in northern Turkey and were assigned several air stations for military purposes. Until 1963 secret NATO bases were maintained to hurl long-range missiles into Soviet Russia had that become necessary.

NATIONHOOD IN AFRICA

Even as European imperial authority in Asia came to an end, so colonial dependencies in Africa swiftly attained their freedom. When the Second World War closed, only Ethiopia and Liberia were fully independent, but a generation later almost all of Africa had been emancipated from alien rule. Nationalist agitations, directed by the small educated classes and attended in places by terrorism, mass disorders, and fighting, yielded the same general results in Africa as in Asia.

Egypt and the Sudan, it may be repeated, became sovereign states in 1956. Even earlier the former Italian holding of Libya had become a free nation, dependent on aid from the United States and Britain until oil was discovered and set huge royalties flowing into the national treasury. Eritrea was merged with Ethiopia, and Italian Somaliland cast off foreign tutelage in 1960. France relinquished her protectorates over Morocco and Tunisia (1956), though keeping military rights in the latter. For eight dreary years, French forces battled with native rebels in Algeria, which in 1962 became a free country.

TROPICAL AFRICA

History pursued a parallel path among the diverse peoples and tribes in tropical Africa, south of the Sahara. Here hunger, disease, and superstitions afflicted the mass of the Negro population. Whereas in an older century, profit-seeking whites had hauled Africans off to New World slavery, Negroes in the colonial era sometimes existed in semiservitude on the soil of their birth. Real or alleged exploitation, coupled with white attitudes of superiority, quickened native passions for independence.

In the British colony of Kenya tribal savagery and superstition, coupled with a small admixture of primitive nationalism, unloosed an irrational rising among the Mau Maus. It required six years for British authorities to put a stop to intimidation, mutilation and killing. That fearsome experience often helped to inspire white repression of natives elsewhere in Africa, but, by the same token, it imparted an impetus to the cause of independence generally.

One after the other, Britain either set her tropical dependencies free or made preparations to do so, and France followed suit. The process proceeded quickly and with remarkable smoothness and with displays of good will on both sides. Without anything approaching adequate preparation, Belgium relinquished (1960) her wardship over the populous and minerally rich Congo Basin colony; anarchy and secessionist movements ensued (p. 851).

Western officials in the larger British and French colonies had trained native administrators for the tasks of self-government before emancipation, yet it was an open question whether Westernized Africans could cope effectively with the heavy challenges confronting them upon winning freedom. Tribalism, poverty, the artificial boundaries of the former colonies bequeathed extremely delicate difficulties to the emerging, nonindustrialized African countries.

Representatives of the new states conferred frequently on proposals for cooperation and unity, on ways and means of avoiding the "Balkanization" of central Africa. But no lasting federations of consequence emerged.

Certain whites lingered on in tropical Africa as administrators or as professional workers and business managers, and assistance was furnished by Western Europe and the United States. Traditionally, official Washington had looked upon Africa as a continent whose guardianship could safely be left to the European powers. Now the United States started to play a positive role in the new nations, sending material and technical aid, and young men and women from a novel institution, the Peace Corps. After preliminary training (sometimes in slum or "disadvantaged neighborhoods" of New York City), college educated Americans proceeded to Africa (and elsewhere) as teachers and as farm and public health workers.

Soviet influences, ideological and political, penetrated into tropical Africa, notably through special agents on mission and through young natives who passed to Communist bloc countries as students. Several prominent native politicians sympathized at least with the Marxist pattern of society, although, in the main, Africa's leaders appeared to be pragmatists, not doctrinaire disciples of Marx. Political confusion and chaotic economic conditions seemed to make central Africa an inviting field in which to sow the seed of Communism.

In the southern reaches of Africa a rather different record unfolded. Despite recurrent nativist uprisings, and criticism from the United Nations, Portugal managed to retain control over its colonies; in the light of what had happened in the tropical zone, however, prophets confidently predicted that the ties with the Portuguese motherland would soon be severed. Self-government prevailed in the British Central African Federation (covering two Rhodesias and Nyasaland), and, regardless of a rising tide of colored protest, public affairs were virtually monopolized by a tiny minority of white settlers. Colored spokesmen clamored vociferously not only for revisions in the complex, discriminatory constitution, but also for the destruction of the Federation itself and in 1963 that happened.

SOUTH AFRICA

The Dominion of South Africa presented yet another picture. Backed by a majority of the three million whites, the government granted only minor concessions to the colored masses and pursued a program of rigid segregation of races, called *apartheid*. Arbitrarily, the Dominion annexed the adjacent territory of Southwest Africa, over which it had exercised a mandate.

By resisting the globe-wide trend toward racial equality, South Africa stirred up powerful emotions in the colored majority, which had expression in recurrent rioting and disorders. Hotheads were plentiful on both sides of the furious struggle. Clear infringements upon human dignity and freedom turned the conscience of the outside world against South Africa. By way of retort, the Dominion seceded from the British Commonwealth and set itself up (1960) as a fully sovereign republic. Yet warm ties of mind and heart with the United Kingdom could not so easily be disrupted.

To compel South Africa to abandon *apartheid*, the General Assembly of the U.N. adopted (1962) by a large majority an Afro-Asian resolution calling upon member states to break off diplomatic relations with the Republic and to impose a boycott upon it. Since Assembly resolutions are not mandatory, and since Great Britain voted against this unique U.N. action, indicating that it intended to ignore the resolution, the measure seemed likely to prove ineffective. However, Great Britain, as well as other nations, independently opposed the sale to South Africa of weapons which could be used to enforce its segregation policies.

CONTAINMENT OF SOVIET RUSSIA

The rapid expansion of Communist territory and influence, the massive military strength of the U.S.S.R., and keener comprehension of basic Soviet ambitions to enthrone the Marxist system everywhere presented a grim challenge to the free nations. Leadership in restraining the Kremlin, in the military containment of Soviet power along the rim of the Communist bloc was undertaken by the United States. No other country possessed the resources or the energy for that herculean task.

The official American posture on the U.S.S.R., set forth in an article in the periodical *Foreign Affairs* (July 1947), asserted, "The main element of any United States policy toward the Soviet Union must be that of a long-term, patient but firm and vigilant containment of Russian expansive tendencies." At that juncture, America, with a monopoly on atomic bombs and overwhelming economic preponderance, more nearly approached omnipotence than any state since the passing of the Roman Empire.

When Communist guerrillas seemed likely in 1947 to overrun Greece, President Harry S Truman proclaimed a principle of foreign policy that bears his name. It affirmed that wherever free people were imperilled "by armed minorities or by outside (Soviet Russian) pressures," the United States would help them to maintain their independence. Congress promptly voted funds to supply military hardware and economic aid to embattled Greece.

Turkey, also, was granted assistance to check Soviet encroachment. Faithful to an ambition of long standing, the Kremlin had demanded the right to construct bases in the Turkish Straits area. Concession on that point would have been tantamount to extending the long arm of Moscow down to the Mediterranean. Upheld by the West, the Turks courageously repulsed Soviet demands.

Secretary of State George Marshall confers with United States Ambassador Lewis Douglas on the Marshall Plan

THE MARSHALL PLAN

Not long after the implementation of the Truman Doctrine, Washington brought forth a farsighted scheme to help Europe in recovering from the material ravages of the war. Called the Marshall Plan in honor of its best-known sponsor, Secretary of State George C. Marshall, the proposal invited the governments of Europe to prepare rehabilitation blueprints and to indicate what aid they would require from America. The Kremlin, however, recoiled in a hostile manner, condemning the Marshall approach as a slick Yankee stratagem to achieve hegemony over the Old World.

Elsewhere the response to the outstretched American hand was enthusiastic. Seventeen nations, West Germany among them, benefited from Marshall Aid. A central agency was formed, the Organization of European Economic Cooperation (OEEC), to supervise allocation of aid and the general execution of the Plan. Advisory missions from the United States worked with the European governments which were being given assistance. By helping Europe to help itself, the United States strengthened friendly nations, arrested the upsurge of Communist sentiment, disposed of some surplus commodities and bettered the prospects for normal commercial exchange once Western Europe had recovered from war-born economic paralysis. Foodstuffs, industrial raw materials, experts with technical "know-how"—all were supplied to the Marshall countries.

When the Plan came to an end in 1952, American assistance had run beyond $12 billion and, along with the energy of the Europeans, this help had brought to pass an impressive recovery in economic activity, much more in industry and transport than in farming. The volume of goods manufactured in Western Europe pushed well beyond pre-war marks, living standards bounded upward, faith in the future was invigorated and the appeal of Communism was parried. After the Marshall Plan expired, Washington adopted (1952) a Mutual Security Program, providing fresh billions in military and financial aid for the defense of free Europe. That was the cheapest way, the logic ran, to assure the safety of America itself.

COLD WAR DUELS

In the meanwhile, Czechoslovakia, which since the end of the war had wavered uncertainly between West and East, had been absorbed (1948) into the circle of Soviet captive satellites. That event convinced many a doubting Thomas in the West that only physical force would halt further expansion of Communist power.

True enough, soon after the Czechoslovak coup, the Soviet bloc suffered diminution by the expulsion of Yugoslavia. Years of quarreling over ideology and Moscow domination provoked passionate personality clashes between the autocratic Stalin and spunky Marshal Tito, dictator of Yugoslavia. A proud national spirit, linked with geographical distance from Moscow, made the Yugoslav defiance and heresy possible. After the sensational rupture, Tito steered his country on a course of national Communism, free of Kremlin authority, and he attracted discipleship in leading circles of the Soviet satellites. The United States furnished aid to Yugoslavia, which, however, clung to the Communist system and professed neutralism in the struggle between the two great power blocs.

That rivalry touched a new high in the summer of 1948 when Stalin imposed a land blockade upon West Berlin, intending to squeeze the Western powers out of the city, perhaps, as the prelude to their expulsion from all of Germany. The United States and Britain countered with a magnificent airlift which provided the necessities of life for over two million beleaguered West Berliners. At the same time, the West cut off trade with the Soviet Zone of Germany. A test of wills persisted for months until the Kremlin retreated, calling off the embargo which had damaged Soviet prestige and had strengthened democratic and Western allegiances among Germans generally. The Western powers had scored handsomely, though there was no assurance that the Soviets would not try again to coerce free Berlin into the Communist fold.

NATO

Given the heightening asperity of the cold war, given the fears and perils which the brute fact of growing Soviet power forced upon the West, given the reasoning that Marshal Stalin understood strength and strength alone, it is easy to perceive why the United States in 1949 united with the free European countries in a military coalition to prevent the advance of the U.S.S.R. deeper into Europe. Negotiation with the Communists was futile unless Western statecraft was prepared to be tough and to take big, calculated risks. Stark necessities of security—the defense of the West—dictated a full-fledged alliance, involving for the United States a momentous departure from classical traditions of national diplomacy. This partnership, called NATO (North Atlantic Treaty Organization), encompassed in its finished form Canada along with the United States and a dozen European countries, from Britain across to Turkey.

The crucial clause in the North Atlantic Pact asserted that an attack upon one or more of the signatories would be interpreted as an attack upon all. Should such an armed attack be made all the partners, the United States among them, would rally to the support of the victim or victims.

Far from being a conspiracy to destroy the Soviet bloc, as was hotly charged by the Kremlin, the Atlantic alliance was a perfectly open partnership answerable to the United Nations. Since that infant organization was incapable of ensuring international security, a North Atlantic regional understanding was imperatively required, sponsors of the Pact contended. It was persuasively argued that the mere existence of the mutual security coalition would discourage a Soviet thrust westward. If that calculation should be mistaken, if Russia should indulge in aggression, NATO forces should be strong enough to hold on until the immense military potential of the United States could be decisively applied. The ultimate guarantee in fact of the freedom of Western Europe, not less than its material well-being, became and continued to be the United States.

Appropriate agencies to implement the treaty were set up: a Council, composed of the principal ministers of the Atlantic powers, and boards of military experts to coordinate organization of the defense forces and to plan for the common security. In 1951, the Council authorized a Supreme Headquarters Allied Powers, Europe (SHAPE). Paris was selected as the seat of this body and General Dwight D. Eisenhower was entrusted with the supreme command. Relations inside NATO were not always tranquil; sharp differences of opinion between major partners sometimes appeared.

Slowly, coordinated Western military forces came into existence, the pace being accelerated by the outbreak of war in Korea (1950). Standing European armies were strengthened with the help of American equipment, and scores of naval installations and air bases were laid out within striking range of the Soviet bloc. Time and again the United States assured its allies that American troops would remain abroad until the Soviet Union had ceased to be a menace.

As one earnest of its intentions, Washington struck a "dollars for bases" bargain (1953) with Franco of Spain, to run for ten years and renewable. In exchange for financial assistance, the United States was allowed to lay out strategic air fields and naval bases in Spain for use against the Soviet Union should that prove necessary. Considerations of security against the U.S.S.R. overrode distaste of the Spanish dictatorship.

Military strategists wished to have Western Germany in the league for security. Proposals for an integrated international army containing German soldiers were vetoed by a fearful France, but Germany was permitted to rearm and was admitted in 1955 to membership in NATO.

Scarcely had NATO been established than consternation spread across the West in the wake of news that the Soviets had exploded (1949) an atom bomb. Thus the United States was robbed of the monopoly on armaments capable of urban devastation, the solidarity of NATO was somewhat shaken, and a furious race began in nuclear weapons. Competition between Washington and Moscow would remain the supreme factor in global affairs.

Instruments of mass destruction in the rival arsenals exercised a sobering, a deterrent, influence upon the other side. Each was too strong to be coerced by the other. Optimists insisted, in the language of Sir John Slessor, Marshal of the British Air Force, that "with the advent of thermonuclear abundance total war has abolished itself." Sooner or later, the pessimist countered, one power would invoke nuclear weapons whether by accident, design, or miscalculation. Whichever view of the future would prove to be accurate, a delicate "balance of terror" governed in international politics.

THE KOREAN WAR

Out in the Orient, in remote Korea, the cold war had turned deadly hot and the young United Nations had been put to a stern test from which it emerged with its flag flying high. America sealed its allegiance to the principles of collective resistance to aggression and the containment of Communism with the lives of thirty-three thousand men and triple that number wounded.

Under wartime agreements, Korea, previously a Japanese colony, was occupied, when hostilities stopped, by Soviet and American troops with the Thirty-Eighth Parallel as the

Vietnamese refugees on their way southward to escape Communist domination in their former homes

dividing line. Obstruction by the Kremlin thwarted plans to unite Korea and restore it to independence. Indeed, backed by a Russian-equipped army, a standard Communist regime was installed in the North. To the South an avowedly democratic Republic was set up, supported by an army supplied with American matériel. Official Washington inastutely intimated that Korea lay outside the American defense perimeter, which encouraged the authorities of North Korea to believe that the United States had washed its hands of the peninsula.

In June of 1950, North Korean troops thrust into the South, plainly challenging the United Nations as the guardian of peace. Prompted by Washington, the Security Council instructed Communist Korea to pull its soldiers back, and, when it declined, the Council summoned U.N. states to compel compliance by force. On order of President Truman, American contingents at once moved into Korea, and subsequently fourteen other states dispatched soldiers to fight under the U.N. flag, General Douglas MacArthur commanding.

Into the autumn of 1950 lines of battle swayed uncertainly to and fro, and then the Red Koreans retreated. It seemed that the fighting was about over. But presently masses of Communist Chinese troops, masquerading as volunteers, crowded into Korea, thrusting the U.N. armies back to the Thirty-Eighth Parallel. Without material and moral support from Soviet Russia, the operations of the Peking Communists would soon have come to a stop.

MacArthur pleaded vigorously for full-scale war upon China, regardless of the risk of armed intervention by U.S.S.R. Reasoning that a drive against China might convert a local struggle into "the Big War," Washington and its European allies flatly rejected the MacArthur recommendation.

After a year of desultory fighting, conversations for a truce were started between the U.N. and the Communists, and, following annoying delays, an armistice was signed in July of 1953, confirming the partition of Korea. The question of a united Korea remained unsettled, and some fifty thousand American troops were kept on duty in the South to forestall any designs the Communists might have of invading again.

Fortitude, firmness and exemplary patience had enabled the U.N. to prevent southern Korea from falling under the domination of the Asiatic Communists. Had that happened, Japan, which had long likened Korea to a pistol pointed at its very heart, would have been put in mortal jeopardy of Communist conquest.

Beyond that, if the U.N. had supinely tolerated the conquest of South Korea, the whole fabric of the newly woven Western defense system would have been gravely imperilled—perhaps fatally weakened. In point of fact, the ghastly conflict in the Orient accelerated the tempo of Western rearmament and tightened the bonds of alliance. Arguably, if the League of Nations in the 1930's had shown the courage, the resolution, and the solidarity displayed by the U.N. in Korea, the Second World War might have been avoided.

WAR IN INDOCHINA

Scarcely had tensions over Korea relaxed when the French Far Eastern colony of Indochina, embracing Cambodia, Laos and Vietnam, crowded into the international spotlight. Communist-led nationalists, bent on terminating French power, had been waging civil war, particularly in Vietnam, since the withdrawal of Japanese armies of occupation in 1945. Paris rebuffed overtures from native leaders for a status similar to that Britain had accorded to India. Then, Communist China stepped up the flow of military assistance to the rebels, and that support was probably decisive in the eventual insurgent success. In line with the "containment of Communism" philosophy, Washington rushed aid in massive quantities to the hard-pressed armies of France, but to little avail.

The savage conflict in southeast Asia was not taken up by the U.N. After French arms suffered a humiliating defeat in 1954, the government in Paris, entangled in great perplexities at home and in its North African holdings, decided to cut its losses. A cease-fire was negotiated with the Communists and for the first time in a generation the globe was freed from war.

Subsequently, France acquiesced in the partition of Vietnam, the northern slice remaining in Communist hands, while South Vietnam, Laos, and Cambodia were proclaimed independent states. They possessed few resources and little spirit to defend themselves from external aggression or from Communist subversion from within. For years to come sporadic guerrilla fighting swept across the rice paddies, the swamps, and jungles of the Indochinese peninsula.

SECURITY PACTS IN ASIA

Communist appetites might very well grow with eating in a manner reminiscent of Hitler in the 1930's and in tune with a newly coined Marxist battlecry of "Asia for the Communists." To counteract this danger, to defend southeast Asia against Communist aggression, the United States, Britain, France, and five Eastern powers signed (1954) a regional security pact, similar in kind to NATO, though more restricted in scope. Called the Southeast Asia Treaty Organization (SEATO), the alliance obligated signatories to act together if any signatory were attacked, and to consult if any member appeared to be endangered by Communist subversion, for example.

It was soon evident that the containment of Communist ambitions in Asia was nearly as desperate a business as defending Western Europe. SEATO helped to bolster up Thailand (Siam) and the Philippine Republic, but the European partners lost interest in the alliance as their colonial possessions in southeast Asia fell away, and Pakistan at best was an uncertain ally.

As another instrument to check the expansion of Communists in southern Asia, Great Britain united (1955) with Pakistan, Iran (Persia), Iraq and Turkey in a Bagdad Pact; proud Iraqi nationalists, four years later, pulled their country out of the coalition, which was then renamed the Central Treaty Organization (CENTO). Members of this defensive alignment promised to integrate their fighting services and their economies. Though not a signatory, the United States "associated" itself with the alliance. The shield against the U.S.S.R. along her extensive southern borders from the Bosporus to Pakistan was not strong, and Moscow could apply military and economic pressures there without much trouble, if it chose to do so.

The United States also entered into mutual defense treaties with Australia and New Zealand (ANZUS) and with resurgent Japan, potentially a very valuable ally in the Far East. Japanese friends of the pact—not to speak of uncompromising opponents—let it be known that Nippon was a reluctant partner, not committed in advance to uphold the actions of Washington in the Orient. In 1960, a revised treaty with Japan obliged America to defend Nippon without a reciprocal pledge by Tokyo.

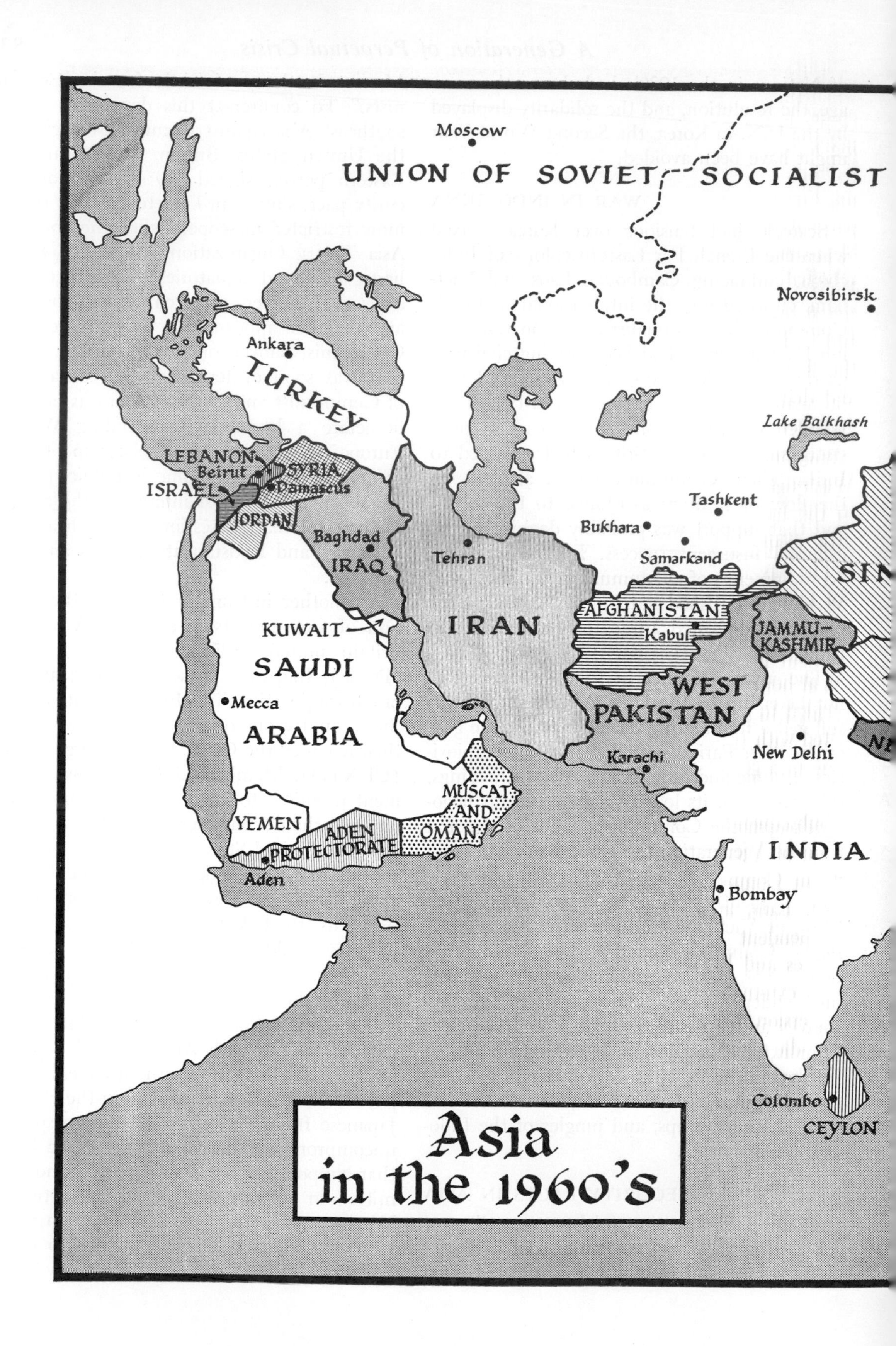

Asia in the 1960's

EPUBLICS
KURILE ISLANDS (U.S.S.R)
SAKHALIN
Lake Baykal
Irkutsk
MANCHURIA
Sea of Japan
JAPAN
Tokyo
Ulan Bator
MONGOLIAN REPUBLIC
Yalu River
NORTH KOREA
INNER MONGOLIA
Peking (Peiping)
Seoul
Hiroshima
SOUTH KOREA
Yellow Sea
NG
CHINESE
Nanking
Shanghai
Wuhan (Hankow)
RYUKYU IS.
OKINAWA
ET
REPUBLIC
Taipei
TAIWAN (FORMOSA)
BHUTAN
Canton
Macao (PORTUGAL)
Hong Kong (BRITAIN)
E. PAKISTAN
Dacca
Hanoi
HAINAN
BURMA
LAOS
NORTH VIETNAM
PHILIPPINE REPUBLIC
Manila
Rangoon
THAILAND
Bangkok
SOUTH VIETNAM
CAMBODIA
Saigon
ANDAMAN ISLANDS (INDIA)
BRUNEI
BRITISH N. BORNEO
SARAWAK
MALAYA
Koala Lumpur
BORNEO
CELEBES
Singapore
SUMATRA
INDONESIA
(PORTUGAL) TIMOR
Djakarta

Considerable left-wing resistance flared up to any alliance with the United States and to the presence of American bases in the islands, but the Japanese parliament ratified the deal.

One thing more. At Bandung, Indonesia, in 1955, representatives of twenty-nine Asian and African countries, independent or on the way to that goal, met in conference. While the delegates affirmed the right of every nation to defend itself, they denounced the SEATO and Bagdad alignments. The broad objectives of the U.N., however, were warmly applauded. Anything savoring of colonialism, racial segregation, and discrimination was condemned. Seeking to quiet apprehensions, the Peking Chinese delegate, in a conciliatory mood, disavowed any desire on the part of his country to infringe upon the integrity of neighboring lands. Seemingly, the Bandung gathering, in spite of outbursts of feuding, fostered a deeper sense of Afro-Asian moral unity. Yet the meeting had no successor.

COMMUNIST INTEGRATION

Taking a leaf from the book of the West, Moscow reinforced the links between the Communist states. To coordinate propaganda activities and to wage unrelenting battle against "Anglo-American imperialism," a Communist Information Bureau or Cominform was created (1947). Bringing together all Communist parties of the world, this agency carried forward the work of the Third International, or Comintern, which had been disbanded by Stalin during the late war as a gesture of good will to the Western allies. Whatever its name, this institution functioned as the principal "foreign missionary society" of Communism.

In direct reply to the Marshall Plan, the Kremlin established (1949) a Council for Mutual Economic Assistance, or Comecon. Countries in the Soviet bloc were pledged to cooperate for economic ends in ways that would be mutually advantageous. In time observers from Red China and other Asiatic Communist states attended meetings of the Council, which were held twice a year. In 1962, Outer Mongolia, an immense, thinly peopled land of yurts and yaks, joined Comecon. A permanent secretariat had—and has—its seat in Moscow.

Up to a point, the diversified resources of the Soviet bloc states complemented each other, and there was much talk about the member countries specializing in making commodities for which their economies best suited them. General planning for the entire Comecon belt, extending from the Elbe River to the Pacific, presented acute difficulties, and it was not always easy to force a member state to accept the program mapped out for it.

After about 1955, the drive for "division of labor" inside the Soviet bloc was intensified and commercial integration was increased, though not as greatly as the Kremlin wished. Russia also set up joint stock companies, half owned by the U.S.S.R., half by a satellite government and administered directly from Moscow. In some instances all the goods produced by these companies and any earnings passed to the Soviet Union. There is little question that the Soviet Union profited the more from trade relations with the captive satellites.

Yet transactions were by no means one-sided, since Russia exported much-needed coal, iron ore, and oil to Comecon partners. Lengthy pipelines to transport oil, electricity supply lines, and improved railway facilities revealed the determination of Moscow to strengthen the economies of the East European states. Cultural exchanges and tourism heightened the sense of solidarity within the Communist bloc.

On the military front, the Soviets devised a counterpart of NATO—the Warsaw Pact (1955). This alliance more or less unified the armed services of the satellite lands under direction of the Supreme Command in Moscow. To fulfill the demands of the Kremlin, the East European states were obliged to maintain large armies, which their treasuries could ill afford, and they had to divert an inordinate amount of their industrial resources to the output of heavy goods that would enlarge military capabilities. Besides, Soviet troops were stationed on the soil of several satellite countries in the name of security, but also to overawe potential dissidents or if necessary to suppress outbreaks. It has been previously pointed out that the Soviet Union possessed a military alliance with Red China.

Apart from regular conferences of the several international Communist organizations, top men of the Communist countries scurried to Moscow for meetings whenever summoned by the Kremlin. Tightening bonds within the Communist bloc widened the gulf separating it from the free nations. Europe was divided more sharply than after the destruction of Christian unity in the age of the Reformation, and, since the secular creeds of East and West shared less in common than the rival versions of Christianity, the division promised to endure.

CHEERING INTERLUDES

For all the bleakness in East-West relationships, shafts of light occasionally pierced through. In 1955, Khrushchev having replaced the inflexible Stalin as captain on the Soviet bridge, the international climate took a turn for the better. The cessation of fighting in Korea and Indochina, the sudden termination of Communist Chinese bombardment of islands adjacent to Formosa (Taiwan) held by Nationalist China, and the recently installed Eisenhower Administration contributed to relaxation of tension.

In that atmosphere, the little German-speaking Republic of Austria regained unfettered sovereignty. Long considered by the wartime allies as a country liberated from Nazi lordship rather than as a conquered land, Austria had been divided into zones for each of the four major allies and garrisoned by their troops. While the Western powers promoted an economic and cultural renaissance in their zones, the Soviets drained off as much wealth as they could from their sector. Understandably, Austria wished to be rid of foreign soldiers and to become the unqualified master of its own house.

For years, at scores of conferences on an Austrian peace treaty, Soviet delegates stubbornly blocked a settlement. So it was a matter of genuine surprise in 1955 when the Kremlin suddenly reversed itself and collaborated in the negotiation of a State Treaty. Thereby, Austria recovered its independence on the condition, promptly incorporated in the national constitution, that it would remain a neutral state somewhat like Switzerland. Though reparations had to be paid for several years to the Soviet Union, all occupying troops straightway withdrew from Austria.

Given free rein, the forces of recovery carried the Republic to unmatched levels of prosperity, and Vienna bloomed as a showplace of freedom, which did not fail to impress those acquainted with the situation in the less favored Communist neighbors. The fact that an Austrian State Treaty had been brought off at all, after a decade of East-West higgling and haggling, suggested that other specific conflicts of interest might yield to patient, dogged, resourceful diplomacy.

Next in line, statesmen of United States, Britain, France and the Soviet Union met at Geneva to discuss outstanding international issues and to explore the possibilities of reducing mutual suspicions which poisoned relations between East and West. At this "summit" meeting, the first gathering of top-level policymakers in ten years, hardy perennials of East-West rivalry came under review. On what terms could the two Germanys be reunited? How could security in Europe be attained? What could be done to limit armaments? How could attitudes between peoples of the contending blocs be improved? Except on the last point, nothing concrete emerged from the Geneva debates, though the comparatively amicable temper of the meeting inspired the press of the world to speak in sanguine tones of the "Spirit of Geneva."

This hypothesis of betterment in East-West relations was blasted, alas, in the autumn of 1955, when the foreign ministers of the West and of Soviet Russia conferred on the same questions that had been ventilated at Geneva. Before adjournment, recriminations between the two sides had resumed traditional levels of asperity. As the only positive results of the meetings of 1955, tourists were more freely admitted to the Soviet Union and cultural and intellectual exchanges between West and East increased and kept on increasing.

UPHEAVAL IN POLAND

Foreign watchers of the times who imagined that Soviet bloc countries were evolving into paradises for wageworkers suffered disillusioning shocks in 1956. Early in the year burly Khrushchev at a party congress shattered the Stalinist myth (p. 793) and inaugurated an energetic destalinization drive. Easing of tyrannical rule in the captive countries of Eastern Europe encouraged unhappy dissidents who were discontented with prevailing conditions of life and labor and with Russian domination.

It was in this environment that rioting broke loose in the Polish industrial community of Poznań. Disorders threatened to spread to other cities and to envelop the Polish countryside as well. Though unrest was harshly suppressed, the ringleaders were let off with only mild punishment. More than that, the Kremlin renounced supervision of the Polish army. Soviet troops were pulled back to frontier districts, and a set of Polish "national" Communists was permitted to undertake the management of public business.

While the new ruling Communists obediently followed the Kremlin line in foreign policy, they were allowed considerable latitude in dealing with home affairs. Shackles upon Polish writers and other intellectuals were loosened, and concessions were granted to the Catholic Church, to which masses of Poles were warmly devoted. The collectivization of farmlands was first stopped and then reversed. "Sit on straw in your own cart and keep your mouth shut" summed up the homespun philosophy of ordinary Poles.

HUNGARIAN REVOLUTION

Up to a point, the victory of "national" Communism in Poland was attributable to a dramatic explosion that rocked Communist Hungary to its very foundations. Broad segments of the population in this "People's Republic" deeply resented Communist economic and religious policies, the overlordship of the Kremlin, and systematic bullying by a Stalinist dictatorship. That regime had been weakened, however, by the anti-Stalinist campaign initiated by Khrushchev.

Emboldened by the troubles in Poland, students and intellectuals of Budapest—the "priviligentsia" in the top brackets of the Communist Party—cut loose in street rioting. Manual workers indulged in work stoppages and participated in popular demonstrations against Communist rule. Police action against the insurgents touched off a mass eruption. Except for hard-core Communists and the politically inarticulate, virtually all Hungarians, not excluding soldiers, joined hands in a spontaneous rebellion. Broadcasts from the free world, implying that help from the outside would be forthcoming, may well have nourished the spirit of revolt.

Insurgent Hungarian spokesmen demanded the withdrawal of Soviet soldiers and arms, cessation of land collectivization, free elections, and an independent, representative government. Under duress the Kremlin temporized, permitted a reformist ministry of moderate Communists to take office and promised general relaxation of controls. Instead of pacifying the insurgents, the prospects of a new Communist deal stoked the fires of freedom. A Budapest mob joyously tore down a monumental statue of Stalin, symbol of the Communist regime, symbol of hated Russian domination.

If Hungary managed to break away from the Soviet bloc, other states might be persuaded to do likewise. To prevent just that, Russian armored columns brutally mowed down the insurrection; gallant citizens of Budapest in particular fought desperately, but they were no match for tanks and artillery. A fresh group of Kremlin puppets, backed by Soviet armed might, was installed in the seats of power.

While the Hungarian rebellion was at a peak, a grave international crisis involving Egypt (described on p. 838) tended to divert world attention from central Europe. Even so, the conscience of the free nations and of neutralist countries was profoundly shocked by naked Russian brutality. Western governments registered verbal protests, yet none sent help to the freedom fighters; to have done so, they

Insurgent mob in Budapest, October 24, 1956. Writing on overturned streetcar reads "Russkies go home"

maintained, might have precipitated a general war.

The United Nations summoned Moscow to stop interfering in Hungarian affairs, but its request that a commission of inquiry be admitted to Hungary to investigate the tragedy on the spot was haughtily and adamantly repulsed. India and some of the smaller unaligned countries censured the Soviets for ruthless suppression of the insurgency, and Soviet loss of intellectual and moral prestige was underscored by the defection of well-known Communists to the West.

Thousands of Hungarian freedom fighters and their families streamed into adjacent countries, especially into Austria, and relief organizations arranged for many to go abroad; some twenty thousand found new homes and old freedoms in the United States. Hungarian rebels in the thousands were imprisoned or shipped off to Siberia, and executions of insurgent leaders, with or without the formality of a drumhead trial, proceeded for many months.

The broad mass of the Hungarians, frustrated, sullenly resigned themselves to conditions which they were powerless to alter. For several years the government maintained strict police surveillance and then eased up a little. The fate of Hungary served as a warning to

President Gamal Abdel Nasser addressing the inhabitants of Beni Yousef in the Upper Nile area

anti-Soviet rebels in other captive countries who longed for national liberation. On the other hand, the ruthlessness with which the rebellion was crushed induced hosts of disillusioned Communists in the West to renounce the faith.

SUEZ AFFAIR

While the tragic events in Hungary unrolled, international attention was diverted to the Suez area of Egypt. In the summer of 1956, President Nasser, embittered by the refusal of the West to aid in the construction of Aswan Dam on the Nile, retaliated by nationalizing the Suez Canal properties and by interfering with the passage of merchant vessels. The governments of London and Paris resolved to invoke military power to restore international ownership of the Canal, and to remove Nasser, who, in his fanatical arrogance, bore some resemblance to Adolf Hitler.

Little Israel, grown weary of border raids from Egypt, of vitriolic abuse pouring from Cairo press and radio, and fearful of a full-bodied Egyptian attack, decided to strike before it was struck. An Israeli expeditionary army thrust aside Egyptian troops without much trouble. British and French forces occupied the Canal Zone. This was war, a clear and present danger to world peace. Molders of opinion, notably the press, in Britain and France were greatly divided over the wisdom of applying force to protect the Canal Zone.

Washington had steadily, though without

full precision, counselled its European allies not to invoke force to bring Nasser to book. On the proposal of the United States, the United Nations ordered the invaders to cease shooting. The Kremlin, heavily involved in the butchery of Hungary, announced that it might dispatch "volunteers" to compel withdrawal of Anglo-French troops.

Reluctantly, invading armies were pulled off Egyptian soil, and a U.N. garrison, recruited from small countries, was posted along a strip of Egypt bordering upon Israel. This contingent served as a barrier to resumption of hostilities, and border affrays dropped off sharply. Popular indignation over the Suez Affair forced a drastic shake-up in the personnel of the British cabinet, Prime Minister Anthony Eden turning over his post to Harold Macmillan.

By its forceful policy, Washington temporarily endangered the existence of the Atlantic Alliance, but, equally, it shored up the moral prestige of the free world among Afro-Asian neutralists and heightened the prestige of the U.N. As for Nasser, the Suez Crisis enhanced his authority in the Arab community of nations, and enheartened him to aid nationalist insurgents in Algeria.

THE RECORD OF THE UNITED NATIONS

As is well known, the Allied powers had consecrated their dearly bought victory in the titanic Second World War by organizing the United Nations. What in fact had this fresh adventure in international cooperation accomplished? What successes had the U.N. achieved in peace-keeping—and where had it failed? At this point it is convenient to review the U.N. record, reiterating certain fragments of the story already touched upon.

As a collective instrument to promote human welfare, the U.N., through its varied subdivisions, performed much useful and little advertised work. For example, millions of hapless refugees, mainly in Europe and the Middle East, were supplied with the basic necessities to live. The Trusteeship Council kept a close eye upon the parcels of territory under its jurisdiction, the number falling rapidly as colonies gained independence. The Council received regular reports from the administering authorities in each trust area, listened to native grievances and periodically dispatched missions to ascertain at first hand how natives were faring. Recommendations for ameliorative reforms were frequently issued.

A good deal was done by U.N. agencies to improve world health conditions. Emergency relief was rushed to victims of mass disasters, and regular campaigns were waged against disease. Malaria was wiped out in Greece and vigorously fought elsewhere. A fearful cholera plague was abruptly arrested in Egypt, venereal diseases and leprosy were combatted, and restrictions were laid upon the transportation of opium. Dentistry was introduced to people hitherto ignorant of care of the teeth, and fellowships enabled physicians and scientific workers from underdeveloped areas to study with specialists in foreign countries.

Valuable humanitarian work was accomplished in immunizing hundreds of thousands of children against tuberculosis, in protection against malaria and other diseases, and in providing health centers and medical training institutions in many lands. From its permanent headquarters at Paris, UNESCO fought illiteracy, spread knowledge on home economics, maintained international work camps, and furnished special forms of assistance to newly independent countries. In the broad realm of economics, technical knowledge was furnished to areas emerging from a colonial status or from centuries of stagnation, the beneficiaries paying part of the cost wherever possible. Projects to raise productivity in agriculture and to spread the benefits of machinofacture were financed by large loans through the International Bank, and an independent agency was set up to promote the use of atomic energy for peaceful purposes. Scientific surveys of the world food situation called attention to the fundamental and alarming fact that population was going up fast in regions where food supplies were most inadequate.

For the benefit of the industrial workers of the world, U.N. agencies collected basic information on conditions and secured adoption

Dag Hammarskjöld

of minimum standards of employment. In shrill accents, the U.N. exposed and condemned exploitation of forced labor in Communist lands, racial discrimination in South Africa, and kindred social iniquities.

Taken all in all, the U.N. had an impressive volume of social and economic betterments to its credit, however modest if measured against globe-wide human needs. When the eight-year tenure of Trygve Lie as Secretary-General ended in 1953, his mantle fell upon another Scandinavian, Dag Hammarskjöld. A Swedish state official, a man of rare intellectual distinction and an expert in economics, he had made a name for himself at international conferences and for firmness in dealings with the Soviets.

With Hammarskjöld at the helm, the U.N. evolved into a vital instrument in global affairs. Patient yet determined, persuasive and courageous, the mild-mannered Secretary-General stood forth as a genuinely supranational civil servant. Yet not merely that, for he claimed a policymaking role for his office.

Because of the recurrent stalemate in the Security Council and of the cumbersome character of the General Assembly after delegates soared beyond a hundred, many of them inexperienced, the effectiveness of the world organization depended more and more upon the diplomatic talents of the Secretary-General. So that the Secretariat, which employed some eighteen thousand workers (1962), would reflect a global geographical basis, some staff members were now recruited from the new nations of Africa and Asia.

Strive as he would to conduct his office with impartiality, Hammarskjöld nonetheless fell afoul of the Kremlin, most strikingly during

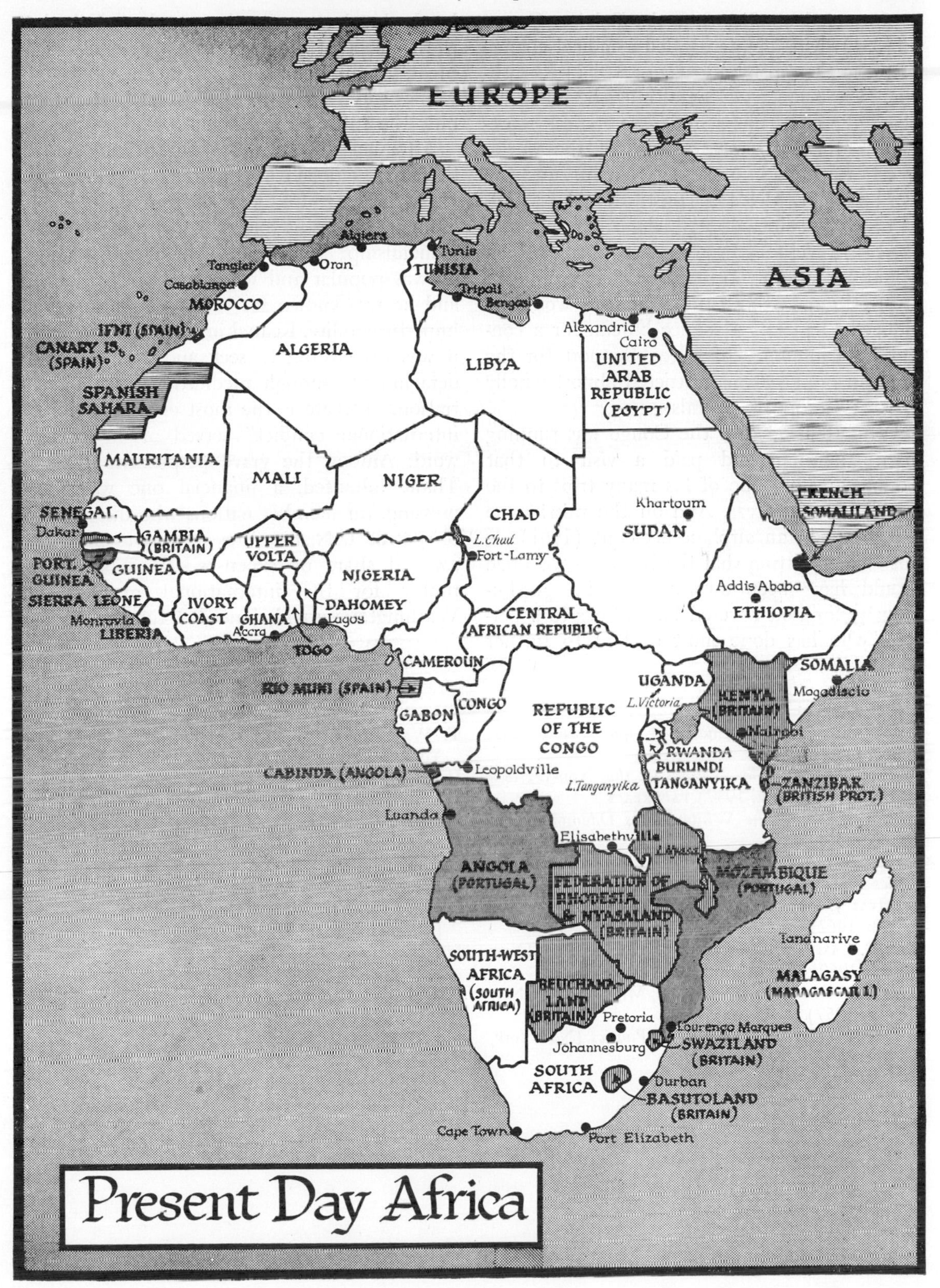

Present Day Africa

a protracted conflict over the Belgian Congo (p. 851). Moscow demanded a radical change in the makeup of the executive. Said Khrushchev, the Secretary-General must be made dependent upon three under-secretaries, representing the three-way division of the world, West, East, and unaligned; (*troika* was the word for it). Were a constitutional revision of that character adopted, the Kremlin could exercise a veto upon executive action which would paralyze, if not wreck, the international organization. At best, the Secretariat would be reduced to merely a service bureau for a continuous conference of states. Support for the Kremlin proposal was restricted almost wholly to East European capitals.

While tension over the Congo was running high, Hammarskjöld paid a visit to that troubled region, one of his many trips to the world's danger areas. And on the mission he met death in an airplane accident (1961). It was entirely fitting that the Nobel Peace Prize should have been awarded to him posthumously, for that coveted honor goes to a person "who has done most or best to further brotherhood amongst the peoples." Whether the concept of the U.N. as a dynamic instrument, as an honest broker in the cold war, would survive the passing of Hammarskjöld only the future could disclose.

After lengthy wrangling, the title of Acting Secretary-General was conferred upon a veteran U.N. delegate, U Thant of Burma, and subsequently he was elected to the Secretary-Generalship. A historian of his native country, he was popular and respected in U.N. circles and he was known for tough-mindedness and imperturbability. Reared in the Buddhist faith, it was his custom to seek and find a certain detachment through meditation and concentration. "Debate is the most civilized form of international conflict" served as his watchword. Among the grave perplexities that U Thant inherited, a financial one was most pressing, for member nations who disapproved of specific U.N. measures refused to pay their assessed share of expenses. To avoid bankruptcy for the international organization, Washington provided needed funds.

FOR FURTHER STUDY

JOHN STRACHEY, *The End of Empire* (New York, 1960)

VERA M. DEAN, *The Nature of the Non-Western World* (New York, 1957) PAPERBACK

LORD BOYD-ORR, *The White Man's Dilemma* (London, 1953)

EUGENE STALEY, *The Future of Underdeveloped Countries* (New York, 1954) PAPERBACK

PERCIVAL J. GRIFFITHS, *Modern India* (new ed., New York, 1962)

JOHN C. CAMPBELL, *Defense of the Middle East* (New York, 1960) PAPERBACK

HARRY B. ELLIS, *Israel and the Middle East* (New York, 1957)

VERNON MCKAY, *Africa in World Politics* (New York, 1962)

T. WALTER WALLBANK, *Contemporary Africa* (New York, 1956) PAPERBACK

HUGH SETON-WATSON, *Neither War Nor Peace* (New York, 1960) PAPERBACK

MASSIMO SALVADORI, *NATO* (New York, 1957) PAPERBACK

GEORGE MODELSKI, *The Communist International System* (Princeton, 1961)

DAVID J. DALLIN, *Soviet Foreign Policy after Stalin* (Philadelphia, 1961)

IVO J. LEDERER, ed., *Russian Foreign Policy: Essays in Historical Perspective* (New Haven, 1962)

FERENC VÁLI, *Rift and Revolt in Hungary* (Cambridge, Mass., 1961)

CHAPTER XXXV

AN ARMED PEACE

U.N. AS A POLITICAL FORCE

USEFUL though the economic and social work of the U.N. was, its higher responsibility was political. As guardian of the peace and guarantor of collective security, the U.N. was obligated to seek pacific adjustments of international disputes. If efforts to settle controversies failed, the U.N. was empowered to halt aggression by the physical coercion of a lawbreaker. So read the Charter. Yet it would be naive to suppose that a babe could hack its way through a dense and dark forest with the strength of a full-grown man. Only if states accepted the decisions of the U.N., or could be forced to do so, would Charter provisions become meaningful.

The U.N. was condemned to impotence in transactions by powers in the Security Council possessing the right of veto. Acrimonious cleavages between the Soviet power bloc and the West, inordinate recourse to the veto by the U.S.S.R., lamed the U.N. from the beginning. Besides, the Soviet Union and its satellites kept aloof from many specialized agencies of the U.N. and declined to pay their full share of the expenses of the international institution.

The admission of many new states to the U.N. enlarged the obstacles to effective action. Yet the organization provided a global forum where the aspirations of the new nations of the colored continents could be laid before the rest of the world. For all its shortcomings, the U.N. proved to be an indispensable reality, without whose activity international anarchy would have raged without restraint. Time might transform the institution into a really effective peacekeeper; in any case, no alternative to the U.N. appeared on the world horizon.

At danger points around the globe, the U.N. posted seasoned observers whose reports furnished objective evidence on which to frame decisions, and their mere presence helped to deter local conflicts from developing into explosions perilous for the whole world.

U.N. BALANCE SHEET

At the outset of its existence, the U.N. was confronted by a quarrel between Iran (Persia) and the Soviet Union. Defying wartime promises, Russian troops lingered in Iran after the war had ended. Appealed to by Iran, the Security Council in 1946 firmly ordered Moscow to evacuate its forces. The Kremlin yielded, chalking up an encouraging success for the infant peace-keeping institution.

Under similar U.N. pressure, Britain and France withdrew (1946) their troops from Syria and Lebanon. Upon the outbreak of hostilities between nationalists of Indonesia and soldiers of the Netherlands, intervention by the Council helped to bring fighting to a stop, and the door was opened for an independent Republic of Indonesia (1949). At the same time, under the aegis of the U.N., an armistice was arranged between Israel and its Arab neighbors, an American, Doctor Ralph J. Bunche, functioning as mediator.

Out in Kashmir, the U.N. halted a war between India and Pakistan and secured approval for a plebiscite to determine the political destiny of the area. However, India stubbornly declined to hold a plebiscite, which Pakistan consistently advocated, and India stationed large bodies of troops close to the frontier of Pakistan. It could be argued, of course, that the U.N. achievements from Iran to Kashmir were relatively minor—but stopping local conflicts removed the possibility that they might evolve into wider conflagrations.

The U.N. proved its mettle and heightened its moral stature by the part it took in the Korean War and by swift, effective moves in the Suez Affair. An emergency U.N. police corps of over five thousand men was posted as a buffer between Egypt and Israel. On three other occasions, U.N. forces were sent into danger zones, ranging from a token team, a mere "presence," dispatched to Laos (1959) up to a regular army of twenty thousand men flown into the chaotic Congo (1960). A proposal that a U.N. team should enter Cuba (1962) to verify the dismantling of Soviet missile facilities there was frustrated by Dictator Fidel Castro (p. 856).

As the supreme forum in which world opinion could be mobilized, the U.N. castigated the Soviet Union for the brutal military repression of the Hungarian rebellion. It likewise upbraided France for its treatment of Algeria. Few items, if indeed any, appeared more frequently on the agenda of the General Assembly than limitation of armaments. More specifically, urgent pleas were raised against an increase in nuclear-weaponed powers and for prohibition on nuclear testing.

RACE IN ARMAMENTS

The arms race between East and West ran a dizzy and alarming course with ever more destructive weapons being stocked in arsenals. Bent on keeping abreast, or better still of outstripping its rival, each competitor laid out colossal sums on instruments of war. Moreover, each side invested vast quantities of scarce scientific talent, managerial skill, and industrial resources in all manner of armaments, especially nuclear bombs and facilities to deliver them.

The bomb unloosed upon Hiroshima in 1945 simply raised the curtain, though it destroyed more lives in a minute than London, for example, lost during almost six years of war. Awesome American hydrogen bombs, exploded in 1953, blotted out distant Pacific islands and reduced the Hiroshima bomb almost to the dimensions of a Christmas tree bauble. In the same year, the Soviets manufactured an H-bomb, restoring parity in nuclear weapons.

From that point onward the pace accelerated. Much information about current developments in armaments was disclosed publicly; more, to be sure, in the West than in the East. Much else remained closely guarded secrets. The Soviet Union, which had a head start on nuclear missiles, produced these weapons for varying ranges, and in 1957 announced the making of an intercontinental ballistic missile. That year, too, the Kremlin fired the first Sputnik, thus demonstrating un-

The Titan intercontinental ballistic missile

expected strength in rocketry. In some American quarters the reaction to Sputnik was pleasingly adult—admiration without envy, a challenge to be mastered—while elsewhere the sentiment prevailed that the Almighty had wantonly deserted his chosen people.

Sputnik caused widespread reverberations in the free nations, from arms technology to the curricula and teaching methods in schools. Spending for defense bounded upward and Washington installed intermediate-range missiles in NATO countries on the periphery of the Soviet Union. Late in the 1950's the terrifying myth circulated in the United States that Russia had jumped far ahead in missile development and that early in the next decade the gap would be so broad that the Kremlin would be able to push the United States around with impunity.

Actually, the United States also perfected a nuclear warhead that could be hurled from one continent to another. It appeared in the early 1960's that the Western power bloc held a healthy lead in intercontinental missiles and in Polaris submarines capable of firing missiles while submerged, but that the advantage in medium-range missiles lay with the Soviets. Equally, while the West possessed overwhelming superiority in bombers that could travel up to five thousand miles, the Soviets had a powerful air force of medium-range bombers suitable for military operations in Europe and Asia. From the U.S.S.R. came claims that a missile had been devised to shoot down other missiles. Save for short pauses, testing of super-bombs above the earth and underground proceeded apace.

Tactical or short-range nuclear arms underwent a steady evolution as did incredibly fast military planes armed with nuclear deterrents. Powerful American fleets stationed in the Mediterranean and in the western Pacific carried aircraft able to deliver missiles, and they, of course, like submarines, required no fixed bases. It was estimated in 1962 that the United States had on hand upwards of forty thousand nuclear warheads! To give prompt warning of an impending attack, networks of Western radar screens were constructed at strategic points.

In the meantime, the "nuclear club" had expanded, Great Britain and France creating nuclear deterrents of their own, though costs ran too high for these nations to do much more than turn out a few bombs for prestige purposes. Rumors suggested that Communist China was engaged in a large nuclear arms program and might manufacture bombs in the near future. While India claimed its nuclear research was directed solely to peaceful ends, no outsider could be positively certain that this was in fact so.

A BALANCE OF TERROR

No matter what damage one belligerent might first do to the other with nuclear warheads, both power blocs possessed the capability of retaliating with swift devastating effect. A nuclear war would yield no victory, no gain, for either contestant—only catastrophic losses. Because of their destructive power, nuclear weapons, it was argued in some responsible circles, provided assurance that they would almost certainly never be used. An effective deterrent policy of East and West, in other language, virtually removed the possibility of a Third World War. On a globe ruled by physical power, an obvious distinction existed between possessing the Bomb and using it—or even rattling it.

For every offensive weapon that had appeared in the past, a defensive answer had been devised; yet, seemingly, no country had come up with an adequate defense against nuclear weaponry. There was much talk (and less action) about measures of civil defense and provision of shelters as protection against fall-out, so that if deterrence failed, the disasters of war would be somewhat lessened.

Year after year, conventional armaments, the weapons that had proved most effective in the Second World War, underwent improvement. Experts insisted that conventional military services were needed to detect aggression or to carry out police tasks anywhere in the world. It appeared that Soviet submarines of conventional types were twice as numerous as the undersea fleets of the Western power bloc.

Millions of men of all tongues were trained and psychologically nerved to fight. The Soviet armed forces of the early 1960's contained about 3,600,000 compared with 2,800,000 serving under the flag of the United States.

DEBATE WITHOUT END

In an imperfect world, competition in armaments proceeded uninterruptedly. Yet, literally hundreds of meetings, under the aegis of the U.N. or directly between governments, discussed limitation on weapons of war, schemes to reduce the likelihood of a surprise attack, and prohibition of atomic bombs and testing. Science had shown that nuclear testing set off radioactive pollution with serious health hazards to the living and to generations yet unborn. Besides, testing poisoned mass emotions on both sides of the Iron Curtain.

Conversations on the regulation of atomic energy under international control started in 1946, three years before the Soviet Union exploded its first nuclear bomb. In the "Baruch plan," Washington proposed international operation of atomic facilities by a veto-free agency. This body would take charge of all known sources of the raw materials required to make nuclear weaponry and would strictly supervise atomic research and development. An international corps of inspectors would guard against violation of agreements.

A large majority of the members of the United Nations bestowed its blessing on the Baruch agenda. Stalin, however, threw away a real strategic advantage by scornfully rejecting any effective form of international control and inspection. His stand remained the law for later autocrats in the Kremlin.

Out of the welter of argumentation, carried on year after year, the salient points in the irreconcilable positions of East and West may be easily defined. Time and again, Soviet spokesmen called for the destruction or the "freezing" of existing nuclear stockpiles and for a ban on manufacturing other bombs. At most, they would agree only to restricted inspection to ascertain whether a country was honestly fulfilling any pledges it might make. They likewise appealed for prompt and unconditional bans on testing nuclear weapons.

The Western power bloc, which meant for most practical purposes, the United States, insisted that first of all an adequate system of on-the site inspection and control would need to be devised and accepted by the Kremlin. That done, the path would lie open to cuts in conventional armaments down to a level deemed necessary to ensure internal order. After that absolute bans might be imposed on all nuclear instruments of war. The character and scope of an international inspectorate to verify that limitation agreements were scrupulously obeyed constituted the real heart of the interminable East-West debate on armaments.

Immense ingenuity was expended by the West in seeking Moscow's approval of balanced, piecemeal, and adequately controlled plans of limitation. Until 1963, at least, it was all without result. Persistently, intransigently, the Kremlin dismissed effective inspection schemes as wily forms of espionage.

With the sanction of Moscow, the Polish Foreign Minister Adam Rapacki brought forward (1957) a novel project for "disengagement," which bears his name. It envisaged a neutralized belt, in which nuclear weapons would be prohibited, extending across the two Germanys, Czechoslovakia, and Poland. Since no formula for inspection was recommended and since by implication West Germany would have to retire from NATO, the Western governments firmly rejected the proposal, describing it as too narrow in scope. Outside of official circles the Rapacki Plan attracted no little applause, although it was not evident whether the Polish overture was anything more than a mere incantation for propaganda ends.

After a generation of fruitless negotiations on armament limitation, popular moods blended a sense of frustration, a feeling of helplessness mixed with plain boredom. Some would define the prevalent attitude as stoical fatalism. However fascinating the complicated problems of "disarmament" might be for experts, many a layman was completely baffled by the technical intricacies involved. The state of mind engendered by armament rivalry might prove calamitous, of course, for one day masses of men, on either side of the Iron Curtain or both, might repeat history by raising the cry "better a fearful end than endless fears."

In 1963, the first hopeful inroads were made toward a resolution of the Great Debate. Representatives of the United States, Great Britain, and the Soviet Union met in Moscow for talks which resulted in the signing of a treaty banning nuclear tests in the air, outer space, and under water. In a Kremlin ceremony televised to Eastern and Western Europe, United States Secretary Dean Rusk, British Foreign Secretary Lord Home, and Soviet Foreign Minister Andrei Gromyko signed the first such control agreement since the age of nuclear warfare began, with Premier Khrushchev and U. N. Secretary-General U Thant witnessing the surprise agreement. Amid the jovial atmosphere of the talks preceding the signing, Khrushchev expressed the belief that the treaty "should contribute to a general relaxation of international tensions," and later, in the face of bitter denunciation from Communist China (p. 857), he praised the United

United States Secretary of State Dean Rusk, Soviet Foreign Minister Andrei Gromyko, and British Foreign Secretary Lord Home sign the nuclear test ban treaty

States and Britain for signing the pact. It is, he said, "a major success for all people of good will."

Although diplomats in Washington and Moscow warned against undue optimism, Secretary of State Rusk proferred the hope that it would be a "turning point" in the cold war, with the possibility of further settlements in sight.

BERLIN IMPASSE

Of all the powder kegs in Europe, Berlin seemed likely most often to explode. It is true that the intensity of the "war of nerves" focusing upon the former German capital fluctuated, even as comparable oscillations occurred in other danger spots of the globe. For several years after the lifting of the Stalinist blockade (1949) relative calm prevailed, but in 1958 Khrushchev threatened, as he would do again and again, to sign a separate peace treaty with the puppet government of East Germany. Berlin became once more a crucial duelling ground between East and West.

This city, it may be recalled, was wholly surrounded by the territory of the German Democratic Republic. Like the rest of Germany, Berlin was partitioned into two sectors, the free West containing over 2,200,000 residents and the Soviet East with half that population.

Governed on the basis of discussion and consent, Social Democrats in the saddle, West Berlin maintained loose political and strong economic bonds with the Bonn Republic and shared in its dazzling prosperity. Only by trade with the West, indeed, could the free sector of Berlin survive. As authorized by understandings with the Soviets, the United States, Britain, and France stationed armed detachments in the area. These forces testified to the determination of the West to protect the liberties of West Berlin and to keep supply routes open. West Berlin stood heroically—an island of freedom in a stormy sea of Communism.

Capital of the Soviet Zone, East Berlin lived under the rigorous Communist dictatorship of Eastern Germany and was garrisoned both by East German and Soviet military units.

In material conditions, the two halves of Berlin vividly reflected the contrast between a free and a Communist society. Abundantly helped by the West, standards of comfort in West Berlin surged to unexampled heights—fine new residential blocks, office and public buildings, busy traffic, gay night life. Small wonder that the community—and West Germany, too—exerted a magnetic attraction upon unhappy East Germans. By way of West Berlin and lesser escape routes, better than three million Germans from the East fled westward by 1961, a large proportion of them young skilled artisans, farmers, and professional workers.

Though the Communists doted on East Berlin as a showcase of their way of life, levels of living were comparatively low and drab, and heaps of wartime rubble and ruins waited to be cleared away. Thousands of East Berliners earned their daily bread in West Berlin and hundreds of youths crossed over regularly to study.

Communists pointed with pride to the Stalin Allee, a long boulevard lined with new apartments and shops, which, after the destalinization process set in, was renamed Karl Marx Allee. The contrast in cultural facilities was less pronounced, for both Berlins boasted first-class theatres, opera houses, and institutions of higher learning. From each side of the divided city, propaganda, spy rings, and other instruments of subversion penetrated to the other half and by extension to the two parts of Germany.

To "solve" the Berlin question various programs attracted partisanship in unofficial quarters outside of Germany. It was proposed, for instance, that the situation would be stabilized if the United Nations, or at least some of its agencies, were transferred to West Berlin. A perfectly fantastic project sketched the building elsewhere of an entirely new spic-and-span city to which the inhabitants of West Berlin would be removed! Communist voices kept calling for a "free and united" Berlin.

In the autumn of 1958 Khrushchev precipitated alarming tensions over Berlin by belligerently announcing that the Kremlin would shortly make a separate peace treaty with East Germany. Were that done the German Communist government would gain in prestige and responsibility and would take control over access to West Berlin. Quite flatly, Khrushchev declared the projected treaty would define West Berlin as a "free city" and would "liquidate the NATO military base there." Once more, as in 1948–49, a blockade might be imposed upon West Berlin, the East German Communists relying for support upon the armed might of the Soviet colossus if that should turn out to be necessary.

Unintimidated, the Western powers firmly indicated that they intended to fulfill oft-repeated promises to protect the liberties of West Berlin, to keep open lines of communication, and to keep military formations there as witness of their resolution. Instead of executing the threat of a separate peace, the Kremlin chiefs agreed to attend a summit conference of top world leaders in Paris to consider the future of Berlin.

Yet before the meeting convened, in May of 1960, Khrushchev and his first lieutenants let it be known that they did not expect anything positive to emerge from the deliberations. Whatever prospects of progress there may have been, exceedingly slim at best, they were shattered when an American U-2 plane on an intelligence mission was shot down on Soviet soil. That dramatic incident, which was handled maladroitly in Washington, afforded the Soviets a convenient pretext to disrupt the Paris summit meeting.

Subsequently, small disputes involving the two Berlins kept the world uneasy. Even so, trading continued between East and West Germany as in years past. The human exodus from the East to West Berlin mounted sharply in 1961, reaching one thousand a day in July and double that in early August. Apparently, the Communist authorities decided that the way to prevent the tottering East Germany regime from collapse was to seal off the Berlin escape hatch.

Without warning, an infamous wall of concrete, surmounted by barbed wire, running twenty-six miles along the boundary of the Soviet sector was erected, cutting Berlin into two parts. This ugly monument to tyranny converted what had been a prison without bars into a prison with bars. Except for foreigners, officials and tourists, travel between East and West Berlin dropped to a mere trickle. Trying to get across the Wall, some East Germans were barbarously murdered, though several thousand luckier ones "made it."

Apart from futile protests against the legality

The Berlin Wall separating East and West Berlin

of the Wall, the Western powers, the United States especially, enlarged their military strength in West Berlin. With rival troops confronting each other at openings along the Wall, the danger of an armed clash was never absent.

While the West proclaimed anew its determination to protect West Berlin, the Allies differed among themselves on what should be done next to counteract Soviet brinkmanship. Here was a fresh test of the solidarity of the Western Alliance, which had endured earlier crises over Berlin. It was commonly understood, moreover, that as West Berlin went so would go West Germany, and as West Germany went so would go the rest of Western Europe. The oracular Lenin himself is said to have remarked, "Whoever holds Berlin, holds Germany. Whoever holds Germany holds Europe." Hesitation concerning an East German peace treaty showed—or seemed to show—that the Kremlin recognized the grave risks of moving too far, too fast.

TROUBLED SOUTHEAST ASIA

If the Berlin question resembled the labors of Sisyphus, the task of preserving peace in southeast Asia—in Laos and South Vietnam—was scarcely less worrisome for the West. Communist pressures, channeled through North Vietnam, caused constant anxiety. Civil war condemned Laos to ferment, Communists and neutralists, abetted from outside, battling against anti-Communists.

Working for a neutral or non-Communist and independent Laos, Washington sent over military supplies and instructors. If suggestions to throw in American troops had been adopted, the sequels might well have been Red Chinese intervention and a second Korea—in a landlocked region of formidable jungle and mountain, fit only for guerrilla warfare.

Diplomacy arranged a cease-fire in 1961 and at a conference in Geneva it was decided that Laos should remain an independent state managed by a coalition ministry. Since Communists held some cabinet posts, opportunities for subversion had not been removed.

Neighboring South Vietnam experienced a creeping war, fought by terrorist bands under Communist inspiration against the pro-Western government. Here, too, Washington poured in arms, cash, and supplies. Communist North Vietnam, whose agents stirred up much of the turmoil in the South, indignantly accused the United States of "imperialistic aggression." For the purpose of encouraging stability in the Indochinese peninsula, and if necessary, to resist Communist pressures, Washington ordered troops temporarily into Thailand (Siam).

CONGO CHAOS

Meanwhile, not peace but the sword had descended upon the former Belgian Congo colony, awarded its freedom in 1960. Spreading over an area more than triple the size of Texas and containing fourteen million people, the Congo became a Republic, though it lacked a workable constitution and had only a small class of educated leaders and few competent native administrators. Acute tribal hostilities and sectional jealousies further darkened the prospects of the new nation.

Hardly had independence been attained than the governing mechanism inherited from the Belgians, accenting old-fashioned paternalism, cracked asunder. Undisciplined native soldiers ran berserk; mobs, intoxicated by the new freedom, indulged in primitive barbarism and anarchic violence. White residents fled, leaving their dead behind, and a large part of the economy that had been Westernized was gripped by paralysis. Unemployment, hunger, and disease tormented town and city. Communist emissaries strummed upon the anticolonial chord and preached the gospel according to Marx.

If the U.N. had not existed, it would have had to have been invented to deal with the desperate Congo situation, the biggest single challenge and burden that had yet confronted the international organization. A U.N. army of twenty thousand colored and white troops was rushed in to restore law and order and to hold as much of the infant Republic as possible together until a corps of trained and honest administrators had been fashioned and effec-

Emperor Haile Selassie greets President of Ghana, Kwame Nkrumah (left) arriving in Addis Ababa to take part in the Africa Heads of State Summit Conference in May, 1962

tive police protection had been established. By way of assistance, foreign civil servants, medical workers, and schoolmasters were sent in.

Charging that the Secretary-General had exceeded his authority in endeavoring to set the Congo house in order, or, alternatively, that he was the willing tool of greedy Western capitalism, the Kremlin demanded a radical alteration in the Secretaryship (p. 842). Some observers surmised that the Soviets were bent in fact upon destroying the U.N. And, by expelling Soviet bloc representatives on grounds of subversive activity, the Congolese authorities embittered tempers in Moscow.

There was more. Native leaders in the Katanga province to the south declared that region a separate state. It was a storehouse of copper and other mineral wealth, and an area where Western, especially Belgian, traditions were deepest rooted. Soldiers of Katanga fought Congolese and U.N. troops alike in the hope of preserving independence.

It was not fanciful to imagine that the ex-colony of Congo, along with other portions of tropical Africa, might degenerate into an array of small, fiercely hostile states on the pattern of the Balkan peninsula. Certainly if Katangan separatism were successful that would set an evil precedent for secessionists in other African states.

In any event, the Congo peoples were probably too disparate to be governed as a tightly integrated, unitary country. As bait to draw Katanga back into the Congo Republic, U.N.

experts cooperated in drafting a constitution providing for a loose federal union, with the component states having a large measure of home rule. Moreover, pressure was applied to Belgian mining interests in Katanga, upon which the secessionist regime depended for finances, to transmit half the revenues to the central Congo government. When these moves failed to produce the desired result, U.N. troops occupied Katanga.

NATIONHOOD FOR ALGERIA

Crowning a prolonged struggle with France, Algeria in 1962 joined the marching throng of independent African countries. Eight years before, Moslem Algerian nationalists banded together in the FLN (*Front de Libération nationale*), had unfurled the banner of revolt. They vowed to go on fighting until French rule was broken. Guerrilla warfare, sometimes waged by rebel groups no more than a dozen strong, pitted against a large French army, produced savage bestialities on both sides. From Tunisia, supplies flowed to the insurgents, and apparently from Sino-Soviet sources also.

Constitutionally and economically, Algeria was more intimately bound to France than her other dependencies, and the presence of a militant European community of a million—one in ten of the population—fundamentally shaped the sweep of events. Apprehensive for their property interests, their civil liberties and indeed their very lives, the European Algerians in the main dreaded the very idea of independence. Shoulder to shoulder with this element stood a large share of the French officers corps and army.

Opinion in France split radically over the question of freedom for Algeria, much the larger, more vocal, part favoring independence either on ideological principle or because it appreciated that the era of colonialism had faded into history or because the warfare was costly in men and money. Strife in Algeria tied down French fighting resources which would have been useful in Europe, and helped to cripple the French parliamentary system.

An attempt by French army units to seize power in Algeria enabled General Charles De Gaulle to take charge of affairs in France (p. 806). He contrived to hold the army intact and to sweep away whatever danger of French civil war there may have been. Pursuing a zigzag course, largely on his own responsibility, without reference to the Paris parliament, and undeterred by two more insurrections of European Algerians and French army personnel (1960, 1961), De Gaulle hammered out a cease-fire with the rebel chiefs and then negotiated a compromise peace.

Freely and fairly conducted referendums in France and in Algeria overwhelmingly ratified the terms of Algerian independence, and the long convulsion abruptly ceased. Guarantees for all European Algerians were prescribed in the treaty settlement. Yet most of the Europeans, and Moslems who had cooperated with them, moved off to France, closing their factories and abandoning vineyards and farms.

In exchange for promises of French financial assistance Algeria permitted the Fifth Republic to retain several military bases and nuclear installations and to participate in the earnings of newly opened oil and gas wells in the Sahara. A leftist faction, not friendly to France and at odds with moderate nationalists, held the tiller as Algeria launched out on the rough sea of independence.

CYCLONE CUBA

Competing in the 1960's with Berlin in Europe, Laos and South Vietnam in Asia, the Congo and Algeria in Africa for the unenviable distinction of the globe's most dangerous spot was the Republic of Cuba. An international confrontation of 1962, involving this island, a mere ninety miles distant from Florida, provoked the most explosive menace to peace since the cannon were silenced in Korea.

Responsibilities elsewhere in the world had led the United States to neglect Latin America somewhat in the 1950's. In 1959, Cuban insurgents broke the back of a benighted, crassly repressive despotism and elevated their bearded revolutionary chieftain, Fidel Castro, to power. The son of a well-to-do family of sugar planters, Castro had been educated for the law but had no fondness for the profession. A congenital rebel, he gathered round him a company of like-minded spirits. They prepared in Mexico to overthrow the Cuban autocrat and then executed their ambitious design. Known as a marathon talker, Premier Castro was as energetic as he was unpredictable. His mood switched abruptly from persuasion to explosion, from youthful charm to red-hot indignation.

Until Castro openly and joyously proclaimed (1961) that he was a Marxist-Leninist and proceeded to create a Communist dictatorship, many a foreign observer interpreted his cause as solely a movement for far-reaching social and political reform. "We are against all dictatorship," Castro had asserted, "whether by a man or a country, or a class, or an oligarchy, or by the military. That is why we are against Communism."

There was a messianic strain in his makeup which inspired Castro to pose as a second Simon Bolivár bent not only upon liberating Cuba, but upon releasing all Latin America from dependence upon Washington. His rhetorical vilification of the United States soared to lyric heights.

For all its comparative backwardness, Cuba at the time of the Castro seizure of control was materially no doubt the best off of the Latin Republics. In office, Castro parcelled out large plantations among peasants, thus winning much popular good will, encouraged industry, and sponsored modest social reforms, though a pledge to eradicate illiteracy seems never to have been implemented. Execution of political opponents, seizures without compensation of foreign-owned property, American for the most part, fiery quarrels with the Roman Catholic hierarchy, and avowal of the Communist creed roused deep resentment and distrust in the United States.

Not less surely, the revolution itself, reformist measures called "Fidelisme," and unbridled denunciation of Wall Street "robber barons" protected by Uncle Sam attracted glad applause from angry young men in many Latin American communities. Rather quickly the generous idealism of the Castro revolution

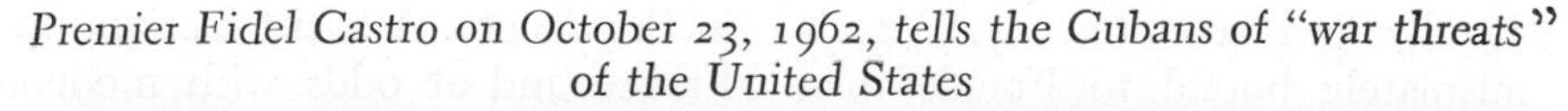

Premier Fidel Castro on October 23, 1962, tells the Cubans of "war threats" of the United States

evaporated; the press was muzzled and a police-style authoritarianism governed the island.

In the longer run, visions of material betterment for the Cuban masses turned out to be illusory. And, when Castro frankly teamed up with international Communism, it was all too evident that he had grossly betrayed his revolutionary movement.

Washington retaliated against the Castro regime by commercial pressures, on the assumption that the government would eventually be strangled, and then severed diplomatic relations. To blunt the appeal of "Fidelisme" in Latin America, Washington sponsored an Alliance for Progress (p. 816). Unlike the Soviets in rebellious Hungary, the United States pursued a relatively moderate policy, without attempting to dictate to Cuba or to smother the Castro system by force.

The Kremlin arranged commercial pacts with Cuba and shipped in hundreds of technicians and substantial quantities of armaments. Castro also welcomed friendly gestures from the Peking Communists. These associations aggravated the specter of Cuba as an outpost of the Sino-Soviet bloc on the threshold of the American continent.

Unhappy Cuban refugees, meantime, had swarmed into the United States. Supported materially and morally by Washington, thirteen hundred refugees staged an ill-starred effort in 1961 to invade their homeland and unhorse the dictator. The calculation that the Cuban populace would rise against Castro proved to be utterly false. The invasion turned into a tragic fiasco. It was announced by the Kremlin that Soviet help would have been rendered to Castro had that been required to ward off the invaders.

Prodded by warnings that the U.S.S.R. had shipped offensive missiles and medium-range bombers to Cuba, President Kennedy dramatically revealed (1962) that the island was

President Kennedy on TV and radio telling the people of the United States of the naval blockade against Cuba, October 22, 1962

in fact being fitted out as a Soviet war base, perilous for the security of the Americas. Under these circumstances, Washington imposed a "quarantine"—a sort of legalism for a naval blockade—around Cuba, so as to intercept ships hauling offensive weapons.

Soviet military installations in Cuba, the President declared, would have to be dismantled forthwith, in a manner satisfactory to Washington, and Soviet bombers called home. Unless offensive armaments were withdrawn, the United States would destroy them. Very large segments of the American defense forces were amassed for action. At the same time, coolness and sanity prevailed over a direct line of communication between Washington and Moscow.

In an impressive display of hemispheric solidarity, the Latin Republics unanimously approved the vigorous Washington diplomacy, and the European allies and many unaligned countries did likewise.

To the immense relief of all concerned, the Soviet strategists recoiled from a direct test of force and retreated from the exposed position in Cuba. Missiles and bombers were promptly pulled out of the island. It was the most striking sacrifice of prestige that Moscow had experienced in the post-Stalin era. Castro, however, adamantly balked at on-site inspection by an international team to verify whether the withdrawal was complete; and although ardent Fidelists thoroughly resented the Moscow policy, Castro's own unwillingness to heed the Kremlin on the international inspection issue threatened to deprive him of indispensable Soviet assistance.

The tense globe-wide fears aroused by the Cuban cyclone quickly subsided. Firmness in Washington lifted morale across the free world, inspiring hope that the showdown in the New World might prove the starting point for adjustment of other East-West controversies.

INSTRUMENTS OF SOVIET POLICY

Soviet dealings with Cuba vividly illustrated the many-faceted nature of Kremlin world policy. The strength of the U.S.S.R. resided not only in military resources, formidable though they were, but also in psychological warfare directed to winning minds and hearts by propaganda. Cultural missions, educational and medical teams actively fostered the drive to gain friends for Communism and its system.

About 1955, the Kremlin added aid to developing nations and economic penetration to its armory of power. Twenty emerging nations —India and Egypt, the Congo and Cuba among them—were beneficiaries of Soviet arms shipments and material assistance. Commercial bonds were tightened in places, as Russian business managers and technicians moved in and industrial plants were built on easy Soviet credit.

Yet, by no means all the emerging states imitated Cuba by entering the Communist camp. Some new governments actually repulsed the wooings of Moscow and dismissed Marxism as a white man's philosophy. Setbacks in Soviet agriculture likewise dimmed interest in the Communist pattern of things. In its disappointment the Kremlin switched its emphasis from uncooperative, established governments in the newly independent states to the local Communist parties. It was hoped that they would prepare the way for a triumphant seizure of power. Moscow never slackened in its conviction that the new states comprised a vital battleground in the secular competition with the West.

As occasion required and opportunity presented itself, the Soviets manipulated foreign trade so as to disturb, if not to upset, markets of Western nations.

On whatever front it operated, the global apparatus of the U.S.S.R. boasted able personnel, well supplied with funds, and buttressed by Communist parties in non-Communist countries. Decisions could be taken by the Kremlin, and indeed were taken, with a minimum of delay, for no effective parliamentary bodies or organs of opinion exercised restraint. On the other hand, fragmentary evidence suggested that on specific points of policy, a division of mind prevailed in the upper echelon at Moscow, though its significance defied exact calculation by outsiders.

And, in any case, the will of Khrushchev appeared to be the decisive factor.

DISCORD IN THE COMMUNIST WORLD

Cuba pointed up another salient aspect of Soviet relations, namely, a puzzling, complicated cleavage with Communist China. Peking assailed Moscow in sharp accents for the ready response to stern warnings on Cuba from Washington. Loud outcries ascended against "appeasement," against wantonly sacrificing brave Cuban revolutionaries placed in jeopardy by "imperialist" enemies. That stand reflected older frictions inside the Marxist household.

A fundamental ideological quarrel had emerged over the inevitability of an armed clash with the Western power bloc. Khrushchev in 1956 had openly repudiated the standard Stalinist doctrine that war with the West was bound to come, and advocated a personal version of "peaceful coexistence" between East and West. As the foregoing pages have recorded, Kremlin words about "peaceful coexistence" seldom found translation into deeds. Yet, the ruling faction in Peking, Stalinist and orthodox, interpreted the newly proclaimed program of the Kremlin as cowardice and heretical betrayal.

From the Chinese viewpoint, it was futile and dangerous to imagine that war with the "imperialist camp" could be permanently averted. Militant Peking wished instead to see the "imperialists" speedily destroyed. Merely to give voice to the coexistence principle, Peking insisted, weakened revolutionary élan in emerging and in developed countries alike. Considering themselves the special protector of colored peoples, the Chinese Reds charged that the coexistence fantasy strengthened the adversaries of Communism in the former colonial areas. Moving several notches farther, Peking implicitly claimed leadership of authentic Communism everywhere.

Polemical speeches and barbed press articles tumbled out, Moscow assailing Peking for "dogmatism," the Chinese condemning the Kremlin as "revisionist." At international Communist gatherings all the European parties—except the Albanian—endorsed "coexistence," while only Albania, north Korea, and, less certainly, North Vietnam lined up with the Chinese. For the Communist Chinese, perhaps the bitterest insult to their faith in the Stalinist creed was the Kremlin's benevolent attitude toward the nuclear test-ban treaty (p. 847). Peking charged the Kremlin with selling out to the "imperialist" United States, and Moscow retaliated with descriptions in its press of the "low levels to which the Chinese leaders have sunk." Khrushchev himself tossed a fiery gauntlet with his statement, "It is not dangerous to mix capitalism and communism."

Thus the split widened, and certain Western observers forecast a rupture in diplomatic relations between the two Communist giants.

Doctrinal disputes tell only part of the vast drama of the Sino-Soviet divergence. Though the Kremlin sturdily championed the admission of Red China into the United Nations and the transfer to it of the permanent seat on the Security Council occupied by Nationalist (Taiwan) China, the U.S.S.R. failed to satisfy fully requests from its Oriental ally for material assistance and for technicians of one sort and another.

Moscow, moreover, resented the movement of Chinese settlers into sparsely peopled Soviet Asia and dreaded the possibility of a tidal wave of emigration sweeping in from a country more than three times as populous as the U.S.S.R. Apparently, too, ill will was fanned by the refusal of the Kremlin to acquiesce in Chinese requests for nuclear armaments, or means to manufacture them.

Be that as it may, Moscow rebuked Peking for recurrent bombardment of islands off the shore of Taiwan (Formosa). Who could tell with certainty that the United States might not one day reply to Chinese shelling with the Bomb? Washington was formally committed to protect Taiwan, the rendezvous of the Nationalist Chinese, against Communist absorption. And, strategically, Taiwan possessed value as a static aircraft carrier. Washington attested its intentions by fertilizing the economy of the island with a substantial volume of material help.

Chinese invasion of India—or of territory claimed by India—in 1962 imposed fresh strains on the Sino-Soviet alignment, since the U.S.S.R. had shipped economic aid and even a little defense equipment to the country of Nehru. Conceivably, Chinese aggression might persuade India to abandon neutralism in favor of identity with the Western power system.

Finally, the coquetting of Moscow with arch-revisionist Tito evoked angry blasts from Peking. That search for a *rapprochement* with Belgrade also alienated the Communist dictator of Albania, Enver Hoxha, who professed undiluted Stalinism and who supposed, rightly or wrongly, that Yugoslavia wished to annex his land. Reviling Hoxha as a Stalin cultist, the Kremlin recalled Soviet advisers, withdrew submarines from pens on the Albanian coast, and in effect excommunicated the country from the Communist bloc.

Scarcely larger than Vermont and having fewer than two million inhabitants, Albania could be pushed around cavalierly, but China was a very, very different proposition. The Oriental dragon in fact took Albania under its tutelage and furnished aid as compensation for the supplies cut off by the U.S.S.R.

As for Tito, he enjoyed the experience of being wooed by two suitors, both ardent, for Washington kept sending over foodstuffs that the United States had stored up in staggering abundance, and strengthened cultural exchanges. Yet Yugoslavia clung to neutralism, Tito aspiring to leadership of the nonaligned nations. With Tito as host, representatives of twenty-four other uncommitted governments converged (1961) upon Belgrade, Nehru and Nasser being notable delegates. Innocuous resolutions begged the competing power blocs to maintain peace, but the conference declined to approve the position of the West on the delicate Berlin question or on cessation of Soviet nuclear tests. Voices in America demanded that Tito be chastised by denying him any more assistance, but Washington responded negatively, preferring to gamble on continued Yugoslav neutralism. An ostentatious visit of Tito to Moscow in 1962 revived clamor in the United States to cut off further supplies.

TOGETHER WE STAND

With friction fermenting in the Communist camp, Western Europe moved along an uncharted trail toward integration. For long generations, men of vision, men of good will, had preached the idea of a voluntary union of the nations of Europe for the common good. Yet national prides and prejudices, age-old blood feuds, the deep-rooted dogma of national sovereignty and lurking fears of economic competition had excluded "the European idea" from the realm of practical politics.

In the post-Hiroshima era, however, strong, fresh winds blew across the Old World. The war had battered Western Europe to her knees and had painfully dramatized the cruel consequences of competitive nationalisms. Besides, the menacing might of Communist Russia, spreading by conquest or by subversion, imperilled the freedoms and attendant values of Western civilization. Joseph Stalin may properly be regarded as the principal architect of the web of West European supranational institutions (that is, possessing powers not subject to control by national parliaments), some of them overlapping, which emerged during the years after the war.

Not least because of the obvious advantages of its own federal union, the United States persistently prodded European statesmen along the road of integration. Little by little, the hesitations of the timid, the prudent, or the skeptical in Western Europe bowed to reason and stark necessity. All ranks of society, all ages, and particularly young men and women, came to share the conviction that amalgamation was essential for progress, prosperity, peace, and for faith in the future.

The carrying out of the Marshall Plan and the establishment of NATO gave decided boosts to the general principle of integration. At French Strasbourg in 1949 a Council of Europe was set up to promote unity. This body, composed of delegates from the free European countries, possessed no executive authority; it was empowered simply to make recommendations to the governments of the member states.

More significant was the organization of a Coal and Steel Community (1953), the child of imaginative French statecraft. France, West Germany, Italy, and the Benelux group—the Six—joined in creating a supranational authority over their coal and steel industries with headquarters in the city of Luxembourg. Administrative officers fixed prices and decided quantities of production and the like for the Community. Sponsors of the project reasoned —and accurately—that the Community would foster greater efficiency in production, anchor Federal Germany more firmly in the free world system, and facilitate the manufacture of conventional armaments. This original pilot project for an economic coalition of Western Europe amply demonstrated its practicality, as soon as quirks in the administrative machinery had been ironed out.

Once the momentum of integration had been built up, it kept rolling along. A European Atomic Energy Community—Euratom—was founded (1957) as a supranational agency to pool resources of nuclear energy for peaceful uses.

THE COMMON MARKET

Big sister of Euratom was the European Economic Community (EEC), popularly known as the Common Market. This combination, which embraced the 160,000,000 inhabitants of the "Six," started to operate in 1958, its scope and management having been defined in an elaborate Treaty of Rome of the preceding year. As the name implied, EEC as a supranational economic institution formed a single big market offering the advantages of mass production and distribution, and forcing inefficient producers out of business through competition. Tariffs and lesser hindrances to trade were to be progressively abandoned, so that by 1970 at the latest the Common Market would become a free trade area for goods and services.

In the meanwhile, a common tariff on commodities entering from outside the EEC would come into force. Management of the Community was entrusted to an executive commission, which employed a powerful supranational civil service. A council of ministers, representing the national interests of the member states, made final policy decisions.

Almost from the beginning EEC was a striking success, vital in the billowing prosperity of the "Six." Trade inside the Community expanded substantially, though it was anticipated that the rate of growth in the late 1960's would be slower than in the first years of the experiment. Trade with outside countries expanded to a much smaller degree than between member states. Yet the EEC participated importantly in furnishing aid to the newly independent countries of Asia and Africa. West Germany, for instance, outpaced Great Britain in helping India and Pakistan, while France allocated more than twice as much of her national income to development aid as did Britain.

The accomplishments of EEC generated schemes for unification in other sectors of economic life. Plans evolved for common standards on basic agricultural and transportation interests, on fuel, on taxation and public finance, and on social welfare legislation.

Yet influential planners of EEC were concerned less with its economic merits, it would seem, than with the political potentialities. Said EEC President Walter Hallstein (who as a prisoner of war had observed the American federal system at firsthand), "We are not in business, we are in politics." The long term, avowed goal was political amalgamation under supranational executive, parliamentary, and judicial bodies.

Stated otherwise, the big objective was the organization of a federal "United States of Western Europe," in one form or another. It would rank with the superpowers, the Soviet bloc and America, and might in fact rival the latter in leadership of the West. There was much talk, though, of some sort of equal partnership between the United States and the European Community.

Among the friends of a united free Europe, no consensus emerged concerning the precise character of the governing institutionalism. While some advocates desired a tightly knit system, others, French President Charles De Gaulle among them, insisted that only a loose political confederation would be acceptable. This school of thought recoiled negatively to proposals that would cut too deeply into rooted traditions of national sovereignty.

So successful was the Common Market that other European countries sought membership in or "association" with it. (Greece entered in 1962 as the first associate member.) Most significant, the British cabinet asked to be admitted and initiated negotiations with the "Six" on terms of entry. Britain was reluctant, however, to take any step that might impair the special relations enjoyed with the Commonwealth nations and the United States. During the Second World War, Winston Churchill told De Gaulle, "Each time we have to choose between Europe and the open sea, we shall always choose the open sea. Each time I have to choose between you and Roosevelt, I shall always choose Roosevelt."

Reverberations set up by the dynamic Common Market were worldwide and promised to intensify if Great Britain joined. It exerted an interest, perhaps an attraction, among the captive countries of Eastern Europe, which partly inspired an offensive against ECC by the Soviet press and radio. The Communist paper *Pravda*, for example, attacked the Common Market as "a criminal plot intended to cure the ulcers and vices of capitalism." Though Khrushchev denounced the Common Market his language was not so unrestrained as might have been expected, and he remarked that economic cooperation between different blocs was possible. At the same time, he pressed for faster development of the Communist counterpart of the Common Market, the Comecon.

A great debate, in the meantime, raged in Great Britain over joining the Common Market (page 804), and experts patiently ironed out many, though not all, British differences with the "Six" on conditions of membership. Then, in 1963, De Gaulle imposed what amounted to a veto upon the entry of the United Kingdom into EEC. That action, while sudden, was not wholly out of character with earlier policy statements of the assertive French President.

It appeared that De Gaulle was incensed over an armaments understanding, called the Nassau agreement, arranged at the end of 1962 by London and Washington. Thereby, the United States would sell Polaris missiles for British submarines, which in turn would be assigned to a multinational NATO nuclear force. Hoping to end an acrimonious quarrel with France over nuclear weaponry, the United States offered to supply Polaris missiles to the Fifth Republic as well. Washington urged, moreover, that the European allies should increase the conventional forces under NATO command and shoulder more of the common defense costs.

At the same time that De Gaulle denied Britain admission to EEC, he rejected the program of the United States for integrated NATO nuclear armaments. Critics decried the biggest foreign policy decision of De Gaulle's presidency as a return to "Bonapartism." The General cherished a grand design: Western Europe should become self-sufficient, both economically and in nuclear weapons, and should advance into the future under the leadership of France. This French-centered "Little Europe" would balance the United States, it was reasoned, in the free world security framework. Beyond that, De Gaulle dreamed of negotiating a deal with the Kremlin which would create a European power bloc as a barrier to possible pressure of Asiatics westward.

By debarring Britain from the Common Market, De Gaulle avoided the likelihood of a serious dispute over ascendancy in that organization. And, by the same token, the General challenged the traditional leadership of Washington in the community of free nations and so strained relations anew inside NATO.

British elements which opposed entry into the Common Market, such as the dominant wing of the Labour Party, welcomed the De Gaulle initiative, while partisans of membership reacted with passionate resentment. All parties cast about for alternatives that promised to stimulate the sluggish British economy and to overcome the mounting volume of unemployment.

However much the associates of France wished Britain to join the "Six"—the cabinets of Italy and the Netherlands were strongly in favor—they could not persuade De Gaulle to change his mind. Some observers felt that pressure from Common Market countries might in time overcome French objections, but that was problematical.

Dissension between the principal free countries, though not so profound as the Soviet-Chinese schism in the opposing camp, was warmly greeted in Communist quarters.

FRANCO-GERMAN RECONCILIATION

Central in the rapidly paced swing in Western Europe toward economic and political partnership was a remarkable *rapprochement* between France and Germany.

On the battlefield of Champagne in 1962, an affair unique in the military annals of the two countries took place. French and German soldiers marched in a joint parade with President De Gaulle and Chancellor Adenauer looking benignly on. That affair, followed directly by mass at the Rheims Cathedral, dramatically symbolized the reconciliation between these ancient and hereditary enemies. Their fierce rivalries and hatreds which had periodically upset the high politics of Europe for centuries appeared to have run their course.

French national pride, so profoundly humiliated by the swift collapse of the armed forces in 1940, had rebounded. That turn of events had consolidated the popularity of De Gaulle with broad layers of the French public and counteracted dissent over measures leading up to the independence of Algeria. Relying upon patriotic sentiment—and apathy induced by national affluence—De Gaulle worked hard to rehabilitate the standing of France in the family of nations.

His ambitious program for French grandeur reached a high point with the denial of British membership in EEC and insistence upon an independent nuclear striking capacity for "Little Europe." This course had disturbing repercussions upon the North Atlantic Alliance and dealt a heavy, though probably not a fatal, blow to an integrated "United States of Western Europe." Be that as it may, the omens appeared favorable for continuing co-operation between the regimes of De Gaulle and that of West Germany.

SUMMARY

Any actively minded person with a preference for the tranquil life has done badly to be born into the tumultuous post-Hiroshima generation. Like the waves of the sea, one emergency followed close upon another. Yet, it may be recalled that long ago a Hebrew sage admonished his fellows that "man is born to trouble as the sparks fly upward." The swift dissolution of the vast white colonial empires or the rapid, relentless upsurge in the world's population would alone have stamped the period with peculiar qualities.

Running through the woof and warp of this anxious era of armed peace was the global struggle, partly ideological, partly power politics, between the Western bloc of free nations and Soviet Communism. Apart from the U.S.S.R. itself, the Soviet bloc embraced 100,000,000 people in the captive lands of Europe from East Germany through Rumania. Communist Yugoslavia, ruled by the apostate Tito, and Albania were expelled from the combination, and when Hungary attempted to break away, the revolution was ruthlessly crushed. On the military side, the Soviet bloc was knitted together by the Warsaw Pact, while Comecon expressed and encouraged economic collaboration.

The Eastern power bloc commanded vast and growing military resources in both conventional and nuclear armaments. In terms of men and firepower, the U.S.S.R. boasted the strongest land power on earth. To the east the Soviet Union had negotiated a formal alliance with Communist China, but fissures inside the Sino-Soviet alignment testified that it was not in fact a solid monolithic structure. Two small Asiatic nations had identified themselves with Peking—North Korea and North Vietnam—and so had Balkan Albania.

Diplomatists and special emissaries of the international Communist conspiracy filtered into neutralist lands, promoting subversion there and in developing and free countries as well. In carefully chosen non-Communist areas, a Communist economic offensive of sorts was carried on to capture markets and to disrupt traditional commercial ties with the West. Similarly, foreign aid in the shape of military equipment and limited amounts of economic assistance (more in the form of loans instead of outright grants) and technical help were dispatched to developing countries. If the Soviet bloc cut off supplies of oil and food to Cuba, for instance, and stopped industrial and technical aid, the Castro economy would probably topple.

As leader of the Communist world and posing as the enemy of colonialism, the U.S.S.R. waged vigorous and resourceful psychological warfare. The principal target of vilification and propaganda was the United States, the supreme obstacle to the worldwide enthronement of Communism.

Faced by the challenge and truculence of Soviet might, the freedom-loving peoples, determined to protect their liberties and to preserve the heritage of Western civilization, built up a formidable bulwark of defense. Implicitly, the West adopted as its motto, "Peace through strength—our guiding star," a choice fragment of Churchillian eloquence. To guard free Europe, to contain Stalinist expansionism, NATO was created and it was presently supplemented by regional defense pacts, notably SEATO and CENTO. Acting on the principle of "divide and rule," Soviet strategy worked tirelessly to sow discord within the Atlantic Alliance, intending if possible to disrupt it utterly. The West expanded its defense capabilities with both conventional and atomic armaments.

By means of foreign aid, or better, mutual security programs, both developed and emergent countries were supplied with Western economic and military help, as well as with technical and educational assistance. Like the Communists, though perhaps with less intensity, the free nations conducted ideological campaigns to win friends and influence people wherever opportunities existed. Another vital phase of the reply to the Soviet challenge were several integration projects in Western Europe, crowned by the Common Market.

Aloof from the contending power blocs were the neutralist or unaligned states extending from Yugoslavia across the newly independent republics of Africa to populous India and Indonesia. Neutralist postures in world politics ranged from passive indifference to undercover alignment with West or East. It appeared that some of the unaligned countries were more and more aware of the Soviet menace to their freedom. Prominent politicians in the uncommitted countries, Marshal Tito for one, dreamed of building a third coalition of power.

Though the United Nations fell short of the expectations of other worldly idealists, it had served the cause of peace and the advancement of human welfare. Under the emblem of the U.N. certain quarrels were resolved (Iran) and aggression was thrown back (Korea; the Suez). To keep the peace, U.N. detachments were planted along the Israel-Egyptian border and in the Congo.

To be sure, failure was recorded, as in Kashmir and in the frustrating warfare in South Vietnam, but the U.N. had to its credit many useful social and humanitarian, educational and scientific accomplishments. It actively encouraged and witnessed the signing of a treaty to suspend nuclear testing, and unceasingly worked toward the regulation of armaments and the establishment of an international police force capable of coping with any possible aggressor, the latter a necessary prerequisite, it was widely believed, for effective armament limitation.

AMERICA IN A CHANGING WORLD

As the core of Western strength and the keystone of the free societies, the United States shouldered its immense, sobering responsibilities in good heart. The English poet, Percy Bysshe Shelley, had the right idea in the "Revolt of Islam" where he portrayed America as the very home of freedom.

> Yes, in the desert there is built a home
> For Freedom. Genius is made strong to rear
> The monuments of man beneath the dome
> Of a new heaven; myriads assemble there
> Whom the proud lords of man, in rage or fear,
> Drive from their wasted homes.

In line with commitments—and to avoid submission to intimidation by the Kremlin—

the United States steadily expanded its own defense capabilities and those of its friends. Conventional weapons, strategic nuclear deterrents, bomber bases and missile sites in allied countries formed the mainsprings of the American defense network. Due to spectacular advances in the making of bombs and of missiles of nearly limitless range and destructive power, the United States started in 1963 to dismantle some of its foreign military facilities.

From Canada around the globe to Japan, Washington had negotiated alliances, diverse in content, with more than two-score other free countries. Taking into account national interests and prides, it was no surprise that perfect harmony did not always prevail inside the several regional groupings for security. Some allies, for example, resented the control that the United States retained over nuclear warheads, and allied diplomatic planners differed on how best to forestall Communist moves against West Berlin. To repel, if necessary, localized "brush fires," substantial bodies of American forces were maintained in Europe.

Consistently, Washington spoke out for integration of Western Europe, and on July 4, 1962 President John F. Kennedy in a memorable address pleaded for "a more perfect union ...with our European friends." This Declaration of Interdependence assumed that Britain would enter the Common Market, setting the stage to organize an Atlantic partnership a broad free trade market. As a first step, the President advocated a series of tariff reductions on industrial commodities on both sides of the Atlantic. Cuts in custom duties by America and by Western Europe would apply not only to imports from each other but also to imports from outside countries.

Unswerving support of the U.N. and its lofty objectives constituted another cardinal point in American world policy; when the international organization was confronted by financial collapse, Washington furnished funds which averted that calamity.

Besides, the United States studiously courted the good will of unaligned countries by furnishing assistance, encouraging ideas of government by consent and of independence, and seeking to demonstrate by faith and works that freedom offered more in spiritual values and material betterment than the Communist pattern of living. Increasingly, aid to developing nations took the form of loans instead of gifts. Prospering allies were urged to bear a larger share of the new version of "the White Man's Burden," so as to reduce deficits in the United States balance of international payments and the drain on American gold reserves.

Through such channels as were open, Washington endeavored to sustain the spirit of resistance to Communist rule in the captive countries of Eastern Europe, to keep green the hope of eventual liberation, and to strengthen abiding bonds of comradeship. Important means to that end were shipments of surplus farm products, cultural exchanges, and the "Voice of America." Among men of Eastern Europe who longed for release from Soviet bondage, faith and confidence in the United States were precious realities, and, conversely, a large volume of discontent with Communist totalitarianism existed.

Though resting reliance for security and peace upon military and economic power and upon the strength of its allies, Washington periodically manifested readiness for negotiation with the Kremlin to reduce tensions and lessen antagonisms. Washington maintained the attitude that although no general settlements of outstanding differences could reasonably be anticipated, determination, patient wisdom, and willingness to compromise might yield an agreement on suspension of nuclear testing, for example, or on limitation of armaments. And, though a little progress was made, certain large sources of discord involving fundamental clashes of interest, such as the two Germanys, possessed a semipermanent character.

In his eloquent Inaugural Address, President Kennedy set forth (1961) the national purpose in the long struggle that stretched ahead. "Let every nation know," he declared, "whether it wishes us well or ill, that we shall pay any price, bear any burden, meet any hardship, support any friend, oppose any foe to assure the survival and success of liberty."

FOR FURTHER STUDY

CLARK M. EICHELBERGER, *U.N.: The First Fifteen Years* (New York, 1960)

Yearbook of the United Nations, (New York, 1947-)

HENRY A. KISSINGER, *Nuclear Weapons and Foreign Policy* (New York, 1957) PAPERBACK

HANSON W. BALDWIN, *The Great Arms Race* (New York, 1958)

HENRY L. ROBERTS, *Russia and America* (New York, 1956) PAPERBACK

JOHN MANDER, *Berlin, Hostage for the West* (London, 1962) PAPERBACK

ROYAL INSTITUTE OF INTERNATIONAL AFFAIRS, *Collective Defense in South East Asia* (London, 1956)

JOAN GILLESPIE, *Algeria: Rebellion and Revolution* (London, 1960)

EDWIN LIEUWEN, *Arms and Politics in Latin America* (New York, 1960) PAPERBACK

CHRISTOPHER M. WOODHOUSE, *British Foreign Policy Since the Second World War* (New York, 1962)

GEOFFREY F. HUDSON, ed., *The Sino-Soviet Dispute* (New York, 1961)

DENYS HAY, *Europe: The Emergence of an Idea* (Chicago, 1957)

ARNOLD J. ZURCHER, *The Struggle to Unite Europe* (New York, 1958)

ISAIAH FRANK, *European Common Market* (New York, 1961)

KURT BIRRENBACH, *The Future of the Atlantic Community* (New York, 1963)

For works on current history, see list at end of Chapter XXXIII.

A List of Significant Dates

WESTERN EUROPE		CENTRAL AND EASTERN EUROPE		OVERSEAS	
1922	Irish Free State	1921	New Economic Policy (N.E.P.)	1922	China Nine Power Treaty
1924	First Labour Ministry	1922	Fascist coup d'état	1925	Death of Sun Yat-sen
1932	British Tariff Legislation	1923	French occupation of the Ruhr	1927	Chiang Kai-shek "unites" China
1931	Statute of Westminster	1924	Death of Lenin—Stalin to the fore	1932	Japan sets up Manchukuo
1931	Spanish Republic	1928	First Five Year Plan	1933	F. D. Roosevelt and New Deal
1934	Stavisky Affair	1933	Hitler enthroned	1935-7	United States Neutrality Acts
1936	French Popular Front	1936	Nazi Occupation of Rhineland	1937	Sino-Japanese War
1936	Spanish Civil War	1936	Stalin Constitution	1941	Pearl Harbor
1940	Churchill Prime Minister	1938	Seizure of Austria	1946	Independence of the Philippines
1945	Labour Ministry	1938	Dismemberment of Czechoslovakia	1947	India: Partitioned and Independent
1946	Fourth French Republic	1945	Partition of Germany	1948	Republic of Israel
1949	Ireland separates from Britain	1946	Italian Republic	1949	Republic of Indonesia
1951	British Conservatives in power	1948	Berlin Airlift	1949	Communist Triumph in China
1956	Macmillan replaces Eden as Prime Minister	1948	Yugoslavia breaks with Russia	1953	Eisenhower, President
1958	Fifth French Republic	1949	Comecon	1954	SEATO
1962	DeGaulle election victory	1949	Two German Republics	1954	U.S.-Japanese Alliance
1963	DeGaulle vetoes British entry into Common Market	1949	Adenauer era	1955	Bagdad Pact (1959 CENTO)
1963	Douglas-Home Prime Minister	1953	Death of Stalin—Khrushchev to the fore	1955	Bandung Conference
		1953	Rising in Soviet Germany	1956	Suez Affair
		1954	Trieste Settlement	1956	Independence African States
		1955	Warsaw Pact	1960	Congo Chaos
		1955	Austria Independent	1960	South Africa, a Republic
		1956	Khrushchev denunciation of Stalin	1961	Kennedy, President
		1956	Hungarian Revolution	1962	Algerian Civil War ends
		1961	Berlin Wall	1962	Kennedy Inter-Continental Declaration
		1962	Albania expelled from Soviet bloc	1962	Cuba-U.S.-Soviet confrontation
		1963	Erhard West German Chancellor	1962	China invades India
				1963	Sino-Soviet Schism
				1963	Kennedy Assassination

A List of Significant Dates

CULTURAL AFFAIRS

1922 *Decline of the West* (Spengler)

1922 *Babbitt* (Lewis)

1923 *Lectures on Psychoanalysis* (Freud)

1926 *Science and the Modern World* (Whitehead)

1926 *The Plough and the Stars* (O'Casey)

1929 Restoration of Papal Sovereignty in Vatican City

1929 *The Quest for Certainty* (Dewey)

1936 *Freedom in the Modern World* (Maritain)

1936 *General Theory of Employment* (Keynes)

1937 "Guernica" (Picasso)

1939 Pope Pius XII

1939 *Grapes of Wrath* (Steinbeck)

1939 "Adam" (Epstein)

1940 *For Whom the Bell Tolls* (Hemingway)

1947, 1957 *Study of History* (abridged, Toynbee)

1947 *Doctor Faustus* (Mann)

1948 *The Plague* (Camus)

1948 *The Caucasian Chalk Circle* (Brecht)

1948 World Council of Churches—Amsterdam

1950 *The Cocktail Party* (Eliot)

1953 New Moscow University

1955 *The Thaw* (Ehrenburg)

1957 *Look Back in Anger* (Osborne)

1958 Pope John XXIII

1958 *Doctor Zhivago* (Pasternak)

1960 Brasilia, capital of Brazil

1962 Lincoln Center for the Performing Arts

1962 Ecumenical (General) Conference

1962 New Coventry Cathedral

1963 Pope Paul VI

GENERAL

1920 League of Nations

1921 Washington Conference

1924 The Dawes Plan

1925 Locarno

1927 Lindbergh Flight to Paris

1929 The Great Depression

1930 Television

1933 Japan and Germany Quit the League

1934 Russia enters the League

1935 Abyssinian War

1936 Rome-Berlin Axis

1939 Soviet-Nazi Pact

1939 Second World War

1941 Nazi invasion of Russia

1941 United States at War

1941 Penicillin

1945 A-bomb

1945 Charter of the United Nations

1947 "Containment" Doctrine

1947 Marshall Plan

1949 NATO

1949 Soviet Atomic Bomb

1950 Korean War

1953 H-Bomb

1953 Hammarskjöld U.N. Secretary-General

1953 Coal and Steel Community

1955 Federal Germany in NATO

1955 Geneva Summit Meeting

1957 Euratom

1957 Sputniks

1957 Intercontinental missiles

1958 European Economic Community (Common Market)

1960 Paris Summit Meeting

1960 Soviet space flights

1960 Discord in Communist World

1961 U Thant U.N. Secretary-General

1962 American space flights

1963 U.S.-Britain-U.S.S.R. Nuclear Test Ban Treaty

ERNEST BARKER, et al., eds., *The European Inheritance* (3 vols., London, 1954)

PRESERVED SMITH, *A History of Modern Culture* (2 vols., New York, 1930–1934) PAPERBACK

WILLIAM C. DAMPIER, *A History of Science* (new ed., New York, 1958)

EDWARD P. CHEYNEY, *The European Background of American History* (New York, 1904) PAPERBACK

HALVDAN KOHT, *The American Spirit in Europe* (Philadelphia, 1949)

GEORGE N. CLARK, *The Seventeenth Century* (new ed., Oxford, 1947) PAPERBACK

FREDERICK L. NUSSBAUM, *The Triumph of Science and Reason* (New York, 1953) PAPERBACK

JOHN B. WOLF, *The Emergence of the Great Powers* (New York, 1951) PAPERBACK

VOLTAIRE, *The Age of Louis XIV* (many editions)

WALTER L. DORN, *Competition for Empire* (New York, 1940)

LEO GERSHOY, *From Despotism to Revolution, 1763–1789* (New York, 1944) PAPERBACK

CARL L. BECKER, *The Heavenly City of the Eighteenth Century Philosophers* (new ed., New Haven, 1955) PAPERBACK

GEORGE LEFEBVRE, *The Coming of the French Revolution* (Eng. trans., Princeton, 1947) PAPERBACK

JAMES THOMPSON, *Napoleon Bonaparte* (New York, 1952)

THOMAS S. ASHTON, *The Industrial Revolution, 1760–1830* (New York, 1948)

GEORGE P. GOOCH, *History and Historians of the Nineteenth Century* (new ed., London, 1952) PAPERBACK

FREDERICK B. ARTZ, *Reaction and Revolution* (New York, 1934)

CARLETON J. H. HAYES, *A Generation of Materialism* (New York, 1941)

WILLIAM L. LANGER, *The Diplomacy of Imperialism* (new ed., New York, 1950)

SIDNEY B. FAY, *The Origins of the World War* (new ed., New York, 1948)

ARTHUR J. MAY, *Europe and Two World Wars* (New York, 1947)

CRANE BRINTON, *The Temper of Western Europe* (Cambridge, Mass., 1953)

GEORGE M. TREVELYAN, *British History in the Nineteenth Century and After* (new ed., New York, 1938)

HEINRICH VON TREITSCHKE, *The History of Germany in the Nineteenth Century* (Eng. ed., 7 vols., New York 1915–1919)

DONALD M. WALLACE, *Russia* (last ed., New York, 1912)

EDWARD H. CARR, *A History of Soviet Russia* (6 vols., New York, 1950–1959. Other volumes to follow)

JOHN F. JAMESON, *The American Revolution Considered as a Social Movement* (new ed., New York, 1950) PAPERBACK

CHARLES A. and MARY BEARD, *The Rise of American Civilization* (4 vols., New York, 1927–1942)

DEXTER PERKINS, *The American Approach to Foreign Policy* (new ed., Cambridge, Mass., 1962)

JOHN B. BURY, *The Idea of Progress* (new ed., New York, 1960) PAPERBACK

STEPHEN KING-HALL, *Our Times, 1900–1960* (London, 1961)

PRINCIPAL RULERS OF CHURCH AND STATE, 1650-1963

A selective list with dates indicating duration of reigns and pontificates

THE PAPACY

Alexander VII, 1655-1667
Clement IX, 1667-1669
Clement X, 1670-1676
Innocent XI, 1676-1689
Alexander VIII, 1689-1691
Innocent XII, 1691-1700
Clement XI, 1700-1721
Innocent XIII, 1721-1724
Benedict XIII, 1724-1730
Clement XII, 1730-1740
Benedict XIV, 1740-1758
Clement XIII, 1758-1769
Clement XIV, 1769-1774
Pius VI, 1775-1799
Pius VII, 1800-1823
Leo XII, 1823-1829
Pius VIII, 1829-1830
Gregory XVI, 1831-1846
Pius IX, 1846-1878
Leo XIII, 1878-1903
Pius X, 1903-1914
Benedict XV, 1914-1922
Pius XI, 1922-1939
Pius XII, 1939-1958
John XXIII, 1958-1963
Paul VI, 1963-

GERMANY

HAPSBURG DYNASTY
Ferdinand III, 1637-1657
Leopold I, 1658-1705
Joseph I, 1705-1711
Charles VI, 1711-1740
Charles VII, 1742-1745
HAPSBURG-LORRAINE DYNASTY
Francis I, 1745-1765
Joseph II, 1765-1790
Leopold II, 1790-1792
Francis II, 1792-1806
Confederation of the Rhine, 1806-1813
German Confederation (Bund), 1815-1866
North German Confederation, 1866-1871
William I, 1871-1888
Frederick III, 1888
William II, 1888-1918
THE REPUBLIC
Friedrich Ebert, 1919-1925
Paul von Hindenburg, 1925-1934
Adolf Hitler, 1934-1945: THIRD REICH
MILITARY OCCUPATION, 1945-1949
WEST GERMAN REPUBLIC, 1949-
GERMAN PEOPLES' REPUBLIC, 1949-

AUSTRIA

HAPSBURG DYNASTY
Ferdinand III, 1637-1657
Leopold I, 1658-1705
Joseph I, 1705-1711
Charles VI, 1711-1740
Maria Theresa, 1740-1780
Joseph II, 1780-1790
Leopold II, 1790-1792
Francis I (Holy Roman Emperor as Francis II, 1792-1804), Emperor, 1804-1835
Ferdinand I, 1835-1848
Francis Joseph, 1848-1916
Charles I, 1916-1918
REPUBLIC, 1918-1938
UNITED TO GERMANY, 1938-1945
SECOND REPUBLIC, 1945-

FRANCE

BOURBON KINGS
Louis XIV, 1643-1715
Louis XV, 1715-1774
Louis XVI, 1774-1792
Louis XVII (nominal king), 1793-1795
THE REPUBLIC, 1792-1799
THE CONSULATE, 1799-1804
FIRST EMPIRE (Napoleon I, Bonaparte, Emperor), 1804-1815
THE BOURBON RESTORATION
Louis XVIII, 1814-1824
Charles X, 1824-1830
Louis Philippe, 1830-1848
THE SECOND REPUBLIC, 1848-1852
THE SECOND EMPIRE, 1852-1870
THE THIRD REPUBLIC, 1871-1940
Marshal Philippe Pétain (Chief of the State), 1940-1944
PROVISIONAL GOVERNMENT, 1944-1946
FOURTH REPUBLIC, 1946-1958
FIFTH REPUBLIC, 1958-

GREAT BRITAIN

THE COMMONWEALTH, 1649-1660
STUART RULERS
Charles II, 1660-1685
James II, 1685-1688
William III and Mary, 1689-1702
Anne, 1702-1714
HANOVER RULERS
George I, 1714-1727
George II, 1727-1760
George III, 1760-1820
George IV, 1820-1830
William IV, 1830-1837
Victoria, 1837-1901
Edward VII, 1901-1910
WINDSOR RULERS
George V, 1910-1936
Edward VIII, 1936
George VI, 1936-1952
Elizabeth II, 1952-

SPAIN

HAPSBURG DYNASTY
Philip IV, 1621-1665
Charles II, 1665-1700
BOURBON DYNASTY
Philip V, 1700-1724
Louis I, 1724
Philip V, 1724-1746
Ferdinand VI, 1746-1759
Charles III, 1759-1788
Charles IV, 1788-1808
Ferdinand VII, 1808
Joseph Bonaparte, 1808-1813
Ferdinand VII (restored), 1814-1833
Isabella II, 1833-1868
SAVOY DYNASTY
Amadeo, 1870-1873
REPUBLIC, 1873-1874
BOURBON DYNASTY
Alphonso XII, 1874-1885
Alphonso XIII, 1886-1931
REPUBLIC, 1931-1939
Francisco Franco, 1938-

THE NETHERLANDS

PRINCES OF ORANGE STADTHOLDERS
William II, 1647-1650
STADTHOLDERSHIP SUSPENDED, 1650-1672
William of Nassau, 1672-1702
STADTHOLDERSHIP SUSPENDED, 1702-1747
William IV, 1747-1751
William V, 1751-1795
BATAVIAN REPUBLIC, 1795-1806
Louis Bonaparte, 1806-1810
UNITED TO FRANCE, 1810-1813
HOUSE OF ORANGE
Willem Frederik, as William I, 1815-1840
William II, 1840-1849
William III, 1849-1890
Wilhelmina, 1890-1948
Juliana, 1948-

ITALY

SAVOY DYNASTY
Victor Amadeus II, 1720-1730
Charles Emmanuel III, 1730-1773
Victor Amadeus III, 1773-1796
Charles Emmanuel IV, 1796-1802
Victor Emmanuel I, 1802-1821
Charles Felix, 1821-1831
Charles Albert, 1831-1849
Victor Emmanuel II, 1849-1878
Humbert, 1878-1900
Victor Emmanuel III, 1900-1946
FASCIST DICTATORSHIP (Benito Mussolini), 1922-1944
Humbert II, 1946
REPUBLIC, 1946-

PRUSSIA

Frederick William, Elector of Brandenburg, 1640-1688
Frederick I (Elector of Brandenburg as Frederick III, 1688-1701), King, 1701-1713
Frederick William I, 1713-1740
Frederick II the Great, 1740-1786
Frederick William II, 1786-1797
Frederick William III, 1797-1840
Frederick William IV, 1840-1861
William I, 1861-1888
United to Germany, 1871

RUSSIA

Romanov Dynasty

Alexis, 1645-1676
Feodor III, 1676-1682
Ivan V and Peter I the Great, 1682-1689
Peter I the Great, 1689-1725
Catherine I, 1725-1727
Peter II, 1727-1730
Anna, 1730-1740
Ivan VI, 1740-1741
Elizabeth, 1741-1762
Peter III, 1762
Catherine II the Great, 1762-1796
Paul I, 1796-1801
Alexander I, 1801-1825
Nicholas I, 1825-1855
Alexander II, 1855-1881
Alexander III, 1881-1894
Nicholas II, 1894-1917

Chairmen of Council of People's Commissars

Nikolai Lenin, 1917-1924
Aleksei Ivanovich Rykov, 1924-1930
Vyacheslav Mikhailovich Molotov, 1930-1941
Joseph Stalin, 1941-1953
Georgi M. Malenkov, 1953-1954
Nikita S. Khrushchev, 1954-

TURKEY

Ottoman Sultans

Mohammed IV, 1648-1687
Suleiman II (or III), 1687-1691
Ahmed, 1691-1695
Mustafa II, 1695-1703
Ahmed III, 1703-1730
Mahmud I, 1730-1754
Osman III, 1754-1757
Mustafa III, 1757-1774
Abdul-Hamid I, 1774-1789
Selim III, 1789-1807
Mustafa IV, 1807-1808
Mahmud II, 1808-1839
Abdul-Medjid, 1839-1861
Abdul-Aziz, 1861-1876
Murad V, 1876
Abdul-Hamid II, 1876-1909
Mohammed V, 1909-1918
Mohammed VI, 1918-1922
REPUBLIC, 1923-

INDEX OF ILLUSTRATIONS

CHAPTER X

CHAPTER XI

CHAPTER XII

CHAPTER XV

CHAPTER XVI

CHAPTER XVII

CHAPTER XVIII

CHAPTER XIX

CHAPTER XX

CHAPTER XXI

CHAPTER XXII

CHAPTER XXV

CHAPTER XXVI

CHAPTER XXVII

CHAPTER XXXII

CHAPTER XXXIII

CHAPTER XXXIV

INDEX OF MAPS

INDEX

A

B

C

D

E

F

G

H

I

J

K

L

M

Q

R

S

W

Y

Z